CIVIL RIGHTS
LEGISLATION AND LITIGATION

CIVIL RIGHTS LEGISLATION AND LITIGATION, THIRD EDITION

Berger Levinson, Rosalie & Bodensteiner, Ivan E.

Published by:

 Vandeplas Publishing, LLC–2019

801 International Parkway, 5th Floor
Lake Mary, FL. 32746
USA

www.vandeplaspublishing.com

ISBN 978-1-60042-503-5

CIVIL RIGHTS
LEGISLATION AND LITIGATION
Third edition

ROSALIE BERGER LEVINSON

AND

IVAN E. BODENSTEINER

PROFESSORS OF LAW
VALPARAISO UNIVERSITY SCHOOL OF LAW

TABLE OF CONTENTS

CHAPTER IV: DISCRIMINATION IN FEDERALLY ASSISTED PROGRAMS   633

Table of Cases

Major cases are printed in capital letters,
with the bold page numbers indicating their primary treatment.

A

B

C

D

E

H

K

L

M

N

O

P

W

Y

Z

The goal of this course is to convey an understanding of key federal statutes available to enforce civil rights. This textbook explores the Reconstruction Era laws that were passed soon after the Civil War as well as several modern civil rights provisions. It is important to remember that there are state constitutions and laws protecting civil rights, which may provide greater protection than that available under the federal Constitution and statutes. It is therefore critical to examine both the state decisions interpreting the state constitution (in particular state due process and equal protection or equal privileges clauses) as well as state and local anti-discrimination statutes in determining a client's best course of action.

Throughout this Textbook we will compare and contrast the Reconstruction Era legislation and the modern legislation. Soon after the Civil War, Congress enacted significant laws aimed at obliterating all vestiges of slavery. Despite enactment of the Thirteenth Amendment abolishing slavery, race discrimination was pervasive. In fact, eight southern states adopted so-called Black Codes that severely restricted the rights of the newly freed slaves, excluding them from various occupations, restricting their movement, and making it a crime for anyone to educate them. In response, Congress, acting under the enforcement provision of the Thirteenth Amendment, enacted the Civil Rights Bill of 1866 (the precursor to 42 U.S.C. § 1981 and § 1982), which prohibited race discrimination primarily with regard to contracts and property rights. Then, in 1871, pursuant to the Fourteenth Amendment that bars states from denying due process and equal protection, Congress enacted § 1983 as part of the Ku Klux Klan Act. Although this provision created no substantive rights, it provided a cause of action against those who violate federal constitutional and statutory rights while acting "under color of state law."* Further, Congress enacted § 1985(3) that, although again creating no substantive rights, prohibits conspiracies to interfere with existing federal rights. These early provisions were brief, consisting of one or two sentences. Unlike the modern civil rights acts, Congress did not provide any explicit type of enforcement scheme or even remedies. For reasons that will become apparent upon reading the early cases, these provisions generally lay dormant until the 1960s. At that time, the Warren Court gave the provisions an expansive interpretation, making § 1983 an effective tool for suing

---

* There is no analogous statutory cause of action for suing federal officials who violate constitutional rights. In *Bivens v. Six Unknown Named Agents of the Federal Bureau of Narcotics*, 403 U.S. 388 (1971), the Supreme Court held that a federal cause of action for money damages may be inferred directly from the Fourth Amendment. However, the Supreme Court in a series of decisions has significantly limited the availability of a *Bivens* action. See Ziglar v. Abbasi, 137 S. Ct. 1843 (2017) (stressing that any extension of Bivens to new factual scenarios is now a "disfavored judicial activity").

state and local government officials and entities that violate federal rights, and holding that §§ 1981 and 1982 reach purely private acts of discrimination. In addition, Congress began enacting new civil rights legislation addressing various forms of discrimination.

In light of the modern civil rights legislation, it is legitimate to ask why the old provisions are still utilized today. You will learn that the old provisions in some instances provide broader remedies than the newer provisions. To be effective, litigants must be able to judge the advantages and disadvantages of the various laws and thus must understand the interrelationship between the old and new provisions. In this textbook, we will explore both the Reconstruction Era statutes as well as the modern civil rights provisions that deal with employment discrimination—Title VII of the Civil Rights Act of 1964, the Age Discrimination in Employment Act (ADEA), and Title I of the Americans with Disabilities Act (ADAAA). Further, the materials will provide an overview of a series of federal statutes that are linked to federal funding—Title VI, which prohibits race discrimination on the part of public and private entities that receive federal funds, Title IX, which prohibits sex discrimination on the part of all educational institutions that receive federal funds, and § 504 of the Rehabilitation Act, which prohibits discrimination based on disability on the part of all entities receiving federal funds.

In general, in analyzing a federal statute the following inquiries should be made:

A. **What is the constitutional source of the federal enactment**, *i.e.*, what gives Congress authority to reach this type of discrimination? Although Congress may not state explicitly the source of its power, this question raises significant issues regarding the constitutional validity of a particular enactment as well as its scope. For example, if Congress acts under § 5 of the Fourteenth Amendment, the enactment is limited by the state action requirement embodied in that Amendment.

B. **How broad is the coverage of a particular enactment**? Sub-questions here include:
   1. Who are appropriate **parties** to the litigation: as to plaintiffs, whose rights are protected by the law and who has standing to enforce the law? As to defendants, who was Congress intending to regulate and what exclusions did it envision?
   2. What types of **conduct** did Congress intend to regulate—what are the elements of a *prima facie* case? A recurring issue is whether a showing of intent, as opposed to a disparate impact, is required in order to establish a claim. Further, even when intent is required, is it sufficient to prove the impermissible bias was "a motivating factor" in the adverse employment action, or must the plaintiff prove "but for" causation, *i.e.*, the harm would not have occurred in the absence of the defendant's impermissible bias.
   3. What **defenses** to alleged misconduct does the Act provide? Here, in addition to explicit statutory defenses, constitutional as well as certain judicially created defenses will be explored.

C. **How is the Act to be enforced?** The enforcement question illustrates a key distinction between the older and newer civil rights provisions; namely, the latter often provide administrative remedies lacking in the Reconstruction legislation. Assuming the existence of administrative remedies, are they optional or mandatory, *i.e.*, is it necessary to exhaust administrative remedies before pursuing relief in court? If judicial remedies are available, are these available to private litigants, *i.e.*, is there a private cause of action, what is the basis for jurisdiction, what is the relevant limitations period, is there a right to a jury trial, and what relief may be obtained in court, *i.e.*, injunction, damages and/or attorney fees?

D. **What is the relationship between this statute and other laws dealing with the same type of discrimination?** Throughout the materials, the relative advantages and disadvantages of pursuing various civil rights remedies will be explored.

The problems that appear throughout the material are designed to help students explore these questions.

CHAPTER I:
CONGRESSIONAL POWER TO ENFORCE EQUAL RIGHTS

A. CIVIL WAR AMENDMENTS: STATE ACTION REQUIREMENT

CIVIL RIGHTS CASES
109 U.S. 3 (1883)

[One of the first major challenges to congressional power to enact civil rights legislation occurred soon after the Civil War when the Court was asked to assess the validity of a federal statute prohibiting race discrimination in public accommodations.]

Mr. Justice BRADLEY delivered the opinion of the Court.

[I]t is the purpose of the law [Civil Rights Act of 1875] to declare that, in the enjoyment of the accommodations and privileges of inns, public conveyances, theatres, and other places of public amusement, no distinction shall be made between citizens of different race or color, or between those who have, and those who have not, been slaves. Its effect is to declare, that in all inns, public conveyances, and places of amusement, colored citizens, whether formerly slaves or not, and citizens of other races, shall have the same accommodations and privileges in all inns, public conveyances, and places of amusement as are enjoyed by white citizens; and *vice versa*.

Has Congress constitutional power to make such a law? Of course, no one will contend that the power to pass it was contained in the Constitution before the adoption of the last three amendments. The power is sought, first, in the Fourteenth Amendment.

The first section of the Fourteenth Amendment (which is the one relied on), after declaring who shall be citizens of the United States, and of the several States, is prohibitory in its character, and prohibitory upon the States. It declares that:

> No State shall make or enforce any law which shall abridge the privileges or immunities of citizens of the United States; nor shall any State deprive any person of life, liberty, or property without due process of law; nor deny to any person within its jurisdiction the equal protection of the laws.

It is State action of a particular character that is prohibited. Individual invasion of individual rights is not the subject-matter of the amendment. It has a deeper and broader scope. It nullifies and makes void all State legislation, and State action of every kind, which impairs the privileges and immunities of citizens of the United States, or which injures them in life, liberty or property without due process of law, or which denies to any of them the equal protection of the laws. It not only does this, but, in order that the national will, thus declared, may not be a mere *brutum fulmen*, the last section of the amendment invests Congress with power to enforce it by appropriate legislation. To enforce what? To enforce the prohibition. To adopt appropriate legislation for correcting the effects of such prohibited State laws and State acts, and thus to render them effectually null, void, and innocuous. This is the legislative power conferred upon Congress, and this is the whole of it. It does not invest Congress with power to legislate upon subjects which are within the domain of State legislation; but to provide modes of relief against State legislation, or State action, of the kind referred to. It does not authorize Congress to create a code of municipal law for the regulation of private rights; but to provide modes of redress against the operation of State laws, and the action of State officers executive or judicial, when these are subversive of the fundamental rights specified in the amendment. Positive rights and privileges are undoubtedly secured by the Fourteenth Amendment; but they are secured by way of prohibition against State laws and State proceedings affecting those rights and privileges, and by power given to Congress to legislate for the purpose of carrying such prohibition into effect: and such legislation must necessarily be predicated upon such supposed State laws or State proceedings, and be directed to the correction of their operation and effect.

And so in the present case, until some State law has been passed, or some State action through its officers or agents has been taken, adverse to the rights of citizens sought to be protected by the Fourteenth Amendment, no legislation of the United States under said amendment, nor any proceeding under such legislation, can be called into activity: for the prohibitions of the amendment are against State laws and acts done under State authority.

An inspection of the law shows that it makes no reference whatever to any supposed or apprehended violation of the Fourteenth Amendment on the part of the States. It is not predicated on any such view. It proceeds *ex directo* to declare that certain acts committed by individuals shall be deemed offenses, and shall be prosecuted and punished by proceedings in the courts of the United States. It does not profess to be corrective of any constitutional wrong committed by the States; it does not make its operation to depend upon any such wrong committed. It applies equally to cases arising in States which have the justest laws respecting the personal rights of citizens, and whose authorities are ever ready to enforce such laws, as to those which arise in States that may have violated the prohibition of the amendment. In other words, it steps into the domain of local jurisprudence, and lays down rules for the conduct of individuals in society towards each other, and imposes sanctions for the enforcement of those rules, without referring in any manner to any supposed action of the State or its authorities.

In this connection it is proper to state that civil rights, such as are guaranteed by the Constitution against State aggression, cannot be impaired by the wrongful acts of individuals, unsupported by State authority in the shape of laws, customs, or judicial or executive proceedings. The wrongful act of an individual, unsupported by any such authority, is simply a private wrong, or a crime of that individual; an invasion of the rights of the injured party, it is true, whether they affect his person, his property, or his reputation; but if not sanctioned in some way by the State, or not done under State authority, his rights remain in full force, and may presumably be vindicated by resort to the laws of the State for redress. An individual cannot deprive a man of his right to vote, to hold property, to buy and sell, to sue in the courts, or to be a witness or a juror; he may, by force or fraud, interfere with the enjoyment of the right in a particular case; he may commit an assault against the person, or commit murder, or use ruffian violence at the polls, or slander the good name of a fellow citizen; but, unless protected in these wrongful acts by some shield of State law or State authority, he cannot destroy or injure the right; he will only render himself amenable to satisfaction or punishment; and amenable therefor to the laws of the State where the wrongful acts are committed. Hence, in all those cases where the Constitution seeks to protect the rights of the citizen against discriminative and unjust laws of the State by prohibiting such laws, it is not individual offenses, but abrogation and denial of rights, which it denounces, and for which it clothes the Congress with power to provide a remedy. This abrogation and denial of rights, for which the States alone were or could be responsible, was the great seminal and fundamental wrong which was intended to be remedied. And the remedy to be provided must necessarily be predicated upon that wrong. It must assume that in the cases provided for, the evil or wrong actually committed rests upon some State law or State authority for its excuse and perpetration.

Of course, these remarks do not apply to those cases in which Congress is clothed with direct and plenary powers of legislation over the whole subject, accompanied with an express or implied denial of such power to the States, as in the regulation of commerce with foreign nations, among the several States, and with the Indian tribes, the coining of money, the establishment of post offices and post roads, the declaring of war, etc. In these cases Congress has power to pass laws for regulating the subjects specified in every detail, and the conduct and transactions of individuals in respect thereof.

If the principles of interpretation which we have laid down are correct, as we deem them to be, it is clear that the law in question cannot be sustained by any grant of legislative power made to Congress by the Fourteenth Amendment. That amendment prohibits the States from denying to any person the equal protection of the laws, and declares that Congress shall have power to enforce, by appropriate legislation, the provisions of the amendment. The law in question, without any reference to adverse State legislation on the subject, declares that all persons shall be entitled to equal accommodations and privileges of inns, public conveyances, and places of public amusement, and imposes a penalty upon any individual who shall deny to any citizen such equal accommodations and privileges. This is not corrective legislation; it is primary and direct; it takes immediate and absolute possession of the subject of the right of admission to inns, public conveyances, and places of amusement. It supersedes and displaces State legislation on the same subject, or only allows it permissive force. It ignores such legislation, and assumes that the matter is one that belongs to the domain of national regulation. Whether it would not have been a more effective protection of the rights of citizens to have clothed Congress with plenary power over the whole subject, is not now the question. What we have to decide is, whether such plenary power has been conferred upon Congress by the Fourteenth Amendment; and in our judgment, it has not.

But the power of Congress to adopt direct and primary, as distinguished from corrective legislation, on the subject in hand, is sought, in the second place, from the Thirteenth Amendment, which abolishes slavery. This amendment declares "that neither slavery, nor involuntary servitude, except as a punishment for crime, whereof the party shall have been duly convicted, shall exist within the United States, or any place subject to their jurisdiction;" and it gives Congress power to enforce the amendment by appropriate legislation.

This amendment, as well as the Fourteenth, is undoubtedly self-executing without any ancillary legislation, so far as its terms are applicable to any existing state of circumstances. By its own unaided force and effect it abolished slavery, and established universal freedom. Still, legislation may be necessary and proper to meet all the various cases and circumstances to be affected by it, and to prescribe proper modes of redress for its violation in letter or spirit. And such legislation may be primary and direct in its character; for the amendment is not a mere prohibition of State laws establishing or upholding slavery, but an absolute declaration that slavery or involuntary servitude shall not exist in any part of the United States.

It is true, that slavery cannot exist without law, any more than property in lands and goods can exist without law: and, therefore, the Thirteenth Amendment may be regarded as nullifying all State laws which establish or uphold slavery. But it has a reflex character also, establishing and decreeing universal civil and political freedom throughout the United States; and it is assumed, that the power vested in Congress to enforce the article by appropriate legislation, clothes Congress with power to pass all laws necessary and proper for abolishing all badges and incidents of slavery in the United States: and upon this assumption it is claimed, that this is sufficient authority for declaring by law that all persons shall have equal accommodations and privileges in all inns, public conveyances, and places of amusement; the argument being, that the denial of such equal accommodation and privileges is, in itself, a subjection to a species of servitude within the meaning of the amendment. Conceding the major proposition to be true, that Congress has a right to enact all necessary and proper laws for the obliteration and prevention of slavery with all its badges and incidents, is the minor proposition also true, that the denial to any person of admission to the accommodations and privileges of an inn, a public conveyance, or a theatre, does subject that person to any form of servitude, or tend to fasten upon him any badge of slavery? If it does not, then power to pass the law is not found in the Thirteenth Amendment.

The long existence of African slavery in this country gave us very distinct notions of what it was, and what were its necessary incidents. Compulsory service of the slave for the benefit of the master, restraint of his movements except by the master's will, disability to hold property, to make contracts, to have a standing in court, to be a witness against a white person, and such like burdens and incapacities, were the inseparable incidents of the institution. Severer punishments for crimes were imposed on the slave than on free persons guilty of the same offenses.

Congress, as we have seen, by the Civil Rights Bill of 1866[1], passed in view of the Thirteenth Amendment before the Fourteenth was adopted, undertook to wipe out these burdens and disabilities, the necessary incidents of slavery, constituting its substance and visible form; and to secure to all citizens of every race and color, and without regard to previous servitude, those fundamental rights which are the essence of civil freedom, namely, the same right to make and enforce contracts, to sue, be parties, give evidence, and to inherit, purchase, lease, sell and convey property, as is enjoyed by white citizens. Whether this legislation was fully authorized by the Thirteenth Amendment alone, without the support which it afterward received from the Fourteenth Amendment, after the adoption of which it was re-enacted with some additions, it is not necessary to inquire. It is referred to for the purpose of showing that at that time (in 1866) Congress did not assume, under the authority given by the Thirteenth Amendment, to adjust what may be called the social rights of men and races in the community; but only to declare and vindicate those fundamental rights which appertain to the essence of citizenship, and the enjoyment or deprivation of which constitutes the essential distinction between freedom and slavery.

The only question under the present head, therefore, is, whether the refusal of any persons of the accommodations of an inn, or a public conveyance, or a place of public amusement, by an individual, and without any sanction or support from any State law or regulation, does inflict upon such persons any manner of servitude, or form of slavery, as those terms are understood in this country?

After giving to these questions all the consideration which their importance demands, we are forced to the conclusion that such an act of refusal has nothing to do with slavery or involuntary servitude, and that if it is violative of any right of the party, his redress is to be sought under the laws of the State; or if those laws are adverse to his rights and do not protect him, his remedy will be found in the corrective legislation which Congress has adopted, or may adopt, for counteracting the effect of State laws, or State action, prohibited by the Fourteenth Amendment. It would be running the slavery argument into the ground to make it apply to every act of discrimination which a person may see fit to make as to the guests he will entertain, or as to the people he will take into his coach or cab or car, or admit to his concert or theatre, or deal with in other matters of intercourse or business. Innkeepers and public carriers, by the laws of all the States, so far as we are aware, are bound, to the extent of their facilities, to furnish proper accommodation to all unobjectionable persons who in good faith apply for them. If the laws themselves make any unjust discrimination, amenable to the prohibitions of the fourteenth amendment, Congress has full power to afford a remedy under that amendment and in accordance with it.

Mr. Justice HARLAN dissenting

The Thirteenth Amendment, it is conceded, did something more than to prohibit slavery as an *institution*, resting upon distinctions of race, and upheld by positive law. My brethren admit

---

1   This Bill was the forerunner for § 1981 and § 1982, which are discussed in Chapter II.

that it established and decreed universal *civil freedom* throughout the United States. But did the freedom thus established involve nothing more than exemption from actual slavery? Was nothing more intended than to forbid one man from owning another as property? Was it the purpose of the nation simply to destroy the institution, and then remit the race, theretofore held in bondage, to the several States for such protection, in their civil rights, necessarily growing out of freedom, as those States, in their discretion, might choose to provide? Were the States against whose protest the institution was destroyed, to be left free, so far as national interference was concerned, to make or allow discriminations against that race, as such, in the enjoyment of those fundamental rights which by universal concession, inhere in a state of freedom?

That there are burdens and disabilities which constitute badges of slavery and servitude, and that the power to enforce by appropriate legislation the Thirteenth Amendment may be exerted by legislation of a direct and primary character, for the eradication, not simply of the institution, but of its badges and incidents, are propositions which ought to be deemed indisputable. They lie at the foundation of the Civil Rights Act of 1866. Whether that act was authorized by the Thirteenth Amendment alone, without the support which it subsequently received from the Fourteenth Amendment, after the adoption of which it was re-enacted with some additions, my brethren do not consider it necessary to inquire. But I submit, with all respect to them, that its constitutionality is conclusively shown by their opinion. They admit, as I have said, that the Thirteenth Amendment established freedom; that there are burdens and disabilities, the necessary incidents of slavery, which constitute its substance and visible form; that Congress, by the act of 1866, passed in view of the Thirteenth Amendment, before the Fourteenth was adopted, undertook to remove certain burdens and disabilities, the necessary incidents of slavery, and to secure to all citizens of every race and color, and without regard to previous servitude, those fundamental rights which are the essence of civil freedom, namely, the same right to make and enforce contracts, to sue, be parties, give evidence, and to inherit, purchase, lease, sell, and convey property as is enjoyed by white citizens; that under the Thirteenth Amendment, Congress has to do with slavery and its incidents; and that legislation, so far as necessary or proper to eradicate all forms and incidents of slavery and involuntary servitude, may be direct and primary, operating upon the acts of individuals, whether sanctioned by State legislation or not. These propositions being conceded, it is impossible, as it seems to me, to question the constitutional validity of the Civil Rights Act of 1866. I do not contend that the Thirteenth Amendment invests Congress with authority, by legislation, to define and regulate the entire body of the civil rights which citizens enjoy, or may enjoy, in the several States. But I hold that since slavery, as the court has repeatedly declared, *Slaughter-House Cases*, 16 Wall. 36; *Strauder v. West Virginia*, 100 U.S. 303, was the moving or principal cause of the adoption of that amendment, and since that institution rested wholly upon the inferiority, as a race, of those held in bondage, their freedom necessarily involved immunity from, and protection against, all discrimination against them, because of their race, in respect of such civil rights as belong to freemen of other races. Congress, therefore, under its express power to enforce that amendment, by appropriate legislation, may enact laws to protect that people against the deprivation, *because of their race*, of any civil rights granted to other freemen in the same State; and such legislation may be of a direct and primary character, operating upon States, their officers and agents, and, also, upon, at least, such individuals and corporations as exercise public functions and wield power and authority under the State.

What has been said is sufficient to show that the power of Congress under the Thirteenth Amendment is not necessarily restricted to legislation against slavery as an institution upheld by positive law, but may be exerted to the extent, at least, of protecting the liberated race against discrimination, in respect of legal rights belonging to freemen, where such discrimination is based upon race.

It remains now to inquire what are the legal rights of colored persons in respect of the accommodations, privileges and facilities of public conveyances, inns and places of public amusement?

* * *

I am of the opinion that such discrimination practiced by corporations and individuals in the exercise of their public or quasi-public functions is a badge of servitude the imposition of which Congress may prevent under its power, by appropriate legislation, to enforce the Thirteenth Amendment; and, consequently, without reference to its enlarged power under the Fourteenth Amendment, the act of March 1, 1875, is not, in my judgment, repugnant to the Constitution.

It remains now to consider these cases with reference to the power Congress has possessed since the adoption of the Fourteenth Amendment. Much that has been said as to the power of Congress under the Thirteenth Amendment is applicable to this branch of discussion, and will not be repeated.

But when, under what circumstances, and to what extent, may Congress, by means of legislation, exert its power to enforce the provisions of this amendment? The theory of the opinion of the majority of the court—the foundation upon which their reasoning seems to rest—is, that the general government cannot, in advance of hostile State laws or hostile State proceedings, actively interfere for the protection of any of the rights, privileges, and immunities secured by the Fourteenth Amendment.

The assumption that this amendment consists wholly of prohibitions upon State laws and State proceedings in hostility to its provisions, is unauthorized by its language. The first clause of the first section—"All persons born or naturalized in the United States, and subject to the jurisdiction thereof, are citizens of the United States, and of the State wherein they reside"—is of a distinctly affirmative character. In its application to the colored race, previously liberated, it created and granted, as well citizenship of the United States, as citizenship of the State in which they respectively resided. It introduced all of that race, whose ancestors had been imported and sold as slaves, at once, into the political community known as the "People of the United States." They became, instantly, citizens of the United States, *and* of their respective States. Further, they were brought, by this supreme act of the nation, within the direct operation of that provision of the Constitution which declares that "the citizens of each State shall be entitled to all privileges and immunities of citizens in the several States." Art. 4, § 2.

The citizenship thus acquired, by that race, in virtue of an affirmative grant from the nation, may be protected, not alone by the judicial branch of the government, but by congressional legislation of a primary direct character; this, because the power of Congress is not restricted to the enforcement of prohibitions upon State laws or State action. It is, in terms distinct and positive, to enforce "the *provisions* of *this article*" of amendment; not simply those of a prohibitive character, but the provisions—*all* of the provisions—affirmative and prohibitive, of the amendment. It is, therefore, a grave misconception to suppose that the fifth section of the amendment has reference exclusively to express prohibitions upon State laws or State action. If any right was created by that amendment, the grant of power, through appropriate legislation, to enforce its provisions, authorizes Congress, by means of legislation, operating throughout the entire Union, to guard, secure, and protect that right.

But what was secured to colored citizens of the United States—as between them and their respective States—by the national grant to them of State citizenship? With what rights, privileges, or immunities did this grant invest them? There is one, if there be no other—exemption from race discrimination in respect of any civil right belonging to citizens of the white race in the same State. That, surely, is their constitutional privilege when within the jurisdiction of other States. And such must be their constitutional right, in their own State, unless the recent amendments be splendid baubles, thrown out to delude those who deserved fair and generous treatment at the hands of the nation. Citizenship in this country necessarily imports at least equality of civil rights among citizens of every race in the same State. It is fundamental in American citizenship that, in respect of such rights, there shall be no discrimination by the State, or its officers, or by individuals or corporations exercising public functions or authority, against any citizen because of his race or previous condition or servitude.

But if it were conceded that the power of Congress could not be brought into activity until the rights specified in the act of 1875 had been abridged or denied by some State law or State action, I maintain that the decision of the court is erroneous. There has been adverse State action within the Fourteenth Amendment as heretofore interpreted by this court.

In every material sense applicable to the practical enforcement of the Fourteenth Amendment, railroad corporations, keepers of inns, and managers of places of public amusement are agents or instrumentalities of the State, because they are charged with duties to the public, and are amenable, in respect of their duties and functions, to governmental regulation. It seems to me that, within the principle settled in *Ex parte Virginia*, a denial, by these instrumentalities of the State, to the citizen, because of his race, of that equality of civil rights secured to him by law, is a denial by the State, within the meaning of the Fourteenth Amendment. If it be not, then that race is left, in respect of the civil rights in question, practically at the mercy of corporations and individuals wielding power under the States.

1. How does the majority describe and limit Congress' power to enact legislation under the Fourteenth Amendment? What about under the Thirteenth Amendment? Under the Commerce Clause?

2. How would Justice Harlan define Congressional power under the Thirteenth and Fourteenth Amendments? Has his view emerged as the "correct" one?

3. In *United States v. Guest*, 383 U.S. 745 (1966), the Court again confronted whether Congress may regulate private conduct under § 5 of the Fourteenth Amendment. The majority opinion avoided the issue, reasoning that: "the indictment in fact contains an express allegation of state involvement sufficient at least to require the denial of a motion to dismiss." In a concurring opinion authored by Justice Clark, three Justices asserted "that there now can be no doubt that the specific language of § 5 empowers the Congress to enact laws punishing all conspiracies—with or without state action— that interfere with Fourteenth Amendment rights."

Justice Brennan, joined by two others, explained that together with Clark's opinion: "A majority of the members of the Court expresses the view today that § 5 empowers Congress to enact laws punishing *all* conspiracies to interfere with the exercise of Fourteenth Amendment rights, whether or not state officers or others acting under the color of state law are implicated in the conspiracy," thereby rejecting the interpretation of § 5 found in the *Civil Rights Cases*: "Viewed in its proper perspective, § 5 of the Fourteenth Amendment appears as a positive grant of legislative power, authorizing Congress to exercise its discretion in fashioning remedies to achieve civil and political equality for all citizens."

Thirty-four years later, however, in **United States v. Morrison**, 529 U.S. 598 (2000), the Supreme Court expressly rejected the argument that *Guest* overruled the *Civil Rights Cases*:

> To accept petitioners' argument, . . . one must add to the three Justices joining Justice Brennan's reasoned explanation for his belief that the *Civil Rights Cases* were wrongly decided, the three Justices joining Justice Clark's opinion who gave no explanation whatever for their similar view. This is simply not the way that reasoned constitutional adjudication proceeds. We accordingly have no hesitation in saying that it would take more than the naked dicta contained in Justice Clark's opinion, when added to Justice Brennan's opinion, to cast any doubt upon the enduring vitality of the *Civil Rights Cases* . . .

JONES V. ALFRED H. MAYER CO.
392 U.S. 409 (1968)

Mr. Justice STEWART delivered the opinion of the Court.

In this case we are called upon to determine the scope and the constitutionality of an Act of Congress, 42 U.S.C. § 1982, which provides that:

> All citizens of the United States shall have the same right, in every State and Territory, as is enjoyed by white citizens thereof to inherit, purchase, lease, sell, hold and convey real and personal property.

The remaining question is whether Congress has power under the Constitution to do what § 1982 purports to do: to prohibit all racial discrimination, private and public, in the sale and rental of property. Our starting point is the Thirteenth Amendment, for it was pursuant to that constitutional provision that Congress originally enacted what is now § 1982. The Amendment consists of two parts. Section 1 states:

> Neither slavery nor involuntary servitude, except as a punishment for crime whereof the party shall have been duly convicted, shall exist within the United States, or any place subject to their jurisdiction.

Section 2 provides: "Congress shall have power to enforce this article by appropriate legislation."

As its text reveals, the Thirteenth Amendment "is not a mere prohibition of State laws establishing or upholding slavery, but an absolute declaration that slavery or involuntary servitude shall not exist in any part of the United States." *Civil Rights Cases*, 109 U.S. 3, 20. It has never been doubted, therefore, "that the power vested in Congress to enforce the article by appropriate legislation," includes the power to enact laws "direct and primary, operating upon the acts of individuals, whether sanctioned by State legislation or not."

Thus, the fact that § 1982 operates upon the unofficial acts of private individuals, whether or not sanctioned by state law, presents no constitutional problem. If Congress has power under the Thirteenth Amendment to eradicate conditions that prevent Negroes from buying and renting property because of their race or color, then no federal statute calculated to achieve that objective can be thought to exceed the constitutional power of Congress simply because it reached beyond state action to regulate the conduct of private individuals. The constitutional question in this case, therefore, comes to this: Does the authority of Congress to enforce the Thirteenth Amendment "by appropriate legislation" include the power to eliminate all racial barriers to the acquisition of real and personal property? We think the answer to that question is plainly yes.

Surely Congress has the power under the Thirteenth Amendment rationally to determine what are the badges and the incidents of slavery, and the authority to translate that determination into effective legislation. Nor can we say that the determination Congress has made is an irrational one. For this Court recognized long ago that, whatever else they may have encompassed, the badges and incidents of slavery—its "burdens and disabilities"—included restraints upon "those fundamental rights which are the essence of civil freedom, namely, the same right ... to inherit, purchase, lease, sell and convey property, as is enjoyed by white citizens." *Civil Rights Cases*, 109 U.S. 3, 22. Just as the Black Codes, enacted after the Civil War to restrict the free exercise of those rights, were substitutes for the slave system, so the exclusion of Negroes from white communities became a substitute for the Black Codes. And when racial discrimination herds men into ghettos and makes their ability to buy property turn on the color of their skin, then it too is a relic of slavery.

Representative Wilson of Iowa was the floor manager in the House for the Civil Rights Act of 1866. In urging that Congress had ample authority to pass the pending bill, he recalled the celebrated words of Chief Justice Marshall in *McCulloch v. Maryland*, 4 Wheat. 316, 421:

> Let the end be legitimate, let it be within the scope of the constitution, and all means which are appropriate, which are plainly adapted to that end, which are not prohibited, but consist with the letter and spirit of the constitution, are constitutional.

"The end is legitimate," the Congressman said, "because it is defined by the Constitution itself. The end is the maintenance of freedom. A man who enjoys the civil rights mentioned in this bill cannot be reduced to slavery. This settles the appropriateness of this measure, and that settles its constitutionality."

NOTES AND QUESTIONS

1. Using the *Jones* analysis, would Congress today have the power under the Thirteenth Amendment to enact the type of public accommodations law invalidated in the *Civil Rights Cases*?

2. In light of its constitutional source, can § 1982 be used to reach racial discrimination directed at Whites? Asian-Americans? Jews? Could Congress legislate under the Thirteenth Amendment to protect women from sex discrimination?

B. THE COMMERCE CLAUSE AS A SOURCE OF CONGRESSIONAL POWER

HEART OF ATLANTA MOTEL, INC. V. UNITED STATES
379 U.S. 241 (1964)

Mr. Justice CLARK delivered the opinion of the Court.

This is a declaratory judgment action attacking the constitutionality of Title II of the Civil Rights Act of 1964 [42 U.S.C. § 2000a].

This Title is divided into seven sections beginning with § 201(a) which provides that:

> All persons shall be entitled to the full and equal enjoyment of the goods, services, facilities, privileges, advantages, and accommodations of any place of public accommodation, as defined in this section, without discrimination or segregation on the ground of race, color, religion, or national origin.

There are listed in § 201(b) four classes of business establishments, each of which "serves the public" and "is a place of public accommodation" within the meaning of § 201(a) "if its operations affect commerce, or if discrimination or segregation by it is supported by State action."

The Senate Commerce Committee made it quite clear that the fundamental object of Title II was to vindicate "the deprivation of personal dignity that surely accompanies denials of equal access to public establishments." At the same time, however, it noted that such an objective has been and could be readily achieved "by congressional action based on the commerce power of the Constitution." S. REP. No. 872. Our study of the legislative record, made in the light of prior cases, has brought us to the conclusion that Congress possessed ample power in this regard, and we have therefore not considered the other grounds relied upon.

5. The Civil Rights Cases and Their Application

In light of our ground for decision, it might be well at the outset to discuss the *Civil Rights Cases*, which declared provisions of the Civil Rights Act of 1875 unconstitutional. We think that decision inapposite, and without precedential value in determining the constitutionality of the present Act. Unlike Title II of the present legislation, the 1875 Act broadly proscribed discrimination in "inns, public conveyances on land or water, theaters, and other places of public amusement," without limiting the categories of affected businesses to those impinging upon interstate commerce. In contrast, the applicability of Title II is carefully limited to enterprises having a direct and substantial relation to the interstate flow of goods and people, except where state action is involved. Further, the fact that certain kinds of businesses may not in 1875 have been sufficiently involved in interstate commerce to warrant bringing them within the ambit of the commerce power is not necessarily dispositive of the same question today. Our populace had not reached its present mobility, nor were facilities, goods and services circulating as readily in interstate commerce as they are today. Although the principles which we apply today are those first formulated by Chief Justice Marshall in *Gibbons v. Ogden*, 9 Wheat. 1 (1824), the conditions of transportation and commerce have changed dramatically, and we must apply those principles to the present state of commerce. The sheer increase in volume of interstate traffic alone would give discriminatory practices which inhibit travel a far larger impact upon the Nation's commerce than such practices had on the economy of another day. Finally, there is language in the *Civil Rights Cases* which indicates that the Court did not fully consider whether the 1875 Act could be sustained as an exercise of the commerce power. Though the Court observed that "no one will contend that the power to pass it was contained in the Constitution before the adoption of the last three amendments [Thirteenth, Fourteenth, and Fifteenth]," the Court went on specifically to note that the Act was not "conceived" in terms of the commerce power.

6. The Basis of Congressional Action

While the Act as adopted carried no congressional findings the record of its passage through each house is replete with evidence of the burdens that discrimination by race or color places upon interstate commerce. This testimony included the fact that our people have become increasingly mobile with millions of people of all races traveling from State to State; that Negroes in particular have been the subject of discrimination in transient accommodations, having to travel great distances to secure the same; that often they have been unable to obtain accommodations and have had to call upon friends to put them up overnight, S. Rep. No. 872; and that these conditions had become so acute as to require the listing of available lodging for Negroes in a special guidebook which was itself "dramatic testimony to the difficulties" Negroes encounter in travel. Senate Commerce Committee Hearings. These exclusionary practices were found to be nationwide, the Under Secretary of Commerce testifying that there is "no question that this discrimination in the North still exists to a large degree" and in the West and Midwest as well. This testimony indicated a qualitative as well as quantitative effect on interstate travel by Negroes. The former was the obvious impairment of the Negro traveler's pleasure and convenience that resulted when he continually was uncertain of finding lodging. As for the latter, there was evidence that this uncertainty stemming from racial discrimination had the effect of discouraging travel on the part of a substantial portion of the Negro community.

7. The Power of Congress over Interstate Travel

The same interest in protecting interstate commerce which led Congress to deal with segregation in interstate carriers and the white-slave traffic has prompted it to extend the exercise of its power to gambling, to criminal enterprises, to deceptive practices in the sale of products, to fraudulent security transactions, to misbranding of drugs, to wages and hours, to members of labor unions, to crop control, to discrimination against shippers, to the protection of small business from injurious price cutting, to resale price maintenance, to professional football, and to racial discrimination by owners and managers of terminal restaurants.

That Congress was legislating against moral wrongs in many of these areas rendered its enactments no less valid. In framing Title II of this Act Congress was also dealing with what is considered a moral problem. But that fact does not detract from the overwhelming evidence of the disruptive effect that racial discrimination has had on commercial intercourse. It was this burden which empowered Congress to enact appropriate legislation, and, given this basis for the exercise of its power, Congress was not restricted by the fact that the particular obstruction to interstate commerce with which it was dealing was also deemed a moral and social wrong.

We, therefore, conclude that the action of the Congress in the adoption of the Act as applied here to a motel which concededly serves interstate travelers is within the power granted it by the Commerce Clause of the Constitution, as interpreted by this Court for 140 years. It may be argued that Congress could have pursued other methods to eliminate the obstructions it found in interstate commerce caused by racial discrimination. But this is a matter of policy that rests entirely with the Congress not with the courts. How obstructions in commerce may be removed—what means are to be employed—is within the sound and exclusive discretion of the Congress. It is subject only to one caveat—that the means chosen by it must be reasonably adapted to the end permitted by the Constitution. We cannot say that its choice here was not so adapted. The Constitution requires no more.

NOTES AND QUESTIONS

1. How is the scope of Title II different from that of the Civil Rights Act of 1875, which was invalidated in the *Civil Rights Cases*?

2. Why did Congress in the 1960's rely upon the Commerce Clause as the basis for enacting anti-discrimination legislation? What does race discrimination in public accommodations have to do with commerce? Would it make any difference in terms of coverage if the source of the Act was § 5 of the Fourteenth Amendment? Or § 2 of the Thirteenth Amendment?

LIMITATIONS ON CONGRESS'S POWER TO REACH PRIVATE CONDUCT UNDER THE COMMERCE CLAUSE:

In *U.S. v. Lopez*, 514 U.S. 549 (1995), the Court held that Congress exceeded its Commerce Clause power in passing the Gun-Free School Zone Act, which prohibited possession of a firearm within 1,000 feet of a school. The Court held that Congress must demonstrate that a regulated activity "substantially affects" interstate commerce, and here the criminal statute had nothing to do with commerce nor was possession of firearms in any way connected with a commercial transaction. The statute lacked a jurisdictional element that would require prosecutors to demonstrate a link to commerce on a case-by-case basis, and it governed in areas historically left to the state, namely criminal law enforcement and education. Further, Congress failed to make sufficient findings linking the regulated activity to interstate commerce.

UNITED STATES V. MORRISON

529 U.S. 598 (2000)

Chief Justice REHNQUIST delivered the opinion of the Court.

In these cases we consider the constitutionality of 42 U.S.C. §13981, which provides a federal civil remedy for the victims of gender- motivated violence.

I

Petitioner Christy Brzonkala enrolled at Virginia Polytechnic Institute (Virginia Tech) in the fall of 1994. In September of that year, Brzonkala met respondents Antonio Morrison and James Crawford, who were both students at Virginia Tech and members of its varsity football team. Brzonkala alleges that, within 30 minutes of meeting Morrison and Crawford, they assaulted and repeatedly raped her.

Section 13981 was part of the Violence Against Women Act of 1994. It states that "[a]ll persons within the United States shall have the right to be free from crimes of violence motivated by gender." 42 U.S.C. § 13981(b). To enforce that right, subsection (c) declares:

> A person (including a person who acts under color of any statute, ordinance, regulation, custom, or usage of any State) who commits a crime of violence motivated by gender and thus deprives another of the right declared in subsection (b) of this section shall be liable to the party injured, in an action for the recovery of compensatory and punitive damages, injunctive and declaratory relief, and such other relief as a court may deem appropriate.

Section 13981 defines a "crim[e] of violence motivated by gender" as "a crime of violence committed because of gender or on the basis of gender, and due, at least in part, to an animus based on the victim's gender." § 13981(d)(1). It also provides that the term "crime of violence" includes any

> (A) ... act or series of acts that would constitute a felony against the person or that would constitute a felony against property if the conduct presents a serious risk of physical injury to another, and that would come within the meaning of State or Federal offenses described in section 16 of Title 18, whether or not those acts have actually resulted in criminal charges, prosecution, or conviction and whether or not those acts were committed in the special maritime, territorial, or prison jurisdiction of the United States; and

(B) includes an act or series of acts that would constitute a felony described in subparagraph (A) but for the relationship between the person who takes such action and the individual against whom such action is taken.

§ 13981(d)(2).

Every law enacted by Congress must be based on one or more of its powers enumerated in the Constitution. Congress explicitly identified the sources of federal authority on which it relied in enacting § 13981. It said that a "federal civil rights cause of action" is established "[p]ursuant to the affirmative power of Congress . . . under section 5 of the Fourteenth Amendment to the Constitution, as well as under section 8 of Article I of the Constitution."

II

As we discussed at length in *Lopez*, our interpretation of the Commerce Clause has changed as our Nation has developed. We need not repeat that detailed review of the Commerce Clause's history here; it suffices to say that, in the years since *Jones & Laughlin Steel Corp.*, Congress has had considerably greater latitude in regulating conduct and transactions under the Commerce Clause than our previous case law permitted.

Lopez emphasized, however, that even under our modern, expansive interpretation of the Commerce Clause, Congress' regulatory authority is not without effective bounds. . . . As we observed in *Lopez*, modern Commerce Clause jurisprudence has "identified three broad categories of activity that Congress may regulate under its commerce power. . . . First, Congress may regulate the use of the channels of interstate commerce. . . . Second, Congress is empowered to regulate and protect the instrumentalities of interstate commerce, or persons or things in interstate commerce, even though the threat may come only from intrastate activities. . . . Finally, Congress' commerce authority includes the power to regulate those activities having a substantial relation to interstate commerce, i.e., those activities that substantially affect interstate commerce."

Petitioners do not contend that these cases fall within either of the first two of these categories of Commerce Clause regulation. They seek to sustain § 13981 as a regulation of activity that substantially affects interstate commerce.

In *Lopez*, we held that the Gun-Free School Zones Act of 1990, 18 U.S.C. § 922(q)(1)(A), which made it a federal crime to knowingly possess a firearm in a school zone, exceeded Congress' authority under the Commerce Clause . . . we observed that § 922(q) was "a criminal statute that by its terms has nothing to do with 'commerce' or any sort of economic enterprise, however broadly one might define those terms." Both petitioners and Justice SOUTER's dissent downplay the role that the economic nature of the regulated activity plays in our Commerce Clause analysis. But a fair reading of *Lopez* shows that the noneconomic, criminal nature of the conduct at issue was central to our decision in that case. *Lopez*'s review of Commerce Clause case law demonstrates that in those cases where we have sustained federal regulation of intrastate activity based upon the activity's substantial effects on interstate commerce, the activity in question has been some sort of economic endeavor.

The second consideration that we found important in analyzing § 922(q) was that the statute contained "no express jurisdictional element which might limit its reach to a discrete set of firearm possessions that additionally have an explicit connection with or effect on interstate commerce." Third, we noted that neither § 922(q) "'nor its legislative history contain[s] express congressional findings regarding the effects upon interstate commerce of gun possession in a school zone.'" Finally, our decision in *Lopez* rested in part on the fact that the link between gun possession and a substantial effect on interstate commerce was attenuated.

With these principles underlying our Commerce Clause jurisprudence as reference points, the proper resolution of the present cases is clear. Gender- motivated crimes of violence are not, in any sense of the phrase, economic activity. While we need not adopt a categorical rule against aggregating the effects of any noneconomic activity in order to decide these cases, thus far in our Nation's history our cases have upheld Commerce Clause regulation of intrastate activity only where that activity is economic in nature.

Like the Gun-Free School Zones Act at issue in *Lopez*, § 13981 contains no jurisdictional element establishing that the federal cause of action is in pursuance of Congress' power to regulate interstate commerce. Although *Lopez* makes clear that such a jurisdictional element would lend support to the argument that § 13981 is sufficiently tied to interstate commerce, Congress elected to cast § 13981's remedy over a wider, and more purely intrastate, body of violent crime.

In contrast with the lack of congressional findings that we faced in *Lopez*, § 13981 *is* supported by numerous findings regarding the serious impact that gender-motivated violence has on victims and their families. But the existence of congressional findings is not sufficient, by itself, to sustain the constitutionality of Commerce Clause legislation. As we stated in *Lopez*, "'[S]imply because Congress may conclude that a particular activity substantially affects interstate commerce does not necessarily make it so.'" Rather, "'[w]hether particular operations affect interstate commerce sufficiently to come under the constitutional power of Congress to regulate them is ultimately a judicial rather than a legislative question, and can be settled finally only by this Court.'"

In these cases, Congress' findings are substantially weakened by the fact that they rely so heavily on a method of reasoning that we have already rejected as unworkable if we are to maintain the Constitution's enumeration of powers. Congress found that gender-motivated violence affects interstate commerce:

> by deterring potential victims from traveling interstate, from engaging in employment in interstate business, and from transacting with business, and in places involved in inter state commerce; . . . by diminishing national productivity, increasing medical and other costs, and decreasing the supply of and the demand for interstate products.

Given these findings and petitioners' arguments, the concern that we expressed in *Lopez* that Congress might use the Commerce Clause to completely obliterate the Constitution's distinction between national and local authority seems well founded. The reasoning that petitioners advance seeks to follow the but-for causal chain from the initial occurrence of violent crime (the suppression of which has always been the prime object of the States' police power) to every attenuated effect upon interstate commerce. If accepted, petitioners' reasoning would allow Congress to regulate any crime as long as the nationwide, aggregated impact of that crime has substantial effects on employment, production, transit, or consumption. Indeed, if Congress may regulate gender-motivated violence, it would be able to regulate murder or any other type of violence since gender- motivated violence, as a subset of all violent crime, is certain to have lesser economic impacts than the larger class of which it is a part.

We accordingly reject the argument that Congress may regulate noneconomic, violent criminal conduct based solely on that conduct's aggregate effect on interstate commerce. The Constitution requires a distinction between what is truly national and what is truly local. In recognizing this fact we preserve one of the few principles that has been consistent since the Clause was adopted. The regulation and punishment of intrastate violence that is not directed at the instrumentalities, channels, or goods involved in interstate commerce has always been the province of the States.

[Justice THOMAS wrote a concurring opinion. He would explicitly reject the "substantial effects" test as inconsistent with the original understanding of Congress's power, and as failing to sufficiently protect state sovereignty.]

Justice SOUTER, with whom Justice STEVENS, Justice GINSBURG, and Justice BREYER join, dissenting.

The business of the courts is to review the congressional assessment, not for soundness but simply for the rationality of concluding that a jurisdictional basis exists in fact. Any explicit findings that Congress chooses to make, though not dispositive of the question of rationality, may advance judicial review by identifying factual authority on which Congress relied.

One obvious difference from *Lopez* is the mountain of data assembled by Congress, here showing the effects of violence against women on interstate commerce. Passage of the Act in 1994 was preceded by four years of hearings, which included testimony from physicians and law professors; from survivors of rape and domestic violence; and from representatives of state law enforcement and private business. The record includes reports on gender bias from task forces in 21 States, and we have the benefit of specific factual findings in the eight separate Reports issued by Congress and its committees over the long course leading to enactment. . . .[T]he sufficiency of the evidence before Congress to provide a rational basis for the finding cannot seriously be questioned. Indeed, the legislative record here is far more voluminous than the record compiled by Congress and found sufficient in two prior cases upholding Title II of the Civil Rights Act of 1964 against Commerce Clause challenges.

The fact that the Act does not pass muster before the Court today is therefore proof, to a degree that *Lopez* was not, that the Court's nominal adherence to the substantial effects test is merely that. Although a new jurisprudence has not emerged with any distinctness, it is clear that some congressional conclusions about obviously substantial, cumulative effects on commerce are being assigned lesser values than the once-stable doctrine would assign them. These devaluations are accomplished not by any express repudiation of the substantial effects test or its application through the aggregation of individual conduct, but by supplanting rational basis scrutiny with a new criterion of review.

Thus, the elusive heart of the majority's analysis in these cases is its statement that Congress' findings of fact are "weakened" by the presence of a disfavored "method of reasoning." This seems to suggest that the "substantial effects" analysis is not a factual enquiry, for Congress in the first instance with subsequent judicial review looking only to the rationality of the congressional conclusion, but one of a rather different sort, dependent upon a uniquely judicial competence.

The collective opinion of state officials that the Act was needed continues virtually unchanged, and when the Civil Rights Remedy was challenged in court, the States came to its defense. Thirty-six of them . . . have filed an amicus brief in support of petitioners in these cases, and only one State has taken respondents' side. It is, then, not the least irony of these cases that the States will be forced to enjoy the new federalism whether they want it or not.

NOTES AND QUESTIONS

1. Can the constitutional defect identified in *Morrison* be cured by restricting the law to gender biased crimes perpetrated with a weapon that has moved in interstate commerce? Or where assailants crossed state lines to attack their victims? Does it make sense to assess federalism concerns by such a wooden measure as the "jurisdictional hook"?

2. Is "federalism" really a problem where the attorneys general of 36 states saw the need for a national law and supported the Act? Does VAWA really intrude on state sovereignty?

PROBLEM: ONE

The 1994 Freedom of Access to Clinic Entrances Act imposes civil and criminal penalties against anyone who: "(1) by force or threat of force or by physical obstruction, intentionally injures, intimidates or interferes with or attempts to injure, intimidate, or interfere with any person because that person is or has been, or in order to intimidate such person or any other person or any class of persons from, obtaining or providing reproductive health services; . . . or (3) intentionally damages or destroys the property of a facility, or attempts to do so, because such a facility provides reproductive health services . . . ." 18 U.S.C. § 248(a).

Congress found that doctors and patients often travel across state lines to provide and receive services; in other words, there is an interstate market both with respect to patients and doctors. In addition, the clinics receive supplies through interstate commerce. Congress further found that violence, and physical obstruction of clinic entrances, threatened interstate commerce in the provision of reproductive services. Thus, FACE protects and regulates commercial enterprises operating in interstate commerce. Set forth briefly the arguments for and against congressional authority to enact this law.

C. CONGRESSIONAL POWER TO EXPAND CONSTITUTIONAL GUARANTEES UNDER THE CIVIL WAR AMENDMENTS

KATZENBACH V. MORGAN
384 U.S. 641 (1966)

Mr. Justice BRENNAN delivered the opinion of the Court.

These cases concern the Constitutionality of § 4(e) of the Voting Rights Act of 1965. That law, in the respects pertinent in these cases, provides that no person who has successfully completed the sixth primary grade in a public school in, or a private school accredited by, the Commonwealth of Puerto Rico in which the language of instruction was other than English shall be denied the right to vote in any election because of his inability to read or write English. Appellees, registered voters in New York City, brought this suit to challenge the constitutionality of § 4(e) insofar as it *pro tanto* prohibits the enforcement of the election laws of New York requiring an ability to read and write English as a condition of voting. Under these laws many of the several hundred thousand New York City residents who have migrated there from the Commonwealth of Puerto Rico had previously been denied the right to vote, and appellees attack § 4(e) insofar as it would enable many of these citizens to vote. Pursuant to § 14(b) of the Voting Rights Act of 1965, appellees commenced this proceeding in the District Court for the District of Columbia seeking a declaration that § 4(e) is invalid and an injunction prohibiting appellants, the Attorney General of the United States and the New York City Board of Elections, from either enforcing or complying with § 4(e).

We hold that, in the application challenged in these cases, § 4(e) is a proper exercise of the powers granted to Congress by § 5 of the Fourteenth Amendment and that by force of the Supremacy Clause, Article VI, the New York English literacy requirement cannot be enforced to the extent that it is inconsistent with § 4(e).

The Attorney General of the State of New York argues that an exercise of congressional power under § 5 of the Fourteenth Amendment that prohibits the enforcement of a state law can only be sustained if the judicial branch determines that the state law is prohibited by the provisions of the Amendment that Congress sought to enforce. More specifically, he urges that § 4(e) cannot be sustained as appropriate legislation to enforce the Equal Protection Clause unless the judiciary decides—even with the guidance of a congressional judgment—that the application of the English literacy requirement prohibited by § 4(e) is forbidden by the Equal Protection Clause itself. We disagree. Neither the language nor history of § 5 supports such a construction. As was said with regard to § 5 in *Ex parte Virginia*, 100 U.S. 339, 345, "It is the power of Congress which has been enlarged. Congress is authorized to *enforce* the prohibitions by appropriate legislation. Some legislation is contemplated to make the amendments fully effective." A construction of § 5 that would require a judicial determination that the enforcement of the state law precluded by Congress violated the Amendment, as a condition of sustaining the congressional enactment, would depreciate both congressional resourcefulness and congressional responsibility for implementing the Amendment. It would confine the legislative power in this context to the insignificant role of abrogating only those state laws that the judicial branch was prepared to adjudge unconstitutional, or of merely informing the judgment of the judiciary by particularizing the "majestic generalities" of § 1 of the Amendment.

Thus our task in this case is not to determine whether the New York English literacy requirement as applied to deny the right to vote to a person who successfully completed the sixth grade in a Puerto Rican school violates the Equal Protection Clause. Accordingly, our decision in *Lassiter v. Northampton Election Bd.*, 360 U.S. 45, sustaining the North Carolina English literacy requirement as not in all circumstances prohibited by the first sections of the Fourteenth and Fifteenth Amendments, is inapposite.

Lassiter did not present the question before us here: Without regard to whether the judiciary would find that the Equal Protection Clause itself nullifies New York's English literacy requirement as so applied, could Congress prohibit the enforcement of the state law by legislating under § 5 of the Fourteenth Amendment? In answering this question, our task is limited to determining whether such legislation is, as required by § 5, appropriate legislation to enforce the Equal Protection Clause.

By including § 5 the draftsmen sought to grant to Congress, by a specific provision applicable to the Fourteenth Amendment, the same broad powers expressed in the Necessary and Proper Clause, Art. I, § 8, cl. 18. The classic formulation of the reach of those powers was established by Chief Justice Marshall in *McCulloch v. Maryland*, 4 Wheat. 316, 421:

> Let the end be legitimate, let it be within the scope of the constitution, and all means which are appropriate, which are plainly adapted to that end, which are not prohibited, but consist with the letter and spirit of the constitution, are constitutional. . . .

We therefore proceed to the consideration whether § 4(e) is "appropriate legislation" to enforce the Equal Protection Clause, that is, under the *McCulloch v. Maryland* standard, whether § 4(e) may be regarded as an enactment to enforce the Equal Protection Clause, whether it is "plainly adapted to that end" and whether it is not prohibited by but is consistent with "the letter and spirit of the constitution."[10]

---

10 Contrary to the suggestion of the dissent, § 5 does not grant Congress power to exercise discretion in the other direction and to enact "statutes so as in effect to dilute equal protection and due process decisions of this Court." We emphasize that Congress' power under § 5 is limited to adopting measures to enforce the guarantees of the Amendment; § 5 grants Congress no power to restrict, abrogate, or dilute these guarantees. Thus, for example, an enactment authorizing the States to establish racially segregated systems of education would not be—as required by § 5—a measure "to enforce" the Equal Protection Clause since that clause of its own force prohibits such state laws.

There can be no doubt that § 4(e) may be regarded as an enactment to enforce the Equal Protection Clause. Congress explicitly declared that it enacted § (4)(e) "to secure the rights under the fourteenth amendment of persons educated in American-flag schools in which the predominant classroom language was other than English." The persons referred to include those who have migrated from the Commonwealth of Puerto Rico to New York and who have been denied the right to vote because of their inability to read and write English, and the Fourteenth Amendment rights referred to include those emanating from the Equal Protection Clause. More specifically, § 4(e) may be viewed as a measure to secure for the Puerto Rican community residing in New York non-discriminatory treatment by government—both in the imposition of voting qualifications and the provision or administration of governmental services, such as public schools, public housing and law enforcement.

Section 4(e) may be readily seen as "plainly adapted" to furthering these aims of the Equal Protection Clause. The practical effect of § 4(e) is to prohibit New York from denying the right to vote to large segments of its Puerto Rican community. Congress has thus prohibited the State from denying to that community the right that is "preservative of all rights." This enhanced political power will be helpful in gaining nondiscriminatory treatment in public services for the entire Puerto Rican community. Section 4(e) thereby enables the Puerto Rican minority better to obtain "perfect equality of civil rights and the equal protection of the laws." It was well within congressional authority to say that this need of the Puerto Rican minority for the vote warranted federal intrusion upon any state interests served by the English literacy requirement. It was for Congress, as the branch that made this judgment, to assess and weigh the various conflicting considerations—the risk or pervasiveness of the discrimination in governmental services, the effectiveness of eliminating the state restriction on the right to vote as a means of dealing with the evil, the adequacy or availability of alternative remedies, and the nature and significance of the state interests that would be affected by the nullification of the English literacy requirement as applied to residents who have successfully completed the sixth grade in a Puerto Rican school. It is not for us to review the congressional resolution of these factors. It is enough that we be able to perceive a basis upon which the Congress might resolve the conflict as it did. There plainly was such a basis to support § 4(e) in the application in question in this case. Any contrary conclusion would require us to be blind to the realities familiar to the legislators.

The result is no different if we confine our inquiry to the question whether § 4(e) was merely legislation aimed at the elimination of an invidious discrimination in establishing voter qualifications. We are told that New York's English literacy requirement originated in the desire to provide an incentive for non-English speaking immigrants to learn the English language and in order to assure the intelligent exercise of the franchise. Yet Congress might well have questioned, in light of the many exemptions provided, and some evidence suggesting that prejudice played a prominent role in the enactment of the requirement, whether these were actually the interests being served. Congress might have also questioned whether denial of a right deemed so precious and fundamental in our society was a necessary or appropriate means of encouraging persons to learn English, or of furthering the goal of an intelligent exercise of the franchise. Finally, Congress might well have concluded that as a means of furthering the intelligent exercise of the franchise, an ability to read or understand Spanish is as effective as ability to read English for those to whom Spanish-language newspapers and Spanish-language radio and television programs are available to inform them of election issues and governmental affairs. Since Congress undertook to legislate so as to preclude the enforcement of the state law, and did so in the context of a general appraisal of literacy requirements for voting to which it brought a specially informed legislative competence, it was Congress' prerogative to weigh these competing considerations. Here again, it is enough that we perceive a basis upon which Congress might predicate a judgment that the application of New York's English literacy requirement to deny the right to vote to a person with a sixth grade education in Puerto Rican schools in which the language of instruction was other than English constituted an invidious discrimination in violation of the Equal Protection Clause.

We therefore conclude that § 4(e), in the application challenged in this case, is appropriate legislation to enforce the Equal Protection Clause.

Mr. Justice HARLAN, whom Mr. Justice STEWART joins, dissenting.

The Court declares that since § 5 of the Fourteenth Amendment gives to the Congress power to "enforce" the prohibitions of the Amendment by "appropriate" legislation, the test for judicial review of any congressional determination in this area is simply one of rationality; that is, in effect, was Congress acting rationally in declaring that the New York statute is irrational? Although § 5 most certainly does give to the Congress wide powers in the field of devising remedial legislation to effectuate the Amendment's prohibition on arbitrary state action, . . . I believe the Court has confused the issue of how much enforcement power Congress possesses under § 5 with the distinct issue of what questions are appropriate for congressional determination and what questions are essentially judicial in nature.

When recognized state violations of federal constitutional standards have occurred, Congress is of course empowered by § 5 to take appropriate remedial measures to redress and prevent the wrongs. But it is a judicial question whether the condition with which Congress has thus sought to deal is in truth an infringement of the Constitution, something that is the necessary prerequisite to bringing the § 5 power into play at all.

The question here is not whether the statute is appropriate remedial legislation to cure an established violation of a constitutional command, but whether there has in fact been an infringement of that constitutional command, that is, whether a particular state practice or, as here, a statute, is so arbitrary or irrational as to offend the command of the Equal Protection Clause of the Fourteenth Amendment. That question is one for the judicial branch ultimately to determine. Were the rule otherwise, Congress would be able to qualify this Court's constitutional decisions under the Fourteenth and Fifteenth Amendments, let alone those under other provisions of the Constitution, by resorting to congressional power under the Necessary and Proper Clause. In view of this Court's holding in *Lassiter* that an English literacy test is a permissible exercise of state supervision over its franchise, I do not think it is open to Congress to limit the effect of that decision as it has undertaken to do by § 4(e). In effect the Court reads § 5 of the Fourteenth Amendment as giving Congress the power to define the *substantive* scope of the Amendment. If that indeed be the true reach of § 5, then I do not see why Congress should not be able as well to exercise its § 5 "discretion" by enacting statutes so as in effect to dilute equal protection and due process decisions of this Court. In all such cases there is room for reasonable men to differ as to whether or not a denial of equal protection or due process has occurred, and the final decision is one of judgment. Until today this judgment has always been one for the judiciary to resolve. . . .

In assessing the deference we should give to this kind of congressional expression of policy, it is relevant that the judiciary has always given to congressional enactments a presumption of validity. However, it is also a canon of judicial review that state statutes are given a similar presumption. Whichever way this case is decided, one statute will be rendered inoperative in whole or in part, and although it has been suggested that this Court should give somewhat more deference to Congress than to a state legislature, such a simple weighing of presumptions is hardly a satisfying way of resolving a matter that touches the distribution of state and federal power in an area so sensitive as that of the regulation of the franchise. Rather it should be recognized that while the Fourteenth Amendment is a "brooding omnipresence" over all state legislation, the substantive matter which it touches are all within the primary legislative competence of the States. Federal authority, legislative no less than judicial, does not intrude unless there has been a denial by state action of Fourteenth Amendment limitations, in this instance a denial of equal protection. At least in the area of primary state concern a state statute that passes constitutional muster under the judicial standard of rationality should not be permitted to be set at naught by a mere contrary congressional pronouncement unsupported by a legislative record justifying that conclusion.

To deny the effectiveness of this congressional enactment is not of course to disparage Congress' exertion of authority in the field of civil rights; it is simply to recognize that the Legislative Branch like the other branches of federal authority is subject to the governmental boundaries set by the Constitution. To hold, on this record, that § 4(e) overrides the New York literacy requirement seems to me tantamount to allowing the Fourteenth Amendment to swallow the State's constitutionally ordained primary authority in this field. For if Congress by what, as here, amounts to mere *ipse dixit* can set that otherwise permissible requirement partially at naught I see no reason why it could not also substitute its judgment for that of the States in other fields of their exclusive primary competence as well.

NOTES AND QUESTIONS

1. Does this decision in effect overrule Lassiter?

2. Assume that there had been a previous challenge to the New York election law by the Puerto Rican community and that the Supreme Court had sustained the use of literacy tests as non-discriminatory. Could Congress have legislated to prohibit this practice? Explain.

3. Does the majority generally support Congressional power to reinterpret the Constitution, e.g., to pass a law which prohibits busing to achieve racial integration or to allow prayer in the schools, contrary to Supreme Court decisions on these questions? The Supreme Court has held that at least certain types of affirmative action programs do not violate the Fourteenth Amendment. Could Congress nonetheless conclude that they violate "the spirit" of the amendment, and thus pass a law prohibiting states from enacting any affirmative action program?

Carefully review footnote 10 in responding to these questions. Is the distinction between "expanding" and "contracting" constitutional rights workable?

CITY OF ROME V. UNITED STATES
446 U.S. 156 (1980)

Mr. Justice MARSHALL delivered the opinion of the Court.

At issue in this case is the constitutionality of the Voting Rights Act of 1965 and its applicability to electoral changes and annexations made by the City of Rome, Ga.

Section 5 of the Voting Rights Act of 1965 requires preclearance by the Attorney General or the United States District Court for the District of Columbia of any change in a "standard, practice, or procedure with respect to voting," 42 U.S.C. § 1973c, made after November 1, 1964, by jurisdictions that fall within the coverage formula set forth in § 4(b) of the Act, 42 U.S.C. § 1973b(b). In 1965, the Attorney General designated Georgia a covered jurisdiction under the Act, and the municipalities of that State must therefore comply with the preclearance procedure.

The District Court found that the disapproved electoral changes and annexations had not been made for any discriminatory purpose, but did have a discriminatory effect. . . . The Court's treatment in *South Carolina v. Katzenbach* of the Act's ban on literacy tests demonstrates that, under the Fifteenth Amendment, Congress may prohibit voting practices that have only a discriminatory effect. The Court has earlier held in *Lassiter* that the use of a literacy test that was fair on its face and was not employed in a discriminatory fashion did not violate § 1 of the Fifteenth Amendment. In upholding the Act's *per se* ban on such tests in *South Carolina v. Katzenbach*, the Court found no reason to overrule *Lassiter*. Instead, the Court recognized that the prohibition was an appropriate method of enforcing the Fifteenth Amendment because for many years most of the covered jurisdictions had imposed such tests to effect voting discrimination and the continued use of even nondiscriminatory, fairly administered literacy tests would "freeze the effect" of past discrimination by allowing white illiterates to remain on the voting rolls while excluding illiterate Negroes. *South Carolina v. Katzenbach*. This holding makes clear that Congress may, under the authority of § 2 of the Fifteenth Amendment, prohibit state action that, though in itself not violative of § 1, perpetuates the effects of past discrimination.

1. If the City of Rome had redrawn its voting districts for racially neutral reasons, could the Court have found a Fifteenth Amendment violation based on adverse effect? If not, how can Congress, acting under the enforcement provision of the Fifteenth Amendment, forbid the City's action?

2. More generally, should Congress be permitted to prohibit practices which the Supreme Court has held do not offend the Constitution? Since the Court has held that the Equal Protection guarantee forbids only intentional discriminatory practices, how is Congress "enforcing" that provision when it bans a practice that lacks such impermissible motivation?

CITY OF BOERNE V. FLORES
521 u.s. 507 (1997).

Justice KENNEDY delivered the opinion of the Court.

A decision by local zoning authorities to deny a church a building permit was challenged under the Religious Freedom Restoration Act of 1993 (RFRA), 42 U.S. C.A. § 2000bb *et. seq.* The case calls into question the authority of Congress to enact RFRA. We conclude the statute exceeds Congress' power.

II

Congress enacted RFRA in direct response to the Court's decision in *Employment Div. Dept. of Human Resources of Ore. v. Smith* (1990). There we considered a Free Exercise Clause Claim brought by members of the Native American Church who were denied unemployment benefits when they lost their jobs because they had used peyote. Their practice was to ingest peyote for sacramental purposes, and they challenged an Oregon statute of general applicability which made use of the drug criminal. In evaluating the claim, we declined to apply the balancing test set forth in *Sherbert v. Verner* (1963), under which we would have asked whether Oregon's prohibition substantially burdened a religious practice, and, if it did, whether the burden was justified by a compelling government interest . . . . The application of the *Sherbert* test, the *Smith* decision explained, would have produced an anomaly in the law, a constitutional right to ignore neutral laws of general applicability . . . *Smith* held that neutral, generally applicable laws may be applied to religious practices even when not supported by a compelling governmental interest.

Four members of the Court disagreed. They argued the law placed a substantial burden on the Native American church members so that it could be upheld only if the law served a compelling state interest and was narrowly tailored to achieve that end. . .

These points of constitutional interpretation were debated by Members of Congress in hearings and floor debates. Many criticized the Court's reasoning, and this disagreement resulted in the passage of RFRA. Congress announced:

(1) [T]he framers of the Constitution, recognizing free exercise of religion as an unalienable right, secured its protection in the First Amendment to the Constitution;

(2) laws 'neutral' toward religion may burden religious exercise as surely as laws intended to interfere with religious exercise;

(3) governments should not substantially burden religious exercise without compelling justification;

(4) in *Employment Division v. Smith*, the Supreme Court virtually eliminated the requirement that the government justify burdens on religious exercise imposed by laws neutral toward religion; and

(5) the compelling interest test as set forth in prior Federal court rulings is a workable test for striking sensible balances between religious liberty and competing prior governmental interests.
42 U.S.C. § 2000bb(a).

The Act's stated purposes are:

(1) to restore the compelling interest test as set forth in Sherbert v. Verner and to guarantee its application in all cases where free exercise of religion is substantially burdened; and

(2) to provide a claim or defense to persons whose religious exercise is substantially burdened by government.

RFRA prohibits "[g]overnment from "substantially burden[ing]" a person's exercise of religion even if the burden results from a rule of general applicability unless the government can demonstrate the burden "(1) is in furtherance of a compelling governmental interest; and (2) is the least restrictive means of furthering that compelling governmental interest." The Act's mandate applies to any "branch, department, agency, instrumentality, and official (or any other person acting under color of law) of the United States," as well as to any "State, or . . . subdivision of a State." The Act's universal coverage is confirmed in § 2000bb-3(a), under which RFRA "applies to all Federal and State law, and the implementation of that law, whether mandatory or otherwise, and whether adopted before or after [RFRA's enactment]." In accordance with RFRA's usage of the term, we shall use "state law" to include local and municipal ordinances.

III

A

. . . Congress relied on its Fourteenth Amendment enforcement power in enacting the most far reaching and substantial of RFRA's provisions, those which impose its requirements on the States . . . . The parties disagree over whether RFRA is a proper exercise of Congress' § 5 power "to enforce" by "appropriate legislation" the constitutional guarantee that no State shall deprive any person of "life, liberty, or property, without due process of law" nor deny any person "equal protection of the laws."

In defense of the Act respondent contends, with support from the United States as *amicus*, that RFRA is permissible enforcement legislation. Congress, it is said, is only protecting by legislation one of the liberties guaranteed by the Fourteenth Amendment's Due Process Clause, the free exercise of religion, beyond what is necessary under *Smith*. It is said the congressional decision to dispense with proof of deliberate or overt discrimination and instead concentrate on a law's effects accords with the settled understanding that § 5 includes the power to enact legislation designed to prevent as well as remedy constitutional violations. It is further contended that Congress' § 5 power is not limited to remedial or preventive legislation.

All must acknowledge that § 5 is "a positive grant of legislative power" to Congress. Legislation which deters or remedies constitutional violations can fall within the sweep of Congress' enforcement power even if in the process it prohibits conduct which is not itself unconstitutional and intrudes into "legislative spheres of autonomy previously reserved to the States." For example, the Court upheld a suspension of literacy tests and similar voting requirements under Congress' parallel power to enforce the provisions of the Fifteenth Amendment, see U.S. Const. amend. XV, § 2, as a measure to combat racial discrimination in voting, *South Carolina v. Katzenbach*, despite the facial constitutionality of the tests under *Lassiter v. Northampton County Bd. of Elections, City of Rome v. United States* (upholding 7-year extension of the Voting Rights Act's requirement that certain jurisdictions preclear any change to a "'standard, practice, or procedure with respect to voting'").

Congress' power under § 5, however, extends only to "enforc[ing]" the provisions of the Fourteenth Amendment. The Court has described this power as "remedial," *South Carolina v. Katzenbach*. The design of the Amendment and the text of § 5 are inconsistent with the suggestion that Congress has the power to decree the substance of the Fourteenth Amendment's restrictions on States. Legislation which alters the meaning of the Free Exercise Clause cannot be said to be enforcing the Clause . . .

While the line between measures that remedy or prevent unconstitutional actions and measures that make a substantive change in the governing law is not easy to discern, and Congress must have wide latitude in determining where it lies, the distinction exists and must be observed. There must be a congruence and proportionality between the injury to be prevented or remedied and the means adopted to that end. Lacking such a connection, legislation may become substantive in operation and effect. History and our case law support drawing the distinction, one apparent from the text of the Amendment . . .

The remedial and preventive nature of Congress' enforcement power, and the limitation inherent in the power, were confirmed in our earliest cases on the Fourteenth Amendment. In the *Civil Rights Cases*, the Court invalidated sections of the Civil Rights Act of 1875 which prescribed criminal penalties for denying to any person "the full enjoyment of" public accommodations and conveyances, on the grounds that it exceeded Congress' power by seeking to regulate private conduct. The Enforcement Clause, the Court said, did not authorize Congress to pass "general legislation upon the rights of the citizen, but corrective legislation; that is, such as may be necessary and proper for counteracting such laws as the States may adopt or enforce, and which, by the amendment, they are prohibited from making or enforcing . . . ."

There is language in our opinion in *Katzenbach v. Morgan* which could be interpreted as acknowledging a power in Congress to enact legislation that expands the rights contained in § 1 of the Fourteenth Amendment. This is not a necessary interpretation, however, or even the best one . . . . If Congress could define its own powers by altering the Fourteenth Amendment's meaning, no longer would the Constitution be "superior paramount law, unchangeable by ordinary means." It would be "on a level with ordinary legislative acts, and, like other acts, . . . alterable when the legislature shall please to alter it." *Marbury v. Madison*. Under this approach, it is difficult to conceive of a principle that would limit congressional power.

B

Respondent contends that RFRA is a proper exercise of Congress' remedial or preventive power. The Act, it is said, is a reasonable means of protecting the free exercise of religion as defined by *Smith*. It prevents and remedies laws which are enacted with the unconstitutional object of targeting religious beliefs and practices. To avoid the difficulty of proving such violations, it is said, Congress can simply invalidate any law which imposes a substantial burden on a religious practice unless it is justified by a compelling interest and is the least restrictive means of accomplishing that interest. If Congress can prohibit laws with discriminatory effects in order to prevent racial discrimination in violation of the Equal Protection Clause, then it can do the same, respondent argues, to promote religious liberty.

While preventive rules are sometimes appropriate remedial measures, there must be a congruence between the means used and the ends to be achieved. The appropriateness of remedial measures must be considered in light of the evil presented. Strong measures appropriate to address one harm may be an unwarranted response to another, lesser one.

A comparison between RFRA and Voting Rights Act is instructive. In contrast to the record which confronted Congress and the judiciary in the voting rights cases, RFRA's legislative record lacks examples of modern instances of generally applicable laws passed because of religious bigotry. The history of persecution in this country detailed in the hearings mentions no episodes occurring in the past 40 years. Rather, the emphasis of the hearings was on laws of general applicability which place incidental burdens on religion. Much of the discussion centered upon anecdotal evidence of autopsies performed on Jewish individuals and Hmong immigrants in violation of their religious beliefs, and on zoning regulations and historic preservation laws (like the one at issue here), which as an incident of their normal operation, have adverse effects on churches and synagogues. It is difficult to maintain that they are examples of legislation enacted or enforced due to animus or hostility to the burdened religious practices or that they indicate some widespread pattern of religious discrimination in this country. Congress' concern was with the incidental burdens imposed, not the object or purpose of the legislation. This lack of support in the legislative record, however, is not RFRA's most serious shortcoming. Judicial deference, in most cases, is based not on the state of the legislative record Congress compiles but "on due regard for the decision of the body constitutionally appointed to decide." *Oregon v. Mitchell* (opinion of Harlan, J.). As a general matter, it is for Congress to determine the method by which it will reach a decision.

Regardless of the state of the legislative record, RFRA cannot be considered remedial, preventive legislation, if those terms are to have any meaning. RFRA is so out of proportion to a supposed remedial or preventive object that it cannot be understood as responsive to, or designed to prevent, unconstitutional behavior. It appears, instead, to attempt a substantive change in constitutional behavior. It appears, instead, to attempt a substantive change in constitutional protections. Preventive measures prohibiting certain types of laws may be appropriate when there is reason to believe that many of the laws affected by the congressional enactment have a significant likelihood of being unconstitutional. *See City of Rome v. United States* (since "jurisdictions with a demonstrable history of intentional racial discrimination . . . create the risk of purposeful discrimination" Congress could "prohibit changes that have a discriminatory impact" in those jurisdictions). Remedial legislation under § 5 "should be adapted to the mischief and wrong which the [Fourteenth] [A]mendment was intended to provide against." *Civil Rights Cases.*

RFRA is not so confined. Sweeping coverage ensures its intrusion at every level of government, displacing laws and prohibiting official actions of almost every description and regardless of subject matter. RFRA's restrictions apply to every agency and official of the Federal, State, and local Governments. 42 U.S.C.A. § 2000bb-2(1). RFRA applies to all federal and state law, statutory or otherwise, whether adopted before or after its enactment. RFRA has no termination date or termination mechanism. Any law is subject to challenge at any time by any individual who alleges a substantial burden on his or her free exercise of religion.

The reach and scope of RFRA distinguish it from other measures passed under Congress' enforcement power, even in the area of voting rights. In *South Carolina v. Katzenbach,* the challenged provisions were confined to those regions of the country where voting discrimination had been most flagrant, and affected a discrete class of state laws, *i.e.,* state voting laws. Furthermore, to ensure that the reach of the Voting Rights Act was limited to those cases in which constitutional violations were most likely (in order to reduce the possibility of overbreadth), the coverage under the Act would terminate "at the behest of States and political subdivisions in which the danger of substantial voting discrimination has not materialized during the preceding five years." The provisions restricting and banning literacy tests, upheld in *Katzenbach v. Morgan,* and *Oregon v. Mitchell,* attacked a particular type of voting qualification, one with a long history as a "notorious means to deny and abridge voting rights on racial grounds." In *City of Rome,* the Court rejected a challenge to the constitutionality of a Voting Rights Act provision which required certain jurisdictions to submit changes in electoral practices to the Department of Justice for preimplementation review. The requirement was placed only on jurisdictions with a history of intentional racial discrimination in voting. Like the provisions at issue in *South Carolina v. Katzenbach,* this provision permitted a covered jurisdiction to avoid preclearance requirements under certain conditions and, moreover, lapsed in seven years. This is not to say, of course, that § 5 legislation requires termination dates, geographic restrictions or egregious predicates. Where, however, a congressional enactment pervasively prohibits constitutional state action in an effort to remedy or to prevent unconstitutional state action, limitations of this kind tend to ensure Congress' means are proportionate to ends legitimate under § 5.

The stringent test RFRA demands of state laws reflects a lack of proportionality or congruence between the means adopted and the legitimate end to be achieved. If an objector can show a substantial burden on his free exercise, the State must demonstrate a compelling governmental interest and show that the law is the least restrictive means of furthering its interest. Claims that a law substantially burdens someone's exercise of religion will often be difficult to contest. Requiring a State to demonstrate a compelling interest and show that it has adopted the least restrictive means of achieving that interest is the most demanding test known to constitutional law . . . Laws valid under *Smith* would fall under RFRA without regard to whether they had the object of stifling or punishing free exercise. We make these observations not to reargue the position of the majority in *Smith* but to illustrate the substantive alteration of its holding attempted by RFRA. Even assuming RFRA would be interpreted in effect to mandate some lesser test, say one equivalent to intermediate scrutiny, the statute nevertheless would require searching judicial scrutiny of state law with the attendant likelihood of invalidation. This is a considerable congressional intrusion into the States' traditional prerogatives and general authority to regulate for the health and welfare of their citizens.

The substantial costs RFRA exacts, both in practical terms of imposing a heavy litigation burden on the States and in terms of curtailing their traditional general regulatory power, far exceed any pattern or practice of unconstitutional conduct under the Free Exercise Clause, as interpreted in *Smith.* Simply put, RFRA is not designed to identify and counteract state laws likely to be unconstitutional because of their treatment of religion. In most cases, the state laws to which RFRA applies are not ones which will have been motivated by religious bigotry. If a state law disproportionately burdened a particular class of religious observers, this circumstance might be evidence of an impermissible legislative motive. RFRA's substantial burden test, however, is not even a discriminatory effects or disparate impact test. It is a reality of the modern regulatory state that numerous state laws, such as the zoning regulations at issue here, impose a substantial burden on a large class of individuals. When the exercise of religion has been burdened in an incidental way by a law of general application, it does not follow that the persons affected have been burdened any more than other citizens, let alone burdened because of their religious beliefs. In addition, the Act imposes in every case a least restrictive means requirement—a requirement that was not used in the pre-*Smith* jurisprudence RFRA purported to codify—which also indicates that the legislation is broader than is appropriate if the goal is to prevent and remedy constitutional violations.

RFRA was designed to control cases and controversies, such as the one before us; but as the provisions of the federal statute here invoked are beyond congressional authority, it is this Court's precedent, not RFRA, which must control. [C]ourts retain the power, as they have since *Marbury v. Madison*, to determine if Congress has exceeded its authority under the Constitution. Broad as the power of Congress is under the Enforcement Clause of the Fourteenth Amendment, RFRA contradicts vital principles necessary to maintain separation of powers and the federal balance. The judgment of the Court of Appeals sustaining the Act's constitutionality is reversed.

NOTES AND QUESTIONS

1. Can a clear line be drawn between laws that "remedy constitutional violations" and laws that "substantially change the law"? What did Congress say its purpose was in enacting RFRA? Does *Boerne* simply mean that Congress should go back and do a better job of factfinding?

2. Does the Court overturn *Katzenbach*? If not, can *Boerne* be squared with *Katzenbach*'s holding that, under § 5 of the Fourteenth Amendment, Congress may pass laws aimed at practices that have a discriminatory effect, even though the Fourteenth Amendment itself bars only intentionally discriminatory practices? The Court took care to distinguish the Voting Rights cases, but a key provision of this Act was later found to be unconstitutional. In *Shelby County, Alabama v. Holder*, 570 U.S. 529 (2013), the Court addressed the formula used in the Voting Rights Act to determine which state and local government entities had a history of race discrimination in voting, triggering the need to seek preclearance by the federal government before pursuing changes in their voting procedures. Contrary to its earlier deferential approach to congressional enforcement of voting rights, the Court held that Congress' 2006 Reauthorization failed to consider current voting conditions in the covered jurisdictions, some of which had achieved racial parity. The majority declared that § 4(b)'s formula "is based on decades-old data and eradicated practices . . . forty-year-old facts having no logical relation to the present day." The four dissenting Justices opined that the Court failed to defer to Congress' decision that the law was still necessary to fight discrimination in voting. Prior to the Reauthorization, Congress held twenty-one hearings and produced a 15,000-page record. The dissent pointed to this record:

> Congress determined, based on a voluminous record, that the scourge of discrimination was not yet extirpated. The question this case presents is who decides whether,

as currently operative, § 5 remains justifiable, this Court, or a Congress charged with the obligation to enforce the post-Civil War Amendments "by appropriate legislation." With overwhelming support in both Houses, Congress concluded that, for two prime reasons, § 5 should continue in force, unabated. First, continuance would facilitate completion of the impressive gains thus far made; and second, continuance would guard against backsliding. Those assessments were well with Congress' province to make and should elicit this Court's unstinting approbation.

In fact, immediately following the decision, the State of Texas adopted a voter ID law for which preclearance had been previously denied. Several states have followed Texas' lead. Although laws that have a disparate impact on racial minorities are prohibited by § 2, challengers must wait to prove a statistically adverse impact or show that the law was enacted for a discriminatory purpose, which could take years.

3. If the Justices' key concern is "state sovereignty," is RFRA constitutional as applied to federal law and actions? Does this ignore the Court's ruling on separation of powers, *i.e.*, Congress usurped the judicial function by reinterpreting the Free Exercise Clause of the First Amendment? In *Gonzales v. O Centro Espirita Beneficente Uniao Do Vegetal*, 546 U.S. 418 (2006), the Court assumed that RFRA was a constitutional enactment as applied to federal law and proceeded to rule that, on the merits, the federal government had failed to sustain its burden of demonstrating a compelling interest for not exempting a religious group from federal drug laws.

UNITED STATES V. MORRISON
529 U.S. 598 (2000)

Chief Justice REHNQUIST delivered the opinion of the Court.

III

Because we conclude that the Commerce Clause does not provide Congress with authority to enact § 13981,[a] we address petitioners' alternative argument that the section's civil remedy should be upheld as an exercise of Congress' remedial power under § 5 of the Fourteenth Amendment.

Petitioners' § 5 argument is founded on an assertion that there is pervasive bias in various state justice systems against victims of gender-motivated violence. This assertion is supported by a voluminous congressional record. Specifically, Congress received evidence that many participants in state justice systems are perpetuating an array of erroneous stereotypes and assumptions. Congress concluded that these discriminatory stereotypes often result in

---

a   Part I of this opinion invalidating VAWA as exceeding Congress' power under the Commerce Clause is discussed, *supra*.

insufficient investigation and prosecution of gender-motivated crime, inappropriate focus on the behavior and credibility of the victims of that crime, and unacceptably lenient punishments for those who are actually convicted of gender-motivated violence. Petitioners contend that this bias denies victims of gender-motivated violence the equal protection of the laws and that Congress therefore acted appropriately in enacting a private civil remedy against the perpetrators of gender-motivated violence to both remedy the States' bias and deter future instances of discrimination in the state courts.

As our cases have established, state-sponsored gender discrimination violates equal protection unless it "'serves "important governmental objectives and . . . the discriminatory "means employed" are "substantially related to the achievement of those objectives."' However, the language and purpose of the Fourteenth Amendment place certain limitations on the manner in which Congress may attack discriminatory conduct. These limitations are necessary to prevent the Fourteenth Amendment from obliterating the Framers' carefully crafted balance of power between the States and the National Government. Foremost among these limitations is the time-honored principle that the Fourteenth Amendment, by its very terms, prohibits only state action.

Petitioners . . . argue that, unlike the situation in the *Civil Rights Cases*, here there has been gender-based disparate treatment by state authorities, whereas in those cases there was no indication of such state action. There is abundant evidence, however, to show that the Congresses that enacted the Civil Rights Acts of 1871 and 1875 had a purpose similar to that of Congress in enacting § 13981: There were state laws on the books bespeaking equality of treatment, but in the administration of these laws there was discrimination against newly freed slaves.

But even if that distinction were valid, we do not believe it would save § 13981's civil remedy. For the remedy is simply not "corrective in its character, adapted to counteract and redress the operation of such prohibited [s]tate laws or proceedings of [s]tate officers." Or, as we have phrased it in more recent cases, prophylactic legislation under § 5 must have a "congruence and proportionality between the injury to be prevented or remedied and the means adopted to that end." Section 13981 is not aimed at proscribing discrimination by officials which the Fourteenth Amendment might not itself proscribe; it is directed not at any State or state actor, but at individuals who have committed criminal acts motivated by gender bias.

In the present cases, for example, § 13981 visits no consequence whatever on any Virginia public official involved in investigating or prosecuting Brzonkala's assault. The section is, therefore, unlike any of the § 5 remedies that we have previously upheld. Section 13981 is also different from these previously upheld remedies in that it applies uniformly throughout the Nation. Congress' findings indicate that the problem of discrimination against the victims of gender-motivated crimes does not exist in all States, or even most States. By contrast, the § 5 remedy upheld in *Katzenbach v. Morgan*, was directed only to the State where the evil found by Congress existed.

1. Is the Court's rigid application of a "congruence and proportionality" test justified? Compare the analysis in *Katzenbach*: "Let the end be legitimate...." On the other hand, will a private civil damage remedy "deter" or remedy the state's biased treatment of domestic violence?

2. *Morrison* reaffirms the *Civil Rights Cases*, which held that civil rights abuses by private parties are outside Congress' authority to enforce equality under the Fourteenth Amendment. The Hate Crimes Prevention Act punishes violent assaults motivated by bias against gays, ethnic minorities and the disabled. Can this Act survive a constitutional challenge after *Morrison*?

3. The **Eleventh Amendment** reads: "The Judicial power of the United States shall not be construed to extend to any suit in law or equity, commenced or prosecuted against one of the United States by Citizens of another state, or by Citizens or Subjects of any foreign state." Although the text of the Eleventh Amendment appears to bar only suits by noncitizens, it has long been interpreted to also preclude a suit against a state by its own citizens. *Hans v. Louisiana*, 134 U.S. 1 (1890). In *Edelman v. Jordan*, 415 U.S. 651 (1974), the Court explained the rule that "a suit by private parties seeking to impose a liability which must be paid from public funds in the state treasury is barred by the Eleventh Amendment," even if the State is not named as a party to the action. Equitable relief (an injunction), even if it may have a significant future impact on state treasuries, is permitted, but a retroactive award of monetary relief is barred by the Eleventh Amendment. Thus, state officials may be sued in their official capacity only for injunctive relief.

FITZPATRICK V. BITZER
427 U.S. 445 (1976)

Mr. Justice REHNQUIST delivered the opinion of the Court.

In the 1972 Amendments to Title VII of the Civil Rights Act of 1964, Congress, acting under § 5 of the Fourteenth Amendment, authorized federal courts to award money damages in favor of a private individual against a state government found to have subjected that person to employment discrimination on the basis of "race, color, religion, sex, or national origin." The principal question presented by these cases is whether, as against the shield of sovereign immunity afforded the State, Congress has the power to authorize federal courts to enter such an award against the State as a means of enforcing the substantive guarantees of the Fourteenth Amendment.

All parties in the instant litigation agree with the Court of Appeals that the suit for retroactive benefits by the petitioners is in fact indistinguishable from that sought to be maintained in Edelman, since what is sought here is a damages award payable to a private party from the state treasury. Our analysis begins where Edelman ended, for in this Title VII case the "threshold fact of congressional authorization," to sue the State as employer is clearly present.

As ratified by the States after the Civil War, that Amendment quite clearly contemplates limitations on their authority. In relevant part, it provides:

"Section 1. . . . No State shall make or enforce any law which shall abridge the privileges or immunities of citizens of the United States; nor shall any State deprive any person of life, liberty, or property, without due process of law; nor deny to any person within its jurisdiction the equal protection of the laws."

"Section 5. The Congress shall have power to enforce by appropriate legislation, the provisions of this article."

The impact of the Fourteenth Amendment upon the relationship between the Federal Government and the States, and the reach of congressional power under § 5, were examined at length by this Court in *Ex parte State of Virginia*, 100 U.S. 339 (1880). A state judge had been arrested and indicted under a federal criminal statute prohibiting the exclusion on the basis of race of any citizen from service as a juror in a state court. The judge claimed that the statute was beyond Congress' power to enact under either the Thirteenth or the Fourteenth Amendment. The Court first observed that these Amendments "were intended to be, what they really are, limitations of the power of the States and enlargements of the power of Congress." It then addressed the relationship between the language of § 5 and the substantive provisions of the Fourteenth Amendment:

> The prohibitions of the Fourteenth Amendment are directed to the States, and they are to a degree restrictions of State power. It is these which Congress is empowered to enforce, and to enforce against State action, however put forth, whether that action be executive, legislative, or judicial. Such enforcement is no invasion of State sovereignty. No law can be, which the people of the States have, by the Constitution of the United States, empowered Congress to enact. It is said the selection of jurors for her courts and the administration of her laws belong to each State; that they are her rights. This is true in the general. But in exercising her rights, a State cannot disregard the limitations which the Federal Constitution has applied to her power.

There can be no doubt that this line of cases has sanctioned intrusions by Congress, acting under the Civil War Amendments, into the judicial, executive, and legislative spheres of autonomy previously reserved to the States. The legislation considered in each case was grounded on the expansion of Congress' powers with the corresponding diminution of state sovereignty found to be intended by the Framers and made part of the Constitution upon the States' ratification of those Amendments. It is true that none of these previous cases presented the question of the relationship between the Eleventh Amendment and the enforcement power granted to

Congress under § 5 of the Fourteenth Amendment. But we think that the Eleventh Amendment, and the principle of state sovereignty which it embodies, are necessarily limited by the enforcement provisions of § 5 of the Fourteenth Amendment. In that section Congress is expressly granted authority to enforce "by appropriate legislation" the substantive provisions of the Fourteenth Amendment, which themselves embody significant limitations on state authority. When Congress acts pursuant to § 5, not only is it exercising legislative authority that is plenary within the terms of the constitutional grant, it is exercising that authority under one section of a constitutional Amendment whose other sections by their own terms embody limitations on state authority. We think that Congress may, in determining what is "appropriate legislation" for the purpose of enforcing the provisions of the Fourteenth Amendment, provide for private suits against States or state officials which are constitutionally impermissible in other contexts.

NOTES AND QUESTIONS

1. Although the Court in *Fitzpatrick* ruled that Congress could authorize suit for monetary damages against state governments if it acts pursuant to Section 5 of the Fourteenth Amendment, in *Seminole Tribe v. Florida*, 517 U.S. 44 (1996), it ruled that when Congress acts under its Article I powers, such as the Commerce Clause, it cannot abrogate the Eleventh Amendment. Further, in *City of Boerne*, the Court narrowed the scope of Congress' Section 5 powers.

2. **Congressional abrogation:** The interrelationship of *Fitzpatrick*'s ruling on the Eleventh Amendment and *Boerne*'s ruling on Section 5 power was first addressed in *Florida Prepaid Postsecondary Education Expense Board v. College Savings Bank*, 527 U.S. 627 (1999). The Court in a 5 to 4 ruling invoked *Boerne* to hold that the Patent and Plant Variety Protection Remedy Clarification Act of 1992, which expressly abrogated the state's immunity from claims of patent infringement, was an unconstitutional exercise of Congress' authority under § 5 of the Fourteenth Amendment. Although finding that Congress unequivocally expressed its intent to abrogate the Eleventh Amendment, the majority reasoned that since Congress' enforcement power is remedial, Congress must identify the conduct transgressing the Fourteenth Amendment's substantive provisions and must tailor its legislative scheme to remedy or prevent such conduct—there must be proportionality between the injury to be prevented or remedied and the means adopted to that end. Looking to the legislative history, the Court found that Congress identified no pattern of patent infringement by states, but rather, the House Report provided only two examples of patent infringement suits against states and the Federal Circuit identified only eight such suits in 110 years. In short, Congress identified no pattern of patent infringements by states, much less a pattern of Constitutional violations. The Court reasoned that a state's infringement of a patent does not violate the Constitution unless the state provides no remedy or only inadequate remedies to injured patent owners. Further, unintentional patent infringements would not violate the Fourteenth

Amendment Due Process Clause. The case suggests that a legislative record must demonstrate a history of "widespread and persistent deprivation of Constitutional rights" in order for Congress to take action under § 5. The Court also concluded that the provisions of the Act were "out of proportion to a supposed remedial or preventive object" since the Act was not limited to cases involving arguable constitutional violations, nor was the remedy limited to certain types of infringement, such as non-negligent infringement or infringement authorized pursuant to state policy.

The next decisions apply this new jurisprudence to modern civil rights statutes.

KIMEL V. FLORIDA BOARD OF REGENTS
528 u.s. 62 (2000)

JUSTICE O'CONNOR delivered the opinion of the Court.

The Age Discrimination in Employment Act of 1967 makes it unlawful for an employer, including a State, "to fail or refuse to hire or to discharge any individual or otherwise discriminate against any individual . . . because of such individual's age." 29 U.S.C. § 623(a)(1). In these cases, three sets of plaintiffs filed suit under the Act, seeking money damages for their state employers' alleged discrimination on the basis of age. In each case, the state employer moved to dismiss the suit on the basis of its Eleventh Amendment immunity. In these cases, we are asked to consider whether the ADEA contains a clear statement of Congress' intent to abrogate the States' Eleventh Amendment immunity and, if so, whether the ADEA is a proper exercise of Congress' constitutional authority. We conclude that the ADEA does contain a clear statement of Congress' intent to abrogate the States' immunity, but that the abrogation exceeded Congress' authority under § 5 of the Fourteenth Amendment.

Since its enactment, the ADEA's scope of coverage has been expanded by amendment. Of particular importance to these cases is the Act's treatment of state employers and employees. When first passed in 1967, the ADEA applied only to private employers. In 1974, in a statute consisting primarily of amendments to the FLSA, Congress extended application of the ADEA's substantive requirements to the States.

To determine whether a federal statute properly subjects States to suits by individuals, we apply a "simple but stringent test: 'Congress may abrogate the States' constitutionally secured immunity from suit in federal court only by making its intention unmistakably clear in the language of the statute.'" Read as a whole, the plain language of these provisions clearly demonstrates Congress' intent to subject the States to suit for money damages at the hands of individual employees.

The statute authorizes employee suits against States "in any *Federal or State* court of competent jurisdiction." § 216(b) (emphasis added). That choice of language sufficiently indicates Congress' intent, in the ADEA, to abrogate the States' Eleventh Amendment immunity to suits by individuals.

IV

A

In *Seminole Tribe*, we held that Congress lacks power under Article I to abrogate the States' sovereign immunity. . . . Under our firmly established precedent then, if the ADEA rests solely on Congress' Article I commerce power, the private petitioners in today's cases cannot maintain their suits against their state employers. . .

Section 5 of the Fourteenth Amendment, however, does grant Congress the authority to abrogate the States' sovereign immunity. In *Fitzpatrick v. Bitzer*, 427 U.S. 445 (1976), we recognized that "the Eleventh Amendment, and the principle of state sovereignty which it embodies, are necessarily limited by the enforcement provisions of § 5 of the Fourteenth Amendment." *Id.* at 456 (citation omitted). Since our decision in *Fitzpatrick*, we have reaffirmed the validity of that congressional power on numerous occasions. . . . Accordingly, the private petitioners in these cases may maintain their ADEA suits against the States of Alabama and Florida if, and only if, the ADEA is appropriate legislation under § 5.

B

Congress' § 5 power is not confined to the enactment of legislation that merely parrots the precise wording of the Fourteenth Amendment. Rather, Congress' power "to enforce" the Amendment includes the authority both to remedy and to deter violation of rights guaranteed thereunder by prohibiting a somewhat broader swath of conduct, including that which is not itself forbidden by the Amendment's text.

Nevertheless, we have also recognized that the same language that serves as the basis for the affirmative grant of congressional power also serves to limit that power. For example, Congress cannot "decree the substance of the Fourteenth Amendment's restrictions on the States. . . . It has been given the power 'to enforce,' not the power to determine what constitutes a constitutional violation." In *City of Boerne*, we noted that the determination whether purportedly prophylactic legislation constitutes appropriate remedial legislation, or instead effects a substantive redefinition of the Fourteenth Amendment right at issue, is often difficult. The line between the two is a fine one. Accordingly, recognizing that "Congress must have wide latitude in determining where [that line] lies," we held that "[t]here must be a congruence and proportionality between the injury to be prevented or remedied and the means adopted to that end."

C

Applying the same "congruence and proportionality" test in these cases, we conclude that the ADEA is not "appropriate legislation" under § 5 of the Fourteenth Amendment. Initially, the substantive requirements the ADEA imposes on state and local governments are disproportionate to any unconstitutional conduct that conceivably could be targeted by the Act. Age classifications, unlike governmental conduct based on race or gender, cannot be characterized as "so seldom relevant to the achievement of any legitimate state interest that laws grounded in such considerations are deemed to reflect prejudice and antipathy." Old age also does not define a discrete and insular minority because all persons, if they live out their normal life spans, will experience it. Accordingly, as we recognized in *Murgia, Bradley*, and *Gregory*, age is not a suspect classification under the Equal Protection Clause. . . . Our Constitution permits States to draw lines on the basis of age when they have a rational basis for doing so at a class-based level, even if it "is probably not true" that those reasons are valid in the majority of cases.

Judged against the backdrop of our equal protection jurisprudence, it is clear that the ADEA is "so out of proportion to a supposed remedial or preventive object that it cannot be understood as responsive to, or designed to prevent, unconstitutional behavior." The Act, through its broad restriction on the use of age as a discriminating factor, prohibits substantially more state employment decisions and practices than would likely be held unconstitutional under the applicable equal protection, rational basis standard.

That the ADEA prohibits very little conduct likely to be held unconstitutional, while significant, does not alone provide the answer to our § 5 inquiry. Difficult and intractable problems often require powerful remedies, and we have never held that § 5 precludes Congress from enacting reasonably prophylactic legislation. Our task is to determine whether the ADEA is in fact just such an appropriate remedy or, instead, merely an attempt to substantively redefine the States' legal obligations with respect to age discrimination. One means by which we have made such a determination in the past is by examining the legislative record containing the reasons for Congress' action.

Congress never identified any pattern of age discrimination by the States, much less any discrimination whatsoever that rose to the level of constitutional violation. The evidence compiled by petitioners to demonstrate such attention by Congress to age discrimination by the States falls well short of the mark. That evidence consists almost entirely of isolated sentences clipped from floor debates and legislative reports.

A review of the ADEA's legislative record as a whole, then, reveals that Congress had virtually no reason to believe that state and local governments were unconstitutionally discriminating against their employees on the basis of age. Although that lack of support is not determinative of the § 5 inquiry, Congress' failure to uncover any significant pattern of unconstitutional discrimination here confirms that Congress had no reason to believe that broad prophylactic legislation was necessary in this field. In light of the indiscriminate scope of the Act's substantive requirements, and the lack of evidence of widespread and unconstitutional age discrimination by the States, we hold that the ADEA is not a valid exercise of Congress' power under § 5 of the Fourteenth Amendment. The ADEA's purported abrogation of the States' sovereign immunity is accordingly invalid.

D

Our decision today does not signal the end of the line for employees who find themselves subject to age discrimination at the hands of their state employers. We hold only that, in the

ADEA, Congress did not validly abrogate the States' sovereign immunity to suits by private individuals. State employees are protected by state age discrimination statutes, and may recover money damages from their state employers, in almost every State of the Union. Those avenues of relief remain available today, just as they were before this decision.

Because the ADEA does not validly abrogate the States' sovereign immunity, however, the present suits must be dismissed. Accordingly, the judgment of the Court of Appeals is affirmed.

Justice STEVENS, with whom Justices SOUTER, GINSBURG and BREYER join, dissenting in part and concurring in part.

Federalism concerns do make it appropriate for Congress to speak clearly when it regulates state action. But when it does so, as it has in these cases, we can safely presume that the burdens the statute imposes on the sovereignty of the several States were taken into account during the deliberative process leading to the enactment of the measure. There is not a word in the text of the Constitution supporting the Court's conclusion that the judge-made doctrine of sovereign immunity limits Congress' power to authorize private parties, as well as federal agencies, to enforce federal law against the States. The importance of respecting the Framers' decision to assign the business of lawmaking to the Congress dictates firm resistance to the present majority's repeated substitution of its own views of federalism for those expressed in statutes enacted by the Congress and signed by the President.

NOTES AND QUESTIONS

1. Based on Kimel, what "test" will the Supreme Court apply in determining whether Congress validly abrogated the Eleventh Amendment in enacting laws passed under § 5 of the Fourteenth Amendment?

2. Does the ADEA fail the test because it reaches a "broader swath of conduct" than the Fourteenth Amendment? Why is it relevant that the Fourteenth Amendment reaches only irrational age discrimination?

BOARD OF TRUSTEES OF UNIV. OF ALA. V. GARRETT
531 U.S. 356 (2001)

Chief Justice REHNQUIST delivered the opinion of the Court.

We decide here whether employees of the State of Alabama may recover money damages by reason of the State's failure to comply with the provisions of Title I of the Americans with Disabilities Act of 1990 (ADA or Act). We hold that such suits are barred by the Eleventh Amendment.

The ADA prohibits certain employers, including the States, from "discriminating against a qualified individual with a disability because of the disability of such individual in regard to job application procedures, the hiring, advancement, or discharge of employees, employee compensation, job training, and other terms, conditions, and privileges of employment." To this end, the Act requires employers to "mak[e] reasonable accommodations to the known physical or mental limitations of an otherwise qualified individual with a disability who is an applicant or employee, unless [the employer] can demonstrate that the accommodation would impose an undue hardship on the operation of the [employer's] business." § 12112(b)(5)(A). . . .

City of Boerne confirmed the long-settled principle that it is the responsibility of this Court, not Congress, to define the substance of constitutional guarantees. Accordingly, § 5 legislation reaching beyond the scope of § 1's actual guarantees must exhibit "congruence and proportionality between the injury to be prevented or remedied and the means adopted to that end."

II

The first step in applying these now familiar principles is to identify with some precision the scope of the constitutional right at issue. Here, that inquiry requires us to examine the limitations § 1 of the Fourteenth Amendment places upon States' treatment of the disabled.

States are not required by the Fourteenth Amendment to make special accommodations for the disabled, so long as their actions towards such individuals are rational. They could quite hard headedly—and perhaps hardheartedly—hold to job-qualification requirements which do not make allowance for the disabled. If special accommodations for the disabled are to be required, they have to come from positive law and not through the Equal Protection Clause.

III

Once we have determined the metes and bounds of the constitutional right in question, we examine whether Congress identified a history and pattern of unconstitutional employment discrimination by the States against the disabled. Just as § 1of the Fourteenth Amendment applies only to actions committed "under color of state law," Congress' § 5 authority is appropriately exercised only in response to state transgressions. . . .

Congress made a general finding in the ADA that "historically, society has tended to isolate and segregate individuals with disabilities, and, despite some improvements, such forms of discrimination against individuals with disabilities continue to be a serious and pervasive social problem." 42 U.S.C. § 12101(a)(2). The record assembled by Congress includes many instances to support such a finding. But the great majority of these incidents do not deal with the activities of States.

Respondents in their brief cite half a dozen examples from the record that did involve States. . . . Several of these incidents undoubtedly evidence an unwillingness on the part of state officials to make the sort of accommodations for the disabled required by the ADA. Whether they were irrational under our decision in *Cleburne* is more debatable, particularly when the incident is described out of context. But even if it were to be determined that each incident upon fuller examination showed unconstitutional action on the part of the State, these incidents taken together fall far short of even suggesting the pattern of unconstitutional discrimination on which § 5 legislation must be based.

Even were it possible to squeeze out of these examples a pattern of unconstitutional discrimination by the States, the rights and remedies created by the ADA against the States would raise the same sort of concerns as to congruence and proportionality as were found in *City of Boerne*. For example, whereas it would be entirely rational (and therefore constitutional) for a state employer to conserve scarce financial resources by hiring employees who are able to use existing facilities, the ADA requires employers to "mak[e] existing facilities used by employees readily accessible to and usable by individuals with disabilities." 42 U.S.C. §§ 12112(5)(B), 12111(9). The ADA does except employers from the "reasonable accommodatio[n]" requirement where the employer "can demonstrate that the accommodation would impose an undue hardship on the operation of the business of such covered entity." However, even with this exception, the accommodation duty far exceeds what is constitutionally required in that it makes unlawful a range of alternate responses that would be reasonable but would fall short of imposing an "undue burden" upon the employer. The Act also makes it the employer's duty to prove that it would suffer such a burden, instead of requiring (as the Constitution does) that the complaining party negate reasonable bases for the employer's decision.

The ADA also forbids "utilizing standards, criteria, or methods of administration" that disparately impact the disabled, without regard to whether such conduct has a rational basis. § 12112(b)(3)(A). Although disparate impact may be relevant evidence of racial discrimination, such evidence alone is insufficient even where the Fourteenth Amendment subjects state action to strict scrutiny.

Congressional enactment of the ADA represents [Congress'] judgment that there should be a "comprehensive national mandate for the elimination of discrimination against individuals with disabilities." 42 U.S.C. § 12101(b)(1). Congress is the final authority as to desirable public policy, but in order to authorize private individuals to recover money damages against the States, there must be a pattern of discrimination by the States which violates the Fourteenth Amendment, and the remedy imposed by Congress must be congruent and proportional to the targeted violation. Those requirements are not met here.

[In a lengthy dissent, Justice BREYER, joined by three other Justices, noted that Congress had compiled "a vast legislative record" documenting massive discrimination against persons with disabilities, including "roughly 300 examples of discrimination by state governments," set forth in an Appendix after the case. The dissent accused the majority of holding Congress "to a strict, judicially created evidentiary standard," and of failing to give Congress proper deference in its choice of an appropriate means to combat disability discrimination: "The Court, through its evidentiary demands, its non-deferential review, and its failure to distinguish between judicial and legislative constitutional competencies, improperly invades a power that the Constitution assigns to Congress."]

1. Why does the Court find that the ADA was not a valid exercise of Congress' § 5 authority?

2. Note that *Kimel and Garrett* do not affect ADEA and ADA claims brought against local government in federal court because the Eleventh Amendment insulates only the state and arms of the state. *See infra*, Chapter II.

NEVADA DEPARTMENT OF HUMAN RESOURCES V. HIBBS
538 U.S. 721 (2003)

Chief Justice REHNQUIST delivered the opinion of the Court.

The Family and Medical Leave Act of 1993 (FMLA or Act) entitles eligible employees to take up to 12 work weeks of unpaid leave annually for any of several reasons, including the onset of a "serious health condition" in an employee's spouse, child, or parent. 29 U.S.C. § 2612(a)(1)(C). The Act creates a private right of action to seek both equitable relief and money damages "against any employer (including a public agency) in any Federal or State court of competent jurisdiction," § 2617(a)(2), should that employer "interfere with, restrain, or deny the exercise of" FMLA rights, § 2615(a)(1). We hold that employees of the State of Nevada may recover money damages in the event of the State's failure to comply with the family-care provision of the Act.

Petitioners include the Nevada Department of Human Resources (Department) and two of its officers. Respondent William Hibbs (hereinafter respondent) worked for the Department's Welfare Division. In April and May 1997, he sought leave under the FMLA to care for his ailing wife, who was recovering from a car accident and neck surgery. The Department granted his request for the full 12 weeks of FMLA leave and authorized him to use the leave intermittently as needed between May and December 1997. Respondent did so until August 5, 1997, after which he did not return to work. In October 1997, the Department informed respondent that he had exhausted his FMLA leave, that no further leave would be granted, and that he must report to work by November 12, 1997. Respondent failed to do so and was terminated.

Respondent sued petitioners in the United States District Court seeking damages and injunctive and declaratory relief for, *inter alia*, violations of 29 U.S.C. § 2612(a)(1)(C). The District Court awarded petitioners summary judgment on the grounds that the FMLA claim was barred by the Eleventh Amendment and that respondent's Fourteenth Amendment rights had not been violated. The Ninth Circuit reversed.

We granted certiorari, to resolve a split among the Courts of Appeals on the question whether an individual may sue a State for money damages in federal court for violation of § 2612(a)(1)(C).

For over a century now, we have made clear that the Constitution does not provide for federal jurisdiction over suits against nonconsenting States. Congress may, however, abrogate such immunity in federal court if it makes its intention to abrogate unmistakably clear in the language of the statute and acts pursuant to a valid exercise of its power under § 5 of the Fourteenth Amendment. The clarity of Congress' intent here is not fairly debatable. The Act enables employees to seek damages "against any employer (including a public agency) in any Federal or State court of competent jurisdiction," and Congress has defined "public agency" to include both "the government of a State or political subdivision thereof" and "any agency of . . . a State, or a political subdivision of a State," §§ 203(x), 2611(4)(A)(iii).

In enacting the FMLA, Congress relied on two of the powers vested in it by the Constitution: its Article I commerce power and its power under § 5 of the Fourteenth Amendment to enforce that Amendment's guarantees. Congress may not abrogate the States' sovereign immunity pursuant to its Article I power over commerce. *Seminole Tribe v. Florida*, 517 U.S. 44 (1996). Congress may, however, abrogate States' sovereign immunity through a valid exercise of its § 5 power, for "the Eleventh Amendment, and the principle of state sovereignty which it embodies, are necessarily limited by the enforcement provisions of § 5 of the Fourteenth Amendment."

Two provisions of the Fourteenth Amendment are relevant here: Section 5 grants Congress the power "to enforce" the substantive guarantees of § 1—among them, equal protection of the laws—by enacting "appropriate legislation." Congress may, in the exercise of its § 5 power, do more than simply proscribe conduct that we have held unconstitutional. "'Congress' power "to enforce" the Amendment includes the authority both to remedy and to deter violation of rights guaranteed thereunder by prohibiting a somewhat broader swath of conduct, including that which is not itself forbidden by the Amendment's text.'" *Garrett*. In other words, Congress may enact so-called prophylactic legislation that proscribes facially constitutional conduct, in order to prevent and deter unconstitutional conduct.

City of Boerne also confirmed, however, that it falls to this Court, not Congress, to define the substance of constitutional guarantees. "The ultimate interpretation and determination of the Fourteenth Amendment's substantive meaning remains the province of the Judicial Branch." *Kimel*. Section 5 legislation reaching beyond the scope of § 1's actual guarantees must be an appropriate remedy for identified constitutional violations, not "an attempt to substantively redefine the States' legal obligations." We distinguish appropriate prophylactic legislation from "substantive redefinition of the Fourteenth Amendment right at issue," by applying the test set forth in *City of Boerne*: Valid § 5 legislation must exhibit "congruence and proportionality between the injury to be prevented or remedied and the means adopted to that end."

The FMLA aims to protect the right to be free from gender-based discrimination in the workplace. We have held that statutory classifications that distinguish between males and females are subject to heightened scrutiny. For a gender-based classification to withstand such scrutiny, it must "serv[e] important governmental objectives," and "the discriminatory means employed [must be] substantially related to the achievement of those objectives." *United States v. Virginia*. The State's justification for such a classification "must not rely on overbroad generalizations about the different talents, capacities, or preferences of males and females." We now inquire whether Congress had evidence of a pattern of constitutional violations on the part of the States in this area.

The history of the many state laws limiting women's employment opportunities is chronicled in—and, until relatively recently, was sanctioned by—this Court's own opinions. For example, in *Bradwell v. State* and *Goesaert v. Cleary,* the Court upheld state laws prohibiting women from practicing law and tending bar, respectively. State laws frequently subjected women to distinctive restrictions, terms, conditions, and benefits for those jobs they could take. In *Muller v. Oregon,* for example, this Court approved a state law limiting the hours that women could work for wages, and observed that 19 States had such laws at the time. Such laws were based on the related beliefs that (1) woman is, and should remain, "the center of home and family life," and (2) "a proper discharge of [a woman's] maternal functions— having in view not merely her own health, but the well-being of the race—justif[ies] legislation to protect her from the greed as well as the passion of man," *Muller.* Until our decision in *Reed v. Reed,* "it remained the prevailing doctrine that government, both federal and state, could withhold from women opportunities accorded men so long as any 'basis in reason'"—such as the above beliefs—"could be conceived for the discrimination." *Virginia.*

Congress responded to this history of discrimination by abrogating States' sovereign immunity in Title VII of the Civil Rights Act of 1964, and we sustained this abrogation in *Fitzpatrick.* But state gender discrimination did not cease. According to evidence that was before Congress when it enacted the FMLA, States continue to rely on invalid gender stereotypes in the employment context, specifically in the administration of leave benefits. Reliance on such stereotypes cannot justify the States' gender discrimination in this area. The long and extensive history of sex discrimination prompted us to hold that measures that differentiate on the basis of gender warrant heightened scrutiny; here, as in *Fitzpatrick,* the persistence of such unconstitutional discrimination by the States justifies Congress' passage of prophylactic § 5 legislation.

As the FMLA's legislative record reflects, a 1990 Bureau of Labor Statistics (BLS) survey stated that 37 percent of surveyed private-sector employees were covered by maternity leave policies, while only 18 percent were covered by paternity leave policies. The corresponding numbers from a similar BLS survey the previous year were 33 percent and 16 percent, respectively. *Ibid.* While these data show an increase in the percentage of employees eligible for such leave, they also show a widening of the gender gap during the same period. Thus, stereotype-based beliefs about the allocation of family duties remained firmly rooted, and employers' reliance on them in establishing discriminatory leave policies remained widespread.[3]

Congress also heard testimony that "[p]arental leave for fathers . . . is rare. Even . . . [w]here child-care leave policies do exist, men, *both in the public and private sectors,* receive notoriously discriminatory treatment in their requests for such leave." Many States offered women extended "maternity" leave that far exceeded the typical 4- to 8-week period of physical disability due to pregnancy and childbirth, but very few States granted men a parallel benefit: Fifteen States provided women up to one year of extended maternity leave, while only four provided men with the same. This and other differential leave policies were not attributable to any differential physical needs of men and women, but rather to the pervasive sex-role stereotype that caring for family members is women's work.

---

3 While this and other material described leave policies in the private sector, a 50-state survey also before Congress demonstrated that "[t]he proportion and construction of leave policies available to public sector employees differs little from those offered private sector employees."

Finally, Congress had evidence that, even where state laws and policies were not facially discriminatory, they were applied in discriminatory ways. It was aware of the "serious problems with the discretionary nature of family leave," because when "the authority to grant leave and to arrange the length of that leave rests with individual supervisors," it leaves "employees open to discretionary and possibly unequal treatment." Testimony supported that conclusion, explaining that "[t]he lack of uniform parental and medical leave policies in the work place has created an environment where [sex] discrimination is rampant."

In sum, the States' record of unconstitutional participation in, and fostering of, gender-based discrimination in the administration of leave benefits is weighty enough to justify the enactment of prophylactic § 5 legislation.

We reached the opposite conclusion in *Garrett* and *Kimel*. In those cases, the § 5 legislation under review responded to a purported tendency of state officials to make age- or disability-based distinctions. Under our equal protection case law, discrimination on the basis of such characteristics is not judged under a heightened review standard, and passes muster if there is "a rational basis for doing so at a class-based level, even if it 'is probably not true' that those reasons are valid in the majority of cases." Thus, in order to impugn the constitutionality of state discrimination against the disabled or the elderly, Congress must identify, not just the existence of age- or disability-based state decisions, but a "widespread pattern" of irrational reliance on such criteria. *Kimel*. We found no such showing with respect to the ADEA and Title I of the Americans with Disabilities Act of 1990 (ADA).

Here, however, Congress directed its attention to state gender discrimination, which triggers a heightened level of scrutiny. Because the standard for demonstrating the constitutionality of a gender-based classification is more difficult to meet than our rational-basis test—it must "serv[e] important governmental objectives" and be "substantially related to the achievement of those objectives,"—it was easier for Congress to show a pattern of state constitutional violations. Congress was similarly successful in *South Carolina v. Katzenbach*, where we upheld the Voting Rights Act of 1965: Because racial classifications are presumptively invalid, most of the States' acts of race discrimination violated the Fourteenth Amendment.

Stereotypes about women's domestic roles are reinforced by parallel stereotypes presuming a lack of domestic responsibilities for men. Because employers continued to regard the family as the woman's domain, they often denied men similar accommodations or discouraged them from taking leave. These mutually reinforcing stereotypes created a self-fulfilling cycle of discrimination that forced women to continue to assume the role of primary family caregiver, and fostered employers' stereotypical views about women's commitment to work and their value as employees. Those perceptions, in turn, Congress reasoned, lead to subtle discrimination that may be difficult to detect on a case-by-case basis.

We believe that Congress' chosen remedy, the family-care leave provision of the FMLA, is "congruent and proportional to the targeted violation." Congress had already tried unsuccessfully to address this problem through Title VII and the amendment of Title VII by the Pregnancy Discrimination Act, 42 U.S.C. § 2000e(k). Here, as in *Katzenbach, supra*, Congress again confronted a "difficult and intractable proble[m]," where previous legislative attempts had failed. Such problems may justify added prophylactic measures in response.

By creating an across-the-board, routine employment benefit for all eligible employees, Congress sought to ensure that family-care leave would no longer be stigmatized as an inordinate drain on the workplace caused by female employees, and that employers could not evade leave obligations simply by hiring men. By setting a minimum standard of family leave for *all* eligible employees, irrespective of gender, the FMLA attacks the formerly state-sanctioned stereotype that only women are responsible for family caregiving, thereby reducing employers' incentives to engage in discrimination by basing hiring and promotion decisions on stereotypes.

The dissent characterizes the FMLA as a "substantive entitlement program" rather than a remedial statute because it establishes a floor of 12 weeks' leave. In the dissent's view, in the face of evidence of gender-based discrimination by the States in the provision of leave benefits, Congress could do no more in exercising its § 5 power than simply proscribe such discrimination. But this position cannot be squared with our recognition that Congress "is not confined to the enactment of legislation that merely parrots the precise wording of the Fourteenth Amendment," but may prohibit "a somewhat broader swath of conduct, including that which is not itself forbidden by the Amendment's text." *Kimel.*

Indeed, in light of the evidence before Congress, a statute mirroring Title VII, that simply mandated gender equality in the administration of leave benefits, would not have achieved Congress' remedial object. Such a law would allow States to provide for no family leave at all. Where "[t]wo-thirds of the nonprofessional caregivers for older, chronically ill, or disabled persons are working women" and state practices continue to reinforce the stereotype of women as caregivers, such a policy would exclude far more women than men from the workplace.

Unlike the statutes at issue in *City of Boerne, Kimel,* and *Garrett,* which applied broadly to every aspect of state employers' operations, the FMLA is narrowly targeted at the fault line between work and family—precisely where sex-based overgeneralization has been and remains strongest—and affects only one aspect of the employment relationship.

We also find significant the many other limitations that Congress placed on the scope of this measure. The FMLA requires only unpaid leave, 29 U.S.C. § 2612(a)(1), and applies only to employees who have worked for the employer for at least one year and provided 1,250 hours of service within the last 12 months, § 2611(2)(A). Employees in high-ranking or sensitive positions are simply ineligible for FMLA leave; of particular importance to the States, the FMLA expressly excludes from coverage state elected officials, their staffs, and appointed policymakers. §§ 2611(2)(B)(i) and (3), 203(e)(2)(C). Employees must give advance notice of foreseeable leave, § 2612(e), and employers may require certification by a health care provider of the need for leave, § 2613. In choosing 12 weeks as the appropriate leave floor, Congress chose "a middle ground, a period long enough to serve 'the needs of families' but not so long that it would upset 'the legitimate interests of employers.'" Moreover, the cause of action under the FMLA is a restricted one: The damages recoverable are strictly defined and measured by actual monetary losses, §§ 2617(a)(1)(A)(i)-(iii), and the accrual period for backpay is limited by the Act's 2-year statute of limitations (extended to three years only for willful violations), §§ 2617(c)(1) and (2).

For the above reasons, we conclude that § 2612(a)(1)(C) is congruent and proportional to its remedial object, and can "be understood as responsive to, or designed to prevent, unconstitutional behavior." *City of Boerne.*

Justice KENNEDY, with whom Justice SCALIA and Justice THOMAS join, dissenting.

Congress does not have authority to define the substantive content of the Equal Protection Clause; it may only shape the remedies warranted by the violations of that guarantee. *City of Boerne.* This requirement has special force in the context of the Eleventh Amendment, which protects a State's fiscal integrity from federal intrusion by vesting the States with immunity from private actions for damages pursuant to federal laws. The Commerce Clause likely would permit the National Government to enact an entitlement program such as this one; but when Congress couples the entitlement with the authorization to sue the States for monetary damages, it blurs the line of accountability the State has to its own citizens. These basic concerns underlie cases such as *Garrett* and *Kimel,* and should counsel far more caution than the Court shows in holding § 2612(a)(1)(C) is somehow a congruent and proportional remedy to an identified pattern of discrimination.

The Court is unable to show that States have engaged in a pattern of unlawful conduct which warrants the remedy of opening state treasuries to private suits. The inability to adduce evidence of alleged discrimination, coupled with the inescapable fact that the federal scheme is not a remedy but a benefit program, demonstrate the lack of the requisite link between any problem Congress has identified and the program it mandated.

The relevant question, as the Court seems to acknowledge, is whether, notwithstanding the passage of Title VII and similar state legislation, the States continued to engage in widespread discrimination on the basis of gender in the provision of family leave benefits. If such a pattern were shown, the Eleventh Amendment would not bar Congress from devising a congruent and proportional remedy. The evidence to substantiate this charge must be far more specific, however, than a simple recitation of a general history of employment discrimination against women. When the federal statute seeks to abrogate state sovereign immunity, the Court should be more careful to insist on adherence to the analytic requirements set forth in its own precedents. Persisting overall effects of gender-based discrimination at the workplace must not be ignored; but simply noting the problem is not a substitute for evidence which identifies some real discrimination the family leave rules are designed to prevent.

Respondents fail to make the requisite showing. . . . Thirty States, the District of Columbia, and Puerto Rico had adopted some form of family-care leave in the years preceding the Act's adoption. Congressional hearings noted that the provision of family leave was "an issue which has picked up tremendous momentum in the States, with some 21 of them having some form of family or medical leave on the books." Congress also acknowledged that many States had implemented leave policies more generous than those envisioned by the Act. At the very least, the history of the Act suggests States were in the process of solving any existing gender-based discrimination in the provision of family leave.

The Court acknowledges that States have adopted family leave programs prior to federal intervention, but argues these policies suffered from serious imperfections. Even if correct, this observation proves, at most, that programs more generous and more effective than those operated by the States were feasible. That the States did not devise the optimal programs is not, however, evidence that the States were perpetuating unconstitutional discrimination. Given that the States assumed a pioneering role in the creation of family leave schemes, it is not surprising these early efforts may have been imperfect. This is altogether different, however, from purposeful discrimination.

Considered in its entirety, the evidence fails to document a pattern of unconstitutional conduct sufficient to justify the abrogation of States' sovereign immunity. The few incidents identified by the Court "fall far short of even suggesting the pattern of unconstitutional discrimination on which § 5 legislation must be based." Juxtaposed to this evidence is the States' record of addressing gender-based discrimination in the provision of leave benefits on their own volition.

Our concern with gender discrimination, which is subjected to heightened scrutiny, as opposed to age- or disability-based distinctions, which are reviewed under rational standard, does not alter this conclusion. The application of heightened scrutiny is designed to ensure gender-based classifications are not based on the entrenched and pervasive stereotypes which inhibit women's progress in the workplace. This consideration does not divest respondents of their burden to show that "Congress identified a history and pattern of unconstitutional employment discrimination by the States."

The paucity of evidence to support the case the Court tries to make demonstrates that Congress was not responding with a congruent and proportional remedy to a perceived course of unconstitutional conduct. Instead, it enacted a substantive entitlement program of its own. If Congress had been concerned about different treatment of men and women with respect to family leave, a congruent remedy would have sought to ensure the benefits of any leave program enacted by a State are available to men and women on an equal basis. Instead, the Act imposes, across the board, a requirement that States grant a minimum of 12 weeks of leave per year. 29 U.S.C. § 2612(a)(1)(C). This requirement may represent Congress' considered judgment as to the optimal balance between the family obligations of workers and the interests of employers, and the States may decide to follow these guidelines in designing their own family leave benefits. It does not follow, however, that if the States choose to enact a different benefit scheme, they should be deemed to engage in unconstitutional conduct and forced to open their treasuries to private suits for damages.

NOTES AND QUESTIONS

1. Note that the author of the opinion, Justice Rehnquist, has been a staunch supporter of the new federalism. On the other hand, he also authored *Fitzpatrick v. Bitzer*, upholding Congress' abrogation of the Eleventh Amendment in Title VII of the

Civil Rights Act of 1964, which prohibits race, gender, religion, and national origin discrimination in employment, and subjects state employers to suit for monetary damages in federal courts.

2. Would Hibbs' termination have violated the Equal Protection Clause? If not, how can Congress make this termination unlawful under the FMLA?

3. How does the FMLA remedy inequality? Has Congress demonstrated "a widespread pattern of constitutional violations" by state officials? What about the statistical evidence that some thirty states had adopted some form of family-care leave prior to the FMLA?

4. Does the Act meet the "congruence and proportionality" test? Is it limited geographically or temporally? Does it just reach only states that have engaged in egregious conduct? Why did Justice Rehnquist nonetheless find this to be a valid, prophylactic measure? Wouldn't prohibiting gender discrimination regarding family leaves be much more proportionate and congruent to the problem?

5. How does the Court distinguish *Garrett* and *Kimel*? Is the distinction a viable one?

6. Distinguishing *Hibbs*, in *Coleman v. Court of Appeals of Maryland*, 566 U.S. 30 (2012), the Court, in a 5–4 ruling, decided Congress does not have the power, under § 5 of the Fourteenth Amendment, to abrogate the states' Eleventh Amendment protection from suits for damages alleging a violation of the "self-care" provision in the FMLA. In a four-Justice plurality opinion, Justice Kennedy said Congress did not have "widespread evidence of sex discrimination or stereotyping in the administration of sick leave." In fact, at the time the FMLA was adopted 95% of full-time state and local government employees had sick leave plans, and 96% had short-term disability plans. Thus, *Hibbs*, which addressed family leave policies, was not controlling. Justice Scalia concurred in the judgment, but did not join the plurality opinion. He argued that the "'congruence and proportionality' test makes no sense," and that, outside race discrimination, he "would limit Congress' § 5 power to the regulation of conduct that *itself* violates the Fourteenth Amendment." Justice Ginsburg, in her dissenting opinion joined by three other Justices, argued that the FMLA, in its entirety, is directed at sex discrimination. Congress made the self-care provision gender neutral to avoid giving employers an incentive to not hire females.

Justice Stevens delivered the opinion of the Court.

Title II of the Americans with Disabilities Act of 1990 (ADA or Act), 104 Stat. 337, 42 U.S.C. §§12131-12165, provides that "no qualified individual with a disability shall, by reason of such disability, be excluded from participation in or be denied the benefits of the services, programs or activities of a public entity, or be subjected to discrimination by any such entity." § 12132. The question presented in this case is whether Title II exceeds Congress' power under § 5 of the Fourteenth Amendment.

I

In August 1998, respondents George Lane and Beverly Jones filed this action against the State of Tennessee and a number of Tennessee counties, alleging past and ongoing violations of Title II. Respondents, both of whom are paraplegics who use wheelchairs for mobility, claimed that they were denied access to, and the services of, the state court system by reason of their disabilities. Lane alleged that he was compelled to appear to answer a set of criminal charges on the second floor of a county courthouse that had no elevator. At his first appearance, Lane crawled up two flights of stairs to get to the courtroom. When Lane returned to the courthouse for a hearing, he refused to crawl again or to be carried by officers to the courtroom; he consequently was arrested and jailed for failure to appear. Jones, a certified court reporter, alleged that she has not been able to gain access to a number of county courthouses, and, as a result, has lost both work and an opportunity to participate in the judicial process. Respondents sought damages and equitable relief.

The State moved to dismiss the suit on the ground that it was barred by the Eleventh Amendment. The District Court denied the motion without opinion, and the State appealed. In *Garrett*, we concluded that the Eleventh Amendment bars private suits seeking money damages for state violations of Title I of the ADA. We left open, however, the question whether the Eleventh Amendment permits suits for money damages under Title II.

II

Invoking "the sweep of congressional authority, including the power to enforce the fourteenth amendment and to regulate commerce," the ADA is designed "to provide a clear and comprehensive national mandate for the elimination of discrimination against individuals with disabilities." §§ 12101(b)(1), (b)(4). It forbids discrimination against persons with disabilities in three major areas of public life: employment, which is covered by Title I of the statute; public services, programs, and activities, which are the subject of Title II; and public accommodations, which are covered by Title III.

Title II, §§ 12131-12134, prohibits any public entity from discriminating against "qualified" persons with disabilities in the provision or operation of public services, programs, or activities. The Act defines the term "public entity" to include state and local governments, as well as their agencies and instrumentalities. § 12131(1). Persons with disabilities are "qualified" if they, "with or without reasonable modifications to rules, policies, or practices, the removal of architectural, communication, or transportation barriers, or the provision of auxiliary aids and services, mee[t] the essential eligibility requirements for the receipt of services or the participation in programs or activities provided by a public entity." § 12131(2). Title II's enforcement provision incorporates by reference §505 of the Rehabilitation Act of 1973, 92 Stat. 2982, as added, 29 U.S.C. § 794a, which authorizes private citizens to bring suits for money damages. 42 U.S.C. § 12133.

III

Applying the *Boerne* test in *Garrett*, we concluded that Title I of the ADA was not a valid exercise of Congress' § 5 power to enforce the Fourteenth Amendment's prohibition on unconstitutional disability discrimination in public employment . . ., we concluded Congress' exercise of its prophylactic § 5 power was unsupported by a relevant history and pattern of constitutional violations. Although the dissent pointed out that Congress had before it a great deal of evidence of discrimination by the States against persons with disabilities, the Court's opinion noted that the "overwhelming majority" of that evidence related to "the provision of public services and public accommodations, which areas are addressed in Titles II and III," rather than Title I.

IV

The first step of the *Boerne* inquiry requires us to identify the constitutional right or rights that Congress sought to enforce when it enacted Title II. In *Garrett* we identified Title I's purpose as enforcement of the Fourteenth Amendment's command that "all persons similarly situated should be treated alike." As we observed, classifications based on disability violate that constitutional command if they lack a rational relationship to a legitimate governmental purpose.

Title II, like Title I, seeks to enforce this prohibition on irrational disability discrimination. But it also seeks to enforce a variety of other basic constitutional guarantees, infringements of which are subject to more searching judicial review. These rights include some, like the right of access to the courts at issue in this case, that are protected by the Due Process Clause of the Fourteenth Amendment. The Due Process Clause and the Confrontation Clause of the Sixth Amendment, as applied to the States via the Fourteenth Amendment, both guarantee to a criminal defendant such as respondent Lane the "right to be present at all stages of the trial where his absence might frustrate the fairness of the proceedings." The Due Process Clause also requires the States to afford certain civil litigants a "meaningful opportunity to be heard" by removing obstacles to their full participation in judicial proceedings.

Whether Title II validly enforces these constitutional rights is a question that "must be judged with reference to the historical experience which it reflects." While § 5 authorizes Congress to enact reasonably prophylactic remedial legislation, the appropriateness of the remedy depends on the gravity of the harm it seeks to prevent. "Difficult and intractable problems often require powerful remedies," *Kimel*, but it is also true that "[s]trong measures appropriate to address one harm may be an unwarranted response to another, lesser one," *Boerne*.

It is not difficult to perceive the harm that Title II is designed to address. Congress enacted Title II against a backdrop of pervasive unequal treatment in the administration of state services and programs, including systematic deprivations of fundamental rights. For example, "[a]s of 1979, most States . . . categorically disqualified 'idiots' from voting, without regard to individual capacity." The majority of these laws remain on the books, and have been the subject of legal challenge as recently as 2001. Similarly, a number of States have prohibited and continue to prohibit persons with disabilities from engaging in activities such as marrying and serving as jurors. The historical experience that Title II reflects is also documented in this Court's cases, which have identified unconstitutional treatment of disabled persons by state agencies in a variety of settings, including unjustified commitment; the abuse and neglect of persons committed to state mental health hospitals; and irrational discrimination in zoning decisions. The decisions of other courts, too, document a pattern of unequal treatment in the administration of a wide range of public services, programs, and activities, including the penal system, public education, and voting. Notably, these decisions also demonstrate a pattern of unconstitutional treatment in the administration of justice.

This pattern of disability discrimination persisted despite several federal and state legislative efforts to address it. In the deliberations that led up to the enactment of the ADA, Congress identified important shortcomings in existing laws that rendered them "inadequate to address the pervasive problems of discrimination that people with disabilities are facing." It also uncovered further evidence of those shortcomings, in the form of hundreds of examples of unequal treatment of persons with disabilities by States and their political subdivisions. As the Court's opinion in *Garrett* observed, the "overwhelming majority" of these examples concerned discrimination in the administration of public programs and services.

With respect to the particular services at issue in this case, Congress learned that many individuals, in many States across the country, were being excluded from courthouses and court proceedings by reason of their disabilities. A report before Congress showed that some 76% of public services and programs housed in state-owned buildings were inaccessible to and unusable by persons with disabilities, even taking into account the possibility that the services and programs might be restructured or relocated to other parts of the buildings. Congress itself heard testimony from persons with disabilities who described the physical inaccessibility of local courthouses. And its appointed task force heard numerous examples of the exclusion of persons with disabilities from state judicial services and programs, including exclusion of persons with visual impairments and hearing impairments from jury service, failure of state and local governments to provide interpretive services for the hearing impaired, failure to permit the testimony of adults with developmental disabilities in abuse cases, and failure to make courtrooms accessible to witnesses with physical disabilities.

Given the sheer volume of evidence demonstrating the nature and extent of unconstitutional discrimination against persons with disabilities in the provision of public services, the dissent's contention that the record is insufficient to justify Congress' exercise of its prophylactic power is puzzling, to say the least. Just last Term in *Hibbs*, we approved the family-care leave provision of the FMLA as valid §5 legislation based primarily on evidence of disparate provision of parenting leave, little of which concerned unconstitutional state conduct. We explained that because the FMLA was targeted at sex-based classifications, which are subject to a heightened standard of judicial scrutiny, "it was easier for Congress to show a pattern of state constitutional violations" than in *Garrett* or *Kimel*, both of which concerned legislation that targeted classifications subject to rational-basis review. Title II is aimed at the enforcement of a variety of basic rights, including the right of access to the courts at issue in this case, that call for a standard of judicial review at least as searching, and in some cases more searching, than the standard that applies to sex-based classifications. And in any event, the record of constitutional violations in this case-including judicial findings of unconstitutional state action, and statistical, legislative, and anecdotal evidence of the widespread exclusion of persons with disabilities from the enjoyment of public services-far exceeds the record in *Hibbs*.

The conclusion that Congress drew from this body of evidence is set forth in the text of the ADA itself: "[D]iscrimination against individuals with disabilities persists in such critical areas as . . . education, transportation, communication, recreation, institutionalization, health services, voting, and *access to public services.*" 42 U.S.C. §12101(a)(3) (emphasis added). This finding, together with the extensive record of disability discrimination that underlies it, makes clear beyond peradventure that inadequate provision of public services and access to public facilities was an appropriate subject for prophylactic legislation.

V

The only question that remains is whether Title II is an appropriate response to this history and pattern of unequal treatment. At the outset, we must determine the scope of that inquiry. Title II—unlike RFRA, the Patent Remedy Act, and the other statutes we have reviewed for validity under § 5—reaches a wide array of official conduct in an effort to enforce an equally wide array of constitutional guarantees. Petitioner urges us both to examine the broad range of Title II's applications all at once, and to treat that breadth as a mark of the law's invalidity. According to petitioner, the fact that Title II applies not only to public education and voting-booth access but also to seating at state-owned hockey rinks indicates that Title II is not appropriately tailored to serve its objectives. But nothing in our case law requires us to consider Title II, with its wide variety of applications, as an undifferentiated whole. Whatever might be said about Title II's other applications, the question presented in this case is not whether Congress can validly subject the States to private suits for money damages for failing to provide reasonable access to hockey rinks, or even to voting booths, but whether Congress had the power under § 5 to enforce the constitutional right of access to the courts. Because we find that Title

II unquestionably is valid § 5 legislation as it applies to the class of cases implicating the accessibility of judicial services, we need go no further.

Congress' chosen remedy for the pattern of exclusion and discrimination described above, Title II's requirement of program accessibility, is congruent and proportional to its object of enforcing the right of access to the courts. The unequal treatment of disabled persons in the administration of judicial services has a long history, and has persisted despite several legislative efforts to remedy the problem of disability discrimination. Faced with considerable evidence of the shortcomings of previous legislative responses, Congress was justified in concluding that this "difficult and intractable proble[m]" warranted "added prophylactic measures in response."

The remedy Congress chose is nevertheless a limited one. Recognizing that failure to accommodate persons with disabilities will often have the same practical effect as outright exclusion, Congress required the States to take reasonable measures to remove architectural and other barriers to accessibility. 42 U.S.C. § 12131(2). But Title II does not require States to employ any and all means to make judicial services accessible to persons with disabilities, and it does not require States to compromise their essential eligibility criteria for public programs. It requires only "reasonable modifications" that would not fundamentally alter the nature of the service provided, and only when the individual seeking modification is otherwise eligible for the service.

This duty to accommodate is perfectly consistent with the well-established due process principle that, "within the limits of practicability, a State must afford to all individuals a meaningful opportunity to be heard" in its courts. *Boddie.* Our cases have recognized a number of affirmative obligations that flow from this principle: the duty to waive filing fees in certain family-law and criminal cases, the duty to provide transcripts to criminal defendants seeking review of their convictions, and the duty to provide counsel to certain criminal defendants. Each of these cases makes clear that ordinary considerations of cost and convenience alone cannot justify a State's failure to provide individuals with a meaningful right of access to the courts. Judged against this backdrop, Title II's affirmative obligation to accommodate persons with disabilities in the administration of justice cannot be said to be "so out of proportion to a supposed remedial or preventive object that it cannot be understood as responsive to, or designed to prevent, unconstitutional behavior." It is, rather, a reasonable prophylactic measure, reasonably targeted to a legitimate end.

For these reasons, we conclude that Title II, as it applies to the class of cases implicating the fundamental right of access to the courts, constitutes a valid exercise of Congress' § 5 authority to enforce the guarantees of the Fourteenth Amendment.

Chief Justice Rehnquist, with whom Justice Kennedy and Justice Thomas join, dissenting.

In *Garrett,* we conducted the three-step inquiry first enunciated in *City of Boerne* to determine whether Title I of the ADA satisfied the congruence-and-proportionality test. A faithful application of that test to Title II reveals that it too "'substantively redefine[s],'" rather than permissibly enforces, the rights protected by the Fourteenth Amendment.

The first step is to "identify with some precision the scope of the constitutional right at issue." In this case, the task of identifying the scope of the relevant constitutional protection is more difficult because Title II purports to enforce a panoply of constitutional rights of disabled persons: not only the equal protection right against irrational discrimination, but also certain rights protected by the Due Process Clause. However, because the Court ultimately upholds Title II "as it applies to the class of cases implicating the fundamental right of access to the courts," the proper inquiry focuses on the scope of those due process rights. The Court cites four access-to-the-courts rights that Title II purportedly enforces: (1) the right of the criminal defendant to be present at all critical stages of the trial; (2) the right of litigants to have a "meaningful opportunity to be heard" in judicial proceedings; (3) the right of the criminal defendant to trial by a jury composed of a fair cross section of the community; and (4) the public right of access to criminal proceedings.

Having traced the "metes and bounds" of the constitutional rights at issue, the next step in the congruence-and-proportionality inquiry requires us to examine whether Congress "identi-fied a history and pattern" of violations of these constitutional rights by the States with respect to the disabled. This step is crucial to determining whether Title II is a legitimate attempt to remedy or prevent actual constitutional violations by the States or an illegitimate attempt to rewrite the constitutional provisions it purports to enforce. Indeed, "Congress' § 5 power is appropriately exercised *only* in response to state transgressions." But the majority identifies nothing in the legislative record that shows Congress was responding to widespread violations of the due process rights of disabled persons.

Rather than limiting its discussion of constitutional violations to the due process rights on which it ultimately relies, the majority sets out on a wide-ranging account of societal discrimi-nation against the disabled. Even if it were proper to consider this broader category of evidence, much of it does not concern *unconstitutional* action by the *States*. We have repeatedly held that such evidence is irrelevant to the inquiry whether Congress has validly abrogated Eleventh Amendment immunity, a privilege enjoyed only by the sovereign States. Moreover, the majority today cites the same congressional task force evidence we rejected in *Garrett*. With respect to the due process "access to the courts" rights on which the Court ultimately relies, Congress' fail-ure to identify a pattern of actual constitutional violations by the States is even more striking. Indeed, there is *nothing* in the legislative record or statutory findings to indicate that disabled persons were systematically denied the right to be present at criminal trials, denied the mean-ingful opportunity to be heard in civil cases, unconstitutionally excluded from jury service, or denied the right to attend criminal trials.

Even if the anecdotal evidence and conclusory statements relied on by the majority could be properly considered, the mere existence of an architecturally "inaccessible" courthouse-i.e., one a disabled person cannot utilize without assistance-does not state a constitutional violation. A violation of due process occurs only when a person is actually denied the constitutional right to access a given judicial proceeding. We have never held that a person has a *constitutional* right to make his way into a courtroom without any external assistance. Nor does an "inaccessible" courthouse violate the Equal Protection Clause, unless it is irrational for the State not to alter the courthouse to make it "accessible." But financial considerations almost always furnish a rational basis for a State to decline to make those alterations. Thus, evidence regarding inaccessible courthouses, because it is not evidence of constitutional violations, provides no basis to abrogate States' sovereign immunity.

The third step of our congruence-and-proportionality inquiry removes any doubt as to whether Title II is valid § 5 legislation. At this stage, we ask whether the rights and remedies created by Title II are congruent and proportional to the constitutional rights it purports to enforce and the record of constitutional violations adduced by Congress. The ADA's findings make clear that Congress believed it was attacking "discrimination" in all areas of public services, as well as the "discriminatory effect" of "architectural, transportation, and communication barriers." §§ 12101(a)(3), (a)(5). In sum, Title II requires, on pain of money damages, special accommodations for disabled persons in virtually every interaction they have with the State.

"Despite subjecting States to this expansive liability," the broad terms of Title II "d[o] nothing to limit the coverage of the Act to cases involving arguable constitutional violations." By requiring special accommodation and the elimination of programs that have a disparate impact on the disabled, Title II prohibits far more state conduct than does the equal protection ban on irrational discrimination. The majority, however, claims that Title II also vindicates fundamental rights protected by the Due Process Clause-in addition to access to the courts-that are subject to heightened Fourteenth Amendment scrutiny. But Title II is not tailored to provide prophylactic protection of these rights; instead, it applies to any service, program, or activity provided by any entity. Its provisions affect transportation, health, education, and recreation programs, among many others, all of which are accorded only rational-basis scrutiny under the Equal Protection Clause. A requirement of accommodation for the disabled at a state-owned amusement park or sports stadium, for example, bears no permissible prophylactic relationship to enabling disabled persons to exercise their fundamental constitutional rights.

The majority concludes that Title II's massive overbreadth can be cured by considering the statute only "as it applies to the class of cases implicating the accessibility of judicial services." I have grave doubts about importing an "as applied" approach into the § 5 context. While the majority is of course correct that this Court normally only considers the application of a statute to a particular case, the proper inquiry under *City of Boerne* and its progeny is somewhat different. In applying the congruence-and-proportionality test, we ask whether Congress has attempted to statutorily redefine the constitutional rights protected by the Fourteenth Amendment. This question can only be answered by measuring the breadth of a statute's coverage against the scope of the constitutional rights it purports to enforce and the record of violations it purports to remedy.

Even in the limited courthouse-access context, Title II does not properly abrogate state sovereign immunity. As demonstrated in depth above, Congress utterly failed to identify any evidence that disabled persons were denied constitutionally protected access to judicial proceedings. Without this predicate showing, Title II, even if we were to hypothesize that it applies only to courthouses, cannot be viewed as a congruent and proportional response to state constitutional violations.

1. How does the majority distinguish *Garrett*? Are the cases irreconcilable, as Justice Rehnquist asserts?

2. Should the Court use an "as applied" standard to assess congressional power under § 5? What are the dangers of this approach? Other than access to courthouses, did Congress validly abrogate the Eleventh Amendment with regard to Title II's application to other "public" facilities and services?

3. The Supreme Court revisited the abrogation question in *U.S. v. Georgia*, 546 U.S. 151 (2006). A disabled inmate in the state prison sued for money damages under Title II of the ADA. Goodman alleged he was unable to move his wheelchair in his cell, and there were several instances in which he was forced to sit in his own bodily waste because prison officials refused to provide assistance. The Eleventh Circuit ruled that Goodman had alleged actual violations of the Eighth Amendment by state agents, and the state did not contest this holding. The Supreme Court, in a unanimous decision by Justice Scalia, ruled that Goodman's claims for money damages against the State, which independently violated the Eighth Amendment, could be brought under Title II: "While the Members of this Court have disagreed regarding the scope of Congress' 'prophylactic' enforcement powers under § 5 of the Fourteenth Amendment, no one doubts that § 5 grants Congress the power to 'enforce . . . the provisions' of the Amendment by creating private remedies against the States for *actual* violations of those provisions. . . . This enforcement power includes the power to abrogate state sovereign immunity by authorizing private suits for damages against the States. Thus, insofar as Title II creates a private cause of action for damages against the States for conduct that *actually* violates the Fourteenth Amendment, Title II validly abrogates state sovereign immunity."

PROBLEM: TWO

The Equal Pay Act ("EPA") of 1963, 29 U.S.C. § 206(d), provides that: "no employer having employees subject to this provision shall discriminate . . . between employees on the basis of sex by paying wages to employees in such establishment at a rate less than the rate at which he pays wages to employees of the opposite sex in such establishment for equal work. . . ." Once an employee proves that she is paid less than a male who performs a job in the same establishment that is substantially similar in terms of skill, effort and responsibility, the employer will be liable for wage discrimination and subject to damages unless it can prove a factor other than sex justifies the wage disparity. The employee need not prove the wage discrimination was intentional in order to recover.

1. What constitutional provision(s) empowers Congress to enact this legislation as applied to **private** employers? Discuss the Civil War Amendments, as well as the Commerce Clause, as possible sources.

2. Did Congress validly abrogate the Eleventh Amendment when, in 1974, it extended the damage remedy of the Equal Pay Act to include state and local government employers? Does it matter whether the constitutional source for this expansion was the Commerce Clause or the Fourteenth Amendment?

3. Since the Supreme Court has held that only intentional discrimination is actionable under the Equal Protection Clause, may Congress acting under § 5 of the Fourteenth Amendment prohibit unintentional gender-based wage disparities? Does it suffice that the legislative record identified a serious and endemic problem of employment discrimination in private industry? (No similar findings with respect to wage discrimination in the public sector were noted in 1974, but can't this be implied?) Does the EPA survive the "congruence and proportionality" test established and explicated in *Boerne, Kimel, Garrett, Morrison, Hibbs,* and *Lane?*

D. THE SPENDING POWER

Article I, § 8, clause 1 provides Congress with the power to "pay debts and provide for the common defense and general welfare of the United States." As described in *United States v. Butler,* 297 U.S. 1 (1936), there were historically two competing interpretations of this provision. James Madison and Thomas Jefferson believed that Congress' power to appropriate funds for the "general welfare" was limited by the enumerated powers set forth in the remainder of Article I, § 8. Alexander Hamilton and James Monroe, on the other hand, adopted a much broader interpretation of the general welfare clause, believing that the scope of permissible spending power extended beyond the enumerated powers to any "national purpose" encompassed within this term.

While the Court in *Butler* adopted the Hamiltonian view, it found that Congress had indeed violated states' rights by invading their power to regulate agricultural production. One year later, however, the Court shifted its position, holding in *Helvering v. Davis,* 301 U.S. 619 (1937), that Congress had broad discretion to decide what was necessary for the general welfare, and that its choice would not be overturned unless "clearly wrong." It further stressed that the concept of general welfare was a dynamic one and thus the broad welfare legislation introduced by the FDR Administration to deal with the depression should indeed be upheld. On the same day, the Court, in *Steward Machine Company v. Davis,* 301 U.S. 548 (1937), upheld the unemployment tax provisions of the Social Security Act which had been challenged as violating state sovereign power contrary to the Tenth Amendment. The Court ruled that this Act did not violate states' rights, but actually freed the states to deal with the problems of unemployment by eliminating fear of economic disadvantage.

Aside from the requirement that Congress be acting to further "national purposes," are there any limitations on Congress' power to regulate by attaching conditions on its monetary grants?

SOUTH DAKOTA V. DOLE
483 U.S. 203 (1987)

[In 1984 Congress enacted 23 U.S.C. § 158, which directs the Secretary of Transportation to withhold a percentage of federal highway funds to states where the drinking age is under 21 years of age. Without explicitly deciding the scope of the Twenty-first Amendment, the Court addressed the Spending Power question.]

Chief Justice REHNQUIST delivered the opinion of the Court.

[W]e need not decide whether [the Twenty-first Amendment] would prohibit an attempt by Congress to legislate directly a national minimum drinking age. Here, Congress has acted indirectly under its spending power to encourage uniformity in the States' drinking ages. As we explain below, we find this legislative effort within constitutional bounds even if Congress may not regulate drinking ages directly.

The Constitution empowers Congress to "lay and collect Taxes, Duties, Imposts, and Excises, to pay the Debts and provide for the common Defence and general Welfare of the United States." Art. I, § 8, cl. 1. Incident to this power, Congress may attach conditions on the receipt of federal funds, and has repeatedly employed the power "to further broad policy objectives by conditioning receipt of federal moneys upon compliance by the recipient with federal statutory and administrative directives." The breadth of this power was made clear in *United States v. Butler*, where the Court, resolving a longstanding debate over the scope of the Spending Clause, determined that "the power of Congress to authorize expenditure of public moneys for public purposes is not limited by the direct grants of legislative power found in the Constitution." Thus, objectives not thought to be within Article I's "enumerated legislative fields," may nevertheless be attained through the use of the spending power and the conditional grant of federal funds.

The spending power is of course not unlimited, but is instead subject to several general restrictions articulated in our cases. The first of these limitations is derived from the language of the Constitution itself: the exercise of the spending power must be in pursuit of "the general welfare." In considering whether a particular expenditure is intended to serve general public purposes, courts should defer substantially to the judgment of Congress. Second, we have required that if Congress desires to condition the States' receipt of federal funds, it "must do so unambiguously, enabl[ing] the States to exercise their choice knowingly, cognizant of the consequences of their participation." *Pennhurst State School v. Halderman*. Third, our cases have suggested (without significant elaboration) that conditions on federal grants might be illegitimate if they are unrelated "to the federal interest in particular national projects or programs."

Finally, we have noted that other constitutional provisions may provide an independent bar to the conditional grant of federal funds.

South Dakota does not seriously claim that § 158 is inconsistent with any of the first three restrictions mentioned above. We can readily conclude that the provision is designed to serve the general welfare, especially in light of the fact that "the concept of welfare or the opposite is shaped by Congress. . . ." Congress found that the differing drinking ages in the States created particular incentives for young persons to combine their desire to drink with their ability to drive, and that this interstate problem required a national solution. The means it chose to address this dangerous situation were reasonably calculated to advance the general welfare. The conditions upon which States receive the funds, moreover, could not be more clearly stated by Congress. And the State itself, rather than challenging the germaneness of the condition of federal purposes, admits that it "has never contended that the congressional action was . . . unrelated to a national concern in the absence of the Twenty-first Amendment." Indeed, the condition imposed by Congress is directly related to one of the main purposes for which highway funds are expended—safe interstate travel. This goal of the interstate highway system had been frustrated by varying drinking ages among the States. A presidential commission appointed to study alcohol-related accidents and fatalities on the Nation's highways concluded that the lack of uniformity in the States' drinking ages created "an incentive to drink and drive" because "young person commut[e] to border States where the drinking age is lower." By enacting § 158, Congress conditioned the receipt of federal funds in a way reasonably calculated to address this particular impediment to a purpose for which the funds are expended.

The remaining question about the validity of § 158—and the basic point of disagreement between the parties—is whether the Twenty-first Amendment constitutes an "independent constitutional bar" to the conditional grant of federal funds. Petitioner, relying on its view that the Twenty-first Amendment prohibits *direct* regulation of drinking ages by Congress, asserts that "Congress may not use the spending power to regulate that which it is prohibited from regulating directly under the Twenty-first Amendment." But our cases show that this "independent constitutional bar" limitation on the spending power is not of the kind petitioner suggests. *Butler*, for example, established that the constitutional limitations on Congress when exercising its spending power are less exacting than those on its authority to regulate directly.

We have also held that a perceived Tenth Amendment limitation on congressional regulation of state affairs did not concomitantly limit the range of conditions legitimately placed on federal grants. In *Oklahoma v. Civil Service Comm'n*, the Court considered the validity of the Hatch Act insofar as it was applied to political activities of state officials whose employment was financed in whole or in part with federal funds. The State contended that an order under this provision to withhold certain federal funds unless a state official was removed invaded its sovereignty in violation of the Tenth Amendment. Though finding that "the United States is not concerned with, and has no power to regulate, local political activities as such of state officials," the Court nevertheless held that the Federal Government "does have power to fix the terms upon which its money allotments to states shall be disbursed." The Court found no violation of the State's sovereignty because the State could, and did, adopt "the `simple expedient' of not yielding to what she urges is federal coercion. The offer of benefits to a state by the United States dependent upon cooperation by the state with federal plans, assumedly for the general welfare, is not unusual."

These cases establish that the "independent constitutional bar" limitation on the spending power is not, as petitioner suggests, a prohibition on the indirect achievement of objectives which Congress is not empowered to achieve directly. Instead, we think that the language in our earlier opinions stands for the unexceptionable proposition that the power may not be used to induce the States to engage in activities that would themselves be unconstitutional. Thus, for example, a grant of federal funds conditioned on invidiously discriminatory state action or the infliction of cruel and unusual punishment would be an illegitimate exercise of the Congress' broad spending power. But no such claim can be or is made here. Were South Dakota to succumb to the blandishments offered by Congress and raise its drinking age to 21, the State's action in so doing would not violate the constitutional rights of anyone.

Our decisions have recognized that in some circumstances the financial inducement offered by Congress might be so coercive as to pass the point at which "pressure turns into compulsion." Here, however, Congress has directed only that a State desiring to establish a minimum drinking age lower than 21 lose a relatively small percentage of certain federal highway funds. Petitioner contends that the coercive nature of this program is evident from the degree of success it has achieved. We cannot conclude, however, that a conditional grant of federal money of this sort is unconstitutional simply by reason of its success in achieving the congressional objective.

When we consider, for a moment, that all South Dakota would lose if she adheres to her chosen course as to a suitable minimum drinking age is 5% of the funds otherwise obtainable under specified highway grant programs, the argument as to coercion is shown to be more rhetoric than fact.

Here Congress has offered relatively mild encouragement to the States to enact higher minimum drinking ages than they would otherwise choose. But the enactment of such laws remains the prerogative of the States not merely in theory but in fact. Even if Congress might lack the power to impose a national minimum drinking age directly, we conclude that encouragement to state action found in § 158 is a valid use of the spending power.

Justice BRENNAN, dissenting

I agree with Justice O'CONNOR that regulation of the minimum age of purchasers of liquor falls squarely within the ambit of those powers reserved to the States by the Twenty-first Amendment. Since States possess this constitutional power, Congress can not condition a federal grant in a manner that abridges this right. The Amendment, itself, strikes the proper balance between federal and state authority. I therefore dissent.

Justice O'CONNOR, dissenting

The Court today upholds the National Minimum Drinking Age Amendment as a valid exercise of the Spending Power conferred by Article I, § 8. But § 158 is not a condition on spending reasonably related to the expenditure of federal funds and cannot be justified on that ground. Rather, it is an attempt to regulate the sale of liquor, an attempt that lies outside Congress' power to regulate commerce because it falls within the ambit of § 2 of the Twenty-first Amendment.

My disagreement with the Court is relatively narrow on the Spending Power issue: it is a disagreement about the application of a principle rather than a disagreement on the principle itself. I agree with the Court that Congress may attach conditions on the receipt of federal funds to further "the federal interest in particular national projects or programs." I also subscribe to the established proposition that the reach of the Spending Power "is not limited by the direct grants of legislative power found in the Constitution." Finally, I agree that there are four separate types of limitations on the Spending Power: the expenditure must be for the general welfare, the conditions imposed must be unambiguous, they must be reasonably related to the purpose of the expenditure, and the legislation may not violate any independent constitutional prohibition. Insofar as two of those limitations are concerned, the Court is clearly correct that § 158 is wholly unobjectionable. Establishment of a national minimum drinking age certainly fits within the broad concept of the general welfare and the statute is entirely unambiguous. I am also willing to assume *arguendo* that the Twenty-first Amendment does not constitute an "independent constitutional bar" to a spending condition.

But the Court's application of the requirement that the condition imposed be reasonably related to the purpose for which the funds are expended, is cursory and unconvincing. We have repeatedly said that Congress may condition grants under the Spending Power only in ways reasonably related to the purpose of the federal program. In my view, establishment of a minimum drinking age of 21 is not sufficiently related to interstate highway construction to justify so conditioning funds appropriated for that purpose.

When Congress appropriates money to build a highway, it is entitled to insist that the highway be a safe one. But it is not entitled to insist as a condition of the use of highway funds that the State impose or change regulations in other areas of the State's social, and economic life because of an attenuated or tangential relationship to highway use or safety. Indeed, if the rule were otherwise, the Congress could effectively regulate almost any area of a State's social, political, or economic life on the theory that use of the interstate transportation system is somehow enhanced.

NOTES AND QUESTIONS

1. Could Congress, acting under the Commerce Clause, have directly ordered the states to raise their drinking age to 21?

2. Did the Court ignore state sovereignty? If Congress threatened loss of *all* federal highway money, would the outcome have been the same?

3. As indicated in *Dole*, the Supreme Court in *Pennhurst State School and Hospital v. Halderman*, 451 U.S. 1 (1981), held that Congress, in acting under the Spending Clause, is bound by a requirement that the terms of its grants be clear. In *Pennhurst*, the Court

was asked to consider whether the Developmentally Disabled Assistance and Bill of Rights Act of 1975 imposed affirmative obligations on states, which accepted the funds, to assure mentally retarded persons a right to "appropriate treatment" in the "least restrictive" environment. The Court's reasoning follows:

> In discerning congressional intent, we necessarily turn to the possible sources of Congress' power to legislate, namely, Congress' power to enforce the Fourteenth Amendment and its power under the Spending Clause to place conditions on the grant of federal funds.
>
> Although this Court has previously addressed issues going to Congress' power to secure the guarantees of the Fourteenth Amendment, we have had little occasion to consider the appropriate test for determining when Congress intends to enforce those guarantees. Because such legislation imposes congressional policy on a State involuntarily, and because it often intrudes on traditional state authority, we should not quickly attribute to Congress an unstated intent to act under its authority to enforce the Fourteenth Amendment. Our previous cases are wholly consistent with that view, since Congress in those cases expressly articulated its intent to legislate pursuant to § 5. Those cases, moreover, involved statutes which simply prohibited certain kinds of state conduct. The case for inferring intent is at its weakest where, as here, the rights asserted impose *affirmative* obligations on the States to fund certain services, since we may assume that Congress will not implicitly attempt to impose massive financial obligations on the States.
>
> Turning to Congress' power to legislate pursuant to the spending power, our cases have long recognized that Congress may fix the terms on which it shall disburse federal money to the States. Unlike legislation enacted under § 5, however, legislation enacted pursuant to the spending power is much in the nature of a contract: in return for federal funds, the States agree to comply with federally imposed conditions. The legitimacy of Congress' power to legislate under the spending power thus rests on whether the State voluntarily and knowingly accepts the terms of the `contract.' There can, of course, be no knowing acceptance if a State is unaware of the conditions or is unable to ascertain what is expected of it. Accordingly, if Congress intends to impose a condition on the grant of federal moneys, it must do so unambiguously.
>
> Indeed, in those instances where Congress has intended the States to fund certain entitlements as a condition of receiving federal funds, it has proved capable of saying so explicitly. We must carefully inquire, then, whether Congress in § 6010 imposed an obligation on the States to spend state money to fund certain rights as a condition of receiving federal moneys under the Act or whether it spoke merely in precatory terms.
>
> Applying those principles to these cases, we find nothing in the Act or its legislative history to suggest that Congress intended to require the States to assume the high cost of

providing 'appropriate treatment' in the 'least restrictive environment' to their mentally retarded citizens.

a. What limitation on the spending power does *Pennhurst* impose on Congress?

b. Could Congress have passed the Developmentally Disabled Assistance and Bill of Rights Act under § 5 of the Fourteenth Amendment? If the Act allowed suit for damages against a non-complying state, would the Eleventh Amendment pose a barrier? Compare *Kimel.* May Congress abrogate the Eleventh Amendment when it invokes its Article I Spending Power? Should the question be abrogation or don't individual states simply waive immunity when they accept federal funds?

c. If the Act had clearly set forth an affirmative obligation on the states to provide rehabilitation services in the least restrictive environment, could the Tenth Amendment have been used to invalidate the law?

4. In Sossamon v. Texas, 563 U.S. 277 (2011), the Court relied on Pennhurst to hold that states, in accepting federal funding, did not consent to waive their sovereign immunity to private suits for monetary damages under the Religious Land Use and Institutionalized Persons Act of 2000 (RLUIPA). This Act was passed in response to the Supreme Court's decision invalidating the Religious Freedom Restoration Act in City of Boerne, supra. Section 3 of the Act targets restrictions on the religious exercise of institutionalized persons, and it provides an express private cause of action for "appropriate relief against a government entity that receives federal financial assistance." The Court ruled that "RLUIPA's authorization of 'appropriate relief against a government,' is not the unequivocal expression of state consent that our precedents require . . . where a statute is susceptible of multiple plausible interpretations, including one preserving immunity, we will not consider a State to have waived its sovereign immunity." Further, the Court, while recognizing that Spending Clause power operates as a form of contract and damages are always available for breach of contract, ruled that ordinary contract principles do not apply where the sovereign is a party: "[the] implied-contract-remedies proposal cannot be squared with our longstanding rule that a waiver of sovereign immunity must be expressly and unequivocally stated in the text of the relevant statute . . . without such a clear statement from Congress and notice to the States, federal courts may not step in and abrogate state sovereign immunity."

If the Act clearly provided for compensatory damages, would it be upheld as a valid exercise of Congress' Spending Power?

[In a 5–4 decision the Court upheld the "individual mandate," which required almost all Americans to purchase health insurance or pay a tax penalty. The Court reasoned that this provision in the Patient Protection and Affordable Care Act (ACA) was a valid exercise of Congress's power to tax. However, five Justices also held that the ACA was not a valid exercise of Congress's Commerce Clause power because, by requiring individuals to purchase health insurance, it was regulating the inactivity of those not engaged in commerce. Finally, in a 7–2 ruling, in an opinion by Chief Justice Roberts, the Court held that the Medicaid expansion provision of the ACA exceeded Congress's power under the Spending Clause. This portion of the decision follows:]

IV

A

The States also contend that the Medicaid expansion exceeds Congress's authority under the Spending Clause. They claim that Congress is coercing the States to adopt the changes it wants by threatening to withhold all of a State's Medicaid grants, unless the State accepts the new expanded funding and complies with the conditions that come with it. This, they argue, violates the basic principle that the "Federal Government may not compel the States to enact or administer a federal regulatory program."

There is no doubt that the Act dramatically increases state obligations under Medicaid. The current Medicaid program requires States to cover only certain discrete categories of needy individuals—pregnant women, children, needy families, the blind, the elderly, and the disabled. There is no mandatory coverage for most childless adults, and the States typically do not offer any such coverage. The States also enjoy considerable flexibility with respect to the coverage levels for parents of needy families. On average States cover only those unemployed parents who make less than 37 percent of the federal poverty level, and only those employed parents who make less than 63 percent of the poverty line.

The Medicaid provisions of the Affordable Care Act, in contrast, require States to expand their Medicaid programs by 2014 to cover *all* individuals under the age of 65 with incomes below 133 percent of the federal poverty line. The Act also establishes a new "[e]ssential health benefits" package, which States must provide to all new Medicaid recipients—a level sufficient to satisfy a recipient's obligations under the individual mandate. The Affordable Care Act provides that the Federal Government will pay 100 percent of the costs of covering these newly eligible individuals through 2016. In the following years, the federal payment level gradually decreases, to a minimum of 90 percent. In light of the expansion in coverage mandated by the Act, the Federal Government estimates that its Medicaid spending will increase by approximately $100 billion per year, nearly 40 percent above current levels.

The Spending Clause grants Congress the power "to pay the Debts and provide for the ... general Welfare of the United States." U.S. Const., Art. I, § 8, cl. 1. We have long recognized that Congress may use this power to grant federal funds to the States, and may condition such a grant upon the States' "taking certain actions that Congress could not require them to take." Such measures "encourage a State to regulate in a particular way, [and] influenc[e] a State's policy choices." The conditions imposed by Congress ensure that the funds are used by the States to "provide for the ... general Welfare" in the manner Congress intended.

At the same time, our cases have recognized limits on Congress's power under the Spending Clause to secure state compliance with federal objectives. "We have repeatedly characterized ... Spending Clause legislation as 'much in the nature of a *contract.*'" The legitimacy of Congress's exercise of the spending power "thus rests on whether the State voluntarily and knowingly accepts the terms of the 'contract.'" *Pennhurst.* Respecting this limitation is critical to ensuring that Spending Clause legislation does not undermine the status of the States as independent sovereigns in our federal system.

That insight has led this Court to strike down federal legislation that commandeers a State's legislative or administrative apparatus for federal purposes. It has also led us to scrutinize Spending Clause legislation to ensure that Congress is not using financial inducements to exert a "power akin to undue influence." Congress may use its spending power to create incentives for States to act in accordance with federal policies. But when "pressure turns into compulsion," the legislation runs contrary to our system of federalism. "[T]he Constitution simply does not give Congress the authority to require the States to regulate." That is true whether Congress directly commands a State to regulate or indirectly coerces a State to adopt a federal regulatory system as its own.

Permitting the Federal Government to force the States to implement a federal program would threaten the political accountability key to our federal system. "[W]here the Federal Government directs the States to regulate, it may be state officials who will bear the brunt of public disapproval, while the federal officials who devised the regulatory program may remain insulated from the electoral ramifications of their decision." Spending Clause programs do not pose this danger when a State has a legitimate choice whether to accept the federal conditions in exchange for federal funds. In such a situation, state officials can fairly be held politically accountable for choosing to accept or refuse the federal offer. But when the State has no choice, the Federal Government can achieve its objectives without accountability, just as in *New York* and *Printz.* Indeed, this danger is heightened when Congress acts under the Spending Clause, because Congress can use that power to implement federal policy it could not impose directly under its enumerated powers.

Congress may attach appropriate conditions to federal taxing and spending programs to preserve its control over the use of federal funds. In the typical case we look to the States to defend their prerogatives by adopting "the simple expedient of not yielding" to federal blandishments when they do not want to embrace the federal policies as their own. The States are separate and independent sovereigns. Sometimes they have to act like it.

The States, however, argue that the Medicaid expansion is far from the typical case. They object that Congress has "crossed the line distinguishing encouragement from coercion," in the way it has structured the funding: Instead of simply refusing to grant the new funds to States that will not accept the new conditions, Congress has also threatened to withhold those States' existing Medicaid funds. The States claim that this threat serves no purpose other than to force unwilling States to sign up for the dramatic expansion in health care coverage effected by the Act.

Given the nature of the threat and the programs at issue here, we must agree. We have upheld Congress's authority to condition the receipt of funds on the States' complying with restrictions on the use of those funds, because that is the means by which Congress ensures that the funds are spent according to its view of the "general Welfare." Conditions that do not here govern the use of the funds, however, cannot be justified on that basis. When, for example, such conditions take the form of threats to terminate other significant independent grants, the conditions are properly viewed as a means of pressuring the States to accept policy changes.

In *South Dakota v. Dole,* we considered a challenge to a federal law that threatened to withhold five percent of a State's federal highway funds if the State did not raise its drinking age to 21. We found that the inducement was not impermissibly coercive, because Congress was offering only "relatively mild encouragement to the States." We observed that "all South Dakota would lose if she adheres to her chosen course as to a suitable minimum drinking age is 5%" of her highway funds. In fact, the federal funds at stake constituted less than half of one percent of South Dakota's budget at the time.

In this case, the financial "inducement" Congress has chosen is much more than "relatively mild encouragement"—it is a gun to the head. Section 1396c of the Medicaid Act provides that if a State's Medicaid plan does not comply with the Act's requirements, the Secretary of Health and Human Services may declare that "further payments will not be made to the State." A State that opts out of the Affordable Care Act's expansion in health care coverage thus stands to lose not merely "a relatively small percentage" of its existing Medicaid funding, but *all* of it. Medicaid spending accounts for over 20 percent of the average State's total budget, with federal funds covering 50 to 83 percent of those costs. The Federal Government estimates that it will pay out approximately $3.3 trillion between 2010 and 2019 in order to cover the costs of *pre*-expansion Medicaid. In addition, the States have developed intricate statutory and administrative regimes over the course of many decades to implement their objectives under existing Medicaid. It is easy to see how the *Dole* Court could conclude that the threatened loss of less than half of one percent of South Dakota's budget left that State with a "prerogative" to reject Congress's desired policy, "not merely in theory but in fact." The threatened loss of over 10 percent of a State's overall budget, in contrast, is economic dragooning that leaves the States with no real option but to acquiesce in the Medicaid expansion.

Justice GINSBURG claims that *Dole* is distinguishable because here "Congress has not threatened to withhold funds earmarked for any other program." But that begs the question: The States contend that the expansion is in reality a new program and that Congress is forcing them to accept it by threatening the funds for the existing Medicaid program. We cannot agree that existing Medicaid and the expansion dictated by the Affordable Care Act are all one program simply because "Congress styled" them as such. If the expansion is not properly viewed as a modification of the existing Medicaid program, Congress's decision to so title it is irrelevant.

Here, the Government claims that the Medicaid expansion is properly viewed merely as a modification of the existing program because the States agreed that Congress could change the terms of Medicaid when they signed on in the first place. The Government observes that the Social Security Act, which includes the original Medicaid provisions, contains a clause expressly reserving "[t]he right to alter, amend, or repeal any provision" of that statute.

The Medicaid expansion, however, accomplishes a shift in kind, not merely degree. The original program was designed to cover medical services for four particular categories of the needy: the disabled, the blind, the elderly, and needy families with dependent children. Previous amendments to Medicaid eligibility merely altered and expanded the boundaries of these categories. Under the Affordable Care Act, Medicaid is transformed into a program to meet the health care needs of the entire nonelderly population with income below 133 percent of the poverty level. It is no longer a program to care for the neediest among us, but rather an element of a comprehensive national plan to provide universal health insurance coverage.

As we have explained, "[t]hough Congress' power to legislate under the spending power is broad, it does not include surprising participating States with post-acceptance or 'retroactive' conditions." A State could hardly anticipate that Congress's reservation of the right to "alter" or "amend" the Medicaid program included the power to transform it so dramatically.

The Court in *Steward Machine* did not attempt to "fix the outermost line" where persuasion gives way to coercion. The Court found it "[e]nough for present purposes that wherever the line may be, this statute is within it." We have no need to fix a line either. It is enough for today that wherever that line may be, this statute is surely beyond it. Congress may not simply "conscript state [agencies] into the national bureaucratic army."

B

Nothing in our opinion precludes Congress from offering funds under the Affordable Care Act to expand the availability of health care, and requiring that States accepting such funds comply with the conditions on their use. What Congress is not free to do is to penalize States that choose not to participate in that new program by taking away their existing Medicaid funding. Section 1396c gives the Secretary of Health and Human Services the authority to do just that. It allows her to withhold *all* "further [Medicaid] payments ... to the State" if she determines that the State is out of compliance with any Medicaid requirement, including those contained in the expansion. In light of the Court's holding, the Secretary cannot apply § 1396c to withdraw existing Medicaid funds for failure to comply with the requirements set out in the expansion.

1. Unlike the Court's ruling on the Commerce Clause, Justice Roberts' judgment on the Medicaid expansion was 7–2. It marks the first time the Supreme Court has invalidated a spending measure based on the Tenth Amendment compulsion argument. However, the Court stressed that a loss of all Medicaid funds, which was the penalty for noncompliance, would result in an average state's budget being cut by 10%. The fact that most states receive more than $1 billion in federal Medicaid funding shows the significance of the dollars involved. This may make this a very unique Spending Power case.

2. Was the majority correct in holding that the expansion of Medicaid was "essentially a new program," and thus a decision to join or not could not affect the state's ability to continue receiving preexisting Medicaid funding? Justice Ginsburg, in dissent, argued that the ACA was not tantamount to a new grant program. Rather, Medicaid, as amended by the ACA, is a single program enacted to enable poor persons to receive basic healthcare. In light of past expansions, plus express statutory warnings that Congress might change the requirements participating states must meet, she rejected the notion that the ACA fails due to lack of notice. The whole coercion argument is premised on Congress' creation of an entirely new program, whereas, in reality, Medicaid "simply reaches more of America's poor than Congress originally covered."

CHAPTER II:
RECONSTRUCTION LEGISLATION

A. SUBSTANTIVE PROVISIONS

1. SECTION 1981: RACE DISCRIMINATION AFFECTING CONTRACTS

a. The Meaning of Race Discrimination

SAINT FRANCIS COLLEGE V. AL-KHAZRAJI
481 U.S. 604 (1987)

Justice WHITE delivered the opinion of the Court.

Respondent, a citizen of the United States born in Iraq, was an associate professor at St. Francis College, one of the petitioners here. In January 1978, he applied for tenure; the Board of Trustees denied his request on February 23, 1978. He accepted a 1-year, nonrenewable contract and sought administrative reconsideration of the tenure decision, which was denied on February 6, 1979.

On October 30, 1980, respondent filed a *pro se* complaint in the District Court alleging a violation of Title VII of the Civil Rights Act of 1964 and claiming discrimination based on national origin, religion, and/or race. Amended complaints were filed, adding claims under the 42 U.S.C. §§ 1981, 1983, 1985(3), 1986, and state law. The District Court dismissed the 1986, 1985(3) and Title VII claims as untimely but held that the §§ 1981 and 1983 claims were not barred by the Pennsylvania 6-year statute of limitations.

II

Although § 1981 does not itself use the word "race," the Court has construed the section to forbid all "racial" discrimination in the making of private as well as public contracts. The petitioner college, although a private institution, was therefore subject to this statutory command. There is no disagreement among the parties on these propositions. The issue is whether respondent has alleged *racial* discrimination within the meaning of § 1981.

Petitioners contend that respondent is a Caucasian and cannot allege the kind of discrimination § 1981 forbids. Petitioner's submission rests on the assumption that all those who might be deemed Caucasians today were thought to be of the same race when § 1981 became law in the 19th century; and it may be that a variety of ethnic groups, including Arabs, are now considered to be within the Caucasian race. The understanding of "race" in the 19th century, however, was different. Plainly, all those who might be deemed Caucasian today were not thought to be of the same race at the time § 1981 became law.

In the middle years of the 19th century, dictionaries commonly referred to race as a "continued series of descendants from a parent who is called the *stock*," N. WEBSTER, AN AMERICAN DICTIONARY OF THE ENGLISH LANGUAGE 666 (New York 1830) (emphasis in original), "[t]he lineage of a family," N. WEBSTER, 2 A DICTIONARY OF THE ENGLISH LANGUAGE 411 (New Haven 1841), or "descendants of a common ancestor," J. DONALD, CHAMBERS'S ETYMOLOGICAL DICTIONARY OF THE ENGLISH LANGUAGE 415 (London 1871). The 1887 edition of Webster's expanded the definition somewhat: "The descendants of a common ancestor; a family, tribe, people or nation, believed or presumed to belong to the same stock." N. WEBSTER, DICTIONARY OF THE ENGLISH LANGUAGE (W. Wheeler ed. 1887). It was not until the 20th century that dictionaries began referring to the Caucasian, Mongolian and Negro races, 8 The CENTURY DICTIONARY AND CYCLOPEDIA 4926 (1911), or to race as involving divisions of mankind based upon different physical characteristics. WEBSTER'S COLLEGIATE DICTIONARY 794 (1916). Even so, modern dictionaries still include among the definitions of race as being "a family, tribe, people, or nation belonging to the same stock." WEBSTER'S THIRD NEW INTERNATIONAL DICTIONARY Mass. 1870 (1971); WEBSTER'S NINTH NEW COLLEGIATE DICTIONARY 969 (Springfield, Mass. 1986).

Encyclopedias of the 19th century also described race in terms of ethnic groups, which is a narrower concept of race than petitioners urge. *Encyclopedia Americana* in 1858, for example, referred in 1854 to various races such as Finns, gypsies, Basques, and Hebrews. The 1863 version of the *New American Cyclopaedia* divided the Arabs into a number of subsidiary races, represented the Hebrews as of the Semitic race, and identified numerous other groups as constituting races, including Swedes, Norwegians, Germans, Greeks, Finns, Italians, Spanish, Mongolians, Russians, and the like. The Ninth edition of the *Encyclopedia Britannica* also referred to Arabs, Jews, and other ethnic groups such as Germans, Hungarians, and Greeks as separate races.

These dictionary and encyclopedic sources are somewhat diverse, but it is clear that they do not support the claim that for the purposes of § 1981, Arabs, Englishmen, Germans and certain other ethnic groups are to be considered a single race. We would expect the legislative history of § 1981, which the Court held in *Runyon v. McCrary* had its source in the Civil Rights Act of 1866, as well as the Voting Rights Act of 1870, to reflect this common understanding, which it surely does. The debates are replete with references to the Scandinavian races, as well as the Chinese, Latin, Spanish, and Anglo-Saxon races. Jews, Mexicans, blacks, and Mongolians were similarly categorized. Gypsies were referred to as a race.

The history of the 1870 Act reflects similar understanding of what groups Congress intended to protect from intentional discrimination. It is clear, for example, that the civil rights sections of the 1870 Act provided protection for immigrant groups such as the Chinese. This view was expressed in the Senate. In the House, Representative Bingham described § 16 of the Act, part of the authority for § 1981, as declaring "that the States shall not hereafter discriminate against the immigrant from China and in favor of the immigrant from Prussia, nor against the immigrant from France and in favor of the immigrant from Ireland."

Based on the history of § 1981, we have little trouble in concluding that Congress intended to protect from discrimination identifiable classes of persons who are subjected to intentional discrimination solely because of their ancestry or ethnic characteristics. Such discrimination is racial discrimination that Congress intended § 1981 to forbid, whether or not it would be classified as racial in terms of modern scientific theory. The Court of Appeals was thus quite right in holding that § 1981, "at a minimum," reaches discrimination against an individual "because he or she is genetically part of an ethnically and physiognomically distinctive subgrouping of *homo sapiens*." It is clear from our holding, however, that a distinctive physiognomy is not essential to qualify for § 1981 protection. If respondent on remand can prove that he was subjected to intentional discrimination based on the fact that he was born an Arab, rather than solely on the place or nation of his origin, or his religion, he will have made out a case under § 1981.

NOTES AND QUESTIONS

1. How on remand can it be determined whether discrimination is based on place of origin or ancestry? Why doesn't § 1981 reach discrimination based "solely on place or nation of origin?" Doesn't the legislative history of the 1870 Act indicate Congressional intent to protect immigrant groups from discrimination?

2. If § 1981 has its source in the Thirteenth Amendment, which was intended to abolish slavery and the "incidents" of slavery, how can § 1981 be used to reach "race" discrimination against groups that do not share the history of slavery involving African-Americans?

SHAARE TEFILA CONGREGATION V. COBB
481 U.S. 615 (1987)

Justice WHITE delivered the opinion of the Court.

On November 2, 1982, the outside walls of the synagogue of the Shaare Tefila Congregation in Silver Spring, Maryland, were sprayed with red and black paint and with large anti-Semitic slogans, phrases and symbols. A few months later, the Congregation and some individual members brought this suit in the Federal District Court, alleging that defendants' desecration of the synagogue has violated 42 U.S.C. §§ 1981, 1982, 1985(3) and the Maryland common law of trespass, nuisance, and intentional infliction of emotional distress. On defendants' motion under FED. RULE CIV. PROC. 12(b)(1) and (6), the District Court dismissed all the claims. The Court of Appeals affirmed in all respects.

Section 1982 guarantees all citizens of the United States, "the same right . . . as is enjoyed by white citizens . . . to inherit, purchase, lease, sell, hold, and convey real and personal property."

The section forbids both official and private racially discriminatory interference with property rights. Petitioners' allegation was that they were deprived of the right to hold property in violation of § 1982 because the defendants were motivated by racial prejudice. They unsuccessfully argued in the District Court and Court of Appeals that Jews are not a racially distinct group, but that defendants' conduct is actionable because they viewed Jews as racially distinct and were motivated by racial prejudice. The Court of Appeals held that § 1982 was not "intended to apply to situations in which a plaintiff is not a member of a racially distinct group but is merely *perceived* to be so by defendants." The Court of Appeals believed that "[b]ecause discrimination against Jews is not racial discrimination," the District Court was correct in dismissing the § 1982 claim.

We agree with the Court of Appeals that a charge of racial discrimination within the meaning of § 1982 cannot be made out by alleging only that the defendants were motivated by racial animus; it is necessary as well to allege that defendants' animus was directed towards the kind of group that Congress intended to protect when it passed the statute. To hold otherwise would unacceptably extend the reach of the statute.

We agree with petitioners, however, that the Court of Appeals erred in holding that Jews cannot state a § 1982 claim against other white defendants. That view rested on the notion that because Jews today are not thought of to be members of a separate race, they cannot make out a claim of racial discrimination within the meaning of § 1982. That construction of the section we have today rejected in *Saint Francis College v. Al-Khazraji.* Our opinion in that case observed that definitions of race when § 1982 was passed were not the same as they are today and concluded that the section was "intended to protect from discrimination identifiable classes of persons who are subjected to intentional discrimination solely because of their ancestry or ethnic characteristics." As *St. Francis* makes clear, the question before us is not whether Jews are considered to be a separate race by today's standards, but whether, at the time § 1982 was adopted, Jews constituted a group of people that Congress intended to protect. It is evident from the legislative history of the section reviewed in *Saint Francis College*, a review that we need not repeat here, that Jews and Arabs were among the peoples then considered to be distinct races and hence within the protection of the statute.

NOTES AND QUESTIONS

1. If the defendant perceives a group as being "racially distinct," why shouldn't § 1982 liability be imposed?

2. Does the Supreme Court limit § 1982 protection to only those groups cited in the legislative debates?

3. If the defendants' action in *Shaare Tefila* is found to have been religiously motivated, must the suit be dismissed? Would Congress have authority to reach this type of private discrimination under the Thirteenth Amendment?

4. Assuming the discrimination is race-based, could Israeli citizens have brought this litigation under § 1982? May they sue under § 1981?

MCDONALD V. SANTA FE TRAIL TRANSPORTATION CO.

427 U.S. 273 (1976)

Mr. Justice MARSHALL delivered the opinion of the Court.

Petitioners, L.N. McDonald and Raymond L. Laird, brought this action in the United States District Court for the Southern District of Texas seeking relief against Santa Fe Trail Transportation Co. and International Brotherhood of Teamsters Local 988, which represented Santa Fe's Houston employees, for alleged violations of the Civil Rights Act of 1866, 42 U.S.C. § 1981, and of Title VII of the Civil Rights Act of 1964, in connection with their discharge from Santa Fe's employment. [W]e must decide whether § 1981, which provides that "[a]ll persons . . . shall have the same right . . . to make and enforce contracts . . . as is enjoyed by white citizens. . . ." affords protection from racial discrimination in private employment to white persons as well as nonwhites.

While neither of the courts below elaborated its reason for not applying § 1981 to racial discrimination against white persons, respondents suggest two lines of argument to support that judgment. First, they argue that by operation of the phrase "as is enjoyed by white citizens," § 1981 unambiguously limits itself to the protection of nonwhite persons against racial discrimination. Second, they contend that such a reading is consistent with the legislative history of the provision, which derives its operative language from § 1 of the Civil Rights Act of 1866. The 1866 statute, they assert, was concerned predominantly with assuring specified civil rights to the former Negro slaves freed by virtue of the Thirteenth Amendment, and not at all with protecting the corresponding civil rights of white persons.

We find neither argument persuasive. Rather, our examination of the language and history of § 1981 convinces us that § 1981 is applicable to racial discrimination in private employment against white persons.

First, we cannot accept the view that the terms of § 1981 exclude its application to racial discrimination against white persons. On the contrary, the statute explicitly applies to "*all* persons" (emphasis added), including white persons. While a mechanical reading of the phrase "as is enjoyed by white citizens" would seem to lend support to respondents' reading of the statute, we have previously described this phrase simply as emphasizing "the racial character of the rights being protected." In any event, whatever ambiguity there may be in the language of § 1981 is clarified by an examination of the legislative history of § 1981's language as it was originally forged in the Civil Rights Act of 1866.

The bill ultimately enacted as the Civil Rights Act of 1866 was introduced by Senator Trumbull of Illinois as a "bill to protect *all* persons in the United States in their civil rights" and was initially described by him as applying to "every race and color." Consistent with the views of its draftsman, and the prevailing view in the Congress as to the reach of its powers under the enforcement section of the Thirteenth Amendment, the terms of the bill prohibited any racial discrimination in the making and enforcement of contracts against whites as well as nonwhites.

While it is, of course, true that the immediate impetus for the bill was the necessity for further relief of the constitutionally emancipated former Negro slaves, the general discussion of the scope of the bill did not circumscribe its broad language to that limited goal. On the contrary, the bill was routinely viewed, by its opponents and supporters alike, as applying to the civil rights of whites as well as nonwhites.

It is clear, thus, that the bill, as it passed the Senate, was not limited in scope to discrimination against nonwhites. Accordingly, respondents pitch their legislative history argument largely upon the House's amendment of the Senate bill to add the "as is enjoyed by white citizens" phrase. But the statutory history is equally clear that that phrase was not intended to have the effect of eliminating from the bill the prohibition of racial discrimination against whites.

Representative Wilson of Iowa, Chairman of the Judiciary Committee and the bill's floor manager in the House, proposed the addition of the quoted phrase immediately upon the introduction of the bill. The change was offered explicitly to technically "perfect" the bill, and was accepted as such without objection or debate.

That Wilson's amendment was viewed simply as a technical adjustment without substantive effect is corroborated by the structure of the bill as it then stood. Even as amended the bill still provided that "there shall be no discrimination in civil rights or immunities among citizens of the United States in any State or Territory of the United States on account of race, color or previous condition of slavery." To read Wilson's amendment as excluding white persons from the particularly enumerated civil rights guarantees of the Act would contradict this more general language; and we would be unwilling to conclude, without further evidence, that in adopting the amendment without debate or discussion, the House so regarded it.

Finally, in later dialogue Wilson made quite clear that the purpose of his amendment was not to affect the Act's protection of white persons. Rather, he states, "the reason for offering [the amendment] was this: it was thought by some persons that unless these qualifying words were incorporated in the bill, those rights might be extended to all citizens, whether male or female, majors or minors." Thus, the purpose of the amendment was simply "to emphasize the racial character of the rights being protected," not to limit its application to nonwhite persons.

The Senate debate on the House version of the bill likewise emphasizes that Representative Wilson's amendment was not viewed as limiting the bill's prohibition of racial discrimination against white persons. Senator Trumbull, still managing the bill on the floor of the Senate, was asked whether there was not an inconsistency between the application of the bill to all "citizens of every race and color" and the statement that they shall have "the same right to make and enforce contracts . . . *as is enjoyed by white persons*," (emphasis supplied) and it was suggested that the emphasized words were superfluous. Senator Trumbull responded in agreement with the view that the words were merely "superfluous. I do not think they alter the bill."

This cumulative evidence of congressional intent makes clear, we think, that the 1866 statute, designed to protect the "same right . . . to make and enforce contracts" of "citizens of every race and color" was not understood or intended to be reduced by Representative Wilson's amendment, or any other provision, to the protection solely of nonwhites. Rather, the Act was meant, by its broad terms, to proscribe discrimination in the making or enforcement of contracts against, or in favor of, any race. Unlikely as it might have appeared in 1866 that white citizens would encounter substantial racial discrimination of the sort proscribed under the Act, the statutory structure and legislative history persuade us that the 39th Congress was intent upon establishing in the federal law a broader principle than would have been necessary simply to meet the particular and immediate plight of the newly freed Negro slaves. And while the statutory language has been somewhat streamlined in re-enactment and codification, there is no indication that § 1981 is intended to provide any less than the Congress enacted in 1866 regarding racial discrimination against white persons. Thus, we conclude that the District Court erred in dismissing petitioners' claims under § 1981 on the ground that the protections of that provision are unavailable to white persons.

NOTES AND QUESTIONS

1. How does the Court justify its interpretation of the "as is enjoyed by white citizens" language as protecting whites?

2. In light of its legislative history, can a white plaintiff utilize § 1981 to challenge an affirmative action program?

3. In *Domino's Pizza, Inc. v. McDonald*, 546 U.S. 470 (2006), the Court ruled that the plaintiff, who was sole shareholder and president of a corporation that had entered into contracts with Domino's Pizza, could not bring a § 1981 claim in his individual capacity as a black man because he did not have any rights under the existing contract. The statute's text could not be read to include a cause of action simply because the plaintiff enforced contracts for a corporation as its agent. Applying basic corporation and agency law, the Court, in a unanimous opinion, concluded that a corporation's shareholder and contracting officer has no rights and is exposed to no liability under the corporation's contracts, and thus lacks standing to sue for impairment of the right to contract under § 1981.

b. Suing Private Defendants Under § 1981

RUNYON V. MCCRARY
427 u.s. 160 (1976)

Mr. Justice STEWART delivered the opinion of the Court.

The principal issue presented by these consolidated cases is whether a federal law, namely 42 U.S.C. § 1981, prohibits private schools from excluding qualified children solely because they are Negroes.

I

The respondents in No. 75-62, Michael McCrary and Colin Gonzales, are Negro children. By their parents, they filed a class action against the petitioners in No. 75-62, Russell and Katheryne Runyon, who are the proprietors of Bobbe's School in Arlington, Va. Their complaint alleged that they had been prevented from attending the school because of the petitioners' policy of denying admission to Negroes, in violation of 42 U.S.C. § 1981 and Title II of the Civil Rights Act of 1964, 42 U.S.C. § 2000a, *et seq.* They sought declaratory and injunctive relief and damages. On the same day Colin Gonzales, the respondent in No. 75-66, filed a similar complaint by his parents against the petitioner in No. 75-66, Fairfax-Brewster School, Inc., located in Fairfax County, Va. The petitioner in No. 75-278, the Southern Independent School Association, sought and was granted permission to intervene as a party defendant in the suit against the Runyons. That organization is a nonprofit association composed of six state private school associations, and represents 395 private schools. It is stipulated that many of these schools deny admission to Negroes.

In response to a mailed brochure addressed "resident" and an advertisement in the "Yellow Pages" of the telephone directory, Mr. and Mrs. Gonzales telephoned and then visited the Fairfax-Brewster School in May of 1969. After the visit, they submitted an application for Colin's admission to the day camp. The school was "unable to accommodate [Colin's] application." Mr. Gonzales telephoned the school. Fairfax-Brewster's Chairman of the Board explained that the reason for Colin's rejection was that the school was not integrated. Mr. Gonzales then telephoned Bobbe's School, from which the family had also received in the mail a brochure addressed to "resident." In response to a question concerning that school's admissions policies, he was told that only members of the Caucasian race were accepted. In August 1972, Mrs. McCrary telephoned Bobbe's School in response to an advertisement in the telephone book. She inquired about nursery school facilities for her son, Michael. She also asked if the school was integrated. The answer was no.

II

It is worth noting at the outset some of the questions that these cases do not present. They do not present any question of the right of a private social organization to limit its membership on racial or any other grounds. They do not present any question of the right of a private school to limit its student body to boys, to girls, or to adherents of a particular religious faith, since 42 U.S.C. § 1981 is in no way addressed to such categories of selectivity. They do not even present the application of § 1981 to private sectarian schools that practice *racial* exclusion on religious grounds. Rather, these cases present only two basic questions: whether § 1981 prohibits private, commercially operated, nonsectarian schools from denying admission to prospective students because they are Negroes, and, if so, whether that federal law is constitutional as so applied.

A. Applicability of § 1981

It is now well established that § 1 of the Civil Rights Act of 1866, 42 U.S.C. § 1981, prohibits racial discrimination in the making and enforcement of private contracts.

In *Jones* [v. *Alfred H. Mayer Co.*], the Court held that the portion of § 1 of the Civil Rights Act of 1866 presently codified as 42 U.S.C. § 1982 prohibits private racial discrimination in the sale or rental of real or personal property. Relying on the legislative history of § 1, from which both § 1981 and § 1982 derive, the Court concluded that Congress intended to prohibit "all racial discrimination, private and public, in the sale . . . of property," and that this prohibition was within Congress' power under § 2 of the Thirteenth Amendment "rationally to determine what are the badges and the incidents of slavery, and to translate that determination into effective legislation."

As the Court indicated in *Jones*, that holding necessarily implied that the portion of § 1 of the 1866 Act presently codified as 42 U.S.C. § 1981 likewise reaches purely private acts of racial discrimination. The statutory holding in *Jones* was that the "[1866] Act was designed to do just what its terms suggest: to prohibit all racial discrimination, whether or not under color of law, with respect to the rights enumerated therein—including the right to purchase or lease property." One of the "rights enumerated" in § 1 is "the same right . . . to make and enforce contracts . . . as is enjoyed by white citizens." Just as in *Jones* a Negro's § 1 right to purchase property on equal terms with whites was violated when a private person refused to sell to the prospective purchaser solely because he was a Negro, so also a Negro's § 1 right to "make and enforce contracts" is violated if a private offeror refuses to extend to a Negro, solely because he is a Negro, the same opportunity to enter into contracts as he extends to white offerees.

It is apparent that the racial exclusion practiced by the Fairfax-Brewster School and Bobbe's Private School amounts to a classic violation of § 1981. The parents of Colin Gonzales and Michael McCrary sought to enter into contractual relationships with Bobbe's School for educational services. Colin Gonzales' parents sought to enter into a similar relationship with the Fairfax-Brewster School. Under those contractual relationships, the schools would have received payments for services rendered, and the prospective students would have received instruction in return for those payments. The educational services of Bobbe's School and the Fairfax-Brewster School were advertised and offered to members of the general public.[10] But neither school offered services on an equal basis to white and nonwhite students. As the Court of Appeals held, "there is ample evidence in the record to support the trial judge's factual determinations . . . [that] Colin [Gonzales] and Michael [McCrary] were denied admission to the schools because of their race." The Court of Appeals' conclusion that § 1981 was thereby violated follows inexorably from the language of that statute, as construed in *Jones, Tillman*, and *Johnson*. The petitioning schools and school association argue principally that § 1981 does not reach private acts of racial discrimination. That view is wholly inconsistent with *Jones*' interpretation of the legislative history of § 1 of the Civil Rights Act of 1866, an interpretation that was reaffirmed in *Sullivan v. Little Hunting Park, Inc.*, and again in *Tillman v. Wheaton-Haven Recreation Ass'n*. And this consistent interpretation of the law necessarily requires the conclusion that § 1981, like § 1982, reaches private conduct.

It is noteworthy that Congress in enacting the Equal Employment Opportunity Act of 1972, specifically considered and rejected an amendment that would have repealed the Civil Rights Act of 1866, as interpreted by this Court in *Jones*, insofar as it affords private-sector employees a right of action based on racial discrimination in employment. There could hardly be a clearer indication of congressional agreement with the view that § 1981 *does* reach private acts of racial discrimination.

Mr. Justice WHITE, with whom Mr. Justice REHNQUIST joins, dissenting.

We are urged here to extend the meaning and reach of 42 U.S.C. § 1981 so as to establish a general prohibition against a private individual's or institution's refusing to enter into a contract with another person because of that person's race.

On its face the statute gives "[a]ll persons" (plainly including Negroes) the "*same right . . . to make . . . contracts . . . as is enjoyed by white citizens*." (Emphasis added.) The words "right . . . enjoyed by white citizens" clearly refer to rights existing apart from this statute. Whites had at the time when § 1981 was first enacted, and have (with a few exceptions mentioned

---

10 These cases do not raise the issue of whether the "private club or other [private] establishment" exemption in § 201(e) of the Civil Rights Act of 1964, 42 U.S.C. § 2000a(e), operates to narrow § 1 of the Civil Rights Act of 1866. As the Court of Appeals implied, that exemption, if applicable at all, comes into play only if the establishment is "not in fact open to the public. . . ." 42 U.S.C. § 2000a(e). Both Bobbe's School and the Fairfax-Brewster School advertised in the "Yellow Pages" of the telephone directory and both used mass mailings in attempting to attract students. As the Court of Appeals observed, these "schools are private only in the sense that they are managed by private persons and they are not direct recipients of public funds. Their actual and potential constituency, however, is more public than private. They appeal to the parents of all children in the area who can meet their academic and other admission requirements. This is clearly demonstrated in this case by the public advertisements."

Moreover, it is doubtful that a plausible "implied repeal" argument could be made in this context in any event. Implied repeals occur if two Acts are in irreconcilable conflict. Title II of the Civil Rights Act of 1964, of which the "private club" exemption is a part, does not by its terms reach private schools. Since there would appear to be no potential for overlapping application of § 1981 and Title II of the 1964 Act with respect to racial discrimination practiced by private schools, there would also appear to be no potential for conflict between § 1981 and Title II's "private club" exemption in this context.

below), no right to make a contract with an unwilling private person, no matter what that person's motivation for refusing to contract. Indeed it is and always has been central to the very concept of a "contract" that there be "assent by the parties who form the contract to the terms thereof," RESTATEMENT OF CONTRACTS § 19(b) (1932). The right to make contracts, enjoyed by white citizens, was therefore always a right to enter into binding agreements only with willing second parties. Since the statute only gives Negroes the "same rights" to contract as is enjoyed by whites, the language of the statute confers no right on Negroes to enter into a contract with an unwilling person no matter what that person's motivation for refusing to contract. What is conferred by 42 U.S.C. § 1981 is the *right*—which was enjoyed by whites—"to make contracts" with other willing parties and to "enforce" those contracts in court. Section 1981 would thus invalidate any state statute or court-made rule of law which would have the effect of disabling Negroes or any other class of persons from making contracts or enforcing contractual obligations or otherwise giving less weight to their obligations than is given to contractual obligations running to whites.

II

The legislative history of 42 U.S.C. § 1981 confirms that the statute means what it says and no more, *i.e.*, that it outlaws any legal rule disabling any person from making or enforcing a contract, but does not prohibit private racially motivated refusals to contract.

Three things emerge unmistakably from this legislative history. First, unlike § 1 of the Civil Rights Act of 1866, which was passed under Congress' Thirteenth Amendment powers to remove from former slaves "'badges and incidents of slavery,'" *Jones v. Alfred H. Mayer Co.*, § 16 of the Voting Rights Act of 1870 was passed under Congress' Fourteenth Amendment powers to prevent the States from denying to "any person . . . equal protection of the laws." U.S. CONST. amend. XIV, § 1. Second, consistent with the scope of that Amendment, § 16 was designed to require "all persons" to be treated "the same" or "equally" under the law and was not designed to require equal treatment at the hands of private individuals. Third, one of the classes of persons for whose benefit the statute was intended was aliens—plainly not a class with respect to which Congress sought to remove badges and incidents of slavery—and not a class protected in any fashion by § 1 of the Civil Rights Act of 1866, since that Act applied only to "citizens."

III

The majority seeks to avoid the construction of 42 U.S.C. § 1981 arrived at above by arguing that it (*i.e.*, § 1977 of the Revised Statutes of 1874) is a re-enactment *both* of § 16 of the Voting Rights Act of 1870—the Fourteenth Amendment statute—*and* of part of § 1 of the Civil Rights Act of 1866—the Thirteenth Amendment statute. The majority argues from this that § 1981 does limit *private* contractual choices because Congress may, under its Thirteenth Amendment powers, proscribe certain kinds of private conduct thought to perpetuate "'badges and incidents of slavery,'" and because this Court has already construed the language "[a]ll citizens of the United

States shall have the same right . . . as is enjoyed by white citizens . . . to . . . *purchase* . . . *real* . . . *property*" (emphasis added), contained in the Thirteenth Amendment statute, to proscribe a refusal by a *private* individual to sell real estate to a Negro because of his race. The majority's position is untenable.

First of all, as noted above, § 1977 of the Revised Statutes was passed by Congress with the Revisers' unambiguous note before it that the section derived solely from the Fourteenth Amendment statute, accompanied by the confirmatory sidenote "Equal rights under the law." Second and more importantly, the majority's argument is logically impossible, because it has the effect of construing the language *"the same right to make . . . contracts . . . as is enjoyed by white citizens,"* contained in § 1977 of the Revised Statutes, to mean one thing with respect to one class of "persons" and another thing with respect to another class of "persons". If § 1981 is held to be a re-enactment of the Thirteenth Amendment statute aimed at private discrimination against "citizens" and the Fourteenth Amendment statute aimed at state-law-created legal disabilities for "all persons," including aliens, then one class of "persons"—Negro citizens—would, under the majority's theory, have a right not to be discriminated against by private individuals and another class—aliens—would be given *by the same language* no such right. The statute draws no such distinction among classes of persons. It logically must be construed either to give "all persons" a right not to be discriminated against by private parties in the making of contracts or to give no persons such a right. Aliens clearly never had such a right under the Fourteenth Amendment statute (or any other statute); § 1977 is concededly derived solely from the Fourteenth Amendment statute so far as coverage of aliens is concerned; and there is absolutely no indication that aliens' rights were expanded by the re-enactment of the Fourteenth Amendment statute in § 1977 of the Revised Statutes of 1874. Accordingly, the statute gives *no* class of persons the right not to be discriminated against by private parties in the making of contracts.

That part of the Thirteenth Amendment statute which gives "[a]ll citizens . . . the same rights to make . . . contracts . . . as is enjoyed by white citizens" was accordingly, not re-enacted as part of § 1977, and, since another portion of the Thirteenth Amendment statute was reenacted as § 1978 of the Revised Statutes, the "right to contract" part of the Thirteenth Amendment statute was repealed in 1874.

Finally, as a matter of common sense, it would seem extremely unlikely that Congress would have intended—without a word in the legislative history addressed to the precise issue—to pass a statute prohibiting every racially motivated refusal to contract by a private individual. It is doubtful that all such refusals could be considered badges or incidents of slavery within Congress' proscriptive power under the Thirteenth Amendment. A racially motivated refusal to hire a Negro or a white babysitter or to admit a Negro or a white to a private association cannot be called a badge of slavery—and yet the construction given by the majority to the Thirteenth Amendment statute attributes to Congress an intent to proscribe them.

Whether such conduct should be condoned or not, whites and blacks will undoubtedly choose to form a variety of associational relationships pursuant to contracts which exclude members of the other race. Social clubs, black and white, and associations designed to further the interests of blacks or whites are but two examples. Lawsuits by members of the other race attempting to gain admittance to such an association are not pleasant to contemplate. As the associational or contractual relationships become more private, the pressures to hold § 1981 inapplicable to them will increase.

NOTES AND QUESTIONS

1. Why do the dissenting Justices reject application of § 1981 to private defendants? Is their review of the statutory history more persuasive? Would it require a different interpretation of the scope of § 1981 as compared to that of § 1982? The Supreme Court in *Patterson v. McLean Credit Union* (1989), *infra* Ch. II, after requesting briefs on the issue, unanimously declined to overrule *Runyon*. Stressing the importance of *stare decisis*, especially in the area of statutory interpretation, the Court found "no special justification" for reversing the decision. It found no "intervening development of the law" and concluded that the prohibition of private race discrimination in the area of contracts "was consistent with our society's deep commitment to the eradication of discrimination based on a person's race or the color of his or her skin."

2. Assuming § 1981 was intended to reach private discrimination, should the Court recognize a right of association or privacy defense, e.g., on the part of a private country club that refuses to contract with a black applicant? Or the family that refuses to hire a babysitter because of race? *See* footnote 10.

3. In light of the history of § 1981 traced in Justice White's dissent, may aliens sue private defendants under § 1981 for race or alienage discrimination?

> Although it would appear that § 1981 reaches only race-based discrimination, two Supreme Court decisions suggest that at least government-sponsored discrimination against aliens, even if not tied to race, may be actionable. In *Takahashi v. Fish & Game Comm.*, 334 U.S. 410 (1948), the Court invalidated a California law that prohibited the issuance of commercial fishing licenses to immigrants who were ineligible for citizenship under federal law. In discussing § 1981, the Court stated:

> The protection of this section has been held to extend to aliens as well as to citizens. Consequently the section and the Fourteenth Amendment on which it rests in part protects "all persons" against state legislation bearing unequally upon them either because of alienage or color. The Fourteenth Amendment and the laws adopted under its authority thus embody a general policy that all persons lawfully in the country shall abide "in any state" on an equality of legal privileges with all citizens under non-discriminatory laws.

> *Id.* at 419-20. Subsequently, in *Graham v. Richardson*, 403 U.S. 365 (1971), the Court invalidated state welfare laws that either denied benefits to non-citizens or that subjected them to

residency requirements different from those of citizens. The Court noted that "state laws that restrict the eligibility of aliens for welfare benefits merely because of their alienage conflict with . . . overriding national policies" set forth in § 1981 and are thus impermissible. *Id.* at 378. Although neither case speaks directly to the scope of § 1981, lower courts have viewed these cases as establishing § 1981 as a prohibition of government discrimination against aliens, even if such is not race-based.

PROBLEM: THREE

Bhandari is a citizen of India and a lawful permanent resident of the United States. In October 1983, Bhandari was employed as an accountant. He applied to First Bankcard Center, an instrumentality of First National, for unsecured revolving consumer credit in the form of a Visa credit card. The application included the question "Are you a U.S. citizen?" Bhandari answered "No."

At the time Bhandari's application was processed, one of First National's credit policy "guidelines" was: "Applicant must be a U.S. citizen unless application is approved by an officer of the Bank." The district court found that the analyst who reviewed Bhandari's application denied it for two reasons: his alienage and his short time of employment in his then-current job. First National sent Bhandari a letter stating only that he was denied credit because he was not a U.S. citizen.

1. Does Saint Francis College assist Bhandari? Does § 1981 reach alienage (not race-based) discrimination? Do Takahashi and Graham support this interpretation?

2. In light of § 1981's legislative history regarding the protection of aliens, even assuming Bhandari is a victim of race discrimination, will he be allowed to sue a private bank under § 1981?

3. The Civil Rights Act of 1991 does not specifically address the alienage dilemma, but 42 U.S.C. § 1981(c) states that the rights protected under § 1981 are "protected against impairment by nongovernment discrimination and impairment under color of state law." Does this now clarify that all plaintiffs—citizens or aliens—may sue private defendants for alienage or race discrimination under § 1981?

c.   Constitutional Defenses

RUNYON V. MCCRARY
427 U.S. 160 (1976)

Mr. Justice STEWART delivered the opinion of the Court.

[After concluding that § 1981 reached private discrimination, see *supra*, the Supreme Court proceeded to discuss the various constitutional defenses raised by the private schools.]

Constitutionality of § 1981 as Applied

The question remains whether § 1981, as applied, violates constitutionally protected rights of free association and privacy, or a parent's right to direct the education of his children.

1. Freedom of Association

In *NAACP v. Alabama*, and similar decisions, the Court has recognized a First Amendment right "to engage in association for the advancement of beliefs and ideas." That right is protected because it promotes and may well be essential to the "[e]ffective advocacy of both public and private points of view, particularly controversial ones" that the First Amendment is designed to foster.

From this principle it may be assumed that parents have a First Amendment right to send their children to educational institutions that promote the belief that racial segregation is desirable, and that the children have an equal right to attend such institutions. But it does not follow that the *practice* of excluding racial minorities from such institutions is also protected by the same principle. As the Court stated in *Norwood v. Harrison*, "the Constitution places no value on discrimination," and while "[i]nvidious private discrimination may be characterized as a form of exercising freedom of association protected by the First Amendment . . . it has never been accorded affirmative constitutional protections. And even some private discrimination is subject to special remedial legislation in certain circumstances under § 2 of the Thirteenth Amendment; Congress has made such discrimination unlawful in other significant contexts." In any event, as the Court of Appeals noted, "there is no showing that discontinuance of [the] discriminatory admission practices would inhibit in any way the teaching in these schools of any ideas or dogma."

2. Parental Rights

In *Meyer v. Nebraska*, the Court held that the liberty protected by the Due Process Clause of the Fourteenth Amendment includes the right "to acquire useful knowledge, to marry, establish a home and bring up children," and, concomitantly, the right to send one's children to a private school that offers specialized training—in that case, instruction in the German language. In *Pierce v. Society of Sisters*, the Court applied "the doctrine of *Meyer v. Nebraska*" to hold unconstitutional an Oregon law requiring the parent, guardian, or other person having custody of a child between 8 and 16 years of age to send that child to public school on pain of criminal liability. The Court thought it "entirely plain that the [statute] unreasonably interferes with the liberty of parents and guardians to direct the upbringing and education of children under their control." In *Wisconsin v. Yoder*, the Court stressed the limited scope of *Pierce*, pointing out that it lent "no support to the contention that parents may replace state educational requirements with their own idiosyncratic views of what knowledge a child needs to be a productive and happy member of society" but rather "held simply that while a State may posit [educational] standards, it may not pre-empt the educational process by requiring children to attend public schools." And in *Norwood v. Harrison*, the Court once again stressed the "limited scope of *Pierce*," which simply "affirmed the right of private schools to exist and to operate."

It is clear that the present application of § 1981 infringes no parental right recognized in *Meyer*, *Pierce*, *Yoder*, or *Norwood*. No challenge is made to the petitioner schools' right to operate or the right of parents to send their children to a particular private school rather than a public school. Nor do these cases involve a challenge to the subject matter which is taught at any private school. Thus, the Fairfax-Brewster School and Bobbe's School and members of the intervenor association remain presumptively free to inculcate whatever values and standards they deem desirable. *Meyer* and its progeny entitle them to no more.

3. The Right of Privacy

The Court has held that in some situations the Constitution confers a right of privacy.

While the application of § 1981 to the conduct at issue here—a private school's adherence to a racially discriminatory admissions policy—does not represent governmental intrusion into the privacy of the home or a similarly intimate setting, it does implicate parental interests. These interests are related to the procreative rights protected in *Roe v. Wade* and *Griswold v. Connecticut*. A person's decision whether to bear a child and a parent's decision concerning the manner in which his child is to be educated may fairly be characterized as exercises of familial rights and responsibilities. But it does not follow that because government is largely or even entirely precluded from regulating the child-bearing decision, it is similarly restricted by the Constitution from regulating the implementation of parental decisions concerning a child's education.

The Court has repeatedly stressed that while parents have a constitutional right to send their children to private schools and a constitutional right to select private schools that offer specialized instruction, they have no constitutional right to provide their children with private school education unfettered by reasonable government regulation. Indeed, the Court in *Pierce* expressly acknowledged "the power of the State reasonably to regulate all schools, to inspect, supervise and examine them, their teachers and pupils."

1. Why did the Court reject all three of the constitutional defenses raised by the two segregated schools?

2. In subsequent decisions involving lawsuits brought under other anti-discrimination laws, the Supreme Court has elaborated on the extent to which the constitution protects associational and privacy rights. In litigation involving the Jaycees and Rotary Clubs (see below), the Supreme Court rejected the argument that the constitution insulates these organizations from state laws prohibiting sex discrimination.

BOARD OF DIRECTORS OF ROTARY INTERNATIONAL V. ROTARY CLUB OF DUARTE
481 U.S. 537 (1987)

[Local rotary club and two of its women members filed a complaint, alleging that actions of Rotary International revoking the charter of the club and terminating its membership in the International for admitting women violated California's Unruh Civil Rights Act. Rotary International argued that the First Amendment trumped the state law.]

Justice POWELL delivered the opinion of the Court.

II

[O]ur cases have afforded constitutional protection to freedom of association in two distinct senses. First, the Court has held that the Constitution protects against unjustified government interference with an individual's choice to enter into and maintain certain intimate or private relationships. Second, the Court has upheld the freedom of individuals to associate for the purpose of engaging in protected speech or religious activities. In many cases, government interference with one form of protected association will also burden the other form of association.

A

The Court has recognized that the freedom to enter into and carry on certain intimate or private relationships is a fundamental element of liberty protected by the Bill of Rights. Such relationships may take various forms, including the most intimate. We have not attempted to mark the precise boundaries of this type of constitutional protection. The intimate relationships to which we have accorded constitutional protection include marriage, the begetting and bearing of children, child rearing and education, and cohabitation with relatives. Of course, we have not held that constitutional protection is restricted to relationships among family members. We have emphasized that the First Amendment protects those relationships, including family relationships, that presuppose "deep attachments and commitments to the necessarily few other individuals with whom one shares not only a special community of thoughts, experiences, and beliefs but also distinctively personal aspects of one's life." *Roberts v. United States Jaycees.* But in *Roberts* we observed that "[d]etermining the limits of state authority over an individual's freedom to enter into a particular association unavoidably entails a careful assessment of where that relationship's objective characteristics locate it on a spectrum from the most intimate to the most attenuated of personal attachments. . . ." In determining whether a particular association is sufficiently personal or private to warrant constitutional protection, we consider factors such as size, purpose, selectivity, and whether others are excluded from critical aspects of the relationship.

The evidence in this case indicates that the relationship among Rotary Club members is not the kind of intimate or private relation that warrants constitutional protection. The size of local Rotary Clubs ranges from fewer than 20 to more than 900. There is no upper limit on the membership of any local Rotary Club. About ten percent of the membership of a typical club moves away or drops out during a typical year. The clubs therefore are instructed to "keep a flow of prospects coming" to make up for the attrition and gradually to enlarge the membership. The purpose of Rotary "is to produce an inclusive, not exclusive, membership, making possible the recognition of all useful local occupations, and enabling the club to be a true cross-section of the business and professional life of the community."

Many of the Rotary Clubs' central activities are carried on in the presence of strangers. Rotary Clubs are required to admit any member of any other Rotary Club to their meetings. Members are encouraged to invite business associates and competitors to meetings. At some Rotary Clubs, the visitors number "in the tens and twenties each week." Joint meetings with the members of other organizations, and other joint activities, are permitted. The clubs are encouraged to seek coverage of their meetings and activities in local newspapers. In sum, Rotary Clubs, rather than carrying on their activities in an atmosphere of privacy, seek to keep their "windows and doors open to the whole world." We therefore conclude that application of the Unruh Act to local Rotary Clubs does not interfere unduly with the members' freedom of private association.

B

The Court also has recognized that the right to engage in activities protected by the First Amendment implies "a corresponding right to associate with others in pursuit of a wide variety of political, social, economic, educational, religious, and cultural ends." *Roberts v. United States Jaycees.* For this reason, "[i]mpediments to the exercise of one's right to choose one's associates can violate the right of association protected by the First Amendment." In this case, however, the evidence fails to demonstrate that admitting women to Rotary Clubs will affect in any significant way the existing members' ability to carry out their various purposes.

As a matter of policy, Rotary Clubs do not take positions on "public questions," including political or international issues. To be sure, Rotary Clubs engage in a variety of commendable service activities that are protected by the First Amendment. But the Unruh Act does not require the clubs to abandon or alter any of these activities. It does not require them to abandon their basic goals of humanitarian service, high ethical standards in all vocations, goodwill, and peace. Nor does it require them to abandon their classification system or admit members who do not reflect a cross-section of the community. Indeed, by opening membership to leading business and professional women in the community, Rotary Clubs are likely to obtain a more representative cross-section of community leaders with a broadened capacity for service.

Even if the Unruh Act does work some slight infringement on Rotary members' right of expressive association, that infringement is justified because it serves the State's compelling interest in eliminating discrimination against women. On its face the Unruh Act, like the Minnesota public accommodations law we considered in *Roberts*, makes no distinctions on the basis of the organization's viewpoint. Moreover, public accommodations laws "plainly serv[e] compelling state interests of the highest order." In *Roberts* we recognized that the State's compelling interest in assuring equal access to women extends to the acquisition of leadership skills and business contacts as well as tangible goods and services. The Unruh Act plainly serves this interest. We therefore hold that application of the Unruh Act to California Rotary Clubs does not violate the right of expressive association afforded by the First Amendment.

NOTES AND QUESTIONS

1. Assume a § 1981 claim is brought against a Kiwanis Club, a community service organization similar to the Rotary, for excluding a black applicant. Does the right to associate provide a defense to this claim? What factors will the Court examine? Should the anti-discrimination principles embodied in § 1981 always outweigh the values of individual or group autonomy and choice?

   Compare *Hurley v. Irish-American Gay, Lesbian and Bi-Sexual Group of Boston*, 517 U.S. 557 (1995), holding that a state could not apply its anti-discrimination statute to require private parade organizers to include marchers who seek to identify themselves as gay. The Court reasoned that a state may not force speakers to alter the expressive content of their parade because the First Amendment guarantees that speakers have autonomy to choose the content of their own messages. Note that this case involves freedom of expressive association, not freedom of intimate association.

2. In *Boy Scouts of America v. Dale*, 530 U.S. 640 (2000), the Court expanded on *Hurley*, finding that application of New Jersey's public accommodations law to require the Boy Scouts to retain an avowed homosexual and gay rights activist as an assistant scout master violates the Boy Scouts' First Amendment right of expressive association. It reasoned that forcing a group to accept a member it does not desire is unconstitutional if the person's presence affects in a significant way the group's ability to advocate public or private viewpoints.

The Court set forth the following three-prong analysis: (1) a court must determine whether the group engages in expressive association: "An association need not associate for the purpose of disseminating a certain message in order to be protected, but must merely engage in expressive activity that could be impaired." Further, "the First Amendment does not require that every member of a group agree on every issue in order for the group's policy to be 'expressive association'." The Boy Scouts met this standard because adult leaders are charged with the task of inculcating youth members with its value system. (2) Second, a court must determine whether the forced membership would significantly affect the group's ability to advocate public or private viewpoints. Giving deference to the Boy Scouts' assertion that it did not want to promote homosexual conduct as a legitimate form of behavior, the Court held that the presence of a gay rights activist would significantly interfere "with the Scouts' choice not to propound a point of view contrary to its beliefs." (3) Third, the Court applied strict scrutiny and concluded that the state's interest in its public accommodations law was not sufficiently compelling to justify this severe intrusion on freedom of expressive association: "[the law] may not interfere with speech for no better reason than promoting an approved message or discouraging a disfavored one, however enlightened either purpose may seem."

BROWN V. DADE CHRISTIAN SCHOOLS
556 F.2D 310 (5TH CIR. 1977)

James C. HILL, Circuit Judge.

Appellant-defendant Dade Christian Schools, Inc. (Dade Christian) appeals from the judgment of the District Court for the Southern District of Florida awarding damages to plaintiffs and enjoining defendant school from barring Valerie and Jacquelin Brown from enrolling in the school because of their race.

It is stipulated that race was the sole reason for the refusal of appellant to enroll the Brown children.

A nonjury trial was conducted and evidence taken consisting of depositions and documents. The first issue was whether or not § 1981 applied to discrimination by a private school. If it were found that 42 U.S.C. § 1981 did apply the court was confronted with the question as to whether or not the conduct of the defendant constituted the exercise of religious belief protected by the Free Exercise of Religion Clause. The defendant asserted that its members sincerely held a religious belief that socialization of the races would lead to racial intermarriage, and that this belief, sanctioned by the Free Exercise Clause, should prevail against private interests created by Congress.

Although the defendant would have us resolve this issue left open in *Runyon*, we are, also, not called upon to balance these potentially conflicting interests. The trial judge, after careful consideration of all the evidence, concluded that the defendant's policy of segregation was not the exercise of religion. Our review of the evidence convinces us that the findings of the trial judge were supported by substantial evidence. The printed card handed to Mrs. Brown at the school expressly stated the racial exclusion to be based on policy. The application for admission to the school contains a list of nine tenets entitled "[w]e believe." While these tenets may constitute religious beliefs, none of them includes anything relating to segregation of schools. Indeed, they do not refer to commingling or separation of the races at all.

We do not hold that a belief must be permanently recorded in written form to be religious in nature. However, the absence of references to school segregation in written literature stating the church's beliefs, distributed to members of the church and the public by leaders of the church and administrators of the school, is strong evidence that school segregation is not the exercise of religion.

Though difficult, it is clearly the duty of the court to decide, as a matter of fact, whether or not an activity constitutes the exercise of religion.

[The court proceeded to find that no institutional religious tenet supported this defense.]

GOLDBERG, Circuit Judge, specially concurring:

Today the plurality embraces the unacceptable principle that beliefs derived from the Bible by members of a Florida Baptist church do not constitute "religion" within the meaning of the first amendment. Its constrictive definition of religion is an egregious departure from the fundamental precept of unswerving religious tolerance that underlies the Constitution's religion clauses. I must respectfully but emphatically record my disagreement with the plurality's approach. This record discloses views that are "religious."

While I agree with the dissenters that appellant raises a free exercise claim that must be considered on its merits, I believe we cannot legitimately delay that consideration, and I therefore reject their suggestion of a remand. I concur in the plurality's result because I believe that appellant's free exercise claim is outweighed by the compelling governmental interest in securing the rights of blacks freely to contract with private schools, thus eradicating one of the badges of slavery against which this nation and this court are firmly committed.

In sum, the record is clear that the relevant beliefs are religious but equally clear that the religious practices are destructive of the undergirding principles of the thirteenth amendment.

Charting the interests of free exercise claimants requires dispassionate dedication to the principle that courts cannot question the veracity of sincerely held religious beliefs. I therefore proceed on the assumption that desegregating Dade Christian would force the principal and at least some of the teachers, students and parents to be disobedient to God. Rejecting the free exercise claim would impinge upon the religious practice of maintaining racial separation in activities that constitute "socialization."

That religious practice was characterized as a "very minor" part of the religion. Departure from the practice, although constituting disobedience to God, would not endanger salvation. While these factors do not sap the free exercise defense of vitality, they make clear that overriding that defense will not endanger the church's survival . . . adherents of the New Testament Baptist Church do not seek to overturn the Civil Rights Act of 1964 or to separate themselves from our integrated society; they merely seek to avoid situations that might lead to interracial marriage.

In this respect it is important to note that no one purports to use § 1981 as a basis for imposing interracial marriages upon anyone. Dade Christian students, like everyone else, remain free to marry whom they choose. Dade Christian parents remain free to teach their children that interracial marriage violates religious commands. That some students may depart their parents' commands and that integrating that school might make it infinitesimally easier for them then to effectuate their disobedience are hardly prospects lending weight to Dade Christian's position. The Constitution has never guaranteed parents an opportunity simultaneously to exist in an urban environment and to exclude every possibility that children will hear and adopt ideas at odds with those of the parents.

I do not mean to suggest that the religious beliefs at issue extend only to interracial marriage. Dade Christian advances a sincere belief that integrated education violates divine command. But that belief occupies a minor position in its adherents' religion and is based largely on the prospect of interracial marriage, a prospect that no government proposes to require.

In sum, Dade Christian's interests, while not minimal, do not rise to the level that has characterized numerous free exercise claims. I find that the government's interests, in comparison, are compelling.

NOTES AND QUESTIONS

1. Was Judge Goldberg correct in asserting in his concurring opinion that the anti-discrimination principle embodied in § 1981 outweighs the institution's free exercise rights?

2. Would the outcome be the same if the school, with a faculty of only five, refused to hire a black school teacher married to a white man? Note that Title VII of the Civil Rights Act of 1964 prohibits race discrimination only on the part of employers who employ fifteen or more employees. Does this suggest a viable privacy defense on the part of smaller institutions? In any event, if the school promotes a segregationist message, could it not argue that hiring a black school teacher opposed to this ideology interferes with its first amendment right of freedom of expressive association? Does *Dale* support this defense?

3. Although the Supreme Court has not yet expressly addressed the question raised in *Dade*, in *Bob Jones University v. United States*, 461 U.S. 574 (1983), it was asked to determine whether non-profit private schools that prescribe and enforce racially discriminatory admission standards on the basis of religious doctrine could qualify as tax exempt organizations under § 501(c)(3) of the Internal Revenue Code of 1954. Although conceding that the purpose of Bob Jones University is "to conduct an institution of learning, giving special emphasis to the Christian religion and the

ethics revealed in the Holy Scriptures," and that it "is dedicated to the teaching and propagation of its fundamentalist Christian religious beliefs," the Court rejected the free exercise defense:

> This Court has long held the Free Exercise Clause of the First Amendment to be an absolute prohibition against governmental regulation of religious beliefs. As interpreted by this Court, moreover, the Free Exercise Clause provides substantial protection for lawful conduct grounded in religious belief. However, "[n]ot all burdens on religion are unconstitutional. The state may justify a limitation on religious liberty by showing that it is essential to accomplish an overriding governmental interest."

> The governmental interest at stake here is compelling. [T]he Government has a fundamental, overriding interest in eradicating racial discrimination in education—discrimination that prevailed, with official approval, for the first 165 years of this Nation's constitutional history. That governmental interest substantially outweighs whatever burden denial of tax benefits places on petitioners' exercise of their religious beliefs. The interests asserted by petitioners cannot be accommodated with that compelling governmental interest, and no "less restrictive means" are available to achieve the governmental interest.

> Petitioner Bob Jones University contends that it is not racially discriminatory. It emphasizes that it now allows all races to enroll, subject only to its restrictions on the conduct of all students, including its prohibitions of association between men and women of different races, and of interracial marriage. Although a ban on intermarriage or interracial dating applies to all races, decisions of this Court firmly establish that discrimination on the basis of racial affiliation and association is a form of racial discrimination. We therefore find that the IRS properly applied Revenue Ruling 71-447 to Bob Jones University.

4. The Supreme Court in *Employment Division, Dep't of Human Resources of Oregon v. Smith*, 494 U.S. 872 (1990), significantly altered its free exercise jurisprudence. It held that a plaintiff seeking religious exemption from a generally applicable law (not targeting only religious institutions or practices) cannot succeed provided the state demonstrates merely a rational basis for its law. Although the Supreme Court addressed the question in the context of a party claiming exemption from a criminal statute (Native American Indians argued that the sacramental use of peyote should be immunized from state drug abuse laws), the lower courts have generally expanded *Smith* to encompass attempts to seek immunity from civil litigation as well. On the other hand, *Smith* distinguished earlier cases as involving Free Exercise plus another constitutional right, *i.e.*, free association, where strict scrutiny would still be triggered.

Assume a student expelled for interracial dating files suit against Bob Jones University under § 1981, seeking reinstatement as a student and significant damages for embarrassment and emotional distress. Does the Free Exercise Clause shield Bob Jones from liability? Isn't the interference with free exercise rights greater than where the institution is only denied a tax benefit? Nonetheless, isn't § 1981 a neutral, generally applicable law? Construct the constitutional defense for religious institutions in a post-*Smith* era.

5. In the context of a suit brought by a teacher alleging violation of the Americans with Disabilities Act, the Supreme Court invoked the Free Exercise and Establishment Clauses to recognize a constitutional defense, which precludes "ministerial" employees from bringing civil rights claims against their employers. *Hosanna-Tabor Evangelical Lutheran Church and School v. EEOC*, discussed *infra* Chapter 3. This defense will apply to all civil rights statutes, including § 1981. *See* Penn v. N.Y. Methodist Hosp., 884 F.3d 416, 424–28 (2d Cir. 2018) (chaplain could not bring § 1981 claim against her hospital employer because, even if the hospital no longer was connected to a church, it kept "Methodist" in its name, it maintained a robust department of pastoral care for its patients, and it employed the plaintiff as a chaplain whose sole job it was to provide religious care to the hospital's patients; joining the Fourth, Sixth, and Eighth Circuits, the court finds that the ministerial exception doctrine applies to pastoral staff members at hospitals and nursing homes because an evaluation of plaintiff's claims would require a court to assess alleged wrongdoing, which involved the plaintiff's choice of a hymn, his insensitivity to non-Christian patients, and his failure to provide spiritual support, all raising serious Establishment Clause problems).

   Further, the Religious Freedom Restoration Act (RFRA), discussed in Chapter One, allows a challenge to any federal statute that operates to "substantially burden religious exercise without compelling justification." In *Burwell v. Hobby Lobby Stores, Inc.,* 573 U.S. 682 (2014), the Supreme Court ruled that even corporations, like Hobby Lobby, may bring suit under RFRA. Hobby Lobby successfully challenged the section in the Affordable Care Act that requires that employers that provide insurance include contraceptive coverage for their female employees. The Court ruled that closely-held for-profit corporations are "persons" within the meaning of RFRA, and that the contraceptive mandate interfered with the religious liberty of Hobby Lobby by forcing it to provide certain methods of contraception that it viewed as abortifacients (or else to pay a penalty).

d. Types of Conduct Regulated

i. Discriminatory Treatment

PATTERSON V. MCLEAN CREDIT UNION
491 U.S. 164 (1989)

Justice KENNEDY delivered the opinion of the Court.

Petitioner Brenda Patterson, a black woman, was employed by respondent McLean Credit Union as a teller and a file coordinator, commencing in May 1972. In July 1982, she was laid off. After the termination, petitioner commenced this action in District Court. She alleged that respondent, in violation of 42 U.S.C. § 1981, had harassed her, failed to promote her to an intermediate accounting clerk position, and then discharged her, all because of her race.

* * *

III

A

By its plain terms, the relevant provision in § 1981 protects two rights: "the same right . . . to make . . . contracts" and "the same right . . . to . . . enforce contracts." The first of these protections extends only to the formation of a contract, but not to problems that may arise later from the conditions of continuing employment. The statute prohibits, when based on race, the refusal to enter into a contract with someone, as well as the offer to make a contract only on discriminatory terms. But the right to make contracts does not extend, as a matter of either logic or semantics, to conduct by the employer after the contract relation has been established, including breach of the terms of the contract or imposition of discriminatory working conditions. Such postformation conduct does not involve the right to make a contract, but rather implicates the performance of established contract obligations and the conditions of continuing employment, matters more naturally governed by state contract law and Title VII.

The second of these guarantees, "the same right . . . to . . . enforce contracts . . . as is enjoyed by white citizens," embraces protection of a legal process, and of a right of access to legal process, that will address and resolve contract-law claims without regard to race. In this respect, it prohibits discrimination that infects the legal process in ways that prevent one from enforcing contract rights, by reason of his or her race, and this is so whether this discrimination is attributed to a statute or simply to existing practices. It also covers wholly private efforts to impede access to the courts or obstruct nonjudicial methods of adjudicating disputes about the force of binding obligations, as well as discrimination by private entities, such as labor unions, in enforcing the terms of a contract. Following this principle and consistent with our holding in *Runyon* that § 1981 applies to private conduct, we have held that certain private entities such as labor unions, which bear explicit responsibilities to process grievances, press claims, and represent members in disputes over the terms of binding obligations that run from the employer to the employee, are subject to liability under § 1981 for racial discrimination in the enforcement of labor contracts.

B

Applying these principles to the case before us, we agree with the Court of Appeals that petitioner's racial harassment claim is not actionable under § 1981. Petitioner also alleges that she was passed over for promotion, not offered training for higher level jobs, and denied wage increases, all because of her race.

With the exception perhaps of her claim that respondent refused to promote her to a position as an accountant, none of the conduct which petitioner alleges as part of the racial harassment against her involves either a refusal to make a contract with her or the impairment of her ability to enforce her established contract rights. Rather, the conduct which petitioner labels as actionable racial harassment is postformation conduct by the employer relating to the terms and conditions of continuing employment.

Interpreting § 1981 to cover postformation conduct unrelated to an employee's right to enforce her contract, such as incidents relating to the conditions of employment, is not only inconsistent with that statute's limitation to the making and enforcement of contracts, but would also undermine the detailed and well-crafted procedures for conciliation and resolution of Title VII claims.

Where conduct is covered by both § 1981 and Title VII, the detailed procedures of Title VII are rendered a dead letter, as the plaintiff is free to pursue a claim by bringing suit under § 1981 without resort to those statutory prerequisites. We agree that, after *Runyon*, there is some necessary overlap between Title VII and § 1981, and that where the statutes do in fact overlap we are not at liberty "to infer any positive preference for one over the other." *Johnson v. Railway Express Agency, Inc., infra.* We should be reluctant, however, to read an earlier statute broadly where the result is to circumvent the detailed remedial scheme constructed in a later statute.

IV

This brings us to the question of the District Court's jury instructions on petitioner's promotion claim. We think the District Court erred when it instructed the jury that petitioner had to prove that she was better qualified than the white employee who allegedly received the promotion. In order to prevail under § 1981, a plaintiff must prove purposeful discrimination. We have developed, in analogous areas of civil rights law, a carefully designed framework of proof to determine, in the context of disparate treatment, the ultimate issue of whether the defendant intentionally discriminated against the plaintiff. We agree with the Court of Appeals that this scheme of proof, structured as a "sensible, orderly way to evaluate the evidence in light of common experience as it bears on the critical question of discrimination," should apply to claims of racial discrimination under § 1981.

Although the Court of Appeals recognized that the *McDonnell Douglas/Burdine* scheme of proof should apply in § 1981 cases such as this one, it erred in describing petitioner's burden. Under our well-established framework, the plaintiff has the initial burden of proving, by the preponderance of the evidence, a *prima facie* case of discrimination. The burden is not onerous. Here, petitioner need only prove by a preponderance of the evidence that she applied for and was qualified for an available position, that she was rejected, and that after she was rejected respondent either continued to seek applicants for the position, or, as is alleged here, filled the position with a white employee.

Once the plaintiff establishes a *prima facie* case, an inference of discrimination arises. In order to rebut this inference, the employer must present evidence that the plaintiff was rejected, or the other applicant was chosen, for a legitimate nondiscriminatory reason. Here, respondent presented evidence that it gave the job to the white applicant because she was better qualified for the position, and therefore rebutted any presumption of discrimination that petitioner may have established. At this point, as our prior cases make clear, petitioner retains the final burden of persuading the jury of intentional discrimination.

Although petitioner retains the ultimate burden of persuasion, our cases make clear that she must also have the opportunity to demonstrate that respondent's proffered reasons for its decision were not its true reasons. In doing so, petitioner is not limited to presenting evidence of a certain type. This is where the District Court erred. The evidence which petitioner can present in an attempt to establish that respondent's stated reasons are pretextual may take a variety of forms. Indeed, she might seek to demonstrate that respondent's claim to have promoted a better-qualified applicant was pretextual by showing that she was in fact better qualified than the person chosen for the position. The District Court erred, however, in instructing the jury that in order to succeed petitioner was required to make such a showing. There are certainly other ways in which petitioner could seek to prove that respondent's reasons were pretextual.

NOTES AND QUESTIONS

1. Does the Court foreclose all § 1981 actions alleging race-based terminations and other post-contract conduct? What about a claim that an employer refused to renew a contract for discriminatory reasons? As to promotions, the Court explained, "Only where the promotion rises to the level of an opportunity for a new and distinct relationship between employee and employer is such a claim actionable under § 1981."

2. Why did the Court reject the jury instructions regarding the plaintiff's rebuttal burden? If Patterson cannot prove that she was better qualified than the white employee promoted, how can she still win her case?

3. The Civil Rights Act of 1991 overturned *Patterson* by defining the term "make and enforce contracts" to include "the making, performance, modification, and termination of contracts, and the enjoyment of all benefits, privileges, terms, and conditions of the contractual relationship?" *See* 42 U.S.C. § 1981(b). Would all of Patterson's claims be actionable under the new Act? What if she alleged that she was fired for complaining about the racially discriminatory treatment of a co-worker? The following case addresses this question.

ii. Retaliation

CBOCS WEST, INC. V. HUMPHRIES
553 U.S. 442 (2008)

BREYER, J., delivered the opinion of the Court.

[Humphries, a black former assistant manager of a Cracker Barrel restaurant alleged in part that he was discharged because he had complained to management that another black employee had been dismissed for race-based reasons.]

II

The question before us is whether § 1981 encompasses retaliation claims. We conclude that it does. And because our conclusion rests in significant part upon principles of *stare decisis,* we begin by examining the pertinent interpretive history.

A

The Court first considered a comparable question in 1969, in *Sullivan v. Little Hunting Park, Inc.* The case arose under 42 U.S.C. § 1982, a statutory provision that Congress enacted just after the Civil War, along with § 1981, to protect the rights of black citizens. The provision was similar to § 1981 except that it focused, not upon rights to make and to enforce contracts, but rights related to the ownership of property.

Paul E. Sullivan, a white man, had rented his house to T.R. Freeman, Jr., a black man. He had also assigned Freeman a membership share in a corporation, which permitted the owner to use a private park that the corporation controlled. Because of Freeman's race, the corporation, Little Hunting Park, Inc., refused to approve the share assignment. And, when Sullivan protested, the association expelled Sullivan and took away his membership shares.

Sullivan sued Little Hunting Park, claiming that its actions violated § 1982. The Court upheld Sullivan's claim. It found that the corporation's refusal "to approve the assignment of the membership share . . . was clearly an interference with Freeman's [the black lessee's] right to 'lease.'" It added that Sullivan, the white lessor, "has standing to maintain this action," because, as the Court had previously said, "the white owner is at times 'the only effective adversary' of the unlawful restrictive covenant." The Court noted that to permit the corporation to punish Sullivan "for trying to vindicate the rights of minorities protected by § 1982" would give "impetus to the perpetuation of racial restrictions on property." And this Court has made clear that *Sullivan* stands for the proposition that § 1982 encompasses retaliation claims. *See Jackson v. Birmingham Bd. of Educ.* ("[I]n *Sullivan* we interpreted a general prohibition on racial discrimination [in § 1982] to cover retaliation against those who advocate the rights of groups protected by that prohibition").

While the *Sullivan* decision interpreted § 1982, our precedents have long construed §§ 1981 and 1982 similarly. In *Runyon v. McCrary,* the Court considered whether § 1981 prohibits private acts of discrimination. Citing *Sullivan,* along with *Jones v. Alfred H. Mayer Co.,* and *Tillman v. Wheaton-Haven Recreation Ass'n, Inc.,* the Court reasoned that this case law "necessarily requires the conclusion that § 1981, like § 1982, reaches private conduct."

As indicated in *Runyon,* the Court has construed §§ 1981 and 1982 alike because it has recognized the sister statutes' common language, origin, and purposes. Like § 1981, § 1982 traces its origin to § 1 of the Civil Rights Act of 1866. Like § 1981, § 1982 represents an immediately post-Civil War legislative effort to guarantee the then newly freed slaves the same legal rights that other citizens enjoy. Like § 1981, § 1982 uses broad language that says "[a]ll citizens of the United States shall have the same right, in every State and Territory, as is enjoyed by white citizens . . . ."

In light of these precedents, it is not surprising that following *Sullivan,* federal appeals courts concluded, on the basis of *Sullivan* or its reasoning, that § 1981 encompassed retaliation claims.

B

In 1989, 20 years after *Sullivan,* this Court in *Patterson v. McLean Credit Union,* significantly limited the scope of § 1981. The Court focused upon § 1981's words "to make and enforce contracts" and interpreted the phrase narrowly. It wrote that the statutory phrase did not apply to "conduct by the employer *after the contract relation has been established,* including breach of the terms of the contract or imposition of discriminatory working conditions." Thus § 1981 did not encompass the claim of a black employee who charged that her employer had violated her employment contract by harassing her and failing to promote her, all because of her race.

Since victims of an employer's retaliation will often have opposed discriminatory conduct taking place *after* the formation of the employment contract, *Patterson's* holding, for a brief time, seems in practice to have foreclosed retaliation claims. In 1991, however, Congress weighed in on the matter. Congress passed the Civil Rights Act of 1991, with the design to supersede *Patterson.* Insofar as is relevant here, the new law changed 42 U.S.C. § 1981 by reenacting the former provision, designating it as § 1981(a), and adding a new subsection, (b), which, says:

"Make and enforce contracts" defined

For purposes of this section, the term 'make and enforce contracts' includes the making, performance, modification, and termination of contracts, and the enjoyment of all benefits, privileges, terms, and conditions of the contractual relationship.

An accompanying Senate Report pointed out that the amendment superseded *Patterson* by adding a new subsection (b) that would "reaffirm that the right 'to make and enforce contracts' includes the enjoyment of all benefits, privileges, terms and conditions of the contractual relationship." Among other things, it would "ensure that Americans may not be harassed, *fired* or otherwise discriminated against in contracts because of their race." An accompanying House Report said that in "cutting back the scope of the rights to 'make' and 'enforce' contracts[,] *Patterson* . . . has been interpreted to eliminate retaliation claims that the courts had previously recognized under section 1981." It added that the protections that subsection (b) provided, in "the context of employment discrimination . . . would include, but not be limited to, claims of harassment, discharge, demotion, promotion, transfer, *retaliation,* and hiring." (emphasis added). It also said that the new law "would restore rights to sue for such retaliatory conduct."

After enactment of the new law, the Federal Courts of Appeals again reached a broad consensus that § 1981, as amended, encompasses retaliation claims. The upshot is this: (1) in 1969, *Sullivan,* as interpreted by *Jackson,* recognized that § 1982 encompasses a retaliation action; (2) this Court has long interpreted §§ 1981 and 1982 alike; (3) in 1989, *Patterson,* without mention of retaliation, narrowed § 1981 by excluding from its scope conduct, namely post-contract-formation conduct, where retaliation would most likely be found; but in 1991, Congress enacted legislation that superseded *Patterson* and explicitly defined the scope of § 1981 to include post-contract-formation conduct; and (4) since 1991, the lower courts have uniformly interpreted § 1981 as encompassing retaliation actions.

C

Sullivan, as interpreted and relied upon by *Jackson,* as well as the long line of related cases where we construe §§ 1981 and 1982 similarly, lead us to conclude that the view that § 1981 encompasses retaliation claims is indeed well embedded in the law. That being so, considerations of *stare decisis* strongly support our adherence to that view. And those considerations impose a considerable burden upon those who would seek a different interpretation that would necessarily unsettle many Court precedents.

III

In our view, CBOCS' several arguments, taken separately or together, cannot justify a departure from what we have just described as the well-embedded interpretation of § 1981. First, CBOCS points to the plain text of § 1981—a text that says that "*[a]ll persons . . . shall have the same right . . . to make and enforce contracts . . . as is enjoyed by white citizens.*" 42 U.S.C.

§ 1981(a) (emphasis added). CBOCS adds that, insofar as Humphries complains of retaliation, he is complaining of a retaliatory action that the employer would have taken against him whether he was black or white, and there is no way to construe this text to cover that kind of deprivation. Thus the text's language, CBOCS concludes, simply "does not provide for a cause of action based on retaliation."

We agree with CBOCS that the statute's language does not expressly refer to the claim of an individual (black or white) who suffers retaliation because he has tried to help a different individual, suffering direct racial discrimination, secure his § 1981 rights. But that fact alone is not sufficient to carry the day. After all, this Court has long held that the statutory text of § 1981's sister statute, § 1982, provides protection from retaliation for reasons related to the *enforcement* of the express statutory right.

Moreover, the Court has recently read another broadly worded civil rights statute, namely, Title IX of the Education Amendments of 1972, as including an antiretaliation remedy. In 2005 in *Jackson,* the Court considered whether statutory language prohibiting "discrimination [on the basis of sex] under any education program or activity receiving Federal financial assistance," § 1681(a), encompassed claims of retaliation for complaints about sex discrimination. Despite the fact that Title IX does not use the word "retaliation," the Court held in *Jackson v. Birmingham Board of Education* that the statute's language encompassed such a claim, in part because: (1) "Congress enacted Title IX just three years after *Sullivan* was decided"; (2) it is "'realistic to presume that Congress was thoroughly familiar'" with *Sullivan;* and (3) Congress consequently "'expected its enactment'" of Title IX "'to be interpreted in conformity with'" *Sullivan.* The Court in *Jackson* explicitly rejected the arguments the dissent advances here-that *Sullivan* was merely a standing case.

Regardless, the linguistic argument that CBOCS makes was apparent at the time the Court decided *Sullivan.* And we believe it is too late in the day in effect to overturn the holding in that case (nor does CBOCS ask us to do so) on the basis of a linguistic argument that was apparent, and which the Court did not embrace at that time.

Second, CBOCS argues that Congress, in 1991 when it reenacted § 1981 with amendments, intended the reenacted statute *not* to cover retaliation. CBOCS rests this conclusion primarily upon the fact that Congress *did not* include an *explicit* antiretaliation provision or the word "retaliation" in the new statutory language-although Congress has included explicit antiretaliation language in other civil rights statutes.

We believe, however, that the circumstances to which CBOCS points find a far more plausible explanation in the fact that, given *Sullivan* and the new statutory language nullifying *Patterson,* there was no need for Congress to include explicit language about retaliation. After all, the 1991 amendments themselves make clear that Congress intended to supersede the result in *Patterson* and embrace pre-*Patterson* law. And pre-*Patterson* law included *Sullivan.* Nothing in the statute's text or in the surrounding circumstances suggests any congressional effort to supersede *Sullivan* or the interpretation that courts have subsequently given that case. To the contrary, the amendments' history indicates that Congress intended to restore that interpretation.

Third, CBOCS points out that § 1981, if applied to employment-related retaliation actions, would overlap with Title VII. It adds that Title VII requires that those who invoke its remedial powers satisfy certain procedural and administrative requirements that § 1981 does not contain. *See, e.g.,*42 U.S.C. § 2000e-5(e)(1) (charge of discrimination must be brought before EEOC within 180 days of the discriminatory act); § 2000e-5(f)(1) (suit must be filed within 90 days of obtaining an EEOC right-to-sue letter). And CBOCS says that permitting a § 1981 retaliation action would allow a retaliation plaintiff to circumvent Title VII's "specific administrative and procedural mechanisms," thereby undermining their effectiveness.

This argument, however, proves too much. Precisely the same kind of Title VII/ § 1981 "overlap" and potential circumvention exists in respect to employment-related direct discrimination. Yet Congress explicitly created the overlap in respect to direct employment discrimination. Nor is it obvious how we can interpret § 1981 to avoid *employment*-related overlap without eviscerating § 1981 in respect to *non*-employment contracts where no such overlap exists.

Regardless, we have previously acknowledged a "necessary overlap" between Title VII and § 1981. We have added that the "remedies available under Title VII and under § 1981, although related, and although directed to most of the same ends, are separate, distinct, and independent." *Johnson v. Transportation Agency*, 480 U.S. 616 (1987). We have pointed out that Title VII provides important administrative remedies and other benefits that § 1981 lacks. And we have concluded that "Title VII was designed to supplement, rather than supplant, existing laws and institutions relating to employment discrimination." In a word, we have previously held that the "overlap" reflects congressional design. We have no reason to reach a different conclusion in this case.

Fourth, CBOCS says it finds support for its position in two of our recent cases, *Burlington N. & S.F.R. Co. v. White* and *Domino's Pizza, Inc. v. McDonald.* In *Burlington*, a Title VII case, we distinguished between discrimination that harms individuals because of "who they are, *i.e.*, their status," for example, as women or as black persons, and discrimination that harms "individuals based on what they do, *i.e.*, their conduct," for example, whistle-blowing that leads to retaliation. CBOCS says that we should draw a similar distinction here and conclude that § 1981 only encompasses status-based discrimination. In *Burlington*, however, we used the status/conduct distinction to help explain why Congress might have wanted its explicit Title VII antiretaliation provision to sweep more broadly (*i.e.*, to include conduct *outside* the workplace) than its substantive Title VII (status-based) antidiscrimination provision. *Burlington* did not suggest that Congress must separate the two in all events.

CBOCS highlights the second case, *Domino's Pizza*, along with *Patterson*, to show that this Court now follows an approach to statutory interpretation that emphasizes text. And that newer approach, CBOCS claims, should lead us to revisit the holding in *Sullivan*, an older case, where the Court placed less weight upon the textual language itself. But even were we to posit for argument's sake that changes in interpretive approach take place from time to time, we could not agree that the existence of such a change would justify reexamination of well-established prior law. Principles of *stare decisis*, after all, demand respect for precedent whether judicial methods of interpretation change or stay the same. Were that not so, those principles would fail to achieve the legal stability that they seek and upon which the rule of law depends.

IV

We conclude that considerations of *stare decisis* strongly support our adherence to *Sullivan* and the long line of related cases where we interpret §§ 1981 and 1982 similarly. CBOCS' arguments do not convince us to the contrary. We consequently hold that 42 U.S.C. § 1981 encompasses claims of retaliation. The judgment of the Court of Appeals is affirmed.

Justice THOMAS, with whom Justice SCALIA joins, dissenting.

It is unexceptional in our case law that "'[s]tatutory construction must begin with the language employed by Congress and the assumption that the ordinary meaning of that language accurately expresses the legislative purpose.'" Today, that rule is honored in the breach: The Court's analysis of the statutory text does not appear until Part III of its opinion, and then only as a potential reason to depart from the interpretation the Court has already concluded, on other grounds, must "carry the day." Unlike the Court, I think it best to begin, as we usually do, with the text of the statute.

Section 1981(a) guarantees "[a]ll persons . . . the same right . . . to make and enforce contracts . . . as is enjoyed by white citizens." It is difficult to see where one finds a cause of action for retaliation in this language. On its face, § 1981(a) is a straightforward ban on racial discrimination in the making and enforcement of contracts. Not surprisingly, that is how the Court has always construed it.

Respondent nonetheless contends that "[t]he terms of section 1981 are significantly different, and broader, than a simple prohibition against discrimination." It is true that § 1981(a), which was enacted shortly after the Civil War, does not use the modern statutory formulation prohibiting "discrimination on the basis of race." But that is the clear import of its terms. Contrary to respondent's contention, nothing in § 1981 evinces a "concer[n] with protecting individuals 'based on what they do,'" as opposed to "'prevent[ing] injury to individuals based on who they are.'" Nor does § 1981 "affirmatively guarante[e]" freestanding "rights to engage in particular conduct." The statute assumes that "white citizens" enjoy certain rights and requires that those rights be extended equally to "[a]ll persons," regardless of their race. That is to say, it prohibits discrimination based on race.

Retaliation is not discrimination based on race. When an individual is subjected to reprisal because he has complained about racial discrimination, the injury he suffers is not on account of his *race;* rather, it is the result of his *conduct.* [A] claim of retaliation is both logically and factually distinct from a claim of discrimination-logically because retaliation based on conduct and discrimination based on status are mutually exclusive categories, and factually because a claim of retaliation does not depend on proof that any status-based discrimination actually occurred. Consider, for example, an employer who fires any employee who complains of race discrimination, regardless of the employee's race. Such an employer is undoubtedly guilty of retaliation, but he has not discriminated on the basis of anyone's race. Because the employer treats all employees-black and white-the same, he does not deny any employee "the same right ... to make and enforce contracts . . . as is enjoyed by white citizens."

Section 1981's silence regarding retaliation is not dispositive, the Court says, because "it is too late in the day" to resort to "a linguistic argument" that was supposedly rejected in *Sullivan*. The Court's reliance on *Sullivan* is entirely misplaced. But it also bears emphasis that the Court does not even purport to identify any basis in the statutory text for the "well-embedded interpretation of § 1981," it adopts for the first time today. Unlike the Court, I find the statute's text dispositive. Because § 1981 by its terms prohibits only discrimination based on race, and because retaliation is not discrimination based on race, § 1981 does not provide an implied cause of action for retaliation.

NOTES AND QUESTIONS

1. The question of whether a civil rights law reaches retaliatory conduct is a critical one for all the laws discussed in this textbook. Some of the modern civil rights laws— most notably Title VII—explicitly create a remedy against employers who retaliate against employees who file claims, assist others in filing discrimination claims or who oppose an employer's unlawful practices. *See infra* Ch. III. However, most of the older provisions as well as the modern "funding" statutes, such as Title IX discussed in this opinion, are silent on this question. *See infra* Chapter IV. As reflected in this decision, the Justices are deeply divided as to the Court's appropriate role in construing federal statutes. Some rely on separation of powers to insist on a strict textualist approach, whereas others assert that congressional intent, as reflected in the legislative history and the underlying purpose of the law, should guide a court. What, if anything, justifies looking beyond the text in ascertaining the will of Congress? Should policy arguments guide the Court's interpretation of federal laws? Was the Court's *stare decisis* argument persuasive?

2. In a companion case, *Gomez-Perez v. Potter*, 553 U.S. 474 (2008), discussed *infra* Ch. III, the Court held that the federal sector provision of the Age Discrimination in Employment Act ("ADEA") should be interpreted to include a retaliation claim on behalf of federal employees who complain of age discrimination. The majority relied on the *Sullivan* and *Jackson* cases discussed in *CBOCS* to reach its decision. Although, in contrast to the public sector, the private sector provision in the ADEA specifically prohibits retaliation, the Court held that this did not preclude "inferring such a cause of action on behalf of federal employees since the two provisions were enacted seven years apart and are couched in very different terms."

3. Note carefully the discussion of overlapping rights in *CBOCS*. If employees can pursue a remedy for retaliatory action under Title VII, why "imply" such a cause of action under § 1981?

e. Intent Requirement and Respondeat Superior

GENERAL BUILDING CONTRACTORS ASS'N V. PENNSYLVANIA
458 U.S. 375 (1982)

Justice REHNQUIST delivered the opinion of the Court.

Respondents, the Commonwealth of Pennsylvania and the representatives of a class of racial minorities who are skilled or seek work as operating engineers in the construction industry in Eastern Pennsylvania and Delaware, commenced this action under a variety of federal statutes protecting civil rights, including 42 U.S.C. § 1981. The complaint sought to redress racial discrimination in the operation of an exclusive hiring hall established in contracts between Local 542 of the International Union of Operating Engineers and construction industry employers doing business within the Union's jurisdiction. Respondents also alleged discrimination in the operation of an apprenticeship program established by Local 542 and several construction trade associations. Named as defendants were Local 542, the trade associations, the organization charged with administering the trade's apprenticeship program, and a class of approximately 1,400 construction industry employers. Petitioners, the defendant contractors and trade associations, seek review of a judgment granting an injunction against them. The questions we resolve are whether liability under 42 U.S.C. § 1981 requires proof of discriminatory intent and whether, absent such proof, liability can nevertheless be imposed vicariously on the employers and trade associations for the discriminatory conduct of the Union.

This action was filed in 1971 by the Commonwealth of Pennsylvania and 12 black plaintiffs representing a proposed class of minority group members residing within the jurisdiction of Local 542. The complaint charged that the Union and the JATC [Joint Apprenticeship and Training Committee] had violated numerous state and federal laws prohibiting employment discrimination, including Title VII of the Civil Rights Act of 1964, 42 U.S.C. § 2000e, *et seq.* and 42 U.S.C. § 1981. The complaint alleged that these defendants had engaged in a pattern and practice of racial discrimination, by systematically denying access to the Union's referral lists, and by arbitrarily skewing referrals in favor of white workers, limiting most minority workers who did gain access to the hiring hall to jobs of short hours and low pay. The contractor employers and trade associations were also named as defendants, although the complaint did not allege a Title VII cause of action against them.[4]

The District Court's opinion in the liability phase of the trial is lengthy. For our purposes, however, the relevant findings and conclusions can be summarized briefly. First, the court found that the hiring hall system established by collective bargaining was neutral on its face. Indeed, after May 1, 1971, the contracts contained a provision expressly prohibiting employment discrimination on the basis of race, religion, color, or national origin. But the court found that Local

---

4   The complaint did not assert a Title VII cause of action against petitioners because they were not named in the complaint filed by the plaintiffs with the Equal Employment Opportunity Commission, a precondition to suit in federal court.

542, in administering the system, "practiced a pattern of intentional discrimination and that union practices in the overall operation of a hiring hall for operating engineers created substantial racial disparities." The court made similar findings regarding the JATC's administration of the job-training program. On the basis of these findings, the District Court held that Local 542 and the JATC had violated Title VII, both because they intentionally discriminated and because they enforced practices that resulted in a disparate racial impact. The court also interpreted 42 U.S.C. § 1981 to permit imposition of liability "on roughly the same basis as a Title VII claim," and therefore concluded that the Union and the JATC had also violated § 1981.

Turning to petitioners' liability under § 1981, the court found that the plaintiffs had failed to prove "that the associations or contractors viewed simply as a class were actually aware of the union discrimination," and had failed to show "intent to discriminate by the employers as a class." Nevertheless, the court held the employers and the associations liable under § 1981 for the purpose of imposing an injunctive remedy "as a result of their contractual relationship to and use of a hiring hall system which in practice effectuated intentional discrimination, whether or not the employers and associations knew or should have known [of the Union's conduct]." The court reasoned that liability under § 1981 "requires no proof of purposeful conduct on the part of any of the defendants." Instead, it was sufficient that "(1) the employers delegated an important aspect of their hiring procedure to the union; [and that] (2) the union, in effectuating the delegation, intentionally discriminated or, alternatively, produced a discriminatory impact." "[P]laintiffs have shown that the requisite relationship exists among employers, associations, and union to render applicable the theory of *respondeat superior*, thus making employers and associations liable injunctively for the discriminatory acts of the union."

The District Court held that petitioners had violated 42 U.S.C. § 1981 notwithstanding its finding that, as a class, petitioners did not intentionally discriminate against minority workers and neither knew nor had reason to know of the Union's discriminatory practices. The first question we address, therefore, is whether liability may be imposed under § 1981 without proof of intentional discrimination.

In determining whether § 1981 reaches practices that merely result in a disproportionate impact on a particular class, or instead is limited to conduct motivated by a discriminatory purpose, we must be mindful of the "events and passions of the time" in which the law was forged. The Civil War had ended in April 1865. The First Session of the Thirty-ninth Congress met on December 4, 1865, some six months after the preceding Congress had sent to the States the Thirteenth Amendment and just two weeks before the Secretary of State certified the Amendment's ratification. On January 5, 1866, Senator Trumbull introduced the bill that would become the 1866 Act.

The principal object of the legislation was to eradicate the Black Codes, laws enacted by Southern legislatures imposing a range of civil disabilities on freedmen. Most of these laws embodied express racial classifications and although others, such as those penalizing vagrancy, were facially neutral, Congress plainly perceived all of them as consciously conceived methods of resurrecting the incidents of slavery.

The immediate evils with which the Thirty-ninth Congress was concerned simply did not include practices that were "neutral on their face, and even neutral in terms of intent," but that had the incidental effect of disadvantaging blacks to a greater degree than whites. Congress instead acted to protect the freedmen from intentional discrimination by those whose object was "to make their former slaves dependent serfs, victims of unjust laws, and debarred from all progress and elevation by organized social prejudices."

Our conclusion that § 1981 reaches only purposeful discrimination is supported by one final observation about its legislative history. As noted earlier, the origins of the law can be traced to both the Civil Rights Act of 1866 and the Enforcement Act of 1870. Both of these laws, in turn, were legislative cousins of the Fourteenth Amendment. The 1866 Act represented Congress' first attempt to ensure equal rights for the freedmen following the formal abolition of slavery effected by the Thirteenth Amendment. As such, it constituted an initial blueprint of the Fourteenth Amendment, which Congress proposed in part as a means of "incorporat[ing] the guaranties of the Civil Rights Act of 1866 in the organic law of the land." The 1870 Act, which contained the language that now appears in § 1981, was enacted as a means of enforcing the recently ratified Fourteenth Amendment. In light of the close connection between these Acts and the Amendment, it would be incongruous to construe the principal object of their successor, § 1981, in a manner markedly different from that of the Amendment itself.

With respect to the latter, "official action will not be held unconstitutional solely because it results in a racially disproportionate impact". "[E]ven if a neutral law has a disproportionately adverse impact upon a racial minority, it is unconstitutional under the Equal Protection Clause only if that impact can be traced to a discriminatory purpose." *Personnel Administrator of Mass. v. Feeney.* The same Congress that proposed the Fourteenth Amendment also passed the Civil Rights Act of 1866, and the ratification of that Amendment paved the way for the Enforcement Act of 1870. These measures were all products of the same milieu and were directed against the same evils. Although Congress might have charted a different course in enacting the predecessors to § 1981 than it did in proposing the Fourteenth Amendment, we have found no convincing evidence that it did so.

We conclude, therefore, that § 1981, like the Equal Protection Clause, can be violated only by purposeful discrimination.

The District Court held petitioners liable under § 1981 notwithstanding its finding that the plaintiffs had failed to prove intent to discriminate on the part of the employers and associations as a class. In light of our holding that § 1981 can be violated only by intentional discrimination, the District Court's judgment can stand only if liability under § 1981 can properly rest on some ground other than the discriminatory motivation of the petitioners themselves. Both the District Court and respondents have relied on such grounds, but we find them unconvincing.

The District Court reasoned that liability could be vicariously imposed upon the employers and associations, based upon the intentional discrimination practiced by Local 542 in its operation of the hiring hall. As applied to the petitioner associations, the District Court's theory is flawed on its own terms. The doctrine of *respondeat superior*, as traditionally conceived and as understood by the District Court, enables the imposition of liability on a principal for the tortious acts of his agent and, in the more common case, on the master for the wrongful acts of his servant.

A master-servant relationship is a form of agency in which the master employs the servant as "an agent to perform service in his affairs" and "controls or has the right to control the physical conduct of the other in the performance of the service." Local 542, in its operation of the hiring hall, simply performed no function as the agent or servant of the associations. The record demonstrates that the associations themselves do not hire operating engineers, and never have. Their primary purpose is to represent certain employers in contract negotiations with the Union. Even if the doctrine of *respondeat superior* were broadly applicable to suits based on § 1981, therefore, it would not support the imposition of liability on a defendant based on the acts of a party with whom it had no agency or employment relationship.

We have similar difficulty in accepting the application of traditional *respondeat superior* doctrine to the class of contractor employers. In the run of cases, the relationship between an employer and the union that represents its employees simply cannot be accurately characterized as one between principal and agent or master and servant. Indeed, such a conception is alien to the fundamental assumptions upon which the federal labor laws are structured.

The District Court also justified its result by concluding that § 1981 imposes a "nondelegable duty" on petitioners "to see that discrimination does not take place in the selection of [their] workforce." The concept of a nondelegable duty imposes upon the principal not merely an obligation to exercise care in his own activities, but to answer for the well-being of those persons to whom the duty runs. In a sense, to characterize such a duty as "nondelegable" is merely to restate the duty. Thus, in this litigation the question is not whether the employers and associations are free to delegate their duty to abide by § 1981, for whatever duty the statute imposes, they are bound to adhere to it. The question is what duty does § 1981 impose. More precisely, does § 1981 impose a duty to refrain from intentionally denying blacks the right to contract on the same basis as whites or does it impose an affirmative obligation to ensure that blacks enjoy such a right? The language of the statute does not speak in terms of duties. It merely declares specific rights held by "[a]ll persons within the jurisdiction of the United States." We are confident that the Thirty-ninth Congress meant to do no more than prohibit the employers and associations in these cases from intentionally depriving black workers of the rights enumerated in the statute, including the equal right to contract. It did not intend to make them the guarantors of the workers' rights as against third parties who would infringe them.

NOTES AND QUESTIONS

1. Why does the Court hold that § 1981 reaches only intentional discrimination? How can the majority's emphasis on the Fourteenth Amendment source of § 1981 be squared with the analysis in *Runyon*, which emphasized the Thirteenth Amendment source?

2. What impact does the decision have on § 1982? Should the same intent requirement be read into that provision or does the different legislative history suggest a different outcome?

3. How may an aggrieved employee satisfy the intent requirement? Isn't it likely that the defendant employers and trade associations knew of the blatantly discriminatory practices of the union? Has the Court allowed an employer to hide behind a veil of ignorance? May an employer assign personnel hiring decisions to an outside employment agency and thereby escape liability for an all-white workforce? Can intentional discrimination be proved through acts of omission?

In *Arlington Heights v. Metropolitan Housing Dev. Corp.*, 429 U.S. 252 (1977), the Court, in the context of an alleged race-based refusal to rezone from single to multiple family units to permit construction of low income housing, lists four factors relevant to assessing claims of intentional discrimination, namely
   (1) disparate impact;
   (2) historical background of the decision;
   (3) the sequence of events leading up to the challenged decision; and
   (4) substantive departures from the normal procedural sequence.

These factors are often invoked by courts, including the Supreme Court, in assessing whether the government has intentionally discriminated against a protected group. *See, e.g.*, Masterpiece Cakeshop v. Colorado Civil Rights, 138 S. Ct. 1719 (2018).

4. In *Goodman v. Lukens Steel*, 482 U.S. 656 (1987), the Court ruled that a Union's decision not to file race-bias grievances demonstrated more than "mere passivity" and thus was actionable under § 1981, even if the Union did not act for racially invidious reasons, but only to avoid "antagonizing" the employer. What is the difference between racial animus and intentional discrimination based on race? If the former is not required, can challenges to affirmative action programs be brought under § 1981?

5. Does *General Building Contractors* totally rule out *respondeat superior* liability? If not, why does the Court reject it here? The Court's apparent refusal to reject *respondeat superior* in the context of a private defendant raised some speculation as to whether *respondeat superior* might also be available to hold a government entity liable under § 1981 for the misconduct of its employees. The question is quite significant because municipal entities cannot be held liable under § 1983, which provides a cause of action for the deprivation "under color of state law" of federal constitutional or statutory rights based on *respondeat superior*.

The Supreme Court, in *Jett v. Dallas Independent School District*, 491 U.S. 701 (1989), held that § 1983, provides the exclusive federal damages remedy for violation of the rights guaranteed by § 1981 when the claim is brought against "state actors." The Civil Rights Act of 1991 appears to overturn *Jett* because it provides that the rights protected under § 1981 are protected against impairment by nongovernmental discrimination as well as impairment "under color of state law." However, the Act does not address the question whether government entities sued under this provision can be held liable on a *respondeat superior* theory. See § 1981(c). The majority of appellate courts have ruled that although § 1981(c) "creates rights," their violation must be pursued under § 1983, because the purpose of § 1981(c) was to codify *Runyon* and *Patterson* with regard to private defendants, not to overturn *Jett*, which is not mentioned in the legislative history. *See* Duplan v. City of New York, 888 F.3d 612, 619–21 (2d Cir. 2018) (court joins nine sister circuits in concluding that § 1981 does not provide a separate right of action against state actors and thus plaintiff's claims against the city were properly dismissed). The Ninth Circuit, taking a strict textualist approach, has found a cause of action against government defendants under § 1981, but it has concluded that when a § 1981 claim is brought against a government defendant, there is no *respondeat superior* liability. Because Congress used the "under color of state law" language from § 1983, the Ninth Circuit reasoned that the same rules regarding liability apply.

f. Relation to Other Acts

JOHNSON V. RAILWAY EXPRESS AGENCY
421 U.S. 454 (1975)

Mr. Justice BLACKMUN delivered the opinion of the Court.

This case presents the issue whether the timely filing of a charge of employment discrimination with the Equal Employment Opportunity Commission (EEOC), pursuant to § 706 of Title VII of the Civil Rights Act of 1964, 42 U.S.C. § 2000e-5, tolls the running of the period of limitation applicable to an action, based on the same facts, instituted under § 1981.

Petitioner, Willie Johnson, Jr., is a Negro. He started to work for respondent Railway Express Agency, Inc., now, by change of name, REA Express, Inc. (REA), in Memphis, Tenn., in the spring of 1964 as an express handler. On May 31, 1967, while still employed by REA, but now as a driver rather than as a handler, petitioner, with others, timely filed with the EEOC a charge that REA was discriminating against its Negro employees with respect to seniority rules and job assignments. Three weeks later, on June 20, REA terminated petitioner's employment. Petitioner then amended his charge to include an allegation that he had been discharged because of his race.

The EEOC issued its "Final Investigation Report" on December 22, 1967. The report generally supported petitioner's claims of racial discrimination. It was not until more than two years later, however, on March 31, 1970, that the Commission rendered its decision finding reasonable cause to believe petitioner's charges. And 9 1/2 more months went by before the EEOC, on January 15, 1971, pursuant to 42 U.S.C. § 2000e-5(e), as it then read, gave petitioner notice of his right to institute a Title VII civil action against the respondents within 30 days.

After receiving this notice, petitioner encountered some difficulty in obtaining counsel. The United States District Court for the Western District of Tennessee, on February 12, 1971, permitted petitioner to file the right-to-sue letter with the court's clerk as a complaint, in satisfaction of the 30-day requirement. The court also granted petitioner leave to proceed *in forma pauperis*, and it appointed counsel to represent him. On March 18, counsel filed a "Supplemental Complaint" against REA and the two unions, alleging racial discrimination on the part of the defendants, in violation of Title VII of the 1964 Act *and of* 42 U.S.C. § 1981. The unions and REA respectively moved for summary judgment or, in the alternative, for dismissal of all claims. The District Court dismissed the § 1981 claims as barred by Tennessee's one-year statute of limitations. Petitioner's remaining claims were dismissed on other grounds.

In his appeal to the United States Court of Appeals for the Sixth Circuit, petitioner, with respect to his § 1981 claims, argued that the running of the one-year period of limitation was suspended during the pendency of his timely filed administrative complaint with the EEOC under Title VII. The Court of Appeals rejected this argument.

Despite Title VII's range and its design as a comprehensive solution for the problem of invidious discrimination in employment, the aggrieved individual clearly is not deprived of other remedies he possesses and is not limited to Title VII in his search for relief. "[T]he legislative history of Title VII manifests a congressional intent to allow an individual to pursue independently his rights under both Title VII and other applicable state and federal statutes." In particular, Congress noted "that the remedies available to the individual under Title VII are co-extensive with the indiv[i]dual's right to sue under the provisions of the Civil Rights Act of 1866, 42 U.S.C. § 1981, and that the two procedures augment each other and are not mutually exclusive." Later, in considering the Equal Employment Opportunity Act of 1972, the Senate rejected an amendment that would have deprived a claimant of any right to sue under § 1981.

Title 42 U.S.C. § 1981, being the present codification of § 16 of the century-old Civil Rights Act of 1870, on its face relates primarily to racial discrimination in the making and enforcement of contracts. Although this Court has not specifically so held, it is well-settled among the Federal Courts of Appeals—and we now join them—that § 1981 affords a federal remedy against discrimination in private employment on the basis of race. An individual who establishes a cause of action under § 1981 is entitled to both equitable and legal relief, including compensatory and, under certain circumstances, punitive damages. And a backpay award under § 1981 is not restricted to the two years specified for backpay recovery under Title VII.

Section 1981 is not coextensive in its coverage with Title VII. The latter is made inapplicable to certain employers. 42 U.S.C. § 2000e(b). Also, Title VII offers assistance in investigation, conciliation, counsel, waiver of court costs, and attorneys' fees, items that are unavailable at least under the specific terms of § 1981.[a]

Petitioner, and the United States as *amicus curiae*, concede, as they must, the independence of the avenues of relief respectively available under Title VII and the older § 1981. Further, it has been noted that the filing of a Title VII charge and resort to Title VII's administrative machinery are not prerequisites for the institution of a § 1981 action.

We are satisfied, also, that Congress did not expect that a § 1981 court action usually would be resorted to only upon completion of Title VII procedures and the Commission's efforts to obtain voluntary compliance. Conciliation and persuasion through the administrative process, to be sure, often constitute a desirable approach to settlement of disputes based on sensitive and emotional charges of invidious employment discrimination. We recognize, too, that the filing of a lawsuit might tend to deter efforts at conciliation, that lack of success in the legal action could weaken the Commission's efforts to induce voluntary compliance, and that a suit is privately oriented and narrow, rather than broad, in application, as successful conciliation tend to be. But these are the natural effects of the choice Congress has made available to the claimant by its conferring upon him independent administrative and judicial remedies. The choice is a valuable one. Under some circumstances, the administrative route may be highly preferred over the litigatory; under others, the reverse may be true. We are disinclined, in the face of congressional emphasis upon the existence and independence of the two remedies, to infer any positive preference for one over the other, without a more definite expression in the legislation Congress has enacted, as, for example, a proscription of a § 1981 action while an EEOC claim is pending.

We generally conclude, therefore, that the remedies available under Title VII and under § 1981, although related, and although directed to most of the same ends, are separate, distinct, and independent. With this base established, we turn to the limitation issue.

Since there is no specifically stated or otherwise relevant federal statute of limitations for a cause of action under § 1981, the controlling period would ordinarily be the most appropriate one provided by state law.

The cause of action asserted by petitioner accrued, if at all, not later than June 20, 1967, the date of his discharge. Therefore, in the absence of some circumstance that suspended the running of the limitation period, petitioner's cause of action under § 1981 was time barred after June 20, 1968, over 2-1/2 years before petitioner filed his complaint.

There is nothing anomalous or novel about this. State law has been followed in a variety of cases that raised questions concerning the overtones and details of application of the state limitation period to the federal cause of action. Nor is there anything peculiar to a federal civil rights action that would justify special reluctance in applying state law. Indeed, the express terms of 42 U.S.C. § 1988[b] suggest that the contrary is true.

---

[a] One year after this decision the Civil Rights Attorney's Fees Awards Act of 1976, 42 U.S.C. § 1988(b), created a right on behalf of the prevailing party in a § 1981 suit to collect fees.

[b] *See* text of § 1988 in Appendix.

Although state law is our primary guide in this area, it is not, to be sure, our exclusive guide. As the Court noted in *Auto Workers v. Hoosier Corp.*, 383 U.S., at 706–07, considerations of state law may be displaced where their application would be inconsistent with the federal policy underlying the cause of action under consideration.

Petitioner argues that a failure to toll the limitation period in this case will conflict seriously with the broad remedial and humane purposes of Title VII. Specifically, he urges that Title VII embodies a strong federal policy in support of conciliation and voluntary compliance as a means of achieving the statutory mandate of equal employment opportunity. He suggests that failure to toll the statute on a § 1981 claim during the pendency of an administrative complaint in the EEOC would force a plaintiff into premature and expensive litigation that would destroy all chances for administrative conciliation and voluntary compliance.

We have noted this possibility above and, indeed, it is conceivable, and perhaps almost to be expected, that failure to toll will have the effect of pressing a civil rights complainant who values his § 1981 claim into court before the EEOC has completed its administrative proceeding. One answer to this, although perhaps not a highly satisfactory one, is that the plaintiff in his § 1981 suit may ask the court to stay proceedings until the administrative efforts at conciliation and voluntary compliance have been completed. But the fundamental answer to petitioner's argument lies in the fact—presumably a happy one for the civil rights claimant—that Congress clearly has retained § 1981 as a remedy against private employment discrimination separate from and independent of the more elaborate and time-consuming procedures of Title VII.

NOTES AND QUESTIONS

1. Does the Court's holding pressure litigants to bypass Title VII and file in federal court, thus obfuscating the informal conciliatory goals of the newer Act? How does the Court resolve this problem?

2. What are the advantages and disadvantages expressed by the Court in utilizing § 1981 rather than Title VII in pursuing relief for race discrimination in employment?

   Compare the differences between the two Acts in terms of coverage, agency versus judicial enforcement, and remedies.

3. **Statute of Limitations:** As *Johnson* suggests, the statute of limitations for § 1981 is considerably longer than that under Title VII. The Supreme Court in *Goodman v. Lukens Steel* (1987) held that a federal court should apply the personal injury statute of limitations for the state in which it sits, which is normally one to three years. Further, Congress enacted a four-year catch-all statute of limitations, 28 U.S.C. § 1658, for civil actions "arising under an Act of Congress enacted after" December 1, 1990. As discussed, the 1991 Civil Rights Act amended § 1981, creating a new right of action for post-contract formation claims, which are therefore subject to § 1658's

four-year statute of limitations: "An amendment to an existing statute is no less an 'Act of Congress' than a new, stand-alone statute." *See Jones v. R.R. Donnelley & Sons Co.*, 541 U.S. 369 (2004). This means that "pre-contract" claims will be governed by the state personal injury statute, whereas "post-contract" violations trigger the federal four-year rule.

2. SECTION 1982: DISCRIMINATION REGARDING PROPERTY RIGHTS

a. Suing Private Individuals under § 1982

JONES V. ALFRED H. MAYER CO.
392 U.S. 409 (1968)

Mr. Justice STEWART delivered the opinion of the Court.

In this case we are called upon to determine the scope and the constitutionality of § 1982, which provides that:

All citizens of the United States shall have the same right, in every State and Territory, as is enjoyed by white citizens thereof to inherit, purchase, lease, sell, hold, and convey real and personal property.

On September 2, 1965, the petitioners filed a complaint alleging that the respondents had refused to sell them a home in the Paddock Woods community of St. Louis County for the sole reason that petitioner Joseph Lee Jones is a Negro. Relying in part upon § 1982, the petitioners sought injunctive and other relief. The District Court sustained the respondents' motion to dismiss the complaint, and the Court of Appeals for the Eighth Circuit affirmed, concluding that § 1982 applies only to state action and does not reach private refusals to sell. For the reasons that follow, we reverse the judgment of the Court of Appeals. We hold that § 1982 bars all racial discrimination, private as well as public, in the sale or rental of property, and that the statute, thus construed, is a valid exercise of the power of Congress to enforce the Thirteenth Amendment.

I

At the outset, it is important to make clear precisely what this case does *not* involve. Whatever else it may be, 42 U.S.C. § 1982 is not a comprehensive open housing law. In sharp contrast to the Fair Housing Title (Title VIII) of the Civil Rights Act of 1968, the statute in this case deals only with racial discrimination and does not address itself to discrimination on grounds of religion or national origin. It does not deal specifically with discrimination in the provision of services or facilities in connection with the sale or rental of a dwelling. It does not prohibit advertising or other representations that indicate discriminatory preferences. It does not refer explicitly to discrimination in financing arrangements or in the provision of brokerage services. It does not empower a federal administrative agency to assist aggrieved parties.

Thus, although § 1982 contains none of the exemptions that Congress included in the Civil Rights Act of 1968, it would be a serious mistake to suppose that § 1982 in any way diminishes the significance of the law recently enacted by Congress. Indeed, the Senate Subcommittee on Housing and Urban Affairs was informed in hearings held after the Court of Appeals had rendered its decision in this case that § 1982 might well be "a presently valid federal statutory ban against discrimination by private persons in the sale or lease of real property." The Subcommittee was told, however, that even if this Court should so construe § 1982, the existence of that statute would not "eliminate the need for congressional action" to spell out "responsibility on the part of the federal government to enforce the rights it protects." The point was made that, in light of the many difficulties confronted by private litigants seeking to enforce such rights on their own, "legislation is needed to establish federal machinery for enforcement of the rights guaranteed under § 1982 of Title 42 even if the plaintiffs in *Jones v. Alfred H. Mayer Company* should prevail in the United States Supreme Court."

We begin with the language of the statute itself. In plain and unambiguous terms, § 1982 grants to all citizens, without regard to race or color, "the same right" to purchase and lease property "as is enjoyed by white citizens." As the Court of Appeals in this case evidently recognized, that right can be impaired as effectively by "those who place property on the market" as by the State itself. For, even if the State and its agents lend no support to those who wish to exclude persons from their communities on racial grounds, the fact remains that, whenever property "is placed on the market for whites only, whites have a right denied to Negroes." So long as a Negro citizen who wants to buy or rent a home can be turned away simply because he is not white, he cannot be said to enjoy "the *same* right as is enjoyed by white citizens to purchase [and] lease real and personal property." 42 U.S.C. § 1982.

On its face, therefore, § 1982 appears to prohibit *all* discrimination against Negroes in the sale or rental of property—discrimination by private owners as well as discrimination by public authorities. Indeed, even the respondents seem to concede that, if § 1982 "means what it says"—to use the words of the respondents' brief—then it must encompass every racially motivated refusal to sell or rent and cannot be confined to officially sanctioned segregation in housing. Stressing what they consider to be the revolutionary implications of so literal a reading of § 1982, the respondents argue that Congress cannot possibly have intended any such result. Our examination of the relevant history, however, persuades us that Congress meant exactly what it said.

In its original form, 42 U.S.C. § 1982 was part of § 1 of the Civil Rights Act of 1866. That section was cast in sweeping terms:

> *Be it enacted by the Senate and House of Representatives of the United States of America in Congress assembled,* That all persons born in the United States and not subject to any foreign power, are hereby declared to be citizens of the United States; and such citizens,

of every race and color, without regard to any previous condition of slavery or involuntary servitude, shall have the same right to inherit, purchase, lease, sell, hold, and convey real and personal property, and to full and equal benefit of all laws and proceedings for the security of person and property, as is enjoyed by white citizens, and shall be subject to like punishment, pains, and penalties, and to none other, any law, statute, ordinance, regulation, or custom, to the contrary notwithstanding.

To the Congress that passed the Civil Rights Act of 1866, it was clear that the right to do these things might be infringed not only by "State or local law" but also by "custom, or prejudice." Thus, when Congress provided in § 1 of the Civil Rights Act that the right to purchase and lease property was to be enjoyed equally throughout the United States by Negro and white citizens alike, it plainly meant to secure that right against interference from any source whatever, whether governmental or private.

In attempting to demonstrate the contrary, the respondents rely heavily upon the fact that the Congress which approved the 1866 statute wished to eradicate the recently enacted Black Codes—laws which had saddled Negroes with "onerous disabilities and burdens, and curtailed their rights . . . to such an extent that their freedom was of little value." *Slaughter-House Cases.* The respondents suggest that the only evil Congress sought to eliminate was that of racially discriminatory laws in the former Confederate States. But the Civil Rights Act was drafted to apply throughout the country, and its language was far broader than would have been necessary to strike down discriminatory statutes.

That broad language, we are asked to believe, was a mere slip of the legislative pen. We disagree. For the same Congress that wanted to do away with the Black Codes *also* had before it an imposing body of evidence pointing to the mistreatment of Negroes by private individuals and unofficial groups, mistreatment unrelated to any hostile state legislation. "Accounts in newspapers North and South, Freedman's Bureau and other official documents, private reports and correspondence were all adduced" to show that "private outrage and atrocity" were "daily inflicted on freedmen. . . ." The congressional debates are replete with references to private injustices against Negroes—references to white employers who refused to pay their Negro workers, white planters who agreed among themselves not to hire freed slaves without the permission of their former masters, white citizens who assaulted Negroes or who combined to drive them out of their communities.

In this setting, it would have been strange indeed if Congress had viewed its task as encompassing merely the nullification of racist laws in the former rebel States.

In light of the concerns that led Congress to adopt it and the contents of the debates that preceded its passage, it is clear that the Act was designed to do just what its terms suggest: to prohibit all racial discrimination, whether or not under color of law, with respect to the rights enumerated therein—including the right to purchase or lease property.

Nor was the scope of the 1866 Act altered when it was re-enacted in 1870, some two years after the ratification of the Fourteenth Amendment. It is quite true that some members of Congress supported the Fourteenth Amendment "in order to eliminate doubt as to the constitutional validity of the Civil Rights Act as applied to the States." But it certainly does not follow that the adoption of the Fourteenth Amendment or the subsequent readoption of the Civil Rights Act were meant somehow to *limit* its application to state action. The legislative history furnishes not the slightest factual basis for any such speculation, and the conditions prevailing in 1870 make it highly implausible. For by that time most, if not all, of the former Confederate States, then under the control of "reconstructed" legislatures, had formally repudiated racial discrimination, and the focus of congressional concern had clearly shifted from hostile statutes to the activities of groups like the Ku Klux Klan, operating wholly outside the law.

Against this background, it would obviously make no sense to assume, without any historical support whatever, that Congress made a silent decision in 1870 to exempt private discrimination from the operation of the Civil Rights Act of 1866.

NOTES AND QUESTIONS

1. How does the majority justify its holding that § 1982 reaches private discrimination? Would the drafters of § 1982 have envisioned a suit against a white homeowner for refusing to sell to a black purchaser when there was widespread segregation at the time of the enactment? Should this matter?

2. Why does the Court begin its discussion by contrasting § 1982 with the Fair Housing Act? What differences does it describe? A brief description of this Act is found *infra*, c. Relation to Other Acts.

b. Types of Conduct Regulated

SULLIVAN V. LITTLE HUNTING PARK
396 U.S. 229 (1969)

Opinion of the Court by Mr. Justice DOUGLAS, announced by Mr. Justice BLACK.

Little Hunting Park, Inc. is a Virginia nonstock corporation organized to operate a community park and playground facilities for the benefit of residents in an area of Fairfax County, Virginia. A membership share entitles all persons in the immediate family of the shareholder to use the corporation's recreation facilities. Under the bylaws, a person owning a membership share is entitled when he rents his home to assign the share to his tenant, subject to approval of the board of directors. Paul E. Sullivan and his family owned a house in this area and lived in it. Later he bought another house in the area and leased the first one to T.R. Freeman, Jr., an employee of the U.S. Department of Agriculture; and assigned his membership share to Freeman. The board refused to approve the assignment because Freeman was a Negro. Sullivan protested that action and was notified that he would be expelled from the corporation by the board. A hearing was accorded him and he was expelled, the board tendering him cash for his two shares.

Sullivan and Freeman sued under 42 U.S.C. §§ 1981 and 1982 for injunctions and monetary damages. Since Freeman no longer resides in the area served by Little Hunting Park, Inc., his claim is limited solely to damages.

The trial court denied relief to each petitioner. We reverse those judgments.

The Virginia trial court rested on its conclusion that Little Hunting Park was a private social club. But we find nothing of the kind on this record. There was no plan or purpose of exclusiveness. It is open to every white person within the geographic area, there being no selective element other than race.

What we have here is a device functionally comparable to a racially restrictive covenant, the judicial enforcement of which was struck down in *Shelley v. Kraemer*, by reason of the Fourteenth Amendment.

In *Jones v. Mayer Co.*, the complaint charged a refusal to sell petitioner a home because he was black. In the instant case the interest conveyed was a leasehold of realty coupled with a membership share in a nonprofit company organized to offer recreational facilities to owners and lessees of real property in that residential area. It is not material whether the membership share be considered realty or personal property, as § 1982 covers both. Section 1982 covers the right "to inherit, purchase, lease, sell, hold, and convey real and personal property." There is a suggestion that transfer on the books of the corporation of Freeman's share is not covered by any of those verbs. The suggestion is without merit. There has never been any doubt but that Freeman paid part of his $129 monthly rental for the assignment of the membership share in Little Hunting Park. The transaction clearly fell within the "lease." The right to "lease" is protected by § 1982 against the actions of third parties, as well as against the actions of the immediate lessor. Respondents' actions in refusing to approve the assignment of the membership share in this case was clearly an interference with Freeman's right to "lease." A narrow construction of the language of § 1982 would be quite inconsistent with the broad and sweeping nature of the protection meant to be afforded by § 1 of the Civil Rights Act of 1866, from which § 1982 was derived.

We turn to Sullivan's expulsion for the advocacy of Freeman's cause. If that sanction, backed by a state court judgment, can be imposed, then Sullivan is punished for trying to vindicate the rights of minorities protected by § 1982. Such a sanction would give impetus to the perpetuation of racial restrictions on property. That is why we said in *Barrows v. Jackson*, that the white owner is at times "the only effective adversary" of the unlawful restrictive covenant. Under the terms of our decision in *Barrows*, there can be no question but that Sullivan has standing to maintain this action.

We held in *Jones v. Mayer Co.* that although § 1982 is couched in declaratory terms and provides no explicit method of enforcement, a federal court has power to fashion an effective equitable remedy.

[A]s to damages, Congress, by 28 U.S.C. § 1343(4), created federal jurisdiction for "damages or . . . equitable or other relief under any Act of Congress providing for the protection of civil rights. . . ." We reserved in *Jones v. Mayer Co.* the question of what damages, if any, might be appropriately recovered for a violation of § 1982.

We had a like problem in *Bell v. Hood*, where suit was brought against federal officers for alleged violations of the Fourth and Fifth Amendments. The federal statute did not in terms at least provide any remedy. We said:

> [W]here federally protected rights have been invaded, it has been the rule from the beginning that courts will be alert to adjust their remedies so as to grant the necessary relief. And it is also well settled that where legal rights have been invaded, and a federal statute provides for a general right to sue for such invasion, federal courts may use any available remedy to make good the wrong done.

Compensatory damages for deprivation of a federal right are governed by federal standards, as provided by Congress in 42 U.S.C. § 1988.

This means, as we read § 1988, that both federal and state rules on damages may be utilized, whichever better serves the policies expressed in the federal statutes. The rule of damages, whether drawn from federal or state sources, is a federal rule responsive to the need whenever a federal right is impaired.

NOTES AND QUESTIONS

1. What was the nature of the property right involved? In *Tillman v. Wheaton-Haven Recreation Association*, 410 U.S. 431 (1973), the Court defined property as follows:
    When an organization links membership benefits to residency in a narrow geographical area, that decision infuses those benefits into the bundle of rights for which an individual pays when buying or leasing within the area. The mandate of 42 U.S.C. § 1982 then operates to guarantee a nonwhite resident, who purchases, leases, or holds this property, the same rights as are enjoyed by a white resident.

2. Do whites who are adversely treated because they advocate the rights of minorities have standing to sue under § 1982? Can they raise the rights of black discriminatees? Was this a standing rather than a retaliation decision, as the dissent argued in *CBOCS*, *supra* Ch. II.?

3. Why did the Supreme Court reject the "private club" defense raised by Little Hunting Park? Should such a defense ever be recognized? Does the Constitution require recognition of such a defense? What if the white owner of a duplex who lived in one of the units refused to rent the other unit to a black family? Could he be subject to § 1982 liability? Does the fact that the Fair Housing Act, described in *Jones v. Alfred Mayer*, exempts this transaction alter your analysis?

PROBLEM: FOUR

The Salisbury Club, located near Richmond, Virginia, was established in 1963 by the developer of the adjacent Salisbury subdivision. It is a privately-owned club which provides tennis, swimming, golf, and dining facilities for the use of its members. At first, residents of the Salisbury subdivision were formally given preference for membership in the club. In recent years the preference has been abolished to permit the club to attract new members without limitation. Currently, somewhat over half the members reside in the Salisbury subdivision, and until 1977, no resident of the Salisbury subdivision had been denied membership. Moreover, the club has encouraged membership by publishing a sub-division newsletter and assisting real estate agents in their advertising of club membership as a distinct advantage of living in the subdivision.

In May, 1977, Thomas and Barbara Wright moved into a house that they had purchased in the Salisbury subdivision. Soon after moving, they twice applied for membership in the Salisbury Club. Their applications were sponsored by two club members, as required by club bylaws. On both occasions, their applications were rejected because they did not win 75% of the Board's vote, as required by the bylaws. It is conceded that the Wrights were denied membership because they are black.

The Wrights then brought suit in district court, seeking injunctive relief and damages for denial of civil rights guaranteed by 42 U.S.C §§ 1981 and 1982. Subsequently, the district court granted summary judgment for the defendants. After examining the club's formation, membership policies, and membership recruitment activities, the district court found that the Salisbury Club was a "truly private" club. The district court ruled that § 1981 does not apply to truly private clubs and therefore rejected the plaintiffs' § 1981 claim.

In addition, the district court rejected the plaintiff's § 1982 argument. It examined the connection between the subdivision and the club, and discovered no formal link between club membership and ownership of a home in the subdivision. Consequently, it concluded that membership in the club did not amount to "property" within the ambit of § 1982.

1. How should the court rule on appeal regarding the private club question? Would application of § 1981 to a truly private club violate the Constitution? What factors should be examined in assessing whether a club is "truly private"? What are the relevant factors in this case?

2. Can club membership be viewed as a property right within the meaning of § 1982?

3. Since all property claims probably implicate contract rights, is § 1982 superfluous? Under what circumstances would it make a difference? Review the fact situation in *Shaare Tefila, supra* Ch. II.. Did the injury alleged fit into a § 1981 cause of action?

c.   Relation to Other Acts: Fair Housing Act (FHA)

The same year the Supreme Court decided *Jones v. Alfred H. Mayer Co.*, 392 U.S. 409 (1968), holding that § 1982 prohibits private race discrimination in housing, Congress passed the Fair Housing Act as Title VIII of the Civil Rights Act of 1968. The purpose of this Act is "to provide, within constitutional limitations, for fair housing throughout the United States." 42 U.S.C. § 3601. The Act, as amended in 1988, prohibits discrimination based on race, color, religion, sex, disability, familial status or national origin.

To the extent that such discrimination is done under color of state law, Congress had the authority to prohibit it under section 5 of the Fourteenth Amendment. However, the Act is not limited to government discrimination in housing; it includes private discrimination as well. While Congress has the power to regulate private race discrimination in housing under section 2 of the Thirteenth Amendment, its authority for regulating private discrimination based on sex, disability, familial status or religion is less clear. Where would you look for such authority if defending the constitutionality of the Act?

Twenty years after it was enacted, the Act was substantially revised by the Fair Housing Amendments Act of 1988, effective in March 1989. The most significant changes include the expansion of prohibited discriminatory housing practices to include discrimination against persons with a disability and discrimination based on familial status, expanded administrative enforcement, expanded enforcement powers vested in the secretary, changes in enforcement by private persons—including an extension of the limitations period to two years, elimination of the $1,000 limit on punitive damages, and removal of the requirement that an applicant for a fee award demonstrate financial inability to assume the cost of an attorney. In the areas indicated, the 1988 amendments substantially affected enforcement of the Act.

i.   Parties and Conduct Prohibited

Generally, an "aggrieved person," defined at 42 U.S.C. § 3602(i), can seek administrative and/or judicial enforcement of the FHA. This includes not only the obvious direct victims of discrimination in housing—those deprived of an opportunity to lease or purchase or subjected to different terms or conditions—but also indirect victims of discriminatory practices, such as cities, open housing organizations, builders/developers, and individuals deprived of the opportunity to live in an integrated community. Further, the United States can initiate enforcement proceedings, either on behalf of an aggrieved person or under the "pattern or practice" provision, 42 U.S.C. § 3614.

Defendants are usually owners, or their agents, governmental entities, as owners or regulators, builders/developers, appraisers, financial institutions, and possibly insurance companies. There are two sources of exemptions—§ 3603(b) and § 3607(a). The former exempts single-family houses, sold or rented by certain owners, and boarding houses with no more than four units and occupied by the owner. Certain religious organizations and private clubs are exempt under the latter provision.

42 U.S.C. §§ 3604-06, as amended, generally specifies the types of discrimination regulated by the FHA. Certain discriminatory practices, such as a refusal to sell or rent or a difference in terms or conditions based on one of the prohibited factors, obviously violate the Act. Other practices, such as "steering" and "blockbusting," are less direct but also violate the Act. In *Havens Realty Corp v. Coleman*, 455 U.S. 363 (1982), the Court defined "racial steering" as a

> practice by which real estate brokers and agents preserve and encourage patterns of racial segregation in available housing by steering members of racial and ethnic groups to buildings occupied primarily by members of such racial and ethnic groups and away from buildings and neighborhoods inhabited primarily by members of other races or groups.

The 1988 amendments to the FHA give the Department of Housing and Urban Development authority to "make rules . . . to carry out [the FHA]." One of the adopted regulations includes, among the conduct prohibited by § 3604, "[r]efusing to provide . . . property or hazard insurance for dwellings or providing such . . . insurance differently because of race." 24 C.F.R. § 100.70(d)(4).

Section 3617 of the FHA makes it "unlawful to coerce, intimidate, threaten, or interfere with any person in the exercise or enjoyment of . . . any right granted or protected by [§§ 3603-06 of the FHA]." Would this section reach conduct, such as a cross burning in the yard of a black family that just moved into a neighborhood, designed to tell the family that it is not wanted in the neighborhood? If so, does the statute violate the First Amendment? In *Virginia v. Black*, 536 U.S. 343 (2003), the Court held that state law may ban cross burnings done with the intent to intimidate because burning a cross is "a particularly virulent form of intimidation," which is unprotected speech.

ii.   Private Enforcement:

An aggrieved person can pursue either administrative relief, pursuant to 42 U.S.C. § 3610, by filing a complaint with HUD within one year of the alleged discrimination, or judicial relief, pursuant to 42 U.S.C. § 3613, by filing a complaint within two years of the alleged discrimination. When an administrative complaint is filed, HUD either refers it to a certified state or local deferral agency or conducts an investigation. If HUD finds reasonable cause, it issues a "charge" and if neither party (charging party or respondent) elects to have the Attorney General bring an action, there is an opportunity for a hearing before an administrative law judge (ALJ), who can issue equitable relief, actual damages, a civil penalty, attorney fees and costs. The ALJ decision is subject to judicial review in a U.S. Court of Appeals.

An administrative complaint is optional, *i.e.*, the aggrieved party can bypass administrative remedies and go directly to court. Even after filing an administrative complaint, the aggrieved party can file a lawsuit at any time prior to commencement of a hearing by the ALJ. The FHA authorizes broad relief in actions pursuant to § 3613, including equitable relief, compensatory and punitive damages, attorney fees and costs.

Courts tend to utilize the Title VII proof schemes, *i.e.*, plaintiffs alleging disparate treatment or intentional discrimination who do not have direct evidence of discrimination may use the indirect method described in *Patterson v. Mclean Credit Union.* Further, in *Texas Department of Housing and Community Affairs v. Inclusive Communities Project, Inc.,* 135 S. Ct. 2507 (2015), the Court resolved a circuit split, ruling five to four that disparate-impact claims are cognizable under the Fair Housing Act.

3. SECTION 1983: DEPRIVATION OF RIGHTS UNDER COLOR OF STATE LAW

Section 1983 was passed as part of the Ku Klux Klan Act of 1871. Its key purpose, as reflected in its title, *i.e.*, "an act to enforce the provisions of the Fourteenth Amendment," was to protect people from unconstitutional conduct taken under color of state law. This Section, as amended in 1996, reads:

> Every person who, under color of any statute, ordinance, regulation, custom, or usage, of any State or Territory or the District of Columbia, subjects, or causes to be subjected, any citizen of the United States or other person within the jurisdiction thereof to the deprivation of any rights, privileges, or immunities secured by the Constitution and laws, shall be liable to the party injured in an action at law, suit in equity, or other proper proceeding for redress, except that in any action brought against a judicial officer for an act or omission taken in such officer's judicial capacity, injunctive relief shall not be granted unless a declaratory decree was violated or declaratory relief was unavailable.

It is significant to note that § 1983 simply provides a cause of action, *i.e.*, a vehicle for enforcing federal rights, but it does not create any new substantive rights. Thus, in order to successfully bring a § 1983 claim, plaintiffs must meet all of the elements of the underlying constitutional or federal statutory right they seek to enforce.

Although § 1983 dates back to the Reconstruction Era following the civil war, it was relatively dormant for its first 100 years. In part this is due to the slow development of the Fourteenth Amendment itself. For example, in the *Slaughter-House Cases,* 83 U.S. (16 Wall.) 36 (1873), the Court gave a narrow interpretation to the Privileges and Immunities Clause, restricting its protection to a limited category of rights of national citizenship, and it also limited the scope of the equal protection and due process clauses. In short, the narrow interpretation given to constitutional safeguards meant that § 1983 was to remain a dead letter. Between 1871 and 1920 there were only 21 reported cases decided under § 1983.[1] Gradually, as the Supreme Court began to expand the reach of due process and equal protection and as Congress started to enact new federal statutory provisions, § 1983 began to take on new significance. A major step in this development was the Supreme Court's holding in *Monroe v. Pape.*

a. The Meaning of "Under Color of State Law"

MONROE V. PAPE
365 U.S. 167 (1961)

Mr. Justice DOUGLAS delivered the opinion of the Court.

This case presents important questions concerning the construction of 42 U.S.C. § 1983.

The complaint alleges that 13 Chicago police officers broke into petitioners' home in the early morning, routed them from bed, and made them stand naked in the living room, and ransacked every room, emptying drawers and ripping mattress covers. It further alleges that Mr. Monroe was then taken to the police and detained on "open" charges for 10 hours, while he was interrogated about a two-day-old murder, that he was not taken before a magistrate, though one was accessible, that he was not permitted to call his family or attorney, that he was subsequently released without criminal charges being preferred against him. It is alleged that the officers had no search warrant and no arrest warrant and that they acted "under color of the statutes, ordinances, regulations, customs, and usages" of Illinois and the City of Chicago.

There can be no doubt that Congress has the power to enforce provisions of the Fourteenth Amendment against those who carry a badge of authority of a State and represent it in some capacity, whether they act in accordance with their authority or misuse it. The question with which we now deal is the narrower one of whether Congress, in enacting § 1983, meant to give a remedy to parties deprived of constitutional rights, privileges and immunities by an official's abuse of his position.

It is argued that "under color of" enumerated state authority excludes acts of an official or policeman who can show no authority under state law, state custom, or state usage to do what he did. In this case it is said that these policemen, in breaking into petitioners' apartment, violated the Constitution and laws of Illinois. It is pointed out that under Illinois law a simple remedy is offered for that violation and that, so far as it appears, the courts of Illinois are available to give petitioners that full redress which the common law affords for violence done to a person; and it is earnestly argued that no "statute, ordinance, regulation, custom or usage" of Illinois bars that redress.

---

1 Comment, The Civil Rights Act: Emergence Of An Adequate Federal Civil Remedy? 26 IND. L.J. 361, 363 (1951).

The legislation—in particular the section with which we are now concerned—had several purposes. There are threads of many thoughts running through the debates. One who reads them in their entirety sees that the present section had three main aims.

First, it might, of course, override certain kinds of state laws.

Second, it provided a remedy where state law was inadequate. That aspect of the legislation was summed up as follows by Senator Sherman of Ohio:

> [I]t is said the reason is that any offense may be committed upon a negro by a white man, and a negro cannot testify in any case against a white man, so that the only way by which any conviction can be had in Kentucky in those cases is in the United States courts, because the United States courts enforce the United States laws by which negroes may testify.

But the purposes were much broader. The *third* aim was to provide a federal remedy where the state remedy, though adequate in theory, was not available in practice. The opposition to the measure complained that "It overrides the reserved powers of the States," just as they argued that the second section of the bill "absorb[ed] the entire jurisdiction of the States over their local and domestic affairs."

The Act of April 20, 1871, sometimes called "the third 'force bill,'" was passed by a Congress that had the Klan "particularly in mind." The debates are replete with references to the lawless conditions existing in the South in 1871. There was available to the Congress during these debates a report, nearly 600 pages in length, dealing with the activities of the Klan and the inability of the state government to cope with it. This report was drawn on by many of the speakers. It was not the unavailability of state remedies but the failure of certain States to enforce the laws with an equal hand that furnished the powerful momentum behind this "force bill." Mr. Lowe of Kansas said:

> While murder is stalking abroad in disguise, while whippings and lynchings and banishment have been visited upon unoffending American citizens, the local administrations have been found inadequate or unwilling to apply the proper corrective. Combinations, darker than the night that hides them, conspiracies, wicked as the worst of felons could devise, have gone unwhipped of justice. Immunity is given to crime, and the records of the public tribunals are searched in vain for any evidence of effective redress.

There was, it was said, no quarrel with the state laws on the books. It was their lack of enforcement that was the nub of the difficulty.

It was precisely that breadth of the remedy which the opposition emphasized. Mr. Kerr of Indiana referring to the section involved in the present litigation said:

> This section gives to any person who may have been injured in any of his rights, privileges, or immunities of person or property, a civil action for damages against the wrongdoer in

the Federal courts. The offenses committed against him may be the common violations of the municipal law of his State. It is a covert attempt to transfer another large portion of jurisdiction from the State tribunals, to which it of right belongs, to those of the United States. It is neither authorized nor expedient, and is not calculated to bring peace, or order, or domestic content and prosperity to the disturbed society of the South. The contrary will certainly be its effect.

The debates were long and extensive. It is abundantly clear that one reason the legislation was passed was to afford a federal right in federal courts because, by reason of prejudice, passion, neglect, intolerance or otherwise, state laws might not be enforced and the claims of citizens to the enjoyment of rights, privileges, and immunities guaranteed by the Fourteenth Amendment might be denied by the state agencies.

Although the legislation was enacted because of the conditions that existed in the South at that time, it is cast in general language and is as applicable to Illinois as it is to the States whose names were mentioned over and again in the debates. It is no answer that the State has a law which if enforced would give relief. The federal remedy is supplementary to the state remedy, and the latter need not be first sought and refused before the federal one is invoked. Hence the fact that Illinois by its constitution and law outlaws unreasonable searches and seizures is no barrier to the present suit in the federal court.

We had before us in *United States v. Classic*, § 20 of the Criminal Code, 18 U.S.C. § 242, which provides a criminal punishment for anyone who "under color of any law, statute, ordinance, regulation, or custom" subjects any inhabitant of a State to the deprivation of "any rights, privileges, or immunities secured or protected by the Constitution or laws of the United States." Section 242 first came into the law as § 2 of the Civil Rights Act, Act of April 9, 1866. After passage of the Fourteenth Amendment, this provision was re-enacted and amended by §§ 17, 18, Act of May 31, 1870.

In an opinion written by Mr. Justice Stone, in which Mr. Justice Roberts, Mr. Justice Reed, and Mr. Justice Frankfurter joined, the Court ruled, "Misuse of power, possessed by virtue of state law and made possible only because the wrongdoer is clothed with the authority of state law, is action taken 'under the color of' state law." There was a dissenting opinion; but the ruling as to the meaning of "under the color of" state law was not questioned.

That view of the meaning of the words "under color of" state law, 18 U.S.C. § 242, was reaffirmed in *Screws v. United States*. The acts there complained of were committed by state officers in performance of their duties, viz., making an arrest effective. It was urged there, as it is here, that "under color of" state law should not be construed to duplicate in federal law what was an offense under state law. It was said there, as it is here, that the ruling in the *Classic* case as to the meaning of "under color of" state law included only action taken by officials pursuant to state law. We rejected that view. We stated:

The construction given § 20 [18 U.S.C. § 242] in the *Classic* case formulated a rule of law which has become the basis of federal enforcement in this important field. The rule adopted in that case was formulated after mature consideration. It should be good for more than one day only.

We conclude that the meaning given "under color of" law in the [prior] cases was the correct one; and we adhere to it.

[The Court declined to follow the *Screws* holding that criminal penalties could be imposed only for acts "wilfully" done. Because § 1983 creates a civil remedy, the Court explained that, **"Section 1983 should be read against the background of tort liability that makes a man responsible for the natural consequences of his actions. . . ."**]

NOTES AND QUESTIONS

1. How can state or local officials who clearly act *contrary* to state law be deemed to be taking action "under color of state law"? How does the Supreme Court interpret the "under color of state law" requirement?

2. Note carefully the analogy to tort law, a theme that is critical in understanding later interpretations of the Act. Although holding that intent is not required as a matter of statutory interpretation, the constitutional provisions being enforced may have their own state of mind requirement.

3. In light of its legislative history, should § 1983 relief be available in a state which does provide adequate remedies for official wrongdoing? Why provide a federal forum today if state courts and state law already adequately protect civil rights? Does "federalism" suggest that state courts be given the first opportunity to correct state official wrongdoing, especially when dealing with a case of isolated abuse of state authority by an official? Should this decision be made by Congress or the courts?

4. Although the Court gave an expansive interpretation to the "under color of state law" provision, it proceeded to rule that the term "person" in § 1983 could not be read to include the city of Chicago, but rather was limited to natural persons. The Supreme Court again addressed and overruled this part of the opinion seventeen years later in *Monell v. Dep't of Social Services*, discussed *infra*.

POLK COUNTY V. DODSON
454 U.S. 312 (1981)

Justice POWELL delivered the opinion of the Court.

The question in this case is whether a public defender acts "under color of state law" when representing an indigent defendant in a state criminal proceeding.

Dodson brought the action in federal court under 42 U.S.C. § 1983. As the factual basis for his lawsuit Dodson alleged that Martha Shepard, an attorney in the Polk County Offender Advocate's Office, had failed to represent him adequately in an appeal to the Iowa Supreme Court.

In *United States v. Classic* this Court held that a person acts under color of state law only when exercising power "possessed by virtue of state law and made possible only because the wrongdoer is clothed with the authority of state law." In this case the Offender Advocate for Polk County assigned Martha Shepard to represent Russell Dodson in the appeal of his criminal conviction. This assignment entailed functions and obligations in no way dependent on state authority. From the moment of her appointment, Shepard became Dodson's lawyer, and Dodson became Shepard's client. Except for the source of payment, their relationship became identical to that existing between any other lawyer and client. "Once a lawyer has undertaken the representation of an accused, the duties and obligations are the same whether the lawyer is privately retained, appointed or serving in a legal aid or defender program." ABA STANDARDS FOR CRIMINAL JUSTICE 4-3.9 (2d ed. 1980).

The respondent argues that a public defender's employment relationship with the State, rather than his function, should determine whether he acts under color of state law. We take a different view.

A

In arguing that the employment relationship establishes that the public defender acts under color of state law, Dodson relies heavily on two cases in which this Court assumed that physicians, whose relationships with their patients have not traditionally depended on state authority, could be held liable under § 1983. *See O'Connor v. Donaldson, Estelle v. Gamble.* These cases, he argues, are analytically identical to this one. Like the physicians in *O'Connor* and *Estelle*, a public defender is paid by the State. Further, like the institutionalized patients in those cases, an indigent convict is unable to choose the professional who will render him traditionally private services. These factors, it is argued, establish that public defenders—like physicians in state hospitals—act under color of state law and are amenable to suit under § 1983.

In our view *O'Connor* and *Estelle* are distinguishable from this case. *O'Connor* involved claims against a psychiatrist who served as the superintendent at a state mental hospital. Although a physician with traditionally private obligations to his patients, he was sued in his capacity as a state custodian and administrator. Unlike a lawyer, the administrator of a state hospital owes no duty of "undivided loyalty" to his patients. On the contrary, it is his function to protect the interest of the public as well as that of his wards. Similarly, *Estelle* involved a physician who was the medical director of the Texas Department of Corrections and also the chief medical officer of a prison hospital. He saw his patients in a custodial as well as a medical capacity.

Because of their custodial and supervisory functions, the state-employed doctors in *O'Connor* and *Estelle* faced their employer in a very different posture than does a public defender. Institutional physicians assume an obligation to the mission that the State, through the institution, attempts to achieve. With the public defender it is different. [I]t is the function of the public defender to enter "not guilty" pleas, move to suppress State's evidence, object to evidence at trial, cross-examine State's witnesses, and make closing arguments in behalf of defendants. All of these are adversarial functions. We find it peculiarly difficult to detect any color of state law in such activities.

B

Despite the public defender's obligation to represent his clients against the State, Dodson argues—and the Court of Appeals concluded—that the status of the public defender differs materially from that of other defense lawyers. Because public defenders are paid by the State, it is argued that they are subject to supervision by persons with interests unrelated to those of indigent clients. Although the employment relationship is certainly a relevant factor, we find it insufficient to establish that a public defender acts under color of State law within the meaning of § 1983.

First, a public defender is not amenable to administrative direction in the same sense as other employees of the State. Administrative and legislative decisions undoubtedly influence the way a public defender does his work. State decisions may determine the quality of his law library or the size of his caseload. But a defense lawyer is not, and by the nature of his function cannot be, the servant of an administrative superior. Held to the same standards of competence and integrity as a private lawyer, a public defender works under canons of professional responsibility that mandate his exercise of independent judgment on behalf of the client.

Second, and equally important, it is the constitutional obligation of the State to respect the professional independence of the public defenders whom it engages. There can be no fair trial unless the accused receives the services of an effective and independent advocate.

In concluding that Shepard did not act under color of state law in exercising her independent professional judgment in a criminal proceeding, we do not suggest that a public defender never acts in that role. In *Branti v. Finkel*, for example, we found that a public defender so acted when making hiring and firing decisions on behalf of the State. It may be—although the question is not present in this case—that a public defender also would act under color of state law while performing certain administrative and possibly investigative functions. And of course we intimate no views as to a public defenders' liability for malpractice in an appropriate case under state tort law. With respect to Dodson's § 1983 claims against Shepard, we decide only that a public defender does not act under color of state law when performing a lawyer's traditional functions as counsel to a defendant in a criminal proceeding. Because it was based on such activities, the complaint against Shepard must be dismissed.

1. Can the Court's holding be reconciled with *Monroe*'s pronouncement that § 1983 applies whenever misuse of power is made possible only because the wrongdoer is clothed with state authority? Hasn't wrongdoing occurred only because the State "clothed" its public defender with power?

2. What if a public defender fires a government-salaried secretary because of gender? Is a § 1983 claim then available?

3. Is all conduct by a government employee actionable? What about a police officer who assaults his wife with his department-issued revolver? What types of evidence would be relevant in deciding whether the conduct is a "personal frolic" or a misuse of government authority?

4. How broad is the *Dodson* exception—do any other government employees occupy a similarly unique position? What about a private physician under contract with the state to provide medical services to inmates?

WEST V. ATKINS
487 u.s. 42 (1988)

Justice BLACKMUN delivered the opinion of the Court.

This case presents the question whether a physician who is under contract with the State to provide medical services to inmates at a state-prison hospital on a part-time basis acts "under color of state law," within the meaning of 42 U.S.C. § 1983, when he treats an inmate.

I

Petitioner, Quincy West, tore his left Achilles tendon in 1983 while playing volleyball at Odom Correctional Center, the Jackson, N.C., state prison in which he was incarcerated. A physician under contract to provide medical care to Odom inmates examined petitioner and directed that he be transferred to Raleigh for orthopedic consultation at Central Prison Hospital, the acute-care medical facility operated by the State for its more than 17,500 inmates. Central Prison Hospital has one full-time staff physician, and obtains additional medical assistance under "Contracts for Professional Services" between the State and area physicians.

Respondent, Samuel Atkins, M.D., a private physician, provided orthopedic services to inmates pursuant to one such contract. Under it, Doctor Atkins was paid approximately $52,000 annually to operate two "clinics" each week at Central Prison Hospital, with additional amounts for surgery. Over a period of several months, he treated West's injury by placing his leg in a series of casts. West alleges that although the doctor acknowledged that surgery would be necessary, he refused to schedule it, and that he eventually discharged West while his ankle was still swollen and painful, and his movement still impeded. Because West was a prisoner in "close custody," he was not free to employ or elect to see a different physician of his own choosing. . . .

Pursuant to 42 U.S.C. § 1983, West, proceeding pro se, commenced this action against Doctor Atkins in the United States District Court for the Eastern District of North Carolina for violation of his Eighth Amendment right to be free from cruel and unusual punishment. West alleged that Atkins was deliberately indifferent to his serious medical needs, by failing to provide adequate treatment.

II

To state a claim under § 1983, a plaintiff must allege the violation of a right secured by the Constitution and laws of the United States, and must show that the alleged deprivation was committed by a person acting under color of state law. The adequacy of West's allegation and the sufficiency of his showing on [the eighth amendment] element of his § 1983 cause of action are not contested here. The only issue before us is whether petitioner has established the second essential element—that respondent acted under color of state law in treating West's injury.

A

The traditional definition of acting under color of state law requires that the defendant in a § 1983 action have exercised power "possessed by virtue of state law and made possible only because the wrongdoer is clothed with the authority of state law." In *Lugar v. Edmondson Oil Co.*, 457 U.S. 922 (1987), the Court made clear that if a defendant's conduct satisfies the state-action requirement of the Fourteenth Amendment, "that conduct [is] also action under color of state law and will support a suit under § 1983." In such circumstances, the defendant's alleged infringement of the plaintiff's federal rights is "fairly attributable to the State."

To constitute state action, "the deprivation must be caused by the exercise of some right or privilege created by the State or by a person for whom the State is responsible," and "the party charged with the deprivation must be a person who may fairly be said to be a state actor." *Ibid.* "[S]tate employment is generally sufficient to render the defendant a state actor." *Id.* at 936 n.18. It is firmly established that a defendant in a § 1983 suit acts under color of state law when he abuses the position given to him by the State. *See* Monroe v. Pape, 365 U.S. at 172. Thus, generally, a public employee acts under color of state law while acting in his official capacity or while exercising his responsibilities pursuant to state law.

Indeed, *Polk County v. Dodson*, relied upon by the Court of Appeals, is the only case in which this Court has determined that a person who is employed by the State and who is sued under § 1983 for abusing his position in the performance of his assigned tasks was not acting under color of state law.

B

We disagree with the Court of Appeals and respondent that Polk County dictates a conclusion that respondent did not act under color of state law in providing medical treatment to petitioner. In contrast to the public defender, Doctor Atkins' professional and ethical obligation to make independent medical judgments did not set him in conflict with the State and other prison authorities. Indeed, his relationship with other prison authorities was cooperative. "Institutional physicians assume an obligation to the mission that the State, through the institution, attempts to achieve." The American Medical Association Standards for Health Services in Prisons (1979) provide that medical personnel and other prison officials are to act in "close cooperation and coordination" in a "joint effort." Doctor Atkins' professional obligations certainly did not oblige him to function as "the State's adversary." We thus find the proffered analogy between respondent and the public defender in Polk County unpersuasive.

The Court of Appeals' approach to determining who is subject to suit under § 1983, wholeheartedly embraced by respondent, cannot be reconciled with this Court's decision in *Estelle v. Gamble*, 429 U.S. 97 (1976), which demonstrates that custodial and supervisory functions are irrelevant to an assessment whether the particular action challenged was performed under color of state law. In *Estelle*, the inmate's Eighth Amendment claim was brought against the physician-employee, Dr. Gray, in his capacity both as treating physician and as medical director of the state prison system. Gray was sued, however, solely on the basis of allegedly substandard medical treatment given to the plaintiff; his supervisory and custodial functions were not at issue. The Court explicitly held that "indifference . . . manifested by prison doctors in their response to the prisoner's needs . . . states a cause of action under § 1983." *Id.* at 104–105.

C

The fact that the State employed respondent pursuant to a contractual arrangement that did not generate the same benefits or obligations applicable to other "state employees" does not alter the analysis. It is the physician's function within the state system, not the precise terms of his employment, that determines whether his actions can fairly be attributed to the State. Whether a physician is on the state payroll or is paid by contract, the dispositive issue concerns the relationship among the State, the physician, and the prisoner. Contracting out prison medical care does not relieve the State of its constitutional duty to provide adequate medical treatment to those in its custody, and it does not deprive the State's prisoners of the means to vindicate their Eighth Amendment rights. The State bore an affirmative obligation to provide adequate medical care to West; the State delegated that function to respondent Atkins; and respondent voluntarily assumed that obligation by contract.

Nor does the fact that Doctor Atkins' employment contract did not require him to work exclusively for the prison make him any less a state actor than if he performed those duties as a full-time, permanent member of the state prison medical staff. It is the physician's function while working for the State, not the amount of time he spends in performance of those duties or the fact that he may be employed by others to perform similar duties, that determines whether he is acting under color of state law. In the State's employ, respondent worked as a physician at the prison hospital fully vested with state authority to fulfill essential aspects of the duty, placed on the State by the Eighth Amendment and state law, to provide essential medical care to those the State had incarcerated. Doctor Atkins must be considered to be a state actor.

III

For the reasons stated above, we conclude that respondent's delivery of medical treatment to West was state action fairly attributable to the State, and that respondent therefore acted under color of state law for purposes of § 1983. Accordingly, we reverse the judgment of the Court of Appeals and remand the case for further proceedings consistent with this opinion.

NOTES AND QUESTIONS

1. How does the Court distinguish *Dodson*?

2. When may private individuals be sued under § 1983? Note that if a plaintiff is alleging a violation of the Fourteenth Amendment, state action must be present. What then is the relationship between "under color of law" and the state action requirement of the Fourteenth Amendment? May a debtor maintain a Fourteenth Amendment Due Process action against a private creditor who acts pursuant to state law in seizing his property? Justice Blackmun's opinion cites the Supreme Court's rule that if the state action requirement is met, the action will be deemed to be "under color of state law." In *Lugar v. Edmondson Oil Co.*, 457 U.S. 922 (1982), the Court explained that a deprivation must be "caused by the exercise of some right or privilege created by the State or by a rule of conduct imposed by the State or by a person for whom the State is responsible." In addition, the defendant must "clearly be said to be a state actor," in the sense that the defendant "has acted together with or has obtained significant aid from state officials." The standard was met because the challenged statute authorized a creditor to file a petition with a court clerk and thus obtain a prejudgment attachment of a debtor's property to be executed by the sheriff. In contrast, in *Flagg Bros., Inc. v. Brooks*, 436 U.S. 149 (1978), the Court held that even if a creditor acting pursuant to the self-help provision of a state statute is acting "under color of state law," there is no Fourteenth Amendment state action. Because § 1983 did not create new rights, all of the elements of the underlying constitutional claim must be satisfied. Thus, all the Supreme Court decisions that have limited the concept of state action in recent years similarly limit the availability of a § 1983 remedy. *See, e.g., Rendall-Baker v. Kohn*, 457 U.S. 830 (1982) (actions of a private school which is heavily funded, supported, and regulated by the state do not constitute state action); *Blum v. Yaretsky*, 457 U.S. 991 (1982) (reaching the same conclusion regarding a private nursing home).

Does a private security guard act "under color of state law" when detaining an alleged shoplifter? By calling the police to effectuate an arrest will the store owner be subjected to § 1983 liability? Is the *Lugar* test met? What if the private security guard is an off-duty police officer wearing his official uniform?

3. In *Brentwood Academy v. Tennessee Secondary School*, 511 U.S. 288 (2001), the Court held that a nominally private statewide voluntary association that governs sports among public and private secondary schools in Tennessee is a state actor. In a 5-4 ruling, the majority reasoned that the state action determination is dependent upon several factors:

> Our cases have identified a host of facts that can bear on the fairness of such an attribution. We have, for example, held that a challenged activity may be state action when it results from the State's exercise of "coercive power," when the State provides "significant encouragement, either overt or covert," or when a private actor operates as a "willful participant in joint activity with the State or its agents." We have treated a nominally private entity as a state actor when it is controlled by an "agency of the State," when it has been delegated a public function by the State, when it is "entwined with governmental policies" or when government is "entwined in [its] management or control."

Relying on the latter theory, the Court determined that the "pervasive entwinement" of public high schools and public officials in the Association's "composition and workings" demanded a finding of state action. The Court reasoned that public schools predominated in the membership (84% of the membership), members of the State Board of Education were assigned ex officio to serve as members of the governing bodies, and the organization's employees were eligible for membership in the state retirement system: "Entwinement will support a conclusion that an ostensibly private organization ought to be charged with a public character and judged by constitutional standards; entwinement to the degree shown here requires it."

TOWER V. GLOVER
467 U.S. 914 (1984)

Justice O'CONNOR delivered the opinion of the Court.

Petitioners are two public defenders working in the State of Oregon. Petitioner Bruce Tower, the Douglas County Public Defender, represented respondent Billy Irl Glover at one of Glover's state trials on robbery charges, at which Glover was convicted. Petitioner Gary Babcock, the Oregon State Public Defender, represented Glover in Glover's unsuccessful state-court appeal from this and at least one other conviction.

In an action brought under 42 U.S.C. § 1983, Glover alleges that petitioners conspired with various state officials, including the trial and appellate court judges and the former Attorney General of Oregon, to secure Glover's conviction. Glover seeks neither reversal of his conviction nor compensatory damages, but asks instead for $5 million in punitive damages to be awarded against each petitioner.

In *Polk County v. Dodson* we held that appointed counsel in a state criminal prosecution, though paid and ultimately supervised by the State, does not act "under the color of" state law in the normal course of conducting the defense. In *Dennis v. Sparks*, however, the Court held that an otherwise private person acts "under color of" state law when engaged in a conspiracy with state officials to deprive another of federal rights. Glover alleges that petitioners conspired with state officials, and his complaint, therefore, includes an adequate allegation of conduct "under color of" state law.

NOTES AND QUESTIONS

1. Why may the public defender in this case be sued under § 1983?

2. In *Dennis v. Sparks*, 449 U.S. 24, 27-28 (1980), the Supreme Court ruled that a § 1983 action could be maintained against a private citizen who bribed a judge to issue a restraining order, provided he was "a willful participant in joint action with the state or its agents." The Court reasoned that, "Private persons jointly engaged with state officials in the challenged action are acting 'under color' of law for purposes of § 1983." Did the Court ignore the "state action" requirement of the Fourteenth Amendment? Why should conspiracies be treated differently?

3. Although federal officials may not be sued under § 1983 because they do not act "under color of *state* law," the Supreme Court has held that § 1983 may be used where federal officials engage in a conspiracy with state officers to violate rights. Dombrowski v. Eastland, 387 U.S. 82 (1967).

PROBLEM: FIVE

Edward Soldal lived with his wife and four children in a trailer home, which he owned, situated on a rented lot in a trailer park in Illinois. The owner of the trailer park decided to evict Soldal, but before securing a court order as required by Illinois law, the trailer park owner decided to go ahead and evict the family forcibly. Anticipating the possibility of resistance, the manager of the trailer park notified the Cook County Sheriff's Office, and, in fact, when trailer office employees arrived at the Soldal's trailer home, they were accompanied by a Cook County Deputy Sheriff who told Soldal that he was there to prevent him from interfering with eviction. Other deputy sheriffs were also at the scene to ensure that the eviction proceeded without interruption. In removing the sewer and water boxes from the side of the trailer home, the employees damaged the home. Much more significantly, the entire eviction violated Illinois law because no court order authorizing it had yet been issued.

The Soldals have filed suit against the trailer park owners as well as the deputy sheriffs alleging violation of their federal constitutional rights.

1. Did the mere presence of police at the scene of the private act transform the private act into one "under color of state law"? Consider this question in light of *Lugar* and *Tower*.

2. Assume the private property owners were acting without police assistance pursuant to a court order when they had the trailer home removed and that Illinois law permitted an ex parte judicial order. Would both elements of *Lugar* be satisfied?

b.   Deprivation of Rights Secured by Federal Law

MAINE V. THIBOUTOT
448 U.S. 1 (1980)

Mr. Justice BRENNAN delivered the opinion of the Court.

The case presents two related questions arising under 42 U.S.C. §§ 1983 and 1988. Respondents brought this suit in the Maine Superior Court alleging that petitioners, the State of Maine and its Commissioner of Human Services, violated § 1983 by depriving respondents of welfare benefits to which they were entitled under the federal Social Security Act. The petitioners present two issues: (1) whether § 1983 encompasses claims based on purely statutory violations of federal law, and (2) if so, whether attorney's fees under § 1988 may be awarded to the prevailing party in such an action.

I

Respondents, Lionel and Joline Thiboutot, are married and have eight children, three of whom are Lionel's by a previous marriage. The Maine Department of Human Services notified Lionel that, in computing the Aid to Families with Dependent Children (AFDC) benefits to which he was entitled for the three children exclusively his, it would no longer make allowance for the money spent to support the other five children, even though Lionel is legally obligated to support them. Respondents, challenging the State's interpretation of 42 U.S.C. § 602(a)(7), exhausted their state administrative remedies and then sought judicial review of the administrative action in the State Superior Court. By amended complaint, respondents also claimed relief under § 1983 for themselves and others similarly situated.

II

Section 1983 provides:

Every person who, under color of any statute, ordinance, regulation, custom, or usage, of any State or Territory, subjects or causes to be subjected, any citizen of the United States or other person within the jurisdiction thereof to the deprivation of any rights, privileges, or immunities secured by the Constitution *and laws*, shall be liable to the party injured in an action at law, suit in equity, or other proper proceeding for redress. (Emphasis added.)

The question before us is whether the phrase "and laws," as used in § 1983, means what it says, or whether it should be limited to some subset of laws. Given that Congress attached no modifiers to the phrase, the plain language of the statute undoubtedly embraces respondents' claim that petitioners violated the Social Security Act.

Even were the language ambiguous, however, any doubt as to its meaning has been resolved by our several cases suggesting, explicitly or implicitly, that the § 1983 remedy broadly encompasses violations of federal statutory as well as constitutional law. *Rosado v. Wyman*, for example, "held that suits in federal court under § 1983 are proper to secure compliance with the provisions of the Social Security Act on the part of participating States."

While some might dismiss as dictum the foregoing statements, numerous and specific as they are, our analysis in several § 1983 cases involving Social Security Act (SSA) claims has relied on the availability of a § 1983 cause of action for statutory claims. Constitutional claims were also raised in these cases, providing a jurisdictional base, but the statutory claims were allowed to go forward, and were decided on the merits under the court's pendent jurisdiction.

In the face of the plain language of § 1983 and our consistent treatment of that provision, petitioners nevertheless persist in suggesting that the phrase "and laws" should be read as limited to civil rights or equal protection laws. Petitioners suggest that when § 1 of the Civil Rights Act of 1871, which accorded jurisdiction and a remedy for deprivations of rights secured by "the Constitution of the United States," was divided by the 1874 statutory revision into a remedial section, REV. STAT. § 1979, and jurisdictional sections, REV. STAT. §§ 563(12) and 629(16), Congress intended that the same change made in § 629(16) be made as to each of the new sections as well. Section 629(16), the jurisdictional provision for the circuit courts and the model for the current jurisdictional provision, 28 U.S.C. § 1343(3), applied to deprivations of rights secured by "the Constitution of the United States, or of any right secured by any law providing for equal rights." On the other hand, the remedial provision, the predecessor of § 1983, was expanded to apply to deprivations of rights secured by "the Constitution and laws," and § 563(12), the provision granting jurisdiction to the district courts, to deprivations of rights secured by "the Constitution of the United States, or of any right secured by any law of the United States."

We need not repeat at length the detailed debate over the meaning of the scanty legislative history concerning the addition of the phrase "and laws." One conclusion which emerges clearly is that the legislative history does not permit a definitive answer. There is no express explanation offered for the insertion of the phrase "and laws." On the one hand, a principal purpose of the added language was to "ensure that federal legislation providing specifically for equality of rights would be brought within the ambit of the civil action authorized by that statute." On the other hand, there are no indications that that was the only purpose, and Congress' attention was specifically directed to this new language. Representative Lawrence, in a speech to the House of Representatives that began by observing that the revisers had very often changed the meaning of existing statutes, referred to the civil rights statutes as "possibly [showing] verbal modifications bordering on legislation." He went on to read to Congress the original and revised versions. In short, Congress was aware of what it was doing, and the legislative history does not demonstrate that the plain language was not intended. Petitioners' arguments amount to the claim that had Congress been more careful, and had it fully thought out the relationship among various sections, it might have acted differently. That argument, however, can best be addressed to Congress, which, it is important to note, has remained quiet in the face of our many pronouncements on the scope of § 1983.

III

Petitioners next argue that, even if this claim is within § 1983, Congress did not intend statutory claims to be covered by the Civil Rights Attorney's Fees Awards Act of 1976, which added the following sentence to 42 U.S.C. § 1988 (emphasis added):

> In *any action* or proceeding *to enforce* a provision of §§ 1981, 1982, 1983, 1985 and 1986 of this title, title IX of Public Law 92-318 [20 U.S.C. 1681 *et seq.*], . . . or title VI of the Civil Rights Act of 1964 [42 U.S.C. 2000d *et seq.*], the court, in its discretion, may allow the prevailing party, other than the United States, a reasonable attorney's fee as part of the costs.

Once again, the plain language provides an answer. The statute states that fees are available in *any* § 1983 action. Since we hold that this statutory action is properly brought under § 1983, § 1988 plainly applies to this suit.

Mr. Justice POWELL, with whom THE CHIEF JUSTICE and Mr. Justice REHNQUIST join, dissenting.

The Court holds today, almost casually, that 42 U.S.C. § 1983 creates a cause of action for deprivations under color of state law of any federal statutory right. Having transformed purely statutory claims into "civil rights" actions under § 1983, the Court concludes that 42 U.S.C. § 1988 permits the "prevailing party" to recover his attorney's fees.

The legislative history alone refutes the Court's assertion that the 43d Congress intended to alter the meaning of § 1983. But there are other compelling reasons to reject the Court's interpretation of the phrase "and laws." First, by reading those words to encompass every federal enactment, the Court extends § 1983 beyond the reach of its jurisdictional counterpart. Second, that reading creates a broad program for enforcing federal legislation that departs significantly from the purposes of § 1983. Such unexpected and plainly unintended consequences should be avoided whenever a statute reasonably may be given an interpretation that is consistent with the legislative purpose.

A

The Court acknowledges that its construction of § 1983 creates federal "civil rights" for which 28 U.S.C. § 1343(3) supplies no federal jurisdiction.[7] The Court finds no "inherent illogic" in this view. But the gap in the Court's logic is wide indeed in light of the history and purpose of the civil rights legislation we consider today. Sections 1983 and 1343(3) derive from the same section of the same Act. As originally enacted, the two sections necessarily were coextensive. And this Court has emphasized repeatedly that the right to a federal forum in every case was viewed as a crucial ingredient in the federal remedy afforded by § 1983.

The Court ignores these perceptions and dismisses without explanation the proposition that § 1983 and § 1343(3) are coextensive. The Court cites no evidence that Congress ever intended to alter so fundamentally its original remedial plan, and I am aware of none. Nearly every commentator who has considered the question has concluded that § 1343(3) was intended to supply federal jurisdiction in all § 1983 actions. Since § 1343(3) covers statutory claims only when they arise under laws providing for the equal rights of citizens, the same limitation necessarily is implicit in § 1983. The Court's decision to apply that statute without regard to the scope of its jurisdictional counterpart is at war with the plainly expressed intent of Congress.

B

The Court's opinion does not consider the nature or scope of the litigation it has authorized. In practical effect, today's decision means that state and local governments, officers, and employees now may face liability whenever a person believes he has been injured by the administration of *any* federal-state cooperative program, whether or not that program is related to equal or civil rights.

Even a cursory survey of the United States Code reveals that literally hundreds of cooperative regulatory and social welfare enactments may be affected. The States now participate in the enforcement of federal laws governing migrant labor, noxious weeds, historic preservation, wildlife conservation, anadromous fisheries, scenic trails, and strip mining. Various statutes authorize federal-state cooperative agreements in most aspects of federal land management. In addition, federal grants administered by state and local governments now are available in virtually every area of public administration. Unemployment, Medicaid, school lunch subsidies, food stamps, and other welfare benefits may provide particularly inviting subjects of litigation. Federal assistance also includes a variety of subsidies for education, housing, health care,

---

7   Section 1343(3) supplies jurisdiction for claims involving rights secured by the Constitution "or by any Act of Congress providing for equal rights of citizens or of all persons within the jurisdiction of the United States." Neither § 1983 itself nor the Social Security Act provides for equal rights within the meaning of this action.

transportation, public works, and law enforcement. Those who might benefit from these grants now will be potential § 1983 plaintiffs.

No one can predict the extent to which litigation arising from today's decision will harass state and local officials; nor can one foresee the number of new filings in our already overburdened courts. But no one can doubt that these consequences will be substantial. And the Court advances no reason to believe that any Congress—from 1874 to the present day—intended this expansion of federally imposed liability on state defendants.

Moreover, state and local governments will bear the entire burden of liability for violations of statutory "civil rights" even when federal officials are involved equally in the administration of the affected program. Section 1983 grants no right of action against the United States, and few of the foregoing cooperative programs provide expressly for private actions to enforce their terms.

Even when a cause of action against federal officials is available, litigants are likely to focus efforts upon state defendants in order to obtain attorney's fees under the liberal standard of 42 U.S.C. § 1988. There is some evidence that § 1983 claims already are being appended to complaints solely for the purpose of obtaining fees in actions where "civil rights" of any kind are at best an afterthought. In this case, for example, the respondents added a § 1983 count to their complaint some years after the action was initiated, apparently in response to the enactment of the Civil Rights Attorney's Fees Awards Act of 1976.

Today's decision confers upon the courts unprecedented authority to oversee state actions that have little or nothing to do with the individual rights defined and enforced by the civil rights legislation of the Reconstruction Era. This result cannot be reconciled with the purposes for which § 1983 was enacted. It also imposes unequal burdens on state and federal officials in the joint administration of federal programs and may expose state defendants to liability for attorney's fees in virtually every case. If any Member of the 43d Congress had suggested legislation embodying these results, the proposal certainly would have been hotly debated. It is simply inconceivable that Congress, while professing a firm intention not to make substantive changes in the law, nevertheless intended to enact a major new remedial program by approving—without discussion—the addition of two words to a statute adopted only three years earlier.

NOTES AND QUESTIONS

1. Was the majority's decision to extend the reach of § 1983 beyond its jurisdictional counterpart persuasive? In light of the language in § 1343(3), could this suit have been pursued in federal court? If not under § 1343(3), what about under § 1331? Note that prior to 1980, claims could not be brought under § 1331 unless they satisfied a jurisdictional amount requirement. At the time this suit was initiated the "lost" social security benefits would not have satisfied the $10,000 jurisdictional amount required, thus foreclosing a federal forum. The elimination of the jurisdictional amount requirement in 1980, coupled with the holding in *Maine*, had the potential of significantly increasing the federal caseload.

2. If § 1983 was intended by Congress to enforce the Fourteenth Amendment, may § 1983 be used to enforce constitutional rights not incorporated through the Due Process Clause of the Fourteenth Amendment?

In *Dennis v. Higgins*, 498 U.S. 439 (1991), the Supreme Court ruled that the Commerce Clause confers rights within the meaning of § 1983. Arguing by analogy to the standard used to "infer" rights from a federal statute, the Court reasoned that the Commerce Clause creates obligations binding on the government, it is neither too vague nor amorphous to be beyond the competence of the judiciary to enforce, and it was intended to benefit those engaged in interstate commerce.

However, in *National Private Truck Council, Inc. v. Oklahoma Tax Commission*, 515 U.S. 582 (1995), the Court unanimously held that state courts may not grant federal remedies under § 1983 and 1988 to successful litigants challenging a state tax as violating Commerce Clause rights. The Court reasoned that in light of the well-established presumption of a "hands-off approach regarding state taxes," Congress never intended to authorize injunctive or declaratory relief under § 1983 in state tax cases where there is an adequate remedy at law. Because an injunction issued by state courts under § 1983 is just as disruptive of state taxation schemes as one entered by a federal court, which would be barred by the Tax Injunction Act, the Court concluded that general federalism principles foreclose the use of § 1983 in this context.

3. Are there any limits as to the federal statutes which may be enforced through § 1983? Should there be? Or, must such limitations come from Congress, rather than the courts? If Congress does not wish a statute to be enforced under § 1983, should it be required to say so?

MIDDLESEX COUNTY SEWERAGE AUTHORITY V. NATIONAL SEA CLAMMERS ASS'N
453 U.S. 1 (1981)

[The plaintiffs alleged that the defendant was damaging their fishing grounds by dumping sewage in the ocean, contrary to two federal statutes—the Federal Water Pollution Control Act (FWPCA) and the Marine Protection, Research, and Sanctuaries Act (MPRSA). After concluding that Congress did not intend to allow a private cause of action under either of these Acts and that a nuisance claim could not be maintained under federal common law, the Court *sua sponte* addressed the possibility of maintaining a § 1983 suit to enforce these federal laws]

Justice POWELL delivered the opinion of the Court.

Although the parties have not suggested it, there remains a possible alternative source of express congressional authorization of private suits under these Acts. Last Term, in *Maine v. Thiboutot*, the Court construed 42 U.S.C. § 1983 as authorizing suits to redress violations by state officials of rights created by federal statutes. Accordingly, it could be argued that respondents may sue the municipalities and sewerage boards under the FWPCA and MPRSA by virtue of a right of action created by § 1983.

The claim brought here arguably falls within the scope of *Maine v. Thiboutot* because it involves a suit by a private party claiming that a federal statute has been violated under color of state law, causing an injury. The Court, however, has recognized two exceptions to the application of § 1983 to statutory violations. In *Pennhurst State School and Hospital v. Halderman*, we remanded certain claims for a determination (i) whether Congress had foreclosed private enforcement of that statute in the enactment itself, and (ii) whether the statute at issue there was the kind that created enforceable "rights" under § 1983. In the present cases, because we find that Congress foreclosed a § 1983 remedy under these Acts, we need not reach the second question whether these Acts created "rights, privileges, or immunities" within the meaning of § 1983.

When the remedial devices provided in a particular act are sufficiently comprehensive, they may suffice to demonstrate congressional intent to preclude the remedy of suits under § 1983. As Justice Stewart stated in *Chapman v. Houston Welfare Rights Organization* (dissenting opinion), when "a state official is alleged to have violated a federal statute which provides its own comprehensive enforcement scheme, the requirements of that enforcement procedure may not be bypassed by bringing suit directly under § 1983." As discussed above, the FWPCA and MPRSA do provide quite comprehensive enforcement mechanisms. It is hard to believe that Congress intended to preserve the § 1983 right of action when it created so many specific statutory remedies, including the two citizen-suit provisions. We therefore conclude that the existence of these express remedies demonstrates not only that Congress intended to foreclose implied private actions but also that it intended to supplant any remedy that otherwise would be available under § 1983.

NOTES AND QUESTIONS

1. If Congress has created a federal right and a comprehensive remedy, does it make sense to allow § 1983 to be used to secure broader relief, e.g., to secure attorneys fees not provided for in the Act?

2. Should the plaintiff have the burden of showing that Congress intended to allow § 1983 enforcement, or must the defendant show that Congress intended to foreclose use of this provision?

3. As to the second exception to *Maine*, how will it be determined whether the statute creates "enforceable rights"? If Congress has not provided a private cause of action under an enactment, may a court nonetheless find that the law creates rights enforceable under § 1983? Note that as to the former, plaintiff has the burden of proving that Congress intended to create a private cause of action, and the Court in recent years has "abandoned its hospitable attitude towards implied rights of action."

Thompson v. Thompson, 448 U.S. 174 (1988). Yet, even if Congress has failed to provide a private cause of action in its enactment, isn't Congress presumed to legislate against the background of § 1983, thus contemplating private enforcement of federal statutes, absent an indication of contrary intent?

WRIGHT V. CITY OF ROANOKE REDEVELOPMENT AND HOUSING AUTHORITY

479 u.s. 418 (1987)

Justice WHITE delivered the opinion of the Court.

Petitioners in this case, tenants living in low-income housing projects owned by respondent, brought suit under 42 U.S.C. § 1983, alleging that respondent overbilled them for their utilities and thereby violated the rent ceiling imposed by the Brooke Amendment to the Housing Act of 1937, and the implementing regulations of the Department of Housing and Urban Development (HUD).

I

Respondent is one of many public housing authorities (PHAs) established throughout the country under the United States Housing Act of 1937, 42 U.S.C. §§ 1401 *et seq.*, to provide affordable housing for low-income people. In 1969, the Housing Act was amended in a fundamental respect: the Brooke Amendment imposed a ceiling for rents charged to low-income people living in public housing projects, and, as later amended, provides that a low-income family "shall pay as rent" a specified percentage of its income. HUD has consistently considered "rent" to include a reasonable amount for the use of utilities, which is defined by regulation as that amount equal to or less than an amount determined by the PHA to be a reasonable part of the rent paid by low-income tenants.

In their suit against respondent, petitioners alleged that respondent had overcharged them for their utilities by failing to comply with the applicable HUD regulations in establishing the amount of utility service to which petitioners were entitled. Thus, according to petitioners, respondent imposed a surcharge for "excess" utility consumption that should have been part of petitioners' rent.

II

Maine v. Thiboutot held that § 1983 was available to enforce violations of federal statutes by agents of the State. *Pennhurst* and *National Sea Clammers Ass'n*, however, recognized two exceptions to the application of § 1983 to remedy statutory violations: where Congress has foreclosed such enforcement of the statute in the enactment itself and where the statute did not create enforceable rights, privileges, or immunities within the meaning of § 1983. In *Pennhurst* a § 1983 action did not lie because the statutory provisions were thought to be only statements of "findings" indicating no more than a congressional preference—at most a "nudge in the preferred directio[n]," and not intended to rise to the level of an enforceable right. In *Sea Clammers*, an intent to foreclose resort to § 1983 was found in the comprehensive remedial scheme provided by Congress, a scheme that itself provided for private actions and left no room for additional private remedies under § 1983. Under these cases, if there is a state deprivation of a "right" secured by a federal statute, § 1983 provides a remedial cause of action unless the state actor demonstrates by express provision or other specific evidence from the statute itself that Congress intended to foreclose such private enforcement.

Here, the Court of Appeals held that the statute and the Brooke Amendment clearly manifested congressional intention to vest in HUD the exclusive power to enforce the benefits due housing project tenants and hence the intention to foreclose both a private cause of action under the Housing Act and any private enforcement under § 1983.

We disagree with the Court of Appeals' rather summary conclusion that the administrative scheme of enforcement foreclosed private enforcement. HUD undoubtedly has considerable authority to oversee the operation of PHAs. We are unconvinced, however, that respondent has overcome its burden of showing that "the remedial devices provided in [the Housing Act] are sufficiently comprehensive to demonstrate congressional intent to preclude the remedy of suits under § 1983." They do not show that "Congress specifically foreclosed a remedy under § 1983." Not only are the Brooke Amendment and its legislative history devoid of any express indication that exclusive enforcement authority was vested in HUD, but there have also been both congressional and agency actions indicating that enforcement authority is not centralized and that private actions were anticipated. Neither, in our view, are the remedial mechanisms provided sufficiently comprehensive and effective to raise a clear inference that Congress intended to foreclose a § 1983 cause of action for the enforcement of tenants' rights secured by federal law.

In both *Sea Clammers* and *Smith v. Robinson* the statutes at issue themselves provided for private judicial remedies, thereby evidencing congressional intent to supplant the § 1983 remedy. There is nothing of that kind found in the Brooke Amendment or elsewhere in the Housing Act. Indeed, the only private remedy provided for is the local grievance procedures which the Act now requires. These procedures are not open to class grievances; and even if tenants may grieve about a PHA's utility allowance schedule, which petitioners dispute, the existence of a state administrative remedy does not ordinarily foreclose resort to § 1983.

Lastly, it is said that tenants may sue on their lease in state courts and enforce their Brooke Amendment rights in that litigation. Perhaps they could, but the state court remedy is hardly a reason to bar an action under § 1983, which was adopted to provide a federal remedy for the enforcement of federal rights.

In sum, we conclude that nothing in the Housing Act or the Brooke Amendment evidences that Congress intended to preclude petitioners' § 1983 claim against respondent.

III

Although the Court of Appeals read the Brooke Amendment as extending to housing project tenants certain rights enforceable only by HUD, respondent asserts that neither the Brooke Amendment nor the interim regulations gave the tenants any specific or definable rights to utilities, that is, no enforceable rights within the meaning of § 1983. We perceive little substance in this claim. The Brooke Amendment could not be clearer: as further amended in 1981, tenants could be charged as rent no more and no less than 30 percent of their income. This was a mandatory limitation focusing on the individual family and its income. The intent to benefit tenants is undeniable. Nor is there any question that HUD interim regulations, in effect when this suit began, expressly required that a "reasonable" amount for utilities be included in rent that PHA was allowed to charge, an interpretation to which HUD has adhered both before and after the adoption of the Brooke Amendment. HUD's view is entitled to deference as a valid interpretation of the statute, and Congress in the course of amending that provision has not disagreed with it.

Respondent nevertheless asserts that the provision for a "reasonable" allowance for utilities is too vague and amorphous to confer on tenants an enforceable "right" within the meaning of § 1983 and that the whole matter of utility allowances must be left to the discretion of the PHA, subject to supervision by HUD. The regulations, however, defining the statutory concept of "rent" as including utilities, have the force of law, they specifically set out guidelines that the PHAs were to follow in establishing utility allowances, and they require notice to tenants and an opportunity to comment on proposed allowances. In our view, the benefits Congress intended to confer on tenants are sufficiently specific and definite to qualify as enforceable rights under *Pennhurst* and § 1983, rights that are not, as respondent suggests, beyond the competence of the judiciary to enforce.

Justice O'CONNOR, with whom THE CHIEF JUSTICE, Justice POWELL, and Justice SCALIA join, dissenting.

The petitioners in this case assert that the Brooke Amendment creates an enforceable right to have "reasonable utilities" included in the limitation on the "rent" they may be charged by a public housing authority (PHA). The Brooke Amendment, as amended, provides that a low-income family "shall pay as rent" a specified percentage of its monthly income for publicly assisted housing.

Assuming, as the Court finds, that Congress intended to create an enforceable right to a limitation on the amount PHAs may charge "as rent," the question remains whether petitioners' claim to reasonable utilities comes within the scope of the right that Congress intended to confer. On the face of the statute, there is nothing to suggest that Congress intended that utilities be included within the statutory entitlement. "Rent" in ordinary usage simply means consideration paid for the use or occupation of property, and the statute does not suggest congressional intent to adopt a broader construction of the term.

The legislative history of the Brooke Amendment, far from indicating an intent to create a statutory right to utilities, shows that Congress was presented with, and ultimately rejected, a proposal to create an enforceable right to "reasonable utilities."

In the absence of an indication in the language, legislative history, or administrative interpretation of the Brooke Amendment that Congress intended to create an enforceable right to utilities, it is necessary to ask whether administrative regulations *alone* could create such a right. This is a troubling issue not briefed by the parties, and I do not attempt to resolve it here. The Court's questionable reasoning that, because for 4 years HUD gave somewhat less discretion to the PHAs in setting reasonable utilities allowances, HUD understood Congress to have *required* enforceable utility standards, apparently allows it to sidestep the question. I am concerned, however, that lurking behind the Court's analysis may be the view that, once it has been found that a statute creates some enforceable right, any regulation adopted within the purview of the statute creates rights enforceable in federal courts, regardless of whether Congress or the promulgating agency ever contemplated such a result. Thus, HUD's frequently changing views on how best to administer the provision of utilities to public housing tenants becomes the focal point for the creation and extinguishment of federal "rights." Such a result, where determination of § 1983 "rights" has been unleashed from any connection to congressional intent, is troubling indeed.

NOTES AND QUESTIONS

1. Did the Supreme Court in *Sea Clammers* find congressional intent to foreclose the use of § 1983 through "specific evidence" or "an express provision" in the federal statutes in question? If not, does *Wright* narrow the holding in that case? Why doesn't HUD's comprehensive enforcement scheme foreclose use of § 1983?

2. As to enforceable rights, how readily should rights be inferred from agency regulations? If such regulations have "the force of law" and can be corrected by Congress, why should the Court hesitate to allow their enforcement under § 1983? Does violation of an agency regulation mean that an individual has been deprived of "rights, privileges, or immunities" secured by federal law within the meaning of § 1983?

3. In *Wilder v. Virginia Hosp. Ass'n*, 496 U.S. 498 (1990), the Court held that the Medicaid Act created a right enforceable by health care providers to reasonable and adequate rates of reimbursement. The Act required that states participating in the Medicaid program adopt a plan with "reasonable and adequate" rates. The statute, as well as the regulations, set forth factors that a state needed to consider in adopting its rates, arguably providing an objective benchmark to determine compliance. The Court held that the requirement was not so vague or amorphous as to be judicially unenforceable, even though the Act gave the states substantial discretion in choosing

among reasonable methods of calculating rates. Further, the Court emphasized that the burden was on the defendant to show by "express provision or other specific evidence from the statute" that Congress intended to foreclose private enforcement through § 1983.

SUTER V. ARTIST M
503 U.S. 347 (1992)

[The Court was asked to determine whether the Adoption and Assistance Child Welfare Act created rights enforceable under § 1983. The Act required states to make "reasonable efforts" to both prevent the placement of children in foster care and to return children as quickly as possible where placement in foster care was necessary. It was undisputed that Illinois' plan, which generally addressed this concern, was approved by the Secretary of Health and Human Services. The plaintiffs were children who claimed that the Illinois Department of Child and Family Services failed to assign caseworkers in a timely fashion, and thereby violated the "reasonable efforts" requirement of the statute. The Seventh Circuit held that the "reasonable efforts" clause created a privately enforceable right that could be pursued by children who resided at home under court supervision. It affirmed the district court order that the state assign a caseworker to each child and his/her family within three days of a juvenile court proceeding. In a 7-2 opinion, the Court reversed.]

THE CHIEF JUSTICE delivered the opinion of the Court.

[The statute in question], 42 U.S.C. § 671(a)(15) requires that to obtain federal reimbursement, a State have a plan which "provides that, in each case, reasonable efforts will be made . . . to prevent or eliminate the need for removal of the child from his home, and . . . to make it possible for the child to return to his home. . . ."

As recognized by petitioners, respondents, and the courts below, the Act is mandatory in its terms. However, in the light shed by *Pennhurst*, we must examine exactly what is required of States by the Act. Here, the terms of § 671(a) are clear . . . therefore the Act does place a requirement on the states, but that requirement only goes so far as to ensure that the State have a plan approved by the Secretary which contains the sixteen listed features.

No further statutory guidance is found as to how "reasonable efforts" are to be measured. This directive is not the only one which Congress has given to the States, and it is a directive whose meaning will obviously vary with the circumstances of each individual case. How the State was to comply with this directive, and with the other provisions of the Act, was, within broad limits, left up to the State.

The regulations promulgated by the Secretary to enforce the Adoption Act do not evidence a view that § 671(a) places any requirement for state receipt of federal funds other than the requirement that the State submit a plan to be approved by the Secretary. What is significant is that the regulations are not specific, and do not provide notice to the States that failure to do anything other than submit a plan with the requisite features, to be approved by the Secretary, is a further condition on the receipt of funds from the Federal Government.

Careful examination of the language relied upon by respondents, in the context of the entire Act, leads us to conclude that the "reasonable efforts" language does not unambiguously confer an enforceable right upon the Act's beneficiaries. The term "reasonable efforts" in this context is at least as plausibly read to impose only a rather generalized duty on the State, to be enforced not by private individuals, but by the Secretary.

NOTES AND QUESTIONS

1. Can Justice Rehnquist's analysis be reconciled with that used in *Wilder* and *Wright*? Is the judicial task, implicated in *Wilder*, of assessing reasonable rates of reimbursement (in light of market rates and other economic factors) different from the task of assessing "reasonable" efforts to keep families intact? Does his requirement that Congress "unambiguously" confer rights reverse the presumption in favor of enforceability, contrary to prior case precedent?

2. In *Blessing v. Freestone*, 520 U.S. 329 (1997), plaintiffs sued under § 1983 to enforce Title IV-D of the Social Security Act, alleging that the state agency failed to take adequate steps to obtain child support payments for them due to structural defects in the state's program—the agency was understaffed and collecting support in less than 5% of its cases. The Court ruled unanimously that Title IV-D did not give parents an enforceable right to demand better performance from the state agency. Justice O'Connor stated that courts should examine three factors in determining whether a statutory provision creates private enforceable rights: **(1) whether the plaintiff is the intended beneficiary of the statute, (2) whether plaintiff's asserted interests are so vague and amorphous as to be beyond the competence of the judiciary to enforce, and (3) whether the statute imposes binding obligations on the state. The plaintiffs never made it beyond the first step:**

    In their complaint, respondents argued that federal law granted them "individual rights to all mandated services delivered in substantial compliance with Title IV-D and its implementing regulations." They sought a broad injunction requiring the director of Arizona's child support agency to achieve "substantial compliance . . . throughout all programmatic operations." Attributing the deficiencies in the State's program primarily to staff shortages and other structural defects, respondents essentially invited the District Court to oversee every aspect of Arizona's Title IV-D program.

    Without distinguishing among the numerous rights that might have been created by this federally funded welfare program, the Court of Appeals agreed in sweeping terms that "Title IV-D creates enforceable rights in families in need of Title IV-D services." The Court of Appeals did not specify exactly which "rights" it was purporting to recognize, but it apparently believed that federal law gave respondents the right to have the State substantially comply with Title IV-D in all respects. We disagree.

As an initial matter, the lower court's holding that Title IV-D "creates enforceable rights" paints with too broad a brush. It was incumbent upon respondents to identify with particularity the rights they claimed, since it is impossible to determine whether Title IV-D, as an undifferentiated whole, gives rise to undefined "rights." Only when the complaint is broken down into manageable analytic bites can a court ascertain whether each separate claim satisfies the various criteria we have set forth for determining whether a federal statute creates rights . . . the requirement that a State operate its child support program in "substantial compliance" with Title IV-D was not intended to benefit individual children and custodial parents, and therefore it does not constitute a federal right. Far from creating an *individual* entitlement to services, the standard is simply a yardstick for the Secretary to measure the *systemwide* performance of a State's Title IV-D program.

We do not foreclose the possibility that some provisions of Title IV-D give rise to individual rights. For example, respondent Madrid alleged that the state agency managed to collect some support payments from her ex-husband but failed to pass through the first $50 of each payment, to which she was purportedly entitled under the pre-1996 version of § 657(b)(1). Although § 657 may give her a federal right to receive a specified portion of the money collected on her behalf by Arizona, she did not explicitly request such relief in the complaint.

GONZAGA UNIVERSITY V. DOE
536 U.S. 273 (2002)

Chief Justice REHNQUIST delivered the opinion of the Court.

The question presented is whether a student may sue a private university for damages under § 1983 to enforce provisions of the Family Educational Rights and Privacy Act of 1974 (FERPA), 20 U.S.C. § 1232g, which prohibit the federal funding of educational institutions that have a policy or practice of releasing education records to unauthorized persons. We hold such an action foreclosed because the relevant provisions of FERPA create no personal rights to enforce under § 1983.

Respondent John Doe is a former undergraduate in the School of Education at Gonzaga University, a private university in Spokane, Washington. He planned to graduate and teach at a Washington public elementary school. Washington at the time required all of its new teachers to obtain an affidavit of good moral character from a dean of their graduating college or university. In October 1993, Roberta League, Gonzaga's "teacher certification specialist," overheard one student tell another that respondent engaged in acts of sexual misconduct against Jane Doe, a female undergraduate. League launched an investigation and contacted the state agency responsible for teacher certification, identifying respondent by name and discussing the allegations against him. Respondent did not learn of the investigation, or that information about him had been disclosed, until March 1994, when he was told by League and others that he would not receive the affidavit required for certification as a Washington schoolteacher.

Respondent then sued Gonzaga and League in state court. He alleged violations of Washington tort and contract law, as well as a pendent violation of § 1983 for the release of personal information to an "unauthorized person" in violation of FERPA.[1] A jury found for respondent on all counts, awarding him $1,155,000, including $150,000 in compensatory damages and $300,000 in punitive damages on the FERPA claim.

Congress enacted FERPA under its spending power to condition the receipt of federal funds on certain requirements relating to the access and disclosure of student educational records. The Act directs the Secretary of Education to withhold federal funds from any public or private "educational agency or institution" that fails to comply with these conditions.

Respondent contends that this statutory regime confers upon any student enrolled at a covered school or institution a federal right, enforceable in suits for damages under § 1983, not to have "education records" disclosed to unauthorized persons without the student's express written consent. But we have never before held, and decline to do so here, that spending legislation drafted in terms resembling those of FERPA can confer enforceable rights.

[I]n *Pennhurst State School and Hospital v. Halderman*, we rejected a claim that the Developmentally Disabled Assistance and Bill of Rights Act of 1975 conferred enforceable rights .... We made clear that unless Congress "speak[s] with a clear voice," and manifests an "unambiguous" intent to confer individual rights, federal funding provisions provide no basis for private enforcement by § 1983.

Since *Pennhurst*, only twice have we found spending legislation to give rise to enforceable rights. In *Wright v. Roanoke Redevelopment and Housing Authority*, we allowed a § 1983 suit by tenants to recover past overcharges under a rent-ceiling provision of the Public Housing Act, on the ground that the provision unambiguously conferred "a mandatory [benefit] focusing on the individual family and its income." The key to our inquiry was that Congress spoke in terms that "could not be clearer," and conferred entitlements "sufficiently specific and definite to qualify as enforceable rights under *Pennhurst*." Also significant was that the federal agency charged with administering the Public Housing Act "ha[d] never provided a procedure by which tenants could complain to it about the alleged failures [of state welfare agencies] to abide by [the Act's rent-ceiling provision]."

Three years later, in *Wilder v. Virginia Hospital Ass'n*, we allowed a § 1983 suit brought by health care providers to enforce a reimbursement provision of the Medicaid Act, on the ground that the provision, much like the rent-ceiling provision in *Wright*, explicitly conferred specific monetary entitlements upon the plaintiffs. Congress left no doubt of its intent for private

---

1 The Washington Court of Appeals and the Washington Supreme Court found petitioners to have acted "under color of state law" for purposes of § 1983 when they disclosed respondent's personal information to state officials in connection with state-law teacher certification requirements. Although the petition for certiorari challenged this holding, we agreed to review only the question posed in the first paragraph of this opinion. We therefore assume without deciding that the relevant disclosures occurred under color of state law.

enforcement, we said, because the provision required States to pay an "objective" monetary entitlement to individual health care providers, with no sufficient administrative means of enforcing the requirement against States that failed to comply.

Our more recent decisions, however, have rejected attempts to infer enforceable rights from Spending Clause statutes. . . [I]n *Blessing v. Freestone*, [w]e found no basis for the suit . . . . Because the provision focused on "the aggregate services provided by the State," rather than "the needs of any particular person," it conferred no individual rights and thus could not be enforced by § 1983.

Some language in our opinions might be read to suggest that something less than an unambiguously conferred right is enforceable by § 1983. *Blessing*, for example, set forth three "factors" to guide judicial inquiry into whether or not a statute confers a right: "Congress must have intended that the provision in question benefit the plaintiff," "the plaintiff must demonstrate that the right assertedly protected by the statute is not so 'vague and amorphous' that its enforcement would strain judicial resources," and "the provision giving rise to the asserted right must be couched in mandatory, rather than precatory, terms." In the same paragraph, however, *Blessing* emphasizes that it is only violations of *rights*, not *laws*, which give rise to § 1983 actions. This confusion has led some courts to interpret *Blessing* as allowing plaintiffs to enforce a statute under § 1983 so long as the plaintiff falls within the general zone of interest that the statute is intended to protect; something less than what is required for a statute to create rights enforceable directly from the statute itself under an implied private right of action.

We now reject the notion that our cases permit anything short of an unambiguously conferred right to support a cause of action brought under § 1983. Section 1983 provides a remedy only for the deprivation of "rights, privileges, or immunities secured by the Constitution and laws" of the United States. Accordingly, it is *rights*, not the broader or vaguer "benefits" or "interests," that may be enforced under the authority of that section. This being so, we further reject the notion that our implied right of action cases are separate and distinct from our § 1983 cases.

We have recognized that whether a statutory violation may be enforced through § 1983 "is a different inquiry than that involved in determining whether a private right of action can be implied from a particular statute." But the inquiries overlap in one meaningful respect—in either case we must first determine whether Congress *intended to create a federal right*. For a statute to create such private rights, its text must be "phrased in terms of the persons benefited." But even where a statute is phrased in such explicit rights-creating terms, a plaintiff suing under an implied right of action still must show that the statute manifests an intent "to create not just a private *right* but also a private *remedy*." *Alexander v. Sandoval*.

Plaintiffs suing under § 1983 do not have the burden of showing an intent to create a private remedy because § 1983 generally supplies a remedy for the vindication of rights secured by federal statutes. Once a plaintiff demonstrates that a statute confers an individual right, the right is presumptively enforceable by § 1983. But the initial inquiry—determining whether a statute confers any right at all—is no different from the initial inquiry in an implied right of action case, the express purpose of which is to determine whether or not a statute "confer[s] rights on a particular class of persons. . . ." Accordingly, where the text and structure of a statute provide no indication that Congress intends to create new individual rights, there is no basis for a private suit, whether under § 1983 or under an implied right of action.

With this principle in mind, there is no question that FERPA's nondisclosure provisions fail to confer enforceable rights. To begin with, the provisions entirely lack the sort of "rights-creating" language critical to showing the requisite congressional intent to create new rights. Unlike the individually focused terminology of Titles VI and IX ("no person shall be subjected to discrimination"), FERPA's provisions speak only to the Secretary of Education, directing that "[n]o funds shall be made available" to any "educational agency or institution" which has a prohibited "policy or practice." This focus is two steps removed from the interests of individual students and parents and clearly does not confer the sort of "*individual* entitlement" that is enforceable under § 1983.

FERPA's nondisclosure provisions further speak only in terms of institutional policy and practice, not individual instances of disclosure. *See* §§ 1232g(b)(1)-(2) (prohibiting the funding of "any educational agency or institution which has a *policy or practice* of permitting the release of education records"). Therefore, as in *Blessing*, they have an "aggregate" focus, they are not concerned with "whether the needs of any particular person have been satisfied," and they cannot "give rise to individual rights." Recipient institutions can further avoid termination of funding so long as they "comply substantially" with the Act's requirements. § 1234c(a). This, too, is not unlike *Blessing*, which found that Title IV-D failed to support a § 1983 suit in part because it only required "substantial compliance" with federal regulations.

Our conclusion that FERPA's nondisclosure provisions fail to confer enforceable rights is buttressed by the mechanism that Congress chose to provide for enforcing those provisions. Congress expressly authorized the Secretary of Education to "*deal with violations*" of the Act, and required the Secretary to "establish or designate [a] review board" for investigating and adjudicating such violations. Pursuant to these provisions, the Secretary created the Family Policy Compliance Office (FPCO) "to act as the Review Board required under the Act and to enforce the Act with respect to all applicable programs." These administrative procedures squarely distinguish this case from *Wright* and *Wilder*, where an aggrieved individual lacked any federal review mechanism, and further counsel against our finding a congressional intent to create individually enforceable private rights.

In sum, if Congress wishes to create new rights enforceable under § 1983, it must do so in clear and unambiguous terms—no less and no more than what is required for Congress to create new rights enforceable under an implied private right of action. FERPA's nondisclosure provisions contain no rights- creating language, they have an aggregate, not individual, focus, and they serve primarily to direct the Secretary of Education's distribution of public funds to educational institutions. They therefore create no rights enforceable under § 1983.

[In a concurring opinion, Justice Breyer, joined by Justice Souter, agreed that congressional intent was key and that FERPA manifested no such intent, but rejected the presumption that Congress intends to create a right only if the text or structure of the statute demonstrates "unambiguous" intent. In dissent, Justice Stevens, joined by Justice Ginsburg, argued that FERPA contained rights-creating language that satisfied the *Blessing* test.]

NOTES AND QUESTIONS

1. In footnote 1, the Court assumed without deciding that the conduct of a private university could be deemed "under color of state law" based on the Gonzaga policy of discussing students with state certification officials. What arguments can be made for and against this conclusion?

2. Does *Blessing*'s three-prong analysis survive this case? If not, what test does the Court substitute? What factors were most critical to the Court's conclusion that FERPA did not create rights enforceable under § 1983?

3. Should the existence of an administrative remedy be used to infer that Congress did not intend to create enforceable rights? In *Wright*, the Court held that the existence of an administrative remedy is generally insufficient to infer congressional foreclosure of a § 1983 claim. Can *Wright* and *Gonzaga* be reconciled?

    Where a federal statute provides its own judicial, not just administrative, enforcement mechanism, the Court is more apt to discover congressional intent to foreclose § 1983 enforcement. In *City of Rancho Palos Verdes, California v. Abrams*, 544 U.S. 113 (2005), the Court ruled that an individual could not enforce the federal Telecommunications Act because of its comprehensive remedial scheme. Although the Court specifically declined to hold that the availability of a private judicial remedy conclusively establishes Congress' intent to foreclose §1983 relief, it stated that an "express, private means of redress in the statute itself is ordinarily an indication that Congress did not intend to leave open a more expansive remedy under § 1983." It noted, however, that the inference that a statutory judicial remedy is exclusive "can surely be overcome by textual indication, express or implicit, that the remedy is to complement, rather than supplant, § 1983." Critical in this case was the fact that the Telecommunications Act provided only thirty days after the local government's final action to seek judicial review, and it did not allow either for compensatory damages or for attorneys' fees and costs. Five Justices, concurring in the judgment, emphasized that "context, not just literal text" should be examined in assessing congressional intent with respect to a particular statute. The context here, however, demonstrated that Congress sought to solve a national problem, while still allowing state and local government authorities to make decisions, subject only to minimal federal judicial review. Allowing enforcement of the Act through Section 1983 would distort the Act's scheme of expedited judicial review and limited remedies that Congress envisioned.

4. How critical was it to the majority in *Gonzaga* that FERPA is a funding measure? Recall *South Dakota v. Dole, supra*: "If Congress desires to condition the State's receipt of federal funds, it must do so unambiguously, enabling the States to exercise their choice knowingly, cognizant of the consequences of their participation." Outside the area of appropriations measures, the Supreme Court has confirmed the availability of § 1983 to enforce federal statutes. In *Livadas v. Bradshaw*, 512 U.S. 107 (1994), a unanimous Court sustained the right of a discharged employee to sue the state labor Commissioner for violating her NLRA right to bargain collectively. The Court reasoned that:

> § 1983 remains a generally and presumptively available remedy for claimed violations of federal law . . . we have no difficulty concluding that the NLRA protects interests of employees and employers against abridgement by a State, as well as by private actors; that the obligations it imposes on government actors are not "vague and amorphous" as to exceed judicial competence to decide; and that Congress had not meant to foreclose relief under § 1983.

How does this standard differ from that adopted by the Court in *Gonzaga*?

5. **Constitutional Rights:** Although § 1983 purportedly provides a remedy for the enforcement of all constitutional rights violations, in the following cases the Court carves out a **congressional preclusion** exception, as well as a special rule where § 1983 is used to enforce procedural due process rights.

SMITH V. ROBINSON
468 U.S. 992 (1983)

Justice BLACKMUN delivered the opinion of the Court.

This case presents questions regarding the award of attorney's fees in a proceeding to secure a "free appropriate public education" for a handicapped child. At various stages in the proceeding, petitioners asserted claims for relief based on state law, on the Education of the Handicapped Act (EHA), on § 504 of the Rehabilitation Act of 1973, and on the Due Process and Equal Protection Clauses of the Fourteenth Amendment to the United States Constitution. The United States Court of Appeals for the First Circuit concluded that because the proceeding, in essence, was one to enforce the provisions of the EHA, a statute that does not provide for the payment of attorney's fees, petitioners were not entitled to such fees.

Resolution of this dispute requires us to explore congressional intent, both in authorizing fees for substantial unaddressed constitutional claims and in setting out the elaborate substantive and procedural requirements of the EHA, with no indication that attorney's fees are available in an action to enforce those requirements. We turn first to petitioners' claim that they were entitled to fees under 42 U.S.C. § 1988 because they asserted substantial constitutional claims.

As petitioners emphasize, their § 1983 claims were not based on alleged violations of the EHA,[11] but on independent claims of constitutional deprivations. As the Court of Appeals recognized, however, petitioners' constitutional claims, a denial of due process and a denial of a free appropriate public education as guaranteed by the Equal Protection Clause, are virtually identical to their EHA claims. The question to be asked, therefore, is whether Congress intended that the EHA be the exclusive avenue through which a plaintiff may assert those claims.

We have little difficulty concluding that Congress intended the EHA to be the exclusive avenue through which a plaintiff may assert an equal protection claim to a publicly financed special education. The EHA is a comprehensive scheme set up by Congress to aid the States in complying with their constitutional obligations to provide public education for handicapped children. Both the provisions of the statute and its legislative history indicate that Congress intended handicapped children with constitutional claims to a free appropriate public education to pursue those claims through the carefully tailored administrative and judicial mechanism set out in the statute.

In the statement of findings with which the EHA begins, Congress noted that there were more than 8 million handicapped children in the country, the special education needs of most of whom were not being fully met. Congress also recognized that in a series of "landmark court cases," the right to an equal education opportunity for handicapped children had been established. The EHA was an attempt to relieve the fiscal burden placed on States and localities by their responsibility to provide education for all handicapped children. At the same time, however, Congress made clear that the EHA is not simply a funding statute. The responsibility for providing the required education remains on the States. And the Act establishes an enforceable substantive right to a free appropriate public education. Finally, the Act establishes an elaborate procedural mechanism to protect the rights of handicapped children. The procedures not only ensure that hearings conducted by the State are fair and adequate. They also effect Congress' intent that each child's individual educational needs be worked out through a process that begins in the local level and includes ongoing parental involvement, detailed procedural safeguards, and a right to judicial review.

In light of the comprehensive nature of the procedures and guarantees set out in the EHA and Congress' express efforts to place on local and state educational agencies the primary responsibility for developing a plan to accommodate the needs of each individual handicapped child, we find it difficult to believe that Congress also meant to leave undisturbed the ability of a handicapped child to go directly to court with an equal protection claim to a free appropriate public education. Not only would such a result render superfluous most of the detailed procedural protections outlined in the statute, but, more important, it would also run counter to Congress' view that the needs of handicapped children are best accommodated by having the parents and the local education agency work together to formulate an individualized plan for

---

11 Courts generally agree that the EHA may not be claimed as the basis for a §1983 action.

each handicapped child's education. No federal district court presented with a constitutional claim to a public education can duplicate that process.

We do not lightly conclude that Congress intended to preclude reliance on § 1983 as a remedy for a substantial equal protection claim. Since 1871, when it was passed by Congress, § 1983 has stood as an independent safeguard against deprivations of federal constitutional and statutory rights. Nevertheless, § 1983 is a statutory remedy and Congress retains the authority to repeal it or replace it with an alternative remedy.[15] The crucial consideration is what Congress intended.

In this case, we think Congress' intent is clear. Allowing a plaintiff to circumvent the EHA administrative remedies would be inconsistent with Congress' carefully tailored scheme. The legislative history gives no indication that Congress intended such a result. Rather, it indicates that Congress perceived the EHA as the most effective vehicle for protecting the constitutional right of a handicapped child to a public education. We conclude, therefore, that where the EHA is available to a handicapped child asserting a right to a free appropriate public education, based either on the EHA or on the Equal Protection Clause of the Fourteenth Amendment, the EHA is the exclusive avenue through which the child and his parents or guardian can pursue their claim.

NOTES AND QUESTIONS

1. If the EHA (now entitled Individuals with Disabilities Education Act) provides comprehensive relief, why did the plaintiffs want to use § 1983?

2. Should the "inference" of congressional intent to foreclose the enforcement of statutory rights be treated the same as congressional foreclosure of constitutional claims? Has the Court permitted Congress to in effect override a constitutional guarantee?

3. Does it make sense to infer that Congress, in seeking to strengthen the right to equal educational opportunity, cut off a very effective remedy under § 1983, *i.e.*, one providing for damages and attorney fees? If Congress feels the Court has misconstrued its intent, may it now overrule the *Smith* decision?

   In fact, in 1986 Congress enacted the Handicapped Children's Protection Act, which provides that nothing in the EHA shall be read to foreclose relief under any other federal law. *See* 20 U.S.C. § 1415(f). Does Congress have authority to override a Supreme Court decision in this manner?

4. The Court, in *Fitzgerald v. Barnstable School Committee*, 555 U.S. 246 (2009), unanimously held that Title IX of the Education Amendments of 1972, which prohibits sex discrimination by educational institutions that receive federal financial assistance, "was not meant to be an exclusive mechanism for addressing gender discrimination in schools, or a substitute for § 1983 suits as a means of enforcing constitutional

rights." *Id.* at 258. Therefore, the plaintiff in a peer-on-peer sexual harassment case is not precluded from asserting a § 1983 claim to redress unconstitutional gender discrimination in schools. The Court posed two questions: (1) whether congressional intent to foreclose could be found in the text or legislative history of Title IX, and (2) whether the rights and protections of Title IX were the same as those protected under § 1983 and the Equal Protection Clause. Distinguishing prior cases, such as *Sea Clammers, supra,* and *Smith, supra,* where the statute at issue required plaintiffs to comply with particular procedures and/or to exhaust particular administrative remedies before filing a lawsuit, the Court noted that Title IX has no administrative exhaustion requirement and no notice provisions. Recognizing "the divergent coverage of Title IX and the Equal Protection Clause, as well as the absence of a comprehensive remedial scheme comparable to those at issue in [prior cases]," the Court ruled that allowing a § 1983 constitutional claim would not thwart an elaborate, comprehensive congressional enforcement scheme, nor would a concurrent § 1983 cause of action circumvent congressionally required procedures.

5. In *Madigan v. Levin,* 692 F.3d 607 (7th Cir. 2012), *certiorari dismissed as improvidently granted,* 571 U.S. 1 (2013), the Seventh Circuit rejected the argument that Congress intended the Age Discrimination in Employment Act to be the exclusive remedy for age bias claims brought by government employees. The Seventh Circuit, contrary to the First, Fourth, Fifth, Ninth, Tenth, and D.C. Circuits, reasoned that the § 1983 equal protection remedy and the ADEA cause of action could coexist, and that it was unlikely that Congress intended the statute to preclude constitutional age bias claims.

PROBLEM: SIX

This is an appeal from the summary judgment granted by the district court to defendant Fort Wayne Community Schools on a teacher's claim, under 42 U.S.C. § 1983, alleging racial and sexual discrimination in her discharge from employment.

The district court held that the plaintiff's complaint stated a claim for employment discrimination, for which the remedy is found exclusively in Title VII, 42 U.S.C. § 2000e, and that plaintiff was bound by Title VII's administrative exhaustion requirements, including the filing of a charge of discrimination with the EEOC and the receipt of notice of a right to sue in federal court. The plaintiff had not satisfied these exhaustion requirements in pursuing her § 1983 claim, and the district court accordingly granted summary judgment against her.

The plaintiff contends that as a state government employee she can base her § 1983 claim on the alleged violations of her Fourteenth Amendment right to equal protection, irrespective of whether the school's conduct also violated Title VII. The defendant asserts that the plaintiff's Fourteenth Amendment rights are not independent of the rights provided her under Title VII, and that Congress intended Title VII to preempt § 1983 in the area of public employment discrimination.

Title VII prohibits employment discrimination based on race or sex. It provides a comprehensive administrative and judicial remedy, including back wages, damages, and attorney's fees. The Fourteenth Amendment's Equal Protection Clause prohibits intentional discrimination based on membership in a particular class, including acts of employment discrimination. The plaintiff contends that the substantive basis of her § 1983 action is the defendant's violation of the Fourteenth Amendment's Equal Protection Clause.

1. May the plaintiff use § 1983 to enforce Title VII rights? How should the court decide this question, and who carries the burden of proof?

2. How is it determined whether the Title VII remedy forecloses the plaintiff's right to bring an equal protection claim under § 1983? Is this different from the issue raised in question one?

3. Can the plaintiff use § 1981, in addition to § 1983 and Title VII, to challenge the racially discriminatory discharge from employment? Review *Johnson v. Railway Express* and *Jett v. Independent School District*. Assuming an action may be brought against a government entity under § 1981, what statute of limitations would govern this claim?

PARRATT V. TAYLOR
451 U.S. 527 (1981)

Justice REHNQUIST delivered the opinion of the Court.

The respondent is an inmate at the Nebraska Penal and Correctional Complex who ordered by mail certain hobby materials valued at $23.50. The hobby materials were lost and respondent brought suit under 42 U.S.C. § 1983 to recover their value. At first blush one might well inquire why respondent brought an action in federal court to recover damages of such a small amount for negligent loss of property, but because 28 U.S.C. § 1343, the predicate for the jurisdiction of the United States District Court, contains no minimum dollar limitation, he was authorized by Congress to bring his action under that section if he met its requirements and if he stated a claim for relief under 42 U.S.C. § 1983. Respondent claimed that his property was negligently lost by prison officials in violation of his rights under the Fourteenth Amendment to the United States Constitution. More specifically, he claimed that he had been deprived of property without due process of law.

The facts underlying this dispute are not seriously contested. Respondent paid for the hobby materials he ordered with two drafts drawn on his inmate account by prison officials. The packages arrived at the complex and were signed for by two employees who worked in the prison hobby center. One of the employees was a civilian and the other was an inmate. Respondent was in segregation at the time and was not permitted to have the hobby materials. Normal prison procedures for the handling of mail packages is that upon arrival they are either delivered to the prisoner who signs a receipt for the package or the prisoner is notified to pick up the package and to sign a receipt. No inmate other than the one to whom the package is addressed is supposed to sign for a package. After being released from segregation, respondent contacted several prison officials regarding the whereabouts of his packages. The officials were never able to locate the packages or to determine what caused their disappearance.

In 1976, respondent commenced this action against the petitioners, the Warden and Hobby Manager of the prison, in the District Court seeking to recover the value of the hobby materials which he claimed had been lost as a result of the petitioners' negligence. Respondent alleged that petitioners' conduct deprived him of property without due process of law in violation of the Fourteenth Amendment of the United States Constitution. Respondent chose to proceed in the United States District Court under 28 U.S.C. § 1343 and 42 U.S.C. § 1983, even though the State of Nebraska had a tort claims procedure which provided a remedy to persons who suffered tortious losses at the hands of the State.

Nothing in the language of § 1983 or its legislative history limits the statute solely to intentional deprivations of constitutional rights. Section 1983, unlike its criminal counterpart, 18 U.S.C. § 242, has never been found by this Court to contain a state-of-mind requirement. The Court recognized as much in *Monroe v. Pape*.

Accordingly, in any § 1983 action the initial inquiry must focus on whether the two essential elements to a § 1983 action are present: (1) whether the conduct complained of was committed by a person acting under color of state law; and (2) whether this conduct deprived a person of rights, privileges, or immunities secured by the Constitution or laws of the United States.

The only deprivation respondent alleges in his complaint is that "his rights under the Fourteenth Amendment of the Constitution of the United State were violated. That he was deprived of his property and Due Process of Law." As such, respondent's claims differ from the claims which were before us in *Monroe v. Pape*, which involved violations of the Fourth Amendment. Respondent here refers to no other right, privilege, or immunity secured by the Constitution or federal laws other than the Due Process Clause of the Fourteenth Amendment *simpliciter*.

Unquestionably, respondent's claim satisfies three prerequisites of a valid due process claim: the petitioners acted under color of state law; the hobby kit falls within the definition of property; and the alleged loss, even though negligently caused, amounted to a deprivation. Standing alone, however, these three elements do not establish a violation of the Fourteenth Amendment. Nothing in that Amendment protects against all deprivations of life, liberty, or property by the State. The Fourteenth Amendment protects only against deprivations "without due process of law." Our inquiry therefore must focus on whether the respondent has suffered a deprivation of property without due process of law. In particular, we must decide whether the tort remedies which the State of Nebraska provides as a means of redress for property deprivations satisfy the requirements of procedural due process.

This Court has never directly addressed the question of what process is due a person when an employee of a State negligently takes his property. In some cases this Court has held that due process requires a predeprivation hearing before the State interferes with any liberty or property interest enjoyed by its citizens. In most of these cases, however, the deprivation of property was pursuant to some established state procedure and "process" could be offered before any actual deprivation took place.

We have, however, recognized that postdeprivation remedies made available by the State can satisfy the Due Process Clause. In such cases, the normal predeprivation notice and opportunity to be heard is pretermitted if the State provides a postdeprivation remedy. In *North American Cold Storage Co. v. Chicago*, we upheld the right of a State to seize and destroy unwholesome food without a preseizure hearing. The possibility of erroneous destruction of property was outweighed by the fact that the public health emergency justified immediate action and the owner of the property could recover his damages in an action at law after the incident. In *Ewing v. Mytinger & Casselberry, Inc.*, we upheld under the Fifth Amendment Due Process Clause the summary seizure and destruction of drugs without a preseizure hearing. These cases recognize that either the necessity of quick action by the State or the impracticality of providing any meaningful predeprivation process, when coupled with the availability of some meaningful means by which to assess the propriety of the State's action at some time after the initial taking, can satisfy the requirements of procedural due process.

The justifications which we have found sufficient to uphold takings of property without any pre-deprivation process are applicable to a situation such as the present one involving a tortious loss of a prisoner's property as a result of a random and unauthorized act by a state employee. In such a case, the loss is not a result of some established state procedure and the State cannot predict precisely when the loss will occur. It is difficult to conceive of how the State could provide a meaningful hearing before the deprivation takes place. The loss of property, although attributable to the State as action under "color of law," is in almost all cases beyond the control of the State. Indeed, in most cases it is not only impracticable, but impossible, to provide a meaningful hearing before the deprivation. That does not mean, of course, that the State can take property without providing a meaningful postdeprivation hearing. The prior cases which have excused the prior-hearing requirement have rested in part on the availability of some meaningful opportunity subsequent to the initial taking for a determination of rights and liabilities.

Application of the principles recited above to this case leads us to conclude the respondent has not alleged a violation of the Due Process Clause of the Fourteenth Amendment. Although he has been deprived of property under color of state law, the deprivation did not occur as a result of some established state procedure. Indeed, the deprivation occurred as a result of the unauthorized failure of agents of the State to follow established state procedure. There is no contention that the procedures themselves are inadequate nor is there any contention that it was practicable for the State to provide a predeprivation hearing. Moreover, the State of Nebraska has provided respondent with the means by which he can receive redress for the deprivation. The State provides a remedy to persons who believe they have suffered a tortious loss at the hands of the State. Through this tort claims procedure the State hears and pays claims of prisoners housed in its penal institutions. This procedure was in existence at the time of the loss here in question but respondent did not use it. It is argued that the State does not adequately protect the respondent's interests because it provides only for an action against the State as opposed to its individual employees, it contains no provisions for punitive damages, and there is no right to a trial by jury. Although the state remedies may not provide the respondent with all the relief which may have been available if he could have proceeded under § 1983, that does not mean that the state remedies are not adequate to satisfy the requirements of due process. The remedies provided could have fully compensated the respondent for the property loss he suffered, and we hold that they are sufficient to satisfy the requirements of due process.

Our decision today is fully consistent with our prior cases. To accept respondent's argument that the conduct of the state officials in this case constituted a violation of the Fourteenth Amendment would almost necessarily result in turning every alleged injury which may have been inflicted by a state official acting under "color of law" into a violation of the Fourteenth Amendment cognizable under § 1983. It is hard to perceive any logical stopping place to such a line of reasoning. Presumably, under this rationale any party who is involved in nothing more than an automobile accident with a state official could allege a constitutional violation under § 1983. Such reasoning "would make of the Fourteenth Amendment a font to tort law to be superimposed upon whatever systems may already be administered by the States." *Paul v. Davis.* We do not think that the drafters of the Fourteenth Amendment intended the Amendment to play such a role in our society.

Justice BLACKMUN, concurring.

While I join the Court's opinion in this case, I write separately to emphasize my understanding of its narrow reach. This suit concerns the deprivation only of property and was brought only against supervisory personnel, whose simple "negligence" was assumed but, on this record, not actually proved. I do not read the Court's opinion as applicable to a case concerning deprivation of life or of liberty. I also do not understand the Court to intimate that the sole content of the Due Process Clause is procedural regularity. I continue to believe that there are certain governmental actions that, even if undertaken with a full panoply of procedural protection, are, in and of themselves, antithetical to fundamental notions of due process.

NOTES AND QUESTIONS

1. Is the Court interpreting the scope of § 1983 or the meaning of procedural due process? Does the availability of state remedies always foreclose a § 1983 claim? If so, has the Court *sub silentio* overruled *Monroe*'s holding that the federal remedy is "supplemental" to the state remedy?

2. In light of *Parratt*, would the plaintiffs in *Monroe*, who claimed Fourth Amendment violations, be denied a federal remedy and be relegated to a state court suit for false arrest and malicious prosecution? Did the deprivation in *Monroe* occur "as a result of some established procedure"? How are the cases distinguishable?

3. How "adequate" must the state remedy be to satisfy due process? Must it be as complete as the § 1983 remedy?

4. What if prison guards had intentionally deprived Parratt of his property? Should the analysis be the same? In *Hudson v. Palmer*, 468 U.S. 517 (1984), the Court reasoned:

> While Parratt is necessarily limited by its facts to negligent deprivations of property, it is evident that its reasoning applies as well to intentional deprivations of property. The underlying rationale of Parratt is that when deprivations of property are effected through random and unauthorized conduct of a state employee, predeprivation procedures are simply "impracticable" since the state cannot know when such deprivations will occur. We can discern no logical distinction between negligent and intentional deprivations of property insofar as the "practicability" of affording predeprivation process is concerned. The state can no more anticipate and control in advance the random and unauthorized intentional conduct of its employees than it can anticipate similar negligent conduct. Arguably, intentional acts are even more difficult to anticipate because one bent on intentionally depriving a person of his property might well take affirmative steps to avoid signaling his intent.
>
> If negligent deprivations of property do not violate the Due Process Clause because predeprivation process is impracticable, it follows that intentional deprivations do not violate that Clause provided, of course, that adequate state postdeprivation remedies are available. Accordingly, we hold that an unauthorized intentional deprivation of property by a state employee does not constitute a violation of the procedural requirements of the Due Process Clause of the Fourteenth Amendment if a meaningful post-deprivation remedy for the loss is available. For intentional, as for negligent deprivations of property by state employees, the state's action is not complete until and unless it provides or refuses to provide a suitable postdeprivation remedy.

DANIELS V. WILLIAMS

474 U.S. 327 (1986)

Justice REHNQUIST delivered the opinion of the Court.

In *Parratt v. Taylor* a state prisoner sued under 42 U.S.C. § 1983, claiming that prison officials had negligently deprived him of his property without due process of law. Petitioner's claim in this case, which also rests on an alleged Fourteenth Amendment "deprivation" caused by the negligent conduct of a prison official, leads us to reconsider our statement in *Parratt* that "the alleged loss, even though negligently caused, amounted to a deprivation." We conclude that the Due Process Clause is simply not implicated by a *negligent* act of an official causing unintended loss of or injury to life, liberty or property.

In this § 1983 action, petitioner seeks to recover damages for back and ankle injuries alleg-edly sustained when he fell on a prison stairway. He claims that, while an inmate at the city jail in Richmond, Virginia, he slipped on a pillow negligently left on the stairs by respondent, a cor-rectional deputy stationed at the jail. Respondent's negligence, the argument runs, "deprived" petitioner of his "liberty" interest in freedom from bodily injury; because respondent maintains that he is entitled to the defense of sovereign immunity in a state tort suit, petitioner is without an "adequate" state remedy. Accordingly, the deprivation of liberty was without "due process of law."

In *Parratt*, we granted certiorari, "to decide whether mere negligence will support a claim for relief under § 1983." After examining the language, legislative history and prior interpreta-tions of the statute, we concluded that § 1983, unlike its criminal counterpart, 18 U.S.C. § 242, contains no state-of-mind requirement independent of that necessary to state a violation of the underlying constitutional right. We adhere to that conclusion. But in any given § 1983 suit, the plaintiff must still prove a violation of the underlying constitutional right; and depending on the right, merely negligent conduct may not be enough to state a claim. *See, e.g., Arlington Heights v. Metropolitan Housing Dev. Corp.* (invidious discriminatory purpose required for claim of racial discrimination under the Equal Protection Clause); *Estelle v. Gamble* ("deliberate indifference" to prisoner's serious illness or injury sufficient to constitute cruel and unusual punishment under the Eighth Amendment).

The only tie between the facts of this case and anything governmental in nature is the fact that respondent was a sheriff's deputy at the Richmond city jail and petitioner was an inmate confined in that jail. But while the Due Process Clause of the Fourteenth Amendment obviously speaks to some facets of this relationship, we do not believe its protections are triggered by lack of due care by prison officials. Where a government official's act causing injury to life, liberty or property is merely negligent, "no procedure for compensation is *constitutionally* required." *Parratt* (Powell, J., concurring in result) (emphasis added.)[1]

Petitioner also suggests that artful litigants, undeterred by a requirement that they plead more than mere negligence, will often be able to allege sufficient facts to support a claim of intentional deprivation. In the instant case, for example, petitioner notes that he could have alleged that the pillow was left on the stairs with the intention of harming him. This invitation to "artful" pleading, petitioner contends, would engender sticky (and needless) disputes over what is fairly pleaded. What's more, requiring complainants to allege something more than neg-ligence would raise serious questions about what "more" than negligence—intent, recklessness or "gross negligence"—is required,[3] and indeed about what these elusive terms mean. But even if accurate, petitioner's observations do not carry the day. In the first place, many branches of

---

[1] Accordingly, we need not decide whether, as petitioner contends, the possibility of a sovereign immunity defense in a Virginia tort suit would render that remedy "inadequate" under Parratt and Hudson v. Palmer.

[3] Despite his claim about what he might have pleaded, petitioner concedes that respondent was at most negligent. Accordingly, this case affords us no occasion to consider whether something less than intentional conduct, such as recklessness or "gross negligence," is enough to trigger the protections of the Due Process Clause.

the law abound in nice distinctions that may be troublesome but have been thought nonetheless necessary. More important, the difference between one end of the spectrum—negligence—and the other—intent—is abundantly clear. In any event, we decline to trivialize the Due Process Clause in an effort to simplify constitutional litigation.

NOTES AND QUESTIONS

1. If the deprivation had been intentional, would *Parratt* have barred plaintiff's claim that he was deprived of a liberty interest without due process of law? Should *Parratt* apply to deprivations of liberty? Is the state more able to predict when random deprivations of liberty will occur?

2. Does the Court clarify what "state of mind" must be pleaded in a procedural due process case? *See* footnote 3.

3. **Substantive Due Process:** Review Justice Blackmun's concurring opinion in *Parratt*. Could the plaintiff have avoided *Parratt* entirely by pleading egregious abuse of government power, *i.e.*, a violation of substantive due process? In *County of Sacramento v. Lewis*, 523 U.S. 833 (1998), the Court reasoned that abuse of executive power must "shock the conscience" to be actionable as a substantive due process violation. However, it noted that sometimes "deliberate indifference" to serious constitutional rights violations may be egregious enough to satisfy this standard, *i.e.*, where medical care is denied to pretrial detainees. On the other hand, in cases where actual deliberation is impossible, *i.e.*, prison officials facing a riot or police officers deciding whether to give chase, "only a purpose to cause harm will satisfy the shocks-the-conscience test." Because there was no evidence that the high speed chase at issue in that case was done with "intent to harm the suspects," it could not give rise to liability under substantive due process.

   The appropriate "state-of-mind" requirement to prove a substantive due process violation returned to the Court in 2015. In *Kingsley v. Hendrickson*, 135 S. Ct. 2466 (2015), a pretrial detainee sued jail guards for their alleged use of excessive force in violation of substantive due process. He challenged the jury instructions, which required him to prove the jail guards actually knew that their use of force presented a risk of serious harm to Kingsley, but they acted "with reckless disregard" for his rights and safety—this is the subjective deliberate indifference test that governs convicted inmates' Eighth Amendment claims. The Court distinguished *Lewis*, which held that in situations where there is no time for deliberation the defendant must intend to commit the challenged acts in question. Here, it was undisputed that the guards intended to tase Kingsley, even after he was lying facedown with his hands cuffed behind his back. The Court held that, in deciding whether force deliberately used is "constitutionally speaking excessive" under substantive due process, courts should apply an *objective* standard. A pretrial detainee, unlike a convicted inmate, need not prove the *subjective* state of mind of the jail guards in a particular case, but must only show "that the force purposefully or knowingly used against him was objectively unreasonable"—the standard required by the Fourth Amendment. Because pretrial detainees are presumed innocent, they cannot be subjected to any punishment, and they need not show intent to punish, but only that the actions are "not rationally related to a legitimate non-punitive governmental purpose" or that the actions "appear excessive in relation to that purpose." *See* Rosalie Berger Levinson, Kingsley *Breathes New Life into Substantive Due Process*, 93 NOTRE DAME L. REV. 357 (2017).

4. Note that the Court leaves open the question whether a sovereign immunity defense renders the state remedy inadequate. *See* footnote 1. How can a "remedy" be considered "adequate" if state immunity precludes relief?

ZINERMON V. BURCH
494 U.S. 113 (1990)

Justice BLACKMUN delivered the opinion of the Court.

Respondent Burch brought this suit under 42 U.S.C. § 1983 against the 11 petitioners, who are physicians, administrators, and staff members at Florida State Hospital (FSH), and others. Respondent alleges that petitioners deprived him of his liberty, without due process of law, by admitting him to FSH as a "voluntary" mental patient when he was incompetent to give informed consent to his admission. Burch contends that in his case petitioners should have afforded him procedural safeguards required by the Constitution before involuntary commitment of a mentally ill person, and that petitioners' failure to do so violated his due process rights.

Petitioners argue that Burch's complaint failed to state a claim under § 1983 because, in their view, it alleged only a random, unauthorized violation of the Florida statutes governing admission of mental patients. Their argument rests on *Parratt v. Taylor* and *Hudson v. Palmer* where this Court held that a deprivation of a constitutionally protected property interest caused by a state employee's random, unauthorized conduct does not give rise to a § 1983 procedural due process claim, unless the State fails to provide an adequate postdeprivation remedy. The Court in those two cases reasoned that in a situation where the State cannot predict and guard in advance against a deprivation, a postdeprivation tort remedy is all the process the State can be expected to provide, and is constitutionally sufficient.

Because this case concerns the propriety of a Rule 12(b)(6) dismissal, the question before us is a narrow one. We decide only whether the *Parratt* rule necessarily means that Burch's complaint fails to allege any deprivation of due process, because he was constitutionally entitled to nothing more than what he received—an opportunity to sue petitioners in tort for his allegedly unlawful confinement. The broader questions of what procedural safeguards the Due Process

Clause requires in the context of an admission to a mental hospital, and whether Florida's statutes meet these constitutional requirements, are not presented in this case. Burch did not frame his action as a challenge to the constitutional adequacy of Florida's mental health statutes. Both before the Eleventh Circuit and in his brief here, he disavowed any challenge to the statutes themselves, and restricted his claim to the contention that petitioners' failure to provide constitutionally adequate safeguards in his case violated his due process rights.

II

A

On December 7, 1981, Burch was found wandering along a Florida highway, appearing to be hurt and disoriented. He was taken to Apalachee Community Mental Health Services (ACMHS) in Tallahassee. ACMHS is a private mental health care facility designated by the State to receive patients suffering from mental illness. Its staff in their evaluation forms stated that, upon his arrival at ACMHS, Burch was hallucinating, confused, psychotic, and believed he was "in heaven." His face and chest were bruised and bloodied, suggesting that he had fallen or had been attacked. Burch was asked to sign forms giving his consent to admission and treatment. He did so. He remained at ACMHS for three days, during which time the facility's staff diagnosed his condition as paranoid schizophrenia and gave him psychotropic medication. On December 10, the staff found that Burch was "in need of longer-term stabilization," and referred him to FSH, a public hospital owned and operated by the State as a mental health treatment facility. Later that day, Burch signed forms requesting admission and authorizing treatment at FSH. He was then taken to FSH by a county sheriff.

Upon his arrival at FSH, Burch signed other forms for voluntary admission and treatment. One form, entitled "Request for Voluntary Admission," recited that the patient requests admission for "observation, diagnosis, care and treatment of [my] mental condition," and that the patient, if admitted, agrees "to accept such treatment as may be prescribed by members of the medical and psychiatric staff in accordance with the provisions of expressed and informed consent."

On December 23, Burch signed a form entitled "Authorization for Treatment." This form stated that he authorized "the professional staff of [FSH] to administer treatment, except electroconvulsive treatment"; that he had been informed of "the purpose of treatment; common side effects thereof; alternative treatment modalities; approximate length of care," and of his power to revoke consent to treatment; and that he had read and fully understood the Authorization. Petitioner Zinermon, a staff physician at FSH, signed the form as the witness.

Burch remained at FSH until May 7, 1982, five months after his initial admission to ACMHS. During that time, no hearing was held regarding his hospitalization and treatment.

After his release, Burch complained that he had been admitted inappropriately to FSH and did not remember signing a voluntary admission form. His complaint reached the Florida Human Rights Advocacy Committee of the State's Department of Health and Rehabilitation Services. The Committee investigated and replied to Burch by letter dated April 4, 1984. The letter stated that Burch in fact had signed a voluntary admission form, but that there was "docu-mentation that you were heavily medicated and disoriented on admission and . . . you were probably not competent to be signing legal documents." The letter also stated that, at a meeting of the Committee with FSH staff on August 4, 1983, "hospital administration was made aware that they were very likely asking medicated clients to make decisions at a time when they were not mentally competent."

B

Burch's complaint thus alleges that he was admitted and detained at FSH for five months under Florida's statutory provisions for "voluntary" admission. These provisions are part of a comprehensive statutory scheme under which a person may be admitted to a mental hospital in several different ways.

First, Florida provides for short-term emergency admission. If there is reason to believe that a person is mentally ill and likely "to injure himself or others" or is in "need of care or treat-ment and lacks sufficient capacity to make a responsible application on his own behalf," he may immediately be detained for up to 48 hours.

Second, under a court order a person may be detained at a mental health facility for up to five days for evaluation, if he is likely "to injure himself or others" or if he is in "need of care or treatment which, if not provided, may result in neglect or refusal to care for himself and . . . such neglect or refusal poses a real and present threat of substantial harm to his well-being."

Third, a person may be detained as an involuntary patient, if he meets the same criteria as for evaluation, and if the facility administrator and two mental health professionals recommend involuntary placement. Before involuntary placement, the patient has a right to notice, a judi-cial hearing, appointed counsel, access to medical records and personnel, and an independent expert examination. If the court determines that the patient meets the criteria for involuntary placement, it then decides whether the patient is competent to consent to treatment. If not, the court appoints a guardian advocate to make treatment decisions. After six months, the facility must either release the patient, or seek a court order for continued placement by stating the reasons therefor, summarizing the patient's treatment to that point, and submitting a plan for future treatment.

Finally, a person may be admitted as a voluntary patient. Mental hospitals may admit for treatment any adult "making application by express and informed consent," if he is "found to show evidence of mental illness and to be suitable for treatment." "Express and informed con-sent" is defined as "consent voluntarily given in writing after sufficient explanation and disclo-sure . . . to enable the person . . . to make a knowing and willful decision without any element of force, fraud, deceit, duress, or other form of constraint or coercion." A voluntary patient may request discharge at any time. If he does, the facility administrator must either release him within three days, or initiate the involuntary placement process. At the time of his admission and each six months thereafter, a voluntary patient and his legal guardian or representatives must be notified in writing of the right to apply for a discharge.

Burch, in apparent compliance with [the section providing for voluntary commitment] was admitted by signing forms applying for voluntary admission. He alleges, however, that petitioners violated this statute in admitting him as a voluntary patient, because they knew or should have known that he was incapable of making an informed decision as to his admission. He claims that he was entitled to receive the procedural safeguards provided by Florida's involuntary placement procedure, and that petitioners violated his due process rights by failing to initiate this procedure. The question presented is whether these allegations suffice to state a claim under § 1983, in light of *Parratt* and *Hudson*.

III

A

Overlapping state remedies are generally irrelevant to the question of the existence of a cause of action under § 1983. A plaintiff, for example, may bring a § 1983 action for an unlawful search and seizure despite the fact that the search and seizure violated the State's Constitution or statutes, and despite the fact that there are common-law remedies for trespass and conversion.

This general rule applies in a straightforward way to two of the three kinds of § 1983 claims that may be brought against the State under the Due Process Clause of the Fourteenth Amendment. First, the Clause incorporates many of the specific protections defined in the Bill of Rights. A plaintiff may bring suit under § 1983 for state officials' violation of his rights to, *e.g.*, freedom of speech or freedom from unreasonable searches and seizures. Second, the Due Process Clause contains a substantive component that bars certain arbitrary, wrongful government actions "regardless of the fairness of the procedures used to implement them." As to these two types of claims, the constitutional violation actionable under § 1983 is complete when the wrongful action is taken. A plaintiff, under *Monroe v. Pape*, may invoke § 1983 regardless of any state-tort remedy that might be available to compensate him for the deprivation of these rights.

The Due Process Clause also encompasses a third type of protection, a guarantee of fair procedure. A § 1983 action may be brought for a violation of procedural due process, but here the existence of state remedies is relevant in a special sense. In procedural due process claims, the deprivation by state action of a constitutionally protected interest in "life, liberty, or property" is not in itself unconstitutional; what is unconstitutional is the deprivation of such an interest without due process of law. The constitutional violation actionable under § 1983 is not complete when the deprivation occurs; it is not complete unless and until the State fails to provide due process. Therefore, to determine whether a constitutional violation has occurred, it is necessary to ask what process the State provided, and whether it was constitutionally adequate. This inquiry would examine the procedural safeguards built into the statutory or administrative procedure of effecting the deprivation, and any remedies for erroneous deprivations provided by statute or tort law.

In this case, Burch does not claim that his confinement at FSH violated any of the specific guarantees of the Bill of Rights. Burch's complaint could be read to include a substantive due process claim, but that issue was not raised in the petition for certiorari, and we express no view on whether the facts Burch alleges could give rise to such a claim. The claim at issue falls within the third, or procedural, category of § 1983 claims based on the Due Process Clause.

B

Due process, as this Court often has said, is a flexible concept that varies with the particular situation. To determine what procedural protections the Constitution requires in a particular case, we weigh several factors:

> First, the private interest that will be affected by the official action; second, the risk of an erroneous deprivation of such interest through the procedures used, and the probable value, if any, of additional or substitute procedural safeguards; and finally, the Government's interest, including the function involved and the fiscal and administrative burdens that the additional or substitute procedural requirement would entail. *Mathews v. Eldridge*.

Applying this test, the Court usually has held that the Constitution requires some kind of a hearing before the State deprives a person of liberty or property. In some circumstances, however, the Court has held that a statutory provision for a postdeprivation hearing, or a common-law tort remedy for erroneous deprivation, satisfies due process.

This is where the *Parratt* rule comes into play. *Parratt* and *Hudson* represent a special case of the general *Mathews v. Eldridge* analysis, in which postdeprivation tort remedies are all the process that is due, simply because they are the only remedies the State could be expected to provide.

C

Petitioners argue that the dismissal under Rule 12(b)(6) was proper because, as in *Parratt* and *Hudson*, the State could not possibly have provided predeprivation process to prevent the kind of "random, unauthorized" wrongful deprivation of liberty Burch alleges, so the postdeprivation remedies provided by Florida's statutory and common law necessarily are all the process Burch was due.

Before turning to that issue, however, we must address a threshold question raised by Burch. He argues that *Parratt* and *Hudson* cannot apply to his situation, because those cases are limited to deprivations of property, not liberty.

Burch alleges that he was deprived of his liberty interest in avoiding confinement in a mental hospital without either informed consent or the procedural safeguards of the involuntary placement process. Petitioners do not seriously dispute that there is a substantial liberty interest in avoiding confinement in a mental hospital. Burch's confinement at FSH for five months without a hearing or any other procedure to determine either that he validly had consented to admission, or that he met the statutory standard for involuntary placement, clearly infringes on this liberty interest.

Burch argues that postdeprivation tort remedies are *never* constitutionally adequate for a deprivation of liberty, as opposed to property, so the *Parratt* rule cannot apply to this case. We, however, do not find support in precedent for a categorical distinction between a deprivation of liberty and one of property. In *Parratt* itself, the Court said that its analysis was "quite consistent with the approach taken" in *Ingraham v. Wright*, a liberty interest case.

It is true that *Parratt* and *Hudson* concerned deprivations of property. It is also true that Burch's interest in avoiding six months' confinement is of an order different from inmate Parratt's interest in mail-order materials valued at $23.50. But the reasoning of *Parratt* and *Hudson* emphasizes the State's inability to provide predeprivation process because of the random and unpredictable nature of the deprivation, not the fact that only property losses were at stake. In situations where the State feasibly can provide a predeprivation hearing before taking property, it generally must do so regardless of the adequacy of a postdeprivation tort remedy to compensate for the taking. Conversely, in situations where a predeprivation hearing is unduly burdensome in proportion to the liberty interest at stake or where the State is truly unable to anticipate and prevent a random deprivation of a liberty interest, postdeprivation remedies might satisfy due process. Thus, the fact that a deprivation of liberty is involved in this case does not automatically preclude application of the *Parratt* rule.

To determine whether, as petitioners contend, the *Parratt* rule necessarily precludes § 1983 liability in this case, we must ask whether predeprivation procedural safeguards could address the risk of deprivations of the kind Burch alleges. To do this, we examine the risk involved. The risk is that some persons who come into Florida's mental health facilities will apparently be willing to sign forms authorizing admission and treatment, but will be incompetent to give the "express and informed consent" required for voluntary placement under § 394.465(1)(a). Indeed, the very nature of mental illness makes it foreseeable that a person needing mental health care will be unable to understand any proffered "explanation and disclosure of the subject matter" of the forms that person is asked to sign, and will be unable "to make a knowing and willful decision" whether to consent to admission. A person who is willing to sign forms but is incapable of making an informed decision is, by the same token, unlikely to benefit from the voluntary patient's statutory right to request discharge. Such a person thus is in danger of being confined indefinitely without benefit of the procedural safeguards of the involuntary placement process, a process specifically designed to protect persons incapable of looking after their own interests.

Persons who are mentally ill and incapable of giving informed consent to admission would not necessarily meet the statutory standard for involuntary placement, which requires either that they are likely to injure themselves or others, or that their neglect or refusal to care for themselves threatens their well-being. The involuntary placement process serves to guard against the confinement of a person who, though mentally ill, is harmless and can live safely outside an institution. Confinement of such a person not only violates Florida law, but also is unconstitutional. Thus, it is at least possible that if Burch had had an involuntary placement hearing, he would not have been found to meet the statutory standard for involuntary placement, and would not have been confined at FSH. Moreover, even assuming that Burch would have met the statutory requirements for involuntary placement, he still could have been harmed by being deprived of other protections built into the involuntary placement procedure, such as the appointment of a guardian advocate to make treatment decisions, and periodic judicial review of placement.

The very risks created by the application of the informed-consent requirement to the special context of mental health care are borne out by the facts alleged in this case. It appears from the exhibits accompanying Burch's complaint that he was simply given admission forms to sign by clerical workers, and, after he signed, was considered a voluntary patient. Burch alleges that petitioners knew or should have known that he was incapable of informed consent. This allegation is supported, at least as to petitioner Zinermon, by the psychiatrist's admission notes, described above, on Burch's mental state. Thus, the way in which Burch allegedly was admitted to FSH certainly did not ensure compliance with the statutory standard for voluntary admission. We now consider whether predeprivation safeguards would have any value in guarding against the kind of deprivation Burch allegedly suffered. Petitioners urge that here, as in *Parratt* and *Hudson*, such procedures could have no value at all, because the State cannot prevent its officials from making random and unauthorized errors in the admission process. We disagree. The Florida statutes, of course, do not allow incompetent persons to be admitted as "voluntary" patients. But the statutes do not direct any member of the facility staff to determine whether a person is competent to give consent, nor to initiate the involuntary placement procedure for every incompetent patient. A patient who is willing to sign forms but incapable of informed consent certainly cannot be relied on to protest his "voluntary" admission and demand that the involuntary placement procedure be followed. The staff are the only persons in a position to take notice of any misuse of the voluntary admission process, and to ensure that the proper procedure is followed.

Florida chose to delegate to petitioners a broad power to admit patients to FSH, *i.e.*, to effect what, in the absence of informed consent, is a substantial deprivation of liberty. Because petitioners had state authority to deprive persons of liberty, the Constitution imposed on them the State's concomitant duty to see that no deprivation occur without adequate procedural protections.

It may be permissible constitutionally for a State to have a statutory scheme like Florida's, which gives state officials broad power and little guidance in admitting mental patients. But when those officials fail to provide constitutionally required procedural safeguards to a person whom they deprive of liberty, the state officials cannot then escape liability by invoking *Parratt* and *Hudson*. It is immaterial whether the due process violation Burch alleges is best described as arising from petitioners' failure to comply with state procedures for admitting involuntary patients, or from the absence of a specific requirement that petitioners determine whether a patient is competent to consent to voluntary admission. Burch's suit is neither an action challenging the facial adequacy of a State's statutory procedures, nor an action based only on state officials' random and unauthorized violation of state laws. Burch is not simply attempting to blame the State for misconduct by its employees. He seeks to hold state officials accountable for their abuse of their broadly delegated, uncircumscribed power to effect the deprivation at issue.

This case, therefore, is not controlled by *Parratt* and *Hudson*, for three basic reasons:

First, petitioners cannot claim that the deprivation of Burch's liberty was unpredictable. Under Florida's statutory scheme, only a person competent to give informed consent may be admitted as a voluntary patient. There is, however, no specified way of determining, before a patient is asked to sign admission forms, whether he is competent. It is hardly unforeseeable that a person requesting treatment for mental illness might be incapable of informed consent, and that state officials with the power to admit patients might take their apparent willingness to be admitted at face value and not initiate involuntary placement procedures. Any erroneous deprivation will occur, if at all, at a specific, predictable point in the admission process—when a patient is given admission forms to sign.

Second, we cannot say that predeprivation process was impossible here. Florida already has an established procedure for involuntary placement. The problem is only to ensure that this procedure is afforded to all patients who cannot be admitted voluntarily, both those who are unwilling and those who are unable to give consent. In *Parratt*, the very nature of the deprivation made predeprivation process "impossible."

Here, in contrast, there is nothing absurd in suggesting that, had the State limited and guided petitioners' power to admit patients, the deprivation might have been averted. Burch's complaint alleges that petitioners "knew or should have known" that he was incompetent, and nonetheless admitted him as a voluntary patient in "willful, wanton, and reckless disregard" of his constitutional rights. Understood in context, the allegation means only that petitioners disregarded their duty to ensure that the proper procedures were followed, not that they, like the prison guard in *Hudson*, were bent upon effecting this substantive deprivation and would have done so despite any and all predeprivation safeguards. Moreover, it would indeed be strange to allow state officials to escape § 1983 liability for failing to provide constitutionally required procedural protections, by assuming that those procedures would be futile because the same state officials would find a way to subvert them.

Third, petitioners cannot characterize their conduct as "unauthorized" in the sense the term is used in *Parratt* and *Hudson*. The State delegated to them the power and authority to effect the very deprivation complained of here, Burch's confinement in a mental hospital, and also delegated to them the concomitant duty to initiate the procedural safeguards set up by state law to guard against unlawful confinement. In *Parratt* and *Hudson*, the state employees had no similar broad authority to deprive prisoners of their personal property, and no similar duty to initiate (for persons unable to protect their own interests) the procedural safeguards required before deprivations occur. The deprivation here is "unauthorized" only in the sense that it was not an act sanctioned by state law, but, instead, was a "depriv[ation] of constitutional rights . . . by an official's abuse of his position."

We conclude that petitioners cannot escape § 1983 liability by characterizing their conduct as a "random, unauthorized" violation of Florida law which the State was not in a position to predict or avert, so that all the process Burch could possibly be due is a postdeprivation damages remedy. Burch, according to the allegations of his complaint, was deprived of a substantial liberty interest without either valid consent or an involuntary placement hearing, by the very state officials charged with the power to deprive mental patients of their liberty and the duty to implement procedural safeguards. Such a deprivation is foreseeable, due to the nature of mental illness, and will occur, if at all, at a predictable point in the admission process. Unlike *Parratt* and *Hudson*, this case does not represent the special instance of the *Mathews* due process analysis where postdeprivation process is all that is due because no predeprivation safeguards would be of use in preventing the kind of deprivation alleged.

We express no view on the ultimate merits of Burch's claim; we hold only that his complaint was sufficient to state a claim under § 1983 for violation of his procedural due process rights.

Justice O'CONNOR, with whom THE CHIEF JUSTICE, Justice SCALIA and Justice KENNEDY join, dissenting.

Without doubt, respondent Burch alleges a serious deprivation of liberty, yet equally clearly he alleges no violation of the Fourteenth Amendment. The Court concludes that an allegation of state actors' wanton, unauthorized departure from a State's established policies and procedures, working a deprivation of liberty, suffices to support a procedural due process claim even though the State provides adequate post-deprivation remedies for that deprivation. The Court's opinion unnecessarily transforms well-established procedural due process doctrine and departs from controlling precedent. I respectfully dissent.

Application of *Parratt* and *Hudson* indicates that respondent has failed to state a claim allowing recovery under 42 U.S.C. § 1983. Petitioners' actions were unauthorized: they are alleged to have wrongly and without license departed from established state practices. Florida officials in a position to establish safeguards commanded that the voluntary admission process be employed only for consenting patients and that the involuntary hearing procedures be used to admit unconsenting patients. Yet it is alleged that petitioners "with willful, wanton and reckless disregard of and indifference to" Burch's rights contravened both commands. As in *Parratt*, the deprivation "occurred as a result of the unauthorized failure of agents of the State to follow established state procedure." The wanton or reckless nature of the failure indicates it to be random. The State could not foresee the particular contravention and was hardly "in a position to provide for predeprivation process" to ensure that officials bent upon subverting the State's requirements would in fact follow those procedures. For this wrongful deprivation resulting from an unauthorized departure from established state practice, Florida provides adequate post-deprivation remedies, as two courts below concluded, and which the Court and respondent do not dispute. *Parratt* and *Hudson* thus should govern this case and indicate that respondent has failed to allege a violation of the Fourteenth Amendment.

1. The Court lists three reasons why this case is not controlled by *Parratt*. Must all three of these distinguishing factors be present to avoid *Parratt*?

2. Why is pre-deprivation process possible in *Zinermon* but not *Parratt*? Is this the critical difference in the two cases?

3. The challenged conduct in *Zinermon* was not "unauthorized" because the responsible officials had been delegated the power and authority to "effect the deprivation" at issue. Is conduct which is contrary to state law or local ordinance always "unauthorized?" Does it depend on the level or rank of the official engaging in the challenged conduct, *i.e.*, would the result in *Parratt* be different if the warden had deprived the inmate of his property?

4. Would mandatory competency hearings safeguard against abuse? If the statute so provided, but the admitting personnel nonetheless found Burch competent to consent, would the existence of state remedies foreclose the federal claim?

PROBLEM: SEVEN

On December 19, 1980, Davidson was threatened by McMillian, a fellow inmate at the New Jersey State Prison at Leesburg. He sent a note reporting the incident that found its way to defendant Cannon, the Assistant Superintendent of the prison, who read the note and sent it on to defendant James, a corrections sergeant. The note, addressed to a civilian hearing officer, said:

> When I went back to the unit after seeing you McMillian was on the steps outside the unit. When I was going past him he told me 'I'll fuck you up you old mother-fucking fag. Go up to your cell, I be right there.' I ignored this and went to another person's cell and thought about it. Then I figured I should tell you so 'if' anything develops you would be aware. I'm quite content to let this matter drop but evidently McMillian isn't. Thank you. R. Davidson.

Cannon subsequently testified that he did not view the situation as urgent because on previous occasions when plaintiff had a serious problem he had contacted Cannon directly.

James received the note at about 2:00 P.M. on December 19, and was informed of its contents. James then attended to other matters, which he described as emergencies, and left the note on his desk unread. By the time he left the prison that evening James had forgotten about the note, and since neither he nor Cannon worked on December 20 or 21, the officers on duty at that time had not been informed of the threat. Davidson took no steps other than writing the note to alert the authorities that he feared an attack, and he did not request protective custody.

He testified that he did not foresee an attack, and that he wrote the note to exonerate himself in the event that McMillian started another fight. He also testified that he wanted officials to reprimand McMillian in order to forestall any future incident. On Sunday, December 21, McMillian attacked plaintiff with a fork, breaking his nose and inflicting other wounds to his face, neck, head and body.

Davidson brought this § 1983 suit in the United States District Court claiming that Cannon and James had violated his constitutional rights under the Eighth Amendment and the Due Process Clause of the Fourteenth Amendment. The relevant state law provides: "Neither a public entity nor a public employee is liable for any injury caused by a prisoner to another prisoner."

Does *Daniels* or *Parratt* foreclose plaintiff's suit? Respond to the following:

1. Does it matter whether the alleged procedural due process deprivation demonstrates intentional wrongdoing or deliberate indifference or negligence? Review Notes and Questions following *Daniels v. Williams*.
   No

2. Is this a challenge to random, unauthorized misconduct or to an official practice, or is this a *Zinermon* situation?

3. Does it matter that this is a deprivation of liberty, rather than property?
   No

4. Will the procedural and substantive due process and the Eighth Amendment claims be treated the same in terms of the relevance of state remedies?

5. Is the state remedy inadequate?

c.   Municipal (Entity) Liability

MONELL V. DEPARTMENT OF SOCIAL SERVICES
436 u.s. 658 (1978)

[The Supreme Court in this case was called upon to reconsider its holding in *Monroe v. Pape* that a city could not be considered a "person" within the meaning of § 1983. A group of female employees sued government officials as well as the department of social services and the city of New York for its official policy of compelling pregnant employees to take unpaid leaves of absence before such were required for medical reasons. The Court reviewed the legislative history surrounding passage of § 1983 which had provided the basis for its earlier holding in *Monroe*.]

Justice BRENNAN delivered the opinion of the Court.

There are three distinct stages in the legislative consideration of the bill which became the Civil Rights Act of 1871. On March 28, 1871, Representative Shellabarger, acting for a House select committee, reported H.R. 320, a bill "to enforce the provisions of the fourteenth amendment to the Constitution of the United States, and for other purposes." H.R. 320 contained four sections. Section 1, now codified as 42 U.S.C. § 1983, was the subject of only limited debate and was passed without amendment. Sections 2 through 4 dealt primarily with the "other purpose" of suppressing Ku Klux Klan violence in the Southern States. The wisdom and constitutionality of these sections—not § 1, now § 1983—were the subject of almost all congressional debate and each of these sections was amended. The House finished its initial debates on H.R. 320 on April 7, 1871, and one week later the Senate also voted out a bill. Again, debate on § 1 of the bill was limited and that section was passed as introduced.

Immediately prior to the vote on H.R. 320 in the Senate, Senator Sherman introduced his amendment. This was *not* an amendment to § 1 of the bill, but was to be added as § 7 at the end of the bill.

On April 18, 1871, the first conference committee completed its work on H.R. 320. The main features of the conference committee draft of the Sherman amendment were these: First, a cause of action was given to persons injured by

> any persons riotously and tumultuously assembled together . . . with intent to deprive any person of any right conferred upon him by the Constitution and laws of the United States, or to deter him or punish him for exercising such right, or by reason of his race, color, or previous condition of servitude. . . .

Second, the bill provided that the action would be against the county, city or parish in which the riot had occurred and that it could be maintained by either the person injured or his legal representative. Third, unlike the amendment as proposed, the conference substitute made the government defendant liable on the judgment if it was not satisfied against individual defendants who had committed the violence.

In the ensuing debate on the first conference report, which was the first debate of any kind on the Sherman amendment, Senator Sherman explained that the purpose of his amendment was to enlist the aid of persons of property in the enforcement of the civil rights law by making their property "responsible" for Ku Klux Klan damage.

The first conference substitute passed the Senate but was rejected by the House. House opponents, within whose ranks were some who had supported § 1, thought the Federal Government could not, consistent with the Constitution, obligate municipal corporations to keep the peace if those corporations were neither so obligated nor so authorized by their state charters. And, because of this constitutional objection, opponents of the Sherman amendment were unwilling to impose damages liability for nonperformance of a duty which Congress could not require municipalities to perform.

The meaning of the legislative history sketched above can most readily be developed by first considering the debate on the report of the first conference committee. This debate shows conclusively that the constitutional objections raised against the Sherman amendment—on which our holding in *Monroe* was based—would not have prohibited congressional creation of a civil remedy against state municipal corporations that infringed federal rights.

C. Debate on § 1 of the Civil Rights Bill

In both Houses, statements of the supporters of § 1 corroborated that Congress, in enacting § 1, intended to give a broad remedy for violations of federally protected civil rights. Moreover, since municipalities through their official acts could, equally with natural persons, create the harms intended to be remedied by § 1, and, further, since Congress intended § 1 to be broadly construed, there is no reason to suppose that municipal corporations would have been excluded from the sweep of § 1. One need not rely on this inference alone, however, for the debates show that Members of Congress understood "persons" to include municipal corporations.

Representative Bingham, for example, in discussing § 1 of the bill, explained that he had drafted § 1 of the Fourteenth Amendment with the case of *Barron v. Mayor of Baltimore* (1833), especially in mind. "In [that] case the city had taken private property for public use, without compensation . . ., and there was no redress for the wrong." Bingham's further remarks clearly indicate his view that such takings by cities, as had occurred in *Barron*, would be redressable under § 1 of the bill. More generally, and as Bingham's remarks confirm, § 1 of the bill would logically be the vehicle by which Congress provided redress for taking, since that section provided the only civil remedy for Fourteenth Amendment violations and that Amendment unequivocally prohibited uncompensated takings.

In addition, by 1871, it was well understood that corporations should be treated as natural persons for virtually all purposes of constitutional and statutory analysis.

That the "usual" meaning of the word "person" would extend to municipal corporations is also evidenced by an Act of Congress which had been passed only months before the Civil Rights Act was passed. This Act provided that

> in all acts hereafter passed . . . the word 'person' may extend and be applied to bodies politic and corporate . . . unless the context shows that such words were intended to be used in a more limited sense. Act of Feb. 25, 1871, § 2, 16 STAT. 431.

Municipal corporations in 1871 were included within the phrase "bodies politic and corporate" and, accordingly, the "plain meaning" of § 1 is that local government bodies were to be included within the ambit of the persons who could be sued under § 1 of the Civil Rights Act.

II

Our analysis of the legislative history of the Civil Rights Act of 1871 compels the conclusion that Congress *did* intend municipalities and other local government units to be included among those persons to whom § 1983 applies.[54] Local governing bodies, therefore, can be sued directly under § 1983 for monetary, declaratory, or injunctive relief where, as here, the action that is alleged to be unconstitutional implements or executes a policy statement, ordinance, regulation, or decision officially adopted and promulgated by that body's officers. Moreover, although the touchstone of the § 1983 action against a government body is an allegation that official policy is responsible for a deprivation of rights protected by the Constitution, local governments, like every other § 1983 "person," by the very terms of the statute, may be sued for constitutional deprivations visited pursuant to governmental "custom" even though such a custom has not received formal approval through the body's official decisionmaking channels. As Mr. Justice Harlan, writing for the Court, said in *Adickes v. S.H. Kress & Co.*: "Congress included customs and usages [in § 1983] because of the persistent and widespread discriminatory practices of state officials. . . . Although not authorized by written law, such practices of state officials could well be so permanent and well settled as to constitute a 'custom or usage' with the force of law."

On the other hand, the language of § 1983, read against the background of the same legislative history, compels the conclusion that Congress did not intend municipalities to be held liable unless action pursuant to official municipal policy of some nature caused a constitutional tort. In particular, we conclude that a municipality cannot be held liable solely because it employs a tortfeasor—or, in other words, a municipality cannot be held liable under § 1983 on a *respondeat superior* theory.

We begin with the language of § 1983 as originally passed:

> *[A]ny person who*, under color of any law, statute, ordinance, regulation, custom, or usage of any State, *shall subject, or cause to be subjected*, any person . . . to the deprivation of any rights, privileges, or immunities secured by the Constitution of the United States, shall, any such law, statute, ordinance, regulation, custom, or usage of the State to the contrary notwithstanding, be liable to the party injured in any action at law, suit in equity, or other proper proceeding for redress. . . . (emphasis added).

The italicized language plainly imposes liability on a government that, under color of some official policy, "causes" an employee to violate another's constitutional rights. At the same time, that language cannot be easily read to impose liability vicariously on governing bodies solely on the basis of the existence of an employer-employee relationship with a tortfeasor.

---

54 There is certainly no constitutional impediment to municipal liability. "The Tenth Amendment's reservation of nondelegated powers to the States is not implicated by a federal-court judgment enforcing the express prohibitions of unlawful state conduct enacted by the Fourteenth Amendment." *Milliken v. Bradley.* Nor is there any basis for concluding that the Eleventh Amendment is a bar to municipal liability.

Equally important, creation of a federal law of *respondeat superior* would have raised all the constitutional problems associated with the obligation to keep the peace, an obligation Congress chose not to impose because it thought imposition of such an obligation unconstitutional. To this day, there is disagreement about the basis for imposing liability on an employer for the torts of an employee when the sole nexus between the employer and the tort is the fact of the employer-employee relationship. Nonetheless, two justifications tend to stand out. First is the common-sense notion that no matter how blameless an employer appears to be in an individual case, accidents might nonetheless be reduced if employers had to bear the cost of accidents. Second is the argument that the cost of accidents should be spread to the community as a whole on an insurance theory.[58]

The first justification is of the same sort that was offered for statutes like the Sherman amendment: "The obligation to make compensation for injury resulting from riot is, by arbitrary enactment of statutes, affirmatory law, and the reason of passing the statute is to secure a more perfect police regulation." This justification was obviously insufficient to sustain the amendment against perceived constitutional difficulties and there is no reason to suppose that a more general liability imposed for a similar reason would have been thought less constitutionally objectionable. The second justification was similarly put forward as a justification for the Sherman amendment: "we do not look upon [the Sherman amendment] as a punishment. It is a mutual insurance." Again, this justification was insufficient to sustain the amendment.

We conclude, therefore that a local government may not be sued under § 1983 for an injury inflicted solely by its employees or agents. Instead, it is when execution of a government's policy or custom, whether made by its lawmakers or by those whose edicts or acts may fairly be said to represent official policy, inflicts the injury that the government as an entity is responsible under § 1983. Since this case unquestionably involves official policy as the moving force of the constitutional violation found by the District Court, we must reverse the judgment below. In so doing, we have no occasion to address, and do not address, what the full contours of municipal liability under § 1983 may be. We have attempted only to sketch so much of the § 1983 cause of action against a local government as is apparent from the history of the 1871 Act and our prior cases, and we expressly leave further development of this action to another day.

NOTES AND QUESTIONS

1. Why does the Court set aside its interpretation of legislative history in *Monroe* to now find that the term "person" includes local government entities?

2. What limitations on municipal liability does the Court delineate? If *Monroe v. Pape* were litigated today, would the City of Chicago be held liable?

---

58   A third justification, often cited but which on examination is apparently insufficient to justify the doctrine of *respondeat superior*, is that liability follows the right to control the actions of a tortfeasor. By our decision in *Rizzo v. Goode*, we would appear to have decided that the mere right to control without any control or direction having been exercised and without any failure to supervise is not enough to support § 1983 liability.

3. Why does the Court reject liability imposed based on a *respondeat superior* theory—does the legislative history support this holding? Isn't there a difference between imposing vicarious liability on a city for the conduct of private citizens and holding the entity liable for the misconduct of its own government officials?

4. In *Los Angeles County, California v. Humphries*, 562 U.S. 29 (2010), the Supreme Court resolved a circuit split as to whether *Monell's* "policy or custom" requirement applies only to claims for monetary relief, or whether it extends to claims for prospective relief, "such as an injunction or declaratory judgment." The Court unanimously reasoned that Congress intended to hold cities liable under § 1983 only for their own violations of federal law and that the "policy or custom" requirement applied irrespective of the nature of the relief sought. Although by the time *Monell* reached the Supreme Court only the plaintiff's damages claim remained alive and the opinion expressed the concern that municipalities might have to pay large damages awards, *Monell's* "rejection of *respondeat superior* liability rested not on the municipality's economic needs," but on the fact that liability "must arise out of a municipality's own wrongful conduct."

5. What if the defendant, Department of Social Agencies, was a state, as opposed to county or municipal, entity? Could it be named as a "person"? The Supreme Court, in *Will v. Michigan Dep't of State Police*, 491 U.S. 58 (1989), held that a state is not a "person" as that term is used in § 1983. The Court reasoned that, unlike the issue in *Monell*, the question of suing a state and its agencies is clouded by the Eleventh Amendment, which was a dominant concern when legislators enacted § 1983. By holding that the term "person" does not include the state, the Court foreclosed a § 1983 suit against a state or an arm of the state even if suit was brought in state court and even if the state consented to suit (both of which are not barred by the Eleventh Amendment). However, the Supreme Court in *Will* then borrowed from Eleventh Amendment jurisprudence in holding that state officials may be sued in their official capacity for injunctive relief. Further, in *Hafer v. Melo*, 502 U.S. 21 (1991), the Court rejected a state official's argument that she could not be held *personally* liable under § 1983 for damages because she took the challenged action—discharging several state employees upon assuming office—in her official capacity. While *Will* precludes a § 1983 damage award against a state official in her official capacity (since this would in reality be a claim against the entity), a state official can be held liable for damages under § 1983 in her personal/individual capacity for action taken in her official capacity. In short, a § 1983 plaintiff who challenges the conduct of a state official and seeks both injunctive and monetary relief should sue the official in her official capacity for an injunction and in her personal/individual capacity for damages. *See also discussion of the Eleventh Amendment, infra.*

6. How is it to be determined whether the actions of a particular government official represent "official policy"?

i.   Liability for Conduct of "Policymakers"

PEMBAUR V. CITY OF CINCINNATI
475 U.S. 469 (1986)

Justice BRENNAN delivered the opinion of the Court, except as to Part II-B.

In *Monell v. New York City Dep't of Social Services* the Court concluded that municipal liability under 42 U.S.C. § 1983 is limited to deprivations of federally protected rights caused by action taken "pursuant to official municipal policy of some nature." The question presented is whether, and in what circumstances, a decision by municipal policymakers on a single occasion may satisfy this requirement.

I

Bertold Pembaur is a licensed Ohio physician and the sole proprietor of the Rockdale Medical Center, located in the city of Cincinnati in Hamilton County. During the spring of 1977, Simon Leis, the Hamilton County Prosecutor, began investigating charges that Pembaur fraudulently had accepted payments from state welfare agencies for services not actually provided to patients. A grand jury was convened, and the case was assigned to Assistant Prosecutor William Whalen. In April, the grand jury charged Pembaur in a six-count indictment.

During the investigation, the grand jury issued subpoenas for the appearance of two of Pembaur's employees. When these employees failed to appear as directed, the prosecutor obtained capiases for their arrest and detention from the Court of Common Pleas of Hamilton County.

On May 19, 1977, two Hamilton County Deputy Sheriffs attempted to serve the capiases at Pembaur's clinic. Pembaur . . . closed the door, which automatically locked from the inside, and wedged a piece of wood between it and the wall. Pembaur refused to let them enter, claiming that the police had no legal authority to be there and requesting that they leave.

Shortly thereafter, several Cincinnati police officers appeared. The Deputy Sheriffs explained the situation to them and asked that they speak to Pembaur. The Cincinnati police told Pembaur that the papers were lawful and that he should allow the Deputy Sheriffs to enter. When Pembaur refused, the Cincinnati police called for a superior officer. When he too failed to persuade Pembaur to open the door, the Deputy Sheriffs decided to call their supervisor for further instructions. Their supervisor told them to call Assistant Prosecutor Whalen and to follow his instructions. The Deputy Sheriffs then telephoned Whalen and informed him of the situation. Whalen conferred with County Prosecutor Leis, who told Whalen to instruct the Deputy

Sheriffs to "go in and get [the witnesses]." Whalen in turn passed these instructions along to the Deputy Sheriffs.

After a final attempt to persuade Pembaur voluntarily to allow them to enter, the Deputy Sheriffs tried unsuccessfully to force the door. City police officers, who had been advised of the County Prosecutor's instructions to "go in and get" the witnesses, obtained an axe and chopped down the door.

On April 20, 1981, Pembaur filed the present action in the United States District Court for the Southern District of Ohio against the city of Cincinnati, the county of Hamilton, the Cincinnati Police Chief, the Hamilton County Sheriff, the members of the Hamilton Board of County Commissioners (in their official capacities only), Assistant Prosecutor Whalen, and nine city and county police officers. Pembaur sought damages under 42 U.S.C. § 1983, alleging that the county and city police had violated his rights under the Fourth and Fourteenth Amendments. His theory was that, absent exigent circumstances, the Fourth Amendment prohibits police from searching an individual's home or business without a search warrant even to execute an arrest warrant for a third person. We agreed with that proposition in *Steagald v. United States*, decided the day after Pembaur filed this lawsuit. Pembaur sought $10 million in actual and $10 million in punitive damages, plus costs and attorney's fees.

II

A

Our analysis must begin with the proposition that "Congress did not intend municipalities to be held liable unless action pursuant to official municipal policy of some nature caused a constitutional tort." *Monell.* The "official policy" requirement was intended to distinguish acts of the *municipality* from acts of *employees* of the municipality, and thereby make clear that municipal liability is limited to action for which the municipality is actually responsible. *Monell* reasoned that recovery from a municipality is limited to acts that are, properly speaking, acts "of the municipality"—that is, acts which the municipality has officially sanctioned or ordered.

With this understanding, it is plain that municipal liability may be imposed for a single decision by municipal policymakers under appropriate circumstances. No one has ever doubted, for instance, that a municipality may be liable under § 1983 for a single decision by its properly constituted legislative body—whether or not that body had taken similar action in the past or intended to do so in the future—because even a single decision by such a body unquestionably constitutes an act of official government policy. *See, e.g., Newport v. Fact Concerts, Inc.* (city council cancelled license permitting concert because of dispute over content of performance); *Owen v. City of Independence* (city council passed resolution firing plaintiff without a pretermination hearing). But the power to establish policy is no more the exclusive province of the legislature at the local level than at the state or national level. *Monell's* language makes clear that it expressly envisioned other officials "whose acts or edicts may fairly be said to represent official policy," and whose decisions therefore may give rise to municipal liability under § 1983.

Indeed, any other conclusion would be inconsistent with the principles underlying § 1983. To be sure, "official policy" often refers to formal rules or understandings—often but not always committed to writing—that are intended to, and do, establish fixed plans of action to be followed under similar circumstances consistently and over time. That was the case in *Monell* itself, which involved a written rule requiring pregnant employees to take unpaid leaves of absence before such leaves were medically necessary. However, as in *Owen* and *Newport*, a government frequently chooses a course of action tailored to a particular situation and not intended to control decisions in later situations. If the decision to adopt that particular course of action is properly made by that government's authorized decisionmakers, it surely represents an act of official government "policy" as that term is commonly understood. More importantly, where action is directed by those who establish governmental policy, the municipality is equally responsible whether that action is to be taken only once or to be taken repeatedly. To deny compensation to the victim would therefore be contrary to the fundamental purpose of § 1983.

B

Having said this much, we hasten to emphasize that not every decision by municipal officers automatically subjects the municipality to § 1983 liability. Municipal liability attaches only where the decisionmaker possesses final authority to establish municipal policy with respect to the action ordered. The fact that a particular official—even a policymaking official—has discretion in the exercise of particular functions does not, without more, give rise to municipal liability based on an exercise of that discretion. *See, e.g., Oklahoma City v. Tuttle.* The official must also be responsible for establishing final government policy respecting such activity before the municipality can be held liable. Authority to make municipal policy may be granted directly by a legislative enactment or may be delegated by an official who possesses such authority, and of course, whether an official had final policymaking authority is a question of state law. However, like other governmental entities, municipalities often spread policymaking authority among various officers and official bodies. As a result, particular officers may have authority to establish binding county policy respecting particular matters and to adjust that policy for the county in changing circumstances. To hold a municipality liable for actions ordered by such officers exercising their policymaking authority is no more an application of the theory of *respondeat superior* than was holding the municipalities liable for the decisions of the city councils in *Owen* and *Newport*. In each case municipal liability attached to a single decision to take unlawful action made by municipal policymakers. We hold that municipal liability under § 1983 attaches where—and only where—a deliberate choice to follow a course of action is made from among various alternatives by the official or officials responsible for establishing final policy with respect to the subject matter in question.

C

Applying this standard to the case before us, we have little difficulty concluding that the Court of Appeals erred in dismissing petitioner's claim against the county. The Deputy Sheriffs who attempted to serve the capiases at petitioner's clinic found themselves in a difficult situation. Unsure of the proper course of action to follow, they sought instructions from their supervisors. The instructions they received were to follow the orders of the County Prosecutor. The Prosecutor made a considered decision based on his understanding of the law and commanded the officers forcibly to enter petitioner's clinic. That decision directly caused the violation of petitioner's Fourth Amendment rights.

Respondent argues that the County Prosecutor lacked authority to establish municipal policy respecting law enforcement practices because only the County Sheriff may establish policy respecting such practices. Respondent suggests that the County Prosecutor was merely rendering "legal advice" when he ordered the Deputy Sheriffs to "go in and get" the witnesses. Consequently, the argument concludes, the action of the individual Deputy Sheriffs in following this advice and forcibly entering petitioner's clinic was not pursuant to a properly established municipal policy.

We might be inclined to agree with respondent if we thought that the Prosecutor had only rendered "legal advice." However, the Court of Appeals concluded, based upon its examination of Ohio law, that both the County Sheriff and the County Prosecutor could establish county policy under appropriate circumstances, a conclusion that we do not question here. In ordering the Deputy Sheriffs to enter petitioner's clinic the County Prosecutor was acting as the final decisionmaker for the county, and the county may therefore be held liable under § 1983.

Justice WHITE, concurring.

The forcible entry made in this case was not then illegal under federal, state, or local law. The City of Cincinnati frankly conceded that forcible entry of third-party property to effect otherwise valid arrests was standard operating procedure. There is no reason to believe that the respondent would abjure using lawful means to execute the capiases issued in this case or had limited the authority of its officers to use force in executing capiases. Further, the county officials who had the authority to approve or disapprove such entries opted for the forceful entry, a choice that was later held to be inconsistent with the Fourth Amendment. Vesting discretion in its officers to use force and its use in this case sufficiently manifested county policy to warrant reversal of the judgment below.

This does not mean that every act of municipal officers with final authority to effect or authorize arrests and searches represents the policy of the municipality. It would be different if *Steagald v. United States* had been decided when the events at issue here occurred, if the state constitution or statutes had forbade forceful entries without a warrant, or if there had been a municipal ordinance to this effect. Local law enforcement officers are expected to obey the law and ordinarily swear to do so when they take office. Where the controlling law places limits on their authority, they cannot be said to have the authority to make contrary policy. Had the sheriff or prosecutor in this case failed to follow an existing warrant requirement, it would be absurd to say that he was nevertheless executing county policy in authorizing the forceful entry in this case and even stranger to say that the county would be liable if the sheriff had secured a warrant and it turned out that he and the magistrate had mistakenly thought there was probable cause for the warrant. If deliberate or mistaken acts like this, admittedly contrary to local law, expose the county to liability, it must be on the basis of *respondeat superior* and not because the officers' acts represents local policy.

Such results would not conform to *Monell* and the cases following it. I do not understand the Court to hold otherwise in stating that municipal liability attaches where "a deliberate choice to follow a course of action is made from among various alternatives by the official or officials responsible for establishing final policy with respect to the subject matter in question." A sheriff, for example, is not the final policy maker with respect to the probable cause requirement for a valid arrest. He has no alternative but to act in accordance with the established standard; and his deliberate or mistaken departure from the controlling law of arrest would not represent municipal policy.

In this case, however, the sheriff and the prosecutor chose a course that was not forbidden by any applicable law, a choice that they then had the authority to make. This was county policy, and it was no less so at the time because a later decision of this Court declared unwarranted forceful entry into third party premises to be violation of the Fourth Amendment. Hence, I join the Court's opinion and judgment.

Justice POWELL, with whom THE CHIEF JUSTICE and Justice REHNQUIST join, dissenting.

The Court today holds Hamilton County liable for the forcible entry in May 1977 by deputy sheriffs into petitioner's office. The entry and subsequent search were pursuant to capiases for third parties—petitioner's employees—who had failed to answer a summons to appear as witnesses before a grand jury investigating petitioner. When petitioner refused to allow the sheriffs to enter, one of them, at the request of his supervisor, called the office of the County Prosecutor for instructions. The Assistant County Prosecutor received the call, and apparently was in doubt as to what advice to give. He referred the question to the County Prosecutor, who advised the deputy sheriffs to "go in and get them" [the witnesses] pursuant to the capiases.

This five word response to a single question over the phone is now found by this Court to have created an official county policy for which Hamilton County is liable under § 1983. This holding is wrong for at least two reasons. First, the prosecutor's response and the deputies' subsequent actions did not violate any constitutional right that existed at the time of the forcible entry. Second, no official county policy could have been created solely by an offhand telephone response from a busy County Prosecutor.

1. Should a single decision of a high level government official bind the entity where it is not a rule of general applicability nor one reached through formal process?

2. Will the single act of a policymaker always trigger entity liability? What limitations does Justice White suggest? If the County Prosecutor's decision was clearly contrary to state or county policy, or well-established federal law at the time it was rendered, should the county be liable?

   In *City of St. Louis v. Praprotnik*, 485 U.S. 112 (1988), the Supreme Court held that where a government agency simply goes along with the discretionary decisions of one of its subordinates, this should not be interpreted as a delegation of final policy making authority. Thus, even if the St. Louis Civil Service Commission gave great deference to the appointing authority's decisions, this was an insufficient basis for holding the city liable. Further, the Court in *Praprotnik* reiterated the cautionary limitation voiced by Justices White and O'Connor in *Pembaur*: "When an official's discretionary decisions are constrained by policies not of that official's making, those policies, rather than the subordinate's departures from them, are the act of the municipality." Thus, a distinction must be drawn between the official who has authority to promulgate policy and the official who merely has discretion to render decisions within the parameters of a policy already established by the government entity.

   The Court in *Praprotnik* specifically left open the question of whether policy making authority is to be decided by judge or jury. The Supreme Court in *Jett v. Dallas Independent School Dist.*, 491 U.S. 701 (1989), clarified that this is a legal question to be resolved by the trial judge before a case is submitted to the jury.

3. How will it be determined whether a government official is the "final repository of power" with respect to the action ordered? What if state law provides an appeal process from the decision of the government official?

4. Can liability be imposed on a government entity if the harm is caused solely by wrongdoing of low level officials, *i.e.*, what if the deputy sheriffs had broken into Dr. Pembaur's office without the consent of the county prosecutor? What if this had been the third such break-in within a month, and policymaking officials were aware of, but did nothing about, the first two?

ii.   Liability for the Misconduct of Non-policymakers

OKLAHOMA CITY V. TUTTLE
471 u.s. 808 (1984)

Justice REHNQUIST announced the judgment of the Court and delivered an opinion with respect to Part III, in which BURGER, C.J., and WHITE and O'CONNOR, J.J., joined.

I

On October 4, 1980, Officer Julian Rotramel, a member of the Oklahoma City police force, shot and killed Albert Tuttle outside the We'll Do Club, a bar in Oklahoma City. Officer Rotramel, who had been on the force for 10 months, had responded to an all points bulletin indicating that there was a robbery in progress at the Club.

Rotramel was the first officer to reach the bar, and the testimony concerning what happened thereafter is sharply conflicting. Rotramel's version was that when he entered the bar Tuttle walked toward him, and Rotramel grabbed Tuttle's arm and requested that he stay within the bar. Tuttle matched the description contained in the bulletin. The barmaid testified that she told Rotramel that no robbery had occurred. Rotramel testified that while he was questioning the barmaid Tuttle kept bending towards his boots, and attempting to squirm from the officer's grip. Tuttle finally broke away from Rotramel, and, ignoring the officer's commands to "halt," went outside. When Rotramel cleared the threshold to the outside door, he saw Tuttle crouched down on the sidewalk, with his hands in or near his boot. Rotramel again ordered Tuttle to halt, but when Tuttle started to come out of his crouch Rotramel discharged his weapon. Rotramel testified at trial that he believed Tuttle had removed a gun from his boot, and that his life was in danger. Tuttle died from the gunshot wound. When his boot was removed at the hospital prior to surgery, a toy pistol fell out.

Respondent Rose Marie Tuttle is Albert Tuttle's widow, and the administratrix of his estate. She brought suit under § 1983 in the United State District Court, Western District of Oklahoma, against Rotramel and the city, alleging that their actions had deprived Tuttle of certain of his constitutional rights. At trial respondent introduced evidence concerning the facts surrounding the incident, and also adduced testimony from an expert in police training practices. The expert testified that, based upon Rotramel's conduct during the incident in question and the expert's review of the Oklahoma City police training curriculum, it was his opinion that Rotramel's training was grossly inadequate. Respondent introduced no evidence that Rotramel or any other member of the Oklahoma City police force had been involved in a similar incident.

The case was presented to the jury on the theory that Rotramel's act had deprived Tuttle of life without due process of law, or that he had violated Tuttle's rights by using "excessive force in his apprehension." With respect to municipal liability the trial judge instructed the jury:

If a police officer denies a person his constitutional rights, the city that employs that officer is not liable for such a denial of the right simply because of the employment relationship. But there are circumstances under which a city is liable for a deprivation of a constitutional right. Where the official policy of the city causes an employee of the city to deprive a person of such rights in the execution of that policy, the city may be liable.

* * *

It is the plaintiff's contention that such a policy existed and she relies upon allegations that the city is grossly negligent in training of police officers, in its failure to review and discipline its officers. The plaintiff has alleged that the failure of the city to adequately supervise, train, review, and discipline the police officers constitutes deliberate indifference to the constitutional rights of the decedent and acquiescence in the probability of serious police misconduct.

* * *

Absent more evidence of supervisory indifference, such as acquiescence in a prior matter of conduct, official policy such as to impose liability . . . under the federal Civil Rights Act cannot ordinarily be inferred from a single incident of illegality such as a first excessive use of force to stop a suspect; but a single, unusually excessive use of force may be sufficiently out of the ordinary to warrant an inference that it was attributable to inadequate training or supervision amounting to 'deliberate indifference' or 'gross negligence' on the part of the officials in charge. The city cannot be held liable for simple negligence. Furthermore, the plaintiff must show a causal link between the police misconduct and the adoption of a policy or plan by the defendant municipality. (Emphasis supplied.)

The jury returned a verdict in favor of Rotramel but against the city, and awarded respondent $1,500,000 in damages.

III

Respondent argue[s] that the question presented by petitioner—whether a single isolated incident of the use of excessive force by a police officer establishes an official custom or policy of a municipality—is in truth not presented by this record because there was more evidence of an official "policy" of "inadequate training" than might be inferred from the incident giving rise to Tuttle's death. But unfortunately for respondent, the instruction given by the District Court allowed the jury to impose liability on the basis of such a single incident without the benefit of the additional evidence. The trial court stated that the jury could "infer," from "a single, unusually excessive use of force . . . that it was attributable to inadequate training or supervision amounting to 'deliberate indifference' or 'gross negligence' on the part of the officials in charge."

We think this inference unwarranted; first, in its assumption that the act at issue arose from inadequate training, and second, in its further assumption concerning the state of mind of the municipal policymakers. But more importantly, the inference allows a § 1983 plaintiff to establish municipal liability without submitting proof of a single action taken by a municipal policymaker. Respondent contends that *Monell* suggests the contrary result, because it "expressly provided that an official 'decision' would suffice to establish liability, although a single decision will often have only a single victim." But this very contention illustrates the wide difference between the municipal "policy" at issue in *Monell* and the "policy" alleged here. The "policy" of the New York City Department of Social Services that was challenged in *Monell* was a policy that by its terms compelled pregnant employees to take mandatory leaves of absence before such leaves were required for medical reasons; this policy in and of itself violated the constitutional rights of pregnant employees by reason of our decision in *Cleveland Board of Education v. LaFleur*. Obviously, it requires only one application of a policy such as this to satisfy fully *Monell*'s requirement that a municipal corporation be held liable only for constitutional violations resulting from the municipality's official policy.

Here, however, the "policy" that respondent seeks to rely upon is far more nebulous, and a good deal further removed from the constitutional violation, than was the policy in *Monell*. To establish the constitutional violation in *Monell* no evidence was needed other than a statement of the policy by the municipal corporation, and its exercise; but the type of "policy" upon which respondent relies, and its causal relation to the alleged constitutional violation, are not susceptible to such easy proof. In the first place, the word "policy" generally implies a course of action consciously chosen from among various alternatives; it is therefore difficult in one sense even to accept the submission that someone pursues a "policy" of "inadequate training," unless evidence be adduced which proves that the inadequacies resulted from conscious choice—that is, proof that the policymakers deliberately chose a training program which would prove inadequate. And in the second place, some limitation must be placed on establishing municipal liability through policies that are not themselves unconstitutional, or the test set out in *Monell* will become a dead letter. At the very least there must be an affirmative link between the policy and the particular constitutional violation alleged.

Here the instructions allowed the jury to infer a thoroughly nebulous "policy" of "inadequate training" on the part of the municipal corporation from the single incident described earlier in this opinion, and at the same time sanctioned the inference that the "policy" was the cause of the incident. Such an approach provides a means for circumventing *Monell*'s limitations altogether. Proof of a single incident of unconstitutional activity is not sufficient to impose liability under *Monell*, unless proof of the incident includes proof that it was caused by an existing, unconstitutional municipal policy, which policy can be attributed to a municipal policymaker. Otherwise the existence of the unconstitutional policy, and its origin, must be separately proved. But where the policy relied upon is not itself unconstitutional, considerably more proof than the single incident will be necessary in every case to establish both the requisite fault on the part of the municipality, and the causal connection between the "policy" and the constitutional deprivation.

1. How did the plaintiff seek to link the City to the official's misconduct?

2. What error did the Court identify in the jury instructions?

3. The Court cautioned that "where the policy relied upon is not itself unconstitutional, considerably more proof than the single incident will be necessary in every case to establish both the requisite fault on the part of the municipality, and the causal connection between the 'policy' and the constitutional deprivation." Based on this statement, several appellate courts imposed a special "heightened pleading requirement" in cases where a plaintiff alleged a constitutional violation was caused by a city's failure to adequately train and supervise its officers. In *Leatherman v. Terrant County Narcotics Intelligence and Coordination Unit*, 507 U.S. 163 (1993), the Supreme Court held that this special pleading rule is contrary to the "notice pleading" imposed by the Federal Rules of Civil Procedure. The Court in *Bell Atlantic v. Twombly*, 550 U.S. 544 (2007), reiterated the notice pleading rule, but also held that to avoid dismissal for failure to state a claim, the plaintiff must plead "enough facts to state a claim to relief that is plausible on its face. . . . Factual allegations must be enough to raise a right to relief above the speculative level, on the assumption that all the allegations in the complaint are true (even if doubtful in fact)." In *Ashcroft v. Iqbal*, 566 U.S. 662 (2009), the Court, while not reversing *Leatherman*, cemented the "plausibility" test as the governing standard necessary to survive a motion to dismiss.

CITY OF CANTON, OHIO V. HARRIS
489 U.S. 378 (1989)

[In this case plaintiff claimed that although she exhibited severe physical illness after her arrest, she was not transported to a hospital nor were medical personnel summoned to examine her. Following her release, she did go to a hospital where for one week she was treated for emotional problems allegedly stemming from the arrest. A jury returned a verdict of $200,000, relying on evidence that a city regulation gave the shift commander sole discretion to determine whether a detainee required medical care, and yet commanders were not provided with any special training to determine when to summon medical care. The Supreme Court rejected the city's position that it can be found liable only where "the policy in question is itself unconstitutional." It determined that there are "limited circumstances in which an allegation of a 'failure to train' can be the basis for liability under § 1983." On the other hand, the Court placed narrow restrictions on the availability of municipal liability based simply on inadequacy of police training.]

Justice WHITE delivered the opinion of the Court.

We hold today that the inadequacy of police training may serve as the basis for § 1983 liability only where the failure to train amounts to deliberate indifference to the rights of persons with whom the police come into contact. Only where a municipality's failure to train its employees in a relevant respect evidences a "deliberate indifference" to the rights of its inhabitants can such a shortcoming be properly thought of as a city "policy or custom" that is actionable under § 1983.

Monell's rule that a city is not liable under § 1983 unless a municipal policy causes a constitutional deprivation will not be satisfied by merely alleging that the existing training program for a class of employees, such as police officers, represents a policy for which the city is responsible. That much may be true. The issue in a case like this one, however, is whether that training program is adequate; and if it is not, the question becomes whether such inadequate training can justifiably be said to represent "city policy." It may seem contrary to common sense to assert that a municipality will actually have a policy of not taking reasonable steps to train its employees. But it may happen that in light of the duties assigned to specific officers or employees the need for more or different training is so obvious, and the inadequacy so likely to result in the violation of constitutional rights, that the policymakers of the city can reasonably be said to have been deliberately indifferent to the need.[10] In that event, the failure to provide proper training may fairly be said to represent a policy for which the city is responsible, and for which the city may be held liable if it actually causes injury.

In resolving the issue of a city's liability, the focus must be on adequacy of the training program in relation to the tasks the particular officers must perform. That a particular officer may be unsatisfactorily trained will not alone suffice to fasten liability on the city, for the officer's shortcomings may have resulted from factors other than a faulty training program. Neither will it suffice to prove that an injury or accident could have been avoided if an officer had had better or more training, sufficient to equip him to avoid the particular injury-causing conduct. Such a claim could be made about almost any encounter resulting in injury, yet not condemn the adequacy of the program to enable officers to respond properly to the usual and recurring situations with which they must deal. And plainly, adequately trained officers occasionally make mistakes; the fact that they do says little about the training program or the legal basis for holding the city liable.

Moreover, for liability to attach in this circumstance, the identified deficiency in a city's training program must be closely related to the ultimate injury. Thus in the case at hand, respondent must still prove that the deficiency in training actually caused the police officers' indifference to her medical needs. Would the injury have been avoided had the employee been trained

---

10   For example, city policy makers know to a moral certainty that their police officers will be required to arrest fleeing felons. The city has armed its officers with firearms, in part to allow them to accomplish this task. Thus, the need to train officers in the constitutional limitations on the use of deadly force, see *Tennessee v. Garner*, can be said to be "so obvious," that failure to do so could properly be characterized as "deliberate indifference" to constitutional rights.

It could also be that the police, in exercising their discretion, so often violate constitutional rights that the need for further training must have been plainly obvious to the city policy makers, who, nevertheless, are "deliberately indifferent" to the need.

under a program that was not deficient in the identified respect? Predicting how a hypothetically well-trained officer would have acted under the circumstances may not be an easy task for the factfinder, particularly since matters of judgment may be involved, and since officers who are well trained are not free from error and perhaps might react very much like the untrained officer in similar circumstances. But judge and jury, doing their respective jobs, will be adequate to the task.

[Although Justices O'Connor, Scalia, and Kennedy agreed with the standard set forth by Justice White that municipal liability may be imposed under certain circumstances, they felt it unnecessary to remand because the complaint simply alleged failure to train officers to diagnose the symptoms of emotional illness. They concluded that there was no obvious need for training that would support a finding of deliberate indifference under the circumstances of this case. Instead a city must be on constructive notice that a particular omission is substantially certain to result in a constitutional violation. Justice O'Connor distinguished this situation from one involving a pattern of constitutional violations that would put the city on notice of potential violations which need to be redressed. Since this case involved only a single incident, the city had no reason to suspect that failure to provide this type of training would lead to injuries.]

NOTES AND QUESTIONS

1. On remand, what will Harris have to prove to win her case against the city? If the allegation is failure to train officers regarding the arrest of misdemeanants with potentially serious emotional problems, can such failure meet the deliberate indifference standard? What about the causality requirement?

2. Read carefully Justice White's analysis in footnote 10. In the absence of a series of incidents that would put policymakers on notice of the need for further training, can municipal liability ever be established?

3. If inadequate training may trigger municipal liability and most errors made by city employees might be averted through better training of its employees, won't cities almost always be held liable? On the other hand, by requiring an established policy that itself is unconstitutional, couldn't a city easily insulate itself from liability by simply adopting ordinances and regulations requiring adherence to constitutional standards? Has the Court in essence adopted a middle ground where inadequacy of training may be a basis for imposing liability, but only where the failure demonstrates flagrant disregard for constitutional wrongdoing and where the link between the lack of training and the constitutional injury is direct?

4. In the typical jail suicide case, the plaintiff challenges government's failure to train jail personnel to recognize psychological screening factors related to suicide risks. If

there is no "constitutional right" to have jail personnel trained in suicide prevention, how can failure to train be viewed as "deliberate indifference"?

On the other hand, if statistical profiles on detainees likely to commit suicide are widely available and used by police departments, does a department's failure to take any precautionary measures demonstrate deliberate indifference? If the city prepares a manual, but a jailer fails to follow the guidelines, is the city insulated from liability?

BOARD OF COUNTY COMMISSIONERS OF BRYAN CTY. V. BROWN
520 U.S. 397 (1997)

Justice O'CONNOR delivered the opinion of the Court.

Respondent Jill Brown brought a claim for damages against petitioner Bryan County under 42 U.S.C. § 1983. She alleged that a county police officer used excessive force in arresting her, and that the county itself was liable for her injuries based on its sheriff's hiring and training decisions. She prevailed on her claims against the county following a jury trial, and the Court of Appeals for the Fifth Circuit affirmed the judgment against the county on the basis of the hiring claim alone. We granted certiorari. We conclude that the Court of Appeals' decision cannot be squared with our recognition that, in enacting § 1983, Congress did not intend to impose liability on a municipality unless *deliberate* action attributable to the municipality itself is the "moving force" behind the plaintiff's deprivation of federal rights.

I

In the early morning hours of May 12, 1991, respondent Jill Brown and her husband were driving from Grayson County, Texas, to their home in Bryan County, Oklahoma. After crossing into Oklahoma, they approached a police checkpoint. Mr. Brown, who was driving, decided to avoid the checkpoint and return to Texas. After seeing the Browns' truck turn away from the checkpoint, Bryan County Deputy Sheriff Robert Morrison and Reserve Deputy Stacy Burns pursued the vehicle.

After he got out of the squad car, Deputy Sheriff Morrison pointed his gun toward the Browns' vehicle and ordered the Browns to raise their hands. Reserve Deputy Burns, who was unarmed, rounded the corner of the vehicle on the passenger's side. Burns twice ordered respondent Jill Brown from the vehicle. When she did not exit, he used an "arm bar" technique, grabbing respondent's arm at the wrist and elbow, pulling her from the vehicle, and spinning her to the ground. Respondent's knees were severely injured, and she later underwent corrective surgery. Ultimately, she may need knee replacements.

Respondent sought compensation for her injuries under 42 U.S.C. § 1983 and state law from Burns, Bryan County Sheriff B.J. Moore, and the county itself. Respondent claimed, among other things, that Bryan County was liable for Burns' alleged use of excessive force based on Sheriff Moore's decision to hire Burns, the son of his nephew. Specifically, respondent claimed that

Sheriff Moore had failed to adequately review Burns' background. Burns had a record of driving infractions and had pleaded guilty to various driving-related and other misdemeanors, including assault and battery, resisting arrest, and public drunkenness. At trial, Sheriff Moore testified that he had obtained Burns' driving record and a report on Burns from the National Crime Information Center, but had not closely reviewed either. Sheriff Moore authorized Burns to make arrests, but not to carry a weapon or to operate a patrol car.

II

The parties join issue on whether, under *Monell* and subsequent cases, a single hiring decision by a county sheriff can be a "policy" that triggers municipal liability. Relying on our decision in *Pembaur*, respondent claims that a single act by a decisionmaker with final authority in the relevant area constitutes a "policy" attributable to the municipality itself. So long as a § 1983 plaintiff identifies a decision properly attributable to the municipality, respondent argues, there is no risk of imposing *respondeat superior* liability.

As our § 1983 municipal liability jurisprudence illustrates, however, it is not enough for a § 1983 plaintiff merely to identify conduct properly attributable to the municipality. The plaintiff must also demonstrate that, through its *deliberate* conduct, the municipality was the "moving force" behind the injury alleged. That is, a plaintiff must show that the municipal action was taken with the requisite degree of culpability and must demonstrate a direct causal link between the municipal action and the deprivation of federal rights.

Sheriff Moore's hiring decision was itself legal, and Sheriff Moore did not authorize Burns to use excessive force. Respondent's claim, rather, is that a single facially lawful hiring decision can launch a series of events that ultimately cause a violation of federal rights. Where a plaintiff claims that the municipality has not directly inflicted an injury, but nonetheless has caused an employee to do so, rigorous standards of culpability and causation must be applied to ensure that the municipality is not held liable solely for the actions of its employee.

In relying heavily on *Pembaur*, respondent blurs the distinction between § 1983 cases that present no difficult questions of fault and causation and those that do. To the extent that we have recognized a cause of action under § 1983 based on a single decision attributable to a municipality, we have done so only where the evidence that the municipality had acted and that the plaintiff had suffered a deprivation of federal rights also proved fault and causation. . . . In *Pembaur*, it was not disputed that the prosecutor had specifically directed the action resulting in the deprivation of petitioner's rights. The conclusion that the decision was that of a final municipal decisionmaker and was therefore properly attributable to the municipality established municipal liability. No questions of fault or causation arose.

Claims not involving an allegation that the municipal action itself violated federal law, or directed or authorized the deprivation of federal rights, present much more difficult problems of proof. That a plaintiff has suffered a deprivation of federal rights at the hands of a municipal employee will not alone permit an inference of municipal culpability and causation; the plaintiff will simply have shown that the *employee* acted culpably. We recognized these difficulties in *Canton v. Harris* where we considered a claim that inadequate training of shift supervisors at a city jail led to a deprivation of a detainee's constitutional rights. We held that, quite apart from the state of mind required to establish the underlying constitutional violation—in that case, a violation of due process—a plaintiff seeking to establish municipal liability on the theory that a facially lawful municipal action has led an employee to violate a plaintiff's rights must demonstrate that the municipal action was taken with "deliberate indifference" as to its known or obvious consequences. A showing of simple or even heightened negligence will not suffice.

We concluded in *Canton* that an "inadequate training" claim could be the basis for § 1983 liability in "limited circumstances." We spoke, however, of a deficient training "program," necessarily intended to apply over time to multiple employees. Existence of a "program" makes proof of fault and causation at least possible in an inadequate training case. If a program does not prevent constitutional violations, municipal decisionmakers may eventually be put on notice that a new program is called for. Their continued adherence to an approach that they know or should know has failed to prevent tortious conduct by employees may establish the conscious disregard for the consequences of their action—the "deliberate indifference"—necessary to trigger municipal liability.

Respondent does not claim that she can identify any pattern of injuries linked to Sheriff Moore's hiring practices. Indeed, respondent does not contend that Sheriff Moore's hiring practices are generally defective. The only evidence on this point at trial suggested that Sheriff Moore had adequately screened the backgrounds of all prior deputies he hired. Respondent instead seeks to trace liability to what can only be described as a deviation from Sheriff Moore's ordinary hiring practices. Where a claim of municipal liability rests on a single decision, not itself representing a violation of federal law and not directing such a violation, the danger that a municipality will be held liable without fault is high. Because the decision necessarily governs a single case, there can be no notice to the municipal decisionmaker, based on previous violations of federally protected rights, that his approach is inadequate. Nor will it be readily apparent that the municipality's action caused the injury in question, because the plaintiff can point to no other incident tending to make it more likely that the plaintiff's own injury flows from the municipality's action, rather than from some other intervening cause.

Respondent purports to rely on *Canton*, arguing that Burns' use of excessive force was the plainly obvious consequence of Sheriff Moore's failure to screen Burns' record. In essence, respondent claims that this showing of "obviousness" would demonstrate both that Sheriff Moore acted with conscious disregard for the consequences of his action and that the Sheriff's action directly caused her injuries, and would thus substitute for the pattern of injuries ordinarily necessary to establish municipal culpability and causation.

The proffered analogy between failure-to-train cases and inadequate screening cases is not persuasive. In leaving open in *Canton* the possibility that a plaintiff might succeed in carrying a failure-to-train claim without showing a pattern of constitutional violations, we simply hypothesized that, in a narrow range of circumstances, a violation of federal rights may be a highly predictable consequence of a failure to equip law enforcement officers with specific tools to handle recurring situations. The likelihood that the situation will recur and the predictability that an officer lacking specific tools to handle that situation will violate citizens' rights could justify a finding that policymakers' decision not to train the officer reflected "deliberate indifference" to the obvious consequence of the policymakers' choice—namely, a violation of a specific constitutional or statutory right. The high degree of predictability may also support an inference of causation—that the municipality's indifference led directly to the very consequence that was so predictable.

Where a plaintiff presents a § 1983 claim premised upon the inadequacy of an official's review of a prospective applicant's record, however, there is a particular danger that a municipality will be held liable for an injury not directly caused by a deliberate action attributable to the municipality itself. Every injury suffered at the hands of a municipal employee can be traced to a hiring decision in a "but-for" sense: But for the municipality's decision to hire the employee, the plaintiff would not have suffered the injury. To prevent municipal liability for a hiring decision from collapsing into *respondeat superior* liability, a court must carefully test the link between the policymaker's inadequate decision and the particular injury alleged.

In attempting to import the reasoning of *Canton* into the hiring context, respondent ignores the fact that predicting the consequence of a single hiring decision, even one based on an inadequate assessment of a record, is far more difficult than predicting what might flow from the failure to train a single law enforcement officer as to a specific skill necessary to the discharge of his duties. As our decision in *Canton* makes clear, "deliberate indifference" is a stringent standard of fault, requiring proof that a municipal actor disregarded a known or obvious consequence of his action. Unlike the risk from a particular glaring omission in a training regimen, the risk from a single instance of inadequate screening of an applicant's background is not "obvious" in the abstract; rather, it depends upon the background of the applicant. A lack of scrutiny may increase the likelihood that an unfit officer will be hired, and that the unfit officer will, when placed in a particular position to affect the rights of citizens, act improperly. But that is only a generalized showing of risk. The fact that inadequate scrutiny of an applicant's background would make a violation of rights more *likely* cannot alone give rise to an inference that a policymaker's failure to scrutinize the record of a particular applicant produced a specific constitutional violation. After all, a full screening of an applicant's background might reveal no cause for concern at all; if so, a hiring official who failed to scrutinize the applicant's background cannot be said to have consciously disregarded an obvious risk that the officer would subsequently inflict a particular constitutional injury.

We assume that a jury could properly find in this case that Sheriff Moore's assessment of Burns' background was inadequate. Sheriff Moore's own testimony indicated that he did not inquire into the underlying conduct or the disposition of any of the misdemeanor charges reflected on Burns' record before hiring him. But this showing of an instance of inadequate screening is not enough to establish "deliberate indifference." In layman's terms, inadequate screening of an applicant's record may reflect "indifference" to the applicant's background. For purposes of a legal inquiry into municipal liability under § 1983, however, that is not the *relevant* "indifference." A plaintiff must demonstrate that a municipal decision reflects deliberate indifference to the risk that a violation of a particular constitutional or statutory right will follow the decision. Only where adequate scrutiny of an applicant's background would lead a reasonable policymaker to conclude that the plainly obvious consequence of the decision to hire the applicant would be the deprivation of a third party's federally protected right can the official's failure to adequately scrutinize the applicant's background constitute "deliberate indifference."

As discussed above, a finding of culpability simply cannot depend on the mere probability that any officer inadequately screened will inflict any constitutional injury. Rather, it must depend on a finding that *this* officer was highly likely to inflict the *particular* injury suffered by the plaintiff. The connection between the background of the particular applicant and the specific constitutional violation alleged must be strong.

Even assuming without deciding that proof of a single instance of inadequate screening could ever trigger municipal liability, the evidence in this case was insufficient to support a finding that, in hiring Burns, Sheriff Moore disregarded a known or obvious risk of injury. To be sure, Burns' record reflected various misdemeanor infractions. Respondent claims that the record demonstrated such a strong propensity for violence that Burns' application of excessive force was highly likely. The primary charges on which respondent relies, however, are those arising from a fight on a college campus where Burns was a student. In connection with this single incident, Burns was charged with assault and battery, resisting arrest, and public drunkenness. In January 1990, when he pleaded guilty to those charges, Burns also pleaded guilty to various driving-related offenses, including nine moving violations and a charge of driving with a suspended license. In addition, Burns had previously pleaded guilty to being in actual physical control of a vehicle while intoxicated.

The fact that Burns had pleaded guilty to traffic offenses and other misdemeanors may well have made him an extremely poor candidate for reserve deputy. Had Sheriff Moore fully reviewed Burns' record, he might have come to precisely that conclusion. But unless he would necessarily have reached that decision *because* Burns' use of excessive force would have been a plainly obvious consequence of the hiring decision, Sheriff Moore's inadequate scrutiny of Burns' record cannot constitute "deliberate indifference" to respondent's federally protected right to be free from a use of excessive force.

III

Cases involving constitutional injuries allegedly traceable to an ill-considered hiring decision pose the greatest risk that a municipality will be held liable for an injury that it did not cause. In the broadest sense, every injury is traceable to a hiring decision. Where a court fails to adhere to rigorous requirements of culpability and causation, municipal liability collapses into *respondeat superior* liability. A failure to apply stringent culpability and causation requirements raises serious federalism concerns, in that it risks constitutionalizing particular hiring requirements that States have themselves elected not to impose. Bryan County is not liable for Sheriff Moore's isolated decision to hire Burns without adequate screening, because respondent has not demonstrated that his decision reflected a conscious disregard for a high risk that Burns would use excessive force in violation of respondent's federally protected right.

[In dissent, four Justices accuse the Court of imposing an impossible standard. Under the majority's test, deliberate indifference exists only when the risk of the subsequent, particular constitutional violation is a "plainly obvious" consequence of not doing a background check on this applicant. They note that this standard appears to be higher than that for reckless fault in criminal law and ignores the fact that some acts of a policymaker present a substantial risk of harm even though the acts are not unconstitutional *per se.* Three Justices (Breyer, Stevens, and Ginsburg) argue that *Monell* should be re-examined to determine whether a vicarious liability standard would not better serve the goals of § 1983. They opine that the confused body of case law is neither readily understandable nor easy to apply and that since many states, in any event, authorize indemnification of employees found liable under § 1983 for actions within the scope of their employment, a vicarious liability principle should be adopted.]

NOTES AND QUESTIONS

1. On what basis did Brown seek to hold the county liable for Officer Burns' use of excessive force?

2. If Sheriff Moore was the policymaker for the county, why doesn't his hiring decision bind the county? How does the Court distinguish *Pembaur*?

3. Did Sheriff Moore's conduct in failing to screen Burns meet the deliberate indifference standard set forth in *Canton*? Is the Court applying the same standard here? If not, why should failure to train claims be treated differently than failure to perform background checks for new hires? Did Brown allege a policy of failing to perform background checks? Would that have made a difference?

4. Does the Court hold that a "single" instance of inadequate screening may never trigger municipal liability? Didn't *Canton* permit liability to be imposed based on a single violation arising from a failure to train? Is it really less predictable that hiring an officer with a spotty background may lead to constitutional rights violations?

5. Is the dissent correct in finding that the majority has ratcheted up the *Canton* standard by requiring plaintiffs to demonstrate that the risk of the *particular* constitutional violation was a plainly obvious consequence of deficient screening? In *Canton*, didn't the Court suggest that the policymaker's action need only be "so likely to result in the violation of constitutional rights that the policymaker . . . can reasonably be said to have been indifferent to the need" to perform certain actions? Will the Court's new stringent standard ever be met? Should it be applied to failure to train cases? Note that on remand the Fifth Circuit reinstated the verdict for Brown based on her failure-to-train claim. 219 F.3d 450 (5th Cir. 2000).

Justice THOMAS delivered the opinion of the Court.

The Orleans Parish District Attorney's Office now concedes that, in prosecuting respondent John Thompson for attempted armed robbery, prosecutors failed to disclose evidence that should have been turned over to the defense under *Brady v. Maryland*, 373 U.S. 83, 83 S. Ct. 1194, 10 L. Ed. 2d 215 (1963). Thompson was convicted. Because of that conviction Thompson elected not to testify in his own defense in his later trial for murder, and he was again convicted. Thompson spent 18 years in prison, including 14 years on death row. One month before Thompson's scheduled execution, his investigator discovered the undisclosed evidence from his armed robbery trial. The reviewing court determined that the evidence was exculpatory, and both of Thompson's convictions were vacated.

After his release from prison, Thompson sued petitioner Harry Connick, in his official capacity as the Orleans Parish District Attorney, for damages under 42 U.S.C. § 1983. Thompson alleged that Connick had failed to train his prosecutors adequately about their duty to produce exculpatory evidence and that the lack of training had caused the nondisclosure in Thompson's robbery case. The jury awarded Thompson $14 million, and the Court of Appeals for the Fifth Circuit affirmed by an evenly divided en banc court. We granted certiorari to decide whether a district attorney's office may be held liable under § 1983 for failure to train based on a single *Brady* violation. We hold that it cannot.

I

A

In early 1985, John Thompson was charged with the murder of Raymond T. Liuzza, Jr. in New Orleans. Publicity following the murder charge led the victims of an unrelated armed robbery to identify Thompson as their attacker. The district attorney charged Thompson with attempted armed robbery.

As part of the robbery investigation, a crime scene technician took from one of the victims' pants a swatch of fabric stained with the robber's blood. Approximately one week before Thompson's armed robbery trial, the swatch was sent to the crime laboratory. Two days before the trial, assistant district attorney Bruce Whittaker received the crime lab's report, which stated that the perpetrator had blood type B. There is no evidence that the prosecutors ever had Thompson's blood tested or that they knew what his blood type was. Whittaker claimed he placed the report on assistant district attorney James Williams' desk, but Williams denied seeing it. The report was never disclosed to Thompson's counsel.

Williams tried the armed robbery case with assistant district attorney Gerry Deegan. On the first day of trial, Deegan checked all of the physical evidence in the case out of the police property room, including the blood-stained swatch. Deegan then checked all of the evidence but the swatch into the courthouse property room. The prosecutors did not mention the swatch or the crime lab report at trial, and the jury convicted Thompson of attempted armed robbery.

A few weeks later, Williams and special prosecutor Eric Dubelier tried Thompson for the Liuzza murder. Because of the armed robbery conviction, Thompson chose not to testify in his own defense. He was convicted and sentenced to death. The State scheduled Thompson's execution for May 20, 1999.

In late April 1999, Thompson's private investigator discovered the crime lab report from the armed robbery investigation in the files of the New Orleans Police Crime Laboratory. Thompson was tested and found to have blood type O, proving that the blood on the swatch was not his. Thompson's attorneys presented this evidence to the district attorney's office, which, in turn, moved to stay the execution and vacate Thompson's armed robbery conviction. The Louisiana Court of Appeals then reversed Thompson's murder conviction, concluding that the armed robbery conviction unconstitutionally deprived Thompson of his right to testify in his own defense at the murder trial. In 2003, the district attorney's office retried Thompson for Liuzza's murder. The jury found him not guilty.

B

Thompson then brought this action against the district attorney's office, Connick, Williams, and others, alleging that their conduct caused him to be wrongfully convicted, incarcerated for 18 years, and nearly executed. The only claim that proceeded to trial was Thompson's claim under § 1983 that the district attorney's office had violated *Brady* by failing to disclose the crime lab report in his armed robbery trial. Thompson alleged liability under two theories: (1) the *Brady* violation was caused by an unconstitutional policy of the district attorney's office; and (2) the violation was caused by Connick's deliberate indifference to an obvious need to train the prosecutors in his office in order to avoid such constitutional violations.

Before trial, Connick conceded that the failure to produce the crime lab report constituted a *Brady* violation. Accordingly, the District Court instructed the jury that the "only issue" was whether the nondisclosure was caused by either a policy, practice, or custom of the district attorney's office or a deliberately indifferent failure to train the office's prosecutors.

Although no prosecutor remembered any specific training session regarding *Brady* prior to 1985, it was undisputed at trial that the prosecutors were familiar with the general *Brady* requirement that the State disclose to the defense evidence in its possession that is favorable to the accused. Prosecutors testified that office policy was to turn crime lab reports and other scientific evidence over to the defense. They also testified that, after the discovery of the undisclosed crime lab report in 1999, prosecutors disagreed about whether it had to be disclosed under *Brady* absent knowledge of Thompson's blood type.

The jury rejected Thompson's claim that an unconstitutional office policy caused the *Brady* violation, but found the district attorney's office liable for failing to train the prosecutors. The jury awarded Thompson $14 million in damages, and the District Court added more than $1 million in attorney's fees and costs.

After the verdict, Connick renewed his objection—which he had raised on summary judgment—that he could not have been deliberately indifferent to an obvious need for more or different *Brady* training because there was no evidence that he was aware of a pattern of similar *Brady* violations. The District Court rejected this argument for the reasons that it had given in the summary judgment order. In that order, the court had concluded that a pattern of violations is not necessary to prove deliberate indifference when the need for training is "so obvious." Relying on *Canton v. Harris*, the court had held that Thompson could demonstrate deliberate indifference by proving that "the DA's office knew to a moral certainty that assistan[t] [district attorneys] would acquire *Brady* material, that without training it is not always obvious what *Brady* requires, and that withholding *Brady* material will virtually always lead to a substantial violation of constitutional rights." A panel of the Court of Appeals for the Fifth Circuit affirmed.

II

The *Brady* violation conceded in this case occurred when one or more of the four prosecutors involved with Thompson's armed robbery prosecution failed to disclose the crime lab report to Thompson's counsel. Under Thompson's failure-to-train theory, he bore the burden of proving both (1) that Connick, the policymaker for the district attorney's office, was deliberately indifferent to the need to train the prosecutors about their *Brady* disclosure obligation with respect to evidence of this type and (2) that the lack of training actually caused the *Brady* violation in this case. Connick argues that he was entitled to judgment as a matter of law because Thompson did not prove that he was on actual or constructive notice of, and therefore deliberately indifferent to, a need for more or different *Brady* training. We agree.

A

Plaintiffs who seek to impose liability on local governments under § 1983 must prove that "action pursuant to official municipal policy" caused their injury. In limited circumstances, a local government's decision not to train certain employees about their legal duty to avoid violating citizens' rights may rise to the level of an official government policy for purposes of § 1983. A municipality's culpability for a deprivation of rights is at its most tenuous where a claim turns on a failure to train. To satisfy the statute, a municipality's failure to train its employees in a relevant respect must amount to "deliberate indifference to the rights of persons with whom the [untrained employees] come into contact."

"'[D]eliberate indifference' is a stringent standard of fault, requiring proof that a municipal actor disregarded a known or obvious consequence of his action." Thus, when city policymakers are on actual or constructive notice that a particular omission in their training program causes city employees to violate citizens' constitutional rights, the city may be deemed deliberately indifferent if the policymakers choose to retain that program. The city's "policy of inaction" in light of notice that its program will cause constitutional violations "is the functional equivalent of a decision by the city itself to violate the Constitution."

B

A pattern of similar constitutional violations by untrained employees is "ordinarily necessary" to demonstrate deliberate indifference for purposes of failure to train. Although Thompson does not contend that he proved a pattern of similar *Brady* violations, he points out that, during the ten years preceding his armed robbery trial, Louisiana courts had overturned four convictions because of *Brady* violations by prosecutors in Connick's office. Those four reversals could not have put Connick on notice that the office's *Brady* training was inadequate with respect to the sort of *Brady* violation at issue here. None of those cases involved failure to disclose blood evidence, a crime lab report, or physical or scientific evidence of any kind. Because those incidents are not similar to the violation at issue here, they could not have put Connick on notice that specific training was necessary to avoid this constitutional violation.[7]

C

Instead of relying on a pattern of similar *Brady* violations, Thompson relies on the "single-incident" liability that this Court hypothesized in *Canton*. He contends that the *Brady* violation in his case was the "obvious" consequence of failing to provide specific *Brady* training, and that this showing of "obviousness" can substitute for the pattern of violations ordinarily necessary to establish municipal culpability. The Court sought not to foreclose the possibility, however rare, that the unconstitutional consequences of failing to train could be so patently obvious that a city could be liable under § 1983 without proof of a pre-existing pattern of violations.

Failure to train prosecutors in their *Brady* obligations does not fall within the narrow range of *Canton*'s hypothesized single-incident liability. The obvious need for specific legal training that was present in the *Canton* scenario is absent here. Armed police must sometimes make split-second decisions with life-or-death consequences. There is no reason to assume that police academy applicants are familiar with the constitutional constraints on the use of deadly force. And, in the absence of training, there is no way for novice officers to obtain the legal knowledge they require. Under those circumstances there is an obvious need for some form of training. In stark contrast, legal "[t]raining is what differentiates attorneys from average public employees."

Attorneys are trained in the law and equipped with the tools to interpret and apply legal principles, understand constitutional limits, and exercise legal judgment. Before they may enter the profession and receive a law license, all attorneys must graduate from law school or pass a substantive examination; attorneys in the vast majority of jurisdictions must do both. These threshold requirements are designed to ensure that all new attorneys have learned how to find, understand, and apply legal rules.

---

7 Thompson also asserts that this case is not about a "single incident" because up to four prosecutors may have been responsible for the nondisclosure of the crime lab report and, according to his allegations, withheld additional evidence in his armed robbery and murder trials. But contemporaneous or subsequent conduct cannot establish a pattern of violations that would provide "notice to the cit[y] and the opportunity to conform to constitutional dictates . . . ." *Canton*.

Nor does professional training end at graduation. Most jurisdictions require attorneys to satisfy continuing-education requirements. Even those few jurisdictions that do not impose mandatory continuing-education requirements mandate that attorneys represent their clients competently and encourage attorneys to engage in continuing study and education.

Attorneys who practice with other attorneys, such as in district attorney's offices, also train on the job as they learn from more experienced attorneys. For instance, here in the Orleans Parish District Attorney's Office, junior prosecutors were trained by senior prosecutors who supervised them as they worked together to prepare cases for trial, and trial chiefs oversaw the preparation of the cases. Senior attorneys also circulated court decisions and instructional memoranda to keep the prosecutors abreast of relevant legal developments.

In addition, attorneys in all jurisdictions must satisfy character and fitness standards to receive a law license and are personally subject to an ethical regime designed to reinforce the profession's standards. Prosecutors have a special "duty to seek justice, not merely to convict." Among prosecutors' unique ethical obligations is the duty to produce *Brady* evidence to the defense. An attorney who violates his or her ethical obligations is subject to professional discipline, including sanctions, suspension, and disbarment.

In light of this regime of legal training and professional responsibility, recurring constitutional violations are not the "obvious consequence" of failing to provide prosecutors with formal in-house training about how to obey the law. Prosecutors are not only equipped but are also ethically bound to know what *Brady* entails and to perform legal research when they are uncertain. A district attorney is entitled to rely on prosecutors' professional training and ethical obligations in the absence of specific reason, such as a pattern of violations, to believe that those tools are insufficient to prevent future constitutional violations in "the usual and recurring situations with which [the prosecutors] must deal." A licensed attorney making legal judgments, in his capacity as a prosecutor, about *Brady* material simply does not present the same "highly predictable" constitutional danger as *Canton*'s untrained officer.

A second significant difference between this case and the example in *Canton* is the nuance of the allegedly necessary training. The *Canton* hypothetical assumes that the armed police officers have no knowledge at all of the constitutional limits on the use of deadly force. But it is undisputed here that the prosecutors in Connick's office were familiar with the general *Brady* rule. Thompson's complaint therefore cannot rely on the utter lack of an ability to cope with constitutional situations that underlies the *Canton* hypothetical, but rather must assert that prosecutors were not trained about particular *Brady* evidence or the specific scenario related to the violation in his case. That sort of nuance simply cannot support an inference of deliberate indifference here.

Thompson suggests that the absence of any *formal* training sessions about *Brady* is equivalent to the complete absence of legal training that the Court imagined in *Canton*. But failure-to-train liability is concerned with the substance of the training, not the particular instructional format. The statute does not provide plaintiffs or courts *carte blanche* to micromanage local governments throughout the United States.

We do not assume that prosecutors will always make correct *Brady* decisions or that guidance regarding specific *Brady* questions would not assist prosecutors. But showing merely that additional training would have been helpful in making difficult decisions does not establish municipal liability. "[P]rov[ing] that an injury or accident could have been avoided if an [employee] had had better or more training, sufficient to equip him to avoid the particular injury-causing conduct" will not suffice. The possibility of single-incident liability that the Court left open in *Canton* is not this case.

The dissent rejects our holding that *Canton*'s hypothesized single-incident liability does not, as a legal matter, encompass failure to train prosecutors in their *Brady* obligation. It would instead apply the *Canton* hypothetical to this case, and thus devotes almost all of its opinion to explaining why the evidence supports liability under that theory. But the dissent's attempt to address our holding—by pointing out that not all prosecutors will necessarily have enrolled in criminal procedure class—misses the point. The reason why the *Canton* hypothetical is inapplicable is that attorneys, unlike police officers, are equipped with the tools to find, interpret, and apply legal principles.

By the end of its opinion, however, the dissent finally reveals that its real disagreement is not with our holding today, but with this Court's precedent. The dissent does not see "any reason," for the Court's conclusion in *Bryan County* that a pattern of violations is "ordinarily necessary" to demonstrate deliberate indifference for purposes of failure to train.

The District Court and the Court of Appeals panel erroneously believed that Thompson had proved deliberate indifference by showing the "obviousness" of a need for additional training. They based this conclusion on Connick's awareness that (1) prosecutors would confront *Brady* issues while at the district attorney's office; (2) inexperienced prosecutors were expected to understand *Brady*'s requirements; (3) *Brady* has gray areas that make for difficult choices; and (4) erroneous decisions regarding *Brady* evidence would result in constitutional violations.

It does not follow that, because *Brady* has gray areas and some *Brady* decisions are difficult, prosecutors will so obviously make wrong decisions that failing to train them amounts to "a decision by the city itself to violate the Constitution." To prove deliberate indifference, Thompson needed to show that Connick was on notice that, absent additional specified training, it was "highly predictable" that the prosecutors in his office would be confounded by those gray areas and make incorrect *Brady* decisions as a result. In fact, Thompson had to show that it was *so* predictable that failing to train the prosecutors amounted to *conscious disregard* for defendants' *Brady* rights.

We conclude that this case does not fall within the narrow range of "single-incident" liability hypothesized in *Canton* as a possible exception to the pattern of violations necessary to prove deliberate indifference in § 1983 actions alleging failure to train. The District Court should have granted Connick judgment as a matter of law on the failure-to-train claim because Thompson did not prove a pattern of similar violations that would "establish that the 'policy of inaction' [was] the functional equivalent of a decision by the city itself to violate the Constitution."

Justice SCALIA, with whom Justice ALITO joins, concurring.

The withholding of evidence in his case was almost certainly caused not by a failure to give prosecutors specific training, but by miscreant prosecutor Gerry Deegan's willful suppression of evidence he believed to be exculpatory, in an effort to railroad Thompson. According to Deegan's colleague Michael Riehlmann, in 1994 Deegan confessed to him—in the same conversation in which Deegan revealed he had only a few months to live—that he had "suppressed blood evidence in the armed robbery trial of John Thompson that in some way exculpated the defendant." I have no reason to disbelieve that account, particularly since Riehlmann's testimony hardly paints a flattering picture of himself: Riehlmann kept silent about Deegan's misconduct for another five years, as a result of which he incurred professional sanctions. And if Riehlmann's story is true, then the "moving force," behind the suppression of evidence was Deegan, not a failure of continuing legal education.

The dissent suspends disbelief about this, insisting that with proper *Brady* training, "surely at least one" of the prosecutors in Thompson's trial would have turned over the lab report and blood swatch. But training must consist of more than mere broad encomiums of *Brady:* We have made clear that "the identified deficiency in a city's training program [must be] closely related to the ultimate injury." So even indulging the dissent's assumption that Thompson's prosecutors failed to disclose the lab report *in good faith*—in a way that could be prevented by training—what sort of training would have prevented the good-faith nondisclosure of a blood report not known to be exculpatory?

Justice GINSBURG, with whom Justice BREYER, Justice SOTOMAYOR, and Justice KAGAN join, dissenting.

The Court holds that the Orleans Parish District Attorney's Office (District Attorney's Office or Office) cannot be held liable, in a civil rights action under 42 U.S.C. § 1983, for the grave injustice Thompson suffered. That is so, the Court tells us, because Thompson has shown only an aberrant *Brady* violation, not a routine practice of giving short shrift to *Brady*'s requirements. The evidence presented to the jury that awarded compensation to Thompson, however, points distinctly away from the Court's assessment. As the trial record in the § 1983 action reveals, the conceded, long-concealed prosecutorial transgressions were neither isolated nor atypical.

From the top down, the evidence showed, members of the District Attorney's Office, including the District Attorney himself, misperceived *Brady*'s compass and therefore inadequately attended to their disclosure obligations. Throughout the pretrial and trial proceedings against Thompson, the team of four engaged in prosecuting him for armed robbery and murder hid from the defense and the court exculpatory information Thompson requested and had a constitutional right to receive. The prosecutors did so despite multiple opportunities, spanning nearly two decades, to set the record straight. Based on the prosecutors' conduct relating to Thompson's trials, a fact trier could reasonably conclude that inattention to *Brady* was standard operating procedure at the District Attorney's Office.

What happened here, the Court's opinion obscures, was no momentary oversight, no single incident of a lone officer's misconduct. Instead, the evidence demonstrated that misperception and disregard of *Brady*'s disclosure requirements were pervasive in Orleans Parish. That evidence, I would hold, established persistent, deliberately indifferent conduct for which the District Attorney's Office bears responsibility under § 1983.

Over 20 years ago, we observed that a municipality's failure to provide training may be so egregious that, even without notice of prior constitutional violations, the failure "could properly be characterized as 'deliberate indifference' to constitutional rights." "[I]n light of the duties assigned to specific officers or employees," *Canton* recognized, "it may happen that . . . the need for more or different training is so obvious, and the inadequacy so likely to result in the violation of constitutional rights, that the policymakers . . . can reasonably be said to have been deliberately indifferent to the need." Thompson presented convincing evidence to satisfy this standard.

Abundant evidence supported the jury's finding that additional *Brady* training was obviously necessary to ensure that *Brady* violations would not occur: (1) Connick, the Office's sole policymaker, misunderstood *Brady*. (2) Other leaders in the Office, who bore direct responsibility for training less experienced prosecutors, were similarly uninformed about *Brady*. (3) Prosecutors in the Office received no *Brady* training. (4) The Office shirked its responsibility to keep prosecutors abreast of relevant legal developments concerning *Brady* requirements. As a result of these multiple shortfalls, it was hardly surprising that *Brady* violations in fact occurred, severely undermining the integrity of Thompson's trials.

Connick was the Office's sole policymaker, and his testimony exposed a flawed understanding of a prosecutor's *Brady* obligations. Connick should have comprehended that Orleans Parish prosecutors lacked essential guidance on *Brady* and its application. In fact, Connick has effectively conceded that *Brady* training in his Office was inadequate. In 1985, Connick acknowledged, many of his prosecutors "were coming fresh out of law school," and the Office's "[h]uge turnover" allowed attorneys with little experience to advance quickly to supervisory positions.

Thompson's expert characterized Connick's supervision regarding *Brady* as "the blind leading the blind." For example, in 1985 trial attorneys "sometimes . . . went to Mr. Connick" with *Brady* questions, "and he would tell them" how to proceed. But Connick acknowledged that he had "stopped reading law books . . . and looking at opinions" when he was first elected District Attorney in 1974.

Prosecutors confirmed that training in the District Attorney's Office, overall, was deficient. Soon after Connick retired, a survey of assistant district attorneys in the Office revealed that more than half felt that they had not received the training they needed to do their jobs.

Louisiana did not require continuing legal education at the time of Thompson's trials. Primary responsibility for keeping prosecutors *au courant* with developments in the law, therefore, resided in the District Attorney's Office. The 1987 Office policy manual was a compilation of memoranda on criminal law and practice circulated to prosecutors from 1974, when Connick became District Attorney, through 1987. The manual contained four sentences, nothing more, on *Brady*. This slim instruction, the jury learned, was notably inaccurate, incomplete, and dated.

In sum, the evidence permitted the jury to reach the following conclusions. First, Connick did not ensure that prosecutors in his Office knew their *Brady* obligations; he neither confirmed their familiarity with *Brady* when he hired them, nor saw to it that training took place on his watch. Second, the need for *Brady* training and monitoring was obvious to Connick. Indeed he so testified. Third, Connick's cavalier approach to his staff's knowledge and observation of *Brady* requirements contributed to a culture of inattention to *Brady* in Orleans Parish.

Connick resisted an effort to hold prosecutors accountable for *Brady* compliance because he felt the effort would "make [his] job more difficult." He never disciplined or fired a single prosecutor for violating *Brady*. In both quantity and quality, then, the evidence canvassed here was more than sufficient to warrant a jury determination that Connick and the prosecutors who served under him were not merely negligent regarding *Brady*. Rather, they were deliberately indifferent to what the law requires.

In *Canton,* this Court spoke of circumstances in which the need for training may be "so obvious," and the lack of training "so likely" to result in constitutional violations, that policymakers who do not provide for the requisite training "can reasonably be said to have been deliberately indifferent to the need" for such training. This case, I am convinced, belongs in the category *Canton* marked out.

The District Court, tracking *Canton*'s language, instructed the jury that Thompson could prevail on his "deliberate indifference" claim only if the evidence persuaded the jury on three points. First, Connick "was certain that prosecutors would confront the situation where they would have to decide which evidence was required by the Constitution to be provided to the accused." Second, "the situation involved a difficult choice[,] or one that prosecutors had a history of mishandling, such that additional training, supervision or monitoring was clearly needed." Third, "the wrong choice by a prosecutor in that situation would frequently cause a deprivation of an accused's constitutional rights."

The jury could reasonably find that *Brady* rights may involve choices so difficult that Connick obviously knew or should have known prosecutors needed more than perfunctory training to make the correct choices.

Based on the evidence presented, the jury could conclude that *Brady* errors by untrained prosecutors would frequently cause deprivations of defendants' constitutional rights. The jury learned of several *Brady* oversights in Thompson's trials and heard testimony that Connick's Office had one of the worst *Brady* records in the country. Because prosecutors faced considerable pressure to get convictions and were instructed to "turn over what was required by state and federal law, but no more," the risk was all too real that they would err by withholding rather than revealing information favorable to the defense.

In sum, the *Brady* violations in Thompson's prosecutions were not singular and they were not aberrational. They were just what one would expect given the attitude toward *Brady* pervasive in the District Attorney's Office. Thompson demonstrated that no fewer than five prosecutors—the four trial prosecutors and Riehlmann—disregarded his *Brady* rights. He established that they kept from him, year upon year, evidence vital to his defense. Their conduct, he showed with equal force, was a foreseeable consequence of lax training in, and absence of monitoring of, a legal requirement fundamental to a fair trial.

1. After this case will plaintiffs in all failure-to-train cases have to show a pattern of prior constitutional violations in order to demonstrate deliberate indifference? If not, how is this case unique? If plaintiffs can show a "pattern" of violations, does this establish a "custom," regardless of the failure to train or supervise?

2. What if Thompson had claimed a failure to supervise or discipline in the face of *Brady* violations, rather than a failure to train? The evidence showed that Connick had never disciplined any prosecutor for violating *Brady*. Would the "obvious" consequence of a failure to discipline be more *Brady* violations?

3. Even assuming a deficient training program, was this the actual cause ("moving force") of Thompson's injury? Is Justice Scalia correct in asserting that no amount of training would have prevented Deegan's deliberate bad faith misconduct?

4. Note that had Connick been sued individually for failing to train prosecutors he would be shielded by absolute prosecutorial immunity. *See Van De Kamp v. Goldstein, infra.*

Problem: Eight

Rymer, a truck driver, participated in a convoy on an interstate in Kentucky. The convoy was stopped by state and local law enforcement officials, including Officer Stillwell of the City of Shepherdsville. Rymer and three other truck drivers were arrested. Officer Stillwell beat and kicked Rymer violently during the arrest. Rymer was treated by an emergency medical technician who recommended that Rymer be taken to a hospital. Officer Stillwell rejected this recommendation. Rymer and the others were jailed for the night. The next morning the arrested individuals were taken to the county court to enter their pleas. They were then released.

The evidence viewed most favorably to Rymer showed that during Rymer's arrest, Stillwell beat and kicked Rymer many times and hit Rymer once in the stomach and head with a nightstick. Stillwell refused to accept an emergency medical technician's suggestion that Rymer needed x-rays. Evidence of the injuries included photographs and the testimony of Rymer, the jailer, and the Bullitt County Sheriff. The evidence further showed that, at the time of the incident, the City had no rules or regulations governing its police force. Nor did the City require any pre-employment training. The initial training received by the officers was on-the-job training. Although the City required the officers to complete forty hours of training each year after being hired, none of the training received by Officer Stillwell instructed him on arrest procedures or treatment of injured persons. The City's police officers used their own discretion in the arrest and medical treatment of persons suspected of criminal activity.

1. If this was the first incident of police brutality in the city of Shepherdsville, could Rymer establish a "custom" of police brutality? May the City nonetheless be held liable for a "policy" of inadequate training? How should the jury instructions read?

2. What if the evidence indicates that Officer Stillwell acted out of a personal vendetta against Rymer—could a policy of inadequate training be a basis for holding the City liable in that situation? Was the officer acting "under color of state law"?

3. What types of discovery should Rymer's counsel pursue?

4. As municipal counsel, what steps would you advise a city to take to avoid liability for police officer misconduct? If the City had had a police manual which set forth the proper instructions regarding arrest procedures, would this have absolved it of liability? What if the Department had brought formal disciplinary proceedings against Stillwell following this incident?

d. Municipal Immunity

OWEN V. CITY OF INDEPENDENCE
445 U.S. 622 (1980)

Mr. Justice BRENNAN delivered the opinion of the Court.

Monell v. New York City Dep't of Social Services overruled *Monroe v. Pape* insofar as *Monroe* held that local governments were not among the "persons" to whom 42 U.S.C. § 1983 applies and were therefore wholly immune from suit under the statute. *Monell* reserved decision, however, on the question whether local governments, although not entitled to an absolute immunity, should be afforded some form of official immunity in § 1983 suits. In this action the Court of Appeals for the Eighth Circuit held that respondent city of Independence, Mo., "is entitled to qualified immunity from liability" based on the good faith of its officials.

I

On February 20, 1967, Robert L. Broucek, then City Manager of respondent city of Independence, Mo., appointed petitioner George D. Owen to an indefinite term as Chief of Police.[2] In 1972, Owen and a new City Manager, Lyle W. Alberg, engaged in a dispute over petitioner's administration of the Police Department's property room. In March of that year, a handgun, which the records

---

2 Under § 3.3(1) of the city's charter, the City Manager has sole authority to "[a]ppoint, and when deemed necessary for the good of the service, lay off, suspend, demote, or remove all directors, or heads of administrative departments and all other administrative officers and employees of the city."

of the Department's property room stated had been destroyed, turned up in Kansas City in the possession of a felon. This discovery prompted Alberg to initiate an investigation of the management of the property room. Although the probe was initially directed by petitioner, Alberg soon transferred responsibility for the investigation to the city's Department of Law, instructing the City Counselor to supervise its conduct and to inform him directly of its findings.

On the evening of April 17, 1972, the City Council held its regularly scheduled meeting. After completion of the planned agenda, Councilman Roberts read a statement he had prepared on the investigation. Among other allegations, Roberts charged that petitioner had misappropriated Police Department property for his own use, that narcotics and money had "mysteriously disappeared" from his office, that traffic tickets had been manipulated, that high ranking police officials had made "inappropriate" requests affecting the police court, and that "things have occurred causing the unusual release of felons." At the close of his statement, Roberts moved that the investigative reports be released to the news media and turned over to the prosecutor for presentation to the grand jury, and that the City Manager "take all direct and appropriate action" against those persons "involved in illegal, wrongful, or gross inefficient activities brought out in the investigative reports." After some discussion, the City Council passed Roberts' motion with no dissents and one abstention.

City Manager Alberg discharged petitioner the very next day. Petitioner was not given any reason for his dismissal; he received only a written notice stating that his employment as Chief of Police was "[t]erminated under the provisions of § 3.3(1) of the City Charter."

II

Petitioner named the city of Independence, City Manager Alberg, and the present members of the City Council in their official capacities as defendants in this suit. Alleging that he was discharged without notice of reasons and without a hearing in violation of his constitutional rights to procedural and substantive due process, petitioner sought declaratory and injunctive relief, including a hearing on his discharge, backpay from the date of discharge, and attorney's fees.

The Court of Appeals held that the municipality's official policy was responsible for the deprivation of petitioner's constitutional rights: "[T]he stigma attached to [petitioner] in connection with his discharge was caused by the official conduct of the City's lawmakers, or by those whose acts may fairly be said to represent official policy. Such conduct amounted to official policy causing the infringement of [petitioner's] constitutional rights, in violation of § 1983."

Nevertheless, the Court of Appeals affirmed the judgment of the District Court denying petitioner any relief against the respondent city, stating:

> The Supreme Court's decisions in *Board of Regents v. Roth*, and *Perry v. Sindermann*, crystallized the rule establishing the right to a name-clearing hearing for a government employee allegedly stigmatized in the course of his discharge. The Court decided those two cases two months after the discharge in the instant case. Thus, officials of the City of Independence could not have been aware of [petitioner's] right to a name-clearing

hearing in connection with the discharge. The City of Independence should not be charged with predicting the future course of constitutional law. . . We extend the limited immunity the district court applied to the individual defendants to cover the City as well, because its officials acted in good faith and without malice. We hold the City not liable for actions it could not reasonably have known violated [petitioner's] constitutional rights.

III

Since colonial times, a distinct feature of our Nation's system of governance has been the conferral of political power upon public and municipal corporations for the management of matters of local concern. As *Monell* recounted, by 1871, municipalities—like private corporations—were treated as natural persons for virtually all purposes of constitutional and statutory analysis. In particular, they were routinely sued in both federal and state courts. Local governmental units were regularly held to answer in damages for a wide range of statutory and constitutional violations, as well as for common-law actions for breach of contract. And although, as we discuss below, a municipality was not subject to suit for all manner of tortious conduct, it is clear that at the time § 1983 was enacted, local governmental bodies did not enjoy the sort of "good-faith" qualified immunity extended to them by the Court of Appeals.

As a general rule, it was understood that a municipality's tort liability in damages was identical to that of private corporations and individuals. Under this general theory of liability, a municipality was deemed responsible for any private losses generated through a wide variety of its operations and functions, from personal injuries due to its defective sewers, thoroughfares, and public utilities, to property damage caused by its trespasses and uncompensated takings.

[I]n the hundreds of cases from that era awarding damages against municipal governments for wrongs committed by them, one searches in vain for much mention of a qualified immunity based on the good faith of municipal officers. Indeed, where the issue was discussed at all, the courts had rejected the proposition that a municipality should be privileged where it reasonably believed its actions to be lawful.

In sum, we can discern no "tradition so well grounded in history and reason" that would warrant the conclusion that in enacting § 1 of the Civil Rights Act, the 42d Congress *sub silentio* extended to municipalities a qualified immunity based on the good faith of their officers. Absent any clearer indication that Congress intended so to limit the reach of a statute expressly designed to provide a "broad remedy for violations of federally protected civil rights," we are unwilling to suppose that injuries occasioned by a municipality's unconstitutional conduct were not also meant to be fully redressable through its sweep.

Our rejection of a construction of § 1983 that would accord municipalities a qualified immunity for their good-faith constitutional violations is compelled both by the legislative purpose in enacting the statute and by considerations of public policy. The central aim of the Civil Rights Act was to provide protection to those persons wronged by the "'[m]isuse of power, possessed by virtue of state law made possible only because the wrongdoer is clothed with the authority of state law.'" *Monroe*. By creating an express federal remedy, Congress sought to "enforce provisions of the Fourteenth Amendment against those who carry a badge of authority of a State and represent it in some capacity, whether they act in accordance with their authority or misuse it."

How "uniquely amiss" it would be, therefore, if the government itself—"the social organ to which all in our society look for the promotion of liberty, justice, fair and equal treatment, and the setting of worthy norms and goals for social conduct"—were permitted to disavow liability for the injury it has begotten. A damages remedy against the offending party is a vital component of any scheme for vindicating cherished constitutional guarantees, and the importance of assuring its efficacy is only accentuated when the wrongdoer is the institution that has been established to protect the very rights it has transgressed. Yet owing to the qualified immunity enjoyed by most government officials,[a] many victims of municipal malfeasance would be left remediless if the city were also allowed to assert a good-faith defense. Unless countervailing considerations counsel otherwise, the injustice of such a result should not be tolerated.

Moreover, § 1983 was intended not only to provide compensation to the victims of past abuses, but to serve as a deterrent against future constitutional deprivations, as well. The knowledge that a municipality will be liable for all of its injurious conduct, whether committed in good faith or not, should create an incentive for officials who may harbor doubts about the lawfulness of their intended actions to err on the side of protecting citizens' constitutional rights. Furthermore, the threat that damages might be levied against the city may encourage those in a policymaking position to institute internal rules and programs designed to minimize the likelihood of unintentional infringements on constitutional rights. Such procedures are particularly beneficial in preventing those "systemic" injuries that result not so much from the conduct of any single individual, but from the interactive behavior of several government officials, each of whom may be acting in good faith.

Our previous decisions conferring qualified immunities on various government officials are not to be read as derogating the significance of the societal interest in compensating the innocent victims of governmental misconduct. Rather, in each case we concluded that overriding considerations of public policy nonetheless demanded that the official be given a measure of protection from personal liability. The concerns that justified those decisions, however, are less compelling, if not wholly inapplicable, when the liability of the municipal entity is at issue.

In *Scheuer v. Rhodes*, THE CHIEF JUSTICE identified the two "mutually dependent rationales" on which the doctrine of official immunity rested: (1) the injustice, particularly in the absence of bad faith, of subjecting to liability an officer who is required, by the legal obligations of his position, to exercise discretion; (2) the danger that the threat of such liability would deter his willingness to execute his office with the decisiveness and the judgment required by the public good.

The first consideration is simply not implicated when the damages award comes not from the official's pocket, but from the public treasury. It hardly seems unjust to require a municipal defendant which has violated a citizen's constitutional rights to compensate him for the injury

---

a   The question of official immunity is discussed infra.

suffered thereby. Indeed, Congress enacted § 1983 precisely to provide a remedy for such abuses of official power. Elemental notions of fairness dictate that one who causes a loss should bear the loss.

The second rationale mentioned in *Scheuer* also loses its force when it is the municipality, in contrast to the official, whose liability is at issue. At the heart of this justification for a qualified immunity for the individual official is the concern that the threat of *personal* monetary liability will introduce an unwarranted and unconscionable consideration into the decisionmaking process, thus paralyzing the governing official's decisiveness and distorting his judgment on matters of public policy. The inhibiting effect is significantly reduced, if not eliminated, however, when the threat of personal liability is removed. First, as an empirical matter, it is questionable whether the hazard of municipal loss will deter a public officer from the conscientious exercise of his duties; city officials routinely make decisions that either require a large expenditure of municipal funds or involve a substantial risk of depleting the public fisc. More important, though, is the realization that consideration of the *municipality's* liability for constitutional violations is quite properly the concern of its elected or appointed officials. Indeed, a decisionmaker would be derelict in his duties if, at some point, he did not consider whether his decision comports with constitutional mandates and did not weigh the risk that a violation might result in an award of damages from the public treasury.

IV

In sum, our decision holding that municipalities have no immunity from damages liability flowing from their constitutional violations harmonizes well with developments in the common law and our own pronouncements on official immunities under § 1983. Doctrines of tort law have changed significantly over the past century, and our notions of governmental responsibility should properly reflect that evolution. No longer is individual "blameworthiness" the acid test of liability; the principle of equitable loss-spreading has joined fault as a factor in distributing the costs of official misconduct.

We believe that today's decision, together with prior precedents in this area, properly allocates these costs among the three principals in the scenario of the § 1983 cause of action: the victim of the constitutional deprivation; the officer whose conduct caused the injury; and the public, as represented by the municipal entity. The innocent individual who is harmed by an abuse of governmental authority is assured that he will be compensated for his injury. The offending official, so long as he conducts himself in good faith, may go about his business secure in the knowledge that a qualified immunity will protect him from personal liability for damages that are more appropriately chargeable to the populace as a whole. And the public will be forced to bear only the costs of injury inflicted by the "execution of a government's policy or custom, whether made by its lawmakers or by those whose edicts or acts may fairly be said to represent official policy."

1. Was there a *respondeat superior* problem here? Why not?

2. Did the Court correctly balance the competing policy concerns—will denial of immunity for government entities, especially in the context of evolving, unsettled constitutional law, deter forceful decision making?

3. Should liability be imposed on a city without proof of fault—isn't this precisely what the Supreme Court rejected in *Monell* in declining to impose vicarious liability? If the Court is now accepting "equitable loss-spreading" as a valid justification for imposing liability "without fault," can it continue to reject liability based on *respondeat superior*?

4. Does the "policy/custom" requirement of *Monell* sufficiently insulate government entities from liability? Recall *Pembaur*, where the Court imposed liability for a single, arguably nondeliberative decision of a policymaker. If the prosecutor in *Pembaur* was following the Fourth Amendment law in effect at the time he issued his "break the door down" order, should the city be held liable for failing to predict a change in the law?

CITY OF NEWPORT V. FACT CONCERTS, INC.
453 U.S. 247 (1981)

Justice BLACKMUN delivered the opinion of the Court.

In *Monell*, this Court for the first time held that a local government was subject to suit as a "person" within the meaning of 42 U.S.C. § 1983. Aside from concluding that a municipal body was not wholly immune from civil liability, the Court had no occasion to explore the nature or scope of any particular municipal immunity under the statute. The question presented by this case is whether a municipality may be held liable for punitive damages under § 1983.

It is by now well settled that the tort liability created by § 1983 cannot be understood in a historical vacuum. In the Civil Rights Act of 1871, Congress created a federal remedy against a person who, acting under color of state law, deprives another of constitutional rights. One important assumption underlying the Court's decisions in this area is that members of the 42d Congress were familiar with common-law principles, including defenses previously recognized in ordinary tort litigation, and that they likely intended these common-law principles to obtain, absent specific provisions to the contrary.

At the same time, the Court's willingness to recognize certain traditional immunities as affirmative defenses has not led it to conclude that Congress incorporated *all* immunities existing at common law. Indeed, because the 1871 Act was designed to expose state and local officials to a new form of liability, it would defeat the promise of the statute to recognize any preexisting immunity without determining both the policies that it serves and its compatibility with the purposes of § 1983. Only after careful inquiry into considerations of both history and policy has the Court construed § 1983 to incorporate a particular immunity defense.

Since *Monell* was decided three years ago, the Court has applied this two-part approach when scrutinizing a claim of immunity proffered by a municipality. In *Owen*, the Court held that neither history nor policy supported a construction of § 1983 that would allow a municipality to assert the good faith of its officers or agents as a defense to liability for damages. *Owen*, however, concerned only compensatory damages, and petitioner contends that with respect to a municipality's liability for punitive damages, an examination of the common-law background and policy considerations yields a very different result.

A

By the time Congress enacted what is now § 1983, the immunity of a municipal corporation from punitive damages at common law was not open to serious question. It was generally understood by 1871 that a municipality, like a private corporation, was to be treated as a natural person subject to suit for a wide range of tortious activity, but this understanding did not extend to the award of punitive or exemplary damages. Indeed, the courts that had considered the issue prior to 1871 were virtually unanimous in denying such damages against a municipal corporation. Judicial disinclination to award punitive damages against a municipality has persisted to the present day in the vast majority of jurisdictions.

In general, courts viewed punitive damages as contrary to sound public policy, because such awards would burden the very taxpayers and citizens for whose benefit the wrongdoer was being chastised. The courts readily distinguished between liability to compensate for injuries inflicted by a municipality's officers and agents, and vindictive damages appropriate as punishment for the bad-faith conduct of those same officers and agents. Compensation was an obligation properly shared by the municipality itself, whereas punishment properly applied only to the actual wrongdoers. The courts thus protected the public from unjust punishment, and the municipalities from undue fiscal constraints.

Given that municipal immunity from punitive damages was well established at common law by 1871, we proceed on the familiar assumption that "Congress would have specifically so provided had it wished to abolish the doctrine." Nothing in the legislative debates suggests that, in enacting § 1 of the Civil Rights Act, the 42d Congress intended any such abolition. Indeed, the limited legislative history relevant to this issue suggests the opposite.

B

Finding no evidence that Congress intended to disturb the settled common-law immunity, we now must determine whether considerations of public policy dictate a contrary result. In doing so, we examine the objectives underlying punitive damages in general, and their relationship to the goals of § 1983.

Punitive damages by definition are not intended to compensate the injured party, but rather to punish the tortfeasor whose wrongful action was intentional or malicious, and to deter him and others from similar extreme conduct. Regarding retribution, it remains true that an award of punitive damages against a municipality "punishes" only the taxpayers, who took no part in the commission of the tort. These damages are assessed over and above the amount necessary to compensate the injured party. Thus, there is no question here of equitably distributing the losses resulting from official misconduct. Indeed, punitive damages imposed on a municipality are in effect a windfall to a fully compensated plaintiff, and are likely accompanied by an increase in taxes or a reduction of public services for the citizens footing the bill. Neither reason nor justice suggests that such retribution should be visited upon the shoulders of blameless or unknowing taxpayers.

The other major objective of punitive damages awards is to prevent future misconduct. Respondent argues vigorously that deterrence is a primary purpose of § 1983, and that because punitive awards against municipalities for the malicious conduct of their policymaking officials will induce voters to condemn official misconduct through the electoral process, the threat of such awards will deter future constitutional violations. Respondent is correct in asserting that the deterrence of future abuses of power by persons acting under color of state law is an important purpose of § 1983. For several reasons, however, we conclude that the deterrence rationale of § 1983 does not justify making punitive damages available against municipalities.

First, it is far from clear that municipal officials, including those at the policymaking level, would be deterred from wrongdoing by the knowledge that large punitive awards could be assessed based on the wealth of their municipality. Indemnification may not be available to the municipality under local law, and even if it were, officials likely will not be able themselves to pay such sizable awards. Thus, assuming, *arguendo*, that the responsible official is not impervious to shame and humiliation, the impact on the individual tortfeasor of this deterrence in the air is at best uncertain.

There also is no reason to suppose that corrective action, such as the discharge of offending officials who were appointed and the public excoriation of those who were elected, will not occur unless punitive damages are awarded against the municipality.

Moreover, there is available a more effective means of deterrence. By allowing juries and courts to assess punitive damages in appropriate circumstances against the offending official, based on his personal financial resources, the statute directly advances the public's interest in preventing repeated constitutional deprivations. In our view, this provides sufficient protection against the prospect that a public official may commit recurrent constitutional violations by reason of his office. The Court previously has found, with respect to such violations, that a damages remedy recoverable against individuals is more effective as a deterrent than the threat of damages against a government employer. We see no reason to depart from that conclusion here, especially since the imposition of additional penalties would most likely fall upon the citizen-taxpayer.

Finally, although the benefits associated with awarding punitive damages against municipalities under § 1983 are of doubtful character, the costs may be very real.

The Court has remarked elsewhere on the broad discretion traditionally accorded to juries in assessing the amount of punitive damages. Because evidence of a tortfeasor's wealth is traditionally admissible as a measure of the amount of punitive damages that should be awarded, the unlimited taxing power of a municipality may have a prejudicial impact on the jury, in effect encouraging it to impose a sizable award. The impact of such a windfall recovery is likely to be both unpredictable and, at times, substantial, and we are sensitive to the possible strain on local treasuries and therefore on services available to the public at large. Absent a compelling reason for approving such an award, not present here, we deem it unwise to inflict the risk.

NOTES AND QUESTIONS

1. How does the Court justify insulating municipalities from punitive damages?

2. Did the Court properly distinguish compensatory from punitive damages and did it accurately weigh the competing policy concerns?

4. SECTION 1985: CONSPIRACY TO INTERFERE WITH CIVIL RIGHTS

a. Depriving Persons of Rights or Privileges

i.   Scope of § 1985(3)

GRIFFIN V. BRECKENRIDGE
403 U.S. 88 (1971)

Mr. Justice STEWART delivered the opinion of the Court.

This litigation began when the petitioners filed a complaint seeking compensatory and punitive damages and alleging, in substantial part, as follows:

2. The plaintiffs are Negro citizens of the United States and residents of Kemper County, Mississippi.

3. The defendants, Lavon Breckenridge and James Calvin Breckenridge, are white adult citizens of the United States residing in DeKalb, Kemper County, Mississippi.

4. On July 2, 1966, the plaintiffs were passengers in an automobile belonging to and operated by R.G. Grady of Memphis, Tennessee. They were travelling upon the federal, state and local highways in and about DeKalb, Mississippi, performing various errands and visiting friends.

5. On July 2, 1966 defendants, acting under a mistaken belief that R.G. Grady was a worker for Civil Rights for Negroes, willfully and maliciously conspired, planned, and agreed to block the passage of said plaintiffs in said automobile upon the public highways, to stop and detain them and to assault, beat and injure them with deadly weapons. Their purpose was to prevent said plaintiffs and other Negro-Americans, through such force, violence and intimidation, from seeking the equal protection of the laws and from enjoying the equal rights, privileges and immunities of citizens under the laws of the United States and the State of Mississippi, including but not limited to their rights to freedom of speech, movement, association and assembly; their right to petition their government for redress of their grievances; their rights to be secure in their persons and their homes; and their rights not to be enslaved nor deprived of life and liberty other than by due process of law.

6. Pursuant to their conspiracy, defendants drove their truck into the path of Grady's automobile and blocked its passage over the public road. Both defendants then forced Grady and said plaintiffs to get out of Grady's automobile and prevented said plaintiffs from escaping while defendant James Calvin Breckenridge clubbed Grady with a blackjack, pipe or other kind of club by pointing firearms at said plaintiffs and uttering threats to kill and injure them if defendants' orders were not obeyed, thereby terrorizing them to the utmost degree and depriving them of their liberty.

The District Court dismissed the complaint for failure to state a cause of action, relying on the authority of this Court's opinion in *Collins v. Hardyman*, which in effect construed the language of § 1985(3) as reaching only conspiracies under color of state law. The Court of Appeals for the Fifth Circuit affirmed the judgment of dismissal.

III

We turn, then, to an examination of the meaning of § 1985(3).[a] On their face, the words of the statute fully encompass the conduct of private persons. The provision speaks simply of "two or more persons in any State or Territory" who "conspire or go in disguise on the highway or on the premises of another." Going in disguise, in particular, is in this context an activity so little associated with official action and so commonly connected with private marauders that this clause could almost never be applicable under the artificially restrictive construction of *Collins*. And since the "going in disguise" aspect must include private action, it is hard to see how the conspiracy aspect, joined by a disjunctive, could be read to require the involvement of state officers.

The provision continues, specifying the motivation required "for the purpose of depriving, either directly or indirectly, any person or class of persons of the equal protection of laws, or of the equal privileges and immunities under the laws." This language is, of course, similar to that of § 1 of the Fourteenth Amendment, which in terms speaks only to the States, and

---

a   Review § 1985(3) in Appendix.

judicial thinking about what can constitute an equal protection deprivation has, because of the Amendment's wording, focused almost entirely upon identifying the requisite "state action" and defining the offending forms of state law and official conduct. A century of Fourteenth Amendment adjudication has, in other words, made it understandably difficult to conceive of what might constitute a deprivation of the equal protection of the laws by private persons. Yet there is nothing inherent in the phrase that requires the action working the deprivation to come from the State. Indeed, the failure to mention any such requisite can be viewed as an important indication of congressional intent to speak in § 1985(3) of *all* deprivations of "equal protection of the laws" and "equal privileges and immunities under the laws," whatever their source.

In construing the exact criminal counterpart of § 1985(3), the Court observed that the statute was "not limited to take effect only in case [of state action]," but "was framed to protect from invasion by private persons, the equal privileges and immunities under the laws, of all persons and classes of persons." *United States v. Harris.*

A like construction of § 1985(3) is reinforced when examination is broadened to take in its companion statutory provisions. There appear to be three possible forms for a state action limitation on § 1985(3)—that there must be action under color of state law, that there must be interference with or influence upon state authorities, or that there must be a private conspiracy so massive and effective that it supplants those authorities and thus satisfies the state action requirement. The Congress that passed the Civil Rights Act of 1871, § 2 of which is the parent of § 1985(3), dealt with each of these three situations in explicit terms in other parts of the same Act. [For example] an element of the cause of action established by the first section, 42 U.S.C. § 1983, is that the deprivation complained of must have been inflicted under color of state law. To read any such requirement into § 1985(3) would thus deprive that section of all independent effect.

The final area of inquiry into the meaning of § 1985(3) lies in its legislative history. As originally introduced in the 42d Congress, the section was solely a criminal provision outlawing certain conspiratorial acts done with intent "to do any act in violation of the rights, privileges, or immunities of another person." Introducing the bill, the House sponsor, Representative Shellabarger, stressed that "the United States always has assumed to enforce, as against the States, *and also persons*, every one of the provisions of the Constitution." The enormous sweep of the original language led to pressures for amendment, in the course of which the present civil remedy was added. The explanations of the added language centered entirely on the animus or motivation that would be required, and there was no suggestion whatever that liability would not be imposed for purely private conspiracies.

Other supporters of the bill were even more explicit in their insistence upon coverage of private action. Shortly before the amendment was introduced, Representative Shanks urged, "I do not want to see [this measure] so amended that there shall be taken out of it the frank assertion of the power of the national Government to protect life, liberty, and property, irrespective of the act of the State." At about the same time, Representative Coburn asked: "Shall we deal with individuals, or with the State as a State? If we can deal with individuals, that is a less radical course, and works less interference with local governments." After the amendment had been proposed in the House, Senator Pool insisted in support of the bill during Senate debate that "Congress must deal with individuals, not States. It must punish the offender against the rights of the citizen. . . ."

It is thus evident that all indicators—text, companion provisions, and legislative history—point unwaveringly to § 1985(3)'s coverage of private conspiracies. That the statute was meant to reach private action does not, however, mean that it was intended to apply to all tortious, conspiratorial interferences with the rights of others. For, though the supporters of the legislation insisted on coverage of private conspiracies, they were equally emphatic that they did not believe, in the words of Representative Cook, "that Congress has a right to punish an assault and battery when committed by two or more persons within a State." The constitutional shoals that would lie in the path of interpreting § 1985(3) as a general federal tort law can be avoided by giving full effect to the congressional purpose—by requiring, as an element of the cause of action, the kind of invidiously discriminatory motivation stressed by the sponsors of the limiting amendment. The language requiring intent to deprive of *equal* protection, or *equal* privileges and immunities, means that there must be some racial, or perhaps otherwise class-based, invidiously discriminatory animus behind the conspirators' action.[9] The conspiracy, in other words, must aim at a deprivation of the equal enjoyment of rights secured by the law to all.

IV

We return to the petitioners' complaint to determine whether it states a cause of action under § 1985(3) as so construed. To come within the legislation a complaint must allege that the defendants did (1) "conspire or go in disguise on the highway or on the premises of another" (2) "for the purpose of depriving, either directly or indirectly, any person or class of persons of the equal protection of the laws, or of equal privileges and immunities under the laws." It must then assert that one or more of the conspirators (3) did, or caused to be done, "any act in furtherance of the object of [the] conspiracy," whereby another was (4a) "injured in his person or property" or (4b) "deprived of having and exercising any right or privilege of a citizen of the United States."

The complaint fully alleges, with particulars, that the respondents conspired to carry out the assault. It further asserts that "[t]heir purpose was to prevent [the] plaintiffs and other Negro-Americans, through . . . force, violence and intimidation, from seeking the equal protection of the laws and from enjoying the equal rights, privileges and immunities of citizens under the laws of the United States and the State of Mississippi," including a long list of enumerated rights such as free speech, assembly, association, and movement. The complaint further alleges that the respondents were "acting under a mistaken belief that R.G. Grady was a worker for Civil Rights for Negroes." These allegations clearly support the requisite animus to deprive the petitioners of the equal enjoyment of legal rights because of their race. The claims of detention, threats, and battery amply satisfy the requirement of acts done in furtherance of the conspiracy. Finally, the petitioners—whether or not the nonparty Grady was the main or only target of

---

9 We need not decide, given the facts of this case, whether a conspiracy motivated by invidiously discriminatory intent other than racial bias would be actionable under the portion of § 1985(3) before us.

the conspiracy—allege personal injury resulting from those acts. The complaint, then, states a cause of action under § 1985(3). Indeed, the conduct here alleged lies so close to the core of the coverage intended by Congress that it is hard to conceive of wholly private conduct that would come within the statute if this does not. We must, accordingly, consider whether Congress had constitutional power to enact a statute that imposes liability under federal law for the conduct alleged in this complaint.

V

[W]e need not find the language of § 1985(3) now before us constitutional in all its possible applications in order to uphold its facial constitutionality and its application to the complaint in this case.

That § 1985(3) reaches private conspiracies to deprive others of legal rights can, of itself, cause no doubts of its constitutionality.

Our inquiry, therefore, need go only to identifying a source of congressional power to reach the private conspiracy alleged by the complaint in this case.

A

[S]urely there has never been any doubt of the power of Congress to impose liability on private persons under § 2 of [the Thirteenth Amendment], "for the amendment is not a mere prohibition of State laws establishing or upholding slavery, but an absolute declaration that slavery or involuntary servitude shall not exist in any part of the United States." *Civil Rights Cases.* Not only may Congress impose such liability, but the varieties of private conduct that it may make criminally punishable or civilly remediable extend far beyond the actual imposition of slavery or involuntary servitude. By the Thirteenth Amendment, we committed ourselves as a Nation to the proposition that the former slaves and their descendants should be forever free. To keep that promise, "Congress has the power under the Thirteenth Amendment rationally to determine what are the badges and the incidents of slavery, and the authority to translate that determination into effective legislation." *Jones v. Alfred H. Mayer Co.* We can only conclude that Congress was wholly within its powers under § 2 of the Thirteenth Amendment in creating a statutory cause of action for Negro citizens who have been the victims of conspiratorial, racially discriminatory private action aimed at depriving them of the basic rights that the law secures to all free men.

B

Our cases have firmly established that the right of interstate travel is constitutionally protected, does not necessarily rest on the Fourteenth Amendment, and is assertable against private as well as governmental interference. The "right to pass freely from State to State" has been explicitly recognized as "among the rights and privileges of National citizenship." That right, like other rights of national citizenship, is within the power of Congress to protect by appropriate legislation.

The complaint in this case alleged that the petitioners "were travelling upon the federal, state and local highways in and about" DeKalb, Kemper County, Mississippi. Kemper County is on the Mississippi-Alabama border. One of the results of the conspiracy, according to the complaint, was to prevent the petitioners and other Negroes from exercising their "rights to travel the public highways without restraint in the same terms as white citizens in Kemper County, Mississippi." Finally, the conspiracy was alleged to have been inspired by the respondents' erroneous belief that Grady, a Tennessean, was a worker for Negro civil rights. Under these allegations it is open to the petitioners to prove at trial that they had been engaging in interstate travel or intended to do so, that their federal right to travel interstate was one of the rights meant to be discriminatorily impaired by the conspiracy, that the conspirators intended to drive out-of-state civil rights workers from the State, or that they meant to deter the petitioners from associating with such persons. This and other evidence could make it clear that the petitioners had suffered from conduct that Congress may reach under its power to protect the right of interstate travel.

C

In identifying these two constitutional sources of congressional power, we do not imply the absence of any other. More specifically, the allegations of the complaint in this case have not required consideration of the scope of the power of Congress under § 5 of the Fourteenth Amendment. By the same token, since the allegations of the complaint bring this cause of action so close to the constitutionally authorized core of the statute, there has been no occasion here to trace out its constitutionally permissible periphery.

NOTES AND QUESTIONS

1. How does the Court justify its conclusion that § 1985(3) reaches private conspiracies?

2. What substantive rights of the plaintiffs were allegedly violated in *Griffin*?

3. Where does the Court find congressional power to reach the private conspiracy alleged here? If congressional power is based on the Thirteenth Amendment, can any group other than blacks seek protection under § 1985? Recall the Supreme Court's interpretation of § 1981 and § 1982.

4. Where in § 1985(3) does the Court find the class-based animus requirement? What is the Court's concern if the statute is not limited to situations where there is a class-based animus?

5. Could these plaintiffs state a claim under § 1981? § 1982? § 1983?

CARPENTERS V. SCOTT

463 U.S. 825 (1983)

Justice WHITE, delivered the opinion of the Court.

This case concerns the scope of the cause of action made available by 42 U.S.C. § 1985(3) to those injured by conspiracies formed "for the purpose of depriving, either directly or indirectly, any person or class of persons of the equal protection of the laws, or of equal privileges and immunities under the laws."

I

A.A. Cross Construction Co., Inc. (Cross), contracted with the Department of the Army to construct the Alligator Bayou Pumping Station and Gravity Drainage Structure on the Taylor Bayou Hurricane Levee near Port Arthur, Tex. In accordance with its usual practice, Cross hired workers for the project without regard to union membership. Some of them were from outside the Port Arthur area. Employees of Cross were several times warned by local residents that Cross' practice of hiring nonunion workers was a matter of serious concern to many in the area and that it could lead to trouble. According to the District Court, the evidence showed that at a January 15, 1975, meeting of the Executive Committee of the Sabine Area Building and Construction Trades Council a citizen protest against Cross' hiring practices was discussed and a time and place for the protest were chosen. On the morning of January 17, a large group assembled at the entrance to the Alligator Bayou construction site. In the Group were union members present at the January 15 meeting. From this gathering several truckloads of men emerged, drove on to the construction site, assaulted and beat Cross employees, and burned and destroyed construction equipment. The District Court found that continued violence was threatened "if the nonunion workers did not leave the area or concede to union policies and principles." The violence and vandalism delayed construction and led Cross to default on its contract with the Army.

The plaintiffs in this case, after amendment of the complaint, were respondents Scott and Matthews—two Cross employees who had been beaten—and the company itself. The Sabine Area Building and Trades Council, 25 local unions, and various individuals were named as defendants. Plaintiffs asserted that defendants had conspired to deprive plaintiffs of their legally protected rights, contrary to 42 U.S.C. § 1985(3). The case was tried to the court. A permanent injunction was entered, and damages were awarded against 11 of the local unions, $5,000 each to the individual plaintiffs and $112,385.44 to Cross, plus attorney's fees in the amount of $25,000.

II

We do not disagree with the District court and the Court of Appeals that there was a conspiracy, an act done in furtherance thereof, and a resultant injury to persons and property. Contrary to the Court of Appeals, however, we conclude that an alleged conspiracy to infringe First Amendment rights is not a violation of § 1985(3) unless it is proved that the State is involved in the conspiracy or that the aim of the conspiracy is to influence the activity of the State. We also disagree with the Court of Appeals' view that there was present here the kind of animus that § 1985(3) requires.

The Equal Protection Clause of the Fourteenth Amendment prohibits any State from denying any person the equal protection of the laws. The First Amendment, which by virtue of the Due Process Clause of the Fourteenth Amendment now applies to state governments and their officials, prohibits either Congress or a State from making any "law . . . abridging the freedom of speech, . . . or the right of the people peaceably to assemble." Had § 1985(3) in so many words prohibited conspiracies to deprive any person of the equal protection of the laws guaranteed by the Fourteenth Amendment or of freedom of speech guaranteed by the First Amendment, it would be untenable to contend that either of those provisions could be violated by a conspiracy that did not somehow involve or affect a State. [Therefore] a conspiracy to violate First Amendment rights is not made out without proof of state involvement.

Griffin v. Breckinridge is not to the contrary. There we held that § 1985(3) reaches purely private conspiracies and, as so interpreted, was not invalid on its face or as there applied.

Griffin did not hold that even when the alleged conspiracy is aimed at a right that is by definition a right only against state interference the plaintiff in a § 1985(3) suit nevertheless need not prove that the conspiracy contemplated state involvement of some sort. The complaint in *Griffin* alleged, among other things, a deprivation of First Amendment rights, but we did not sustain the action on the basis of that allegation and paid it scant attention. Instead, we upheld the application of § 1985(3) to private conspiracies aimed at interfering with rights constitutionally protected against private, as well as official, encroachment.

Neither is respondents' position helped by the assertion that even if the Fourteenth Amendment does not provide authority to proscribe exclusively private conspiracies, precisely the same conduct could be proscribed by the Commerce Clause. That is no doubt the case; but § 1985(3) is not such a provision, since it "provides no substantive rights itself" to the class conspired against. The rights, privileges, and immunities that § 1985(3) vindicates must be found elsewhere, and here the right claimed to have been infringed has its source in the First Amendment. Because that Amendment restrains only official conduct, to make out their § 1985(3) case, it was necessary for respondents to prove that the State was somehow involved in or affected by the conspiracy.

The Court of Appeals accordingly erred in holding that § 1985(3) prohibits wholly private conspiracies to abridge the right of association guaranteed by the First Amendment. Because of that holding the Court of Appeals found it unnecessary to determine whether respondent's action could be sustained under § 1985(3) as involving a conspiracy to deprive respondents of rights, privileges, or immunities under state law or those protected against private action by the Federal Constitution or federal statutory law. Conceivably, we could remand for consideration of these possibilities, or we ourselves could consider them. We take neither course, for in our view the Court of Appeals should also be reversed on the dispositive ground that § 1985(3)'s requirement that there must be "some racial, or perhaps otherwise class-based, invidiously discriminatory animus behind the conspirators' action," was not satisfied in this case.

Because the facts in *Griffin* revealed an animus against Negroes and those who supported them, a class-based, invidious discrimination which was the central concern of Congress in enacting § 1985(3), the Court expressly declined to decide "whether a conspiracy motivated by invidiously discriminatory intent other than racial bias would be actionable under the portion of § 1985(3) before us." Both courts below answered that question; both held that the section not only reaches conspiracies other than those motivated by racial bias but also forbids conspiracies against workers who refuse to join a union. We disagree with the latter conclusion and do not affirm the former.

The Court of Appeals arrived at its result by first describing the Reconstruction-era Ku Klux Klan as a political organization that sought to deprive a large segment of the Southern population of political power and participation in the governance of those States and of the Nation. The Court of Appeals then reasoned that because Republicans were among the objects of the Klan's conspiratorial activities, Republicans in particular and political groups in general were to be protected by § 1985(3). Finally, because it believed that an animus against an economic group such as those who preferred nonunion association is "closely akin" to the animus against political association, the Court of Appeals concluded that the animus against nonunion employees in the Port Arthur area was sufficiently similar to the animus against a political party to satisfy the requirements of § 1985(3).

We are unpersuaded. In the first place, it is a close question whether § 1985(3) was intended to reach any class-based animus other than the animus against Negroes and those who championed their cause, most notably Republicans. The central theme of the bill's proponents was that the Klan and others were forcibly resisting efforts to emancipate Negroes and give them equal access to political power. The predominant purpose of § 1985(3) was to combat the prevalent animus against Negroes and their supporters. The latter included Republicans generally, as well as others, such as Northerners who came South with sympathetic views towards the Negro. Although we have examined with some care the legislative history that has been marshaled in support of the position that Congress meant to forbid wholly nonracial, but politically motivated conspiracies, we find difficult the question whether § 1985(3) provided a remedy for every concerted effort by one political group to nullify the influence of or do other injury to a competing group by use of otherwise unlawful means. To accede to that view would go far toward making the federal courts, by virtue of § 1985(3), the monitors of campaign tactics in both state and federal elections, a role that the courts should not be quick to assume. If respondents' submission were accepted, the proscription of § 1985(3) would arguably reach the claim that a political party has interfered with the freedom of speech of another political party by encouraging the heckling of its rival's speakers and the disruption of the rival's meetings.

We realize that there is some legislative history to support the view that § 1985(3) has a broader reach. Senator Edmunds' statement on the floor of the Senate is the clearest expression of this view. He said that if a conspiracy were formed against a man "because he was a Democrat, if you please, or because he was a Catholic, or because he was a Methodist, or because he was a Vermonter, . . . then this section could reach it." The provision that is now § 1985(3), however, originated in the House. The narrowing amendment, which changed § 1985(3) to its present form, was proposed, debated, and adopted there, and the Senate made only technical changes to the bill. Senator Edmund's views, since he managed the bill on the floor of the Senate, are not without weight. But we were aware of his views in *Griffin* and still withheld judgment on the question whether § 1985(3), as enacted, went any farther than its central concern—combating the violent and other efforts of the Klan and its allies to resist and to frustrate the intended effects of the Thirteenth, Fourteenth, and Fifteenth Amendments. Lacking other evidence of congressional intention, we follow the same course here.

D

Even if the section must be construed to reach conspiracies aimed at any class or organization on account of its political views or activities, or at any other classes posited by Senator Edmunds, we find no convincing support in the legislative history for the proposition that the provision was intended to reach conspiracies motivated by bias towards others on account of their *economic* views, status, or activities. Such a construction would extend § 1985(3) into the economic life of the country in a way that we doubt that the 1871 Congress would have intended when it passed the provision in 1871.

Respondents submit that Congress intended to protect two general classes of Republicans, Negroes and Northern immigrants, the latter because the Klan resented carpetbagger efforts to dominate the economic life of the South. Respondents rely on a series of statements made during the debates on the Civil Rights Act of 1871, of which § 1985 was a part, indicating that Northern laborers and businessmen who had come from the North had been the targets of Klan conspiracies. As we understand these remarks, however, the speakers believed that these Northerners were viewed as suspect because they were Republicans and were thought to be sympathetic to Negroes. We do not interpret these parts of the debates as asserting that the Klan had a general animus against either labor or capital, or against persons from other States as such. Nor is it plausible that the Southern Democrats were prejudiced generally against enterprising persons trying to better themselves, even if those enterprising persons were from the Northern States. The animus was against Negroes and their sympathizers, and perhaps against Republicans as a class, but not against economic groups as such.

We thus cannot construe § 1985(3) to reach conspiracies motivated by economic or commercial animus. Were it otherwise, for example, § 1985(3) could be brought to bear on any act of violence resulting from union efforts to organize an employer or from the employer's efforts to resist it, so long as the victim merely asserted and proved that the conduct involved a conspiracy motivated by an animus in favor of unionization, or against it, as the case may be. The National Labor Relations Act addresses in great detail the relationship between employer, employee, and union in a great variety of situations, and it would be an unsettling event to rule that strike and picket-line violence must now be considered in the light of the strictures of § 1985(3). Economic and commercial conflicts, we think, are best dealt with by statutes, federal or state, specifically addressed to such problems, as well as by the general law proscribing injuries to persons and property. If we have misconstrued the intent of the 1871 Congress, or, in any event, if Congress now prefers to take a different tack, the Court will, of course, enforce any statute within the power of Congress to enact.

NOTES AND QUESTIONS

1. Why were plaintiffs precluded from enforcing their First Amendment rights under § 1985(3)? How was *Griffin* distinguished?

2. The Court has never answered the question posed in *Griffin, supra,* at n.9, "whether a conspiracy motivated by invidiously discriminatory intent other than racial bias would be actionable under the portion of § 1985(3) before us," and *Scott* simply describes this as a "close question."

BRAY V. ALEXANDRIA WOMEN'S HEALTH CLINIC
506 U.S. 263 (1993)

Justice SCALIA delivered the opinion of the Court.

This case presents the question whether the first clause of 42 U.S.C. § 1985(3)—the surviving version of § 2 of the Civil Rights Act of 1871—provides a federal cause of action against persons obstructing access to abortion clinics. Respondents are clinics that perform abortions, and organizations that support legalized abortion and that have members who may wish to use abortion clinics. Petitioners are Operation Rescue, an unincorporated association whose members oppose abortion, and six individuals. Among its activities, Operation Rescue organizes antiabortion demonstrations in which participants trespass on, and obstruct general access to, the premises of abortion clinics. The individual petitioners organize and coordinate these demonstrations.

Respondents sued to enjoin petitioners from conducting demonstrations at abortion clinics in the Washington, D.C., metropolitan area. Following an expedited trial, the District Court ruled that petitioners had violated § 1985(3) by conspiring to deprive women seeking abortions of their right to interstate travel. The court also ruled for respondents on their pendent state-law claims of trespass and public nuisance. As relief on these three claims, the court enjoined petitioners from trespassing on, or obstructing access to, abortion clinics in specified Virginia counties and cities in the Washington, D.C., metropolitan area.

I

Our precedents establish that in order to prove a private conspiracy in violation of the first clause of § 1985(3), a plaintiff must show, inter alia, (1) that "some racial, or perhaps otherwise class-based, invidiously discriminatory animus [lay] behind the conspirators' action," *Griffin v.*

Breckenridge, and (2) that the conspiracy "aimed at interfering with rights" that are "protected against private, as well as official, encroachment," *Carpenters v. Scott*. We think neither showing has been made in the present case.

A

To begin with, we reject the apparent conclusion of the District Court (which respondents make no effort to defend) that opposition to abortion constitutes discrimination against the "class" of "women seeking abortion." Whatever may be the precise meaning of a "class" for purposes of *Griffin*'s speculative extension of § 1985(3) beyond race, the term unquestionably connotes something more than a group of individuals who share a desire to engage in conduct that the § 1985(3) defendant disfavors. Otherwise, innumerable tort plaintiffs would be able to assert causes of action under § 1985(3) by simply defining the aggrieved class as those seeking to engage in the activity the defendant has interfered with. This definitional ploy would convert the statute into the "general federal tort law" it was the very purpose of the animus requirement to avoid.

Respondents' contention, however, is that the alleged class-based discrimination is directed not at "women seeking abortion" but at women in general. We find it unnecessary to decide whether that is a qualifying class under § 1985(3), since the claim that petitioners' opposition to abortion reflects an animus against women in general must be rejected. We do not think that the "animus" requirement can be met only by maliciously motivated, as opposed to assertedly benign (though objectively invidious), discrimination against women. It does demand, however, at least a purpose that focuses upon women by reason of their sex—for example (to use an illustration of assertedly benign discrimination), the purpose of "saving" women because they are women from a combative, aggressive profession such as the practice of law. The record in this case does not indicate that petitioners' demonstrations are motivated by a purpose (malevolent or benign) directed specifically at women as a class; to the contrary, the District Court found that petitioners define their "rescues" not with reference to women, but as physical intervention "'between abortionists and the innocent victims,'" and that "all [petitioners] share a deep commitment to the goals of stopping the practice of abortion and reversing its legalization." Given this record, respondents' contention that a class-based animus has been established can be true only if one of two suggested propositions is true: (1) that opposition to abortion can reasonably be presumed to reflect a sex-based intent, or (2) that intent is irrelevant, and a class-based animus can be determined solely by effect. Neither proposition is supportable.

As to the first: Some activities may be such an irrational object of disfavor that, if they are targeted, and if they also happen to be engaged in exclusively or predominantly by a particular class of people, an intent to disfavor that class can readily be presumed. A tax on wearing yarmulkes is a tax on Jews. But opposition to voluntary abortion cannot possibly be considered such an irrational surrogate for opposition to (or paternalism towards) women. Whatever one thinks of abortion, it cannot be denied that there are common and respectable reasons for opposing it, other than hatred of or condescension toward (or indeed any view at all concerning) women as a class—as is evident from the fact that men and women are on both sides of the issue, just as men and women are on both sides of petitioners' unlawful demonstrations.

Respondents' case comes down, then, to the proposition that intent is legally irrelevant; that since voluntary abortion is an activity engaged in only by women, to disfavor it is ipso facto to discriminate invidiously against women as a class. Our cases do not support that proposition. In *Geduldig v. Aiello*, we rejected the claim that a state disability insurance system that denied coverage to certain disabilities resulting from pregnancy discriminated on the basis of sex in violation of the Equal Protection Clause of the Fourteenth Amendment. "While it is true," we said, "that only women can become pregnant, it does not follow that every legislative classification concerning pregnancy is a sex-based classification." We reached a similar conclusion in *Personnel Administrator of Mass. v. Feeney*, sustaining against an Equal Protection Clause challenge a Massachusetts law giving employment preference to military veterans, a class which in Massachusetts was over 98% male. "'Discriminatory purpose,'" we said, "implies more than intent as volition or intent as awareness of consequences. It implies that the decisionmaker . . . selected or reaffirmed a particular course of action at least in part 'because of,' not merely 'in spite of,' its adverse effects upon an identifiable group." The same principle applies to "class-based, invidiously discriminatory animus" requirement of § 1985(3).

The nature of the "invidiously discriminatory animus" *Griffin* had in mind is suggested both by the language used in that phrase and by the company in which the phrase is found. Whether one agrees or disagrees with the goal of preventing abortion, that goal in itself (apart from the use of unlawful means to achieve it, which is not relevant to our discussion of animus) does not remotely qualify for such harsh description, and for such derogatory association with racism.

B

Respondents' federal claim fails for a second, independent reason: A § 1985(3) private conspiracy "for the purpose of depriving . . . any person or class of persons of the equal protection of the laws, or of equal privileges and immunities under the laws," requires an intent to deprive persons of a right guaranteed against private impairment. No intent to deprive of such a right was established here.

Respondents, like the courts below, rely upon the right to interstate travel—which we have held to be, in at least some contexts, a right constitutionally protected against private interference. But all that respondents can point to by way of connecting petitioners' actions with that particular right is the District Court's finding that "[s]ubstantial numbers of women seeking the services of [abortion] clinics in the Washington Metropolitan area travel interstate to reach the clinics." That is not enough.

Our discussion in *Carpenters* makes clear that it does not suffice for application of § 1985(3) that a protected right be incidentally affected. A conspiracy is not "for the purpose" of denying equal protection simply because it has an effect upon a protected right. The right must be "aimed at," its impairment must be a conscious objective of the enterprise. Just as the invidiously discriminatory animus" requirement, discussed above, requires that the defendant have taken his action "at least in part 'because of,' not merely 'in spite of,' its adverse effects upon an identifiable group," so also the "intent to deprive of a right" requirement demands that the defendant do more than merely be aware of a deprivation of right that he causes, and more than merely accept it; he must act at least in part for the very purpose of producing it. That was not shown to be the case here, and is on its face implausible. Petitioners oppose abortion, and it is irrelevant to their opposition whether the abortion is performed after interstate travel.

Respondents have failed to show a conspiracy to violate the right of interstate travel for yet another reason: petitioners' proposed demonstrations would not implicate that right. The federal guarantee of interstate travel does not transform state-law torts into federal offenses when they are intentionally committed against interstate travelers. Rather, it protects interstate travelers against two sets of burdens: "the erection of actual barriers to interstate movement" and "being treated differently" from intrastate travelers. As far as appears from this record, the only "actual barriers to movement" that would have resulted from Petitioners' proposed demonstrations would have been in the immediate vicinity of the abortion clinics, restricting movement from one portion of the Commonwealth of Virginia to another. Such a purely intrastate restriction does not implicate the right of interstate travel, even if it is applied intentionally against travelers from other States, unless it is applied discriminatorily against them. That would not be the case here, as respondents conceded at oral argument.

The other right alleged by respondents to have been intentionally infringed is the right to abortion. The District Court declined to rule on this contention, relying exclusively upon the right-of-interstate-travel theory; in our view it also is an inadequate basis for respondents' § 1985(3) claim. Whereas, unlike the right of interstate travel, the asserted right to abortion was assuredly "aimed at" by the petitioners, deprivation of that federal right (whatever its contours) cannot be the object of a purely private conspiracy. In *Carpenters*, we rejected a claim that an alleged private conspiracy to infringe First Amendment rights violated § 1985(3). The statute does not apply, we said, to private conspiracies that are "aimed at a right that is by definition a right only against state interference," but applies only to such conspiracies as are "aimed at interfering with rights . . . protected against private, as well as official, encroachment." There are few such rights (we have hitherto recognized only the Thirteenth Amendment right to be free from involuntary servitude, and, in the same Thirteenth Amendment context, the right of interstate travel). The right to abortion is not among them.

[Three dissenters argued that class-based animus against women exists because the defendants oppose exercise of a right that is unique to women.]

NOTES AND QUESTIONS

1. Does the Court rule out gender-biased claims under § 1985(3)? Some appellate courts have "included sex discrimination within the categories of animus condemned by § 1985(3)." *See, e.g., Novotny v. Great American Federal Savings & Loan Ass'n*, 584 F.2d 1235 (3d Cir. 1978), *rev'd on other grounds*, 442 U.S. 366 (1979), *see infra*.

2. Why does the Court reject the interstate travel and abortion rights claims?

PROBLEM: NINE

Plaintiff Taylor took up residence in the monastery of the Holy Protection of the Blessed Virgin Mary, a local religious organization, in Oklahoma City, Oklahoma. Taylor's parents were opposed to his joining the religion and in July of 1976 they took the action which led to this cause. They employed an organization called the Freedom of Thought Foundation, a corporation which carries on the business of deprogramming religious zealots. Deprogramming is a process of attempting a psychological shock treatment on members of nonmainstream religious sects in an effort to sever their involvement with a religious cult lifestyle.

As part of the program, Taylor's father, through Freedom of Thought, applied to the Oklahoma County District Court to be appointed as "temporary" guardian of Taylor. Defendants Howard and Trauscht, lawyers for Dr. Taylor, the father of plaintiff, visited Judge John A. Benson, an Oklahoma state district judge who was temporarily assigned in Oklahoma City, and conferred with him ex parte. They asked him to hear the case. Benson contacted the Probate Judge who would ordinarily hear such a matter and obtained permission to hear it. Only after that was the petition for guardianship filed. Judge Benson ordered the temporary guardian of plaintiff's person be appointed in order to determine whether plaintiff was under the influence of a religious cult. Judge Benson said that he wanted the plaintiff taken into custody "so that (plaintiff) could be given notice of a [permanent] guardianship hearing." Plaintiff was at the monastery when the deputies came for him. He offered no resistance. The hearing occurred before Judge Benson as soon as Taylor was brought into court. Although Judge Benson found him to be normal, he formally entered an "order appointing Taylor's father as Temporary Guardian of the Person."

The July 15, 1976 order provided that Dr. Walter Taylor be appointed the Temporary Guardian of the Person of the plaintiff with power to take him into custody and have him examined, counseled and treated by a variety of health professionals.

On the basis of this order, plaintiff was taken that same day from Oklahoma City, Oklahoma to Akron, Ohio. He was not examined by physicians or psychiatrists. The only examination occurred on July 24 which was performed by Dr. Gilmartin, a psychologist, with apparently some experience in treating cult members. Taylor was held for approximately one week in Akron where he was kept at a motel and under constant guard. There followed the deprogramming. Taylor testified that he was physically and mentally abused, subjected to shock treatment, threatened with jail if he escaped, and told the pressure would stop if he would renounce his religion.

Around July 23, 1976, plaintiff was taken from Akron to Phoenix, Arizona, where apparently his mother was staying. He was held, still under guard, for the rehabilitation phase of the deprogramming. However, he escaped July 31, 1976, and returned to Oklahoma City and to the seminary. He has been there ever since. The record does not indicate that any effort was made to remove him from the seminary after this. Subsequently, Taylor instituted this present suit in the United States District Court for the Eastern District of Oklahoma against not only the deprogrammers, but also his parents and his brother. However, the Taylor family members were dismissed by an agreement prior to trial. The deprogrammers remain.

1. The complaint asserts a claim against the deprogrammers under § 1985(3): (a) Is there a class-based animus? (b) What substantive right(s) should be asserted by the plaintiff and are those rights enforceable through § 1985(3)?

2. Could the plaintiff state a claim under § 1983, and thereby avoid the class-based animus and conspiracy requirements? Review *Lugar* and *Tower v. Glover, supra* Ch. II. If yes, does § 1985(3) add anything not already provided through § 1983?

ii.   Rights Enforceable Through § 1985(3)

GREAT AMERICAN FEDERAL SAVINGS & LOAN ASS'N V. NOVOTNY
442 U.S. 366 (1979)

Mr. Justice STEWART delivered the opinion of the Court.

I

The respondent, John R. Novotny, began his career with the Great American Federal Savings and Loan Association (hereinafter Association) in Allegheny County, Pa., in 1950. By 1975, he was secretary of the Association, a member of its board of directors, and a loan officer. According to the allegations of the complaint in this case the Association "intentionally and deliberately embarked upon and pursued a course of conduct the effect of which was to deny to female employees equal employment opportunity. . . ." When Novotny expressed support for the female employees at a meeting of the board of directors, his connection with the Association abruptly ended. He was not re-elected as secretary; he was not re-elected to the board; and he was fired. His support for the Association's female employees, he alleges, was the cause of the termination of his employment.

Novotny filed a complaint with the Equal Employment Opportunity Commission under Title VII of the Civil Rights Act of 1964. After receiving a right-to-sue letter, he brought this lawsuit against the Association and its directors. He claimed damages under 42 U.S.C. § 1985(3), contending that he had been injured as the result of a conspiracy to deprive him of equal protection of and equal privileges and immunities under the laws. The District Court granted the defendant's motion to dismiss. It held that § 1985(3) could not be invoked because the directors of a single corporation could not, as a matter of law and fact, engage in a conspiracy.

Novotny appealed. The Court of Appeals ruled that Novotny had stated a cause of action under § 1985(3). It held that conspiracies motivated by an invidious animus against women fall within the § 1985(3), and that Novotny, a male allegedly injured as a result of such a conspiracy, had standing to bring suit under that statutory provision. It ruled that Title VII could be the source of a right asserted in an action under § 1985(3), and that intracorporate conspiracies come within the intendment of the section. Finally, the court concluded that its construction of § 1985(3) did not present any serious constitutional problem.

II

Section 1985(3) provides no substantive rights itself; it merely provides a remedy for violation of the rights it designates. The primary question in the present case, therefore, is whether a person injured by a conspiracy to violate § 704(a) of Title VII of the Civil Rights Act of 1964 is deprived of "the equal protection of the laws, or of equal privileges and immunities under the laws" within the meaning of § 1985(3).[11]

Under Title VII, cases of alleged employment discrimination are subject to detailed administrative and judicial process designed to provide an opportunity for nonjudicial and nonadversary resolution of claims.

The Act provides for injunctive relief, specifically including backpay relief. The majority of the federal courts have held that the Act does not allow a court to award general or punitive damages.[a] The Act expressly allows the prevailing party to recover his attorney's fees, and, in some cases, provides that a district court may appoint counsel for a plaintiff. Because the Act expressly authorizes only equitable remedies, the courts have consistently held that neither party has a right to a jury trial.

If a violation of Title VII could be asserted through § 1985(3), a complainant could avoid most if not all of these detailed and specific provisions of the law. Section 1985(3) expressly authorizes compensatory damages; punitive damages might well follow. The plaintiff or defendant might demand a jury trial. The short and precise time limitations of Title VII would be grossly altered. Perhaps most importantly, the complainant could completely bypass the administrative process, which plays in the scheme established by Congress in Title VII.

The problem in this case is closely akin to that in *Brown v. GSA*. There, we held that § 717 of Title VII provides the exclusive remedy for employment discrimination claims of those federal employees that it covers. Our conclusion was based on the proposition that

> [t]he balance, completeness, and structural integrity of § 717 are inconsistent with the petitioner's contention that the judicial remedy afforded by § 717(c) was designed merely to supplement other putative judicial relief.

---

11 For the purposes of this question we assume but certainly do not decide that the directors of a single corporation can form a conspiracy within the meaning of § 1985(3).

2a The Civil Rights Act of 1991 added a damage provision, albeit with caps, for Title VII litigants. See *infra* Ch. III.

Here, the case is even more compelling. In *Brown*, the Court concluded that § 717 displaced other causes of action arguably available to assert substantive rights similar to those granted by § 717. Section 1985(3), by contrast, *creates* no rights. It is a purely remedial statute, providing a civil cause of action when some otherwise defined federal rights—to equal protection of the laws or equal privileges and immunities under the laws—is breached by a conspiracy in the manner defined by the section. Thus, we are not faced in this case with a question of implied repeal. The right Novotny claims under § 704(a) did not even arguably exist before the passage of Title VII. The only question here, therefore, is whether the rights created by Title VII may be asserted within the *remedial* framework of § 1985(3).

This case thus differs markedly from the cases recently decided by this Court that have related the substantive provisions of last century's Civil Rights Acts to contemporary legislation conferring similar substantive rights. In those cases we have held that substantive rights conferred in the 19th century were not withdrawn, *sub silentio*, by the subsequent passage of the modern statutes. Thus, in *Jones v. Alfred H. Mayer Co.*, we considered the effect of the fair housing provisions of the Civil Rights Act of 1968 on the property rights guaranteed by the Civil Rights Act of 1866, now codified at 42 U.S.C. § 1982. And in *Johnson v. Railway Express Agency* we held that the passage of Title VII did not work an implied repeal of the substantive rights to contract conferred by the same 19th-century statute and now codified at 42 U.S.C. § 1981.

This case, by contrast, does not involve two "independent" rights, and for the same basic reasons that underlay the Court's decision in *Brown v. GSA*, reinforced by the other considerations discussed in this opinion, we conclude that § 1985(3) may not be invoked to redress violations of Title VII. It is true that a § 1985(3) remedy would not be coextensive with Title VII, since a plaintiff in an action under § 1985(3) must prove both a conspiracy and a group animus that Title VII does not require. While this incomplete congruity would limit the damage that would be done to Title VII, it would not eliminate it. Unimpaired effectiveness can be given to the plan put together by Congress in Title VII only by holding that deprivation of a right created by Title VII cannot be the basis for a cause of action under § 1985(3).

[Three dissenting Justices argued that "Because § 1985(3) provides a remedy for *any person* injured as a result of deprivation of a substantive federal right, it must be seen as itself creating rights in persons other than those to whom the underlying federal right extends."]

NOTES AND QUESTIONS

1. Why is this case not governed by *Jones* or *Johnson*? Is it analogous to *National Sea Clammers, supra* Ch. II? If this action had been allowed, would all Title VII plaintiffs be able to expand relief by suing under § 1985(3)?

2. Could a state or local government employee alleging sex discrimination sue under § 1983 to enforce Fourteenth Amendment rights in lieu of, or in addition to, bringing

suit under Title VII? Review *Smith v. Robinson, supra* Ch. II, and Problem Six, *supra.* Could she sue under § 1985(3) to enforce the same rights?

3. In light of the limiting interpretations of § 1985(3), can you think of situations which can be litigated under § 1985(3) but not §§ 1981, 1982 or 1983?

B. GENERAL ENFORCEMENT ISSUES

The civil rights legislation passed during the reconstruction era lacks the detail found in modern legislation. Very little is stated in the statutes about enforcement issues, such as limitations period, exhaustion of other remedies, relief and defenses. Federal court jurisdiction was addressed in what is now 28 U.S.C. § 1343 and, since elimination of the amount in controversy requirement in 1980, is also available under the general federal question provision, 28 U.S.C. § 1331.

1. ADOPTION OF STATE LAW

a. General

ROBERTSON V. WEGMANN
436 U.S. 584 (1978)

Mr. Justice MARSHALL delivered the opinion of the Court.

In early 1970, Clay L. Shaw filed a civil rights action under 42 U.S.C. § 1983 in the United States District Court for the Eastern District of Louisiana. Four years later, before trial had commenced, Shaw died. The question presented is whether the District Court was required to adopt as federal law a Louisiana survivorship statute, which would have caused this action to abate, or was free instead to create a federal common-law rule allowing the action to survive. Resolution of this question turns on whether the state statute is "inconsistent with the Constitution and laws of the United States." 42 U.S.C. § 1988.

I

In 1969, Shaw was tried in a Louisiana state court on charges of having participated in a conspiracy to assassinate President John F. Kennedy. He was acquitted by a jury but within days was arrested on charges of having committed perjury in his testimony at the conspiracy trial. Alleging that these prosecutions were undertaken in bad faith, Shaw's § 1983 complaint named as defendants the then District Attorney of Orleans Parish, Jim Garrison, and five other persons. Trial was set for November 1974, but in August 1974 Shaw died. The executor of his estate, respondent Edward F. Wegmann (hereafter respondent), moved to be substituted as plaintiff, and the District Court granted the motion. Petitioner and other defendants then moved to dismiss the action on the ground that it had abated on Shaw's death.[a]

II

As both courts below held, and as both parties here have assumed, the decision as to the applicable survivorship rule is governed by 42 U.S.C. § 1988. This statute recognizes that in certain areas "federal law is unsuited or insufficient 'to furnish suitable remedies'"; federal law simply does not "cover every issue that may arise in the context of a federal civil rights action." *Moor v. County of Alameda*, quoting 42 U.S.C. § 1988. When federal law is thus "deficient," § 1988 instructs us to turn to "the common law, as modified and changed by the constitution and statutes of the [forum] State," as long as these are "not inconsistent with the Constitution and laws of the United States." Regardless of the source of the law applied in a particular case, however, it is clear that the ultimate rule adopted under § 1988 "'is a federal rule responsive to the need whenever a federal right is impaired.'"

III

In resolving questions of inconsistency between state and federal law raised under § 1988, courts must look not only at particular federal statutes and constitutional provisions, but also at "the policies expressed in [them]." Of particular importance is whether application of state law "would be inconsistent with the federal policy underlying the cause of action under consideration." The instant cause of action arises under 42 U.S.C. § 1983, one of the "Reconstruction civil rights statutes" that this Court had accorded "'a sweep as broad as [their] language.'"

Despite the broad sweep of § 1983, we can find nothing in the statute or its underlying policies to indicate that a state law causing abatement of a particular action should invariably be ignored in favor of a rule of absolute survivorship. The policies underlying § 1983 include compensation of persons injured by deprivation of federal rights and prevention of abuses of power by those acting under color of state law. No claim is made here that Louisiana's survivorship laws are in general inconsistent with these policies, and indeed most Louisiana actions survive the plaintiff's death.

It is therefore difficult to see how any of § 1983's policies would be undermined if Shaw's action were to abate. The goal of compensating those injured by a deprivation of rights provides no basis for requiring compensation of one who is merely suing as the executor of the deceased's estate. And, given that most Louisiana actions survive the plaintiff's death, the fact

---

[a] Under Louisiana law the cause of action abated upon the death of the plaintiff, where death was not caused by the challenged conduct, unless the plaintiff is survived by a spouse, children, parents or siblings.

that a particular action might abate surely would not adversely affect § 1983's role in preventing official illegality, at least in situations in which there is no claim that the illegality caused the plaintiff's death. A state official contemplating illegal activity must always be prepared to face the prospect of a § 1983 action being filed against him. In light of this prospect, even an official aware of the intricacies of Louisiana survivorship law would hardly be influenced in his behavior by its provisions.

It is true that § 1983 provides "a uniquely federal remedy against incursions under the claimed authority of state law upon rights secured by the Constitution and laws of the Nation." That a federal remedy should be available, however, does not mean that a § 1983 plaintiff (or his representative) must be allowed to continue an action in disregard of the state law to which § 1988 refers us. A state statute cannot be considered "inconsistent" with federal law merely because the statute causes the plaintiff to lose the litigation. If success of the § 1983 action were the only benchmark, there would be no reason at all to look to state law, for the appropriate rule would then always be the one favoring the plaintiff, and its source would be essentially irrelevant. But § 1988 quite clearly instructs us to refer to state statutes; it does not say that state law is to be accepted or rejected based solely on which side is advantaged thereby. Under the circumstances presented here, the fact that Shaw was not survived by one of several close relatives should not itself be sufficient to cause the Louisiana survivorship provisions to be deemed "inconsistent with the Constitution and laws of the United States." 42 U.S.C. § 1988.

IV

Our holding today is a narrow one, limited to situations in which no claim is made that state law generally is inhospitable to survival of § 1983 actions and in which the particular application of state survivorship law, while it may cause abatement of the action, has no independent adverse effect on the policies underlying § 1983. A different situation might well be presented, as the District Court noted, if state law "did not provide for survival of any tort actions," or if it significantly restricted the types of actions that survive. We intimate no view, moreover, about whether abatement based on state law could be allowed in a situation in which deprivation of federal rights caused death.

Here it is agreed that Shaw's death was not caused by the deprivation of rights for which he sued under § 1983, and Louisiana law provides for the survival of most tort actions. Respondent's only complaint about Louisiana law is that it would cause Shaw's action to abate. We conclude that the mere fact of abatement of a particular lawsuit is not sufficient ground to declare state law "inconsistent" with federal law.

NOTES AND QUESTIONS

1. Where was the alleged "deficiency" that led the Court to examine state law?

2. Would the result have been different if Shaw's death resulted from the alleged civil rights violation and such an action did not survive under Louisiana law?

b. Statute of Limitations

WILSON V. GARCIA
471 U.S. 261 (1985)

Justice STEVENS delivered the opinion of the Court.

In this case we must determine the most appropriate state statute of limitations to apply to claims enforceable under 42 U.S.C. § 1983.

On January 28, 1982, respondent brought this § 1983 action in the United States District Court for the District of New Mexico seeking "money damages to compensate him for the deprivation of his civil rights guaranteed by the Fourth, Fifth and Fourteenth Amendments to the United States Constitution and for the personal injuries he suffered which were caused by the acts and omissions of the [petitioners] acting under color of law." The complaint alleged that on April 27, 1979, petitioner Wilson, a New Mexico State Police officer, unlawfully arrested the respondent, "brutally and viciously" beat him, and sprayed his face with tear gas; that petitioner Vigil, the Chief of the New Mexico State Police, had notice of Officer Wilson's allegedly "violent propensities," and had failed to reprimand him for committing other unprovoked attacks on citizens; and that Vigil's training and supervision of Wilson was seriously deficient.

The respondent's complaint was filed two years and nine months after the claim purportedly arose. Petitioners moved to dismiss on the ground that the action was barred by the 2-year statute of limitations contained in § 41-4-15(A) of the New Mexico Tort Claims Act.[b] The petitioners' motion was supported by a decision of the New Mexico Supreme Court which squarely held that the Tort Claims Act provides "the most closely analogous state cause of action" to § 1983, and that its 2-year statute of limitations is therefore applicable to actions commenced under § 1983 in the state courts. In addition to the 2-year statute of limitations in the Tort Claims Act, two other New Mexico statutes conceivably could apply to § 1983 claims: § 37-1-8, which provides a 3-year limitation period for actions "for an injury to the person or reputation of any person"; and § 37-1-4, which provides a 4-year limitation period for "all other actions not herein otherwise provided for." If either of these longer statutes applied to the respondent's § 1983 claim, the complaint was timely filed.

---

b   That section provides:

   Actions against a governmental entity or a public employee for torts shall be forever barred, unless such action is commenced within two years after the date of occurrence resulting in loss, injury or death. . . .

I

The Reconstruction Civil Rights Acts do not contain a specific statute of limitations governing § 1983 actions—"a void which is commonplace in federal statutory law." When Congress has not established a time limitation for a federal cause of action, the settled practice has been to adopt a local time limitation as federal law if it is not inconsistent with federal law or policy to do so. In 42 U.S.C. § 1988, Congress has implicitly endorsed this approach with respect to claims enforceable under the Reconstruction Civil Rights Acts.

The language of § 1988, directs the courts to follow "a three-step process" in determining the rules of decision applicable to civil rights claims:

> First, courts are to look to the laws of the United States 'so far as such laws are suitable to carry [the civil and criminal civil rights statutes] into effect.' If no suitable federal rule exists, courts undertake the second step by considering application of state 'common law, as modified and changed by the constitution and statutes' of the forum state. A third step asserts the predominance of the federal interest: courts are to apply state law only if it is not 'inconsistent with the Constitution and laws of the United States.' *Burnett v. Grattan.*

This case principally involves the second step in the process: the selection of "the most appropriate," or "the most analogous" state statute of limitations to apply to this § 1983 claim.

In order to determine the most "most appropriate" or "most analogous" New Mexico statute to apply to the respondent's claim, we must answer three questions. We must first consider whether state law or federal law governs the characterization of a § 1983 claim for statute of limitations purposes. If federal law applies, we must next decide whether all § 1983 claims should be characterized in the same way, or whether they should be evaluated differently depending upon the varying factual circumstances and legal theories presented in each individual case. Finally, we must characterize the essence of the claim in the pending case, and decide which statute provides the most appropriate limiting principle. Although the text of neither § 1983 nor § 1988 provides a pellucid answer to any of these questions, all three parts of the inquiry are, in the final analysis, questions of statutory construction.

II

Our identification of the correct source of law properly begins with the text of § 1988. Congress' first instruction in the statute is that the law to be applied in adjudicating civil rights claims shall be in "conformity with the laws of the United States, so far as such laws are suitable." This mandate implies that resort to state law—the second step in the process—should not be undertaken before principles of federal law are exhausted. The characterization of § 1983 for statute of limitations purposes is derived from the elements of the cause of action, and Congress' purpose in providing it. These, of course, are matters of federal law. Since federal law is available to decide the question, the language of § 1988 directs that the matter of characterization should be treated as a federal question. Only the length of the limitations period, and closely related questions of tolling and application, are to be governed by state law.

This interpretation is also supported by Congress' third instruction in § 1988: state law shall only apply "so far as the same is not inconsistent with" federal law. This requirement emphasizes "the predominance of the federal interest" in the borrowing process, taken as a whole. Even when principles of state law are borrowed to assist in the enforcement of this federal remedy, the state rule is adopted as "a federal rule responsive to the need whenever a federal right is impaired." The importation of the policies and purposes of the States on matters of civil rights is not the primary office of the borrowing provision in § 1988; rather, the statute is designed to assure that neutral rules of decision will be available to enforce the civil rights actions, among them § 1983. Congress surely did not intend to assign to state courts and legislatures a conclusive role in the formative function of defining and characterizing the essential elements of a federal cause of action.

In borrowing statutes of limitations for other federal claims, this Court has generally recognized that the problem of characterization "is ultimately a question of federal law." In *DelCostello v. Teamsters*, for example, we recently declined to apply a state statute of limitations when we were convinced that a federal statute of limitations for another cause of action better reflected the balance that Congress would have preferred between the substantive policies underlying the federal claim and the policies of repose. So here, the federal interest in uniformity and the interest in having "firmly defined, easily applied rules," support the conclusion that Congress intended the characterization of § 1983 to be measured by federal rather than state standards.

III

[I]n considering whether all § 1983 claims should be characterized in the same way for limitations purposes, it is useful to recall that § 1983 provides "a uniquely federal remedy against incursions under the claimed authority of state law upon rights secured by the Constitution and laws of the Nation." The high purposes of this unique remedy make it appropriate to accord the statute "a sweep as broad as its language." Because the § 1983 remedy is one that can "override certain kinds of state laws," *Monroe v. Pape*, and is, in all events, "supplementary to any remedy any State might have," *McNeese v. Board of Education*, it can have no precise counterpart in state law. Therefore, it is "the purest coincidence" when state statutes or the common law provide for equivalent remedies; any analogies to those causes of action are bound to be imperfect.

In this light, practical considerations help to explain why a simple, broad characterization of all § 1983 claims best fits the statute's remedial purpose. The experience of the courts that have predicated their choice of the correct statute of limitations on an analysis of the particular facts of each claim demonstrates that their approach inevitably breeds uncertainty and time-consuming litigation that is foreign to the central purposes of § 1983. Almost every § 1983 claim can be favorably analogized to more than one of the ancient common-law forms of action, each of which may be governed by a different statute of limitations. In the case before us, for example, the respondent alleges that he was injured by a New Mexico State Police officer who used excessive force to carry out an unlawful arrest. This § 1983 claim is arguably analogous to distinct state tort claims for false arrest, assault and battery, or personal injuries. Moreover, the claim could also be characterized as one arising under a statute, or as governed by the special New Mexico statute authorizing recovery against the State for the torts of its agents.

A catalog of other constitutional claims that have been alleged under § 1983 would encompass numerous and diverse topics and subtopics: discrimination in public employment on the basis of race or the exercise of First Amendment rights, discharge or demotion without procedural due process, mistreatment of school children, deliberate indifference to the medical needs of prison inmates, the seizure of chattels without advance notice or sufficient opportunity to be heard—to identify only a few. If the choice of the statute of limitations were to depend upon the particular facts or the precise legal theory of each claim, counsel could almost always argue, with considerable force, that two or more periods of limitations should apply to each § 1983 claim. Moreover, under such an approach different statutes of limitations would be applied to the various § 1983 claims arising in the same State, and multiple periods of limitations would often apply to the same case. There is no reason to believe that Congress would have sanctioned this interpretation of its statute.

When § 1983 was enacted, it is unlikely that Congress actually foresaw the wide diversity of claims that the new remedy would ultimately embrace. The simplicity of the admonition in § 1988 is consistent with the assumption that Congress intended the identification of the appropriate statute of limitations to be an uncomplicated task for judges, lawyers, and litigants, rather than a source of uncertainty, and unproductive and ever increasing litigation. Moreover, the legislative purpose to create an effective remedy for the enforcement of federal civil rights is obstructed by uncertainty in the applicable statute of limitations, for scarce resources must be dissipated by useless litigation on collateral matters.

Although the need for national uniformity "has not been held to warrant the displacement of state statutes of limitations for civil rights actions," uniformity within each State is entirely consistent with the borrowing principle contained in § 1988. We conclude that the statute is fairly construed as a directive to select, in each State, the one most appropriate statute of limitations for all § 1983 claims. The federal interests in uniformity, certainty, and the minimization of unnecessary litigation all support the conclusion that Congress favored this simple approach.

IV

After exhaustively reviewing the different ways that § 1983 claims have been characterized in every Federal Circuit, the Court of Appeals concluded that the tort action for the recovery of damages for personal injuries is the best alternative available. We agree that this choice is supported by the nature of the § 1983 remedy, and by the federal interest in ensuring that the borrowed period of limitations not discriminate against the federal civil rights remedy.

The specific historical catalyst for the Civil Rights Act of 1871 was the campaign of violence and deception in the South, fomented by the Ku Klux Klan, which was denying decent citizens their civil and political rights. The debates on the Act chronicle the alarming insecurity of life, liberty, and property in the Southern States, and the refuge that local authorities extended to the authors of these outrageous incidents. By providing a remedy for the violation of constitutional rights, Congress hoped to restore peace and justice to the region through the subtle power of civil enforcement.

The atrocities that concerned Congress in 1871 plainly sounded in tort. Relying on this premise we have found tort analogies compelling in establishing the elements of a cause of action under § 1983, and in identifying the immunities available to defendants. As we have noted, however, the § 1983 remedy encompasses a broad range of potential tort analogies, from injuries to property to infringements of individual liberty.

Among the potential analogies, Congress unquestionably would have considered the remedies established in the Civil Rights Act to be more analogous to tort claims for personal injury than, for example, to claims for damages to property or breach of contract. The unifying theme of the Civil Rights Act of 1871 is reflected in the language of the Fourteenth Amendment that unequivocally recognizes the equal status of every "*person*" subject to the jurisdiction of any of the several States. The Constitution's command is that all "*persons*" shall be accorded the full privileges of citizenship; no *person* shall be deprived of life, liberty, or property without due process of law or be denied the equal protection of the laws. A violation of that command is an injury to the individual rights of the person.

Finally, we are satisfied that Congress would not have characterized § 1983 as providing a cause of action analogous to state remedies for wrongs committed by public officials. It was the very ineffectiveness of state remedies that led Congress to enact the Civil Rights Acts in the first place. Congress therefore intended that the remedy provided in § 1983 be independently enforceable whether or not it duplicates a parallel state remedy. The characterization of all § 1983 actions as involving claims for personal injuries minimizes the risk that the choice of a state statute of limitations would not fairly serve the federal interests vindicated by § 1983. General personal injury actions, sounding in tort, constitute a major part of the total volume of civil litigation in the state courts today, and probably did so in 1871 when § 1983 was enacted. It is most unlikely that the period of limitations applicable to such claims ever was, or ever would be, fixed in a way that would discriminate against federal claims, or be inconsistent with federal law in any respect.

V

In view of our holding that § 1983 claims are best characterized as personal injury actions, the Court of Appeals correctly applied the 3-year statute of limitations governing actions "for an injury to the person or reputation of any person."

NOTES AND QUESTIONS

1. Does *Garcia* establish a uniform statute of limitations for § 1983 actions? Has the Court accomplished its goal of promoting the federal interest in uniformity and certainty?

2. Would the outcome in *Garcia* have been different if New Mexico had a six-month limitations period for personal injury actions?

3. Indiana has a five-year statute of limitations for actions against government officials and a two-year statute for personal injury actions. Before *Garcia* the Seventh Circuit held that the five-year statute governs § 1983 actions. Will this control § 1983 actions after *Garcia*?

4. If a state has multiple statutes of limitations for personal injury actions, e.g., one for intentional torts and another general or residual provision, which should control § 1983 cases? *See Owens v. Okure*, 488 U.S. 235 (1989) (general or residual personal injury statute controls rather than specific provision for intentional torts).

5. If state law tolls the personal injury statute of limitations while one is incarcerated, should this apply in a § 1983 action? *See Hardin v. Straub*, 490 U.S. 536 (1989) (Michigan tolling provision applied to inmate's § 1983 action). *Compare Wallace v. Kato*, 548 U.S. 384 (2007) (statute of limitations for § 1983 false arrest claim accrues at the time of arrest, not when conviction is set aside; accrual presents an issue of federal, not state, law).

GOODMAN V. LUKENS STEEL CO.
482 U.S. 656 (1987)

Justice WHITE delivered the opinion of the Court.

I

Because § 1981, like §§ 1982 and 1983, does not contain a statute of limitations, federal courts should select the most appropriate or analogous state statute of limitations. In *Wilson* [v. *Garcia*], the reach of which is at issue in this case, there were three holdings: for the purpose of characterizing a claim asserted under § 1983, federal law, rather than state law, is controlling; a single state statute of limitations should be selected to govern all § 1983 suits; and because claims under § 1983 are in essence claims for personal injury, the state statute applicable to such claims should be borrowed. Petitioners agree with the Court of Appeals that the first two *Garcia* holdings apply in § 1981 cases, but insist that the third does not. Their submission is that § 1981 deals primarily with economic rights, more specifically the execution and enforcement of contracts, and that the appropriate limitations period to borrow is the one applicable to suits for interference with contractual rights, which in Pennsylvania was six years.

The Court of Appeals properly rejected this submission. Section 1981 has a much broader focus than contractual rights. The section speaks not only of personal rights to contract, but personal rights to sue, to testify, and to equal rights under all laws for the security of persons and property; and all persons are to be subject to like punishments, taxes and burdens of every kind. Section 1981 of the present Code was § 1977 of the Revised Statutes of 1874. Its heading was and is "Equal rights under the law" and is contained in a chapter entitled "Civil Rights." Insofar as it deals with contracts, it declares the personal right to make and enforce contracts, a right, as the section has been construed, that may not be interfered with on racial grounds. The provision asserts, in effect, that competence and capacity to contract shall not depend upon race. It is thus part of a federal law barring racial discrimination, which, as the Court of Appeals said, is a fundamental injury to the individual rights of a person. *Wilson*'s characterization of § 1983 claims is thus equally appropriate here, particularly since § 1983 would reach state action that encroaches on the rights protected by § 1981. That § 1981 had far-reaching economic consequences does not change this conclusion, since such impact flows from guaranteeing the personal right to engage in economically significant activity free from racially discriminatory interference. The Court of Appeals was correct in selecting the Pennsylvania 2-year limitations period governing personal injury actions.

NOTES AND QUESTIONS

1. Is the Court's reasoning—which leads to the conclusion that actions under § 1981, like those under § 1983, should be governed by the personal injury limitations period—persuasive? Would the limitations period for contract actions be more appropriate?

2. Should the forum state's limitations period for personal injury actions apply to § 1982 cases? § 1985(3) cases? Would the state limitations period for civil conspiracy actions be more appropriate for 1985(3) cases?

3. In 1990, Congress passed 28 U.S.C. § 1658, which states:

   [e]xcept as otherwise provided by law, a civil action arising under an Act of Congress enacted after the date of the enactment of this section may not be commenced later than 4 years after the cause of action accrues.

   The Civil Rights Act of 1991 adds a new section, 42 U.S.C. § 1981(b), which defines the right to be free from discrimination to include "termination of contracts," as well as other post-contract discriminatory conduct. Is an action under this section controlled by 28 U.S.C. § 1658? *See Jones v. R.R. Donnelley,* discussed *supra* Ch. II (§ 1658 governs post-hiring discrimination claims that were not actionable under § 1981 prior to the 1991 amendment).

2. APPLICABILITY OF STATE ADMINISTRATIVE REMEDIES AND NOTICE REQUIREMENTS

PATSY V. FLORIDA BOARD OF REGENTS
457 U.S. 496 (1982)

Justice MARSHALL delivered the opinion of the Court.

This case presents the question whether exhaustion of state administrative remedies is a prerequisite to an action under 42 U.S.C. § 1983. Petitioner Georgia Patsy filed this action, alleging that her employer, Florida International University (FIU), had denied her employment opportunities solely on the basis of her race and sex. By a divided vote, the United States Court of Appeals for the Fifth Circuit found that petitioner was required to exhaust "adequate and appropriate" administrative remedies, and remanded the case to the District Court to consider the adequacy of the administrative procedures.

II

The question whether exhaustion of administrative remedies should ever be required in a § 1983 action has prompted vigorous debate and disagreement. Our resolution of this issue, however, is made much easier because we are not writing on a clean slate. This Court has addressed this issue, as well as related issues, on several prior occasions.

Respondent suggests that our prior precedents do not control our decision today, arguing that these cases can be distinguished on their facts or that this Court did not "fully" consider the question whether exhaustion should be required. This contention need not detain us long. Beginning with *McNeese v. Board of Education*, we have on numerous occasions rejected the argument that a § 1983 action should be dismissed where the plaintiff has not exhausted state administrative remedies. Respondent may be correct in arguing that several of these decisions could have been based on traditional exceptions to the exhaustion doctrine. Nevertheless, this Court has stated categorically that exhaustion is not a prerequisite to an action under § 1983, and we have not deviated from that position in the 19 years since *McNeese*. Therefore, we do not address the question presented in this case as one of first impression.

III
A

In determining whether our prior decisions misconstrued the meaning of § 1983, we begin with a review of the legislative history to § 1 of the Civil Rights Act of 1871, the precursor to § 1983. Although we recognize that the 1871 Congress did not expressly contemplate the exhaustion question, we believe that the tenor of the debates over § 1 supports our conclusion that exhaustion of administrative remedies in § 1983 actions should not be judicially imposed.

The Civil Rights Act of 1871, along with the Fourteenth Amendment it was enacted to enforce, were crucial ingredients in the basic alteration of our federal system accomplished during the Reconstruction Era. During that time, the Federal Government was clearly established as a guarantor of the basic federal rights of individuals against incursions by state power. As we recognized in *Mitchum v. Foster*, "[t]he very purpose of § 1983 was to interpose the federal courts between the States and the people, as guardians of the people's federal rights—to protect the people from unconstitutional action under color of state law, 'whether that action be executive, legislative, or judicial.'"

At least three recurring themes in the debates over § 1 cast serious doubt on the suggestion that requiring exhaustion of state administrative remedies would be consistent with the intent of the 1871 Congress. First, in passing § 1, Congress assigned to the federal courts a paramount role in protecting constitutional rights.

A second theme in the debates further suggests that the 1871 Congress would not have wanted to impose an exhaustion requirement. A major factor motivating the expansion of federal jurisdiction through §§ 1 and 2 of the bill was the belief of the 1871 Congress that the state authorities had been unable or unwilling to protect the constitutional rights of individuals or to punish those who violated these rights. Of primary importance to the exhaustion question was the mistrust that the 1871 Congress held for the fact finding processes of state institutions. This Congress believed that federal courts would be less susceptible to local prejudice and to the existing defects in the factfinding processes of the state courts. This perceived defect in the State's factfinding processes is particularly relevant to the question of exhaustion of administrative remedies: exhaustion rules are often applied in deference to the superior factfinding ability of the relevant administrative agency.

A third feature of the debates relevant to the exhaustion question is the fact that many legislators interpreted the bill to provide dual or concurrent forums in the state and federal system, enabling the plaintiff to choose the forum in which to seek relief.

This legislative history supports the conclusion that our prior decisions, holding that exhaustion of state administrative remedies is not a prerequisite to an action under § 1983, did not misperceive the statutory intent: it seems fair to infer that the 1871 Congress did not intend that an individual be compelled in every case to exhaust state administrative remedies before filing an action under § 1 of the Civil Rights Act. We recognize, however, that drawing such a conclusion from this history alone is somewhat precarious: the 1871 Congress was not presented with the question of exhaustion of administrative remedies, nor was it aware of the potential role of state administrative agencies. Therefore, we do not rely exclusively on this legislative history in deciding the question presented here. Congress addressed the question of exhaustion under § 1983 when it recently enacted 42 U.S.C. § 1997e. The legislative history of § 1997e provides strong evidence of congressional intent on this issue.

B

The Civil Rights of Institutionalized Persons Act, 42 U.S.C. § 1997, *et seq.*, was enacted primarily to ensure that the United States Attorney General has "legal standing to enforce existing constitutional rights and Federal statutory rights of institutionalized persons." In § 1997e, Congress also created a specific, limited exhaustion requirement for adult prisoners bringing actions pursuant to § 1983.[a] Section 1997e and its legislative history demonstrate that Congress understood that exhaustion is not generally required in § 1983 actions, and that it decided to carve out only a narrow exception to this rule. A judicially imposed exhaustion requirement would be inconsistent with Congress' decision to adopt § 1997e and would usurp policy judgments that Congress has reserved for itself.

[T]he exhaustion provisions of the Act make sense, and are not superfluous, only if exhaustion could not be required before its enactment and if Congress intended to carve out a narrow exception to this no-exhaustion rule. The legislative history of § 1997e demonstrates that Congress had taken the approach of carving our specific exceptions to the general rule that federal courts cannot require exhaustion under § 1983. It is not our province to alter the balance struck by Congress in establishing the procedural framework for bringing actions under § 1983.

C

Respondent and the Court of Appeals argue that exhaustion of administrative remedies should be required because it would further various policies. They argue that an exhaustion requirement would lessen the perceived burden that § 1983 actions impose on federal courts; would further the goal of comity and improve federal-state relations by postponing federal-court review until after the state administrative agency had passed on the issue; and would enable the agency, which presumably has expertise in the area at issue, to enlighten the federal court's ultimate decision.

As we noted earlier, policy consideration alone cannot justify judicially imposed exhaustion unless exhaustion is consistent with congressional intent. Furthermore, as the debates over incorporating the exhaustion requirement in § 1997e demonstrate, the relevant policy considerations do not invariably point in one direction, and there is vehement disagreement over the validity of the assumptions underlying many of them. The very difficulty of these policy considerations, and Congress' superior institutional competence to pursue this debate, suggest that legislative not judicial solutions are preferable.

Beyond the policy issues that must be resolved in deciding *whether* to require exhaustion, there are equally difficult questions concerning the design and scope of an exhaustion requirement. These questions include how to define those categories of § 1983 claims in which

---

a 42 U.S.C. § 1997e is part of the Prison Litigation Reform Act and has resulted in several Supreme Court decisions attempting to clarify its meaning. See, e.g., Jones v. Bock, 549 U.S. 199 (2007) (holding that the failure to exhaust is an affirmative defense to be raised by the defendant and allowing exhausted claims to proceed even though the complaint includes an unexhausted claim).

exhaustion might be desirable; how to unify and centralize the standards for judging the kinds of administrative procedures that should be exhausted; what tolling requirements and time limitations should be adopted; what is the *res judicata* and collateral estoppel effect of particular administrative determinations; what consequences should attach to the failure to comply with procedural requirements of administrative proceedings; and whether federal courts could grant necessary interim injunctive relief and hold the action pending exhaustion, or proceed to judgment without requiring exhaustion even though exhaustion might otherwise be required, where the relevant administrative agency is either powerless or not inclined to grant such interim relief. These and similar questions might be answered swiftly and surely by legislation, but would create costly, remedy-delaying, and court-burdening litigation if answered incrementally by the judiciary in the context of diverse constitutional claims relating to thousands of different state agencies.

IV

Based on the legislative histories of both § 1983 and § 1997e, we conclude that exhaustion of state administrative remedies should not be required as a prerequisite to bringing an action pursuant to § 1983. We decline to overturn our prior decisions holding that such exhaustion is not required.

NOTES AND QUESTIONS

1. The Court in *Patsy* decided that exhaustion should not be required unless Congress adopts such a requirement. Should § 1983 plaintiffs ever exhaust state administrative remedies, even though it is not required? Consider the potential impact on municipal liability if an administrative agency validates the challenged misconduct, *supra* Ch. II, but also the concern that the agency's factual findings might be binding in future litigation discussed *infra*.

2. Can *Patsy* be reconciled with *Parratt, supra* Ch. II, where the Court held that the existence of state remedies foreclosed relief on the federal claim?

3. Is it necessary to exhaust state judicial remedies before bringing a § 1983 action in federal court? Review *Monroe, supra* Ch. II.

4. If a § 1983 plaintiff seeks to enforce a federal statute, and it requires exhaustion, does *Patsy* control? Recall that § 1983 just creates a cause of action.

5. Should *Patsy* govern a § 1983 action filed in state court? Explain.

Justice BRENNAN delivered the opinion of the Court.

I

On July 4, 1981, Milwaukee police officers stopped petitioner Bobby Felder for questioning while searching his neighborhood for an armed suspect. The interrogation proved to be hostile and apparently loud, attracting the attention of petitioner's family and neighbors, who succeeded in convincing the police that petitioner was not the man they sought. According to the police reports, the officers then directed petitioner to return home, but he continued to argue and allegedly pushed one of them, thereby precipitating his arrest for disorderly conduct. Petitioner alleges that in the course of this arrest the officers beat him about the head and face with batons, dragged him across the ground, and threw him, partially unconscious, into the back of a paddy wagon face first, all in full view of his family and neighbors. Petitioner, who is black, alleges that various members of the Police Department conspir[ed] to cover up the misconduct of the arresting officers, all of whom are white. The Department took no disciplinary action against any of the officers, and the City Attorney subsequently dropped the disorderly conduct charge against petitioner.

Nine months after the incident, petitioner filed this action in the Milwaukee County Circuit Court against the city of Milwaukee and certain of its police officers, alleging that the beating and arrest were unprovoked and racially motivated, and violated his rights under the Fourth and Fourteenth Amendments to the United States Constitution. He sought redress under 42 U.S.C. § 1983, as well as attorneys fees pursuant to § 1988. The officers moved to dismiss the suit based on petitioner's failure to comply with the State's notice-of-claim statute. That statute provides that no action may be brought or maintained against any state governmental subdivision, agency, or officer unless claimant either provides written notice of claim within 120 days of the alleged injury, or demonstrates that the relevant subdivision, agency, or officer had actual notice of claim and was not prejudiced by the lack of written notice. The statute further provides that the party seeking redress must also submit an itemized statement of the relief sought to the governmental subdivision or agency, which then has 120 days to grant or disallow the requested relief. Finally, claimants must bring suit within six months of receiving notice that their claim has been disallowed.

II

No one disputes the general and unassailable proposition relied upon by the Wisconsin Supreme Court below that States may establish the rules of procedure governing litigation in their own courts. By the same token, however, where state courts entertain a federally created cause of action, the "federal right cannot be defeated by the forms of local practice." The question before us today, therefore, is essentially one of pre-emption: is the application of the State's notice-of-claim provision to § 1983 actions brought in state courts consistent with the goals of the federal civil rights laws, or does the enforcement of such a requirement instead "'stan[d] as an obstacle to the accomplishment and execution of the full purposes and objectives of Congress'"? Under the Supremacy Clause of the Federal Constitution, "[t]he relative importance to the State of its own law is not material when there is a conflict with a valid federal law," for "any state law, however clearly within a State's acknowledged power, which interferes with or is contrary to federal law, must yield." Because the notice-of-claim statute at issue here conflicts both in its purpose and effects with the remedial objectives of § 1983, and because its enforcement in such actions will frequently and predictably produce different outcomes in § 1983 litigation based solely on whether the claim is asserted in state or federal court, we conclude that the state law is pre-empted when the § 1983 action is brought in a state court.

A

Section 1983 creates a species of liability in favor of persons deprived of their federal civil rights by those wielding state authority.

Any assessment of the applicability of a state law to federal civil rights litigation, therefore, must be made in light of the purpose and nature of the federal right. This is so whether the question of state-law applicability arises in § 1983 litigation brought in state courts, which possess concurrent jurisdiction over such actions, or in federal-court litigation, where, because the federal civil rights law fails to provide certain rules of decision thought essential to the orderly adjudication of rights, courts are occasionally called upon to borrow state law. *See* 42 U.S.C. § 1988. Accordingly, we have held that a state law that immunizes government conduct otherwise subject to suit under § 1983 is preempted, even where the federal civil rights litigation takes place in state court, because the application of the state immunity law would thwart the congressional remedy, which of course already provides certain immunities for state officials. Similarly, in actions brought in federal courts, we have disapproved the adoption of state statutes of limitation that provide only a truncated period of time within which to file suit, because such statutes inadequately accommodate the complexities of federal civil rights litigation and are thus inconsistent with Congress' compensatory aims. And we have directed the lower federal courts in § 1983 cases to borrow the state-law limitations period for personal injury claims because it is "most unlikely that the period of limitations applicable to such claims ever was, or ever would be, fixed [by the forum State] in a way that would discriminate against federal claims, or be inconsistent with federal law in any respect."

Although we have never passed on the question, the lower federal courts have all, with but one exception, concluded that notice-of-claim provisions are inapplicable to § 1983 actions brought in federal court. These courts have reasoned that, unlike the lack of statutes of limitations in the federal civil rights laws, the absence of any notice-of-claim provision is not a deficiency requiring the importation of such statutes into the federal civil rights scheme. Because statutes of limitation are among the universally familiar aspects of litigation considered indispensable to any scheme of justice, it is entirely reasonable to assume that Congress did not intend to create a right enforceable in perpetuity. Notice-of-claim provisions, by contrast, are neither universally familiar nor in any sense indispensable prerequisites to litigation, and there is thus no reason to suppose that Congress intended federal courts to apply such rules, which "significantly inhibit the ability to bring federal actions."

While we fully agree with this near unanimous consensus of the federal courts, that judgment is not dispositive here, where the question is not one of adoption but of pre-emption. Nevertheless, this determination that notice-of-claim statutes are inapplicable to federal-court § 1983 litigation informs our analysis in two crucial respects. First, it demonstrates that the application of the notice requirement burdens the exercise of the federal right by forcing civil rights victims who seek redress in state courts to comply with a requirement that is entirely absent from civil rights litigation in federal courts. This burden, as we explain below, is inconsistent in both design and effect with the compensatory aims of the federal civil rights laws. Second, it reveals that the enforcement of such statutes in § 1983 actions brought in state court will frequently and predictably produce different outcomes in federal civil rights litigation based solely on whether that litigation takes place in state or federal court. States may not apply such an outcome-determinative law when entertaining substantive federal rights in their courts.

B

As we noted above, the central purpose of the Reconstruction-Era laws is to provide compensatory relief to those deprived of their federal rights by state actors. Section 1983 accomplishes this goal by creating a form of liability that, by its very nature, runs only against a specific class of defendants: government bodies and their officials. Wisconsin's notice-of-claim statute undermines this "uniquely federal remedy," in several interrelated ways. First, it conditions the right of recovery that Congress has authorized, and does so for a reason manifestly inconsistent with the purposes of the federal statute: to minimize governmental liability. Nor is this condition a neutral and uniformly applicable rule of procedure; rather, it is a substantive burden imposed only upon those who seek redress for injuries resulting from the use or misuse of governmental authority. Second, the notice provision discriminates against the federal right. While the State affords the victim of an intentional tort two years to recognize the compensable nature of his or her injury, the civil rights victim is given only four months to appreciate that he or she has been deprived of a federal constitutional of statutory rights. Finally, the notice provision operates, in part, as an exhaustion requirement, in that it forces claimants to seek satisfaction in the first instance from the governmental defendant. We think it plain that Congress never intended that those injured by governmental wrongdoers could be required, as a condition of recovery, to submit their claims to the government responsible for their injuries.

(1)

Wisconsin's notice-of-claim statute is part of a broader legislative scheme governing the rights of citizens to sue the State's subdivisions. The statute, both in its earliest and current forms, provides a circumscribed waiver of local governmental immunity that limits the amount recoverable in suits against local governments and imposes the notice requirements at issue here.

In sum, as respondents explain, the State has chosen to expose its subdivisions to large liability and defense costs, and, in light of that choice, has made the concomitant decision to impose conditions that "assis[t] municipalities in controlling those costs." The decision to subject state subdivisions to liability for violations of federal rights, however, was a choice that Congress, not the Wisconsin legislature, made, and it is a decision that the State has no authority to override. Thus, however understandable or laudable the State's interest in controlling liability expenses might otherwise be, it is patently incompatible with the compensatory goals of the federal legislation, as are the means the State has chosen to effectuate it.

This incompatibility is revealed by the design of the notice-of-claim statute itself, which operates as a condition precedent to recovery in all actions brought in state court against governmental entities or officers. "Congress," we have previously noted, "surely did not intend to assign to state courts and legislatures a conclusive role in the formative function of defining and characterizing the essential elements of a federal cause of action."

This burdening of a federal right, moreover, is not the natural or permissible consequence of an otherwise neutral, uniformly applicable state rule. Although it is true that the notice-of-claim statute does not discriminate between state and federal causes of action against local governments, the fact remains that the law's protection extends only to governmental defendants and thus conditions the right to bring suit against the very persons and entities Congress intended to subject to liability.

(2)

While respondents and *amici* suggest that prompt investigation of claims inures to the benefit of claimants and local governments alike, by providing both with an accurate factual picture of the incident, such statutes "are enacted *primarily* for the benefit of governmental defendants," and are intended to afford such defendants an opportunity to prepare a stronger case. Sound notions of public administration may support the prompt notice requirement, but those policies necessarily clash with the remedial purposes of the federal civil rights laws. Here, the notice-of-claim provision most emphatically does discriminate in a manner detrimental to the federal right: only those persons who wish to sue governmental defendants are required to provide notice within such an abbreviated time period. Many civil rights victims, however, will fail to appreciate the compensable nature of their injuries within the 4-month window provided by the notice-of-claim provision, and will thus be barred from asserting their federal right to recovery in state court unless they can show that the defendant had actual notice of the injury, the circumstances giving rise to it, and the claimant's intent to hold the defendant responsible—a showing which, as the facts of this case vividly demonstrate, is not easily made in Wisconsin.

(3)

Finally, the notice provision imposes an exhaustion requirement on persons who choose to assert their federal right in state courts, inasmuch as the § 1983 plaintiff must provide the requisite notice of injury within 120 days of the civil rights violation, then wait an additional 120 days while the governmental defendant investigates the claim and attempts to settle it. In *Patsy v. Board of Regents of Florida*, we held that plaintiffs need not exhaust state administrative remedies before instituting § 1983 suits in federal court. The Wisconsin Supreme Court, however, deemed that decision inapplicable to this state-court suit on the theory that States retain the authority to prescribe the rules and procedures governing suits in their courts. As we have just explained, however, that authority does not extend so far as to permit States to place conditions on the vindication of a federal right. Moreover, as we noted in *Patsy*, Congress enacted § 1983 in response to the widespread deprivations of civil rights in the Southern States and the inability or unwillingness of authorities in those States to protect those rights or punish wrongdoers. Although it is true that the principal remedy Congress chose to provide injured persons was immediate access to *federal* courts, it did not leave the protection of such rights exclusively in the hands of the federal judiciary, and instead conferred concurrent jurisdiction on state courts as well. Given the evil at which the federal civil rights legislation was aimed, there is simply no reason to suppose that Congress meant "to provide these individuals immediate access to the federal courts notwithstanding any provision of state law to the contrary," yet contemplated that those who sought to vindicate their federal rights in state courts could be required to seek redress in the first instance from the very state officials whose hostility to those rights precipitated their injuries.

C

Respondents and their supporting *amici* urge that we approve the application of the notice-of-claim statute to § 1983 actions brought in state court as a matter of equitable federalism. They note that "'[t]he general rule, bottomed deeply in belief in the importance of state control of state judicial procedure, is that federal law takes the state courts as it finds them.'" Litigants who chose to bring their civil rights actions in state courts presumably do so in order to obtain the benefit of certain procedural advantages in those courts, or to draw their juries from urban populations. Having availed themselves of these benefits, civil rights litigants must comply as well with those state rules they find less to their liking.

However equitable this bitter-with-the-sweet argument may appear in the abstract, it has no place under our Supremacy Clause analysis. Federal law takes state courts as it finds them only insofar as those courts employ rules that do not "impose unnecessary burdens upon rights of recovery authorized by federal laws." States may make the litigation of federal rights as congenial as they see fit—not as a *quid pro quo* for compliance with other, incongenial rules, but because such congeniality does not stand as an obstacle to the accomplishment of Congress' goals. As we have seen, enforcement of the notice-of-claim statute in § 1983 actions brought in state court so interferes with and frustrates the substantive right Congress created that, under the Supremacy Clause, it must yield to the federal interest.

Under *Erie R. Co. v. Tompkins,* when a federal court exercises diversity or pendent jurisdiction over state-law claims, "the outcome of the litigation in the federal court should be substantially the same, so far as legal rules determine the outcome of a litigation, as it would be if tried in a State court." *Guaranty Trust Co. v. York.* Accordingly, federal courts entertaining state-law claims against Wisconsin municipalities are obligated to apply the notice-of-claim provision. Just as federal courts are constitutionally obligated to apply state law to state claims, so too the Supremacy Clause imposes on state courts a constitutional duty "to proceed in such manner that all the substantial rights of the parties under controlling federal law [are] protected."

III

In enacting § 1983, Congress entitled those deprived of their civil rights to recover full compensation from the governmental officials responsible for those deprivations. A state law that conditions that right of recovery upon compliance with a rule designed to minimize governmental liability, and that directs injured persons to seek redress in the first instance from the very targets of the federal legislation, is inconsistent in both purpose and effect with the remedial objectives of the federal civil rights law. Principles of federalism, as well as the Supremacy Clause, dictate that such a state law must give way to vindication of the federal right when that right is asserted in state court.

NOTES AND QUESTIONS

1. Does *Felder* eliminate all differences between § 1983 litigation in federal court and § 1983 litigation in state court? In *Howlett v. Rose,* 496 U.S. 356 (1990), the Court held that state conferred sovereign immunity could not insulate a local school board from a § 1983 action in state court, where the board would be amenable to such suit in federal court. The Court explained "that once a state opens its courts to hear § 1983 actions, it may not selectively exclude certain § 1983 actions by denominating state policies as jurisdictional."

2. New York's Correction Law Section 24 divested its trial courts, which are courts of general jurisdiction, of jurisdiction over § 1983 cases, as well as cases arising under state law, that seek money damages from correction officers for actions taken in the scope of their employment. Section 24 was "[m]otivated by the belief that damages suits filed by prisoners against state correction officers were by and large frivolous and vexatious." In *Haywood v. Drown,* 556 U.S. 729 (2009), the Court ruled that,

even though Section 24 treated federal claims identical to state claims, "equality of treatment does not ensure that a state law will be deemed a neutral rule of judicial administration and therefore a valid excuse for refusing to entertain a federal cause of action." Because the State of New York created courts of general jurisdiction that routinely heard analogous § 1983 actions, it was not necessary for the Court "to decide whether Congress may compel a State to offer a forum, otherwise unavailable under state law, to hear suits brought pursuant to § 1983." But, it ruled that "having made the decision to create courts of general jurisdiction that regularly sit to entertain analogous suits, New York is not at liberty to shut the courthouse door to federal claims that it considers at odds with its local policy." *Id.* at 740. Four dissenting Justices argued that state courts should be permitted to refuse to exercise jurisdiction over federal actions provided they do so on an even-handed basis. Justice Thomas, writing only for himself, argued that neither the U.S. Constitution nor the Court's precedent requires a state to open its courts to § 1983 actions.

3. Will a state "notice of tort claim" statute apply to a pendent state claim (or "supplemental" claim under 28 U.S.C. § 1367) brought with a § 1983 claim in federal court?

Problem: Ten

1. Based on § 1988, would the following state laws control a § 1983 action in federal court?
   (a) a law setting a $300,000 limit on judgments against governmental entities;
   (b) a law eliminating punitive damages in tort actions brought by survivors;
   (c) a law requiring that 75% of any punitive damages award go into a state fund;
   (d) a law prohibiting punitive damages in the absence of compensatory damages;
   (e) a law requiring proof "beyond a reasonable doubt" for punitive damages.

2. Would any of your answers change if the § 1983 suit is filed in state court?

WILLIAMSON PLANNING COMM'N V. HAMILTON BANK
473 U.S. 172 (1985)

Justice BLACKMUN delivered the opinion of the Court.

I

B

Respondent filed this suit in the United States District Court for the Middle District of Tennessee, pursuant to 42 U.S.C. § 1983, alleging that the Commission had taken its property without just compensation and asserting that the Commission should be estopped under state law from denying approval of the project.

As the Court has made clear in several recent decisions, a claim that the application of government regulations effects a taking of a property interest is not ripe until the government entity charged with implementing the regulations has reached a final decision regarding the application of the regulations to the property at issue.

III

A

Respondent argues that it "did everything possible to resolve the conflict with the commission," and that the Commission's denial of approval for respondent's plat was equivalent to a denial of variances. The record does not support respondent's claim, however. There is no evidence that respondent applied to the Board of Zoning Appeals for variances from the zoning ordinance. As noted, the developer sought a ruling that the ordinance in effect in 1973 should be applied, but neither respondent nor the developer sought a variance from the requirements of either the 1973 or 1980 ordinances. Further, although the subdivision regulations in effect in 1981 required that applications to the Commission for variances be in writing, and that notice of the application be given to owners of adjacent property, the record contains no evidence that respondent ever filed a written request for variances from the cul-de-sac, road-grade, or frontage requirements of the subdivision regulations, or that respondent ever gave the required notice.

[I]n the face of respondent's refusal to follow the procedures for requesting a variance, and its refusal to provide specific information about the variances it would require, respondent hardly can maintain that the Commission's disapproval of the preliminary plat was equivalent to a final decision that no variances would be granted.

[R]espondent has not yet obtained a final decision regarding how it will be allowed to develop its property. Our reluctance to examine taking claims until such a final decision has been made is compelled by the very nature of the inquiry required by the Just Compensation Clause. Although "[t]he question of what constitutes a 'taking' for purposes of the Fifth Amendment has proved to be a problem of considerable difficulty," this Court consistently has indicated that among the factors of particular significance in the inquiry are the economic impact of the challenged action and the extent to which it interferes with reasonable investment-backed expectations. Those factors simply cannot be evaluated until the administrative agency has arrived at a final, definitive position regarding how it will apply the regulations at issue to the particular land in question.

Respondent asserts that it should not be required to seek variances from the regulations because its suit is predicated upon 42 U.S.C. § 1983, and there is no requirement that a plaintiff exhaust administrative remedies before bringing a § 1983 action. *Patsy v. Florida Board of Regents.* The question whether administrative remedies must be exhausted is conceptually distinct, however, from the question whether an administrative action must be final before it is judicially reviewable. While the policies underlying the two concepts often overlap, the finality requirement is concerned with whether the initial decisionmaker has arrived at a definitive position on the issue that inflicts an actual, concrete injury; the exhaustion requirement generally refers to administrative and judicial procedures by which an injured party may seek review of an adverse decision and obtain a remedy if the decision is found to be unlawful or otherwise inappropriate. *Patsy* concerned the latter, not the former.

The difference is best illustrated by comparing the procedure for seeking a variance with the procedures that, under *Patsy*, respondent would not be required to exhaust. While it appears that the State provides procedures by which an aggrieved property owner may seek a declaratory judgment regarding the validity of zoning and planning actions taken by county authorities, respondent would not be required to resort to those procedures before bringing its § 1983 action, because those procedures clearly are remedial. Similarly, respondent would not be required to appeal the Commission's rejection of the preliminary plat to the Board of Zoning Appeals, because the Board was empowered, at most, to review that rejection, not to participate in the Commission's decisionmaking.

Resort to those procedures would result in a judgment whether the Commission's actions violated any of respondent's rights. In contrast, resort to the procedure for obtaining variances would result in a conclusive determination by the Commission whether it would allow respondent to develop the subdivision in the manner respondent proposed. The Commission's refusal to approve the preliminary plat does not determine that issue; it prevents respondent from developing its subdivision without obtaining the necessary variances, but leaves open the possibility that respondent may develop the subdivision according to its plat after obtaining the variances. In short, the Commission's denial of approval does not conclusively determine whether respondent will be denied all reasonable beneficial use of its property, and therefore is not a final, reviewable decision.

B

A second reason the taking claim is not yet ripe is that respondent did not seek compensation through the procedures the State has provided for doing so. The Fifth Amendment does not proscribe the taking of property; it proscribes taking without just compensation. Nor does the Fifth Amendment require that just compensation be paid in advance of, or contemporaneously with, the taking; all that is required is that a "'reasonable, certain and adequate provision for obtaining compensation'" exist at the time of the taking. If the government has provided an adequate process for obtaining compensation, and if resort to that process "yield[s] just compensation," then the property owner "has no claim against the Government" for a taking. Thus, we have held that taking claims against the Federal Government are premature until the property owner has availed itself of the process provided by the Tucker Act, 28 U.S.C. § 1491. Similarly, if a State provides an adequate procedure for seeking just compensation, the property owner cannot claim a violation of the Just Compensation Clause until it has used the procedure and been denied just compensation.

The recognition that a property owner has not suffered a violation of the Just Compensation Clause until the owner has unsuccessfully attempted to obtain just compensation through the procedures provided by the State for obtaining such compensation is analogous to the Court's holding in *Parratt v. Taylor*. There, the Court ruled that a person deprived of property through a random and unauthorized act by a state employee does not state a claim under the Due Process Clause merely by alleging the deprivation of property. In such a situation, the Constitution does not require predeprivation process because it would be impossible or impracticable to provide a meaningful hearing before the deprivation. Instead, the Constitution is satisfied by the provision of meaningful postdeprivation process. Thus, the State's action is not "complete" in the sense of causing a constitutional injury "unless or until the state fails to provide an adequate postdeprivation remedy for the property loss." *Hudson v. Palmer*. Likewise, because the Constitution does not require pretaking compensation, and is instead satisfied by a reasonable and adequate provision for obtaining compensation after the taking, the State's action here is not "complete" until the State fails to provide adequate compensation for the taking.

Under Tennessee law, a property owner may bring an inverse condemnation action to obtain just compensation for an alleged taking of property under certain circumstances. The statutory scheme for eminent domain proceedings outlines the procedures by which government entities must exercise the right of eminent domain. The State is prohibited from "enter[ing] upon [condemned] land" until these procedures have been utilized and compensation has been paid the owner, but if a government entity does take possession of the land without following the required procedures,

> the owner of such land may petition for a jury of inquest, in which case the same proceedings may be had, as near as may be, as hereinbefore provided; or he may sue for damages in the ordinary way. . . .

The Tennessee state courts have interpreted § 29-16-123 to allow recovery through inverse condemnation where the "taking" is effected by restrictive zoning laws or development regulations. Respondent has not shown that the inverse condemnation procedure is unavailable or inadequate, and until it has utilized that procedure, its taking claim is premature.

NOTES AND QUESTIONS

1. Why is this case analogous to *Parratt* and not controlled by *Patsy*?

2. Assume a landowner seeks the variances but is denied. He then brings an inverse condemnation action seeking "just compensation" for the taking. Dissatisfied with the amount awarded in state court, he now brings a § 1983 action in federal court claiming a violation of the Fifth Amendment. Can he relitigate the "just compensation" issue? Does *Williamson* effectively preclude § 1983 actions to enforce the "just compensation" clause, at least as to the amount of compensation rather than

the procedures utilized? *See San Remo Hotel, L.P. v. City & County of San Francisco,* 545 U.S. 323 (2005) (even though the plaintiffs' resort to state court was not entirely voluntary, they must specifically reserve the federal takings claim in state court to avoid preclusion).

3. PRECLUSION: EFFECT OF STATE PROCEEDINGS ON FEDERAL COURT ACTIONS

a. State Judicial Proceedings

ALLEN V. MCCURRY
449 U.S. 90 (1980)

Justice STEWART delivered the opinion of the Court.

At a hearing before his criminal trial in a Missouri court, the respondent, Willie McCurry, invoked the Fourth and Fourteenth Amendments to suppress evidence that had been seized by the police. The trial court denied the suppression motion in part, and McCurry was subsequently convicted after a jury trial. The conviction was later affirmed on appeal. Because he did not assert that the state courts had denied him a "full and fair opportunity" to litigate his search and seizure claim, McCurry was barred from seeking a writ of habeas corpus in a federal district court.[a] Nevertheless, he sought federal-court redress for the alleged constitutional violation by bringing a damages suit under 42 U.S.C. § 1983 against the officers who had entered his home and seized the evidence in question. We granted certiorari to consider whether the unavailability of federal habeas corpus prevented the police officers from raising the state court's partial rejection of McCurry's constitutional claim as a collateral estoppel defense to the § 1983 suit against them for damages.

I

In April 1977, several undercover police officers, following an informant's tip that McCurry was dealing in heroin, went to his house in St. Louis, Mo., to attempt a purchase. Two officers, petitioners Allen and Jacobsmeyer, knocked on the front door, while the other officers hid nearby. When McCurry opened the door, the two officers asked to buy some heroin "caps." McCurry went back into the house and returned soon thereafter, firing a pistol at and seriously wounding Allen and Jacobsmeyer. After a gun battle with the other officers and their reinforcements, McCurry retreated into the house; he emerged again when the police demanded that he surrender. Several

---

a   In Stone v. Powell, 428 U.S. 465 (1976), the Court held that a state prisoner could not obtain federal habeas corpus relief, on the ground that evidence obtained in violation of the Fourth Amendment was used at trial, if the state provided a full and fair opportunity to litigate the Fourth Amendment issue.

officers then entered the house without a warrant, purportedly to search for other persons inside. One of the officers seized drugs and other contraband that lay in plain view, as well as additional contraband he found in dresser drawers and in auto tires on the porch.

McCurry was charged with possession of heroin and assault with intent to kill. At the pretrial suppression hearing, the trial judge excluded the evidence seized from the dresser drawers and tires, but denied suppression of the evidence found in plain view. McCurry was convicted of both the heroin and assault offenses.

McCurry subsequently filed the present § 1983 action for $1 million in damages against petitioners Allen and Jacobsmeyer, other unnamed individual police officers, and the city of St. Louis and its police department. The complaint alleged a conspiracy to violate McCurry's Fourth Amendment rights, an unconstitutional search and seizure of his house, and an assault on him by unknown police officers after he had been arrested and handcuffed.

II

The federal courts have traditionally adhered to the related doctrines of *res judicata* and collateral estoppel. Under *res judicata*, a final judgment on the merits of an action precludes the parties or their privies from relitigating issues that were or could have been raised in that action. Under collateral estoppel, once a court has decided an issue of fact or law necessary to its judgment, that decision may preclude relitigation of the issue in a suit on a different cause of action involving a party to the first case. As this Court and other courts have often recognized, *res judicata* and collateral estoppel relieve parties of the cost and vexation of multiple lawsuits, conserve judicial resources, and, by preventing inconsistent decisions, encourage reliance on adjudication.

III

This Court has never directly decided whether the rules of res judicata and collateral estoppel are generally applicable to § 1983 actions. But in *Preiser v. Rodriguez* the Court noted with implicit approval the view of other federal courts that res judicata principles fully apply to civil rights suits brought under that statute.

Because the requirement of mutuality of estoppel was still alive in the federal courts until well into this century, the drafters of the 1871 Civil Rights Act, of which § 1983 is a part, may have had less reason to concern themselves with rules of preclusion than a modern Congress would. Nevertheless, in 1871 res *judicata* and collateral estoppel could certainly have applied in federal suits following state-court litigation between the same parties or their privies, and nothing in the language of § 1983 remotely expresses any congressional intent to contravene the common-law rules of preclusion or to repeal the express statutory requirements of the predecessor of

28 U.S.C. § 1738.[b] Section 1983 creates a new federal cause of action. It says nothing about the preclusive effect of state court judgments.

Moreover, the legislative history of § 1983 does not in any clear way suggest that Congress intended to repeal or restrict the traditional doctrines of preclusion. The main goal of the Act was to override the corrupting influence of the Ku Klux Klan and its sympathizers on the governments and law enforcement agencies of the Southern States and of course the debates show that one strong motive behind its enactment was grave congressional concern that the state courts had been deficient in protecting federal rights. But in the context of the legislative history as a whole, this congressional concern lends only the most equivocal support to any argument that, in cases where the state courts have recognized the constitutional claims asserted and provided fair procedures for determining them, Congress intended to override § 1738 or the common-law rules of collateral estoppel and *res judicata*.

As the Court has understood the history of the legislation, Congress realized that in enacting § 1983 it was altering the balance of judicial power between the state and federal courts. But in doing so, Congress was adding to the jurisdiction of the federal courts, not subtracting from that of the state courts. *See Monroe v. Pape* ("The federal remedy is supplementary to the state remedy. . . ."). The debates contain several references to the concurrent jurisdiction of the state courts over federal questions, and numerous suggestions that the state courts would retain their established jurisdiction so that they could, when the then current political passions abated, demonstrate a new sensitivity to federal rights.

To the extent that it did intend to change the balance of power over federal questions between the state and federal courts, the 42d Congress was acting in a way thoroughly consistent with the doctrines of preclusion. In reviewing the legislative history of § 1983 in *Monroe v. Pape*, the Court inferred that Congress had intended a federal remedy in three circumstances: where state substantive law was facially unconstitutional, where state procedural law was inadequate to allow full litigation of a constitutional claim, and where state procedural law, though adequate in theory, was inadequate in practice. In short, the federal courts could step in where the state courts were unable or unwilling to protect federal rights. This understanding of § 1983 might well support an exception to *res judicata* and collateral estoppel where state law did not provide fair procedures for the litigation of constitutional claims, or where a state court failed to even acknowledge the existence of the constitutional principle on which a litigant based his claim. Such an exception, however, would be essentially the same as the important general limit on rules of preclusion that already exists: Collateral estoppel does not apply where the party against whom an earlier court decision is asserted did not have a full and fair opportunity to litigate the claim or issue decided by the first court. But the Court's view of § 1983 in *Monroe* lends no strength to any argument that Congress intended to allow relitigation of federal issues decided after a full and fair hearing in a state court simply because the state court's decision may have been erroneous.

---

b   This section provides that "judicial proceedings . . . shall have the same full faith and credit in every court within the United States . . . as they have by law or usage in the courts of such State . . . from which they are taken."

The actual basis of the Court of Appeals' holding appears to be a generally framed principle that every person asserting a federal right is entitled to one unencumbered opportunity to litigate that right in a federal district court, regardless of the legal posture in which the federal claim arises. But the authority for this principle is difficult to discern. It cannot lie in the Constitution, which makes no such guarantee, but leaves the scope of the jurisdiction of the federal district courts to the wisdom of Congress. And no such authority is to be found in § 1983 itself. For reasons already discussed at length, nothing in the language or legislative history of § 1983 proves any congressional intent to deny binding effect to a state-court judgment or decision when the state court, acting within its proper jurisdiction, has given the parties a full and fair opportunity to litigate federal claims, and thereby has shown itself willing and able to protect federal rights. And nothing in the legislative history of § 1983 reveals any purpose to afford less deference to judgments in state criminal proceedings than to those in state civil proceedings. There is, in short, no reason to believe that Congress intended to provide a person claiming a federal right an unrestricted opportunity to relitigate an issue already decided in state court simply because the issue arose in a state proceeding in which he would rather not have been engaged at all.

Justice BLACKMUN, with whom Justice BRENNAN and Justice MARSHALL join, dissenting.

The Court today holds that notions of collateral estoppel apply with full force to this suit brought under 42 U.S.C. § 1983. In my view, the Court, in so ruling, ignores the clear import of the legislative history of that statute and disregards the important federal policies that underlie its enforcement.

The following factors persuade me to conclude that this respondent should not be precluded from asserting his claim in federal court. First, at the time § 1983 was passed, a nonparty's ability, as a practical matter, to invoke collateral estoppel was nonexistent. Thus, the 42d Congress could not have anticipated or approved that a criminal defendant, tried and convicted in state court, would be precluded from raising against police officers a constitutional claim arising out of his arrest.

Also, the process of deciding in a state criminal trial whether to exclude or admit evidence is not at all the equivalent of a § 1983 proceeding. The remedy sought in the latter is utterly different. In bringing the civil suit the criminal defendant does not seek to challenge his conviction collaterally. At most, he wins damages. In contrast, the exclusion of evidence may prevent a criminal conviction. A trial court, faced with the decision whether to exclude relevant evidence, confronts institutional pressures that may cause it to give a different shape to the Fourth Amendment right from what would result in civil litigation of a damages claim. Also, the issue whether to exclude evidence is subsidiary to the purpose of a criminal trial, which is to determine the guilt or innocence of the defendant, and a trial court, at least subconsciously, must weigh the potential damage to the truth-seeking process caused by excluding relevant evidence.

A state criminal defendant cannot be held to have chosen "voluntarily" to litigate his Fourth Amendment claim in the state court. The risk of conviction puts pressure upon him to raise all possible defenses. He also faces uncertainty about the wisdom of forgoing litigation on any issue, for there is the possibility that he will be held to have waived his right to appeal on that issue. The "deliberate bypass" of state procedures, which the imposition of collateral estoppel under these circumstances encourages, surely is not a preferred goal. To hold that a criminal defendant who raises a Fourth Amendment claim at his criminal trial "freely and without reservation submits his federal claims for decision by the state courts," is to deny reality. The criminal defendant is an involuntary litigant in the state tribunal, and against him all the forces of the State are arrayed. To force him to a choice between forgoing either a potential defense or a federal forum for hearing his constitutional civil claim is fundamentally unfair.

NOTES AND QUESTIONS

1. Is this decision inconsistent with *Monroe*, *Patsy* and *Felder*, i.e., does it force the federal constitutional issue into state court? Doesn't it give the state prosecutor control over where a person with a Fourth Amendment claim will litigate that claim?

2. Do you agree with the suggestion in the dissent that the Fourth Amendment issue might be decided differently, by the same judge, in a civil action because of the "institutional pressures" in a criminal action? Aside from whether the same judge would decide the issue differently, in a civil action the parties would have a right to trial by jury.

3. Could the accused in a state criminal proceeding, who anticipates civil litigation, avoid preclusion by simply not raising the Fourth Amendment issue in state court? Would the civil case, based on the Fourth Amendment, be barred because the issue could have been raised?

4. Will McCurry, in his § 1983 action, be able to use the portion of the state court ruling which excluded certain evidence? Explain.

5. In *Richards v. Jefferson County, Ala.*, 517 U.S. 793 (1996), the Court held that the plaintiffs, who were challenging an occupation tax imposed by the county, could not be bound by the decision in a consolidated case, brought by the director of finance for the city of Birmingham, the city and three county taxpayers. While the state courts generally are free to develop their own preclusion rules, precluding these plaintiffs would violate due process because (i) they had no notice that another suit was pending in which their legal rights could be conclusively resolved, and (ii) there was no indication that the plaintiffs in the earlier case represented the interests of these plaintiffs. Therefore, Alabama cannot constitutionally preclude these plaintiffs from

litigating their challenge to the occupation tax. Relying in part on the due process concerns addressed in *Richards*, in *Taylor v. Sturgell*, 553 U.S. 880 (2008), the Court rejected a broad "virtual representation" exception to the general rule against non-party claim preclusion.

HARING V. PROSISE
462 U.S. 306 (1983)

Justice MARSHALL delivered the opinion of the Court.

The trial court accepted respondent Prosise's plea of guilty to one count of manufacturing a controlled substance—phencyclidine. At the hearing at which respondent pleaded guilty, a police officer gave a brief account of the search of respondent's apartment that led to the discovery of material typically used in manufacturing this substance. Thereafter, Prosise brought a damages action under 42 U.S.C. § 1983 in Federal District Court against petitioner Haring and the other officers who participated in the search of his apartment.

II

We must decide whether Prosise's § 1983 action to redress an alleged Fourth Amendment violation is barred by the judgment of conviction entered in state court following his guilty plea. Petitioners' initial argument is that under principles of collateral estoppel generally applied by the Virginia courts, Prosise's conviction would bar his subsequent civil challenge to police conduct, and that a federal court must therefore give the state judgment the same effect under 28 U.S.C. § 1738.

[T]he doctrine of collateral estoppel would not be invoked in this case by the Virginia courts for at least three reasons. First, the legality of the search of Prosise's apartment was not actually litigated in the criminal proceedings. Indeed, no issue was "actually litigated" in the state proceeding since Prosise declined to contest his guilt in any way. Second, the criminal proceedings did not actually decide against Prosise any issue on which he must prevail in order to establish his § 1983 claim. The only question raised by the criminal indictment and determined by Prosise's guilty plea in Arlington Circuit Court was whether Prosise unlawfully engaged in the manufacture of a controlled substance. This question is simply irrelevant to the legality of the search under the Fourth Amendment or to Prosise's right to compensation from state officials under § 1983.

Finally, none of the issues in the § 1983 action could have been "necessarily" determined in the criminal proceeding. Specifically, a determination that the county police officers engaged in no illegal police conduct would not have been essential to the trial court's acceptance of Prosise's guilty plea. Indeed, a determination that the search of Prosise's apartment was illegal would have been entirely irrelevant in the context of the guilty plea proceeding. Neither state nor federal law requires that a guilty plea in state court be supported by legally admissible evidence where the accused's valid waiver of his right to stand trial is accompanied by a confession of guilt.

We therefore conclude that Virginia law would not bar Prosise from litigating the validity of the search conducted by petitioners. Accordingly, the issue is not foreclosed under 28 U.S.C. § 1738.

III

We turn next to petitioners' contention that even if Prosise's claim is not precluded under § 1738, this Court should create a special rule of preclusion which nevertheless would bar litigation of his § 1983 claim. As a general matter, even when issues have been raised, argued, and decided in a prior proceeding, and are therefore preclusive under state law, "[r]edetermination of [the] issues [may nevertheless be] warranted if there is reason to doubt the quality, extensiveness, or fairness of procedures followed in prior litigation." Yet petitioners maintain that Prosise should be barred from litigating an issue that was never raised, argued, or decided simply because he had an opportunity to raise the issue in a previous proceeding. Petitioners reason that by pleading guilty Prosise should be deemed to have either admitted the legality of the search or waived any Fourth Amendment claim, thereby precluding him from asserting that claim in any subsequent suit. According to petitioners, such a federal rule of preclusion imposed in addition to the requirements of § 1738 is necessary to further important interests in judicial administration.

There is no justification for creating such an anomalous rule. To begin with, Prosise's guilty plea in no way constituted an admission that the search of his apartment was proper under the Fourth Amendment. During the course of proceedings in Arlington County Circuit Court, Prosise made no concession with respect to the Fourth Amendment claim.

We similarly reject the view, argued by petitioners and accepted by the District Court, that by pleading guilty Prosise "waived" any claim involving an antecedent Fourth Amendment violation.

Under our past decisions, as the District Court correctly recognized, a guilty plea results in the defendant's loss of any meaningful opportunity he might otherwise have had to challenge the admissibility of evidence obtained in violation of the Fourth Amendment. It does not follow, however, that a guilty plea is a "waiver" of antecedent Fourth Amendment claims that may be given effect outside the confines of the criminal proceeding. The defendant's rights under the Fourth Amendment are not among the trial rights that he necessarily waives when he knowingly and voluntarily pleads guilty.

Adoption of petitioners' rule of preclusion would threaten important interests in preserving federal courts as an available forum for the vindication of constitutional rights. Under petitioners' rule, whether or not a state judgment would be accorded preclusive effect by state courts, a federal court would be barred from entertaining a § 1983 claim. The rule would require "an otherwise unwilling party to try [Fourth Amendment] questions to the hilt" and prevail in state court "in order to [preserve] the mere possibility" of later bringing a § 1983 claim in federal court. Defendants who have pleaded guilty and who wish to bring a § 1983 claim would be forced to bring that claim in state court, if at all. Not only have petitioners failed to advance any compelling justification for a rule confining the litigation of constitutional claims to a state forum, but such a rule would be wholly contrary to one of the central concerns which motivated the enactment of § 1983, namely, the "grave congressional concern that the state courts had been deficient in protecting federal rights."

IV

We conclude that respondent's conviction in state court does not preclude him from now seeking to recover damages under 42 U.S.C. § 1983 for an alleged Fourth Amendment violation that was never considered in the state proceedings.

NOTES AND QUESTIONS

1. If Virginia preclusion law barred a civil action for damages after a plea of guilty, under the theory that the Fourth Amendment claim could have been raised as a defense to the state criminal charge, should Prosise's § 1983 action in federal court be barred? Construct an argument against preclusion.

2. In § III of the opinion in *Prosise*, the Court rejected the request that it "create a special rule of preclusion." What was the basis for this request in light of the determination that § 1738 does not preclude the action?

3. Would the result in *Prosise* be the same if Prosise had pleaded not guilty in state court, without raising the Fourth Amendment issue, and then filed a § 1983 action in federal court?

4. Does an agreement in which the defendant in a criminal case releases all § 1983 claims in exchange for dismissal of pending criminal charges or a favorable plea bargain preclude a subsequent § 1983 action? In *Newton v. Rumery*, 480 U.S. 386 (1987), the Court held such a waiver was binding and not necessarily against public policy. Does this give a prosecutor the ability to foreclose civil rights actions against police officers by filing questionable criminal charges? Is such a release truly voluntary?

Justice BLACKMUN delivered the opinion of the Court.

This case raises issues concerning the claim preclusive effect of a state-court judgment in the context of a subsequent suit, under 42 U.S.C. §§ 1983 and 1985 in federal court.

I

Petitioner, Dr. Ethel D. Migra, was employed by the Warren (Ohio) City School District Board of Education from August 1976 to June 1979. She served as supervisor of elementary education. Her employment was on an annual basis under written contracts for successive school years.

On April 17, 1979, at a regularly scheduled meeting, the Board, with all five of its members present, unanimously adopted a resolution renewing Dr. Migra's employment as supervisor for the 1979-1980 school year. Being advised of this, she accepted the renewed appointment by letter dated April 18 delivered to a member of the Board on April 23. Early the following morning her letter was passed on to the Superintendent of Schools and to the Board's President.

The Board, however, held a special meeting, called by its President, on the morning of April 24. The President first read Dr. Migra's acceptance letter. Then, after disposing of other business, a motion was made and adopted, by a vote of 3 to 1, not to renew petitioner's employment for the 1979-1980 school year. Dr. Migra was given written notice of this nonrenewal and never received a written contract of employment for that year.

Petitioner brought suit in the Court of Common Pleas of Trumbull County, Ohio, against the Board and its three members who had voted not to renew her employment. The complaint, although in five counts, presented what the parties now accept as essentially two causes of action, namely, breach of contract by the Board, and wrongful interference by the individual members with petitioner's contract of employment. The state court, after a bench trial, "reserved and continued" the "issue of conspiracy" and did not reach the question of the individual members' liability. It ruled that under Ohio law petitioner had accepted the employment proffered for 1979-1980, that this created a binding contract between her and the Board, and that the Board's subsequent action purporting not to renew the employment relationship had no legal effect. The court awarded Dr. Migra reinstatement to her position and compensatory damages. Thereafter, petitioner moved the state trial court to dismiss without prejudice "the issue of the conspiracy and individual board member liability." That motion was granted.

In July 1980, Dr. Migra filed the present action in the United States District Court for the Northern District of Ohio against the Board, its then individual members, and the Superintendent of Schools. Her complaint alleged that she had become the director of a commission appointed by the Board to fashion a voluntary plan for the desegregation of the District's elementary schools; that she had prepared a social studies curriculum; that the individual defendants objected to and opposed the curriculum and resisted the desegregation plan; that hostility and ill will toward petitioner developed; and that, as a consequence, the individual defendants determined not to renew petitioner's contract of employment. Many of the alleged facts had been proved in the earlier state-court litigation. Dr. Migra claimed that the Board's actions were intended to punish her for the exercise of her First Amendment rights. She also claimed that the actions deprived her of property without due process and denied her equal protection. Her federal claim thus arose under the First, Fifth and Fourteenth Amendments and 42 U.S.C. §§ 1983 and 1985. She requested injunctive relief and compensatory and punitive damages. Answers were filed in due course and shortly thereafter the defendants moved for summary judgment on the basis of *res judicata* and the bar of the statute of limitations.

II

It is now settled that a federal court must give to a state court judgment the same preclusive effect as would be given that judgment under the law of the State in which the judgment was rendered. In *Allen v. McCurry* this Court . . . made clear that issues actually litigated in a state-court proceeding are entitled to the same preclusive effect in a subsequent federal § 1983 suit as they enjoy in the courts of the State where the judgment was rendered.

The Court in *Allen* left open the possibility, however, that the preclusive effect of a state-court judgment might be different as to a federal issue that a § 1983 litigant could have raised but did not raise in the earlier state-court proceeding. That is the central issue to be resolved in the present case. Petitioner did not litigate her § 1983 claim in state court, and she asserts that the state-court judgment should not preclude her suit in federal court simply because her federal claim could have been litigated in the state-court proceeding. Thus, petitioner urges this Court to interpret the interplay of § 1738 and § 1983 in such a way as to accord state-court judgments preclusive effect in § 1983 suits only as to issues actually litigated in state court.

It is difficult to see how the policy concerns underlying § 1983 would justify a distinction between the issue preclusive and claim preclusive effects of state-court judgments. The argument that state-court judgments should have less preclusive effect in § 1983 suits than in other federal suits is based on Congress' expressed concern over the adequacy of state courts as protectors of federal rights. *Allen* recognized that the enactment of § 1983 was motivated partially out of such concern, but *Allen* nevertheless held that § 1983 did not open the way to relitigation of an issue that had been determined in a state criminal proceeding. Any distrust of state courts that would justify a limitation on the preclusive effect of state judgments in § 1983 suits would presumably apply equally to issues that actually were decided in a state court as well as to those that could have been. If § 1983 created an exception to the general preclusive effect accorded to state-court judgments, such an exception would seem to require similar treatment of both issue preclusion and claim preclusion. Having rejected in *Allen* the view that state-court judgments have no issue preclusive effect in § 1983 suits, we must reject the view that § 1983 prevents the judgment in petitioner's state-court proceeding from creating a claim preclusion bar in this case.

Petitioner suggests that to give state-court judgments full issue preclusive effect but not claim preclusive effect would enable litigants to bring their state claims in state court and their federal claims in federal court, thereby taking advantage of the relative expertise of both forums. Although such a division may seem attractive from a plaintiff's perspective, it is not the system established by § 1738. That statute embodies the view that it is more important to give full faith and credit to state-court judgments than to ensure separate forums for federal and state claims. This reflects a variety of concerns, including notions of comity, the need to prevent vexatious litigation, and a desire to conserve judicial resources.

In the present litigation, petitioner does not claim that the state court would not have adjudicated her federal claims had she presented them in her original suit in state court. Alternatively, petitioner could have obtained a federal forum for her federal claim by litigating it first in a federal court. Section 1983, however, does not override state preclusion law and guarantee petitioner a right to proceed to judgment in state court on her state claims and then turn to federal court for adjudication of her federal claims. We hold, therefore, that petitioner's state-court judgment in this litigation has the same claim preclusive effect in federal court that the judgment would have in the Ohio state courts.

NOTES AND QUESTIONS

1. In view of the decision in *Migra*, how would you advise a similarly situated plaintiff to litigate the case? Could Dr. Migra have proceeded in federal and state court simultaneously?

2. Assume a plaintiff first files suit in federal court, but the judge refuses to take pendent or supplemental jurisdiction over a state law claim. Is the plaintiff barred from bringing a second action in state court, raising only the state claim?

3. The federal court plaintiff in *Prosise* had an opportunity to raise the federal issue in state court, but chose not to do so and yet he was not barred from raising it in a § 1983 action. Is the decision in *Prosise* inconsistent with *Migra*? Review Question 3 following *McCurry, supra*.

4. There may be circumstances where the party invoking preclusion would prefer to have the federal court apply federal preclusion law because it is more favorable. As noted by Justice White in his concurring opinion in *Migra*, § 1738 has been interpreted by the Court to require application of state preclusion law to state court judgments, even where federal preclusion law would give them greater effect than state law. This construction, according to Justice White, is unfortunate.

Justice WHITE delivered the opinion of the Court.

As one of its first acts, Congress directed that all United States courts afford the same full faith and credit to state court judgments that would apply in the State's own courts. 28 U.S.C. § 1738. More recently, Congress implemented the national policy against employment discrimination by creating an array of substantive protections and remedies which generally allows federal courts to determine the merits of a discrimination claim. Title VII of the Civil Rights Act of 1964, 42 U.S.C § 2000e, *et seq.* The principal question presented by this case is whether Congress intended Title VII to supersede the principles of comity and repose embodied in § 1738. Specifically, we decide whether a federal court in a Title VII case should give preclusive effect to a decision of a state court upholding a state administrative agency's rejection of an employment discrimination claim as meritless when the state court's decision would be *res judicata* in the State's own courts.

I

Petitioner Rubin Kremer emigrated from Poland in 1970 and was hired in 1973 by respondent Chemical Construction Corp. (Chemico) as an engineer. Two years later he was laid off, along with a number of other employees. Some of these employees were later rehired, but Kremer was not although he made several applications. In May 1976, Kremer filed a discrimination charge with the Equal Employment Opportunity Commission (EEOC), asserting that his discharge and failure to be rehired were due to his national origin and Jewish faith. Because the EEOC may not consider a claim until a state agency having jurisdiction over employment discrimination complaints has had at least 60 days to resolve the matter, the Commission referred Kremer's charge to the New York State Division of Human Rights (NYHRD), the agency charged with enforcing the New York law prohibiting employment discrimination.

After investigating Kremer's complaint, the NYHRD concluded that there was no probable cause to believe that Chemico had engaged in the discriminatory practices complained of. The NYHRD explicitly based its determination on the findings that Kremer was not rehired because one employee who was rehired had greater seniority, that another employee who was rehired filled a lesser position than that previously held by Kremer, and that neither Kremer's creed nor age was a factor considered in Chemico's failure to rehire him. The NYHRD's determination was upheld by its Appeal Board as "not arbitrary, capricious or an abuse of discretion." Kremer again brought his complaint to the attention of the EEOC and also filed, on December 6, 1977, a petition with the Appellate Division of the New York Supreme Court to set aside the adverse administrative determination. On February 27, 1978, five justices of the Appellate Division unanimously affirmed the Appeal Board's order. Kremer could have sought, but did not seek, review by the New York Court of Appeals.

Subsequently, a District Director of the EEOC ruled that there was no reasonable cause to believe that the charge of discrimination was true and issued a right-to-sue notice. The District Director refused a request for reconsideration, noting that he had reviewed the case files and considered the EEOC's disposition as "appropriate and correct in all respects."

Kremer then brought this Title VII action in District Court, claiming discrimination on the basis of national origin and religion. Chemico argued from the outset that Kremer's Title VII action was barred by the doctrine of *res judicata*.

II

Section 1738 requires federal courts to give the same preclusive effect to state court judgments that those judgments would be given in the courts of the State from which the judgments emerged. Here the Appellate Division of the New York Supreme Court has issued a judgment affirming the decision of the NYHRD Appeals Board that the discharge and failure to rehire Kremer were not the product of the discrimination that he had alleged. There is no question that this judicial determination precludes Kremer from bringing "any other action, civil or criminal, based upon the same grievance" in the New York courts. By its terms, therefore, § 1738 would appear to preclude Kremer from relitigating the same question in federal court.

Kremer offers two principal reasons why § 1738 does not bar this action. First, he suggests that in Title VII cases Congress intended that federal courts be relieved of their usual obligation to grant finality to state court decisions. Second, he urges that the New York administrative and judicial proceedings in this case were so deficient that they are not entitled to preclusive effect in federal courts and, in any event, the rejection of a state employment discrimination claim cannot by definition bar a Title VII action. We consider this latter contention in Part III.

A

Allen v. McCurry made clear that an exception to § 1738 will not be recognized unless a later statute contains an express or implied partial repeal. There is no claim here that Title VII expressly repealed § 1738; if there has been a partial repeal, it must be implied.

No provision of Title VII requires claimants to pursue in state court an unfavorable state administrative action, nor does the Act specify the weight a federal court should afford a final judgment by a state court if such a remedy is sought.

Since an implied repeal must ordinarily be evident from the language or operation of a statute, the lack of such manifest incompatibility between Title VII and § 1738 is enough to answer our inquiry. No different conclusion is suggested by the legislative history of Title VII. Although no inescapable conclusions can be drawn from the process of enactment, the legislative debates surrounding the initial passage of Title VII in 1964 and the substantial amendment adopted in 1972 plainly do not demonstrate that Congress intended to override the historic respect that federal courts accord state court judgments.

It is sufficiently clear that Congress, both in 1964 and 1972, though wary of assuming the adequacy of state employment discrimination remedies, did not intend to supplant such laws. We conclude that neither the statutory language nor the congressional debates suffice to repeal § 1738's longstanding directive to federal courts.

<h2 style="text-align:center">III</h2>

The petitioner nevertheless contends that the judgment should not bar his Title VII action because the New York courts did not resolve the issue that the District Court must hear under Title VII—whether Kremer had suffered discriminatory treatment—and because the procedures provided were inadequate. Neither contention is persuasive. Although the claims presented to the NYHRD and subsequently reviewed by the Appellate Division were necessarily based on New York law, the alleged discriminatory acts are prohibited by both federal and state laws. The elements of a successful employment discrimination claim are virtually identical; petitioner could not succeed on a Title VII claim consistently with the judgment of the NYHRD that there is no reason to believe he was terminated or not rehired because of age or religion. The Appellate Division's affirmance of NYHRD's dismissal necessarily decided that petitioner's claim under New York law was meritless, and thus it also decided that a Title VII claim arising from the same events would be equally meritless.

The more serious contention is that even though administrative proceedings and judicial review are legally sufficient to be given preclusive effect in New York, they should be deemed so fundamentally flawed as to be denied recognition under § 1738. We have previously recognized that the judicially created doctrine of collateral estoppel does not apply when the party against whom the earlier decision is asserted did not have a "full and fair opportunity" to litigate the claim or issue. "Redetermination of issues is warranted if there is reason to doubt the quality, extensiveness, or fairness of procedures followed in prior litigation."

Our previous decisions have not specified the source or defined the content of the requirement that the first adjudication offer a full and fair opportunity to litigate. But for present purposes, where we are bound by the statutory directive of § 1738, state proceedings need do no more than satisfy the minimum procedural requirements of the Fourteenth Amendment's Due Process Clause in order to qualify for the full faith and credit guaranteed by federal law. A State may not grant preclusive effect in its own courts to a constitutionally infirm judgment, and other state and federal courts are not required to accord full faith and credit to such a judgment. Section 1738 does not suggest otherwise; other state and federal courts would still be providing a state court judgment with the "same" preclusive effect as the courts of the State from which the judgment emerged. In such a case, there could be no constitutionally recognizable preclusion at all.

We have little doubt that Kremer received all the process that was constitutionally required in rejecting his claim that he had been discriminatorily discharged contrary to the statute. We must bear in mind that no single model of procedural fairness, let alone a particular form of procedure, is dictated by the Due Process Clause. Under New York law, a claim of employment discrimination requires the NYHRD to investigate whether there is "probable cause" to believe that the complaint is true. Before this determination of probable cause is made, the claimant is entitled to a "full opportunity to present on the record, though informally, his charges against his employer or other respondent, including the right to submit all exhibits which he wishes to present and testimony of witnesses in addition to his own testimony." The complainant also is entitled to an opportunity "to rebut evidence submitted by or obtained from the respondent." He may have an attorney assist him and may ask the division to issue subpoenas.

If the investigation discloses probable cause and efforts at conciliation fail, the NYHRD must conduct a public hearing to determine the merits of the complaint. A public hearing must also be held if the Human Rights Appeal Board finds "there has not been a full investigation and opportunity for the complainant to present his contentions and evidence, with a full record." Finally, judicial review in the Appellate Division is available to assure that a claimant is not denied any of the procedural rights to which he was entitled and that the NYHRD's determination was not arbitrary and capricious.

We have no hesitation in concluding that this panoply of procedures, complemented by administrative as well as judicial review, is sufficient under the Due Process Clause.

NOTES AND QUESTIONS

1. Given the mandatory deferral of EEOC charges to the state or local agency, how can charging parties who want to litigate their Title VII cases in federal court avoid the holding in *Kremer*? Could Kremer have avoided the whole exhaustion/preclusion problem by suing Chemico under § 1981 challenging the discharge and the refusal to rehire? Assuming it is after the enactment of the Civil Rights Act of 1991, what statute of limitation would govern his two § 1981 claims?

2. Under *Kremer*, what constitutes a "full and fair opportunity to litigate" a claim?

3. Assume an employee alleging discrimination prevails at a state agency hearing and then loses in state court on the employer's petition for judicial review. Is the employee precluded from litigating *de novo* in federal court under Title VII? Would it make a difference if the state court simply reviews agency decisions for "egregious" error? Has the employee been denied a fair and full opportunity to litigate?

4. If Kremer had been provided a judicial type hearing before the state agency and lost, would that determination be binding in a subsequent federal court Title VII action, assuming the agency decision was not reviewed in state court? *See Elliott, infra.*

b. State Administrative Proceedings

UNIVERSITY OF TENNESSEE V. ELLIOTT
478 U.S. 788 (1986)

Justice WHITE delivered the opinion of the Court.

A state Administrative Law Judge determined that petitioner was not motivated by racial prejudice in seeking to discharge respondent. The question presented is whether this finding is entitled to preclusive effect in federal court, where respondent has raised discrimination claims under various civil rights laws, including Title VII of the Civil Rights Act of 1964, 42 U.S.C. § 2000e *et seq.*, and 42 U.S.C. § 1983.

I

In 1981, the petitioner University of Tennessee informed respondent, a black employee of the University's Agricultural Extension Service, that he would be discharged for inadequate work performance and misconduct on the job. Respondent requested a hearing under Tennessee Uniform Administrative Procedures Act to contest his proposed termination. Prior to the start of the hearing, respondent also filed suit in the United States District Court for the Western District of Tennessee, alleging that his proposed discharge was racially motivated and seeking relief under Title VII and other civil rights statutes, including 42 U.S.C. § 1983. The relief sought included damages, an injunction prohibiting respondent's discharge, and classwide relief from alleged patterns of discrimination by petitioner.

After hearing extensive evidence, the ALJ found that the University had proved some but not all of the charges against respondent, and that the charges were not racially motivated. Concluding that the proposed discharge of respondent was too severe a penalty, the ALJ ordered him transferred to a new assignment with supervisors other than those with whom he had experienced conflicts. Respondent appealed to the University's Vice President for Agriculture, who affirmed the ALJ's ruling. The Vice President stated that his review of the record persuaded him that the proposed discharge of respondent had not been racially motivated.

Respondent did not seek review of these administrative proceedings in the Tennessee courts; instead, he returned to federal court to pursue his civil rights claims. There, petitioner moved for summary judgment on the ground that respondent's suit was an improper collateral attack on the ALJ's ruling, which petitioner contended was entitled to preclusive effect.

II

Title 28 U.S.C. § 1738 governs the preclusive effect to be given the judgments and records of state courts, and is not applicable to the unreviewed state administrative factfinding at issue in this case. However, we have frequently fashioned federal common-law rules of preclusion in the absence of a governing statute. Although § 1738 is a governing statute with regard to the judgments and records of state courts, because § 1738 antedates the development of administrative agencies it clearly does not represent a congressional determination that the decisions of state administrative agencies should not be given preclusive effect. Accordingly, we will consider whether a rule of preclusion is appropriate, first with respect to respondent's Title VII claim, and next with respect to his claims under the Constitution and the Reconstruction civil rights statutes.

III

Under 42 U.S.C. § 2000e-5(b), the Equal Employment Opportunity Commission (EEOC), in investigating discrimination charges, must give "substantial weight to final findings and orders made by State or local authorities in proceedings commenced under State or local [employment discrimination] law." As we noted in *Kremer*, it would make little sense for Congress to write such a provision if state agency findings were entitled to preclusive effect in Title VII actions in federal court.

Moreover, our decision in *Chandler v. Roudebush* strongly supports respondent's contention that Congress intended one in his position to have a trial *de novo* on his Title VII claim. In *Chandler*, we held that a federal employee whose discrimination claim was rejected by her employing agency after an administrative hearing was entitled to a trial *de novo* in federal court on her Title VII claim. After reviewing in considerable detail the language of Title VII and the history of the 1972 amendments to the statute, we concluded:

> The legislative history of the 1972 amendments reinforces the plain meaning of the statute and confirms that Congress intended to accord federal employees the same right to a trial *de novo* [following administrative proceedings] as is enjoyed by private-sector employees and employees of state governments and political subdivisions under the amended Civil Rights Act of 1964.

Like the plaintiff in *Chandler*, the respondent in this case pursued his Title VII action following an administrative proceeding at which the employing agency rejected a discrimination claim. It would be contrary to the rationale of *Chandler* to apply *res judicata* to deny respondent a trial *de novo* on his Title VII claim.

IV

This Court has held that § 1738 requires that state-court judgments be given both issue and claim preclusive effect in subsequent actions under 42 U.S.C. § 1983. Those decisions are not controlling in this case, where § 1738 does not apply; nonetheless, they support the view that Congress, in enacting the Reconstruction civil rights statutes, did not intend to create an exception to general rules of preclusion.

We have previously recognized that it is a sound policy to apply principles of issue preclusion to the factfinding of administrative bodies acting in a judicial capacity. [G]iving preclusive effect to administrative factfinding serves the value underlying general principles of collateral estoppel: enforcing repose. This value, which encompasses both the parties' interest in avoiding the cost and vexation of repetitive litigation and the public's interest in conserving judicial resources is equally implicated whether factfinding is done by a federal or state agency.

Having federal courts give preclusive effect to the factfinding of state administrative tribunals also serves the value of federalism. Significantly, all of the opinions in *Thomas v. Washington Gas Light Co.* express the view that the Full Faith and Credit Clause compels the States to give preclusive effect to the factfindings of an administrative tribunal in a sister State. The Full Faith and Credit Clause is of course not binding on federal courts, but we can certainly look to the policies underlying the Clause in fashioning federal common-law rules of preclusion. "Perhaps the major purpose of the Full Faith and Credit Clause is to act as a nationally unifying force," and this purpose is served by giving preclusive effect to state administrative factfinding rather than leaving the courts of a second forum, state or federal, free to reach conflicting results. Accordingly, we hold that when a state agency "acting in a judicial capacity . . . resolves disputed issues of fact properly before it which the parties have had an adequate opportunity to litigate," federal courts must give the agency's factfinding the same preclusive effect to which it would be entitled in the State's courts.

NOTES AND QUESTIONS

1. In this situation, what public policy is served by precluding the § 1983 claim while the Title VII claim is allowed to proceed? Why does the Court exempt the Title VII claim, but not the § 1983 claim, from the federal common law preclusion rule?

2. Could the plaintiff have avoided this result, and preserved the right to proceed with both claims in federal court, if he had not asked for a hearing under the state Administrative Procedures Act? Wouldn't he still have to "exhaust" administrative remedies before litigating his Title VII claim?

3. Under what circumstances will agency factfinding be given preclusive effect in § 1983 actions?

PROBLEM: ELEVEN

A female employee of the local school corporation contacts you after filing a sexual harassment charge with the State Civil Rights Commission (CRC) alleging a violation of Title VII. She informs you that the CRC has scheduled a "hearing" for next week. The person harassing her is a co-worker, who occasionally has supervisory authority. Assume you are considering a claim against the co-worker under § 1983 to enforce the equal protection clause of the Fourteenth Amendment and a Title VII claim against the school corporation.

1. What are the advantages and risks of going ahead with the CRC hearing? What do you need to know about the CRC proceedings? Discuss both the Title VII and § 1983 claims.

2. Assume you attend the CRC hearing with your client, but are not allowed to examine witnesses. After the CRC finds no discrimination, you file an action in federal court with both § 1983 and Title VII claims. The defendants argue issue preclusion. Evaluate this argument.

3. Assume you can prove harassment, but the individual responsible does not have the resources to satisfy a judgment. The school corporation has a policy prohibiting sex discrimination and sexual harassment. What would you need to know to determine whether you can hold the corporation liable under § 1983?

MCDONALD V. CITY OF WEST BRANCH, MICHIGAN
466 U.S. 284 (1984)

Justice BRENNAN delivered the opinion of the Court.

The question presented in this § 1983 action is whether a federal court may accord preclusive effect to an unappealed arbitration award in a case brought under that statute.

I

On November 26, 1976, petitioner Gary McDonald, then a West Branch, Mich., police officer, was discharged. McDonald filed a grievance pursuant to the collective-bargaining agreement then in force between West Branch and the United Steelworkers of America (the Union), contending that there was "no proper cause" for his discharge, and that, as a result, the discharge violated the collective-bargaining agreement. After the preliminary steps in the contractual grievance procedure had been exhausted, the grievance was taken to arbitration. The arbitrator ruled against McDonald, however, finding that there was just cause for his discharge.

McDonald did not appeal the arbitrator's decision. Subsequently, however, he filed this § 1983 action against the city of West Branch and certain of its officials, including its Chief of Police, Paul Longstreet. In his complaint, McDonald alleged that he was discharged for exercising his First Amendment rights of freedom of speech, freedom of association, and freedom to petition the government for redress of grievances. The case was tried to a jury which returned a verdict against Longstreet, but in favor of the remaining defendants.

II

A

At the outset, we must consider whether federal courts are obligated by statute to accord *res judicata* or collateral estoppel effect to the arbitrator's decision. Respondents contend that the Federal Full Faith and Credit Statute, 28 U.S.C. § 1738, requires that we give preclusive effect to the arbitration award.

Our cases establish that § 1738 obliges federal courts to give the same preclusive effect to a state-court judgment as would the courts of the State rendering the judgments. As we explained in *Kremer*, however, "[a]rbitration decisions . . . are not subject to the mandate of § 1738." This conclusion follows from the plain language of § 1738 which provides in pertinent part that the "*judicial proceedings* [of any court of any State] shall have the same full faith and credit in every court within the United States and its Territories and Possessions as they have by law or usage in the courts of such State . . . from which they are taken." Arbitration is not a "judicial proceeding" and, therefore, § 1738 does not apply to arbitration awards.

B

Because federal courts are not required by statute to give *res judicata* or collateral-estoppel effect to an unappealed arbitration award, any rule of preclusion would necessarily be judicially fashioned. We therefore consider the question whether it was appropriate for the Court of Appeals to fashion such a rule.

Because § 1983 creates a cause of action, there is, of course, no question that Congress intended it to be judicially enforceable. Indeed, as we explained in *Mitchum v. Foster*, "[t]he very purpose of § 1983 was to interpose the federal courts between the States and the people, as guardians of the people's federal rights—to protect the people from unconstitutional action under color of state law." And, although arbitration is well suited to resolving contractual disputes, it cannot provide an adequate substitute for a judicial proceeding in protecting the federal statutory and constitutional rights that § 1983 is designed to safeguard. As a result, according preclusive effect to an arbitration award in a subsequent § 1983 action would undermine that statute's efficacy in protecting federal rights. We need only briefly reiterate the considerations that support this conclusion.

First, an arbitrator's expertise "pertains primarily to the law of the shop, not the law of the land." An arbitrator may not, therefore, have the expertise required to resolve the complex legal questions that arise in § 1983 actions.

Second, because an arbitrator's authority derives solely from the contract, an arbitrator may not have the authority to enforce § 1983.

Third, when, as is usually the case, the union has exclusive control over the "manner and extent to which an individual grievance is presented," there is an additional reason why arbitration is an inadequate substitute for judicial proceedings. The union's interests and those of the individual employee are not always identical or even compatible. As a result, the union may present the employee's grievance less vigorously, or make different strategic choices, than would the employee. Thus, were an arbitration award accorded preclusive effect, an employee's opportunity to be compensated for a constitutional deprivation might be lost merely because it was not in the union's interest to press his claim vigorously.

Finally, arbitral factfinding is generally not equivalent to judicial factfinding. As we explained in *Gardner-Denver*, "[t]he record of the arbitration proceedings is not as complete; the usual rules of evidence do not apply; and rights and procedures common to civil trials, such as discovery, compulsory process, cross-examination, and testimony under oath, are often severely limited or unavailable."

It is apparent, therefore, that in a § 1983 action, an arbitration proceeding cannot provide an adequate substitute for a judicial trial. Consequently, according preclusive effect to arbitration awards in § 1983 actions would severely undermine the protection of federal rights that the statute is designed to provide. We therefore hold that in a § 1983 action, a federal court should not afford *res judicata* or collateral-estoppel effect to an award in an arbitration proceeding brought pursuant to the terms of a collective bargaining agreement.[13]

NOTES AND QUESTIONS

1. What issue was decided adverse to McDonald by the arbitrator?

2. Evaluate the four considerations which the Court lists in support of its conclusion. Are arbitrators, as a group, less reliable or qualified than the ALJ involved in *Elliott*? Why not treat decisions of arbitrators, like those of the ALJ, on a case-by-case basis?

3. How significant is the difference between admissibility, discussed in footnote 13, and preclusion? Would an agency finding of "no good cause to discharge," made in an unemployment compensation proceeding, be admissible? Would it be given preclusive effect?

---

13 Consistent with our [earlier] decisions, an arbitral decision may be admitted as evidence in a §1983 action. As in those cases:

We adopt no standards as to the weight to be accorded an arbitral decision, since this must be determined in the court's discretion with regard to the facts and circumstances of each case. Relevant factors include the existence of provisions in the collective-bargaining agreement that conform substantially with [the statute or constitution], the degree of procedural fairness in the arbitral forum, adequacy of the record with respect to the issue [in the judicial proceeding], and the special competence of particular arbitrators. Where an arbitral determination gives full consideration to an employee's [statutory or constitutional] rights, a court may properly accord it great weight. This is especially true where the issue is solely one of fact, specifically addressed by the parties and decided by the arbitrator on the basis of an adequate record. But the courts should ever be mindful that Congress . . . thought it necessary to provide a judicial forum for the ultimate resolution of [these] claims. It is the duty of the courts to assure the full availability of this forum.

4. REMEDIES

a. Damages

i. Compensatory

CAREY V. PIPHUS
435 U.S. 247 (1978)

Mr. Justice POWELL delivered the opinion of the Court.

In this case, brought under 42 U.S.C. § 1983, we consider the elements and prerequisites for recovery of damages by students who were suspended from public elementary and secondary schools without procedural due process.

I

The District Court held that both students had been suspended without procedural due process. It also held that petitioners were not entitled to qualified immunity from damages because they "should have known that a lengthy suspension without any adjudicative hearing of any type" would violate procedural due process. Despite these holdings, the District Court declined to award damages because:

> Plaintiffs put no evidence in the record to quantify their damages, and the record is completely devoid of any evidence which could even form the basis of a speculative inference measuring the extent of their injuries. Plaintiffs' claims for damages therefore fail for complete lack of proof.

On respondents' appeal, the Court of Appeals reversed and remanded. It first held that the District Court erred in not granting declaratory and injunctive relief. It also held that the District Court should have considered evidence submitted by respondents after judgment that tended to prove the pecuniary value of each day of school that they missed while suspended. The court said, however, that respondents would not be entitled to recover damages representing the value of missed school time if petitioners showed on remand "that there was just cause for the suspension[s] and that therefore [respondents] would have been suspended even if a proper hearing had been held."

Finally, the Court of Appeals held that even if the District Court found on remand that respondents' suspensions were justified, they would be entitled to recover substantial "non-punitive" damages simply because they had been denied procedural due process. We granted certiorari to consider whether, in an action under § 1983 for the deprivation of procedural due process, a plaintiff must prove that he actually was injured by the deprivation before he may recover substantial "nonpunitive" damages.

II

A

Insofar as petitioners contend that the basic purpose of a § 1983 damages award should be to compensate persons for injuries caused by the deprivation of constitutional rights, they have the better of the argument. Rights, constitutional and otherwise, do not exist in a vacuum. Their purpose is to protect persons from injuries to particular interests, and their contours are shaped by the interests they protect.

Our legal system's concept of damages reflects this view of legal rights. "The cardinal principle of damages in Anglo-American law is that of *compensation* for the injury caused to plaintiff by defendant's breach of duty."

The Members of the Congress that enacted § 1983 did not address directly the question of damages, but the principle that damages are designed to compensate persons for injuries caused by the deprivation of rights hardly could have been foreign to the many lawyers in Congress in 1871. Two other sections of the Civil Rights Act of 1871 appear to incorporate this principle, and no reason suggests itself for reading § 1983 differently. To the extent that Congress intended that awards under § 1983 should deter the deprivation of constitutional rights, there is no evidence that it meant to establish a deterrent more formidable than that inherent in the award of compensatory damages.[11]

B

It is less difficult to conclude that damages awards under § 1983 should be governed by the principle of compensation than it is to apply this principle to concrete cases. But over the centuries the common law of torts has developed a set of rules to implement the principle that a person should be compensated fairly for the injuries caused by the violation of his legal rights. These rules, defining the elements of damages and the prerequisites for their recovery, provide the appropriate starting point for the inquiry under § 1983 as well.[13]

It is not clear, however, that common-law tort rules of damages will provide a complete solution to the damages issues in every § 1983 case. In some cases, the interests protected by a particular branch of the common law of torts may parallel closely the interests protected by

---

11 This is not to say that exemplary or punitive damages might not be awarded in a proper case under § 1983 with the specific purpose of deterring or punishing violations of constitutional rights.

We also note that the potential liability of § 1983 defendants for attorney's fees, *see* Civil Rights Attorney's Fees Awards Act of 1976, amending 42 U.S.C. § 1988, provides additional—and by no means inconsequential—assurance that agents of the State will not deliberately ignore due process rights.

13 The Court has looked to the common law of torts in similar fashion in constructing immunities under § 1983. Title 42 U.S.C. § 1988 authorizes courts to look to the common law of the States where this is "necessary to furnish suitable remedies" under § 1983.

a particular constitutional right. In such cases, it may be appropriate to apply the tort rules of damages directly to the § 1983 action. In other cases, the interests protected by a particular constitutional right may not also be protected by an analogous branch of the common law of torts. In those cases, the task will be the more difficult one of adapting common-law rules of damages to provide fair compensation for injuries caused by the deprivation of a constitutional right.

Although this task of adaptation will be one of some delicacy—as this case demonstrates—it must be undertaken. The purpose of § 1983 would be defeated if injuries caused by the deprivation of constitutional rights went uncompensated simply because the common law does not recognize an analogous cause of action. In order to further the purpose of § 1983, the rules governing compensation for injuries caused by the deprivation of constitutional rights should be tailored to the interests protected by the particular right in question—just as the common-law rules of damages themselves were defined by the interests protected in the various branches of tort law.

C

The Due Process Clause of the Fourteenth Amendment provides:

> [N]or shall any State deprive any person of life, liberty, or property, without due process of law. . . .

This Clause "raises no impenetrable barrier to the taking of a person's possessions," or liberty, or life. Procedural due process rules are meant to protect persons not from the deprivation, but from the mistaken or unjustified deprivation of life, liberty, or property. Thus, in deciding what process constitutionally is due in various contexts, the Court repeatedly has emphasized that "procedural due process rules are shaped by the risk of error inherent in the truth-finding process. . . ." Such rules "minimize substantively unfair or mistaken deprivations of" life, liberty or property by enabling persons to contest the basis upon which a State proposes to deprive them of protected interests.

In this case, the Court of Appeals held that if petitioners can prove on remand that "[respondents] would have been suspended even if a proper hearing had been held," then respondents will not be entitled to recover damages to compensate them for injuries caused by the suspensions. The court thought that in such a case, the failure to accord procedural due process could not properly be viewed as the cause of suspensions. The court suggested that in such circumstances, an award of damages for injuries caused by the suspensions would constitute a windfall, rather than compensation, to respondents. We do not understand the parties to disagree with this conclusion. Nor do we.

The parties do disagree as to the further holding of the Court of Appeals that respondents are entitled to recover substantial—although unspecified—damages to compensate them for "the injury which is 'inherent in the nature of the wrong,'" even if their suspensions were justified and even if they fail to prove that the denial of procedural due process actually caused them some real, if intangible, injury. Respondents, elaborating on this theme, submit that the holding is correct because injury fairly may be "presumed" to flow from every denial of procedural due process. Their argument is that in addition to protecting against unjustified deprivations, the Due Process Clause also guarantees the "feeling of just treatment" by the government. They contend that the deprivation of protected interests without procedural due process, even where the premise for the deprivation is not erroneous, inevitably arouses strong feelings of mental and emotional distress in the individual who is denied this "feeling of just treatment." They analogize their case to that of defamation *per se*, in which "the plaintiff is relieved from the necessity of producing any proof whatsoever that he has been injured" in order to recover substantial compensatory damages.

Petitioners do not deny that a purpose of procedural due process is to convey to the individual a feeling that the government has dealt with him fairly, as well as to minimize the risk of mistaken deprivations of protected interests. They go so far as to concede that, in a proper case, persons in respondents' position might well recover damages for mental and emotional distress caused by the denial of procedural due process. Petitioners' argument is the more limited one that such injury cannot be presumed to occur, and that plaintiffs at least should be put to their proof on the issue, as plaintiffs are in most tort actions.

We agree with petitioners in this respect. As we have observed in another context, the doctrine of presumed damages in the common law of defamation *per se* "is an oddity of tort law, for it allows recovery of purportedly compensatory damages without evidence of actual loss." The doctrine has been defended on the grounds that those forms of defamation that are actionable *per se* are virtually certain to cause serious injury to reputation, and that this kind of injury is extremely difficult to prove. Moreover, statements that are defamatory *per se* by their very nature are likely to cause mental and emotional distress, as well as injury to reputation, so there arguably is little reason to require proof of this kind of injury either. But these considerations do not support respondents' contention that damages should be presumed to flow from every deprivation of procedural due process.

First, it is not reasonable to assume that every departure from procedural due process, no matter what the circumstances or how minor, inherently is as likely to cause distress as the publication of defamation *per se* is to cause injury to reputation and distress. Where the deprivation of a protected interest is substantively justified but procedures are deficient in some respect, there may well be those who suffer no distress over the procedural irregularities. Indeed, in contrast to the immediately distressing effect of defamation *per se*, a person may not even know that procedures *were* deficient until he enlists the aid of counsel to challenge a perceived substantive deprivation.

Moreover, where a deprivation is justified but procedures are deficient, whatever distress a person feels may be attributable to the justified deprivation rather than to deficiencies in procedure. But as the Court of Appeals held, the injury caused by a justified deprivation, including distress, is not properly compensable under § 1983. This ambiguity in causation, which is absent in the case of defamation *per se*, provides additional need for requiring the plaintiff to convince the trier of fact that he actually suffered distress because of the denial of procedural due process itself.

Finally, we foresee no particular difficulty in producing evidence that mental and emotional distress actually was caused by the denial of procedural due process itself. Distress is a personal injury familiar to the law, customarily proved by showing the nature and circumstances of the wrong and its effect on the plaintiff.[20] In sum, then, although mental and emotional distress caused by the denial of procedural due process itself is compensable under § 1983, we hold that neither the likelihood of such injury nor the difficulty of proving it is so great as to justify awarding compensatory damages without proof that such injury actually was caused.

D

The Court of Appeals believed, and respondents urge, that cases dealing with awards of damages for racial discrimination, the denial of voting rights, and the denial of Fourth Amendment rights support a presumption of damages where procedural due process is denied. Many of the cases relied upon do not help respondents because they held or implied that some actual, if intangible, injury must be proved before compensatory damages may be recovered. Others simply did not address the issue. More importantly, the elements and prerequisites for recovery of damages appropriate to compensate injuries caused by the deprivation of one constitutional right are not necessarily appropriate to compensate injuries caused by the deprivation of another. As we have said, these issues must be considered with reference to the nature of the interests protected by the particular constitutional right in question. For this reason, and without intimating an opinion as to their merits, we do not deem the cases relied upon to be controlling.

III

Even if respondents' suspensions were justified, and even if they did not suffer any other actual injury, the fact remains that they were deprived of their right to procedural due process. "It is enough to invoke the procedural safeguards of the Fourteenth Amendment that a significant property interest is at stake, whatever the ultimate outcome of a hearing. . . ."

Common-law courts traditionally have vindicated deprivations of certain "absolute" rights that are not shown to have caused actual injury through the award of a nominal sum of money. By making the deprivation of such rights actionable for nominal damages without proof of actual injury, the law recognizes the importance to organized society that those rights be scrupulously observed; but at the same time, it remains true to the principle that substantial damages should be awarded only to compensate actual injury or, in the case of exemplary or punitive damages, to deter or punish malicious deprivations of rights.

Because the right to procedural due process is "absolute" in the sense that it does not depend upon the merits of a claimant's substantive assertions, and because of the importance to organized society that procedural due process be observed, we believe that the denial of procedural

---

20 We use the term "distress" to include mental suffering or emotional anguish. Although essentially subjective, genuine injury in this respect may be evidenced by one's conduct and observed by others. Juries must be guided by appropriate instructions, and an award of damages must be supported by competent evidence concerning the injury.

due process should be actionable for nominal damages without proof of actual injury. We therefore hold that if, upon remand, the District Court determines that respondents' suspensions were justified, respondents nevertheless will be entitled to recover nominal damages not to exceed one dollar from petitioners.

NOTES AND QUESTIONS

1. As counsel for the plaintiff in a case like *Piphus*, how would you attempt to prove damages resulting from the violation of due process where the suspension was found to be justified? What are the chances of success?

2. The Court rejects the plaintiffs' "contention that damages should be presumed to flow from every deprivation of procedural due process." Does it preclude an award of presumed damages in procedural due process cases?

3. Why did the Court look to federal law to control the damage issue, rather than Illinois law pursuant to § 1988, which the Court refers to in footnote 13?

4. Does the plaintiff have to prove actual damages in order to receive nominal damages? What is the significance of the one dollar nominal damage award? Has the plaintiff who obtains no relief other than nominal damages accomplished anything? Is such a plaintiff entitled to fees as the "prevailing" party? *See Farrar v. Hobby, infra* Ch. II.

5. Is the analysis in *Carey* limited to procedural due process, *i.e.*, will presumed damages be allowed for violations of substantive constitutional rights?

MEMPHIS COMMUNITY SCHOOL DISTRICT V. STACHURA
477 U.S. 299 (1986)

Justice POWELL delivered the opinion of the Court.

This case requires us to decide whether 42 U.S.C. § 1983 authorizes an award of compensatory damages based on the factfinder's assessment of the value or importance of a substantive constitutional right.

I

Respondent Stachura is a tenured teacher in the Memphis, Michigan, public schools. When the events that led to this case occurred, respondent taught seventh-grade life science, using a textbook that had been approved by the school board. The textbook included a chapter on human reproduction. During the 1978-1979 school year, respondent spent six weeks on this chapter. As part of their instruction, students were shown pictures of respondent's wife during her pregnancy. Respondent also showed the students two films concerning human growth and sexuality. These films were provided by the county health department, and the principal of respondent's school had approved their use. Both films had been shown in past school years without incident.

After the showing of the pictures and the films, a number of parents complained to school officials about respondent's teaching methods. These complaints, which appear to have been based largely on inaccurate rumors about the allegedly sexually explicit nature of the pictures and films, were discussed at an open school board meeting held on April 23, 1979. Following the advice of the school superintendent, respondent did not attend the meeting, during which a number of parents expressed the view that the respondent should not be allowed to teach in the Memphis school system. The day after the meeting, respondent was suspended with pay. The school board later confirmed the suspension, and notified respondent that an "administration evaluation" of his teaching methods was underway. No such evaluation was ever made. Respondent was reinstated the next fall, after filing this lawsuit.

Respondent sued the school district, the board of education, various board members and school administrators, and two parents who had participated in the April 23 school board meeting. The complaint alleged that respondent's suspension deprived him of both liberty and property without due process of law and violated his First Amendment right to academic freedom. Respondent sought compensatory and punitive damages under 42 U.S.C. § 1983 for these constitutional violations.

At the close of the trial on these claims, the District Court instructed the jury as to the law governing the asserted bases for liability. Turning to damages, the court instructed the jury that on finding liability it should award a sufficient amount to compensate respondent for the injury caused by petitioners' unlawful actions:

> You should consider in this regard any lost earnings; loss of earning capacity; out-of-pocket expenses; and any mental anguish or emotional distress that you find the Plaintiff to have suffered as a result of conduct by the Defendants depriving him of his civil rights.

In addition to this instruction on the standard elements of compensatory damages, the court explained that punitive damages could be awarded, and described the standards governing punitive awards. Finally, at respondent's request and over petitioners' objection, the court charged that damages also could be awarded based on the value or importance of the constitutional rights that were violated:

> If you find that the Plaintiff has been deprived of a Constitutional right, you may award damages to compensate him for the deprivation. Damages for this type of injury are more difficult to measure than damages for a physical injury or injury to one's property. There are no medical bills or other expenses by which you can judge how much compensation is appropriate. In one sense, no monetary value we place upon Constitutional rights can measure their importance in our society or compensate a citizen adequately for

their deprivation. However, just because these rights are not capable of precise evaluation does not mean that an appropriate monetary amount should not be awarded.

The precise value you place upon any Constitutional right which you find was denied to Plaintiff is within your discretion. You may wish to consider the importance of the right in our system of government, the role which this right has played in the history of our republic, [and] the significance of the right in the context of the activities which the Plaintiff was engaged in at the time of the violation of the right.

The jury found petitioners liable, and awarded a total of $275,000 in compensatory damages and $46,000 in punitive damages.

II

Petitioners challenge the jury instructions authorizing damages for violation of constitutional rights on the ground that those instructions permitted the jury to award damages based on its own unguided estimation of the value of such rights. Respondent disagrees with this characterization of the jury instructions, contending that the compensatory damages instructions taken as a whole focused solely on respondent's injury and not on the abstract value of the rights he asserted.

We believe petitioners more accurately characterize the instructions. The damages instructions were divided into three distinct segments: (i) compensatory damages for harm to respondent, (ii) punitive damages, and (iii) additional "compensat[ory]" damages for violations of constitutional rights. No sensible juror could read the third of these segments to modify the first. On the contrary, the damages instructions plainly authorized—in addition to punitive damages—two distinct types of "compensatory" damages: one based on respondent's actual injury according to ordinary tort law standards, and another based on the "value" of certain rights. We therefore consider whether the latter category of damages was properly before the jury.

III

A

The instructions at issue here cannot be squared with *Carey* [*v. Piphus*], or with the principles of tort damages on which *Carey* and § 1983 are grounded. The jurors in this case were told that, in determining how much was necessary to "compensate [respondent] for the deprivation" of his constitutional rights, they should place a money value on the "rights" themselves by considering such factors as the particular right's "importance . . . in our system of government," its role in American history, and its "significance . . . in the context of the activities" in which respondent was engaged. These factors focus, not on compensation for provable injury, but on the jury's subjective perception of the importance of constitutional rights as an abstract matter. *Carey* establishes that such an approach is impermissible. The constitutional right transgressed in *Carey*—the right to due process of law—is central to our system of ordered liberty. We nevertheless held that no compensatory damages could be awarded for violation of that right absent proof of actual injury. *Carey* thus makes clear that the abstract value of a constitutional right may not form the basis for § 1983 damages.[11]

Respondent nevertheless argues that *Carey* does not control here, because in this case a substantive constitutional right—respondent's First Amendment right to academic freedom—was infringed. The argument misperceives our analysis in *Carey*. That case does not establish a two-tiered system of constitutional rights, with substantive rights afforded greater protection than "mere" procedural safeguards. We did acknowledge in *Carey* that "the elements and prerequisites for recovery of damages" might vary depending on the interests protected by the constitutional right at issue. But we emphasized that, whatever the constitutional basis for § 1983 liability, such damages must always be designed "to *compensate injuries* caused by the [constitutional] deprivation." That conclusion simply leaves no room for noncompensatory damages measured by the jury's perception of the abstract "importance" of a constitutional right.

Nor do we find such damages necessary to vindicate the constitutional rights that § 1983 protects. *See* n. 11, *supra*. Section 1983 presupposes that damages that compensate for actual harm ordinarily suffice to deter constitutional violations.

Moreover, damages based on the "value" of constitutional rights are an unwieldy tool for ensuring compliance with the Constitution. History and tradition do not afford any sound guidance concerning the precise value that juries should place on constitutional protections. Accordingly, were such damages available, juries would be free to award arbitrary amounts without any evidentiary basis, or to use their unbounded discretion to punish unpopular defendants. Such damages would be too uncertain to be of any great value to plaintiffs, and would inject caprice into determinations of damages in § 1983 cases. We therefore hold that damages based on the abstract "value" or "importance" of constitutional rights are not a permissible element of compensatory damages in such cases.

B

Respondent further argues that the challenged instructions authorized a form of "presumed" damages— a remedy that is both compensatory in nature and traditionally part of the range of tort law remedies. Alternatively, respondent argues that the erroneous instructions were at worst harmless error.

Neither argument has merit. Presumed damages are a *substitute* for ordinary compensatory damages, not a *supplement* for an award that fully compensates the alleged injury. When a plaintiff seeks compensation for an injury that is likely to have occurred but difficult to establish, some form of presumed damages may possibly be appropriate.

In those circumstances, presumed damages may roughly approximate the harm that the plaintiff suffered and thereby compensate for harms that may be impossible to measure. As we

---

11 We did approve an award of nominal damages for the deprivation of due process in *Carey*. Our discussion of that issue makes clear that nominal damages, and not damages based on some undefinable "value" of infringed rights, are the appropriate means of "vindicating" rights whose deprivation has not caused actual, provable injury.

earlier explained, the instructions at issue in this case did not serve this purpose, but instead called on the jury to measure damages based on a subjective evaluation of the importance of particular constitutional values. Since such damages are wholly divorced from any compensatory purpose, they cannot be justified as presumed damages.[14] Moreover, no rough substitute for compensatory damages was required in this case, since the jury was fully authorized to compensate respondent for both monetary and non-monetary harms caused by petitioners' conduct.

Nor can we find that the erroneous instructions were harmless. The jury was authorized to award three categories of damages: (i) compensatory damages for injury to respondent, (ii) punitive damages, and (iii) damages based on the jury's perception of the "importance" of two provisions of the Constitution. The submission of the third of these categories was error. Although the verdict specified an amount for punitive damages, it did not specify how much of the remaining damages was designed to compensate respondent for his injury and how much reflected the jury's estimation of the value of the constitutional rights that were infringed. For these reasons, the case must be remanded for a new trial on compensatory damages.

Justice MARSHALL, with whom Justice BRENNAN, Justice BLACKMUN, and Justice STEVENS join, concurring in the judgment.

I agree with the Court that this case must be remanded for a new trial on damages. Certain portions of the Court's opinion, however, can be read to suggest that damages in the § 1983 cases are necessarily limited to "out-of-pocket loss," "other monetary harms," and "such injuries as 'impairment of reputation . . ., personal humiliation, and mental anguish and suffering.'" I do not understand the Court so to hold, and I write separately to emphasize that the violation of a constitutional right, in proper cases, may itself constitute a compensable injury.

The instructions given the jury in this case were improper because they did not require the jury to focus on the loss actually sustained by respondent. Rather, they invited the jury to base its award on speculation about "the importance of the right in our system of government" and "the role which this right has played in the history of our republic," guided only by the admonition that "[i]n one sense, no monetary value we place on Constitutional rights can measure their importance in our society or compensate a citizen adequately for their deprivation." These instructions invited the jury to speculate on matters wholly detached from the real injury

---

14 For the same reason, *Nixon v. Herndon*, 273 U.S. 536 (1927), and similar cases do not support the challenged instructions. In Nixon, the Court held that a plaintiff who was illegally prevented from voting in a state primary election suffered compensable injury. This holding did not rest on the "value" of the right to vote as an abstract matter; rather, the Court recognized that the plaintiff had suffered a particular injury—his inability to vote in a particular election—that might be compensated through substantial money damages.

Nixon followed a long line of cases. Although these decisions sometimes speak of damages for the value of the right to vote, their analysis shows that they involve nothing more than an award of presumed damages for a non-monetary harm that cannot easily be quantified:

The "value of the right" in the context of these decisions is the money value of the particular loss that the plaintiff suffered—a loss of which "each member of the jury had personal knowledge." It is *not* the value of the right to vote as a general, abstract matter, based on its role in our history or system of government. Thus, whatever the wisdom of these decisions in the context of the changing scope of compensatory damages over the course of this century, they do not support awards of non-compensatory damages such as those authorized in this case.

occasioned respondent by the deprivation of the right. Further, the instructions might have led the jury to grant respondent damages based on the "abstract value" of the rights to procedural due process—a course directly barred by our decision in *Carey*.

The Court therefore properly remands for a new trial on damages. I do not understand the Court, however, to hold that deprivations of constitutional rights can never themselves constitute compensable injuries. Such a rule would be inconsistent with the logic of *Carey*, and would defeat the purpose of § 1983 by denying compensation for genuine injuries caused by the deprivation of constitutional rights.

NOTES AND QUESTIONS

1. Does the Court in *Stachura* simply extend *Carey* to cases seeking damages for violations of substantive constitutional provisions—*i.e.*, are presumed damages now unavailable in all civil rights cases? Under what circumstances are such damages available? *See* footnote 14. Does evidence of the plaintiff's actual intangible injuries eliminate presumed damages?

2. How much of an impact will *Stachura* have on litigating civil rights cases, *i.e.*, will it significantly affect the amount of recovery or simply the jury instructions? Is it likely that the jury would have awarded the same compensatory damages in *Stachura* even without the improper instruction?

3. Can a § 1983 plaintiff ever recover damages, beyond compensatory damages, based on the abstract value of a constitutional right? Would damages based on abstract value really give juries unbounded discretion "to award arbitrary amounts without any evidentiary basis" or to "punish unpopular defendants?" Don't judges have authority to reduce excessive awards?

4. Does Justice Marshall's concurring opinion clarify the majority opinion?

PROBLEM: TWELVE

In *Lewis v. Harrison School Dist. No. 1*, 805 F.2d 310, 317 (8th Cir. 1986), the plaintiff sued under § 1983 claiming he had been fired as a school principal in violation of his right to free speech. The jury, in response to an interrogatory, found that his speech "was a substantial or motivating factor in the school board's decision to terminate his employment" and that he "would not have been fired had he not made the speech." Lewis was awarded $25,348 for lost wages and $5000 for "violation of [his] first amendment right to freedom of speech."

Regarding the latter, the Eighth Circuit stated:

Because no specific evidence was introduced to support this award of constitutional damages, it falls into the category of "presumed" damages. The district court vacated this award, holding that presumed damages are not available in a § 1983 action based on a first amendment violation.

A recent decision of the United States Supreme Court casts considerable doubt on the availability of presumed damages in the present case. In *Stachura*, which was decided while appeal of this case was pending, the Court held that there is "no room for noncompensatory damages measured by the jury's perception of the abstract 'importance' of a constitutional right.

Although the concurring opinion in *Stachura* attempted to narrow the majority's holding, we read the Court's decision as foreclosing Lewis' claim for presumed damages. The majority held that "[p]resumed damages are a *substitute* for ordinary compensatory damages, not a *supplement* for an award that fully compensates an alleged injury." This language controls our decision. Any door left open by *Stachura* is not for plaintiffs like Lewis, whose damages are readily measurable.

1. Did the district court accurately describe the law? Does the court of appeals accurately apply the holding in *Stachura* regarding presumed damages?

2. Would the following jury instructions, taken from *Bolen v. Knox Community School Corp.*, be appropriate in a case like *Lewis*? As counsel for the plaintiff, would you suggest any changes in the instructions? How about as counsel for the defendants?

    You shall award the actual damages only for those injuries which you find that the plaintiff has proven by a preponderance of the evidence. Moreover, you shall award actual damages only for those injuries which you find the plaintiff has proven by a preponderance of evidence to have been the direct result of conduct by the defendants in violation of the plaintiff's First Amendment rights.

    Actual damages must not be based on speculation or sympathy. They must be based on the evidence presented at trial and only on that evidence.

    If you find that the plaintiff has proven that the defendants violated the plaintiff's First Amendment rights, and the defendants' conduct caused harm or injury to the plaintiff, then the plaintiff is entitled to damages in an amount sufficient to compensate him for his losses and injuries, mental anguish, emotional distress, humiliation, embarrassment, and pain and suffering caused by the defendants' conduct.

    Damages based on the abstract "value" or "importance" of the constitutional rights violated are not a permissible element of compensatory damages.

3. Would the following additional instruction be consistent with *Stachura*:

    If you determine there was a violation of the plaintiff's first amendment rights and it is likely the plaintiff was injured as a result of the violation, but the injury is difficult to establish and you cannot determine the actual value of a particular type of harm, you can presume injury and award damages, as a substitute for ordinary compensatory damages, in an amount which you believe will roughly approximate the harm suffered by the plaintiff and thereby compensate him for that harm.

As counsel for the plaintiff, would you want this instruction given? Explain.

ii.   Punitive

SMITH V. WADE
461 U.S. 30 (1983)

Justice BRENNAN delivered the opinion of the Court.

I

The petitioner, William H. Smith, is a guard at Algoa Reformatory, a unit of the Missouri Division of Corrections for youthful first offenders. The respondent, Daniel R. Wade, was assigned to Algoa as an inmate in 1976. In the summer of 1976 Wade voluntarily checked into Algoa's protective custody unit. Because of disciplinary violations during his stay in protective custody, Wade was given a short term in punitive segregation and then transferred to administrative segregation. On the evening of Wade's first day in administrative segregation, he was placed in a cell with another inmate. Later, when Smith came on duty in Wade's dormitory, he placed a third inmate in Wade's cell. According to Wade's testimony, his cellmates harassed, beat, and sexually assaulted him.

Wade brought suit under 42 U.S.C. § 1983 against Smith and four other guards and correctional officials, alleging that his Eighth Amendment rights had been violated. At trial his evidence showed that he had placed himself in protective custody because of prior incidents of violence against him by other inmates. The third prisoner whom Smith added to the cell had been placed in administrative segregation for fighting. Smith had made no effort to find out whether another cell was available; in fact there was another cell in the same dormitory with only one occupant. Further, only a few weeks earlier, another inmate had been beaten to death in the same dormitory during the same shift, while Smith had been on duty. Wade asserted that Smith and the other defendants knew or should have known that an assault against him was likely under the circumstances.

During the trial, the District Judge entered a directed verdict for two of the defendants. He instructed the jury that Wade could make out an Eighth Amendment violation only by showing "physical abuse of such base, inhumane and barbaric proportions as to shock the sensibilities."

The District Judge also charged the jury that it could award punitive damages on a proper showing:

> In addition to actual damages, the law permits the jury, under certain circumstances, to award the injured person punitive and exemplary damages, in order to punish the wrongdoer for some extraordinary misconduct, and to serve as an example or warning to others not to engage in such conduct.

If you find the issues in favor of the plaintiff, and if the conduct of one or more of the defendants is shown to be *a reckless or callous disregard of, or indifference to, the rights or safety of others*, then you may assess punitive or exemplary damages in addition to any award of actual damages.

. . . The amount of punitive or exemplary damages assessed against any defendant may be such sum as you believe will serve to punish that defendant and to deter him and others from like conduct.

The jury returned verdicts for two of the three remaining defendants. It found Smith liable, however, and awarded $25,000 in compensatory damages and $5,000 in punitive damages.

II

Smith correctly concedes that "punitive damages are available in a 'proper' § 1983 action. . . ." [A]lthough the precise issue of the availability of punitive damages under § 1983 has never come squarely before us, we have had occasion more than once to make clear our view that they are available; indeed, we have rested decisions on related questions on the premise of such availability.

Smith argues, nonetheless, that this was not a "proper" case in which to award punitive damages. More particularly, he attacks the instruction that punitive damages could be awarded on a finding of reckless or callous disregard of or indifference to Wade's rights or safety. Instead, he contends that the proper test is one of actual malicious intent—"ill will, spite, or intent to injure." He offers two arguments for this position: first, that actual intent is the proper standard for punitive damages in all cases under § 1983; and second, that even if intent is not always required, it should be required here because the threshold for punitive damages should always be higher than that for liability in the first instance. We address these in turn.

III

Smith does not argue that the common law, either in 1871 or now, required or requires a showing of actual malicious intent for recovery of punitive damages.

Perhaps not surprisingly, there was significant variation (both terminological and substantive) among American jurisdictions in the latter 19th century on the precise standard to be applied in awarding punitive damages—variation that was exacerbated by the ambiguity and slipperiness of such common terms as "malice" and "gross negligence." Most of the confusion, however, seems to have been over the degree of negligence, recklessness, carelessness, or culpable indifference that should be required—not over whether actual intent was essential. On the contrary, the rule in a large majority of jurisdictions was that punitive damages (also called exemplary damages, vindictive damages, or smart money) could be awarded without a showing of actual ill will, spite, or intent to injure.

The same rule applies today. Most cases under state common law, although varying in their precise terminology, have adopted more or less the same rule, recognizing that punitive damages in tort cases may be awarded not only for actual intent to injure or evil motive, but also for recklessness, serious indifference to or disregard for the rights of others, or even gross negligence.

Smith's argument, which he offers in several forms, is that an actual-intent standard is preferable to a recklessness standard because it is less vague. He points out that punitive damages, by their very nature, are not awarded to compensate the injured party. He concedes, of course, that deterrence of future egregious conduct is a primary purpose of both § 1983, and of punitive damages. But deterrence, he contends, cannot be achieved unless the standard of conduct sought to be deterred is stated with sufficient clarity to enable potential defendants to conform to the law and to avoid the proposed sanction. Recklessness or callous indifference, he argues, is too uncertain a standard to achieve deterrence rationally and fairly. A prison guard, for example, can be expected to know whether he is acting with actual ill will or intent to injure, but not whether he is being reckless or callously indifferent.

Smith's argument, if valid, would apply to ordinary tort cases as easily as to § 1983 suits; hence, it hardly presents an argument for adopting a different rule under § 1983. In any event, the argument is unpersuasive. While, *arguendo*, an intent standard may be easier to understand and to apply to particular situations than a recklessness standard, we are not persuaded that a recklessness standard is too vague to be fair or useful.

More fundamentally, Smith's argument for certainty in the interest of deterrence overlooks the distinction between a standard for punitive damages and a standard of liability in the first instance. Smith seems to assume that prison guards and other state officials look mainly to the standard for punitive damages in shaping their conduct. We question the premise; we assume, and hope, that most officials are guided primarily by the underlying standards of federal substantive law—both out of devotion to duty, and in the interest of avoiding liability for compensatory damages. At any rate, the conscientious officer who desires clear guidance on how to do his job and avoid lawsuits can and should look to the standard for actionability in the first instance. The need for exceptional clarity in the standard for punitive damages arises only if one assumes that there are substantial numbers of officers who will not be deterred by compensatory damages; only such officers will seek to guide their conduct by the punitive damages standard. The presence of such officers constitutes a powerful argument *against* raising the threshold for punitive damages.

In this case, the jury was instructed to apply a high standard of constitutional right ("physical abuse of such base, inhumane and barbaric proportions as to shock the sensibilities"). Smith's contention that this recklessness standard is too vague to provide clear guidance and reasonable deterrence might more properly be reserved for a challenge seeking different standards of liability in the first instance. As for punitive damages, however, in the absence of any persuasive argument to the contrary based on the policies of § 1983, we are content to adopt the policy judgment of the common law—that reckless or callous disregard for the plaintiff's rights, as well as intentional violations of federal law, should be sufficient to trigger a jury's consideration of the appropriateness of punitive damages.

IV

Smith contends that even if § 1983 does not ordinarily require a showing of actual malicious intent for an award of punitive damages, such a showing should be required in this case. He argues that the deterrent and punitive purposes of punitive damages are served only if the threshold for punitive damages is higher in every case than the underlying standard for liability in the first instance. In this case, while the District Judge did not use the same precise terms to explain the standards of liability for compensatory and punitive damages, the parties agree that there is no substantial difference between the showings required by the two instructions; both apply a standard of reckless or callous indifference to Wade's rights. Hence, Smith argues, the District Judge erred in not requiring a higher standard for punitive damages, namely actual malicious intent.

This argument incorrectly assumes that, simply because the instructions specified the same *threshold* of liability for punitive and compensatory damages, the two forms of damages were equally available to the plaintiff. The argument overlooks a key feature of punitive damages—that they are never awarded as of right, no matter how egregious the defendant's conduct. Compensatory damages, by contrast, are mandatory; once liability is found, the jury is required to award compensatory damages in an amount appropriate to compensate the plaintiff for his loss. Hence, it is not entirely accurate to say that punitive and compensatory damages were awarded in this case on the same standard. To make its punitive award, the jury was required to find not only that Smith's conduct met the recklessness threshold (a question of ultimate fact), but also that his conduct merited a punitive award of $5,000 in addition to the compensatory award (a discretionary moral judgment).

Moreover, the rules of ordinary tort law are once more against Smith's argument. There has never been any general common-law rule that the threshold for punitive damages must always be higher than that for compensatory liability. On the contrary, both the FIRST and SECOND RESTATEMENTS OF TORTS have pointed out that "in torts like malicious prosecution that require a particular antisocial state of mind, the improper motive of the tortfeasor is both a necessary element in the cause of action and a reason for awarding punitive damages." Accordingly, in situations where the standard for compensatory liability is as high as or higher than the usual threshold for punitive damages, most courts will permit awards of punitive damages without requiring any extra showing.

This common-law rule makes sense in terms of the purposes of punitive damages. Punitive damages are awarded in the jury's discretion "to punish [the defendant] for his outrageous conduct and to deter him and others like him from similar conduct in the future." RESTATEMENT (SECOND) OF TORTS § 908(1) (1979). The focus is on the character of the tortfeasor's conduct—whether it is of the sort that calls for deterrence and punishment over and above that provided by compensatory awards. If it is of such a character, then it is appropriate to allow a jury to assess punitive damages; and that assessment does not become less appropriate simply because the plaintiff in the case faces a more demanding standard of actionability. To put it differently, society has an interest in deterring and punishing *all* intentional or reckless invasions of the rights of others, even though it sometimes chooses not to impose any liability for lesser degrees of fault.[21]

V

We hold that a jury may be permitted to assess punitive damages in an action under § 1983 when the defendant's conduct is shown to be motivated by evil motive or intent, or when it involved reckless or callous indifference to the federally protected rights of others. We further hold that this threshold applies even when the underlying standard of liability for compensatory damages is one of recklessness.

NOTES AND QUESTIONS

1. Could Wade have named the Missouri Division of Corrections under § 1983?

2. Under the Court's standard for punitive damages, would a plaintiff who proves intentional discrimination usually be eligible for punitive damages?

3. Why didn't the Court, pursuant to § 1988, adopt the punitive damages standard of the forum state? Compare *Wilson v. Garcia, supra* Ch. II. Is there a "deficiency" in § 1983? Is the standard utilized here a federal standard?

4. Could the plaintiff in *Carey* recover punitive damages? Should punitive damages be available where a plaintiff is not entitled to compensatory damages? If the forum state forecloses punitive damages absent an award of compensatory damages, should this rule control § 1983 actions in a state court? in federal court? Review Problem 10, *supra.*

5. Section 102 of the Civil Rights Act of 1991 adds a new section, 42 U.S.C. § 1981a, which makes available compensatory and punitive damages where a plaintiff proves intentional discrimination in violation of Title VII of the Civil Rights Act of 1964, but cannot recover damages under § 1981a. Punitive damages are available where a defendant acted with "malice or with reckless indifference to the federally protected rights" of the plaintiff. However, governmental agencies and political subdivisions are never liable for punitive damages.

   In *Kolstad v. American Dental Association*, 527 U.S. 526 (1999), the Court held that § 1981a(b)(1) does not require a plaintiff to prove egregious or outrageous acts in order to recover punitive damages. However, an employer may not be held vicariously

---

21 "Moreover, after *Carey* punitive damages may be the only significant remedy available in some § 1983 actions where constitutional rights are maliciously violated but the victim cannot prove compensable injury." *Carlson v. Green*, 446 U.S. 14, 22 n.9 (1980).

liable for punitive damages where decisions of its managerial agents are contrary to its good faith efforts to comply with the employment discrimination statutes. The limitation on vicarious liability affects § 1981 actions for punitive damages against private defendants. *See, e.g.*, Wiercinski v. Mangia 57, Inc., 787 F.3d 106 (2d Cir. 2015); Ash v. Tyson Foods, Inc., 664 F.3d 883 (11th Cir. 2011). It will not affect most § 1983 actions because municipal entities are always insulated from punitive damages. *See City of Newport, supra* Ch. II.

6. **Constitutional Limits:** In a series of decisions, the Supreme Court has considered constitutional limitations on awards of punitive damages. A due process challenge to the "common-law method for assessing punitive damages" was rejected in *Pacific Mut. Life Ins. v. Haslip*, 449 U.S. 1 (1991); however, the Court indicated that unlimited jury or judicial discretion in fixing punitive damages could "cross the line into the area of constitutional impropriety." Later, in *Honda Motor Co., Ltd., v. Oberg*, 512 U.S. 415 (1994), the Court held that the Oregon constitution, which prohibits judicial review of the amount of punitive damages awarded by a jury "unless the court can affirmatively say there is no evidence to support the verdict," violates the due process clause of the Fourteenth Amendment. Subsequently, in *BMW of North America, Inc. v. Gore*, 517 U.S. 559 (1996), the Court imposed another due process limitation on punitive damages awards, holding that lawful conduct of the automobile manufacturer outside the state of Alabama could not be considered by an Alabama court in determining the appropriate amount of punitive damages in a fraud action. In addition, the Court decided that an award of $2 million in punitive damages for BMW's failure to inform the plaintiff that his "new" car had been repainted was grossly excessive in light of three factors that serve as guideposts in determining the reasonableness of punitive damages awards: the degree of reprehensibility of the defendant's conduct, the disparity between the punitive damages award and the actual harm to the plaintiff (plaintiff was awarded $4,000 in compensatory damages), and the comparison with civil and criminal penalties that could be imposed for comparable misconduct.

In *State Farm Mut. Auto Ins. Co. v. Campbell*, 538 U.S. 408 (2003), the Court reviewed the Utah Supreme Court's application of the *Gore* guideposts regarding a jury verdict awarding $145 million in punitive damages and $1 million in compensatory damages. The Supreme Court found several problems with the Utah Court's application of *Gore*. First, it erred in relying on State Farm's out-of-state conduct, much of which was lawful where it occurred, that had no nexus to the specific injury suffered by the plaintiffs and was not similar to that which harmed them. Second, while refusing "to impose a bright-line ratio," the Court noted that "[s]ingle-digit multipliers are more likely to comport with due process, while still achieving the State's goals of deterrence and retribution, than awards with ratios in the range of 500 to 1," particularly where, as here, compensatory damages awarded for a year and a half of emotional distress arising from an economic transaction are substantial.

There is a presumption against an award that has a 145-to-1 ratio. Third, the most relevant civil sanction under Utah law is limited to a $10,000 fine. The judgment was reversed and the case was remanded to permit the principles to be applied in the first instance by the Utah courts.

Further, in *Philip Morris USA v. Williams*, 549 U.S. 346 (2007), the Court ruled that a punitive damages award based on a jury's desire to punish a defendant for harming non-parties amounts to a deprivation of property without due process. In a 5-4 opinion, Justice Breyer asserted that the case raised a procedural concern, namely lack of fair notice, in that a defendant cannot be punished for allegedly injuring other smokers. The Court stated that evidence of harm to non-parties could be introduced to demonstrate reprehensibility, *i.e.*, that the conduct that harmed the plaintiff also posed a substantial risk to the general public. However, courts must be wary that a jury is not using this evidence improperly to assess punitive damages and thus punish the defendant for harm inflicted on non-parties. The case means that defense attorneys will not be permitted to keep out evidence of harm to non-parties since the Court says it is relevant to reprehensibility. However, it is likely that the opinion will lead to considerable controversy related to the jury instructions in such cases.

b. Attorney Fees

i. Prevailing Party

A 1976 amendment to 42 U.S.C. § 1988 makes attorney fees available to the "prevailing party" in civil rights cases brought under a number of different statutes. Therefore, parties seeking fees must first show that they prevailed. Difficult questions arise where a party prevails only in part or claims success without court ordered relief.

TEXAS STATE TEACHERS V. GARLAND INDEPENDENT SCHOOL DISTRICT
489 U.S. 782 (1989)

Justice O'CONNOR delivered the opinion of the Court.

We must decide today the proper standard for determining whether a party has "prevailed" in an action brought under certain civil rights statutes such that the party is eligible for an award of attorney's fees under 42 U.S.C. § 1988. This is an issue which has divided the Courts of Appeals both before and after our decision in *Hensley v. Eckerhart.* The Courts of Appeals for the Fifth and Eleventh Circuits require that a party succeed on the "central issue" in the litigation and achieve the "primary relief sought" to be eligible for an award of attorney's fees under § 1988. Most of the other Federal Courts of Appeals have applied a less demanding standard, requiring only that a party succeed on a significant issue and receive some of the relief sought in the lawsuit to qualify for a fee award. In this case, the Court of Appeals for the Fifth Circuit applied the "central issue" test and concluded that petitioners here were not prevailing parties under § 1988.

I

On March 31, 1981, petitioners, the Texas State Teacher's Association, its local affiliate the Garland Education Association, and several individual members and employees of both organizations brought suit under 42 U.S.C. § 1983 against respondent Garland Independent School District and various school district officials. Petitioners' complaint alleged that the school district's policy of prohibiting communications by or with teachers during the school day concerning employee organizations violated petitioners' First and Fourteenth Amendment rights. In particular, petitioners focused their attack on the school district's Administrative Regulation 412, which prohibits employee organizations access to school facilities during school hours and proscribes the use of school mail and internal communications systems by employee organizations. The school district's regulations do permit employee organizations to meet with or recruit teachers on school premises before or after the school day "upon request and approval by the local school principal."

On cross motions for summary judgment, the District Court rejected petitioners' claims in almost all respects. The court found that under *Perry Education Ass'n v. Perry Local Educators' Ass'n* the prohibitions on union access to teachers themselves and to internal communication media during school hours were constitutional. The District Court also rejected petitioners' claim that the school district's policies were unconstitutional in that they prohibited teachers' discussion or promotion of employee organizations among themselves during school hours. As to teacher discussion of employee organizations, the court found that even if some school officials interpreted the regulations to prohibit such speech, there had been no attempt to enforce such an interpretation. As to teacher-to-teacher speech promoting employee organizations, the court found that the record indicated that the school district did prohibit such speech, but concluded that this prohibition was constitutional. The District Court did find for petitioners on one issue: it held that the requirement of school principal approval of teacher meetings with union representatives after school hours was unconstitutionally vague in that no guidelines limited the discretion of the principal's decision to grant or deny access to the campus. The District Court found that this issue was of "minor significance," since there was no evidence in the record to indicate that school officials had ever denied employee organizations the use of school premises during nonschool hours.

On appeal, the Court of Appeals for the Fifth Circuit affirmed in part, reversed in part and remanded. The Court of Appeals agreed with the District Court that petitioners' claim that the First Amendment required the school district to allow union representatives access to school facilities during school hours was foreclosed by our decision in *Perry*. The Court of Appeals affirmed the entry of summary judgment for the school district on this claim. The Court of Appeals, however, disagreed with the District Court's analysis of petitioners' claims relating to teacher-to-teacher discussion of employee organizations during the school day. It found that the prohibition of teacher speech promoting union activity during school hours was unconstitutional. It also found that there was a distinct possibility that the school district would discipline teachers who engaged in any discussion of employee organizations during the school day, and that such a policy had a chilling effect on teachers' First Amendment rights. Finally, the Court of Appeals held that the prohibition on teacher use of internal mail and billboard facilities to discuss employee organizations was unconstitutional. The school district allowed teachers to use these facilities for personal messages of all kinds, and the school district had not shown that the discussion of union activity in these media would be disruptive of its educative mission. As to these claims, the Court of Appeals granted petitioners' motion for summary judgment.

Petitioners then filed the instant application for an award of attorney's fees pursuant to 42 U.S.C. § 1988. The District Court found that under Fifth Circuit precedent petitioners here were not "prevailing parties" within the meaning of § 1988 and thus were ineligible for any fee award. The court recognized that petitioners had achieved "partial success," but indicated that "[i]n this circuit the test for prevailing party status is whether the plaintiff prevailed on the central issue by acquiring the primary relief sought."

A divided panel of the Court of Appeals for the Fifth Circuit affirmed the District Court's judgment denying petitioners prevailing party status under § 1988.

II

As amended, 42 U.S.C. § 1988, provides in pertinent part:

> In any action or proceeding to enforce a provision of sections 1981, 1982, 1983, 1985, and 1986 of this title, title IX of Public Law 92-318, or title VI of the Civil Rights Act of 1964, the court, in its discretion, may allow the prevailing party, other than the United States, a reasonable attorney's fee as part of the costs.

In *Hensley* this Court sought to clarify "the proper standard for setting a fee award where the plaintiff has achieved only limited success." At the outset we noted that no fee award is permissible until the plaintiff has crossed the "statutory threshold" of prevailing party status. In this regard, the Court indicated that "[a] typical formulation is that 'plaintiffs may be considered "prevailing parties" for attorney's fees purposes if they succeed on any significant issue in litigation which achieves some of the benefit the parties sought in bringing the suit.' " The Court then went on to establish certain principles to guide the discretion of the lower courts in setting fee awards in cases where plaintiffs have not achieved complete success.

We think it clear that the "central issue" test applied by the lower courts here is directly contrary to the thrust of our decision in *Hensley*. Although respondents are correct in pointing out that *Hensley* did not adopt one particular standard for determining prevailing party status, *Hensley* does indicate that the degree of the plaintiff's success in relation to the other goals of the lawsuit is a factor critical to the determination of the size of a reasonable fee, not to eligibility for a fee award at all.

Our decision in *Hensley* is consistent with congressional intent in this regard. Congress clearly contemplated that interim fee awards would be available "where a party has prevailed on an important matter in the course of litigation, even when he ultimately does not prevail on all issues." S. Rep. No. 94-1011, p. 5 (1976). In discussing the availability of fees pendente lite under § 1988, we have indicated that such awards are proper where a party "has established his entitlement to some relief on the merits of his claims, either in the trial court or on appeal." *Hanrahan v. Hampton.* The incongruence of the "central issue" test in light of the clear congressional intent that interim fee awards be available to partially prevailing civil rights plaintiffs is readily apparent.

Nor does the central issue test have much to recommend it from the viewpoint of judicial administration of § 1988 and other fee shifting provisions. By focusing on the subjective importance of an issue to the litigants, it asks a question which is almost impossible to answer. Is the "primary relief sought" in a disparate treatment action under Title VII reinstatement, backpay, or injunctive relief? This question, the answer to which appears to depend largely on the mental state of the parties, is wholly irrelevant to the purposes behind the fee shifting provisions, and promises to mire district courts entertaining fee applications in an inquiry which one commentator has described as "excruciating." In sum, the search for the "central" and "tangential" issues in the lawsuit, or for the "primary" as opposed to the "secondary" relief sought, much like the search for the Golden Fleece, distracts the district court from the primary purposes behind § 1988 and is essentially unhelpful in defining the term "prevailing party."

If the plaintiff has succeeded on "any significant issue in litigation which achieve[d] some of the benefit the parties sought in bringing suit" the plaintiff has crossed the threshold to a fee award of some kind. The floor in this regard is provided by our decision in *Hewitt v. Helms.* As we noted there, "[r]espect for ordinary language requires that a plaintiff receive at least some relief on the merits of his claim before he can be said to prevail." Thus, at a minimum, to be considered a prevailing party within the meaning of § 1988 the plaintiff must be able to point to a resolution of the dispute which changes the legal relationship between itself and the defendant. Beyond this absolute limitation, a technical victory may be so insignificant as to be insufficient to support prevailing party status. For example, in the context of this litigation, the District Court found that the requirement that nonschool hour meetings be conducted only with prior approval from the local school principal was unconstitutionally vague. The District Court characterized this issue as "of minor significance" and noted that there was "no evidence that the plaintiffs were ever refused permission to use school premises during non-school hours." If this had been petitioners' only success in the litigation, we think it clear that this alone would not have rendered them "prevailing parties" within the meaning of § 1988. Where the plaintiff's success on a legal claim can be characterized as purely technical or de minimis,* a district court would be justified in concluding that even the "generous formulation" we adopt today has not been satisfied. The touchstone of the prevailing party inquiry must be the material alteration of

---

* Compare Farrar v. Hobby, infra Ch. II.

the legal relationship of the parties in a manner which Congress sought to promote in the fee statute. Where such a change has occurred, the degree of the plaintiff's overall success goes to the reasonableness of the award under *Hensley*, not to the availability of a fee award vel non.

III

Application of the principles enunciated above to the case at hand is not difficult. Petitioners here obtained a judgment vindicating the First Amendment rights of public employees in the workplace. Their success has materially altered the school district's policy limiting the rights of teachers to communicate with each other concerning employee organizations and union activities. Petitioners have thus served the "private attorney general" role which Congress meant to promote in enacting the Civil Rights Attorney's Fees Awards Act of 1976. They prevailed on a significant issue in the litigation and have obtained some of the relief they sought and are thus "prevailing parties" within the meaning of § 1988. We therefore reverse the judgment of the Court of Appeals and remand this case for a determination of a reasonable attorney's fee consistent with the principles established by our decision in *Hensley*.

NOTES AND QUESTIONS

1. In *Hewitt v. Helms*, 482 U.S. 755 (1987), where the Court of Appeals determined that the plaintiff suffered a denial of due process when convicted as a result of prison disciplinary proceedings, the Court decided the plaintiff was not a prevailing party because he never obtained any relief. The Court stated:

   Whatever the outer boundaries of that term [prevailing party] may be, Helms does not fit within them. Respect for ordinary language requires that a plaintiff receive at least some relief on the merits of his claim before he can be said to prevail. Helms obtained no relief. Because of the defendants' official immunity he received no damages award. No injunction or declaratory judgment was entered in his favor. Nor did Helms obtain relief without benefit of a formal judgment—for example, through a consent decree or settlement. The most that he obtained was an interlocutory ruling that his complaint should not have been dismissed for failure to state a constitutional claim. That is not the stuff of which legal victories are made.

   Id. at 759-60. Would the plaintiff in *Hewitt* have prevailed, for fee purposes, if he had obtained a declaratory judgment concerning his misconduct conviction and an order requiring prison officials to expunge any reference to the conviction from his prison records?

2. In *Sole v. Wyner*, 551 U.S. 74 (2007), the Court ruled that winning a preliminary injunction that dissolves with an adverse final decision on the merits is not enough to make a plaintiff a "prevailing party" eligible for attorney fees. In this case a nudist organization relied on an earlier settlement agreement that allowed it to conduct a play with nude performers on the beach, provided a cloth screen was placed in a semicircle around the performance area to shield beachgoers not wishing to see it. The district court granted the preliminary injunction to the plaintiffs on the condition that the group use the cloth screen. However, the next day the group performed the peace sign display, but strayed outside the screen and participants entered the water nude. At the hearing for a permanent injunction the district court found that the group's failure to remain behind the screen demonstrated that the bathing suit rule's ban on nudity was after all "no greater than is essential . . . to protect the experiences of the visiting public."

The Court in a unanimous decision explained that "the touchstone of the prevailing party inquiry [is] the material alteration of a legal relationship of the parties in a manner which Congress sought to promote in the fee statute." At the preliminary injunction stage of the case, the court assessed the plaintiff's probability of success on the merits and the determination was "necessarily hasty and abbreviated." The "controlling" factor, however, was the eventual ruling in favor of the defendants on the merits, rejecting the plaintiff's claim "that the state law banning nudity in the parks was unconstitutional as applied to expressive, nonerotic nudity."

> [The plaintiff's] fleeting success, however, did not establish that she prevailed on the gravamen of her plea for injunctive relief, *i.e.*, her charge that the state officials had denied her and other participants in the peace symbol display "the right to engage in constitutionally protected expressive activities. Prevailing party status, we hold, does not attend achievement of a preliminary injunction that is reversed, dissolved, or otherwise undone by the final decision in the same case."

3. **Catalyst Theory:** For years, lower courts awarded attorney fees to plaintiffs who achieve the desired result of their litigation, even though they did not obtain a judgment on the merits or a court-ordered consent decree. This was done under the "catalyst theory," upon a showing of a causal link between the litigation and the defendants' "voluntary" change in the challenge practice, policy or conduct, and a determination that the plaintiffs' legal claims are not frivolous or groundless. The catalyst theory was rejected by the Supreme Court in *Buckhannon Bd. v. West Virginia D.H.H.R.*, 532 U.S. 598 (2001), where the Court held that a "defendant's voluntary change in conduct, although perhaps accomplishing what the plaintiff sought to achieve by the lawsuit, lacks the necessary judicial *imprimatur* on the change." Therefore, the Court concluded that plaintiffs who obtain relief with "no judicially sanctioned change in the legal relationship of the parties," are not prevailing parties for purposes of the attorney fee statutes. Will this ruling deter plaintiffs with meritorious but expensive cases from bringing suit?

4. **Prevailing Defendant:** Although the statute makes fees available to a "prevailing party," the Court has not allowed prevailing defendants to recover fees as routinely as prevailing plaintiffs. In *Hensley, infra*, the Court noted that "A prevailing defendant may recover an attorney's fee only where the suit was vexatious, frivolous, or brought to harass or embarrass the defendant."

The Court revisited *Hensley*'s rule for prevailing defendants in *Fox v. Vice*, 563 U.S. 826 (2011). When plaintiff decided to run for police chief, the incumbent, Vice, engaged in numerous "dirty tricks," including sending an anonymous letter to Fox in which he threatened to publicize false, defamatory material against him. After the election, Fox brought suit against Vice claiming defamation and extortion under state law as well as violation of his First Amendment and due process rights under federal law. Vice removed the action to federal court and then moved for summary judgment on the § 1983 claims. The magistrate judge entered an order dismissing the civil rights claims and remanding the state claims back to state court. A second magistrate judge then awarded the defendant all of the fees incurred in defending the federal case for almost two years, namely $54,481.

The Supreme Court unanimously reversed, finding that the lower federal courts applied the wrong standard: "We hold today that a court may grant reasonable fees to the defendant in this circumstance, but only for costs that the defendant would not have incurred but for the frivolous claims." Because the "relevant purpose of § 1988 is to relieve defendants of the burdens associated with fending off frivolous litigation," only hours spent defending frivolous litigation are compensable. The lower courts failed to take into account the overlap between the frivolous federal and nonfrivolous state claims, and they applied a standard permitting fees "for any work useful to defending against a frivolous claim, even if lawyers would have done that work regardless." The Court explained that the "but for" standard may sometimes allow compensation to a defendant for attorney work relating to both frivolous and nonfrivolous claims, but only if the frivolous claim required the attorney to do more work because of the defendant's greater financial exposure on that claim. In short, the dispositive question is not whether the attorney's fees related to the nonfrivolous claim, but whether the costs would have been incurred even in the absence of the frivolous allegation. The district court erred in suggesting that the defense attorney would have done much of the same work even if Fox had not brought his frivolous § 1983 claim. Because the defense of the federal claim entailed proof or denial of essentially the same set of facts underlying the state law claims, Vice's attorney would have taken many of the same depositions anyway. Further, in remanding Fox's remaining claims to state court, the federal district court said that the materials "unearthed during discovery were usable in the state court proceedings."

Assume Fox had filed two lawsuits, a federal suit regarding § 1983 claims exclusively and a state court action regarding state law claims only. If the federal court found the federal claims frivolous in that scenario, would defendants be entitled to all their attorney's fees?

5. Successful *pro se* litigants have sought fee awards under § 1988. In *Kay v. Ehrler*, 499 U.S. 432 (1991), the Court held that because "the overriding statutory concern [reflected in § 1988] is the interest in obtaining independent counsel for victims of civil rights violations," a *pro se* litigant who is also an attorney is not entitled to a fee award. The Court also expressed its agreement with those circuits holding that a non-attorney *pro se* litigant is not entitled to a fee award.

ii.   Determining Amount of Fee Award

HENSLEY V. ECKERHART
461 U.S. 424 (1983)

Justice POWELL delivered the opinion of the Court.

The issue in this case is whether a partially prevailing plaintiff may recover an attorney's fee for legal services on unsuccessful claims.

I

A

Respondents brought this lawsuit on behalf of all persons involuntarily confined at the Forensic Unit of the Fulton State Hospital in Fulton, Mo. The Forensic Unit consists of two residential buildings for housing patients who are dangerous to themselves or others. Maximum-security patients are housed in the Marion O. Biggs Building for the Criminally Insane. The rest of the patients reside in the less restrictive Rehabilitation Unit.

In 1972 respondents filed a three-count complaint in the District Court for the Western District of Missouri against petitioners, who are officials at the Forensic Unit and members of the Missouri Mental Health Commission. Count I challenged the constitutionality of treatment and conditions at the Forensic Unit. Count II challenged the placement of patients in the Biggs Building without procedural due process. Count III sought compensation for patients who performed institution-maintaining labor.

Count II was resolved by a consent decree in December 1983. Count III largely was mooted in August 1974 when petitioners began compensating patients for labor pursuant to the Fair Labor Standards Act. In April 1975 respondents voluntarily dismissed the lawsuit and filed a new two-count complaint. Count I again related to the constitutionality of treatment and conditions at the Forensic Unit. Count II sought damages, based on the Thirteenth Amendment, for the value of past patient labor. In July 1976 respondents voluntarily dismissed this backpay count. Finally, in August 1977 respondents filed an amended one-count complaint specifying the conditions that allegedly violated their constitutional right to treatment.

In August 1979, following a three-week trial, the District Court held that an involuntarily committed patient has a constitutional right to minimally adequate treatment. The court then found constitutional violations in five of six general areas: physical environment; individual treatment plans; least restrictive environment; visitation, telephone, and mailing privileges; and seclusion and restraint. With respect to staffing, the sixth general area, the District Court found that the Forensic Unit's staffing levels, which had increased during the litigation, were minimally adequate. Petitioners did not appeal the District Court's decision on the merits.

B

In February 1980 respondents filed a request for attorney's fees for the period from January 1975 through the end of the litigation. Their four attorneys claimed 2,985 hours worked and sought payment at rates varying form $40 to $65 per hour. This amounted to approximately $150,000. Petitioners opposed the request on numerous grounds, including inclusion of hours spent in pursuit of unsuccessful claims.

The District Court first determined that respondents were prevailing parties under 42 U.S.C. § 1988 even though they had not succeeded on every claim. It then refused to eliminate from the award hours spent on unsuccessful claims. Finding that respondents "have obtained relief of significant import," the District Court awarded a fee of $133,332.25.

II

In *Alyeska Pipeline Service Co. v. Wilderness Society*, this Court reaffirmed the "American Rule" that each party in a lawsuit ordinarily shall bear its own attorney's fees unless there is express statutory authorization to the contrary. In response Congress enacted the Civil Rights Attorney's Fees Awards Act of 1976, 42 U.S.C. § 1988, authorizing the district courts to award a reasonable attorney's fee to prevailing parties in civil rights litigation. The purpose of § 1988 is to ensure "effective access to the judicial process" for persons with civil rights grievances. Accordingly, a prevailing plaintiff "'should ordinarily recover an attorney's fee unless special circumstances would render such an award unjust.'"

The amount of the fee, of course, must be determined on the facts of each case. On this issue the House Report simply refers to 12 factors set forth in *Johnson v. Georgia Highway Express*, Inc., 488 F.2d 714 (CA5 1974).[3] One of the factors in *Johnson*, "the amount involved and the

---

3   The 12 factors are: (1) the time and labor required; (2) the novelty and difficulty of the questions; (3) the skill requisite to perform the legal service properly; (4) the preclusion of employment by the attorney due to acceptance of the case; (5) the customary fee; (6) whether the fee is fixed or contingent; (7) time limitations imposed by the client or the circumstances; (8) the amount involved and the results obtained; (9) the experience, reputation, and ability of the attorneys; (10) the "undesirability" of the case; (11) the nature and length of the professional relationship with the client; and (12) awards in similar cases. These factors derive directly from the AMERICAN BAR ASSOCIATION CODE OF PROFESSIONAL RESPONSIBILITY, *Disciplinary Rule* 2-106 (1980).

results obtained," indicates that the level of a plaintiff's success is relevant to the amount of fees to be awarded.

The legislative history, [however] does not provide a definitive answer as to the proper standard for setting a fee award where the plaintiff has achieved only limited success. Consistent with the legislative history, Courts of Appeals generally have recognized the relevance of the results obtained to the amount of a fee award. They have adopted varying standards, however, for applying this principle in cases where the plaintiffs did not succeed on all claims asserted.

III

A

The most useful starting point for determining the amount of a reasonable fee is the number of hours reasonably expended on the litigation multiplied by a reasonable hourly rate. This calculation provides an objective basis on which to make an initial estimate of the value of a lawyer's services. The party seeking an award of fees should submit evidence supporting the hours worked and rates claimed. Where the documentation of hours is inadequate, the district court may reduce the award accordingly.

The district court also should exclude from this initial fee calculation hours that were not "reasonably expended." Cases may be overstaffed, and the skill and experience of lawyers vary widely. Counsel for the prevailing party should make a good-faith effort to exclude from a fee request hours that are excessive, redundant, or otherwise unnecessary, just as a lawyer in private practice ethically is obligated to exclude such hours from his fees submission. "In the private sector, 'billing judgment' is an important component in fee setting. It is no less important here. Hours that are not properly billed to one's *client* also are not properly billed to one's *adversary* pursuant to statutory authority."

B

The product of reasonable hours times a reasonable rate does not end the inquiry. There remain other considerations that may lead the district court to adjust the fee upward or downward, including the important factor of the "results obtained." This factor is particularly crucial where a plaintiff is deemed "prevailing" even though he succeeded on only some of his claims for relief. In this situation two questions must be addressed. First, did the plaintiff fail to prevail on claims that were unrelated to the claims on which he succeeded? Second, did the plaintiff achieve a level of success that makes the hours reasonably expended a satisfactory basis for making a fee award?

In some cases a plaintiff may present in one lawsuit distinctly different claims for relief that are based on different facts and legal theories. In such a suit, even where the claims are brought against the same defendants—often an institution and its officers, as in this case—counsel's work on one claim will be unrelated to his work on another claim. Accordingly, work on an unsuccessful claim cannot be deemed to have been "expended in pursuit of the ultimate result achieved." The congressional intent to limit awards to prevailing parties requires that these unrelated claims be treated as if they had been raised in separate lawsuits, and therefore no fee may be awarded for services on the unsuccessful claim.

It may well be that cases involving such unrelated claims are unlikely to arise with great frequency. Many civil rights cases will present only a single claim. In other cases the plaintiff's claims for relief will involve a common core of facts or will be based on related legal theories. Much of counsel's time will be devoted generally to the litigation as a whole, making it difficult to divide the hours expended on a claim-by-claim basis. Such a lawsuit cannot be viewed as a series of discrete claims. Instead the district court should focus on the significance of the overall relief obtained by the plaintiff in relation to the hours reasonably expended on the litigation.

Where a plaintiff has obtained excellent results, his attorney should recover a fully compensatory fee. Normally this will encompass all hours reasonably expended on the litigation, and indeed in some cases of exceptional success an enhanced award may be justified. In these circumstances the fee award should not be reduced simply because the plaintiff failed to prevail on every contention raised in the lawsuit. Litigants in good faith may raise alternative legal grounds for a desired outcome, and the court's rejection of or failure to reach certain grounds is not a sufficient reason for reducing a fee. The result is what matters.

If, on the other hand, a plaintiff has achieved only partial or limited success, the product of hours reasonably expended on the litigation as a whole times a reasonable hourly rate may be an excessive amount. This will be true even where the plaintiff's claims were interrelated, nonfrivolous, and raised in good faith. Congress has not authorized an award of fees whenever it was reasonable for a plaintiff to bring a lawsuit or whenever conscientious counsel tried the case with devotion and skill. Again, the most critical factor is the degree of success obtained.

Application of this principle is particularly important in complex civil rights litigation involving numerous challenges to institutional practices or conditions. This type of litigation is lengthy and demands many hours of lawyers' services. Although the plaintiff often may succeed in identifying some unlawful practices or conditions, the range of possible success is vast. That the plaintiff is a "prevailing party" therefore may say little about whether the expenditure of counsel's time was reasonable in relation to the success achieved. In this case, for example, the District Court's award of fees based on 2,557 hours worked may have been reasonable in light of the substantial relief obtained. But had respondents prevailed on only one of their six general claims, for example the claim that petitioners' visitation, mail, and telephone policies were overly restrictive, a fee award based on the claimed hours clearly would have been excessive.

There is no precise rule or formula for making these determinations. The district court may attempt to identify specific hours that should be eliminated, or it may simply reduce the award to account for the limited success. The court necessarily has discretion in making this equitable judgment. This discretion, however, must be exercised in light of the considerations we have identified.

C

A request for attorney's fees should not result in a second major litigation. Ideally, of course, litigants will settle the amount of a fee. Where settlement is not possible, the fee applicant bears the burden of establishing entitlement to an award and documenting the appropriate hours expended and hourly rates. The applicant should exercise "billing judgment" with respect to hours worked and should maintain billing time records in a manner that will enable a reviewing court to identify distinct claims.[12]

We reemphasize that the district court has discretion in determining the amount of a fee award. This is appropriate in view of the district court's superior understanding of the litigation and the desirability of avoiding frequent appellate review of what essentially are factual matters. It remains important, however, for the district court to provide a concise but clear explanation of its reasons for the fee award. When an adjustment is requested on the basis of either the exceptional or limited nature of the relief obtained by the plaintiff, the district court should make clear that it has considered that relationship between the amount of the fee awarded and the results obtained.

IV

In this case the District Court began by finding that "[t]he relief [respondents] obtained at trial was substantial and certainly entitles them to be considered prevailing . . ., without the need of examining those issues disposed of prior to trial in order to determine which went in [respondents'] favor." It then declined to divide the hours worked between winning and losing claims, stating that this fails to consider "the relative importance of various issues, the inter-relation of the issues, the difficulty in identifying issues, or the extent to which a party may prevail on various issues." Finally, the court assessed the "amount involved/results obtained" and declared: "Not only should [respondents] be considered prevailing parties, they are parties who have obtained relief of significant import. [Respondents'] relief affects not only them, but also numerous other institutionalized patients similarly situated. The extent of this relief clearly justifies the award of a reasonable attorney's fee."

These findings represent a commendable effort to explain the fee award. Given the inter-related nature of the facts and legal theories in this case, the District Court did not err in refusing to apportion the fee award mechanically on the basis of respondents' success or failure on particular issues. And given the findings with respect to the level of respondents' success, the District Court's award may be consistent with our holding today.

We are unable to affirm the decisions below, however, because the District Court's opinion did not properly consider the relationship between the extent of success and the amount of the fee award. The court's finding that "the [significant] extent of the relief clearly justifies the

---

12 We recognize that there is no certain method of determining when claims are "related" or "unrelated." Plaintiff's counsel, of course, is not required to record in great detail how each minute of his time was expended. But at least counsel should identify the general subject matter of his time expenditures.

award of a reasonable attorney's fee" does not answer the question of what is "reasonable" in light of that level of success. We emphasize that the inquiry does not end with a finding that the plaintiff obtained significant relief. A reduced fee award is appropriate if the relief, however significant, is limited in comparison to the scope of the litigation as a whole.

V

We hold that the extent of a plaintiff's success is a crucial factor in determining the proper amount of an award of attorney's fees under 42 U.S.C. § 1988. Where the plaintiff has failed to prevail on a claim that is distinct in all respects from his successful claims, the hours spent on the unsuccessful claim should be excluded in considering the amount of a reasonable fee. Where a lawsuit consists of related claims, a plaintiff who has won substantial relief should not have his attorney's fee reduced simply because the district court did not adopt each contention raised. But where the plaintiff achieved only limited success, the district court should award only that amount of fees that is reasonable in relation to the results obtained. On remand the District Court should determine the proper amount of the attorney's fee award in light of these standards.

NOTES AND QUESTIONS

1. Assume you represent two persons, both claiming they were wrongfully discharged by a governmental employer in retaliation for exercising First Amendment rights. The two join as plaintiffs in the same case, the case proceeds to trial and one plaintiff prevails while the other loses. Defendant argues that fees should be awarded for only one half of the time spent by counsel for the two plaintiffs. Evaluate this argument in light of *Hensley*.

2. Where a plaintiff prevails on one claim and loses an unrelated claim, how does counsel for the plaintiff establish the amount of time spent on the successful claim? Should the documentation filed in support of the fee petition reflect the time spent on the unrelated, unsuccessful claim? In light of *Hensley*, how detailed should an attorney's time records be? Review *Hensley, supra*, note 12.

3. Assume that before going to federal court you unsuccessfully sought relief for your client before a state administrative body (one that was not sufficiently judicial-like to trigger preclusion). If you eventually succeed in federal court, will you be compensated for the hours spent pursuing relief before the administrative body? The Court in *Webb v. Board of Educ. of Dyer County*, 471 U.S. 234 (1985), ruled that fees could not be recovered under § 1988 for time spent seeking to enforce tenure rights in a state administrative proceeding since (a) there was no need to exhaust administrative remedies and (b) the work done was not related to the § 1983 enforcement proceeding.

It noted, however, that if the work product "was both useful and of a type ordinarily necessary to advance the civil rights litigation," it would be compensable.

BLUM V. STENSON
465 U.S. 886 (1984)

Justice POWELL delivered the opinion of the Court.

The two issues in this case are whether Congress intended fee awards to nonprofit legal service organizations to be calculated according to cost or to prevailing market rates, and whether, and under what circumstances, an upward adjustment of an award based on prevailing market rates is appropriate under § 1988.

I

A

This suit was brought in 1978 by respondent on behalf of a statewide class of Medicaid recipients pursuant to 42 U.S.C. § 1983 in the District Court for the Southern District of New York. Under New York law, one who is eligible to receive benefits under the Supplemental Security Income (SSI) program automatically is eligible to receive Medicaid benefits. Prior to this suit, persons who qualified for Medicaid in this fashion automatically lost their benefits if they thereafter became ineligible for SSI payments. The case was decided on cross-motions for summary judgment after only one set of plaintiff's interrogatories had been served and answered. On these motions, the District Court certified the class and rendered final judgment in favor of the class.

The court enjoined the prior practice of automatic termination of benefits, and prescribed procedural rights for the certified class that included "(a) an *ex parte* determination of continued eligibility for Medicaid, independent of eligibility for SSI; (b) timely and adequate notice of such termination; (c) an opportunity for a hearing." The Court of Appeals for the Second Circuit affirmed. Respondent's subsequent request for an award of reasonable attorney's fees under § 1988 is the subject of the present case.

B

Throughout this litigation, respondent was represented by attorneys from the Legal Aid Society of New York, a private nonprofit law office. In November 1980, respondent filed a request for attorney's fees for the period December 1978 through the end of the litigation. Her three attorneys sought payment for some 809 hours of work at rates varying from $95 to $105 per hour. This amounted to approximately $79,312. Respondent's total fee request, however, reflected a 50% increase in that fee. In her brief to the District Court, respondent explained that such an increase was necessary to compensate for the complexity of the case, the novelty of the issues, and the "great benefit" achieved. The total requested fee amounted to approximately $118,968.

The District Court held that both the hours expended and the rates charged were reasonable. It also held that the fee calculated by multiplying the number of hours times the hourly rates should be increased by the requested 50% because of the quality of representation, the complexity of the issues, the riskiness of success, and the "great benefit to a large class" that was achieved. The District Court awarded the plaintiff class the requested fee of $118,968.

II

Petitioner argues that the use of prevailing market rates to calculate attorney's fees under § 1988 leads to exorbitant fee awards and provides windfalls to civil rights counsel contrary to the express intent of Congress. To avoid this result, petitioner urges this Court to require that all fee awards under § 1988 be calculated according to the cost of providing legal services rather than according to the prevailing market rate. The Solicitor General, for the United States as *amicus curiae*, urges the Court to adopt a cost-related standard only for fee awards made to nonprofit legal aid organizations. He argues that market rates reflect the level of compensation necessary to attract profit making attorneys, but that such rates provide excessive fees to nonprofit counsel. Because market rates incorporate operating expenses that may exceed the expenses of nonprofit legal services organizations, and include an element of profit unnecessary to attract nonprofit counsel, the Solicitor General argues that fee awards based on market rates "confer an unjustified windfall or subsidy upon legal services organizations."

Resolution of these two arguments begins and ends with an interpretation of the attorney's fee statute. In enacting the statute, Congress directed that attorney's fees be calculated according to standards currently in use under other fee-shifting statutes. In the cases cited [with approval] by the Senate Report, fee awards were calculated according to prevailing market rates. None of these cases made any mention of a cost-based standard. Petitioner's argument that the use of market rates violates congressional intent, therefore, is flatly contradicted by the legislative history of § 1988.

It is also clear from the legislative history that Congress did not intend the calculation of fee awards to vary depending on whether plaintiff was represented by private counsel or by a nonprofit legal services organization.

III

We address now the second question presented: whether a 50% upward adjustment in the fee was—as petitioner argues—an abuse of discretion by the District Court. Petitioner makes two separate but related arguments. First, she asserts that a reasonable attorney's fee is calculated by multiplying the reasonable number of hours expended times a reasonable hourly rate and that any upward adjustment of that fee is improper. In the alternative, she argues that the 50% upward adjustment in this case constitutes a clear abuse of discretion.

A

In *Hensley v. Eckerhart*, we reviewed the cases cited in the legislative history of § 1988 and concluded that the "product of reasonable hours times a reasonable rate" normally provides a "reasonable" attorney's fee within the meaning of the statute. *Hensley* also recognized that "in some cases of exceptional success an enhanced award may be justified." In view of our recognition that an enhanced award may be justified "in some cases of exceptional success," we cannot agree with petitioner's argument that an "upward adjustment" is never permissible. The statute requires a "reasonable fee," and there may be circumstances in which the basic standard of reasonable rates multiplied by reasonably expended hours results in a fee that is either unreasonably low or unreasonably high. When, however, the applicant for a fee has carried his burden of showing that the claimed rate and number of hours are reasonable, the resulting product is presumed to be the reasonable fee contemplated by § 1988.

B

The issue remaining is the appropriateness of an upward adjustment to the fee award in this case. The burden of proving that such an adjustment is necessary to the determination of a reasonable fee is on the fee applicant. The record before us contains no evidence supporting an upward adjustment to fees calculated under the basic standard of reasonable rates times reasonable hours. The affidavits of respondent's attorneys do not claim, or even mention, entitlement to a bonus or upward revision. Respondent's brief to the District Court merely states in conclusory fashion that an upward adjustment to the fee is necessary because the issues were novel, the litigation was complex, and the results were of far-reaching significance to a large class of people. The District Court, without elaboration, accepted these conclusory reasons for approving the upward adjustment and supplied additional reasons of its own. In awarding the 50% increase, the court referred to the complexity of the litigation, the novelty of the issues, the high quality of representation, the "great benefit" to the class, and the "riskiness" of the lawsuit. The Court of Appeals, in affirming, shed no light on why it thought this substantial upward adjustment was appropriate. In a single sentence, it simply repeated the unsupported conclusions of the District Court.

The reasons offered by the District Court to support the upward adjustment do not withstand examination. The novelty and complexity of the issues presumably were fully reflected in the number of billable hours recorded by counsel and thus do not warrant an upward adjustment in a fee based on the number of billable hours times reasonable hourly rates. There may be cases, of course, where the experience and special skill of the attorney will require the expenditure of fewer hours than counsel normally would be expected to spend on a particularly novel or complex issue. In those cases, the special skill and experience of counsel should be reflected in the reasonableness of the hourly rates. Neither complexity nor novelty of the issues, therefore, is an appropriate factor in determining whether to increase the basic fee award.

The District Court, having tried the case, was in the best position to conclude that "the quality of representation was high." In view of the reputation of the Legal Aid Society and its staff, we have no doubt that this was true. The "quality of representation," however, generally is reflected in the reasonable hourly rate. It, therefore, may justify an upward adjustment only in the rare case where the fee applicant offers specific evidence to show that the quality of service rendered was superior to that one reasonably should expect in light of the hourly rates charged and that the success was "exceptional." Respondent offered no such evidence in this case, and on this record the District Court's rationale for providing an upward adjustment for quality of representation is a clear example of double counting.

The 50% upward adjustment also was based in part on the District Court's determination that the ultimate outcome of the litigation "was of great benefit to a large class of needy people." The court did not explain, however, exactly how this determination affected the fee award. "Results obtained" is one of the 12 factors identified in *Johnson v. Georgia Highway Express* as relevant to the calculation of a reasonable attorney's fee. It is "particularly crucial where a plaintiff is deemed 'prevailing' even though he succeeded on only some of his claims for relief." Because acknowledgment of the "results obtained" generally will be subsumed within other factors used to calculate a reasonable fee, it normally should not provide an independent basis for increasing the fee award. Neither the District Court's opinion nor respondent's briefs have identified record evidence that shows that the benefit achieved requires an upward adjustment to the fee.

Finally, the District Court included among its reasons for an upward adjustment a statement that the "issues presented were novel and the undertaking therefore risky." Absent any claim in the affidavits or briefs submitted in support of respondent's fee request, seeking such an adjustment, we cannot be sure what prompted the court's statement. Nowhere in the affidavits submitted in support of respondent's fee request, nor in her brief to the District Court, did respondent identify any risks associated with the litigation or claim that the risk of nonpayment required an upward adjustment to provide a reasonable fee. On this record, therefore, any upward adjustment for the contingent nature of the litigation was unjustified.

In sum, we reiterate what was said in *Hensley*: "[w]here a plaintiff has obtained excellent results, his attorney should recover a fully compensatory fee. Normally this will encompass all hours reasonably expended on the litigation, and indeed in some cases of exceptional success an enhanced award may be justified." We therefore reject petitioner's argument that an upward adjustment to an attorney's fee is never appropriate under § 1988. On the record before us, however, respondent established only that hourly rates ranging from $95 per hour to $105 per hour for the full 809.75 hours billed were reasonable. This resulted in a charge of $79,312. Respondent introduced no evidence that enhancement was necessary to provide fair and reasonable compensation. She therefore has failed to carry her burden of justifying entitlement to an upward adjustment. On this record, we conclude that the fee of $79,312 was "fully compensatory." Accordingly, the judgment below is reversed only insofar as the fee award was increased by the sum of $39,656, and is otherwise affirmed.

1. Why award market rate fees in a case where the prevailing plaintiff is represented by a staff attorney employed by a legal services program which receives its operating money from the federally funded Legal Services Corporation? Who should receive the fees paid by the defendant?

2. What is the significance of this decision as it relates to upward adjustments? Does it simply suggest that counsel for the prevailing plaintiff should use all of the factors which might support an upward adjustment to enhance the base hourly rate?

3. How is an attorney who represents plaintiffs in personal injury cases compensated for the risk of not prevailing? If an attorney can bill his clients for a 40-hour week at $250 per hour, will he or she take a contingent case where at most the recovery will be $250 per hour?

4. The Court again faced the issue whether Congress intended upward adjustments to compensate for the contingent nature of success, and thus for the risk of nonpayment, in *Pennsylvania v. Delaware Valley Citizens' Counsel*, 483 U.S. 711 (1987). This case arose under the Clean Air Act, which contains a fee provision similar to § 1988. An upward adjustment by the lower court was reversed, without a majority opinion. Four members of the Court indicated such adjustments "should be reserved for exceptional cases where the need and justification for such enhancement are readily apparent and are supported by evidence in the record and specific findings by the courts." Justice O'Connor concurred in the judgment, and would allow such upward adjustments only upon a showing by the applicant that the relevant market compensates for risk in contingent fee cases as a class in order to attract competent counsel.

   In dissent, four Justices argued that Congress did intend to allow an upward adjustment, in appropriate circumstances, "to place contingent employment *as a whole* on roughly the same economic footing as noncontingent practice."

5. The Court, in *Perdue v. Kenny A.*, 559 U.S. 542 (2010), reiterated that enhancements are permissible, but (1) the lodestar is presumed sufficient to induce a capable attorney to undertake representation of a meritorious civil rights case, (2) the Court has never affirmed an enhancement for performance, (3) enhancements cannot be awarded based on a factor already subsumed in the lodestar calculation, such as complexity of the case or quality of an attorney's performance, and (4) the burden of proving enhancement is borne by the fee applicant, who must produce specific evidence that supports the award. The fee petition here asked only whether a reasonable fee could ever be enhanced based on quality of performance and results obtained. The Court unanimously held that there may be rare circumstances where "superior attorney

performance" is not adequately accounted for in the lodestar, such as where a single or too few factors are used in determining the hourly rate to adequately measure the attorney's true market value or where the attorney makes an extraordinary outlay for expenses in unusually protracted litigation, or where there is exceptional delay in payment of fees.

Five Justices then proceeded to hold that the district court failed to justify its 75% enhancement, despite its one hundred-page detailed opinion finding that the plaintiffs' attorneys exhibited "a higher degree of skill, commitment, dedication, and professionalism than the Court has seen displayed by the attorneys in any other case during its twenty-seven years on the bench." The Court reversed an award of an extra $4.5 million in attorney's fees above the lodestar fee of $6 million because the district court failed to calculate how much of the enhancement was because of outlays for litigation expenses, it did not determine whether delay in receiving fees was extraordinary or unwarranted, and it improperly considered the contingent nature of the case: "Unjustified enhancements that serve only to enrich attorneys are not consistent with the statute's aim." This despite the fact that counsel spent $1.7 million in litigation expenses over three years with no ongoing reimbursement. In short, although nine Justices agreed that an increase in fees beyond the lodestar is permitted in extraordinary circumstances, five Justices sent a clear message that it will be an exceedingly rare case in which the lodestar may be enhanced based upon superior performance by the prevailing plaintiff's attorney. As a general principle, according to the majority, the lodestar will have already taken account of this factor.

6. In a case involving the fee provisions of the Solid Waste Disposal Act and the Clean Water Act, the Court further closed the door to enhancement of the lodestar, i.e., the product of reasonable hours times a reasonable rate, holding that "enhancement for contingency is not permitted under fee-shifting statutes at issue." *City of Burlington v. Dague*, 505 U.S. 557 (1992). Apparently the Court intended to foreclose such enhancements in civil rights cases too: "[t]his language [in the two statutes involved] is similar to that of many other federal fee-shifting statutes, *see, e.g.,* 42 U.S.C. §§ 1988, 2000e-5(k), 7604(d); our case law construing what is a 'reasonable' fee applies uniformly to all of them." *Id.* at 562. *Compare Guam Soc. of Obstetricians & Gynecologists v. ADA*, 100 F.3d 691, 697–99 (9th Cir. 1996) (*Dague* does not preclude the use of a multiplier based on the unavailability of willing local counsel to handle the case due to fear of ostracization and concern for personal safety).

7. In *Missouri v. Jenkins*, 491 U.S. 274 (1989), the Court adopted its dicta from *Delaware Valley Citizens' Counsel, supra,* holding that courts can award an enhancement for delay in payment, either by basing the award on current rates or by an upward adjustment of historical rates. The Court in *Jenkins* also held that the work of law

clerks and paralegals should be compensated under 1988 at the prevailing market rates for such services.

8. Based on *West Virginia University Hospitals, Inc. v. Casey*, 499 U.S. 83 (1991), expert witness fees cannot be recovered by the prevailing party as part of attorney fees under § 1988. However, § 113 of the Civil Rights Act of 1991 amends § 1988 to "include expert fees as part of the attorney's fee" in actions to enforce § 1981 and § 1981a. It also amends the fee provision in Title VII, 42 U.S.C. § 2000e-5(k), to include expert fees. Note that the 1991 amendment to § 1988 does not include all actions covered by the fee provision of § 1988.

CITY OF RIVERSIDE V. RIVERA
477 U.S. 561 (1986)

Justice BRENNAN announced the judgment of the Court and delivered an opinion in which Justice MARSHALL, Justice BLACKMUN, and Justice STEVENS join.

The issue presented in this case is whether an award of attorney's fees under 42 U.S.C. § 1988 is *per se* "unreasonable" within the meaning of the statute if it exceeds the amount of damages recovered by the plaintiff in the underlying civil rights action.

I

Respondents, eight Chicano individuals, attended a party on the evening of August 1, 1975, at the Riverside, California, home of respondents Santos and Jennie Rivera. A large number of unidentified police officers, acting without a warrant, broke up the party using tear gas and, as found by the District Court, "unnecessary physical force." Many of the guests, including four of the respondents, were arrested. The District Court later found that "[t]he party was not creating a disturbance in the community at the time of the break-in." Criminal charges against the arrestees were ultimately dismissed for lack of probable cause.

On June 4, 1976, respondents sued the city of Riverside, its chief of police, and 30 individual police officers under 42 U.S.C. §§ 1981, 1983, 1985(3), and 1986 for allegedly violating their First, Fourth and Fourteenth Amendment rights. The complaint, which also alleged numerous state-law claims, sought damages, and declaratory and injunctive relief. On August 5, 1977, 23 of the individual police officers moved for summary judgment; the District Court granted summary judgment in favor of 17 of these officers. The case against the remaining defendants proceeded to trial in September 1980. The jury returned a total of 37 individual verdicts in favor of the respondents and against the city and five individual officers, finding 11 violations of § 1983, four instances of false arrest and imprisonment, and 22 instances of negligence. Respondents were awarded $33,350 in compensatory and punitive damages: $13,300 for their federal claims, and $20,050 for their state-law claims.

Respondents also sought attorney's fees and costs under § 1988. They requested compensation for 1,946.75 hours expended by their two attorneys at a rate of $125 per hour, and for 84.5 hours expended by law clerks at a rate of $25.00 per hour, a total of $245,456.25. The District Court found both the hours and rates reasonable, and awarded respondents $245,456.25 in attorney's fees. The court rejected respondents' request for certain additional expenses, and for a multiplier sought by respondents to reflect the contingent nature of their success and the high quality of their attorneys' efforts.

II

Petitioners argue that the District Court failed properly to follow *Hensley* in calculating respondent's fee award. We disagree. The District Court carefully considered the results obtained by respondents pursuant to the instructions set forth in *Hensley*, and concluded that respondents were entitled to recover attorney's fees for all hours expended on the litigation.

Based on our review of the record, we agree with the Court of Appeals that the District Court's findings were not clearly erroneous. We conclude that the District Court correctly applied the factors announced in *Hensley* in calculating respondents' fee award, and that the court did not abuse its discretion in awarding attorney's fees for all time reasonably spent litigating the case.

III

Petitioners, joined by the Solicitor General as *amicus curiae*, maintain that *Hensley*'s lodestar approach is inappropriate in civil rights cases where a plaintiff recovers only monetary damages. In these cases, so the argument goes, use of the lodestar may result in fees that exceed the amount of damages recovered and that are therefore unreasonable. Likening such cases to private tort actions, petitioners and the Solicitor General submit that attorney's fees in such cases should be proportionate to the amount of damages a plaintiff recovers. Specifically, they suggest that fee awards in damages cases should be modeled upon the contingent fee arrangements commonly used in personal injury litigation. In this case, assuming a 33% contingency rate, this would entitle respondents to recover approximately $11,000 in attorney's fees.

The amount of damages a plaintiff recovers is certainly relevant to the amount of attorney's fees to be awarded under § 1988. It is, however, only one of many factors that a court should consider in calculating an award of attorney's fees. We reject the proposition that fee awards under § 1988 should necessarily be proportionate to the amount of damages a civil rights plaintiff actually recovers.

A

As an initial matter, we reject the notion that a civil rights action for damages constitutes nothing more than a private tort suit benefiting only the individual plaintiffs whose rights were violated. Unlike most private tort litigants, a civil rights plaintiff seeks to vindicate important civil and constitutional rights that cannot be valued solely in monetary terms. And, Congress has determined that "the public as a whole has an interest in the vindication of the rights conferred by the statutes enumerated in § 1988, over and above the value of a civil rights remedy to a particular plaintiff. . . ." Regardless of the form of relief he actually obtains, a successful civil rights plaintiff often secures important social benefits that are not reflected in nominal or relatively small damages awards. In this case, for example, the District Court found that many of petitioners' unlawful acts were "motivated by a general hostility to the Chicano community" and that this litigation therefore served the public interest. In addition, the damages a plaintiff recovers contributes significantly to the deterrence of civil rights violations in the future. This deterrent effect is particularly evident in the area of individual police misconduct, where injunctive relief generally is unavailable.

Congress expressly recognized that a plaintiff who obtains relief in a civil rights lawsuit "does so not for himself alone but also as a 'private attorney general,' vindicating a policy that Congress 'considered of the highest importance.'"

Because damages awards do not reflect fully the public benefit advanced by civil rights litigation, Congress did not intend for fees in civil rights cases, unlike most private law cases, to depend on obtaining substantial monetary relief. Rather, Congress made clear that it "intended that the amount of fees awarded under [§ 1988] be governed by the same standards which prevail in other types of equally complex Federal litigation, such as antitrust cases and *not be reduced because the rights involved may be nonpecuniary in nature*." Thus, Congress recognized that reasonable attorney's fees under § 1988 are not conditioned upon and need not be proportionate to an award of money damages. The lower courts have generally eschewed such a requirement.

B

A rule that limits attorney's fees in civil rights cases to a proportion of the damages awarded would seriously undermine Congress' purpose in enacting § 1988. Congress enacted § 1988 specifically because it found that the private market for legal services failed to provide many victims of civil rights violations with effective access to the judicial process. These victims ordinarily cannot afford to purchase legal services at the rates set by the private market.

Moreover, the contingent fee arrangements that make legal services available to many victims of personal injuries would often not encourage lawyers to accept civil rights case, which frequently involve substantial expenditures of time and effort but produce only small monetary recoveries. As the House Report states:

[W]hile damages are theoretically available under the statutes covered by [§ 1988], it should be observed that, in some cases, immunity doctrines and special defenses, available only to public officials, preclude or *severely limit the damage remedy*. Consequently, awarding counsel fees to prevailing plaintiffs in such litigation is particularly important and necessary if Federal civil and constitutional rights are to be adequately protected.

A rule of proportionality would make it difficult, if not impossible, for individuals with meritorious civil rights claims but relatively small potential damages to obtain redress from the courts. This is totally inconsistent with the Congress' purpose in enacting § 1988. Congress recognized that private-sector fee arrangements were inadequate to ensure sufficiently vigorous enforcement of civil rights. In order to ensure that lawyers would be willing to represent persons with legitimate civil rights grievances, Congress determined that it would be necessary to compensate lawyers for all time reasonably expended on a case.

This case illustrates why the enforcement of civil rights cannot be entrusted to private-sector fee arrangements. The District Court observed that "[g]iven the nature of this lawsuit and the type of defense presented, many attorneys in the community would have been reluctant to institute and to continue to prosecute this action." The court concluded, moreover, that "[c]ounsel for plaintiffs achieved excellent results for their clients, and their accomplishment in this case was outstanding. The amount of time expended by counsel in conducting this litigation was reasonable and reflected sound legal judgment under the circumstances." Nevertheless, petitioners suggest that respondents' counsel should be compensated for only a small fraction of the actual time spent litigating the case. In light of the difficult nature of the issues presented by this lawsuit and the low pecuniary value of the many of the rights respondents sought to vindicate, it is highly unlikely that the prospect of a fee equal to a fraction of the damages respondents might recover would have been sufficient to attract competent counsel. Moreover, since counsel might not have found it economically feasible to expend the amount of time respondents' counsel found necessary to litigate the case properly, it is even less likely that counsel would have achieved the excellent results that respondents' counsel obtained here. Thus, had respondents had to rely on private-sector fee arrangements, they might well have been unable to obtain redress for their grievances. It is precisely for this reason that Congress enacted § 1988.

IV

We agree with petitioners that Congress intended that statutory fee awards be "adequate to attract competent counsel, but . . . not produce windfalls to attorneys." However, we find no evidence that Congress intended that, in order to avoid "windfalls to attorneys," attorney's fees be proportionate to the amount of damages a civil rights plaintiff might recover.

In the absence of any indication that Congress intended to adopt a strict rule that attorney's fees under § 1988 be proportionate to damages recovered, we decline to adopt such a rule ourselves.

Justice POWELL, concurring in the judgment.

I join only the Court's judgment. The plurality opinion reads our decision in *Hensley v. Eckerhart* more expansively than I would, and more expansively than is necessary to decide this case. For me affirmance —quite simply—is required by the District Court's detailed findings of fact, which were approved by the Court of Appeals. On its face, the fee award seems unreasonable. But I find no basis for this Court to reject the findings made and approved by the courts below.

Petitioners argue for a rule of proportionality between the fee awarded and the damages recovered in a civil rights case. Neither the decisions of this Court nor the legislative history of § 1988 support such a "rule." The facts and circumstances of litigation are infinitely variable. Under *Hensley*, of course, "the most critical factor [in the final determination of fee awards] is the degree of success obtained." Where recovery of private damages is the purpose of a civil rights litigation, a district court, in fixing fees, is obligated to give primary consideration to the amount of damages awarded as compared to the amount sought. In some civil rights cases, however, the court may consider the vindication of constitutional rights in addition to the amount of damages recovered. In this case, for example, the District Court made an explicit finding that the "public interest" had been served by the jury's verdict that the warrantless entry was lawless and unconstitutional. Although the finding of a Fourth Amendment violation hardly can be considered a new constitutional ruling, in the special circumstances of this case, the vindication of the asserted Fourth Amendment right may well have served a public interest, supporting the amount of the fees awarded. As the District Court put it, there were allegations that the police misconduct was "motivated by a general hostility to the Chicano community in the area. . . ." The record also contained evidence of racial slurs by some of the police.

NOTES AND QUESTIONS

1. Does Justice Brennan foreclose looking to the amount of damages in determining a reasonable attorney fee award? How does Justice Powell's position (the critical fifth vote) differ from the position taken in the plurality opinion?

2. Assume a plaintiff in a procedural due process case prevails but recovers only $1.00 in nominal damages, per *Carey v. Piphus*. Should the plaintiff recover full compensation for all time reasonably expended by counsel even though broad compensatory damages were sought? Is it reasonable for counsel to invest several hundred hours in such a case when it is quite clear that the plaintiff will not receive more than $1? Will it depend on whether the case forces a change in the challenged practice or policy? If the plaintiff initially sought only declaratory relief and nominal damages, hasn't she achieved "excellent results" within the meaning of *Hensley* for which a "fully compensatory" fee is available?

In *Farrar v. Hobby*, 506 U.S. 103 (1992), the Court held that a plaintiff who recovers only nominal damages is a prevailing party under § 1988: "Now that we are confronted with the question whether a nominal damages award is the sort of "technical," "insignificant" victory that cannot confer prevailing party status [*see Garland, supra*], we hold that the prevailing party inquiry does not turn on the magnitude of the relief obtained." However, this plaintiff, who sought $17 million in damages, but failed to prove an essential element (actual, compensatory injury) of his claim for damages, is not entitled to a fee award because the most critical factor in determining a reasonable fee is the degree of overall success obtained. In short, a reasonable fee in this case was zero dollars.

As noted by Justice O'Connor in her concurring opinion, this plaintiff filed suit demanding $17 million from six defendants and after ten years of litigation, including two trips to the Court of Appeals, got one dollar from one defendant. Justice O'Connor identified three "relevant indicia of success—the extent of relief, the significance of the legal issue on which the plaintiff prevailed, and the public purpose served—" to be considered in determining whether a victory is de minimis. The four dissenting justices, who agreed that the plaintiff is a prevailing party and would have remanded for a determination of whether any fees should be awarded, stressed that this decision does not preclude an award of fees in all cases where a plaintiff recovers only nominal damages.

Thus, the case leaves open the possibility that a plaintiff who recovers only nominal damages was sufficiently successful to recover fees. For example, could a plaintiff who seeks compensatory damages in the amount of $1000 but recovers only nominal damages, as the result of the use of excessive force by a police officer, recover fees— assuming the plaintiff seeks fees of $20,000 instead of $280,000, as in *Farrar*? Could the plaintiff in *Carey v. Piphus, supra*, recover attorney fees after *Farrar*?

3. What is the significance of a fee agreement between counsel and the plaintiff, setting either a contingent fee or a fairly low hourly rate, when the prevailing plaintiff seeks fees under § 1988? In *Blanchard v. Bergeron*, 489 U.S. 87 (1989), the Court held a 40% contingent-fee arrangement did not serve as a ceiling on the amount of fees the court could award under § 1988, but it is a factor which can be considered in determining a reasonable fee. Also, a statutory fee award does not limit an attorney's entitlement under a contingent fee agreement. *Venegas v. Mitchell*, 495 U.S. 82 (1990).

4. 4. *Rivera* is an extreme example of how the fee provision in § 1988 changes a defendant's exposure in civil rights litigation. It also stresses the importance of an accurate evaluation of the case on the part of counsel for the defendant for settlement purposes. The following section will focus on defense strategy.

iii. Impact of Fees on Settlement

EVANS V. JEFF D.
475 u.s. 717 (1986)

Justice STEVENS delivered the opinion of the Court.

In *Maher v. Gagne*, we held that fees *may* be assessed against state officials after a case has been settled by the entry of a consent decree. In this case, we consider the question whether attorney's fees *must* be assessed when the case has been settled by a consent decree granting prospective relief to the plaintiff class but providing that the defendants shall not pay any part of the prevailing party's fees or costs. We hold that the District Court has the power, in its sound discretion, to refuse to award fees.

I

The petitioners are the Governor and other public officials of the State of Idaho responsible for the education and treatment of children who suffer from emotional and mental handicaps. Respondents are a class of such children who have been or will be placed in petitioners' care.

On August 4, 1980, respondents commenced this action by filing a complaint against petitioners in the United States District Court for the District of Idaho. The factual allegations in the complaint described deficiencies in both the educational programs and the health care services provided respondents. These deficiencies allegedly violated the United States Constitution, the Idaho Constitution, four federal statutes, and certain provisions of the Idaho Code. The complaint prayed for injunctive relief and for an award of costs and attorney's fees, but it did not seek damages.

On the day the complaint was filed, the District Court entered two orders, one granting the respondents leave to proceed *in forma pauperis*, and a second appointing Charles Johnson as their next friend for the sole purpose of instituting and prosecuting the action. At that time Johnson was employed by the Idaho Legal Aid Society, Inc., a private, non-profit corporation that provides free legal services to qualified low-income persons. Because the Idaho Legal Aid Society is prohibited from representing clients who are capable of paying their own fees, it made no agreement requiring any of the respondents to pay for the costs of litigation or the legal services it provided through Johnson. Moreover, the special character of both the class and its attorney-client relationship with Johnson explains why it did not enter into any agreement covering the various contingencies that might arise during the course of settlement negotiations of a class action of this kind.

Shortly after petitioners filed their answer, and before substantial work had been done on the case, the parties entered into settlement negotiations. They were able to reach agreement concerning that part of the complaint relating to educational services with relative ease and, on October 14, 1981, entered into a stipulation disposing of that part of the case. The stipulation provided that each party would bear its "own attorney's fees and costs thus far incurred." The District Court promptly entered an order approving the partial settlement.

Negotiations concerning the treatment claims broke down, however, and the parties filed cross-motions for summary judgment. Although the District Court dismissed several of respondents' claims, it held that the federal constitutional claims raised genuine issues of fact to be resolved at trial. Thereafter, the parties stipulated to the entry of a class certification order, engaged in discovery, and otherwise prepared to try the case in the spring of 1983.

In March of 1983, one week before the trial, petitioners presented respondents with a new settlement proposal. As respondents themselves characterize it, the proposal "offered virtually all of the injunctive relief [they] had sought in their complaint." The Court of Appeals agreed with this characterization, and further noted that the proposed relief was "more than the district court in earlier hearings had indicated it was willing to grant." As was true of the earlier partial settlement, however, petitioners' offer included a provision for a waiver by respondents of any claim to fees or costs. Originally, this waiver was unacceptable to the Idaho Legal Aid Society, which had instructed Johnson to reject any settlement offer conditioned upon a waiver of fees, but Johnson ultimately determined that his ethical obligation to his clients mandated acceptance of the proposal. The parties conditioned the waiver on approval by the District Court.

After the stipulation was signed, Johnson filed a written motion requesting the District Court to approve the settlement "except for the provision on costs and attorney's fees," and to allow the respondents to present a bill of costs and fees for consideration by the court. At the oral argument on that motion, Johnson contended that petitioners' offer had exploited his ethical duty to his clients—that he was "forced," by an offer giving his clients "the best result [they] could have gotten in this court or any other court," to waive his attorney's fees. The District Court, however, evaluated the waiver in the context of the entire settlement and rejected the ethical underpinnings of Johnson's argument. The Court of Appeals invalidated the fee waiver and left standing the remainder of the settlement; it then instructed the District Court to "make its own determination of the fees that are reasonable" and remanded for that limited purpose.

II

The question this case presents, then, is whether the Fees Act requires a district court to disapprove a stipulation seeking to settle a civil rights class action under Rule 23 when the offered relief equals or exceeds the probable outcome at trial but is expressly conditioned on waiver of statutory eligibility for attorney's fees. For reasons set out below, we are not persuaded that Congress has commanded that all such settlements must be rejected by the District Court. Moreover, on the facts of record in this case, we are satisfied that the District Court did not abuse its discretion by approving the fee waiver.

III

The text of the Fees Act provides no support for the proposition that Congress intended to ban all fee waivers offered in connection with substantial relief on the merits. On the contrary, the language of the Act, as well as its legislative history, indicates that Congress bestowed on the "prevailing *party*" (generally plaintiffs) a statutory eligibility for a discretionary award of attorney's fees in specified civil rights actions. It did not prevent the party from waiving this eligibility anymore than it legislated against assignment of this right to an attorney, such as effectively occurred here. Instead, Congress enacted the fee-shifting provision as "an integral part of the remedies necessary to obtain" compliance with civil rights laws, to further the same general purpose—promotion of respect for civil rights—that led it to provide damages and injunctive relief. The statute and its legislative history nowhere suggest that Congress intended to forbid all waivers of attorney's fees—even those insisted upon by a civil rights plaintiff in exchange for some other relief to which he is indisputably not entitled—anymore than it intended to bar a concession on damages to secure broader injunctive relief. Thus, while it is undoubtedly true that Congress expected fee-shifting to attract competent counsel to represent citizens deprived of their civil rights, it neither bestowed fee awards upon attorneys nor rendered them nonwaivable or nonnegotiable; instead, it added them to the arsenal of remedies available to combat violations of civil rights, a goal not invariably inconsistent with conditioning settlement on the merits on a waiver of statutory attorney's fees.

In fact, we believe that a general proscription against negotiated waiver of attorney's fees in exchange for a settlement on the merits would itself impede vindication of civil rights, at least in some cases, by reducing the attractiveness of settlement. Of particular relevance in this regard is our recent decision in *Marek v. Chesny*. In that case, which admittedly was not a class action and therefore did not implicate the court's approval power under Rule 23(e), we specifically considered and rejected the contention that civil rights actions should be treated differently from other civil actions for purposes of settlement. As the Chief Justice explained in his opinion for the Court, the settlement of litigation provides benefits for civil rights plaintiffs as well as defendants and is consistent with the purposes of the Fees Act. To promote both settlement and civil rights, we implicitly acknowledged in *Marek v. Chesny* the possibility of a tradeoff between merits relief and attorney's fees when we upheld the defendant's lump-sum offer to settle the entire civil rights action, including any liability for fees and costs.

In approving the package offer in *Marek v. Chesny* we recognized that a rule prohibiting the comprehensive negotiation of all outstanding issues in a pending case might well preclude the settlement of a substantial number of cases:

> If defendants are not allowed to make lump-sum offers that would, if accepted, represent their total liability, they would understandably be reluctant to make settlement offers. As the Court of Appeals observed, 'many a defendant would be unwilling to make a binding settlement offer on terms that left it exposed to liability for attorney's fees in whatever amount the court might fix on motion of the plaintiff.'

Most defendants are unlikely to settle unless the cost of the predicted judgment, discounted by its probability, plus the transaction costs of further litigation, are greater than the cost of the settlement package. If fee waivers cannot be negotiated, the settlement package must either contain an attorney's fee component of potentially large and typically uncertain magnitude, or else the parties must agree to have the fee fixed by the court. Although either of these alternatives may well be acceptable in many cases, there surely is a significant number in which neither alternative will be as satisfactory as a decision to try the entire case.

The adverse impact of removing attorney's fees and costs from bargaining might be tolerable if the uncertainty introduced into settlement negotiations were small. But it is not. The defendants' potential liability for fees in this kind of litigation can be as significant as, and sometimes even more significant than, their potential liability on the merits.

The consequence of this succession of necessarily judgmental decisions for the ultimate fee award is inescapable: a defendants' liability for his opponent's attorney's fees in a civil rights action cannot be fixed with a sufficient degree of confidence to make defendants indifferent to their exclusion from negotiation. It is therefore not implausible to anticipate that parties to a significant number of civil rights cases will refuse to settle if liability for attorney's fees remains open, thereby forcing more cases to trial, unnecessarily burdening the judicial system, and disserving civil rights litigants. Respondents' own waiver of attorney's fees and costs to obtain settlement of their educational claims is eloquent testimony to the utility of fee waivers in vindicating civil rights claims. We conclude, therefore, that it is not necessary to construe the Fees Act as embodying a general rule prohibiting settlements conditioned on the waiver of fees in order to be faithful to the purposes of that Act.

IV

The question remains whether the District Court abused its discretion in this case by approving a settlement which included a complete fee waiver. As noted earlier, Rule 23(e) wisely requires court approval of the terms of any settlement of a class action. The potential conflict among members of the class—in this case, for example, the possible conflict between children primarily interested in better educational programs and those primarily interested in improved health care—fully justifies the requirement of court approval.

In light of the record, respondents must—to sustain the judgment in their favor—confront the District Court's finding that the extensive structural relief they obtained constituted an adequate *quid pro quo* for their waiver of attorney's fees. The Court of Appeals did not overturn this finding. Indeed, even that court did not suggest that the option of rejecting the entire settlement and requiring the parties either to try the case or to attempt to negotiate a different settlement would have served the interests of justice. Only by making the unsupported assumption that the respondent class was entitled to retain the favorable portions of the settlement while rejecting the fee waiver could the Court of Appeals conclude that the District Court had acted unwisely.

What the outcome of this settlement illustrates is that the Fees Act has given the victims of civil rights violations a powerful weapon that improves their ability to employ counsel, to obtain access to the courts, and thereafter to vindicate their rights by means of settlement or trial. For aught that appears, it was the "coercive" effect of respondents' statutory right to seek a fee award that motivated petitioners' exceptionally generous offer. Whether this weapon might be even more powerful if fee waivers were prohibited in cases like this is another question, but it is in any event a question that Congress is best equipped to answer. Thus far, the Legislature has not commanded that fees be paid whenever a case is settled. Unless it issues such a command, we shall rely primarily on the sound discretion of the district courts to appraise the reasonableness of particular class-action settlements on a case-by-case basis, in the light of all the relevant circumstances. In this case, the District Court did not abuse its discretion in upholding a fee waiver which secured broad injunctive relief, relief greater than that which plaintiffs could reasonably have expected to achieve at trial.

NOTES AND QUESTIONS

1. As private counsel representing civil rights plaintiffs, can you do anything to avoid a forced waiver of fees, as in *Jeff D.*? Consider the following:

   a. In a case seeking only injunctive relief, have the plaintiff sign a retainer agreement which includes a clause requiring the plaintiff to pay a reasonable hourly rate for your services if the case is settled without payment of fees by the defendant;

   b. In a case seeking damages, have the plaintiff sign a retainer agreement which includes a clause requiring the plaintiff to pay counsel a percentage of any award obtained through settlement and, if this does not equal a reasonable hourly rate, a supplemental hourly rate.

2. Absent a "*quid pro quo*" for the fee waiver, is it an abuse of discretion for a court to approve a settlement offer which excludes fees? Should a district court approve a settlement offer which includes a waiver of fees where the defendant has no realistic defense on the merits?

3. Rule 68, FED. R. CIV. PRO., Offer of Judgment, reads as follows:

   (a) At least 14 days before the date set for trial, a party defending against a claim may serve on an opposing party an offer to allow judgment on specific terms, with the costs then accrued. If, within 14 days after being served, the opposing party serves written notice accepting the offer, either party may then file the offer and notice of acceptance, plus proof of service. The clerk must then enter judgment. (b) An unaccepted offer is considered withdrawn, but it does not preclude a later offer. Evidence of an unaccepted offer is not admissible except in a proceeding to determine costs. (c) When one party's liability to another has been determined but the extent of liability remains to be determined by further proceedings, the party held liable may make an offer of judgment. It must be served within a reasonable time—but at least 14 days—before the date set for a hearing to determine the extent of liability. (d) If the judgment that the offeree finally obtains is not more favorable than the unaccepted offer, the offeree must pay the costs incurred after the offer was made.

In *Marek v. Chesny*, 473 U.S. 1 (1985), discussed in *Jeff D.*, the Court held that a valid Rule 68 offer ($100,000), which was more favorable than the judgment ultimately obtained by the plaintiff ($60,000) plus the fees and costs accrued prior to the offer ($32,000), precluded the plaintiff from obtaining an award of fees under § 1988 for work done *after* the offer was made. Thus defendants were liable for only $32,000 in fees and costs, instead of the $171,000 sought at the end of trial. Does *Marek* deter attorneys from bringing good faith actions because of the prospect of losing their entitlement to fees if the settlement offer proves to be more favorable than the ultimate recovery? Did the Court strike the appropriate balance?

Rule 68 does not provide a basis for a prevailing defendant, who made an offer of judgment, to recover costs. *See Delta Air Lines v. August*, 450 U.S. 346 (1981) (Rule 68 is inapplicable in cases in which the defendant obtained a favorable judgment; Rule 54(d), FRCP, gives the court discretion to award costs to such defendant). Where the plaintiff wins, but recovers less than the amount offered, some courts have allowed the defendant to recover post-offer costs, but not fees.

4. Assume you represent the city in a case like *Rivera*, and when the case is filed you promptly determine the plaintiffs have a good chance of establishing liability, but that attorney fees far exceeded any damages likely to be awarded. Further assume the plaintiffs seek only damages. How should you proceed if you want to use Rule 68 to limit liability?

PROBLEM: THIRTEEN

The plaintiff, Ms. Felton, was arrested at the scene of an automobile accident and later charged with driving without liability insurance. After she was brought to the police station, Ms. Felton was subjected to a strip search, including her body cavities.

Ms. Felton filed a § 1983 action in federal court alleging that the police used excessive force in making the arrest and conducted an unreasonable strip search, all in violation of the Fourth Amendment. In addition, she asserted a supplemental (pendent) state tort claim challenging both the arrest and the search.

Prior to trial, the judge dismissed the state tort claim for failure to comply with the notice requirement. At trial the jury returned a verdict in Ms. Felton's favor on the strip search claim, awarding $30,000 in compensatory damages, but ruled in favor of the police on the excessive force claim arising out of the arrest.

1. Is Ms. Felton entitled to fees for all time spent litigating her Fourth Amendment claims? Make the arguments for both plaintiff and defendants.

2. Assume the plaintiff's attorney spent 10 hours on the state tort claim before it was dismissed. Does the court have discretion to award fees for this time?

3. If the plaintiff had prevailed on all claims, including the state tort claim, would she be entitled to fees for 15 hours researching the state claim? Explain.

4. Assume that the defendants, early in the litigation, made a valid Rule 68 offer of judgment "in the amount of $40,000, including costs and fees accrued to the date of the offer." Prior to the date of the offer, the plaintiff incurred fees and costs in the amount of $9,500, and after the date of the offer she incurred an additional $25,000. Based on the jury verdict, should the plaintiff's award of costs and fees be limited to $9,500? Explain.

c. Equitable Relief

Section 1983 expressly provides that persons who deprive others of rights protected by the federal constitution and laws "shall be liable to the party injured in [a] . . . suit in equity." While §§ 1981 and 1982 do not expressly provide for equitable relief, the Supreme Court has made it clear that such relief is available. *See Johnson v. Railway Express Agency*, 421 U.S. 454, 461 (1975) (§ 1981); *Jones v. Alfred H. Mayer Co.*, 392 U.S. 409, 414 n.13 (1968) (§ 1982); *Sullivan v. Little Hunting Park, Inc.*, 396 U.S. 229, 238 (1969) (§ 1982). Lower courts have also held that injunctive relief is available under § 1985(3). *See, e.g., Martinez v. Winner*, 771 F.2d 424, 441 (10th Cir. 1985). The usual rules governing injunctions apply to requests for equitable relief under the civil rights statutes. There are, however, some judicially created limitations on granting equitable relief, particularly in actions under § 1983. These are generally addressed under the doctrines of abstention and equitable restraint. Another limitation, based on standing, is demonstrated by the following case.

CITY OF LOS ANGELES V. LYONS

5. 461 U.S. 95 (1983)

Justice WHITE delivered the opinion of the Court.

The issue here is whether respondent Lyons satisfied the prerequisites for seeking injunctive relief in the Federal District Court.

I

This case began on February 7, 1977, when respondent, Adolph Lyons, filed a complaint for damages, injunction, and declaratory relief in the United States District Court for the Central District of California. The defendants were the City of Los Angeles and four of its police officers. The complaint alleged that on October 6, 1976, at 2 a.m., Lyons was stopped by the defendant officers for a traffic or vehicle code violation and that although Lyons offered no resistance or threat whatsoever, the officers, without provocation or justification, seized Lyons and applied a "chokehold"—either the "bar arm control" hold or the "carotid-artery control" hold or both—rendering him unconscious and causing damage to his larynx. Counts I through IV of the complaint sought damages against the officers and the City. Count V, with which we are principally concerned here, sought a preliminary and permanent injunction against the City barring the use of the control holds. That count alleged that the City's police officers, "pursuant to the authorization, instruction and encouragement of Defendant City of Los Angeles, regularly and routinely apply these choke holds in innumerable situations where they are not threatened by the use of any deadly force whatsoever," that numerous persons have been injured as the result of the application of the chokeholds, that Lyons and others similarly situated are threatened with irreparable injury in the form of bodily injury and loss of life, and that Lyons "justifiably fears that any contact he has with Los Angeles Police officers may result in his being choked and strangled to death without provocation, justification or other legal excuse." Lyons alleged the threatened impairment of rights protected by the First, Fourth, Eighth, and Fourteenth Amendments. Injunctive relief was sought against the use of the control holds "except in situations where the proposed victim of said control reasonably appears to be threatening the immediate use of deadly force." Count VI sought declaratory relief against the City, *i.e.*, a judgment that use of the chokeholds absent the threat of immediate use of deadly force is a *per se* violation of various constitutional rights.

The District Court, by order, granted the City's motion for partial judgment on the pleadings and entered judgment for the City on Counts V and VI. The Court of Appeals reversed the judgment for the City on Counts V and VI, holding over the City's objection that despite our decisions in *O'Shea v. Littleton* and *Rizzo v. Goode* Lyons had standing to seek relief against the application of the chokeholds. We denied certiorari.

On remand, Lyons applied for a preliminary injunction. Lyons pressed only the Count V claim at this point. The District Court found that Lyons had been stopped for a traffic infringement and that without provocation or legal justification the officers involved had applied a "Department-authorized chokehold which resulted in injuries to the plaintiff." The court further found that the department authorizes the use of the holds in situations where no one is threatened by death or grievous bodily harm, that officers are insufficiently trained, that the use of the holds involves a high risk of injury or death as then employed, and that their continued use in situations where neither death nor serious bodily injury is threatened "is unconscionable in a civilized society." The court concluded that such use violated Lyons' substantive due process rights under the Fourteenth Amendment. A preliminary injunction was entered enjoining "the use of both the carotid-artery and bar arm holds under circumstances which do not threaten death or serious bodily injury." An improved training program and regular reporting and record-keeping were also ordered. The Court of Appeals affirmed in a brief *per curiam* opinion stating that the District Court had not abused its discretion in entering a preliminary injunction.

II

Since our grant of certiorari, circumstances pertinent to the case have changed. Originally, Lyons' complaint alleged that at least two deaths had occurred as a result of the application of chokeholds by the police. His first amended complaint alleged that 10 chokehold-related deaths had occurred. By May 1982, there had been five more such deaths. On May 6, 1982, the Chief of Police in Los Angeles prohibited the use of the bar-arm chokehold in any circumstances. A few days later, on May 12, 1982, the Board of Police Commissioners imposed a 6-month moratorium on the use of the carotid-artery chokehold except under circumstances where deadly force is authorized.

III

It goes without saying that those who seek to invoke the jurisdiction of the federal courts must satisfy the threshold requirement imposed by Art. III of the Constitution by alleging an actual case or controversy. Plaintiffs must demonstrate a "personal stake in the outcome" in order to "assure that concrete adverseness which sharpens the presentation of issues" necessary for the proper resolution of constitutional questions. Abstract injury is not enough. The plaintiff must show that he "has sustained or is immediately in danger of sustaining some direct injury" as the result of the challenged official conduct and the injury or threat of injury must be both "real and immediate," not "conjectural" or "hypothetical."

In *O'Shea v. Littleton*, we dealt with a case brought by a class of plaintiffs claiming that they had been subjected to discriminatory enforcement of the criminal law. Among other things, a county magistrate and judge were accused of discriminatory conduct in various respects, such as sentencing members of plaintiff's class more harshly than other defendants. The Court of Appeals reversed the dismissal of the suit by the District Court, ruling that if the allegations were proved, an appropriate injunction could be entered.

We reversed for failure of the complaint to allege a case or controversy. Although it was claimed in that case that particular members of the plaintiff class had actually suffered from the alleged unconstitutional practices, we observed that "[p]ast exposure to illegal conduct does not in itself show a present case or controversy regarding injunctive relief . . . if unaccompanied by any continuing, present adverse effects." Past wrongs were evidence bearing on "whether there is a real and immediate threat of repeated injury." But the prospect of future injury rested "on the likelihood that [plaintiffs] will again be arrested for and charged with violations of the criminal law and will again be subjected to bond proceedings, trial, or sentencing before petitioners." The most that could be said for plaintiffs' standing was "that *if* [plaintiffs] proceed to violate an unchallenged law and *if* they are charged, held to answer, and tried in any proceedings before petitioners, they will be subjected to the discriminatory practices that petitioners are alleged to have followed." We could not find a case or controversy in those circumstances: the threat to the plaintiffs was not "sufficiently real and immediate to show an existing controversy simply because they anticipate violating lawful criminal statutes and being tried for their offenses. . . ." It was to be assumed that "[plaintiffs] will conduct their activities within the law and so avoid prosecution and conviction as well as exposure to the challenged course of conduct said to be followed by petitioners."

We further observed that case-or-controversy considerations "obviously shade into those determining whether the complaint states a sound basis for equitable relief," and went on to hold that even if the complaint presented an existing case or controversy, an adequate basis for equitable relief against petitioners had not been demonstrated:

> [Plaintiffs] have failed, moreover, to establish the basic requisites of the issuance of equitable relief in these circumstances—the likelihood of substantial and immediate irreparable injury, and the inadequacy of remedies at law. We have already canvassed the necessarily conjectural nature of the threatened injury to which [plaintiffs] are allegedly subjected. And if any of the [plaintiffs] are ever prosecuted and face trial, or if they are illegally sentenced, there are available state and federal procedures which could provide relief from the wrongful conduct alleged.

Another relevant decision for present purposes is *Rizzo v. Goode*, a case in which plaintiffs alleged widespread illegal and unconstitutional police conduct aimed at minority citizens and against city residents in general. The Court reiterated the holding in *O'Shea* that past wrongs do not in themselves amount to that real and immediate threat of injury necessary to make out a case or controversy. The claim of injury rested upon "what one of a small, unnamed minority of policemen might do to them in the future because of that unknown policeman's perception" of departmental procedures. This hypothesis was "even more attenuated than those allegations of future injury found insufficient in *O'Shea* to warrant [the] invocation of federal jurisdiction." The Court also held that plaintiffs' showing at trial of a relatively few instances of violations by individual police officers, without any showing of a deliberate policy on behalf of the named defendants, did not provide a basis for equitable relief.

IV

No extension of *O'Shea* and *Rizzo* is necessary to hold that respondent Lyons has failed to demonstrate a case or controversy with the City that would justify the equitable relief sought. Lyons' standing to seek the injunction requested depended on whether he was likely to suffer future injury from the use of the chokeholds by police officers. Count V of the complaint alleged the traffic stop and choking incident five months before. That Lyons may have been illegally choked by the police on October 6, 1976, while presumably affording Lyons standing to claim damages against the individual officers and perhaps against the City, does nothing to establish a real and immediate threat that he would again be stopped for a traffic violation, or for any other offense, by an officer or officers who would illegally choke him into unconsciousness without any provocation or resistance on his part. The additional allegation in the complaint that the police in Los Angeles routinely apply chokeholds in situations where they are not threatened by the use of deadly force falls far short of the allegations that would be necessary to establish a case or controversy between these parties.

In order to establish an actual controversy in this case, Lyons would have had not only to allege that he would have another encounter with the police but also to make the incredible assertion either (1) that *all* police officers in Los Angeles *always* choke any citizen with whom they happen to have an encounter, whether for the purpose of arrest, issuing a citation, or for questioning, or (2) that the City ordered or authorized police officers to act in such manner. Although Count V alleged that the City authorized the use of the control holds in situations where deadly force was not threatened, it did not indicate why Lyons might be realistically threatened by police officers who acted within the strictures of the City's policy. If, for example, chokeholds were authorized to be used only to counter resistance to an arrest by a suspect, or to thwart an effort to escape, any future threat to Lyons from the City's policy or from the conduct of police officers would be no more real than the possibility that he would again have an encounter with the police and that either he would illegally resist arrest or detention or the officers would disobey their instructions and again render him unconscious without any provocation.

First, the Court of Appeals thought that Lyons was more immediately threatened than the plaintiffs in those cases since, according to the Court of Appeals, Lyons need only be stopped for a minor traffic violation to be subject to the strangleholds. But even assuming that Lyons would again be stopped for a traffic or other violation in the reasonably near future, it is untenable to assert, and the complaint made no such allegation, that strangleholds are applied by the Los Angeles police to every citizen who is stopped or arrested regardless of the conduct of the person stopped. We cannot agree that the "odds" that Lyons would not only again be stopped for a traffic violation but would also be subjected to a chokehold without any provocation whatsoever are sufficient to make out a federal case for equitable relief. We note that five months elapsed between October 6, 1976, and the filing of the complaint, yet there was no allegation of further unfortunate encounters between Lyons and the police.

Of course, it may be that among the countless encounters between the police and the citizens of a great city such as Los Angeles, there will be certain instances in which strangleholds will be illegally applied and injury and death unconstitutionally inflicted on the victim. As we have said, however, it is no more than conjecture to suggest that in every instance of a traffic stop, arrest, or other encounter between the police and a citizen, the police will act unconstitutionally and inflict injury without provocation or legal excuse. And it is surely no more than speculation to assert either that Lyons himself will again be involved in one of those unfortunate instances, or that he will be arrested in the future and provoke the use of a chokehold by resisting arrest, attempting to escape, or threatening deadly force or serious bodily injury.

... The City's policy was described as authorizing the use of the strangleholds "under circumstances where no one is threatened with death or grievous bodily harm." That policy was not further described, but the record before the court contained the department's existing policy with respect to the employment of chokeholds. Nothing in that policy, contained in a Police Department manual, suggests that the chokeholds, or other kinds of force for that matter, are authorized absent some resistance or other provocation by the arrestee or other suspect. On the contrary, police officers were instructed to use chokeholds only when lesser degrees of force do not suffice and then only "to gain control of a suspect who is violently resisting the officer or trying to escape."

Our conclusion is that the Court of Appeals failed to heed *O'Shea*, *Rizzo*, and other relevant authority, and that the District Court was quite right in dismissing Count V.

V

Lyons fares no better if it be assumed that his pending damages suit affords him Art. III standing to seek an injunction as a remedy for the claim arising out of the October 1976 events. The equitable remedy is unavailable absent a showing of irreparable injury, a requirement that cannot be met where there is no showing of any real or immediate threat that the plaintiff will be wronged again—a "likelihood of substantial and immediate irreparable injury." The speculative nature of Lyons' claim of future injury requires a finding that this prerequisite of equitable relief has not been fulfilled.

Nor will the injury that Lyons allegedly suffered in 1976 go unrecompensed; for that injury, he has an adequate remedy at law. Contrary to the view of the Court of Appeals, it is not at all "difficult" under our holding "to see how anyone can ever challenge police or similar administrative practices." The legality of the violence to which Lyons claims he was once subjected is at issue in his suit for damages and can be determined there.

Absent a sufficient likelihood that he will again be wronged in a similar way, Lyons is no more entitled to an injunction than any other citizen of Los Angeles; and a federal court may not entertain a claim by any or all citizens who no more than assert that certain practices of law enforcement officers are unconstitutional.

[W]ithholding injunctive relief does not mean that the "federal law will exercise no deterrent effect in these circumstances." If Lyons has suffered an injury barred by the Federal Constitution, he has a remedy for damages under § 1983. Furthermore, those who deliberately deprive a citizen of his constitutional rights risk conviction under the federal criminal laws. [*See* 42 U.S.C. §§ 241 and 242.]

Beyond these considerations the state courts need not impose the same standing or remedial requirements that govern federal-court proceedings. The individual States may permit their courts to use injunctions to oversee the conduct of law enforcement authorities on a continuing basis. But this is not the role of a federal court, absent far more justification than Lyons has proffered in this case.

Justice MARSHALL, with whom Justice BRENNAN, Justice BLACKMUN, and Justice STEVENS join, dissenting.

The District Court found that the city of Los Angeles authorizes its police officers to apply life-threatening chokeholds to citizens who pose no threat of violence, and that respondent, Adolph Lyons, was subjected to such a chokehold. The Court today holds that a federal court is without power to enjoin the enforcement of the city's policy, no matter how flagrantly unconstitutional it may be. Since no one can show that he will be choked in the future, no one—not even a person who, like Lyons, has almost been choked to death—has standing to challenge the continuation of the policy. The city is free to continue the policy indefinitely as long as it is willing to pay damages for the injuries and deaths that result. I dissent from this unprecedented and unwarranted approach to standing.

Although the city instructs its officers that use of a chokehold does not constitute deadly force, since 1975 no less then 16 persons have died following the use of a chokehold by an LAPD police officer. Twelve have been Negro males.[3] The evidence submitted to the District Court established that for many years it has been the official policy of the city to permit police officers to employ chokeholds in a variety of situations where they face no threat of violence. In reported "altercations" between LAPD officers and citizens the chokeholds are used more frequently than any other means of physical restraint. Between February 1975 and July 1980, LAPD officers applied chokeholds on at least 975 occasions, which represented more than three-quarters of the reported altercations.

Although there has been no occasion to determine the precise contours of the city's chokehold policy, the evidence submitted to the District Court provides some indications. LAPD Training Officer Terry Speer testified that an officer is authorized to deploy a chokehold whenever he "*feels* that there's about to be a bodily attack made on him." A training bulletin states that "[c]ontrol holds . . . allow officers to subdue *any* resistance by the suspects." In the proceedings below the city characterized its own policy as authorizing the use of chokeholds "'to gain control of a suspect who is violently resisting the officer *or trying to escape*,'" to "subdue any resistance by the suspects," and to permit an officer, "where . . . resisted, but *not necessarily threatened with serious bodily harm or death*, . . . to subdue a suspect who forcibly resists an officer."

The Court's decision removes an entire class of constitutional violations from the equitable relief powers of a federal court. It immunizes from prospective equitable relief any policy that authorizes persistent deprivations of constitutional rights as long as no individual can establish with substantial certainty that he will be injured, or injured again, in the future. THE CHIEF JUSTICE asked in *Bivens v. Six Unknown Fed. Narcotics Agents* (dissenting opinion), "what would be the judicial response to a police order authorizing 'shoot to kill' with respect to every fugitive"? His answer was that it would be "easy to predict our collective wrath and outrage." We now learn that wrath and outrage cannot be translated into an order to cease the unconstitutional

---

3   Thus in a city where Negro males constitute 9% of the population, they have accounted for 75% of the deaths resulting from the use of chokeholds. In addition to his other allegations, Lyons alleged racial discrimination in violation of the Equal Protection Clause of the Fourteenth Amendment.

practice, but only an award of damages to those who are victimized by the practice and live to sue and the survivors of those who are not so fortunate. Under the view expressed by the majority today, if the police adopt a policy of "shoot to kill," or a policy of shooting 1 out of 10 suspects, the federal courts will be powerless to enjoin its continuation. The federal judicial power is now limited to levying a toll for such a systematic constitutional violation.

NOTES AND QUESTIONS

1. Assume a city ordinance provides for chokeholds, but limits the use to women; would a woman who had been subjected to a chokehold have standing to seek an injunction? What if the ordinance limited the use of chokeholds to black males—would a victim have standing to seek an injunction?

2. Would a federal court be powerless to enjoin a "shoot to kill" policy, as suggested in the dissenting opinion?

3. Would the outcome in *Lyons* have been different if the plaintiff had filed a class action? Explain. Does the decision in *Lyons* foreclose standing to seek a declaratory judgment in a similar situation? *See Robinson v. City of Chicago*, 868 F.2d 959 (7th Cir. 1989) (applying *Lyons* to a request for declaratory relief).

4. If Lyons succeeds in his damage claim and obtains a declaration that the practice or policy is unconstitutional, would this have the practical effect of an injunction? If the city continues to enforce the policy, would an injunction then be available to enforce the declaratory judgment? *See* 28 U.S.C. § 2202 which provides that "[f]urther necessary or proper relief based on a declaratory judgment or decree may be granted . . . against any adverse party whose rights have been determined by such judgment."

5. Would the decision in *Lyons* govern a similar § 1983 action filed in state court?

PROBLEM: FOURTEEN

This appeal involves the constitutionality under the First and Fourteenth Amendments to the Constitution of a city ordinance that prohibits an individual from in any manner opposing, molesting, abusing, or interrupting a policeman in the execution of his duty. An individual who has been arrested several times for violating the ordinance, and who has never been found guilty, challenges its constitutionality as violating his right to freedom of speech.

The relevant ordinance of the City of Houston, Texas, provides:

Section 34-11. Assaulting or interfering with policemen.

(a) It shall be unlawful for any person to assault, strike or in any manner oppose, molest, abuse or interrupt any policeman in the execution of his duty, or any person summoned to aid in making an arrest.

While Houston police officers Kelley and Holtsclaw were making a traffic arrest at the intersection of Westheimer and Whitney streets in Houston, they noticed Charles Jones directing traffic and stopping vehicles, including a city bus, in a heavily travelled lane of traffic on Westheimer. Officer Kelley approached Jones and began speaking with him about his behavior. The testimony about what happened next is conflicting. Raymond Hill[a] testified that, after a short conversation between Officer Kelley and Jones, Jones attempted to leave, but Officer Kelley grabbed him by the shoulder and began yelling at him. Hill further testified that, after Officer Kelley permitted Jones to leave, Kelley chased him, and upon catching him and being joined by his partner, challenged Jones to fight. The district court, however, disregarded this testimony, and found that "Officer Kelley approached Jones and began speaking with him." Such a finding is supported by the record.

At this point, Hill yelled to the policemen, in an admitted attempt to divert their attention from Jones, "Leave him alone. Why don't you pick on somebody your own size?" or words to that effect. According to Officer Kelley's testimony, after Hill yelled to him, Kelley turned towards Hill and asked, "Are you interrupting me in my official capacity as a Houston police officer?" He testified that Hill, who was standing with a crowd of people behind him, put his hands on his hips and replied, "Yes. Why don't you pick on somebody my size?" Officer Kelley then arrested Hill and charged him with violating the ordinance. After a trial in municipal court Hill was found not guilty.

This was not the first time Hill had been charged with violating the ordinance. In 1975, Hill approached Officers Stoffel and Strodman while they were making a traffic arrest. Hill first wrote down the identification numbers on the officers' vehicle, and then walked to within arm's length of one of the officers on the side nearest the officer's revolver. Officer Stoffel asked Hill to move along. Instead of complying, Hill moved closer to the officers, and was then arrested. He was later tried and found not guilty.

In 1977, Hill was standing near the Asylum Bookstore, an adult arcade in which the police suspected illegal activities were in progress. When Hill observed vice squad cars parked nearby, he entered the bookstore and announced over the public address system that police officers were present and that the patrons should be prepared to produce identification. The patrons fled upon hearing the announcement, and Hill was arrested for interfering with the investigation. The case was subsequently dismissed.

---

a   Mr. Hill, who was disturbed by what he perceived to be police harassment of homosexuals, made a practice of deliberately confronting police while making arrests and he intended to continue this conduct.

Finally, in October, 1982, eight months after he was arrested for the incident involving Jones, Hill was arrested for violating the ordinance when he refused to leave the immediate area where two police officers were investigating a car parked with an unknown, unconscious person inside. The charges were later dismissed when the arresting officers failed to appear in Municipal Court.

After hearing testimony from Hill and Officer Kelley, as well as testimony from other individuals who had been arrested under the ordinance and other Houston police officers who have made arrests under the ordinance, the court entered judgment for the City of Houston. The court first found that Hill lacked standing to challenge the constitutionality of the ordinance.

1. On behalf of Hill, construct an argument for reversal of the standing decision.

2. Would it make any difference if, despite Hill's behavior, he had never been arrested? Explain.

3. Can Hill avoid *Lyons* by arguing he suffered continuing injury because of the "chilling effect" on the exercise of his First Amendment rights? Are all First Amendment cases exempt from the holding in *Lyons*? Was Lyons "at risk" while engaged in protected activity?

5. IMMUNITY DEFENSE

Although the text of § 1983 does not mention defenses, the Supreme Court, looking to the common law as it existed in 1871 when § 1983 was enacted, has recognized two types of immunity to shield officials from personal liability. Depending on the task or function being performed when engaged in the challenged conduct, public officials sued for damages in their individual capacity may establish an **absolute immunity** defense. This defense insulates them from having to defend the claim for damages. If not absolute immunity, officials might be entitled to **qualified immunity**, which also insulates them from defending the claim for damages. A qualified immunity is available, however, only where the right asserted by the plaintiff was not "clearly established" at the time of the challenged conduct.

Suits against governmental officials in their **official capacity** are simply another way of pleading actions against the entities of which the officials are agents. *Kentucky v. Graham*, 473 U.S. 159, 165 (1985). Injunctive relief should be sought against the appropriate officers in their official capacity. The immunity doctrines come into play when damages are sought against government officers in their **individual or personal capacity**, *i.e.*, to be paid by the individuals. *See also Hafer v. Melo*, 502 U.S. 21 (1991).

The availability of the immunity defense highlights the importance of the decision in *Owen v. City of Independence, supra* Ch. II, holding that municipalities do not enjoy a "good faith" defense. States and state agencies have a form of immunity in federal court resulting from the

Eleventh Amendment which limits the jurisdiction of the federal courts. Further, states and state agencies are not "persons" for § 1983 purposes.

a.   Absolute Immunity of Government Officials

CLEAVINGER V. SAXNER

474 U.S. 193 (1985)

Justice BLACKMUN delivered the opinion of the Court.

This case presents the issue whether members of a federal prison's Institution Discipline Committee, who hear cases in which inmates are charged with rules infractions, are entitled to absolute, as distinguished from qualified, immunity from personal damages liability for actions violative of the United States Constitution.

II

A. This Court has observed: "Few doctrines were more solidly established at common law than the immunity of judges from liability for damages for acts committed within their judicial jurisdiction." *Pierson v. Ray.* The Court specifically has pronounced and followed this doctrine of the common law for more than a century. In *Bradley v. Fisher*, it ruled that a federal judge may not be held accountable in damages for a judicial act taken within his court's jurisdiction. Such immunity applies, "however erroneous the act may have been, and however injurious in its consequences it may have proved to the plaintiff. . . Nor can this exemption of the judges from civil liability be affected by the motives with which their judicial acts are performed." In *Pierson v. Ray*, the Court held that absolute immunity shielded a municipal judge who was sued for damages under 42 U.S.C. § 1983 by clergymen who alleged that he had convicted them unconstitutionally for a peaceful protest against racial segregation. The Court stressed that such immunity was essential to protect the integrity of the judicial process. And in *Stump v. Sparkman*, the Court once again enunciated this principle, despite any "informality with which [the judge] proceeded," and despite any *ex parte* feature of the proceeding.

With this judicial immunity firmly established, the Court has extended absolute immunity to certain others who perform functions closely associated with the judicial process. The federal hearing examiner and administrative law judge have been afforded absolute immunity. "There can be little doubt that the role of a modern federal hearing examiner or administrative law judge . . . is 'functionally comparable' to that of a judge." *Butz v. Economou.* Full immunity also has been given to federal and state prosecutors. *Imbler v. Pachtman.* The same is true for witnesses, including police officers, who testify in judicial proceedings. Witnesses are "integral parts of the judicial process" and, accordingly, are shielded by absolute immunity. *Briscoe v.*

LaHue. And the Court has noted the adoption in this country of the principle of immunity for grand jurors. *See Imbler v. Pachtman.*

Although this Court has not decided whether state parole officials enjoy absolute immunity as a matter of federal law, *see Martinez v. California*, federal appellate courts have so held.

B. The Court has extended absolute immunity to the President when damages liability is predicated on his official act. *Nixon v. Fitzgerald.* "For executive officials in general, however, our cases make plain that qualified immunity represents the norm." In any event, "federal officials who seek absolute exemption from personal liability for unconstitutional conduct must bear the burden of showing that public policy requires an exemption of that scope."[a]

C. The Court has said that "in general our cases have followed a 'functional' approach to immunity law. . . . [Our] cases clearly indicate that immunity analysis rests on functional categories, not on the status of the defendant." Absolute immunity flows not from rank or title or "location within the Government," but from the nature of the responsibilities of the individual official. And in *Butz* the Court mentioned the following factors, among others, as characteristic of the judicial process and to be considered in determining absolute as contrasted with qualified immunity: (a) the need to assure that the individual can perform his functions without harassment or intimidation; (b) the presence of safeguards that reduce the need for private damages actions as a means of controlling unconstitutional conduct; (c) insulation from political influence; (d) the importance of precedent; (e) the adversary nature of the process; and (f) the correctability of error on appeal.

III

We turn to the application of these principles to the facts of the present case.

When we evaluate the claim of immunity for the committee members, we bear in mind that immunity status is for the benefit of the public as well as for the individual concerned. The committee members, in a sense, do perform an adjudicatory function in that they determine whether the accused inmate is guilty or innocent of the charge leveled against him; in that they hear testimony and receive documentary evidence; in that they evaluate credibility and weigh evidence; and in that they render a decision. We recognize, too, the presence of some societal importance in this dispute-resolution function. The administration of a prison is a difficult undertaking at best, for it concerns persons many of whom have demonstrated a proclivity for antisocial, criminal, and violent conduct. We also acknowledge that many inmates do not refrain from harassment and intimidation. The number of nonmeritorious prisoners' cases that come

---

[a] In a case raising a related issue, *Clinton v. Jones*, 520 U.S. 681 (1997), the Court rejected the argument that the Constitution affords the President temporary immunity in a civil action seeking damages for conduct (alleged sexual harassment of a government employee while he was governor of Arkansas) that occurred before he took office. President Clinton sought, on immunity grounds, an order dismissing the case and tolling the statute of limitations until he is no longer President. While the trial judge denied the motion to dismiss and ruled that discovery could go forward, she ordered any trial stayed until the end of Clinton's presidency. The Court held there is no constitutionally-required temporary immunity from such civil actions and deferral of the case until after the President leaves office was an abuse of discretion. However, the "high respect that is owed to the office of the Chief Executive . . . should inform the conduct of the entire proceeding, including the timing and scope of discovery."

to this Court's notice is evidence of this. Tension between prison officials and inmates has been described as "unremitting. . . . Retaliation is much more than a theoretical possibility." And we do not underestimate the fact, stressed by petitioners, that committee members usually are persons of modest means and, if they are usable and unprotected, perhaps would be disinclined to serve on a discipline committee.

We conclude, nonetheless, that these concerns, to the extent they are well grounded, are overstated in the context of constitutional violations. We do not perceive the discipline committee's function as a "classic" adjudicatory one, as petitioners would describe it. Surely, the members of the committee, unlike a federal or state judge, are not "independent"; to say that they are is to ignore reality. They are not professional hearing officers, as are administrative law judges. They are, instead, prison officials, albeit no longer of the rank and file, temporarily diverted from their usual duties. They are employees of the Bureau of Prisons and they are the direct subordinates of the warden who reviews their decision. They work with the fellow employee who lodges the charge against the inmate upon whom they sit in judgment. The credibility determination they make often is one between a co-worker and an inmate. They thus are under obvious pressure to resolve a disciplinary dispute in favor of the institution and their fellow employee. It is the old situational problem of the relationship between the keeper and the kept, a relationship that hardly is conducive to a truly adjudicatory performance.

Neither do we equate this discipline committee membership to service upon a traditional parole board. The board is a "neutral and detached" hearing body. The parole board member has been described as an impartial professional serving essentially "'as an arm of the sentencing judge.'" And in the penalty context, the parole board is constitutionally required to provide greater due process protection than is the institution discipline committee.

We relate this committee membership, instead, to the school board service the Court had under consideration in *Wood v. Strickland*. The school board members were to function as "adjudicators in the school disciplinary process," and they were to "judge whether there have been violations of school regulations and, if so, the appropriate sanction for the violations." Despite the board's adjudicative function, the Court concluded that the board members were to be protected by only qualified immunity. After noting the suggestion of the presence of a deterrence-from-service factor, the Court concluded "that absolute immunity would not be justified since it would not sufficiently increase the ability of school officials to exercise their discretion in a forthright manner to warrant the absence of a remedy for students subjected to intentional or otherwise inexcusable deprivations."

Petitioners assert with some vigor that procedural formality is not a prerequisite for absolute immunity. They refer to well-known summary and *ex parte* proceedings, such as the issuance of search warrants and temporary restraining orders, and the setting of bail. And they sound a note of practicality by stating that recasting prison disciplinary tribunals in the mold of formal administrative bodies would be inimical to the needs of prison discipline and security. It is said that committee procedures fully comply with, and indeed exceed, what [due process] requires, that they are sufficiently "judicial" to qualify for absolute immunity, and that [decisions establishing due process requirements] "would be undone" as a practical matter if absolute immunity were not afforded. In any event, it is asserted, committee proceedings contain ample safeguards to ensure the avoidance or correction of constitutional errors. Among these are the qualifications for committee service; prior notice to the inmate; representation by a staff member; the right to present certain evidence at the hearing; the right to be present; the requirement for a detailed record; the availability of administrative review at three levels (demonstrated by the relief obtained on review by these respondents at the first two levels); and the availability of ultimate review in federal court under 28 U.S.C. § 2241. Finally, it is said that qualified immunity would provide insufficient protection for committee members.

We are not persuaded. To be sure, the line between absolute immunity and qualified immunity often is not an easy one to perceive and structure. That determination in this case, however, is not difficult, and we readily conclude that these committee members fall on the qualified-immunity side of the line.

Under the Bureau's disciplinary policy in effect at the time of respondents' hearings, few of the procedural safeguards contained in the Administrative Procedure Act under consideration in *Butz* were present. The prisoner was to be afforded neither a lawyer nor an independent staff representative. There was no right to compel the attendance of witnesses or to cross-examine. There was no right to discovery. There was no cognizable burden of proof. No verbatim transcript was afforded. Information presented often was hearsay or self-serving. The committee members were not truly independent. In sum, the members had no identification with the judicial process of the kind and depth that has occasioned absolute immunity.

Qualified immunity, however, is available to these committee members. That, we conclude, is the proper point at which to effect the balance between the opposing considerations.

NOTES AND QUESTIONS

1. What justifications(s) does the Court suggest for absolute immunity and what type of "functions" trigger its application?

2. Closely review the factors the Court cited in determining whether absolute or only qualified immunity applies. As the Court explains, the government official carries the burden to justify the immunity defense, which is treated as an affirmative defense under Rule 8(c), FRCP, that should be raised in the answer with a subsequent motion for summary judgment to determine its validity.

3. Is there a correlation between preclusion and judicial immunity, *i.e.*, should hearing officers whose decisions are given preclusive effect by the courts enjoy absolute immunity? Would a decision of the prison discipline committee in *Cleavenger* be given preclusive effect in a subsequent § 1983 action? Review *Elliott, supra* Ch. II. Compare the factors relevant to the preclusion determination with those assessed in determining absolute immunity.

4. **Legislative Functions:** State legislators enjoy an absolute immunity, from both damages and injunctive relief, when performing their legislative functions. *Supreme Court of Virginia v. Consumers Union*, 446 U.S. 718, 732-33 (1980). In *Bogan v. Scott-Harris*, 523 U.S. 44 (1998), the Court extended absolute legislative immunity to the legislative acts of local legislators, as well as the mayor, who introduced the budget eliminating the plaintiff's position and signed the ordinance into law. The plaintiff alleged that the elimination of her position was motivated by racial animus and a desire to retaliate against her for exercising first amendment rights.

5. **Prosecutorial Functions:** The Court, in *Imbler v. Pachtman*, 424 U.S. 409 (1976), held that prosecutors are absolutely immune from liability in § 1983 cases challenging prosecutorial actions that are "intimately associated with the judicial phase of the criminal process," *id.* at 430. The significance of function, rather than title, is demonstrated by *Burns v. Reed*, 500 U.S. 478 (1991), in which a prosecutor gave legal advice to the police regarding the use of hypnosis and later, during a probable cause hearing to obtain a search warrant, presented testimony of a confession without mentioning the use of hypnosis. Because it is so "intimately associated with the judicial phase of the criminal process," the prosecutor's conduct during the probable cause hearing is protected by absolute immunity, but his role in advising the police is part of the investigative phase of a criminal case, not "intimately associated with the judicial phase," and protected only by the qualified immunity.

   Relying upon *Burns*, the Court in *Buckley v. Fitzsimmons*, 509 U.S. 259 (1993), rejected the prosecutors' claim to absolute immunity as to two separate functions. First, the plaintiff alleged that the prosecutors conspired, before the grand jury was impaneled, to manufacture false evidence linking his boot with the boot print left on the front door by the murderer. Because the prosecutors at this point were attempting to establish probable cause, they were acting as detectives rather than advocates and, therefore, entitled to only a qualified immunity. Second, the plaintiff alleged that during the public announcement of the indictment the prosecutor made false statements and released mug shots to the press, resulting in the denial of a fair trial. Here too the Court rejected the absolute immunity defense, indicating that "[c]omments to the media have no functional tie to the judicial process just because they are made by a prosecutor." While press conferences may be an integral part of a prosecutor's job and serve a vital public function, they are not within the prosecutor's role as advocate.

   Finally, in *Van de Kamp v. Goldstein*, 555 U.S. 335 (2009), the Court addressed the circumstances under which even administrative tasks may fall within the scope of absolute prosecutorial immunity. Goldstein, after a successful habeas corpus action resulting in his release from prison, brought a § 1983 action alleging that the prosecution's failure to disclose impeachment material in his criminal trial resulted from a failure properly to train prosecutors, a failure properly to supervise prosecutors, and a failure to establish an information system containing potential impeachment material about informants. Rejecting an automatic exception for management tasks, the Court held that the management tasks at issue in this case concern how and when to make impeachment information available at trial and, therefore, are directly connected with a "prosecutor's basic trial advocacy duties." *Id.* at 346. The Court was reluctant to allow a § 1983 plaintiff to avoid absolute immunity by suing supervisors, rather than the actual trial prosecutor, and casting the claim as a failure of training or supervision. Similarly, the Court determined that subjecting prosecutors to liability based on the failure to adopt an effective information system would undermine the necessary independence and integrity of the prosecutorial decisionmaking process because such a claim requires review of the office's legal judgments that are "intimately associated with the judicial phase of the criminal process." *Imbler,* 424 U.S. at 430. In short, the defendants "are entitled to absolute immunity in respect to Goldstein's claims that their supervision, training, or information-system management was constitutionally inadequate." *Van de Kamp,* 555 U.S. at 349.

FORRESTER V. WHITE
484 U.S. 219 (1988)

Justice O'CONNOR delivered the opinion of the Court.

This case requires us to decide whether a state-court judge has absolute immunity from a suit for damages under 42 U.S.C. § 1983 for his decision to dismiss a subordinate court employee. The employee, who had been a probation officer, alleged that she was demoted and discharged on account of her sex, in violation of the Equal Protection Clause of the Fourteenth Amendment. We conclude that the judge's decisions were not judicial acts for which he should be held absolutely immune.

I

Respondent Howard Lee White served as Circuit Judge of the Seventh Judicial Circuit of the State of Illinois and Presiding Judge of the Circuit Court in Jersey County. Under Illinois law, Judge White had the authority to hire adult probation officers, who were removable in his discretion. In addition, as designee of the Chief Judge of the Seventh Judicial Circuit, Judge White had the authority to appoint juvenile probation officers to serve at his pleasure.

In April 1977, Judge White hired petitioner Cynthia A. Forrester as an adult and juvenile probation officer. Forrester prepared presentence reports for Judge White in adult offender cases, and recommendations for disposition and placement in juvenile cases. She also supervised persons on probation and recommended revocation when necessary. In July 1979, Judge White appointed Forrester as Project Supervisor of the Jersey County Juvenile Court Intake and Referral Services Project, a position that carried increased supervisory responsibilities. Judge

White demoted Forrester to a nonsupervisory position in the summer of 1980. He discharged her on October 1, 1980.

Forrester alleged violations of Title VII of the Civil Rights Act of 1964, 42 U.S.C. § 2000e *et seq.*, and 42 U.S.C. § 1983. A jury found that Judge White had discriminated against Forrester on account of her sex, in violation of the Equal Protection Clause of the Fourteenth Amendment. The jury awarded her $81,818.80 in compensatory damages under § 1983. Forrester's other claims were dismissed in the course of the law suit.

II

Suits for monetary damages are meant to compensate the victims of wrongful actions and to discourage conduct that may result in liability. Special problems arise, however, when government officials are exposed to liability for damages. To the extent that the threat of liability encourages these officials to carry out their duties in a lawful and appropriate manner, and to pay their victims when they do not, it accomplishes exactly what it should. By its nature, however, the threat of liability can create perverse incentives that operate to *inhibit* officials in the proper performance of their duties. In many contexts, government officials are expected to make decisions that are impartial or imaginative, and that above all are informed by considerations other than the personal interests of the decisionmaker. Because government officials are engaged by definition in governing, their decisions will often have adverse effects on other persons. When officials are threatened with personal liability for acts taken pursuant to their official duties, they may well be induced to act with an excess of caution or otherwise to skew their decisions in ways that result in less than full fidelity to the objective and independent criteria that ought to guide their conduct. In this way, exposing government officials to the same legal hazards faced by other citizens may detract from the rule of law instead of contributing to it.

III

As a class, judges have long enjoyed a comparatively sweeping form of immunity, though one not perfectly well-defined. The purposes served by judicial immunity from liability in damages have been variously described. In [earlier decisions] the Court emphasized that the nature of the adjudicative function requires a judge frequently to disappoint some of the most intense and ungovernable desires that people can have. If judges were personally liable for erroneous decisions, the resulting avalanche of suits, most of them frivolous but vexatious, would provide powerful incentives for judges to avoid rendering decisions likely to provoke such suits. The resulting timidity would be hard to detect or control, and it would manifestly detract from independent and impartial adjudication. Nor are suits against judges the only available means through which litigants can protect themselves from the consequences of judicial error. Most judicial mistakes or wrongs are open to correction through ordinary mechanisms of review, which are largely free of the harmful side-effects inevitably associated with exposing judges to personal liability.

When applied to the paradigmatic judicial acts involved in resolving disputes between parties who have invoked the jurisdiction of a court, the doctrine of absolute judicial immunity has not been particularly controversial. Difficulties have arisen primarily in attempting to draw the line between truly judicial acts, for which immunity is appropriate, and acts that simply happen to have been done by judges. Here, as in other contexts, immunity is justified and defined by the *functions* it protects and serves, not by the person to whom it attaches.

This Court has never undertaken to articulate a precise and general definition of the class of acts entitled to immunity. The decided cases, however, suggest an intelligible distinction between judicial acts and the administrative, legislative, or executive functions that judges may on occasion be assigned by law to perform.

IV

In the case before us, we think it clear that Judge White was acting in an administrative capacity when he demoted and discharged Forrester. Those acts—like many others involved in supervising court employees and overseeing the efficient operation of a court—may have been quite important in providing the necessary conditions of a sound adjudicative system. The decisions at issue, however, were not themselves judicial or adjudicative. As Judge Posner pointed out below, a judge who hires or fires a probation officer cannot meaningfully be distinguished from a district attorney who hires and fires assistant district attorneys, or indeed from any other executive branch official who is responsible for making such employment decisions. Such decisions, like personnel decisions made by judges, are often crucial to the efficient operation of public institutions (some of which are at least as important as the courts), yet no one suggests that they give rise to absolute immunity from liability in damages under § 1983.

The majority below thought that the threat of vexatious lawsuits by disgruntled ex-employees could interfere with the quality of a judge's decisions:

> The evil to be avoided is the following: A judge loses confidence in his probation officer, but hesitates to fire him because of the threat of litigation. He then retains the officer, in which case the parties appearing before the court are the victims, because the quality of the judge's decision-making will decline.

There is considerable force in this analysis, but it in no way serves to distinguish judges from other public officials who hire and fire subordinates. Indeed, to the extent that a judge is less free than most executive branch officials to delegate decision-making authority to subordinates, there may be somewhat less reason to cloak judges with absolute immunity from such suits than there would be to protect such other officials. This does not imply that qualified immunity, like that available to executive branch officials who make similar discretionary decisions, is unavailable to judges for their employment decisions. Absolute immunity, however, is "strong medicine, justified only when the danger of [officials' being] deflect[ed] from the effective performance of their duties] is very great." The danger here is not great enough. Nor do we think it significant that, under Illinois law, only a judge can hire or fire probation officers. To conclude that, because a judge acts within the scope of his authority, such employment decisions are brought within the court's "jurisdiction," or converted into "judicial acts," would lift form above substance.

We conclude that Judge White was not entitled to absolute immunity for his decisions to demote and discharge Forrester. In so holding, we do not decide whether Judge White is entitled to a new trial, or whether he may be able to claim a qualified immunity for the acts complained of in Forrester's suit.

NOTES AND QUESTIONS

1. Is a state court judge, who refuses to issue arrest warrants against whites when the victims are black, absolutely immune from damages in an action brought by the black victim of a crime committed by a white person? Would *Lyons, supra* Ch. II, foreclose an action to enjoin the judge engaged in this practice?

   In *Stump v. Sparkman*, 435 U.S. 349 (1978), the judge approved an *ex parte* petition brought by a mother to authorize performance of a tubal ligation on her minor daughter. The Court concluded that Judge Stump was absolutely immune from damages in an action by the daughter and her husband because under Indiana law he had the power to entertain and act on such petitions.

   The scope of the absolute immunity enjoyed by judicial officers was emphasized by the Court in a per curiam opinion in *Mireles v. Waco*, 502 U.S. 9 (1991), holding that a state judge who ordered police officers "to forcibly and with excessive force seize and bring plaintiff [a public defender] into his courtroom" acted in his judicial capacity and is therefore absolutely immune from damages under § 1983. Assuming it is a normal function of a judge to order persons to appear in court, should a judge be insulated when he orders use of excessive force?

2. In *Pulliam v. Allen*, 466 U.S. 522 (1984), the Court held that a magistrate's practice of imposing bail on persons arrested for nonjailable offenses under Virginia law and of incarcerating those persons if they could not meet the bail was unconstitutional. Relying on the common law and the text of the fee provision, the Court rejected the judge's claim that the injunction and the award of attorney's fees against her should have been barred by principles of judicial immunity.

   In response to the *Pulliam* decision, Congress enacted Title III of the Federal Courts Improvement Act of 1996, which amended § 1983 to generally preclude injunctive relief against a judicial officer in an action challenging "judicial capacity" acts or omissions, and § 1988(b), precluding liability for fees and costs for "judicial capacity" actions, unless clearly in excess of the court's jurisdiction.

3. **Derivative Immunity:** The Court in *Antoine v. Byers & Anderson, Inc.*, 509 U.S. 429 (1993), held that a court reporter, sued for damages resulting from her delay in preparing the transcript of a federal criminal trial, is protected only by qualified immunity. Applying the functional approach, the Court noted that court reporters do not exercise the kind of discretion and judgment protected by judicial immunity. Further, there is no common law tradition of protection for court reporters.

Assume a state police officer presents erroneous information to a judge for the purpose of obtaining an arrest warrant. Does the officer enjoy absolute immunity in a § 1983 damage action, brought by a person arrested pursuant to the warrant, alleging that the officer in applying for the warrant violated Fourth and Fourteenth Amendment rights?

In *Malley v. Briggs*, 475 U.S. 335 (1986), the Court found that no such immunity existed at common law and rejected the analogy to a prosecutor, stating:

> Even were we to overlook the fact that petitioner is inviting us to expand what was a qualified immunity at common law into an absolute immunity, we would find his analogy between himself and a prosecutor untenable. We have interpreted § 1983 to give absolute immunity to functions "intimately associated with the *judicial* phase of the criminal process," *Imbler*, not from an exaggerated esteem for those who perform these functions, and certainly not from a desire to shield abuses of office, but because any lesser degree of immunity could impair the judicial process itself. We intend no disrespect to the officer applying for a warrant by observing that his action, while a vital part of the administration of criminal justice, is further removed from the judicial phase of criminal proceedings than the act of a prosecutor in seeking an indictment. Furthermore, petitioner's analogy, while it has some force, does not take account of the fact that the prosecutor's act in seeking an indictment is but the first step in the process of seeking a conviction. Exposing the prosecutor to liability for the initial phase of his prosecutorial work could interfere with his exercise of independent judgment at every phase of his work, since the prosecutor might come to see later decisions in terms of their effect on his potential liability. Thus, we shield the prosecutor seeking an indictment because any lesser immunity could impair the performance of a central actor in the judicial process.
>
> In the case of the officer applying for a warrant, it is our judgment that the judicial process will on the whole benefit from a rule of qualified rather than absolute immunity. We do not believe that the *Harlow* standard, which gives ample room for mistaken judgments, will frequently deter an officer from submitting an affidavit when probable cause to make an arrest is present. True, an officer who knows that objectively unreasonable decisions will be actionable may be motivated to reflect, before submitting a request for a warrant, whether he has a reasonable basis for believing that his affidavit establishes probable cause. But such reflection is desirable, because it reduces the likelihood that the officer's request for a warrant will be premature. Premature requests for warrants are at

best a waste of judicial resources; at worst, they lead to premature arrests, which may injure the innocent or, by giving the basis for a suppression motion, benefit the guilty.

A similar issue was addressed in *Kalina v. Fletcher*, 522 U.S. 118 (1997), where the Court held that the activities of a prosecutor in preparing and filing an information and a motion for an arrest warrant were protected by absolute immunity. However, in preparing a sworn certificate designed to establish probable cause for an arrest warrant, the prosecutor was acting as a complaining witness not protected by absolute immunity. The plaintiff alleged that the prosecutor made false statements in the certificate.

REHBERG V. PAULK
566 U.S. 356 (2012)

Justice ALITO delivered the opinion of the Court.

This case requires us to decide whether a "complaining witness" in a grand jury proceeding is entitled to the same immunity in an action under 42 U.S.C. § 1983 as a witness who testifies at trial. We see no sound reason to draw a distinction for this purpose between grand jury and trial witnesses.

I

Petitioner Charles Rehberg, a certified public accountant, sent anonymous faxes to several recipients, including the management of a hospital in Albany, Georgia, criticizing the hospital's management and activities. In response, the local district attorney's office, with the assistance of its chief investigator, respondent James Paulk, launched a criminal investigation of petitioner, allegedly as a favor to the hospital's leadership.

Respondent testified before a grand jury, and petitioner was then indicted for aggravated assault, burglary, and six counts of making harassing telephone calls. The indictment charged that petitioner had assaulted a hospital physician, Dr. James Hotz, after unlawfully entering the doctor's home. Petitioner challenged the sufficiency of the indictment, and it was dismissed. A few months later, respondent returned to the grand jury, and petitioner was indicted again, this time for assaulting Dr. Hotz and for making harassing phone calls. Petitioner challenged the sufficiency of this second indictment . . . . Again, the indictment was dismissed. While the second indictment was still pending, respondent appeared before a grand jury for a third time, and yet another indictment was returned. Petitioner was charged with assault and making harassing phone calls. This final indictment was ultimately dismissed as well.

Petitioner then brought this action against respondent under § 1983. Petitioner alleged that respondent conspired to present and did present false testimony to the grand jury. Respondent moved to dismiss, arguing, among other things, that he was entitled to absolute immunity for his grand jury testimony.

II

Recognizing that "Congress intended [§ 1983] to be construed in the light of common-law principles," the Court has looked to the common law for guidance in determining the scope of the immunities available in a § 1983 action. We take what has been termed a "functional approach." We consult the common law to identify those governmental functions that were historically viewed as so important and vulnerable to interference by means of litigation that some form of absolute immunity from civil liability was needed to ensure that they are performed "'with independence and without fear of consequences. . . .'"

While the Court has looked to the common law in determining the scope of the absolute immunity available under § 1983, the Court has not suggested that § 1983 is simply a federalized amalgamation of pre-existing common-law claims, an all-in-one federal claim encompassing the torts of assault, trespass, false arrest, defamation, malicious prosecution, and more. The new federal claim created by § 1983 differs in important ways from those pre-existing torts. It is broader in that it reaches constitutional and statutory violations that do not correspond to any previously known tort. Thus, both the scope of the new tort and the scope of the absolute immunity available in § 1983 actions differ in some respects from the common law.

III

At common law, trial witnesses enjoyed a limited form of absolute immunity for statements made in the course of a judicial proceeding: They had complete immunity against slander and libel claims, even if it was alleged that the statements in question were maliciously false.

In *Briscoe v. Lahue*, 460 U.S. 325 (1983), however, this Court held that the immunity of a trial witness sued under § 1983 is broader: In such a case, a trial witness has absolute immunity with respect to *any* claim based on the witness' testimony. When a witness is sued because of his testimony, the Court wrote, "'the claims of the individual must yield to the dictates of public policy.'" Without absolute immunity for witnesses, the Court concluded, the truth-seeking process at trial would be impaired. Witnesses "might be reluctant to come forward to testify," and even if a witness took the stand, the witness "might be inclined to shade his testimony in favor of the potential plaintiff" for "fear of subsequent liability."

The factors that justify absolute immunity for trial witnesses apply with equal force to grand jury witnesses. In both contexts, a witness' fear of retaliatory litigation may deprive the tribunal of critical evidence. And in neither context is the deterrent of potential civil liability needed to prevent perjurious testimony. In *Briscoe*, the Court concluded that the possibility of civil liability was not needed to deter false testimony at trial because other sanctions—chiefly prosecution for perjury—provided a sufficient deterrent. Since perjury before a grand jury, like perjury at trial, is a serious criminal offense, there is no reason to think that this deterrent is any less effective in preventing false grand jury testimony.

Neither is there any reason to distinguish law enforcement witnesses from lay witnesses. In *Briscoe,* it was argued that absolute immunity was not needed for police-officer witnesses, but the Court refused to draw that distinction. The *Briscoe* Court rebuffed two arguments for distinguishing between law enforcement witnesses and lay witnesses for immunity purposes: first, that absolute immunity is not needed for law enforcement witnesses because they are less likely to be intimidated by the threat of suit and, second, that such witnesses should not be shielded by absolute immunity because false testimony by a police officer is likely to be more damaging than false testimony by a lay witness. The Court observed that there are other factors not applicable to lay witnesses that weigh in favor of extending absolute immunity to police officer witnesses.

First, police officers testify with some frequency. If police officer witnesses were routinely forced to defend against claims based on their testimony, their "'energy and attention would be diverted from the pressing duty of enforcing the criminal law.'" Second, a police officer witness' potential liability, if conditioned on the exoneration of the accused, could influence decisions on appeal and collateral relief. Needless to say, such decisions should not be influenced by the likelihood of a subsequent civil rights action. But the possibility that a decision favorable to the accused might subject a police officer witness to liability would create the "'risk of injecting extraneous concerns'" into appellate review and postconviction proceedings. In addition, law enforcement witnesses face the possibility of sanctions not applicable to lay witnesses, namely, loss of their jobs and other employment-related sanctions.

For these reasons, we conclude that grand jury witnesses should enjoy the same immunity as witnesses at trial. This means that a grand jury witness has absolute immunity from any § 1983 claim based on the witness' testimony. In addition, as the Court of Appeals held, this rule may not be circumvented by claiming that a grand jury witness conspired to present false testimony or by using evidence of the witness' testimony to support any other § 1983 claim concerning the initiation or maintenance of a prosecution. Were it otherwise, "a criminal defendant turned civil plaintiff could simply reframe a claim to attack the preparation instead of the absolutely immune actions themselves." In the vast majority of cases involving a claim against a grand jury witness, the witness and the prosecutor conducting the investigation engage in preparatory activity, such as a preliminary discussion in which the witness relates the substance of his intended testimony. We decline to endorse a rule of absolute immunity that is so easily frustrated.

IV

Petitioner's main argument is that our cases, chiefly *Malley* and *Kalina,* already establish that a "complaining witness" is not shielded by absolute immunity. In those cases, law enforcement officials who submitted affidavits in support of applications for arrest warrants were denied absolute immunity because they "performed the function of a complaining witness." Relying on these cases, petitioner contends that certain grand jury witnesses—namely, those who qualify as "complaining witnesses"—are not entitled to absolute immunity. Petitioner's argument is based on a fundamental misunderstanding of the distinctive function played by a "complaining witness" during the period when § 1983's predecessor was enacted.

At that time, the term "complaining witness" was used to refer to a party [a private citizen] who procured an arrest and initiated a criminal prosecution. A "complaining witness" might not actually ever testify, and thus the term "'witness' in 'complaining witness' is misleading." . . . testifying, whether before a grand jury or at trial, was not the distinctive function performed by a complaining witness. It is clear—and petitioner does not contend otherwise—that a complaining witness cannot be held liable for perjurious *trial* testimony. And there is no more reason why a complaining witness should be subject to liability for testimony before a grand jury.

Once the distinctive function performed by a "complaining witness" is understood, it is apparent that a law enforcement officer who testifies before a grand jury is not at all comparable to a "complaining witness." By testifying before a grand jury, a law enforcement officer does not perform the function of applying for an arrest warrant; nor does such an officer make the critical decision to initiate a prosecution. It is of course true that a detective or case agent who has performed or supervised most of the investigative work in a case may serve as an important witness in the grand jury proceeding and may very much want the grand jury to return an indictment. But such a witness, unlike a complaining witness at common law, does not make the decision to press criminal charges.

Instead, it is almost always a prosecutor who is responsible for the decision to present a case to a grand jury, and in many jurisdictions, even if an indictment is handed up, a prosecution cannot proceed unless the prosecutor signs the indictment. It would thus be anomalous to permit a police officer who testifies before a grand jury to be sued for maliciously procuring an unjust prosecution when it is the prosecutor, who is shielded by absolute immunity, who is actually responsible for the decision to prosecute.

Petitioner contends that the deterrent effect of civil liability is more needed in the grand jury context because trial witnesses are exposed to cross-examination, which is designed to expose perjury. This argument overlooks the fact that a critical grand jury witness is likely to testify again at trial and may be cross-examined at that time. But in any event, the force of petitioner's argument is more than offset by a special problem that would be created by allowing civil actions against grand jury witnesses—subversion of grand jury secrecy.

"'We consistently have recognized that the proper functioning of our grand jury system depends upon the secrecy of grand jury proceedings.'" Allowing § 1983 actions against grand jury witnesses would compromise this vital secrecy. If the testimony of witnesses before a grand jury could provide the basis for, or could be used as evidence supporting, a § 1983 claim, the identities of grand jury witnesses could be discovered by filing a § 1983 action and moving for the disclosure of the transcript of grand jury proceedings. Especially in cases involving violent criminal organizations or other subjects who might retaliate against adverse grand jury witnesses, the threat of such disclosure might seriously undermine the grand jury process.

For these reasons, we hold that a grand jury witness is entitled to the same immunity as a trial witness.

1. Why did the Court unanimously reject the historical argument that complaining witnesses did not enjoy absolute immunity at common law? Can *Kalina* be distinguished?

1. Did the Court properly weigh the competing policy arguments? Doesn't the decision leave plaintiffs, like Rehberg, without a remedy against clear, repetitive abuse of investigatory and prosecutorial power? Isn't there a compelling public interest in deterring malicious prosecution?

Problem: Fifteen

Assume a state court judge appoints private attorneys, on a case-by-case basis, to represent indigent defendants in criminal cases and the attorneys are paid an hourly rate for their services. Further assume the judge refuses to appoint female attorneys.

1. Is the judge absolutely immune from injunctive relief and damages in a sex discrimination action brought by a female attorney?

2. Is a judge's decision not to appoint counsel, on grounds that the accused is not indigent, shielded by absolute immunity?

b.   Qualified Immunity of Government Officials

HARLOW V. FITZGERALD
457 u.s. 800 (1982)

Justice POWELL delivered the opinion of the Court.

The issue in this case is the scope of the immunity available to the senior aides and advisors of the President of the United States in a suit for damages based upon their official acts.

I

In this suit for civil damages petitioners Harlow and Butterfield are alleged to have participated in a conspiracy to violate the constitutional and statutory rights of the respondent Fitzgerald. Respondent avers that petitioners entered the conspiracy in their capacities as senior White House aides to former President Richard M. Nixon.

IV

Even if they cannot establish that their official functions require absolute immunity,[a] petitioners assert that public policy at least mandates an application of the qualified immunity standard that would permit the defeat of insubstantial claims without resort to trial. We agree.

A

The resolution of immunity questions inherently requires a balance between the evils inevitable in any available alternative. In situations of abuse of office, an action for damages may offer the only realistic avenue for vindication of constitutional guarantees. It is this recognition that has required the denial of absolute immunity to more public officers. At the same time, however, it cannot be disputed seriously that claims frequently run against the innocent as well as the guilty—at a cost not only to the defendant officials, but to society as a whole. These social costs include the expenses of litigation, the diversion of official energy from pressing public issues, and the deterrence of able citizens from acceptance of public office. Finally, there is the danger that fear of being sued will "dampen the ardor of all but the most resolute, or the most irresponsible [public officials], in the unflinching discharge of their duties."

In identifying qualified immunity as the best attainable accommodation of competing values, we relied on the assumption that this standard would permit "[i]nsubstantial lawsuits [to] be quickly terminated." Yet petitioners advance persuasive arguments that the dismissal of insubstantial lawsuits without trial—a factor presupposed in the balance of competing interests struck by our prior cases—requires an adjustment of the "good faith" standard established by our decisions.

B

Qualified or "good faith" immunity is an affirmative defense that must be pleaded by a defendant official. *Gomez v. Toledo*.[24] Decisions of this Court have established that the "good faith" defense has both an "objective" and a "subjective" aspect. The objective element involves a presumptive knowledge of and respect for "basic, unquestioned constitutional rights." *Wood v. Strickland.* The subjective component refers to "permissible intentions." Characteristically the Court has defined these elements by identifying the circumstances in which qualified immunity would *not* be available. Referring both to the objective and subjective elements, we have held that qualified immunity would be defeated if an official "*knew or reasonably should have known*

---

a   The defendants argued they were entitled to absolute immunity "as an incident of their offices as Presidential aides." The Court rejected the argument that public policy requires a "blanket protection," *i.e.*, full "derivative" immunity, for such officials, but left open the possibility that the defendants could show on remand that their responsibilities included a function so sensitive as to require absolute immunity and that the challenged conduct involved such a function.

24 Although *Gomez* presented the question in the context of an action under 42 U.S.C. § 1983, the Court's analysis indicates that "immunity" must also be pleaded as a defense in actions under the Constitution and laws of the United States. *Gomez* did not decide which party bore the burden of proof on the issue of good faith.

that the action he took within his sphere of official responsibility would violate the constitutional rights of the [plaintiff], *or* if he took the action *with the malicious intention* to cause a deprivation of constitutional rights or other injury. . . ."

The subjective element of the good-faith defense frequently has proved incompatible with our admonition in *Butz* [*v. Economou*] that insubstantial claims should not proceed to trial. Rule 56 of the Federal Rules of Civil Procedure provides that disputed questions of fact ordinarily may not be decided on motion for summary judgment. And an official's subjective good faith has been considered to be a question of fact that some courts have regarded as inherently requiring resolution by a jury.

In the context of *Butz'* attempted balancing of competing values, it now is clear that substantial costs attend the litigation of the subjective good faith of government officials. Not only are there risks of trial—distraction of officials from their governmental duties, inhibition of discretionary action, and deterrence of able people from public service. There are special costs to "subjective" inquiries of this kind. Immunity generally is available only to officials performing discretionary functions. In contrast with the thought processes accompanying "ministerial" tasks, the judgments surrounding discretionary action almost inevitably are influenced by the decisionmaker's experiences, values, and emotions. These variables explain why questions of subjective intent so rarely can be decided by summary judgment. Yet they also frame a background in which there often is no clear end to the relevant evidence. Judicial inquiry into subjective motivation therefore may entail broad-ranging discovery and the deposing of numerous persons, including an official's professional colleagues. Inquires of this kind can be peculiarly disruptive of effective government.

Consistently with the balance at which we aimed in *Butz*, we conclude today that bare allegations of malice should not suffice to subject government officials either to the costs of trial or to the burdens of broad-reaching discovery. We therefore hold that government officials performing discretionary functions, generally are shielded from liability for civil damages insofar as their conduct does not violate clearly established statutory or constitutional rights of which a reasonable person would have known.

Reliance on the objective reasonableness of an official's conduct, as measured by reference to clearly established law, should avoid excessive disruption of government and permit the resolution of many insubstantial claims on summary judgment. On summary judgment, the judge appropriately may determine, not only the currently applicable law, but whether that law was clearly established at the time an action occurred.[32] If the law at that time was not clearly established, an official could not reasonably be expected to anticipate subsequent legal developments, nor could he fairly be said to "know" that the law forbade conduct not previously identified as unlawful. Until this threshold immunity question is resolved, discovery should not be allowed. If the law was clearly established, the immunity defense ordinarily should fail, since a reasonably competent public official should know the law governing his conduct. Nevertheless, if the

---

32 As in Procunier v. Navarette, we need not define here the circumstances under which "the state of the law" should be "evaluated by reference to the opinions of this Court, of the Courts of Appeals, or of the local District Court."

official pleading the defense claims extraordinary circumstances and can prove that he neither knew nor should have known of the relevant legal standard, the defense should be sustained. But again, the defense would turn primarily on objective factors.

By defining the limits of qualified immunity essentially in objective terms, we provide no license to lawless conduct. The public interest in deterrence of unlawful conduct and in compensation of victims remains protected by a test that focuses on the objective legal reasonableness of an official's acts. Where an official could be expected to know that certain conduct would violate statutory or constitutional rights, he should be made to hesitate; and a person who suffers injury caused by such conduct may have a cause of action. But where an official's duties legitimately require action in which clearly established rights are not implicated, the public interest may be better served by action taken "with independence and without fear of consequences."[34]

NOTES AND QUESTIONS

1. *Harlow* was not a § 1983 action; why did the plaintiff not utilize § 1983? What is the source of the qualified immunity doctrine?

2. How does the Supreme Court modify the *Wood v. Strickland* test and why? Does the defendant who acts with clear malice and ill will escape liability merely because the federal right being violated is not clearly established? In *Davis v. Scherer*, 468 U.S. 183 (1984), the Court stated that *Harlow* "rejected the inquiry into state of mind in favor of a wholly objective standard." Thus, even though the defendant knowingly and willfully violated state regulations that protected the plaintiff, because the conduct did not violate clearly established federal rights, the misconduct was insulated by qualified immunity.

3. What is the purpose of the qualified immunity doctrine? If government indemnifies its officials, does public policy support this defense? In a case where the plaintiff seeks injunctive relief as well as damages, what has the defendant government official accomplished by prevailing on the qualified immunity issue through summary judgment?

4. Which party has the burden of proof on the immunity issue? Review n.24.

5. If the defendant's motion for summary judgment is denied because the law was clearly established, is the plaintiff automatically entitled to summary judgment on liability? Under what "extraordinary circumstances" should a defendant be entitled

---

34 We emphasize that our decision applies only to suits for civil damages arising from actions within the scope of an official's duties and in "objective" good faith. We express no view as to the conditions in which injunctive or declaratory relief might be available.

to qualified immunity even though the law is clearly established? What if the official relied on the advice of counsel?

6. **Clearly Established:** Can the law be "clearly established" without a Supreme Court decision on point? What if only the circuit court of appeals, or the district court, has ruled in favor of the plaintiff's position? What if a case is one of first impression in the circuit where it is pending and the other circuits are divided on the relevant legal issue? The Court, in *Wilson v. Layne*, 526 U.S. 603 (1999), held "it is a violation of the Fourth Amendment for police to bring members of the media or other third parties into a home during the execution of a search warrant when the presence of the third parties in the home was not in aid of the execution of the warrant." However, that right was not clearly established in April 1992 because the constitutional right was not "obvious," there were no judicial opinions holding the practice unlawful, and the formal ride-along policies of the officers' employers allowed third parties to enter private homes. Noting a split among the circuits developed between the date of the challenged conduct and its decision, the Court indicated "it is unfair to subject police to monetary damages for picking the losing side of the controversy" where judges disagree on a constitutional issue.

In contrast, in *Hope v. Pelzer*, 536 U.S. 730 (2002), the Court held that the Eleventh Circuit erred in conferring qualified immunity on prison guards who handcuffed an inmate to a hitching post for several hours in the hot sun without providing water or bathroom breaks. The Court rejected the Eleventh Circuit's requirement that the facts of a previous case must be "materially similar" to plaintiff's situation in order to avoid qualified immunity. The critical question instead is whether the state of the law would have provided fair warning to officials that their alleged treatment of an inmate was unconstitutional. The Court found "fair warning" here, because this was an "obvious" violation of the Eighth Amendment. In addition, the guards acted contrary to state Department of Corrections' regulations, and the Department of Justice had also advised state officials of the unconstitutionality of its practice before the incidents in this case took place.

Despite *Hope*, most Supreme Court cases have emphasized the importance of defining the constitutional right *specifically* and *narrowly*. For example, in *Safford Unified School District # 1 v. Redding*, 557 U.S. 364 (2009), the issue was "whether a 13-year-old student's Fourth Amendment right was violated when she was subjected to a search of her bra and underpants by school officials acting on reasonable suspicion that she had brought forbidden prescription and over-the-counter drugs to school." *Id.* at 368. Based on the factual record, the Court determined "there were no reasons to suspect the drugs presented a danger or were concealed in her underwear" and, therefore, the search violated the Fourth Amendment. *Id.* More specifically, "what was missing from the suspected facts that pointed to [Ms. Redding] was any indication of danger to the students from the power of the drugs or their quantity, and any reason to suppose that [she] was carrying pills in her underwear." *Id.* at 376–77. Twenty-four years earlier, in *New Jersey v. T.L.O.*, 469 U.S. 325 (1985), the Court recognized that the school setting demands "some modification of the level of suspicion of illicit activity needed to justify a search," and so it adopted a "reasonable suspicion" standard and held that a school search "will be permissible in its scope when the measures adopted are reasonably related to the objectives of the search and not excessively intrusive in light of the age and sex of the student and the nature of the infraction." Nonetheless, the Court in *Safford* held that the school officials responsible for the search were entitled to qualified immunity because of the "disuniform," "divergent conclusions," regarding the application of the *T.L.O.* standard to searches by school officials. *Id.* at 378 (citing three court of appeals decisions). While qualified immunity does not necessarily follow "disuniform views of the law," it is warranted here, according to the Court, because "the cases viewing school strip searches differently from the ways we see them are numerous enough with well-reasoned majority and dissenting opinions, to counsel doubt that we were sufficiently clear in the prior statement of law." *Id.* at 378–79. Justices Stevens and Ginsburg dissented on the qualified immunity issue, stating that "the clarity of a well-established right should not depend on whether jurists have misread our precedents." *Id.* at 380. Why isn't this an "obvious" constitutional rights violation case (like *Hope*), which requires no factual analogy to established precedent?

7. The meaning of clearly established law has been particularly problematic in the context of Fourth Amendment violations. In *Anderson v. Creighton*, 483 U.S. 635 (1987), the Court held that a law enforcement officer who participates in a search that violates the Fourth Amendment may be held personally liable for money damages "if a reasonable officer could have believed that the search comported with the Fourth Amendment." It explained "that the right the official is alleged to have violated must have been 'clearly established' in a more particularized, and hence more relevant, sense: The contours of the right must be sufficiently clear that a reasonable official would understand that what he is doing violates that right. This is not to say that an official action is protected by qualified immunity unless the very action in question has previously been held unlawful, but it is to say that in the light of preexisting law the unlawfulness must be apparent."

Thus, although "the right to be free from warrantless searches of one's home unless the searching officers have probable cause and there are exigent circumstances was clearly established," this does not necessarily defeat qualified immunity: "We have recognized that it is inevitable that law enforcement officials will in some cases reasonably but mistakenly conclude that probable cause is present, as we have indicated that in such cases those officials—like other officials who act in ways they reasonably believe to be lawful—should not be held personally liable. The same is true of their conclusions regarding exigent circumstances."

Should an officer who is found to have acted without probable cause in making an arrest be deemed to have engaged in "objectively unreasonable" conduct? If the jury finds no probable cause and no exigent circumstances, how can the officer establish that the search was "objectively" reasonable? In *City and County of San Francisco v. Sheehan*, 135 S. Ct. 1765 (2015), reiterated that "qualified immunity is no immunity at all if 'clearly established' law can simply be defined as the right to be free from unreasonable searches and seizures." In this case a group home resident who suffered from mental illness alleged that the police violated her Fourth Amendment rights by failing to accommodate her mental illness before reentering her room and shooting her after she threatened to kill a social worker and threatened officers with a knife. The Court assumed, without deciding, that dealing with the mentally ill might require some modification of Fourth Amendment principles. However, it concluded that no legal precedent clearly established that plaintiff had a right to accommodation of her disability, even if the officers acted contrary to their training, which taught them to employ a "de-escalation" strategy and to wait for back-up. There was no Supreme Court precedent establishing that the Fourth Amendment required officers to treat an armed, mentally ill individual differently, nor did a "robust consensus of cases of persuasive authority" put the officers on notice that their conduct violated clearly established law.

Further, in *Aschcroft v. al-Kidd*, 563 U.S. 731 (2011), the Supreme Court expanded protection for government officials by changing the test to ask whether "every reasonable official," rather than Anderson's "a reasonable official," would understand the conduct violated clearly established law. The former test looks to objective reasonableness, whereas "every reasonable official" provides greater leeway to assess reasonableness. Id. at 741. This has made it much more difficult for plaintiffs to survive summary judgment based on qualified immunity.

For example, in *District of Columbia v. Wesby*, 138 S. Ct. 577 (2018), the Court held that, even assuming officers lacked actual probable cause to arrest partygoers for unlawfully entering vacant home, they enjoyed qualified immunity because, under the circumstances they confronted, they reasonably could have believed probable cause existed. No controlling case held that a suspect's bona fide belief of a right to enter a private residence necessarily defeats probable cause or that officers must accept suspects' "innocent explanation at face value." Further, there was no case precedent finding a Fourth Amendment violation "under similar circumstances," and this was not an "obvious case" where a body of relevant case law is unnecessary.

Similarly, in *Kisela v. Hughes*, 138 S. Ct. 1148 (2018) (per curiam), the Court explained that because the use of excessive force depends on the specific facts of each case, qualified immunity should be afforded unless existing precedent "squarely governs" the specific facts at issue. The Ninth Circuit erred in ruling that an officer responding to a 911 call who shot a knife-wielding woman violated clearly established law, because this was not an "obvious" case where every competent officer would have known that shooting the plaintiff under these specific circumstances would violate the Fourth Amendment. Rather, the officer believed the plaintiff posed a threat to another woman, and he had to make a split-second decision.

The following decision provides a summary of the principles the Supreme Court established in these cases:

CITY OF ESCONDIDO, CALIFORNIA V. EMMONS
139 S. CT. 500 (2019)

PER CURIAM.

The question in this qualified immunity case is whether two police officers violated clearly established law when they forcibly apprehended a man at the scene of a reported domestic violence incident.

The record, viewed in the light most favorable to the plaintiff, shows the following. In April 2013, Escondido police received a 911 call from Maggie Emmons about a domestic violence incident at her apartment. Emmons lived at the apartment with her husband, her two children, and a roommate, Ametria Douglas. Officer Jake Houchin responded to the scene and eventually helped take a domestic violence report from Emmons about injuries caused by her husband. The officers arrested her husband. He was later released.

A few weeks later, on May 27, 2013, at about 2:30 p.m., Escondido police received a 911 call about another possible domestic disturbance at Emmons' apartment. That 911 call came from Ametria Douglas' mother, Trina Douglas. Trina Douglas was not at the apartment, but she was on the phone with her daughter Ametria, who was at the apartment. Trina heard her daughter Ametria and Maggie Emmons yelling at each other and heard her daughter screaming for help. The call then disconnected, and Trina Douglas called 911.

Officer Houchin again responded, along with Officer Robert Craig. The dispatcher informed the officers that two children could be in the residence and that calls to the apartment had gone unanswered.

Police body-camera video of the officers' actions at the apartment is in the record.

The officers knocked on the door of the apartment. No one answered. But a side window was open, and the officers spoke with Emmons through that window, attempting to convince her to open the door to the apartment so that they could conduct a welfare check. A man in the apartment also told Emmons to back away from the window, but the officers said they could not identify the man. At some point during this exchange, Sergeant Kevin Toth, Officer Joseph Leffingwell, and Officer Huy Quach arrived as backup.

A few minutes later, a man opened the apartment door and came outside. At that point, Officer Craig was standing alone just outside the door. Officer Craig told the man not to close the door, but the man closed the door and tried to brush past Officer Craig. Officer Craig stopped the man, took him quickly to the ground, and handcuffed him. Officer Craig did not hit the man or display any weapon. The video shows that the man was not in any visible or audible pain as a result of the takedown or while on the ground. Within a few minutes, officers helped the man up and arrested him for a misdemeanor offense of resisting and delaying a police officer.

The man turned out to be Maggie Emmons' father, Marty Emmons. Marty Emmons later sued Officer Craig and Sergeant Toth, among others, under 42 U.S.C. § 1983. He raised several claims, including, as relevant here, a claim of excessive force in violation of the Fourth Amendment. The suit sought money damages for which Officer Craig and Sergeant Toth would be personally liable.

The District Court granted summary judgment to Officer Craig. According to the District Court, the law did not clearly establish that Officer Craig could not take down an arrestee in these circumstances. The court explained that the officers were responding to a domestic dispute, and that the encounter had escalated when the officers could not enter the apartment to conduct a welfare check. The District Court also noted that when Marty Emmons exited the apartment, none of the officers knew whether he was armed or dangerous, or whether he had injured any individuals inside the apartment.

The Court of Appeals reversed and remanded for trial on the excessive force claims against both Officer Craig and Sergeant Toth. The Ninth Circuit's entire relevant analysis of the qualified immunity question consisted of the following: "The right to be free of excessive force was clearly established at the time of the events in question. *Gravelet–Blondin v. Shelton*, 728 F.3d 1086, 1093 (9th Cir. 2013)." *Id.*, at 726.

As we have explained many times: "Qualified immunity attaches when an official's conduct does not violate clearly established statutory or constitutional rights of which a reasonable person would have known." *Kisela v. Hughes, District of Columbia v. Wesby; White v. Pauly* (per curiam); *Mullenix v. Luna* (per curiam).

Under our cases, the clearly established right must be defined with specificity. "This Court has repeatedly told courts . . . not to define clearly established law at a high level of generality." *Kisela*, 138 S. Ct., at 1152. That is particularly important in excessive force cases, as we have explained:

> Specificity is especially important in the Fourth Amendment context, where the Court has recognized that it is sometimes difficult for an officer to determine how the relevant legal doctrine, here excessive force, will apply to the factual situation the officer confronts. Use of excessive force is an area of the law in which the result depends very much on the facts of each case, and thus police officers are entitled to qualified immunity unless existing precedent squarely governs the specific facts at issue....

> [I]t does not suffice for a court simply to state that an officer may not use unreasonable and excessive force, deny qualified immunity, and then remit the case for a trial on the question of reasonableness. An officer cannot be said to have violated a clearly established right unless the right's contours were sufficiently definite that any reasonable official in the defendant's shoes would have understood that he was violating it.

Id. at 1153.

In this case, the Court of Appeals contravened those settled principles. The Court of Appeals should have asked whether clearly established law prohibited the officers from stopping and taking down a man in these circumstances. Instead, the Court of Appeals defined the clearly established right at a high level of generality by saying only that the "right to be free of excessive force" was clearly established. With the right defined at that high level of generality, the Court of Appeals then denied qualified immunity to the officers and remanded the case for trial.

Under our precedents, the Court of Appeals' formulation of the clearly established right was far too general. To be sure, the Court of Appeals cited the *Gravelet–Blondin* case from that Circuit, which described a right to be "free from the application of non-trivial force for engaging in mere passive resistance. . . ." 728 F.3d, at 1093. Assuming without deciding that a court of appeals decision may constitute clearly established law for purposes of qualified immunity, see *City and County of San Francisco v. Sheehan*, the Ninth Circuit's *Gravelet–Blondin* case law involved police force against individuals engaged in *passive* resistance. The Court of Appeals made no effort to explain how that case law prohibited Officer Craig's actions in this case. That is a problem under our precedents:

> [W]e have stressed the need to identify a case where an officer acting under similar circumstances was held to have violated the Fourth Amendment.... While there does not have to be a case directly on point, existing precedent must place the lawfulness of the particular [action] beyond debate. . . . Of course, there can be the rare obvious case, where the unlawfulness of the officer's conduct is sufficiently clear even though existing precedent does not address similar circumstances. . . . But a body of relevant case law is usually necessary to clearly establish the answer. . . ." *Wesby*, 138 S. Ct., at 581.

The Court of Appeals failed to properly analyze whether clearly established law barred Officer Craig from stopping and taking down Marty Emmons in this manner as Emmons exited the apartment. Therefore, we remand the case for the Court of Appeals to conduct the analysis required by our precedents with respect to whether Officer Craig is entitled to qualified immunity.

The petition for certiorari is granted, the judgment of the Court of Appeals is reversed in part and vacated in part, and the case is remanded for further proceedings consistent with this opinion.

NOTES AND QUESTIONS

1. What errors did the Court find in the Ninth Circuit's analysis of the qualified immunity question? Why wasn't the earlier Ninth Circuit decision sufficient to provide officers "notice"?

2. How will the immunity issue be resolved on remand?

3. Assume (a) the defendant is not entitled to summary judgment on the factual allegations in the complaint, (b) the defendant's affidavit supporting summary judgment gives a version of the facts which would establish an objectively reasonable search, and (c) the plaintiff's affidavit opposing summary judgment reiterates the facts in the complaint and contests the defendant's version of the facts. Can the trial court resolve the immunity issue on summary judgment? If not, how should it proceed?

4. **Reliance on a Warrant:** In *Malley v. Briggs*, 475 U.S. 335 (1986), the Court rejected the argument that "the act of applying for a warrant is *per se* objectively reasonable:

> It is true that in an ideal system an unreasonable request for a warrant would be harmless, because no judge would approve it. But ours is not an ideal system, and it is possible that a magistrate, working under docket pressures, will fail to perform as a magistrate should. We find it reasonable to require the officer applying for the warrant to minimize this danger by exercising reasonable professional judgment.

Subsequently, in *Messerschmidt v. Millender*, 565 U.S. 535 (2012), the Supreme Court granted officers qualified immunity for conducting a home search pursuant to an allegedly unconstitutionally overbroad warrant. After receiving a report that the suspect shot at his girlfriend with a sawed-off shotgun, officers conducted a detailed investigation that verified that the suspect was a member of two gangs, and that he had been arrested and convicted for numerous violent and firearm-related offenses. The Court reiterated the basic rule that where a Fourth Amendment violation involves a search pursuant to a warrant, a neutral magistrate's issuance of the warrant is a strong indication that the officers acted in an objectively reasonable manner unless "it is obvious that no reasonably competent officer would have concluded that a warrant should issue." The majority accepted the lower court's finding that the warrant, which authorized search for all firearms and ammunition, as well as evidence indicating gang membership, was so overbroad that it violated the Fourth Amendment. Nonetheless, the Court granted qualified immunity, reasoning that an officer could reasonably conclude that the sawed-off shotgun was not the only firearm the suspect owned and that seizing firearms was necessary to prevent further assaults on the complainant. Further, authorization to search for gang-related materials was reasonable to demonstrate a possible motive for the attack or to later impeach the suspect. The fact that the officers sought and obtained approval from supervisory officials and a deputy district attorney before submitting the warrant request to the magistrate further supported the conclusion that the officer could reasonably have believed that the scope of the warrant was supported by probable cause. The Court reasoned that an arguable defect in the breadth of the warrant would have been apparent only upon a "close parsing of the warrant application" to determine whether the affidavits established probable cause to search for all the items listed. Thus, even if the warrant was unconstitutionally overbroad, the officers were protected by qualified immunity.

5. **Private Defendants:** In *Wyatt v. Cole*, 504 U.S. 158 (1992), the Court held that private defendants who conspire with state officials to violate constitutional rights are not protected by the qualified immunity doctrine enunciated in *Harlow*. After noting that "the reasons for recognizing such an immunity were based not simply on the existence of a good-faith defense at common law, but on the special policy concerns involved in suing government officials," the Court concluded that "the rationales mandating qualified immunity for public officials are not applicable to private parties." Why is this true?

Relying on *Wyatt*, the Court in *Richardson v. McKnight*, 521 U.S. 399 (1997), held that prison guards, who are employed by a private prison management firm, are not entitled to a qualified immunity from suit by inmates alleging the use of excessive force. First, the Court noted that "[h]istory does *not* reveal a 'firmly rooted' tradition of immunity applicable to privately employed prison guards," and second it found that the purposes of the immunity doctrine do not warrant immunity for private prison guards. In closing, the Court issued three caveats: (i) it did not address whether the private guards acted under color of state law, (ii) the immunity issue presented was addressed in the context in which it arose, *i.e.*, "one in which a private firm, systematically organized to assume a major lengthy administrative task . . . with limited direct supervision by the government, undertakes that task for profit and potentially in competition with other firms," and (iii) it was not deciding whether the private defendants could assert a special "good faith" defense.

The Supreme Court revisited the question of qualified immunity for private defendants who act under color of state law in *Filarsky v. Delia*, 566 U.S. 377 (2012). In this case a private attorney was hired by the city to conduct an internal investigation of a firefighter (Delia), who the department suspected was inappropriately taking sick leave after evidence surfaced that Delia purchased building supplies from a home improvement store. After Delia refused to allow search of his home, Filarsky persuaded the chief to order the firefighter to bring the materials outside onto his front yard to prove he was not doing home improvement. After he did so, he was exonerated. Delia then sued Filarsky as well as several government officials for violating his Fourth Amendment rights. The Supreme Court unanimously held that private individuals hired to perform work on a temporary or part-time basis for the government are eligible to seek qualified immunity. The Court relied upon the fact that, at common law, immunity was granted regardless of whether an employee worked full-time or part-time, because, in fact, at the time § 1983 was adopted most government employees worked on a part-time basis. Further, the Court explained that three policy rationales favored the extension of immunity. First, it was necessary to extend qualified immunity so that those privately hired to carry out a government task will not act with unwarranted timidity because of a fear of litigation. Second, fear of liability would deter private individuals, including those well qualified and well experienced, like the defendant here, from offering their services. Third, the concern that without immunity government officials will be distracted by lawsuits applies here in that if Filarsky does not enjoy immunity, fire department officials will be called to testify in the case. Finally, the Court noted that it would be unjust for those who work for smaller government entities to be denied qualified immunity, whereas large government entities can afford to hire full-time investigators who would partake of that immunity.

The Court distinguished *Richardson* as an exceptional, narrow decision involving a private firm operating with limited direct supervision by the government and undertaking a task for profit, where the normal concerns underlying recognition of governmental immunity did not apply. The Court suggested that, despite *Richardson*, there will be a strong presumption in favor of granting qualified immunity where individuals are hired by the government to assist in carrying out its work.

c. Procedural Issues:

1. Sequence of Analysis:

In *Saucier v. Katz*, 533 U.S. 194 (2001), the plaintiff alleged the use of excessive force by a federal officer. First, the Court emphasized the need for the lower courts, in considering the qualified immunity defense, to consider the threshold question—"[t]aken in the light most favorable to the party asserting the injury, do the facts alleged show the officer's conduct violated a constitutional right?" If the answer is no, there is no necessity for further inquiry relating to the qualified immunity defense. However, if the answer is yes, then the Court must determine "whether the force used violated a clearly established Fourth Amendment protection so that [the officer] was not entitled to immunity." In addressing this issue, the Court stated: "[a]n officer might correctly perceive all of the relevant facts but have a mistaken understanding as to whether a particular amount of force is legal in those circumstances. If the officer's mistake as to what the law requires is reasonable, however, the officer is entitled to the immunity defense." Here, the Court concluded, the officer "could have believed that hurrying [the plaintiff] away from the scene, where the Vice President was speaking and [the officer] had just approached the fence designed to separate the public from the speakers, was within the bounds of appropriate police responses."

Eight years after *Saucier* was decided, the Court reexamined its two-step procedure in *Pearson v. Callahan*, 555 U.S. 223 (2009), and unanimously decided it should be modified. First, the Court recognized the benefits of the two-step process—in some cases a discussion of why the relevant facts do not violate clearly established law makes it apparent that the facts do not make out a constitutional violation, and the two-step process promotes the development of constitutional precedent. Government actors benefit because they can then better conform their behavior to constitutional standards and future plaintiffs benefit because they can overcome qualified immunity and recover damages for injuries. However, the Court noted that these benefits are offset by the often unnecessary litigation of constitutional issues that waste both judicial and parties' resources. The consideration of whether there is a constitutional violation may be short-changed where the court has already determined there was not a violation of clearly established law. Further, the two-step process departs from the general rule that courts should not decide constitutional questions unless it is necessary. The Court concluded that the benefits of the two-step process can be retained and the disadvantages avoided by allowing lower court judges "to determine the order of decisionmaking [that] will best facilitate the fair and efficient disposition of each case." *Id.* at 242. In sum, "while the sequence set forth [in *Saucier*] is often appropriate, it should no longer be regarded as mandatory."

In *Ashcroft v. al-Kidd*, 563 U.S. 731 (2011), the Court revisited the sequence question. While reaffirming that lower courts have discretion to decide which of the two prongs of qualified immunity to tackle first, the Court explained:

> Courts should think carefully before expending "scarce judicial resources" to resolve difficult and novel questions of constitutional or statutory interpretation that will "have no effect on the outcome of the case." When, however, a Court of Appeals does address both prongs of qualified-immunity analysis, we have discretion to correct its errors at each step. Although not necessary to reverse an erroneous judgment, doing so ensures that courts do not insulate constitutional decisions at the frontiers of the law from our review or inadvertently undermine the values qualified immunity seeks to promote. The former occurs when the constitutional-law question is wrongly decided; the latter when what is not clearly established is held to be so. In this case, the Court of Appeals' analysis at both steps of the qualified-immunity inquiry needs correction.

Similarly, in *Camreta v. Greene*, 563 U.S. 692 (2011), the Court ruled that defendants who are granted summary judgment based on qualified immunity may nonetheless be permitted to appeal an unfavorable constitutional ruling. In this case the district court ruled that a caseworker and local sheriff violated plaintiff's rights by not securing a warrant before seizing a nine-year-old while she was in school and questioning her about allegations that her father was sexually abusing her. However, the defendants did not violate clearly settled law and were thus entitled to qualified immunity. Although normally judicial restraint requires courts to avoid reaching constitutional questions unnecessarily, a decision that a government official violated the Constitution, but is entitled to qualified immunity because the right was not clearly established, is reviewable in the Supreme Court at the behest of an immunized official.

The Court reasoned that the constitutional ruling would govern the official's behavior and denying review "would undermine the very purpose served by the two-step process, 'which is to clarify constitutional rights without undue delay.'" The Court emphasized that it was address-ing only its own authority to review cases in this procedural posture and not whether appellate courts have the same leeway. In addition, the Court emphasized that it retains discretion to decide whether to review: "Our decision today does no more than exempt one special category of cases from our usual rule against considering prevailing parties' petitions. Going forward, we will consider these petitions one by one in accord with our usual standards."

Ultimately the Court did not reach the constitutional issue because it decided that the case should be dismissed because it was moot. After cert was granted, the child's family moved to Florida and there was no possibility that she would be seized in the Ninth Circuit's jurisdiction as part of a child abuse investigation. In their concurring opinions Justices Kennedy and Scalia suggest that the Court should "end the extraordinary practice of ruling upon constitutional questions unnecessarily when the defendant possesses qualified immunity."

2.   **Special Pleading Rules:**

In *Crawford-El v. Britton*, 523 U.S. 574 (1998), an inmate alleged that a corrections officer retal-iated against him in violation of his First Amendment rights, a constitutional claim that requires proof of improper motive. The Court of Appeals held that "in order to prevail in an unconstitu-tional-motive case, the plaintiff must establish that motive by clear and convincing evidence," reasoning that "because an official's state of mind is 'easy to allege and hard to disprove,' insub-stantial claims that turn on improper intent may be less amenable to summary disposition than other types of claims against government officials. This category of claims therefore implicates obvious concerns with the social costs of subjecting public officials to discovery and trial, as well as liability for damages." The Supreme Court rejected this analysis:

> Neither the text of § 1983 or any other federal statute, nor the Federal Rules of Civil Procedure, provides any support for imposing the clear and convincing burden of proof on plaintiffs either at the summary judgment stage or in the trial itself. . . . [T]he Court of Appeals adopted a heightened proof standard in large part to reduce the availability of discovery in actions that require proof of motive. To the extent that the court was con-cerned with this procedural issue, our cases demonstrate that questions regarding plead-ing, discovery, and summary judgment are most frequently and most effectively resolved either by the rulemaking process or the legislative process.

In *Harlow* we noted that a "'firm application of the Federal Rules of Civil Procedure' is fully warranted" and may lead to the prompt disposition of insubstantial claims. Though we have rejected the Court of Appeals' solution, we are aware of the potential problem that troubled the court. It is therefore appropriate to add a few words on some of the existing procedures available to federal trial judges in handling claims that involve examination of an official's state of mind.

When a plaintiff files a complaint against a public official alleging a claim that requires proof of wrongful motive, the trial court must exercise its discretion in a way that protects the substance of the qualified immunity defense. It must exercise its discretion so that officials are not subjected to unnecessary and burdensome discovery or trial proceedings. The district judge has two primary options prior to permitting any discovery at all. First, the court may order a reply to the defendant's or a third party's answer under Federal Rule of Civil Procedure 7(a), or grant the defendant's motion for a more definite statement under Rule 12(e). Thus, the court may insist that the plaintiff "put forward specific, nonconclusory factual allegations" that establish improper motive causing cognizable injury in order to survive a prediscovery motion for dismissal or summary judgment. This option exists even if the official chooses not to plead the affirmative defense of qualified immunity. Second, if the defendant does plead the immunity defense, the district court should resolve that threshold question before permitting discovery. To do so, the court must determine whether, assuming the truth of the plaintiff's allegations, the official's conduct violated clearly established law. Because the former option of demanding more specific allegations of intent places no burden on the defendant-official, the district judge may choose that alternative before resolving the immunity question, which sometimes requires complicated analysis of legal issues.

If the plaintiff's action survives these initial hurdles and is otherwise viable, the plaintiff ordinarily will be entitled to some discovery. Rule 26 vests the trial judge with broad discretion to tailor discovery narrowly and to dictate the sequence of discovery. On its own motion, the trial court

> may alter the limits in [the Federal Rules] on the number of depositions and interrogatories and may also limit the length of depositions under Rule 30 and the number of requests under Rule 36. The frequency or extent of use of the discovery methods otherwise permitted under these rules . . . shall be limited by the court if it determines that . . . (iii) the burden or expense of the proposed discovery outweighs its likely benefit, taking into account the needs of the case, the amount in controversy, the parties' resources, the importance of the issues at stake in the litigation, and the importance of the proposed discovery in resolving the issues. Rule 26(b)(2).
>
> Additionally, upon motion the court may limit the time, place, and manner of discovery, or even bar discovery altogether on certain subjects, as required "to protect a party or person from annoyance, embarrassment, oppression, or undue burden or expense." Rule 26(c). And the court may also set the timing and sequence of discovery. Rule 26(d).
>
> These provisions create many options for the district judge. For instance, the court may at first permit the plaintiff to take only a focused deposition of the defendant before allowing any additional discovery. Alternatively, the court may postpone all inquiry regarding the official's subjective motive until discovery has been had on objective factual questions such as whether the plaintiff suffered any injury or whether the plaintiff actually engaged in protected conduct that could be the object of unlawful retaliation. The trial judge can therefore manage the discovery process to facilitate prompt and efficient resolution of the lawsuit; as the evidence is gathered, the defendant-official may move for partial summary judgment on objective issues that are potentially dispositive

and are more amenable to summary disposition than disputes about the official's intent, which frequently turn on credibility assessments. Of course, the judge should give priority to discovery concerning issues that bear upon the qualified immunity defense, such as the actions that the official actually took, since that defense should be resolved as early as possible.

Beyond these procedures and others that we have not mentioned, summary judgment serves as the ultimate screen to weed out truly insubstantial lawsuits prior to trial. At that stage, if the defendant-official has made a properly supported motion, the plaintiff may not respond simply with general attacks upon the defendant's credibility, but rather must identify affirmative evidence from which a jury could find that the plaintiff has carried his or her burden of proving the pertinent motive. Finally, federal trial judges are undoubtedly familiar with two additional tools that are available in extreme cases to protect public officials from undue harassment: Rule 11, which authorizes sanctions for the filing of papers that are frivolous, lacking in factual support, or "presented for any improper purpose, such as to harass"; and 28 U.S.C.A. 1915(e)(2) (Supp.1997), which authorizes dismissal "at any time" of *in forma pauperis* suits that are "frivolous or malicious."

It is the district judges rather than appellate judges like ourselves who have had the most experience in managing cases in which an official's intent is an element. Given the wide variety of civil rights and "constitutional tort" claims that trial judges confront, broad discretion in the management of the fact finding process may be more useful and equitable to all the parties than the categorical rule imposed by the Court of Appeals.

In the following case, without overturning *Crawford-El*, the Court (1) altered pleading rules and (2) rejected well-established principles regarding supervisory liability.

ASHCROFT V. IQBAL
556 U.S. 662 (2009)

Justice KENNEDY delivered the opinion of the Court.

Respondent Javaid Iqbal is a citizen of Pakistan and a Muslim. In the wake of the September 11, 2001, terrorist attacks he was arrested in the United States on criminal charges and detained by federal officials. Respondent claims he was deprived of various constitutional protections while in federal custody. To redress the alleged deprivations, respondent filed a complaint against numerous federal officials, including John Ashcroft, the former Attorney General of the United States, and Robert Mueller, the Director of the Federal Bureau of Investigation (FBI). Ashcroft and Mueller are the petitioners in the case now before us. As to these two petitioners, the complaint alleges that they adopted an unconstitutional policy that subjected respondent to harsh conditions of confinement on account of his race, religion, or national origin.

Respondent's account of his prison ordeal could, if proved, demonstrate unconstitutional misconduct by some governmental actors. But the allegations and pleadings with respect to these actors are not before us here. This case instead turns on a narrower question: Did respondent, as the plaintiff in the District Court, plead factual matter that, if taken as true, states a claim that petitioners deprived him of his clearly established constitutional rights. We hold respondent's pleadings are insufficient.

<h1 style="text-align:center">I</h1>

Following the 2001 attacks, the FBI and other entities within the Department of Justice began an investigation of vast reach to identify the assailants and prevent them from attacking anew.

In the ensuing months the FBI questioned more than 1,000 people with suspected links to the attacks in particular or to terrorism in general. Of those individuals, some 762 were held on immigration charges; and a 184-member subset of that group was deemed to be "of 'high interest'" to the investigation. The high-interest detainees were held under restrictive conditions designed to prevent them from communicating with the general prison population or the outside world.

Respondent was one of the detainees. According to his complaint, in November 2001 agents of the FBI and Immigration and Naturalization Service arrested him on charges of fraud in relation to identification documents and conspiracy to defraud the United States. Pending trial for those crimes, respondent was housed at the Metropolitan Detention Center (MDC) in Brooklyn, New York. Respondent was designated a person "of high interest" to the September 11 investigation and in January 2002 was placed in a section of the MDC known as the Administrative Maximum Special Housing Unit (ADMAX SHU). As the facility's name indicates, the ADMAX SHU incorporates the maximum security conditions allowable under Federal Bureau of Prison regulations. ADMAX SHU detainees were kept in lockdown 23 hours a day, spending the remaining hour outside their cells in handcuffs and leg irons accompanied by a four-officer escort.

Respondent pleaded guilty to the criminal charges, served a term of imprisonment, and was removed to his native Pakistan. He then filed a *Bivens* action in the United States District Court against 34 current and former federal officials and 19 "John Doe" federal corrections officers. The 21-cause-of-action complaint does not challenge respondent's arrest or his confinement in the MDC's general prison population. Rather, it concentrates on his treatment while confined to the ADMAX SHU. The complaint sets forth various claims against defendants who are not before us. For instance, the complaint alleges that respondent's jailors "kicked him in the stomach, punched him in the face, and dragged him across" his cell without justification, subjected him to serial strip and body-cavity searches when he posed no safety risk to himself or others, and refused to let him and other Muslims pray because there would be "[n]o prayers for terrorists."

The allegations against petitioners are the only ones relevant here. The complaint contends that petitioners designated respondent a person of high interest on account of his race, religion, or national origin, in contravention of the First and Fifth Amendments to the Constitution. The complaint alleges that "the [FBI], under the direction of Defendant MUELLER, arrested and detained thousands of Arab Muslim men ... as part of its investigation of the events of September 11." It further alleges that "[t]he policy of holding post-September-11th detainees in highly restrictive conditions of confinement until they were 'cleared' by the FBI was approved by Defendants Ashcroft and Mueller in discussions in the weeks after September 11, 2001." Lastly, the complaint posits that petitioners "each knew of, condoned, and willfully and maliciously agreed to subject" respondent to harsh conditions of confinement "as a matter of policy, solely on account of [his] religion, race, and/or national origin and for no legitimate penological interest." The pleading names Ashcroft as the "principal architect" of the policy, and identifies Mueller as "instrumental in [its] adoption, promulgation, and implementation."

Petitioners moved to dismiss the complaint for failure to state sufficient allegations to show their own involvement in clearly established unconstitutional conduct. The District Court denied their motion. Accepting all of the allegations in respondent's complaint as true, the court held that "it cannot be said that there [is] no set of facts on which [respondent] would be entitled to relief as against" petitioners. Invoking the collateral-order doctrine petitioners filed an interlocutory appeal in the Second Circuit. While that appeal was pending, this Court decided *Bell Atlantic Corp. v. Twombly,* 550 U.S. 544 (2007), which discussed the standard for evaluating whether a complaint is sufficient to survive a motion to dismiss.

The Court of Appeals considered *Twombly*'s applicability to this case. Acknowledging that *Twombly* retired the *Conley* no-set-of-facts test relied upon by the District Court, the Court of Appeals' opinion discussed at length how to apply this Court's "standard for assessing the adequacy of pleadings." It concluded that *Twombly* called for a "flexible 'plausibility standard,' which obliges a pleader to amplify a claim with some factual allegations in those contexts where such amplification is needed to render the claim *plausible*." The court found that petitioners' appeal did not present one of "those contexts" requiring amplification. As a consequence, it held respondent's pleading adequate to allege petitioners' personal involvement in discriminatory decisions which, if true, violated clearly established constitutional law.

III

In *Twombly*, the Court found it necessary first to discuss the antitrust principles implicated by the complaint. Here too we begin by taking note of the elements a plaintiff must plead to state a claim of unconstitutional discrimination against officials entitled to assert the defense of qualified immunity.

In *Bivens*—proceeding on the theory that a right suggests a remedy—this Court "recognized for the first time an implied private action for damages against federal officers alleged to have violated a citizen's constitutional rights." Because implied causes of action are disfavored, the Court has been reluctant to extend *Bivens* liability "to any new context or new category of defendants."

In the limited settings where *Bivens* does apply, the implied cause of action is the "federal analog to suits brought against state officials under 42 U.S.C. § 1983." Based on the rules our precedents establish, respondent correctly concedes that Government officials may not be held liable for the unconstitutional conduct of their subordinates under a theory of *respondeat superior.* Because vicarious liability is inapplicable to *Bivens* and § 1983 suits, a plaintiff must plead that each Government-official defendant, through the official's own individual actions, has violated the Constitution.

The factors necessary to establish a *Bivens* violation will vary with the constitutional provision at issue. Where the claim is invidious discrimination in contravention of the First and Fifth Amendments, our decisions make clear that the plaintiff must plead and prove that the defendant acted with discriminatory purpose. Under extant precedent purposeful discrimination requires more than "intent as volition or intent as awareness of consequences." It instead involves a decisionmaker's undertaking a course of action "'because of,' not merely 'in spite of,' [the action's] adverse effects upon an identifiable group." It follows that, to state a claim based on a violation of a clearly established right, respondent must plead sufficient factual matter to show that petitioners adopted and implemented the detention policies at issue not for a neutral, investigative reason but for the purpose of discriminating on account of race, religion, or national origin.

Respondent disagrees. He argues that, under a theory of "supervisory liability," petitioners can be liable for "knowledge and acquiescence in their subordinates' use of discriminatory criteria to make classification decisions among detainees." That is to say, respondent believes a supervisor's mere knowledge of his subordinate's discriminatory purpose amounts to the supervisor's violating the Constitution. We reject this argument. Respondent's conception of "supervisory liability" is inconsistent with his accurate stipulation that petitioners may not be held accountable for the misdeeds of their agents. In a § 1983 suit or a *Bivens* action—where masters do not answer for the torts of their servants—the term "supervisory liability" is a misnomer. Absent vicarious liability, each Government official, his or her title notwithstanding, is only liable for his or her own misconduct. In the context of determining whether there is a violation of clearly established right to overcome qualified immunity, purpose rather than knowledge is required to impose *Bivens* liability on the subordinate for unconstitutional discrimination; the same holds true for an official charged with violations arising from his or her superintendent responsibilities.

IV

A

We turn to respondent's complaint. Under Federal Rule of Civil Procedure 8(a)(2), a pleading must contain a "short and plain statement of the claim showing that the pleader is entitled to relief." As the Court held in *Twombly*, the pleading standard Rule 8 announces does not require "detailed factual allegations," but it demands more than an unadorned, the-defendant-unlawfully-harmed-me accusation. A pleading that offers "labels and conclusions" or "a formulaic recitation of the elements of a cause of action will not do." Nor does a complaint suffice if it tenders "naked assertion[s]" devoid of "further factual enhancement."

To survive a motion to dismiss, a complaint must contain sufficient factual matter, accepted as true, to "state a claim to relief that is plausible on its face." A claim has facial plausibility when the plaintiff pleads factual content that allows the court to draw the reasonable inference that the defendant is liable for the misconduct alleged. The plausibility standard is not akin to a "probability requirement," but it asks for more than a sheer possibility that a defendant has acted unlawfully. Where a complaint pleads facts that are "merely consistent with" a defendant's liability, it "stops short of the line between possibility and plausibility of 'entitlement to relief.'"

Two working principles underlie our decision in *Twombly*. First, the tenet that a court must accept as true all of the allegations contained in a complaint is inapplicable to legal conclusions. Threadbare recitals of the elements of a cause of action, supported by mere conclusory statements, do not suffice. Rule 8 marks a notable and generous departure from the hyper-technical, code-pleading regime of a prior era, but it does not unlock the doors of discovery for a plaintiff armed with nothing more than conclusions. Second, only a complaint that states a plausible claim for relief survives a motion to dismiss. Determining whether a complaint states a plausible claim for relief will, as the Court of Appeals observed, be a context-specific task that requires the reviewing court to draw on its judicial experience and common sense. But where the well-pleaded facts do not permit the court to infer more than the mere possibility of misconduct, the complaint has alleged-but it has not "show[n]"-"that the pleader is entitled to relief."

In keeping with these principles a court considering a motion to dismiss can choose to begin by identifying pleadings that, because they are no more than conclusions, are not entitled to the assumption of truth. While legal conclusions can provide the framework of a complaint, they must be supported by factual allegations. When there are well-pleaded factual allegations, a court should assume their veracity and then determine whether they plausibly give rise to an entitlement to relief.

B

Under *Twombly*'s construction of Rule 8, we conclude that respondent's complaint has not "nudged [his] claims" of invidious discrimination "across the line from conceivable to plausible."

We begin our analysis by identifying the allegations in the complaint that are not entitled to the assumption of truth. Respondent pleads that petitioners "knew of, condoned, and willfully and maliciously agreed to subject [him]" to harsh conditions of confinement "as a matter of policy, solely on account of [his] religion, race, and/or national origin and for no legitimate penological interest." The complaint alleges that Ashcroft was the "principal architect" of this invidious policy, and that Mueller was "instrumental" in adopting and executing it. These bare assertions . . . amount to nothing more than a "formulaic recitation of the elements" of a constitutional discrimination claim, namely, that petitioners adopted a policy "'because of,' not merely 'in spite of,' its adverse effects upon an identifiable group." As such, the allegations are conclusory and not entitled to be assumed true. To be clear, we do not reject these bald allegations on the ground that they are unrealistic or nonsensical. It is the conclusory nature of respondent's allegations, rather than their extravagantly fanciful nature, that disentitles them to the presumption of truth.

We next consider the factual allegations in respondent's complaint to determine if they plausibly suggest an entitlement to relief. The complaint alleges that "the [FBI], under the direction of Defendant MUELLER, arrested and detained thousands of Arab Muslim men ... as part of its investigation of the events of September 11." It further claims that "[t]he policy of holding post-September-11th detainees in highly restrictive conditions of confinement until they were 'cleared' by the FBI was approved by Defendants ASHCROFT and MUELLER in discussions in the weeks after September 11, 2001." Taken as true, these allegations are consistent with petitioners' purposefully designating detainees "of high interest" because of their race, religion, or national origin. But given more likely explanations, they do not plausibly establish this purpose.

The September 11 attacks were perpetrated by 19 Arab Muslim hijackers who counted themselves members in good standing of al Qaeda, an Islamic fundamentalist group. Al Qaeda was headed by another Arab Muslim-Osama bin Laden-and composed in large part of his Arab Muslim disciples. It should come as no surprise that a legitimate policy directing law enforcement to arrest and detain individuals because of their suspected link to the attacks would produce a disparate, incidental impact on Arab Muslims, even though the purpose of the policy was to target neither Arabs nor Muslims. On the facts respondent alleges the arrests Mueller oversaw were likely lawful and justified by his nondiscriminatory intent to detain aliens who were illegally present in the United States and who had potential connections to those who committed terrorist acts. As between that "obvious alternative explanation" for the arrests and the purposeful, invidious discrimination respondent asks us to infer, discrimination is not a plausible conclusion.

But even if the complaint's well-pleaded facts give rise to a plausible inference that respondent's arrest was the result of unconstitutional discrimination, that inference alone would not entitle respondent to relief. It is important to recall that respondent's complaint challenges neither the constitutionality of his arrest nor his initial detention in the MDC. Respondent's constitutional claims against petitioners rest solely on their ostensible "policy of holding post-September-11th detainees" in the ADMAX SHU once they were categorized as "of high interest." To prevail on that theory, the complaint must contain facts plausibly showing that petitioners purposefully adopted a policy of classifying post-September-11 detainees as "of high interest" because of their race, religion, or national origin.

This the complaint fails to do. Though respondent alleges that various other defendants, who are not before us, may have labeled him a person of "of high interest" for impermissible reasons, his only factual allegation against petitioners accuses them of adopting a policy approving "restrictive conditions of confinement" for post-September-11 detainees until they were "'cleared' by the FBI." Accepting the truth of that allegation, the complaint does not show, or even intimate, that petitioners purposefully housed detainees in the ADMAX SHU due to their race, religion, or national origin. All it plausibly suggests is that the Nation's top law enforcement officers, in the aftermath of a devastating terrorist attack, sought to keep suspected terrorists in the most secure conditions available until the suspects could be cleared of terrorist activity. Respondent does not argue, nor can he, that such a motive would violate petitioners' constitutional obligations. He would need to allege more by way of factual content to "nudg[e]" his claim of purposeful discrimination "across the line from conceivable to plausible."

V

We hold that respondent's complaint fails to plead sufficient facts to state a claim for purposeful and unlawful discrimination against petitioners. The Court of Appeals should decide in the first instance whether to remand to the District Court so that respondent can seek leave to amend his deficient complaint.

The judgment of the Court of Appeals is reversed, and the case is remanded for further proceedings consistent with this opinion.

It is so ordered.

Justice SOUTER, with whom Justice STEVENS, Justice GINSBURG, and Justice BREYER join, dissenting.

I

The District Court denied Ashcroft and Mueller's motion to dismiss Iqbal's discrimination claim, and the Court of Appeals affirmed. Ashcroft and Mueller then asked this Court to grant certiorari on two questions:

> "1. Whether a conclusory allegation that a cabinet-level officer or other high-ranking official knew of, condoned, or agreed to subject a plaintiff to allegedly unconstitutional acts purportedly committed by subordinate officials is sufficient to state individual-capacity claims against those officials under *Bivens*.

> "2. Whether a cabinet-level officer or other high-ranking official may be held personally liable for the allegedly unconstitutional acts of subordinate officials on the ground that, as high-level supervisors, they had constructive notice of the discrimination allegedly carried out by such subordinate officials."

The Court granted certiorari on both questions. The first is about pleading; the second goes to the liability standard.

In the first question, Ashcroft and Mueller did not ask whether "a cabinet-level officer or other high-ranking official" who "knew of, condoned, or agreed to subject a plaintiff to allegedly unconstitutional acts committed by subordinate officials" was subject to liability under *Bivens*. In fact, they conceded in their petition for certiorari that they would be liable if they had "actual knowledge" of discrimination by their subordinates and exhibited "'deliberate indifference'" to that discrimination. Instead, they asked the Court to address whether Iqbal's allegations against them (which they call conclusory) were sufficient to satisfy Rule 8(a)(2), and in particular whether the Court of Appeals misapplied our decision in *Twombly* construing that rule.

In the second question, Ashcroft and Mueller asked this Court to say whether they could be held personally liable for the actions of their subordinates based on the theory that they had constructive notice of their subordinates' unconstitutional conduct.

Without acknowledging the parties' agreement as to the standard of supervisory liability, the Court asserts that it must *sua sponte* decide the scope of supervisory liability here. But deciding the scope of supervisory *Bivens* liability in this case is uncalled for. There are several reasons, starting with the position Ashcroft and Mueller have taken and following from it.

First, Ashcroft and Mueller have, as noted, made the critical concession that a supervisor's knowledge of a subordinate's unconstitutional conduct and deliberate indifference to that conduct are grounds for *Bivens* liability. Iqbal seeks to recover on a theory that Ashcroft and Mueller at least knowingly acquiesced (and maybe more than acquiesced) in the discriminatory acts of their subordinates; if he can show this, he will satisfy Ashcroft and Mueller's own test for supervisory liability.

Second, because of the concession, we have received no briefing or argument on the proper scope of supervisory liability, much less the full-dress argument we normally require. We consequently are in no position to decide the precise contours of supervisory liability here, this issue being a complicated one that has divided the Courts of Appeals.

Finally, the Court's approach is most unfair to Iqbal. He was entitled to rely on Ashcroft and Mueller's concession, both in their petition for certiorari and in their merits briefs, that they could be held liable on a theory of knowledge and deliberate indifference. By overriding that concession, the Court denies Iqbal a fair chance to be heard on the question.

The majority, however, does ignore the concession. The majority says that in a *Bivens* action, "where masters do not answer for the torts of their servants," "the term 'supervisory liability' is a misnomer," and that "[a]bsent vicarious liability, each Government official, his or her title notwithstanding, is only liable for his or her own misconduct." Lest there be any mistake, in these words the majority is not narrowing the scope of supervisory liability; it is eliminating *Bivens* supervisory liability entirely. The nature of a supervisory liability theory is that the supervisor may be liable, under certain conditions, for the wrongdoing of his subordinates, and it is this very principle that the majority rejects. ("[P]etitioners cannot be held liable unless they themselves acted on account of a constitutionally protected characteristic").

The dangers of the majority's readiness to proceed without briefing and argument are apparent in its cursory analysis, which rests on the assumption that only two outcomes are possible here: *respondeat superior* liability, in which "an employer is subject to liability for torts committed by employees while acting within the scope of their employment," or no supervisory liability at all. In fact, there is quite a spectrum of possible tests for supervisory liability: it could be imposed where a supervisor has actual knowledge of a subordinate's constitutional violation and acquiesces; or where supervisors "'know about the conduct and facilitate it, approve it, condone it, or turn a blind eye for fear of what they might see'"; or where the supervisor has no actual knowledge of the violation but was reckless in his supervision of the subordinate. I am unsure what the general test for supervisory liability should be, and in the absence of briefing and argument I am in no position to choose or devise one.

II

Given petitioners' concession, the complaint satisfies Rule 8(a)(2). Ashcroft and Mueller admit they are liable for their subordinates' conduct if they "had actual knowledge of the assertedly discriminatory nature of the classification of suspects as being 'of high interest' and they were deliberately indifferent to that discrimination." Iqbal alleges that after the September 11 attacks the Federal Bureau of Investigation (FBI) "arrested and detained thousands of Arab Muslim men," that many of these men were designated by high-ranking FBI officials as being "'of high interest,'" and that in many cases, including Iqbal's, this designation was made "because of the race, religion, and national origin of the detainees, and not because of any evidence of the detainees' involvement in supporting terrorist activity." The complaint further alleges that Ashcroft was the "principal architect of the policies and practices challenged" and that Mueller "was instrumental in the adoption, promulgation, and implementation of the policies and practices challenged." According to the complaint, Ashcroft and Mueller "knew of, condoned, and willfully and maliciously agreed to subject [Iqbal] to these conditions of confinement as a matter of policy, solely on account of [his] religion, race, and/or national origin and for no legitimate penological interest." The complaint thus alleges, at a bare minimum, that Ashcroft and Mueller knew of and condoned the discriminatory policy their subordinates carried out. Actually, the complaint goes further in alleging that Ashcroft and Muller affirmatively acted to create the discriminatory detention policy. If these factual allegations are true, Ashcroft and Mueller were, at the very least, aware of the discriminatory policy being implemented and deliberately indifferent to it.

Ashcroft and Mueller argue that these allegations fail to satisfy the "plausibility standard" of *Twombly*. They contend that Iqbal's claims are implausible because such high-ranking officials "tend not to be personally involved in the specific actions of lower-level officers down the bureaucratic chain of command." But this response bespeaks a fundamental misunderstanding of the enquiry that *Twombly* demands. *Twombly* does not require a court at the motion-to-dismiss stage to consider whether the factual allegations are probably true. We made it clear, on the contrary, that a court must take the allegations as true, no matter how skeptical the court may be. The sole exception to this rule lies with allegations that are sufficiently fantastic to defy reality as we know it: claims about little green men, or the plaintiff's recent trip to Pluto, or experiences in time travel. That is not what we have here.

Under *Twombly*, the relevant question is whether, assuming the factual allegations are true, the plaintiff has stated a ground for relief that is plausible. That is, in *Twombly*'s words, a plaintiff must "allege facts" that, taken as true, are "suggestive of illegal conduct." Here, by contrast, the allegations in the complaint are neither confined to naked legal conclusions nor consistent with legal conduct. The complaint alleges that FBI officials discriminated against Iqbal solely on account of his race, religion, and national origin, and it alleges the knowledge and deliberate indifference that, by Ashcroft and Mueller's own admission, are sufficient to make them liable for the illegal action. Iqbal's complaint therefore contains "enough facts to state a claim to relief that is plausible on its face."

By my lights, there is no principled basis for the majority's disregard of the allegations link-ing Ashcroft and Mueller to their subordinates' discrimination.

NOTES AND QUESTIONS

1. What two-step analysis does the Court establish for determining whether pleadings are sufficient to survive a Motion to Dismiss? Why didn't Iqbal's complaint meet this standard?

2. The dissent opines that the defendants conceded they could be held liable if they had actual knowledge of the discriminatory conduct of their subordinates and yet acted with deliberate indifference to that knowledge. They contested only a "constructive knowledge" standard followed by some circuits at this time. Does the Court eliminate "knowledge and acquiescence" in a subordinate's wrongdoing as a basis for imposing supervisory liability? What test for supervisory liability does the Court adopt, and why didn't Iqbal's complaint meet that standard?

MITCHELL V. FORSYTH
472 u.s. 511 (1985)

Justice WHITE delivered the opinion of the Court.

This is a suit for damages stemming from a warrantless wiretap authorized by petitioner, a former Attorney General of the United States.

I

In 1970, the Federal Bureau of Investigation learned that members of an antiwar group known as the East Coast Conspiracy to Save Lives had made plans to blow up heating tunnels linking federal office buildings in Washington, D.C., and had also discussed the possibility of kidnapping then National Security Adviser Henry Kissinger. On November 6, 1970, acting on the basis of this information, the then Attorney General John Mitchell authorized a warrantless wiretap on the telephone of William Davidon, a Haverford College physics professor who was a member of the group. According to the Attorney General, the purpose of the wiretap was the gathering of intelligence in the interest of national security.

The FBI installed the tap in late November 1970, and it stayed in place until January 6, 1971. During that time, the Government intercepted three conversations between Davidon and respondent Keith Forsyth. The record before us does not suggest that the intercepted conversa-tions, which appear to be innocuous, were ever used against Forsyth in any way.

Shortly thereafter, this Court ruled that the Fourth Amendment does not permit the use of warrantless wiretaps in cases involving domestic threats to the national security.

[The trial court ruled against the defendant on the immunity issue and he sought immediate review of this order as an appealable "final decision."]

III

Although 28 U.S.C. § 1291 vests the courts of appeals with jurisdiction over appeals only from "final decisions" of the district courts, "a decision 'final' within the meaning of § 1291 does not necessarily mean the last order possible to be made in a case." Thus, a decision of a district court is appealable if it falls within "that small class which finally determine claims of right separable from, and collateral to, rights asserted in the action, too important to be denied review and too independent of the cause itself to require that appellate consideration be deferred until the whole case is adjudicated."

A major characteristic of the denial or granting of a claim appealable under *Cohen*'s "collateral order" doctrine is that "unless it can be reviewed before [the proceedings terminate], it can never be reviewed at all." When a district court has denied a defendant's claim of right not to stand trial, on double jeopardy grounds, for example, we have consistently held the court's decision appealable, for such a right cannot be effectively vindicated after the trial has occurred. Thus, the denial of a substantial claim of absolute immunity is an order appealable before final judgment, for the essence of absolute immunity is its possessor's entitlement not to have to answer for his conduct in a civil damages action.

At the heart of the issue before us is the question whether qualified immunity shares this essential attribute of absolute immunity—whether qualified immunity is in fact an entitlement not to stand trial under certain circumstances. The conception animating the qualified immunity doctrine as set forth in *Harlow v. Fitzgerald* is that "where an official's duties legitimately require action in which clearly established rights are not implicated, the public interest may be better served by action taken 'with independence and without fear of consequences.'" [T]he "consequences" with which we were concerned in *Harlow* are not limited to liability for money damages; they also include "the general costs of subjecting officials to the risks of trial—distraction of officials from their governmental duties, inhibition of discretionary action, and deterrence of able people from public service." Indeed, *Harlow* emphasizes that even such pretrial matters as discovery are to be avoided if possible, as "[i]nquiries of this kind can be peculiarly disruptive of effective government."

With these concerns in mind, the *Harlow* Court refashioned the qualified immunity doctrine in such a way as to "permit the resolution of many insubstantial claims on summary judgment" and to avoid "subject[ing] government officials either to the costs of trial or to the burdens of broad-reaching discovery" in cases where the legal norms the officials are alleged to have violated were not clearly established at the time. Unless the plaintiff's allegations state a claim of violation of clearly established law, a defendant pleading qualified immunity is entitled to dismissal before the commencement of discovery. Even if the plaintiff's complaint adequately alleges the commission of acts that violated clearly established law, the defendant is entitled to summary judgment if discovery fails to uncover evidence sufficient to create a genuine issue as to whether the defendant in fact committed those acts. *Harlow* thus recognized an entitlement not to stand trial or face the other burdens of litigation, conditioned on the resolution of the essentially legal question whether the conduct of which the plaintiff complains violated clearly established law. The entitlement is an *immunity from suit* rather then a mere defense to liability; and like an absolute immunity, it is effectively lost if a case is erroneously permitted to go to trial. Accordingly, the reasoning that underlies the immediate appealability of an order denying absolute immunity indicates to us that the denial of qualified immunity should be similarly appealable: in each case, the district court's decision is effectively unreviewable on appeal from a final judgment.

An appealable interlocutory decision must satisfy two additional criteria: it must "conclusively determine the disputed question" and that question must involve a "clai[m] of right separable from, and collateral to, rights asserted in the action." The denial of a defendant's motion for dismissal or summary judgment on the ground of qualified immunity easily meets these requirements. Such a decision is "conclusive" in either of two respects. In some cases, it may represent the trial court's conclusion that even if the facts are as asserted by the defendant, the defendant's actions violated clearly established law and are therefore not within the scope of the qualified immunity. In such a case, there will be nothing in the subsequent course of the proceedings in the district court that can alter the court's conclusion that the defendant is not immune. Alternatively, the trial judge may rule only that if the facts are as asserted by the plaintiff, the defendant is not immune. At trial, the plaintiff may not succeed in proving his version of the facts, and the defendant may thus escape liability. Even so, the court's denial of summary judgment finally and conclusively determines the defendant's claim of right not to *stand trial* on the plaintiff's allegations, and because "[t]here are simply no further steps that can be taken in the District Court to avoid the trial the defendant maintains is barred," it is apparent that "*Cohen*'s threshold requirement of a fully consummated decision is satisfied" in such a case.

Similarly, it follows from the recognition that qualified immunity is in part an entitlement not to be forced to litigate the consequences of official conduct that a claim of immunity is conceptually distinct from the merits of the plaintiff's claim that his rights have been violated. An appellate court reviewing the denial of the defendant's claim of immunity need not consider the correctness of the plaintiff's version of the facts, nor even determine whether the plaintiff's allegations actually state a claim. All it need determine is a question of law: whether the legal norms allegedly violated by the defendant were clearly established at the time of the challenged actions or, in cases where the district court has denied summary judgment for the defendant on the ground that even under the defendant's version of the facts the defendant's conduct violated clearly established law, whether the law clearly proscribed the actions the defendant claims he took. To be sure, the resolution of these legal issues will entail consideration of the factual allegations that make up the plaintiff's claim for relief; the same is true, however, when a court must consider whether a prosecution is barred by a claim of former jeopardy or whether a Congressman is absolutely immune from suit because the complained of conduct falls within the protections of the Speech and Debate Clause. In the case of a double jeopardy claim, the court must compare the facts alleged in the second indictment with those in the first to determine whether the prosecutions are for the same offense, while in evaluating a claim of immunity under the Speech and Debate Clause, a court must analyze the plaintiff's complaint to determine whether the plaintiff seeks to hold a Congressman liable for protected legislative actions or for other, unprotected conduct. In holding these and similar issues of absolute immunity to be appealable under the collateral order doctrine, the Court has recognized that a question of immunity is separate from the merits of the underlying action for purposes of the *Cohen* test even though a reviewing court must consider the plaintiff's factual allegations in resolving the immunity issue.

Accordingly, we hold that a district court's denial of a claim of qualified immunity, to the extent that it turns on an issue of law, is an appealable "final decision" within the meaning of 28 U.S.C. § 1291 notwithstanding the absence of a final judgment.

NOTES AND QUESTIONS

1. In *Johnson v. Jones*, 515 U.S. 304 (1995), the Court limited *Forsyth*, holding that an order denying police officers' motion for summary judgment, raising the qualified immunity defense, was not immediately appealable because the court simply decided that there were genuine issues of fact for trial. Here there was a factual dispute over whether the officers stood by and allowed others to beat the plaintiff. *Forsyth* does not control this situation because the order denying summary judgment was not a "final decision" within the meaning of the relevant statute, *i.e.*, the court decided it could not determine the qualified immunity issue because of a factual dispute.

   In *Behrens v. Pelletier*, 516 U.S. 299 (1996), the Court "clarified" *Johnson*, stating "[it] held, simply, that determinations of evidentiary sufficiency at summary judgment are not immediately appealable merely because they happen to arise in a qualified-immunity case; if what is at issue in the sufficiency determination is nothing more than whether the evidence could support a finding that particular conduct occurred, the question decided is not truly 'separable' from the plaintiff's claim, and hence there is no 'final decision' under *Cohen* and *Mitchell*." *Id.* at 842. However, where the trial court determines that certain conduct attributed to the defendant (which was controverted) constitutes a violation of clearly established law, the defendant may argue on appeal that all of the conduct deemed sufficiently supported for summary judgment purposes meets the standard of "objective legal reasonableness."

2. A defendant filed an immediate appeal of an order denying his motion to dismiss, based on qualified immunity. After this ruling was affirmed on appeal, the defendant filed a motion for summary judgment, again raising the qualified immunity defense. The trial court denied summary judgment and the defendant filed another immediate appeal, which was dismissed by the court of appeals. In *Behrens, supra*, the Court rejected the "one-interlocutory-appeal" rule, holding that rejection of the qualified immunity defense at either the motion to dismiss or summary judgment stage is a

final judgment subject to immediate appeal. This is true even if, as here, it results in two interlocutory appeals because the factors determinative of the qualified immunity issue are different at the summary judgment stage than at the motion to dismiss stage where the court considers only the allegations in the complaint must be accepted.

Why should a defendant, who has the option of filing for summary judgment on the qualified immunity defense, be given two opportunities to delay a trial on the merits?

The Supreme Court considered the appealability of qualified immunity decisions in *Ortiz v. Jordan*, 532 U.S. 180 (2011), holding that summary judgment orders denying qualified immunity based on disputed facts are not appealable after a full trial on the merits. The defendant prison officials did not appeal the district court's denial of their pretrial qualified immunity motion for summary judgment, where the denial was based on disputed facts. After a verdict was entered for the prisoner, the officials sought to appeal the denial of their summary judgment motion, but the Court ruled that after a trial, the "full record developed in court supersedes the record existing at the time of the summary judgment motion." The defendants failed to renew their motion for judgment as a matter of law after the verdict against them, which left the court of appeals "powerless" to review their claim that the plaintiff's evidence was insufficient to establish a constitutional violation. As a result, the Sixth Circuit erred in upsetting the jury's decision on the officials' liability. Although the defendants tried to argue that a qualified immunity plea raising a "purely legal" issue is preserved for appeal by an unsuccessful summary judgment motion even if the plea is not reiterated in a Rule 50(b) motion, the Court reasoned that here the dispositive facts were in dispute and the immunity defense did not raise "neat abstract issues of law."

3. Does the rationale of *Forsyth* apply where the plaintiff, in addition to damages, seeks injunctive relief which will require a trial even if the defendant official enjoys a qualified immunity?

In *Behrens, supra*, the Court held that the "right to immunity is a right to immunity *from certain claims*, not from litigation in general." *Id.* at 841. Therefore, the fact that a defendant will have to endure discovery and a trial on other claims does not affect the right to an immediate appeal on the qualified immunity issue. Note, however, that unless the appeal on the qualified immunity issue is frivolous, it will normally result in a stay of proceedings in the trial court. *Apostol v. Gallion*, 870 F.2d 1335 (7th Cir. 1989).

4. The "collateral order" doctrine applied in *Forsyth* does not control § 1983 actions in state court. In *Johnson v. Fankell*, 520 U.S. 911 (1997), the Court held there is no federal right to an interlocutory appeal from a state court order rejecting the qualified immunity defense because (i) the "collateral order" doctrine is based on an

interpretation of a federal statute and is not binding on the states, and (ii) the Idaho Appellate Rule, which does not provide for an such an appeal, is not pre-empted by § 1983. Pre-emption was rejected because dismissal of the appeal was based on a "neutral state rule" and the nature of the interest protected by the immunity defense, *i.e.*, "the ultimate purpose of qualified immunity is to protect the state and its officials from overenforcement of federal rights." Reliance on *Felder v. Casey* (*supra* Ch. II) was misplaced because the denial of an interlocutory appeal does not affect the "ultimate outcome of the case."

Problem: Sixteen

Defendant McLaughlin was employed as a child protective services (CPS) worker by defendant-appellee, the Department of Social and Health Services, State of Washington (DSHS). Her duties included investigating and reporting cases of alleged child abuse and neglect. Prior to September 1978, a fellow CPS worker informed McLaughlin that plaintiff Coverdell had moved into McLaughlin's service region, that Coverdell was pregnant with her third child, and that the court had already terminated Coverdell's parental rights to her eldest child. Coverdell's rights were terminated because she and her husband, Roscoe, were emotionally unstable, easily angered, violent, and a danger to the child.

After receiving this information, McLaughlin attempted to visit the Coverdell residence to determine whether conditions there were suitable for the expected child. Coverdell denied McLaughlin admission to the residence.

The expected child, Christina, was born on September 27, 1978. Later that day, McLaughlin received a telephone call from an employee of the hospital at which Coverdell was confined. The employee informed McLaughlin that Coverdell had given birth to a girl and that Coverdell had requested that the hospital refrain from notifying the DSHS of the birth.

The following day, September 28, 1978, McLaughlin provided the Columbia County Prosecutor with an affidavit stating that the court had previously deprived Roscoe and Alice Coverdell of permanent custody of their eldest child, Angel, because of hazardous living conditions; that Union County, Oregon was currently seeking to deprive the Coverdells of permanent custody of their second child, James; that McLaughlin had personal contact with the Coverdells and believed them to be emotionally unstable; that McLaughlin had requested admission to the Coverdell residence but had been denied access; and that McLaughlin believed that the newborn Christina would be in danger if she were to reside with the Coverdells.

The next day, on the basis of McLaughlin's affidavit, the Columbia County Prosecutor filed a motion in state court for an order to take Christina into custody. Coverdell received no notice of the motion, nor was she represented at the hearing. On the same day, the court issued an order authorizing the DSHS to take immediate custody of Christina. The next day, September 30, 1978, McLaughlin executed the court's order by removing Christina from the hospital and placing her in temporary shelter care. On October 27, 1978, the state court ordered that Christina remain in shelter care until further court order.

In March 1980, Coverdell petitioned the state court to regain custody of Christina. At the hearing on the petition, McLaughlin testified in opposition to Christina's placement with Coverdell, as did defendant Langston, the foster mother who was then caring for Christina. Langston filed a motion to permit her to intervene in this proceeding and requested a hearing. The court denied these requests but stayed its order pending Langston's appeal. Langston then instituted a separate action in state court seeking custody of Christina.

Shortly after Coverdell filed her petition, DSHS petitioned the court for termination of Coverdell's parental rights to Christina. During the pendency of that proceeding, DSHS did not permit Coverdell to visit with Christina. Coverdell sought and obtained a court order permitting visitation. Langston again filed a motion to intervene and asked for reconsideration of the order permitting Coverdell to visit Christina. Langston's motion was denied. Sometime after Coverdell began exercising her court ordered visitation rights, Langston reported to DSHS her suspicion that Coverdell had been sexually abusing Christina. In February 1982, after hearings on the matter, Coverdell's visitation rights were terminated by the state court.

The various state court proceedings culminated on December 20, 1984, when the court ordered termination of the parental rights of Alice and Roscoe Coverdell over Christina. That order is now final.

On May 31, 1985, Coverdell filed a § 1983 action in federal court, alleging that the actions of DSHS and McLaughlin, under color of state law, deprived Coverdell of her rights under the United States Constitution and the laws of the United States. More specifically, Coverdell alleged that DSHS, McLaughlin, and Langston acted individually and in concert to prevent the return of Christina to Coverdell, thereby denying Coverdell her right to due process and equal protection, in that the defendants' actions were predicated on their belief that Coverdell was "of an inferior intellectual capacity and of an inferior personality and otherwise mentally handicapped."

1. Is McLaughlin absolutely immune from damages based on her conduct in:

   a. providing an affidavit that triggers the initiation of child dependency proceedings in state court;

   b. removing Christina from the hospital, pursuant to court order;

   c. testifying at the hearing in court?

2. Assume McLaughlin is not absolutely immune and apply the qualified immunity doctrine to her conduct referred to in question 1 a. above.

3. Is Langston, the foster mother, subject to suit under § 1983? If yes, is Langston entitled to either absolute or qualified immunity if she is included as a defendant?

4. Ms. Coverdell has two other children. Does she have standing to seek an injunction to prohibit McLaughlin from seizing these children without prior notice and an opportunity for a hearing?

5. May Coverdell sue DSHS directly under § 1983 for its conduct in seeking to terminate her parental rights? If so, does DSHS enjoy immunity?

6. GOVERNMENTAL ENTITY IMMUNITY

a. Local Government

Local governmental entities do not enjoy the absolute or qualified immunities which protect government officials. *See Owen v. City of Independence*, 445 U.S. 622 (1980), *supra* Ch. II. Furthermore, such entities are not protected by the Eleventh Amendment, discussed in the following section. Therefore, plaintiffs can avoid absolute and qualified immunity problems by suing local governmental officials' employers for damages, if they can overcome the fact that they cannot rely upon *respondeat superior*.

Generally local governmental entities are not liable for punitive damages. *City of Newport v. Fact Concerts, Inc.*, 453 U.S. 247 (1981). However, if a state statute which indemnifies government officials for individual liability does not exclude indemnity for punitive damages, this has been held to constitute a waiver of the protection against punitive damages. *Kolar v. County of Sangamon of State of Illinois*, 756 F.2d 564, 567 (7th Cir. 1985). Illinois subsequently amended its statute to foreclose the waiver argument.

Liability and jurisdictional questions will often turn on whether an entity is considered a branch of state or local government, but the determination is not always readily apparent. In *Mt. Healthy City School Dist. v. Doyle*, 429 U.S. 274, 280 (1977), the Court noted that the answer depends at least in part of the "nature of the entity created by state law." The most important factor seems to be whether a judgment against the entity is in effect a judgment against the state treasury. When determining whether an entity is "an arm of the State," courts look at the particular function of the entity at issue; this means that an entity may be "an arm of the State" when performing some functions, but not when performing others.

b. State Government—Eleventh Amendment

[Review earlier discussion of *Fitzpatrick v. Bitzer, supra*, discussing congressional abrogation of the Eleventh Amendment.]

Justice POWELL delivered the opinion of the Court.

This case presents the question whether a federal court may award injunctive relief against state officials on the basis of state law.

II

A

Article III, § 2, of the Constitution provides that the federal judicial power extends, *inter alia*, to controversies "between a State and Citizens of another State." Relying on this language, this Court in 1793 assumed original jurisdiction over a suit brought by a citizen of South Carolina against the State of Georgia. *Chisholm v. Georgia.* The decision "created such a shock of surprise that the Eleventh Amendment was at once proposed and adopted." The Amendment provides:

> The Judicial power of the United States shall not be construed to extend to any suit in law or equity, commenced or prosecuted against one of the United States by Citizens of another State, or by Citizens or Subjects of any Foreign State.

The Amendment's language overruled the particular result in *Chisholm*, but this Court has recognized that its greater significance lies in its affirmation that the fundamental principle of sovereign immunity limits the grant of judicial authority in Art. III. Thus, in *Hans v. Louisiana*, 134 U.S. 1 (1890), the Court held that, despite the limited terms of the Eleventh Amendment, a federal court could not entertain a suit brought by a citizen against his own State. After reviewing the constitutional debates concerning the scope of Art. III, the Court determined that federal jurisdiction over suits against unconsenting States "was not contemplated by the Constitution when establishing the judicial power of the United States."

A sovereign's immunity may be waived, and the Court consistently has held that a State may consent to suit against it in federal court. We have insisted, however, that the State's consent be unequivocally expressed. Similarly, although Congress has power with respect to the rights protected by the Fourteenth Amendment to abrogate the Eleventh Amendment immunity, *see Fitzpatrick v. Bitzer*, we have required an unequivocal expression of congressional intent to "overturn the constitutionally guaranteed immunity of the several States." *Quern v. Jordan* (holding that 42 U.S.C. § 1983 does not override States' Eleventh Amendment immunity). Our reluctance to infer that a State's immunity from suit in the federal courts has been negated stems from recognition of the vital role of the doctrine of sovereign immunity in our federal system. A State's constitutional interest in immunity encompasses not merely *whether* it may be sued, but *where* it may be sued. Accordingly, in deciding this case we must be guided by "[t]he principles of federalism that inform Eleventh Amendment doctrine."

B

This Court's decisions thus establish that "an unconsenting State is immune from suits brought in federal courts by her own citizens as well as by citizens of another state." There may be a question, however, whether a particular suit in fact is a suit against a State. It is clear, of course, that in the absence of consent a suit in which the State or one of its agencies or departments is named as the defendant is proscribed by the Eleventh Amendment. This jurisdictional bar applies regardless of the nature of the relief sought.

When the suit is brought only against state officials, a question arises as to whether that suit is a suit against the State itself. Although prior decisions of this Court have not been entirely consistent on this issue, certain principles are well established. The Eleventh Amendment bars a suit against state officials when "the state is the real, substantial party in interest." Thus, "[t]he general rule is that relief sought nominally against an officer is in fact against the sovereign if the decree would operate against the latter." And, as when the State itself is named as the defendant, a suit against state officials that is in fact a suit against a State is barred regardless of whether it seeks damages or injunctive relief.

The Court has recognized an important exception to this general rule: a suit challenging the constitutionality of a state official's action is not one against the State. This was the holding in *Ex parte Young*, in which a federal court enjoined the Attorney General of the State of Minnesota from bringing suit to enforce a state statute that allegedly violated the Fourteenth Amendment. This Court held that the Eleventh Amendment did not prohibit issuance of this injunction. The theory of the case was that an unconstitutional enactment is "void" and therefore does not "impart to [the officer] any immunity from responsibility to the supreme authority of the United States." Since the State could not authorize the action, the officer was "stripped of his official or representative character and [was] subjected in his person to the consequences of his individual conduct."

While the rule permitting suits alleging conduct contrary to "the supreme authority of the United States" has survived, the theory of *Young* has not been provided an expansive interpretation. Thus, in *Edelman v. Jordan*, the Court emphasized that the Eleventh Amendment bars some forms of injunctive relief against state officials for violation of federal law. In particular, *Edelman* held that when a plaintiff sues a state official alleging a violation of federal law, the federal court may award an injunction that governs the official's future conduct, but not one that awards retroactive monetary relief. Under the theory of *Young*, such a suit would not be one against the State since the federal-law allegation would strip the state officer of his official authority. Nevertheless, retroactive relief was barred by the Eleventh Amendment.

III

With these principles in mind, we now turn to the question whether the claim that petitioners violated *state law* in carrying out their official duties at Pennhurst is one against the State and therefore barred by the Eleventh Amendment. Respondents advance two principal arguments in support of the judgment below. First, they contend that under the doctrine of *Edelman v. Jordan* the suit is not against the State because the courts below ordered only prospective injunctive relief. Second, they assert that the state-law claim properly was decided under the doctrine of pendent jurisdiction. Respondents rely on decisions of this Court awarding relief against state officials on the basis of a pendent state-law claim.

We first address the contention that respondents' state-law claim is not barred by the Eleventh Amendment because it seeks only prospective relief as defined in *Edelman*. The Court of Appeals held that if the judgment below rested on federal law, it could be entered against petitioner state officials under the doctrine established in *Edelman* and *Young* even though the prospective financial burden was substantial and ongoing. The court assumed, and respondents assert, that this reasoning applies as well when the official acts in violation of state law. This argument misconstrues the basis of the doctrine established in *Young* and *Edelman*.

As discussed above, the injunction in *Young* was justified, notwithstanding the obvious impact on the State itself, on the view that sovereign immunity does not apply because an official who acts unconstitutionally is "stripped of his official or representative character." This rationale, of course, created the "well-recognized irony" that an official's unconstitutional conduct constitutes state action under the Fourteenth Amendment but not the Eleventh Amendment. Nonetheless, the *Young* doctrine has been accepted as necessary to permit the federal courts to vindicate federal rights and hold state officials responsible to "the supreme authority of the United States." Our decisions repeatedly have emphasized that the *Young* doctrine rests on the need to promote the vindication of federal rights.

The Court also has recognized, however, that the need to promote the supremacy of federal law must be accommodated to the constitutional immunity of the States. This is the significance of *Edelman*. We recognized that the prospective relief authorized by *Young* "has permitted the Civil War Amendments to the Constitution to serve as a sword, rather than merely a shield, for those whom they were designed to protect." But we declined to extend the fiction of *Young* to encompass retroactive relief, for to do so would effectively eliminate the constitutional immunity of the States. Accordingly, we concluded that although the difference between permissible and impermissible relief "will not in many instances be that between day and night," an award of retroactive relief necessarily "'falls[s] afoul of the Eleventh Amendment if that basic constitutional provision is to be conceived of as having any present force.'" In sum, *Edelman*'s distinction between prospective and retroactive relief fulfills the underlying purpose of *Ex parte Young* while at the same time preserving to an important degree the constitutional immunity of the States.

This need to reconcile competing interests is wholly absent, however, when a plaintiff alleges that a state official has violated *state* law. In such a case the entire basis for the doctrine of *Young* and *Edelman* disappears. A federal court's grant of relief against state officials on the basis of state law, whether prospective or retroactive, does not vindicate the supreme authority of federal law. On the contrary, it is difficult to think of a greater intrusion on state sovereignty than when a federal court instructs state officials on how to conform their conduct to state law. Such a result conflicts directly with the principles of federalism that underlie the Eleventh

Amendment. We conclude that *Young* and *Edelman* are inapplicable in a suit against state officials on the basis of state law.

NOTES AND QUESTIONS

1. Why did the Court refuse to extend the *Ex parte Young* doctrine to claims for an injunction based on a violation of state law? Does the Court foreclose a declaratory judgment based on state law?

    In *Virginia Office for Protection and Advocacy v. Stewart*, 563 U.S. 247 (2011) the Court ruled that *Ex Parte Young* permits a federal court to hear a lawsuit for prospective relief against state officials even where suit is brought by an agency of the same state.

2. Even though the Eleventh Amendment does not apply to actions in state court, the Court relied in part on the scope of the Eleventh Amendment in holding that neither a state nor its officials acting in their official capacity is a "person" within the meaning of § 1983. *Will v. Michigan Dep't of State Police*, 491 U.S. 58 (1989) ("[t]his does not mean that we think that the scope of the Eleventh Amendment and the scope of § 1983 are not separate issues;" but "in deciphering congressional intent as to the scope of § 1983, the scope of the Eleventh Amendment is a consideration"). The Court did note, however, that state officials acting in their official capacity can be sued under § 1983 for prospective injunctive relief.

    Since § 1983 actions can be filed in state court, why should the Eleventh Amendment be a factor in interpreting the scope of the term "person" as used in § 1983?

3. Keeping in mind the preclusion principles discussed *supra* Ch. II, consider the litigation options available to a plaintiff challenging conditions in a state institution and seeking injunctive relief and damages based on both federal and state law. Note that the Eleventh Amendment does not apply to litigation in state court. Further, it does not bar an award of damages against a state official in her personal or individual capacity. *Hafer v. Melo*, 502 U.S. 21 (1991).

Problem: Seventeen

1. Does the Eleventh Amendment provide protection in the following situations, assuming litigation in federal court:

    a. Suit against a state or state agency, seeking either damages or injunctive relief, with the plaintiff's claim based on (a) state law? (b) federal law?

b. Suit for injunctive relief against a state official, in his or her official capacity, with the plaintiff's claim based on (a) state law? (b) federal law?

c. Suit for damages against a state official, in his or her official capacity, with the plaintiff's claim based on (a) state law? (b) federal law?

d. Suit for damages against a state official in his or her individual capacity, with the plaintiff's claim based on (a) state law? (b) federal law?

2. Now assume a § 1983 action is brought in state court against a state or state agency, seeking both damages and injunctive relief. How would you respond on behalf of the defendant?

ATASCADERO STATE HOSPITAL V. SCANLON
473 U.S. 234 (1985)

Justice POWELL delivered the opinion of the Court.

This case presents the question whether States and state agencies are subject to suit in federal court by litigants seeking retroactive monetary relief under § 504 of the Rehabilitation Act of 1973, 29 U.S.C. § 794, or whether such suits are proscribed by the Eleventh Amendment.

I

Respondent, Douglas James Scanlon, suffers from diabetes mellitus and has no sight in one eye. In November 1979, he filed this action against petitioners, Atascadero State Hospital and the California Department of Mental Health, in the United States District Court for the Central District of California, alleging that in 1978 the hospital denied him employment as a graduate student assistant recreational therapist solely because of his physical handicaps. Respondent charged that the hospital's discriminatory refusal to hire him violated § 504 of the Rehabilitation Act of 1973 and certain state fair employment laws. Respondent sought compensatory, injunctive, and declaratory relief.

II

In this case, we are asked to decide whether the State of California is subject to suit in federal court for alleged violations of § 504 of the Rehabilitation Act. Respondent makes three arguments in support of his view that the Eleventh Amendment does not bar such a suit: first, that the State has waived its immunity by virtue of Art. III, § 5, of the California Constitution; second, that in enacting the Rehabilitation Act, Congress has abrogated the constitutional immunity of the States; third, that by accepting federal funds under the Rehabilitation Act, the State has consented to suit in federal court. Under the prior decisions of this Court, none of these claims has merit.

III

Respondent argues that the State of California has waived its immunity to suit in federal court, and thus the Eleventh Amendment does not bar this suit. Respondent relies on Art. III, § 5, of the California Constitution, which provides: "Suits may be brought against the State in such manner and in such courts as shall be directed by law." In respondent's view, unless the California Legislature affirmatively imposes sovereign immunity, the State is potentially subject to suit in any court, federal as well as state.

The test for determining whether a State has waived its immunity from federal-court jurisdiction is a stringent one. Although a State's general waiver of sovereign immunity may subject it to suit in state court, it is not enough to waive the immunity guaranteed by the Eleventh Amendment. As we explained just last Term, "a State's constitutional interest in immunity encompasses not merely *whether* it may be sued, but *where* it may be sued." Thus, in order for a state statute or constitutional provision to constitute a waiver of Eleventh Amendment immunity, it must specify the State's intention to subject itself to suit in *federal court.*

In view of these principles, we do not believe that Art. III, § 5, of the California Constitution constitutes a waiver of the State's constitutional immunity. This provision does not specifically indicate the State's willingness to be sued in federal court. Indeed, the provision appears simply to authorize the legislature to waive the State's sovereign immunity. In the absence of an unequivocal waiver specifically applicable to federal-court jurisdiction, we decline to find that California has waived its constitutional immunity.

IV

Respondent also contends that in enacting the Rehabilitation Act, Congress abrogated the States' constitutional immunity. In making this argument, respondent relies on the pre- and post-enactment legislative history of the Act and inferences from general statutory language. To reach respondent's conclusion, we would have to temper the requirement, well established in our cases, that Congress unequivocally express its intention to abrogate the Eleventh Amendment bar to suits against the States in federal court. We decline to do so, and affirm that Congress may abrogate the States' constitutionally secured immunity from suit in federal court only by making its intention unmistakably clear in the language of the statute. The fundamental nature of the interests implicated by the Eleventh Amendment dictates this conclusion.

Congress' power to abrogate a State's immunity means that in certain circumstances the usual constitutional balance between the States and the Federal Government does not obtain. "Congress may, in determining what is 'appropriate legislation' for the purpose of enforcing the provisions of the Fourteenth Amendment, provide for private suits against States or state officials which are constitutionally impermissible in other contexts." *Fitzpatrick.* In view of this fact, it is incumbent upon the federal courts to be certain of Congress' intent before finding that federal law overrides the guarantees of the Eleventh Amendment. The requirement that Congress unequivocally express this intention in the statutory language ensures such certainty.

For these reasons, we hold that Congress must express its intention to abrogate the Eleventh Amendment in unmistakable language in the statute itself.

In light of this principle, we must determine whether Congress, in adopting the Rehabilitation Act, has chosen to override the Eleventh Amendment. Section 504 of the Rehabilitation Act provides in pertinent part:

> No otherwise qualified handicapped individual in the United States, as defined in section 706(7) of this title, shall, solely by reason of his handicap, be excluded from the participation in, be denied the benefits of, or be subjected to discrimination under any program or activity receiving Federal financial assistance or under any program or activity conducted by any Executive agency or by the United States Postal Service."

Section 505, which was added to the Act in 1978, as set forth in 29 U.S.C. § 794a, describes the available remedies under the Act, including the provisions pertinent to this case:

> (a)(2) The remedies, procedures, and rights set forth in Title VI of the Civil Rights Act of 1964 [42 U.S.C. 2000d *et seq.*] shall be available to any person aggrieved by any act or failure to act by any recipient of Federal assistance or Federal provider of such assistance under section 794 of this title.

The statute thus provides remedies for violations of § 504 by "*any* recipient of Federal assistance." There is no claim here that the State of California is not a recipient of federal aid under the statute. But given their constitutional role, the States are not like any other class of recipients of federal aid. A general authorization for suit in federal court is not the kind of unequivocal statutory language sufficient to abrogate the Eleventh Amendment. When Congress chooses to subject the States to federal jurisdiction, it must do so specifically. Accordingly, we hold that the Rehabilitation Act does not abrogate the Eleventh Amendment bar to suits against the States.

V

Finally, we consider the position adopted by the Court of Appeals that the State consented to suit in federal court by accepting funds under the Rehabilitation Act.

The court properly recognized that the mere receipt of federal funds cannot establish that a State has consented to suit in federal court. The court erred, however, in concluding that because various provisions of the Rehabilitation Act are addressed to the States, a State necessarily consents to suit in federal court by participating in programs funded under the statute. We have decided today that the Rehabilitation Act does not evince an unmistakable congressional purpose, pursuant to § 5 of the Fourteenth Amendment, to subject unconsenting States to the jurisdiction of the federal courts. The Act likewise falls far short of manifesting a clear intent to condition participation in the programs funded under the Act on a State's consent to waive its constitutional immunity. Thus, were we to view this statute as an enactment pursuant to the Spending Clause, Art. I, § 8, we would hold that there was no indication that the State of California consented to federal jurisdiction.

NOTES AND QUESTIONS

1. Could Scanlon have avoided the Eleventh Amendment problem by naming as defendants the heads of the state hospital and the state department of mental health?

2. Notice that the Court considers three theories—waiver and consent by the state and abrogation by Congress. Review 42 U.S.C. § 2000d-7 (*see* Appendix), passed in 1986.

   a. Has Congress now abrogated Eleventh Amendment protection in federal suits to enforce § 504?

   b. What limitation on Congress' Spending Power has the Court recognized? See Chapter I.

3. In *Fitzpatrick v. Bitzer*, 427 U.S. 445 (1976), the Court considered whether Congress had the power, in passing the 1972 amendments to Title VII, which extended its coverage to state employers, to authorize federal courts to award back pay and attorney fees in actions finding discrimination in employment by state government. It held that Congress, acting under § 5 of the Fourteenth Amendment, could abrogate the states' Eleventh Amendment protection:

   It is true that none of [the] previous cases presented the question of the relationship between the Eleventh Amendment and the enforcement power granted to Congress under § 5 of the Fourteenth Amendment. But we think that the Eleventh Amendment, and the principle of state sovereignty which it embodies, are necessarily limited by the enforcement provisions of § 5 of the Fourteenth Amendment. In that section Congress is expressly granted authority to enforce "by appropriate legislation" the substantive provisions of the Fourteenth Amendment, which themselves embody significant limitations on state authority. When Congress acts pursuant to § 5, not only is it exercising legislative authority that is plenary within the terms of the constitutional grant, it is exercising that authority under one section of a constitutional Amendment whose other sections by their own terms embody limitations on state authority. We think that Congress may, in determining what is "appropriate legislation" for the purpose of enforcing the provisions of the Fourteenth Amendment, provide for private suits against States or state officials which are constitutionally impermissible in other contexts.

Two terms later the Court faced the question whether the Eleventh Amendment bars an award of attorney fees under § 1988, to be paid by a state agency. Relying on *Bitzer* and the legislative history of the Fee Act, the Court upheld such a fee award in *Hutto v. Finney*, 437 U.S. 678 (1978), stating:

> As this Court made clear in *Fitzpatrick v. Bitzer*, Congress has plenary power to set aside the States' immunity from retroactive relief in order to enforce the Fourteenth Amendment. When it passed the Act, Congress undoubtedly intended to exercise that power and to authorize fee awards payable by the States when their officials are sued in their official capacities. The Act itself could not be broader. It applies to "any" action brought to enforce certain civil rights laws. It contains no hint of an exception for States defending injunction actions; indeed, the Act primarily applies to laws passed specifically to restrain state action.
>
> The legislative history is equally plain: "[I]t is intended that the attorneys' fees, like other items of costs, will be collected either directly from the official, in his official capacity, from funds of his agency or under his control, or from the State or local government (whether or not the agency or government is a named party.)" The House Report is in accord: "The greater resources available to governments provide an ample base from which fees can be awarded to the prevailing plaintiff in suits against governmental officials or entities." The Report adds in a footnote that: "Of course, the 11th Amendment is not a bar to the awarding of counsel fees against state governments. *Fitzpatrick v. Bitzer*." Congress' intent was expressed in deeds as well as words. It rejected at least two attempts to amend the Act and immunize state and local governments from awards.
>
> The Act imposes attorney's fees "as part of the costs." Costs have traditionally been awarded without regard for the States' Eleventh Amendment immunity. The practice of awarding costs against the States goes back to 1849 in this Court. The Court has never viewed the Eleventh Amendment as barring such awards, even in suits between States and individual litigants.

In *Missouri v. Jenkins*, 491 U.S. 274 (1989), the Court clarified its holding in *Hutto* in rejecting an Eleventh Amendment defense to a fee award enhanced for delay in payment. It indicated that the application of § 1988 to states did not depend on congressional abrogation of the Eleventh Amendment because the immunity it provides does not extend to an award of fees ancillary to a grant of prospective relief.

4. In a 5–4 decision the Court ruled that Congress has the authority to abrogate states' Eleventh Amendment immunity when passing legislation pursuant to its power

under the Commerce Clause. *Pennsylvania v. Union Gas Co.*, 491 U.S. 1 (1989). Since the Eleventh Amendment was passed *after* the Commerce Clause, shouldn't it be interpreted as a limitation on congressional power to abrogate the states' protection when legislating under the Commerce Clause? Does the Commerce Clause, like the Fourteenth Amendment, impose substantive limits on state power?

In another 5–4 decision, *Seminole Tribe of Florida v. Florida*, 517 U.S. 44 (1996), *Union Gas Co.* was overruled, with the Court referring to it as "a solitary departure from established law." While affirming that Congress was granted the power to abrogate by § 5 of the Fourteenth Amendment, the Court concludes that neither the interstate commerce clause nor the Indian commerce clause grants Congress such power. Review note 2, *supra*; does *Seminole Tribe* affect abrogation of Eleventh Amendment immunity when Congress acts pursuant to the spending clause?

Since the decision in *Seminole Tribe*, the Court has decided two bankruptcy cases raising state sovereign immunity issues. First, in *Tennessee Student Assistance Corp. v. Hood*, 541 U.S. 440 (2004), the Court held that "a bankruptcy court's discharge of a student loan debt does not implicate a State's Eleventh Amendment immunity" because the "discharge of a debt by a bankruptcy court is . . . an *in rem* proceeding" in which a debtor seeks a discharge of his debts, not "monetary damages or any affirmative relief from a State." Therefore, a bankruptcy court's exercise of its in rem jurisdiction to discharge a student loan debt does not infringe upon state sovereignty. Second, in *Central Virginia Community College v. Katz*, 546 U.S. 356 (2006), the Court considered a related question: "whether a proceeding initiated by a bankruptcy trustee to set aside preferential transfers by the debtor to state agencies is barred by sovereign immunity." Instead of addressing the question it had identified in granting certiorari, whether Congress had validly abrogated state sovereign immunity in enacting Chapter 11 of the Bankruptcy Code, the Court found that "the Framers, in adopting the Bankruptcy Clause, plainly intended to give Congress the power to redress the rampant injustice resulting from States' refusal to respect one another's discharge orders." By ratifying the Clause the States "acquiesced in a subordination of whatever sovereign immunity they might otherwise have asserted in proceedings necessary to effectuate the *in rem* jurisdiction of the bankruptcy courts." Therefore, it was not necessary to determine whether Congress had validly abrogated the States' immunity; the "relevant 'abrogation' is the one effected in the plan of the Convention, not by statute," and Congress was free to choose to treat States the same as other creditors with respect to preferences.

Several attempts by Congress to abrogate Eleventh Amendment immunity pursuant to its power under §5 of the Fourteenth Amendment have been struck down by the Court. *See, e.g., Bd. of Trustees, Univ. of Ala v. Garrett*, 531 U.S. 356 (2001) (Title I of Americans with Disabilities Act); *Kimel v. Florida Bd. of Regents*, 528 U.S. 62 (2000) (Age Discrimination in Employment Act); *College Savings Bank v. Florida Prepaid Postsecondary Education Expense Board*, 527 U.S. 666 (1999) (Trademark Remedy

Clarification Act); *Florida Prepaid Postsecondary Education Expense Board v. College Savings Bank*, 527 U.S. 627 (1999) (Patent Remedy Act). Each of these Acts was found to be beyond the remedial power of Congress when acting pursuant to §5 of the Fourteenth Amendment. *Compare Tennessee v. Lane*, 541 U.S. 509 (2004) (Title II of Americans with Disabilities Act); *Nevada Dep't of Human Resources v. Hibbs*, 538 U.S. 721 (2003) (Family and Medical Leave Act). *See* discussion of §5 power, *supra*, Ch. I.

5. In *Puerto Rico Aqueduct & Sewer Auth. v. Metcalf & Eddy*, 506 U.S. 139 (1993), the Court held that states and state agencies can take advantage of the collateral order doctrine to appeal a district court order denying a claim of Eleventh Amendment immunity. *See Mitchell v. Forsyth, supra* Ch. II.

6. Removal as Waiver: The plaintiff in *Wisconsin Department of Corrections v. Schacht*, 524 U.S. 381 (1998), sued the Department and several of its employees, both in their personal and in their official capacity, in state court alleging a violation of the fourteenth amendment. After the defendants removed to federal court, they raised an eleventh amendment defense to the claim against the Department and the official capacity claims for damages against the employees. The Court held that the state's invocation of the eleventh amendment placed certain claims beyond the power of the federal court, but it did not destroy removal jurisdiction over the entire case.

   In addition, the Court said the Eleventh Amendment does not automatically destroy federal court jurisdiction. Rather, it gives the state the right to raise a waivable defense. Unless the state raises the defense, the court can ignore it.

7. Continuing its expansion of state sovereign immunity, the Court in *Fed. Maritime Comm'n v. S.C. State Ports Auth.*, 535 U.S. 743 (2002), held that the sovereign immunity enjoyed by the states extends beyond the literal text of the Eleventh Amendment and bars federal agency adjudication of a complaint by a private party claiming an arm of the state violated a federal statute. Noting that the "preeminent purpose of state sovereign immunity is to accord States the dignity that is consistent with their status as sovereign entities," the Court indicated "if the Framers thought it an impermissible affront to a State's dignity to be required to answer the complaints of private parties in federal courts, we cannot imagine that they would have found it acceptable to compel a State to do exactly the same thing before the administrative tribunal of an agency."

CHAPTER III:
MODERN CIVIL RIGHTS LEGISLATION

The second major civil rights movement in this country (the first having its roots in the Civil War) culminated in passage of the Civil Rights Act of 1964. This Chapter explores Title VII of this Act, which reaches various types of discrimination in employment, the Age Discrimination in Employment Act of 1967, as well as Title I of the Americans with Disabilities Act. Unlike the Reconstruction Era statutes covered in Chapter II, these Acts are quite detailed in terms of coverage, remedies, and enforcement. They invoke the assistance of federal, and sometimes state, administrative agencies to carry out their goals. Unlike §§ 1983 and 1985(3), these laws create substantive rights on behalf of covered persons. Following the format established in Chapter II, this Chapter will address the constitutional source of each statute, who can be plaintiffs and defendants, the conduct prohibited by the legislation, the method of proving claims, statutory and other defenses, the means of enforcement, remedies and the relationship to the earlier acts where applicable.

A. TITLE VII: EMPLOYMENT DISCRIMINATION

Title VII was enacted in 1964 and took effect in July of 1965. Passed as part of the broad Civil Rights Act of 1964,[1] its purpose was to eliminate the existing economic barriers against blacks in the area of employment.[2] However, it also covers discrimination based on sex, religion or national origin. It reaches employers, labor unions, and employment agencies.

Congress in enacting Title VII looked to the Commerce Clause as the basis for reaching private employers, and thus the main statutory provisions of the Act refer to employers engaged in interstate commerce or in an industry affecting interstate commerce. The Supreme Court's decision in *Katzenbach v. McClung*, 379 U.S. 294 (1964), upholding the validity of Title II of the Civil Rights Act of 1964, which also has the commerce clause as its source, confirms the constitutional validity of Title VII.

The Equal Protection Clause of the Fourteenth Amendment provided the basis for extending coverage to include state and local government employers in 1972. This extension was upheld by the Supreme Court as against an Eleventh Amendment state sovereignty claim in *Fitzpatrick v.*

---

1   The Civil Rights Act of 1964 also covers discrimination in the area of voting rights, public facilities, public education, as well as federally funded private entities. Title II was considered *supra* in Chapter I and Title VI is covered in Chapter IV.

2   Vaas, *Title VII: Legislative History*, 7 B.C. Indus. & Com. L. Rev. 431, 441 (1966).

Bitzer, supra Ch. II. The Court found that Congress had abrogated the states' Eleventh Amendment immunity and thus state employers can be sued in federal court for back wages and attorney fees.

1.   COVERAGE

Carefully read §§ 701(a), (b) and (f), § 702(a), §§ 703(a)(1) and (2) and (e)(2), § 704(a), and § 717. Make a list of all potential plaintiffs and defendants as well as statutorily exempt employers and answer the following:

1. Must a plaintiff be an employee to file suit? Although it was generally understood that applicants denied employment may file suit, some question was raised as to whether **former** employees who, following their termination, are provided negative references in retaliation for their having filed with the Equal Employment Opportunity Commission (EEOC), may pursue claims. The Supreme Court in *Robinson v. Shell Oil Company*, 519 U.S. 337 (1997), held that the term "employee" includes former employees and thus they may sue for allegedly retaliatory post-employment actions. The Supreme Court reasoned that although the statutory text and its context were ambiguous, several of the provisions in the statute plainly contemplate that former employees can make use of the remedial mechanism of Title VII and that such an interpretation is more consistent with the statute and its goals.

2. Are **independent contractors** protected? For example, may a physician who was denied staff privileges at a hospital for racially discriminatory reasons pursue a claim under Title VII? In *Clackamas Gastroenterology Ass'n v. Wells*, 538 U.S. 440 (2003), the Court considered whether physicians practicing in a professional corporation could be counted as employees in order to satisfy the fifteen-employee threshold required for coverage under the Americans with Disabilities Act. The Court cited with approval the EEOC's Compliance Manual,[1] which focuses on the extent of control an employer has in order to distinguish between employees/servants and independent contractors: "We think that the common-law element of control is the principal guidepost that should be followed in this case." The Court cited with approval the six-factor test set forth by the EEOC—namely whether the organization can hire or fire the individual or determine the rules and regulations of his work, whether the organization supervises the individual's work, whether the individual reports to someone higher in the organization, whether, and if so, to what extent the individual is able to influence the organization, whether the parties intended that the individual be an employee, as expressed in written agreements or contracts, and

---

[3]   This Manual does not have the force of law, but is entitled to deference "only to the extent that [it has] the power to persuade." *Christensen v. Harris Cty.*, 529 U.S. 576 (2000).

whether the individual shares in the profits, losses, and liabilities of the organization. The Court cautioned that titles are not determinative, nor is the mere existence of a document designated as an "employment agreement" conclusive. Rather, courts must examine all incidents of the relationship. Although the Court remanded the case for reconsideration under these guidelines, it noted that the trial court's findings appeared to weigh heavily in favor of finding that the four physicians who owned the professional corporation and constituted its Board of Directors were not clinic employees. Would the partners of a law firm be viewed as employees under EEOC standards?

3. What types of discrimination are covered? Does the Act provide protection from discrimination based on sexual preference? The Act reaches discrimination "based on sex," but the circuits are divided as to whether this should be interpreted to include discrimination based on homosexuality or gender identity.

4. When may federal employees bring employment discrimination claims? Note that in *Brown v. General Services Admin.*, 425 U.S. 820 (1976), the Supreme Court held that § 717 of Title VII provides the exclusive remedy for employment discrimination claims brought against the United States. Further, § 302 of the Civil Rights Act of 1991 extends the Act's coverage to include Senate employees.[4]

5. May all state and local government employees sue their employer? Study carefully § 701(f), which includes language also found in the Equal Pay Act and the Age Discrimination in Employment Act. Compare *Gregory v. Ashcroft*, 501 U.S. 452 (1991), holding that non-elected state court judges are policy makers who fall within the exemption in 29 U.S.C. § 630(f) and are thus not protected by the ADEA from state mandatory retirement laws. The legislative history of § 701(f) indicates the exclusion was intended to apply "only to those individuals who are in highly intimate and sensitive positions of responsibility on the staff of the elected official."

   Title III, § 321 of the Civil Rights Act of 1991, 2 U.S.C. § 1220, referred to as the "Government Employee Rights Act of 1991," creates a statutory right on behalf of persons who work as personal staff members, policymakers, or legal advisors of those elected to public office in any state or political subdivision of any state. The Act sets up a procedural mechanism somewhat different from that available under Title VII, but the Act incorporates Title VII's remedial provisions.

6. The Supreme Court has clarified that the requirement that an employer have 15 employees "for each working day" for 20 weeks is satisfied by looking to the

---

4 Although employees of the House of Representatives are not covered, the House has codified a fair employment practices policy which has been used internally for several years. Contrary to Title VII, however, the policy does not provide for judicial review, liability of the employer is not personal, nor are compensatory or punitive damages available.

employer's payroll, rather than examining physical presence of employees. *Walters v. Metropolitan Educational Enterprises*, 519 U.S. 202 (1997). The rule applies to both private sector and government employers. *Mount Lemmon Fire Dist. v. Guido*, 139 S. Ct. 22 (2018). However, in *Arbaugh v. Y & H Corp.*, 546 U.S. 500 (2006), the Court held that Title VII's numerical threshold is not jurisdictional, but rather relates to the substantive adequacy of the Title VII claim, and thus it cannot be raised defensively late in a lawsuit. The Court reasoned that "when Congress does not rank a statutory limitation on coverage as jurisdictional, courts should treat the restriction as non-jurisdictional in character."

2. TYPES OF CONDUCT REGULATED AND METHODS OF PROOF

a. Disparate Treatment

MCDONNELL DOUGLAS CORPORATION V. GREEN
411 U.S. 792 (1973)

Mr. Justice POWELL delivered the opinion of the Court.

The case before us raises significant questions as to the proper order and nature of proof in actions under Title VII of the Civil Rights Act of 1964.

Petitioner, McDonnell Douglas Corp., is an aerospace and aircraft manufacturer headquartered in St. Louis, Missouri, where it employs over 30,000 people. Respondent, a black citizen of St. Louis, worked for petitioner as a mechanic and laboratory technician from 1956 until August 28, 1964, when he was laid off in the course of a general reduction in petitioner's work force.

Respondent, a long-time activist in the civil rights movement, protested vigorously that his discharge and the general hiring practices of petitioner were racially motivated. As part of this protest, respondent and other members of the Congress on Racial Equality illegally stalled their cars on the main roads leading to petitioner's plant for the purpose of blocking access to it at the time of the morning shift change. The District Judge described the plan for, and respondent's participation in, the "stall-in" as follows:

> Acting under the 'stall-in' plan, plaintiff [respondent in the present action] drove his car onto Brown Road, a McDonnell access road, at approximately 7:00 a.m., at the start of the morning rush hour. Plaintiff was aware of the traffic problems that would result. He stopped his car with the intent to block traffic. The police arrived shortly and requested plaintiff to move his car. He refused to move his car voluntarily. Plaintiff's car was towed away by the police, and he was arrested for obstructing traffic. Plaintiff pleaded guilty to the charge of obstructing traffic and was fined.

On July 2, 1965, a "lock-in" took place wherein a chain and padlock were placed on the front door of a building to prevent the occupants, certain of petitioner's employees, from leaving. Though respondent apparently knew beforehand of the "lock-in," the full extent of his involvement remains uncertain.

Some three weeks following the "lock-in," on July 25, 1965, petitioner publicly advertised for qualified mechanics, respondent's trade, and respondent promptly applied for re-employment. Petitioner turned down respondent, basing its rejection on respondent's participation in the "stall-in" and "lock-in". Shortly thereafter, respondent filed a formal complaint with the Equal Employment Opportunity Commission, claiming that petitioner had refused to rehire him because of his race and persistent involvement in the civil rights movement, in violation of §§ 703(a)(1) and 704(a) of the Civil Rights Act of 1964, 42 U.S.C. §§ 2000e-2(a)(1) and 2000e-3(a). The former section generally prohibits racial discrimination in any employment decision while the latter forbids discrimination against applicants or employees for attempting to protest or correct allegedly discriminatory conditions of employment.

The Commission made no finding on respondent's allegation of racial bias under § 703(a)(1), but it did find reasonable cause to believe petitioner had violated § 704(a) by refusing to rehire respondent because of his civil rights activity. On April 15, 1968, respondent brought the present action, claiming initially a violation of § 704(a) and, in an amended complaint, a violation of § 703(a)(1) as well. The District Court dismissed the latter claim of racial discrimination in petitioner's hiring procedures on the ground that the Commission had failed to make a determination of reasonable cause to believe that a violation of that section had been committed. The District Court also found that petitioner's refusal to rehire respondent was based solely on his participation in the illegal demonstrations and not on his legitimate civil rights activities. The court concluded that nothing in Title VII or § 704 protected "such activity as employed by the plaintiff in the 'stall in' and 'lock in' demonstrations."

On appeal, the Eighth Circuit affirmed that unlawful protests were not protected activities under § 704(a) but reversed the dismissal of respondent's § 703(a)(1) claim relating to racially discriminatory hiring practices, holding that a prior Commission determination of reasonable cause was not a jurisdictional prerequisite to raising a claim under that section in federal court.

I

We agree with the Court of Appeals that absence of a Commission finding of reasonable cause cannot bar suit under an appropriate section of Title VII and that the District Judge erred in dismissing respondent's claim of racial discrimination under § 703(a)(1). Respondent satisfied the jurisdictional prerequisites to a federal action (i) by filing timely charges of employment discrimination with the Commission and (ii) by receiving and acting upon the Commission's statutory notice of the right to sue, 42 U.S.C. §§ 2000e-5(a) and 2000e-5(e). The Act does not restrict a complainant's right to sue to those charges as to which the Commission has made findings of reasonable cause, and we will not engraft on the statute a requirement which may inhibit the review of claims of employment discrimination in the federal courts. The Commission itself does not consider the absence of a "reasonable cause" determination as providing employer immunity from similar charges in a federal court, 29 C.F.R. § 1601.30, and the courts of appeal have held that, in view of the large volume of complaints before the Commission and the non-adversary character of many of its proceedings, "court actions under Title VII are *de novo* proceedings and . . . a Commission 'no reasonable cause' finding does not bar a lawsuit in the case."

II

The critical issue before us concerns the order and allocation of proof in a private, non-class action challenging employment discrimination. The language of Title VII makes plain the purpose of Congress to assure equality of employment opportunities and to eliminate those discriminatory practices and devices which have fostered racially stratified job environments to the disadvantage of minority citizens.

The complainant in a Title VII trial must carry the initial burden under the statute of establishing a *prima facie* case of racial discrimination. This may be done by showing (i) that he belongs to a racial minority; (ii) that he applied and was qualified for a job for which the employer was seeking applicants; (iii) that, despite his qualifications, he was rejected; and (iv) that, after his rejection, the position remained open and the employer continued to seek applicants from persons of complainant's qualifications. In the instant case, we agree with the Court of Appeals that respondent proved a *prima facie* case. Petitioner sought mechanics, respondent's trade, and continued to do so after respondent's rejection. Petitioner, moreover, does not dispute respondent's qualifications and acknowledges that his past work performance in petitioner's employ was "satisfactory."

The burden then must shift to the employer to articulate some legitimate, nondiscriminatory reason for the employee's rejection. We need not attempt in the instant case to detail every matter which fairly could be recognized as a reasonable basis for a refusal to hire. Here petitioner has assigned respondent's participation in unlawful conduct against it as the cause for his rejection. We think that this suffices to discharge petitioner's burden of proof at this stage and to meet respondent's *prima facie* case of discrimination. Respondent admittedly had taken part in a carefully planned "stall-in," designed to tie up access to and egress from petitioner's plant at a peak traffic hour. Nothing in Title VII compels an employer to absolve and rehire one who has engaged in such deliberate, unlawful activity against it.

Petitioner's reason for rejection thus suffices to meet the *prima facie* case, but the inquiry must not end here. While Title VII does not, without more, compel rehiring of respondent, neither does it permit petitioner to use respondent's conduct as a pretext for the sort of discrimination prohibited by § 703(a)(1). On remand, respondent must, as the Court of Appeals recognized, be afforded a fair opportunity to show that petitioner's stated reason for respondent's rejection was in fact pretext. Especially relevant to such a showing would be evidence that white employees involved in acts against petitioner of comparable seriousness to the "stall-in" were nevertheless retained or rehired. Petitioner may justifiably refuse to rehire one who was engaged in unlawful, disruptive acts against it, but only if this criterion is applied alike to members of all races.

Other evidence that may be relevant to any showing of pretext includes facts as to the petitioner's treatment of respondent during his prior term of employment; petitioner's reaction, if any, to respondent's legitimate civil rights activities; and petitioner's general policy and practice with respect to minority employment. On the latter point, statistics as to petitioner's employment policy and practice may be helpful to a determination of whether petitioner's refusal to rehire respondent in this case conformed to a general pattern of discrimination against blacks. In short, on the retrial respondent must be given a full and fair opportunity to demonstrate by competent evidence that the presumptively valid reasons for his rejection were in fact a coverup for a racially discriminatory decision.

NOTES AND QUESTIONS

1. **Preclusion:** What preclusive effect, if any, does an adverse EEOC determination have on a Title VII litigant? May its finding be introduced into evidence? Note that Rule 803(8)(C), FRE, allows admission of investigative reports made by government agencies in civil trials "unless the sources of information or other circumstances indicate untrustworthiness." Further, even if evidence meets Rule 803, judges will decide under Rule 403 whether the probative value of the evidence is substantially out-weighed by its prejudicial effect.

2. ***Prima facie* case:** What must Green show to establish a *prima facie* case? How can Green prove that the employer's asserted justifications were "pretextual"? Note that on remand, the plaintiff introduced evidence that the employer had not disciplined striking white employees who had engaged in illegal activity, but the court found the evidence insufficient to prove pretext and discounted by favorable statistics regarding minority representation in the employer's labor force. *Green v. McDonnell*, 528 F.2d 1102 (8th Cir. 1972).

3. **Intent:** The key thrust of the disparate treatment theory is that the plaintiff must prove that she is a victim of intentional race discrimination. The Supreme Court's decision in *McDonnell* allows the plaintiff to survive summary judgment by providing evidence of each of its elements. The *McDonnell* approach has been adapted for use in a variety of Title VII charges, including discrimination regarding hiring, promotion, demotion, discharge, lay-offs and retaliation. Further it has been used to establish claims of sex discrimination, religious discrimination and discrimination based on national origin. It has also been adopted by federal courts considering claims under §§ 1981, 1982, and Equal Protection claims brought under 1983 as well as under Title VIII (the Fair Housing Act) and the Age Discrimination in Employment Act. In short, it is the starting point for analyzing claims of intentional discrimination.

4. In *Swierkiewicz v. Sorema*, 534 U.S. 506 (2002), the Court held that an employment discrimination complaint need not contain specific facts establishing a *prima facie* case under the *McDonnell-Douglas* framework to avoid dismissal but instead must contain only "a short and plain statement of the claim showing that the pleader is entitled to relief." FRCP 8(a)(2). The *McDonnell-Douglas* framework, which requires plaintiff to show membership in a protected group, qualification for job in question, adverse employment action, and circumstances supporting an inference of discrimination, is an evidentiary standard, not a pleading requirement. Imposing a heightened pleading standard conflicts with Rule 8(a)'s express language, which requires simply that the complaint "give defendant fair notice of what plaintiff's claim is and the grounds upon which it rests." A complaint may be dismissed only if it is clear that no relief could be granted under any set of facts that could be proved consistent with the allegations. The Court notes that the elements of a *prima facie* case may be difficult to establish before discovery and concludes that plaintiff's complaint easily satisfied the more liberal pleading rule. *Compare Ashcroft v. Iqbal, supra* Ch. II, imposing a "plausibility" requirement necessary for all federal claims to survive a motion to dismiss.

TEXAS DEPARTMENT OF COMMUNITY AFFAIRS V. BURDINE
450 U.S. 248 (1981)

Justice POWELL delivered the opinion of the Court.

This case requires us to address again the nature of the evidentiary burden placed upon the defendant in an employment discrimination suit brought under Title VII of the Civil Rights Act of 1964. The narrow question presented is whether, after the plaintiff has proved a *prima facie* case of discriminatory treatment, the burden shifts to the defendant to persuade the court by a preponderance of the evidence that legitimate, nondiscriminatory reasons for the challenged employment action existed.

I

The [Court of Appeals] reaffirmed its previously announced views that the defendant in a Title VII case bears the burden of proving by a preponderance of the evidence the existence of legitimate nondiscriminatory reasons for the employment action and that the defendant also must prove by objective evidence that those hired or promoted were better qualified than the plaintiff.

II

The nature of the burden that shifts to the defendant should be understood in light of the plaintiff's ultimate and intermediate burdens. The ultimate burden of persuading the trier of fact that the defendant intentionally discriminated against the plaintiff remains at all times with the plaintiff. The *McDonnell Douglas* division of intermediate evidentiary burdens serves to bring the litigants and the court expeditiously and fairly to this ultimate question.

The burden of establishing a *prima facie* case of disparate treatment is not onerous. The plaintiff must prove by a preponderance of the evidence that she applied for an available position for which she was qualified, but was rejected under circumstances which give rise to an inference of unlawful discrimination. The *prima facie* case serves an important function in the litigation: it eliminates the most common nondiscriminatory reasons for the plaintiff's rejection. As the Court explained in *Furnco Construction Corp. v. Waters* (1978), the *prima facie* case "raises an inference of discrimination only because we presume these acts, if otherwise unexplained, are more likely than not based on the consideration of impermissible factors." Establishment of the *prima facie* case in effect creates a presumption that the employer unlawfully discriminated against the employee. If the trier of fact believes the plaintiff's evidence, and if the employer is silent in the face of the presumption, the court must enter judgment for the plaintiff because no issue of fact remains in the case.

The burden that shifts to the defendant, therefore, is to rebut the presumption of discrimination by producing evidence that the plaintiff was rejected, or someone else was preferred, for a legitimate, nondiscriminatory reason. The defendant need not persuade the court that it was actually motivated by the proffered reasons. It is sufficient if the defendant's evidence raises a genuine issue of fact as to whether it discriminated against the plaintiff. To accomplish this, the defendant must clearly set forth, through the introduction of admissible evidence, the reasons for the plaintiff's rejections.[9] The explanation provided must be legally sufficient to justify a judgment for the defendant. If the defendant carries this burden of production, the presumption raised by the *prima facie* case is rebutted,[10] and the factual inquiry proceeds to a new level of specificity. Placing this burden of production on the defendant thus serves simultaneously to meet the plaintiff's *prima facie* case by presenting a legitimate reason for the action and to frame the factual issue with sufficient clarity so that the plaintiff will have a full and fair opportunity to demonstrate pretext. The sufficiency of the defendant's evidence should be evaluated by the extent to which it fulfills these functions.

The plaintiff retains the burden of persuasion. She now must have the opportunity to demonstrate that the proffered reason was not the true reason for the employment decision. This burden now merges with the ultimate burden of persuading the court that she has been the victim of intentional discrimination. She may succeed in this either directly by persuading the

---

9 An articulation not admitted into evidence will not suffice. Thus, the defendant cannot meet its burden merely through an answer to the complaint or by argument of counsel.

10 *See generally* J. THAYER, PRELIMINARY TREATISE ON EVIDENCE 346 (1898). In saying that the presumption drops from the case, we do not imply that the trier of fact no longer may consider evidence previously introduced by the plaintiff to establish a prima facie case. A satisfactory explanation by the defendant destroys the legally mandatory inference of discrimination arising from the plaintiff's initial evidence. Nonetheless, this evidence and inferences properly drawn therefrom may be considered by the trier of fact on the issue of whether the defendant's explanation is pretextual. Indeed, there may be some cases where the plaintiff's initial evidence, combined with effective cross-examination of the defendant, will suffice to discredit the defendant's explanation.

court that a discriminatory reason more likely motivated the employer or indirectly by showing that the employer's proffered explanation is unworthy of credence.

III

A

The Court of Appeals has misconstrued the nature of the burden that *McDonnell Douglas* and its progeny place on the defendant.

The court placed the burden of persuasion on the defendant apparently because it feared that "[i]f an employer need only *articulate*—not prove—a legitimate, nondiscriminatory reason for his action, he may compose fictitious, but legitimate, reasons for his actions." We do not believe, however, that limiting the defendant's evidentiary obligation to a burden of production will unduly hinder the plaintiff. First, as noted above, the defendant's explanation of its legitimate reasons must be clear and reasonably specific. This obligation arises both from the necessity of rebutting the inference of discrimination arising from the *prima facie* case and from the requirement that the plaintiff be afforded "a full and fair opportunity" to demonstrate pretext. Second, although the defendant does not bear a formal burden of persuasion, the defendant nevertheless retains an incentive to persuade the trier of fact that the employment decision was lawful. Thus, the defendant normally will attempt to prove the factual basis for its explanation. Third, the liberal discovery rules applicable to any civil suit in federal court are supplemented in a Title VII suit by the plaintiff's access to the Equal Employment Opportunity Commission's investigatory files concerning her complaint. Given these factors, we are unpersuaded that the plaintiff will find it particularly difficult to prove that a proffered explanation lacking a factual basis is a pretext. We remain confident that the *McDonnell Douglas* framework permits the plaintiff meriting relief to demonstrate intentional discrimination.

B

The Court of Appeals also erred in requiring the defendant to prove by objective evidence that the person hired or promoted was more qualified than the plaintiff. *McDonnell Douglas* teaches that it is the plaintiff's task to demonstrate that similarly situated employees were not treated equally. The Court of Appeals' rule would require the employer to show that the plaintiff's objective qualifications were inferior to those of the person selected. If it cannot, a court would, in effect, conclude that it has discriminated.

The court's procedural rule harbors a substantive error. Title VII prohibits all discrimination in employment based upon race, sex, and national origin. Title VII, however, does not demand that an employer give preferential treatment to minorities or women. 42 U.S.C. § 2000e-2(j). The statute was not intended to "diminish traditional management prerogatives." It does not require the employer to restructure his employment practices to maximize the number of minorities and women hired.

1. In establishing a *prima facie* case, must the plaintiff prove that she is as qualified as the person hired? What about at the "pretext" stage? *See Patterson v. McLean, supra* Ch. II. *See also Ash v. Tyson Foods, Inc.,* 546 U.S. 454 (2006) (per curiam), holding that a plaintiff's evidence of superior qualifications might show that an employer's articulated reasons for its failure-to-promote decision were pretextual. The Eleventh Circuit had stated that pretext can be established based on comparative qualifications only when "the disparity in qualifications is so apparent as virtually to jump off the page and slap you in your face." The Court reasoned that this standard was "unhelpful and imprecise," but it declined to give a precise definition of what standard courts should apply in pretext cases based on superior qualifications.

2. On remand the appellate court ruled that the employer's duty was only to produce admissible evidence that would allow the trier of fact to conclude that the employment decision had not been motivated by discriminatory animus, and it held that the standard was met by evidence that the plaintiff did not work well with others. *Burdine v. Texas Dep't of Community Affairs,* 647 F.2d 513 (5th Cir. 1981). What types of evidence would Burdine introduce in trying to establish pretext? If she can show that this proffered explanation is unworthy of credence, does this establish intentional discrimination as a matter of law? Or is it possible for a court to conclude that neither the employer's reason nor impermissible discrimination was the basis for the employment decision?

    In *St. Mary's Honor Center v. Hicks,* 509 U.S. 502 (1993), the Court rejected the argument that the factfinder's disbelief of the reason(s) advanced by an employer for the challenged employment decision *compels* a judgment for the plaintiff. Rather,

    > [t]he factfinder's disbelief of the reasons put forward by the defendant (particularly if disbelief is accompanied by a suspicion of mendacity) may, together with the elements of the *prima facie* case, suffice to show intentional discrimination. Thus, rejection of the defendant's proffered reasons, will *permit* the trier of fact to infer the ultimate fact of intentional discrimination [without additional proof of discrimination].

    To compel a judgment for the plaintiff, the Court said, would disregard the fundamental principle of Rule 301, FRE, that a presumption does not shift the burden of persuasion, and ignore the repeated holding in Title VII cases that the plaintiff at all times bears the "ultimate burden of persuasion."

    > . . . nothing in law would permit us to substitute for the required finding that the employer's action was the product of unlawful discrimination, the much different

(and much lesser) finding that the employer's explanation of its action was not believable...

... That the employer's proffered reason is unpersuasive, or even obviously contrived, does not necessarily establish that the plaintiff's proffered reason of race is correct.

The Court explained *Burdine*'s allusions to proving pretext as referring to "pretext for discrimination." Thus, the district court could conclude that even though the employer's stated reasons were not the real reasons for the discharge, plaintiff nonetheless is not entitled to judgment because he has not shown the conduct "was racially rather than personally motivated."

Does this, as the dissent contends, allow the factfinder "to roam the record, searching for some nondiscriminatory explanation that the defendant has not raised and that the plaintiff has had no opportunity to disprove?"

3. Despite *Hicks*, the appellate courts remained divided on the amount and types of evidence necessary to create a jury question on intentional discrimination. The Court revisited these issues in the following age discrimination case:

REEVES V. SANDERSON
530 U.S. 133 (2000)

Justice O'CONNOR delivered the opinion of the Court.

This case concerns the kind and amount of evidence necessary to sustain a jury's verdict that an employer unlawfully discriminated on the basis of age. Specifically, we must resolve whether a defendant is entitled to judgment as a matter of law when the plaintiff's case consists exclusively of a *prima facie* case of discrimination and sufficient evidence for the trier of fact to disbelieve the defendant's legitimate, nondiscriminatory explanation for its action. We must also decide whether the employer was entitled to judgment as a matter of law under the particular circumstances presented here.

I

In October 1995, petitioner Roger Reeves was 57 years old and had spent 40 years in the employ of respondent, Sanderson Plumbing Products, Inc., a manufacturer of toilet seats and covers. Petitioner worked in a department known as the "Hinge Room," where he supervised the "regular line." Joe Oswalt, in his mid-thirties, supervised the Hinge Room's "special line," and Russell Caldwell, the manager of the Hinge Room and age 45, supervised both petitioner and Oswalt. Petitioner's responsibilities included recording the attendance and hours of those under his supervision, and reviewing a weekly report that listed the hours worked by each employee.

In the summer of 1995, Caldwell informed Powe Chesnut, the director of manufacturing and the husband of company president Sandra Sanderson, that "production was down" in the Hinge Room because employees were often absent and were "coming in late and leaving early." Because the monthly attendance reports did not indicate a problem, Chesnut ordered an audit of the Hinge Room's time sheets for July, August, and September of that year. According to Chesnut's testimony, that investigation revealed "numerous timekeeping errors and misrepresentations on the part of Caldwell, Reeves, and Oswalt." Following the audit, Chesnut, along with Dana Jester, vice president of human resources, and Tom Whitaker, vice president of operations, recommended to company president Sanderson that petitioner and Caldwell be fired. In October 1995, Sanderson followed the recommendation and discharged both petitioner and Caldwell.

In June 1996, petitioner filed suit . . . contending that he had been fired because of his age in violation of the Age Discrimination in Employment Act of 1967 (ADEA). At trial, respondent contended that it had fired petitioner due to his failure to maintain accurate attendance records, while petitioner attempted to demonstrate that respondent's explanation was pretext for age discrimination. Petitioner introduced evidence that he had accurately recorded the attendance and hours of the employees under his supervision, and that Chesnut, whom Oswalt described as wielding "absolute power" within the company, had demonstrated age-based animus in his dealings with petitioner.

[T]he jury returned a verdict in favor of petitioner, awarding him $35,000 in compensatory damages, and found that respondent's age discrimination had been "willfu[l]." The District Court accordingly entered judgment for petitioner in the amount of $70,000, which included $35,000 in liquidated damages based on the jury's findings of willfulness.

The Court of Appeals for the Fifth Circuit reversed, holding that petitioner had not introduced sufficient evidence to sustain the jury's finding of unlawful discrimination. After noting respondent's proffered justification for petitioner's discharge, the court acknowledged that petitioner "very well may" have offered sufficient evidence for "a reasonable jury [to] have found that [respondent's] explanation for its employment decision was pretextual." The court explained, however, that this was "not dispositive" of the ultimate issue—namely, "whether Reeves presented sufficient evidence that his age motivated [respondent's] employment decision."

II

In this case, the evidence supporting the respondent's explanation for petitioner's discharge consisted primarily of testimony by Chesnut and Sanderson and documentation of petitioner's alleged "shoddy record keeping." Sanderson testified that she accepted the recommendation to discharge petitioner because he had 'intentionally falsif[ied] company records."

Petitioner, however, made a substantial showing that respondent's explanation was false. Petitioner similarly cast doubt on whether he was responsible for any failure to discipline late and absent employees. First, petitioner offered evidence that he had properly maintained the attendance records. Petitioner testified that his job only included reviewing the daily and weekly attendance reports, and that disciplinary writeups were based on the monthly reports, which were reviewed by Caldwell. Sanderson admitted that Caldwell, and not petitioner, was responsible for citing employees for violations of the company's attendance policy. Finally, petitioner stated that on previous occasions that employees were paid for hours they had not worked, the company had simply adjusted those employee's next paychecks to correct the errors.

Based on this evidence, the Court of Appeals concluded that petitioner "very well may be correct" that "a reasonable jury could have found that [respondent's] explanation for its employment decision was pretextual. Nonetheless, the court held that this showing, standing alone, was insufficient to sustain the jury's finding of liability." [T]he Court of Appeals proceeded from the assumption that a *prima facie* case of discrimination, combined with sufficient evidence for the trier of fact to disbelieve the defendant's legitimate, nondiscriminatory reason for its decision, is insufficient as a matter of law to sustain a jury's finding of intentional discrimination.

In so reasoning, the Court of Appeals misconceived the evidentiary burden borne by plaintiffs who attempt to prove intentional discrimination through indirect evidence. This much is evident from our decision in *St. Mary's Honor Center*. There we held that the fact-finder's rejection of the employer's legitimate, nondiscriminatory reason for its action does not *compel* judgment for the plaintiff. The ultimate question is whether the employer intentionally discriminated, and proof that "the employer's proffered reason is unpersuasive, or even obviously contrived, does not necessarily establish that the plaintiff's proffered reason . . . is correct." In other words, "[i]t is not enough . . . to *dis*believe the employer; the fact-finder must *believe* the plaintiff's explanation of intentional discrimination."

In reaching this conclusion, however, we reasoned that it is *permissible* for the trier of fact to infer the ultimate fact of discrimination from the falsity of the employer's explanation. Proof that the defendant's explanation is unworthy of credence is simply one form of circumstantial evidence that is probative of intentional discrimination, and it may be quite persuasive. In appropriate circumstances, the trier of fact can reasonably infer from the falsity of the explanation that the employer is dissembling to cover up a discriminatory purpose. Such an inference is consistent with the general principle of evidence law that the fact-finder is entitled to consider a party's dishonesty about a material fact as "affirmative evidence of guilt." Moreover, once the employer's justification has been eliminated, discrimination may well be the most likely alternative explanation, especially since the employer is in the best position to put forth the actual reason for its decision. Thus, a plaintiff's *prima facie* case, combined with sufficient evidence to find that the employer's asserted justification is false, may permit the trier of fact to conclude that the employer unlawfully discriminated.

This is not to say that such a showing by the plaintiff will *always* be adequate to sustain a jury's finding of liability. Certainly there will be instances where, although the plaintiff has established a *prima facie* case and set forth sufficient evidence to reject the defendant's explanation, no rational fact-finder could conclude that the action was discriminatory. For instance, an employer would be entitled to judgment as a matter of law if the record conclusively revealed some other, nondiscriminatory reason for the employer's decision, or if the plaintiff created only a weak issue of fact as to whether the employer's reason was untrue and there was abundant and uncontroverted independent evidence that no discrimination had occurred. To hold otherwise would be effectively to insulate an entire category of employment discrimination cases from review under Rule 50, and we have reiterated that trial courts should not "treat discrimination differently from other ultimate questions of fact."

Whether judgment as a matter of law is appropriate in any particular case will depend on a number of factors. Those include the strength of the plaintiff's *prima facie* case, the probative value of the proof that the employer's explanation is false, and any other evidence that supports the employer's case and that properly may be considered on a motion for judgment as a matter of law. For purposes of this case, we need not—and could not—resolve all of the circumstances in which such factors would entitle an employer to judgment as a matter of law. It suffices to say that, because a *prima facie* case and sufficient evidence to reject the employer's explanation may permit a finding of liability, the Court of Appeals erred in proceeding from the premise that a plaintiff must always introduce additional, independent evidence of discrimination.

III

A

The remaining question is whether, despite the Court of Appeals' misconception of petitioner's evidentiary burden, respondent was nonetheless entitled to judgment as a matter of law. Under Rule 50, a court should render judgment as a matter of law when "a party has been fully heard on an issue and there is no legally sufficient evidentiary basis for a reasonable jury to find for that party on that issue." In the analogous context of summary judgment under rule 56, we have stated that the court must review the record "taken as a whole." And the standard for granting summary judgment "mirrors" the standard for judgment as a matter of law, such that "the inquiry under each is the same." It therefore follows that, in entertaining a motion for judgment as a matter of law, the court should review all of the evidence in the record. In doing so, however, the court must draw all reasonable inferences in favor of the nonmoving party, and it may not make credibility determinations or weigh the evidence. Thus, although the court should review the record as a whole, it must disregard all evidence favorable to the moving party that the jury is not required to believe. That is, the court should give credence to the evidence favoring the nonmovant as well as that "evidence supporting the moving party that is uncontradicted and unimpeached, at least to the extent that that evidence comes from disinterested witnesses."

B

Applying this standard here, it is apparent that respondent was not entitled to judgment as a matter of law. In this case, in addition to establishing a *prima facie* case of discrimination and creating a jury issue as to the falsity of the employer's explanation, petitioner introduced additional evidence that Chesnut was motivated by age-based animus and was principally responsible for petitioner's firing. Petitioner testified that Chesnut had told him that he "was so old

[he] must have come over on the Mayflower" and, on one occasion when petitioner was having difficulty starting a machine, that he "was too damn old to do [his] job." According to petitioner, Chesnut would regularly "cuss at me and shake his finger in my face." Oswalt, roughly 24 years younger than petitioner, corroborated that there was an "obvious difference" in how Chesnut treated them. Oswalt explained that Chesnut "tolerated quite a bit" from him even though he "defied" Chesnut "quite often," but that Chesnut treated petitioner "[i]n a manner, as you would … treat … a child when … you're angry with [him]." Petitioner also demonstrated that, according to company records, he and Oswalt had nearly identical rates of productivity in 1993. Yet respondent conducted an efficiency study of only the regular line, supervised by petitioner, and placed only petitioner on probation.

In holding that the record contained insufficient evidence to sustain the jury's verdict, the Court of Appeals misapplied the standard of review dictated by Rule 50. Again, the court disregarded critical evidence favorable to petitioner—namely, the evidence supporting petitioner's *prima facie* case and undermining respondent's nondiscriminatory explanation. The court also failed to draw all reasonable inferences in favor of petitioner. For instance, while acknowledging "the potentially damning nature" of Chesnut's age-related comments, the court discounted them on the ground that they "were not made in the direct context of Reeve's termination." And the court discredited petitioner's evidence that Chesnut was the actual decision maker by giving weight to the fact that there was "no evidence to suggest that any of the other decision makers were motivated by age." Moreover, the other evidence on which the court relied—that Caldwell and Oswalt were also cited for poor record keeping, and that respondent employed many managers over age 50—although relevant, is certainly not dispositive. In concluding that these circumstances so overwhelmed the evidence favoring petitioner that no rational trier of fact could have found that petitioner was fired because of his age, the Court of Appeals impermissibly substituted its judgment concerning the weight of the evidence for the jury's.

Justice GINSBURG, concurring.

The Court today holds that an employment discrimination plaintiff *may* survive judgment as a matter of law by submitting two categories of evidence: first, evidence establishing a "*prima facie* case," and second, evidence from which a rational fact-finder could conclude that the employer's proffered explanation for its actions was false. Because the Court of Appeals in this case plainly, and erroneously, required the plaintiff to offer some evidence beyond those two categories, no broader holding is necessary to support reversal.

[E]vidence suggesting that a defendant accused of illegal discrimination has chosen to give a false explanation for its actions gives rise to a rational inference that the defendant could be masking its actual, illegal motivation. Whether the defendant was in fact motivated by discrimination is of course for the finder of fact to decide. But the inference remains—unless it is conclusively demonstrated, by evidence the district court is required to credit on a motion for judgment as a matter of law, that discrimination could not have been the defendant's true motivation. If such conclusive demonstrations are (as I suspect) atypical, it follows that the ultimate question of liability ordinarily should not be taken from the jury once the plaintiff has introduced the two categories of evidence described above. Because the Court's opinion leaves room for such further elaboration in an appropriate case, I join it in full.

NOTES AND QUESTIONS

1. The Court's unanimous ruling clarifies that plaintiffs need not introduce "additional" or "direct" evidence to avoid summary judgment or ultimately to succeed. Under what circumstances, however, will a *prima facie* case plus evidence of pretext be *insufficient* to support a jury verdict of intentional discrimination? Compare Justice Ginsburg's view.

2. What evidentiary principles does the Court set forth for reviewing motions brought under Rules 50 and 56, FRCP? How did the Court of Appeals violate these principles?

3. Although this was an ADEA case, its rejection of the so-called "pretext plus" requirement, as well as its procedural holding regarding the appropriate standard to review jury decisions, extends to other claims of discrimination.

4. Evidentiary questions as to the admissibility of alleged discrimination against other employees or by other supervisors often arise when plaintiffs seek to establish pretext. The Court, in the context of an ADEA claim, addressed the admissibility of testimony of other employees who alleged bias, but who were not working with the same supervisor as the plaintiff. In *Sprint/United Management Co. v. Mendelsohn*, 552 U.S. 379 (2008), the Court held that a *per se* rule excluding such evidence was contrary to the "fact-intensive, context-specific inquiry" that is required: "[W]hether evidence of discrimination by other supervisors is relevant in an individual ADEA case is fact based and depends on many factors, including how closely related the evidence is to the plaintiff's circumstances and theory of the case."

i.   Mixed Motive Case

The *McDonnell-Douglas/Burdine* analysis described in the previous section is used where the plaintiff's case consists of circumstantial evidence that the plaintiff argues supports an inference of discrimination. Although most employers today are too sophisticated to engage in blatant acts of discrimination, there continue to be cases where the plaintiff can present evidence that directly supports a finding of illegal motive. Oftentimes the evidence presented in these cases suggests that the employment decision was motivated by both unlawful and lawful reasons, and thus they have been referred to as "mixed motive" cases.

Outside the context of Title VII litigation, the Supreme Court held that where a plaintiff introduces evidence that directly proves the defendant has engaged in unconstitutional conduct, the burden shifts to the defendant to prove by a preponderance of the evidence that it would have reached the same decision even in the absence of the protected conduct. *Mt. Healthy City School Dist. Bd. of Educ. v. Doyle*, 429 U.S. 274 (1977).

If the plaintiff's evidence establishes that the employer's decision was motivated at least in part by unlawful reasons, should an employer nonetheless escape liability by establishing that it would have made the same decision for lawful reasons? The Supreme Court stated in *McDonald v. Santa Fe Trail Transp. Co.*, 427 U.S. 273 (1976), that a plaintiff in a Title VII case is required to show "that race was the 'but for' cause" of an impermissible employment decision. If an employer proves that the adverse action would have been taken anyway, was discriminatory animus the "cause" of the adverse employment decision? On the other hand, if racial reasons were a "motivating factor" in an employment decision, hasn't Title VII been violated?

PRICE WATERHOUSE V. HOPKINS
490 U.S. 228 (1989)

BRENNAN, J., announced the judgment of the Court and delivered an opinion, in which MARSHALL, BLACKMUN, and STEVENS, JJ., joined. WHITE, J., and O'CONNOR, J., filed opinions concurring in the judgment. KENNEDY, J., filed a dissenting opinion, in which REHNQUIST, C.J., and SCALIA, J., joined.

Ann Hopkins was a senior manager in an office of Price Waterhouse when she was proposed for partnership in 1982. She was neither offered nor denied admission to the partnership; instead, her candidacy was held for reconsideration the following year. When the partners in her office later refused to repropose her for partnership, she sued Price Waterhouse under Title VII of the Civil Rights Act of 1964, charging that the firm had discriminated against her on the basis of sex in its decisions regarding partnership. Judge Gesell in the District Court for the District of Columbia ruled in her favor on the question of liability, and the Court of Appeals for the District of Columbia Circuit affirmed. We granted certiorari to resolve a conflict among the Courts of Appeals concerning the respective burdens of proof of a defendant and plaintiff in a suit under Title VII when it has been shown that an employment decision resulted from a mixture of legitimate and illegitimate motives.

I

Ann Hopkins had worked at Price Waterhouse's Office of Government Services in Washington, D.C., for five years when the partners in that office proposed her as a candidate for partnership. Of the 662 partners at the firm at that time, 7 were women. Of the 88 persons proposed for partnership that year, only 1—Hopkins—was a woman. Forty-seven of these candidates were admitted to the partnership, 21 were rejected, and 20—including Hopkins—were "held" for reconsideration the following year.

In a jointly prepared statement supporting her candidacy, the partners in Hopkins' office showcased her successful 2-year effort to secure a $25 million contract with the Department of State, labeling it "an outstanding performance" and one that Hopkins carried out "virtually at the partner level." Despite Price Waterhouse's attempt at trial to minimize her contribution to this project, Judge Gesell specifically found that Hopkins had "played a key role in Price Waterhouse's successful effort to win a multi-million dollar contract with the Department of State." Indeed, he went on, "[n]one of the other partnership candidates at Price Waterhouse that year had a comparable record in terms of successfully securing major contracts for the partnership."

The partners in Hopkins' office praised her character as well as her accomplishments, describing her in their joint statement as "an outstanding professional" who had a "deft touch," a "strong character, independence and integrity." Clients appear to have agreed with these assessments. At trial, one official from the State Department described her as "extremely competent, intelligent, strong and forthright, very productive, energetic and creative." Another high-ranking official praised Hopkins' decisiveness, broadmindedness, and "intellectual clarity"; she was, in his words, "a stimulating conversationalist." Evaluations such as these led Judge Gesell to conclude that Hopkins "had no difficulty dealing with clients and her clients appear to have been very pleased with her work" and that she "was generally viewed as a highly competent project leader who worked long hours, pushed vigorously to meet deadlines and demanded much from the multidisciplinary staffs with which she worked."

On too many occasions, however, Hopkins' aggressiveness apparently spilled over into abrasiveness. Staff members seem to have borne the brunt of Hopkins' brusqueness. Long before her bid for partnership, partners evaluating her work had counseled her to improve her relations with staff members. Although later evaluations indicate an improvement, Hopkins' perceived shortcomings in this important area eventually doomed her bid for partnership. Virtually all of the partners' negative remarks about Hopkins—even those of partners supporting her—had to do with her "interpersonal skills." Both "[s]upporters and opponents of her candidacy," stressed Judge Gesell, "indicated that she was sometimes overly aggressive, unduly harsh, difficult to work with and impatient with staff."

There were clear signs, though, that some of the partners reacted negatively to Hopkins' personality because she was a woman. One partner described her as "macho"; another suggested that she "overcompensated for being a woman"; a third advised her to take "a course at charm school". Several partners criticized her use of profanity; in response, one partner suggested that those partners objected to her swearing only "because it[']s a lady using foul language." But it was the man who, as Judge Gesell found, bore responsibility for explaining to Hopkins the reasons for the Policy Board's decision to place her candidacy on hold who delivered the coup de grace: in order to improve her chances for partnership, Thomas Beyer advised, Hopkins should "walk more femininely, talk more femininely, dress more femininely, wear make-up, have her hair styled, and wear jewelry."

In previous years, other female candidates for partnership also had been evaluated in sex-based terms. As a general matter, Judge Gesell concluded, "[c]andidates were viewed favorably if partners believed they maintained their femin[in]ity while becoming effective professional managers"; in this environment, "[t]o be identified as a 'women's lib[b]er' was regarded as [a] negative comment." In fact, the judge found that in previous years "[o]ne partner repeatedly commented that he could not consider any woman seriously as a partnership candidate and believed that women were not even capable of functioning as senior managers—yet the firm took no action to discourage his comments and recorded his vote in the overall summary of the evaluations."

Judge Gesell found that Price Waterhouse legitimately emphasized interpersonal skills in its partnership decisions, and also found that the firm had not fabricated its complaints about Hopkins' interpersonal skills as a pretext for discrimination. Moreover, he concluded, the firm did not give decisive emphasis to such traits only because Hopkins was a woman; although there were male candidates who lacked these skills but who were admitted to partnership, the judge found that these candidates possessed other, positive traits that Hopkins lacked.

The judge went on to decide, however, that some of the partners' remarks about Hopkins stemmed from an impermissibly cabined view of the proper behavior of women, and that Price Waterhouse had done nothing to disavow reliance on such comments. He held that Price Waterhouse had unlawfully discriminated against Hopkins on the basis of sex by consciously giving credence and effect to partners' comments that resulted from sex stereotyping.

II

The specification of the standard of causation under Title VII is a decision about the kind of conduct that violates that statute. According to Price Waterhouse, an employer violates Title VII only if it gives decisive consideration to an employee's gender, race, national origin, or religion in making a decision that affects that employee. On Price Waterhouse's theory, even if a plaintiff shows that her gender played a part in an employment decision, it is still her burden to show that the decision would have been different if the employer had not discriminated. In Hopkins' view, on the other hand, an employer violates the statute whenever it allows one of these attributes to play any part in an employment decision. Once a plaintiff shows that this occurred, according to Hopkins, the employer's proof that it would have made the same decision in the absence of discrimination can serve to limit equitable relief but not to avoid a finding of liability. We conclude that, as often happens, the truth lies somewhere in-between.

A

Congress' intent to forbid employers to take gender into account in making employment decisions appears on the face of the statute. In now-familiar language, the statute forbids an employer to "fail or refuse to hire or to discharge any individual, or otherwise to discriminate with respect to his compensation, terms, conditions, or privileges of employment," or to "limit, segregate, or classify his employees or applicants for employment in any way which would deprive or tend to deprive any individual of employment opportunities or otherwise adversely affect his status as an employee, *because* of such individual's . . . sex." 42 U.S.C. §§ 2000e-2(a)(1), (2) (emphasis added). We take these words to mean that gender must be irrelevant to employment decisions. To construe the words "because of" as colloquial shorthand for "but-for causation," as does Price Waterhouse, is to misunderstand them.

To say that an employer may not take gender into account is not, however, the end of the matter, for that describes only one aspect of Title VII. The other important aspect of the statute is its preservation of an employer's remaining freedom of choice. We conclude that the preservation of this freedom means that an employer shall not be liable if it can prove that, even if it had not taken gender into account, it would have come to the same decision regarding a particular person. The statute's maintenance of employer prerogatives is evident from the statute itself and from its history, both in Congress and in this Court.

Our holding casts no shadow on *Burdine*, in which we decided that, even after a plaintiff has made out a *prima facie* case of discrimination under Title VII, the burden of persuasion does not shift to the employer to show that its stated legitimate reason for the employment decision was the true reason. We stress, first, that neither court below shifted the burden of persuasion to Price Waterhouse on this question, and in fact, the District Court found that Hopkins had not shown that the firm's stated reason for its decision was pretextual. Moreover, since we hold that the plaintiff retains the burden of persuasion on the issue whether gender played a part in the employment decision, the situation before us is not the one of "shifting burdens" that we addressed in *Burdine*. Instead, the employer's burden is most appropriately deemed an affirmative defense: the plaintiff must persuade the factfinder on one point, and then the employer, if it wishes to prevail, must persuade it on another. Where a decision was the product of a mixture of legitimate and illegitimate motives, it simply makes no sense to ask whether the legitimate reason was "*the* 'true reason'" (emphasis added) for the decision—which is the question asked by *Burdine*.[12]

C

In saying that gender played a motivating part in an employment decision, we mean that, if we asked the employer at the moment of the decision what its reasons were and if we received a truthful response, one of those reasons would be that the applicant or employee was a woman. In the specific context of sex stereotyping, an employer who acts on the basis of a belief that a woman cannot be aggressive, or that she must not be, has acted on the basis of gender.

Although the parties do not overtly dispute this last proposition, the placement by Price Waterhouse of "sex stereotyping" in quotation marks throughout its brief seems to us an insinuation either that such stereotyping was not present in this case or that it lacks legal relevance. We reject both possibilities. As to the existence of sex stereotyping in this case, we are not inclined to quarrel with the District Court's conclusion that a number of the partners' comments showed sex stereotyping at work. As for the legal relevance of sex stereotyping, we are beyond the day when an employer could evaluate employees by assuming or insisting that they matched the stereotype associated with their group, for "'[i]n forbidding employers to discriminate against individuals because of their sex, Congress intended to strike at the entire spectrum of disparate treatment of men and women resulting from sex stereotypes.'" *Los Angeles Dep't of*

Water & Power v. Manhart. An employer who objects to aggressiveness in women but whose positions require this trait places women in an intolerable and impermissible Catch-22: out of a job if they behave aggressively and out of a job if they don't. Title VII lifts women out of this bind.

Remarks at work that are based on sex stereotypes do not inevitably prove that gender played a part in a particular employment decision. The plaintiff must show that the employer actually relied on her gender in making its decision. In making this showing, stereotyped remarks can certainly be evidence that gender played a part. In any event, the stereotyping in this case did not simply consist of stray remarks. On the contrary, Hopkins proved that Price Waterhouse invited partners to submit comments; that some of the comments stemmed from sex stereotypes; that an important part of the Policy Board's decision on Hopkins was an assessment of the submitted comments; and that Price Waterhouse in no way disclaimed reliance on the sex-linked evaluations.

As to the employer's proof, in most cases, the employer should be able to present some objective evidence as to its probable decision in the absence of an impermissible motive. Moreover, proving "that the same decision would have been justified . . . is not the same as proving that the same decision would have been made." An employer may not, in other words, prevail in a mixed-motives case by offering a legitimate and sufficient reason for its decision if that reason did not motivate it at the time of the decision. The employer instead must show that its legitimate reason, standing alone, would have induced it to make the same decision.

V

We hold that when a plaintiff in a Title VII case proves that her gender played a motivating part in an employment decision, the defendant may avoid a finding of liability only by proving by a preponderance of the evidence that it would have made the same decision even if it had not taken the plaintiff's gender into account. Because the courts below erred by deciding that the defendant must make this proof by clear and convincing evidence, we reverse the Court of Appeals' judgment against Price Waterhouse on liability and remand the case to that court for further proceedings.

Justice O'CONNOR, concurring in the judgment.

The evidentiary rule the Court adopts today should be viewed as a supplement to the careful framework established by our unanimous decisions in *McDonnell Douglas Corp.* and *Burdine,* for use in cases such as this one where the employer has created uncertainty as to causation by knowingly giving substantial weight to an impermissible criterion. I write separately to explain why I believe such a departure from the *McDonnell Douglas* standard is justified in the circumstances presented by this and like cases, and to express my views as to when and how the strong medicine of requiring the employer to bear the burden of persuasion on the issue of causation should be administered.

As the Court of Appeals characterized it, Ann Hopkins proved that Price Waterhouse "permitt[ed] stereotypical attitudes towards women to play a significant, though unquantifiable, role in its decision not to invite her to become a partner." At this point Ann Hopkins had taken her proof as far as it could go. She had proved discriminatory input into the decisional process, and had proved that participants in the process considered her failure to conform to the stereotypes credited by a number of the decisionmakers had been a substantial factor in the decision.

Particularly in the context of the professional world, where decisions are often made by collegial bodies on the basis of largely subjective criteria, requiring the plaintiff to prove that any one factor was the definitive cause of the decisionmakers' action may be tantamount to declaring Title VII inapplicable to such decisions.

In my view, in order to justify shifting the burden on the issue of causation to the defendant, a disparate treatment plaintiff must show by direct evidence that an illegitimate criterion was a substantial factor in the decision. . . . Thus, stray remarks in the workplace, while perhaps probative of sexual harassment, cannot justify requiring the employer to prove that its hiring or promotion decisions were based on legitimate criteria. Nor can statements by nondecisionmakers, or statements by decisionmakers unrelated to the decisional process itself suffice to satisfy the plaintiff's burden in this regard. What is required is what Ann Hopkins showed here: direct evidence that decisionmakers placed substantial negative reliance on an illegitimate criterion in reaching their decision.

It should be obvious that the threshold standard I would adopt for shifting the burden of persuasion to the defendant differs substantially from that proposed by the plurality, the plurality's suggestion to the contrary notwithstanding. The plurality proceeds from the premise that the words "because of" in the statute do not embody any causal requirement at all. Under my approach, the plaintiff must produce evidence sufficient to show that an illegitimate criterion was a substantial factor in the particular employment decision such that a reasonable factfinder could draw an inference that the decision was made "because of" the plaintiff's protected status. Only then would the burden of proof shift to the defendant to prove that the decision would have been justified by other, wholly legitimate considerations.

NOTES AND QUESTIONS

1. How would Hopkins' case have been analyzed under *McDonnell-Douglas/Burdine*?

2. If Hopkins establishes that impermissible sex discrimination played a part in the employment decision, hasn't she proved a Title VII violation triggering the right to a declaratory judgment and attorneys fees, *i.e.*, shouldn't the "same decision" inquiry only affect relief? or is the *Mt. Healthy*/First Amendment analogy persuasive? Compare the Court's decision in *Carey v. Piphus*, awarding nominal damages based on a finding that procedural due process was violated. Does Title VII prohibit consideration of illegal factors, or only adverse action that was based on illegal factors?

3. How does Justice O'Connor's opinion differ from that of the plurality? Ultimately, Congress resolved the conflict. The **Civil Rights Act of 1991** overturned *Price Waterhouse* in part by providing that once an employee establishes that discrimination was a "motivating factor" in an employment decision, the employer is liable for violating Title VII, even where it can show the same action would have been taken in the absence of the impermissible motivating factor. 42 U.S.C. § 2000e-2(m). The Act, however, significantly limited relief where an employer can meet the "same decision" standard. § 2000e-5(g)(2)(B). The next case addresses these provisions:

DESERT PALACE, INC. V. COSTA
539 U.S. 90 (2003)

Justice THOMAS delivered the opinion of the Court.

The question before us in this case is whether a plaintiff must present direct evidence of discrimination in order to obtain a mixed-motive instruction under Title VII of the Civil Rights Act of 1964, as amended by the Civil Rights Act of 1991 (1991 Act). We hold that direct evidence is not required.

I

A

Since 1964, Title VII has made it an "unlawful employment practice for an employer . . . to discriminate against any individual . . ., *because of* such individual's race, color, religion, sex, or national origin." 42 U.S.C. § 2000e-2(a)(1) (emphasis added). In *Price Waterhouse*, the Court considered whether an employment decision is made "because of" sex in a "mixed- motive" case, *i.e.*, where both legitimate and illegitimate reasons motivated the decision. The Court concluded that, under § 2000e-2(a)(1), an employer could "avoid a finding of liability . . . by proving that it would have made the same decision even if it had not allowed gender to play such a role." The Court was divided, however, over the predicate question of when the burden of proof may be shifted to an employer to prove the affirmative defense.

Justice BRENNAN, writing for a plurality of four Justices, would have held that "when a plaintiff . . . proves that her gender played a *motivating* part in an employment decision, the defendant may avoid a finding of liability only by proving by a preponderance of the evidence that it would have made the same decision even if it had not taken the plaintiff's gender into account." (emphasis added). The plurality did not, however, "suggest a limitation on the possible ways of proving that [gender] stereotyping played a motivating role in an employment decision."

Justice WHITE and Justice O'CONNOR both concurred in the judgment. Justice O'CONNOR, like Justice WHITE, would have required the plaintiff to show that an illegitimate consideration was a "substantial factor" in the employment decision. But, under Justice O'CONNOR's view, "the burden on the issue of causation" would shift to the employer only where "a disparate treatment plaintiff [could] show by *direct evidence* that an illegitimate criterion was a substantial factor in the decision." (emphasis added).

Two years after *Price Waterhouse*, Congress passed the 1991 Act "in large part [as] a response to a series of decisions of this Court interpreting the Civil Rights Acts of 1866 and 1964." In particular, § 107 of the 1991 Act, which is at issue in this case, "respond[ed]" to *Price Waterhouse* by "setting forth standards applicable in 'mixed motive' cases" in two new statutory provisions.[1] The first establishes an alternative for proving that an "unlawful employment practice" has occurred:

> "'Except as otherwise provided in this subchapter, an unlawful employment practice is established when the complaining party demonstrates that race, color, religion, sex, or national origin was a motivating factor for any employment practice, even though other factors also motivated the practice.'" 42 U.S.C. § 2000e-2(m).

The second provides that, with respect to "'a claim in which an individual proves a violation under section 2000e-2(m),'" the employer has a limited affirmative defense that does not absolve it of liability, but restricts the remedies available to a plaintiff. The available remedies include only declaratory relief, certain types of injunctive relief, and attorney's fees and costs. 42 U.S.C. § 2000e-5(g)(2)(B). In order to avail itself of the affirmative defense, the employer must "demonstrat[e] that [it] would have taken the same action in the absence of the impermissible motivating factor." Relying primarily on Justice O'CONNOR's concurrence in *Price Waterhouse*, a number of courts have held that direct evidence is required to establish liability under § 2000e-2(m).

B

Petitioner Desert Palace, Inc., employed respondent Catharina Costa as a warehouse worker and heavy equipment operator. Respondent was the only woman in this job and in her local Teamsters bargaining unit.

Respondent experienced a number of problems with management and her co-workers that led to an escalating series of disciplinary sanctions, including informal rebukes, a denial of privileges, and suspension. Petitioner finally terminated respondent after she was involved in a physical altercation in a warehouse elevator with fellow Teamsters member Herbert Gerber. Petitioner disciplined both employees because the facts surrounding the incident were in dispute, but Gerber, who had a clean disciplinary record, received only a 5-day suspension.

Respondent subsequently filed this lawsuit against petitioner in the United States District Court for the District of Nevada, asserting claims of sex discrimination and sexual harassment under Title VII. The District Court dismissed the sexual harassment claim, but allowed the claim for sex discrimination to go to the jury. At trial, respondent presented evidence that (1) she was

---

1   This case does not require us to decide when, if ever, § 107 applies outside of the mixed-motive context.

singled out for "intense 'stalking'" by one of her supervisors, (2) she received harsher discipline than men for the same conduct, (3) she was treated less favorably than men in the assignment of overtime, and (4) supervisors repeatedly "stack[ed]" her disciplinary record and "frequently used or tolerated" sex-based slurs against her.

The District Court gave the jury the following mixed-motive instruction:

> "'You have heard evidence that the defendant's treatment of the plaintiff was motivated by the plaintiff's sex and also by other lawful reasons. If you find that the plaintiff's sex was a motivating factor in the defendant's treatment of the plaintiff, the plaintiff is entitled to your verdict, even if you find that the defendant's conduct was also motivated by a lawful reason.

> "'However, if you find that the defendant's treatment of the plaintiff was motivated by both gender and lawful reasons, you must decide whether the plaintiff is entitled to damages. The plaintiff is entitled to damages unless the defendant proves by a preponderance of the evidence that the defendant would have treated plaintiff similarly even if the plaintiff's gender had played no role in the employment decision.'"

Petitioner unsuccessfully objected to this instruction, claiming that respondent had failed to adduce "direct evidence" that sex was a motivating factor in her dismissal or in any of the other adverse employment actions taken against her. The jury rendered a verdict for respondent, awarding backpay, compensatory damages, and punitive damages.

II

This case provides us with the first opportunity to consider the effects of the 1991 Act on jury instructions in mixed-motive cases. Specifically, we must decide whether a plaintiff must present direct evidence of discrimination in order to obtain a mixed-motive instruction under 42 U.S.C. § 2000e-2(m).

Our precedents make clear that the starting point for our analysis is the statutory text. And where, as here, the words of the statute are unambiguous, the "'judicial inquiry is complete.'" Section 2000e-2(m) unambiguously states that a plaintiff need only "demonstrat[e]" that an employer used a forbidden consideration with respect to "any employment practice." On its face, the statute does not mention, much less require, that a plaintiff make a heightened showing through direct evidence. Indeed, petitioner concedes as much.

Moreover, Congress explicitly defined the term "demonstrates" in the 1991 Act, leaving little doubt that no special evidentiary showing is required. Title VII defines the term "'demonstrates'" as to "mee[t] the burdens of production and persuasion." § 2000e(m). If Congress intended the term "'demonstrates'" to require that the "burdens of production and persuasion" be met by direct evidence or some other heightened showing, it could have made that intent clear by including language to that effect in § 2000e(m). Its failure to do so is significant, for Congress has been unequivocal when imposing heightened proof requirements in other circumstances, including in other provisions of Title 42.

In addition, Title VII's silence with respect to the type of evidence required in mixed-motive cases also suggests that we should not depart from the "[c]onventional rul[e] of civil litigation [that] generally appl[ies] in Title VII cases." *Ibid.* That rule requires a plaintiff to prove his case "by a preponderance of the evidence," *ibid.* using "direct or circumstantial evidence," *Postal Service Bd. of Governors v. Aikens.* We have often acknowledged the utility of circumstantial evidence in discrimination cases. For instance, in *Reeves v. Sanderson Plumbing Products, Inc.*, we recognized that evidence that a defendant's explanation for an employment practice is "unworthy of credence" is "one form of circumstantial evidence that is probative of intentional discrimination." The reason for treating circumstantial and direct evidence alike is both clear and deep-rooted: "Circumstantial evidence is not only sufficient, but may also be more certain, satisfying and persuasive than direct evidence."

Finally, the use of the term "demonstrates" in other provisions of Title VII tends to show further that § 2000e2(m) does not incorporate a direct evidence requirement. *See, e.g.,* 42 U.S.C. §§ 2000e-2(k)(1)(A)(i), 2000e- 5(g)(2)(B). For instance, § 2000e-5(g)(2)(B) requires an employer to "demonstrat[e] that [it] would have taken the same action in the absence of the impermissible motivating factor" in order to take advantage of the partial affirmative defense. Due to the similarity in structure between that provision and § 2000e-2(m), it would be logical to assume that the term "demonstrates" would carry the same meaning with respect to both provisions. But when pressed at oral argument about whether direct evidence is required before the partial affirmative defense can be invoked, petitioner did not "agree that . . . the defendant or the employer has any heightened standard" to satisfy. Absent some congressional indication to the contrary, we decline to give the same term in the same Act a different meaning depending on whether the rights of the plaintiff or the defendant are at issue.

In order to obtain an instruction under § 2000e-2(m), a plaintiff need only present sufficient evidence for a reasonable jury to conclude, by a preponderance of the evidence, that "race, color, religion, sex, or national origin was a motivating factor for any employment practice." Because direct evidence of discrimination is not required in mixed-motive cases, the Court of Appeals correctly concluded that the District Court did not abuse its discretion in giving a mixed-motive instruction to the jury. Accordingly, the judgment of the Court of Appeals is affirmed.

NOTES AND QUESTIONS

1. How would Costa's case have been analyzed under *McDonnell Douglas*? Could she have survived summary judgment or a directed verdict?

2. What was Desert Palace's grounds for objecting to the jury instructions? If an employee can shift the burden of proof onto the employer by showing that it may have used a forbidden factor with respect to its decision, has *McDonnell Douglas* been

eviscerated? What does footnote 1 suggest? Does § 703(m) mention mixed-motive? If direct evidence is not necessary, how is mixed-motive distinguishable from other kinds of cases? Will this decision make it tougher for an employer to avoid summary judgment in all disparate treatment cases, or to ultimately avoid liability?

3. Questions have arisen as to when a subordinate's bias will satisfy the "a motivating factor" standard where an independent, unbiased person makes the ultimate employment decision, but that decision is influenced by the subordinate's bias. Some circuits held that the subordinate's animus is relevant only if that person exerted "significant influence over the decision," such that the animus can be imputed to the decisionmaker. Others required that the decisionmaker must actually be motivated by discriminatory animus. The Supreme Court, in *Staub v. Proctor Hospital*, 562 U.S. 411 (2011), resolved this issue in the context of a suit brought under the Uniformed Services Employment and Re-employment Rights Act (USERRA), which imposes liability if military service is "a motivating factor" in an adverse job action. Rejecting the notion that the ultimate decisionmaker must act with discriminatory animus, the Supreme Court held that an employer may be liable if a biased supervisor's discriminatory intent was a "proximate cause" in the termination, even if the ultimate decisionmaker was unbiased: "[I]f a supervisor performs an act motivated by an anti-military animus that is *intended* by the supervisor to cause an adverse employment action, and if that act is a proximate cause of the ultimate employment action, then the employer is liable." Thus, an employee must present evidence both that the biased supervisor intended the ultimate adverse employment action and that the bias was a "proximate cause" of the action, which requires "some direct relation between the injury asserted and the injurious conduct alleged." Further, the Court rejected the argument that if an unbiased decisionmaker conducts an independent investigation, the employer is necessarily insulated from liability. The Court reasoned that a biased supervisor's report may still be "a causal factor" if the investigation takes it into account. Only if the investigation results in termination for reasons unrelated to the biased report can the causal link be broken.

Significantly, the Court rejected not only the view that the decisionmaker must have discriminatory animus, but also the less onerous requirement, followed in some circuits, that the biased supervisor have "a singular influence" on the decisionmaker. The Court's opinion explicitly noted the similarities between USERRA and Title VII, in particular, the "a motivating factor" language. Thus, *Staub* governs Title VII litigation.

4. Questions regarding mixed-motive analysis have been raised in other contexts. Significantly, the Supreme Court in *Gross v. FBL Financial Services, Inc.*, 557 U.S. 167 (2009), discussed *infra*, ruled that Age Discrimination in Employment Act claims are governed by "but for" causation and are outside the scope of the 1991 mixed-motive

amendment. In *University of Texas Southwest Medical Center v. Nassar*, 570 U.S. 338 (2013), discussed *infra*, the Supreme Court in a 5–4 decision held that Congress' new "mixed-motive" provision did not apply to Title VII retaliation claims. Congress' reference to "unlawful employment practice" in the 1991 amendment encompassed only discrimination claims, not retaliation claims.

Problem: Eighteen

Jane Fields was an English professor at Aimes University who was recently denied tenure. The decision was made by a panel of six tenured English professors in her department. During the course of discussion with two of the six decision-makers, Fields was informed that "refusing sexual advances was no way to get tenure." The other tenured faculty member present nodded his head in agreement. The University vehemently argues that Fields was not qualified for tenure—that she had not published the quality articles necessary, and, thus, the University was justified in giving Fields a terminal contract.

1. How would Fields' case be analyzed under the *McDonnell Douglas/Burdine* approach? Can she even establish a *prima facie* case of gender discrimination? If she presents evidence that she did publish "quality" articles, can she survive summary judgment?

2. Has Fields sufficiently proved that gender was a "motivating factor" in the university's adverse tenure decision within the meaning of the Civil Rights Act of 1991? If so, could the University, nonetheless, avoid liability?

ii.   After-Acquired Evidence

MCKENNON V. NASHVILLE BANNER PUBLISHING COMPANY
513 u.s. 352 (1995)

Justice KENNEDY delivered the opinion of the Court.

The question before us is whether an employee discharged in violation of the Age Discrimination in Employment Act of 1967 is barred from all relief when, after her discharge, the employer discovers evidence of wrongdoing that, in any event, would have led to the employee's termination on lawful and legitimate grounds.

I

For some 30 years, petitioner Christine McKennon worked for respondent Nashville Banner Publishing Company. She was discharged, the Banner claimed, as part of a work force reduction plan necessitated by cost considerations. McKennon, who was 62 years old when she lost her job, thought another reason explained her dismissal: her age.

In preparation of the case, the Banner took McKennon's deposition. She testified that, during her final year of employment, she had copied several confidential documents bearing upon the company's financial condition. She had access to these records as secretary to the Banner's comptroller. McKennon took the copies home and showed them to her husband. Her motivation, she averred, was an apprehension she was about to be fired because of her age. . . . A few days after these deposition disclosures, the Banner sent McKennon a letter declaring that removal and copying of the records was in violation of her job responsibilities and advising her (again) that she was terminated. The Banner's letter also recited that had it known of McKennon's misconduct it would have discharged her at once for that reason.

II

We shall assume, as summary judgment procedures require us to assume, that the sole reason for McKennon's initial discharge was her age, a discharge violative of the ADEA. Our further premise is that the misconduct revealed by the deposition was so grave that McKennon's immediate discharge would have followed its disclosure in any event.

The Court of Appeals considered McKennon's misconduct, in effect, to be supervening grounds for termination. That may be so, but it does not follow, as the Court of Appeals said in citing one of its own earlier cases, that the misconduct renders it "'irrelevant whether or not [McKennon] was discriminated against.'" We conclude that a violation of the ADEA cannot be so altogether disregarded.

The ADEA and Title VII share common substantive features and also a common purpose: "the elimination of discrimination in the workplace." Congress designed the remedial measures in these statutes to serve as a "spur or catalyst" to cause employers "to self-examine and to self-evaluate their employment practices and to endeavor to eliminate, so far as possible, the last vestiges" of discrimination. Deterrence is one object of these statutes. Compensation for injuries caused by the prohibited discrimination is another. It would not accord with this scheme if after-acquired evidence of wrongdoing that would have resulted in termination operates, in every instance, to bar all relief for an earlier violation of the Act.

The objectives of the ADEA are furthered when even a single employee establishes that an employer has discriminated against him or her. The disclosure through litigation of incidents or practices which violate national policies respecting nondiscrimination in the work force is itself important, for the occurrence of violations may disclose patterns of noncompliance resulting from a misappreciation of the Act's operation or entrenched resistance to its commands, either of which can be of industry-wide significance. The efficacy of its enforcement mechanisms becomes one measure of the success of the Act.

In *Mt. Healthy* we addressed a mixed-motives case, in which two motives were said to be operative in the employer's decision to fire an employee. One was lawful, the other (an alleged constitutional violation) unlawful. We held that if the lawful reason alone would have sufficed to justify the firing, the employee could not prevail in a suit against the employer. The case was controlled by the difficulty, and what we thought was the lack of necessity, of disentangling the proper motive from the improper one where both played a part in the termination and the former motive would suffice to sustain the employer's action.

That is not the problem confronted here. As we have said, the case comes to us on the express assumption that an unlawful motive was the sole basis for the firing. McKennon's misconduct was not discovered until after she had been fired. The employer could not have been motivated by knowledge it did not have and it cannot now claim that the employee was fired for the nondiscriminatory reason. Mixed motive cases are inapposite here, except to the important extent they underscore the necessity of determining the employer's motives in ordering the discharge, an essential element in determining whether the employer violated the federal antidiscrimination law.

Our inquiry is not at an end, however, for even though the employer has violated the Act, we must consider how the after-acquired evidence of the employee's wrongdoing bears on the specific remedy to be ordered. Equity's maxim that a suitor who engaged in his own reprehensible conduct in the course of the transaction at issue must be denied equitable relief because of unclean hands, a rule which in conventional formulation operated in limine to bar the suitor from invoking the aid of the equity court, has not been applied where Congress authorizes broad equitable relief to serve important national policies. We have rejected the unclean hands defense "where a private suit serves important public purposes." That does not mean, however, the employee's own misconduct is irrelevant to all the remedies otherwise available under the statute. The statute controlling this case provides that "the court shall have jurisdiction to grant such legal or equitable relief as may be appropriate to effectuate the purposes of this chapter, including without limitation judgments compelling employment, reinstatement or promotion, or enforcing the liability for [amounts owing to a person as a result of a violation of this chapter]." 29 U.S.C. § 626(b); *see also* § 216(b). In giving effect to the ADEA, we must recognize the duality between the legitimate interests of the employer and the important claims of the employee who invokes the national employment policy mandated by the Act. The employee's wrongdoing must be taken into account, we conclude, lest the employer's legitimate concerns be ignored. In determining appropriate remedial action, the employee's wrongdoing becomes relevant not to punish the employee, or out of concern "for the relative moral worth of the parties," but to take due account of the lawful prerogatives of the employer in the usual course of its business and the corresponding equities that it has arising from the employee's wrongdoing.

The proper boundaries of remedial relief in the general class of cases where, after termination, it is discovered that the employee has engaged in wrongdoing must be addressed by the judicial system in the ordinary course of further decisions, for the factual permutations and the equitable considerations they raise will vary from case to case. We do conclude that here, and as a general rule in cases of this type, neither reinstatement nor front pay is an appropriate remedy. It would be both inequitable and pointless to order the reinstatement of someone the employer would have terminated, and will terminate, in any event and upon lawful grounds.

The proper measure of backpay presents a more difficult problem. Resolution of this question must give proper recognition to the fact that an ADEA violation has occurred which must be deterred and compensated without undue infringement upon the employer's rights and prerogatives. The object of compensation is to restore the employee to the position he or she would have been in absent the discrimination, *Franks v. Bowman Transportation Co.*, but that principle is difficult to apply with precision where there is after-acquired evidence of wrongdoing that would have led to termination on legitimate grounds had the employer known about it. Once an employer learns about employee wrongdoing that would lead to a legitimate discharge, we cannot require the employer to ignore the information, even if it is acquired during the course of discovery in a suit against the employer and even if the information might have gone undiscovered absent the suit. The beginning point in the trial court's formulation of a remedy should be calculation of backpay from the date of the unlawful discharge to the date the new information was discovered. In determining the appropriate order for relief, the court can consider taking into further account extraordinary equitable circumstances that affect the legitimate interests of either party. An absolute rule barring any recovery of backpay, however, would undermine the ADEA's objective of forcing employers to consider and examine their motivations, and of penalizing them for employment decisions that spring from age discrimination.

Where an employer seeks to rely upon after-acquired evidence of wrongdoing, it must first establish that the wrongdoing was of such severity that the employee in fact would have been terminated on those grounds alone if the employer had known of it at the time of the discharge. The concern that employers might as a routine matter undertake extensive discovery into an employee's background or performance on the job to resist claims under the Act is not an insubstantial one, but we think the authority of the courts to award attorney's fees, mandated under the statute, 29 U.S.C. §§ 216(b), 626(b), and in appropriate cases to invoke the provisions of Rule 11 of the Federal Rules of Civil Procedure will deter most abuses.

NOTES AND QUESTIONS

1. How does the issue here differ from that in *Price Waterhouse*? Should it be resolved in the same way? Why shouldn't the employer have to prove it would have discovered the information even in the absence of the discrimination? Wouldn't McKennon still be working for Banner today "but for" the discrimination?

2. Because the opinion generally contemplates back pay until the "new information" is discovered, what advice would you give to employers who receive an EEOC charge? Employees should be advised that their employment history may be closely scrutinized for misconduct—and that job applications often state that misrepresentation is grounds for automatic discharge.

3. What "test" must an employer meet to bar relief based on after-acquired evidence? What if the issue is gross incompetence, rather than misconduct?

b.   Disproportionate Impact

In addition to disparate treatment cases wherein the plaintiffs must eventually prove intentional discrimination, the Supreme Court has also interpreted Title VII to prohibit practices which although facially neutral have a disparate impact on a protected group.

GRIGGS V. DUKE POWER CO.
401 U.S. 424 (1971)

Mr. Chief Justice BURGER delivered the opinion of the Court.

[The Court addressed the question of whether requiring a high school diploma or a passing grade on a standardized general intelligence test could be used as a condition of employment.]

The objective of Congress in the enactment of Title VII is plain from the language of the statute. It was to achieve equality of employment opportunities and remove barriers that have operated in the past to favor an identifiable group of white employees over other employees. Under the Act, practices, procedures, or tests neutral on their face, and even neutral in terms of intent, cannot be maintained if they operate to "freeze" the status quo of prior discriminatory employment practices.

The Court of Appeals' opinion, and the partial dissent, agreed that, on the record in the present case, "whites register far better on the Company's alternative requirements" than Negroes. This consequence would appear to be directly traceable to race. Basic intelligence must have the means of articulation to manifest itself fairly in a testing process. Because they are Negroes, petitioners have long received inferior education in segregated schools. Congress did not intend by Title VII, however, to guarantee a job to every person regardless of qualifications. In short, the Act does not command that any person be hired simply because he was formerly the subject of discrimination, or because he is a member of a minority group. Discriminatory preference for any group, minority or majority, is precisely and only what Congress has proscribed. What is required by Congress is the removal of artificial, arbitrary, and unnecessary barriers to employment when the barriers operate invidiously to discriminate on the basis of racial or other impermissible classification.

The Act proscribes not only overt discrimination but also practices that are fair in form, but discriminatory in operation. The touchstone is business necessity. If an employment practice which operates to exclude Negroes cannot be shown to be related to job performance, the practice is prohibited.

On the record before us, neither the high school completion requirement nor the general intelligence test is shown to bear a demonstrable relationship to successful performance of the jobs for which it was used. Both were adopted, as the Court of Appeals noted, without meaningful study of their relationship to job-performance ability. Rather, a vice president of the Company testified, the requirements were instituted on the Company's judgment that they generally would improve the overall quality of the work force.

The Court of Appeals held that the Company had adopted the diploma and test requirements without any "intention to discriminate against Negro employees." We do not suggest that either the District Court or the Court of Appeals erred in examining the employer's intent; but good intent or absence of discriminatory intent does not redeem employment procedures or testing mechanisms that operate as "built-in headwinds" for minority groups and are unrelated to measuring job capability.

The Company's lack of discriminatory intent is suggested by special efforts to help the undereducated employees through Company financing of two-thirds the cost of tuition for high school training. But Congress directed the thrust of the Act to the *consequences* of employment practices, not simply the motivation. More than that, Congress has placed on the employer the burden of showing that any given requirement must have a manifest relationship to the employment in question.

The Company contends that its general intelligence tests are specifically permitted by § 703(h) of the Act. That section authorizes the use of "any professionally developed ability test" that is not "designed, intended *or used* to discriminate because of race. . .." (Emphasis added.)

The Equal Employment Opportunity Commission, having enforcement responsibility, has issued guidelines interpreting § 703(h) to permit only the use of job-related tests. The administrative interpretation of the Act by the enforcing agency is entitled to great deference. Since the Act and its legislative history support the Commission's construction, this affords good reason to treat the guidelines as expressing the will of Congress.

NOTES AND QUESTIONS

1. Could the plaintiffs in *Griggs* have established a *prima facie* case under *Burdine*?

2. Does *Griggs* allow a court to invalidate a facially neutral practice without any showing of intentional discrimination? Is it fair to infer that an employer who uses a test which is not job related is engaging in intentional discrimination? Is such an inference necessary to prove a violation of Title VII?

3. Since the language of § 703(a)(2) prohibits discrimination "because of race," how does the Court find that Congress intended to reach "unintentional" conduct? In prohibiting unintentional discrimination by state and local government employers, and subjecting them to liability for damages, did Congress exceed its Fourteenth Amendment power in light of the Court's holding that only intentional discrimination violates the Equal Protection Clause? If Congress was concerned with practices which freeze "the status quo of prior discriminatory employment practices," must a plaintiff present evidence that a state employer engaged in such discriminatory practices in order to prove a Title VII violation? If not, is this a valid remedial measure as applied to government employers? *See Katzenbach* and *Boerne, supra* Chapter One.

4. After *Griggs*, may an employer require a high school diploma simply to upgrade the quality of its workforce? What if a comparison of the relevant workforce showed that a significantly larger percentage of whites in the relevant population had a high school diploma as compared to blacks? What would the employer have to "show" to justify such a requirement?

5. Does the employer in an impact case have a burden of production or a burden of persuasion, and what is plaintiff's "ultimate burden"? Consider *Albemarle Paper Co. v. Moody*, 422 U.S. 405 (1975), in which the Court described *Griggs* as follows:

> . . . this Court unanimously held that Title VII forbids the use of employment tests that are discriminatory in effect unless the employer meets "the burden of showing that any given requirement [has] . . . a manifest relationship to the employment in question." This burden arises, of course, only after the complaining party or class has made out a *prima facie* case of discrimination, *i.e.*, has shown that the tests in question select applicants for hire or promotion in a racial pattern significantly different from that of the pool of applicants. If an employer does then meet the burden of proving that its tests are "job related," it remains open to the complaining party to show that other tests or selection devices, without a similarly undesirable racial effect, would also serve the employer's legitimate interest in "efficient and trustworthy workmanship." Such a showing would be evidence that the employer was using its tests merely as a "pretext" for discrimination.

NEW YORK TRANSIT AUTHORITY V. BEAZER
440 U.S. 568 (1979)

Mr. Justice STEVENS delivered the opinion of the Court.

The Transit Authority (TA) operates the subway system and certain bus lines in New York City. It employs about 47,000 persons, of whom many—perhaps most—are employed in positions that involve danger to themselves or to the public. For example, some 12,300 are subway motormen, towermen, conductors, or bus operators. The District Court found that these jobs are attended by unusual hazards and must be performed by "persons of maximum alertness and competence." Certain other jobs, such as operating cranes and handling high-voltage equipment, are also considered "critical" or "safety sensitive," while still others, though classified as "noncritical," have a potentially important impact on the overall operation of the transportation system.

TA enforces a general policy against employing persons who use narcotic drugs. The policy is reflected in Rule 11(b) of TA's Rules and Regulations. Methadone is regarded as a narcotic within the meaning of Rule 11(b).

About 40,000 persons receive methadone maintenance treatment in New York City, of whom about 26,000 participate in the five major public or semipublic programs, and 14,000 are involved in about 25 private programs. The sole purpose of all these programs is to treat the addiction of persons who have been using heroin for at least two years.

The evidence indicates that methadone is an effective cure for the physical aspects of heroin addiction. But the District Court also found "that many persons attempting to overcome heroin addiction have psychological or life-style problems which reach beyond what can be cured by the physical taking of doses of methadone." The crucial indicator of successful methadone maintenance is the patient's abstinence from the illegal or excessive use of drugs and alcohol. The District Court found that the risk of reversion to drug or alcohol abuse declines dramatically after the first few months of treatment. Indeed, "the strong majority" of patients who have been on methadone maintenance for at least a year are free from illicit drug use. But a significant number are not. On this critical point, the evidence relied upon by the District Court reveals that even among participants with more than 12 months' tenure in methadone maintenance programs, the incidence of drug and alcohol abuse may often approach and even exceed 25%.

This litigation was brought by the four respondents as a class action on behalf of all persons who have been, or would in the future be, subject to discharge or rejection as employees of TA by reason of participation in a methadone maintenance program. Their complaint alleged that TA's blanket exclusion of all former heroin addicts receiving methadone treatment was illegal under the Civil Rights Act of 1866, 42 U.S.C. § 1981, Title VII of the Civil Rights Act of 1964, and the Equal Protection Clause of the Fourteenth Amendment.

The trial record contains extensive evidence concerning the success of methadone maintenance programs, the employability of persons taking methadone, and the ability of prospective employers to detect drug abuse or other undesirable characteristics of methadone users. In general, the District Court concluded that there are substantial numbers of methadone users who are just as employable as other members of the general population and that normal personnel-screening procedures—at least if augmented by some method of obtaining information from the staffs of methadone programs—would enable TA to identify the unqualified applicants on an individual basis. On the other hand, the District Court recognized that at least one-third of the persons receiving methadone treatment—and probably a good many more—would unquestionably be classified as unemployable.

After extensively reviewing the evidence, the District Court briefly stated its conclusion that TA's methadone policy is unconstitutional.

Almost a year later the District Court filed a supplemental opinion allowing respondents to recover attorney's fees under 42 U.S.C. § 2000e-5(k). This determination was premised on the court's additional holding that TA's drug policy violated Title VII. Having already concluded that the blanket exclusion was not rationally related to any business needs of TA, the court reasoned that the statute is violated if the exclusionary policy has a discriminatory effect against blacks and Hispanics. That effect was proved, in the District Court's view, by two statistics: (1) of the employees referred to TA's medical consultant for suspected violation of its drug policy, 81% are black or Hispanic; (2) between 62% and 65% of all methadone-maintained persons in

New York City are black or Hispanic. The court, however, did not find that TA's policy was motivated by any bias against blacks or Hispanics; indeed, it expressly found that the policy was not adopted with a discriminatory purpose.

The District Court's findings do not support its conclusion that TA's regulation prohibiting the use of narcotics, or its interpretation of that regulation to encompass users of methadone, violated Title VII of the Civil Rights Act.

A *prima facie* violation of the Act may be established by statistical evidence showing that an employment practice has the effect of denying the members of one race equal access to employment opportunities. Even assuming that respondents have crossed this threshold, when the entire record is examined it is clear that the two statistics on which they and the District Court relied do not prove a violation of Title VII.

First, the District Court noted that 81% of the employees referred to TA's medical director for suspected violation of its narcotics rule were either black or Hispanic. But respondents have only challenged the rule to the extent that it is construed to apply to methadone users, and that statistic tells us nothing about the racial composition of the employees suspected of using methadone. Nor does the record give us any information about the number of black, Hispanic, or white persons who were dismissed for using methadone.

Second, the District Court noted that about 63% of the persons in New York City receiving methadone maintenance in *public* programs—*i.e.*, 63% of the 65% of all New York City methadone users who are in such programs—are black or Hispanic. We do not know, however, how many of these persons ever worked or sought to work for TA. This statistic therefore reveals little if anything about the racial composition of the class of TA job applicants and employees receiving methadone treatment. More particularly, it tells us nothing about the class of otherwise-qualified applicants and employees who have participated in methadone maintenance programs for over a year—the only class improperly excluded by TA's policy under the District Court's analysis. The record demonstrates, in fact, that the figure is virtually irrelevant because a substantial portion of the persons included in it are either unqualified for other reasons—such as the illicit use of drugs and alcohol—or have received successful assistance in finding jobs with employers other than TA. Finally, we have absolutely no data on the 14,000 methadone users in the *private* programs, leaving open the possibility that the percentage of blacks and Hispanics in the class of methadone users is not significantly greater than the percentage of those minorities in the general population of New York City.

At best, respondents' statistical showing is weak; even if it is capable of establishing a *prima facie* case of discrimination, it is assuredly rebutted by TA's demonstration that its narcotics rule (and the rule's application to methadone users) is "job related." The District Court's express finding that the rule was not motivated by racial animus forecloses any claim in rebuttal that it was merely a pretext for intentional discrimination. We conclude that respondents failed to prove a violation of Title VII.

1. Why did the Court reject the general population data? What data would have established a *prima facie* case? Is it fair to restrict plaintiffs to applicant data where the challenged practice deters minority group members using methadone from applying and where the general population is presumptively qualified for the "at issue" jobs?

2. How does the Court characterize the employer's burden? How significant was the safety factor?

3. As to plaintiff's rebuttal, is the majority requiring proof of intent to establish a violation of Title VII once the defendant satisfies its burden? Does an employer's persistent use of a test where less discriminatory alternatives are available allow an inference of intentional discrimination? What if plaintiffs' suggested alternative— "augmented" personnel screening procedures—would be more costly?

4. In *Wards Cove Packing Co., Inc. v. Atonio*, 490 U.S. 642 (1989), the Court issued several rulings addressing disparate impact analysis. First, it held that to make out a *prima facie* case, "a plaintiff must demonstrate that it is the application of a specific or particular employment practice that has created the disparate impact under attack." Simply demonstrating that a group of factors, taken together, had a disparate impact on minority applicants is insufficient. Instead, plaintiffs must isolate each particular practice that caused the disparate impact.

    Second, the Court changed the general understanding of who bears the burden of proving "business necessity." It held that although "the employer carries the burden of producing evidence of a business justification for his employment practice . . . the burden of persuasion remains with the disparate-impact plaintiff." Further, it described the "dispositive issue" as "whether a challenged practice serves, in a significant way, the legitimate employment goals of the employer," emphasizing that there was "no requirement that the challenged practice be 'essential' or 'indispensable' to the employer's business for it to pass muster."

    Further, if plaintiffs cannot persuade the trier of fact on the question of business necessity, they can prevail only by persuading the factfinder that "other tests or selection devices, without a similarly undesirable racial effect, would also serve the employer's legitimate [hiring] interest[s]," thereby proving that the "tests were merely used as a 'pretext' for discrimination."

    The Court stressed that any alternative practices must be equally effective in achieving the employer's legitimate employment goals, looking to factors such as costs or other burdens of proposed alternative selection devices, and that courts should "proceed with care" before mandating that an employer adopt a plaintiff's alternate selection or hiring practice.

One of the key purposes of the **Civil Rights Act of 1991** was to overrule *Wards Cove*. Read carefully §§ 2000e-2(k) (rules governing disparate impact analysis) and 2000e-m (defining the term "demonstrate"). What aspects of *Wards Cove* has Congress addressed? Has it reinstated the *Griggs* analysis?

5. The Uniform Guidelines on Employee Selection Procedures (29 C.F.R. § 1607) address the problem of identifying the particular practice that causes the adverse impact. The regulations require:

   (a) that employers break down their hiring process into component parts. [§ 1607.3(A)]

   (b) that they analyze the adverse impact of each component part, i.e., do a demographic analysis of each element. [§ 1607.4(B)]

   (c) if an adverse impact is shown, the employer must "validate" its practice; identify possible less discriminatory alternatives, and show either that the other alternatives are less effective or more costly. [§ 1607.4(B)]

   The rules specify that where the employer fails to maintain data on adverse impact, "the federal enforcement agencies may draw an inference of adverse impact of the selection process . . . if the user has a underutilization of a group in the job category, as compared to the group's representation in the relevant labor market or, in the case of jobs filled from within, the applicable workforce." § 1607.4(D). What is the plaintiffs' "ultimate" burden in winning a disparate impact case? When will the existence of "less discriminatory" alternatives prove that Title VII has been violated?

PROBLEM: NINETEEN

Prepare a chart setting forth the analysis of:

   a. *prima facie* case

   b. the employer's response

   c. the employee's rebuttal

under (1) *Griggs/Albemarle Paper Co.*; (2) *Wards Cove*; and (3) the Civil Rights Act of 1991.

Justice BRENNAN delivered the opinion of the Court.

We consider here whether an employer sued for violation of Title VII of the Civil Rights Act of 1964 may assert a "bottom-line" theory of defense. Under that theory, as asserted in this case, an employer's acts of racial discrimination in promotions—effected by an examination having disparate impact—would not render the employer liable for the racial discrimination suffered by employees barred from promotion if the "bottom-line" result of the promotional process was an appropriate racial balance. We hold that the "bottom line" does not preclude respondent employees from establishing a *prima facie* case, nor does it provide petitioner employer with a defense to such a case.

I

To attain permanent status as supervisors respondents had to participate in a selection process that required, as the first step, a passing score on a written examination. This written test was administered on December 2, 1978, to 329 candidates. Of these candidates, 48 identified themselves as black and 259 identified themselves as white. The results of the examination were announced in March 1979. With the passing score set at 65, 54.17 percent of the identified black candidates passed. This was approximately 68 percent of the passing rate for the identified white candidates. The four respondents were among the blacks who failed the examination, and they were thus excluded from further consideration for permanent supervisory positions. In April 1979, respondents instituted this action in the United States District Court for the District of Connecticut against petitioners, the State of Connecticut, two state agencies, and two state officials. Respondents alleged, *inter alia*, that petitioners violated Title VII by imposing, as an absolute condition for consideration for promotion, that applicants pass a written test that excluded blacks in disproportionate numbers and that was not job related.

More than a year after this action was instituted, and approximately one month before trial, petitioners made promotions from the eligibility list generated by the written examination. In choosing persons from that list, petitioners considered past work performance, recommendations of the candidates' supervisors and, to a lesser extent, seniority. Petitioners then applied what the Court of Appeals characterized as an affirmative-action program in order to ensure a significant number of minority supervisors. Forty-six persons were promoted to permanent supervisory positions, 11 of whom were black and 35 of whom were white. The over-all result of the selection process was that, of the 48 identified black candidates who participated in the selection process, 22.9 percent were promoted and of the 259 identified white candidates, 13.5 percent were promoted. It is this "bottom-line" result, more favorable to blacks than to whites, that petitioners urge should be adjudged to be a complete defense to respondents' suit.

II

A

Petitioners' examination, which barred promotion and had a discriminatory impact on black employees, clearly falls within the literal language of § 703(a)(2), as interpreted by *Griggs*. The statute speaks, not in terms of jobs and promotions, but in terms of *limitations* and *classifications* that would deprive any individual of employment *opportunities*. A disparate-impact claim reflects the language of § 703(a)(2) and Congress' basic objectives in enacting the statute: "to achieve equality of employment *opportunities* and remove barriers that have operated in the past to favor an identifiable group of white employees over other employees." When an employer uses a non-job-related barrier in order to deny a minority or woman applicant employment or promotion, and that barrier has a significant adverse effect on minorities or women, then the applicant has been deprived of an employment *opportunity* "because of . . . race, color, religion, sex, or national origin." In other words, § 703(a)(2) prohibits discriminatory "artificial, arbitrary, and unnecessary barriers to employment," that "limit . . . or classify . . . applicants for employment . . . in any way which would deprive or tend to deprive any individual of employment *opportunities*."

The suggestion that disparate impact should be measured only at the bottom line ignores the fact that Title VII guarantees these individual respondents the *opportunity* to compete equally with white workers on the basis of job-related criteria. Title VII strives to achieve equality of opportunity by rooting out "artificial, arbitrary, and unnecessary" employer-created barriers to professional development that have a discriminatory impact upon individuals.

B

The United States, in its brief as *amicus curiae*, apparently recognizes that respondents' claim in this case falls within the affirmative commands of Title VII. But it seeks to support the District Court's judgment in this case by relying on the defenses provided to the employer in § 703(h). Section 703(h) provides in pertinent part:

> Notwithstanding any other provision of this subchapter, it shall not be an unlawful employment practice for an employer . . . to give and to act upon the results of any professionally developed ability test provided that such test, its administration or action upon the results is not designed, intended or used to discriminate because of race, color, religion, sex or national origin.

The Government argues that the test administered by the petitioners was not "used to discriminate" because it did not actually deprive disproportionate numbers of blacks of promotions. But the Government's reliance on § 703(h) as offering the employer some special haven for discriminatory tests is misplaced. We considered the relevance of this provision in *Griggs*. After examining the legislative history of § 703(h), we concluded that Congress, in adding § 703(h), intended only to make clear that tests that were *job related* would be permissible despite their disparate impact. A non-job-related test that has a disparate racial impact, and is used to "limit" or "classify" employees, is "used to discriminate" within the meaning of Title VII, whether or not it was "designed or intended" to have this effect and despite an employer's efforts to compensate for its discriminatory effect.

In sum, respondents' claim of disparate impact from the examination, a pass-fail barrier to employment opportunity, states a *prima facie* case of employment discrimination under § 703(a)(2), despite their employer's nondiscriminatory "bottom line," and that "bottom-line" is no defense to this *prima facie* case under § 703(h).

III

It is clear that Congress never intended to give an employer license to discriminate against some employees on the basis of race or sex merely because he favorably treats other members of the employees' group. Every *individual* employee is protected against both discriminatory treatment and "practices that are fair in form, but discriminatory in operation." *Griggs*. Requirements and tests that have a discriminatory impact are merely some of the more subtle, but also the more pervasive, of the "practices and devices which have fostered racially stratified job environments to the disadvantage of minority citizens." *McDonnell Douglas Corp.*

NOTES AND QUESTIONS

1. What if, unlike the situation here, the selection device did not exclude anyone, but was simply one factor among others in the selection process? Would the "bottom line" data then preclude finding a Title VII violation? Or should an employer be required to validate each component of a multi-factor test, such as the interview process?

2. Is "bottom line" data relevant in disparate treatment cases? Why should there be a difference? If an employer's workforce is 50% female, is this probative evidence that a refusal to hire was not based on impermissible sex discrimination?

PROBLEM: TWENTY

The New Bedford Police Department makes appointments for police officers from a list of eligible applicants that is certified to it by the state civil service personnel division. The lists at issue in this case were derived from a 1972 written examination for the position of police officer. Applicants' names appear on the list in order of their scores on the exam, adjusted for various statutory and court-ordered preferences. Mary Marky took the 1972 examination and was notified in 1973 that her score was 93.3%. She passed the city's physical fitness examination in May, 1974, and was placed on the "certified" list.

Prior to June, 1974, New Bedford had two distinct police categories: males were police officers and females were police women. Male applicants were ineligible for positions as police officers if they failed to meet a minimum height requirement of five feet six inches. In June, 1974, the city abandoned these separate job categories, and thereafter both men and women competed for positions as police officers. Women applicants were also required to meet the five feet six-inch height minimum.

In July, 1974, a woman police officer retired. Because the city needed a female officer to perform special duties, related for example, to female prisoners, it sought special permission from state authorities to engage in sex-specific hiring using the list of female applicants already certified.

In August, 1974, Marky was interviewed for a position as a police officer in New Bedford, but was rejected because she failed to meet the five feet six-inch height requirement.

Two women who placed third and fourth on the list satisfied the height requirement and were appointed to positions as police officers. The woman appearing second on the list was also disqualified because of the height requirement.

1. Does application of a 5'6" height requirement violate Title VII in light of statistics that 80% of the male population is 5'6" or over, whereas less than 20% of the female population meets this standard? May Marky rely on general population data, or should she be restricted to the actual applicant pool?

2. Did the use of the height requirement have a disparate impact on women at any stage of this selection process? Does the "bottom line," i.e., a female was hired by the Department, defeat Marky's Title VII claim even though, absent the height requirement, she would have been hired?

c.   Retaliation Claims

BURLINGTON NORTHERN & SANTA FE RAILWAY CO. V. WHITE
548 U.S. 53 (2006)

Justice BREYER delivered the opinion of the Court.

Title VII of the Civil Rights Act of 1964 forbids employment discrimination against "any individual" based on that individual's "race, color, religion, sex, or national origin." 42 U.S.C. § 2000e-2(a). A separate section of the Act—its anti-retaliation provision—forbids an employer from "discriminat[ing] against" an employee or job applicant because that individual "opposed any practice" made unlawful by Title VII or "made a charge, testified, assisted, or participated in" a Title VII proceeding or investigation. § 2000e-3(a).

The Courts of Appeals have come to different conclusions about the scope of the Act's anti-retaliation provision, particularly the reach of its phrase "discriminate against." Does that provision confine actionable retaliation to activity that affects the terms and conditions of employment? And how harmful must the adverse actions be to fall within its scope?

We conclude that the anti-retaliation provision does not confine the actions and harms it forbids to those that are related to employment or occur at the workplace. We also conclude that the provision covers those (and only those) employer actions that would have been materially adverse to a reasonable employee or job applicant. In the present context that means that the employer's actions must be harmful to the point that they could well dissuade a reasonable worker from making or supporting a charge of discrimination.

I
A

This case arises out of actions that supervisors at petitioner Burlington Northern & Santa Fe Railway Company took against respondent Sheila White, the only woman working in the Maintenance of Way department at Burlington's Tennessee Yard. In June 1997, Burlington's roadmaster, Marvin Brown, interviewed White and expressed interest in her previous experience operating forklifts. Burlington hired White as a "track laborer," a job that involves removing and replacing track components, transporting track material, cutting brush, and clearing litter and cargo spillage from the right-of-way. Soon after White arrived on the job, a co-worker who had previously operated the forklift chose to assume other responsibilities. Brown immediately assigned White to operate the forklift. While she also performed some of the other track laborer tasks, operating the forklift was White's primary responsibility.

In September 1997, White complained to Burlington officials that her immediate supervisor, Bill Joiner, had repeatedly told her that women should not be working in the Maintenance of Way department. Joiner, White said, had also made insulting and inappropriate remarks to her in front of her male colleagues. After an internal investigation, Burlington suspended Joiner for 10 days and ordered him to attend a sexual-harassment training session.

On September 26, Brown told White about Joiner's discipline. At the same time, he told White that he was removing her from forklift duty and assigning her to perform only standard track laborer tasks. Brown explained that the reassignment reflected co-worker's complaints that, in fairness, a "'more senior man'" should have the "less arduous and cleaner job" of forklift operator.

On October 10, White filed a complaint with the Equal Employment Opportunity Commission (EEOC or Commission). She claimed that the reassignment of her duties amounted to unlawful gender-based discrimination and retaliation for her having earlier complained about Joiner. In early December, White filed a second retaliation charge with the Commission, claiming that Brown had placed her under surveillance and was monitoring her daily activities.

A few days later, White and her immediate supervisor, Percy Sharkey, disagreed about which truck should transport White from one location to another. The specific facts of the disagreement are in dispute, but the upshot is that Sharkey told Brown later that afternoon that White had been insubordinate. Brown immediately suspended White without pay. White invoked internal grievance procedures. Those procedures led Burlington to conclude that White had *not* been insubordinate. Burlington reinstated White to her position and awarded her back-pay for the 37 days she was suspended. White filed an additional retaliation charge with the EEOC based on the suspension.

B

After exhausting administrative remedies, White filed this Title VII action against Burlington in federal court. As relevant here, she claimed that Burlington's actions—(1) changing her job responsibilities, and (2) suspending her for 37 days without pay—amounted to unlawful retaliation in violation of Title VII. § 2000e-3(a). A jury found in White's favor on both of these claims. It awarded her $43,500 in compensatory damages, including $3,250 in medical expenses.

II

Title VII's anti-retaliation provision forbids employer actions that "discriminate against" an employee (or job applicant) because he has "opposed" a practice that Title VII forbids or has "made a charge, testified, assisted, or participated in" a Title VII "investigation, proceeding, or hearing." § 2000e-3(a). No one doubts that the term "discriminate against" refers to distinctions or differences in treatment that injure protected individuals. But different Circuits have come to different conclusions about whether the challenged action has to be employment or workplace related and about how harmful that action must be to constitute retaliation.

A

The language of the substantive provision differs from that of the anti-retaliation provision in important ways. Section 703(a) sets forth Title VII's core anti-discrimination provision in the following terms:

> "It shall be an unlawful employment practice for an employer—
>
> "(1) *to fail or refuse to hire or to discharge any individual,* or otherwise to discriminate against any individual *with respect to his compensation, terms, conditions, or privileges of employment,* because of such individual's race, color, religion, sex, or national origin; or
>
> "(2) to limit, segregate, or classify his employees or applicants for employment in any way *which would deprive or tend to deprive any individual of employment opportunities or otherwise adversely affect his status as an employee,* because of such individual's race, color, religion, sex, or national origin." § 2000e-2(a) (emphasis added).

Section 704(a) sets forth Title VII's anti-retaliation provision in the following terms:

"It shall be an unlawful employment practice for an employer *to discriminate against* any of his employees or applicants for employment . . . because he has opposed any practice made an unlawful employment practice by this subchapter, or because he has made a charge, testified, assisted, or participated in any manner in an investigation, proceeding, or hearing under this subchapter." § 2000e-3(a) (emphasis added).

The underscored words in the substantive provision—"hire," "discharge," "compensation, terms, conditions, or privileges of employment," "employment opportunities," and "status as an employee"—explicitly limit the scope of that provision to actions that affect employment or alter the conditions of the workplace. No such limiting words appear in the anti-retaliation provision. Given these linguistic differences, the question here is not whether identical or similar words should be read in *pari materia* to mean the same thing. Rather, the question is whether Congress intended its different words to make a legal difference. We normally presume that, where words differ as they differ here, "'Congress acts intentionally and purposely in the disparate inclusion or exclusion.'"

There is strong reason to believe that Congress intended the differences that its language suggests, for the two provisions differ not only in language but in purpose as well. The anti-discrimination provision seeks a workplace where individuals are not discriminated against because of their racial, ethnic, religious, or gender-based status. The anti-retaliation provision seeks to secure that primary objective by preventing an employer from interfering (through retaliation) with an employee's efforts to secure or advance enforcement of the Act's basic guarantees. The substantive provision seeks to prevent injury to individuals based on who they are, *i.e.*, their status. The anti-retaliation provision seeks to prevent harm to individuals based on what they do, *i.e.*, their conduct.

To secure the first objective, Congress did not need to prohibit anything other than employment-related discrimination. The substantive provision's basic objective of "equality of employment opportunities" and the elimination of practices that tend to bring about "stratified job environments," would be achieved were all employment-related discrimination miraculously eliminated.

But one cannot secure the second objective by focusing only upon employer actions and harm that concern employment and the workplace. Were all such actions and harms eliminated, the anti-retaliation provision's objective would *not* be achieved. An employer can effectively retaliate against an employee by taking actions not directly related to his employment or by causing him harm *outside* the workplace. A provision limited to employment-related actions would not deter the many forms that effective retaliation can take. Hence, such a limited construction would fail to fully achieve the anti-retaliation provision's "primary purpose," namely, "[m]aintaining unfettered access to statutory remedial mechanisms." *Robinson v. Shell Oil Co.*

Title VII depends for its enforcement upon the cooperation of employees who are willing to file complaints and act as witnesses. "Plainly, effective enforcement could thus only be expected if employees felt free to approach officials with their grievances." Interpreting the anti-retaliation provision to provide broad protection from retaliation helps assure the cooperation upon which accomplishment of the Act's primary objective depends.

For these reasons, we conclude that Title VII's substantive provision and its anti-retaliation provision are not coterminous. The scope of the anti-retaliation provision extends beyond workplace-related or employment-related retaliatory acts and harm. We therefore reject the standards applied in the Courts of Appeals that have treated the anti-retaliation provision as forbidding the same conduct prohibited by the anti-discrimination provision and that have limited actionable retaliation to so-called "ultimate employment decisions."

B

The anti-retaliation provision protects an individual not from all retaliation, but from retaliation that produces an injury or harm. As we have explained, the Courts of Appeals have used differing language to describe the level of seriousness to which this harm must rise before it becomes actionable retaliation. We agree with the formulation set forth by the Seventh and the District of Columbia Circuits. In our view, a plaintiff must show that a reasonable employee would have found the challenged action materially adverse, "which in this context means it well might have 'dissuaded a reasonable worker from making or supporting a charge of discrimination.'"

We speak of *material* adversity because we believe it is important to separate significant from trivial harms. An employee's decision to report discriminatory behavior cannot immunize that employee from those petty slights or minor annoyances that often take place at work and that all employees experience. The anti-retaliation provision seeks to prevent employer interference with "unfettered access" to Title VII's remedial mechanisms. It does so by prohibiting employer actions that are likely "to deter victims of discrimination from complaining to the EEOC," the courts, and their employers. And normally petty slights, minor annoyances, and simple lack of good manners will not create such deterrence. We refer to reactions of a *reasonable* employee because we believe that the provision's standard for judging harm must be objective. An objective standard is judicially administrable. It avoids the uncertainties and unfair discrepancies that can plague a judicial effort to determine a plaintiff's unusual subjective feelings. We have emphasized the need for objective standards in other Title VII contexts, and those same concerns animate our decision here.

We phrase the standard in general terms because the significance of any given act of retaliation will often depend upon the particular circumstances. Context matters. A schedule change in an employee's work schedule may make little difference to many workers, but may matter enormously to a young mother with school age children. A supervisor's refusal to invite an employee to lunch is normally trivial, a nonactionable petty slight. But to retaliate by excluding an employee from a weekly training lunch that contributes significantly to the employee's professional advancement might well deter a reasonable employee from complaining about discrimination. Hence, a legal standard that speaks in general terms rather than specific prohibited acts is preferable, for an "act that would be immaterial in some situations is material in others." By focusing on the materiality of the challenged action and the perspective of a reasonable person in the plaintiff's position, we believe this standard will screen out trivial conduct while effectively capturing those acts that are likely to dissuade employees from complaining or assisting in complaints about discrimination.

III

Applying this standard to the facts of this case, we believe that there was a sufficient evidentiary basis to support the jury's verdict on White's retaliation claim. *See Reeves v. Sanderson Plumbing Products, Inc.* The jury found that two of Burlington's actions amounted to retaliation: the reassignment of White from forklift duty to standard track laborer tasks and the 37-day suspension without pay.

First, Burlington argues that a reassignment of duties cannot constitute retaliatory discrimination where, as here, both the former and present duties fall within the same job description. We do not see why that is so. Almost every job category involves some responsibilities and duties that are less desirable than others. Common sense suggests that one good way to discourage an employee such as White from bringing discrimination charges would be to insist that she spend more time performing the more arduous duties and less time performing those that are easier or more agreeable. That is presumably why the EEOC has consistently found "[r]etaliatory work assignments" to be a classic and "widely recognized" example of "forbidden retaliation."

To be sure, reassignment of job duties is not automatically actionable. Whether a particular reassignment is materially adverse depends upon the circumstances of the particular case, and "should be judged from the perspective of a reasonable person in the plaintiff's position, considering 'all the circumstances.'" But here, the jury had before it considerable evidence that the track labor duties were "by all accounts more arduous and dirtier"; that the "forklift operator position required more qualifications, which is an indication of prestige"; and that "the forklift operator position was objectively considered a better job and the male employees resented White for occupying it." Based on this record, a jury could reasonably conclude that the reassignment of responsibilities would have been materially adverse to a reasonable employee.

Second, Burlington argues that the 37-day suspension without pay lacked statutory significance because Burlington ultimately reinstated White with backpay. Burlington says that "it defies reason to believe that Congress would have considered a rescinded investigatory suspension with full back pay" to be unlawful, particularly because Title VII, throughout much of its history, provided no relief in an equitable action for victims in White's position. White did receive backpay. But White and her family had to live for 37 days without income. They did not know during that time whether or when White could return to work. Many reasonable employees would find a month without a paycheck to be a serious hardship. And White described to the jury the physical and emotional hardship that 37 days of having "no income, no money" in fact caused. ("That was the worst Christmas I had out of my life. No income, no money, and that made all of us feel bad. . . . I got very depressed"). Indeed, she obtained medical treatment for her emotional distress. A reasonable employee facing the choice between retaining her job (and paycheck) and filing a discrimination complaint might well choose the former. That is to say, an indefinite suspension without pay could well act as a deterrent, even if the suspended employee eventually received backpay. Thus, the jury's conclusion that the 37-day suspension without pay was materially adverse was a reasonable one.

NOTES AND QUESTIONS

1. How does the Court justify the use of different elements for establishing violations of the disparate treatment and the retaliation provisions of Title VII?

2. Are employers given sufficient guidance as to when actionable retaliation will be found, i.e., what if retaliation takes the form of "shunning" or harassment by coworkers? Does adoption of the objective "reasonable employee" standard satisfy this concern?

3. Why didn't it suffice that the company "remedied" the suspension by making full restitution to White?

4. Note that this decision makes it more likely that an employee can prevail on a retaliation claim, even while losing the underlying discrimination claim. Indeed, in this case the jury dismissed White's sexual discrimination claim, but ruled favorably on her retaliation claim.

5. **Opposition Clause:** A human resources officer, who is investigating rumors of sexual harassment by the employer's employee relations director, asked Ms. Crawford whether she had witnessed any inappropriate behavior on his part and she responded by describing several instances of sexually harassing behavior. Subsequently, she was discharged and she filed an action under Title VII claiming retaliation in violation of 42 U.S.C. § 2000e-3(a). The Supreme Court, in *Crawford v. Metropolitan Government of Nashville*, 555 U.S. 271 (2009), determined that the opposition clause in § 2000e-3(a) "extends to an employee who speaks out about discrimination not on her own initiative, but in answering questions during an employer's internal investigation." *Id.* at 273. After looking at the ordinary meaning of "oppose," as well as the EEOC Compliance Manual, the Court concluded there is "no reason to doubt that a person can 'oppose' by responding to someone else's question just as surely as by provoking the discussion, and nothing in the statute requires a freakish rule protecting an employee who reports discrimination on her own initiative but not one who reports the same discrimination in the same words when her boss asks a question." *Id.* at 277–78.

6. In *Gross v. FBL Financial Services, Inc.*, 557 U.S. 167 (2009), discussed *infra*, the Court reasoned that the phrase "because of," which is found in the ADEA at issue in *Gross*, requires that plaintiff prove retaliation was the "but for" cause of the adverse action. The application of *Gross* to Title VII retaliation cases is addressed in the next decision:

UNIVERSITY OF TEXAS SOUTHWESTERN MEDICAL CENTER V. NASSAR
570 U.S. 338 (2013)

Justice KENNEDY delivered the opinion of the Court.

Title VII is central to the federal policy of prohibiting wrongful discrimination in the Nation's workplaces and in all sectors of economic endeavor. This opinion discusses the causation rules for two categories of wrongful employer conduct prohibited by Title VII. The first type is called, for purposes of this opinion, status-based discrimination. The term is used here to refer to basic workplace protection such as prohibitions against employer discrimination on the basis of race, color, religion, sex, or national origin, in hiring, firing, salary structure, promotion and the like. *See* § 2000e–2(a). The second type of conduct is employer retaliation on account of an employee's having opposed, complained of, or sought remedies for, unlawful workplace discrimination. *See* § 2000e–3(a).

An employee who alleges status-based discrimination under Title VII need not show that the causal link between injury and wrong is so close that the injury would not have occurred but for the act. So-called but-for causation is not the test. It suffices instead to show that the motive to discriminate was one of the employer's motives, even if the employer also had other, lawful motives that were causative in the employer's decision. The question the Court must answer here is whether that lessened causation standard is applicable to claims of unlawful employer retaliation under § 2000e–3(a).

Respondent is a medical doctor of Middle Eastern descent who specializes in internal medicine and infectious diseases. In 1995, he was hired to work both as a member of the University's faculty and a staff physician at the Hospital. In 2004, Dr. Beth Levine was hired as the University's Chief of Infectious Disease Medicine. In that position Levine became respondent's ultimate (though not direct) superior. Respondent alleged that Levine was biased against him on account of his religion and ethnic heritage, a bias manifested by undeserved scrutiny of his billing practices and productivity, as well as comments that "'Middle Easterners are lazy.'" On different occasions during his employment, respondent met with Dr. Gregory Fitz, the University's Chair of Internal Medicine and Levine's supervisor, to complain about Levine's alleged harassment. Despite obtaining a promotion with Levine's assistance in 2006, respondent continued to believe that she was biased against him. So he tried to arrange to continue working at the Hospital without also being on the University's faculty. After preliminary negotiations with the Hospital suggested this might be possible, respondent resigned his teaching post in July 2006 and sent a letter to Dr. Fitz (among others), in which he stated that the reason for his departure was harassment by Levine. That harassment, he asserted, "'stems from . . . religious, racial and cultural bias against Arabs and Muslims.'" After reading that letter, Dr. Fitz expressed consternation at respondent's accusations, saying that Levine had been "publicly humiliated by th[e] letter" and that it was "very important that she be publicly exonerated."

On learning of [the Hospital's] offer, Dr. Fitz protested to the Hospital, asserting that the offer was inconsistent with the affiliation agreement's requirement that all staff physicians also be members of the University faculty. The Hospital then withdrew its offer.

After exhausting his administrative remedies, respondent filed this Title VII suit in the United States District Court for the Northern District of Texas. He alleged two discrete violations of Title VII. The first was a status-based discrimination claim under § 2000e–2(a). Respondent alleged that Dr. Levine's racially and religiously motivated harassment had resulted in his constructive discharge from the University. Respondent's second claim was that Dr. Fitz's efforts to prevent the Hospital from hiring him were in retaliation for complaining about Dr. Levine's harassment, in violation of § 2000e–3(a). The jury found for respondent on both claims. It awarded him over $400,000 in backpay and more than $3 million in compensatory damages. The District Court later reduced the compensatory damages to $300,000.

II

This case requires the Court to define the proper standard of causation for Title VII retaliation claims. . . . In the usual course, this standard requires the plaintiff to show "that the harm would not have occurred" in the absence of—that is, but for—the defendant's conduct. . . . Since the statute's passage in 1964, it has prohibited employers from discriminating against their employees on any of seven specified criteria. Five of them—race, color, religion, sex, and national origin—are personal characteristics and are set forth in § 2000e–2. And then there is a point of great import for this case: The two remaining categories of wrongful employer conduct—the employee's opposition to employment discrimination, and the employee's submission of or support for a complaint that alleges employment discrimination—are not wrongs based on personal traits but rather types of protected employee conduct. These latter two categories are covered by a separate, subsequent section of Title VII, § 2000e–3(a).

Under the status-based discrimination provision, it is an "unlawful employment practice" for an employer "to discriminate against any individual . . . because of such individual's race, color, religion, sex, or national origin." § 2000e–2(a). . . . [T]he 1991 Act substituted a new burden-shifting framework for the one endorsed by *Price Waterhouse.* Under that new regime, a plaintiff could obtain declaratory relief, attorney's fees and costs, and some forms of injunctive relief based solely on proof that race, color, religion, sex, or nationality was a motivating factor in the employment action; but the employer's proof that it would still have taken the same employment action would save it from monetary damages and a reinstatement order.

III

As noted, Title VII's antiretaliation provision, which is set forth in § 2000e–3(a), appears in a different section from Title VII's ban on status-based discrimination. This enactment, like the statute at issue in *Gross,* makes it unlawful for an employer to take adverse employment action against an employee "because" of certain criteria. Given the lack of any meaningful textual difference between the text in this statute and the one in *Gross,* the proper conclusion here, as in *Gross,* is that Title VII retaliation claims require proof that the desire to retaliate was the but-for cause of the challenged employment action.

The principal counterargument offered by respondent and the United States relies on their different understanding of the motivating-factor section, which—on its face—applies only to status discrimination, discrimination on the basis of race, color, religion, sex, and national origin. In substance, they contend that: (1) retaliation is defined by the statute to be an unlawful employment practice; (2) § 2000e–2(m) allows unlawful employment practices to be proved based on a showing that race, color, religion, sex, or national origin was a motivating factor for—and not necessarily the but-for factor in—the challenged employment action; and (3) the Court has, as a matter of course, held that "retaliation for complaining about race discrimination *is* 'discrimination based on race.'"

There are three main flaws in this reading of § 2000e–2(m). The first is that it is inconsistent with the provision's plain language. It must be acknowledged that because Title VII defines "unlawful employment practice" to include retaliation, the question presented by this case would be different if § 2000e–2(m) extended its coverage to all unlawful employment practices. As actually written, however, the text of the motivating-factor provision, while it begins by referring to "unlawful employment practices," then proceeds to address only five of the seven prohibited discriminatory actions—actions based on the employee's status, *i.e.,* race, color, religion, sex, and national origin. This indicates Congress' intent to confine that provision's coverage to only those types of employment practices. The text of § 2000e–2(m) says nothing about retaliation claims. Given this clear language, it would be improper to conclude that what Congress omitted from the statute is nevertheless within its scope.

The second problem with this reading is its inconsistency with the design and structure of the statute as a whole. When Congress wrote the motivating-factor provision in 1991, it chose to insert it as a subsection within § 2000e–2, which contains Title VII's ban on status-based discrimination, and says nothing about retaliation.

The third problem with respondent's and the Government's reading of the motivating-factor standard is in its submission that this Court's decisions interpreting federal antidiscrimination law have, as a general matter, treated bans on status-based discrimination as also prohibiting retaliation. In support of this proposition, both respondent and the United States rely upon decisions in which this Court has "read [a] broadly worded civil rights statute ... as including an antiretaliation remedy." In *CBOCS West, Inc. v. Humphries,* 553 U.S. 442 (2008), for example, the Court held that 42 U.S.C. § 1981—which declares that all persons "shall have the same right ... to make and enforce contracts ... as is enjoyed by white citizens"—prohibits not only racial discrimination but also retaliation against those who oppose it. And in *Gómez–Pérez v. Potter*, 553 U.S. 474 (2008), the Court likewise read a bar on retaliation into the broad wording of the federal-employee provisions of the ADEA.

These decisions are not controlling here. It is true these cases do state the general proposition that Congress' enactment of a broadly phrased antidiscrimination statute may signal a concomitant intent to ban retaliation against individuals who oppose that discrimination, even where the statute does not refer to retaliation in so many words. What those cases do not support, however, is the quite different rule that every reference to race, color, creed, sex, or nationality in an antidiscrimination statute is to be treated as a synonym for "retaliation." For one thing, § 2000e–2(m) is not itself a substantive bar on discrimination. Rather, it is a rule that establishes the causation standard for proving a violation defined elsewhere in Title VII. The cases cited by respondent and the Government do not address rules of this sort, and those precedents are of limited relevance here.

If Title VII had likewise been phrased in broad and general terms, respondent's argument might have more force. But that is not how Title VII was written, which makes it incorrect to infer that Congress meant anything other than what the text does say on the subject of retaliation. Unlike Title IX, § 1981, § 1982, and the federal-sector provisions of the ADEA, Title VII is a detailed statutory scheme. Congress has in explicit terms altered the standard of causation for one class of claims but not another, despite the obvious opportunity to do so in the 1991 Act.

The proper interpretation and implementation of § 2000e–3(a) and its causation standard have central importance to the fair and responsible allocation of resources in the judicial and litigation systems. This is of particular significance because claims of retaliation are being made with ever-increasing frequency. The number of these claims filed with the Equal Employment Opportunity Commission (EEOC) has nearly doubled in the past 15 years—from just over 16,000 in 1997 to over 31,000 in 2012. Indeed, the number of retaliation claims filed with the EEOC has now outstripped those for every type of status-based discrimination except race.

In addition lessening the causation standard could also contribute to the filing of frivolous claims, which would siphon resources from efforts by employer, administrative agencies, and courts to combat workplace harassment. Consider in this regard the case of an employee who knows that he or she is about to be fired for poor performance, given a lower pay grade, or even just transferred to a different assignment or location. To forestall that lawful action, he or she might be tempted to make an unfounded charge of racial, sexual, or religious discrimination; then, when the unrelated employment action comes, the employee could allege that it is retaliation. If respondent were to prevail in his argument here, that claim could be established by a lessened causation standard, all in order to prevent the undesired change in employment circumstances. Even if the employer could escape judgment after trial, the lessened causation standard would make it far more difficult to dismiss dubious claims at the summary judgment stage.

In sum, Title VII defines the term "unlawful employment practice" as discrimination on the basis of any of seven prohibited criteria: race, color, religion, sex, national origin, opposition to employment discrimination, and submitting or supporting a complaint about employment discrimination. The text of § 2000e–2(m) mentions just the first five of these factors, the status-based ones; and it omits the final two, which deal with retaliation. When it added § 2000e–2(m) to Title VII in 1991, Congress inserted it within the section of the statute that deals only with those same five criteria, not the section that deals with retaliation claims or one of the sections that apply to all claims of unlawful employment practices. And while the Court has inferred a congressional intent to prohibit retaliation when confronted with broadly worded antidiscrimination statutes, Title VII's detailed structure makes that inference inappropriate here. Based on these textual and structural indications, the Court now concludes as follows: Title VII retaliation claims must be proved according to traditional principles of but-for causation, not the lessened causation test stated in § 2000e–2(m). This requires proof that the unlawful retaliation would not have occurred in the absence of the alleged wrongful action or actions of the employer.

NOTES AND QUESTIONS

1. Why did the Court adopt a "but for" causation standard for retaliation claims? Was Justice Kennedy's reliance on the "huge" increase in retaliation cases, "many frivolous," a valid justification?

2. By rejecting the "a motivating" standard, the Court also denied the burdenshifting provision, even though originally the burdenshifting standard came as a result of Price-Waterhouse, not the codification. Justice Kennedy reasoned that the codification displaced Price-Waterhouse and thus there would be no burdenshifting. Some appellate courts have made it more difficult for plaintiffs to survive summary judgment, reasoning that they must have enough evidence from which a jury could find but-for causation.

3. In *Thompson v. North American Stainless, LP*, 562 U.S. 170 (2011), the plaintiff was fired after his coworker/fiancé filed a sex discrimination claim against the company with the EEOC. The Court held that "a reasonable worker might be dissuaded from engaging in protected activity if she knew that her fiancé would be fired," and it found " no textual basis for making an exception . . . for third-party reprisals." Applying the *Burlington* standard, the Court explained that "the significance of any given act of retaliation will often depend upon the particular circumstances," and courts should examine both the nature of the relationship with a third party and the severity of the reprisal.

3. SPECIAL ISSUES REGARDING SEX DISCRIMINATION

The legislative history regarding Title VII's prohibition of sex discrimination is very sparse. The ban was actually inserted by an opponent to Title VII who hoped that by expanding the

Act's coverage, it would be defeated. This lack of guidance eventually necessitated further congressional action as reflected in the cases and materials which follow.

a. Pregnancy

GENERAL ELECTRIC CO. V. GILBERT
429 U.S. 125 (1976)

Mr. Justice REHNQUIST delivered the opinion of the Court.

Petitioner, General Electric Co., provides for all of its employees a disability plan which pays weekly non-occupational sickness and accident benefits. Excluded from the plan's coverage, however, are disabilities arising from pregnancy. Respondents, on behalf of a class of women employees, brought this action seeking, a declaration that this exclusion constitutes sex discrimination in violation of Title VII of the Civil Rights Act of 1964.

I

As part of its total compensation package, General Electric provides nonoccupational sickness and accident benefits to all employees under its Weekly Sickness and Accident Insurance Plan (Plan) in an amount equal to 60% of an employee's normal straight-time weekly earnings. These payments are paid to employees who become totally disabled as a result of a nonoccupational sickness or accident.

The individual named respondents are present or former hourly paid production employees at General Electric's plant in Salem, Va. Each of these employees was pregnant during 1971 or 1972, while employed by General Electric, and each presented a claim to the company for disability benefits under the Plan to cover the period while absent from work as a result of the pregnancy. These claims were routinely denied on the ground that the Plan did not provide disability-benefit payments for any absence due to pregnancy.

Between the date on which the District Court's judgment was rendered and the time this case was decided by the Court of Appeals, we decided *Geduldig v. Aiello*, where we rejected a claim that a very similar disability program established under California law violated the Equal Protection Clause of the Fourteenth Amendment because that plan's exclusion of pregnancy disabilities represented sex discrimination.

II

Section 703(a)(1) provides in relevant part that it shall be an unlawful employment practice for an employer to discriminate against any individual with respect to his compensation, terms, conditions, or privileges of employment, because of such individual's race, color, religion, sex, or national origin.

While there is no necessary inference that Congress, in choosing this language, intended to incorporate into Title VII the concepts of discrimination which have evolved from court decisions construing the Equal Protection Clause of the Fourteenth Amendment, the similarities between the congressional language and some of those decisions surely indicate that the latter are a useful starting point in interpreting the former. Particularly in the case of defining the term "discrimination," which Congress has nowhere in Title VII defined, those cases afford an existing body of law analyzing and discussing that term in a legal context not wholly dissimilar to the concerns which Congress manifested in enacting Title VII. We think, therefore, that our decision in *Geduldig*, dealing with a strikingly similar disability plan, is quite relevant in determining whether or not the pregnancy exclusion did discriminate on the basis of sex.

We rejected appellee's equal protection challenge to this statutory scheme. We first noted:

> We cannot agree that the exclusion of this disability from coverage amounts to invidious discrimination under the Equal Protection Clause. California does not discriminate with respect to the persons or groups which are eligible for disability insurance protection under the program. The classification challenged in this case relates to the asserted underinclusiveness of the set of risks that the State has selected to insure.

We recognized in *Geduldig*, of course, that the fact that there was no sex-based discrimination as such was not the end of the analysis, should it be shown "that distinctions involving pregnancy are mere pretexts designed to effect an invidious discrimination against the members of one sex or the other." But we noted that no semblance of such a showing had been made. Since it is a finding of sex-based discrimination that must trigger, in a case such as this, the finding of an unlawful employment practice under § 703(a)(1), *Geduldig* is precisely on point in its holding that an exclusion of pregnancy from a disability-benefits plan providing general coverage is not a gender-based discrimination at all.

The instant suit was grounded on Title VII rather than the Equal Protection Clause, and our cases recognize that a *prima facie* violation of Title VII can be established in some circumstances upon proof that the *effect* of an otherwise facially neutral plan or classification is to discriminate against members of one class or another.

As in *Geduldig*, respondents have not attempted to meet the burden of demonstrating a gender-based discriminatory effect resulting from the exclusion of pregnancy related disabilities from coverage. Whatever the ultimate probative value of the evidence introduced before the District Court on this subject in the instant case, at the very least it tended to illustrate that the selection of risks covered by the Plan did not operate, in fact, to discriminate against women. As in *Geduldig*, we start from the indisputable baseline that "[t]he fiscal and actuarial benefits of the program . . . accrue to members of both sexes." We need not disturb the findings of the District

Court to note that neither is there a finding, nor was there any evidence which would support a finding, that the financial benefits of the Plan "worked to discriminate against any definable group or class in terms of the aggregate risk protection derived by that group or class from the program." The Plan, in effect (and for all that appears), is nothing more than an insurance package, which covers some risks, but excludes others. The "package" going to relevant identifiable groups we are presently concerned with—General Electric's male and female employees—covers exactly the same categories of risk, and is facially nondiscriminatory in the sense that "[t]here is no risk from which men are protected and women are not. Likewise, there is no risk from which women are protected and men are not." As there is no proof that the package is in fact worth more to men than to women, it is impossible to find any gender-based discriminatory effect in this scheme simply because women disabled as a result of pregnancy do not receive benefits; that is to say, gender-based discrimination does not result simply because an employer's disability-benefits plan is less than all-inclusive. For all that appears, pregnancy-related disabilities constitute an *additional* risk, unique to women, and the failure to compensate them for this risk does not destroy the presumed parity of the benefits, accruing to men and women alike, which results from the facially evenhanded *inclusion* of risks. To hold otherwise would endanger the common sense notion that an employer who has no disability benefits program at all does not violate Title VII even though the "underinclusion" of risks impacts, as a result of pregnancy-related disabilities, more heavily upon one gender than upon the other. Just as there is not facial gender-based discrimination in that case, so, too, there is none here.

NOTES AND QUESTIONS

1. Should discrimination based on pregnancy-related disabilities be analyzed as a disparate treatment or disparate impact problem? Is cost a defense under either scheme? Note that an amicus brief filed by AT&T contended that it would cost their company $20 million a year to add pregnancy coverage to their policy.

2. How can it be shown that the exclusion is a "pretext" for sex discrimination? Note that the district court made findings that General Electric had a history of sex discrimination regarding pregnant employees, *i.e.*, forced maternity leave in the sixth month and a prohibition on returning to work until six weeks after birth, and that this discriminatory attitude was a motivating factor in the insurance policy. Why wasn't this enough to establish pretext? What about the fact that male-only disabilities, such as vasectomies, prostatectomies and circumcisions, were covered by the policy? Can pregnancy be distinguished as a "voluntary" disability?

3. In light of the Court's reasoning in *Gilbert*, could a disability plan exclude coverage for sickle cell anemia or Tay Sachs disease (the former affects almost exclusively blacks, whereas the latter is found predominately in Jews of Eastern European origin)? Does

the fact that only a subclass of women, *i.e.*, pregnant women, is affected make the classification any less sex-based?

4. What if Gilbert had been terminated due to her pregnancy? Or denied accumulated seniority benefits? The Supreme Court, in *Nashville Gas Co. v. Satty*, 434 U.S. 136 (1977), found that the employer's policy of denying accumulated seniority to female workers who return from a pregnancy leave did violate § 703(a)(2). Distinguishing *Gilbert*, the Court reasoned:

> Petitioner had not merely refused to extend to women a benefit that men cannot and do not receive, but has imposed on women a substantial burden that men need not suffer. The distinction between benefits and burdens is more than one of semantics. We held in *Gilbert* that § 703(a)(1) did not require that greater economic benefits be paid to one sex or the other . . . but that holding does not allow us to read § 703(a)(2) to permit an employer to burden female employees in such a way as to deprive them of employment opportunities because of their different role.

5. Since the Supreme Court held in *Geduldig* that discrimination based on pregnancy is not sex-based discrimination within the meaning of the Fourteenth Amendment equal protection guarantee, may Congress acting under § 5 of the Fourteenth Amendment redefine the term "sex discrimination" used in Title VII to encompass pregnancy claims? In response to *Gilbert*, Congress in 1978, in fact, amended Title VII to include the Pregnancy Discrimination Act (PDA), found at 42 U.S.C. § 2000e(k). Read this provision carefully. Does it require that employers now cover the costs of pregnancy? May an employer refuse to hire a pregnant woman? Will an employer have to hold a job open for a pregnant employee until she is able to return to work? May an employer fire a woman for having an abortion? Must it pay for the abortion?

NEWPORT NEWS SHIPBUILDING & DRY DOCK V. EEOC
462 U.S. 669 (1983)

Justice STEVENS delivered the opinion of the Court.

In 1978 Congress decided to overrule our decision in *General Electric Co.*, by amending Title VII of the Civil Rights Act of 1964 "to prohibit sex discrimination on the basis of pregnancy." On the effective date of the Act, petitioner amended its health insurance plan to provide its female employees with hospitalization benefits for pregnancy-related conditions to the same extent as for other medical conditions. The plan continued, however, to provide less favorable pregnancy benefits for spouses of male employees. The question presented is whether the amended plan complies with the amended statute.

After the passage of the Pregnancy Discrimination Act, and before the amendment to petitioner's plan became effective, the Equal Employment Opportunity Commission issued "interpretive guidelines" in the form of questions and answers. Two of those questions, numbers 21 and 22, made it clear that the EEOC would consider petitioner's amended plan unlawful. Number 21 read as follows:

> 21. Q. Must an employer provide health insurance coverage for the medical expenses of pregnancy-related conditions of the spouses of male employees? Of the dependents of all employees?
>
> A. Where an employer provides no coverage for dependents, the employer is not required to institute such coverage. However, if an employer's insurance program covers the medical expenses of spouses of female employees, then it must equally cover the medical expenses of spouses of male employees, including those arising from pregnancy-related conditions.
> But the insurance does not have to cover the pregnancy-related conditions of non-spouse dependents as long as it excludes the pregnancy-related conditions of such non-spouse dependents of male and female employees equally.

Ultimately the question we must decide is whether petitioner has discriminated against its male employees with respect to their compensation, terms, conditions, or privileges of employment because of *their* sex within the meaning of § 703(a)(1) of Title VII. Although the Pregnancy Discrimination Act has clarified the meaning of certain terms in this section, neither that Act nor the underlying statute contains a definition of the word "discriminate." In order to decide whether petitioner's plan discriminates against male employees because of their sex, we must therefore go beyond the bare statutory language. Accordingly, we shall consider whether Congress, by enacting the Pregnancy Discrimination Act, not only overturned the specific holding in *General Electric Co. v. Gilbert*, but also rejected the test of discrimination employed by the Court in that case. We believe it did. Under the proper test petitioner's plan is unlawful, because the protection it affords to married male employees is less comprehensive than the protection it affords to married female employees.

Section 703(a) makes it an unlawful employment practice for an employer to "discriminate against any individual with respect to his compensation, terms, conditions, or privileges of employment, because of such individual's race, color, religion, sex, or national origin. . . ." 42 U.S.C. § 2000e-2(a)(1). Health insurance and other fringe benefits are "compensation, terms, conditions, or privileges of employment." Male as well as female employees are protected against discrimination. Thus, if a private employer were to provide complete health insurance coverage for the dependents of its female employees, and no coverage at all for the dependents of its male employees, it would violate Title VII. Petitioner's practice is just as unlawful. Its plan provides limited pregnancy-related benefits for employees' wives, and affords more extensive coverage for employees' spouses for all other medical conditions requiring hospitalization. Thus the husbands of female employees receive a specified level of hospitalization coverage for all conditions; the wives of male employees receive such coverage except for pregnancy-related conditions. Although *Gilbert* concluded that an otherwise inclusive plan that singled out pregnancy-related benefits for exclusion was nondiscriminatory on its face, because only women can become pregnant, Congress has unequivocally rejected that reasoning. The 1978 Act makes clear that it is discriminatory to treat pregnancy-related conditions less favorably than other medical conditions. Thus petitioner's plan unlawfully gives married male employees a benefit package for their dependents that is less inclusive than the dependency coverage provided to married female employees.

There is no merit to petitioner's argument that the prohibitions of Title VII do not extend to discrimination against pregnant spouses because the statute applies only to discrimination in employment. A two-step analysis demonstrates the fallacy in this contention. The Pregnancy Discrimination Act has now made clear that, for all Title VII purposes, discrimination based on a woman's pregnancy is, on its face, discrimination because of her sex. And since the sex of the spouse is always the opposite of the sex of the employee, it follows inexorably that discrimination against female spouses in the provision of fringe benefits is also discrimination against the male employees.

NOTES AND QUESTIONS

1. If the purpose of the Pregnancy Discrimination Act (PDA) was to protect female employees, why does the Court find that it reaches female spouses of male employees?

2. Must spouses of male employees be given the same pregnancy benefits as female employees? May an employer refuse to provide pregnancy coverage to dependents of employees if it provides coverage of female employees?

3. Does a benefit plan that excludes birth control pills violate the PDA? What if the plan excludes all contraceptives?

4. Questions about an employer's duty to accommodate pregnant women raise difficult issues regarding the meaning of the PDA's second clause. The Supreme Court confronted this in the following case:

YOUNG V. UNITED PARCEL SERVICE, INC.

135 S. CT. 1338 (2015)

Justice BREYER delivered the opinion of the Court.

The Pregnancy Discrimination Act makes clear that Title VII's prohibition against sex discrimination applies to discrimination based on pregnancy. It also says that employers must treat "women affected by pregnancy ... the same for all employment-related purposes ... as other persons not so affected but similar in their ability or inability to work." 42 U.S.C. § 2000e(k). We must decide how this latter provision applies in the context of an employer's policy that accommodates many, but not all, workers with nonpregnancy-related disabilities.

In our view, the Act requires courts to consider the extent to which an employer's policy treats pregnant workers less favorably than it treats nonpregnant workers similar in their ability or inability to work. And here—as in all cases in which an individual plaintiff seeks to show disparate treatment through indirect evidence—it requires courts to consider any legitimate, nondiscriminatory, nonpretextual justification for these differences in treatment. *See McDonnell Douglas Corp. v. Green.* Ultimately the court must determine whether the nature of the employer's policy and the way in which it burdens pregnant women shows that the employer has engaged in intentional discrimination.

I

The petitioner, Peggy Young, worked as a part-time driver for the respondent, United Parcel Service (UPS). Her responsibilities included pickup and delivery of packages that had arrived by air carrier the previous night. In 2006, after suffering several miscarriages, she became pregnant. Her doctor told her that she should not lift more than 20 pounds during the first 20 weeks of her pregnancy or more than 10 pounds thereafter. UPS required drivers like Young to be able to lift parcels weighing up to 70 pounds (and up to 150 pounds with assistance). UPS told Young she could not work while under a lifting restriction. Young consequently stayed home without pay during most of the time she was pregnant and eventually lost her employee medical coverage.

Young subsequently brought this federal lawsuit. We focus here on her claim that UPS acted unlawfully in refusing to accommodate her pregnancy-related lifting restriction. Young said that her co-workers were willing to help her with heavy packages. She also said that UPS accommodated other drivers who were "similar in their . . . inability to work." She accordingly concluded that UPS must accommodate her as well.

UPS responded that the "other persons" whom it had accommodated were (1) drivers who had become disabled on the job, (2) those who had lost their Department of Transportation (DOT) certifications, and (3) those who suffered from a disability covered by the Americans with Disabilities Act of 1990 (ADA). UPS said that, since Young did not fall within any of those categories, it had not discriminated against Young on the basis of pregnancy but had treated her just as it treated all "other" relevant "persons."

In 1978, Congress enacted the Pregnancy Discrimination Act, which added new language to Title VII's definitions subsection. The first clause of the 1978 Act specifies that Title VII's "ter[m] 'because of sex' . . . include[s] . . . because of or on the basis of pregnancy, childbirth, or related medical conditions." § 2000e(k). The second clause says that:

"women affected by pregnancy, childbirth, or related medical conditions shall be treated the same for all employment-related purposes . . . as other persons not so affected but similar in their ability or inability to work. . . ."

This case requires us to consider the application of the second clause to a "disparate-treatment" claim—a claim that an employer intentionally treated a complainant less favorably than employees with the "complainant's qualifications" but outside the complainant's protected class.

We note that employment discrimination law also creates what is called a "disparate-impact" claim. In evaluating a disparate-impact claim, courts focus on the effects of an employment practice, determining whether they are unlawful irrespective of motivation or intent. But Young has not alleged a disparate-impact claim.

II

The parties disagree about the interpretation of the Pregnancy Discrimination Act's second clause. Does this clause mean that courts must compare workers only in respect to the work limitations that they suffer? Does it mean that courts must ignore all other similarities or differences between pregnant and nonpregnant workers? Or does it mean that courts, when deciding who the relevant "other persons" are, may consider other similarities and differences as well? If so, which ones?

The parties propose very different answers to this question. Young and the United States believe that the second clause of the Pregnancy Discrimination Act "requires an employer to provide the same accommodations to workplace disabilities caused by pregnancy that it provides to workplace disabilities that have other causes but have a similar effect on the ability to work." Young contends that the second clause means that whenever "an employer accommodates only a subset of workers with disabling conditions," a court should find a Title VII violation if "pregnant workers who are similar in the ability to work" do not "receive the same [accommodation] even if still other non-pregnant workers do not receive accommodations."

UPS takes an almost polar opposite view. It contends that the second clause does no more than define sex discrimination to include pregnancy discrimination. Under this view, courts would compare the accommodations an employer provides to pregnant women with the accommodations it provides to others within a facially neutral category (such as those with off-the-job injuries) to determine whether the employer has violated Title VII.

We cannot accept either of these interpretations. The problem with Young's approach is that it proves too much. It seems to say that the statute grants pregnant workers a "most-favored-nation" status. As long as an employer provides one or two workers with an accommodation— say, those with particularly hazardous jobs, or those whose workplace presence is particularly needed, or those who have worked at the company for many years, or those who are over the age of 55—then it must provide similar accommodations to all pregnant workers (with comparable physical limitations), irrespective of the nature of their jobs, the employer's need to keep them working, their ages, or any other criteria.

We doubt that Congress intended to grant pregnant workers an unconditional most-favored-nation status. We find it similarly difficult to accept the opposite interpretation of the Act's second clause. UPS says that the second clause simply defines sex discrimination to include pregnancy discrimination. The first clause accomplishes that objective when it expressly amends Title VII's definitional provision to make clear that Title VII's words "because of sex" and "on the basis of sex" "include, but are not limited to, because of or on the basis of pregnancy, childbirth, or related medical conditions." Moreover, the interpretation espoused by UPS and the dissent would fail to carry out an important congressional objective. As we have noted, Congress' "unambiguou[s]" intent in passing the Act was to overturn "both the holding and the reasoning of the Court in the Gilbert decision." Simply including pregnancy among Title VII's protected traits would not overturn Gilbert in full—in particular, it would not respond to Gilbert's determination that an employer can treat pregnancy less favorably than diseases or disabilities resulting in a similar inability to work.

III

In our view, an individual pregnant worker who seeks to show disparate treatment through indirect evidence may do so through application of the McDonnell Douglas framework. That framework requires a plaintiff to make out a prima facie case of discrimination. But it is "not intended to be an inflexible rule." Rather, an individual plaintiff may establish a prima facie case by "showing actions taken by the employer from which one can infer, if such actions remain unexplained, that it is more likely than not that such actions were based on a discriminatory criterion illegal under" Title VII. The burden of making this showing is "not onerous." In particular, making this showing is not as burdensome as succeeding on "an ultimate finding of fact as to" a discriminatory employment action. Neither does it require the plaintiff to show that those whom the employer favored and those whom the employer disfavored were similar in all but the protected ways.

Thus, a plaintiff alleging that the denial of an accommodation constituted disparate treatment under the Pregnancy Discrimination Act's second clause may make out a prima facie case by showing, as in McDonnell Douglas, that she belongs to the protected class, that she sought accommodation, that the employer did not accommodate her, and that the employer did accommodate others "similar in their ability or inability to work."

The employer may then seek to justify its refusal to accommodate the plaintiff by relying on "legitimate, nondiscriminatory" reasons for denying her accommodation. But, consistent with the Act's basic objective, that reason normally cannot consist simply of a claim that it is more expensive or less convenient to add pregnant women to the category of those ("similar in their ability or inability to work") whom the employer accommodates. After all, the employer in Gilbert could in all likelihood have made just such a claim.

If the employer offers an apparently "legitimate, non-discriminatory" reason for its actions, the plaintiff may in turn show that the employer's proffered reasons are in fact pretextual. We believe that the plaintiff may reach a jury on this issue by providing sufficient evidence that the employer's policies impose a significant burden on pregnant workers, and that the employer's "legitimate, nondiscriminatory" reasons are not sufficiently strong to justify the burden, but rather—when considered along with the burden imposed—give rise to an inference of intentional discrimination.

The plaintiff can create a genuine issue of material fact as to whether a significant burden exists by providing evidence that the employer accommodates a large percentage of nonpregnant workers while failing to accommodate a large percentage of pregnant workers. Here, for example, if the facts are as Young says they are, she can show that UPS accommodates most nonpregnant employees with lifting limitations while categorically failing to accommodate pregnant employees with lifting limitations. Young might also add that the fact that UPS has multiple policies that accommodate nonpregnant employees with lifting restrictions suggests that its reasons for failing to accommodate pregnant employees with lifting restrictions are not sufficiently strong—to the point that a jury could find that its reasons for failing to accommodate pregnant employees give rise to an inference of intentional discrimination.

This approach, though limited to the Pregnancy Discrimination Act context, is consistent with our longstanding rule that a plaintiff can use circumstantial proof to rebut an employer's apparently legitimate, nondiscriminatory reasons for treating individuals within a protected class differently than those outside the protected class. In particular, it is hardly anomalous that a plaintiff may rebut an employer's proffered justifications by showing how a policy operates in practice. In McDonnell Douglas itself, we noted that an employer's "general policy and practice with respect to minority employment"—including "statistics as to" that policy and practice—could be evidence of pretext. Moreover, the continued focus on whether the plaintiff has introduced sufficient evidence to give rise to an inference of intentional discrimination avoids confusing the disparate-treatment and disparate-impact doctrines.

IV

Under this interpretation of the Act, the judgment of the Fourth Circuit must be vacated. A party is entitled to summary judgment if there is "no genuine dispute as to any material fact and the movant is entitled to judgment as a matter of law." Viewing the record in the light most favorable to Young, there is a genuine dispute as to whether UPS provided more favorable treatment to at least some employees whose situation cannot reasonably be distinguished from Young's. In other words, Young created a genuine dispute of material fact as to the fourth prong of the McDonnell Douglas analysis.

Young also introduced evidence that UPS had three separate accommodation policies (on-the-job, ADA, DOT). Taken together, Young argued, these policies significantly burdened pregnant women. See shop steward's testimony that "the only light duty requested [due to physical] restrictions that became an issue" at UPS "were with women who were pregnant." The Fourth Circuit did not consider the combined effects of these policies, nor did it consider the strength of UPS' justifications for each when combined. That is, why, when the employer accommodated so many, could it not accommodate pregnant women as well?

We do not determine whether Young created a genuine issue of material fact as to whether UPS' reasons for having treated Young less favorably than it treated these other nonpregnant employees were pretextual. We leave a final determination of that question for the Fourth Circuit to make on remand, in light of the interpretation of the Pregnancy Discrimination Act that we have set out above.

NOTES AND QUESTIONS:

1. Why does Justice Breyer reject both parties' interpretations of the PDA? Are pregnant employees similar to workers who suffer short-term disabilities, and thus they must be treated the same with regard to "light duty" work?

2. How can pregnant employees prove disparate treatment? How is the Court's approach different from the traditional McDonnell Douglas analysis, and how does the Court justify the "modifications"? As to the prima facie case, who are the relevant "comparators" and how many are required to support an inference of discrimination? As to the employer's rebuttal, what counts as a "legitimate nondiscriminatory reason," and what proof is required to show pretext?

3. What must Young and UPS prove on remand to win their cases? Does Young have to prove UPS acted with hostility towards pregnant women?

   In a stinging dissent, Justice Scalia attacked the majority's "newfangled balancing test" that allows a pregnant woman to prove discriminatory motive "by showing that the effects of her employer's policy fall more harshly on pregnant women" and "are inadequately justified"—thereby "bungling the dichotomy between claims of disparate treatment and claims of disparate impact." Is this critique accurate?

4. How would you advise a client who asks whether it must provide a pregnant employee with light duty? When does an employer's refusal to accommodate establish intentional discrimination?

5. In a portion of the opinion omitted here, the Court discusses the possible implications of the amendments to the Americans with Disabilities Act: "We note that statutory changes made after the time of Young's pregnancy may limit the future significance of our interpretation of the Act. In 2008, Congress expanded the definition of "disability" under the ADA to make clear that "physical or mental impairment[s] that substantially limi[t]" an individual's ability to lift, stand, or bend are ADA-covered disabilities. ADA Amendments Act of 2008. As interpreted by the EEOC, the new statutory definition requires employers to accommodate employees whose temporary lifting restrictions originate off the job. We express no view on these statutory and regulatory changes."

Although the definition of disability in the ADA specifically excludes pregnancy, how will the ADA amendments affect the situation presented by the facts of this case?

Problem: Twenty-One

On June 30, 1975, Graphic Arts International Union entered into a contract with the Department of Labor, pursuant to which the Department provided the union with funds to operate an on-the-job training program—the "Project for Equal Progression" (PEP)—for women entering the graphic arts industry. This financial support included salaries for two full-time employees, a project coordinator and an administrative assistant, to manage the program.

In February, 1977, Ms. Abraham, who worked as an administrative assistant, informed her superior that she was pregnant and that she expected her child in September. She reiterated this in June and inquired as to the permissible length of maternity leave, but never got a definite answer. On August 5 she departed on what she believed to be a leave.

The contract between the union and the Department of Labor provided that employees engaged in the PEP project would have ten days of sick leave and ten days of vacation leave, and the union declares that it had no policy allowing such employees any amount of additional leave for any purpose. Since Ms. Abraham was off for 25 days, she was terminated from her position. The union endeavors to defend ten days as the unyielding maximum leave entitlement of PEP employees on the ground that the short duration of the project could tolerate no more.

An EEOC regulation, 29 C.F.R. § 1604.10(c), provides:

> [w]here the termination of an employee who is temporarily disabled is caused by an employment policy under which insufficient or no leave is available, such a termination violates the Act if it has a disparate impact on employment of one sex and is not justified by business necessity.

1. Does the union's leave policy violate the PDA? Does it violate the EEOC regulation? Does the EEOC regulation impermissibly extend the PDA by reaching beyond the "equal treatment" concern in the Act?

2. Analyze the disparate impact claim under the Civil Rights Act of 1991.

3. If a male PEP employee had a heart attack which required him to miss more than ten days, would his job be protected under Title VII? What if a prostatectomy kept him from returning to work beyond the 10 days allowed?

4. What if the contract provided *no* disability leave for anyone? Would this violate either Title VII or the regulation?

5. If the union had simply refused to pay for the additional leave, would Ms. Abraham have had a claim against it?

NOTE ON FAMILY MEDICAL LEAVE ACT

In light of statistical data that 90% of all women in the workforce will get pregnant at some point in their working careers, did Congress go far enough in protecting female workers when it enacted the Pregnancy Discrimination Act?

Responding to these concerns, Congress enacted the Family and Medical Leave Act of 1993, which requires private employers of 50 or more employees to provide eligible employees up to 12 weeks of unpaid leave for their own serious illness, the birth or adoption of a child, or the care of a seriously ill child, spouse, or parent. Federal civil service employees, state and local government employees, and congressional employees also are covered by the law. In *Nevada Department of Human Resources v. Hibbs, supra* Ch. I, the Supreme Court upheld the Act as a valid exercise of Congress' power under § 5 of the Fourteenth Amendment. *See* 29 U.S.C. §§ 2601-2654. However, in *Coleman v. Maryland, supra* Ch. I, the Court ruled that damage claims under the "self-care" provision of the FMLA may not be brought against state employers, because Congress did not validly abrogate the Eleventh Amendment.

Highlights of the law include:

1. Employees must be employed for at least one year and have worked at least 1,250 hours within the previous 12-month period to be eligible for leave.

2. Employees are entitled to take 12 weeks of leave for these reasons in any 12-month period.

3. Employees taking leave are entitled to receive health benefits while they are on unpaid leave under the same terms and conditions as when they were on the job.

4. Employers must guarantee employees the right to return to their previous or an equivalent position with no loss of benefits at the end of the leave, although the law provides a limited exception from the restoration provision to certain highly paid employees.

5. Local education agencies are permitted to provide more limited family and medical leave to teachers.

6. The law allows civil suits by employees and also allows the Secretary of Labor to sue for damages on behalf of employees whose employers have violated the Act.

b. Pension Benefits

Assume that you represent an employer whose labor force consists of almost an equal number of men and women employees. The employer wishes to provide pension benefits for its employees and it learns that in order to secure the same benefits it will cost approximately twenty dollars per month for the female workers as compared to only fifteen dollars per month for the male workers. This is based on actuarial tables that women live longer and thus will be receiving on the average more benefits. The employer wants to know whether it can deduct the twenty dollars from the salary of female employees and fifteen dollars from that of male employees or whether instead it should be deducting seventeen dollars and fifty cents from all of the employees. If it does the latter, are male employees then being forced to subsidize female workers contrary to the rights of male employees?

LOS ANGELES DEPARTMENT OF WATER & POWER V. MANHART
435 U.S. 702 (1978)

Mr. Justice STEVENS delivered the opinion of the Court.

As a class, women live longer than men. For this reason, the Los Angeles Department of Water and Power required its female employees to make larger contributions to its pension fund than its male employees. We granted certiorari to decide whether this practice discriminated against individual female employees because of their sex in violation of § 703(a)(1) of the Civil Rights Act of 1964, as amended.

Based on a study of mortality tables and its own experience, the Department determined that its 2,000 female employees, on the average, will live a few years longer than its 10,000 male employees. The cost of a pension for the average retired female is greater than for the average male retiree because more monthly payments must be made to the average woman. The Department therefore required female employees to make monthly contributions to the fund which were 14.84% higher than the contributions required of comparable male employees. Because employee contributions were withheld from paychecks, a female employee took home less pay than a male employee earning that same salary.[5]

The Department and various *amici curiae* contend that: (1) the differential in take-home pay between men and women was not discrimination within the meaning of § 703(a)(1) because it was offset by a difference in the value of the pension benefits provided to the two classes of employees; (2) the differential was based on a factor "other than sex" within the meaning of the Equal Pay Act of 1963 and was therefore protected by the so-called Bennett Amendment; (3) the rationale of *General Electric Co. v. Gilbert* requires reversal; and (4) in any event, the retroactive monetary recovery is unjustified. We consider these contentions in turn.

---

[5] The significance of the disparity is illustrated by the record of one woman whose contributions to the fund (including interest on the amount withheld each month) amounted to $18,171.40; a similarly situated male would have contributed only $12,843.53.

I

It is now well recognized that employment decisions cannot be predicated on mere "stereo-typed" impressions about the characteristics of males or females. Myths and purely habitual assumptions about a woman's inability to perform certain kinds of work are no longer accept-able reasons for refusing to employ qualified individuals, or for paying them less. This case does not, however, involve a fictional difference between men and women. It involves a generaliza-tion that the parties accept as unquestionably true: Women, as a class, do live longer than men. The Department treated its women employees differently from its men employees because the two classes are in fact different. It is equally true, however, that all individuals in the respec-tive classes do not share the characteristic that differentiates the average class representatives. Many women do not live as long as the average man and many men outlive the average woman. The question, therefore, is whether the existence or nonexistence of "discrimination" is to be determined by comparison of class characteristics or individual characteristics. A "stereotyped" answer to that question may not be the same as the answer that the language and purpose of the statute command.

The statute makes it unlawful "to discriminate against any *individual* with respect to his compensation, terms, conditions, or privileges of employment, because of such *individual's* race, color, religion, sex, or national origin." 42 U.S.C. § 2000e-2(a)(1) (emphasis added). The statute's focus on the individual is unambiguous. It precludes treatment of individuals as simply compo-nents of a racial, religious, sexual, or national class. If height is required for a job, a tall woman may not be refused employment merely because, on the average, women are too short. Even a true generalization about the class is an insufficient reason for disqualifying an individual to whom the generalization does not apply.

That proposition is of critical importance in this case because there is no assurance that any individual woman working for the Department will actually fit the generalization on which the Department's policy is based. Many of those individuals will not live as long as the average man. While they were working, those individuals received smaller paychecks because of their sex, but they will receive no compensating advantage when they retire.

It is true, of course, that while contributions are being collected from the employees, the Department cannot know which individuals will predecease the average woman. Therefore, unless women as a class are assessed an extra charge, they will be subsidized, to some extent, by the class of male employees. It follows, according to the Department, that fairness to its class of male employees justifies the extra assessment against all of its female employees.

But the question of fairness to various classes affected by the statute is essentially a matter of policy for the legislature to address. Congress has decided that classifications based on sex, like those based on national origin or race, are unlawful. Actuarial studies could unquestionably identify differences in life expectancy based on race or national origin, as well as sex.[15] But a

---

15 For example, the life expectancy of a white baby in 1973 was 72.2 years; a non-white baby could expect to live 65.9 years, a difference of 6.3 years.

statute that was designed to make race irrelevant in the employment market could not reasonably be construed to permit a take-home-pay differential based on a racial classification.

Even if the statutory language were less clear, the basic policy of the statute requires that we focus on fairness to individuals rather than fairness to classes. Practices that classify employees in terms of religion, race, or sex tend to preserve traditional assumptions about groups rather than thoughtful scrutiny of individuals. The generalization involved in this case illustrates the point. Separate mortality tables are easily interpreted as reflecting innate differences between the sexes; but a significant part of the longevity differential may be explained by the social fact that men are heavier smokers than women.

Finally, there is no reason to believe that Congress intended a special definition of discrimination in the context of employee group insurance coverage. It is true that insurance is concerned with events that are individually unpredictable, but that is characteristic of many employment decisions. Individual risks, like individual performance, may not be predicted by resort to classifications proscribed by Title VII. Indeed, the fact that this case involves a group insurance program highlights a basic flaw in the Department's fairness argument. For when insurance risks are grouped, the better risks always subsidize the poorer risks. Healthy persons subsidize medical benefits for the less healthy; unmarried workers subsidize the pensions of married workers; persons who eat, drink, or smoke to excess may subsidize pension benefits for persons whose habits are more temperate. Treating different classes of risks as though they were the same for purposes of group insurance is a common practice that has never been considered inherently unfair. To insure the flabby and the fit as though they were equivalent risks may be more common than treating men and women alike; but nothing more than habit makes one "subsidy" seem less fair than the other.

An employment practice that requires 2,000 individuals to contribute more money into a fund than 10,000 other employees simply because each of them is a woman, rather than a man, is in direct conflict with both the language and the policy of the Act. Such a practice does not pass the simple test of whether the evidence shows "treatment of a person in a manner which but for that person's sex would be different." It constitutes discrimination and is unlawful unless exempted by the Equal Pay Act of 1963 or some other affirmative justification.

II

Shortly before the enactment of Title VII in 1964, Senator Bennett proposed an amendment providing that a compensation differential based on sex would not be unlawful if it was authorized by the Equal Pay Act, which had been passed a year earlier.[a] The Equal Pay Act requires employers to pay members of both sexes the same wages for equivalent work, except when the differential is pursuant to one of four specified exceptions. The Department contends that the fourth exception applies here. That exception authorizes a "differential based on any other factor other than sex."

---

a   *See* 42 U.S.C. § 2000e-2(h) and 29 U.S.C § 206(d) in the Appendix.

The Department argues that the different contributions exacted from men and women were based on the factor of longevity rather than sex. It is plain, however, that any individual's life expectancy is based on a number of factors of which sex is only one. The record contains no evidence that any factor other than the employee's sex was taken into account in calculating the 14.84% differential between the respective contributions by men and women. We agree with Judge Duniway's observation that one cannot "say that an actuarial distinction based entirely on sex is 'based on any other factor other than sex.' Sex is exactly what it is based on."

III

In essence, the Department is arguing that the *prima facie* showing of discrimination based on evidence of different contributions for the respective sexes is rebutted by its demonstration that there is a like difference in the cost of providing benefits for the respective classes. That argument might prevail if Title VII contained a cost-justification defense comparable to the affirmative defense available in a price discrimination suit. But neither Congress nor the courts have recognized such a defense under Title VII.

Although we conclude that the Department's practice violated Title VII, we do not suggest that the statute was intended to revolutionize the insurance and pension industries. All that is at issue today is a requirement that men and women make unequal contributions to an employer-operated pension fund. Nothing in our holding implies that it would be unlawful for an employer to set aside equal retirement contributions for each employee and let each retiree purchase the largest benefit which his or her accumulated contributions could command in the open market. Nor does it call into question the insurance industry practice of considering the composition of an employer's work force in determining the probable cost of a retirement or death benefit plan.

NOTES AND QUESTIONS

1. If the established greater longevity of women results in higher pension costs, why is an employer's reliance on this fact impermissible sex discrimination? Why isn't cost a legitimate, non-discriminatory reason for disparate treatment? What if statistics also indicate that 84% of all women live no longer than the average male?

2. If the insurance industry provides no unisex pension plan, is there any way for an employer to avoid Title VII liability?

3. Could an employer justify deducting more from a black employee's paycheck to purchase life insurance, based on actuarial tables that the life expectancy for blacks is less than that of whites? *See* footnote 15.

4. What does the Equal Pay Act have to do with this Title VII challenge? Is longevity a "factor other than sex" within the meaning of the Equal Pay Act?

5. If an employer makes the same contribution to a pension fund for male and female employees, but the monthly benefit that retired female employees will receive is less due to actuarial tables, does this violate Title VII? Is this sex discrimination or just discrimination based on longevity? In *Arizona Governing Committee v. Norris*, 463 U.S. 1073 (1983), the Court ruled that Title VII prohibits an employer from offering its employees the option of receiving retirement benefits from one of several companies selected by the employer, all of which pay lower monthly retirement benefits to a woman than to a man who has made the same contributions, reasoning that:

> "the classification of employees on the basis of sex is no more permissible at the pay-out stage of a retirement plan than at the pay-in stage." It is no defense that all annuities immediately available in the open market may have been based on sex-segregated actuarial tables. Having created a plan whereby employees can obtain the advantages of using deferred compensation to purchase an annuity only if they invest in one of the companies specifically selected by the State, the State cannot disclaim responsibility for the discriminatory features of the insurers' options. It would be inconsistent with the broad remedial purposes of Title VII to hold that an employer who adopts a discriminatory fringe-benefit plan can avoid liability on the ground that he could not find a third party willing to treat his employees on a nondiscriminatory basis. An employer who confronts such a situation must either supply the fringe benefit himself, without the assistance of any third party, or not provide it at all.

May insurance companies be sued by non-employees for using gender-based tables under Title VII? Or assume that an insurance company offered life insurance plans where premiums were calculated according to race-based actuarial tables. Could a black applicant forced to pay more for his policy than a white applicant maintain a suit against the insurance company under § 1981?

c. Wage Discrimination: The Equal Pay Act and the Bennett Amendment

COUNTY OF WASHINGTON V. GUNTHER
452 U.S. 161 (1981)

Justice BRENNAN delivered the opinion of the Court.

The question present is whether § 703(h) of Title VII of the Civil Rights Acts of 1964, restricts Title VII's prohibition of sex-based wage discrimination to claims of equal pay for equal work.

I

This case arises over the payment by petitioner County of Washington, Ore., of substantially lower wages to female guards in the female section of the county jail than it paid to male guards in the male section of the jail. Respondents are four women who were employed to guard female prisoners and to carry out certain other functions in the jail.

Respondents filed suit against petitioners in Federal District Court under Title VII, seeking backpay and other relief. They alleged that they were paid unequal wages for work substantially equal to that performed by male guards, and in the alternative, that part of the pay differential was attributable to intentional sex discrimination. The latter allegation was based on a claim that, because of intentional discrimination, the county set the pay scale for female guards, but not for male guards, at a level lower than that warranted by its own survey of outside markets and the worth of the jobs.

After trial, the District Court found that the male guards supervised more than 10 times as many prisoners per guard as did the female guards, and that the females devoted much of their time to less valuable clerical duties. It therefore held that respondents' jobs were not substantially equal to those of the male guards, and that respondents were thus not entitled to equal pay. The Court of Appeals affirmed on that issue, and respondents do not seek review of the ruling.

The District Court also dismissed respondents' claim that the discrepancy in pay between the male and female guards was attributable in part to intentional sex discrimination. It held as a matter of law that a sex-based wage discrimination claim cannot be brought under Title VII unless it would satisfy the equal work standard of the Equal Pay Act of 1963, 29 U.S.C. § 206(d).

We emphasize at the outset the narrowness of the question before us in this case. Respondents' claim is not based on the controversial concept of "comparable worth," under which plaintiffs might claim increased compensation on the basis of a comparison of the intrinsic worth or difficulty of their job with that of other jobs in the same organization or community. Rather, respondents seek to prove, by direct evidence, that their wages were depressed because of intentional sex discrimination, consisting of setting the wage scale for female guards, but not for male guards, at a level lower than its own survey of outside markets and the worth of the job warranted.

II

Title VII makes it an unlawful employment practice for an employer "to discriminate against any individual with respect to his compensation, terms, conditions, or privileges of employment, because of such individual's . . . sex. . . ." 42 U.S.C. § 2000e-2(a). The Bennett Amendment to Title VII, however, provides:

> It shall not be an unlawful employment practice under this subchapter for any employer to differentiate upon the basis of sex in determining the amount of the wages or compensation paid or to be paid to employees of such employer if such differentiation is authorized by the provisions of section 206(d) of title 29. 42 U.S.C. § 2000e-2(h).

To discover what practices are exempted from Title VII's prohibitions by the Bennett Amendment, we must turn to § 206(d)—the Equal Pay Act—which provides in relevant part:

> No employer having employees subject to any provisions of this section shall discriminate, within any establishment in which such employees are employed, between employees on the basis of sex by paying wages to employees in such establishment at a rate less than the rate at which he pays wages to employees of the opposite sex in such establishment for equal work on jobs the performance of which requires equal skill, effort, and responsibility, and which are performed under similar working conditions, except where such payment is made pursuant to

> (i)   a seniority system;
> (ii) a merit system;
> (iii) a system which measures earnings by quantity or quality of production; or
> (iv) a differential based on any other factor other than sex.
> 29 U.S.C. § 206(d)(1).

On its face, the Equal Pay Act contains three restrictions pertinent to this case. First, its coverage is limited to those employers subject to the Fair Labor Standards Act. Thus, the Act does not apply, for example, to certain businesses engaged in retail sales, fishing, agriculture, and newspaper publishing. Second, the Act is restricted to cases involving "equal work on jobs the performance of which requires equal skill, effort, and responsibility, and which are performed under similar working conditions." 29 U.S.C. § 206(d)(1). Third, the Act's four affirmative defenses exempt any wage differentials attributable to seniority, merit, quantity or quality of production, or "any other factor other than sex."

The language of the Bennett Amendment suggests an intention to incorporate only the affirmative defenses of the Equal Pay Act into Title VII. The Amendment bars sex-based wage discrimination claims under Title VII where the pay differential is "authorized" by the Equal Pay Act. Although the word "authorize" sometimes means simply "to permit," it ordinarily denotes affirmative enabling action. The question, then, is what wage practices have been affirmatively authorized by the Equal Pay Act.

The Equal Pay Act is divided into two parts: a definition of the violation, followed by four affirmative defenses. The first part can hardly be said to "authorize" anything at all: it is purely prohibitory. The second part, however, in essence "authorizes" employers to differentiate in pay on the basis of seniority, merit, quantity or quality of production, or any other factor other than sex, even though such differentiation might otherwise violate the Act. It is to these provisions, therefore, that the Bennett Amendment must refer. . . . The Bennett Amendment was offered as a "technical amendment" designed to resolve any potential conflicts between Title VII and the Equal Pay Act. Thus, with respect to the first three defenses, the Bennett Amendment has the effect of guaranteeing that courts and administrative agencies adopt a consistent interpretation of like provisions in both statutes. Otherwise, they might develop inconsistent bodies of case law interpreting two sets of nearly identical language.

More importantly, incorporation of the fourth affirmative defense could have significant consequences for Title VII litigation. Title VII's prohibition of discriminatory employment practices was intended to be broadly inclusive, proscribing "not only overt discrimination but also practices that are fair in form, but discriminatory in operation." *Griggs.* The structure of Title VII litigation, including presumptions, burdens of proof, and defenses, has been designed to reflect this approach. The fourth affirmative defense of the Equal Pay Act, however, was designed differently, to confine the application of the Act to wage differentials attributable to sex discrimination. Equal Pay Act litigation, therefore, has been structured to permit employers to defend against charges of discrimination where their pay differentials are based on a bona fide use of "other factors other than sex." Under the Equal Pay Act, the courts and administrative agencies are not permitted to "substitute their judgment for the judgment of the employer . . . who [has] established and applied a bona fide job rating system," so long as it does not discriminate on the basis of sex. Although we do not decide in this case how sex-based wage discrimination litigation under Title VII should be structured to accommodate the fourth affirmative defense of the Equal Pay Act, we consider it clear that the Bennett Amendment, under this interpretation, is not rendered superfluous.

We therefore conclude that only differentials attributable to the four affirmative defenses of the Equal Pay Act are "authorized" by that Act within the meaning of § 703(h) of Title VII.

III

Petitioner argues strenuously that the approach of the Court of Appeals places "the pay structure of virtually every employer and the entire economy . . . at risk and subject to scrutiny by the federal courts." They raise the specter that "Title VII plaintiffs could draw any type of comparison imaginable concerning job duties and pay between any job predominantly performed by women and any job predominantly performed by men." But whatever the merit of petitioners' arguments in other contexts, they are inapplicable here, for claims based on the type of job comparisons petitioners describe are manifestly different from respondents' claim. Respondents contend that the County of Washington evaluated the worth of their jobs; that the county determined that they should be paid approximately 95% as much as the male correctional officers; that it paid them only about 70% as much, while paying the male officers the full evaluated worth of their jobs; and that the failure of the county to pay respondents the full evaluated worth of their jobs can be proved to be attributable to intentional sex discrimination. Thus, respondents' suit does not require a court to make its own subjective assessment of the value of the male and female guard jobs, or to attempt by statistical technique or other method to quantify the effect of sex discrimination on the wage rates.

We do not decide in this case the precise contours of lawsuits challenging sex discrimination in compensation under Title VII. It is sufficient to note that respondents' claims of discriminatory undercompensation are not barred by § 703(h) of Title VII merely because respondents do not perform work equal to that of male jail guards.

NOTES AND QUESTIONS

1. If the county had not conducted a job evaluation study, would the plaintiff's Title VII claim have been successful? Why is the Court reluctant to embrace the "comparable worth" theory?

   A 1985 EEOC ruling states that sex-based wage discrimination violates Title VII only where the plaintiff can prove (1) discriminatory application of a wage policy or system or the discriminatory use of wage setting techniques such as job evaluation or market surveys, (2) the existence of barriers to equal access to jobs, or (3) the preponderance of direct or circumstantial evidence that wages are intentionally depressed because of the occupants of the job.

   If an employer is generally aware of a comparable worth problem but does nothing, is this intentional suppression of wages?

2. **"Factor Other than Sex":** Could this suit have been maintained under the Equal Pay Act? If not, how does the EPA affect the Title VII analysis? Is the "market demand" for jobs a "factor other than sex" which justifies paying nurses, most of whom are female, significantly less than physicians, most of whom are male? Since the Bennett Amendment incorporates this Equal Pay Act defense, can a "comparable" worth claim ever be successfully litigated under Title VII? May an all-female faculty in a University's nursing school successfully challenge the significantly higher salaries paid to the predominantly male faculty in the engineering school?

   What if the wage difference is based on the applicant's "prior salary"? The Ninth Circuit, in a 6–5 en banc ruling, held that reliance on prior salary perpetuates "the very gender-based assumptions about the value of work that the Equal Pay Act was designed to end." This opinion, however, was vacated and remanded by the Supreme Court because one of the judges in the majority opinion died before the decision was filed, and thus his vote could not be counted. *Yovino v. Rizo*, 139 S. Ct. 706 (2019).

3. Are there litigation advantages to bringing suit under the EPA instead of Title VII? Consider the following:

   a. In a disparate treatment case brought under Title VII, the burden of proving that the defendant intentionally discriminated remains at all times with the plaintiff. Under the EPA, once plaintiff proves she performed work requiring substantially equal levels of skill, effort and responsibility under substantially equal working conditions as male coworkers, the burden shifts to the employer to establish one of the affirmative defenses.

   b. Although the EPA does not impose Title VII's 15-employee restriction, the list of statutory exemptions is quite lengthy. The most significant exemptions are small retail and service businesses and those whose business is predominantly intrastate. 29 U.S.C. § 203.

   c. Under the EPA the EEOC has the power to initiate judicial proceedings, but unlike Title VII, a litigant may, but need not, first pursue EEOC remedies before filing a lawsuit. 29 U.S.C. § 216(b).

   d. The EPA statute of limitations is two years, or three years for willful violations, 29 U.S.C. § 255(a), compared to 180-300 days for filing a charge with the EEOC under Title VII (discussed *infra*).

   e. While Title VII limits a back pay award to sums accruing up to two years prior to filing the EEOC charge, § 2000e-5(g)(1), under the EPA an award of back wages may be extended to three years for willful violations, 29 U.S.C. § 255(a). More significantly, if the plaintiff proves a willful violation, the Act provides for an award of liquidated damages in the amount of the back pay award unless the employer can prove that the challenged conduct "was in good faith and that he had reasonable grounds for believing that his act or omission was not a violation." 29 U.S.C. § 260.

   f. While Title VII permits fees for the prevailing party, the EPA's fee provision limits attorney fees to the prevailing plaintiff only.

Carol Cole and Linda Long are female athletic coaches in the Madison, Wisconsin school district who claim they are paid substantially less for coaching girls' teams than males coaching the same sport boys' team. Although the boys' track and tennis teams are no different from the girls' teams that Carol coaches in terms of number of students, length of season, or number of practice sessions, the boys' teams play almost twice as many matches as the girls' teams. As to the basketball teams, which Linda coaches, there is some indication that the boys' teams are sometimes larger and play longer seasons; however, this is arguably offset by the fact that the head coaches of the boys' teams have more assistants than their female counterparts. The women also argue that they are discouraged from applying to coach boys' teams and that only one woman has ever been hired to coach a male team, although she was paid the same as her male counterpart. Further after the complaint was filed, the school district began appointing more men to coach girls' teams for the same pay as the women coaches received.

The Madison school district argues that the coaching jobs of boys' and girls' teams are not the same. It notes, for example, that the boys' teams are greater revenue producers than the girls' teams, and that because of the larger size of at least some of the boy's teams, the head coach has the additional task of supervising more assistant coaches. Further, it argues that it has never engaged in intentional discrimination against female coaches and that, in any event, the sex of the teams is a "factor other than sex."

Long and Cole have filed suit under Title VII, the Equal Pay Act, and 42 U.S.C. § 1983, alleging violation of the Equal Protection Clause.

1. Prepare a chart setting forth the proof scheme that will govern the Equal Pay Act and Title VII disparate impact (post-Civil Rights Act of 1991) claims? Could the court find a violation of one, but not the other?

2. What will Cole and Long have to prove to succeed on the sex discrimination claim under the Equal Protection Clause of the Fourteenth Amendment?

d. Sexual Harassment

MERITOR SAVINGS BANK V. VINSON
477 U.S. 57 (1986)

Justice REHNQUIST delivered the opinion of the Court.

This case presents important questions concerning claims of workplace "sexual harassment" brought under Title VII of the Civil Rights Act of 1964.

I

In 1974, respondent Mechelle Vinson met Sidney Taylor, a vice president of what is now petitioner Meritor Savings Bank (the bank) and manager of one of its branch offices. When respondent asked whether she might obtain employment at the bank, Taylor gave her an application, which she completed and returned the next day; later that same day Taylor called her to say that she had been hired. With Taylor as her supervisor, respondent started as a teller-trainee, and thereafter was promoted to teller, head teller, and assistant branch manager. She worked at the same branch for four years and it is undisputed that her advancement there was based on merit alone. In September 1978, respondent notified Taylor that she was taking sick leave for an indefinite period. On November 1, 1978, the bank discharged her for excessive use of that leave.

Respondent brought this action against Taylor and the bank, claiming that during her four years at the bank she had "constantly been subjected to sexual harassment" by Taylor in violation of Title VII. She sought injunctive relief, compensatory and punitive damages against Taylor and the bank, and attorney's fees.

At the 11-day bench trial, the parties presented conflicting testimony about Taylor's behavior during respondent's employment. Respondent testified that during her probationary period as a teller-trainee, Taylor treated her in a fatherly way and made no sexual advances. Shortly thereafter, however, he invited her out to dinner and, during the course of the meal suggested that they go to a motel to have sexual relations. At first she refused, but out of what she described as fear of losing her job she eventually agreed. According to respondent, Taylor thereafter made repeated demands upon her for sexual favors, usually at the branch, both during and after business hours; she estimated that over the next several years she had intercourse with him some 40 or 50 times. In addition, respondent testified that Taylor fondled her in front of other employees and followed her into the women's restroom when she went there alone, exposed himself to her, and even forcibly raped her on several occasions. These activities ceased after 1977, respondent stated, when she started going with a steady boyfriend.

Respondent also testified that Taylor touched and fondled other women employees of the bank, and she attempted to call witnesses to support this charge. Finally, respondent testified that because she was afraid of Taylor she never reported his harassment to any of his supervisors and never attempted to use the bank's complaint procedure.

Taylor denied respondent's allegations of sexual activity, testifying that he never fondled her, never made suggestive remarks to her, never engaged in sexual intercourse with her and never asked her to do so. He contended instead that respondent made her accusations in response to a business-related dispute. The bank also denied respondent's allegations and asserted that any sexual harassment by Taylor was unknown to the bank and engaged in without its consent or approval.

II

Title VII of the Civil Rights Act of 1964 makes it "an unlawful employment practice for an employer . . . to discriminate against any individual with respect to his compensation, terms, conditions, or privileges of employment, because of such individual's race, color, religion, sex, or national origin." 42 U.S.C. § 2000e-2(a)(1). The prohibition against discrimination based on sex was added to Title VII at the last minute on the floor of the House of Representatives. The principal argument in opposition to the amendment was that "sex discrimination" was sufficiently different from other types of discrimination that it ought to receive separate legislative treatment. This argument was defeated, the bill quickly passed as amended, and we are left with little legislative history to guide us in interpreting the Act's prohibition against discrimination based on "sex."

Respondent argues, and the Court of Appeals held, that unwelcome sexual advances that create an offensive or hostile working environment violate Title VII. Without question, when a supervisor sexually harasses a subordinate because of the subordinate's sex, that supervisor "discriminate[s]" on the basis of sex. Petitioner apparently does not challenge this proposition. It contends instead that in prohibiting discrimination with respect to "compensation, terms, conditions, or privileges" of employment, Congress was concerned with what petitioner describes as "tangible loss" of "an economic character," not "purely psychological aspects of the workplace environment." In support of this claim petitioner observes that in both the legislative history of Title VII and this Court's Title VII decisions, the focus has been on tangible, economic barriers erected by discrimination.

We reject petitioner's view. First, the language of Title VII is not limited to "economics" or "tangible" discrimination. The phrase "terms, conditions, or privileges of employment" evinces a congressional intent "'to strike at the entire spectrum of disparate treatment of men and women'" in employment. *Los Angeles Department of Water and Power v. Manhart*. Petitioner has pointed to nothing in the Act to suggest that Congress contemplated the limitation urged here.

Second, in 1980 the EEOC issued guidelines specifying that "sexual harassment," as there defined, is a form of sex discrimination prohibited by Title VII. As an "administrative interpretation of the Act by the enforcing agency" these guidelines, "'while not controlling upon the courts by reason of their authority, do constitute a body of experience and informed judgment to which courts and litigants may properly resort for guidance,'" *General Electric Co. v. Gilbert*. The EEOC guidelines fully support the view that harassment leading to noneconomic injury can violate Title VII.

In defining "sexual harassment," the guidelines first describe the kinds of workplace conduct that may be actionable under Title VII. These include "[u]nwelcome sexual advances, requests for sexual favors, and other verbal or physical conduct of a sexual nature." 29 C.F.R. § 1604.11(a) (1985). Relevant to the charges at issue in this case, the guidelines provide that such sexual misconduct constitutes prohibited "sexual harassment," whether or not it is directly linked to the grant or denial of an economic *quid pro quo*, where "such conduct has the purpose or effect of unreasonably interfering with an individual's work performance or creating an intimidating, hostile, or offensive working environment." § 1604.11(a)(3).

In concluding that so-called "hostile environment" (*i.e.*, non *quid pro quo*) harassment violated Title VII, the EEOC drew upon a substantial body of judicial decisions and EEOC precedent holding that Title VII affords employees the right to work in an environment free from discriminatory intimidation, ridicule and insult [based on race, religion and national origin]. Nothing in Title VII suggests that a hostile environment based on discriminatory *sexual* harassment should not be likewise prohibited. The guidelines thus appropriately drew from, and were fully consistent with, the existing case law.

Since the guidelines were issued, courts have uniformly held, and we agree, that a plaintiff may establish a violation of Title VII by proving that discrimination based on sex has created a hostile or abusive work environment. As the Court of Appeals for the Eleventh Circuit wrote in *Henson v. Dundee*, 682 F.2d 897, 902 (1982):

> Sexual harassment which creates a hostile or offensive environment for members of one sex is every bit the arbitrary barrier to sexual equality at the workplace that racial harassment is to racial equality. Surely, a requirement that a man or woman run a gauntlet of sexual abuse in return for the privilege of being allowed to work and make a living can be as demeaning and disconcerting as the harshest of racial epithets.

Of course, as [other] courts [have] recognized, not all workplace conduct that may be described as 'harassment' affects a "term, condition or privilege" of employment within the meaning of Title VII. For sexual harassment to be actionable, it must be sufficiently severe or pervasive "to alter the conditions of [the victim's] employment and create an abusive working environment." Respondent's allegations in this case—which include not only pervasive harassment but also criminal conduct of the most serious nature—are plainly sufficient to state a claim for "hostile environment" sexual harassment.

The question remains, however, whether the District Court's ultimate finding that respondent "was not the victim of sexual harassment," effectively disposed of the respondent's claim. The Court of Appeals recognized, we think correctly, that this ultimate finding was likely based on one or both of two erroneous views of the law. First, the District Court apparently believed that a claim for sexual harassment will not lie absent an *economic* effect on the complainant's employment.

Second, the District Court's conclusion that no actionable harassment occurred might have rested on its earlier "finding" that "[i]f [respondent] and Taylor did engage in an intimate or sexual relationship . . ., that relationship was a voluntary one." But the fact that sex-related conduct was "voluntary," in the sense that the complainant was not forced to participate against her will, is not a defense to a sexual harassment suit brought under Title VII. The gravamen of any sexual harassment claim is that the alleged sexual advances were "unwelcome." 29 C.F.R. § 1604.11(a) (1985). The correct inquiry is whether respondent by her conduct indicated that the alleged sexual advances were unwelcome, not whether her actual participation in sexual intercourse was voluntary.

Petitioner contends that even if this case must be remanded to the District Court, the Court of Appeals erred in one of the terms of its remand. Specifically, the Court of Appeals stated that testimony about respondent's "dress and personal fantasies," which the District Court apparently admitted into evidence, "had no place in this litigation." The apparent ground for this conclusion was that respondent's voluntariness *vel non* in submitting to Taylor's advances was immaterial to her sexual harassment claim. While "voluntariness" in the sense of consent is not a defense to such a claim, it does not follow that a complainant's sexually provocative speech or dress is irrelevant as a matter of law in determining whether he or she found particular sexual advances unwelcome. To the contrary, such evidence is obviously relevant. The EEOC guidelines emphasize that the trier of fact must determine the existence of sexual harassment in light of "the record as a whole" and "the totality of circumstances, such as the nature of the sexual advances and the context in which the alleged incidents occurred." 29 C.F.R. § 1604.11(b) (1985). Respondent's claim that any marginal relevance of the evidence in question was outweighed by the potential for unfair prejudice is the sort of argument properly addressed to the District Court. In this case the District Court concluded that the evidence should be admitted, and the Court of Appeals' contrary conclusion was based upon the erroneous, categorical view that testimony about provocative dress and publicly expressed sexual fantasies "had no place in this litigation." While the District Court must carefully weigh the applicable considerations in deciding whether to admit evidence of this kind, there is no *per se* rule against its admissibility.

III

We decline the parties' invitation to issue a definitive rule on employer liability, but we do agree with the EEOC that Congress wanted courts to look to agency principles for guidance in this area. While such common-law principles may not be transferable in all their particulars to Title VII, Congress' decision to define "employer" to include any "agent" of an employer, 42 U.S.C. § 2000e(b), surely evinces an intent to place some limits on the acts of employees for which employers under Title VII are to be held responsible. For this reason, we hold that the Court of Appeals erred in concluding that employers are always automatically liable for sexual harassment by their supervisors. For the same reason, absence of notice to an employer does not necessarily insulate that employer from liability.

Finally, we reject petitioner's view that the mere existence of a grievance procedure and a policy against discrimination, coupled with respondent's failure to invoke that procedure, must insulate petitioner from liability. While those facts are plainly relevant, the situation before us demonstrates why they are not necessarily dispositive. Petitioner's general nondiscrimination policy did not address sexual harassment in particular, and thus did not alert employees to their employer's interest in correcting that form of discrimination. Moreover, the bank's grievance procedure apparently required an employee to complain first to her supervisor, in this case Taylor. Since Taylor was the alleged perpetrator, it is not altogether surprising that respondent failed to invoke the procedure and report her grievance to him. Petitioner's contention that respondent's failure should insulate it from liability might be substantially stronger if its procedures were better calculated to encourage victims of harassment to come forward.

IV

In sum, we hold that a claim of "hostile environment" sex discrimination is actionable under Title VII, that the District Court's findings were insufficient to dispose of respondent's hostile environment claim, and that the District Court did not err in admitting testimony about respondent's sexually provocative speech and dress. As to employer liability, we conclude that the Court of Appeals was wrong to entirely disregard agency principles and impose absolute liability on employers for the acts of their supervisors, regardless of the circumstances of a particular case.

Accordingly, the judgment of the Court of Appeals reversing the judgment of the District Court is affirmed, and the case is remanded for further proceedings consistent with this opinion.

NOTES AND QUESTIONS

1. What language in Title VII addresses hostile environment claims?

2. Why is the distinction between "unwelcome" and "involuntary" critical? If conduct appears welcome to a supervisor, but is really unwelcome and the victim is afraid to express this, should it be actionable? Is the victim's sexually provocative dress or conduct admissible on this issue?

    Rule 412(a), FRE, provides that the "following evidence is not admissible in a civil or criminal proceeding involving alleged sexual misconduct: (1) evidence offered to prove that a victim engaged in other sexual behavior; or (2) evidence offered to prove a victim's sexual predisposition." However, Rule 412(b)(2) states an exception: "[i]n a civil case, the court may admit evidence offered to prove a victim's sexual behavior or sexual disposition if its probative value substantially outweighs the danger of harm to any victim and of unfair prejudice to any party." Contrary to the Rule 403 balance, the probative value must substantially outweigh the "danger of harm to any victim and of unfair prejudice to any party" under Rule 412, and the burden is shifted to the employer to demonstrate admissibility, rather than requiring the victim to establish grounds for excluding the evidence. *See also* Rule 415, FRE, allowing use of similar acts by the perpetrator in a case alleging sexual assault.

3. In a *quid pro quo* case, should the employer be automatically liable for a supervisor's conduct? Isn't absolute liability imposed when a supervisor decides to discharge an employee because of race or sex?

4. In a hostile environment case, should the existence of a policy and complaint procedure relating to sexual harassment affect the analysis?

5. If Taylor wins on remand, what relief is available? Note that prior to the Civil Rights Act of 1991, Title VII did not provide for damages. Compare the *quid pro quo* and hostile environment situations.

6. Does a victim of sexual harassment in the workplace have a tort claim under state law? Does a federal court have the power to entertain such a claim?

HARRIS V. FORKLIFT SYSTEMS, INC.
510 U.S. 17 (1993)

Justice O'CONNOR delivered the opinion of the Court.

In this case we consider the definition of a discriminatorily "abusive work environment" (also known as a "hostile work environment") under Title VII of the Civil Rights Act of 1964.

I

Teresa Harris worked as a manager at Forklift Systems, Inc., an equipment rental company, from April 1985 until October 1987. Charles Hardy was Forklift's president. The Magistrate found that, throughout Harris' time at Forklift, Hardy often insulted her because of her gender and often made her the target of sexual innuendos. Hardy told Harris on several occasions, in the presence of other employees, "You're a woman, what do you know" and "We need a man as the rental manager"; at least once, he told her she was "a dumb ass woman." Again in front of others, he suggested that the two of them "go to the Holiday Inn to negotiate [Harris'] raise." Hardy occasionally asked Harris and other female employees to get coins from his front pants pocket. He threw objects on the ground in front of Harris and other women, and asked them to pick the objects up. He made sexual innuendos about Harris' and other women's clothing.

In mid-August 1987, Harris complained to Hardy about his conduct. Hardy said he was surprised that Harris was offended, claimed he was only joking, and apologized. He also promised he would stop, and based on this assurance Harris stayed on the job. But in early September, Hardy began anew: While Harris was arranging a deal with one of Forklift's customers, he asked her, again in front of other employees, "What did you do promise the guy . . . some [sex] Saturday night?" On October 1, Harris collected her paycheck and quit.

Harris then sued Forklift, claiming that Hardy's conduct had created an abusive work environment for her because of her gender. The United States District Court for the Middle District of Tennessee, adopting the report and recommendation of the Magistrate, found this to be "a close case," but held that Hardy's conduct did not create an abusive environment. The court found that some of Hardy's comments "offended [Harris], and would offend the reasonable woman," but that they were not

> so severe as to be expected to seriously affect [Harris'] psychological well-being. A reasonable woman manager under like circumstances would have been offended by Hardy, but his conduct would not have risen to the level of interfering with that person's work performance.
>
> Neither do I believe that [Harris] was subjectively so offended that she suffered injury... Although Hardy may at times have genuinely offended [Harris], I do not believe that he created a working environment so poisoned as to be intimidating or abusive to [Harris].

II

Title VII of the Civil Rights Act of 1964 makes it "an unlawful employment practice for an employer . . . to discriminate against any individual with respect to his compensation, terms, conditions, or privileges of employment, because of such individual's race, color, religion, sex, or national origin." When the workplace is permeated with "discriminatory intimidation, ridicule, and insult," that is "sufficiently severe or pervasive to alter the conditions of the victim's employment and create an abusive working environment," Title VII is violated.

This standard, which we reaffirm today, takes a middle path between making actionable any conduct that is merely offensive and requiring the conduct to cause a tangible psychological injury. As we pointed out in *Meritor*, "mere utterance of an . . . epithet which engenders offensive feelings in a employee," does not sufficiently affect the conditions of employment to implicate Title VII. Conduct that is not severe or pervasive enough to create an objectively hostile or abusive work environment—an environment that a reasonable person would find hostile or abusive—is beyond Title VII's purview. Likewise, if the victim does not subjectively perceive the environment to be abusive, the conduct has not actually altered the conditions of the victim's employment, and there is no Title VII violation.

But Title VII comes into play before the harassing conduct leads to a nervous breakdown. A discriminatorily abusive work environment, even one that does not seriously affect employees' psychological well-being, can and often will detract from employees' job performance, discourage employees from remaining on the job, or keep them from advancing in their careers. Moreover, even without regard to these tangible effects, the very fact that the discriminatory conduct was so severe or pervasive that it created a work environment abusive to employees because of their race, gender, religion, or national origin offends Title VII's broad rule of workplace equality. The appalling conduct alleged in *Meritor*, and the reference in that case to environments "'so heavily polluted with discrimination as to destroy completely the emotional and psychological stability of minority group workers,'" merely present some especially egregious examples of harassment. They do not mark the boundary of what is actionable.

We therefore believe the District Court erred in relying on whether the conduct "seriously affect[ed] plaintiff's psychological well-being" or led her to "suffe[r] injury." Such an inquiry may needlessly focus the factfinder's attention on concrete psychological harm, an element Title VII does not require. Certainly Title VII bars conduct that would seriously affect a reasonable person's psychological well-being, but the statute is not limited to such conduct. So long as the environment would reasonably be perceived, and is perceived, as hostile or abusive, *Meritor*, there is no need for it also to be psychologically injurious.

This is not, and by its nature cannot be, a mathematically precise test. We need not answer today all the potential questions it raises, nor specifically address the EEOC's new regulations on this subject. But we can say that whether an environment is "hostile" or "abusive" can be determined only by looking at all the circumstances. These may include the frequency of the discriminatory conduct; its severity; whether it is physically threatening or humiliating, or a mere offensive utterance; and whether it unreasonably interferes with an employee's work performance. The effect on the employee's psychological well-being is, of course, relevant to determining whether the plaintiff actually found the environment abusive. But while psychological harm, like any other relevant factor, may be taken into account, no single factor is required.

Justice GINSBURG, concurring

Today the Court reaffirms the holding of *Meritor Savings Bank*: "[A] plaintiff may establish a violation of Title VII by proving that discrimination based on sex has created a hostile or abusive work environment." The critical issue, Title VII's text indicates, is whether members of one sex are exposed to disadvantageous terms or conditions of employment to which members of the other sex are not exposed. As the Equal Employment Opportunity Commission emphasized, the adjudicator's inquiry should center, dominantly, on whether the discriminatory conduct has unreasonably interfered with the plaintiff's work performance. To show such interference, "the plaintiff need not prove that his or her tangible productivity has declined as a result of the harassment." It suffices to prove that a reasonable person subjected to the discriminatory conduct would find, as the plaintiff did, that the harassment so altered working conditions as to "ma[k]e it more difficult to do the job."

NOTES AND QUESTIONS

1. Does the Court adopt an objective or subjective test in deciding whether an employee has been subjected to a hostile work environment?

2. Must the plaintiff prove that the harassing conduct interfered with her work performance?

3. If a supervisor's conduct, *e.g.*, posting sexually offensive photos or telling sexually offensive jokes, is equally offensive to both males and females, is there sex

discrimination? Do threats of physical violence and acts of physical aggression directed at females, because they are female, constitute sex discrimination?

4. When is sexual harassment "sufficiently severe or pervasive 'to alter the conditions of [the victim's] employment and create an abusive working environment,'" and therefore actionable? Must there be physical touching? Can one incident be enough? What "factors" does the Court provide?

5. In *Clark County School Dist. v. Breeden*, 532 U.S. 268 (2001), the Court emphasized that simple teasing, offhand comments, and isolated incidents will not amount to discriminatory changes in the "terms and conditions of employment." Breeden, a Human Resources Director, claimed that her supervisor read aloud from an application stating that the applicant had once commented, "I hear making love to you is like making love to the Grand Canyon." The supervisor looked at Breeden and stated, "I don't know what that means," and another male employee responded "Well, I'll tell you later," and both men chuckled. This was the extent of the alleged harassment, and the Court reasoned that, at worst, the comments constituted an isolated incident "that cannot remotely be considered 'extremely serious,'" as required by the Court's previous decisions.

The plaintiff could not establish a *prima facie* case of retaliation, because she could not prove that her complaint to her supervisors constituted "protected activity." The Court determined that no reasonable person could have believed the comments in question violated Title VII, and thus the plaintiff's complaint about the comments was not protected activity. Many lower federal courts have read *Breeden* as requiring that plaintiffs show an objectively reasonable belief that she was opposing an unlawful employment practice. A good faith, but unreasonable, belief is not protected.

ONCALE V. SUNDOWNER OFFSHORE SERVICES, INC.
523 U.S. 75 (1998)

Justice Scalia delivered the opinion of the Court.

This case presents the question whether workplace harassment can violate Title VII's prohibition against "discrimination . . . because of . . . sex," 42 U.S.C. § 2000e-2(a)(1), when the harasser and the harassed employee are of the same sex.

I

The District Court having granted summary judgment for respondent, we must assume the facts to be as alleged by petitioner Joseph Oncale. The precise details are irrelevant to the legal point we must decide, and in the interest of both brevity and dignity we shall describe them only generally. In late October 1991, Oncale was working for respondent Sundowner Offshore Services on a Chevron U.S.A., Inc., oil platform in the Gulf of Mexico. He was employed as a roustabout on an eight-man crew which included respondents John Lyons, Danny Pippen, and Brandon Johnson. Lyons, the crane operator, and Pippen, the driller, had supervisory authority. On several occasions, Oncale was forcibly subjected to sex-related, humiliating actions against him by Lyons, Pippen and Johnson in the presence of the rest of the crew. Pippen and Lyons also physically assaulted Oncale in a sexual manner, and Lyons threatened him with rape.

Oncale's complaints to supervisory personnel produced no remedial action; in fact, the company's Safety Compliance Clerk, Valent Hohen, told Oncale that Lyons and Pippen "picked [on] him all the time too," and called him a name suggesting homosexuality. Oncale eventually quit—asking that his pink slip reflect that he "voluntarily left due to sexual harassment and verbal abuse." When asked at his deposition why he left Sundowner, Oncale stated "I felt that if I didn't leave my job, that I would be raped or forced to have sex."

II

Title VII's prohibition of discrimination "because of . . . sex" protects men as well as women, and in the related context of racial discrimination in the workplace we have rejected any conclusive presumption that an employer will not discriminate against members of his own race. "Because of the many facets of human motivation, it would be unwise to presume as a matter of law that human beings of one definable group will not discriminate against other members of that group." *Castaneda v. Partida*. If our precedents leave any doubt on the question, we hold today that nothing in Title VII necessarily bars a claim of discrimination "because of . . . sex" merely because the plaintiff and the defendant (or the person charged with acting on behalf of the defendant) are of the same sex.

We see no justification in the statutory language or our precedents for a categorical rule excluding same-sex harassment claims from the coverage of Title VII. As some courts have observed, male-on-male sexual harassment in the workplace was assuredly not the principal evil Congress was concerned with when it enacted Title VII. But statutory prohibitions often go beyond the principal evil to cover reasonably comparable evils, and it is ultimately the provisions of our laws rather than the principal concerns of our legislators by which we are governed. Title VII prohibits "discrimination . . . because of . . . sex" in the "terms" or "conditions" of employment. Our holding that this includes sexual harassment must extend to sexual harassment of any kind that meets the statutory requirements.

Respondents and their *amici* contend that recognizing liability for same-sex harassment will transform Title VII into a general civility code for the American workplace. But that risk is no greater for same-sex than for opposite-sex harassment, and is adequately met by careful attention to the requirements of the statute. Title VII does not prohibit all verbal or physical harassment in the workplace; it is directed only at "discrimination . . . because of . . . sex." We have never held that workplace harassment, even harassment between men and women, is automatically discrimination because of sex merely because the words used have sexual content or connotations. "The critical issue, Title VII's text indicates, is whether members of one sex are exposed to disadvantageous terms or conditions of employment to which members of the other sex are not exposed." *Harris* (GINSBURG, J., concurring).

Courts and juries have found the inference of discrimination easy to draw in most male-female sexual harassment situations, because the challenged conduct typically involves explicit or implicit proposals of sexual activity; it is reasonable to assume those proposals would not have been made to someone of the same sex. The same chain of inference would be available to a plaintiff alleging same-sex harassment, if there were credible evidence that the harasser was homosexual. But harassing conduct need not be motivated by sexual desire to support an inference of discrimination on the basis of sex. A trier of fact might reasonably find such discrimination, for example, if a female victim is harassed in such sex-specific and derogatory terms by another woman as to make it clear that the harasser is motivated by general hostility to the presence of women in the workplace. A same-sex harassment plaintiff may also, of course, offer direct comparative evidence about how the alleged harasser treated members of both sexes in a mixed-sex workplace. Whatever evidentiary route the plaintiff chooses to follow, he or she must always prove that the conduct at issue was not merely tinged with offensive sexual connotations, but actually constituted "*discrimina[tion]* . . . because of . . . sex."

And there is another requirement that prevents Title VII from expanding into a general civility code: As we emphasized in *Meritor* and *Harris*, the statute does not reach genuine but innocuous differences in the ways men and women routinely interact with members of the same sex and of the opposite sex. The prohibition of harassment on the basis of sex requires neither asexuality nor androgyny in the workplace; it forbids only behavior so objectively offensive as to alter the "conditions" of the victim's employment. "Conduct that is not severe or pervasive enough to create an objectively hostile or abusive work environment—an environment that a reasonable person would find hostile or abusive—is beyond Title VII's purview." *Harris*. We have always regarded that requirement as crucial, and as sufficient to ensure that courts and juries do not mistake ordinary socializing in the workplace—such as male-on-male horseplay or inter-sexual flirtation—for discriminatory "conditions of employment."

We have emphasized, moreover, that the objective severity of harassment should be judged from the perspective of a reasonable person in the plaintiff's position, considering "all the circumstances." *Harris*. In same-sex (as in all) harassment cases, that inquiry requires careful consideration of the social context in which particular behavior occurs and is experienced by its target. A professional football player's working environment is not severely or pervasively abusive, for example, if the coach smacks him on the buttocks as he heads onto the field-even if the same behavior would reasonably be experienced as abusive by the coach's secretary (male or female) back at the office. The real social impact of workplace behavior often depends on a constellation of surrounding circumstances, expectations, and relationships which are not fully captured by a simple recitation of the words used or the physical acts performed. Common sense, and an appropriate sensitivity to social context, will enable courts and juries to distinguish between simple teasing or roughhousing among members of the same sex, and conduct which a reasonable person in the plaintiff's position would find severely hostile or abusive.

1. How can Oncale establish on remand that he was subjected to discrimination "because of sex"? Was he singled out because he is male? If his harassers are not homosexual and the workplace is all male, how can he prove that "members of one sex are exposed to disadvantageous terms or conditions . . . to which members of the other sex are not exposed"?

2. By focusing on social context, does the Court suggest that women in blue-collar, traditionally male occupations should tolerate harassment more than women who have white-collar jobs?

3. **Sexual orientation and gender identity discrimination:** What if Oncale was singled out because he was perceived as effeminate or gay? Is this discrimination "because of sex"? The Court in *Price Waterhouse, supra,* ruled that sex stereotyping by an employer based on a person's gender nonconforming behavior is a form of impermissible sex discrimination. Ann Hopkins alleged she was denied a promotion because Price-Waterhouse officials felt she was too assertive and lacked femininity. A plurality of the Court reasoned that under Title VII "gender must be irrelevant to employment decisions" and that "[i]n the specific context of sex stereotyping, an employer who acts on the basis of a belief that a woman cannot be aggressive, or that she must not be, has acted on the basis of gender."

   Although discrimination based on sexual orientation is not explicitly covered under Title VII's prohibition of sex discrimination, some appellate courts have invoked *Price-Waterhouse* to hold that discrimination based on a homosexual employee's effeminacy or a lesbian employee's masculinity is a form of impermissible gender-stereotyping. *See, e.g., Christiansen v. Omnicom Group, Incorporated,* 852 F.3d 195 (2d Cir. 2017) (sexual orientation discrimination is not actionable under Title VII, but district court erred in dismissing plaintiff's claim based on gender stereotyping; although complaint alleged fewer allegations about gay employee's effeminacy than about his sexual orientation, the gender-stereotyping allegations that he was perceived as too effeminate and submissive were sufficient to withstand dismissal). Other appellate courts have held that *Price Waterhouse*'s reasoning encompasses discrimination based on gender identity, because transsexuals present a paradigm example of discrimination based on nonconformity to sexual stereotypes. *See, e.g., Barnes v. City of Cincinnati,* 401 F.3d 729 (6th Cir. 2005) (police officer, a preoperative male-to-female transsexual who alleged his failure to conform to sex stereotypes concerning how a man should look and behave was the driving force behind defendant's actions, stated a claim for relief under Title VII's prohibition of sex discrimination).

   Further, two appellate courts have held that sexual orientation discrimination is **directly** prohibited by Title VII, without the necessity of proving sex stereotyping.

In *Hively v. Ivy Tech Community College*, 853 F.3d 339 (7th Cir. 2017) (en banc), the Seventh Circuit ruled that discrimination based on sexual orientation is itself a form of sex discrimination actionable under Title VII. The plaintiff, an openly lesbian professor, did not rely on the gender nonconformity/stereotyping theory of *Price Waterhouse*, but the court reasoned that she was treated differently on the basis of sex because a male attracted to a female would not have suffered an adverse employment action. The court also invoked the Supreme Court's Title VII opinions in *Price Waterhouse* and *Oncale*, as well as "the common sense reality that it is actually impossible to discriminate on the basis of sexual orientation without discriminating on the basis of sex." The Second Circuit, in *Zarda v. Altitude Express, Inc.*, 883 F.3d 100 (2d Cir. 2018) (en banc), *cert. granted*, 139 S. Ct. ____ (2019), agreed with the Seventh Circuit, explaining that sexual orientation is a subset of sex discrimination actionable under Title VII for three reasons: (1) "sexual orientation is defined by one's sex in relation to the sex of those to whom one is attracted," and thus sex is taken into account when an employer discriminates on the basis of sexual orientation; (2) sexual orientation bias is "almost invariably rooted in stereotypes about which sex men and women should be physically attracted to"; and (3) sexual orientation discrimination is "associational discrimination because an adverse employment action that is motivated by the employer's opposition to association between members of particular sexes discriminates against an employee on the basis of sex." The Fifth and Eleventh Circuits have rejected this analysis, reasoning that when Congress enacted Title VII, it never intended to reach sexual orientation discrimination. *Wittmer v. Phillips 66 Co.*, 915 F.3d 328 (5th Cir. 2019) (reaffirming its earlier circuit ruling that Title VII does not apply to discrimination based on sexual orientation); *Bostock v. Clayton County Board of Commissioners*, 723 Fed. App'x 964 (11th Cir. 2018), *cert. granted*, 139 S. Ct. ____ (2019) (Title VII does not prohibit discrimination based on sexual preference).

As to gender identity discrimination, the Sixth Circuit has ruled that transgender individuals may sue directly under Title VII both because an individual's transgender status is always based on gender-stereotypes **and** because "it is analytically impossible to fire an employee based on that employee's status as a transgender person without being motivated, at least in part, by the employee's sex." *E.E.O.C. v. R.G. & G.R. Harris Funeral Homes, Inc.*, 884 F.3d 560 (6th Cir. 2018), *cert. granted*, 139 S. Ct. ____ (2019). Notably, the Sixth Circuit rejected the employer's argument that continuing to employ a transgender person would substantially burden its religious freedom rights under the Religious Freedom Restoration Act of 1993, 42 U.S.C.A. § 2000bb et seq. *E.E.O.C. v. R.G. & G.R. Harris Funeral Homes, Inc.*, 884 F.3d 560, 585–97 (6th Cir. 2018). A funeral home director argued that permitting the plaintiff to wear attire that comports with her conception of gender was at odds with his religious belief that sex is an immutable God-given gift and not a changeable social construct. The court held, as a matter of law, that tolerating an employee's understanding of her sex and gender identity is not tantamount to supporting it, and thus cannot be viewed as a substantial burden. Further, even if retaining the plaintiff imposed a substantial burden, the government has a compelling interest in eliminating sex discrimination in the workplace, and Title VII constitutes the least restrictive means for eradicating this discrimination. *Cf. Wittmer v. Phillips, supra* (invoking circuit's "binding" precedent to reject Title VII's application to discrimination based on transgender status).

BURLINGTON INDUSTRIES V. ELLERTH
524 U.S. 742 (1998)

JUSTICE KENNEDY delivered the opinion of the Court.

We decide whether, under Title VII of the Civil Rights Act of 1964, an employee who refuses the unwelcome and threatening sexual advances of a supervisor, yet suffers no adverse, tangible job consequences, can recover against the employer without showing the employer is negligent or otherwise at fault for the supervisor's actions.

I

Summary judgment was granted for the employer, so we must take the facts alleged by the employee to be true. The employer is Burlington Industries, the petitioner. The employee is Kimberly Ellerth, the respondent. From March 1993 until May 1994, Ellerth worked as a salesperson in one of Burlington's divisions in Chicago, Illinois. During her employment, she alleges, she was subjected to constant sexual harassment by her supervisor, one Ted Slowik. In the hierarchy of Burlington's management structure, Slowik was a mid-level manager. He had authority to make hiring and promotion decisions subject to the approval of his supervisor, who signed the paperwork.

Against a background of repeated boorish and offensive remarks and gestures which Slowik allegedly made, Ellerth places particular emphasis on three alleged incidents where Slowik's comments could be construed as threats to deny her tangible job benefits. In the summer of 1993, while on a business trip, Slowik invited Ellerth to the hotel lounge, an invitation Ellerth felt compelled to accept because Slowik was her boss. When Ellerth gave no encouragement to remarks Slowik made about her breasts, he told her to 'loosen up' and warned, '[y]ou know, Kim, I could make your life very hard or very easy at Burlington.'

In March 1994, when Ellerth was being considered for a promotion, Slowik expressed reservations during the promotion interview because she was not 'loose enough.' The comment was followed by his reaching over and rubbing her knee. Ellerth did receive the promotion; but when Slowik called to announce it, he told Ellerth, 'you're gonna be out there with men who work in factories, and they certainly like women with pretty butts/legs.'

In May 1994, Ellerth called Slowik, asking permission to insert a customer's logo into a fabric sample. Slowik responded, 'I don't have time for you right now, Kim—unless you want to tell me what you're wearing.' Ellerth told Slowik she had to go and ended the call. A day or two later, Ellerth called Slowik to ask permission again. This time he denied her request, but added something along the lines of, 'are you wearing shorter skirts yet, Kim, because it would make your job a whole heck of a lot easier.'

A short time later, Ellerth's immediate supervisor cautioned her about returning telephone calls to customers in a prompt fashion. In response, Ellerth quit. She faxed a letter giving reasons unrelated to the alleged sexual harassment we have described. About three weeks later, however, she sent a letter explaining she quit because of Slowik's behavior. During her tenure at Burlington, Ellerth did not inform anyone in authority about Slowik's conduct, despite knowing Burlington had a policy against sexual harassment. In fact, she chose not to inform her immediate supervisor (not Slowik) because "it would be his duty as my supervisor to report any incidents of sexual harassment." On one occasion, she told Slowik a comment he made was inappropriate.

II

At the outset, we assume an important proposition yet to be established before a trier of fact. It is a premise assumed as well, in explicit or implicit terms, in the various opinions by the judges of the Court of Appeals. The premise is: a trier of fact could find in Slowik's remarks numerous threats to retaliate against Ellerth if she denied some sexual liberties. The threats, however, were not carried out or fulfilled. Cases based on threats which are carried out are referred to often as *quid pro quo* cases, as distinct from bothersome attentions or sexual remarks that are sufficiently severe or pervasive to create a hostile work environment. The terms *quid pro quo* and hostile work environment are helpful, perhaps, in making a rough demarcation between cases in which threats are carried out and those where they are not or are absent altogether, but beyond this are of limited utility. '*Quid pro quo*' and 'hostile work environment' do not appear in the statutory text. The terms appeared first in the academic literature, found their way into decisions of the Courts of Appeals, and were mentioned in this Court's decision in *Meritor*.

In *Meritor*, the terms served a specific and limited purpose. There we considered whether the conduct in question constituted discrimination in the terms or conditions of employment in violation of Title VII. We assumed, and with adequate reason, that if an employer demanded sexual favors from an employee in return for a job benefit, discrimination with respect to terms or conditions of employment was explicit. Less obvious was whether an employer's sexually demeaning behavior altered terms or conditions of employment in violation of Title VII. We distinguished between quid pro quo claims and hostile environment claims, and said both were cognizable under Title VII, though the latter requires harassment that is severe or pervasive. The principal significance of the distinction is to instruct that Title VII is violated by either explicit or constructive alterations in the terms or conditions of employment and to explain the latter must be severe or pervasive. The distinction was not discussed for its bearing upon an employer's liability for an employee's discrimination. On this question *Meritor* held, with no further specifics, that agency principles controlled.

We do not suggest the terms quid pro quo and hostile work environment are irrelevant to Title VII litigation. To the extent they illustrate the distinction between cases involving a threat which is carried out and offensive conduct in general, the terms are relevant when there is a threshold question whether a plaintiff can prove discrimination in violation of Title VII. When a plaintiff proves that a tangible employment action resulted from a refusal to submit to a supervisor's sexual demands, he or she establishes that the employment decision itself constitutes a change in the terms and conditions of employment that is actionable under Title VII. For any sexual harassment preceding the employment decision to be actionable, however, the conduct must be severe or pervasive. Because Ellerth's claim involves only unfulfilled threats, it should be categorized as a hostile work environment claim which requires a showing of severe or pervasive conduct. For purposes of this case, we accept the District Court's finding that the alleged conduct was severe or pervasive. The case before us involves numerous alleged threats, and we express no opinion as to whether a single unfulfilled threat is sufficient to constitute discrimination in the terms or conditions of employment.

When we assume discrimination can be proved, however, the factors we discuss below, and not the categories *quid pro quo* and hostile work environment, will be controlling on the issue of vicarious liability. That is the question we must resolve.

III

We must decide, then, whether an employer has vicarious liability when a supervisor creates a hostile work environment by making explicit threats to alter a subordinate's terms or conditions of employment, based on sex, but does not fulfill the threat. We return to principles of agency law, for the term 'employer' is defined under Title VII to include 'agents.' 42 U.S.C. § 2000e(b); *see Meritor*. In express terms, Congress has directed federal courts to interpret Title VII based on agency principles.

As *Meritor* acknowledged, the Restatement (Second) of Agency (1957) (hereinafter Restatement), is a useful beginning point for a discussion of general agency principles. Section 219(1) of the Restatement sets out a central principle of agency law: 'A master is subject to liability for the torts of his servants committed while acting in the scope of their employment.' [A] supervisor acting out of gender-based animus or a desire to fulfill sexual urges may not be actuated by a purpose to serve the employer. The harassing supervisor often acts for personal motives, motives unrelated and even antithetical to the objectives of the employer. The general rule is that sexual harassment by a supervisor is not conduct within the scope of employment.

Scope of employment does not define the only basis for employer liability under agency principles. In limited circumstances, agency principles impose liability on employers even where employees commit torts outside the scope of employment. The principles are set forth in the much-cited § 219(2) of the Restatement:

(2) A master is not subject to liability for the torts of his servants acting outside the scope of their employment, unless:

  (a) the master intended the conduct or the consequences, or

  (b) the master was negligent or reckless, or

  (c) the conduct violated a non-delegable duty of the master, or

  (d) the servant purported to act or to speak on behalf of the principal and there was reliance upon apparent authority, or he was aided in accomplishing the tort by the existence of the agency relation.

Subsection (a) addresses direct liability, where the employer acts with tortious intent, and indirect liability, where the agent's high rank in the company makes him or her the employer's alter ego. None of the parties contend Slowik's rank imputes liability under this principle. There is no contention, furthermore, that a nondelegable duty is involved. *See* § 219(2)(c). So, for our purposes here, subsections (a) and (c) can be put aside. Subsections (b) and (d) are possible grounds for imposing employer liability on account of a supervisor's acts and must be considered. Under subsection (b), an employer is liable when the tort is attributable to the employer's own negligence. § 219(2)(b). Thus, although a supervisor's sexual harassment is outside the scope of employment because the conduct was for personal motives, an employer can be liable, nonetheless, where its own negligence is a cause of the harassment. An employer is negligent with respect to sexual harassment if it knew or should have known about the conduct and failed to stop it. Negligence sets a minimum standard for employer liability under Title VII; but Ellerth seeks to invoke the more stringent standard of vicarious liability.

Subsection 219(2)(d) concerns vicarious liability for intentional torts committed by an employee when the employee uses apparent authority (the apparent authority standard), or when the employee 'was aided in accomplishing the tort by the existence of the agency relation' (the aided in the agency relation standard).

As a general rule, apparent authority is relevant where the agent purports to exercise a power which he or she does not have, as distinct from where the agent threatens to misuse actual power. In the usual case, a supervisor's harassment involves misuse of actual power, not the false impression of its existence. Apparent authority analysis therefore is inappropriate in this context. If, in the unusual case, it is alleged there is a false impression that the actor was a supervisor, when he in fact was not, the victim's mistaken conclusion must be a reasonable one. When a party seeks to impose vicarious liability based on an agent's misuse of delegated authority, the Restatement's aided in the agency relation rule, rather than the apparent authority rule, appears to be the appropriate form of analysis.

We turn to the aided in the agency relation standard. In a sense, most workplace tortfeasors are aided in accomplishing their tortious objective by the existence of the agency relation: Were this to satisfy the aided in the agency relation standard, an employer would be subject to vicarious liability not only for all supervisor harassment, but also for all co-worker harassment, a result enforced by neither the EEOC nor any court of appeals to have considered the issue.

At the outset, we can identify a class of cases where, beyond question, more than the mere existence of the employment relation aids in commission of the harassment: when a supervisor takes a tangible employment action against the subordinate. Every Federal Court of Appeals to have considered the question has found vicarious liability when a discriminatory act results in a tangible employment action. In *Meritor*, we acknowledged this consensus. Although few courts have elaborated how agency principles support this rule, we think it reflects a correct application of the aided in the agency relation standard.

In the context of this case, a tangible employment action would have taken the form of a denial of a raise or a promotion. The concept of a tangible employment action appears in numerous cases in the Courts of Appeals discussing claims involving race, age, and national origin discrimination, as well as sex discrimination. Without endorsing the specific results of those decisions, we think it prudent to import the concept of a tangible employment action for resolution of the vicarious liability issue we consider here. A tangible employment action constitutes a significant change in employment status, such as hiring, firing, failing to promote, reassignment with significantly different responsibilities, or a decision causing a significant change in benefits. *Compare Crady v. Liberty Nat. Bank & Trust Co. of Ind.*, 993 F.2d 132, 136 (CA7 1993) ('A materially adverse change might be indicated by a termination of employment, a demotion evidenced by a decrease in wage or salary, a less distinguished title, a material loss of benefits, significantly diminished material responsibilities, or other indices that might be unique to a particular situation'), with *Flaherty v. Gas Research Institute*, 31 F.3d 451, 456 (CA7 1994) (a 'bruised ego' is not enough); *Kocsis v. Multi-Care Management, Inc.*, 97 F.3d 876, 887 (CA6 1996) (demotion without change in pay, benefits, duties, or prestige insufficient) and *Harlston v. McDonnell Douglas* Corp., 37 F.3d 379, 382 (CA8 1994) (reassignment to more inconvenient job insufficient).

When a supervisor makes a tangible employment decision, there is assurance the injury could not have been inflicted absent the agency relation. A tangible employment action in most cases inflicts direct economic harm. As a general proposition, only a supervisor, or other person acting with the authority of the company, can cause this sort of injury. A co-worker can break a co- worker's arm as easily as a supervisor, and anyone who has regular contact with an employee can inflict psychological injuries by his or her offensive conduct. But one co-worker (absent some elaborate scheme) cannot dock another's pay, nor can one co-worker demote another. Tangible employment actions fall within the special province of the supervisor. The supervisor has been empowered by the company as a distinct class of agent to make economic decisions affecting other employees under his or her control.

Tangible employment actions are the means by which the supervisor brings the official power of the enterprise to bear on subordinates. A tangible employment decision requires an official act of the enterprise, a company act. The decision in most cases is documented in official company records, and may be subject to review by higher level supervisors. The supervisor often must obtain the imprimatur of the enterprise and use its internal processes.

For these reasons, a tangible employment action taken by the supervisor becomes for Title VII purposes the act of the employer. Whatever the exact contours of the aided in the agency relation standard, its requirements will always be met when a supervisor takes a tangible employment action against a subordinate. In that instance, it would be implausible to interpret agency principles to allow an employer to escape liability, as *Meritor* itself appeared to acknowledge.

Whether the agency relation aids in commission of supervisor harassment which does not culminate in a tangible employment action is less obvious. Application of the standard is made difficult by its malleable terminology, which can be read to either expand or limit liability in the context of supervisor harassment. On the one hand, a supervisor's power and authority invests his or her harassing conduct with a particular threatening character, and in this sense, a supervisor always is aided by the agency relation. On the other hand, there are acts of harassment a supervisor might commit which might be the same acts a co-employee would commit, and there may be some circumstances where the supervisor's status makes little difference.

Although *Meritor* suggested the limitation on employer liability stemmed from agency principles, the Court acknowledged other considerations might be relevant as well. For example, Title VII is designed to encourage the creation of antiharassment policies and effective grievance mechanisms. Were employer liability to depend in part on an employer's effort to create such procedures, it would effect Congress' intention to promote conciliation rather than litigation in the Title VII context, and the EEOC's policy of encouraging the development of grievance procedures. To the extent limiting employer liability could encourage employees to report harassing conduct before it becomes severe or pervasive, it would also serve Title VII's deterrent purpose. As we have observed, Title VII borrows from tort law the avoidable consequences doctrine, and the considerations which animate that doctrine would also support the limitation of employer liability in certain circumstances.

In order to accommodate the agency principles of vicarious liability for harm caused by misuse of supervisory authority, as well as Title VII's equally basic policies of encouraging forethought by employers and saving action by objecting employees, we adopt the following holding in this case and in *Faragher v. Boca Raton*, also decided today. An employer is subject to vicarious liability to a victimized employee for an actionable hostile environment created by a supervisor with immediate (or successively higher) authority over the employee. When no tangible employment action is taken, a defending employer may raise an affirmative defense to liability or damages, subject to proof by a preponderance of the evidence, *see* Fed. Rule Civ. Proc. 8(c). The defense comprises two necessary elements: (a) that the employer exercised reasonable care to prevent and correct promptly any sexually harassing behavior, and (b) that the plaintiff employee unreasonably failed to take advantage of any preventive or corrective opportunities provided by the employer or to avoid harm otherwise. While proof that an employer had promulgated an anti- harassment policy with complaint procedure is not necessary in every instance as a matter of law, the need for a stated policy suitable to the employment circumstances may appropriately be addressed in any case when litigating the first element of the defense. And while proof that an employee failed to fulfill the corresponding obligation of reasonable care to avoid harm is not limited to showing any unreasonable failure to use any complaint procedure provided by the employer, a demonstration of such failure will normally suffice to satisfy the employer's burden under the second element of the defense. No affirmative defense is available, however, when the supervisor's harassment culminates in a tangible employment action, such as discharge, demotion, or undesirable reassignment.

IV

Although Ellerth has not alleged she suffered a tangible employment action at the hands of Slowik, which would deprive Burlington of the availability of the affirmative defense, this is not dispositive. In light of our decision, Burlington is still subject to vicarious liability for Slowik's activity, but Burlington should have an opportunity to assert and prove the affirmative defense to liability.

For these reasons, we will affirm the judgment of the Court of Appeals, reversing the grant of summary judgment against Ellerth. On remand, the District Court will have the opportunity to decide whether it would be appropriate to allow Ellerth to amend her pleading or supplement her discovery.

Justice THOMAS, with whom Justice SCALIA joins, dissenting.

The Court today manufactures a rule that employers are vicariously liable if supervisors create a sexually hostile work environment, subject to an affirmative defense that the Court barely attempts to define. This rule applies even if the employer has a policy against sexual harassment, the employee knows about that policy, and the employee never informs anyone in a position of authority about the supervisor's conduct. An employer should be liable if, and only if, the plaintiff proves that the employer was negligent in permitting the supervisor's conduct to occur.

Under a negligence standard, Burlington cannot be held liable for Slowick's conduct. Although respondent alleged a hostile work environment, she never contended that Burlington had been negligent in permitting the harassment to occur, and there is no question that Burlington acted reasonably under the circumstances. The company had a policy against sexual harassment, and respondent admitted that she was aware of the policy but nonetheless failed to tell anyone with authority over Slowick about his behavior. Burlington therefore cannot be charged with knowledge of Slowick's alleged harassment or with a failure to exercise reasonable care in not knowing about it.

Rejecting a negligence standard, the Court instead imposes a rule of vicarious employer liability, subject to a vague affirmative defense, for the acts of supervisors who wield no delegated authority in creating a hostile work environment. This rule is a whole-cloth creation that draws no support from the legal principles on which the Court claims it is based. Compounding its error, the Court fails to explain how employers can rely upon the affirmative defense, thus ensuring a continuing reign of confusion in this important area of the law.

What these statements mean for district courts ruling on motions for summary judgment—the critical question for employers now subject to the vicarious liability rule—remains a mystery. Moreover, employers will be liable notwithstanding the affirmative defense, even though they acted reasonably, so long as the plaintiff in question fulfilled her duty of reasonable care to avoid harm. In practice, therefore, employer liability very well may be the rule. But as the Court acknowledges, this is the one result that it is clear Congress did not intend.

The Court's holding does guarantee one result: There will be more and more litigation to clarify applicable legal rules in an area in which both practitioners and the courts have long been begging for guidance. It thus truly boggles the mind that the Court can claim that its holding will effect 'Congress' intention to promote conciliation rather than litigation in the Title VII context.' All in all, today's decision is an ironic result for a case that generated eight separate opinions in the Court of Appeals on a fundamental question, and in which we granted certiorari 'to assist in defining the relevant standards of employer liability.'

NOTES AND QUESTIONS

1. Ellerth's supervisor threatened her with unfavorable tangible employment actions, yet the Court rejects absolute vicarious liability. Why? Does the Court draw a clear line between tangible loss and hostile work environment claims? How should courts treat a demotion without salary change? a reassignment to a more inconvenient job? denial of a bonus?

2. Will the affirmative defense be available where the supervisor's harassment culminates in a tangible job action, but the employer promptly investigates and reverses the adverse decision? Has the Court accepted absolute liability as the standard in all quid pro quo cases?

3. What will Ellerth have to prove on remand? Will an employee who has been threatened by a harassing supervisor with adverse employment action always satisfy the Court's requirement that "the conduct must be severe or pervasive" to constitute a hostile work environment? What will Burlington have to prove to avoid liability? Is the dissent correct in asserting that "the Court barely attempts to define" the defense? What standard would the dissent adopt?

FARAGHER V. CITY OF BOCA RATON
524 u.s. 775 (1998)

JUSTICE SOUTER delivered the opinion of the Court.

This case calls for identification of the circumstances under which an employer may be held liable under Title VII for the acts of a supervisory employee whose sexual harassment of subordinates has created a hostile work environment amounting to employment discrimination. We hold that an employer is vicariously liable for actionable discrimination caused by a supervisor, but subject to an affirmative defense looking to the reasonableness of the employer's conduct as well as that of a plaintiff victim.

I

Between 1985 and 1990, while attending college, petitioner Beth Ann Faragher worked part time and during the summers as an ocean lifeguard for the Marine Safety Section of the Parks and Recreation Department of respondent, the City of Boca Raton, Florida (City). During this period, Faragher's immediate supervisors were Bill Terry, David Silverman, and Robert Gordon. In June 1990, Faragher resigned.

In 1992, Faragher brought an action against Terry, Silverman, and the City, asserting claims under Title VII, 42 U.S.C. § 1983, and Florida law. So far as it concerns the Title VII claim, the complaint alleged that Terry and Silverman created a 'sexually hostile atmosphere' at the beach by repeatedly subjecting Faragher and other female lifeguards to 'uninvited and offensive touching,' by making lewd remarks, and by speaking of women in offensive terms. The complaint contained specific allegations that Terry once said that he would never promote a woman to the rank of lieutenant, and that Silverman had said to Faragher, 'Date me or clean the toilets for a year.'

In February 1986, the City adopted a sexual harassment policy, which it stated in a memorandum from the City Manager addressed to all employees. In May 1990, the City revised the policy and reissued a statement of it. Although the City may actually have circulated the memos and statements to some employees, it completely failed to disseminate its policy among employees of the Marine Safety Section, with the result that Terry, Silverman, Gordon, and many lifeguards were unaware of it.

From time to time over the course of Faragher's tenure at the Marine Safety Section, between 4 and 6 of the 40 to 50 lifeguards were women. During that 5-year period, Terry repeatedly touched the bodies of female employees without invitation, would put his arm around Faragher, with his hand on her buttocks, and once made contact with another female lifeguard in a motion of sexual simulation. He made crudely demeaning references to women generally, and once commented disparagingly on Faragher's shape. During a job interview with a woman he hired as a lifeguard, Terry said that the female lifeguards had sex with their male counterparts and asked whether she would do the same.

Silverman behaved in similar ways. He once tackled Faragher and remarked that, but for a physical characteristic he found unattractive, he would readily have had sexual relations with her. Another time, he pantomimed an act of oral sex. Within earshot of the female lifeguards, Silverman made frequent, vulgar references to women and sexual matters, commented on the bodies of female lifeguards and beachgoers, and at least twice told female lifeguards that he would like to engage in sex with them.

Faragher did not complain to higher management about Terry or Silverman. . . . In April 1990, however, two months before Faragher's resignation, Nancy Ewanchew, a former lifeguard, wrote to Richard Bender, the City's Personnel Director, complaining that Terry and Silverman had harassed her and other female lifeguards. Following investigation of this complaint, the City found that Terry and Silverman had behaved improperly, reprimanded them, and required them to choose between a suspension without pay or the forfeiture of annual leave.

On the basis of these findings, the District Court concluded that the conduct of Terry and Silverman was discriminatory harassment sufficiently serious to alter the conditions of Faragher's employment and constitute an abusive working environment. A panel of the Court of Appeals for the Eleventh Circuit reversed the judgment against the City.

II

A

[The] standards for judging hostility are sufficiently demanding to ensure that Title VII does not become a 'general civility code.' Properly applied, they will filter out complaints attacking 'the ordinary tribulations of the workplace, such as the sporadic use of abusive language, gender-related jokes, and occasional teasing.' We have made it clear that conduct must be extreme to amount to a change in the terms and conditions of employment, and the Courts of Appeals have heeded this view.

While indicating the substantive contours of the hostile environments forbidden by Title VII, our cases have established few definite rules for determining when an employer will be liable for a discriminatory environment that is otherwise actionably abusive.

B

The Court of Appeals rejected vicarious liability on the part of the City insofar as it might rest on the concluding principle set forth in § 219(2)(d) of the Restatement, that an employer 'is not subject to liability for the torts of his servants acting outside the scope of their employment unless . . . the servant purported to act or speak on behalf of the principal and there was reliance on apparent authority, or he was aided in accomplishing the tort by the existence of the agency relation.' Faragher points to several ways in which the agency relationship aided Terry and Silverman in carrying out their harassment. She argues that in general offending supervisors can abuse their authority to keep subordinates in their presence while they make offensive statements, and that they implicitly threaten to misuse their supervisory powers to deter any resistance or complaint. Thus, she maintains that power conferred on Terry and Silverman by the City enabled them to act for so long without provoking defiance or complaint.

We agree with Faragher that in implementing Title VII it makes sense to hold an employer vicariously liable for some tortious conduct of a supervisor made possible by abuse of his supervisory authority, and that the aided-by-agency-relation principle embodied in § 219(2)(d) of the Restatement provides an appropriate starting point for determining liability for the kind of harassment presented here. Several courts, indeed, have noted what Faragher has argued, that there is a sense in which a harassing supervisor is always assisted in his misconduct by the supervisory relationship. The agency relationship affords contact with an employee subjected to a supervisor's sexual harassment, and the victim may well be reluctant to accept the risks of blowing the whistle on a superior.

When a person with supervisory authority discriminates in the terms and conditions of subordinates' employment, his actions necessarily draw upon his superior position over the people who report to him, or those under them, whereas an employee generally cannot check a supervisor's abusive conduct the same way that she might deal with abuse from a co-worker. When a fellow employee harasses, the victim can walk away or tell the offender where to go, but it may be difficult to offer such responses to a supervisor, whose 'power to supervise— [which may be] to hire and fire, and to set work schedules and pay rates—does not disappear . . . when he chooses to harass through insults and offensive gestures rather than directly with threats of firing or promises of promotion.' Estrich, *Sex at Work*, 43 STAN. L. REV. 813, 854 (1991). Recognition of employer liability when discriminatory misuse of supervisory authority alters the terms and conditions of a victim's employment is underscored by the fact that the employer has a greater opportunity to guard against misconduct by supervisors than by common workers; employers have greater opportunity and incentive to screen them, train them, and monitor their performance. In sum, there are good reasons for vicarious liability for misuse of supervisory authority.

Although Title VII seeks 'to make persons whole for injuries suffered on account of unlawful employment discrimination,' its 'primary objective,' like that of any statute meant to influence primary conduct, is not to provide redress but to avoid harm. As long ago as 1980, the Equal Employment Opportunity Commission (EEOC), charged with the enforcement of Title VII, adopted regulations advising employers to 'take all steps necessary to prevent sexual harassment from occurring, such as . . . informing employees of their right to raise and how to raise the issue of harassment.'. . . and in 1990 the Commission issued a policy statement enjoining employers to establish a complaint procedure 'designed to encourage victims of harassment to come forward [without requiring] a victim to complain first to the offending supervisor.' EEOC Policy Guidance on Sexual Harassment, 8 FEP Manual 405:6699 (Mar. 19, 1990). It would therefore implement clear statutory policy and complement the Government's Title VII enforcement efforts to recognize the employer's affirmative obligation to prevent violations and give credit here to employers who make reasonable efforts to discharge their duty. Indeed, a theory of vicarious liability for misuse of supervisory power would be at odds with the statutory policy if it failed to provide employers with some such incentive.

The requirement to show that the employee has failed in a coordinate duty to avoid or mitigate harm reflects an equally obvious policy imported from the general theory of damages, that a victim has a duty 'to use such means as are reasonable under the circumstances to avoid or minimize the damages' that result from violations of the statute. An employer may, for example, have provided a proven, effective mechanism for reporting and resolving complaints of sexual harassment, available to the employee without undue risk or expense. If the plaintiff unreasonably failed to avail herself of the employer's preventive or remedial apparatus, she should not recover damages that could have been avoided if she had done so. If the victim could have avoided harm, no liability should be found against the employer who had taken reasonable care, and if damages could reasonably have been mitigated no award against a liable employer should reward a plaintiff for what her own efforts could have avoided.

In order to accommodate the principle of vicarious liability for harm caused by misuse of supervisory authority, as well as Title VII's equally basic policies of encouraging forethought by employers and saving action by objecting employees, we adopt the following holding in this case and in *Burlington Industries, Inc. v. Ellerth*, also decided today. An employer is subject to vicarious liability to a victimized employee for an actionable hostile environment created by a supervisor with immediate (or successively higher) authority over the employee. When no tangible employment action is taken, a defending employer may raise an affirmative defense to liability or damages, subject to proof by a preponderance of the evidence, *see* FED. RULE. CIV. PROC. 8(c). The defense comprises two necessary elements: (a) that the employer exercised reasonable care to prevent and correct promptly any sexually harassing behavior, and (b) that the plaintiff employee unreasonably failed to take advantage of any preventive or corrective opportunities provided by the employer or to avoid harm otherwise. While proof that an employer had promulgated an antiharassment policy with complaint procedure is not necessary in every instance as a matter of law, the need for a stated policy suitable to the employment circumstances may appropriately be addressed in any case when litigating the first element of the defense. And while proof that an employee failed to fulfill the corresponding obligation of reasonable care to avoid harm is not limited to showing an unreasonable failure to use any complaint procedure provided by the employer, a demonstration of such failure will normally suffice to satisfy the employer's burden under the second element of the defense. No affirmative defense is available, however, when the supervisor's harassment culminates in a tangible employment action, such as discharge, demotion, or undesirable reassignment.

Applying these rules here, we believe that the judgment of the Court of Appeals must be reversed. The District Court found that the degree of hostility in the work environment rose to the actionable level and was attributable to Silverman and Terry. It is undisputed that these supervisors 'were granted virtually unchecked authority' over their subordinates, 'directly controll[ing] and supervis[ing] all aspects of [Faragher's] day-to-day activities.' It is also clear that Faragher and her colleagues were 'completely isolated from the City's higher management.' The City did not seek review of these findings.

While the City would have an opportunity to raise an affirmative defense if there were any serious prospect of its presenting one, it appears from the record that any such avenue is closed. The District Court found that the City had entirely failed to disseminate its policy against sexual harassment among the beach employees and that its officials made no attempt to keep track of the conduct of supervisors like Terry and Silverman. The record also makes clear that the City's policy did not include any assurance that the harassing supervisors could be bypassed in registering complaints. Under such circumstances, we hold as a matter of law that the City could not be found to have exercised reasonable care to prevent the supervisors' harassing conduct. Unlike the employer of a small workforce, who might expect that sufficient care to prevent tortious behavior could be exercised informally, those responsible for city operations could not reasonably have thought that precautions against hostile environments in any one of many departments in far-flung locations could be effective without communicating some formal policy against harassment, with a sensible complaint procedure.

The City points to nothing that might justify a conclusion by the District Court on remand that the City had exercised reasonable care. Nor is there any reason to remand for consideration of Faragher's efforts to mitigate her own damages, since the award to her was solely nominal.

NOTES AND QUESTIONS

1. What agency theory does the Court rely upon in imposing vicarious liability on an employer for a supervisor's harassing conduct? What rationale does the Court give for adopting an affirmative defense?

2. Why couldn't the city utilize the affirmative defense in this case? If an employer has no sexual harassment policy, but it acts promptly to correct a supervisor's misconduct, will liability still be imposed? Has such an employer taken steps to "prevent" harassment? If the employer acts reasonably both to prevent and to correct harassment, but the employee has also acted reasonably in promptly reporting the harassment, may the employer nonetheless be held liable for a supervisor's misconduct?

3. What will Faragher have to prove to succeed on her §1983 suit against her supervisors and the city?

4. **Supervisors:** In *Faragher*, the Court noted that "an employee who controls work assignments and schedules certainly may possess 'immediate,' day-to-day authority over a victim notwithstanding a lack of power to take tangible employment actions." Despite this language, the Supreme Court in *Vance v. Ball State University*, 570 U.S. 421 (2013), narrowly defined the term "supervisor" as someone "empowered by the employer to take tangible employment actions against the victim." Rejecting the EEOC Enforcement Guidance, which tied a supervisor's status to her ability to exercise significant direction over another's daily work, the Court reasoned that the EEOC definition was "murky" and filled with "ambiguity." In contrast, its bright-line rule ensured that decisions as to the status of the harasser are made before litigation has commenced or possibly at summary judgment.

Defending his ruling, Justice Alito explained that the statements in *Faragher* were not intended to provide a definitive answer as to who qualified as a supervisor, Congress did not use the term "supervisor" in Title VII, and the focus in *Ellerth* on vicarious liability was tied to the theory that only the conduct of harassers who can effect "a significant change in employment status such as hiring, firing, failing to promote, reassignment with significantly different responsibilities, or a decision causing a significant change in benefits," justifies the vicarious liability rule. In a footnote,

Justice Alito suggested that Silverman's comment to Faragher, "Date me or clean the toilets for a year," likely would have constituted significantly different responsibilities for a lifeguard, whose job is to guard the beach, and if that reassignment had "economic consequences" it might constitute a tangible employment action. Thus, the definition of supervisor will not leave employees unprotected against harassment because they can still utilize the vicarious liability rule where threats translate into economic consequences.

5. **Coworker harassment:** Justice Alito, in *Vance*, noted that his definition of "supervisor" "will not leave employees unprotected against harassment by coworkers who possess the authority to inflict psychological injury by assigning unpleasant tasks or by altering the work environment in objectionable ways." Rather, victims could still prevail by showing that an employer was negligent in permitting this harassment to occur: "Evidence that an employer did not monitor the workplace, failed to respond to complaints, failed to provide a system for registering complaints, or effectively discouraged complaints from being filed would be relevant." Further, "the jury should be instructed that the nature and degree of authority wielded by the harasser is an important fact to be considered in determining whether the employer was negligent."

The EEOC Guidelines instruct that negligence will be found "where the employer or its agents or supervisory employees, knows or should have known of the conduct unless it can show that it took immediate and appropriate corrective action." Thus, it is necessary for an employee to complain to someone within the company who has authority to address complaints to give the employer the opportunity to take corrective action. Many questions have arisen as to what constitutes an appropriate response. In general, remedial action will be deemed deficient if it is untimely or if it is not reasonably calculated to end the harassment.

The negligence standard has also been used by courts where the harassment is perpetrated by non-employees, such as customers, suppliers, clients, or independent contractors. If an employer knows or should know of the harassment, yet takes no action to stop it, it may be held liable.

PENNSYLVANIA STATE POLICE V. SUDERS
542 U.S. 129 (2004)

Justice GINSBURG delivered the opinion of the Court.

Plaintiff-respondent Nancy Drew Suders alleged sexually harassing conduct by her supervisors, officers of the Pennsylvania State Police (PSP), of such severity she was forced to resign. The question presented concerns the proof burdens parties bear when a sexual harassment/

constructive discharge claim of that character is asserted under Title VII of the Civil Rights Act of 1964.

To establish hostile work environment, plaintiffs like Suders must show harassing behavior "sufficiently severe or pervasive to alter the conditions of [their] employment." Beyond that, we hold, to establish "constructive discharge," the plaintiff must make a further showing: She must show that the abusive working environment became so intolerable that her resignation qualified as a fitting response. An employer may defend against such a claim by showing both (1) that it had installed a readily accessible and effective policy for reporting and resolving complaints of sexual harassment, and (2) that the plaintiff unreasonably failed to avail herself of that employer-provided preventive or remedial apparatus. This affirmative defense will not be available to the employer, however, if the plaintiff quits in reasonable response to an employer-sanctioned adverse action officially changing her employment status or situation, for example, a humiliating demotion, extreme cut in pay, or transfer to a position in which she would face unbearable working conditions. In so ruling today, we follow the path marked by our 1998 decisions in *Burlington Industries* and *Faragher*.

I

In March 1998, the PSP hired Suders as a police communications operator for the McConnellsburg barracks. Suders' supervisors were Sergeant Eric D. Easton, Station Commander at the McConnellsburg barracks, Patrol Corporal William D. Baker, and Corporal Eric B. Prendergast. Those three supervisors subjected Suders to a continuous barrage of sexual harassment that ceased only when she resigned from the force.

Easton "would bring up [the subject of] people having sex with animals" each time Suders entered his office. He told Prendergast, in front of Suders, that young girls should be given instruction in how to gratify men with oral sex. Easton also would sit down near Suders, wearing spandex shorts, and spread his legs apart. Apparently imitating a move popularized by television wrestling, Baker repeatedly made an obscene gesture in Suders' presence by grabbing his genitals and shouting out a vulgar comment inviting oral sex. Baker made this gesture as many as five-to-ten times per night throughout Suders' employment at the barracks.

In June 1998, Prendergast accused Suders of taking a missing accident file home with her. After that incident, Suders approached the PSP's Equal Employment Opportunity Officer, Virginia Smith-Elliott, and told her she "might need some help." Smith-Elliott gave Suders her telephone number, but neither woman followed up on the conversation. On August 18, 1998, Suders contacted Smith-Elliott again, this time stating that she was being harassed and was afraid. Smith-Elliott told Suders to file a complaint, but did not tell her how to obtain the necessary form. Smith-Elliott's response and the manner in which it was conveyed appeared to Suders insensitive and unhelpful.

Two days later, Suders' supervisors arrested her for theft, and Suders resigned from the force. The theft arrest occurred in the following circumstances. Suders had several times taken a computer-skills exam to satisfy a PSP job requirement. Each time, Suders' supervisors told her that she had failed. Suders one day came upon her exams in a set of drawers in the women's locker room. She concluded that her supervisors had never forwarded the tests for grading and that their reports of her failures were false. Regarding the tests as her property, Suders removed them from the locker room. Upon finding that the exams had been removed, Suders' supervisors devised a plan to arrest her for theft. The officers dusted the drawer in which the exams had been stored with a theft-detection powder that turns hands blue when touched. As anticipated by Easton, Baker, and Prendergast, Suders attempted to return the tests to the drawer, whereupon her hands turned telltale blue. The supervisors then apprehended and handcuffed her, photographed her blue hands, and commenced to question her. Suders had previously prepared a written resignation, which she tendered soon after the supervisors detained her. Nevertheless, the supervisors initially refused to release her. Instead, they brought her to an interrogation room, gave her warnings under *Miranda*, and continued to question her. Suders reiterated that she wanted to resign, and Easton then let her leave. The PSP never brought theft charges against her.

In September 2000, Suders sued the PSP in Federal District Court, alleging that she had been subjected to sexual harassment and constructively discharged, in violation of Title VII of the Civil Rights Act of 1964.

II

Under the constructive discharge doctrine, an employee's reasonable decision to resign because of unendurable working conditions is assimilated to a formal discharge for remedial purposes. The inquiry is objective: Did working conditions become so intolerable that a reasonable person in the employee's position would have felt compelled to resign?

Although this Court has not had occasion earlier to hold that a claim for constructive discharge lies under Title VII, we have recognized constructive discharge in the labor-law context. Furthermore, we have stated that "Title VII is violated by either explicit or constructive alterations in the terms or conditions of employment." *Ellerth*. We agree with the lower courts and the EEOC that Title VII encompasses employer liability for a constructive discharge.

This case concerns an employer's liability for one subset of Title VII constructive discharge claims: constructive discharge resulting from sexual harassment, or "hostile work environment," attributable to a supervisor. . . . The constructive discharge here at issue stems from, and can be regarded as an aggravated case of, sexual harassment or hostile work environment. For an atmosphere of sexual harassment or hostility to be actionable, the offending behavior "must be sufficiently severe or pervasive to alter the conditions of the victim's employment and create an abusive working environment." A hostile-environment constructive discharge claim entails something more: A plaintiff who advances such a compound claim must show working conditions so intolerable that a reasonable person would have felt compelled to resign.

Suders' claim is of the same genre as the hostile work environment claims the Court analyzed in *Ellerth* and *Faragher*. Essentially, Suders presents a "worse case" harassment scenario, harassment ratcheted up to the breaking point. Like the harassment considered in our pathmarking decisions, harassment so intolerable as to cause a resignation may be effected through co-worker conduct, unofficial supervisory conduct, or official company acts. Unlike an actual termination, which is *always* effected through an official act of the company, a constructive discharge need not be. A constructive discharge involves both an employee's decision to leave and precipitating conduct: The former involves no official action; the latter, like a harassment claim without any constructive discharge assertion, may or may not involve official action.

To be sure, a constructive discharge is functionally the same as an actual termination in damages-enhancing respects. But when an official act does not underlie the constructive discharge, the *Ellerth* and *Faragher* analysis, we here hold, calls for extension of the affirmative defense to the employer. As those leading decisions indicate, official directions and declarations are the acts most likely to be brought home to the employer, the measures over which the employer can exercise greatest control. Absent "an official act of the enterprise," as the last straw, the employer ordinarily would have no particular reason to suspect that a resignation is not the typical kind daily occurring in the work force. And as *Ellerth* and *Faragher* further point out, an official act reflected in company records—a demotion or a reduction in compensation, for example—shows "beyond question" that the supervisor has used his managerial or controlling position to the employee's disadvantage. Absent such an official act, the extent to which the supervisor's misconduct has been aided by the agency relation, is less certain. That uncertainty, our precedent establishes, justifies affording the employer the chance to establish, through the *Ellerth/Faragher* affirmative defense, that it should not be held vicariously liable.

Following *Ellerth* and *Faragher,* the plaintiff who alleges no tangible employment action has the duty to mitigate harm, but the defendant bears the burden to allege and prove that the plaintiff failed in that regard. The plaintiff might elect to allege facts relevant to mitigation in her pleading or to present those facts in her case in chief, but she would do so in anticipation of the employer's affirmative defense, not as a legal requirement.

We agree with the Third Circuit that the case, in its current posture, presents genuine issues of material fact concerning Suders' hostile work environment and constructive discharge claims.[11] We hold, however, that the Court of Appeals erred in declaring the affirmative defense described in *Ellerth* and *Faragher* never available in constructive discharge cases. Accordingly, we vacate the Third Circuit's judgment and remand the case for further proceedings consistent with this opinion.

NOTES AND QUESTIONS

1. Was Suders subjected to a hostile work environment? What factors will be examined in making this determination? Review *Harris, supra.*

---

11 Although most of the discriminatory behavior Suders alleged involved unofficial conduct, the events surrounding her computer-skills exams were less obviously unofficial.

2. **Constructive discharge:** How will it be decided whether a "constructive discharge" has occurred? Some courts had required proof of the employer's intent to force the employee to resign. However, in *Green v. Brennan*, 136 S. Ct. 1769 (2016), the Court rejected this "intent" requirement, holding it suffices that an employee prove circumstances of discrimination so intolerable that a reasonable person would resign, i.e., an objective intolerability standard.

3. Assuming Suders was constructively discharged, will PSP be permitted to assert an affirmative defense? Was Suders subjected to an "official" act before her resignation? *See* footnote 11. Did Suders act reasonably in not pursing relief internally before tendering her resignation? Who will carry the burden of proof on this issue?

4. **Equal Protection:** The appellate courts have unanimously ruled that sexual harassment by a state employer constitutes sex discrimination for purposes of the equal protection clause of the Fourteenth Amendment. Creating abusive conditions for female employees and not for male employees is discrimination. The courts have generally applied Title VII standards in determining whether the harassment is sufficiently severe or pervasive to be actionable. There are, however, some differences:

First, the ultimate inquiry is whether the sexual harassment constitutes intentional discrimination. This differs from the inquiry under Title VII as to whether or not the sexual harassment altered the conditions of the victim's employment. That standard comes from the regulations promulgated under Title VII. *See Vinson.* Second, a plaintiff can make an ultimate showing of sex discrimination either by showing that sexual harassment that is attributable to the employer under § 1983 amounted to intentional sex discrimination or by showing that the conscious failure of the employer to protect the plaintiff from the abusive conditions created by fellow employees amounted to intentional discrimination. It is a good defense if the employer can show that the harassment suffered by the plaintiff was directed at the plaintiff because of factors personal to her and not because she is a woman.

Under § 1983, actions of a state entity's employees are attributed to the state entity itself if those actions are in furtherance of the entity's "policy or custom." A single act of a sufficiently high-ranking policy-maker is sufficient to establish an entity's policy or custom. A policy or custom may also be established by proving that the conduct complained of is a "well-settled . . . practice . . . even though such a custom has not received formal approval through the body's decision making channels." An entity may be liable even for "informal actions, if they reflect a general policy, custom, or pattern of official conduct which even tacitly encourages conduct depriving citizens of their constitutionally protected rights."

Bohen v. City of East Chicago, Indiana, 799 F.2d 1180 (7th Cir. 1986). How does the employer liability issue discussed in *Vinson* differ from that in a § 1983 equal protection case? May a supervisor or co-worker who engaged in harassment be held individually liable for damages under § 1983? Will qualified immunity shield these defendants? When is a city liable under Title VII, as compared to § 1983, for harassment by a supervisor or a coworker? How does the existence of a policy prohibiting harassment affect the issue?

Problem: Twenty-Three

Sparks was employed by Pilot Freight as a billing clerk in its Duluth, Georgia trucking terminal from May 1983 until March 1984. In February 1984, Pilot Freight promoted Dennis Long, a former sales manager in the Atlanta terminal, to the position of terminal manager of the Duluth terminal. As terminal manager, Long held the highest position in the Duluth terminal and, according to Sparks, had authority to exercise virtually unfettered discretion over personnel matters, including the hiring and firing of employees. The only Pilot Freight employees superior to Long were stationed in Pilot Freight's headquarters in North Carolina.

Sparks alleges that shortly after Long arrived in Duluth he began to harass her. One of the earliest instances occurred when Long called her into his office and asked her if she was married or had a boyfriend, and if she could become pregnant. Sparks claims that after she was promoted to general secretary, with Long as her boss, in March 1984, Long's unwelcomed sexual harassment of her continued. This harassment included such acts as: putting his hands on Sparks to rub her shoulders or "fool with" and smell her hair; repeatedly inquiring into Sparks' personal life; on one occasion asking her if he could come to her house with a bottle of wine, and, having been refused, calling out to her over the public address system as she was leaving the office stating that this was her "last chance;" making threatening remarks to Sparks, such as "you'd better be nice to me," "your fate is in my hands," "revenge is the name of the game;" and at least one other remark that the district court concluded was "too sexually explicit" to repeat. Sparks did not notify any of Long's superiors at Pilot Freight that he was harassing her.

In May 1984, Pilot Freight closed its Duluth terminal. Long was transferred to Atlanta where he resumed his former job as sales manager. Sparks and several other employees also were transferred to the Atlanta terminal. The manager of the Atlanta terminal was Carl Connell.

Sparks was given a job as a billing clerk on the night shift where she worked for three days. On the fourth day Sparks allegedly called the office and asked Connell's secretary, Hilda Tatum, whether she could change her working hours. Later that day Tatum called Sparks back to tell Sparks that she could not change her hours. Sparks allegedly responded that she could not come in that night because she was sick. Curtis Turner, a male billing clerk, also called in sick that day. The following day, Connell called Sparks at home several hours before her shift was to begin and fired her. Turner was not fired. Sparks was replaced by John Briscoe, a billing clerk who had been laid off when the Duluth terminal was closed.

Sparks filed the instant action against Pilot Freight, alleging three violations of Title VII. Her first claim is that during her tenure at the Duluth terminal she was subject to hostile working environment sexual harassment by her boss, Dennis Long. Her second two claims relate to her discharge: the first being that Connell engaged in unlawful disparate treatment because of sex when he discharged her and not Turner; the second is that her discharge resulted from *quid pro quo* sexual harassment in that Long induced Connell to fire her in retaliation for her refusal to accede to his sexual demands.

The district court granted summary judgment for Pilot Freight on all three claims.

1. Under *Meritor*, will Sparks survive summary judgment on her hostile environment sexual harassment claim? Apply the *Harris* factors. Is the standard under *Harris* an objective or subjective one—if objective, should the standard be that of a reasonable person or the reasonable woman? In *Oncale, supra*, Justice Scalia looked to the "reasonable person in plaintiff's position."

2. The trial court granted summary judgment against Sparks on both her hostile environment and discharge claims, holding that she failed to establish Pilot Freight's liability for Long's action because she never notified anyone of the harassment. Evaluate this ruling.

3. What steps would you take as a manager to reduce exposure to liability for sexual harassment claims?

4. DEFENSES

a. Bona Fide Occupational Qualification

DOTHARD V. RAWLINSON
433 U.S. 321 (1977)

Mr. Justice STEWART delivered the opinion of the Court.

Appellee Dianne Rawlinson sought employment with the Alabama Board of Corrections as a prison guard, called in Alabama a "correctional counselor." After her application was rejected, she brought this class suit under Title VII of the Civil Rights Act of 1964, and under 42 U.S.C. § 1983, alleging that she had been denied employment because of her sex in violation of federal law.

[The Court initially invalidated height and weight requirements which had a disparate impact on women, but which were not shown to constitute a business necessity.]

Unlike the statutory height and weight requirements, Regulation 204 explicitly discriminates against women on the basis of their sex.16 In defense of this overt discrimination, the appellants rely on § 703(e) of Title VII, which permits sex-based discrimination "in those certain instances where . . . sex . . . is a bona fide occupational qualification reasonably necessary to the normal operation of that particular business or enterprise."

The District Court rejected the bona-fide-occupational qualification (BFOQ) defense, relying on the virtually uniform view of the federal courts that § 703(e) provides only the narrowest of exceptions to the general rule requiring equality of employment opportunities. In *Diaz v. Pan American World Airways*, 442 F.2d 385, 388, the Court of Appeals for the Fifth Circuit held that "discrimination based on sex is valid only when the *essence* of the business operation would be undermined by not hiring members of one sex exclusively." In an earlier case, the same court said that an employer should rely on the BFOQ exception only by proving "that he had reasonable cause to believe, that is, a factual basis for believing, that all or substantially all women would be unable to perform safely and efficiently the duties of the job involved." But whatever the verbal formulation, the federal courts have agreed that it is impermissible under Title VII to refuse to hire an individual woman or man on the basis of stereotyped characterizations of the sexes, and the District Court in the present case held in effect that Regulation 204 is based on just such stereotypical assumptions.

We are persuaded—by the restrictive language of § 703(e), the relevant legislative history, and the consistent interpretation of the Equal Employment Opportunity Commission—that the BFOQ exception was in fact meant to be an extremely narrow exception to the general prohibition of discrimination on the basis of sex. In the particular factual circumstances of this case, however, we conclude that the District Court erred in rejecting the State's contention that Regulation 204 falls within the narrow ambit of the BFOQ exception.

The environment in Alabama's penitentiaries is a peculiarly inhospitable one for human beings of whatever sex. Indeed, a Federal District Court has held that the conditions of confinement in the prisons of the State, characterized by "rampant violence" and a "jungle atmosphere," are constitutionally intolerable. The record in the present case shows that because of inadequate staff and facilities, no attempt is made in the four maximum-security male penitentiaries to classify or segregate inmates according to their offense or level of dangerousness—a procedure that, according to expert testimony, is essential to effective penological administration. Consequently, the estimated 20% of the male prisoners who are sex offenders are scattered throughout the penitentiaries' dormitory facilities.

In this environment of violence and disorganization, it would be an oversimplification to characterize Regulation 204 as an exercise in "romantic paternalism." In the usual case, the argument that a particular job is too dangerous for women may appropriately be met by the rejoinder that it is the purpose of Title VII to allow the individual woman to make that choice for herself. More is at stake in this case, however, than an individual woman's decision to weigh and accept the risks of employment in a "contact" position in a maximum-security male prison.

The essence of a correctional counselor's job is to maintain prison security. A woman's relative ability to maintain order in a male, maximum-security, unclassified penitentiary of the type Alabama now runs could be directly reduced by her womanhood. There is a basis in fact for expecting that sex offenders who have criminally assaulted women in the past would be moved to do so again if access to women were established within the prison. There would also be a real risk that other inmates, deprived of a normal heterosexual environment, would assault women guards because they were women. In a prison system where violence is the order of the day, where inmate access to guards is facilitated by dormitory living arrangements, where every institution is understaffed, and where a substantial portion of the inmate population is composed of sex offenders mixed at random with other prisoners, there are few visible deterrents to inmate assault on women custodians.

Appellee Rawlinson's own expert testified that dormitory housing for aggressive inmates poses a greater security problem than single-cell lockups, and further testified that it would be unwise to use women as guards in a prison where even 10% of the inmates had been convicted of sex crimes and were not segregated from other prisoners.[23] The likelihood that inmates would assault a woman because she was woman would pose a real threat not only to the victim of the assault but also to the basic control of the penitentiary and protection of its inmates and the other personnel. The employee's very womanhood would thus directly undermine her capacity to provide the security that is the essence of a correctional counselor's responsibility.

There was substantial testimony from experts on both sides of this litigation that the use of women as guards in "contact" positions under existing conditions in Alabama maximum-security male penitentiaries would pose a substantial security problem, directly linked to the sex of the prison guard. On the basis of that evidence, we conclude that the District Court was in error in ruling that being male is not a bona fide occupational qualification for the job of correctional counselor in a "contact" position in an Alabama male maximum-security penitentiary.

NOTES AND QUESTIONS

1. Assume Ms. Rawlinson stands 6'2" and weighs 200 lbs. Should it suffice that an employer can show that "substantially" all women would be unable to perform a job safely? What happened to the focus in *Manhart* and *Teal* on the individual? What if a woman is willing to assume the risks entailed with the job and is physically able to do so?

2. Should an employer be able to rely upon its failure to provide a safe work environment as a justification for discrimination? *See* footnote 23. Isn't there a reasonable non-discriminatory alternative means to accomplish the state's safety goal, *i.e.*, segregation of sex offenders from the general prison population? Is this required by Title VII?

   Note that under disproportionate impact analysis once the employer establishes that the qualification is job-related or a business necessity, the employee may still prevail if it is demonstrated that the justifications are pretextual, and this may be done by showing the existence of less discriminatory alternatives. Is this also true under a BFOQ defense? If not, doesn't the statutory language, which requires that the qualification be "reasonably necessary" to the normal operation of the business,

---

23 Alabama's penitentiaries are evidently not typical. Appellee Rawlinson's two experts testified that in a normal, relatively stable maximum security prison—characterized by control over the inmates, reasonable living conditions, and segregation of dangerous offenders—women guards could be used effectively and beneficially. Similarly, an *amicus* brief filed by the State of California attests to that State's success in using women guards in all-male penitentiaries.

incorporate this restriction, *i.e.*, is a flat ban on women "reasonably necessary" where a segregated prison population would substantially reduce the problem?

3. Based on the statutory language in 42 U.S.C. § 2000e-2(e), may **race** ever be a BFOQ? What about a situation involving an all-white prison population which would react violently to an African-American guard, causing security problems? Could the prison survive a Title VII challenge? What analysis would the Court use? What about a claim under § 1983 and the equal protection clause?

4. Can **religion** ever be a BFOQ? Note that in light of the general exemption for religious discrimination on the part of religious institutions, this becomes an issue only where a secular employer wishes to discriminate for arguably bona fide reasons. Consider, for example, the helicopter company that refuses to hire non-Muslims to fly into Mecca due to the practice of beheading those who enter their Holy City. *See Kern v. Dynalectron Co.*, 577 F. Supp. 1196 (N.D. Tex. 1983).

5. In *Hardin v. Stynchcombe*, 691 F.2d 1364 (11th Cir. 1982), plaintiffs challenged a policy of assigning only male deputy sheriffs to work in the male section of the jail and hiring female deputy sheriffs only when contact positions were available in the female section of the jail. Defendants claimed that this assignment policy served to protect the privacy rights of the inmates. In rejecting this defense, the court explained that

> Sex based discrimination is valid only if the essence of the business would be undermined by not hiring members of one sex exclusively. Defendants can satisfy that burden only by proving they had a factual basis for believing that all or substantially all women would be unable to safely and efficiently perform the duties of the job. In addition, defendants bear the burden of proving that because of the nature of the operation of the business they could not rearrange job responsibilities in a way that would eliminate the clash between the privacy interests of the inmates and the employment opportunities of female deputy sheriffs.

The court determined that assignments could be rotated or modified to "avoid the clash between privacy rights and equal employment opportunities." Did the court give sufficient weight to privacy concerns? Isn't it the "essence" of a prison to secure offenders without violating their constitutional rights, including the right to privacy? Did the Supreme Court in *Dothard* consider the existence of alternatives? Should an employer have to accommodate a woman's request for special duties so as to protect inmate privacy?

6. Outside the prison context, should more serious weight be given to individual privacy? May a hospital, for example, exclude male nurses from the obstetrics department?

May a residential home for women deny employment to a male aide where 22 of the 30 residents object to having their personal needs attended to by a male? Since male patients are frequently subjected to invasions of privacy by female nurses, and female patients experience the same from male doctors, do any of these arguments merit much credence? Do they simply perpetuate gender stereotypes?

7. Should "customer preference" ever be a BFOQ? What about a company that denies a woman a position which involves substantial dealings with South American businesses, because of foreign prejudice against women in business? Or an airline which presents psychological data showing that both male and female passengers feel more safe and more comfortable with female rather than male attendants? *See Diaz v. Pan American World Airways* cited in *Criswell, infra* n. 18. Does the gender-based job qualification go to "the essence of the business" in either case? Does pleasing customers go to the essence of a for-profit business?

Compare the Supreme Court's interpretation of the identical BFOQ defense in the Age Discrimination in Employment Act:

WESTERN AIR LINES V. CRISWELL
472 u.s. 400 (1984)

Justice STEVENS delivered the opinion of the Court.

The petitioner, Western Air Lines, Inc., requires that its flight engineers retire at age 60. Although the Age Discrimination in Employment Act of 1967 (ADEA), 29 U.S.C. §§ 621-634, generally prohibits mandatory retirement before age 70, the Act provides an exception "where age is a bona fide occupational qualification [BFOQ] reasonably necessary to the normal operation of the particular business." A jury concluded that Western's mandatory retirement rule did not qualify as a BFOQ even though it purportedly was adopted for safety reasons. The question here is whether the jury was properly instructed on the elements of the BFOQ defense.

I

In its commercial airline operations, Western operates a variety of aircraft, including the Boeing 727 and the McDonnell-Douglas DC-10. These aircraft require three crew members in the cockpit: a captain, a first officer, and a flight engineer. "The 'captain' is the pilot and controls the aircraft. He is responsible for all phases of its operation. The 'first officer' is the copilot and assists the captain. The 'flight engineer' usually monitors a side-facing instrument panel. He does not operate the flight controls unless the captain and the first officer become incapacitated."

A regulation of the Federal Aviation Administration (FAA) prohibits any person from serving as a pilot or first officer on a commercial flight "if that person has reached his 60th birthday." The FAA has justified the retention of mandatory retirement for pilots on the theory that "incapacitating medical events" and "adverse psychological, emotional, and physical changes" occur as a consequence of aging. "The inability to detect or predict with precision an individual's risk of sudden or subtle incapacitation, in the face of known age-related risks, counsels against relaxation of the rule."

At the same time, the FAA has refused to establish a mandatory retirement age for flight engineers. "While a flight engineer has important duties which contribute to the safe operation of the airplane, he or she may not assume the responsibilities of the pilot in command." Moreover, available statistics establish that flight engineers have rarely been a contributing cause or factor in commercial aircraft "accidents" or "incidents."

In 1978, respondents Criswell and Starley were captains operating DC-10s for Western. Both men celebrated their 60th birthdays in July 1978. Under the collective-bargaining agreement in effect between Western and the union, cockpit crew members could obtain open positions by bidding in order of seniority. In order to avoid mandatory retirement under the FAA's under-age-60 rule for pilots, Criswell and Starley applied for reassignment as flight engineers. Western denied both requests, ostensibly on the ground that both employees were members of the company's retirement plan which required all crew members to retire at age 60. For the same reason, respondent Ron, a career flight engineer, was also retired in 1978 after his 60th birthday.

Criswell, Starley, and Ron brought this action against Western contending that the under-age-60 qualification for the position of flight engineer violated the ADEA. In the District Court, Western defended, in part, on the theory that the age-60 rule is a BFOQ "reasonably necessary" to the safe operation of the airline. All parties submitted evidence concerning the nature of the flight engineer's tasks, the physiological traits required to perform them, and the availability of those traits among persons over age 60.

As the District Court summarized, the evidence at trial established that the flight engineer's "normal duties are less critical to the safety of flight than those of a pilot." The flight engineer, however, of course, might cause considerable disruption in the event of his own medical emergency.

The actual capabilities of persons over age 60, and the ability to detect disease or a precipitous decline in their faculties, were the subject of conflicting medical testimony. Western's expert witness, a former FAA Deputy Federal Air Surgeon, was especially concerned about the possibility of a "cardiovascular event" such as a heart attack. He testified that "with advancing age the likelihood of onset of disease increases and that in persons over age 60 it could not be predicted whether and when such diseases would occur."

The plaintiff's experts, on the other hand, testified that physiological deterioration is caused by disease, not aging, and that "it was feasible to determine on the basis of individual medical examinations whether flight deck crew members including those over age 60, were physically qualified to continue to fly."

III

In *Usery v. Tamiami Trail Tours, Inc.*, the Court of Appeals for the Fifth Circuit was called upon to evaluate the merits of a BFOQ defense to a claim of age discrimination. Tamiami Trail Tours, Inc., had a policy of refusing to hire persons over age 40 as intercity bus drivers. At trial, the bus company introduced testimony supporting its theory that the hiring policy was a BFOQ based upon safety considerations—the need to employ persons who have a low risk of accidents. In evaluating this contention, the Court of Appeals drew on its Title VII precedents, and concluded that two inquiries were relevant.

First, the court recognized that some job qualifications may be so peripheral to the central mission of the employer's business that no age discrimination can be "reasonably *necessary* to the normal operation of the particular business."18 The bus company justified the age qualification for hiring its drivers on safety considerations, but the court concluded that this claim was to be evaluated under an objective standard:

> [T]he job qualifications which the employer invokes to justify his discrimination must be *reasonably necessary* to the essence of his business—here, the *safe* transportation of bus passengers from one point to another. The greater the safety factor, measured by the likelihood of harm and the probable severity of that harm in case of an accident, the more stringent may be the job qualifications designed to insure safe driving.

This inquiry "adjusts to the safety factor" by ensuring that the employer's restrictive job qualifications are "reasonably necessary" to further the overriding interest in public safety.

Second, the court recognized that the ADEA requires that age qualifications be something more than "convenient" or "reasonable"; they must be "reasonably necessary . . . to the particular business," and this is only so when the employer is compelled to rely on age as a proxy for the safety-related job qualifications validated in the first inquiry. This showing could be made in two ways. The employer could establish that it "'had reasonable cause to believe, that is, a factual basis for believing, that all or substantially all [persons over the age qualifications] would be unable to perform safely and efficiently the duties of the job involved.'" In *Tamiami*, the employer did not seek to justify its hiring qualification under this standard.

Alternatively, the employer could establish that age was a legitimate proxy for the safety-related job qualifications by proving that it is "'impossible or highly impractical'" to deal with the older employees on an individual basis. "One method by which the employer can carry this burden is to establish that some members of the discriminated-against class possess a trait precluding safe and efficient job performance that cannot be ascertained by means other than knowledge of the applicant's membership in the class." In *Tamiami*, the medical evidence on this point was conflicting, but the District Court had found that individual examinations could not determine which individuals over the age of 40 would be unable to operate the buses safely. The Court of Appeals found that this finding of fact was not "clearly erroneous," and affirmed the District Court's judgment for the bus company on the BFOQ defense.

Congress, in considering the 1978 Amendments, implicitly endorsed the two-part inquiry identified by the Fifth Circuit in the *Tamiami* case. The Senate Committee Report expressed concern that the amendment prohibiting mandatory retirement in accordance with pension plans might imply that mandatory retirement could not be a BFOQ:

> For example, in certain types of particularly arduous law enforcement activity, there may be a factual basis for believing that substantially all employees above a specified age would be unable to continue to perform safely and efficiently the duties of their particular jobs, and it may be impossible or impractical to determine through medical examinations, periodic reviews of current job performance and other objective tests the employees' capacity or ability to continue to perform the jobs safely and efficiently.

Every Court of Appeals that has confronted a BFOQ defense based on safety considerations has analyzed the problem consistently with the *Tamiami* standard. An EEOC regulation embraces the same criteria.[24] Considering the narrow language of the BFOQ exception, the parallel treatment of such questions under Title VII, and the uniform application of the standard by the federal courts, the EEOC and Congress, we conclude that this two-part inquiry properly identifies the relevant considerations for resolving a BFOQ defense to an age-based qualification purportedly justified by considerations of safety.

IV

[Western proposed in a jury instruction that it should succeed on the BFOQ defense by simply proving that it had a "rational basis in fact" for believing the use of flight attendants over age 60 would increase the likelihood of risk to its passengers. Relying on the language and legislative history of the ADEA, the Court rejected use of the "rational basis" standard in favor of a more stringent test.]

Unless an employer can establish a substantial basis for believing that all or nearly all employees above an age lack the qualifications required for the position, the age selected for mandatory retirement less than 70 must be an age at which it is highly impractical for the employer to insure by individual testing that its employees will have the necessary qualifications for the job.

When an employee covered by the Act is able to point to reputable businesses in the same industry that choose to eschew reliance on mandatory retirement earlier than age 70, when the employer itself relies on individualized testing in similar circumstances, and when the

---

24 46 Fed. Reg. 47727 (1981), 29 C.F.R. §1625.6(b) (1984):
An employer asserting a BFOQ defense has the burden of proving that (1) the age limit is reasonably necessary to the essence of the business, and either (2) that all or substantially all individuals excluded from the job involved are in fact disqualified, or (3) that some of the individuals so excluded possess a disqualifying trait that cannot be ascertained except by reference to age. If the employer's objective in asserting a BFOQ is the goal of public safety, the employer must prove that the challenged practice does indeed effectuate that goal and that there is no acceptable alternative which would better advance it or equally advance it with less discriminatory impact.

administrative agency with primary responsibility for maintaining airline safety has determined that individualized testing is not impractical for the relevant position, the employer's attempt to justify its decision on the basis of the contrary opinion of experts—solicited for the purposes of litigation—is hardly convincing on any objective standard short of complete deference. Even in cases involving public safety, the ADEA plainly does not permit the trier of fact to give complete deference to the employer's decision.

NOTES AND QUESTIONS

1. What standard does the Supreme Court adopt regarding the BFOQ defense? Does it differ from the test enunciated in *Dothard*?

2. Study the EEOC Regulation at footnote 24. Must an employer also prove the absence of less discriminatory alternatives to succeed on a BFOQ defense? Note again that the statutory language requires the restriction be "reasonably necessary" to the business. Does the existence of reasonable alternatives always negate the "necessity" requirement? If so, would it be a "reasonable alternative" to require Western to conduct costly medical examinations every month to assure the continued physical ability of older employees to perform?

3. Should the standard be relaxed where safety concerns are implicated? Compare *New York Transit Authority v. Beazer, supra* Ch. III, where the Supreme Court appeared to use a more deferential approach to the business necessity defense where the employer argued a safety justification for its exclusionary policy.

PROBLEM: TWENTY-FOUR

Plaintiffs Ute Harriss and Margaret Feather brought this class action against Pan American World Airways charging it with violations of §§ 703(a)(1) and (2) of Title VII of the Civil Rights Act of 1964. They sued on behalf of themselves and other Pan Am female flight attendants. They contend that Pan Am violated Title VII by: (1) requiring that female flight attendants take maternity leave immediately upon learning of their pregnancy; (2) requiring that they not return to work until sixty days after the birth of the child; and (3) denying them accrual of seniority after the first ninety days of their leave.

Pan Am introduced evidence that a pregnant flight attendant during the first and second trimesters was more likely than a non-pregnant female to be incapacitated during an emergency evacuation, *i.e.*, her ability to respond might be impaired by fatigue, nausea, vomiting, or spontaneous abortion. Further, medical data indicates that it generally takes at least six (6) weeks for the body to recover from childbirth and for normal bodily functions to resume.

Pan Am classifies pregnancy leave as a discretionary leave of absence, which is granted by Pan Am for personal reasons. Employees on discretionary leave accrue seniority for a maximum of ninety days while those on non-discretionary medical leave may accrue seniority for as long as three years. Feather and Harriss lost approximately 130 days of seniority as a result of their mandatory maternity leaves.

1. What standard must the employer meet to justify this maternity policy? Consider the mandatory leave policy, the 60-day post-delivery rule, and the loss of seniority benefits.

1. Should the Airline be required to assign a cabin attendant ground duties even if it proves that non-pregnancy is a BFOQ for flight duty?

INTERNATIONAL UNION, UNITED AUTOMOBILE, AEROSPACE & AGRICULTURAL WORKERS OF AMERICA, UAW V. JOHNSON CONTROLS, INC.

499 U.S. 187 (1991)

Justice BLACKMUN delivered the opinion of the Court.

In this case we are concerned with an employer's gender-based fetal-protection policy. May an employer exclude a fertile female employee from certain jobs because of its concern for the health of the fetus the woman might conceive?

I

Respondent Johnson Controls, Inc., manufactures batteries. In the manufacturing process, the element lead is a primary ingredient. Occupational exposure to lead entails health risks, including the risk of harm to any fetus carried by a female employee.

Before the Civil Rights Act of 1964 became law, Johnson Controls did not employ any woman in a battery-manufacturing job. In June 1977, however, it announced its first official policy concerning its employment of women in lead-exposure work: "[P]rotection of the health of the unborn child is the immediate and direct responsibility of the prospective parents. While the medical profession and the company can support them in the exercise of this responsibility, it cannot assume it for them without simultaneously infringing their rights as persons."

Consistent with that view, Johnson Controls "stopped short of excluding women capable of bearing children from lead exposure," but emphasized that a woman who expected to have a child should not choose a job in which she would have such exposure.

Five years later, in 1982, Johnson Controls shifted from a policy of warning to a policy of exclusion. Between 1979 and 1983, eight employees became pregnant while maintaining blood lead levels in excess of 30 micrograms per deciliter. This appeared to be the critical level noted by the Occupational Health and Safety Administration (OSHA) for a worker who was planning to have a family. *See* 29 C.F.R. § 1910.1025 (1989). The company responded by announcing a broad exclusion of women from jobs that exposed them to lead:

[I]t is [Johnson Controls'] policy that women who are pregnant or who are capable of bearing children will not be placed into jobs involving lead exposure or which could expose them to lead through the exercise of job bidding, bumping, transfer or promotion rights.

The policy defined "women . . . capable of bearing children" as "[a]ll women except those whose inability to bear children is medically documented."

III

The bias in Johnson Controls' policy is obvious. Fertile men, but not fertile women, are given a choice as to whether they wish to risk their reproductive health for a particular job. Section 703(a) of the Civil Rights Act of 1964, as amended, 42 U.S.C. § 2000e-2(a), prohibits sex-based classifications in terms and conditions of employment, in hiring and discharging decisions, and in other employment decisions that adversely affect an employee's status. Respondent's fetal-protection policy explicitly discriminates against women on the basis of their sex. The policy excludes women with childbearing capacity from lead-exposed jobs and so creates a facial classification based on gender.

Nevertheless, the Court of Appeals assumed, as did the two appellate courts who already had confronted the issue, that sex-specific fetal-protection policies do not involve facial discrimination. These courts analyzed the policies as though they were facially neutral, and had only a discriminatory effect upon the employment opportunities of women. Consequently, the courts looked to see if each employer in question had established that its policy was justified as a business necessity. The business necessity standard is more lenient for the employer than the statutory BFOQ defense. The court assumed that because the asserted reason for the sex-based exclusion (protecting women's unconceived offspring) was ostensibly benign, the policy was not sex-based discrimination. That assumption, however, was incorrect.

First, Johnson Controls' policy classifies on the basis of gender and childbearing capacity, rather than fertility alone. Respondent does not seek to protect the unconceived children of all its employees. Despite evidence in the record about the debilitating effect of lead exposure on the male reproductive system, Johnson Controls is concerned only with the harms that may befall the unborn offspring of its female employees. Johnson Controls' policy is facially discriminatory because it requires only a female employee to produce proof that she is not capable of reproducing.

Our conclusion is bolstered by the Pregnancy Discrimination Act of 1978 (PDA), 42 U.S.C. § 2000e(k), in which Congress explicitly provided that, for purposes of Title VII, discrimination "on the basis of sex" includes discrimination "because of or on the basis of pregnancy, childbirth, or related medical conditions." In its use of the words "capable of bearing children" in the 1982 policy statement as the criterion for exclusion, Johnson Controls explicitly classifies on the basis of potential for pregnancy. Under the PDA, such a classification must be regarded, for Title VII purposes, in the same light as explicit sex discrimination. Respondent has chosen to treat all its female employees as potentially pregnant; that choice evinces discrimination on the basis of sex.

We concluded above that Johnson Controls' policy is not neutral because it does not apply to the reproductive capacity of the company's male employees in the same way as it applies to that of the females. Moreover, the absence of a malevolent motive does not convert a facially discriminatory policy into a neutral policy with a discriminatory effect. Whether an employment practice involves disparate treatment through explicit facial discrimination does not depend on why the employer discriminates but rather on the explicit terms of the discrimination.

We hold that Johnson Controls' fetal-protection policy is sex discrimination forbidden under Title VII unless respondent can establish that sex is a "bona fide occupational qualification."

IV

The BFOQ defense is written narrowly, and this Court has read it narrowly. Our emphasis on the restrictive scope of the BFOQ defense is grounded on both the language and the legislative history of § 703.

The wording of the BFOQ defense contains several terms of restriction that indicate that the exception reaches only special situations. The statute thus limits the situations in which discrimination is permissible to "certain instances" where sex discrimination is "reasonably necessary" to the "normal operation" of the "particular" business. Each one of these terms—certain, normal, particular—prevents the use of general subjective standards and favors an objective, verifiable requirement. But the most telling term is "occupational"; this indicates that these objective, verifiable requirements must concern job-related skills and aptitudes.

The concurrence defines "occupational" as meaning related to a job. According to the concurrence, any discriminatory requirement imposed by an employer is "job-related" simply because the employer has chosen to make the requirement a condition of employment. In effect, the concurrence argues that sterility may be an occupational qualification for women because Johnson Controls has chosen to require it. This reading of "occupational" renders the word mere surplusage. "Qualification" by itself would encompass an employer's idiosyncratic requirements. By modifying "qualification" with "occupational," Congress narrowed the term to qualifications that affect an employee's ability to do the job.

Johnson Controls argues that its fetal-protection policy falls within the so-called safety exception to the BFOQ. Our cases have stressed that discrimination on the basis of sex because of safety concerns is allowed only in narrow circumstances. In *Dothard v. Rawlinson*, this Court indicated that danger to a woman herself does not justify discrimination. We there allowed the employer to hire only male guards in contact areas of maximum security male penitentiaries only because more was at stake than the "individual woman's decision to weigh and accept the risks of employment." We found sex to be a BFOQ inasmuch as the employment of a female guard would create real risks of safety to others if violence broke out because the guard was a woman. Sex discrimination was tolerated because sex was related to the guard's ability to do the job—maintaining prison security. We also required in *Dothard* a high correlation between sex and ability to perform job functions and refused to allow employers to use sex as a proxy for strength although it might be a fairly accurate one.

The concurrence ignores the "essence of the business" test and so concludes that "the safety to fetuses in carrying out the duties of battery manufacturing is as much a legitimate concern as is safety to third parties in guarding prisons (*Dothard*) or flying airplanes (*Criswell*)." By limiting its discussion to cost and safety concerns and rejecting the "essence of the business" test that our case law has established, the concurrence seeks to expand what is now the narrow BFOQ defense. Third-party safety considerations properly entered into the BFOQ analysis in *Dothard* and *Criswell* because they went to the core of the employee's job performance. The unconceived fetuses of Johnson Controls' female employees, however, are neither customers nor third parties whose safety is essential to the business of battery manufacturing. No one can disregard the possibility of injury to future children; the BFOQ, however, is not so broad that it transforms this deep social concern into an essential aspect of batterymaking.

Our case law, therefore, makes clear that the safety exception is limited to instances in which sex or pregnancy actually interferes with the employee's ability to perform the job. This approach is consistent with the language of the BFOQ provision itself, for it suggests that permissible distinctions based on sex must relate to ability to perform the duties of the job.

The PDA's amendment to Title VII contains a BFOQ standard of its own: unless pregnant employees differ from others "in their ability or inability to work," they must be "treated the same" as other employees "for all employment-related purposes." 42 U.S.C. § 2000e(k). This language clearly sets forth Congress' remedy for discrimination on the basis of pregnancy and potential pregnancy. Women who are either pregnant or potentially pregnant must be treated like others "similar in their ability . . . to work." In other words, women as capable of doing their jobs as their male counterparts may not be forced to choose between having a child and having a job.

We conclude that the language of both the BFOQ provision and the PDA which amended it, as well as the legislative history and the case law, prohibit an employer from discriminating against a woman because of her capacity to become pregnant unless her reproductive potential prevents her from performing the duties of her job. We reiterate our holdings in *Criswell* and *Dothard* that an employer must direct its concerns about a woman's ability to perform her job safely and efficiently to those aspects of the woman's job-related activities that fall within the "essence" of the particular business.

V

We have no difficulty concluding that Johnson Controls cannot establish a BFOQ. Fertile women, as far as appears in the record, participate in the manufacture of batteries as efficiently as anyone else. Johnson Controls' professed moral and ethical concerns about the welfare of the next generation do not suffice to establish a BFOQ of female sterility. Decisions about the welfare of future children must be left to the parents who conceive, bear, support, and raise them rather than to the employers who hire those parents. Congress has mandated this choice through Title VII, as amended by the Pregnancy Discrimination Act. Johnson Controls has attempted to exclude women because of their reproductive capacity. Title VII and the PDA simply do not allow a woman's dismissal because of her failure to submit to sterilization.

Johnson Controls argues that it must exclude all fertile women because it is impossible to tell which women will become pregnant while working with lead. This argument is somewhat academic in light of our conclusion that the company may not exclude fertile women at all; it perhaps is worth noting, however, that Johnson Controls has shown no "factual basis for believing that all or substantially all women would be unable to perform safely and efficiently the duties of the job involved." Even on this sparse record, it is apparent that Johnson Controls is concerned about only a small minority of women. Of the eight pregnancies reported among the female employees, it has not been shown that any of the babies have birth defects or other abnormalities. The record does not reveal the birth rate for Johnson Controls' female workers but national statistics show that approximately nine percent of all fertile women become pregnant each year. The birthrate drops to two percent for blue collar workers over age 30. Johnson Controls' fear of prenatal injury, no matter how sincere, does not begin to show that substantially all of its fertile women employees are incapable of doing their jobs.

VI

A word about tort liability and the increased cost of fertile women in the workplace is perhaps necessary. One of the dissenting judges in this case expressed concern about an employer's tort liability and concluded that liability for a potential injury to a fetus is a social cost that Title VII does not require a company to ignore.

More than 40 States currently recognize a right to recover for a prenatal injury based either on negligence or on wrongful death. According to Johnson Controls, however, the company complies with the lead standard developed by OSHA and warns its female employees about the damaging effects of lead. It is worth noting that OSHA gave the problem of lead lengthy consideration and concluded that "there is no basis whatsoever for the claim that women of childbearing age should be excluded from the workplace in order to protect the fetus or the course of pregnancy." 43 Fed. Reg. 52952, 52966 (1978). Without negligence, it would be difficult for a court to find liability on the part of the employer. If, under general tort principles, Title VII bans sex-specific fetal-protection policies, the employer fully informs the woman of the risk, and the employer has not acted negligently, the basis for holding an employer liable seems remote at best.

The tort-liability argument reduces to two equally unpersuasive propositions. First, Johnson Controls attempts to solve the problem of reproductive health hazards by resorting to an exclusionary policy. Title VII plainly forbids illegal sex discrimination as a method of diverting attention from an employer's obligation to police the workplace. Second, the specter of an award of damages reflects a fear that hiring fertile women will cost more. The extra cost of employing members of one sex, however, does not provide an affirmative Title VII defense for a discriminatory refusal to hire members of that gender. *See Manhart.* Indeed, in passing the PDA,

Congress considered at length the considerable cost of providing equal treatment of pregnancy and related conditions, but made the "decision to forbid special treatment of pregnancy despite the social costs associated therewith."

We, of course, are not presented with, nor do we decide, a case in which costs would be so prohibitive as to threaten the survival of the employer's business. We merely reiterate our prior holdings that the incremental cost of hiring women cannot justify discriminating against them.

VII

Our holding today that Title VII, as so amended, forbids sex-specific fetal-protection policies is neither remarkable nor unprecedented. Concern for a woman's existing or potential offspring historically has been the excuse for denying women equal employment opportunities. Congress in the PDA prohibited discrimination on the basis of a woman's ability to become pregnant. We do no more than hold that the Pregnancy Discrimination Act means what it says.

It is no more appropriate for the courts than it is for individual employers to decide whether a woman's reproductive role is more important to herself and her family than her economic role. Congress has left this choice to the woman as hers to make.

NOTES AND QUESTIONS

1. Does discrimination against "fertile women" fall within the definition of sex discrimination, as modified by the PDA? If discrimination based on "potential for pregnancy" is a PDA violation, does the exclusion of prescription birth control from an employer's health insurance plan that offers comprehensive coverage for other prescription drugs violate the PDA? Review *Newport News v. EEOC, supra.*

2. Should the Court have remanded to allow Johnson Controls to substantiate its claim that lead exposure disproportionately affects fetuses as compared to adult reproductive capacity, thus justifying a gender-based policy?

3. Has the majority precluded an employer's claim that the exclusion of fertile women from certain jobs is reasonably necessary to avoid substantial tort liability? Doesn't the "normal operation" of a business entail concerns regarding injury to third parties? Should increased cost of doing business not be a defense unless so prohibitive as to threaten a company's survival? Note that four Justices, concurring in the Court's holding, specifically rejected this restrictive interpretation of the BFOQ defense.

4. If this was a government-operated plant sued under the equal protection clause, would discrimination against fertile women be actionable? *See General Electric v. Gilbert, supra.* Could the government meet the "fair and substantial relation to an important government interest" test imposed by the Equal Protection Clause?

5. What if Johnson amends its policy to limit the restriction to pregnant women? Does this alter the Title VII analysis?

6. What if the policy is amended to bar all fertile employees—a facially neutral policy? What analysis would be used?

7. It is estimated that, had the Court sustained the Johnson Controls policy, as many as twenty million hazardous jobs could be closed to fertile women. Feminists argue that employers are not appropriate decisionmakers because they tend to exclude women from hazardous jobs only when women are "marginal" workers. If employers can decide when to restrict women's job opportunities because of fetal risk, women will continue to face identical or equivalent risks in women's jobs, *i.e.*, as nurses and dental hygienists exposed to anesthetic gases or teachers and hospital workers exposed to bacteria and viruses which may cause congenital abnormalities in children. They will simply be exposed to such risks for the lower pay and weaker medical benefits typically associated with female positions. In deciding the risk to future potential fetuses, shouldn't a woman be permitted to weigh not only her own needs for income and medical insurance, but also those of her living children and her other economic responsibilities? Arguably, it is not in the interest of living or potential children to have their mothers working in low paid, hazardous women's jobs with weak medical benefits rather than higher paid, hazardous men's jobs with more significant benefits. *See* Wendy Williams, *Title VII and Fetal Health*, 69 GEO. L.J. 641 (1981).

b.   Bona Fide Seniority System

INTERNATIONAL BROTHERHOOD OF TEAMSTERS V. UNITED STATES
431 U.S. 324 (1977)

Mr. Justice STEWART delivered the opinion of the Court.

This litigation brings here several important questions under Title VII of the Civil Rights Act of 1964. The issues grow out of alleged unlawful employment practices engaged in by an employer and a union. The employer is a common carrier of motor freight with nationwide operations, and the union represents a large group of its employees. The District Court and the Court of Appeals held that the employer had violated Title VII by engaging in a pattern and practice of employment discrimination against Negroes and Spanish-surnamed Americans, and that the union had violated the Act by agreeing with the employer to create and maintain a seniority system that perpetuated the effects of past racial and ethnic discrimination.

II

For purposes of calculating benefits, such as vacations, pensions, and other fringe benefits, an employee's seniority under this system runs from the date he joins the company, and takes into account his total service in all jobs and bargaining units. For competitive purposes, however, such as determining the order in which employees may bid for particular jobs, are laid off, or are recalled from layoff, it is bargaining-unit seniority that controls. Thus, a line driver's seniority, for purposes of bidding for particular runs and protection against layoff, takes into account only the length of time he has been a line driver at a particular terminal. The practical effect is that a city driver or serviceman who transfers to a line-driver job must forfeit all the competitive seniority he has accumulated in his previous bargaining unit and start at the bottom of the line drivers' "board."

The vice of this arrangement, as found by the District Court and the Court of Appeals, was that it "locked" minority workers into inferior jobs and perpetuated prior discrimination by discouraging transfers to jobs as line drivers. While the disincentive applied to all workers, including whites, it was Negroes and Spanish-surnamed persons who, those courts found, suffered the most because many of them had been denied the equal opportunity to become line drivers when they were initially hired, whereas whites either had not sought nor were refused line-driver positions for reasons unrelated to their race or national origin.

The linchpin of the theory embraced by the District Court and the Court of Appeals was that a discriminatee who must forfeit his competitive seniority in order finally to obtain a line-driver job will never be able to "catch up" to the seniority level of his contemporary who was not subject to discrimination.[27] Accordingly, this continued, built-in disadvantage to the prior discriminatee who transfers to a line-driver job was held to constitute a continuing violation of Title VII, for which both the employer and the union who jointly created and maintain the seniority system were liable.

The union, while acknowledging that the seniority system may in some sense perpetuate the effects of prior discrimination, asserts that the system is immunized from a finding of illegality by reason of § 703(h) of Title VII, 42 U.S.C. § 2000e-2(h), which provides in part:

> Notwithstanding any other provision of this subchapter, it shall not be an unlawful employment practice for an employer to apply different standards of compensation, or different terms, conditions, or privileges of employment pursuant to a bona fide seniority system, provided that such differences are not the result of an intention to discriminate because of race or national origin.

---

27 An example would be a Negro who was qualified to be a line driver in 1958 but who, because of his race, was assigned instead a job as a city driver, and is allowed to become a line driver only in 1971. Because he loses his competitive seniority when he transfers jobs, he is forever junior to white line drivers hired between 1958 and 1970. The whites, rather than the Negro, will henceforth enjoy the preferable runs and the greater protection against layoff. Although the original discrimination occurred in 1958—before the effective date of Title VII—the seniority system operates to carry the effects of the earlier discrimination into the present.

It argues that the seniority system in this case is "bona fide" within the meaning of § 703(h) when judged in light of its history, intent, application and all of the circumstances under which it was created and is maintained. More specifically, the union claims that the central purpose of § 703(h) is to ensure that mere perpetuation of *pre-Act* discrimination is not unlawful under Title VII. And, whether or not § 703(h) immunizes the perpetuation of post-Act discrimination, the union claims that the seniority system in this litigation has no such effect. Its position in this Court, as has been its position throughout this litigation, is that the seniority system presents no hurdle to post-Act discriminatees who seek retroactive seniority to the date they would have become line drivers but for the company's discrimination. Indeed, the union asserts that under its collective-bargaining agreements the union will itself take up the cause of the post-Act victim and attempt, through grievance procedures, to gain for him full "make whole" relief, including appropriate seniority.

The Government responds that a seniority system that perpetuates the effects of prior discrimination—pre-Act or post-Act—can never be "bona fide" under § 703(h); at a minimum Title VII prohibits those applications of a seniority system that perpetuate the effects on incumbent employees of prior discriminatory job assignments.

The issues thus joined are open ones in this Court. We considered § 703(h) in *Franks v. Bowman Transportation Co.*, but there decided only that § 703(h) does not bar the award of retroactive seniority to job applicants who seek relief from an employer's post-Act hiring discrimination. We stated that "the thrust of [§ 703(h)] is directed toward defining what is and what is not an illegal discriminatory practice in instances in which the post-Act operation of a seniority system is challenged as perpetuating the effects of discrimination occurring prior to the effective date of the Act." Beyond noting the general purpose of the statute, however, we did not undertake the task of statutory construction required in this litigation.

(1)

Because the company discriminated both before and after the enactment of Title VII, the seniority system is said to have operated to perpetuate the effects of both pre-and post-Act discrimination. Post-Act discriminatees, however, may obtain full "make whole" relief, including retroactive seniority under *Franks v. Bowman*, without attacking the legality of the seniority system as applied to them. *Franks* made clear and the union acknowledges that retroactive seniority may be awarded as relief from an employer's discriminatory hiring and assignment policies even if the seniority system agreement itself makes no provision for such relief. Here the Government has proved that the company engaged in a post-Act pattern of discriminatory hiring, assignment, transfer, and promotion policies. Any Negro or Spanish-surnamed American injured by those policies may receive all appropriate relief as a direct remedy for this discrimination.

(2)

What remains for review is the judgment that the seniority system unlawfully perpetuated the effects of *pre-Act* discrimination. We must decide, in short, whether § 703(h) validates otherwise bona fide seniority systems that afford no constructive seniority to victims discriminated against prior to the effective date of Title VII, and it is to that issue that we now turn.

The primary purpose of Title VII was "to assure equality of employment opportunities and to eliminate those discriminatory practices and devices which have fostered racially stratified job environments to the disadvantage of minority citizens." To achieve this purpose, Congress "proscribe[d] not only overt discrimination but also practices that are fair in form, but discriminatory in operation." Thus, the Court has repeatedly held that a *prima facie* Title VII violation may be established by policies or practices that are neutral on their face and in intent but that nonetheless discriminate in effect against a particular group.

One kind of practice "fair in form, but discriminatory in operation" is that which perpetuates the effects of prior discrimination. As the Court held in *Griggs*: "Under the Act, practices, procedures, or tests neutral on their face, and even neutral in terms of intent, cannot be maintained if they operate to 'freeze' the status quo of prior discriminatory employment practices."

Were it not for § 703(h), the seniority system in this case would seem to fall under the *Griggs* rationale. The heart of the system is its allocation of the choicest jobs, the greatest protection against layoffs, and other advantages to those employees who have been line drivers for the longest time. Where, because of the employer's prior intentional discrimination, the line drivers with the longest tenure are without exception white, the advantages of the seniority system flow disproportionately to them and away from Negro and Spanish-surnamed employees who might by now have enjoyed those advantages had not the employer discriminated before the passage of the Act. This disproportionate distribution of advantages does in a very real sense "operate to 'freeze' the status quo of prior discriminatory employment practices." But both the literal terms of § 703(h) and the legislative history of Title VII demonstrate that Congress considered this very effect of many seniority systems and extended a measure of immunity to them.

Throughout the initial consideration of H.R. 7152, later enacted as the Civil Rights Act of 1964, critics of the bill charged that it would destroy existing seniority rights. The consistent response of Title VII's congressional proponents and of the Justice Department was that seniority rights would not be affected, even where the employer had discriminated prior to the Act.

> Title VII would have no effect on seniority rights existing at the time it takes effect. If, for example, a collective bargaining contract provides that in the event of layoffs, those who were hired last must be laid off first, such a provision would not be affected in the least by title VII. *This would be true even in the case where owing to discrimination prior to the effective date of the title, white workers had more seniority than Negroes.* (emphasis added).

While these statements were made before § 703(h) was added to Title VII, they are authoritative indicators of that section's purpose. Section 703(h) was enacted as part of the

Mansfield-Dirksen compromise substitute bill that cleared the way for the passage of Title VII. The drafters of the compromise bill stated that one of its principal goals was to resolve the ambiguities in the House-passed version of H.R. 7152. It is inconceivable that § 703(h), as part of a compromise bill, was intended to vitiate the earlier representations of the Act's supporters by increasing Title VII's impact on seniority systems.

To be sure, § 703(h) does not immunize all seniority systems. It refers only to "bona fide" systems, and a proviso requires that any differences in treatment not be "the result of an intention to discriminate because of race . . . or national origin. . . ." But our reading of the legislative history compels us to reject the Government's broad argument that no seniority system that tends to perpetuate pre-Act discrimination can be "bona fide." To accept the argument would require us to hold that a seniority system becomes illegal simply because it allows the full exercise of the pre-Act seniority rights of employees of a company that discriminated before Title VII was enacted. It would place an affirmative obligation on the parties to the seniority agreement to subordinate those rights in favor of the claims of pre-Act discriminatees without seniority. The consequence would be a perversion of the congressional purpose. We cannot accept the invitation to disembowel § 703(h) by reading the words "bona fide" as the Government would have us do. Accordingly, we hold that an otherwise neutral, legitimate seniority system does not become unlawful under Title VII simply because it may perpetuate pre-Act discrimination. Congress did not intend to make it illegal for employees with vested seniority rights to continue to exercise those rights, even at the expense of pre-Act discriminatees.

(3)

The seniority system in this litigation is entirely bona fide. It applies equally to all races and ethnic groups. To the extent that it "locks" employees into non-line driver jobs, it does so for all. The city drivers and servicemen who are discouraged from transferring to line-driver jobs are not all Negroes or Spanish-surnamed Americans; to the contrary, the overwhelming majority are white. The placing of line drivers in a separate bargaining unit from other employees is rational, in accord with the industry practice, and consistent with National Labor Relations Board precedents. It is conceded that the seniority system did not have its genesis in racial discrimination, and that it was negotiated and has been maintained free from any illegal purpose. In these circumstances, the single fact that the system extends no retroactive seniority to pre-Act discriminatees does not make it unlawful.

NOTES AND QUESTIONS

1. How can a system which locks in past discrimination be "bona fide?" What did Congress intend by this language? Does the Court's holding in *Franks* that retroactive seniority may be awarded as a remedy for a Title VII violation comport with this intent?

2. Will a seniority system which locks in past discrimination ever be held to violate Title VII? What types of evidence will the plaintiff introduce, and who carries the burden of proof? Is this an affirmative defense, similar to a BFOQ, requiring the employer to prove that its seniority system is bona fide?

3. What if the seniority system had been adopted in 1970, six years after the effective date of Title VII? Following the *Teamsters* decision (in May of 1977), the EEOC on July 12, 1977, issued a Memorandum stating that "discriminatory intent" would be inferred if a discriminatory system is maintained or renegotiated after 1964 when an alternative, less discriminatory system is available. However, the Supreme Court in *American Tobacco Co. v. Patterson*, 456 U.S. 63 (1982), rejected this interpretation:

> On its face § 703(h) makes no distinction between pre- and post-Act seniority systems, just as it does not distinguish between pre- and post Act merit systems or pre- and post Act ability tests. The section does not take the form of a saving clause or a grandfather clause designed to exclude existing practices from the operation of a new rule. Other sections of Title VII enacted by the same Congress contain grandfather clauses, see § 701(b), a difference which increases our reluctance to transform a provision that we have previously described as "defining what is and what is not an illegal discriminatory practice," *Franks v. Bowman Transportation Co.*, from a definitional clause into a grandfather clause.
>
> Under the EEOC's interpretation of the statute, plaintiffs who file a timely challenge to the adoption of a seniority system arguably would prevail in a Title VII action if they could prove that the system would have a discriminatory impact even if it was not purposefully discriminatory. On the other hand, employees who seek redress under Title VII more than 180 days after the adoption of a seniority system—for example, all persons whose employment begins more than 180 days after an employer adopts a seniority system—would have to prove the system was intentionally discriminatory. Yet employees who prevailed by showing that a bona fide seniority system had a discriminatory impact although not adopted with discriminatory intent would not be entitled to an injunction forbidding the application of the system: § 703(h) plainly allows the application of such a seniority system.
>
> A further result of the EEOC's theory would be to discourage unions and employers from modifying pre-Act seniority systems or post-Act systems whose adoption was not timely challenged. Any modification, if timely challenged, would be subject to the *Griggs* standard—even if it benefited persons covered by Title VII—thereby creating an incentive to retain existing systems which enjoy the protection of § 703(h).
>
> Statutes should be interpreted to avoid untenable distinctions and unreasonable results whenever possible. The EEOC's reading of § 703(h) would make it

illegal to adopt, and in practice to apply, seniority systems that fall within the class of systems protected by the provision. We must, therefore, reject such a reading.

In adopting or altering a seniority system post-1964, should an employer be required to establish that a new system that has an adverse impact on a protected group is job-related? If an employer adopts a seniority system, which he knows will perpetuate past discrimination, has he engaged in purposefully discriminatory action? Compare *Personnel Administrator of Mass. v. Feeney*, 442 U.S. 256 (1979), holding that even though the state of Massachusetts adopted an absolute preference for veterans with full knowledge of the adverse impact this would have on women in the state (less than 2% of all women were veterans), it is not guilty of intentional sex discrimination prohibited by the equal protection clause of the Fourteenth Amendment unless the veterans' preference was adopted "because of" and not merely "in spite of" its discriminatory effect on women.

4. Assuming a plaintiff claims a seniority system "had its genesis in intentional race discrimination," how will the statute of limitations question be construed? In *Lorance v. AT&T Technologies, Inc.*, 490 U.S. 900 (1989), the Court held that the statute of limitations for challenging an alleged discriminatorily adopted seniority system begins to run from the date of the signing of an otherwise facially neutral seniority system, even though the effects of that system may not be felt until a later point in time.

This holding was overturned by the Civil Rights Act of 1991, which provides that the triggering date for challenging a seniority system which was adopted for an intentionally discriminatory purpose is either when the system is adopted, or when the individual becomes subject to or is injured by application of the system. *See* 42 U.S.C. § 2000e - 5(e)(2).

PROBLEM: TWENTY-FIVE

Assume you represent a black city driver who was assigned his position in 1968 even though his qualifications were the same as those of a white applicant who was hired on into the higher paid line driver position. This occurred less than a month ago so you are able to file a timely charge of race discrimination regarding this hiring decision. It takes two years to resolve this matter, but eventually the court finds your client was a victim of race discrimination and awards him the line driver position.

1. May the court award your client retroactive seniority back to the 1968 hiring decision? Does § 703(h) and its protection for bona fide seniority systems preclude this result? *See* discussion of *Franks v. Bowman Transportation Co.*

2. What if your client doesn't come to you until one year *after* the hiring decision and thus suit is foreclosed by the statute of limitations? He learns, however, of an opening for line driver, but his transfer will cost him accumulated seniority based on the terms of a seniority system adopted in 1960. Will he be able to successfully challenge the seniority system which has operated to lock blacks into lower paid city driver positions? What analysis under the *Griggs* disparate impact theory? What analysis under § 703(h)?

3. If the employer had simply adopted a flat rule in 1960 prohibiting all transfers, what would the analysis be under Title VII? Analyze post-Civil Rights Act of 1991.

4. Could a black employee terminated because of a departmental seniority rule use § 1981, as amended by the Civil Rights Act of 1991, to challenge a seniority system which locks in past race discrimination?

c.   Reasonable Accommodation of Religious Beliefs

Section 703(a) of title VII prohibits discrimination on the basis of religion. In 1972 Congress added § 701(j), which defines religion to include all aspects of religious observance and practice, and which creates an affirmative defense where an employer can demonstrate that it is unable to reasonably accommodate the employee's religious observance without undue hardship to its business. This provision raises both statutory and constitutional questions. The statutory language raises the question of how much accommodation is reasonable and the related problem of what constitutes undue hardship. In addition, § 701(j) triggers a difficult constitutional question, *i.e.*, at what point does government-required accommodation of religion violate the Establishment Clause? Note the interrelationship between these two issues in that the more accommodation the Act is interpreted to require, the stronger the argument that the Establishment Clause has been violated. As you read the next case, ask whether the underlying constitutional difficulties have affected the Court's interpretation of the statute.

TRANS WORLD AIRLINES, INC. V. HARDISON
432 u.s. 63 (1977)

Mr. Justice WHITE delivered the opinion of the Court.

Section 703(a)(1) of the Civil Rights Act of 1964 makes it an unlawful employment practice for an employer to discriminate against an employee or a prospective employee on the basis of his or her religion. At the time of the events involved here, a guideline of the Equal Employment Opportunity Commission (EEOC), 29 C.F.R. § 1605.1(b) (1968), required, as the Act itself now does, 42 U.S.C. § 2000e(j), that an employer, short of "undue hardship," make "reasonable accommodations" to the religious needs of its employees. The issue in this case is the extent of the employer's obligation under Title VII to accommodate an employee whose religious beliefs prohibit him from working on Saturdays.

I

Petitioner Trans World Airlines (TWA) operates a large maintenance and overhaul base in Kansas City, Mo. On June, 5, 1967, respondent Larry G. Hardison was hired by TWA to work as a clerk in the Stores Department at its Kansas City base. Because of its essential role in the Kansas City operation, the Stores Department must operate 24 hours per day, 365 days per year, and whenever an employee's job in that department is not filled, an employee must be shifted from another department, or a supervisor must cover the job, even if the work in other areas may suffer.

Hardison, like other employees at the Kansas City base, was subject to a seniority system contained in a collective bargaining agreement that TWA maintains with petitioner International Association of Machinists and Aerospace Workers (IAM). The seniority system is implemented by the union steward through a system of bidding by employees for particular shift assignments as they become available. The most senior employees have first choice for job and shift assignments, and the most junior employees are required to work when the union steward is unable to find enough people willing to work at a particular time or in a particular job to fill TWA's needs.

In the spring of 1968 Hardison began to study the religion known as the Worldwide Church of God. One of the tenets of that religion is that one must observe the Sabbath by refraining from performing any work from sunset on Friday until sunset on Saturday. The religion also proscribes work on certain specified religious holidays.

When Hardison informed Everett Kussman, the manager of the Stores Department, of his religious conviction regarding observance of the Sabbath, Kussman agreed that the union steward should seek a job swap for Hardison or a change of days off; that Hardison would have his religious holidays off whenever possible if Hardison agreed to work the traditional holidays when asked; and that Kussman would try to find Hardison another job that would be more compatible with his religious beliefs. The problem was temporarily solved when Hardison transferred to the 11 p.m.-7 a.m. shift. Working this shift permitted Hardison to observe his Sabbath.

The problem soon reappeared when Hardison bid for and received a transfer from Building 1, where he had been employed, to Building 2, where he would work the day shift. The two buildings had entirely separate seniority lists; and while in Building 1 Hardison had sufficient seniority to observe the Sabbath regularly, he was second from the bottom on the Building 2 seniority list.

In Building 2 Hardison was asked to work Saturdays when a fellow employee went on vacation. TWA agreed to permit the union to seek a change of work assignments for Hardison, but the union was not willing to violate the seniority provisions set out in the collective-bargaining contract, and Hardison had insufficient seniority to bid for a shift having Saturdays off.

A proposal that Hardison work only four days a week was rejected by the company. Hardison's job was essential, and on weekends he was the only available person on his shift to perform it. To leave the position empty would have impaired supply shop functions, which were critical to airline operations; to fill Hardison's position with a supervisor or an employee from another area would simply have undermanned another operation; and to employ someone not regularly assigned to work Saturdays would have required TWA to pay premium wages.

When an accommodation was not reached, Hardison refused to report for work on Saturdays. After a hearing, Hardison was discharged on grounds of insubordination for refusing to work during his designated shift.

III

The Court of Appeals held that TWA had not made reasonable efforts to accommodate Hardison's religious needs under the 1967 EEOC guidelines in effect at the time the relevant events occurred. In its view, TWA had rejected three reasonable alternatives, any one of which would have satisfied its obligation without undue hardship. First, within the framework of the seniority system, TWA could have permitted Hardison to work a four-day week, utilizing in his place a supervisor or another worker on duty elsewhere. That this would have caused other shop functions to suffer was insufficient to amount to undue hardship in the opinion of the Court of Appeals. Second—according to the Court of Appeals, also within the bounds of the collective-bargaining contract—the company could have filled Hardison's Saturday shift from other available personnel competent to do the job, of which the court said there were at least 200. That this would have involved premium overtime pay was not deemed an undue hardship. Third, TWA could have arranged a "swap between Hardison and another employee either for another shift or for the Sabbath days." In response to the assertion that this would have involved a breach of the seniority provisions of the contract, the court noted that it had not been settled in the courts whether the required statutory accommodation to religious needs stopped short of transgressing seniority rules, but found it unnecessary to decide the issue because, as the Court of Appeals saw the record, TWA had not sought, and the union had therefore not declined to entertain, a possible variance from the seniority provisions of the collective-bargaining agreement. The company had simply left the entire matter to the union steward who the Court of Appeals said "likewise did nothing."

We disagree with the Court of Appeals in all relevant respects. It is our view that TWA made reasonable efforts to accommodate and that each of the Court of Appeals' suggested alternatives would have been an undue hardship within the meaning of the statute as construed by the EEOC guidelines.

A

It might be inferred from the Court of Appeals' opinion and from the brief of the EEOC in this Court that TWA's efforts to accommodate were no more than negligible. The findings of the

District Court, supported by the record, are to the contrary. In summarizing its more detailed findings, the District Court observed:

> TWA established as a matter of fact that it did take appropriate action to accommodate as required by Title VII. It held several meetings with plaintiff at which it attempted to find a solution to plaintiff's problems. It did accommodate plaintiff's observance of his special religious holidays. It authorized the union steward to search for someone who would swap shifts, which apparently was normal procedure.

It is also true that TWA itself attempted without success to find Hardison another job. The District Court's view was that TWA had done all that could reasonably be expected within the bounds of the seniority system: "Any shift or change was impossible within the seniority framework and the union was not willing to violate the seniority provisions set out in the contract to make a shift or change." As the record shows, Hardison himself testified that Kussman was willing, but the union was not, to work out a shift or job trade with another employee.

B

TWA itself cannot be faulted for having failed to work out a shift or job swap for Hardison. Both the union and TWA had agreed to the seniority system; the union was unwilling to entertain a variance over the objections of men senior to Hardison; and for TWA to have arranged unilaterally for a swap would have amounted to a breach of the collective-bargaining agreement.

Hardison and the EEOC insist that the statutory obligation to accommodate religious needs takes precedence over both the collective-bargaining contract and the seniority rights of TWA's other employees. We agree that neither a collective-bargaining contract nor a seniority system may be employed to violate the statute, but we do not believe that the duty to accommodate requires TWA to take steps inconsistent with the otherwise valid agreement. Collective bargaining, aimed at effecting workable and enforceable agreements between management and labor, lies at the core of our national labor policy, and seniority provisions are universally included in these contracts. Without a clear and express indication from Congress, we cannot agree with Hardison and the EEOC that an agreed-upon seniority system must give way when necessary to accommodate religious observances. The issue is important and warrants some discussion.

Had TWA circumvented the seniority system by relieving Hardison of Saturday work and ordering a senior employee to replace him, it would have denied the latter his shift preference so that Hardison could be given his. The senior employee would also have been deprived of his contractual rights under the collective-bargaining agreement.

Title VII does not contemplate such unequal treatment. The repeated, unequivocal emphasis of both the language and the legislative history of Title VII is on eliminating discrimination in employment, and such discrimination is proscribed when it is directed against majorities as well as minorities. Indeed, the foundation of Hardison's claim is that TWA and IAM engaged in religious *discrimination* in violation of 703(a)(1) when they failed to arrange for him to have

Saturdays off. It would be anomalous to conclude that by "reasonable accommodation" Congress meant that an employer must deny the shift and job preference of some employees, as well as deprive them of their contractual rights, in order to accommodate or prefer the religious needs of others, and we conclude that Title VII does not require an employer to go that far.

Our conclusion is supported by the fact that seniority systems are afforded special treatment under Title VII itself. "[T]he unmistakable purpose of § 703(h) was to make clear that the routine application of a bona fide seniority system would not be unlawful under VII." *Teamsters.* Thus, absent a discriminatory purpose, the operation of a seniority system cannot be an unlawful employment practice even if the system has some discriminatory consequences.

There has been no suggestion of discriminatory intent in this case. "The seniority system was not designed with the intention to discriminate against religion nor did it act to lock members of any religion into a pattern wherein their freedom to exercise their religion was limited. It was coincidental that in plaintiff's case the seniority system acted to compound his problems in exercising his religion."

C

The Court of Appeals also suggested that TWA could have permitted Hardison to work a four-day week if necessary in order to avoid working on his Sabbath. Recognizing that this might have left TWA short-handed on the one shift each week that Hardison did not work, the court still concluded that TWA would suffer no undue hardship if it were required to replace Hardison either with supervisory personnel or with qualified personnel from other departments. Alternatively, the Court of Appeals suggested that TWA could have replaced Hardison on his Saturday shift with other available employees through the payment of premium wages. Both of these alternatives would involve costs to TWA, either in the form of lost efficiency in other jobs or higher wages.

To require TWA to bear more than a *de minimis* cost in order to give Hardison Saturdays off is an undue hardship. Like abandonment of the seniority system, to require TWA to bear additional costs when no such costs are incurred to give other employees the days off that they want would involve unequal treatment of employees on the basis of their religion. By suggesting that TWA should incur certain costs in order to give Hardison Saturdays off the Court of Appeals would in effect require TWA to finance an additional Saturday off and then to choose the employee who will enjoy it on the basis of his religious beliefs. While incurring extra costs to secure a replacement for Hardison might remove the necessity of compelling another employee to work involuntarily in Hardison's place, it would not change the fact that the privilege of having Saturdays off would be allocated according to religious beliefs.

As we have seen, the paramount concern of Congress in enacting Title VII was the elimination of discrimination in employment. In the absence of clear statutory language or legislative history to the contrary, we will not readily construe the statute to require an employer to discriminate against some employees in order to enable others to observe their Sabbath.

1. What steps did TWA actually take to accommodate Hardison's religious needs?

2. How does the Court define "undue hardship"? Why couldn't TWA simply pass the overtime costs onto Hardison—or allow him to transfer back to the first department where he had sufficient seniority to avoid the conflict? Should it matter that such options violate the terms of the collective-bargaining contract? Are all such terms insulated or just the seniority aspects?

3. In the absence of seniority rights protected by a collective-bargaining contract, may an employer show "undue hardship" by pointing to the potential or actual complaints of disgruntled co-employees that mandatory swapping would trigger? Should *Hardison* be read as sounding a death knell to the employer's duty to respect an employee's religious observance?

4. Why does the Court give such a restrictive interpretation to the accommodation requirement? At what point does government-required "accommodation" violate the Establishment Clause? Note that in *Thornton v. Caldor*, 472 U.S. 702 (1985), the Supreme Court held that a Connecticut statute prohibiting an employer from firing an employee for refusing to work on his Sabbath was unconstitutional. The Court reasoned that the law impermissibly advanced a particular religious practice—namely Sabbath observance, and it provided absolute protection without according similar protection for religious and/or ethical beliefs of other employees. In a concurring opinion, Justice O'CONNOR explained that because § 701(j) "calls for reasonable rather than absolute accommodation," it should not be viewed as an unconstitutional "endorsement of religion."

29 C.F.R. PART 1605—GUIDELINES ON DISCRIMINATION BECAUSE OF RELIGION

§ 1605.2—Reasonable accommodation without undue hardship as required by Section 701(j) of Title VII of the Civil Rights Act of 1964.

(c) Reasonable accommodation.

(1) After an employee or prospective employee notifies the employer or labor organization of his or her need for a religious accommodation, the employer or labor organization has an obligation to reasonably accommodate the individual's religious practices. A refusal to accommodate is justified only when an employer or labor organization can demonstrate that an undue hardship would in fact

result from each available alternative method of accommodation. A mere assumption that many more people, with the same religious practices as the person being accommodated, may also need accommodation is not evidence of undue hardship.

(2) When there is more than one method of accommodation available which would not cause undue hardship, the Commission will determine whether the accommodation offered is reasonable by examining:

(i) The alternatives for accommodation considered by the employer or labor organization; and

(ii) The alternatives for accommodation, if any, actually offered to the individual requiring accommodation. Some alternatives for accommodating religious practices might disadvantage the individual with respect to his or her employment opportunities, such as compensation, terms, conditions, or privileges of employment. Therefore, when there is more than one means of accommodation which would not cause undue hardship, the employer or labor organization must offer the alternative which least disadvantages the individual with respect to his or her employment opportunities.

(e) Undue hardship.

(1) Cost. An employer may assert undue hardship to justify a refusal to accommodate an employee's need to be absent from his or her scheduled duty hours if the employer can demonstrate that the accommodation would require "more than a de minimis cost". The Commission will determine what constitutes "more than a de minimis cost" with due regard given to the identifiable cost in relation to the size and operating cost of the employer, and the number of individuals who will in fact need a particular accommodation. In general, the Commission interprets this phrase as it was used in the Hardison decision to mean that costs similar to the regular payment of premium wages of substitutes, which was at issue in Hardison, would constitute undue hardship. However, the Commission will presume that the infrequent payment of premium wages while a more permanent accommodation is being sought are costs which an employer can be required to bear as a means of providing a reasonable accommodation. Further, the Commission will presume that generally, the payment of administrative costs necessary for providing the accommodation will not constitute more than a de minimis cost. Administrative costs, for example, include those costs involved in rearranging schedules and recording substitutions for payroll purposes.

(2) Seniority Rights. Undue hardship would also be shown where a variance from a bona fide seniority system is necessary in order to accommodate an employee's religious practices when doing so would deny another employee his or her job or shift preference guaranteed by that system. Hardison. Arrangements for

voluntary substitutes and swaps (see paragraph (d)(1)(i) of this section) do not constitute an undue hardship to the extent the arrangements do not violate a bona fide seniority system.

Do the guidelines accurately reflect the Court's decision in *Hardison*? Does the duty to accommodate require the employer to adopt the least burdensome alternative? The Court addressed this issue in the following case.

ANSONIA BOARD OF EDUCATION V. PHILBROOK
479 u.s. 60 (1986)

Chief Justice REHNQUIST delivered the opinion of the Court.

Petitioner Ansonia Board of Education has employed respondent Ronald Philbrook since 1962 to teach high school business and typing classes in Ansonia, Connecticut. In 1968, Philbrook was baptized into the Worldwide Church of God. The tenets of the church require members to refrain from secular employment during designated holy days, a practice that has caused respondent to miss approximately six school days each year.

Since the 1967-1968 school year, the school board's collective-bargaining agreements with the Ansonia Federation of Teachers have granted to each teacher 18 days of leave per year for illness, cumulative to 150 and later to 180 days. Accumulated leave may be used for purposes other than illness as specified in the agreement. A teacher may accordingly use five days' leave for a death in the immediate family, one day for attendance at a wedding, three days per year for attendance as an official delegate to a national veterans organization, and the like. With the exception of the agreement covering the 1967-1968 school, each contract has specifically provided three days' annual leave for observance of mandatory religious holidays, as defined in the contract.

The school board has also agreed that teachers may use up to three days of accumulated leave each school year for "necessary personal business." Recent contracts limited permissible personal leave to those uses not otherwise specified in the contract. This limitation dictated, for example, that an employee who wanted more than three leave days to attend the convention of a national veterans organization could not use personal leave to gain extra days for that purpose. Likewise, an employee already absent three days for mandatory religious observances could not later use personal leave for "[a]ny religious activity," or "[a]ny religious observance."

The limitations on the use of personal business leave spawned this litigation. Until the 1976-1977 year, Philbrook observed mandatory holy days by using the three days granted in the contract and then taking unauthorized leave. His pay was reduced accordingly. In 1976, however, respondent stopped taking unauthorized leave for religious reasons, and began scheduling required hospital visits on church holy days. He also worked on several holy days. Dissatisfied with this arrangement, Philbrook repeatedly asked the school board to adopt one of two alternatives. His preferred alternative would allow use of personal business leave for religious observance, effectively giving him three additional days of paid leave for that purpose. Short of this arrangement, respondent suggested that he pay the cost of a substitute and receive full pay for additional days off for religious observances. Petitioner has consistently rejected both proposals.

In addressing this question, the Court of Appeals assumed that the employer had offered a reasonable accommodation of Philbrook's religious beliefs. This alone, however, was insufficient in that court's view to allow resolution of the dispute. The court observed that the duty to accommodate "cannot be defined without reference to undue hardship." It accordingly determined that the accommodation obligation includes a duty to accept "the proposal the employee prefers unless that accommodation causes undue hardship on the employer's conduct of his business."

We find no basis in either the statute or its legislative history for requiring an employer to choose any particular reasonable accommodation. By its very terms the statute directs that any reasonable accommodation by the employer is sufficient to meet its accommodation obligation. The employer violates the statute unless it "demonstrates that [it] is unable to reasonably accommodate . . . an employee's . . . religious observance or practice without undue hardship on the conduct of the employer's business." Thus, where the employer has already reasonably accommodated the employee's religious needs, the statutory inquiry is at an end. The employer need not further show that each of the employee's alternative accommodations would result in undue hardship. As *Hardison* illustrates, the extent of undue hardship on the employer's business is at issue only where the employer claims that it is unable to offer any reasonable accommodation without such hardship. Once the Court of Appeals assumed that the school board had offered to Philbrook a reasonable alternative, it erred by requiring the board to nonetheless demonstrate the hardship of Philbrook's alternatives.

Under the approach articulated by the Court of Appeals, the employee is given every incentive to hold out for the most beneficial accommodation, despite the fact that an employer offers a reasonable resolution of the conflict. This approach, we think, conflicts with both the language of the statute and the views that led to its enactment. We accordingly hold that an employer has met its obligation under § 701(j) when it demonstrates that it has offered a reasonable accommodation to the employee.[6]

The remaining issue in the case is whether the school board's leave policy constitutes a reasonable accommodation of Philbrook's religious beliefs. Because both the District Court and the Court of Appeals applied what we hold to be an erroneous view of the law, neither explicitly considered this question. We think that there are insufficient factual findings as to the manner

---

6 The Court of Appeals found support for its decision in the EEOC's guidelines on religious discrimination. Specifically, the guidelines provide that "when there is more than one means of accommodation which would not cause undue hardship, the employer . . . must offer the alternative which least disadvantages the individual with respect to his or her employment opportunities." 29 C.F.R. §1605.2(c)(2)(ii)(1986). Though superficially consistent with the burden imposed by the Court of Appeals, this guideline, by requiring the employer to choose the option that least disadvantages an individual's employment opportunities, contains a significant limitation not found in the court's standard. To the extent that the guideline, like the approach of the Court of Appeals, requires the employer to accept any alternative favored by the employee short of undue hardship, we find the guideline simply inconsistent with the plain meaning of the statute. We have, of course, noted that EEOC guidelines are properly accorded less weight than administrative regulations declared by Congress to have the force of law.

in which the collective bargaining agreement has been interpreted in order for us to make that judgment initially. We think that the school board policy in this case, requiring respondent to take unpaid leave for holy day observance that exceeded the amount allowed by the collective-bargaining agreement, would generally be a reasonable one. In enacting § 701(j), Congress was understandably motivated by a desire to assure the individual additional opportunity to observe religious practices, but it did not impose a duty on the employer to accommodate at all costs. The provision of unpaid leave eliminates the conflict between the employment requirements and religious practices by allowing the individual to observe fully religious holy days and requires him only to give up compensation for a day that he did not in fact work.

But unpaid leave is not a reasonable accommodation when paid leave is provided for all purposes *except* religious ones. Such an arrangement would display a discrimination against religious practices that is the antithesis of reasonableness. Whether the policy here violates this teaching turns on factual inquiry into past and present administration of the personal business leave provisions of the collective-bargaining agreement. The school board contends that the necessary personal business category in the agreement, like other leave provisions, defines a limited purpose leave. Philbrook, on the other hand, asserts that the necessary personal leave category is not so limited, operating as an open-ended leave provision that may be used for a wide range of secular purposes in addition to those specifically provided for in the contract, but not for similar religious purposes. We do not think that the record is sufficiently clear on this point for us to make the necessary factual findings, and we therefore affirm the judgment of the Court of Appeals remanding the case to the District Court.

NOTES AND QUESTIONS

1. Has the employer "reasonably" accommodated an employee's religious beliefs where it rejects an alternative that would not cause it "undue" hardship? Does the absence of hardship suggest the unreasonableness of the employer's accommodationist efforts? How does the Court interpret the interplay between the concepts of "reasonable accommodation" and "undue hardship"?

2. Is the employer's refusal to allow use of paid "personal business" days for religious observance unreasonable if "personal days" may be used for a wide range of secular purposes? Note that on remand, the court found no evidence to support this claim. 925 F.2d 47 (2d Cir. 1991).

3. The lower courts have held that a *prima facie* case is established when an employee shows that:
   a. he or she has a bona fide religious belief that conflicts with an employment requirement;
   b. he or she informed the employer of this belief;

c. he or she was disciplined for failure to comply with the conflicting employment requirement.

Based on *Philbrook*, once this showing is made, what is the nature of the burden which shifts to the employer? Should this be treated the same as a "direct evidence" case, a disparate treatment case or a disparate impact case?

4. Assume an employer refuses to hire a person because it suspects it will then have to accommodate that individual's religious beliefs. The prima facie case analysis for disparate treatment in the context of religious discrimination differs from the prima facie case analysis where the employee alleges failure to accommodate. These differences were highlighted in the following case:

EQUAL EMPLOYMENT OPPORTUNITY COMMISSION V. ABERCROMBIE & FITCH STORES, INC.
135 s. ct. 2028 (2015)

Justice SCALIA delivered the opinion of the Court.

Title VII of the Civil Rights Act of 1964 prohibits a prospective employer from refusing to hire an applicant in order to avoid accommodating a religious practice that it could accommodate without undue hardship. The question presented is whether this prohibition applies only where an applicant has informed the employer of his need for an accommodation.

I

Respondent Abercrombie & Fitch Stores, Inc., operates several lines of clothing stores, each with its own "style." Consistent with the image Abercrombie seeks to project for each store, the company imposes a Look Policy that governs its employees' dress. The Look Policy prohibits "caps"—a term the Policy does not define—as too informal for Abercrombie's desired image.

Samantha Elauf is a practicing Muslim who, consistent with her understanding of her religion's requirements, wears a headscarf. She applied for a position in an Abercrombie store, and was interviewed by Heather Cooke, the store's assistant manager. Using Abercrombie's ordinary system for evaluating applicants, Cooke gave Elauf a rating that qualified her to be hired; Cooke was concerned, however, that Elauf's headscarf would conflict with the store's Look Policy.

Cooke sought the store manager's guidance to clarify whether the headscarf was a forbidden "cap." When this yielded no answer, Cooke turned to Randall Johnson, the district manager. Cooke informed Johnson that she believed Elauf wore her headscarf because of her faith. Johnson told Cooke that Elauf's headscarf would violate the Look Policy, as would all other headwear, religious or otherwise, and directed Cooke not to hire Elauf.

The EEOC sued Abercrombie on Elauf's behalf, claiming that its refusal to hire Elauf violated Title VII. The District Court granted the EEOC summary judgment on the issue of liability, held a trial on damages, and awarded $20,000. The Tenth Circuit reversed and awarded Abercrombie summary judgment. It concluded that ordinarily an employer cannot be liable under Title VII for failing to accommodate a religious practice until the applicant (or employee) provides the employer with actual knowledge of his need for an accommodation.

II

Abercrombie's primary argument is that an applicant cannot show disparate treatment without first showing that an employer has "actual knowledge" of the applicant's need for an accommodation. We disagree. Instead, an applicant need only show that his need for an accommodation was a motivating factor in the employer's decision.

The disparate-treatment provision forbids employers to: (1) "fail ... to hire" an applicant (2) "because of" (3) "such individual's ... religion" (which includes his religious practice). Here, of course, Abercrombie (1) failed to hire Elauf. The parties concede that (if Elauf sincerely believes that her religion so requires) Elauf's wearing of a headscarf is (3) a "religious practice." All that remains is whether she was not hired (2) "because of" her religious practice.

The term "because of" appears frequently in antidiscrimination laws. It typically imports, at a minimum, the traditional standard of but-for causation. Title VII relaxes this standard, however, to prohibit even making a protected characteristic a "motivating factor" in an employment decision. 42 U.S.C. § 2000e–2(m). "Because of" in § 2000e–2(a)(1) links the forbidden consideration to each of the verbs preceding it; an individual's actual religious practice may not be a motivating factor in failing to hire, in refusing to hire, and so on.

It is significant that § 2000e–2(a)(1) does not impose a knowledge requirement. As Abercrombie acknowledges, some antidiscrimination statutes do. Instead, the intentional discrimination provision prohibits certain motives, regardless of the state of the actor's knowledge. Motive and knowledge are separate concepts. An employer who has actual knowledge of the need for an accommodation does not violate Title VII by refusing to hire an applicant if avoiding that accommodation is not his motive. Conversely, an employer who acts with the motive of avoiding accommodation may violate Title VII even if he has no more than an unsubstantiated suspicion that accommodation would be needed.

Thus, the rule for disparate-treatment claims based on a failure to accommodate a religious practice is straightforward: An employer may not make an applicant's religious practice, confirmed or otherwise, a factor in employment decisions. For example, suppose that an employer thinks (though he does not know for certain) that a job applicant may be an orthodox Jew who will observe the Sabbath, and thus be unable to work on Saturdays. If the applicant actually requires an accommodation of that religious practice, and the employer's desire to avoid the prospective accommodation is a motivating factor in his decision, the employer violates Title VII.

Abercrombie argues that a claim based on a failure to accommodate an applicant's religious practice must be raised as a disparate-impact claim, not a disparate-treatment claim. We think not. That might have been true if Congress had limited the meaning of "religion" in Title VII to religious belief—so that discriminating against a particular religious practice would not be disparate treatment though it might have disparate impact. In fact, however, Congress defined "religion," for Title VII's purposes, as "includ[ing] all aspects of religious observance and practice, as well as belief." 42 U.S.C. § 2000e(j). Thus, religious practice is one of the protected characteristics that cannot be accorded disparate treatment and must be accommodated.

Nor does the statute limit disparate-treatment claims to only those employer policies that treat religious practices less favorably than similar secular practices. Abercrombie's argument that a neutral policy cannot constitute "intentional discrimination" may make sense in other contexts. But Title VII does not demand mere neutrality with regard to religious practices—that they be treated no worse than other practices. Rather, it gives them favored treatment, affirmatively obligating employers not "to fail or refuse to hire or discharge any individual ... because of such individual's" "religious observance and practice." An employer is surely entitled to have, for example, a no-headwear policy as an ordinary matter. But when an applicant requires an accommodation as an "aspec[t] of religious ... practice," it is no response that the subsequent "fail[ure] ... to hire" was due to an otherwise-neutral policy. Title VII requires otherwise-neutral policies to give way to the need for an accommodation.

NOTES AND QUESTIONS

1. How does Justice Scalia define "intentional" religious bias, and why does he reject a "knowledge" requirement? Explain the difference between "knowledge" and "motive."

2. If, during her interview, Elauf had informed A & F that she needed a religious accommodation and was told that the company strictly adhered to a look policy, because it relied on customers' "in-store experience" to promote its products, would Elauf have won her case? Is injury to public image sufficient to prove more than "de minimis" hardship? Compare Cloutier v. Costco Wholesale Corp., 390 F.3d 126 (1st Cir. 2004) (upholding an employer's public image defense against an employee's religious request to wear body piercings); Webb v. Philadelphia, 562 F.3d 256 (3d Cir. 2009) (holding that permitting an exception to a police uniform policy for a Muslim officer seeking to wear a headscarf while on duty would be an undue hardship because of damage to the department's esprit de corps). Assuming a grooming policy is neutrally enforced, should employers be permitted to rely on "company image" or "naked customer preference" to deny employment?

3. In his dissent, Justice Thomas argued that Elauf's case should be assessed under a disparate impact theory because the company maintained a facially neutral practice.

Why does Justice Scalia reject disparate impact analysis? How would the case be analyzed under the disparate impact theory?

4. How can employers avoid liability in these situations? Does the case dictate that employers ask applicants about their need for religious accommodation or does this invite claims for religious discrimination? During oral argument, Justice Roberts posed the hypothetical of an applicant who wears a beard to a job interview. Assuming the employer has a policy prohibiting beards, would the hiring official be required to ask if the beard was for religious reasons? If so, does this "cause more problems," as Justice Roberts surmised?

<h3 align="center">PROBLEM: TWENTY-SIX</h3>

Joe Nottelson was a production worker at Smith Steel Workers (SSW) from October 30, 1997, to April 24, 2005, and a member of the Union from October 30, 1997, to April 15, 2005. The Union is the exclusive bargaining agent for the collective bargaining unit in which plaintiff was employed, and the collective bargaining agreement between SSW and the Union contains a union security clause requiring membership in the Union as a condition of continued employment with SSW.

In May 1998, Nottelson joined the Seventh-day Adventist Church, which teaches that it is morally wrong to be a member of or pay dues to a labor organization. Five years later, Nottelson informed the Union that he could no longer in good conscience support it financially because of his religious convictions and requested the Union to accommodate his religious objection to the payment of union dues by permitting him to pay an equivalent sum to a non-religious, non-union charity. He ceased paying his dues on January 1, 2005, and, to show his good faith, began making contributions to the American Cancer Society. The Union refused the requested accommodation and in March, 2005, notified Nottelson that he would have to pay his delinquent dues or be discharged from SSW pursuant to the union security clause in the collective bargaining agreement. SSW indicated that it was willing to make an accommodation but not without the Union's approval.

On April 15, the Union expelled Nottelson from its membership for failure to pay dues, and on April 24, at the insistence of the Union, SSW discharged him.

In his complaint, Nottelson alleges that SSW and the Union discriminated against him because of his religion in violation of §§ 703(a) and 703(c) of Title VII in that they had failed to show that they could not reasonably accommodate Nottelson's religious observance "without undue hardship" as required by § 701(j) of the Act. The Union was also alleged to have violated the Act by enforcing the union security provision of the collective bargaining agreement so as to cause SSW to discriminate against Nottelson on the basis of religion.

The Union in its responsive pleadings and at trial took the position that enforcement of the union security clause against plaintiff was protected under the National Labor Relations Act (NLRA) and that Title VII's § 701(j), as sought to be applied, violated the Establishment Clause of the First Amendment. SSW asserted the affirmative defense of undue hardship, claiming that it had done all it could to accommodate plaintiff without causing the Union to initiate arbitration proceedings to enforce the union security clause and to file an unfair labor practice charge to the same effect under the NLRA.

1. Has Nottelson established a *prima facie* case?

2. Would accommodation of plaintiff's charity substitute proposal subject the Union and/or SSW to "undue hardship"? If the evidence demonstrates that a charity substitute would require the Union to raise dues by 24 cents per member annually, is this cost more than "*de minimis*"? May the union rely on its fear that this will lead to multiple requests for substitute payments?

Should SSW be held liable for violating Title VII, or does the collective bargaining agreement with the union provide a valid defense? Is the cost of defending a grievance proceeding more than "*de minimis*"?

5. CONSTITUTIONAL DEFENSES

Constitutional defenses may include freedom of association or freedom of religion. As to the former, the Supreme Court has recognized two types of associational freedom, namely intimate association protected under substantive due process and expressive association protected by the First Amendment. *See Board of Directors of Rotary International, supra* Ch. II. As the cases in Chapter Two reveal, a constitutional privacy-type (substantive due process) defense has been limited to groups that are small, selective and exclusive. Because Title VII already exempts bona fide private clubs, 42 U.S.C. § 2000e(b), it is unlikely that such a constitutional defense will succeed. As to an expressive association defense, the group must show that it is an "expressive" organization and that forced association will impair the group's ability to convey its message. In *Hishon v. King & Spaulding*, 467 U.S. 69 (1984), the Court rejected a free association defense to a sex discrimination suit brought under Title VII. The Court reasoned that the law firm/employer was neither an intimate group, nor would its expressive function be inhibited by a requirement that it consider women for partnership positions based on their merit, rather than on their sex.

Although Title VII exempts religious institutions from Title VII claims alleging religious discrimination, *see* §§ 702 and 703, it does not exempt these institutions from discrimination claims based on other grounds, such as race, sex, or national origin, thus raising a question as to whether the First Amendment's Religion Clauses, which protect the free exercise of religion and prohibit excessive entanglement between church and state, provide a defense.

As discussed in Chapter Two, the Free Exercise Clause is not violated where a facially neutral, generally applicable law, such as Title VII, is applied to individuals who object on religious grounds. Some question has been raised, however, as to whether religious institutions, as opposed to individuals, may still assert viable free exercise claims, even where the law is neutral and generally applicable. Further, the Establishment Clause has been interpreted to prohibit civil courts from reviewing internal church disputes involving matters of faith, doctrine and church governance. The Supreme Court addressed both of the Religion Clauses in a case brought under the ADA, which has the same statutory exemptions as Title VII.

HOSANNA–TABOR EVANGELICAL LUTHERAN CHURCH AND SCHOOL V. EQUAL EMPLOYMENT OPPORTUNITY COMMISSION
565 u.s. 171 (2012)

Chief Justice ROBERTS delivered the opinion of the Court.

Certain employment discrimination laws authorize employees who have been wrongfully terminated to sue their employers for reinstatement and damages. The question presented is whether the Establishment and Free Exercise Clauses of the First Amendment bar such an action when the employer is a religious group and the employee is one of the group's ministers.

I

Petitioner Hosanna–Tabor Evangelical Lutheran Church and School is a member congregation of the Lutheran Church–Missouri Synod, the second largest Lutheran denomination in America. Hosanna–Tabor operated a small school in Redford, Michigan, offering a "Christ-centered education" to students in kindergarten through eighth grade.

The Synod classifies teachers into two categories: "called" and "lay." "Called" teachers are regarded as having been called to their vocation by God through a congregation. To be eligible to receive a call from a congregation, a teacher must satisfy certain academic requirements. One way of doing so is by completing a "colloquy" program at a Lutheran college or university. The program requires candidates to take eight courses of theological study, obtain the endorsement of their local Synod district, and pass an oral examination by a faculty committee. A teacher who meets these requirements may be called by a congregation. Once called, a teacher receives the formal title "Minister of Religion, Commissioned."

"Lay" or "contract" teachers, by contrast, are not required to be trained by the Synod or even to be Lutheran. At Hosanna–Tabor, they were appointed by the school board, without a vote of the congregation, to one-year renewable terms. Although teachers at the school generally performed the same duties regardless of whether they were lay or called, lay teachers were hired only when called teachers were unavailable.

Respondent Cheryl Perich was first employed by Hosanna–Tabor as a lay teacher in 1999. After Perich completed her colloquy later that school year, Hosanna–Tabor asked her to become a called teacher. Perich accepted the call and received a "diploma of vocation" designating her a commissioned minister.

Perich taught kindergarten during her first four years at Hosanna–Tabor and fourth grade during the 2003–2004 school year. She taught math, language arts, social studies, science, gym, art, and music. She also taught a religion class four days a week, led the students in prayer and devotional exercises each day, and attended a weekly school-wide chapel service. Perich led the chapel service herself about twice a year.

Perich became ill in June 2004 with what was eventually diagnosed as narcolepsy. Because of her illness, Perich began the 2004–2005 school year on disability leave. On January 27, 2005, however, Perich notified the school principal, Stacey Hoeft, that she would be able to report to work the following month. Hoeft responded that the school had already contracted with a lay teacher to fill Perich's position for the remainder of the school year.

On January 30, Hosanna–Tabor held a meeting of its congregation at which school administrators stated that Perich was unlikely to be physically capable of returning to work that school year or the next. The congregation voted to offer Perich a "peaceful release" from her call, whereby the congregation would pay a portion of her health insurance premiums in exchange for her resignation as a called teacher. Perich refused to resign and produced a note from her doctor stating that she would be able to return to work on February 22.

On the morning of February 22 Perich presented herself at the school. Hoeft asked her to leave but she would not do so until she obtained written documentation that she had reported to work. Later that afternoon, Hoeft called Perich at home and told her that she would likely be fired. Perich responded that she had spoken with an attorney and intended to assert her legal rights.

Following a school board meeting that evening, board chairman Scott Salo sent Perich a letter stating that Hosanna–Tabor was reviewing the process for rescinding her call in light of her "regrettable" actions. As grounds for termination, the letter cited Perich's "insubordination and disruptive behavior" on February 22, as well as the damage she had done to her "working relationship" with the school by "threatening to take legal action."

The EEOC brought suit against Hosanna–Tabor, alleging that Perich had been fired in retaliation for threatening to file an ADA [Americans with Disabilities Act] lawsuit. Hosanna–Tabor moved for summary judgment. Invoking what is known as the "ministerial exception," the Church argued that the suit was barred by the First Amendment because the claims at issue concerned the employment relationship between a religious institution and one of its ministers. According to the Church, Perich was a minister, and she had been fired for a religious reason—namely, that her threat to sue the Church violated the Synod's belief that Christians should resolve their disputes internally.

II

[After tracing the controversy between church and state over religious officers, the Court concludes: "The Establishment Clause prevents the Government from appointing ministers, and the Free Exercise Clause prevents it from interfering with the freedom of religious groups to select their own."]

Until today, we have not had occasion to consider whether this freedom of a religious organization to select its ministers is implicated by a suit alleging discrimination in employment. The Courts of Appeals, in contrast, have had extensive experience with this issue. Since the passage of Title VII, and other employment discrimination laws, the Courts of Appeals have uniformly recognized the existence of a "ministerial exception," grounded in the First Amendment, that precludes application of such legislation to claims concerning the employment relationship between a religious institution and its ministers.

We agree that there is such a ministerial exception. The members of a religious group put their faith in the hands of their ministers. Requiring a church to accept or retain an unwanted minister, or punishing a church for failing to do so, intrudes upon more than a mere employment decision. Such action interferes with the internal governance of the church, depriving the church of control over the selection of those who will personify its beliefs. By imposing an unwanted minister, the state infringes the Free Exercise Clause, which protects a religious group's right to shape its own faith and mission through its appointments. According the state the power to determine which individuals will minister to the faithful also violates the Establishment Clause, which prohibits government involvement in such ecclesiastical decisions.

The EEOC and Perich acknowledge that employment discrimination laws would be unconstitutional as applied to religious groups in certain circumstances. They grant, for example, that it would violate the First Amendment for courts to apply such laws to compel the ordination of women by the Catholic Church or by an Orthodox Jewish seminary. According to the EEOC and Perich, religious organizations could successfully defend against employment discrimination claims in those circumstances by invoking the constitutional right to freedom of association—a right "implicit" in the First Amendment.

We find this position untenable. The right to freedom of association is a right enjoyed by religious and secular groups alike. It follows under the EEOC's and Perich's view that the First Amendment analysis should be the same, whether the association in question is the Lutheran Church, a labor union, or a social club. That result is hard to square with the text of the First Amendment itself, which gives special solicitude to the rights of religious organizations. We cannot accept the remarkable view that the Religion Clauses have nothing to say about a religious organization's freedom to select its own ministers.

The EEOC and Perich also contend that our decision in *Employment Div., Dept. of Human Resources of Ore. v. Smith*, 494 U.S. 872 (1990), precludes recognition of a ministerial exception. In *Smith*, two members of the Native American Church were denied state unemployment benefits after it was determined that they had been fired from their jobs for ingesting peyote, a crime under Oregon law. We held that this did not violate the Free Exercise Clause, even though the peyote had been ingested for sacramental purposes, because the "right of free exercise does not relieve an individual of the obligation to comply with a valid and neutral law of general applicability on the ground that the law proscribes (or prescribes) conduct that his religion prescribes (or proscribes)."

It is true that the ADA's prohibition on retaliation, like Oregon's prohibition on peyote use, is a valid and neutral law of general applicability. But a church's selection of its ministers is unlike an individual's ingestion of peyote. *Smith* involved government regulation of only outward physical acts. The present case, in contrast, concerns government interference with an internal church decision that affects the faith and mission of the church itself. The contention that *Smith* forecloses recognition of a ministerial exception rooted in the Religion Clauses has no merit.

III

Having concluded that there is a ministerial exception grounded in the Religion Clauses of the First Amendment, we consider whether the exception applies in this case. We hold that it does.

Every Court of Appeals to have considered the question has concluded that the ministerial exception is not limited to the head of a religious congregation, and we agree. We are reluctant, however, to adopt a rigid formula for deciding when an employee qualifies as a minister. It is enough for us to conclude, in this our first case involving the ministerial exception, that the exception covers Perich, given all the circumstances of her employment.

To begin with, Hosanna–Tabor held Perich out as a minister, with a role distinct from that of most of its members. When Hosanna–Tabor extended her a call, it issued her a "diploma of vocation" according her the title "Minister of Religion, Commissioned." She was tasked with performing that office "according to the Word of God and the confessional standards of the Evangelical Lutheran Church as drawn from the Sacred Scriptures." In a supplement to the diploma, the congregation undertook to periodically review Perich's "skills of ministry" and "ministerial responsibilities," and to provide for her "continuing education as a professional person in the ministry of the Gospel."

Perich's title as a minister reflected a significant degree of religious training followed by a formal process of commissioning. To be eligible to become a commissioned minister, Perich had to complete eight college-level courses in subjects including biblical interpretation, church doctrine, and the ministry of the Lutheran teacher. It took Perich six years to fulfill these requirements. And when she eventually did, she was commissioned as a minister only upon election by the congregation, which recognized God's call to her to teach. At that point, her call could be rescinded only upon a supermajority vote of the congregation—a protection designed to allow her to "preach the Word of God boldly."

Perich held herself out as a minister of the Church by accepting the formal call to religious service, according to its terms. She did so in other ways as well. For example, she claimed a special housing allowance on her taxes that was available only to employees earning their compensation "'in the exercise of the ministry.'"

Perich's job duties reflected a role in conveying the Church's message and carrying out its mission. Hosanna–Tabor expressly charged her with "lead[ing] others toward Christian maturity" and "teach[ing] faithfully the Word of God, the Sacred Scriptures, in its truth and purity and as set forth in all the symbolical books of the Evangelical Lutheran Church." In fulfilling these responsibilities, Perich taught her students religion four days a week, and led them in prayer three times a day. Once a week, she took her students to a school-wide chapel service, and—about twice a year—she took her turn leading it, choosing the liturgy, selecting the hymns, and delivering a short message based on verses from the Bible. As a source of religious instruction, Perich performed an important role in transmitting the Lutheran faith to the next generation.

In light of these considerations—the formal title given Perich by the Church, the substance reflected in that title, her own use of that title, and the important religious functions she performed for the Church—we conclude that Perich was a minister covered by the ministerial exception.

In reaching a contrary conclusion, the Court of Appeals committed three errors. First, the Sixth Circuit failed to see any relevance in the fact that Perich was a commissioned minister. Although such a title, by itself, does not automatically ensure coverage, the fact that an employee has been ordained or commissioned as a minister is surely relevant, as is the fact that significant religious training and a recognized religious mission underlie the description of the employee's position.

Second, the Sixth Circuit gave too much weight to the fact that lay teachers at the school performed the same religious duties as Perich. We express no view on whether someone with Perich's duties would be covered by the ministerial exception in the absence of the other considerations we have discussed. But though relevant, it cannot be dispositive that others not formally recognized as ministers by the church perform the same functions—particularly when, as here, they did so only because commissioned ministers were unavailable.

Third, the Sixth Circuit placed too much emphasis on Perich's performance of secular duties. It is true that her religious duties consumed only 45 minutes of each workday, and that the rest of her day was devoted to teaching secular subjects. The heads of congregations themselves often have a mix of duties, including secular ones such as helping to manage the congregation's finances, supervising purely secular personnel, and overseeing the upkeep of facilities.

Because Perich was a minister within the meaning of the exception, the First Amendment requires dismissal of this employment discrimination suit against her religious employer. The EEOC and Perich originally sought an order reinstating Perich to her former position as a called teacher. By requiring the Church to accept a minister it did not want, such an order would have plainly violated the Church's freedom under the Religion Clauses to select its own ministers.

Perich no longer seeks reinstatement, having abandoned that relief before this Court. But that is immaterial. Perich continues to seek frontpay in lieu of reinstatement, backpay, compensatory and punitive damages, and attorney's fees. An award of such relief would operate as a penalty on the Church for terminating an unwanted minister, and would be no less prohibited by the First Amendment than an order overturning the termination. Such relief would depend on a determination that Hosanna–Tabor was wrong to have relieved Perich of her position, and it is precisely such a ruling that is barred by the ministerial exception.

The EEOC and Perich suggest that Hosanna–Tabor's asserted religious reason for firing Perich—that she violated the Synod's commitment to internal dispute resolution—was pretextual. That suggestion misses the point of the ministerial exception. The purpose of the exception is not to safeguard a church's decision to fire a minister only when it is made for a religious reason. The exception instead ensures that the authority to select and control who will minister to the faithful—a matter "strictly ecclesiastical,"—is the church's alone.

IV

The case before us is an employment discrimination suit brought on behalf of a minister, challenging her church's decision to fire her. Today we hold only that the ministerial exception bars such a suit. We express no view on whether the exception bars other types of suits, including actions by employees alleging breach of contract or tortious conduct by their religious employers. There will be time enough to address the applicability of the exception to other circumstances if and when they arise.

The interest of society in the enforcement of employment discrimination statutes is undoubtedly important. But so too is the interest of religious groups in choosing who will preach their beliefs, teach their faith, and carry out their mission. When a minister who has been fired sues her church alleging that her termination was discriminatory, the First Amendment has struck the balance for us. The church must be free to choose those who will guide it on its way.

[In a concurring opinion, Justice Thomas reasoned that courts must "defer to a religious organization's good faith understanding of who qualifies as its minister," whereas Justices Alito and Kagan, in a separate concurrence, argue that the term "minister" should apply to "any employee who leads a religious organization, conducts worship services or important religious ceremonies or rituals, or serves as a messenger or teacher of its faith." They urge that the "Court's opinion . . . should not be read to upset [the] consensus" in the appellate courts that recognizes this "functional approach."]

NOTES AND QUESTIONS

1. Assume a church related college refuses to hire a black man to serve as chaplain for the college's predominantly white student body. Does the ministerial exception categorically bar a claim of race discrimination? Does the government's compelling interest in halting race discrimination, recognized in *Bob Jones University, supra* Ch. II, survive *Hosanna-Tabor*? Does the Court in *Hosanna-Tabor* adequately distinguish *Smith*?

2. Did the Court clarify who qualifies as a minister? Should courts be permitted to decide whether the employee in question is a minister? In a footnote, the Supreme Court characterized the ministerial exception as an affirmative defense, which means a religious organization must plead and prove its applicability. Why isn't this very inquiry an assault on church autonomy? Note that Jehovah's Witnesses consider all baptized disciples to be ministers—is this characterization binding on the courts?

3. Assume a ***non-minister*** employee alleges she was terminated because she was pregnant. The religious school claims her termination was due to the fact that she was artificially inseminated, contrary to religious doctrine. May a court delve into whether the asserted religious-based reason is a pretext for pregnancy discrimination? What does the Supreme Court say about the pretext inquiry in the context of the ministerial exception? Should it matter whether a discrimination claim requires inquiry into church doctrine?

4. Assume that Cheryl Perich claimed she was subjected to sexual harassment by the school principal and was then dismissed after she filed a Title VII action against her church employer, in violation of the Lutheran doctrine that disputes among Christians should be resolved internally without resort to the civil court system. Does *Hosanna-Tabor* require dismissal of both her sexual harassment and retaliation claims? What if she seeks only damages, not reinstatement? *See* Rosalie Berger Levinson, *Gender Equality vs. Religious Autonomy: Suing Religious Employers for Sexual Harassment After* Hosanna-Tabor, 11 STANFORD J. C.R. & C.L. 89 (2015).

5. In *Masterpiece Cake Shop, Ltd. v. Colo. Civil Rights Comm'n*, 138 S. Ct. 1719 (2018), the Court conceded that allowing "a vendor who provides goods and services for marriages and weddings to refuse similar services for gay persons would result in 'a community-wide stigma inconsistent with the history and dynamics of civil rights laws that ensure equal access to goods, services, and public accommodations.'" However, without deciding how to resolve the clash between a state civil rights law that barred sexual orientation discrimination and a baker's refusal on religious grounds to prepare a cake for the couple, the Supreme Court narrowly ruled that in this case there was evidence that the state commission that originally considered the dispute demonstrated "clear and impermissible hostility" towards plaintiff's religious beliefs, thereby violating the First Amendment Free Exercise Clause, which requires that plaintiff receive "neutral and respectful consideration of his claims."

6. ENFORCEMENT

Before any litigation may be brought under Title VII, a plaintiff must comply with the administrative exhaustion requirements of the Act. A plaintiff must initially file a charge with the Equal Employment Opportunity Commission on a form which is provided by the EEOC regional offices. In addition, Title VII provides that the EEOC cannot exercise its jurisdiction unless it allows a minimum of sixty days for a state or local deferral agency to pursue the discrimination claim. The EEOC has certified over 42 state-wide deferral agencies as well as a substantial number of municipal and county agencies, which are listed at 29 C.F.R. § 1601.74. Thus, plaintiffs may file their claim with either the state agency or the EEOC, requesting that the latter assume jurisdiction after sixty days or earlier if the state proceedings are terminated. This deferral scheme has created difficult questions regarding the applicable statute of limitations. Although § 706(e) provides a 180-day statute of limitations, it also states that 300 days will be provided where a litigant initially files a complaint in a state with a deferral agency. The inter-relationship between these provisions is addressed in the next case.

a.   Limitations Periods

MOHASCO CORPORATION V. SILVER
447 U.S. 807 (1979)

Mr. Justice STEVENS delivered the opinion of the Court.

The question in this Title VII case is whether Congress intended the word "filed" to have the same meaning in subsections (c) and (e) of § 706 of the Civil Rights Act of 1964. The former subsection prohibits the filing of an unfair employment practice charge with the federal Equal Employment Opportunity Commission (EEOC) until after a state fair employment practices agency has had an opportunity to consider it. The latter subsection requires that in all events the charge must be filed with the EEOC within 300 days of the occurrence. We hold that a literal reading of the two subsections gives full effect to the several policies reflected in the statute.

On August 29, 1975, Mohasco Corp. discharged the respondent from his position as senior marketing economist. On June 15, 1976—291 days later—the EEOC received a letter from respondent asserting that Mohasco had discriminated against him because of his religion. The letter was promptly referred to the New York State Division of Human Rights. That state agency reviewed the matter and, in due course, determined that there was no merit in the charge.

Meanwhile, on August 20, 1976—a date more than 60 days after respondent's letter had been submitted to the EEOC and 357 days after respondent's discharge—the EEOC notified Mohasco that respondent had filed a charge of employment discrimination.

Section 706(e) begins with the general rule that a "charge under this section shall be filed within one hundred and eighty days after the alleged unlawful employment practice occurred." Since respondent's letter was submitted to the EEOC 291 days after the occurrence, he plainly did not exercise the diligence required by that general rule. Nor, as we shall explain, did he have to; but it should be pointed out that had he sent his charge to either the state agency or the EEOC within the 180 days, he would have had no difficulty in complying with the terms of the exception to that general rule allowing a later filing with the EEOC in deferral States.

That exception allows a filing with the EEOC after 180 days if "the person aggrieved has initially instituted proceedings with a State or local agency with authority to grant or seek relief from such practice. . . ." When respondent submitted his letter to the EEOC, he had not yet instituted any state proceedings. Under the literal terms of the statute, it could therefore be argued that he did not bring himself within the exception to the general 180-day requirement.

But in *Love v. Pullman Co.*, we held that "[n]othing in the Act suggests that the state proceedings may not be initiated by the EEOC acting on behalf of the complainant rather than by the complainant himself." Here state proceedings were instituted by the EEOC when it immediately forwarded his letter to the state agency on June 15, 1976. Accordingly, we treat the state proceeding as having been instituted on that date. Since the EEOC could not proceed until either state proceedings had ended or 60 days had passed, the proceedings were "initially instituted with a State . . . agency" prior to their official institution with the EEOC. Therefore, respondent came within § 706(e)'s exception allowing a federal filing more than 180 days after the occurrence.

That exception states that "such charge shall be filed by or on behalf of the person aggrieved within three hundred days after the alleged unlawful employment practice occurred, or within thirty days after receiving notice that the State or local agency has terminated the proceedings under the State or local law, whichever is earlier." Since the state proceedings did not terminate until well after the expiration of the 300-day period, the 300-day limitations period is the one applicable to respondent's charge. The question, then, is whether the June 15, 1976, letter was "filed" when received by the EEOC within the meaning of subsection (e) of § 706.

The answer is supplied by subsection (c), which imposes a special requirement for cases arising in deferral States: "no charge may be filed under subsection [(b)] by the person aggrieved before the expiration of sixty days after proceedings have been commenced under the State and local law, unless such proceedings have been earlier terminated. . . ." Thus, in terms, the statute prohibited the EEOC from allowing the charge to be filed on the date the letter was received. Although, as the Court held in *Love v. Pullman Co.*, it was proper for the EEOC to hold respondent's "complaint in 'suspended animation,' *automatically filing it upon termination of the State proceedings*," (emphasis added), that means that the charge was filed on the 351st day, not the 291st. By that time, however, the 300-day period had run and the filing was therefore untimely.

NOTES AND QUESTIONS

1. If the plaintiff had filed a charge with the state agency instead of the EEOC on June 15, 1976, would his claim have been deemed timely? Why may a complainant take advantage of the 300-day rule even if he or she never institutes state proceedings? If the state has a 180-day statute of limitations for filing employment discrimination claims, and it has been 200 days since the alleged violation, is the Title VII action barred?

2. Although Title VII makes reference to a 180 and 300-day limitations period, it has been said that 240 days is the critical time period in light of *Mohasco*. Why? If a client does not seek your advice until 270 days after the alleged wrongdoing, is it too late to take action?

3. If the state agency in this case had sent the charge back to the EEOC within the 300-day period, would the statutory requirement of § 706(c) be satisfied? Several state

and local deferral agencies have in fact signed work-sharing agreements with the EEOC whereby they agree to waive processing of complaints filed after the 240-day period or to complete proceedings within the 300 days. Do these violate the statutory mandate? What if the state agency retains the right to review the file after the EEOC completes its investigation? Has it "terminated" its proceedings within the meaning of § 706(c)? The next case discusses these issues.

EEOC V. COMMERCIAL OFFICE PRODUCTS
486 U.S. 107 (1988)

Justice MARSHALL delivered the opinion of the Court.

This case raises two questions regarding the time limits for filing charges of employment discrimination with the Equal Employment Opportunity Commission (EEOC) under Title VII of the Civil Rights Act of 1964. The primary question presented is whether a state agency's decision to waive its exclusive 60-day period for initial processing of a discrimination charge, pursuant to a worksharing agreement with the EEOC, "terminates" the agency's proceedings within the meaning of § 706(c) of Title VII, 42 U.S.C. § 2000e-5(c), so that the EEOC immediately may deem the charge filed. In addition, we must decide whether a complainant who files a discrimination charge that is untimely under state law is nonetheless entitled to the extended 300-day federal filing period of § 706(e) of Title VII, 42 U.S.C. § 2000e-5(e).

I

In order to give States and localities an opportunity to combat discrimination free from premature federal intervention, the Act provides that no charge may be filed with the EEOC until 60 days have elapsed from initial filing of the charge with an authorized state or local agency, unless that agency's proceedings "have been earlier terminated." § 706(c), 42 U.S.C. § 2000e-5(c). The EEOC's referral of a charge initially filed with the EEOC to the appropriate state or local agency properly institutes the agency's proceedings within the meaning of the Act, and the EEOC may hold the charge in 'suspended animation' during the agency's 60-day period of exclusive jurisdiction.

The central question in this case is whether a state agency's waiver of the 60-day deferral period, pursuant to a worksharing agreement with the EEOC, constitutes a "termination" of its proceedings so as to permit the EEOC to deem a charge filed and to begin to process it immediately. This question is of substantial importance because the EEOC has used its statutory authority to enter into worksharing agreements with approximately three-quarters of the 109 state and local agencies authorized to enforce state and local employment discrimination laws.

These worksharing agreements typically provide that the state or local agency will process certain categories of charges and that the EEOC will process others, with the state or local agency waiving the 60-day deferral period in the latter instance. In either instance, the non-processing party to the worksharing agreement generally reserves the right to review the initial processing party's resolution of the charge and to investigate the charge further after the initial processing party has completed its proceedings. Whether a waiver of the 60-day deferral period pursuant to a worksharing agreement constitutes a "termination" of a state or local agency's proceedings will determine not only when the EEOC may initiate its proceedings, but also whether an entire class of charges may be timely filed with the EEOC in the first instance.

II

First and foremost, respondent defends the judgment of the Court of Appeals on the ground that the language of the statute unambiguously precludes the conclusion that the CCRD's waiver of the deferral period "terminated" its proceedings. According to respondent, "terminated" means only "'completed'" or "'ended.'" Respondent urges that this definition is met only when a state agency, in the words of the Court of Appeals, "completely relinquish[es] its authority to act on the charge at that point *or in the future.*"

We cannot agree with respondent and the Court of Appeals that "terminate" must mean "to end for all time." Rather, we find persuasive the determination of the First Circuit that the definition of "termination" also includes "cessation in time."

To be sure, "terminate" also may bear the meaning proposed by respondent. Indeed, it may bear that meaning more naturally or more frequently in common usage. But it is axiomatic that the EEOC's interpretation of Title VII, for which it has primary enforcement responsibility, need not be the best one by grammatical or any other standards. Rather, the EEOC's interpretation of ambiguous language need only be reasonable to be entitled to deference. The reasonableness of the EEOC's interpretation of "terminate" in its statutory context is more than amply supported by the legislative history of the deferral provisions of Title VII, the purposes of those provisions, and the language of other sections of the Act, as described in detail below. Deference is therefore appropriate.

The legislative history of the deferral provisions of Title VII demonstrates that the EEOC's interpretation of § 706(c) is far more consistent with the purposes of the Act than respondent's contrary construction.

The deferral provisions of § 706 were enacted as part of a compromise forged during the course of one of the longest filibusters in the Senate's history. The bill that had passed the House provided for "deferral" to state and local enforcement efforts only in the sense that it directed the EEOC to enter into agreements with state agencies providing for the suspension of federal enforcement in certain circumstances.

The proponents of the Dirksen-Mansfield substitute identified two goals of the deferral provisions, both of which fully support the EEOC's conclusion that States may, if they choose, waive the 60-day deferral period but retain jurisdiction over discrimination charges by entering into worksharing agreements with the EEOC. First, the proponents of the substitute deferral provisions explained that the 60-day deferral period was meant to give States a "reasonable opportunity to act under State law before the commencement of any Federal proceedings."

Nothing in the waiver provisions of the worksharing agreements impinges on the opportunity of the States to have an exclusive 60-day period for processing a discrimination charge. The waiver of that opportunity in specified instances is a voluntary choice made through individually negotiated agreements, not an imposition by the Federal Government.

In contrast, respondent's argument that States should not be permitted to waive the deferral period because its creation reflected a congressional preference for state as opposed to federal enforcement is entirely at odds with the voluntarism stressed by the proponents of deferral. Congress clearly foresaw the possibility that States might decline to take advantage of the opportunity for enforcement afforded them by the deferral provisions. It therefore gave the EEOC the authority and responsibility to act when a State is "unable or unwilling" to provide relief.

III

In the alternative, respondent argues in support of the result below that the extended 300-day federal filing period is inapplicable to this case because the complainant failed to file her discrimination charge with the CCRD within Colorado's 180-day limitations period. Respondent reasons that the extended 300-day filing period applies only when "the person aggrieved has initially instituted proceedings with a state or local agency with authority to grant or seek relief" from the practice charged, § 706(e), 42 U.S.C. § 2000e-5(e), and that in the absence of a timely filing under state law, a state agency lacks the requisite "authority to grant or seek relief." The Tenth Circuit rejected this argument below, as has every other Circuit court to consider the question, on the ground that the words "authority to grant or seek relief" refer merely to enabling legislation that establishes state or local agencies, not to state limitations requirements. We join the Circuits in concluding that state time limits for filing discrimination claims do not determine the applicable federal time limit.

The importation of state limitations periods into § 706(e) not only would confuse lay complainants, but also would embroil the EEOC in complicated issues of state law. In order for the EEOC to determine the timeliness of a charge filed with it between 180 and 300 days, it first would have to determine whether the charge had been timely filed under state law, because the answer to the latter question would establish which of the two federal limitations periods should apply. This state-law determination is not a simple matter. The EEOC first would have to determine whether a state limitations period was jurisdictional or nonjurisdictional. And if the limitations period was nonjurisdictional, like Colorado's in this case, the EEOC would have to decide whether it was waived or equitably tolled. The EEOC has neither the time nor the expertise to make such determinations under the varying laws of the many deferral States and has accordingly construed the extended 300-day period to be available regardless of the state filing.

Because we find that the extended 300-day federal limitations period is applicable to this case and that the CCRD's waiver of the 60-day deferral period "terminated" its proceedings within that 300-day limit, we conclude that Leerssen's claim was timely filed under Title VII. We therefore reverse the decision of the Court of Appeals and remand the case for further proceedings consistent with this opinion.

NOTES AND QUESTIONS

1. **Limitations Period for Agency Filing**: Questions relating to the timeliness of EEOC charges have been litigated extensively. The Court in *Zipes v. Trans World Airlines*, 455 U.S. 385 (1982), held that "filing a timely charge of discrimination with the EEOC is not a jurisdictional prerequisite to suit in federal court, but a requirement that, like a statute of limitations, is subject to waiver, estoppel, and equitable tolling." This enables a plaintiff, whose EEOC charge was not filed within the 180-day or 300-day period, to argue that equity requires a tolling of the limitations period. Plaintiffs have been successful in a variety of situations, the most common being where the conduct of an employer lulls a plaintiff into a delay in filing the charge.

2. **State Limitations Periods**: Does the holding in *Commercial Office Products* mean that a plaintiff can totally ignore the state agency process by waiting for the state limitations period to run? Why would a plaintiff do this? If the state agency, operating functionally as the equivalent of a judicial proceeding, found against an employee, would its decision have a preclusive effect in a subsequent Title VII action? Would it have a preclusive effect in a subsequent suit brought under § 1981 or § 1983? Review *Kremer v. Chemical Construction Corp., supra* Ch. II, and *University of Tennessee v. Elliott, supra* Ch. II.

3. **Verification Requirement**: In addition to requiring that a charge be filed with the EEOC within a specified number of days, a separate provision, § 706(b), mandates that the charge "be in writing under oath or affirmation." The EEOC has interpreted these two requirements to allow a filing party to verify a charge even if the time for filing has expired, *i.e.*, the verification will relate back to the original filing date. In *Edelman v. Lynchburg College*, 535 U.S. 106 (2002), the Court upheld the validity of this relation-back regulation. In a unanimous decision, the Court held that this was a valid interpretation of § 706 because nothing in the "charge" section required an oath and § 706(b) did not stipulate when the charge had to be verified. Moreover, the two provisions serve different objectives, namely the time limitation is meant "to encourage a potential charging party to raise a discrimination claim before it gets stale," whereas the verification requirement is intended to protect employers "from the disruption and expense of responding to a claim unless a complainant is serious enough and sure enough to support it by oath subject to liability for perjury." Because it is essential only that the verification occur prior to the time the employer is obliged to respond to the charge, it is unnecessary that the initial charge be under oath. The Court also noted that complainants, who often are without lawyers at this

point in time, may not know enough to verify at the time of filing. In a concurring opinion, Justices O'Connor and Scalia emphasized that since the EEOC had not been given rule-making authority to interpret the substantive provisions of Title VII, its substantive regulations were not entitled to "controlling weight" deference. Here, however, the Court was addressing a procedural, rather than a substantive, regulation and thus greater deference was appropriate.

4. **Continuing Violation**: The Supreme Court has recognized a continuing violation theory where a plaintiff "challenges not just one incident of conduct violative of the Act, but an unlawful practice that continues into the limitations period," and the complaint is filed within the required number of days "of the last asserted occurrence of that practice." *Havens Realty Corp. v. Coleman*, 455 U.S. 363, 380-381 (1982).

Further, the Supreme Court has held that salary disparities, which originated prior to Title VII's effective date but which perpetuate past discrimination, violate the Act. In *Bazemore v. Friday*, 478 U.S. 385 (1986), it explained in a unanimous decision:

> The error of the Court of Appeals with respect to salary disparities created prior to 1972[a] and perpetuated thereafter is too obvious to warrant extended discussion: that the Extension Service discriminated with respect to salaries prior to the time it was covered by Title VII does not excuse perpetuating that discrimination *after* the Extension Service became covered by Title VII. To hold otherwise would have the effect of exempting from liability those employers who were historically the greatest offenders of the rights of blacks. A pattern or practice that would have constituted a violation of Title VII, but for the fact that the statute had not yet become effective, became a violation upon Title VII's effective date, and to the extent an employer continued to engage in that act or practice, he is liable under that statute. While recovery may not be permitted for pre-1972 acts of discrimination, to the extent that this discrimination was perpetuated after 1972, liability may be imposed.
>
> Each week's pay check that delivers less to a black than to a similarly situated white is a wrong actionable under Title VII, regardless of the fact that this pattern was begun prior to the effective date of Title VII. The Court of Appeals plainly erred in holding that the pre-Act discriminatory difference in salaries did not have to be eliminated.

However, in *National R.R. Passenger Corp. v. Morgan*, 536 U.S. 101 (2002), the Court rejected use of the continuing violation doctrine where plaintiff challenges a discrete act, such as termination, denial of promotion, or demotion. As to discrete acts, the Court reasoned that the discriminatory or retaliatory act triggers the applicable limitations period. A failure to file on time cannot be avoided by invoking the so-called

---

a   Title VII was extended to cover Government employers in 1972.

"serial violation" doctrine, which allows otherwise time-barred conduct to trigger liability provided there are a series of related acts, one or more of which fall within the limitations period. The Court explained, however, that an employee may file a charge, even though there was prior knowledge of past discrete acts, so long as the timely charge alleges conduct that is independently discriminatory. Further, an employee may use prior acts as background evidence in support of a timely claim. The Court also held that as to **hostile environment claims**, provided one act contributing to the claim occurs within the filing period, the entire time period of the hostile environment may be considered for purposes of determining liability. The Court explained that incidents comprising a hostile work environment are part of one "unlawful employment practice" within the statutory language. Thus, the statute does not bar a plaintiff from recovering damages for that portion of the hostile environment claim that falls outside the period for filing a timely charge. The Court cautioned, however, that all claims, including hostile work environment, are subject to equitable estoppel, tolling, and possibly laches, which bars a plaintiff from maintaining a suit if he unreasonably delays in filing and, as a result, harms the defendant.

5. In *Ledbetter v. The Goodyear Tire & Rubber Co., Inc.*, 550 U.S. 618 (2007), the Court rejected the *Bazemore* analysis and held: "Because a pay-setting decision is a 'discrete act,' it follows that the period for filing an EEOC charge begins when the act occurs.... A new violation does not occur, and a new charging period does not commence, upon the occurrence of subsequent nondiscriminatory acts that entail adverse effects resulting from the past discrimination."

   In January, 20019, the **Lily Ledbetter Fair Pay Act** was signed into law. *See* 42 U.S.C. § 2000e-5(e)(3)(A) in the Appendix. The Act amends Title VII, as well as the Age Discrimination in Employment Act, the Americans with Disabilities Act, and the Rehabilitation Act, to specify that the time limit for filing pay discrimination claims begins to run each time an employee receives a paycheck that manifests discrimination, not just when the employer makes a discriminatory pay decision. Those opposing the bill argued that this would permit an employee to bring a claim against an employer decades after the initial act of discrimination occurred, conceivably allowing employees to seek damages against a company now led by executives who had nothing to do with the initial act of alleged discrimination. Supporters responded that the doctrine of laches provided employers sufficient protection.

6. Prior to the Pregnancy Discrimination Act (PDA), which was passed in 1978, AT&T treated pregnancy leave as personal leave, rather than disability leave. As a result, employees who took a pregnancy leave received maximum service credit of 30 days. In 1979, after passage of the PDA, AT&T treated pregnancy leave as disability/medical leave and provided service credit on the same basis as other temporary disabilities. However, it did not make retroactive adjustments to the service credit of women

who were subject to pre-PDA personnel policies. Treating the benefit calculation rule as part of a bona fide seniority system, the Court, in *AT&T Corp. v. Hulteen*, 556 U.S. 701 (2009), held that AT&T did not violate the PDA by paying "pension benefits calculated in part under an accrual rule, applied only prior to the PDA, that gave less retirement credit for pregnancy leave than for medical leave generally." According to the majority, this case is controlled by *Teamsters* because the service credit scheme was not illegal prior to the PDA and the AT&T seniority system "did not have its genesis in . . . discrimination, and . . . has been maintained free from any illegal purpose." *Id.* at 710, *quoting Teamsters*, 431 U.S. at 356. *Compare Lewis v. Chicago*, 560 U.S. 205 (2010), holding that the City of Chicago's use of a written test that had a disparate impact on African-American applicants was not time barred. Although the time had lapsed for challenging the City's creation of a hiring list based on scores from the test, Title VII specifically prohibits an employer from *using* a particular employment practice that causes a disparate impact, and thus the City committed a new violation each time it filled a new class of firefighters from the tainted eligibility list. Unlike disparate-treatment claims where discriminatory intent is required, Congress allowed impact claims to be brought against an employer who "uses" a practice that causes disparate impact, whatever the employer's motives. In short, even if a plaintiff fails to file a timely charge challenging the adoption of a practice, he may assert a disparate-impact claim in a timely charge challenging the employer's later application of that practice.

7. **Limitations Period for Judicial Filing**: Read § 706(f)(1). Assuming plaintiff complies with the initial administrative filing requirements, what is the limitations period for filing in federal or state court? Like agency filing, equitable principles also govern judicial filing. The Supreme Court, in *Irwin v. Veterans Administration*, 498 U.S. 89 (1990), noted that equitable tolling may be used in situations in which the claimant diligently sought judicial relief by filing a defective pleading during the statutory period, as well as in cases in which the complainant has been induced by his adversary to allow the filing deadline to pass.

What if a plaintiff does not receive a right to sue letter even though several months have elapsed since the initial filing? What recourse, if any, does the Act provide? *See* § 706(f)(1).

8. **Concurrent Jurisdiction**: Does the Act envision state court suits brought under Title VII? Note that § 706(f)(2) allows a temporary restraining order to be filed in accordance with Rule 65, FRCP, and § 706(j) provides that appeals be taken subject to 28 U.S.C. §§ 1291 and 1292. Do these sections indicate that Congress intended exclusive federal court jurisdiction for Title VII litigation? *See Yellow Freight System Inc. v. Donnelly*, 494 U.S. 820 (1990) (suit may be brought in state court because the

presumption in favor of concurrent jurisdiction was not overcome by the statutory language in Title VII).

b.   Remedies

Title VII authorizes trial courts to enjoin unlawful employment practices and to issue "any other equitable relief as the court deems appropriate." 42 U.S.C. § 2000e-5(g). Further, the Civil Rights Act of 1991 provides, with certain exceptions and limitations, for both compensatory and punitive damages as a remedy for intentional discrimination. 42 U.S.C. § 1981a. Be careful not to confuse this with 42 U.S.C. § 1981(a), which amended the Reconstruction Era Civil Rights Act.

i.   Injunctions and Back Pay

ALBEMARLE PAPER CO. V. MOODY
422 u.s. 405 (1975)

Justice STEWART delivered the opinion of the Court.

Whether a particular member of the plaintiff class should have been awarded any back pay and, if so, how much, are questions not involved in this review. The equities of individual cases were never reached. Though at least some of the members of the plaintiff class obviously suffered a loss of wage opportunities on account of Albemarle's unlawfully discriminatory system of job seniority, the District Court decided that no backpay should be awarded to *anyone* in the class.[8]

The petitioners contend that the statutory scheme provides no guidance, beyond indicating that backpay awards are within the District Court's discretion. We disagree. It is true that backpay is not an automatic or mandatory remedy; like all other remedies under the Act, it is one which the courts "may" invoke. The scheme implicitly recognizes that there may be cases calling for one remedy but not another, and—owing to the structure of the federal judiciary—these choices are, of course, left in the first instance to the district courts. However, such discretionary choices are not left to a court's "inclination, but to its judgment; and its judgment is to be guided by sound legal principles." The power to award backpay was bestowed by Congress, as part of a complex legislative design directed at a historic evil of national proportions. That the court's discretion is equitable in nature hardly means that it is unfettered by meaningful standards or shielded from thorough appellate review.

---

8   The petitioners also contend that no backpay can be awarded to those unnamed parties in the plaintiff class who have not themselves filed charges with the EEOC. We reject this contention. The Courts of Appeals that have confronted the issue are unanimous in recognizing that backpay may be awarded on a class basis under Title VII without exhaustion of administrative procedures by the unnamed class members.

The District Court's decision must therefore be measured against the purposes which inform Title VII. As the Court observed in *Griggs v. Duke Power Co.*, the primary objective was a prophylactic one:

> It was to achieve equality of employment opportunities and remove barriers that have operated in the past to favor an identifiable group of white employees over other employees.

Backpay has an obvious connection with this purpose. If employers faced only the prospect of an injunctive order, they would have little incentive to shun practices of dubious legality. It is the reasonably certain prospect of backpay award that "provide[s] the spur or catalyst which causes employers and unions to self-examine and to self-evaluate their employment practices and to endeavor to eliminate, so far as possible, the last vestiges of an unfortunate and ignominious page in this country's history."

It is also the purpose of Title VII to make persons whole for injuries suffered on account of unlawful employment discrimination. This is shown by the very fact that Congress took care to arm the courts with full equitable powers. Title VII deals with legal injuries of an economic character occasioned by racial or other antiminority discrimination. The terms "complete justice" and "necessary relief" have acquired a clear meaning in such circumstances. Where racial discrimination is concerned, "the [district] court has not merely the power but the duty to render a decree which will so far as possible eliminate the discriminatory effects of the past as well as bar like discrimination in the future." *Louisiana v. United States.* And where a legal injury is of an economic character,

> [t]he general rule is, that when a wrong has been done, and the law gives a remedy, the compensation shall be equal to the injury. The latter is the standard by which the former is to be measured. The injured party is to be placed, as near as may be, in the situation he would have occupied if the wrong had not been committed. *Wicker v. Hoppock*, 6 Wall. 94, 99 (1867).

The "make whole" purpose of Title VII is made evident by the legislative history. It follows that, given a finding of unlawful discrimination, backpay should be denied only for reasons which, if applied generally, would not frustrate the central statutory purposes of eradicating discrimination throughout the economy and making persons whole for injuries suffered through past discrimination. The courts of appeals must maintain a consistent and principled application of the backpay provision, consonant with the twin statutory objectives, while at the same time recognizing that the trial court will often have the keener appreciation of those facts and circumstances peculiar to particular cases.

The District Court's stated grounds for denying backpay in this case must be tested against these standards. The first ground was that Albemarle's breach of Title VII had not been in "bad faith." This is not a sufficient reason for denying backpay. Where an employer *has* shown bad faith—by maintaining a practice which he knew to be illegal or of highly questionable legality—he can make no claims whatsoever on the Chancellor's conscience. But, under Title VII, the mere absence of bad faith simply opens the door to equity; it does not depress the scales in the employer's favor. If backpay were awardable only upon a showing of bad faith, the remedy would become a punishment for moral turpitude, rather than a compensation for workers' injuries. This would read the "make whole" purpose right out of Title VII, for a worker's injury is not less real simply because his employer did not inflict it in "bad faith." Title VII is not concerned with the employer's "good intent or absence of discriminatory intent" for "Congress directed the thrust of the Act to the *consequences* of employment practices, not simply the motivation."

NOTES AND QUESTIONS

1. How does the Court describe the remedial purpose of § 706(g)? What is "make-whole" relief? Should it include pension benefits and medical benefits? What about pre-judgment interest? In *Loeffler v. Frank*, 486 U.S. 549 (1988), the Court cited with approval those circuit decisions awarding pre-judgment interest as "a normal incident" of suits brought under this Act.

2. Will reinstatement always be ordered? What if such would significantly interfere with the operation of the employer's business, *i.e.*, displacing innocent employees? Is front pay, based on an estimation of future earnings, a viable alternative to compensate a victim for continuing future effects of discrimination? If so, how is the "ending date" ascertained—when has the victim been made whole?

3. **No exemption from taxes:** Although the Internal Revenue Code excludes from income damages for injuries that are "tort-like" in nature (those received "on account of personal injury"), the I.R.C. was amended on August 20, 1996, to restrict the exemption to damages from physical injury, *i.e.*, emotional distress "shall not be treated as a physical injury." 26 U.S.C.A. § 104(b). Thus, most awards under Title VII will likely be subject to taxation. Note, however, the Civil Rights Tax Relief Act of 2004, which prohibits taxation of the fee portion of the award.

4. **Injunctive Relief:** Section 706(g) allows the court to issue "any other equitable relief as the court deems appropriate." When coupled with *Albemarle's* focus on "make whole" relief, the lower courts have exercised broad discretion in ordering injunctions to remedy Title VII violations. They have invoked their equitable power to grant tenure, to remove adverse evaluations from an employee's personnel file, and to order other forms of affirmative relief. Questions regarding court-ordered retroactive seniority and quotas are discussed *infra*.

5. **Duty to mitigate:** What limitations does § 706(g) impose on back pay awards? What is the meaning of "amounts earnable with reasonable diligence"? Must a discharged employee accept any type of employment in order to mitigate a backpay award? The appellate courts have generally held that once the employee introduces evidence regarding inability to find comparable work, the employer carries the burden of proving the employee failed to exert reasonable efforts to mitigate damages, and that with reasonable diligence, comparable work would have been found. This is viewed as an affirmative defense subject to waiver.

FORD MOTOR CO. V. EEOC
458 U.S. 219 (1982)

Justice O'CONNOR delivered the opinion of the Court.

This case presents the question whether an employer charged with discrimination in hiring can toll the continuing accrual of backpay liability under § 706(g) of Title VII, simply by unconditionally offering the claimant the job previously denied, or whether the employer also must offer seniority retroactive to the date of the alleged discrimination.

I

A

In June and July 1971, Judy Gaddis, Rebecca Starr, and Zettie Smith applied at a Ford Motor Co. (Ford) parts warehouse located in Charlotte, N.C., for jobs as "picker-packers," "picking" ordered parts from storage, and "packing" them for shipment. At the time, no woman had ever worked in that capacity at the Ford warehouse. All three women were qualified for the positions: Gaddis and Starr recently had been laid off from equivalent jobs at a nearby General Motors (GM) warehouse, and Smith had comparable prior experience. Smith applied before any of the openings were filled, and Gaddis and Starr applied while at least two positions remained available. Ford, however, filled the three vacant positions with men, and Gaddis filed a charge with the federal Equal Employment Opportunity Commission (EEOC), claiming that Ford had discriminated against her because of her sex.

In January 1973, GM recalled Gaddis and Starr to their former positions at its warehouse. The following July, while they were still working at GM, a single vacancy opened up at Ford. Ford offered the job to Gaddis, without seniority retroactive to her 1971 application. Ford's offer, however, did not require Gaddis to abandon or compromise her Title VII claim against Ford. Gaddis did not accept the job, in part because she did not want to be the only woman working at the warehouse, and in part because she did not want to lose the seniority she had earned at GM. Ford then made the same unconditional offer to Starr, who declined for the same reasons. Gaddis and Starr continued to work at the GM warehouse, but in 1974 the warehouse was closed and they were laid off. They then unsuccessfully sought new employment until September 1975, when they entered a Government training program for the unemployed.

Smith applied again for work at Ford in 1973, but was never hired. She worked elsewhere, though at lower wages then she would have earned at Ford, during much of the time between 1971 and the District Court's decision in 1977.

In contrast to Gaddis', Starr's, and Smith's difficulties, at least two of the three men hired by Ford in 1971 were still working at the warehouse at the time of the trial in 1977.

B

In July 1975, the EEOC sued Ford in the United States District Court for the Western District of North Carolina, alleging that Ford had violated Title VII of the Civil Rights Act of 1964, by refusing to hire women at the Charlotte warehouse. The Commission sought injunctive relief and backpay for the victims. After trial, the District Court found that Ford had discriminated against the three women on the basis of their sex and awarded them backpay in an amount equal to "the difference between the amount they would have earned had they been hired in August 1971, and the amounts actually earned or reasonably earnable by them" between that date and the date of the court's order.

II

In this case, Ford and the EEOC offer competing standards to govern backpay liability. Ford argues that if an employer unconditionally offers a claimant the job for which he previously applied, the claimant's rejection of that offer should toll the continuing accrual of backpay liability. The EEOC, on the other hand, defends the lower court's rule, contending that backpay liability should be tolled only by the rejection of an offer that includes seniority retroactive to the date on which the alleged discrimination occurred. Our task is to determine which of these standards better coincides with the "large objectives" of Title VII.

III

The "primary objective" of Title VII is to bring employment discrimination to an end, *Albemarle Paper*, by "'achiev[ing] equality of employment opportunities and remov[ing] barriers that have operated in the past to favor an identifiable group . . . over other employees.'"

To accomplish this objective, the legal rules fashioned to implement Title VII should be designed, consistent with other Title VII policies, to encourage Title VII defendants promptly to make curative, unconditional job offers to Title VII claimants, thereby bringing defendants into "voluntary compliance" and ending discrimination far more quickly than could litigation proceeding at its often ponderous pace.

The rule tolling the further accrual of backpay liability if the defendant offers the claimant the job originally sought well serves the objective of ending discrimination through voluntary compliance, for it gives an employer a strong incentive to hire the Title VII claimant. While the claimant may be not more attractive than the other job applicants, a job offer to the claimant will free the employer of the threat of liability for further backpay damages. Since paying backpay damages is like paying an extra worker who never came to work, Ford's proposed rule gives the Title VII claimant a decided edge over other competitors for the job he seeks.

The rule adopted by the court below, on the other hand, fails to provide the same incentive, because it makes hiring the Title VII claimant more costly than hiring one of the other applicants for the same job. To give the claimant retroactive seniority before an adjudication of liability, the employer must be willing to pay the additional costs of the fringe benefits that come with the seniority that newly hired workers usually do not receive. More important, the employer must also be prepared to cope with the deterioration in morale, labor unrest, and reduced productivity that may be engendered by inserting the claimant into the seniority ladder over the heads of the incumbents who have earned their places through their work on the job. In many cases, moreover, disruption of the existing seniority system will violate a collective-bargaining agreement, with all that such a violation entails for the employer's labor relations. Under the rule adopted by the court below, the employer must be willing to accept all these additional costs if he hopes to toll his backpay liability by offering the job to the claimant. As a result, the employer will be less, rather than more, likely to hire the claimant.

IV

If Gaddis and Starr had rejected an unconditional offer from Ford before they were recalled to their jobs at GM, tolling Ford's backpay liability from the time of Ford's offer plainly would be consistent with providing Gaddis and Starr full compensation for their injuries. An unemployed or underemployed claimant, like all other Title VII claimants, is subject to the statutory duty to minimize damages set out in § 706(g). This duty, rooted in an ancient principle of law, requires the claimant to use reasonable diligence in finding other suitable employment. Although the unemployed or underemployed claimant need not go into another line of work, accept a demotion, or take a demeaning position, he forfeits his right to backpay if he refuses a job substantially equivalent to the one he was denied. Consequently, an employer charged with unlawful discrimination often can toll the accrual of backpay liability by unconditionally offering the claimant the job he sought, and thereby providing him with an opportunity to minimize damages.

An employer's unconditional offer of the job originally sought to an unemployed or underemployed claimant, moreover, need not be supplemented by an offer of retroactive seniority to be effective, lest a defendant's offer be irrationally disfavored relative to other employers' offers of substantially similar jobs. The claimant, after all, plainly would be required to minimize his damages by accepting another employer's offer even though it failed to grant the benefits of seniority not yet earned. Of course, if the claimant fulfills the requirement that he minimize damages by accepting the defendant's unconditional offer, he remains entitled to full compensation if he wins his case. A court may grant him backpay accrued prior to the effective date of the offer, retroactive seniority, and compensation for any losses suffered as a result of his lesser seniority before the court's judgment.

In short, the unemployed or underemployed claimant's statutory obligation to minimize damages requires him to accept an unconditional offer of the job originally sought, even without retroactive seniority. Acceptance of the offer preserves, rather than jeopardizes, the claimant's right to be made whole; in the case of an unemployed or underemployed claimant, Ford's suggested rule merely embodies the existing requirement of § 706(g) that the claimant minimize damages, without affecting his right to compensation.

The sole question that can be raised regarding whether the rule adequately compensates claimants arises in that narrow category of cases in which the claimant believes his replacement job to be superior to the defendant's job without seniority, but inferior to the defendant's job with the benefits of seniority. In the present case, for example, it is possible that Gaddis and Starr considered their GM jobs more attractive than the jobs offered by Ford, but less satisfactory than the positions they would have held at Ford if Ford had hired them initially. If so, they were confronted with two options. They could have accepted Ford's unconditional offer, preserving their right to full compensation if they prevailed on their Title VII claims, but forfeiting their favorable positions at GM. Alternatively, they could have kept their jobs at GM, retaining the possibility of continued employment there, but, under the operation of the rule advocated here by Ford, losing the right to claim further backpay from Ford after the date of Ford's offer. The court below concluded that under these circumstances Ford's rule would present Gaddis and Starr with an "intolerable choice," depriving them of the opportunity to receive full compensation.

We agree that Gaddis and Starr had to choose between two alternatives. We do not agree, however, that their opportunity to choose deprived them of compensation. After all, they had the option of accepting Ford's unconditional offer and retaining the right to seek full compensation at trial, which would comport fully with Title VII's goal of making discrimination victims whole. Therefore, we conclude that, when a claimant rejects the offer of the job he originally sought, as supplemented by a right to full court-ordered compensation, his choice can be taken as establishing that he considers the ongoing injury he has suffered at the hands of the defendant to have been ended by the availability of better opportunities elsewhere. For this reason, we find that, absent special circumstances, the simple rule that the ongoing accrual of backpay liability is tolled when a Title VII claimant rejects the job he originally sought comports with Title VII's policy of making discrimination victims whole.

V

Although Title VII remedies depend primarily upon the objectives discussed above, the statute also permits us to consider the rights of "innocent third parties." The lower court's rule places a particularly onerous burden on the innocent employees of an employer charged with discrimination. Under the court's rule, an employer may cap backpay liability only by forcing his incumbent employees to yield seniority to a person who has not proved, and may never prove, unlawful discrimination. As we have acknowledged on numerous occasions, seniority plays a central role in allocating benefits and burdens among employees. In light of the "over-riding importance" of these rights we should be wary of any rule that encourages job offers that compel innocent workers to sacrifice their seniority to a person who has only claimed, but not yet proved, unlawful discrimination.

NOTES AND QUESTIONS

1. Assume Ford offered plaintiffs a job which paid less or where the job responsibilities differed from those in the position sought. Would refusal to accept the job toll a backpay award? What about an offer conditioned on dropping the Title VII case?

2. Will the majority opinion allow employers to limit their backpay liability by making unfair job offers? Has the Court imposed an "intolerable" choice on plaintiffs?

ii.   Damages

Title I of the Civil Rights Act of 1991 adds a new statutory section, 42 U.S.C. § 1981a, which allows for compensatory and punitive damages, as well as trial by jury, with the following caveats:

(a) The damage provisions apply only to intentional, not to disparate-impact, discrimination.

(b) Damages are available only where "the complaining party cannot recover" under § 1981. Although literally this would appear to foreclose all race discrimination claims, the Sponsors' Interpretive Memorandum explains that the purpose of this provision is to prevent duplicative damage awards where employees sue under both provisions, not to cut off relief where employees fail to prove they could not have litigated under § 1981.

(c) Punitive damages are available where a private employer acts with malice or with reckless or callous indifference to the federally protected rights of the aggrieved employee, but government employers are exempt from any punitive damages award.

(d) The sum of punitive and compensatory damages, defined to exclude back wages and other types of relief previously available under Title VII, may not exceed, for each complaining party, $50,000 for employers with 15-100 employees, $100,000 for employers with 101-200 employees, $200,000 for employers with 201-500 employees, and $300,000 for employers with more than 500 employees.

In *Kolstad v. American Dental Ass'n*, 527 U.S. 526 (1999), the Court rejected the argument that a defendant's conduct must exhibit "egregiousness" in order to trigger punitive damages. Looking to the statutory language, the Court ruled that the focus is on the actor's state of mind, not on the egregiousness of the defendant's misconduct. The only question is whether an employer has discriminated "in the face of a perceived risk that its actions will violate federal law." Although egregious misconduct may be evidence of this mental state, there is no need to show egregiousness or outrageous discrimination independent of the employer's state of mind. The Court noted, however, that there may be instances where an employer engages in intentional discrimination but cannot be held liable for punitive damages because it is unaware of the relevant federal prohibition or it discriminates with the distinct belief that its discrimination is lawful.

On the other hand, the Court ruled 5–4 that there are limits to imputing punitive damages liability for the bad acts of the agent onto the employer. The Court reasoned that an employer may be held liable for punitive damages only in four instances: (1) when the agent has been authorized by the principal to commit the misconduct in question; (2) when the principal recklessly employed the unfit agent; (3) when the agent, acting in a managerial capacity, committed the misconduct within the scope of the of the employment; or (4) when the agent's bad act was subsequently approved by the principal. As to the third situation, the Court held that an employer would be insulated from punitive damages liability if it made a good-faith effort to comply with the requirements of Title VII. The Court reasoned that this is in tension with Title VII's objective of encouraging employers to take prophylactic action. Thus, it concluded that "in the punitive damages context, an employer may not be vicariously liable for the discriminatory employment decisions of managerial agents where these decisions are contrary to the employer's good faith efforts to comply with Title VII." After *Kolstad*, unless the agent is the alter ego of the company, *i.e.* the owner, or the company fails to make a good faith attempt to comply with the Act, punitive damages may not be awarded.

NOTES AND QUESTIONS

1. May a plaintiff pursuing race discrimination claims recover under both §§ 1981(a) and 1981a? How is the relief available under the two provisions different?

2. If a plaintiff raises both disparate impact and disparate treatment claims, will the entire case be tried by a jury, or may the judge retain the right to decide the impact claim? See *Lytle v. Household Mfg.*, 494 U.S. 545 (1990), holding that where a pre-Civil Rights Act of 1991 Title VII action (no damages) is joined with a § 1981 claim, a judge is required to first allow the jury to determine the legal claims so as not to deprive plaintiff of his Seventh Amendment right to jury trial.

3. May punitive damages be awarded in the absence of an award of compensatory damages or back pay? If state law imposes this restriction, will it govern a Title VII action?

4. If front pay is awarded as part of the relief, must the amount be counted towards the statutory cap? See 42 U.S.C. § 1981a(b)(2).

In *Pollard v. E.I. du Pont de Nemours & Co.*, 532 U.S. 843 (2001), the Court ruled that front pay awards are not subject to the 1991 Civil Rights Act's compensatory damages caps. The new Act explicitly created remedies "in addition to" relief already available by Section 706(g) of the 1964 Civil Rights Act. Because front pay was already available under 706(g), it could not be considered "compensatory damages" covered by the 1991 Act's damages caps.

5. Are the "caps" rationally related to any legitimate government interest so as to survive an equal protection challenge? Does the number of employees in a company reflect its economic status? May a company with 505 employees limit its exposure by simply reducing its workforce to 500? *See* § 1981a(b)(3).

6. If an employer is a government entity, what advantages are there to pursuing relief under § 1983? Will punitive damages be available under either provision?

iii. Attorney's Fees

Section 706(k) specifically provides that attorney's fees are available for the prevailing party in Title VII litigation. The statutory language served as the model for the subsequent Civil Rights Attorney's Fees Act, 42 U.S.C. § 1988, and thus the cases interpreting § 1988 basically control Title VII litigation as well. Although § 706(k) provides that fees "may" be awarded to prevailing plaintiffs or defendants, the statutory language has been interpreted in light of the purpose of the fees provision, which is to encourage private vindication of Title VII rights. Thus, the general rule is that a court *should* award fees to a prevailing plaintiff unless "special circumstances" render them unjust. The concept of prevailing party has also been broadly construed to include cases which culminate in a consent decree or where partial relief has been awarded. In contrast, the Court has held that fees will be awarded to a prevailing defendant only where the plaintiff has pursued the action in bad faith or to harass. *EEOC v. Christianberg*, 434 U.S. 412 (1978).

The Supreme Court has held that in light of the mandatory exhaustion provisions in Title VII, requiring resort to state administrative agencies as well as to the EEOC, attorney's fees are available for hours spent handling administrative proceedings, even if the litigation ends at the administrative level. *New York Gaslight v. Carey*, 447 U.S. 54 (1980).

In addition, although § 706(k) allows for fees and costs, the Supreme Court in *West Virginia University Hospitals, Inc. v. Casey*, 499 U.S. 83 (1991), held that the per diem limit of $40 imposed on expert witness fees by 28 U.S.C. §§ 1821(b) and 1920(3) governs § 1988 suits and thus, by implication, Title VII litigation. The Civil Rights Act of 1991 overturned this result by specifically providing for the recovery of expert fees as part of the attorney's fees for actions brought to enforce §§ 1981 and 1981a of the Act. *See* 42 U.S.C. § 1988(c) and 42 U.S.C. § 2000e-5(k).

Finally, Title VII is unique in that §706(g)(2)(b) specifically authorizes an award of fees when it is proved that discrimination was a motivating factor in a challenged employment decision even if the employer demonstrates that the same decision would have been reached in the absence of discrimination. Thus, in a mixed-motive situation, fees should be awarded even in the absence of monetary damages or injunctive relief. On the other hand, relying on *Farrar v. Hobby*, *supra* Ch. II, several appellate courts have ruled that in mixed-motive employment discrimination cases, the award of fees should be proportional to plaintiff's success and to the public purposes served by resolving the dispute, which may mean that no fee is available.

iv.   Retroactive Seniority

In *Franks v. Bowman Transportation Co.*, 424 U.S. 747 (1976), the Supreme Court held that "identifiable applicants who were denied employment because of race after the effective date and in violation of Title VII of the Civil Rights Act of 1964 may be awarded seniority status retroactive to the dates of their employment applications." In reversing the holding of the Court of Appeals that § 703(h) barred this relief, the Court reasoned as follows:

> On its face, § 703(h) appears to be only a definitional provision; as with the other provisions of § 703, subsection(h) delineates which employment practices are illegal and thereby prohibited and which are not. Section 703(h) certainly does not expressly purport to qualify or proscribe relief otherwise appropriate under the remedial provisions of Title VII, § 706(g), 42 U.S.C. § 2000e-5(g), in circumstances where an illegal discriminatory act or practice is found. Further, the legislative history of § 703(h) plainly negates its reading as limiting or qualifying the relief authorized under § 706(g).

Stressing the broad language of § 706(a) and its "make whole" objective, the Court held that retroactive seniority could validly be awarded victims of discrimination.

Does the award of retroactive seniority impose an unduly harsh burden on innocent employees—why should they suffer for their employer's wrongdoing? Why isn't § 703(h) a barrier? The next case addresses a court's power to order retroactive seniority as part of a Title VII remedy in a class action suit.

FIREFIGHTERS LOCAL UNION NO. 1784 V. STOTTS
467 U.S. 561 (1984)

Justice WHITE delivered the opinion of the Court.

Petitioners challenge the Court of Appeals' approval of an order enjoining the City of Memphis from following its seniority system in determining who must be laid off as a result of a budgetary shortfall. Respondents contend that the injunction was necessary to effectuate the terms of a Title VII consent decree in which the City agreed to undertake certain obligations in order to remedy past hiring and promotional practices. Because we conclude that the order cannot be justified, either as an effort to enforce the consent decree or as a valid modification, we reverse.

I

In 1977 respondent Carl Stotts, a black holding the position of firefighting captain in the Memphis, Tennessee, Fire Department, filed a class-action complaint in the United States District Court for the Western District of Tennessee. The complaint charged that the Memphis Fire Department and certain city officials were engaged in a pattern or practice of making hiring and promotion decisions on the basis of race in violation of Title VII of the Civil Rights Act of 1964, as well as 42 U.S.C. §§ 1981 and 1983. Discovery proceeded, settlement negotiations ensued, and, in due course, a consent decree was approved and entered by the District Court on April 25, 1980.

The stated purpose of the decree was to remedy the hiring and promotion practices "of the Department with respect to the employment of blacks." Accordingly, the City agreed to promote 13 named individuals and to provide backpay to 81 employees of the Fire Department. It also adopted the long-term goal of increasing the proportion of minority representation in each job classification in the Fire Department to approximately the proportion of blacks in the labor force in Shelby County, Tenn. However, the City did not, by agreeing to the decree, admit "any violations of law, rule, or regulation with respect to the allegations" in the complaint. The plaintiffs waived any further relief save to enforce the decree, and the District Court retained jurisdiction "for such further orders as may be necessary or appropriate to effectuate the purposes of this decree."

The long-term hiring goal outlined in the decree paralleled the provisions of a 1974 consent decree, which settled a case brought against the City by the United States and which applied citywide. Like the 1974 decree, the 1980 decree also established an interim hiring goal of filling on an annual basis 50 percent of the job vacancies in the Department with qualified black applicants. The 1980 decree contained an additional goal with respect to promotions: the Department was to attempt to ensure that 20 percent of the promotions in each job classification be given to blacks. Neither decree contained provisions for layoffs or reductions in rank, and neither awarded any competitive seniority. The 1974 decree did require that for purposes of promotion, transfer, and assignment, seniority was to be computed "as the total seniority of that person with the City."

In early May, 1981, the City announced that projected budget deficits required a reduction of nonessential personnel throughout the city government. Layoffs were to be based on the "last hired, first fired" rule under which citywide seniority, determined by each employee's length of continuous service from the latest date of permanent employment, was the basis for deciding who would be laid off. If a senior employee's position were abolished or eliminated, the employee could "bump down" to a lower ranking position rather than be laid off. As the Court of Appeals later noted, this layoff policy was adopted pursuant to the seniority system "mentioned in the 1974 Decree and . . . incorporated in the City's memorandum of understanding with the Union."

On May 4, at respondents' request, the District Court entered a temporary restraining order forbidding the layoff of any black employee. The Union, which previously had not been a party to either of these cases, was permitted to intervene. At the preliminary injunction hearing, it appeared that 55 then-filled positions in the Department were to be eliminated and that 39 of these positions were filled with employees having "bumping" rights. It was estimated that 40 least-senior employees in the firefighting bureau of the Department would be laid off and that of these 25 were white and 15 black. It also appeared that 56 percent of the employees hired in the Department since 1974 had been black and that the percentage of black employees had increased from approximately 3 or 4 percent in 1974 to 11.5 percent in 1980.

On May 18, the District Court ordered that the City "not apply the seniority policy proposed insofar as it will decrease the percentage of black lieutenants, drivers, inspectors and privates that are presently employed. . ." On June 23, the District Court broadened its order to include three additional classifications. A modified layoff plan, aimed at protecting black employees in seven classifications so as to comply with the court's order, was presented and approved.

[The Court found that the district court's power to issue the injunction was neither explicit nor implicit in the consent decree, since the terms of the decree did not contemplate seniority rights and the City, without input from the union, would not have purported to bargain away non-minority rights. The Court then turned to the inherent power of federal district courts to modify bona fide seniority systems.]

III

Section 703(h) of Title VII provides that it is not an unlawful employment practice to apply different standards of compensation, or different terms, conditions, or privileges of employment pursuant to a bona fide seniority system, provided that such differences are not the result of an intention to discriminate because of race. It is clear that the City had a seniority system, that its proposed layoff plan conformed to that system, and that in making the settlement the City had not agreed to award competitive seniority to any minority employee whom the City proposed to lay off. The District Court held that the City could not follow its seniority system in making its proposed layoffs because its proposal was discriminatory in effect and hence not a bona fide plan. Section 703(h), however, permits the routine application of a seniority system absent proof of an intention to discriminate. Here, the District Court itself found that the layoff proposal was not adopted with the purpose or intent to discriminate on the basis of race. Nor had the City in agreeing to the decree admitted in any way that it had engaged in intentional discrimination. The Court of Appeals was therefore correct in disagreeing with the District Court's holding that the layoff plan was not a bona fide application of the seniority system, and it would appear that the City could not be faulted for following the seniority plan expressed in its agreement with the Union. The Court of Appeals nevertheless held that the injunction was proper even though it conflicted with the seniority system. This was error.

[T]he Court of Appeals in support of the conclusion that the injunction could be entered notwithstanding its conflict with the seniority system assert[ed] that "[i]t would be incongruous to hold that the use of the preferred means of resolving an employment discrimination action decreased the power of a court to order relief which vindicates the policies embodied within Title VII and 42 U.S.C. §§ 1981 and 1983." The court concluded that if the allegations in the complaint had been proved, the District Court could have entered an order overriding the seniority provisions. Therefore, the court reasoned, "[t]he trial court had authority to override the Firefighter's Union seniority provisions to effectuate the purpose of the 1980 Decree."

The difficulty with this approach is that it overstates the authority of the trial court to disregard a seniority system in fashioning a remedy after a plaintiff has successfully proved that an employer has followed a pattern or practice having a discriminatory effect on black applicants or employees. If individual members of a plaintiff class demonstrate that they have been actual victims of the discriminatory practice, they may be awarded competitive seniority and given their rightful place on the seniority roster. This much is clear from *Franks v. Bowman Transportation Co.* and *Teamsters v. United States. Teamsters*, however, also made clear that mere membership in the disadvantaged class is insufficient to warrant a seniority award; each individual must prove that the discriminatory practice had an impact on him. Even when an individual shows that the discriminatory practice has had an impact on him, he is not automatically entitled to have a nonminority employee laid off to make room for him. He may have to wait until a vacancy occurs, and if there are nonminority employees on layoff, the court must balance the equities in determining who is entitled to the job. Here, there was no finding that any of the blacks protected from lay off had been a victim of discrimination and no award of competitive seniority to any of them. Nor had the parties in formulating the consent decree purported to identify any specific employee entitled to particular relief other than those listed in the exhibits attached to the decree. It therefore seems to us that in light of *Teamsters*, the Court of Appeals imposed on the parties as an adjunct of settlement something that could not have been ordered had the case gone to trial and the plaintiffs proved that a pattern or practice of discrimination existed.

Our ruling in *Teamsters* that a court can award competitive seniority only when the beneficiary of the award had actually been a victim of illegal discrimination is consistent with the policy behind § 706(g) of Title VII, which affects the remedies available in Title VII litigation. That policy, which is to provide make-whole relief only to those who have been actual victims of illegal discrimination, was repeatedly expressed by the sponsors of the Act during the congressional debates. Opponents of the legislation that became Title VII charged that if the bill were enacted, employers could be ordered to hire and promote persons in order to achieve a racially balanced work force even though those persons had not been victims of illegal discrimination. Responding to these charges, Senator Humphrey explained the limits on a court's remedial powers as follows:

> No court order can require hiring, reinstatement, admission to membership, or payment of backpay for anyone who was not fired, refused employment or advancement or admission to a union by an act of discrimination forbidden by this title. This is stated expressly in the last sentence of section 707(e) [enacted without relevant change as § 706(g)]. . . . Contrary to the allegations of some opponents of this title, there is nothing in it that will give any power to the Commission or to any court to require . . . firing . . . of employees

in order to meet a racial 'quota' or to achieve a certain racial balance. That bugaboo has been brought up a dozen times; but it is nonexistent. 110 CONG. REC. 6549 (1964).

The Court of Appeals holding that the District Court's order was permissible as a valid Title VII remedial order ignores not only our ruling in *Teamsters* but the policy behind § 706(g) as well. Accordingly, that holding cannot serve as a basis for sustaining the District Court's order.

Finally, the Court of Appeals was of the view that the District Court ordered no more than that which the City unilaterally could have done by way of adopting an affirmative action program. Whether the City, a public employer, could have taken this course without violating the law is an issue we need not decide. The fact is that in these cases the City took no such action and that the modification of the decree was imposed over its objection.

We thus are unable to agree either that the order entered by the District Court was a justifiable effort to enforce the terms of the decree to which the City had agreed or that it was a legitimate modification of the decree that could be imposed on the City without its consent. Accordingly, the judgment of the Court of Appeals is reversed.

NOTES AND QUESTIONS

1. Does this decision have any effect on the *Franks* holding that federal courts may award retroactive seniority on behalf of individual victims of discrimination?

2. If instead of a consent decree, this case had gone to trial and the Union had been found guilty of race discrimination, could the court have ordered retroactive seniority to the plaintiff class? Could the court have modified the decree to provide retroactive seniority to those who could prove they were actual victims of discrimination?

3. What if the evidence had suggested that the Mayor, in making his lay-off decisions, had chosen those ranks where the greatest impact would be felt by recently hired minorities?

4. Could lay-off protection have been validly provided for in the original consent decree? Should the consent decree be treated the same as "voluntary" affirmative action and is this then permissible? Or would layoff protection still have to be limited to identified victims of discrimination? Does it matter whether the Union is a party to the negotiations? In *W.R. Grace and Co. v. Local Union* 759, 461 U.S. 757 (1983), the Court held that it would not violate any Title VII policy to allow an arbitrator's award imposing back pay damages on an employer for pursuing an affirmative action plan which breached a seniority provision in a collective bargaining agreement, because it is the employer and not union members who should bear the burden of rectifying past discrimination. The Court reasoned that absent a judicial determination, the

employer could not alter the collective bargaining agreement without the union's consent.

5. What impact generally does *Stotts* have on the use of quotas in class action suits? Are goals and quotas foreclosed by the statement in *Stotts* suggesting that "make-whole" relief may be awarded only to actual victims of discrimination? Was the 1980 decree, which set the interim 50% hiring and 20% promotion goals, invalid because it was not limited to actual victims of discrimination? Note that the Justice Department, reacting to the *Stotts* holding, issued a statement that *Stotts* should be read as a sweeping indictment of any plan—court-ordered, through a consent decree, or after full litigation—that provides favored treatment for minorities who have not been found to be victims of discrimination. The Chief of the Justice Department's Civil Rights Division ordered a Justice Department reassessment of hundreds of court-ordered affirmative action programs, stating that Title VII does not tolerate race preferences in employment that benefit non-victims of discrimination at the expense of wholly innocent non-minority employees or potential employees. Did the Justice Department accurately interpret the holding in *Stotts*?

v. Court-ordered Quotas and Goals

LOCAL 28 OF SHEET METAL WORKERS V. EEOC
478 u.s. 421 (1986)

Justice BRENNAN announced the judgment of the Court and delivered the opinion of the Court with respect to Parts I, II, III and VI, and an opinion with respect to Parts IV, V, and VII in which Justice MARSHALL, Justice BLACKMUN, and Justice STEVENS join.

In 1975, petitioners were found guilty of engaging in a pattern and practice of discrimination against black and Hispanic individuals (nonwhites) in violation of Title VII of the Civil Rights Act of 1964, and ordered to end their discriminatory practices, and to admit a certain percentage of nonwhites to union membership by July 1981. In 1982 and again in 1983, petitioners were found guilty of civil contempt for disobeying the District Court's earlier orders. They now challenge the District Court's contempt finding, and also the remedies the court ordered both for the Title VII violation and for contempt. Principally, the issue presented is whether the remedial provision of Title VII, *see* 42 U.S.C. § 2000e-5(g), empowers a district court to order race-conscious relief that may benefit individuals who are not identified victims of unlawful discrimination.

I

In 1964, the New York State Commission for Human Rights determined that petitioners had excluded blacks from the union and the apprenticeship program in violation of state law. The State Commission found, among other things, that Local 28 had never had any black members or apprentices, and that "admission to apprenticeship is conducted largely on a nepot[is]tic basis involving sponsorship by incumbent union members," creating an impenetrable barrier for nonwhite applicants. Petitioners were ordered to "cease and desist" their racially discriminatory practices.

In 1971, the United States initiated this action under Title VII and Executive Order 11246 to enjoin petitioners from engaging in a pattern and practice of discrimination against black and Hispanic individuals (nonwhites). Following a trial in 1975, the District Court concluded that petitioners had violated both Title VII and New York law by discriminating against nonwhite workers in recruitment, selection, training, and admission to the union. The District Court entered an order and judgment (O & J) enjoining petitioners from discriminating against nonwhites, and enjoining the specific practices the court had found to be discriminatory. Recognizing that "the record in both state and federal court against these defendants is replete with instances of . . . bad faith attempts to prevent or delay affirmative action," the court concluded that "the imposition of a remedial racial goal in conjunction with an admission preference in favor of non-whites is essential to place the defendants in a position of compliance with [Title VII]." The court established a 29% nonwhite membership goal, based on the percentage of nonwhites in the relevant labor pool in New York City, for the union to achieve by July 1, 1981. The parties were ordered to devise and to implement recruitment and admission procedures designed to achieve this goal under the supervision of a court-appointed administrator.

[Over the next decade the district court twice found the defendants in contempt for failing to meet the goals and it imposed fines. In 1983 it entered an Amended Affirmative Action Plan and Order (AAAPO), which established a 29.23% minority membership goal to be met by August 31, 1987. The new goal was based on the labor pool in the area covered by the newly expanded union.]

IV

Petitioners, joined by the Solicitor General, argue that the membership goal, the Fund order, and other orders which require petitioners to grant membership preferences to nonwhites are expressly prohibited by § 706(g), which defines the remedies available under Title VII. Petitioners and the Solicitor General maintain that § 706(g) authorizes a district court to award preferential relief only to the actual victims of unlawful discrimination. They maintain that the membership goal and the Fund violate this provision, since they require petitioners to admit to membership, and otherwise to extend benefits to black and Hispanic individuals who are not the identified victims of unlawful discrimination. We reject this argument, and hold that § 706(g) does not prohibit a court from ordering, in appropriate circumstances, affirmative race-conscious relief as a remedy for past discrimination. Specifically, we hold that such relief may be appropriate where an employer or a labor union has engaged in persistent or egregious discrimination, or where necessary to dissipate the lingering effects of pervasive discrimination.

The language of § 706(g) plainly expresses Congress's intent to vest district courts with broad discretion to award "appropriate" equitable relief to remedy unlawful discrimination. Nevertheless, petitioners and the Solicitor General argue that the last sentence of § 706(g) prohibits a court from ordering an employer or labor union to take affirmative steps to eliminate discrimination which might incidentally benefit individuals who are not the actual victims of discrimination. This reading twists the plain language of the statute.

The last sentence of § 706(g) prohibits a court from ordering a union to admit an individual who was "refused admission . . . for any reason other than discrimination." It does not, as petitioners and the Solicitor General suggest, say that a court may order relief only for the actual victims of past discrimination. The sentence on its face addresses only the situation where a plaintiff demonstrates that a union (or an employer) has engaged in unlawful discrimination, but the union can show that a particular individual would have been refused admission even in the absence of discrimination, for example, because that individual was unqualified. In these circumstances, § 706(g) confirms that a court could not order the union to admit that unqualified individual. In this case, neither the membership goal nor the Fund order required petitioners to admit to membership individuals who have been refused admission for reasons unrelated to discrimination. Thus, we do not read § 706(g) to prohibit a court from ordering the kind of affirmative relief the District Court awarded in this case.

In order to foster equal employment opportunities, Congress gave the lower courts broad power under § 706(g) to fashion "the most complete relief possible" to remedy past discrimination. In most cases, the court need only order the employer or union to cease engaging in discriminatory practices, and award make-whole relief to the individuals victimized by those practices. In some instances, however, it may be necessary to require the employer or union to take affirmative steps to end discrimination effectively to enforce Title VII. Where an employer or union has engaged in particularly longstanding or egregious discrimination, an injunction simply reiterating Title VII's prohibition against discrimination will often prove useless and will only result in endless enforcement litigation. In such cases, requiring recalcitrant employers or unions to hire and to admit qualified minorities roughly in proportion to the number of qualified minorities in the work force may be the only effective way to ensure the full enjoyment of the rights protected by Title VII.

Further, even where the employer or union formally ceases to engage in discrimination, informal mechanisms may obstruct equal employment opportunities. An employer's reputation for discrimination may discourage minorities from seeking available employment. In these circumstances, affirmative race-conscious relief may be the only means available "to assure equality of employment opportunities and to eliminate those discriminatory practices and devices which have fostered racially stratified job environments to the disadvantage of minority citizens."

Finally, petitioners and the Solicitor General find support for their reading of § 706(g) in several of our decisions applying that provision. Petitioners refer to several cases for the proposition that court-ordered remedies under § 706(g) are limited to make-whole relief benefiting actual victims of past discrimination.

Petitioners claim to find their strongest support in *Firefighters Local Union v. Stotts*. Relying on *Teamsters*, we observed that a court may abridge a bona fide seniority system in fashioning a Title VII remedy only to make victims of intentional discrimination whole; that is, a court may award competitive seniority to individuals who show that they had been discriminated against.

Stotts discussed the "policy" behind § 706(g) in order to supplement the holding that the District Court could not have interfered with the city's seniority system in fashioning a Title VII remedy. This "policy" was read to prohibit a court from awarding make-whole relief, such as competitive seniority, backpay, or promotion, to individuals who were denied employment opportunities for reasons unrelated to discrimination. The District Court's injunction was considered to be inconsistent with this "policy" because it was tantamount to an award of make-whole relief (in the form of competitive seniority) to individual black firefighters who had not shown that the proposed layoffs were motivated by racial discrimination. However, this limitation on *individual* make-whole relief does not affect a court's authority to order race-conscious affirmative action. The purpose of affirmative action is not to make identified victims whole, but rather to dismantle prior patterns of employment discrimination and to prevent discrimination in the future. Such relief is provided to the class as a whole rather than to individual members; no individual is entitled to relief, and beneficiaries need not show that they were themselves victims of discrimination. In this case, neither the membership goal nor the Fund order required the petitioners to indenture or train particular individuals, and neither required them to admit to membership individuals who were refused admission for reasons unrelated to discrimination. We decline petitioners' invitation to read *Stotts* to prohibit a court from ordering any kind of race-conscious affirmative relief that might benefit nonvictims. This reading would distort the language of § 706(g), and would deprive the courts of an important means of enforcing Title VII's guarantee of equal employment opportunity.

Although we conclude that § 706(g) does not foreclose a district court from instituting some sorts of racial preferences where necessary to remedy past discrimination, we do not mean to suggest that such relief is always proper. While the fashioning of "appropriate" remedies for a particular Title VII violation invokes the "equitable discretion of the district courts," we emphasize that a court's judgment should be guided by sound legal principles. In particular, the court should exercise its discretion with an eye toward Congress' concern that race-conscious affirmative measures not be invoked simply to create a racially balanced work force. In the majority of Title VII cases, the court will not have to impose affirmative action as a remedy for past discriminatory practices and award make-whole relief to the individuals victimized by those practices. However, in some cases, affirmative action may be necessary in order effectively to enforce Title VII. As we noted before, a court may have to resort to race-conscious affirmative action when confronted with an employer or labor union that has engaged in persistent or egregious discrimination. Or, such relief may be necessary to dissipate the lingering effects of pervasive discrimination. Whether there might be other circumstances that justify the use of court-ordered affirmative action is a matter that we need not decide here. We note only that a court should consider whether affirmative action is necessary to remedy past discrimination in a particular case before imposing such measures, and that the court should also take care to tailor its orders to fit the nature of the violation it seeks to correct. In this case, several factors lead us to conclude that the relief ordered by the District Court was proper.

First, both the District Court and the Court of Appeals agreed that the membership goal and Fund order were necessary to remedy petitioners' pervasive and egregious discrimination. The District Court set the original 29% membership goal upon observing that "[t]he record in both state and federal courts against [petitioners] is replete with instances of their bad faith attempts to prevent or delay affirmative action."

Both the membership goal and Fund order were similarly necessary to combat the lingering effects of past discrimination. In light of the District Court's determination that the union's reputation for discrimination operated to discourage nonwhites from even applying for membership, it is unlikely that an injunction would have been sufficient to extend to nonwhites equal opportunities for employment.

Second, the District Court's flexible application of the membership goal gives strong indication that it is not being used simply to achieve and maintain racial balance, but rather as a benchmark against which the court could gauge petitioners' efforts to remedy past discrimination. The court has twice adjusted the deadline for achieving the goal, and has continually approved the changes in the size of the apprenticeship classes to account for the fact that economic conditions prevented petitioners from meeting their membership targets; there is every reason to believe that both the court and the administrator will continue to accommodate *legitimate* explanations for the petitioners' failure to comply with the court's orders.

Third, both the membership goal and the Fund order are temporary measures. Under AAAPO "[p]referential selection of union members [w]ill end as soon as the percentage of [minority union members] approximates the percentage of [minorities] in the local labor force." Similarly, the Fund is scheduled to terminate when petitioners achieve the membership goal, and the court determines that it is no longer needed to remedy past discrimination. The District Court's orders thus operate "as a temporary tool for remedying past discrimination without attempting to 'maintain' a previously achieved balance."

Finally, we think it significant that neither the membership goal nor the Fund order "unnecessarily trammel the interests of white employees." Petitioners concede that the District Court's orders did not require any member of the union to be laid off, and did not discriminate against *existing* union members. While whites seeking admission into the union may be denied benefits extended to their nonwhite counterparts, the court's orders do not stand as an absolute bar to such individuals; indeed, a majority of new union members have been white.

[Justice POWELL's fifth vote upholding the membership goal and Fund order stressed that affirmative relief must be limited to particularly egregious conduct where an injunction alone is insufficient. He also stressed that any specific program be necessary as well as flexible, temporary, not unduly destructive of the interests of non-minorities, and that the quotas chosen reasonably relate to the percentage of minorities in the relevant workforce.]

NOTES AND QUESTIONS

1. How does the Supreme Court distinguish and limit *Stotts*? If the distinction is between prospective and retroactive relief, may a court order class-wide retroactive back pay?

2. What is the justification for awarding class-wide relief which extends beyond those who have been actual victims of discrimination? Without such relief, wouldn't the worst offender—an employer who has successfully discouraged minority applicants—be in the best position to avoid future integration of its workforce?

3. In *United States v. Paradise*, 480 U.S. 149 (1987), the Court addressed the validity of a district court order that at least 50% of the promotions to corporal be awarded to black troopers, if qualified black candidates were available. This order would remain in effect until the Alabama Department of Safety developed and implemented a promotion policy that would not adversely affect blacks, who had been excluded from the Department for four decades, despite previous Court orders. The Court reiterated the factors that must be examined in determining whether race-conscious remedies are appropriate—namely "the necessity for the relief and the efficacy of alternative remedies, the flexibility and duration of the relief, including the availability of waiver provisions; the relationship of the numerical goals to the relevant labor market; and the impact of the relief on rights of third parties." It concluded that the District Court was plainly justified in imposing the remedy chosen: "Any order allowing further delay by the Department was entirely unacceptable. Not only was the immediate promotion of blacks to the rank of corporal essential, but, if the need for continuing judicial oversight was to end, it was also essential that the Department be required to develop a procedure without adverse impact on blacks, and that the effect of past delays be eliminated."

   Further, "the one-for-one requirement and its actual operation indicate that it is flexible in application at all ranks. The requirement may be waived if no qualified black candidates are available. . . . The requirement endures only until the Department comes up with a procedure that does not have a discriminatory impact on blacks."

   In addition, the Court found the 50% order appropriate even though blacks represented only 25% of the relevant workforce since "the 50% figure is not itself the goal; rather it represents the speed at which the goal of 25% will be achieved. . . . To achieve the goal of 25% black representation in the upper ranks, the court was not limited to ordering the promotion of only 25% blacks at any one time. Some promptness in the administration of relief was plainly justified in this case, and use of deadlines or end-dates had proven ineffective."

Finally, "the one-for-one requirement did not impose an unacceptable burden on innocent third parties . . . [t]he temporary and extremely limited nature of the requirement substantially limits any potential burden on white applicants for promotion."

vi. Voluntary Affirmative Action: Constitutional and Statutory Limits

Where private employers voluntarily adopt race- or gender-based affirmative action programs, a Title VII reverse discrimination challenge may be brought. Government employers may face both statutory and constitutional claims. The constitutional and statutory tests both examine the affirmative action programs as to purpose and means, and there is significant overlap in the analysis. There are, however, important differences.

In *City of Richmond v. J.A. Croson Co.*, 488 U.S. 469 (1989), the Supreme Court held that strict scrutiny must be used in evaluating state and local government affirmative action programs. It reasoned that:

> the purpose of strict scrutiny is to "smoke out" illegitimate uses of race by assuring that the legislative body is pursuing a goal important enough to warrant use of a highly suspect tool. The test also ensures that the means chosen "fit" this compelling goal so closely that there is little or no possibility that the motive for the classification was illegitimate racial prejudice or stereotype. Classifications based on race carry a danger of stigmatic harm. Unless they are strictly reserved for remedial settings, they may in fact promote notions of racial inferiority and lead to a politics of racial hostility.

Ultimately, the Court ruled that Richmond's requirement that prime contractors to whom the city awarded construction contracts subcontract 30% of the dollar amount to Minority Business Enterprises failed to meet strict scrutiny. However, the Court cautioned:

> Nothing we say today precludes a state or local entity from taking action to rectify the effects of identified discrimination within its jurisdiction. If the city of Richmond had evidence before it that nonminority contractors were systematically excluding minority businesses from subcontracting opportunities, it could take action to end the discriminatory exclusion. Where there is a significant statistical disparity between the number of qualified minority contractors willing and able to perform a particular service and the number of such contractors actually engaged by the locality or the locality's prime contractors, an inference of discriminatory exclusion could arise. Under such circumstances, the city could act to dismantle the closed business system by taking appropriate measures against those who discriminate on the basis of race or other illegitimate criteria. In the extreme case, some form of narrowly tailored racial preference might be necessary to break down patterns of deliberate exclusion.

In *Adarand Constructors, Inc. v. Pena*, 515 U.S. 200 (1995), the Court held that racial classifications imposed by Congress are also subject to strict scrutiny, and thus must be narrowly tailored to further compelling governmental interests. In her 5-4 opinion, Justice O'Connor, writing for the majority, specifically noted that strict scrutiny does not necessarily mean the end to affirmative action; rather, government may act in response to the "unhappy persistence of both the practice and the lingering effects of racial discrimination against minority groups" provided the race-based action is necessary and the program satisfies the "narrow tailoring" test set out in previous cases.

UNITED STEELWORKERS OF AMERICA V. WEBER
443 U.S. 193 (1979)

Mr. Justice BRENNAN delivered the opinion of the Court.

Challenged here is the legality of an affirmative action plan—collectively bargained by an employer and a union—that reserves for black employees 50% of the openings in an in-plant craft-training program until the percentage of black craftworkers in the plant is commensurate with the percentage of blacks in the local labor force. The question for decision is whether Congress, in Title VII of the Civil Rights Act of 1964, left employers and unions in the private sector free to take such race-conscious steps to eliminate manifest racial imbalances in traditionally segregated job categories. We hold that Title VII does not prohibit such race-conscious affirmative action plans.

I

In 1974, petitioner United Steelworkers of America (USWA) and petitioner Kaiser Aluminum & Chemical Corp. (Kaiser) entered into a master collective-bargaining agreement covering terms and conditions of employment at 15 Kaiser plants. The agreement contained, *inter alia*, an affirmative action plan designed to eliminate conspicuous racial imbalances in Kaiser's then almost exclusively white craftwork forces. Black craft-hiring goals were set for each Kaiser plant equal to the percentage of blacks in the respective local labor forces. To enable plants to meet these goals, on-the-job training programs were established to teach unskilled production workers—black and white—the skills necessary to become craftworkers. The plan reserved for black employees 50% of the openings in these newly created in-plant training programs.

This case arose from the operation of the plan at Kaiser's plant in Gramercy, La. Until 1974, Kaiser hired as craftworkers for that plant only persons who had had prior craft experience. Because blacks had long been excluded from craft unions, few were able to present such credentials. As a consequence, prior to 1974 only 1.83% (5 out of 273) of the skilled craftworkers at the Gramercy plant were black, even though the work force in the Gramercy area was approximately 39% black.

Pursuant to the national agreement Kaiser altered its craft-hiring practice in the Gramercy plant. Rather than hiring already trained outsiders, Kaiser established a training program to train its production workers to fill craft openings. Selection of craft trainees was made on the basis of seniority, with the proviso that at least 50% of the new trainees were to be black until the percentage of black skilled craftworkers in the Gramercy plant approximated the percentage of blacks in the local labor force.

During 1974, the first year of the operation of the Kaiser USWA affirmative action plan, 13 craft trainees were selected from Gramercy's production work force. Of these, seven were black and six white. The most senior black selected into the program had less seniority than several white production workers whose bids for admission were rejected. Thereafter one of those white production workers, respondent Brian Weber (hereafter respondent), instituted this class action in the United States District Court for the Eastern District of Louisiana.

II

We emphasize at the outset the narrowness of our inquiry. Since the Kaiser-USWA plan does not involve state action, this case does not present an alleged violation of the Equal Protection Clause of the Fourteenth Amendment. Further since the Kaiser-USWA plan was adopted voluntarily, we are not concerned with what Title VII requires or with what a court might order to remedy a past proved violation of the Act. The only question before us is the narrow statutory issue of whether Title VII forbids private employers and unions from voluntarily agreeing upon bona fide affirmative action plans that accord racial preferences in the manner and for the purpose provided in the Kaiser-USWA plan. That question was expressly left open in *McDonald v. Santa Fe Trail Transp. Co.*, which held, in a case not involving affirmative action, that Title VII protects whites as well as blacks from certain forms of racial discrimination.

Respondent argues that Congress intended in Title VII to prohibit all race-conscious affirmative action plans. Respondent's argument rests upon a literal interpretation of §§ 703(a) and (d) of the Act. Those sections make it unlawful to "discriminate . . . because of . . . race" in hiring and in the selection of apprentices for training programs. Since, the argument runs, *McDonald* settled that Title VII forbids discrimination against whites as well as blacks, and since the Kaiser-USWA affirmative action plan operates to discriminate against white employees solely because they are white, it follows that the Kaiser-USWA plan violates Title VII.

Respondent's argument is not without force. But it overlooks the significance of the fact that the Kaiser-USWA plan is an affirmative action plan voluntarily adopted by private parties to eliminate traditional patterns of racial segregation. In this context respondent's reliance upon a literal construction of §§ 703(a) and (d) and upon *McDonald* is misplaced. It is a "familiar rule, that a thing may be within the letter of the statute and yet not within the statute, because not within its spirit, nor within the intention of its makers." The prohibition against racial discrimination in §§ 703(a) and (d) of Title VII must therefore be read against the background of the legislative history of Title VII and the historical context from which the Act arose. Examination of those sources makes clear that an interpretation of the sections that forbade all race-conscious affirmative action would "bring about an end completely at variance with the purpose of the statute" and must be rejected.

Congress' primary concern in enacting the prohibition against racial discrimination in Title VII of the Civil Rights Act of 1964 was with "the plight of the Negro in our economy." 110 Cong. Rec. 6548 (1964) (remarks of Sen. Humphrey). Before 1964, blacks were largely relegated to "unskilled and semi-skilled jobs." Accordingly, it was clear to Congress that "[t]he crux of the problem [was] to open employment opportunities for Negroes in occupations which have been traditionally closed to them," and it was to this problem that Title VII's prohibition against racial discrimination in employment was primarily addressed.

It plainly appears from the House Report accompanying the Civil Rights Act that Congress did not intend wholly to prohibit private and voluntary affirmative action efforts as one method of solving this problem. The Report provides:

> No bill can or should lay claim to eliminating all of the causes and consequences of racial and other types of discrimination against minorities. There is reason to believe, however, that national leadership provided by the enactment of Federal legislation dealing with the most troublesome problems *will create an atmosphere conducive to voluntary or local resolution of other forms of discrimination.*

Given this legislative history, we cannot agree with respondent that Congress intended to prohibit the private sector from taking effective steps to accomplish the goal that Congress designed Title VII to achieve.

Our conclusion is further reinforced by examination of the language and legislative history of § 703(j) of Title VII. Opponents of Title VII raised two related arguments against the bill. First, they argued that the Act would be interpreted to *require* employers with racially imbalanced work forces to grant preferential treatment to racial minorities in order to integrate. Second, they argued that employers with racially imbalanced work forces would grant preferential treatment to racial minorities, even if not required to do so by the Act. Had Congress meant to prohibit all race-conscious affirmative action, as respondent urges, it easily could have answered both objections by providing that Title VII would not require or *permit* racially preferential integration efforts. But Congress did not choose such a course. Rather, Congress added § 703(j) which addresses only the first objection. The section provides that nothing contained in Title VII "shall be interpreted to *require* any employer . . . to grant preferential treatment . . . to any group because of the race . . . of such . . . group on account of" a *de facto* racial imbalance in the employer's work force. The section does not state that "nothing in Title VII shall be interpreted to *permit*" voluntary affirmative efforts to correct racial imbalances. The natural inference is that Congress chose not to forbid all voluntary race-conscious affirmative action.

The reasons for this choice are evident from the legislative record. Title VII could not have been enacted into law without substantial support from legislators in both Houses who traditionally resisted federal regulation of private business. Those legislators demanded as a price for their support that "management prerogatives, and union freedoms . . . be left undisturbed to the greatest extent possible." Section 703(j) was proposed by Senator Dirksen to allay any fears that the Act might be interpreted in such a way as to upset this compromise. Clearly, a prohibition against all voluntary, race-conscious, affirmative action efforts would disserve these ends. Such a prohibition would augment the powers of the Federal Government and diminish traditional management prerogatives while at the same time impeding attainment of the ultimate statutory goals. In view of this legislative history and in view of Congress' desire to avoid undue federal regulation of private businesses, use of the word "require" rather than the phrase "require or permit" in § 703(j) fortifies the conclusion that Congress did not intend to limit traditional business freedom to such a degree as to prohibit all voluntary, race-conscious affirmative action.

We therefore hold that Title VII's prohibition in §§ 703(a) and (d) against racial discrimination does not condemn all private, voluntary, race-conscious affirmative action plans.

III

We need not today define in detail the line of demarcation between permissible and impermissible affirmative action plans. It suffices to hold that the challenged Kaiser-USWA affirmative action plan falls on the permissible side of the line. The purposes of the plan mirror those of the statute. Both were designed to breakdown old patterns of racial segregation and hierarchy. Both were structured to "open employment opportunities for Negroes in occupations which have been traditionally closed to them."

At the same time, the plan does not unnecessarily trammel the interests of the white employees. The plan does not require the discharge of white workers and their replacement with new black hires. Nor does the plan create an absolute bar to the advancement of white employees; half of those trained in the program will be white. Moreover, the plan is a temporary measure; it is not intended to maintain racial balance, but simply to eliminate a manifest racial imbalance. Preferential selection of craft trainees at the Gramercy plant will end as soon as the percentage of black skilled craftworkers in the Gramercy plant approximates the percentage of blacks in the local labor force.

We conclude, therefore, that the adoption of the Kaiser-USWA plan for the Gramercy plant falls within the area of discretion left by Title VII to the private sector voluntarily to adopt affirmative action plans designed to eliminate conspicuous racial imbalance in traditionally segregated job categories.

NOTES AND QUESTIONS

1. Was the affirmative action program intended to remedy past discrimination on the part of Kaiser Aluminum? Is this a necessary prerequisite to a valid affirmative action program?

    Why shouldn't the Court require proof of "egregious violations of law" as a prerequisite to the adoption of goals and quotas as it did in *Paradise* and *Sheet Metal Workers*? If this had been court-ordered, would the 50% quota have been sustained?

2. What if there had *never* been race discrimination in the craft industry? Does *Weber* allow a private voluntary affirmative action plan whenever such is reasonably necessary to correct a statistical disparity in the labor force? Is an employer limited to correcting imbalance in "traditionally segregated" job categories? Doesn't § 703(j) forbid the use of quotas to achieve "race balance"?

   Should it matter that minorities who benefit from the program have never been victims of discrimination? Is past societal discrimination a sufficient justification for private voluntary affirmative action?

3. How "voluntary" was the affirmative action program adopted by Kaiser Aluminum? Was the statistical data (only 1.83% of the craft workers at Kaiser's Gramercy plant were black even though the workforce was 39% black) sufficient to create a *prima facie* case of discrimination? Note that Kaiser was under pressure from the Office of Federal Contract Compliance to comply with Executive Order 11246, which requires those who contract with the federal government to institute affirmative action programs. Further, black workers in another plant had already sued Kaiser for violating Title VII. What if Kaiser had adopted its affirmative action program as part of a consent decree? Are consent decrees to be treated as voluntary affirmative action programs or as court-ordered affirmative relief?

   In *Local No. 93 v. City of Cleveland*, 478 U.S. 501 (1986), the Court rejected the argument that the remedial provision of Title VII, § 706(g) foreclosed entry of a consent decree that benefitted individuals who are not actual victims of the defendant's discriminatory practices. It reasoned that "the voluntary nature of a consent decree is its most fundamental characteristic," and thus a federal court is not barred from entering a consent decree simply because the decree provides broader relief than a court could have awarded. How does the analysis of court-ordered affirmative action differ from that of voluntary plans?

4. What if Kaiser, in order to speed up the process of bringing blacks into the craft workers industry, had required that the first fifty openings in the training program go to blacks, and that thereafter the fifty percent quota would be used. Would such a program violate Title VII? What limitations on affirmative action programs does *Weber* suggest?

5. How can an employer protect itself against claims of reverse discrimination? Recognizing the dilemma, the EEOC in 1979 issued guidelines which set forth in detail the elements of a valid affirmative action program. 29 C.F.R. § 1608.4. The guidelines provide a three-step process requiring (1) that the employer conduct a reasonable self-analysis; (2) that the analysis reveal a reasonable basis for taking affirmative action; and (3) that the program implemented be reasonable in relation to the problems disclosed by the self-analysis. As to the second requirement, the

guidelines state that it suffices that facts are revealed showing that an employer's practices have an actual or potential adverse impact on minority groups or that an employer is trying to overcome problems resulting from historical restrictions against minorities. The guidelines state that if these requirements are satisfied, an employer can make a good faith defense based on § 713(b), which insulates employer actions taken "in good faith, in conformity with, and in reliance on any written interpretation or opinion of the Commission." Note, however, that this will insulate the affirmative action program only from Title VII challenges; government employers still face the possibility of an equal protection claim. If Kaiser had been a state employer, would the program have been upheld against a constitutional challenge?

JOHNSON V. TRANSPORTATION AGENCY, SANTA CLARA COUNTY, CAL.
480 U.S. 616 (1987)

Justice BRENNAN delivered the opinion of the Court, in which MARSHALL, BLACKMUN, POWELL, and STEVENS, J.J., joined. O'CONNOR, J., filed an opinion concurring in the judgment. WHITE, SCALIA, and REHNQUIST, J.J. dissented.

I

In December 1978, the Santa Clara County Transit District Board of Supervisors adopted an Affirmative Action Plan (Plan) for the County Transportation Agency. The Plan implemented a County Affirmative Action Plan, which had been adopted, declared the County, because "mere prohibition of discriminatory practices is not enough to remedy the effects of past practices and to permit attainment of an equitable representation of minorities, women and handicapped persons."

The Agency stated that its Plan was intended to achieve "a statistically measurable yearly improvement in hiring, training and promotion of minorities and women throughout the Agency in all major job classifications where they are underrepresented." As a benchmark by which to evaluate progress, the Agency stated that its long term goal was to attain a work force whose composition reflected the proportion of minorities and women in the area labor force.

The Plan acknowledged that a number of factors might make it unrealistic to rely on the Agency's long-term goals in evaluating the Agency's progress in expanding job opportunities for minorities and women. As a result, the Plan counseled that short-range goals be established and annually adjusted to serve as the most realistic guide for actual employment decisions.

The Agency's Plan thus set aside no specific number of positions for minorities or women, but authorized the consideration of ethnicity or sex as a factor when evaluating qualified candidates for jobs in which members of such groups were poorly represented. One such job was the road dispatcher position that is the subject of the dispute in this case.

On December 12, 1979, the Agency announced a vacancy for the promotional position of road dispatcher in the Agency's Roads Division. Twelve County employees applied for the promotion, including Joyce and Johnson. Joyce had worked for the County since 1970, serving as an account clerk until 1975. She had applied for a road dispatcher position in 1974, but was deemed ineligible because she had not served as a road maintenance worker. In 1975, Joyce transferred from a senior account clerk position to a road maintenance worker position, becoming the first woman to fill such a job. During her four years in that position, she occasionally worked out of class as a road dispatcher.

Petitioner Johnson began with the county in 1967 as a road yard clerk, after private employment that included working as supervisor and dispatcher. He had also unsuccessfully applied for the road dispatcher opening in 1974. In 1977, his clerical position was downgraded, and he sought and received a transfer to the position of road maintenance worker. He also occasionally worked out of class as a dispatcher while performing that job.

Nine of the applicants, including Joyce and Johnson, were deemed qualified for the job, and were interviewed by a two-person board. Seven of the applicants scored above 70 on this interview, which meant that they were certified as eligible for selection by the appointing authority. The scores awarded ranged from 70 to 80. Johnson was tied for second with a score of 75, while Joyce ranked next with a score of 73. A second interview was conducted by three Agency supervisors, who ultimately recommended that Johnson be promoted. Prior to the second interview, Joyce had contacted the County's Affirmative Action Office because she feared that her application might not receive disinterested review. The Office in turn contacted the Agency's Affirmative Action Coordinator, whom the Agency's Plan makes responsible for, *inter alia*, keeping the Director informed of opportunities for the Agency to accomplish its objectives under the Plan. At the time, the Agency employed no women in any Skilled Craft position, and had never employed a woman as a road dispatcher. The Coordinator recommended to the Director of the Agency, James Graebner, that Joyce be promoted.

Graebner, authorized to choose any of the seven persons deemed eligible, thus had the benefit of suggestions by the second interview panel and by the Agency Coordinator in arriving at his decision. After deliberation, Graebner concluded that the promotion should be given to Joyce. As he testified: "I tried to look at the whole picture, the combination of her qualifications and Mr. Johnson's qualifications, their test scores, their expertise, their background, affirmative action matters, things like that . . . I believe it was a combination of all those." Graebner testified that he did not regard as significant the fact that Johnson scored 75 and Joyce 73 when interviewed by the two-person board.

II

As a preliminary matter, we note that petitioner bears the burden of establishing the invalidity of the Agency's Plan. This case fits readily within the analytical framework set forth in *McDonnell Douglas Corp. v. Green*. Once a plaintiff establishes a *prima facie* case that race or sex has been taken into account in an employer's employment decision, the burden shifts to the employer to articulate a nondiscriminatory rationale for its decision. The existence of an affirmative action plan provides such a rationale. If such a plan is articulated as the basis for the employer's decision, the burden shifts to the plaintiff to prove that the employer's justification is pretextual and the plan is invalid. As a practical matter, of course, an employer will generally seek to avoid a charge of pretext by presenting evidence in support of its plan. That does not mean, however, as petitioner suggests, that reliance on an affirmative action plan is to be treated as an affirmative defense requiring the employer to carry the burden of proving the validity of the plan. The burden of proving its invalidity remains on the plaintiff.

The assessment of the legality of the Agency Plan must be guided by our decision in *Weber*.[6] In that case, the Court addressed the question whether the employer violated Title VII by adopting a voluntary affirmative action plan designed to "eliminate manifest racial imbalances in traditionally segregated job categories." We upheld the employer's decision to select less senior black applicants over the white respondent, for we found that taking race into account was consistent with Title VII's objective of "break[ing] down old patterns of racial segregation and hierarchy."

The first issue is whether consideration of the sex of applicants for skilled craft jobs was justified by the existence of a "manifest imbalance" that reflected underrepresentation of women in "traditionally segregated job categories." The requirement that the "manifest imbalance" relate to a "traditionally segregated job category" provides assurance both that sex or race will be taken into account in a manner consistent with Title VII's purpose of eliminating the effects of employment discrimination, and that the interests of those employees not benefitting from the plan will not be unduly infringed.

A manifest imbalance need not be such that it would support a *prima facie* case against the employer, as suggested in Justice O'CONNOR's concurrence, since we do not regard as identical the constraints of Title VII and the federal constitution on voluntarily adopted affirmative action plans. Application of the "*prima facie*" standard in Title VII cases would be inconsistent with *Weber*'s focus on statistical imbalance, and could inappropriately create a significant disincentive for employers to adopt an affirmative action plan.

It is clear that the decision to hire Joyce was made pursuant to an Agency plan that directed that sex or race be taken into account for the purpose of remedying underrepresentation. The Agency Plan acknowledged the "limited opportunities that have existed in the past" for women to find employment in certain job classifications "where women have not been traditionally employed in significant numbers." As a result, observed the Plan, women were concentrated in traditionally female jobs in the Agency, and represented a lower percentage in other job classifications than would be expected if such traditional segregation had not occurred. Specifically, 9 of the 10 Para-Professionals and 110 of the 145 office and clerical workers were women. By

---

6   The dissent maintains that the obligations of a public employer under Title VII must be identical to its obligations under the Constitution, and that a public employer's adoption of an affirmative action plan therefore should be governed by *Wygant*. While public employers were not added to the definition of "employer" in Title VII until 1972, there is no evidence that this mere addition to the definitional section of the statute was intended to transform the substantive standard governing employer conduct. The fact that a public employer must also satisfy the Constitution does not negate the fact that the *statutory* prohibition with which that employer must contend was not intended to extend as far as that of the Constitution.

contrast, women were only 2 of the 28 Officials and Administrators, 5 of the 58 Professionals, 12 of the 124 Technicians, none of the Skilled Craft Workers, and 1—who was Joyce—of the 110 Road Maintenance Workers. The Plan sought to remedy these imbalances through "hiring, training and promotion of women throughout the Agency in all major job classifications where they are underrepresented."

We next consider whether the Agency Plan unnecessarily trammeled the rights of male employees or created an absolute bar to their advancement. In contrast to the plan in *Weber*, which provided that 50% of the positions in the craft training program were exclusively for blacks, the Plan sets aside no positions for women. The Plan expressly states that "[t]he 'goals' established for each Division should not be construed as 'quotas' that must be met." Rather, the Plan merely authorizes that consideration be given to affirmative action concerns when evaluating qualified applicants. As the Agency Director testified, the sex of Joyce was but one of the numerous factors he took into account in arriving at his decision.

In addition, petitioner had no absolute entitlement to the road dispatcher position. Seven of the applicants were classified as qualified and eligible, and the Agency Director was authorized to promote any of the seven. Thus, denial of the promotion unsettled no legitimate firmly rooted expectation on the part of the petitioner. Furthermore, while the petitioner in this case was denied a promotion, he retained his employment with the Agency, at the same salary and with the same seniority, and remained eligible for other promotions.

Finally, the Agency's Plan was intended to *attain* a balanced work force, not to maintain one. [S]ubstantial evidence shows that the Agency has sought to take a moderate, gradual approach to eliminating the imbalance in its work force, one which establishes realistic guidance for employment decisions, and which visits minimal intrusion on the legitimate expectations of other employees. Given this fact, as well as the Agency's express commitment to "attain" a balanced work force, there is ample assurance that the Agency does not seek to use its Plan to maintain a permanent racial and sexual balance.

III

We therefore hold that the Agency appropriately took into account as one factor the sex of Diane Joyce in determining that she would be promoted to the road dispatcher position. The decision to do so was made pursuant to an affirmative action plan that represents a moderate, flexible, case-by-case approach to effecting a gradual improvement in the representation of minorities and women in the Agency's work force. Such a plan is fully consistent with Title VII, for it embodies the contribution that voluntary employer action can make in eliminating the vestiges of discrimination in the workplace.

1. Five Justices in note 6 assert that the constraints of Title VII are not identical to the limitations imposed by the Constitution on voluntary affirmative action programs adopted by government employers. How are the standards different?

2. If an equal protection challenge had been added to Johnson's complaint, would he have been successful? Note that under the Fourteenth Amendment, claims of gender discrimination, whether male or female, are tested under an intermediate standard, *i.e.*, requiring that the classification bear a fair and substantial relation to an important government interest, rather than the strict scrutiny used for race discrimination. Further, in *Mississippi Univ. v. Hogan*, 458 U.S. 718 (1982), the Court suggested that a gender-based classification designed to redress discrimination against women in a particular field would pass muster under the important-government-goal test. Could the Transportation Agency meet this standard? Does *Croson*, decided six years after *Hogan*, require that gender-based affirmative action programs survive strict, rather than intermediate, scrutiny? Does it make sense to subject race-based programs to greater scrutiny? *See* Rosalie Berger Levinson, *Gender-Based Affirmative Action and Reverse Gender Bias*, 34 HARV. J.L & GENDER 1 (2011) (discussing the anomaly that under current Supreme Court precedent, affirmative action for women is easier to justify than race-based affirmative action).

3. Why does the Court use the *McDonnell Douglas* analysis? If the employer concedes that the affirmative action program was a "motivating" factor, should the employer carry the burden of justifying the validity of its gender-based program? What effect, if any, does the Civil Rights Act of 1991 have on voluntary affirmative action programs? *See* 42 U.S.C. § 2000e-2(l). The Civil Rights Act of 1991 states that none of its provisions should be construed to affect affirmative action programs that are in accordance with the law.

4. Does the "traditionally segregated" work force requirement suggest active, conscious discrimination by the industry or will statistical underrepresentation due to cultural bias justify an affirmative action program? Can judges separate societal attitudes from conscious gender discrimination in determining the reason for the stark statistical underrepresentation of women in a particular field? If relying solely upon a statistical disparity, does such have to be sufficient to establish a *prima facie* case of discrimination under Title VII? Should statistics comparing the percentage of minorities in the city's workforce with their percentage in the general population suffice?

5. **Disparate Impact Defense:** In *Ricci v. DeStefano*, 557 U.S. 557 (2009), the Court held that New Haven, Connecticut could not ignore the results of a promotion examination administered to city firefighters, despite its concern that use of the test would have excluded almost all minority candidates. A five-Justice majority reasoned that avoiding disparate-impact liability under Title VII did not justify what otherwise would be prohibited reverse race discrimination. Borrowing from its constitutional affirmative action jurisprudence, the Court held that because the City could not establish a "strong basis in evidence" for believing its use of the promotion test would actually expose it to disparate impact liability, its "racially motivated" action in disregarding the test scores violated Title VII:

> Even if respondents were motivated as a subjective matter by a desire to avoid committing disparate-impact discrimination, the record makes clear there is no support for the conclusion that respondents had an objective, strong basis in evidence to find the tests inadequate, with some consequent disparate-impact liability in violation of Title VII.
>
> The racial adverse impact here was significant, and petitioners do not dispute that the City was faced with a prima facie case of disparate-impact liability. . . . The problem for respondents is that a prima facie case of disparate-impact liability—essentially, a threshold showing of a significant statistical disparity, and nothing more—is far from a strong basis in evidence that the City would have been liable under Title VII had it certified the results. That is because the City could be liable for disparate-impact discrimination only if the examinations were not job related and consistent with business necessity, or if there existed an equally valid, less-discriminatory alternative that served the City's needs but that the City refused to adopt. We conclude there is no strong basis in evidence to establish that the test was deficient in either of these respects.

PROBLEM: TWENTY-SEVEN

This dispute has its genesis in the voluntary adoption by the South Bend Community School Corporation Board of Trustees (Board) of an affirmative action plan (Resolution 1020) designed to increase the percentage of minorities in the teaching force. The plaintiffs are white teachers who were laid off by the South Bend Community School Corporation (School Corporation) on June 7, 1982. Resolution 1020 was adopted on December 18, 1978, after several discussions at Board meetings focusing on the recruiting and hiring practices of the School Corporation.

Resolution 1020, as finally adopted, provides that the School Corporation will strive to increase the percentage of minorities in its teaching force until that percentage equals the percentage of minorities in its student body. The Board deemed it essential that the student population, both black and white, have a sufficient number of minority teachers to act as role models.

During the next three school years, (1978-79, 1979-80, and 1980-81), the School Corporation hired a greater percentage of black teachers than it had hired in any prior three-year period since records have been kept regarding the racial composition of the teaching force. Acting pursuant to a mandate that 40% of all openings go to black applicants, 63 out of the 161 teachers hired from the 1978-1979 school year to the 1981-82 school year were black. The percentage of black teachers in the teaching force increased from 10.4% in the 1978-79 school year to 13% in the 1981-82 school year. The percentage of black pupils in the School Corporation in the 1981-82 school year was 25.42%, and the population in the city at the time was approximately 20% black.

On February 8, 1980, Resolution 1020 was incorporated into the Consent Order entered in United States of America v. South Bend Community School Corporation. The United States Department of Justice had commenced an action claiming that the School Corporation had engaged in acts of discrimination which were intended to segregate, and had the effect of segregating, students and faculty on the basis of race within the school system.

The Consent Order required the School Corporation to formulate a specific desegregation plan for student assignment by September 1, 1980. In addition, the Order required the School Corporation to continue to pursue its present affirmative action hiring policies. The Consent Order, however, contained the School Corporation's denial that it ever engaged in intentional discrimination. At no time were findings made that the School Corporation had engaged in intentional discrimination against any black applicant or teacher.

On May 16, 1980, the School Corporation entered into a three-year Collective Bargaining Agreement with the NEA-South Bend, the exclusive bargaining representative for the School Corporation's teachers. Prior to and during the negotiations, the administration and the Board anticipated that the Board might have to lay off teachers during the term of the 1980-83 Collective Bargaining Agreement. Thus, the School Corporation negotiating team proposed an affirmative retention clause to maintain the success it had achieved in recruiting minority teachers pursuant to Resolution 1020.

On April 26, 1982, the Board determined by resolution to eliminate 232 teaching positions, necessitating an actual reduction in force of 188 teachers. Pursuant to the Collective Bargaining Agreement which defined affirmative retention as "maintaining the same percentage of minority teachers in each minority classification throughout a period of reduction in force as were employed prior to such a reduction," white school teachers with greater seniority lost their positions. They allege that they were laid off in violation of the equal protection clause of the Fourteenth Amendment of the Constitution of the United States enforced via §1983, 42 U.S.C. § 1981, and Title VII of the Civil Rights Act of 1964, as amended by the Civil Rights Act of 1991.

1. Was Resolution 1020's 40% goal, which provided preferential treatment in hiring, lawful? Analyze the statutory as well as the constitutional claims.

2. Will the "affirmative retention" clause be upheld against challenges brought under § 1981, § 1983, and Title VII?

3. What are the advantages and disadvantages to pursuing relief under each? Be sure to explore differences in burden of proof, enforcement procedures, as well as remedies and defenses.

B. AGE DISCRIMINATION IN EMPLOYMENT ACT (ADEA)

In 1967 Congress passed the Age Discrimination in Employment Act (ADEA) relying on its power under the Commerce Clause. The purpose of the Act is "to promote employment of older persons based on their ability rather than age; to prohibit arbitrary age discrimination in employment; to help employers and workers find ways of meeting problems arising from the impact of age on employment." 29 U.S.C. § 621(b).

As originally passed, the Act did not apply to the federal government, the states or their political subdivisions. In 1974 Congress amended the ADEA, 29 U.S.C. § 630(b), to include state and political subdivisions as an "employer," and in *Mount Lemmon Fire Dist. v. Guido*, 139 S. Ct. 22 (2018), the Court held that states and their political subdivisions are "employers" covered by the ADEA regardless of the number of employees. The constitutionality of this extension to include state and local governments was upheld as a valid exercise of Congress' power under the Commerce Clause, not precluded by the Tenth Amendment, in *EEOC v. Wyoming*, 460 U.S. 226 (1983). However, the extension to states was revisited in *Kimel v. State of Florida Board of Regents*, 528 U.S. 62 (2000). The Court ruled that although Congress, in enacting the ADEA, expressed "unmistakably clear legislative intent" to abrogate the Eleventh Amendment, it exceeded its power under §5 of the Fourteenth Amendment. Since *Kimel* does not disturb *EEOC v. Wyoming*, the ADEA is a valid enactment under the Commerce Clause, except insofar as it permits suits against states for damages in federal court. Did Congress intend for state employers to be sued for age discrimination, but only in state court? Review *Kimel* in Ch. I.

As amended in 1986, the ADEA prohibits age discrimination in employment against "individuals who are at least forty years of age." The term "employee" excludes "any person elected to public office . . . or any person chosen by such officer to be on such officer's personal staff, or an appointee on the policymaking level or an immediate advisor. . . ." 29 U.S.C. § 630(f). In *Gregory v. Ashcroft*, 501 U.S. 452 (1991), the Court held that this exception extends to appointed state court judges and thus upheld Missouri's mandatory retirement provision for judges at age 70. However, Title III of the Civil Rights Act of 1991 provides a cause of action for the personal staff and advisor, but not the elected official.

The Act reaches employers with "twenty or more employees." Administrative enforcement of the Act, originally vested in the Secretary of Labor, was transferred to the Equal Employment Opportunity Commission effective July 1, 1979.

Because Congress, in passing the ADEA, was guided by Title VII, cases interpreting Title VII have been relied upon in interpreting the ADEA. However, in part because the ADEA was passed as an amendment to the Fair Labor Standards Act, there are some significant differences. The following material will explore some of these differences between the two Acts.

Federal employment is governed by a separate section of the ADEA, 29 U.S.C. § 633a. Treatment of federal employment is different in a few respects: (1) while the EEOC is the enforcement agency, it is not necessary to file a formal charge with the EEOC before filing a civil action, but EEOC regulations address the use of administrative procedures and appeals to the EEOC; (2) in civil actions, there is no right to trial by jury and there is no express provision for attorney fees; and (3) § 633a does not expressly provide for retaliation claims, but the Court in *Gomez-Perez, supra* Ch. II and III, held that the ADEA's prohibition of "discrimination based on age" includes retaliation.

1. PROOF OF CLAIMS

a. **Disparate Treatment**

A plaintiff claiming intentional age discrimination can rely on direct or circumstantial evidence that age was a determining factor in the challenged decision or utilize the indirect method of proof developed under Title VII. Although use of the latter method has not been addressed by the Supreme Court, the circuits have adopted it.

One of the elements of a *prima facie* case under *McDonnell Douglas* was addressed in an ADEA case, *O'Connor v. Consolidated Coin Caterers Corp.*, 517 U.S. 308 (1966). Because the plaintiff, who was fired at age 56, was replaced by someone 40 years old, the lower courts concluded he could not establish a *prima facie* case. In reversing, the Court assumed that the *McDonnell Douglas* evidentiary framework applies to ADEA cases and held the plaintiff need show only that he was replaced by someone younger. Because the ADEA bans discrimination because of age, "[t]he fact that one person in the protected class has lost out to another person in the protected class is thus irrelevant, so long as he has lost out *because of his age.*" However, an inference of age discrimination should "not be drawn from the replacement of one worker with another worker insignificantly younger."

Does *O'Connor* mean that a discharged female, who was replaced by another female, can establish a prima facie case of sex discrimination under Title VII, assuming she satisfies the other elements?

Age discrimination claims may arise as a result of a reduction-in-force (RIF) that leads to the discharge of employees whose performance is satisfactory and who are not replaced. This leads to a modification of the *McDonnell-Douglas prima facie* case. For example, in *Oxman v. WLS-TV,* 846 F.2d 448 (7th Cir. 1988), the court said the plaintiff could establish a *prima facie* case by "showing that he was within the protected age group, that he was performing according to his employer's legitimate expectations, that he was terminated, and that others not in the protected class were treated more favorably." *Id.* at 455. *See also Schoonmaker v. Spartan Graphics Leasing, LLC,* 595 F.3d 261, 265 (6th Cir. 2010) (where the plaintiff was discharged as part of a RIF, the fourth element of a *prima facie* case is modified and the plaintiff must provide "additional direct, circumstantial or statistical evidence tending to indicate that the employer singled out the plaintiff for discharge for impermissible reasons," *quoting Barnes v. GenCorp Inc.*, 896 F.2d 1457, 1465 (6th Cir. 1990)); *Raymond v. Ameritech Corp.*, 442 F.3d 600, 610–11 (7th Cir. 2006) (in a RIF case, the plaintiff must show "at a minimum that the [allegedly similarly situated] employees possessed analogous attributes, experience, education, and qualifications relevant to the position sought, and that the younger employees obtained the desired positions around the same time as the RIF," *quoting Radue v. Kimberly-Clark Corp.*, 218 F.3d 612, 618 (7th Cir. 3000); *Jones v. Unisys Corp.*, 54 F.3d 624, 630 (10th Cir. 1995) (the fourth element in a RIF case requires the plaintiff to present direct or circumstantial evidence from which a jury could find that the employer intended to discriminate in reaching the challenged decision; this is satisfied by circumstantial evidence that the plaintiff was treated less favorably than younger employees).

In the following case, the Court resolved a split in the circuits over whether the ADEA forbids a discriminatory preference for the old over the young.

GENERAL DYNAMICS LAND SYSTEMS, INC. V. CLINE
540 U.S. 581 (2004)

Justice SOUTER delivered the opinion of the Court.

The Age Discrimination in Employment Act forbids discriminatory preference for the young over the old. The question in this case is whether it also prohibits favoring the old over the young. We hold it does not.

I

In 1997, a collective-bargaining agreement between petitioner General Dynamics and the United Auto Workers eliminated the company's obligation to provide health benefits to subsequently retired employees, except as to then-current workers at least 50 years old. Respondents (collectively, Cline) were then at least 40 and thus protected by the Act, but under 50 and so without promise of the benefits. All of them objected to the new terms, although some had retired before the change in order to get the prior advantage, some retired afterwards with no benefit, and some worked on, knowing the new contract would give them no health coverage when they were through.

Cline brought this action against General Dynamics, combining claims under the ADEA and state law. The District Court called the federal claim one of "reverse age discrimination," upon which, it observed, no court had ever granted relief under the ADEA. A divided panel of the Sixth Circuit reversed, with the majority reasoning that the prohibition of § 623(a)(1), covering discrimination against "any individual . . . because of such individual's age," is so clear on its face that if Congress had meant to limit its coverage to protect only the older worker against the younger, it would have said so.

II

The common ground in this case is the generalization that the ADEA's prohibition covers "discriminat[ion] . . . because of [an] individual's age," that helps the younger by hurting the older. In the abstract, the phrase is open to an argument for a broader construction, since reference to "age" carries no express modifier and the word could be read to look two ways. This more expansive possible understanding does not, however, square with the natural reading of the whole provision prohibiting discrimination, and in fact Congress's interpretive clues speak almost unanimously to an understanding of discrimination as directed against workers who are older than the ones getting treated better.

Congress chose not to include age within discrimination forbidden by Title VII of the Civil Rights Act of 1964, being aware that there were legitimate reasons as well as invidious ones for making employment decisions on age. Instead it called for a study of the issue by the Secretary of Labor, who concluded that age discrimination was a serious problem, but one different in kind from discrimination on account of race.[2] The Secretary spoke of disadvantage to older individuals from arbitrary and stereotypical employment distinctions (including then-common policies of age ceilings on hiring), but he examined the problem in light of rational considerations of increased pension cost and, in some cases, legitimate concerns about an older person's ability to do the job. When the Secretary ultimately took the position that arbitrary discrimination against older workers was widespread and persistent enough to call for a federal legislative remedy, he placed his recommendation against the background of common experience that the potential cost of employing someone rises with age, so that the older an employee is, the greater the inducement to prefer a younger substitute. The report contains no suggestion that reactions to age level off at some point, and it was devoid of any indication that the Secretary had noticed unfair advantages accruing to older employees at the expense of their juniors.

Congress then asked for a specific proposal, which the Secretary provided in January 1967. Extensive House and Senate hearings ensued. The testimony at both hearings dwelled on unjustified assumptions about the effect of age on ability to work. The hearings specifically addressed higher pension and benefit costs as heavier drags on hiring workers the older they got. The record thus reflects the common facts that an individual's chances to find and keep a job get worse over time; as between any two people, the younger is in the stronger position, the older more apt to be tagged with demeaning stereotype. Not surprisingly, from the voluminous records of the hearings, we have found (and Cline has cited) nothing suggesting that any workers were registering complaints about discrimination in favor of their seniors. The statutory objects were "to promote employment of older persons based on their ability rather than age; to

---

2 That report found that "[e]mployment discrimination because of race is identified . . . with . . . feelings about people entirely unrelated to their ability to do the job. There is no significant discrimination of this kind so far as older workers are concerned. The most closely related kind of discrimination in the non-employment of older workers involves their rejection because of assumptions about the effect of age on their ability to do a job when there is in fact no basis for these assumptions."

prohibit arbitrary age discrimination in employment; [and] to help employers and workers find ways of meeting problems arising from the impact of age on employment."

Such is the setting of the ADEA's core substantive provision, prohibiting employers and certain others from "discriminat[ion] . . . because of [an] individual's age," whenever (as originally enacted) the individual is "at least forty years of age but less than sixty-five years of age."[a] The prefatory provisions and their legislative history make a case that we think is beyond reasonable doubt, that the ADEA was concerned to protect a relatively old worker from discrimination that works to the advantage of the relatively young.

This same, idiomatic sense of the statutory phrase is confirmed by the statute's restriction of the protected class to those 40 and above. If Congress had been worrying about protecting the younger against the older, it would not likely have ignored everyone under 40. The youthful deficiencies of inexperience and unsteadiness invite stereotypical and discriminatory thinking about those a lot younger than 40, and prejudice suffered by a 40-year-old is not typically owing to youth, as 40-year-olds sadly tend to find out. The enemy of 40 is 30, not 50. Even so, the 40-year threshold was adopted over the objection that some discrimination against older people begins at an even younger age; female flight attendants were not fired at 32 because they were too young. Thus, the 40-year threshold makes sense as identifying a class requiring protection against preference for their juniors, not as defining a class that might be threatened by favoritism toward seniors.

The federal reports are as replete with cases taking this position as they are nearly devoid of decisions like the one reviewed here. To start closest to home, the best example is *Hazen Paper Co. v. Biggins*, in which we held there is no violation of the ADEA in firing an employee because his pension is about to vest, a basis for action that we took to be analytically distinct from age, even though it would never occur without advanced years. We said that "the very essence of age discrimination [is] for an older employee to be fired because the employer believes that productivity and competence decline with old age," whereas discrimination on the basis of pension status "would not constitute discriminatory treatment on the basis of age [because t]he prohibited stereotype [of the faltering worker] would not have figured in this decision, and the attendant stigma would not ensue." And we have relied on this same reading of the statute in other cases. While none of these cases directly addresses the question presented here, all of them show our consistent understanding that the text, structure, and history point to the ADEA as a remedy for unfair preference based on relative youth, leaving complaints of the relatively young outside the statutory concern.

III

Cline and amicus EEOC proffer three rejoinders in favor of their competing view that the prohibition works both ways. First, they say (as does Justice THOMAS) that the statute's

---

a   Although the Act initially imposed an age sixty-five cap, a 1978 amendment raised the upper limit of the protected class to seventy except for tenured faculty at universities. In 1986 the coverage was extended to all persons over age forty. The exemption for compulsory retirement of tenured professors over seventy was retained until December 31, 1993 when, by its own terms, it was repealed.

meaning is plain when the word "age" receives its natural and ordinary meaning and the statute is read as a whole giving "age" the same meaning throughout. And even if the text does not plainly mean what they say it means, they argue that the soundness of their version is shown by a colloquy on the floor of the Senate involving Senator Yarborough, a sponsor of the bill that became the ADEA. Finally, they fall back to the position (fortified by Justice SCALIA's dissent) that we should defer to the EEOC's reading of the statute. On each point, however, we think the argument falls short of unsettling our view of the natural meaning of the phrase speaking of discrimination, read in light of the statute's manifest purpose.

A

The first response to our reading is the dictionary argument that "age" means the length of a person's life, with the phrase "because of such individual's age" stating a simple test of causation: "discriminat[ion] . . . because of [an] individual's age" is treatment that would not have occurred if the individual's span of years had been longer or shorter.

As Justice THOMAS agrees, the word "age" standing alone can be readily understood either as pointing to any number of years lived, or as common shorthand for the longer span and concurrent aches that make youth look good. Which alternative was probably intended is a matter of context; we understand the different choices of meaning that lie behind a sentence like "Age can be shown by a driver's license," and the statement, "Age has left him a shut-in." The point here is that we are not asking an abstract question about the meaning of "age"; we are seeking the meaning of the whole phrase "discriminate . . . because of such individual's age," where it occurs in the ADEA. As we have said, social history emphatically reveals an understanding of age discrimination as aimed against the old, and the statutory reference to age discrimination in this idiomatic sense is confirmed by legislative history. For the very reason that reference to context shows that "age" means "old age" when teamed with "discrimination," the provision of an affirmative defense when age is a bona fide occupational qualification readily shows that "age" as a qualification means comparative youth. As context tells us that "age" means one thing in § 623 (a)(1) and another in § 623(f), so it also tells us that the presumption of uniformity cannot sensibly operate here.

The comparisons Justice THOMAS urges to *McDonald* and *Oncale* serve to clarify our position. Both cases involved Title VII of the Civil Rights Act of 1964 and its prohibition on employment discrimination "because of [an] individual's race . . .[or] sex." The term "age" employed by the ADEA is not, however, comparable to the terms "race" or "sex" employed by Title VII. "Race" and "sex" are general terms that in every day usage require modifiers to indicate any relatively narrow application. We do not commonly understand "race" to refer only to the black race, or "sex" to refer only to the female. But the prohibition of age discrimination is readily read more narrowly than analogous provisions dealing with race and sex. That narrower reading is the more natural one in the textual setting, and it makes perfect sense because of Congress's demonstrated concern with distinctions that hurt older people.

B

The second objection has more substance than the first, but still not enough. The record of congressional action reports a colloquy on the Senate floor between two of the legislators most active in pushing for the ADEA, Senators Javits and Yarborough. Senator Javits began the exchange by raising a concern mentioned by Senator Dominick, that "the bill might not forbid discrimination between two persons each of whom would be between the ages of 40 and 65." Senator Javits then gave his own view that, "if two individuals ages 52 and 42 apply for the same job, and the employer selected the man aged 42 solely . . . because he is younger than the man 52, then he will have violated the act," and asked Senator Yarborough for his opinion. Senator Yarborough answered that "[t]he law prohibits age being a factor in the decision to hire, as to one age over the other, whichever way [the] decision went."

Although in the past we have given weight to Senator Yarborough's views on the construction of the ADEA because he was a sponsor, his side of this exchange is not enough to unsettle our reading of the statute. It is not merely that the discussion was prompted by the question mentioned in *O'Connor v. Consolidated Coin Caterers Corp.*, the possibility of a 52-year-old suing over a preference for someone younger but in the over-40 protected class. What matters is that the Senator's remark, "whichever way [the] decision went," is the only item in all the 1967 hearings, reports, and debates going against the grain of the common understanding of age discrimination. Even from a sponsor, a single outlying statement cannot stand against a tide of context and history, not to mention 30 years of judicial interpretation producing no apparent legislative qualms.

C

The third objection relies on a reading consistent with the Yarborough comment, adopted by the agency now charged with enforcing the statute, as set out at 29 CFR § 1625.2(a) (2003). When the EEOC adopted § 1625.2(a) in 1981, shortly after assuming administrative responsibility for the ADEA, it gave no reasons for the view expressed, beyond noting that the provision was carried forward from an earlier Department of Labor regulation; that earlier regulation itself gave no reasons.

The parties contest the degree of weight owed to the EEOC's reading. Although we have devoted a fair amount of attention lately to the varying degrees of deference deserved by agency pronouncements of different sorts, the recent cases are not on point here. In *Edelman v. Lynchburg College*, we found no need to choose between *Skidmore* and *Chevron*, or even to defer, because the EEOC was clearly right; today, we neither defer nor settle on any degree of deference because the Commission is clearly wrong.

Even for an agency able to claim all the authority possible under *Chevron*, deference to its statutory interpretation is called for only when the devices of judicial construction have been tried and found to yield no clear sense of congressional intent. Here, regular interpretive method leaves no serious question, not even about purely textual ambiguity in the ADEA. The word "age" takes on a definite meaning from being in the phrase "discriminat[ion] . . . because of such individual's age," occurring as that phrase does in a statute structured and manifestly intended to protect the older from arbitrary favor for the younger.

IV

We see the text, structure, purpose, and history of the ADEA, along with its relationship to other federal statutes, as showing that the statute does not mean to stop an employer from favoring an older employee over a younger one. The judgment of the Court of Appeals is reversed.

NOTES AND QUESTIONS

1. Are you persuaded by Justice Souter's analysis? Did Congress intend to prohibit "favoring the old over the young?"

2. The plaintiff in *Hazen Paper Co. v. Biggins*, 507 U.S. 604 (1993), a disparate treatment case, claimed he was fired at age 62, just a few weeks before his pension vested, in order to prevent his pension benefits from vesting. A jury verdict in favor of the plaintiff was upheld by the First Circuit, with the court of appeals holding that the jury could have "reasonably found that age was inextricably intertwined with the decision to fire [the plaintiff]" because "[i]f it were not for [his] age, sixty-two, his pension rights would not have been within a hairbreadth of vesting." The Court rejected this reasoning:

> In a disparate treatment case, liability depends on whether the protected trait (under the ADEA, age) actually motivated the employer's decision. The employer may have relied upon a formal, facially discriminatory policy requiring adverse treatment of the employees with that trait. Or the employer may have been motivated by the protected trait on an ad hoc, informal basis. Whatever the employer's decisionmaking process, a disparate treatment claim cannot succeed unless the employee's protected trait actually played a role in that process and had a determinative influence on the outcome.
>
> Disparate treatment, thus defined, captures the essence of what Congress sought to prohibit in the ADEA. It is the very essence of age discrimination for an older employee to be fired because the employer believes that productivity and competence decline with age. As we explained in *EEOC v. Wyoming*, Congress' promulgation of the ADEA was prompted by its concern that older workers were being deprived of employment on the basis of inaccurate and stigmatizing stereotypes. Thus the ADEA commands that "employers are to evaluate [older] employees . . . on their merits and not their age." The employer cannot rely on age as a proxy for an employee's remaining characteristics, such as productivity, but must instead focus on those factors directly.

When the employer's decision is wholly motivated by factors other than age, the problem of inaccurate and stigmatizing stereotypes disappears. This is true even if the motivating factor is correlated with age, as pension status typically is. Pension plans typically provide that an employee's accrued benefits will become non-forfeitable, or "vested", once the employee completes a certain number of years of service with the employer. On average, an older employee has had more years in the work force than a younger employee, and thus may well have accumulated more years of service with a particular employer. Yet an employee's age is analytically distinct from his years of service. An employee who is younger than 40, and therefore outside the class of older workers as defined by the ADEA, may have worked for a particular employer his entire career, while an older worker may have been newly hired. Because age and years of service are analytically distinct, an employer can take account of one while ignoring the other, and thus it is incorrect to say that a decision based on years of service is necessarily "age-based."

The instant case is illustrative. Under the Hazen Paper pension plan, as construed by the Court of Appeals, an employee's pension benefits vest after the employee completes 10 years of service with the company. Perhaps it is true that older employees of Hazen Paper are more likely to be "close to vesting" than younger employees. Yet a decision by the company to fire an older employee solely because he has nine-plus years of service and therefore is "close to vesting" would not constitute discriminatory treatment on the basis of age. The prohibited stereotype ("Older employees are likely to be ___") would not have figured in this decision, and the attendant stigma would not ensue. The decision would not be the result of an inaccurate and denigrating generalization about age, but would rather represent an *accurate* judgment about the employee—that he indeed is "close to vesting."

* * *

We do not preclude the possibility that an employer who targets employees with a particular pension status on the assumption that these employees are likely to be older thereby engages in age discrimination. Pension status may be a proxy for age, not in the same sense that the ADEA makes the two factors equivalent, but in the sense that the employer may suppose a correlation between the two factors and act accordingly. Nor do we rule out the possibility of dual liability under ERISA and the ADEA where the decision to fire the employee was motivated by the employee's age and by his pension status. Finally, we do not consider the special case where an employee is about to vest in pension benefits as a result of his age, rather than years of service, and the employer fires the employee in order to prevent vesting. That case is not present here. Our holding is simply that an employer does not violate the ADEA just by interfering with an older employee's pension benefits that would have vested by virtue of the employee's years of service.

3. In *Kentucky Retirement Systems v. E.E.O.C.*, 554 U.S. 135 (2008), the Court relied on *Hazen Paper* and held that the Kentucky retirement plan, which treats some workers who become seriously disabled before they are otherwise eligible to retire more generously than it treats some workers who become disabled only after becoming eligible for retirement based on age, does not discriminate because of age. Kentucky allowed two separate routes to "normal retirement" benefits: (a) 20 years of service, or (b) 5 years of service, provided the employee has attained the age of 55. The actual pension is calculated by multiplying the years of service times 2.5% times final preretirement pay. A special provision for hazardous position workers, who become disabled before they are eligible for normal retirement, allows them to retire if they have worked for 5 years or became disabled in the line of duty and, in calculating the benefit, Kentucky adds a certain number of years to the actual years of service in an amount equal to the number of years they would have had to continue working to become eligible for normal retirement benefits. Thus, a 48-year-old employee who is disabled after 17 years of service will have 3 years of service added (to reach the 20-year requirement) in computing benefits. The plaintiff worked until age 61 when he retired due to disability. In computing his benefits, no extra years of service were added. He argued that, on the face of the pension plan, being 55 affected whether additional years of service would be added in computing pension benefits. The EEOC asserted that such a plan, which makes age in part a condition of pension eligibility and which treats workers differently based on their pension status, automatically discriminates "because of age."

   The Supreme Court rejected the EEOC argument because (1) age and pension status remain analytically distinct concepts, (2) circumstances eliminate the possibility that pension status is a proxy for age, (3) there is a clear rationale for the challenged disparity (pension eligibility) that is not age-related, (4) the plan sometimes works to the benefit of older workers, (5) the plan does not rely on stereotypical assumptions about older workers, and (6) of the lack of alternative ways of achieving the goal of providing disabled workers with a sufficient retirement benefit. Thus, the Court reasoned that the evidence failed to prove that age "actually motivated the employer's decision" or "actually played a role in that [decisionmaking] process and had a determinative influence on the outcome." Was the dissent correct in its argument that "benign motive" should not be a defense to a facially discriminatory law?

4. Assume a plaintiff, one of a company's most senior and thus highest paid employees, was managing the company's satellite plant and was its only permanent, full-time employee at that plant. A determining factor in the decision to discharge the plaintiff, and replace him with a younger, lower paid employee from the main plant, was a desire to save the cost of the plaintiff's higher salary because the satellite plant was losing money. Another factor in the decision was the fact that the replacement also provided greater flexibility in moving personnel.

a. Based on these facts, did the plaintiff, age 55, establish a *prima facie* case under the ADEA?

b. Does the salary savings constitute a permissible, non-discriminatory justification for the discharge? Does it have a disparate impact on older workers?

c. Could the company have offered the plaintiff continued employment at a lower salary in order to realize a savings at the satellite plant without violating the ADEA?

5. Application of the mixed-motive analysis adopted in *Price-Waterhouse v. Hopkins, supra*, to ADEA claims was at issue in the following case:

GROSS V. FBL FINANCIAL SERVICES, INC.
557 U.S. 167 (2009)

Justice THOMAS delivered the opinion of the Court.

The question presented by the petitioner in this case is whether a plaintiff must present direct evidence of age discrimination in order to obtain a mixed-motives jury instruction in a suit brought under the Age Discrimination in Employment Act of 1967 (ADEA). Because we hold that such a jury instruction is never proper in an ADEA case, we vacate the decision below.

I

Petitioner Jack Gross began working for respondent FBL Financial Group, Inc. (FBL), in 1971. As of 2001, Gross held the position of claims administration director. But in 2003, when he was 54 years old, Gross was reassigned to the position of claims project coordinator. At that same time, FBL transferred many of Gross' job responsibilities to a newly created position-claims administration manager. That position was given to Lisa Kneeskern, who had previously been supervised by Gross and who was then in her early forties. Although Gross (in his new position) and Kneeskern received the same compensation, Gross considered the reassignment a demotion because of FBL's reallocation of his former job responsibilities to Kneeskern.

In April 2004, Gross filed suit in District Court, alleging that his reassignment to the position of claims project coordinator violated the ADEA, which makes it unlawful for an employer to take adverse action against an employee "because of such individual's age." The case proceeded to trial, where Gross introduced evidence suggesting that his reassignment was based at least in part on his age. FBL defended its decision on the grounds that Gross' reassignment was part of a corporate restructuring and that Gross' new position was better suited to his skills.

At the close of trial, and over FBL's objections, the District Court instructed the jury that it must return a verdict for Gross if he proved, by a preponderance of the evidence, that FBL "demoted [him] to claims projec[t] coordinator" and that his "age was a motivating factor" in FBL's decision to demote him. The jury was further instructed that Gross' age would qualify as a "'motivating factor,' if [it] played a part or a role in [FBL]'s decision to demote [him]." The jury was also instructed regarding FBL's burden of proof. According to the District Court, the "verdict must be for [FBL] ... if it has been proved by the preponderance of the evidence that [FBL] would have demoted [Gross] regardless of his age." The jury returned a verdict for Gross, awarding him $46,945 in lost compensation.

FBL challenged the jury instructions on appeal. The United States Court of Appeals for the Eighth Circuit reversed and remanded for a new trial, holding that the jury had been incorrectly instructed under the standard established in *Price Waterhouse*. In accordance with Circuit precedent, the Court of Appeals identified Justice O'Connor's opinion as controlling. Applying that standard, the Court of Appeals found that Gross needed to present "[d]irect evidence ... sufficient to support a finding by a reasonable fact finder that an illegitimate criterion actually motivated the adverse employment action." Because Gross conceded that he had not presented direct evidence of discrimination, the Court of Appeals held that the District Court should not have given the mixed-motives instruction.

II

The parties have asked us to decide whether a plaintiff must "present direct evidence of discrimination in order to obtain a mixed-motive instruction in a non-Title VII discrimination case." Before reaching this question, however, we must first determine whether the burden of persuasion ever shifts to the party defending an alleged mixed-motives discrimination claim brought under the ADEA.

Petitioner relies on this Court's decisions construing Title VII for his interpretation of the ADEA. Because Title VII is materially different with respect to the relevant burden of persuasion, however, these decisions do not control our construction of the ADEA.

In *Price Waterhouse*, a plurality of the Court and two Justices concurring in the judgment determined that once a "plaintiff in a Title VII case proves that [the plaintiff's membership in a protected class] played a motivating part in an employment decision, the defendant may avoid a finding of liability only by proving by a preponderance of the evidence that it would have made the same decision even if it had not taken [that factor] into account." But as we explained in *Desert Palace, Inc.*, Congress has since amended Title VII by explicitly authorizing discrimination claims in which an improper consideration was "a motivating factor" for an adverse employment decision. See 42 U.S.C. § 2000e-2(m).

This Court has never held that this burden-shifting framework applies to ADEA claims. And, we decline to do so now. When conducting statutory interpretation, we "must be careful not to apply rules applicable under one statute to a different statute without careful and critical examination." Unlike Title VII, the ADEA's text does not provide that a plaintiff may establish discrimination by showing that age was simply a motivating factor. Moreover, Congress neglected to add such a provision to the ADEA when it amended Title VII, even though it contemporaneously amended the ADEA in several ways.

We cannot ignore Congress' decision to amend Title VII's relevant provisions but not make similar changes to the ADEA. When Congress amends one statutory provision but not another, it is presumed to have acted intentionally. Furthermore, "negative implications raised by disparate provisions are strongest" when the provisions were "considered simultaneously when the language raising the implication was inserted." As a result, the Court's interpretation of the ADEA is not governed by Title VII decisions such as *Desert Palace* and *Price Waterhouse*.

Our inquiry therefore must focus on the text of the ADEA to decide whether it authorizes a mixed-motives age discrimination claim. It does not. "Statutory construction must begin with the language employed by Congress and the assumption that the ordinary meaning of that language accurately expresses the legislative purpose." The ADEA provides, in relevant part, that "[i]t shall be unlawful for an employer … to fail or refuse to hire or to discharge any individual or otherwise discriminate against any individual with respect to his compensation, terms, conditions, or privileges of employment, *because of* such individual's age."

The words "because of" mean "by reason of: on account of." Thus, the ordinary meaning of the ADEA's requirement that an employer took adverse action "because of" age is that age was the "reason" that the employer decided to act. To establish a disparate-treatment claim under the plain language of the ADEA, therefore, a plaintiff must prove that age was the "but-for" cause of the employer's adverse decision.

It follows, then, that under § 623(a)(1), the plaintiff retains the burden of persuasion to establish that age was the "but-for" cause of the employer's adverse action. Hence, the burden of persuasion necessary to establish employer liability is the same in alleged mixed-motives cases as in any other ADEA disparate-treatment action. A plaintiff must prove by a preponderance of the evidence (which may be direct or circumstantial), that age was the "but-for" cause of the challenged employer decision.

III

Finally, we reject petitioner's contention that our interpretation of the ADEA is controlled by *Price Waterhouse,* which initially established that the burden of persuasion shifted in alleged mixed-motives Title VII claims. In any event, it is far from clear that the Court would have the same approach were it to consider the question today in the first instance.

Whatever the deficiencies of *Price Waterhouse* in retrospect, it has become evident in the years since that case was decided that its burden-shifting framework is difficult to apply. For example, in cases tried to a jury, courts have found it particularly difficult to craft an instruction to explain its burden-shifting framework. Thus, even if *Price Waterhouse* was doctrinally sound, the problems associated with its application have eliminated any perceivable benefit to extending its framework to ADEA claims.

IV

We hold that a plaintiff bringing a disparate-treatment claim pursuant to the ADEA must prove, by a preponderance of the evidence, that age was the "but-for" cause of the challenged adverse employment action. The burden of persuasion does not shift to the employer to show that it would have taken the action regardless of age, even when a plaintiff has produced some evidence that age was one motivating factor in that decision. Accordingly, we vacate the judgment of the Court of Appeals and remand the case for further proceedings consistent with this opinion.

NOTES AND QUESTIONS

1. Why did the majority reject *Price-Waterhouse*, despite the Court's interpretation of identical language in Title VII to mean "a motivating factor"? Review *University of Texas Southwestern Medical Center v. Nassar, supra*, where the Court relied on this decision to hold that "but for" causation must be proved by employees bringing retaliation claims under Title VII.

2. Will the decision in *Gross* affect the outcome in many ADEA cases? Explain.

b. Disparate Impact

Until the Supreme Court decision in *Smith*, it was not clear whether a disparate impact theory of liability is available under the ADEA. The disparate impact analysis developed in *Griggs v. Duke Power, supra*, was utilized in some ADEA cases, but after *Griggs* was modified by *Wards Cove Packing Co. v. Atonio, supra*, which was then modified by §§ 104 and 105 of the Civil Rights Act of 1991, 42 U.S.C. §§ 2000e(m) and 2000e-2(k), there was confusion over which version of the disparate impact analysis should govern ADEA cases.

SMITH V. CITY OF JACKSON, MISSISSIPPI
544 U.S. 228 (2005)

Justice STEVENS announced the judgment of the Court and delivered the opinion of the Court with respect to Parts I, II, and IV, and an opinion with respect to Part III, in which Justice SOUTER, Justice GINSBURG, and Justice BREYER join.

Petitioners, police and public safety officers employed by the city of Jackson, Mississippi (hereinafter City), contend that salary increases received in 1999 violated the Age Discrimination in Employment Act of 1967 (ADEA) because they were less generous to officers over the age of

40 than to younger officers. Their suit raises the question whether the "disparate-impact" theory of recovery announced in *Griggs*, for cases brought under Title VII of the Civil Rights Act of 1964, is cognizable under the ADEA. Despite the age of the ADEA, it is a question that we have not yet addressed.

I

On October 1, 1998, the City adopted a pay plan granting raises to all City employees. The stated purpose of the plan was to "attract and retain qualified people, provide incentive for performance, maintain competitiveness with other public sector agencies and ensure equitable compensation to all employees regardless of age, sex, race and/or disability." On May 1, 1999, a revision of the plan, which was motivated, at least in part, by the City's desire to bring the starting salaries of police officers up to the regional average, granted raises to all police officers and police dispatchers. Those who had less than five years of tenure received proportionately greater raises when compared to their former pay than those with more seniority. Although some officers over the age of 40 had less than five years of service, most of the older officers had more.

Petitioners are a group of older officers who filed suit under the ADEA claiming both that the City deliberately discriminated against them because of their age (the "disparate-treatment" claim) and that they were "adversely affected" by the plan because of their age (the "disparate-impact" claim). The District Court granted summary judgment to the City on both claims. The Court of Appeals held that the ruling on the former claim was premature because petitioners were entitled to further discovery on the issue of intent, but it affirmed the dismissal of the disparate-impact claim. Over one judge's dissent, the majority concluded that disparate-impact claims are categorically unavailable under the ADEA. Both the majority and the dissent assumed that the facts alleged by petitioners would entitle them to relief under the reasoning of *Griggs*.

We granted the officers' petition for certiorari, and now hold that the ADEA does authorize recovery in "disparate-impact" cases comparable to *Griggs*. Because, however, we conclude that petitioners have not set forth a valid disparate-impact claim, we affirm.

II

During the deliberations that preceded the enactment of the Civil Rights Act of 1964, Congress considered and rejected proposed amendments that would have included older workers among the classes protected from employment discrimination. Congress did, however, request the Secretary of Labor to "make a full and complete study of the factors which might tend to result in discrimination in employment because of age and of the consequences of such discrimination on the economy and individuals affected." The Secretary's report, submitted in response to Congress' request, noted that there was little discrimination arising from dislike or intolerance of older people, but that "arbitrary" discrimination did result from certain age limits.

Moreover, the report observed that discriminatory effects resulted from "[i]nstitutional arrangements that indirectly restrict the employment of older workers."

In response to that report Congress directed the Secretary to propose remedial legislation, and then acted favorably on his proposal. As enacted in 1967, § 4(a)(2) of the ADEA, now codified as 29 U.S.C. § 623(a)(2), provided that it shall be unlawful for an employer "to limit, segregate, or classify his employees in any way which would deprive or tend to deprive any individual of employment opportunities or otherwise adversely affect his status as an employee, because of such individual's age . . . ." Except for substitution of the word "age" for the words "race, color, religion, sex, or national origin," the language of that provision in the ADEA is identical to that found in § 703(a)(2) of the Civil Rights Act of 1964 (Title VII). Other provisions of the ADEA also parallel the earlier statute. Unlike Title VII, however, § 4(f)(1) of the ADEA, contains language that significantly narrows its coverage by permitting any "otherwise prohibited" action "where the differentiation is based on reasonable factors other than age" (hereinafter RFOA provision).

III

In determining whether the ADEA authorizes disparate-impact claims, we begin with the premise that when Congress uses the same language in two statutes having similar purposes, particularly when one is enacted shortly after the other, it is appropriate to presume that Congress intended that text to have the same meaning in both statutes. We have consistently applied that presumption to language in the ADEA that was "derived *in haec verba* from Title VII." Our unanimous interpretation of § 703(a)(2) of the Title VII in *Griggs* is therefore a precedent of compelling importance.

While our opinion in *Griggs* relied primarily on the purposes of [Title VII], buttressed by the fact that the EEOC had endorsed the same view, we have subsequently noted that our holding represented the better reading of the statutory text as well. Neither § 703(a)(2) nor the comparable language in the ADEA simply prohibits actions that "limit, segregate, or classify" persons; rather the language prohibits such actions that "deprive any individual of employment opportunities or otherwise adversely affect his status as an employee, because of such individual's" race or age. Thus the text focuses on the effects of the action on the employee rather than the motivation for the action of the employer.

Griggs, which interpreted the identical text at issue here, thus strongly suggests that a disparate-impact theory should be cognizable under the ADEA. Indeed, for over two decades after our decision in *Griggs*, the Courts of Appeal uniformly interpreted the ADEA as authorizing recovery on a "disparate-impact" theory in appropriate cases. It was only after our decision in *Hazen Paper Co. v. Biggins*, that some of those courts concluded that the ADEA did not authorize a disparate-impact theory of liability. Our opinion in *Hazen Paper*, however, did not address or comment on the issue we decide today. In that case, we held that an employee's allegation that he was discharged shortly before his pension would have vested did not state a cause of action under a disparate-treatment theory. The motivating factor was not, we held, the employee's age, but rather his years of service, a factor that the ADEA did not prohibit an employer from considering when terminating an employee. While we noted that disparate-treatment "captures the essence of what Congress sought to prohibit in the ADEA," we were careful to explain that we were not deciding "whether a disparate impact theory of liability is available under the ADEA . . . ." In sum, there is nothing in our opinion in *Hazen Paper* that precludes an interpretation of the ADEA that parallels our holding in *Griggs*.

The Court of Appeals' categorical rejection of disparate-impact liability, like Justice O'CONNOR's, rested primarily on the RFOA provision and the majority's analysis of legislative history. As we have already explained, we think the history of the enactment of the ADEA, with particular reference to the Wirtz Report, supports the pre-*Hazen Paper* consensus concerning disparate-impact liability. And *Hazen Paper* itself contains the response to the concern over the RFOA provision.

The RFOA provision provides that it shall not be unlawful for an employer "to take any action otherwise prohibited under subsectio[n] (a) . . . where the differentiation is based on reasonable factors other than age discrimination . . . ." In most disparate-treatment cases, if an employer in fact acted on a factor other than age, the action would not be prohibited under subsection (a) in the first place. In those disparate-treatment cases, such as in *Hazen Paper* itself, the RFOA provision is simply unnecessary to avoid liability under the ADEA, since there was no prohibited action in the first place.

In disparate-impact cases, however, the allegedly "otherwise prohibited" activity is not based on age. It is, accordingly, in cases involving disparate-impact claims that the RFOA provision plays its principal role by precluding liability if the adverse impact was attributable to a nonage factor that was "reasonable." Rather than support an argument that disparate impact is unavailable under the ADEA, the RFOA provision actually supports the contrary conclusion.

Finally, we note that both the Department of Labor, which initially drafted the legislation, and the EEOC, which is the agency charged by Congress with responsibility for implementing the statute, have consistently interpreted the ADEA to authorize relief on a disparate-impact theory. The initial regulations, while not mentioning disparate impact by name, nevertheless permitted such claims if the employer relied on a factor that was not related to age.

The text of the statute, as interpreted in *Griggs*, the RFOA provision, and the EEOC regulations all support petitioners' view. We therefore conclude that it was error for the Court of Appeals to hold that the disparate-impact theory of liability is categorically unavailable under the ADEA.

IV

Two textual differences between the ADEA and Title VII make it clear that even though both statutes authorize recovery on a disparate-impact theory, the scope of disparate-impact liability under ADEA is narrower than under Title VII. The first is the RFOA provision, which we have already identified. The second is the amendment to Title VII contained in the Civil Rights Act of 1991. One of the purposes of that amendment was to modify the Court's holding in *Wards Cove*, a case in which we narrowly construed the employer's exposure to liability on a disparate-impact theory. While the relevant 1991 amendments expanded the coverage of Title VII, they did not amend the ADEA or speak to the subject of age discrimination. Hence, *Wards Cove's* pre-1991 interpretation of Title VII's identical language remains applicable to the ADEA.

Congress' decision to limit the coverage of the ADEA by including the RFOA provision is consistent with the fact that age, unlike race or other classifications protected by Title VII, not uncommonly has relevance to an individual's capacity to engage in certain types of employment. To be sure, Congress recognized that this is not always the case, and that society may perceive those differences to be larger or more consequential than they are in fact. However, as Secretary Wirtz noted in his report, "certain circumstances . . . unquestionably affect older workers more strongly, as a group, than they do younger workers." Thus, it is not surprising that certain employment criteria that are routinely used may be reasonable despite their adverse impact on older workers as a group. Moreover, intentional discrimination on the basis of age has not occurred at the same levels as discrimination against those protected by Title VII. While the ADEA reflects Congress' intent to give older workers employment opportunities whenever possible, the RFOA provision reflects this historical difference.

Turning to the case before us, we initially note that petitioners have done little more than point out that the pay plan at issue is relatively less generous to older workers than to younger workers. They have not identified any specific test, requirement, or practice within the pay plan that has an adverse impact on older workers. As we held in *Wards Cove*, it is not enough to simply allege that there is a disparate impact on workers, or point to a generalized policy that leads to such an impact. Rather, the employee is "responsible for isolating and identifying the *specific* employment practices that are allegedly responsible for any observed statistical disparities." Petitioners have failed to do so. Their failure to identify the specific practice being challenged is the sort of omission that could "result in employers being potentially liable for 'the myriad of innocent causes that may lead to statistical imbalances . . . .'" In this case not only did petitioners thus err by failing to identify the relevant practice, but it is also clear from the record that the City's plan was based on reasonable factors other than age.

The plan divided each of five basic positions—police officer, master police officer, police sergeant, police lieutenant, and deputy police chief—into a series of steps and half-steps. The wage for each range was based on a survey of comparable communities in the Southeast. Employees were then assigned a step (or half-step) within their position that corresponded to the lowest step that would still give the individual a 2% raise. Most of the officers were in the three lowest ranks; in each of those ranks there were officers under age 40 and officers over 40. In none did their age affect their compensation. The few officers in the two highest ranks are all over 40. Their raises, though higher in dollar amount than the raises given to junior officers, represented a smaller percentage of their salaries, which of course are higher than the salaries paid to their juniors. They are members of the class complaining of the "disparate impact" of the award.

Petitioners' evidence established two principal facts: First, almost two-thirds (66.2%) of the officers under 40 received raises of more than 10% while less than half (45.3%) of those over 40 did. Second, the average percentage increase for the entire class of officers with less than five years of tenure was somewhat higher than the percentage for those with more seniority.

Because older officers tended to occupy more senior positions, on average they received smaller increases when measured as a percentage of their salary. The basic explanation for the differential was the City's perceived need to raise the salaries of junior officers to make them competitive with comparable positions in the market.

Thus, the disparate impact is attributable to the City's decision to give raises based on seniority and position. Reliance on seniority and rank is unquestionably reasonable given the City's goal of raising employees' salaries to match those in surrounding communities. In sum, we hold that the City's decision to grant a larger raise to lower echelon employees for the purpose of bringing salaries in line with that of surrounding police forces was a decision based on a "reasonable factor other than age" that responded to the City's legitimate goal of retaining police officers.

While there may have been other reasonable ways for the City to achieve its goals, the one selected was not unreasonable. Unlike the business necessity test, which asks whether there are other ways for the employer to achieve its goals that do not result in a disparate impact on a protected class, the reasonableness inquiry includes no such requirement.

Accordingly, while we do not agree with the Court of Appeals' holding that the disparate-impact theory of recovery is never available under the ADEA, we affirm its judgment.

Justice SCALIA, concurring in part and concurring in the judgment.

I concur in the judgment of the Court, and join all except Part III of its opinion. As to that Part, I agree with all of the Court's reasoning, but would find it a basis, not for independent determination of the disparate-impact question, but for deferral to the reasonable views of the Equal Employment Opportunity Commission (EEOC or Commission).

This is an absolutely classic case for deference to agency interpretation. The ADEA confers upon the EEOC authority to issue "such rules and regulations as it may consider necessary or appropriate for carrying out the" ADEA.

The statement of the EEOC which accompanied publication of the agency's final interpretation of the ADEA said the following regarding this regulation: "Paragraph (d) of § 1625.7 has been rewritten to make it clear that employment criteria that are age-neutral on their face but which nevertheless have a disparate impact on members of the protected age group must be justified as a business necessity." The regulation affirmed, moreover, what had been the longstanding position of the Department of Labor, the agency that previously administered the ADEA. And finally, the Commission has appeared in numerous cases in the lower courts, both as a party and as amicus curiae, to defend the position that the ADEA authorizes disparate-impact claims. Even under the unduly constrained standards of agency deference recited in *United States v. Mead Corp.*, the EEOC's reasonable view that the ADEA authorizes disparate-impact claims is deserving of deference.

Justice O'CONNOR, with whom Justice KENNEDY and Justice THOMAS join, concurring in the judgment.

"Disparate treatment . . . captures the essence of what Congress sought to prohibit in the ADEA. It is the very essence of age discrimination for an older employee to be fired because the employer believes that productivity and competence decline with old age." In the nearly four decades since the ADEA's enactment, however, we have never read the statute to impose liability upon an employer without proof of discriminatory intent. I decline to join the Court in doing so today.

I would instead affirm the judgment below on the ground that disparate impact claims are not cognizable under the ADEA. The ADEA's text, legislative history, and purposes together make clear that Congress did not intend the statute to authorize such claims. Moreover, the significant differences between the ADEA and Title VII of the Civil Rights Act of 1964 counsel against transposing to the former our construction of the latter in *Griggs*. Finally, the agencies charged with administering the ADEA have never authoritatively construed the statute's prohibitory language to impose disparate impact liability. Thus, on the precise question of statutory interpretation now before us, there is no reasoned agency reading of the text to which we might defer.

NOTES AND QUESTIONS

1. Based on *Smith*, explain the proof scheme to be utilized in an ADEA disparate impact case.

2. How does RFOA affect disparate impact analysis?

MEACHAM V. KNOLLS ATOMIC POWER LABORATORY
554 u.s. 84 (2008)

Justice SOUTER delivered the opinion of the Court.

A provision of the Age Discrimination in Employment Act of 1967 (ADEA) creates an exemption for employer actions "otherwise prohibited" by the ADEA but "based on reasonable factors other than age" (RFOA). § 623(f)(1). The question is whether an employer facing a disparate-impact claim and planning to defend on the basis of RFOA must not only produce evidence raising the defense, but also persuade the factfinder of its merit. We hold that the employer must do both.

I

The National Government pays private companies to do some of the work maintaining the Nation's fleet of nuclear-powered warships. One such contractor is respondent KAPL, Inc.

(Knolls), the operator of the Government's Knolls Atomic Power Laboratory, which has a history dating back to the first nuclear-powered submarines in the 1940s and 1950s. The demands for naval nuclear reactors changed with the end of the Cold War, and for fiscal year 1996 Knolls was ordered to reduce its work force. Even after a hundred or so employees chose to take the company's ensuing buyout offer, Knolls was left with thirty-some jobs to cut. [Plaintiffs] (Meacham, for short) are among those laid off in the resulting "involuntary reduction in force." In order to select those for layoff, Knolls told its managers to score their subordinates on three scales, "performance," "flexibility," and "critical skills." The scores were summed, along with points for years of service, and the totals determined who should be let go.

Of the 31 salaried employees laid off, 30 were at least 40 years old. Twenty-eight of them sued, raising both disparate-treatment (discriminatory intent) and disparate-impact (discriminatory result) claims under the ADEA and state law, alleging that Knolls "designed and implemented its workforce reduction process to eliminate older employees and that, regardless of intent, the process had a discriminatory impact on ADEA-protected employees." To show a disparate impact, the workers relied on a statistical expert's testimony to the effect that results so skewed according to age could rarely occur by chance; and that the scores for "flexibility" and "criticality," over which managers had the most discretionary judgment, had the firmest statistical ties to the outcomes.

[The Court of Appeals, after the case was remanded by the Supreme Court in light of *City of Jackson*, ruled in favor of Knolls, reasoning that Meacham had not carried the burden of persuasion on the "reasonableness" test. The appellate court explained that even if there were other reasonable ways for Knolls to achieve its goal, the one selected was not unreasonable, and the plaintiff failed to disprove this. A dissenting judge took issue with the majority for confusing business justifications under *Wards Cove* with the statutory RFOA exemption, which she read to be an affirmative defense with the burden of persuasion falling on the defendant.]

II

The ADEA's general prohibitions against age discrimination, 29 U.S.C. §§ 623(a)-(c), (e), are subject to a separate provision, § 623(f), creating exemptions for employer practices "otherwise prohibited under subsections (a), (b), (c), or (e)." The RFOA exemption is listed in § 623(f) alongside one for bona fide occupational qualifications (BFOQ): "It shall not be unlawful for an employer . . . to take any action otherwise prohibited under subsections (a), (b), (c), or (e) . . . where age is a bona fide occupational qualification reasonably necessary to the normal operation of the particular business, or where the differentiation is based on reasonable factors other than age . . . ." § 623(f)(1).

Given how the statute reads, with exemptions laid out apart from the prohibitions (and expressly referring to the prohibited conduct as such), it is no surprise that we have already spoken of the BFOQ and RFOA provisions as being among the ADEA's "five affirmative defenses," *Trans World Airlines, Inc. v. Thurston.* After looking at the statutory text, most lawyers would accept that characterization as a matter of course, thanks to the familiar principle that "[w]hen a proviso . . . carves an exception out of the body of a statute or contract those who set up such exception must prove it." That longstanding convention is part of the backdrop against which the Congress writes laws, and we respect it unless we have compelling reasons to think that Congress meant to put the burden of persuasion on the other side.

We have likewise given the affirmative defense construction to the exemption in the Equal Pay Act of 1963 for pay differentials based on "any other factor other than sex," and there, we took account of the particular weight given to the interpretive convention already noted, when enforcing the Fair Labor Standards Act of 1938. This focus makes the principle of construction the more instructive in ADEA cases: "[i]n enacting the ADEA, Congress exhibited both a detailed knowledge of the FLSA provisions and their judicial interpretation and a willingness to depart from those provisions regarded as undesirable or inappropriate for incorporation." *Lorillard v. Pons.* And we have remarked and relied on the "significant indication of Congress' intent in its directive that the ADEA be enforced in accordance with the 'powers, remedies, and procedures' of the FLSA." As against this interpretive background, there is no hint in the text that Congress meant § 623(f)(1) to march out of step with either the general or specifically FLSA default rules placing the burden of proving an exemption on the party claiming it.

With these principles and prior cases in mind, we find it impossible to look at the text and structure of the ADEA and imagine that the RFOA clause works differently from the BFOQ clause next to it. Both exempt otherwise illegal conduct by reference to a further item of proof, thereby creating a defense for which the burden of persuasion falls on the "one who claims its benefits," the "party seeking relief," and here, "the employer."

Knolls ventures that, regardless, the RFOA provision should be read as mere elaboration on an element of liability. Because it bars liability where action is taken for reasons "other than age," the argument goes, the provision must be directed not at justifying age discrimination by proof of some extenuating fact but at negating the premise of liability under § 623(a)(2), "because of age."

The answer to this argument, however, is *City of Jackson,* where we confirmed that the prohibition in § 623(a)(2) extends to practices with a disparate impact, inferring this result in part from the presence of the RFOA provision at issue here. We drew on the recognized distinction between disparate-treatment and disparate-impact forms of liability, and explained that "the very definition of disparate impact" was that "an employer who classifies his employees without respect to age may still be liable under the terms of this paragraph if such classification adversely affects the employee because of that employee's age." We emphasized that these were the kinds of employer activities, "otherwise prohibited" by § 623(a)(2), that were mainly what the statute meant to test against the RFOA condition: because "[i]n disparate-impact cases . . . the allegedly 'otherwise prohibited' activity is not based on age," it is "in cases involving disparate-impact claims that the RFOA provision plays its principal role by precluding liability if the adverse impact was attributable to a nonage factor that was 'reasonable.'"

Thus, in *City of Jackson,* we made it clear that in the typical disparate-impact case, the employer's practice is "without respect to age" and its adverse impact (though "because of age") is "attributable to a nonage factor"; so action based on a "factor other than age" is the very premise for disparate-impact liability in the first place, not a negation of it or a defense to it. The RFOA defense in a disparate-impact case, then, is not focused on the asserted fact that a non-age factor was at work; we assume it was. The focus of the defense is that the factor relied upon was a "reasonable" one for the employer to be using. Reasonableness is a justification categorically distinct from the factual condition "because of age" and not necessarily correlated with it in any particular way: a reasonable factor may lean more heavily on older workers, as against younger ones, and an unreasonable factor might do just the opposite.

III

The Court of Appeals majority rejected the affirmative defense reading and arrived at its position on the burden of proof question by a different route: because it read our decision in *City of Jackson* as ruling out the so-called "business necessity" enquiry in ADEA cases, the court concluded that the RFOA defense "replaces" it and therefore must conform to its burden of persuasion resting on the complaining party. But the court's premise (that *City of Jackson* modified the "business necessity" enquiry) is mistaken; this alone would be reason enough to reject its approach. And although we are now satisfied that the business necessity test should have no place in ADEA disparate-impact cases, we agree with the Government that this conclusion does not stand in the way of our holding that the RFOA exemption is an affirmative defense.

Although *City of Jackson* contains the statement that "*Wards Cove*'s pre-1991 interpretation of Title VII's identical language remains applicable to the ADEA," *City of Jackson* made only two specific references to aspects of the *Wards Cove* interpretation of Title VII that might have "remain[ed] applicable" in ADEA cases. One was to the existence of disparate-impact liability, which *City of Jackson* explained was narrower in ADEA cases than under Title VII. The other was to a plaintiff-employee's burden of identifying which particular practices allegedly cause an observed disparate impact, which is the employee's burden under both the ADEA and the pre-1991 Title VII. Neither of these references, of course, is at odds with the view of RFOA as an affirmative defense.

If, indeed, *City of Jackson*'s reference to *Wards Cove* could be read literally to include other aspects of the latter case, beyond what mattered in *City of Jackson* itself, the untoward consequences of the broader reading would rule it out. One such consequence is embraced by Meacham, who argues both that the Court of Appeals was wrong to place the burden of persuasion for the RFOA defense on the employee, and that the court was right in thinking that *City of Jackson* adopted the *Wards Cove* burden of persuasion on what Meacham views as one element of an ADEA impact claim. For Meacham takes the position that an impact plaintiff like himself has to negate business necessity in order to show that the employer's actions were "otherwise prohibited"; only then does the RFOA (with the burden of persuasion on the employer) have a role to play. To apply both tests, however, would force the parties to develop (and the court or jury to follow) two overlapping enquiries: first, whether the employment practice at issue (based on a factor other than age) is supported by a business justification; and second, whether that factor is a reasonable one. Depending on how the first enquiry proceeds, a plaintiff might directly contest the force of the employer's rationale, or else try to show that the employer invoked it as a pretext by pointing (for example) to alternative practices with less of a disparate impact. But even if the plaintiff succeeded at one or the other, in Meacham's scheme the employer could still avoid liability by proving reasonableness.

Here is what is so strange: as the Government says, "[i]f disparate-impact plaintiffs have already established that a challenged practice is a pretext for intentional age discrimination, it makes little sense then to ask whether the discriminatory practice is based on reasonable factors *other than age.*" Conversely, proving the reasonableness defense would eliminate much of the point a plaintiff would have had for showing alternatives in the first place: why make the effort to show alternative practices with a less discriminatory effect (and besides, how would that prove pretext?), when everyone knows that the choice of a practice relying on a "reasonable" non-age factor is good enough to avoid liability? At the very least, developing the reasonableness defense would be substantially redundant with the direct contest over the force of the business justification, especially when both enquiries deal with the same, narrowly specified practice. It is not very fair to take the remark about *Wards Cove* in *City of Jackson* as requiring such a wasteful and confusing structure of proof.

IV

As mentioned, where *City of Jackson* did get help from our prior reading of Title VII was in relying on *Wards Cove* to repeat that a plaintiff falls short by merely alleging a disparate impact, or "point[ing] to a generalized policy that leads to such an impact." The plaintiff is obliged to do more: to "isolat[e] and identif[y] the *specific* employment practices that are allegedly responsible for any observed statistical disparities." The aim of this requirement, as *City of Jackson* said, is to avoid the "result [of] employers being potentially liable for 'the myriad of innocent causes that may lead to statistical imbalances.'" And as the outcome in that case shows, the requirement has bite: one sufficient reason for rejecting the employees' challenge was that they "ha[d] done little more than point out that the pay plan at issue [was] relatively less generous to older workers than to younger workers," and "ha[d] not identified any specific test, requirement, or practice within the pay plan that ha[d] an adverse impact on older workers."

Identifying a specific practice is not a trivial burden, and it ought to allay some of the concern raised by Knolls's *amici,* who fear that recognizing an employer's burden of persuasion on an RFOA defense to impact claims will encourage strike suits or nudge plaintiffs with marginal cases into court, in turn inducing employers to alter business practices in order to avoid being sued. It is also to the point that the only thing at stake in this case is the gap between production and persuasion; nobody is saying that even the burden of production should be placed on the plaintiff. And the more plainly reasonable the employer's "factor other than age" is, the shorter the step for that employer from producing evidence raising the defense, to persuading the factfinder that the defense is meritorious. It will be mainly in cases where the reasonableness of the non-age factor is obscure for some reason, that the employer will have more evidence to reveal and more convincing to do in going from production to persuasion.

That said, there is no denying that putting employers to the work of persuading factfinders that their choices are reasonable makes it harder and costlier to defend than if employers merely bore the burden of production; nor do we doubt that this will sometimes affect the way employers do business with their employees. But at the end of the day, *amici*'s concerns have to be directed at Congress, which set the balance where it is, by both creating the RFOA exemption and writing it in the orthodox format of an affirmative defense. We have to read it the way Congress wrote it.

* * *

As we have said before, Congress took account of the distinctive nature of age discrimination, and the need to preserve a fair degree of leeway for employment decisions with effects that correlate with age, when it put the RFOA clause into the ADEA, "significantly narrow[ing] its coverage." *City of Jackson*. And as the outcome for the employer in *City of Jackson* shows, "it is not surprising that certain employment criteria that are routinely used may be reasonable despite their adverse impact on older workers as a group." In this case, we realize that the Court of Appeals showed no hesitation in finding that Knolls prevailed on the RFOA defense, though the court expressed its conclusion in terms of Meacham's failure to meet the burden of persuasion. Whether the outcome should be any different when the burden is properly placed on the employer is best left to that court in the first instance. The judgment of the Court of Appeals is vacated, and the case is remanded for further proceedings consistent with this opinion.

NOTES AND QUESTIONS

1. The Court says its decision will make it "harder and costlier" for employers to defend such cases and that it "will sometimes affect the way employers do business with their employees." Explain what the Court means. Do you agree with the Court?

2. In a disparate impact case, what is the relationship between a business justification and a RFOA? Could an impact claim have been successful in challenging the "vesting policy" in *Biggins*?

c.   Retaliation

Like Title VII, the ADEA prohibits retaliation against those who complain of age discrimination or assist others who challenge such discrimination. 29 U.S.C. § 623(d). Although the section covering federal employment does not address retaliation expressly, the Court in *Gomez-Perez v. Potter*, 553 U.S. 474 (2008), held that retaliation in federal employment is prohibited by the ADEA. As stated by the Court, the "key question in this case is whether the statutory phrase 'discrimination based on age' includes retaliation based on the filing of an age discrimination complaint." After discussing its holdings in *Sullivan v. Little Hunting Park, supra* Ch. II (§ 1982), and *Jackson v. Birmingham Board of Education, infra* Ch. IV (Title IX), the Court said:

> Following the reasoning of *Sullivan* and *Jackson*, we interpret the ADEA federal-sector provision's prohibition of "discrimination based on age" as likewise proscribing retaliation. The statutory language at issue here ("discrimination based on age") is not materially different from the language at issue in *Jackson* ("'discrimination'" "'on the basis of sex'") and is the functional equivalent of the language at issue in *Sullivan*, see *Jackson* (describing *Sullivan* as involving "discrimination on the basis of race"). And the context in which the statutory language appears is the same in all three cases; that is, all three cases involve remedial provisions aimed at prohibiting discrimination.

2. STATUTORY DEFENSES

The ADEA lists several defenses available to employers, 29 U.S.C. § 623(f). In addition to the RFOA discussed in *Meachum,* the first, and most significant, is the bona fide occupational qualification (BFOQ) which was at issue in *Western Airlines v. Criswell,* 472 U.S. 400 (1985), *supra* Ch. III. It is frequently used as the justification for a mandatory retirement age. For example, in *Johnson v. Mayor and City Council of Baltimore,* 472 U.S. 353 (1985), the plaintiff challenged Baltimore's mandatory retirement age of 55 for firefighters. The issue was whether a federal statute generally requiring federal firefighters to retire at age 55 establishes, as a matter of law, that age 55 is a BFOQ for nonfederal firefighters. The Court held that the civil service provision which applies to federal firefighters was not intended by Congress as a BFOQ and was intended to serve purposes unrelated to the BFOQ defense provided in the ADEA. Thus, the federal retirement provision did not provide the city with an absolute defense in an ADEA action.

NOTES AND QUESTIONS

1. Under *Criswell,* what will the City of Baltimore have to show on remand to establish a BFOQ?

2. Some police departments refuse to hire applicants above a certain age, usually age 35. Is such an age requirement a BFOQ? Would a 38-year old applicant rejected because of age have an ADEA claim? a 40-year old applicant? The ADEA, 29 U.S.C. § 623(j), generally provides an exemption for state and local government units with a hiring or retirement age requirement for firefighters and law enforcement officers in effect on March 3, 1983.

   Could the 38-year-old applicant state a claim under § 1983 and the equal protection clause? In *Massachusetts Board of Retirement v. Murgia,* 427 U.S. 307 (1976), the

Court held that a classification based on age is not suspect and only a rational basis is needed to uphold such a classification. Would it be rational to preclude hiring applicants between ages 35-39, if the ADEA requires that a 40-year old applicant be considered?

3.   ENFORCEMENT

Review the ADEA, particularly 29 U.S.C. § 626, to understand the enforcement proceedings, both administrative and judicial. How does it differ from Title VII with respect to the prerequisites for a civil action, the limitations period for civil actions, the relief available and right to jury trial? Note that § 626(e) was amended by § 115 of the Civil Rights Act of 1991 to eliminate the two and three-year limitations periods for civil actions. The deadline for filing a civil action under the ADEA is now comparable to Title VII in that it must be filed within 90 days of receipt of a notice from the EEOC indicating the charge was dismissed or proceedings otherwise terminated. However, after filing an ADEA charge with the EEOC, the charging party may file a civil action 60 days later without waiting for a "right-to-sue" notice from the EEOC.

The Court in *Federal Express Corp. v. Holowecki,* 552 U.S. 389 (2008), discussed *supra,* concluded that Form 283 "Intake Questionnaire" submitted to the EEOC constitutes a "charge" of age discrimination. "In addition to the information required by the regulations, *i.e.,* an allegation and the name of the charged party, if a filing is to be deemed a charge it must be reasonably construed as a request for the agency to take remedial action to protect the employee's rights or otherwise settle a dispute between the employer and the employee." Having determined that the EEOC "acted within its authority in formulating the rule that a filing is deemed a charge if the document reasonably can be construed to request agency action and appropriate relief on the employee's behalf," the Court concluded that one of the plaintiff's completed intake forms— which included (i) her name, address and telephone number, as well as those of the employer, (ii) an allegation that she and other employees had been the victims of age discrimination, (iii) the number of employees who worked at the employer's facility at which she worked, and (iv) a statement indicating she had not sought the assistance of any government agency regarding the matter—meets the test.

The findings of state administrative bodies that are not judicially reviewed should not be given preclusive effect in subsequent ADEA litigation. *Astoria Federal S & L Ass'n v. Solimino,* 501 U.S. 104 (1991).

4.   RELIEF

a.   The relief available under the ADEA differs from Title VII in that the ADEA provides for liquidated damages, if there is a willful violation, but not compensatory and punitive damages. In addition, only a prevailing plaintiff can recover attorney fees under the ADEA. 29 U.S.C. § 216(b). As with Title VII, the plaintiff has a duty to mitigate damages, but the defendant has the burden of showing a failure to mitigate. Wages earned through mitigation are generally deducted from the wages lost as a result of the challenged action.

b. The preferred remedy for future lost compensation is an injunction requiring the employer to hire or reinstate the plaintiff. However, if such relief is not feasible, the court can award front pay. Determining the amount of front pay requires a projection of how long the plaintiff would have continued to work for the defendant, absent the wrongful action, and the amount of compensation. Once the amount is determined, it should be reduced to present value. The duty to mitigate applies to front pay.

c. Frequently employers will attempt to avoid ADEA claims by providing older workers with a financial incentive to "retire" in exchange for a waiver of ADEA claims. The Older Worker Benefit Protection Act of 1990 added 29 U.S.C. § 626(f) and provides several procedural safeguards that must be met before an individual can waive any right or claim under the ADEA. Waivers are not valid unless "knowing and voluntary" and will not be treated as such unless, among other things, there is a written agreement that specifically refers to ADEA claims, there is consideration in addition to anything of value to which the individual is already entitled, the individual is advised to consult an attorney and given at least 21 days to consider the agreement, and the individual has at least 7 days following execution of the agreement to revoke it.

d. If a release does not comply with the requirements of the Act, it does not bar an ADEA claim even where the employee refuses to return any money paid pursuant to the agreement. *Oubre v. Entergy Operations, Inc.*, 522 U.S. 422 (1998).

TRANS WORLD AIRLINES, INC. V. THURSTON
469 U.S. 111 (1985)

Justice POWELL delivered the opinion of the Court.

Trans World Airlines, Inc. (TWA), a commercial airline, permits captains disqualified from serving in that capacity for reasons other than age to transfer automatically to the position of flight engineer. In this case, we must decide whether the Age Discrimination in Employment Act of 1967 (ADEA), 29 U.S.C. § 621 *et seq.*, requires the airline to afford this same "privilege of employment" to those captains disqualified by their age. We also must decide what constitutes a "willful" violation of the ADEA, entitling a plaintiff to "liquidated" or double damages.

[Before reaching the liquidated damages issue, the Court held that the transfer policy discriminated against the disqualified captains on the basis of age, that age was not a BFOQ, and that the transfer policy was not part of a "bona fide seniority system."]

III

A

Section 7(b) of the ADEA, 29 U.S.C. § 626(b), provides that the rights created by the Act are to be "enforced in accordance with the powers, remedies, and procedures" of the Fair Labor Standards Act. But the remedial provisions of the two statutes are not identical. Congress declined to incorporate into the ADEA several FLSA sections. Moreover, § 16(b) of the FLSA, which makes the award of liquidated damages mandatory, is significantly qualified in ADEA § 7(b) by a proviso that a prevailing plaintiff is entitled to double damages "only in cases of willful violations." 29 U.S.C. § 626(b). In this case, the Court of Appeals held that TWA's violation of the ADEA was "willful," and that the respondents therefore were entitled to double damages.

The legislative history of the ADEA indicates that Congress intended for liquidated damages to be punitive in nature. The original bill proposed by the administration incorporated § 16(a) of the FLSA, which imposes criminal liability for a willful violation. Senator Javits found "certain serious defects" in the administration bill. He stated that "difficult problems of proof . . . would arise under a criminal provision," and that the employer's invocation of the Fifth Amendment might impede investigation, conciliation, and enforcement. Therefore, he proposed that "the [FLSA's] criminal penalty in cases of willful violation . . . [be] eliminated and a double damage liability substituted." Senator Javits argued that his proposed amendment would "furnish an effective deterrent to willful violations [of the ADEA]," and it was incorporated into the ADEA with only minor modification.

This Court has recognized that in enacting the ADEA, "Congress exhibited . . . a detailed knowledge of the FLSA provisions and their judicial interpretation . . ." The manner in which FLSA § 16(a) has been interpreted therefore is relevant. In general, courts have found that an employer is subject to criminal penalties under the FLSA when he "wholly disregards the law . . . without making any reasonable effort to determine whether the plan he is following would constitute a violation of the law." This standard is substantially in accord with the interpretation of "willful" adopted by the Court of Appeals in interpreting the liquidated damages provision of the ADEA. The court below stated that a violation of the Act was "willful" if "the employer . . . knew or showed reckless disregard for the matter of whether its conduct was prohibited by the ADEA." Given the legislative history of the liquidated damages provision, we think the "reckless disregard" standard is reasonable.

We are unpersuaded by respondents' argument that a violation of the Act is "willful" if the employer simply knew of the potential applicability of the ADEA. [T]he broad standard proposed by the respondents would result in an award of double damages in almost every case. As employers are required to post ADEA notices, it would be virtually impossible for an employer to show that he was unaware of the Act and its potential applicability. Both the legislative history and the structure of the statute show that Congress intended a two-tiered liability scheme. We decline to interpret the liquidated damages provision of ADEA § 7(b) in a manner that frustrates this intent.

B

As noted above, the Court of Appeals stated that a violation is "willful" if "the employer either knew or showed reckless disregard for the matter of whether its conduct was prohibited by the ADEA." Although we hold that this is an acceptable way to articulate a definition of "willful," the court below misapplied this standard. TWA certainly did not "know" that its conduct violated the Act. Nor can it fairly be said that TWA adopted its transfer policy in "reckless disregard" of the Act's requirements. The record makes clear that TWA officials acted reasonably and in good faith in attempting to determine whether their plan would violate the ADEA.

Shortly after the ADEA was amended, TWA officials met with their lawyers to determine whether the mandatory retirement policy violated the Act. Concluding that the company's existing plan was inconsistent with the ADEA, David Crombie, the airline's Vice President for Administration, proposed a new policy. Despite opposition from the Union, the company adopted a modified version of this initial proposal. Under the plan adopted on August 10, 1978, any pilot in "flight engineer status" on his 60th birthday could continue to work for the airline. On the day the plan was adopted, the union filed suit against the airline claiming that the new retirement policy constituted a "major" change in the collective-bargaining agreement, and thus was barred by the § 6 of the Railway Labor Act. Nevertheless, TWA adhered to its new policy.

There simply is no evidence that TWA acted in "reckless disregard" of the requirements of the ADEA. The airline had obligations under the collective-bargaining agreement with the Air Line Pilots Association. In an attempt to bring its retirement policy into compliance with the ADEA, while at the same time observing the terms of the collective-bargaining agreement, TWA sought legal advice and consulted with the Union. Despite opposition from the Union, a plan was adopted that permitted cockpit employees to work as "flight engineers" after reaching age 60. Apparently TWA officials and the airline's attorneys failed to focus specifically on the effect of each aspect of the new retirement policy for cockpit personnel. It is reasonable to believe that the parties involved, in focusing on the larger overall problem, simply overlooked the challenged aspect of the new plan. We conclude that TWA's violation of the Act was not willful within the meaning of § 7(b), and that respondents therefore are not entitled to liquidated damages.

NOTES AND QUESTIONS

1. How does the standard adopted in *Thurston* compare with the standard for punitive damages in § 1983 actions? *See Smith v. Wade*, 461 U.S. 30 (1983), *supra* Ch. II.

2. Does an award of liquidated damages serve the same purposes (punish and deter) as an award of punitive damages? If so, is the defendant's net worth relevant?

3. Is there a right to trial by jury if the plaintiff does not seek liquidated damages? *See* § 626(c)(2).

4. Will the *Thurston* standard for liquidated damages lead to such awards in most cases where the plaintiff establishes intentional age discrimination? In *Hazen Paper Co. v. Biggins*, 507 U.S. 604 (1993), the Court refused to impose a requirement that plaintiffs show "outrageous" conduct on the part of the employer, or that age was the predominant factor, in order to obtain liquidated damages.

5. In *Commissioner of Internal Revenue v. Schleier*, 515 U.S. 523 (1995), the Court held that any monetary recovery under the ADEA is taxable as income because the Act does not provide "tort or tort type rights," and damages under the Act are not received "on account of personal injuries or sickness." *See* discussion of tax issue under Title VII, *supra* Ch. III.

Problem: Twenty-Eight

This case is before us on appeal from a summary judgment finding that defendant, The Gamewell Corporation (Gamewell), did not violate the Age Discrimination in Employment Act (ADEA) when it terminated plaintiff Holt's employment as part of a general reduction in force. At the time of the discharge, Holt was 63 years old and he was earning an annual salary of $43,825 as purchasing manager of Gamewell.

Holt's discharge occurred in the following manner: On June 29, 1984, Alan Walters (Walters), president of Gamewell, was informed by the board of directors of its parent corporation, that it was necessary to reduce the company's yearly payroll expense by $500,000. This decision was reached because Gamewell had experienced large net operating losses since the time of its acquisition in April 1981. There was general agreement among those meeting on the matter that, in order to reach that figure with a minimum negative effect on Gamewell's ability to operate efficiently, it would be necessary to eliminate several high-level as well as low-level positions. It was Walters' goal to meet the budget cut through the elimination of twenty positions in all. Walters, in turn, notified Eugene Zorn (Zorn), the company's vice-president and technical director, that he would have to layoff from 10-12 employees from his area of operations. Zorn was also told that the criteria to use in selecting employees for layoff was to focus on those persons whose positions could be eliminated or whose duties could be absorbed by others without significantly impairing Gamewell's operating capacity.

Zorn in turn called upon Frederick Hayes (Hayes), the director of manufacturing operations, to make recommendations for the layoff of two higher salaried and three lower salaried employees. Hayes was told that it was critical to ensure that the duties of any person discharged could be covered by other employees or eliminated altogether. He was further instructed that $30,000 per year was the dividing line of those considered to be the higher salaried group. Out of a group of six selected for review, Hayes chose to discharge Holt and Frank DeLoreto, the chief industrial engineer, as within the higher salaried group.

Holt does not argue with the company's position that the criteria for discharge was both high salary and the ability of other employees to take on the duties of the discharged employee. Rather, it is his contention that a higher salary is directly related to seniority and is, therefore a function of age, an illegal criterion for discharge.

Holt compares himself to the three buyers who worked under him, all of whom were younger than he was, and whose salaries were below $30,000. He suggests that they were not subject to possible discharge because of their lower salary, and implies that they were doing the same work that he did, and that he occupied, more or less, the same position. The record reveals otherwise.

Holt was the purchasing manager. He was the only person who occupied this position. He trained and supervised the buyers and evaluated their performances. He and Hayes jointly determined their salaries. While it is true that Holt was capable of performing all the duties of his section, and that he in fact substituted for them when one of the buyers was absent, he nevertheless had a wide range of responsibilities not delegatable to his subordinates.

Gamewell chose to eliminate this management position. Holt does not challenge this decision. Rather, he implies that Gamewell should have discharged one of the buyers instead and given that position to him.

1. Did Holt establish a *prima facie* case of age discrimination using disparate treatment analysis? What would he have to prove to ultimately win his case?

2. Did Holt establish a *prima facie* case using disparate impact analysis? Does consideration of salary, with a higher salary treated as a negative factor, in selecting employees to be discharged necessarily have an adverse impact on older workers?

3. If the decision is reversed and Holt prevails at trial, what relief is available to him?

C. AMERICANS WITH DISABILITIES ACT (ADA)—TITLE I

1. CONGRESSIONAL AUTHORITY

The Americans with Disabilities Act (ADA), 42 U.S.C. § 12101, *et seq.*, was passed in 1990, pursuant to the power of Congress provided by the Commerce Clause and § 5 of the Fourteenth Amendment. As discussed in Chapter I, the power of Congress to pass the ADA pursuant to § 5 was questioned in three cases decided by the Supreme Court: *Garrett* (holding that Congress does not have § 5 power to pass Title I of the ADA and, therefore, its attempt in § 12202 to abrogate Eleventh Amendment immunity is not valid); *Lane* (holding that Title II of the ADA, at least as it applies to the class of cases implicating the fundamental right of access to the courts, is valid legislation pursuant to § 5); and *U.S. v. Georgia* (holding that "insofar as Title II of the ADA creates a private cause of action for damages against the States for conduct that actually violates the Fourteenth Amendment, Title II validly abrogates state sovereign immunity").

Title I of the ADA is valid Commerce Clause legislation, as applied to all covered employers, including the states, but the decision in *Garrett* places limits on enforcement against state employers.

2. COVERAGE QUESTIONS

After several Supreme Court decisions, between 1999 and 2002, that limited significantly the coverage of the ADA by narrowing the meaning of "disability," Congress amended the Act, ADA Amendments Act of 2008 (ADAAA), effective January 1, 2009.

Critical to the scope of the ADA is the meaning of disability: "[t]he term 'disability' means, with respect to an individual—(A) a physical or mental impairment that substantially limits one or more major life activities of such individual; (B) a record of such an impairment; or (C) being regarded as having such an impairment." "[M]ajor life activities include, but are not limited to, caring for oneself, performing manual tasks, seeing, hearing, eating, sleeping, walking, standing, lifting, bending, speaking, breathing, learning, reading, concentrating, thinking, communicating, and working." Further, "a major life activity also includes the operation of a major bodily function, including but not limited to, functions of the immune system, normal cell growth, digestive, bowel, bladder, neurological, brain, respiratory, circulatory, endocrine, and reproductive functions." § 12102, as amended.

Title I of the ADA, 42 U.S.C. § 12111–12117, effective July 26, 1992 for employers with 25 or more employees and July 26, 1994 for employers with 15 or more employees, prohibits discrimination in employment "against a qualified individual on the basis of disability." § 12112(a), as amended. In addition to a general prohibition against discrimination found in § 12112(a), the ADA sets out specific discriminatory acts in § 12112(b), including the failure to make "reasonable accommodations" unless the employer can "demonstrate that the accommodation would impose an undue hardship."

Reasonable accommodation is defined in § 12111(9) and includes job restructuring, modified work schedules and reassignment. Undue hardship, defined in § 12111(10), "means an action requiring significant difficulty or expense" in light of the nature and cost of the accommodation, the resources of the employer, the number of persons employed, etc. The use of medical examinations and inquiries is limited by § 12112(d).

A "qualified individual with a disability" shall not "include any employee or applicant who is currently engaging in the illegal use of drugs," if the employer acts on the basis of such use. § 12114, as amended. In *Chevron USA, Inc. v. Echazabal*, 536 U.S. 73 (2002), the Court held that employers can refuse to employ disabled workers whose disabilities pose a direct threat to their own health, not just that of their co-workers, upholding an EEOC regulation that expands the scope of the statutory defense.

Three 1999 decisions of the Supreme Court substantially limited the number of persons protected by the ADA. The plaintiffs in *Sutton v. United Air Lines, Inc.*, 527 U.S. 471 (1999), were twin sisters with severe myopia, resulting in uncorrected visual acuity of 20/200 or worse in their right eyes and 20/400 or worse in their left eyes, but with corrective lenses each had vision of 20/20 or better. However, they were excluded from consideration for employment as commercial airline pilots because of United's policy requiring uncorrected visual acuity of 20/100 or better, a requirement more stringent than that imposed by the FAA. Their complaint was dismissed and the Supreme Court affirmed because the "determination of whether an individual is disabled should be made with references to measures that mitigate the individual's impairment" and the plaintiffs "failed to allege adequately that their poor eyesight is regarded as an impairment that substantially limits them in the major life activity of working." As to the latter deficiency, they alleged only that United regarded their poor vision as precluding them from holding positions as a "global airline pilot," and this did not substantially limit them in the major life activity of working.

The mitigation issue was also presented in *Murphy v. United Parcel Service*, 527 U.S. 516 (1999), where the plaintiff-mechanic had hypertension (high blood pressure) but, when medicated, the high blood pressure did not substantially limit him in any major life activity. Based on *Sutton*, the Court summarily concluded the disability determination must be made with reference to the mitigating measures Murphy employs. The next question, whether Murphy was disabled "due to limitations that persist despite his medication or the negative side effects of his medication," was not presented. Murphy's "regarded as" argument was unsuccessful because, even though he was fired due to a physical impairment that prevented him from obtaining Department of Transportation (DOT) certification to drive commercial motor vehicles, he was unable to show that he was regarded as unable to perform a class of jobs. At most, the evidence showed he was generally employable in any mechanic job not requiring a DOT certification, but could not perform the particular job requiring such certification. As with the Sutton twins, he was not regarded as substantially limited in the major life activity of working.

In the third case, *Albertsons, Inc. v. Kirkingburg*, 527 U.S. 555 (1999), the plaintiff was a truck driver with monocular vision whose employer required as a job qualification that the drivers meet DOT certification requirements. After hiring Kirkingburg by mistake, the employer fired him two years later because he could not obtain DOT certification. Consistent with *Sutton* and *Murphy*, the Court held that an individual's ability to compensate for an impairment, in this case the body's subconscious mechanism for coping with visual impairment, must be taken into account in determining whether Kirkingburg's monocular vision alone substantially limits the major life activity of seeing. Kirkingburg may, in fact, have a disability if he shows a substantial impairment despite the compensation. More importantly, the Court held that an employer is entitled to enforce a government standard, such as the DOT standard here, as defining an essential job function of the position. Because Kirkingburg could not satisfy the DOT vision requirement, he was not a *qualified* individual with a disability. The fact that the DOT was experimenting with a waiver program did not undermine its basic safety regulation.

These three cases substantially reduced the number of persons with a disability under the Act. The 2008 amendments expressly target this narrow construction of the protected class. Two stated purposes are (a) "to reject the requirement enunciated [in *Sutton*] and its companion cases that whether an impairment substantially limits a major life activity is to be determined with reference to the ameliorative effects of mitigating measures," and (b) "to reject the [Court's reasoning in *Sutton*] with regard to coverage under the third prong of the definition of disability and to reinstate the reasoning of the Supreme Court in *School Board of Nassau County v. Arline*, 480 U.S. 273 (1987) which set forth a broad view of the third prong of the definition of handicap under the Rehabilitation Act of 1973." More specifically, the ADA Amendments Act of 2008 amends § 12102 by adding "rules of construction regarding the definition of disability," including the following: (a) "[t]he definition of disability in this Act shall be construed in favor of broad coverage of individuals under this Act, to the maximum extent permitted by the terms of this Act;" and (b) "[t]he determination of whether an impairment substantially limits a major life activity shall be made without regard to the ameliorative effects of mitigating measures such as—. . . [but] [t]he ameliorative effects of the mitigating measures of ordinary eyeglasses or contact lenses shall be considered in determining whether an impairment substantially limits a major life activity."

In addition to the *Sutton* trilogy, the 2008 amendments also target the Supreme Court's decision in *Toyota Motor Manufacturing v. Williams*, 534 U.S. 184 (2002). The Court considered whether an automobile assembly line worker with carpal tunnel syndrome was substantially limited in the major live activity of performing manual tasks. This required the Court to address an issue not addressed in EEOC regulations: "what a plaintiff must demonstrate to establish a substantial limitation in the major life activity of performing manual tasks." After looking at the dictionary definitions of "substantial" and "major," and determining that the terms "need to be interpreted strictly to create a demanding standard for qualifying as disabled," the Court held "that to be substantially limited in performing manual tasks, an individual must have an impairment that prevents or severely restricts the individual from doing activities that are of central importance to most people's daily lives. The impairment's impact must also be permanent or long-term." When an "impairment is one whose symptoms vary widely from person to person," an individualized assessment of the effect of an impairment is necessary. The Court also rejected the lower court's use of a "class-based framework" when addressing a major life activity other than working and consideration of the individual's inability to perform the tasks associated with her specific job in determining whether she was substantially limited in performing manual tasks. In making the disability determination in this type of case, the courts should consider the individual's ability to tend to her personal hygiene and perform household chores.

One of the purposes of the 2008 amendments is "to reject the standards enunciated by the Supreme Court in [*Toyota Motor*] that the terms 'substantially' and 'major' in the definition of disability under the ADA 'need to be interpreted strictly to create a demanding standard for qualifying as disabled,' and that to be substantially limited in performing a major life activity under the ADA 'an individual must have an impairment that prevents or severely restricts the individual from doing activities that are of central importance to most people's daily lives.'" *See also* § 12102, as amended. Another purpose of the amendments is "to convey congressional intent that the standard created by the Supreme Court in the case of [*Toyota Motor*] for 'substantially limits' . . . has created an inappropriately high level of limitation necessary to obtain coverage under the ADA, to convey that it is the intent of Congress that the primary object of attention in cases brought under the ADA should be whether entities covered under the ADA have compolied with their obligations, and to convey that the question of whether an individual's impairment is a disability under the ADA should not demand extensive analysis." *See also* § 12102, as amended.

In short, Congress has expressed its disagreement with much of the Court's limiting construction of the ADA. The 2008 amendments should make Title I of the ADA more effective in addressing employment discrimination based on disability. *See, e.g., Hilton v. Wright*, 673 F.3d 120 (3d Cir. 2012). However, that remains to be seen.

Two other cases interpreting the ADA remain good law. In *U.S. Airways, Inc. v. Barnett*, 535 U.S. 391 (2002), the plaintiff invoked his seniority rights and transferred to a less physically demanding mail room position after he injured his back while working in a cargo-handling position. After he was in the mail room position for several months, at least two employees with more seniority expressed their intent to bid for the mail room job and Barnett then asked the employer to accommodate his disability. More specifically, Barnett asked the employer to make an exception to the seniority-based bidding system that would allow him to remain in the mail room, but the employer decided not to make such an exception and Barnett lost his job. Four Justices joined Justice Breyer's majority opinion, holding that a seniority system will prevail in most cases, *i.e.*, "to show that a requested accommodation conflicts with the rules of a seniority system is ordinarily to show that the accommodation is not 'reasonable.'" However, the plaintiff has an opportunity to present evidence of special circumstances that would make an exception to the seniority policy a "reasonable accommodation," such as a showing "that the employer, having retained the right to change the seniority system unilaterally, exercises that right fairly frequently, reducing employee expectations that the system will be followed–to the point where one more departure, needed to accommodate an individual with a disability, will not likely make a difference." While she joined Justice Breyer's opinion, Justice O'Connor expressed concern indicating that "the effect of a seniority system on the reasonableness of a reassignment as an accommodation for purposes of the ADA depends on whether the seniority system is legally enforceable." While troubled by the Court's reasoning, she joined Breyer's opinion because she believed his approach for evaluating seniority systems will often lead to the same outcome as the test she would have adopted, *i.e.*, plaintiffs will be able to show that an exception to an unenforceable seniority system is a reasonable accommodation.

Another case, *Cleveland v. Policy Management Systems Corp.*, 526 U.S. 795 (1999), resulted in a slight victory for ADA plaintiffs. Here the Court held that an application for disability benefits under the Social Security Act, in which a claimant essentially states she is unable to work, is not so inherently in conflict with an ADA claim that there should be a special negative presumption against the ADA claim. This is true because of (a) differences in the two acts relating to reasonable accommodation, (b) the fact that the Social Security Administration (SSA) has certain presumptions about disabilities, job availability and the interrelation, (c) the SSA sometimes awards benefits to individuals who not only can, but are working, and (d) one who has applied for, but has not been awarded, Social Security benefits is simply "pleading " alternative theories in the same manner we tolerate under the rules of civil procedure. However, in cases where there appears to be a genuine conflict between an earlier application submitted to the SSA and an ADA claim, the ADA plaintiff will have to explain the apparent inconsistency.

The ADA prohibits retaliation and coercion. *See* 42 U.S.C. § 12203. It prohibits discrimination "against any individual because such individual has opposed any act or practice made unlawful by [the ADA] or because such individual made a charge, testified, assisted, or participated in any manner in an investigation, proceeding, or hearing under [the ADA]." This section also makes it unlawful "to coerce, intimidate, threaten, or interfere with any individual in the exercise or enjoyment of, or on account of his or her having aided or encouraged any other individual in the exercise or enjoyment of, any right granted or protected by [the ADA]." Section 12203 is similar to the prohibition found in Title VII, and it incorporates Title VII "remedies and procedures." *See* 42 U.S.C. § 12203(c).

3. METHOD OF PROOF

The federal circuits generally utilize the Title VII proof scheme in cases alleging intentional discrimination based on disability. Therefore, plaintiffs can utilize either the direct method, relying on direct or circumstantial evidence of discrimination, or the indirect method established in *McDonnell-Douglas.* However, in one respect, proof of intentional discrimination in violation of the ADA may be more analogous to ADEA claims than Title VII claims. In *Gross v. FBL Financial Services, Inc., supra* Ch. III, the Court interpreted the "because of" language in the ADEA differently than those words are interpreted in the context of Title VII, *i.e.,* in an ADEA case the plaintiff must show that age was the "but-for" cause of the challenged employment decision. In contrast, the plaintiff in a Title VII case need only show that the prohibited factor, such as race or sex, was a motivating factor, which leads to "mixed motive" analysis. *See Desert Palace, Inc. v. Costa, supra* Ch. III. Since *Gross,* the trend in ADA cases is to require "but-for" causation, but that does not mean disability has to be the sole cause of the challenged adverse employment action. *See, e.g., Monroe v. Indiana Department of Transportation,* 871 F.3d 495, 503–09 (7th Cir. 2017); *Lewis v. Humboldt Acquisition Corp., Inc.,* 681 F.3d 312, 314-21 (6th Cir. 2012); *Serwatka v. Rockwell Automation, Inc.,* 591 F.3d 957, 959-63 (7th Cir. 2010).

The ADA reaches unintentional discriminatory effects, 42 U.S.C. § 12112(b)(3), (6) & (7), but the case law addressing such claims is not well-developed. Title VII cases should provide guidance for such claims under the ADA.

4. RELIEF

Enforcement of Title I is in accordance with the "powers, remedies, and procedures" of Title VII, including administrative enforcement by the EEOC. 42 U.S.C. § 12117. Therefore, Title VII cases provide guidance. However, there is one difference in that 42 U.S.C. § 1981a(a)(3) insulates an employer from damages if it demonstrates good faith efforts, in consultation with the complaining party who informed the employer of the need for accommodation, to make reasonable accommodation.

CHAPTER IV:
DISCRIMINATIONIN FEDERALLY ASSISTED PROGRAMS

A. INTRODUCTION—COMMON ISSUES

This Chapter deals with three federal statutes aimed at the discriminatory practices of public and private entities that receive federal financial assistance. The first such law to be enacted was Title VI of the Civil Rights Act of 1964, 42 U.S.C. § 2000d, *et seq.*, which bars discrimination in federally funded programs on the basis of race, color or national origin. Federal agencies that disburse funds are given primary responsibility for enforcing the Acts.

All of the enactments discussed in this Chapter were passed by Congress pursuant to its spending power, which is set forth in Article I, § 8, cl. 1. As discussed in Chapter I, the Supreme Court has determined that Congress' spending power is at least as broad as its regulatory power. In *Lau v. Nichols*, 414 U.S. 563 (1974), the Court stated, "[t]he Federal Government has the power to fix the terms on which its money allotments to the state shall be disbursed." On the other hand, the Court in *Pennhurst, supra* Ch. I, reasoned that because a spending provision is similar to a type of contract, the recipient of federal dollars must know in clear terms what the "contract" demands. Thus, if Congress did not clarify that receipt of federal dollars would impose certain affirmative obligations on the states, no cause of action will be found. This contract analysis becomes important in interpreting the remedial aspect of these provisions.

Title VI provided the model for later statutes aimed at other types of discriminatory practices on the part of entities receiving federal financial assistance. For example, Title IX of the Education Amendments of 1972, 20 U.S.C. § 1681, *et seq.*, prohibits sex discrimination in educational institutions, and § 504 of Title V of the Rehabilitation Act of 1973, 28 U.S.C. § 794, *et seq.*, bans discrimination based on disability. What all three Acts have in common is that they are aimed at public and private entities receiving federal financial assistance, the receipt of which is conditioned on compliance with specific antidiscrimination provisions in the funding statutes. Agencies distributing federal funds are required by the Act to promulgate regulations and to terminate funding to any entities that continue to discriminate. Unlike the prohibitions in §§ 1981, 1982, 1983 and Title VII, an entity can avoid these acts by foregoing federal dollars if it wishes. Congress' key concern was to make sure that no federal dollars were spent in support of entities that discriminate.

Several common legal questions are raised with regard to all of these spending provisions:

1.   **Coverage**: All of the Acts are aimed at recipients of federal funding, raising the common question of statutory interpretation as to what types of aid constitute "federal financial assistance." Further, all of these Acts are written in terms of "program" coverage. Although the Supreme Court gave the concept of "program" a narrow interpretation, Congress responded by amending all of these Acts to generally provide for institution-wide coverage; *i.e.*, if any part of an establishment receives federal funds, all of the operations of the entity will be bound by the law. The Civil Rights Restoration Act, 42 U.S.C. § 2000d-4a, which became effective in 1988, broadened the reach of the Acts, but it apparently left intact the remedial provisions of these Acts which state that funding termination is limited to the "specific program or part thereof" receiving the federal financial assistance.

To understand then the significance of the Civil Rights Restoration Act, it is necessary to know that the Supreme Court has recognized a private cause of action on behalf of individual victims of discrimination. *See Cannon v. University of Chicago, infra* Ch. IV. Thus, even though funding may not be terminated where the so-called "pinpoint" provision (42 U.S.C. § 2000d-1) is not satisfied, an individual may bring suit to stop the discriminatory practice of a "program" if any of its operations receive federal financial assistance. In short, it is necessary to distinguish between the coverage question, which is now controlled by the Civil Rights Restoration Act, and the administrative remedy question, which continues to be limited in part by the pinpoint provision.

2.   **Intent/Impact**: As has been discussed with regard to other federal statutes, a question arises as to whether these Acts prohibit only purposeful discrimination or whether it suffices that the entity engages in a practice with a discriminatory impact on a protected group.

3.   **Remedies**: Congress provided explicitly that the enforcement of these Acts would be through the agencies distributing the federal funds. Nonetheless, the Supreme Court held that private individuals may bring lawsuits against recipients that discriminate against them and against the governmental agency that is not enforcing the statute. Although the Court has generally upheld private causes of action on the part of individuals who are victims of discrimination, difficult questions remain as to what types of relief should be awarded.

1. COVERAGE: MEANING OF "RECIPIENT" AND "PROGRAM SPECIFICITY"

GROVE CITY COLLEGE V. BELL
465 U.S. 555 (1984)

Justice WHITE delivered the opinion of the Court.

We must decide, first, whether Title IX applies at all to Grove City College, which accepts no direct assistance but enrolls students who receive federal grants that must be used for educational purposes. If so, we must identify the "education program or activity" at Grove City that is "receiving Federal financial assistance" and determine whether federal assistance to that program may be terminated solely because the College violates the Department's regulations by refusing to execute an Assurance of Compliance with Title IX.

I

Petitioner Grove City College is a private, coeducational, liberal arts college that has sought to preserve its institutional autonomy by consistently refusing state and federal financial assistance. Grove City's desire to avoid federal oversight has led it to decline to participate, not only in direct institutional aid programs, but also in federal student assistance programs under which the College would be required to assess students' eligibility and to determine the amounts of loans, work-study funds, or grants they should receive. Grove City has, however, enrolled a large number of students who receive Basic Educational Opportunity Grants (BEOG's), 20 U.S.C. § 1070a, under the Department of Education's Alternate Disbursement System (ADS).[1]

The Department concluded that Grove City was a "recipient" of "Federal financial assistance" as those terms are defined in the regulations implementing Title IX, 34 C.F.R. §§ 106.2(g)(1),(h) (1982), and, in July 1977, it requested that the College execute the Assurance of Compliance required by 34 C.F.R. § 106.4 (1983). If Grove City had signed the Assurance, it would have agreed to

> [c]omply, to the extent applicable to it, with Title IX . . . and all applicable requirements imposed by or pursuant to the Department's regulation . . . to the end that . . . no person shall, on the basis of sex, be . . . subjected to discrimination under any education program

---

[1] The Secretary, in his discretion, has established two procedures for computing and disbursing BEOGs. Under the Regular Disbursement System (RDS), the Secretary estimates the amount that an institution will need for grants and advances that sum to the institution, which itself selects eligible students, calculates awards, and distributes the grants by either crediting students' accounts or issuing checks. 34 C.F.R. §§ 690.71-.85 (1983). Most institutions whose students receive BEOGs participate in the RDS, but the ADS is an option made available by the Secretary to schools that wish to minimize their involvement in the administration of the BEOG program. Institutions participating in the program through the ADS must make appropriate certifications to the Secretary, but the Secretary calculates awards and makes disbursements directly to eligible students. 34 C.F.R. §§ 690.91-.96 (1983).

or activity for which [it] receives or benefits from Federal financial assistance from the Department.

When Grove City persisted in refusing to execute an Assurance, the Department initiated proceedings to declare the College and its students ineligible to receive BEOGs. The Administrative Law Judge held that the federal financial assistance received by Grove City obligated it to execute an Assurance of Compliance and entered an order terminating assistance until Grove City "corrects its noncompliance with Title IX and satisfies the Department that it is in compliance" with the applicable regulations.

II

In defending its refusal to execute the Assurance of Compliance required by the Department's regulations, Grove City first contends that neither it nor any "education program or activity" of the College receives any federal financial assistance within the meaning of Title IX by virtue of the fact that some of its students receive BEOG's and use them to pay for their education. We disagree.

Grove City provides a well-rounded liberal arts education and a variety of educational programs and student services. The question is whether any of those programs or activities "receiv[es] Federal financial assistance" within the meaning of Title IX when students finance their education with BEOG's. The structure of the Education Amendments of 1972, in which Congress both created the BEOG program and imposed Title IX's nondiscrimination requirement, strongly suggests an affirmative conclusion. BEOG's were aptly characterized as a "centerpiece of the bill," and Title IX "relate[d] directly to [its] central purpose." In view of this connection and Congress' express recognition of discrimination in the administration of student financial aid programs, it would indeed be anomalous to discover that one of the primary components of Congress' comprehensive "package of federal aid" was not intended to trigger coverage under Title IX.

It is not surprising to find, therefore, that the language of § 901(a) contains no hint that Congress perceived a substantive difference between direct institutional assistance and aid received by a school through its students. The linchpin of Grove City's argument that none of its programs receives any federal assistance is a perceived distinction between direct and indirect aid, a distinction that finds no support in the text of § 901(a). Nothing in § 901(a) suggests that Congress elevated form over substance by making the application of the nondiscrimination principle dependent on the manner in which a program or activity receives federal assistance. There is no basis in the statute for the view that only institutions that themselves apply for federal aid or receive checks directly from the federal government are subject to regulation.

Congress' awareness of the purpose and effect of its student aid programs also is reflected in the sparse legislative history of Title IX itself. Title IX was patterned after Title VI of the Civil Rights Act of 1964. The drafters of Title VI envisioned that the receipt of student aid funds would trigger coverage, and, since they approved identical language, we discern no reason to believe that the Congressmen who voted for Title IX intended a different result.

With the benefit of clear statutory language, powerful evidence of Congress' intent, and a longstanding and coherent administrative construction of the phrase "receiving Federal financial assistance," we have little trouble concluding that Title IX coverage is not foreclosed because federal funds are granted to Grove City's students rather than directly to one of the College's educational programs. There remains the question, however, of identifying the "education program or activity" of the College that can properly be characterized as "receiving" federal assistance through grants to some of the students attending the College.

III

An analysis of Title IX's language and legislative history led us to conclude in *North Haven Board of Education v. Bell*, that "an agency's authority under Title IX both to promulgate regulations and to terminate funds is subject to the program-specific limitations of §§ 901 and 902." Although the legislative history contains isolated suggestions that entire institutions are subject to the nondiscrimination provision whenever one of their programs receives federal assistance, we cannot accept the Court of Appeals' conclusion that in the circumstances present here Grove City itself is a "program or activity" that may be regulated in its entirety. Nevertheless, we find no merit in Grove City's contention that a decision treating BEOG's as "Federal financial assistance" cannot be reconciled with Title IX's program-specific language since BEOG's are not tied to any specific "education program or activity."

If Grove City participated in the BEOG program through the RDS, we would have no doubt that the "education program or activity receiving Federal financial assistance" would not be the entire College; rather, it would be its student financial aid program. RDS institutions receive federal funds directly, but can use them only to subsidize or expand their financial aid programs and to recruit students who might otherwise be unable to enroll. In short, the assistance is earmarked for the recipient's financial aid program. Only by ignoring Title IX's program-specific language could we conclude that funds received under the RDS, awarded to eligible students, and paid back to the school when tuition comes due represent federal aid to the entire institution.

We see no reason to reach a different conclusion merely because Grove City has elected to participate in the ADS. Although Grove City does not itself disburse students' awards, BEOG's clearly augment the resources that the College itself devotes to financial aid. As is true of the RDS, however, the fact that federal funds eventually reach the College's general operating budget cannot subject Grove City to institutionwide coverage. Grove City's choice of administrative mechanisms, we hold, neither expands nor contracts the breadth of the "program or activity"—the financial aid program—that receives federal assistance and that may be regulated under Title IX.

The Court of Appeals' analogy between student financial aid received by an educational institution and nonearmarked direct grants provides a more plausible justification for its holding, but it too is faulty. Student financial aid programs, we believe, are *sui generis*. In neither purpose nor effect can BEOG's be fairly characterized as unrestricted grants that institutions may use for whatever purpose they desire. The BEOG program was designed, not merely to increase the total resources available to educational institutions, but to enable them to offer their services to students who had previously been unable to afford higher education. It is true, of course, that substantial portions of the BEOG's received by Grove City's students ultimately find their way into the College's general operating budget and are used to provide a variety of services to the students through whom the funds pass. However, we have found no persuasive evidence suggesting that Congress intended that the Department's regulatory authority follow federally aided students from classroom to classroom, building to building, or activity to activity. In addition, as Congress recognized in considering the Education Amendments of 1972, the economic effect of student aid is far different from the effect of nonearmarked grants to institutions themselves since the former, unlike the latter, increases both an institution's resources and its obligations. In that sense, student financial aid more closely resembles many earmarked grants. We conclude that the receipt of BEOG's by some of Grove City's students does not trigger institution-wide coverage under Title IX. In purpose and effect, BEOG's represent federal financial assistance to the College's own financial aid program, and it is that program that may properly be regulated under Title IX.

IV

Since Grove City operates an "education program or activity receiving Federal financial assistance," the Department may properly demand that the College execute an Assurance of Compliance with Title IX. Grove City contends, however, that the Assurance it was requested to sign was invalid, both on its face and as interpreted by the Department, in that it failed to comport with Title IX's program-specific character. Whatever merit that objection might have had at the time, it is not now a valid basis for refusing to execute an Assurance of Compliance.

The Assurance of Compliance regulation itself does not, on its face, impose institution-wide obligations. Recipients must provide assurance only that "each education program or activity operated by . . . [them] *and to which this part applies* will be operated in compliance with this part." 34 C.F.R. § 106.4 (1983) (emphasis added). The regulations apply, by their terms, "to every recipient and to *each education program or activity* operated by such recipient *which receives or benefits from Federal financial assistance.*" 34 C.F.R. § 106.11 (1983) (emphasis added). These regulations, like those at issue in *North Haven Board of Education v. Bell*, "conform with the limitations Congress enacted in §§ 901 and 902."

NOTES AND QUESTIONS

1. What made Grove City a "recipient of federal financial assistance"?

2. Since student loan money is "non-earmarked," why didn't the Court find the whole institution subject to coverage? Since the student loan money did not subject the entire institution to Title IX coverage, why did the Court sustain the requirement that Grove City College sign the assurance?

3. What if the only federal assistance to Grove City was its tax exempt status? Would it be considered a "recipient" and, if so, would institution-wide coverage be triggered? If the IRS allows a charitable contribution deduction, is a court more likely to find the entity to be a recipient of federal financial assistance?

4. In 1988, Congress passed the Civil Rights Restoration Act, which has been referred to as the "Grove City Bill." Read 42 U.S.C. § 2000d-4a. Title IX (20 U.S.C. § 1687) and § 504 (29 U.S.C. § 794(b)) incorporate the same language. Note that the funding termination provision, 42 U.S.C. § 2000d-1, was not altered by the Act.

   a. Could the Department of Education require Grove City to execute an Assurance of Compliance covering all of its operations? Could BEOGs be cut off today due to sex discrimination in Grove City's athletic department?

   b. Review the introductory note regarding coverage, *supra*. Could a victim of sex discrimination in the athletic department bring a private cause of action against Grove City to stop this discrimination? In light of Title IX's legislative history, which expresses a concern for innocent beneficiaries, does it make sense to interpret the Civil Rights Restoration Act to allow termination of BEOGs to qualifying students due to discrimination with regard to one of the college's operations? On the other hand, does it make sense to impose entity-wide coverage but only program-specific termination of funds?

BOARD OF PUBLIC INSTRUCTION OF TAYLOR COUNTY V. FINCH
414 F.2D 1068 (5TH CIR. 1969)

GOLDBERG, Circuit Judge

Nominally, this case involves a challenge to the validity of an order by the Department of Health, Education and Welfare (HEW) terminating the payment of federal funds to the Board of Public Instruction of Taylor County, Florida, for violating Title VI of the Civil Rights Act of 1964. Underlying this challenge, however, is a broader question concerning the character and reach of the limitations which Congress has placed upon the power of an administrative agency to cut off federal funds and the Congressional policy behind such limitations.

The facts of this case are undisputed. Appellant, the Board of Public Instruction of Taylor County, Florida (hereafter the School Board) operates a small district of eight public schools attended in recent years by approximately 2900 white students and 975 Negro students. Prior to the 1965-1966 school year, the Board maintained these schools on an entirely segregated basis. No white child attended class with any Negro child and no Negro child attended class with any white child.

Following the passage of the Civil Rights Act of 1964, the School Board adopted a 'freedom of choice' plan and submitted it to the Commissioner of Education for approval. Thereafter the School Board complied with the formal requirements of the original and revised Guidelines for the adoption of a freedom of choice plan, *i.e.*, the notification of parents and students, the giving of public notice, etc., but did not, in HEW's view, comply with the Guideline requirements specifying an acceptable pace of desegregation. The record tends to confirm HEW's position.

After a period of delay agreed upon by both sides, hearings were held on January 16 and January 17, 1968. On April 4, 1968, the HEW hearing examiner ruled that the Taylor County School Board was in violation of Title VI of the Civil Rights Act and no longer entitled to federal funds. He found that the School District's "progress toward student desegregation was inadequate," that it "had not made adequate progress toward teacher desegregation," and that the District was "seeking to perpetuate the dual school system through its construction program." Based on these findings, the examiner entered an order terminating "any classes of Federal financial assistance" to the Taylor County School District "arising under any Act of Congress" administered by HEW, the National Science Foundation, and the Department of the Interior until such time as the School District corrected its noncompliance with the Act.

[One of the] questions tendered for consideration on this appeal [is] whether the order entered by HEW in the proceedings below violates 42 U.S.C.A. 2000d-1 (§ 602, Title VI) of the Civil Rights Act. That statute provides in relevant part that the termination of federal financial assistance shall be limited to programs or parts thereof found not in compliance with the Act.

Three separate and distinct federal programs are here involved. One concerns federal aid for the education of children of low income families; one involves grants for supplementary educational centers; the third provides special grants for the education of adults who have not received a college education. Each of the programs has a different objective; each requires a separate plan and separate administrative approval; and each has an individual provision for appellate review. Under these circumstances it is not possible to say on the basis of segregation of faculty and students that all programs in the schools in Taylor County are constitutionally defective. It is perfectly possible that the federal grant for supplementary educational centers would have been used for a facility entirely separate from the rest of the school system. It is also possible that the grant for adult educational classes supported a program that was administered in an entirely desegregated manner even if the elementary and high school classes were not. HEW's failure to make findings of fact on these issues has deprived this court of the means with which to properly discharge its reviewing function. In order to affirm HEW's action, we would have to assume, contrary to the express mandate of 42 U.S.C.A. § 2000d-1, that defects in one part of a school system automatically infect the whole. Such an assumption in disregard of statutory requirements is inconsistent with both fundamental justice and with our judicial responsibilities.

The action of HEW in the proceedings below was clearly disruptive of the legislative scheme. The legislative history of 42 U.S.C.A. 2000d-1 indicates a Congressional purpose to avoid a punitive as opposed to a therapeutic application of the termination power. The procedural limitations placed on the exercise of such power were designed to insure that termination would be "pinpoint[ed] to the situation where discriminatory practices prevail." As said by Senator Long during the Senate debate:

> Proponents of the bill have continually made it clear that it is the intent of Title VI not to require wholesale cutoffs of Federal Funds from all Federal programs in entire States, but instead to require a careful case-by-case application of the principle of nondiscrimination to those particular activities which are actually discriminatory or segregated.

It is important to note that the purpose of limiting the termination power to "activities which are actually discriminatory or segregated" was not for the protection of the political entity whose funds might be cut off, but for the protection of the innocent beneficiaries of programs not tainted by discriminatory practices.

We note finally that the purpose of the Title VI cutoff is best effectuated by separate consideration of the use or intended use of federal funds under each grant statute. If the funds provided by the grant are administered in a discriminatory manner, or if they support a program which is infected by a discriminatory environment, then termination of such funds is proper. But there will also be cases from time to time where a particular program, within a state, within a county, within a district, even within a school (in short, within a "political entity or part thereof"), is effectively insulated from otherwise unlawful activities. Congress did not intend that such a program suffer for the sins of others. HEW was denied the right to condemn programs by association.

NOTES AND QUESTIONS

1. What rationale does this case provide for the "pinpoint" provision? What would HEW have to prove to cut off funds to the adult education program? Is federal aid for the education of children of low income families in jeopardy?

2. Does the expanded definition of "program" in the Civil Rights Restoration Act overrule *Finch*? Under the Civil Rights Restoration Act, would the whole school district now simply be viewed as the covered "program"? Does this mean that all three forms of assistance would then have to be terminated in light of the school's failure to desegregate? On the other hand, assuming that program specificity survives the new Act with regard to termination, wouldn't an agency still be justified in cutting off funds if it proves that segregation in the school system infects a federally supported program?

3. Assume a university supports an all-male prestigious honor society. While the university receives federal funds, it does not use them to support the society. A female student challenges her exclusion from the honor society in a private lawsuit against the university under Title IX. Does she have a valid claim? Could the federal agency terminate federal funds to the university based on its support of the all-male honor society?

4. Some of these issues were specifically addressed in the Senate Committee Report when the 1988 Civil Rights Restoration Act was debated:

FUND TERMINATION

S. 557 will leave in effect the enforcement structure common to each of these statutes. The section in each statute states that the termination of assistance "shall be limited . . . to the particular program, or part thereof, in which such noncompliance has been so found." The bill defines "program" in the same manner as "program or activity", and leaves intact the "or part thereof" pinpointing language.

The seminal case dealing with fund termination is *Board of Public Institution of Taylor County v. Finch*, a Title VI case. Under the *Taylor* ruling, Federal funds earmarked for a specific purpose would not be terminated unless discrimination was found in the use of those funds or the use of the funds was infected with the discrimination elsewhere in the operation of the recipient. In the case of Grove City College, for example, if there is discrimination in the math department, a fund termination remedy would be available because the funds from BEOG's flow throughout the institution and support all of its programs.

U.S. DEP'T OF TRANSPORTATION V. PARALYZED VETERANS
477 U.S. 597 (1986)

Justice POWELL delivered the opinion of the Court.

Section 504 of the Rehabilitation Act of 1973 prohibits discrimination against handicapped persons in any program or activity receiving federal financial assistance. The United States provides financial assistance to airport operators through grants from a Trust Fund created by the Airport and Airway Development Act of 1970. The Government also operates a nationwide air traffic control system. This case presents the question whether, by virtue of such federal assistance, § 504 is applicable to commercial airlines.[1]

---

1 As used herein, the term "airport operator" refers to the various entities that own or manage airports and that have authority to apply for planning or development grants from the Trust Fund. "Commercial airlines" refers to all passenger carriers formerly certificated by the Civil Aeronautics Board.

I

Respondents Paralyzed Veterans of America and two other organizations representing handicapped individuals (collectively PVA) brought this action in the Court of Appeals for the District of Columbia Circuit. PVA contended that CAB's [the Civil Aeronautics Board's] interpretation of the scope of its rulemaking authority under § 504 was inconsistent with congressional intent and controlling legal precedent.

The Court of Appeals agreed with PVA's position. In the court's view, § 504 gave CAB jurisdiction over all air carriers by virtue of the extensive program of federal financial assistance to airports under the Airport and Airway Development Act of 1970, 49 U.S.C. § 1714. The Court of Appeals found an additional source of financial assistance to airlines in the form of the air traffic control system in place at all major airports. It instructed DOT [Department of Transportation]—CAB's successor agency after CAB was disbanded—to issue new regulations that would apply to all commercial airlines.

II
A

The starting point of any inquiry into the application of a statute is the language of the statute itself. By its terms § 504 limits its coverage to the "program or activity" that "receiv[es]" federal financial assistance. At the outset, therefore, § 504 requires us to identify the recipient of the federal assistance. We look to the terms of the underlying grant statute.

The grant statutes relied on by the Court of Appeals are the Airport and Airway Improvement Act of 1982 (the 1982 Act), 49 U.S.C. App. § 2201 *et seq.*, and its predecessor statutes, particularly the Airport and Airway Development Act of 1970. The 1970 Act established the Airport and Airway Trust Fund, appropriations from which are used to fund airport development. The purpose of disbursements from the Trust Fund is to establish "a nationwide system of public airports adequate to meet the present and future needs of civil aeronautics." In the 1982 Act Congress authorized disbursements from the Trust Fund for the Airport Improvement Program (AIP). Under AIP airport operators submit project grant applications for "airport development or airport planning." Funds are disbursed for a variety of airport construction projects: *e.g.*, land acquisition, runway paving, and buildings, sidewalks, and parking, § 151.93.

It is not difficult to identify the recipient of federal financial assistance under these Acts: Congress has made it explicitly clear that these funds are to go to airport operators. Not a single penny of the money is given to the airlines. Thus, the recipient for purposes of § 504 is the *operator* of the airport and not its users.

Congress limited the scope of § 504 to those who actually "receive" federal financial assistance because it sought to impose § 504 coverage as a form of contractual cost of the recipient's agreement to accept the federal funds. We relied on this same rationale in *Grove City College v. Bell*, where we noted that the recipient of the federal assistance—the College—was free to terminate its participation in the federal grant program and thus avoid the requirements of Title

IX. Under the program specific statutes, Title VI, Title IX, and § 504, Congress enters into an arrangement in the nature of a contract with the recipients of the funds: the recipient's acceptance of the funds triggers coverage under the nondiscrimination provision. By limiting coverage to recipients, Congress imposes the obligations of § 504 upon those who are in a position to accept or reject those obligations as a part of the decision whether or not to "receive" federal funds. In this case, the only parties in that position are the airport operators.

B

Respondents attempt to avoid the straightforward conclusion that airlines are not recipients within the meaning of § 504 by arguing that airlines are "indirect recipients" of the aid to airports. They contend that the money given to airports is simply converted by the airports into nonmoney grants to airlines. Under this reasoning, federal assistance is disbursed to airport operators in the form of cash. The airport operators convert the cash into runways and give the federal assistance—now in the form of a runway—to the airlines. In support of this position, respondents point to the fact that many of the structures constructed at airports with aid from the Trust Fund are particularly beneficial to airlines, e.g., runways, taxiways and ramps. They also find support for their position in *Grove City*'s recognition that federal financial assistance could be either direct or indirect. This argument confuses intended *beneficiaries* with intended *recipients*. While we observed in *Grove City* that there is no "distinction between direct and indirect aid" and that "[t]here is no basis in the statute for the view that only institutions that themselves apply for federal aid or receive checks directly from the Federal Government are subject to regulation," we made these statements in the context of determining whom Congress intended to receive the federal money, and thereby be covered by Title IX. It was clear in *Grove City* that Congress' intended recipient was the College, not the individual students to whom the checks were sent from the Government. It was this unusual disbursement pattern of money from the Government through an intermediary (the students) to the intended recipient that caused us to recognize that federal financial assistance could be received indirectly. While *Grove City* stands for the proposition that Title IX coverage extends to Congress' intended recipient, whether receiving the aid directly or indirectly, it does not stand for the proposition that federal coverage follows the aid past the recipient to those who merely benefit from the aid. In this case, it is clear that the airlines do not actually receive the aid; they only benefit from the airports' use of the aid.

Respondents do not contend that airlines actually receive or are intended to receive money from the Trust Fund. Nor can they argue that the airport operators are, like the students in *Grove City*, mere conduits of the aid to its intended recipient, since, unlike the students, the airports are the intended recipients of the funds. Rather, respondents assert that the economic benefit to airlines from the aid to airports is a form of federal financial assistance. This position ignores the very distinction made by Congress in § 504, and recognized in *Grove City*. The statute covers those who receive the aid, but does not extend as far as those who benefit from it. In *Grove City* we recognized that most federal assistance has "economic ripple effects." We rejected the argument that those indirect economic benefits can trigger statutory coverage. Congress tied the regulatory authority to those programs or activities that receive federal financial assistance; the key is to identify the recipient of that assistance. In this case, it is clear that the recipients of the financial assistance extended by Congress under the Trust Fund are the airport operators.[11]

IV

The Court of Appeals also held that the federally-provided air traffic control system is a form of federal financial assistance to airlines. The Federal Government spends some two billion dollars annually to run this system 24 hours a day nation-wide and in various spots around the world. The air traffic controllers are federal employees and the Federal Government finances operation of the terminal control facilities. In short, the air traffic control system is "owned and operated" by the United States. For that reason, the air traffic control system is not "federal financial assistance" at all. Rather, it is a federally conducted program that has many beneficiaries but no recipients. The legislative history of Title VI makes clear that such programs do not constitute federal financial assistance to anyone. As then-Deputy Attorney General Katzenbach explained:

> Activities wholly carried out by the United States with Federal funds, such as river and harbor improvements and other public works, defense installations, veterans' hospitals, mail service, etc., are not included in the list [of federally assisted programs]. Such activities, being wholly owned by, and operated by or for, the United States, cannot fairly be described as receiving Federal assistance. While they may result in general economic benefit to neighboring communities, such benefit is not considered to be financial assistance to a program or activity within the meaning of Title VI.

That reasoning, of course, applies with equal force to § 504. The federal air traffic control system is a public program that does not involve "financial assistance" to anyone.

NOTES AND QUESTIONS

1. Why didn't *Grove City*'s holding that funding need not be "direct" control this situation? Didn't the airlines substantially benefit from the Airport and Airway Improvement Act? Does discrimination by the airlines against disabled travelers "infect" the federally funded airport development program? For example, would the lack of an accessible restroom on an airplane "infect" the airport program?

2. Who is the recipient of the multi-billion dollar air traffic control system?

3. Does the grant of a federal operating certificate to the airline trigger coverage? *See* fn. 11.

4. Does the Civil Rights Restoration Act, 29 U.S.C. § 794(b), affect this decision?

5. The National Collegiate Athletic Association (NCAA), a private association of nearly all public and private universities and four-year colleges with major athletic programs, receives substantial dues from the member institutions, most of which receive federal financial assistance. Relying on *Grove City College* and *Paralyzed Veterans*, the Court in *National Collegiate Athletic Ass'n v. Smith*, 525 U.S. 459 (1999), concluded the NCAA is not a recipient of federal financial assistance because absent evidence the member schools paid their dues with federal funds, at most the NCAA indirectly benefits from the federal assistance afforded to its members. Such an indirect benefit does not trigger Title IX coverage.

PROBLEM: TWENTY-NINE

The Chicago Fire Department did not allow plaintiff Richard Foss to return to work following a blackout on the job and terminated him when his medical leave expired. Foss alleges that he is fully qualified for his job and so the Department's treatment of him is discrimination because of a disability, in violation of § 504 of the Rehabilitation Act of 1973, 29 U.S.C. § 794.

After discovery, the parties agreed to a stipulation on federal financial assistance, which may be summarized as follows: The City of Chicago receives federal revenue-sharing funds but none of these funds is allocated to the Chicago Fire Department. The Fire Department does, however, receive Federal Community Development Block Grant Funds for a First Aid Care Team (FACT) Program. That program, administered for the Department by Hull House Association, trains unemployed low income residents of a Chicago housing project in first aide skills and employs them as emergency medical technicians in the area of their project. Also, the City's Office of Emergency Preparedness and Disaster Services (EPDS), which develops the City's disaster plan, is administratively part of the Fire Department. That office additionally maintains auxiliary firefighting equipment and trains volunteers to run it for use in very large fires. Its operations are 50 per cent reimbursed by Federal Emergency Management Assistance Funds. Foss had no duties relating either to FACT or EPDS. Each Chicago firefighter is covered by the Public Safety Officers' Benefits Act, 42 U.S.C. § 3796, providing $50,000 to dependents if the fireman is killed in the line of duty. In addition, firefighters who reach the rank of Fire Lieutenant or Paramedic Field Officer may apply to the National Fire Academy, established by 15 U.S.C. § 2206, for professional education and training. If successful, the training is provided at no cost to either the Department or the firefighter.

There are, therefore three kinds of funding programs upon which the plaintiff relies. Through revenue sharing the City receives undesignated funds which it can commingle with its general revenues or which it, in its sole discretion, can earmark for particular programs. FACT and EPDS involve funds earmarked by the federal government and received by the Department. Federal death benefits and education grants are paid to individual firefighters.

Foss argues that for purposes of his claim the Chicago Fire Department should be characterized as a federally funded program or activity. It could have received revenue sharing funds, and
it did receive funds for FACT and EDPS, as well as benefits from the federal programs directed
to firefighters. If the entire department is a federal program, then employment discrimination by
the department would have the relationship to federal funds which § 504 requires.

Defendants urge, however, that the specific use of federal funds governs characterization of
the relevant program or activity. They point out that no revenue-sharing funds reached the Fire
Department, and maintain therefore that the entire Department cannot be a federally funded
program or activity. They further note that Foss was not employed in either the FACT or EDPS
programs, did not die, and was not a lieutenant eligible to go to the National Fire Academy.
Therefore, they maintain that even if his allegations are true, his termination implicated no
federally funded program.

1. Does Foss have a viable lawsuit under § 504 of the Rehabilitation Act, as amended by
   the Civil Rights Restoration Act? Review carefully 42 U.S.C. § 2000d-4a, and consider
   all three forms of assistance in your response.

2. Could the Federal Government terminate any of these forms of assistance due to the
   Fire Department's discriminatory employment practices? *See* 42 U.S.C. § 2000d-1.

2.   ENFORCEMENT

a.   **Private Cause of Action**

CANNON V. UNIVERSITY OF CHICAGO
441 U.S. 677 (1979)

Mr. Justice STEVENS delivered the opinion of the Court.

Petitioner's complaints allege that her applications for admission to medical school were
denied by the respondents because she is a woman. Accepting the truth of those allegations
for the purpose of its decision, the Court of Appeals held that petitioner has no right of action
against respondents that may be asserted in a federal court.

As our recent cases—particularly *Cort v. Ash*—demonstrate, the fact that a federal statute
has been violated and some person harmed does not automatically give rise to a private cause
of action in favor of that person. Instead, before concluding that Congress intended to make a
remedy available to a special class of litigants, a court must carefully analyze the four factors
that *Cort* identifies as indicative of such an intent. Our review of those factors persuades us,
however, that the Court of Appeals reached the wrong conclusion and that petitioner does have

a statutory right to pursue her claim that respondents rejected her application on the basis of her sex.

First, the threshold question under *Cort* is whether the statute was enacted for the benefit of a special class of which the plaintiff is a member. That question is answered by looking to the language of the statute itself.

The language in these statutes—which expressly identifies the class Congress intended to benefit—contrasts sharply with statutory language customarily found in criminal statutes, such as that construed in *Cort*, and other laws enacted for the protection of the general public. There would be far less reason to infer a private remedy in favor of individual persons if Congress, instead of drafting Title IX with an unmistakable focus on the benefited class, had written it simply as a ban on discriminatory conduct by recipients of federal funds or as a prohibition against the disbursement of public funds to educational institutions engaged in discriminatory practices.

Unquestionably, therefore, the first of the four factors identified in *Cort* favors the implication of a private cause of action. Title IX explicitly confers a benefit on persons discriminated against on the basis of sex, and petitioner is clearly a member of that class for whose special benefit the statute was enacted.

Second, the *Cort* analysis requires consideration of legislative history. We must recognize, however, that the legislative history of a statute that does not expressly create or deny a private remedy will typically be equally silent or ambiguous on the question. Therefore, in situations such as the present one "in which it is clear that federal law has granted a class of persons certain rights, it is not necessary to show an intention to *create* a private cause of action, although an explicit purpose to *deny* such cause of action would be controlling." But this is not the typical case. Far from evidencing any purpose to *deny* a private cause of action, the history of Title IX rather plainly indicates that Congress intended to create such a remedy.

Title IX was patterned after Title VI of the Civil Rights Act of 1964. The drafters of Title IX explicitly assumed that it would be interpreted and applied as Title VI had been during the preceding eight years. In 1972 when Title IX was enacted, the critical language in Title VI had already been construed as creating a private remedy. Most particularly, in 1967, a distinguished panel of the Court of Appeals for the Fifth Circuit squarely decided this issue in an opinion that was repeatedly cited with approval and never questioned during the ensuing five years. In addition, at least a dozen other federal courts reached similar conclusions in the same or related contexts during those years. It is always appropriate to assume that our elected representatives, like other citizens, know the law; in this case, because of their repeated references to Title VI and its modes of enforcement, we are especially justified in presuming both that those representatives were aware of the prior interpretation of Title VI and that that interpretation reflects their intent with respect to Title IX.

Third, under *Cort*, a private remedy should not be implied if it would frustrate the underlying purpose of the legislative scheme. On the other hand, when that remedy is necessary or at least helpful to the accomplishment of the statutory purpose, the Court is decidedly receptive to its implication under the statute.

Title IX, like its model Title VI, sought to accomplish two related, but nevertheless somewhat different, objectives. First, Congress wanted to avoid the use of federal resources to support discriminatory practices; second, it wanted to provide individual citizens effective protection against those practices. Both of these purposes were repeatedly identified in the debates on the two statutes.

The first purpose is generally served by the statutory procedure for the termination of federal financial support for institutions engaged in discriminatory practices. That remedy is, however, severe and often may not provide an appropriate means of accomplishing the second purpose if merely an isolated violation has occurred. In that situation, the violation might be remedied more efficiently by an order requiring an institution to accept an applicant who had been improperly excluded. Moreover, in that kind of situation it makes little sense to impose on an individual, whose only interest is in obtaining a benefit for herself, or on HEW, the burden of demonstrating that an institution's practices are so pervasively discriminatory that a complete cut-off of federal funding is appropriate. The award of individual relief to a private litigant who has prosecuted her own suit is not only sensible but is also fully consistent with—and in some cases even necessary to—the orderly enforcement of the statute.

[As to the fourth factor in *Cort*—whether the cause of action is one traditionally relegated to state law in an area basically the concern of the states—the Court concluded that the federal government had been the primary protector against discrimination since the Civil War. Thus, federalism concerns were minimal.]

In sum, there is no need in this case to weigh the four *Cort* factors; all of them support the same result. Not only the words and history of Title IX, but also its subject matter and underlying purposes, counsel implication of a cause of action in favor of private victims of discrimination.

NOTES AND QUESTIONS

1. Assuming a private litigant may sue to enforce the federal financial assistance Acts, what types of relief should be available?

   In light of the stated second purpose of Title IX, *i.e.,* "to provide individual citizens effective protection against [discriminatory] practices," does it make sense to impose a damage remedy—or will private entities simply forego federal funds and continue to practice discrimination rather than face the risk of damages which might easily exceed the value of the federal assistance?

2. Could Cannon maintain a private cause of action against the federal agency for disbursing funds to a non-complying entity? Note that in *United States Dep't of Transportation v. Paralyzed Veterans of America, supra,* the Court appeared to assume that such an action may be brought.

b.   Proof of Claims

LAU V. NICHOLS
414 U.S. 563 (1973)

Mr. Justice DOUGLAS delivered the opinion of the Court.

[The plaintiffs in this case challenge the failure on the part of the San Francisco, California, school system to provide students of Chinese ancestry with supplemental courses in the English language. This failure was challenged as violating both the Equal Protection Clause as well as Title VI.]

Basic English skills are at the very core of what these public schools teach. Imposition of a requirement that, before a child can effectively participate in the educational program, he must already have acquired those basic skills is to make a mockery of public education. We know that those who do not understand English are certain to find their classroom experiences wholly incomprehensible and in no way meaningful. We do not reach the Equal Protection Clause argument which has been advanced but rely solely on § 601 of the Civil Rights Act of 1964.

That section bans discrimination based "on the ground of race, color, or national origin," in "any program or activity receiving Federal financial assistance." The school district involved in this litigation receives large amounts of federal financial assistance. The Department of Health, Education, and Welfare (HEW), which has authority to promulgate regulations prohibiting discrimination in federally assisted school systems, in 1968 issued one guideline that "[s]chool systems are responsible for assuring that students of a particular race, color, or national origin are not denied the opportunity to obtain the education generally obtained by other students in the system." 33 FED. REG. 4956.

Discrimination among students on account of race or national origin that is prohibited includes "discrimination . . . in the availability or use of any academic . . . or other facilities of the grantee or other recipient." 45 C.F.R. § 80.5(b). Discrimination is barred which has that *effect* even though no purposeful design is present: a recipient "may not . . . utilize criteria or methods of administration which have the effect of subjecting individuals to discrimination" or have "the effect of defeating or substantially impairing accomplishment of the objectives of the program as respect individuals of a particular race, color, or national origin." *Id.* § 80.3(b)(2).

It seems obvious that the Chinese-speaking minority receive fewer benefits than the English-speaking majority from respondents' school system which denies them a meaningful opportunity to participate in the educational program—all earmarks of the discrimination banned by the regulations. In 1970 HEW issued clarifying guidelines, 35 FED. REG. 11595, which include the following:

> Where inability to speak and understand the English language excludes national origin-minority group children from effective participation in the educational program offered

by a school district, the district must take affirmative steps to rectify the language deficiency in order to open its instructional program to these students.

Respondent school district contractually agreed to "comply with Title VI of the Civil Rights Act of 1964 . . . and all requirements imposed by or pursuant to the Regulation" of HEW (45 C.F.R. pt. 80) which are "issued pursuant to that title. . . ." and also immediately to "take any measures necessary to effectuate this agreement." The Federal Government has power to fix the terms on which its money allotments to the States shall be disbursed. Whatever may be the limits of that power, they have not been reached here.

NOTES AND QUESTIONS

1. Could this suit have succeeded under the Equal Protection Clause? Did the school system intentionally deny equal educational opportunity to anyone?

2. If the plaintiffs could not have succeeded under the Equal Protection Clause, are the agency regulations which reach beyond the constitutional prohibition valid?

REGENTS OF THE UNIVERSITY OF CALIFORNIA V. BAKKE
438 U.S. 265 (1978)

[In this case the plaintiff Alan Bakke challenged a special admissions program of the medical school of the University of California that designated a certain number of slots for minority applicants. The affirmative action program was challenged as violating both Title VI of the Civil Rights Act of 1964, as well as the Equal Protection Clause of the Fourteenth Amendment. A majority of the Court reasoned that Title VI proscribes only those racial classifications that would violate the Equal Protection Clause if employed by a state or its agencies, and it struck down the University's admissions program. Thus, the decision casts some doubt on whether Title VI extends protection beyond that afforded under the Equal Protection Clause, as the Supreme Court had indicated in *Lau*. Relevant excerpts from a concurring opinion follow.]

Opinion of Justices BRENNAN, WHITE, MARSHALL and BLACKMUN, concurring in the Judgment in part and dissenting in part.

II

The threshold question we must decide is whether Title VI of the Civil Rights Act of 1964 bars recipients of federal funds from giving preferential consideration to disadvantaged members of racial minorities as part of a program designed to enable such individuals to surmount the obstacles imposed by racial discrimination.

In our view, Title VI prohibits only those uses of racial criteria that would violate the Fourteenth Amendment if employed by a State or its agencies; it does not bar the preferential treatment of racial minorities as a means of remedying past societal discrimination to the extent that such action is consistent with the Fourteenth Amendment. The legislative history of Title VI, administrative regulations interpreting the statute, subsequent congressional and executive action, and the prior decisions of this Court compel this conclusion. None of these sources lends support to the proposition that Congress intended to bar all race-conscious efforts to extend the benefits of federally financed programs to minorities who have been historically excluded from the full benefits of American life.

The history of Title VI—from President Kennedy's request that Congress grant executive departments and agencies authority to cut off federal funds to programs that discriminate against Negroes through final enactment of legislation incorporating his proposals—reveals one fixed purpose: to give the Executive Branch of Government clear authority to terminate federal funding of private programs that use race as a means of disadvantaging minorities in a manner that would be prohibited by the Constitution if engaged in by government.

We recognize that *Lau*, especially when read in light of our subsequent decision in *Washington v. Davis*, which rejected the general proposition that governmental action is unconstitutional solely because it has a racially disproportionate impact, may be read as being predicated upon the view that, at least under some circumstances, Title VI proscribes conduct which might not be prohibited by the Constitution. Since we are now of the opinion, for the reasons set forth above, that Title VI's standard, applicable alike to public and private recipients of federal funds, is no broader than the Constitution's, we have serious doubts concerning the correctness of what appears to be the premise of that decision. However, even accepting *Lau's* implication that impact alone is in some contexts sufficient to establish a *prima facie* violation of Title VI, contrary to our view that Title VI's definition of racial discrimination is absolutely coextensive with the Constitution's, this would not assist the respondent in the least. First, regardless of whether Title VI's prohibitions extend beyond the Constitution's, the evidence fails to establish, and, indeed, compels the rejection of, the proposition that Congress intended to prohibit recipients of federal funds from voluntarily employing race-conscious measures to eliminate the effects of past societal discrimination against racial minorities such as Negroes. Secondly, *Lau* itself, for the reasons set forth in the immediately preceding paragraph, strongly supports the view that voluntary race-conscious remedial action is permissible under Title VI. If discriminatory racial impact alone is enough to demonstrate at least a *prima facie* Title VI violation, it is difficult to believe that the Title would forbid the Medical School from attempting to correct the racially exclusionary effects of its initial admissions policy during the first two years of the School's operation.

1. Can *Lau* survive the ruling in *Bakke* that Title VI prohibits only the use of racial criteria that would violate the Fourteenth Amendment if employed by the State? Did the Court in *Lau* hold that Title VI itself reached impact claims? If only intentional discrimination is prohibited by the Fourteenth Amendment, isn't the same true of Title VI?

2. Can the cases be reconciled by focusing on the unique nature of "reverse" discrimination claims? Did Congress in enacting Title VI contemplate that its law could be used to invalidate voluntary affirmative action programs?

3. Justice Powell's opinion in *Bakke*, announcing the judgment of the Court in the splintered decision and taking the view that student body diversity is a compelling state interest, was cited extensively by the majority in *Grutter v. Bollinger*, 539 U.S. 306 (2003), to support its conclusion that the University of Michigan law school had a compelling interest in attaining a diverse student body and that its admissions policy was narrowly tailored to achieve that interest. Therefore, the challenge to the admissions policy, based on the Equal Protection Clause, 42 U.S.C. § 1981, and Title VI, failed. However, the University's undergraduate admissions policy was struck down in *Gratz v. Bollinger*, 539 U.S. 244 (2003), as a violation of equal protection because it was not narrowly tailored. The Court noted "that the admissions policy also violates Title VI and [§ 1981]."

4.

5.

6.

7. In *Guardians Association v. Civil Service Commission*, 463 U.S. 582 (1983), the Court addressed the issue of "whether private plaintiffs need to prove discriminatory intent to establish a violation of Title VI of the Civil Rights Act of 1964, and administrative implementing regulations promulgated thereunder." Five Justices, in separate opinions, held that the Court of Appeals erred in requiring proof of discriminatory intent. Justice Stevens, joined by Justice Brennan and Justice Blackmun, reasoned that, although Title VI itself requires proof of discriminatory intent, the administrative regulations incorporating a disparate impact standard are valid. Justice Marshall would hold that, under Title VI itself, proof of disparate impact discrimination is all that is necessary. Justice White agreed with Justice Marshall that discriminatory animus is not an essential element of a violation of Title VI, and that the regulations

are valid, even assuming arguendo that Title VI, in and of itself, does not proscribe disparate impact discrimination. Justice White went on to conclude, however, that "in the absence of proof of discriminatory animus, compensatory relief should not be awarded to private Title VI plaintiffs; unless discriminatory intent is shown, declaratory and limited injunctive relief should be the only available private remedies for Title VI violations." In footnote 27 Justice White summarized the ruling:

> Despite the numerous opinions, the views of at least five Justices on two issues are identifiable. The dissenters, Justices BRENNAN, MARSHALL, BLACKMUN, and STEVENS, join with me to form a majority for upholding the validity of the regulations incorporating a disparate-impact standard. A different majority, however, would not allow compensatory relief in the absence of proof of discriminatory intent. Justice REHNQUIST and I reach this conclusion directly. Justice POWELL, joined by THE CHIEF JUSTICE, believe that no private relief should ever be granted under Title VI under any circumstances. Justice O'CONNOR, would hold that all relief should be denied unless discriminatory intent is proven. It follows from the views of these three latter Justices that no compensatory relief should be awarded if discriminatory animus is not shown.

Justice Powell expressed concern that:

> a majority of the Court would hold that proof of discriminatory effect suffices to establish liability only when the suit is brought to enforce the regulations rather than the statute itself. And it would seem that the regulations may be enforced only in a suit pursuant to 42 U.S.C. § 1983; anyone invoking the implied right of action under Title VI would be limited by the discriminatory-intent standard required to prove violations of Title VI. Thus, the apparent result is that a suit against governmental recipients of federal funds—who may be sued under § 1983— will be governed by a different standard of liability than a suit against private recipients of federal funds. One would have difficulty explaining this result in terms of the legislative history of Title VI.

Three Justices disagreed with this: "Whether a cause of action against private parties exists directly under the regulations and, if so, what the standard of liability in such an action would be, are questions that are not presented by this case." Can § 1983 be used to enforce Title VI regulations? Review *Gonzaga, supra.*

Justice MARSHALL delivered the opinion of the Court.

I

Faced in 1980-1981 with projected state Medicaid costs of $42 million more than the State's Medicaid budget of $388 million, the directors of the Tennessee Medicaid program decided to institute a variety of cost-saving measures. Among these changes was a reduction from 20 to 14 in the number of inpatient hospital days per fiscal year that Tennessee Medicaid would pay hospitals on behalf of a Medicaid recipient. Before the new measures took effect, respondents, Tennessee Medicaid recipients, brought a class action for declaratory and injunctive relief in which they alleged, *inter alia*, that the proposed 14-day limitation on inpatient coverage would have a discriminatory effect on the handicapped. Statistical evidence, which petitioners do not dispute, indicated that in the 1979-1980 fiscal year, 27.4% of all handicapped users of hospital services who received Medicaid required more than 14 days of care, while only 7.8% of non-handicapped users required more than 14 days of inpatient care.

Respondents' position was twofold. First, they argued that the change from 20 to 14 days of coverage would have a disproportionate effect on the handicapped and hence was discriminatory. The second, and major, thrust of respondents' attack was directed at the use of any annual limitation on the number of inpatient days covered, for respondents acknowledged that, given the special needs of the handicapped for medical care, any such limitation was likely to disadvantage the handicapped disproportionately.

II

The first question the parties urge on the Court is whether proof of discriminatory animus is always required to establish a violation of § 504 and its implementing regulations, or whether federal law also reaches action by a recipient of federal funding that discriminates against the handicapped by effect rather than by design. The State of Tennessee argues that § 504 reaches only purposeful discrimination against the handicapped. As support for this position, the State relies heavily on our recent decision in *Guardians Ass'n v. Civil Service Comm'n of New York City*.

In *Guardians*, we confronted the question whether Title VI of the Civil Rights Act of 1964 reaches both intentional and disparate-impact discrimination. No opinion commanded a majority in *Guardians*, and members of the Court offered widely varying interpretations of Title VI. Nonetheless, a two-pronged holding on the nature of the discrimination proscribed by Title VI emerged in that case. First, the Court held that Title VI itself directly reached only instances of intentional discrimination. Second, the Court held that actions having an unjustifiable disparate impact on minorities could be redressed through agency regulations designed to implement the purposes of Title VI. In essence, then, we held that Title VI had delegated to the agencies in the first instance the complex determination of what sorts of disparate impacts upon minorities constituted sufficiently significant social problems, and were readily enough remediable, to warrant altering the practices of the federal grantees that had produced those impacts.

Guardians, therefore, does not support petitioners' blanket proposition that federal law proscribes only intentional discrimination against the handicapped. Indeed, to the extent our holding in *Guardians* is relevant to the interpretation of § 504, *Guardians* suggests that the regulations implementing § 504, upon which respondents in part rely, could make actionable the disparate impact challenged in this case. Moreover, there are reasons to pause before too quickly extending even the first prong of *Guardians* to § 504.

Discrimination against the handicapped was perceived by Congress to be most often the product, not of invidious animus, but rather of thoughtlessness and indifference—of benign neglect. Thus, Representative Vanik, introducing the predecessor to § 504 in the House, described the treatment of the handicapped as one of the country's "shameful oversights," which caused the handicapped to live among society "shunted aside, hidden, and ignored." And Senator Cranston, the Acting Chairman of the Subcommittee that drafted § 504, described the Act as a response to "previous societal neglect." Federal agencies and commentators on the plight of the handicapped similarly have found that discrimination against the handicapped is primarily the result of apathetic attitudes rather than affirmative animus.

In addition, much of the conduct that Congress sought to alter in passing the Rehabilitation Act would be difficult if not impossible to reach were the Act construed to proscribe only conduct fueled by a discriminatory intent. For example, elimination of architectural barriers was one of the central aims of the Act, yet such barriers were clearly not erected with the aim or intent of excluding the handicapped. Similarly, Senator Williams, the chairman of the Labor and Public Welfare Committee that reported out § 504, asserted that the handicapped were the victims of "[d]iscrimination in access to public transportation" and "[d]iscrimination because they do not have the simplest forms of special educational and rehabilitation services they need. . . ." These statements would ring hollow if the resulting legislation could not rectify the harms resulting from action that discriminated by effect as well as by design.

At the same time, the position urged by respondents—that we interpret § 504 to reach all action disparately affecting the handicapped—is also troubling. Because the handicapped typically are not similarly situated to the non-handicapped, respondents' position would in essence require each recipient of federal funds first to evaluate the effect on the handicapped of every proposed action that might touch the interests of the handicapped, and then to consider alternatives for achieving the same objectives with less severe disadvantage to the handicapped. The formalization and policing of this process could lead to a wholly unwieldy administrative and adjudicative burden. Had Congress intended § 504 to be a National Environmental Policy Act for the handicapped, requiring the preparation of "Handicapped Impact Statements" before any action was taken by a grantee that affected the handicapped, we would expect some indication of that purpose in the statute or its legislative history. Yet there is nothing to suggest that such was Congress' purpose. Thus, just as there is reason to question whether Congress intended

§ 504 to reach only intentional discrimination, there is similarly reason to question whether Congress intended § 504 to embrace all claims of disparate-impact discrimination.

Any interpretation of § 504 must therefore be responsive to two powerful but countervailing considerations—the need to give effect to the statutory objectives and the desire to keep § 504 within manageable bounds. Given the legitimacy of both of these goals and the tension between them, we decline the parties' invitation to decide today that one of these goals so overshadows the other as to eclipse it. While we reject the boundless notion that all disparate-impact showings constitute *prima facie* cases under § 504, we assume without deciding that § 504 reaches at least some conduct that has an unjustifiable disparate impact upon the handicapped.

NOTES AND QUESTIONS

1. Why is the Court reluctant to adopt an "impact" standard, as it did in Title VII litigation? Does the Court provide any guidance as to when impact analysis may be used?

2. Does the 14-day limit have an impermissible disparate impact on persons with a disability? If so, should § 504 be interpreted to foreclose government from imposing any limitation on the number of hospital days covered by Medicaid?

3. May a plaintiff state a claim under Title IX for "unintentional" discrimination? Is sex discrimination more likely the result of invidious animus or "benign neglect?" If a medical school's policy of excluding all applicants over age 35 adversely affects women who are more likely to seek admission at a later point in their lives, is Title IX violated?

4. Does Justice Marshall's discussion of the impact regulations support recognition of a separate source of rights not provided by the statute?

ALEXANDER V. SANDOVAL
532 U.S. 275 (2001)

Justice SCALIA delivered the opinion of the Court.

This case presents the question whether private individuals may sue to enforce disparate-impact regulations promulgated under Title VI of the Civil Rights Act of 1964.

I

The Alabama Department of Public Safety (Department), of which petitioner James Alexander is the Director, accepted grants of financial assistance from the United States Department of

Justice (DOJ) and Department of Transportation (DOT) and so subjected itself to the restrictions of Title VI of the Civil Rights Act of 1964. Section 601 of that Title provides that no person shall, "on the ground of race, color, or national origin, be excluded from participation in, be denied the benefits of, or be subjected to discrimination under any program or activity" covered by Title VI. Section 602 authorizes federal agencies "to effectuate the provisions of [§ 601] . . . by issuing rules, regulations, or orders of general applicability," and the DOJ in an exercise of this authority promulgated a regulation forbidding funding recipients to "utilize criteria or methods of administration which have the effect of subjecting individuals to discrimination because of their race, color, or national origin . . . ."

The State of Alabama amended its Constitution in 1990 to declare English "the official language of the state of Alabama." Pursuant to this provision and, petitioners have argued, to advance public safety, the Department decided to administer state driver's license examinations only in English. Respondent Sandoval, as representative of a class, brought suit in the United States District Court for the Middle District of Alabama to enjoin the English-only policy, arguing that it violated the DOJ regulation because it had the effect of subjecting non-English speakers to discrimination based on their national origin. The District Court agreed. It enjoined the policy and ordered the Department to accommodate non-English speakers. Petitioners appealed to the Court of Appeals for the Eleventh Circuit, which affirmed. Both courts rejected petitioners' argument that Title VI did not provide respondents a cause of action to enforce the regulation.

We do not inquire here whether the DOJ regulation was authorized by § 602, or whether the courts below were correct to hold that the English-only policy had the effect of discriminating on the basis of national origin. The petition for writ of certiorari raised, and we agreed to review, only the question posed in the first paragraph of this opinion: whether there is a private cause of action to enforce the regulation.

II

Although Title VI has often come to this Court, it is fair to say (indeed, perhaps an understatement) that our opinions have not eliminated all uncertainty regarding its commands. For purposes of the present case, however, it is clear from our decisions, from Congress's amendments of Title VI, and from the parties' concessions that three aspects of Title VI must be taken as given. First, private individuals may sue to enforce § 601 of Title VI and obtain both injunctive relief and damages.

Second, it is similarly beyond dispute—and no party disagrees—that § 601 prohibits only intentional discrimination.

Third, we must assume for purposes of deciding this case that regulations promulgated under § 602 of Title VI may validly proscribe activities that have a disparate impact on racial groups, even though such activities are permissible under § 601. Though no opinion of this Court has held that, five Justices in *Guardians* voiced that view of the law at least as alternative grounds for their decisions. These statements are in considerable tension with the rule of *Bakke* and *Guardians* that § 601 forbids only intentional discrimination, but petitioners have not challenged the regulations here. We therefore assume for the purposes of deciding this case that the DOJ and DOT regulations proscribing activities that have a disparate impact on the basis of race are valid.

Respondents assert that the issue in this case, like the first two described above, has been resolved by our cases. To reject a private cause of action to enforce the disparate-impact regulations, they say, we would "[have] to ignore the actual language of *Guardians* and *Cannon*." The language in *Cannon* to which respondents refer does not in fact support their position. But in any event, this Court is bound by holdings, not language. *Cannon* was decided on the assumption that the University of Chicago had intentionally discriminated against petitioner. It therefore *held* that Title IX created a private right of action to enforce its ban on intentional discrimination, but had no occasion to consider whether the right reached regulations barring disparate-impact discrimination. In *Guardians*, the Court *held* that private individuals could not recover compensatory damages under Title VI except for intentional discrimination. Five Justices in addition voted to uphold the disparate-impact regulations (four would have declared them invalid), but of those five, three expressly reserved the question of a direct private right of action to enforce the regulations, saying that "[w]hether a cause of action against private parties exists directly under the regulations . . . [is a] questio[n] that [is] not presented by this case." Thus, only two Justices had cause to reach the issue that respondents say the "actual language" of *Guardians* resolves. Neither that case, nor any other in this Court, has held that the private right of action exists.

Nor does it follow straightaway from the three points we have taken as given that Congress must have intended a private right of action to enforce disparate-impact regulations. We do not doubt that regulations applying § 601's ban on intentional discrimination are covered by the cause of action to enforce that section. Such regulations, if valid and reasonable, authoritatively construe the statute itself, and it is therefore meaningless to talk about a separate cause of action to enforce the regulations apart from the statute. A Congress that intends the statute to be enforced through a private cause of action intends the authoritative interpretation of the statute to be so enforced as well.

It is clear now that the disparate-impact regulations do not simply apply § 601—since they indeed forbid conduct that § 601 permits—and therefore clear that the private right of action to enforce § 601 does not include a private right to enforce these regulations. That right must come, if at all, from the independent force of § 602. As stated earlier, we assume for purposes of this decision that § 602 confers the authority to promulgate disparate-impact regulations; the question remains whether it confers a private right of action to enforce them. If not, we must conclude that a failure to comply with regulations promulgated under § 602 that is not also a failure to comply with § 601 is not actionable.

Implicit in our discussion thus far has been a particular understanding of the genesis of private causes of action. Like substantive federal law itself, private rights of action to enforce federal law must be created by Congress. The judicial task is to interpret the statute Congress has passed to determine whether it displays an intent to create not just a private right but also a private remedy. Statutory intent on this latter point is determinative. Without it, a cause of action does not exist and courts may not create one, no matter how desirable that might be as a policy matter, or how compatible with the statute.

We therefore begin (and find that we can end) our search for Congress's intent with the text and structure of Title VI. Section 602 authorizes federal agencies "to effectuate the provisions of [§ 601] . . . by issuing rules, regulations, or orders of general applicability." It is immediately clear that the "rights-creating" language so critical to the Court's analysis in *Cannon* of § 601, is completely absent from § 602. Whereas § 601 decrees that "[n]o person . . . shall . . . be subjected to discrimination," the text of § 602 provides that "[e]ach Federal department and agency . . . is authorized and directed to effectuate the provisions of [§ 601]." Far from displaying congressional intent to create new rights, § 602 limits agencies to "effectuat[ing]" rights already created by § 601. And the focus of § 602 is twice removed from the individuals who will ultimately benefit from Title VI's protection. Statutes that focus on the person regulated rather than the individuals protected create "no implication of an intent to confer rights on a particular class of persons." Section 602 is yet a step further removed: it focuses neither on the individuals protected nor even on the funding recipients being regulated, but on the agencies that will do the regulating. When this is true, "[t]here [is] far less reason to infer a private remedy in favor of individual persons." So far as we can tell, this authorizing portion of § 602 reveals no congressional intent to create a private right of action.

Nor do the methods that § 602 goes on to provide for enforcing its authorized regulations manifest an intent to create a private remedy; if anything, they suggest the opposite. Section 602 empowers agencies to enforce their regulations either by terminating funding to the "particular program, or part thereof," that has violated the regulation or "by any other means authorized by law." No enforcement action may be taken, however, "until the department or agency concerned has advised the appropriate person or persons of the failure to comply with the requirement and has determined that compliance cannot be secured by voluntary means." And every agency enforcement action is subject to judicial review. § 2000d-2. If an agency attempts to terminate program funding, still more restrictions apply. The agency head must "file with the committees of the House and Senate having legislative jurisdiction over the program or activity involved a full written report of the circumstances and the grounds for such action." And the termination of funding does not "become effective until thirty days have elapsed after the filing of such report." Whatever these elaborate restrictions on agency enforcement may imply for the private enforcement of rights created *outside* of § 602, they tend to contradict a congressional intent to create privately enforceable rights through § 602 itself. The express provision of one method of enforcing a substantive rule suggests that Congress intended to preclude others. Sometimes the suggestion is so strong that it precludes a finding of congressional intent to create a private right of action, even though other aspects of the statute (such as language making the would-be plaintiff "a member of the class for whose benefit the statute was enacted") suggest the contrary. And as our § 1983 cases show, some remedial schemes foreclose a private cause of action to enforce even those statutes that admittedly create substantive private rights. In the present case, the claim of exclusivity for the express remedial scheme does not even have to overcome such obstacles. The question whether § 602's remedial scheme can overbear other evidence of congressional intent is simply not presented, since we have found no evidence anywhere in the text to suggest that Congress intended to create a private right to enforce regulations promulgated under § 602.

Both the Government and respondents argue that the *regulations* contain rights-creating language and so must be privately enforceable, but that argument skips an analytical step. Language in a regulation may invoke a private right of action that Congress through statutory text created, but it may not create a right that Congress has not. Thus, when a statute has provided a general authorization for private enforcement of regulations, it may perhaps be correct that the intent displayed in each regulation can determine whether or not it is privately enforceable. But it is most certainly incorrect to say that language in a regulation can conjure up a private cause of action that has not been authorized by Congress. Agencies may play the sorcerer's apprentice but not the sorcerer himself.

NOTES AND QUESTIONS

1. Based on *Sandoval*, what is the status of Title VI regulations that reach discriminatory impact? May federal agencies enforce them?

2. Could suit have been brought against the Director of Public Safety under § 1983 to enforce the impact regulations? Review *Gonzaga*, *supra* Ch. II, wherein the Court reasoned that the question of whether a statute creates a private cause of action is identical to the initial question used to determine whether a statute creates rights that may be enforced under § 1983, i.e., whether "Congress intends to create new individual rights." Did Congress in enacting Title VI "make its intention [to create rights] 'unmistakably clear'"? Does *Sandoval* definitively answer this question?

   May § 1983 be used to enforce Title VI itself? Although Title VI creates enforceable substantive rights, has Congress "impliedly" indicated its intent to foreclose the use of § 1983 by creating a comprehensive administrative remedy? In analyzing this question, should we examine the remedy actually provided for in the statute or the remedy that the Court has "implied"? Would there be any litigation advantage to using § 1983?

3. Do any of the following statutes—Title VI, Title IX, and § 504—reach facially neutral rules, policies or practices with a disparate impact, absent a showing of discriminatory intent?

PROBLEM: THIRTY

This litigation challenges New York City's decision to close Sydenham Hospital, one of its 17 municipal hospitals, on the ground that the City's proposed action would constitute racial discrimination in the use of federal funds in violation of Title VI of the Civil Rights Act of 1964. Like most American cities, New York has struggled mightily to provide adequate municipal services with limited financial resources. Its difficulties have become particularly severe since its budget crisis that began in the mid-1979s. Closing Sydenham is one of the many painful steps that the City has undertaken or proposed in an effort to maintain financial stability. The discrimination claim in this case arises from the fact that Sydenham, located in central Harlem, serves a population that is 98% minority (Black and Hispanic).

In April, 1979, Mayor Koch appointed a Health Policy Task Force to examine ways of reducing costly excess hospital capacity while maintaining access to high quality health services. The Task Force report, issued June 20, 1979, recommended a series of steps that the City's Health and Hospital Corporation (HHC) estimated would save $30 million in fiscal year 1981. With respect to the 17 hospitals of the municipal hospital system, the report proposed that some hospitals be replaced, that some hospitals reduce the number of beds, and that two hospitals, Sydenham and Metropolitan, both located in Harlem, be closed, since their operation caused the greatest financial strain on the City. The HHC approved the report on June 28, 1979.

1. Can the plaintiffs state a claim under either Title VI or agency regulations prohibiting government action that adversely affects racial minorities? Could the plaintiffs establish the closings were racially motivated? What other evidence is needed?

2. May plaintiffs sue under § 1983 to enforce the regulation? May they sue the Agency to enforce the regulation? What relief is available?

3. What defenses regarding liability should be raised by New York City? If the plaintiffs establish a *prima facie* case of discriminatory impact, what burden shifts to the defendant? What if the plaintiffs could show alternatives with a less adverse impact on minorities?

4. Could the plaintiffs have stated a claim against the City under §1981? Under the Equal Protection Clause and § 1983?

c. Remedies

CONSOLIDATED RAIL CORP. V. DARRONE
465 U.S. 624 (1984)

Justice POWELL delivered the opinion of the Court.

This case requires us to clarify the scope of the private right of action to enforce § 504 of the Rehabilitation Act of 1973, that prohibits discrimination against the handicapped by federal grant recipients. There is a conflict among the Circuits.

In 1978, Congress amended the Rehabilitation Act to specify the means of enforcing its ban on discrimination. In particular, § 505(a)(2), as added, 29 U.S.C. §§ 794a(a)(2), made available the "remedies, procedure, and rights set forth in Title VI of the Civil Rights Acts of 1964" to victims of discrimination in violation of § 504 of the Act.

In 1979, Thomas LeStrange filed suit against petitioner for violation of rights conferred by § 504 of the Rehabilitation Act. The complaint alleged that the Erie Lackawanna Railroad, to which Conrail is the successor in interest, had employed the plaintiff as a locomotive engineer; that an accident had required amputation of plaintiff's left hand and forearm in 1971; and that, after LeStrange was disabled, the Erie Lackawanna Railroad, and then Conrail, had refused to employ him although it had no justification for finding him unfit to work.

Facts

We are met initially by petitioner's contention that the death of the plaintiff LeStrange has mooted the case and deprives the Court of jurisdiction for that reason. Petitioner concedes, however, that there remains a case or controversy if LeStrange's estate may recover money that would have been owed to LeStrange. Without determining the extent to which money damages are available under § 504, we think it clear that § 504 authorizes a plaintiff who alleges intentional discrimination to bring an equitable action for backpay. The case therefore is not moot.

In *Guardians Association v. Civil Service Commission*, 463 U.S. 582 (1983), a majority of the Court expressed the view that a private plaintiff under Title VI could recover backpay; and no member of the Court contended that backpay was unavailable, at least as a remedy for intentional discrimination. It is unnecessary to review here the grounds for this interpretation of Title VI. It suffices to state that we now apply this interpretation to § 505(a)(2), that, as we have noted, provides to plaintiffs under § 504 the remedies set forth in Title VI. Therefore, respondent, having alleged intentional discrimination, may recover backpay in the present § 504 suit.

NOTES AND QUESTIONS

1. Does the Court establish that equitable retroactive relief is available for intentional violations of all of the funding provisions?

2. What relief, other than back pay, will be available to victims of intentional discrimination under Title VI, Title IX and the Rehabilitation Act? What arguments

should be made for and against the availability of compensatory damages for humiliation and mental anguish suffered as a result of discriminatory treatment? What about punitive damages?

3. Does § 2000d-7, wherein Congress eliminated an Eleventh Amendment defense for state defendants, suggest that claims for monetary relief were assumed to exist under Title VI, Title IX and § 504? *See* discussion *infra*, regarding this defense.

FRANKLIN V. GWINNETT COUNTY PUBLIC SCHOOLS
503 U.S. 60 (1992)

Justice WHITE delivered the opinion of the Court.

This case presents the question whether the implied right of action under Title IX of the Education Amendments of 1972, 20 U.S.C. §§ 1681-1688 (Title IX), which this Court recognized in *Cannon v. University of Chicago* supports a claim for monetary damages.

I

Christine Franklin was a student at North Gwinnett High School in Gwinnett County, Georgia, between September 1985 and August 1989. Gwinnett County School District operates the high school and receives federal funds. According to the complaint, Franklin was subjected to continual sexual harassment beginning in the autumn of her tenth grade year (1986) from Andrew Hill, a sports coach and teacher employed by the district. Among other allegations, Franklin avers that Hill engaged her in sexually-oriented conversations in which he asked about her sexual experiences with her boyfriend and whether she would consider having sexual intercourse with an older man, that Hill forcibly kissed her on the mouth in the school parking lot, that he telephoned her at her home and asked if she would meet him socially, and that, on three occasions in her junior year, Hill interrupted a class, requested that the teacher excuse Franklin, and took her to a private office where he subjected her to coercive intercourse. The complaint further alleges that though they became aware of and investigated Hill's sexual harassment of Franklin and other female students, teachers and administrators took no action to halt it and discouraged Franklin from pressing charges against Hill. On April 14, 1988, Hill resigned on the condition that all matters pending against him be dropped. The school thereupon closed its investigation.

In this action, the District Court dismissed the complaint on the ground that Title IX does not authorize an award of damages. The Court of Appeals affirmed.

II

In *Cannon v. University of Chicago*, the Court held that Title IX is enforceable through an implied right of action. We have no occasion here to reconsider that decision. Rather, in this case we must decide what remedies are available in a suit brought pursuant to this implied right. As we have often stated, the question of what remedies are available under a statute that provides a private right of action is "analytically distinct" from the issue of whether such a right exists in the first place. Thus, although we examine the text and history of a statute to determine whether Congress intended to create a right of action, we presume the availability of all appropriate remedies unless Congress has expressly indicated otherwise. This principle has deep roots in our jurisprudence.

A

"[W]here legal rights have been invaded, and a federal statute provides for a general right to sue for such invasion, federal courts may use any available remedy to make good the wrong done." *Bell v. Hood*. The Court explained this longstanding rule as jurisdictional, and upheld the exercise of the federal courts' power to award appropriate relief so long as a cause of action existed under the Constitution or laws of the United States. The foundation upon which the *Bell v. Hood* Court articulated this traditional presumption, therefore, was well settled.

B

[Defendants] and the United States as *amicus curiae*, however, maintain that whatever the traditional presumption may have been when the Court decided *Bell v. Hood*, it has disappeared in succeeding decades. We do not agree. . . .

Contrary to arguments by respondents and the United States that *Guardians Ass'n v. Civil Service Comm'n of New York City* and *Consolidated Rail Corp. v. Darrone* eroded this traditional presumption, those cases in fact support it. Though the multiple opinions in *Guardians* suggest the difficulty of inferring the common ground among the Justices in that case, a clear majority expressed the view that damages were available under Title VI in an action seeking remedies for an intentional violation, and no Justice challenged the traditional presumption in favor of a federal court's power to award appropriate relief in a cognizable cause of action. The correctness of this inference was made clear the following Term when the Court unanimously held that the 1978 amendment to § 504 of the Rehabilitation Act of 1973—which had expressly incorporated the "remedies, procedures, and rights set forth in Title VI"—authorizes an award of backpay. In *Darrone*, the Court observed that a majority in *Guardians* had "agreed that retroactive relief is available to private plaintiffs for all discrimination . . . that is actionable under Title VI." The general rule, therefore, is that absent clear direction to the contrary by Congress, the federal courts have the power to award any appropriate relief in a cognizable cause of action brought pursuant to a federal statute.

III

We now address whether Congress intended to limit application of this general principle in the enforcement of Title IX. Because the cause of action was inferred by the Court in *Cannon,* the usual recourse to statutory text and legislative history in the period prior to that decision necessarily will not enlighten our analysis. Since the Court in *Cannon* concluded that this statute supported no express right of action, it is hardly surprising that Congress also said nothing about the applicable remedies for an implied right of action.

During the period prior to the decision in *Cannon,* the inquiry in any event is not "'basically a matter of statutory construction,'" as the United States asserts. Rather, in determining Congress's intent to limit application of the traditional presumption in favor of all appropriate relief, we evaluate the state of the law when the legislature passed Title IX. In the years before and after Congress enacted this statute, the Court "follow[ed] a common-law tradition [and] regarded the denial of a remedy as the exception rather than the rule."

In the years after the announcement of *Cannon,* on the other hand, a more traditional method of statutory analysis is possible, because Congress was legislating with full cognizance of that decision. Our reading of the two amendments to Title IX enacted after *Cannon* leads us to conclude that Congress did not intend to limit the remedies available in a suit brought under Title IX. In the Civil Rights Remedies Equalization Amendment of 1986, 42 U.S.C. § 2000d-7, Congress abrogated the States' Eleventh Amendment immunity under Title IX, Title VI, § 504 of the Rehabilitation Act of 1973, and the Age Discrimination Act of 1975. This statute cannot be read except as a validation of *Cannon*'s holding. A subsection of the 1986 law provides that in a suit against a State, "remedies (including remedies both at law and in equity) are available for such a violation to the same extent as such remedies are available for such a violation in the suit against any public or private entity other than a State." 42 U.S.C. § 2000d-7(a)(2).

In addition to the Civil Rights Remedies Equalization Amendment of 1986, Congress also enacted the Civil Rights Restoration Act of 1987. Without in any way altering the existing rights of action and the corresponding remedies permissible under Title IX, Title VI, § 504 of the Rehabilitation Act, and the Age Discrimination Act, Congress broadened the coverage of these antidiscrimination provisions in this legislation. In seeking to correct what it considered to be an unacceptable decision on our part in *Grove City College v. Bell,* Congress made no effort to restrict the right of action recognized in *Cannon* and ratified in the 1986 Act or to alter the traditional presumption in favor of any appropriate relief for violation of a federal right. We cannot say, therefore, that Congress has limited the remedies available to a complainant in a suit brought under Title IX.

IV

Respondents and the United States nevertheless suggest three reasons why we should not apply the traditional presumption in favor of appropriate relief in this case.

First, respondents argue that an award of damages violates separation of powers principles because it unduly expands the federal courts' power into a sphere properly reserved to the Executive and Legislative Branches. In making this argument, respondents misconceive the difference between a cause of action and a remedy. Unlike the finding of a cause of action, which authorizes a court to hear a case or controversy, the discretion to award appropriate relief involves no such increase in judicial power. Federal courts cannot reach out to award remedies when the Constitution or laws of the United States do not support a cause of action. Indeed, properly understood, respondents' position invites us to abdicate our historic judicial authority to award appropriate relief in cases brought in our court system.

Next, consistent with the Court of Appeals' reasoning, respondents and the United States contend that the normal presumption in favor of all appropriate remedies should not apply because Title IX was enacted pursuant to Congress's Spending Clause power. In *Pennhurst* the Court observed that remedies were limited under such Spending Clause statutes when the alleged violation was unintentional. Respondents and the United States maintain that this presumption should apply equally to intentional violations. We disagree. The point of not permitting monetary damages for an unintentional violation is that the receiving entity of federal funds lacks notice that it will be liable for a monetary award. This notice problem does not arise in a case such as this, in which intentional discrimination is alleged. Unquestionably, Title IX placed on the Gwinnett County Schools the duty not to discriminate on the basis of sex, and "when a supervisor sexually harasses a subordinate because of the subordinate's sex, that supervisor 'discriminate[s]' on the basis of sex." *Meritor Savings Bank*. We believe the same rule should apply when a teacher sexually harasses and abuses a student. Congress surely did not intend for federal monies to be expended to support the intentional actions it sought by statute to proscribe. Moreover, the notion that Spending Clause statutes do not authorize monetary awards for intentional violations is belied by our unanimous holding in *Darrone*. Respondents and the United States characterize the backpay remedy in *Darrone* as equitable relief, but this description is irrelevant to their underlying objection: that application of the traditional rule in this case will require state entities to pay monetary awards out of their treasuries for intentional violations of federal statutes.

C

Finally, the United States asserts that the remedies permissible under Title IX should nevertheless be limited to backpay and prospective relief. In addition to diverging from our traditional approach to deciding what remedies are available for violation of a federal right, this position conflicts with sound logic. First, both remedies are equitable in nature, and it is axiomatic that a court should determine the adequacy of a remedy in law before resorting to equitable relief. Under the ordinary convention, the proper inquiry would be whether monetary damages provided an adequate remedy, and if not, whether equitable relief would be appropriate. Moreover, in this case the equitable remedies suggested by respondent and the Federal Government are clearly inadequate. Backpay does nothing for petitioner, because she was a student when the alleged discrimination occurred. Similarly, because Hill—the person she claims subjected her to sexual harassment—no longer teaches at the school and she herself no longer attends a school in the Gwinnett system, prospective relief accords her no remedy at all. The government's answer that administrative action helps other similarly-situated students in effect acknowledges that its approach would leave [plaintiff] remediless.

V

In sum, we conclude that a damages remedy is available for an action brought to enforce Title IX. The judgment of the Court of Appeals, therefore, is reversed and the case is remanded for further proceedings consistent with this opinion.

[Justice SCALIA, with whom THE CHIEF JUSTICE and Justice THOMAS join, concurred in the judgment.]

NOTES AND QUESTIONS

1. Does the Court adequately address the Spending Clause argument in part IV-B of its opinion? Will the result in *Franklin* cause schools to forego federal funds rather than subject themselves to damage actions in which the awards might exceed the amount of the federal funds?

     In *Sossamon v. Texas*, 563 U.S. 277 (2011), *supra* Ch. I, the Court found that the "appropriate relief against the government" language in RLUPA was not an unequivocal expression of state consent to be subjected to a damage action. The Court distinguished *Franklin* as a case involving an implied cause of action against municipal entities where the question is whether Congress has given clear direction to exclude a damages remedy. In contrast, the question regarding abrogation of the Eleventh Amendment is whether Congress has given clear direction that it intends to include a damages remedy. Does this distinction make sense?

2. Are compensatory damages now available in actions brought under Title VI or § 504? Where liability is based on discriminatory impact, does *Franklin* authorize an award of compensatory damages?

3. Does *Franklin* authorize an award of punitive damages?

     In *Barnes v. Gorman*, 536 U.S. 181 (2002), the Court held that punitive damages may not be awarded in private suits against public entities under Title II of the ADA and § 504 of the Rehabilitation Act. Noting the importance of the recipient of federal financial assistance being on notice of the remedies it will be subjected to if it accepts the federal funding, the Court recognized that the recipient is generally on notice of not only the remedies explicitly provided in the legislation, but also those remedies traditionally available in suits for breach of contract, where punitive damages, unlike compensatory damages and equitable relief, are generally not available. Further, the Court indicated that punitive damages cannot be implied because it is doubtful that funding recipients "would even have accepted the funding if punitive damages liability was a required condition."

Justice Scalia concurred in the judgment in *Franklin*, but only because of the post-*Cannon* legislation referred to in part III of the opinion. He points out that where a statutory cause of action is implied, as here, there will never be an express indication from Congress that remedies should be limited.

4. Could Ms. Franklin have pursued a § 1983 claim against the school for damages? What would she have to prove to hold the school liable? What if she had been attending a private school?

d.　Attorneys Fees

NORTH CAROLINA DEP'T OF TRANSPORTATION V. CREST STREET
479 U.S. 6 (1986)

Justice O'CONNOR delivered the opinion of the Court.

This case presents the question whether a court may award attorney's fees under the Civil Rights Attorney's Fees Awards Act of 1976, 42 U.S.C. § 1988, in a separate federal action not to enforce any of the civil rights laws listed in § 1988, but solely to recover attorney's fees.

I

In 1957, the Durham City Council advised the North Carolina State Highway Commission of the need for a major east-west expressway in the city. Over the years parts of this highway were completed. In 1976, petitioner North Carolina Department of Transportation (NCDOT) resumed planning an extension of the east-west highway. The proposed extension was to run through the Crest Street community, an established, predominantly black neighborhood in Durham. The extension would have displaced the community park and church and many of the residents of the neighborhood. Respondents, Residents of Crest Street Community and the Save Our Church and Community Committee, two unincorporated associations, retained the North Central Legal Assistance Program to represent them in regard to the proposed highway extension.

The costs of the proposed extension were to be covered in large part by federal funds. Pursuant to Title VI, the Department of Transportation (DOT) promulgated regulations requiring recipients of federal funds to provide assurances of compliance, periodic compliance reports, and access to information relevant to compliance.

In September 1978, respondents filed a complaint with DOT. Respondents challenged petitioner's proposed extension as violative of Title VI, and requested that NCDOT be prohibited from planning or constructing the proposed highway through the Crest Street community. DOT conducted an investigation, met with representatives of the petitioners and of the respondents, and obtained documents from petitioners and respondents. In February 1980 the DOT Director of Civil Rights informed NCDOT that based on DOT's "preliminary judgments," there was "reasonable cause to believe that the construction of the Expressway along the alignment proposed in the Draft [Environmental Impact Statement] would constitute a *prima facie* violation of Title VI and, in particular, § 21.5(b)(3) of our Departmental Title VI regulation." DOT urged petitioners to attempt to negotiate a resolution to the controversy. After negotiations spanning 15 months, in February 1982, petitioners, respondents and the city of Durham reached a preliminary agreement on the highway design and mitigation of the adverse impact of the project, but continued to negotiate toward a final plan.

Since 1973, construction of the highway extension had been enjoined by an order entered in the unrelated proceedings in *ECOS, Inc. v. Brinegar.* The plaintiffs in ECOS were a nonprofit educational ecological organization, an association of Duke University students and some of its members, and two Durham residents. The action alleged violations of the Federal-Aid Highway Act, the Department of Transportation Act of 1966, and the National Environmental Policy Act of 1969. The order enjoined construction until the defendants, state and federal transportation officials and a construction company, achieved full compliance with the above statutes. In August 1982 NCDOT moved to dissolve the ECOS injunction. Respondent Crest Street Community Council, Inc., and an individual Crest Street resident moved to intervene in the ECOS action and filed a proposed complaint asserting Title VI violations. While the motion to intervene was pending, petitioners and respondents continued negotiations, and reached agreement on a Final Mitigation Plan. On December 14, 1982, the District Court entered a consent judgment in the ECOS action. The consent judgment dissolved the injunction and dismissed the action. It also dismissed with prejudice respondents' Title VI claims on the condition that petitioners implement the Final Mitigation Plan, although the District Court had never ruled on the Crest Street Community Council, Inc., motion to intervene. The following day the Final Mitigation Plan was formally executed by petitioners, respondents, and the city of Durham.

The Plan set out comprehensive requirements for NCDOT and the city of Durham to mitigate the impact of the highway. Under the Plan NCDOT agreed to move the proposed highway right-of-way and modify an interchange so as to preserve the community church and park. The Plan also required NCDOT and the city of Durham to develop and provide a new park and community site in the same area. Respondents' counsel had spent more than 12,000 hours over the course of five years on this project, preparing the administrative complaint, assisting the DOT investigation, actively participating in negotiations to resolve the dispute, and informing DOT on the progress of those negotiations. The result of this diligent labor was both substantial and concrete.

Under the Plan, respondents stated that they did not waive any right to attorney's fees, and the city of Durham and NCDOT denied liability for attorney's fees. Respondents filed an action in District Court for attorney's fees under 42 U.S.C. § 1988.

II

In cases in which civil rights litigation was preceded by administrative proceedings, this Court has had occasion to consider whether the court in the civil rights action could award attorney's fees for time spent in the particular administrative processes. *Webb v. Dyer County Board of Education* (state tenure rights hearing is not a proceeding to enforce § 1983); *New York Gaslight Club, Inc. v. Carey* (mandatory state employment discrimination proceedings are proceedings to enforce Title VII). This case presents a question similar to those raised in *Webb and Carey*: whether negotiations subsequent to the filing of a Title VI administrative complaint are, under § 1988, "proceedings to enforce" Title VI. This case also presents a question that had not been posed by our prior § 1988 cases: whether attorney's fees under § 1988 can be sought in a court action other than litigation in which a party seeks to enforce the civil rights laws listed in § 1988. Because our resolution of the latter question resolves this case, we do not reach the former.

In pertinent part, the Civil Rights Attorney's Fees Awards Act of 1976, 42 U.S.C. § 1988, provides:

> In any action or proceeding to enforce a provision of . . . Title VI of the Civil Rights Act of 1964, the court, in its discretion, may allow the prevailing party, other than the United States, a reasonable attorney's fee as part of the costs.

The plain language of § 1988 suggests the answer to the question of whether attorney's fees may be awarded in an independent action which is not to enforce any of the civil rights laws listed in § 1988. The section states that *in the action or proceeding to enforce* the civil rights laws listed—42 U.S.C. §§ 1981, 1982, 1983, 1985, 1986, Title IX, or Title VI—*the court* may award attorney's fees. The case before us is not, and was never, an action to enforce any of these laws. On its face, § 1988 does not authorize a court to award attorney's fees except in an action to enforce the listed civil rights laws.

The legislative history of § 1988 supports the plain import of the statutory language. As we have noted before, the legislative history is replete with references to "the enforcement of the civil rights statutes 'in suits,' 'through the courts' and by 'judicial process.'"

Moreover, we now believe that the paradoxical nature of this result may have been exaggerated. There are many types of behavior that may lead others to comply with civil rights laws. For example, an employee, after talking to his lawyer, may choose to discuss hiring or promotion practices with an employer, and as a result of this discussion the employer may alter those practices to comply more fully with employment discrimination laws. In some sense it may be considered anomalous that this employee's initiative would not be awarded with attorney's fees. But an award of attorney's fees under § 1988 depends not only on the results obtained, but also on what actions were needed to achieve those results. It is entirely reasonable to limit the award of attorney's fees to those parties who, in order to obtain relief, found it necessary to file a complaint in court.

We have also suggested in past cases that today's holding would create an incentive to file protective lawsuits in order to obtain attorney's fees. Upon reflection, however, we think that the better view was expressed by our conclusion in *Webb*, that "competent counsel will be motivated by the interests of the client to pursue . . . administrative remedies when they are available and counsel believes that they may prove successful." An interpretation of § 1988 cannot be based on the assumption that "an attorney would advise the client to forgo an available avenue of relief solely because § 1988 does not provide for attorney's fees. . . ." Moreover, our holding creates a legitimate incentive for potential civil rights defendants to resolve disputes expeditiously, rather than risk the attorney's fees liability connected to civil rights litigation.

A court hearing one of the civil rights claims covered by § 1988 may still award attorney's fees for time spent on administrative proceedings to enforce the civil rights claim prior to the litigation. Moreover, even if the prior proceeding is not a "proceeding to enforce" one of the § 1988 civil rights laws, the "discrete portion of the work product from the administrative proceedings" that "was both useful and of a type ordinarily necessary to advance the civil rights litigation to the stage it reached before settlement" can be part of the attorney's fees awarded under § 1988. Under the plain language and legislative history of § 1988, however, only a court in an action to enforce one of the civil rights laws listed in § 1988 may award attorney's fees.

NOTES AND QUESTIONS

1. Didn't the Crest Street group initiate "proceedings" under Title VI by filing an administrative complaint with the Secretary as contemplated by the Regulations? Why then no fees?

2. Didn't the Crest Street group initiate "proceedings" to intervene in the ECOS suit? If leave had been granted, could fees have been awarded for time spent negotiating with the Department prior to the intervention ruling?

3. In light of *Crest*, how can plaintiff's counsel protect their right to recover fees?

   In his dissent, Justice Brennan advises counsel to preserve their right to fees by initially filing a federal civil action, pursuing the available administrative agency remedy, obtaining a stay from the federal district court, and then returning to court to file a fee petition after prevailing before the agency. Could Congress have intended this awkward procedure?

4. Although § 1988 does not mention the Rehabilitation Act, Congress in 1978 amended that Act to include a fee provision, 29 U.S.C. § 794a(b).

For each of the three funding statutes—Title VI, Title IX, and § 504—indicate:

a. whether it reaches neutral practices with a disparate impact, as well as intentional discrimination;

b. the relief available upon a showing of intentional discrimination; and

c. the relief available, if any, upon a showing of a disparate impact. Carefully review the questions following Sandoval.

3. DEFENSES

a. Eleventh Amendment and Official Immunity

As discussed previously in Ch. II, the Supreme Court ruled in *Atascadero State Hosp. v. Scanlon*, 473 U.S. 234 (1985), that the Eleventh Amendment foreclosed suit in federal court against the State of California for violation of the Rehabilitation Act. The impact of this case, however, was short-lived. Congress in 1986 amended the Rehabilitation Act to provide that the Eleventh Amendment does not immunize government defendants as to "all violations which occur in whole or in part after October 21, 1986." See 42 U.S.C. § 2000d-7. The Act makes specific reference to Title VI, Title IX, and § 504, and then refers generally to other federal funding measures that prohibit discrimination.

Does the decision in *Seminole Tribe of Florida v. Florida,* 517 U.S. 44 (1996), *supra* Ch. II, holding that the commerce clause does not grant Congress the power to abrogate Eleventh Amendment immunity, affect the 1986 amendment? Does *Kimel v. State of Florida Board of Regents, supra* Ch. I, cast doubt on the application of these laws to state government—especially the Rehabilitation Act since it protects a non-suspect class? *Compare Lapides v. Bd. of Regents of Univ. System,* 535 U.S. 613 (2002), holding that where a state removes state law claims, to which the state has explicitly waived immunity from state court proceedings, its act of removal constitutes a waiver of Eleventh Amendment immunity.

May officials who are not really the "recipients" of the financial assistance be sued in their individual capacity, *e.g.,* could the teacher in *Franklin* be subjected to damages under Title IX?

Although § 504 of the Rehabilitation Act prohibits discrimination "by any Executive agency," in *Lane v. Pena*, 518 U.S. 187 (1996), the Court held that Congress has not waived the federal government's sovereign immunity from awards of monetary damages for violations of this provision. May agencies nonetheless be sued for prospective injunctive relief for allegedly failing to enforce the Acts? *See Paralyzed Veterans.*

b. Statute of Limitations

None of the three federal funding statutes—Title VI, Title IX, and § 504—contains its own statute of limitations. Although § 1988 does not apply to these enactments (aside from the 1976 amendment which provides for attorney fees), some courts have borrowed the § 1988 analysis requiring an inquiry into the most analogous state law. Note, e.g., the reasoning in *Alexopulos v. San Francisco United School Dist.*, 817 F.2d 551, 554 (9th Cir. 1987):

> Mrs. Alexopulos brings her claim under § 504 of the Rehabilitation Act. She alleges the District denied Alexis a free public education. Section 504 was enacted as a general civil rights provision "to prevent discrimination against all handicapped individuals . . . in employment, housing, transportation, education, health services, or any other Federally-aided programs."
>
> Because § 504 contains no statute of limitations for filing an action, we borrow the statute of limitations governing an analogous California cause of action. California Code of Civil Procedure § 338(1) provides a three-year limitation period "upon a liability created by statute." This court has applied § 338(1) to an action for violations of civil rights under 42 U.S.C. § 1983. Analogous to 42 U.S.C. § 1983, § 504 is a civil rights statute that creates statutory liabilities and thus is also governed by the three year limitation period of § 338(1).

NOTES AND QUESTIONS

1. If the discrimination had arisen in the context of employment, could a contract limitation period (often up to 10 years) have been used? Should a court impose the 6-month statute of limitations provided in Title VI Regulations for administrative complaints? Compare *Burnett v. Grattan*, 468 U.S. 42 (1984), holding it inappropriate to apply a six-month statute of limitations used for administrative complaints in employment cases, because of the difference in goals reflected in the state administrative process and the § 1983 action.

2. Because *Wilson v. Garcia* and *Goodman v. Lukens Steel*, *supra* Ch. II, relied on § 1988 in applying state limitations periods, was the Ninth Circuit correct in using a § 1983 analogy? Should the courts generally adopt the forum state's personal injury limitations period in cases brought under the funding statutes? Several circuits have done so, but litigants should always check the law in the relevant circuit.

B. TITLE IX

Title IX protects applicants from gender bias by educational institutions that receive federal financial assistance, as well as the students and employees of such institutions. As noted previously, Title IX reaches employment discrimination even where the primary purpose of the financial assistance is not to provide employment. *North Haven Board of Education v. Bell*, 456 U.S. 512, 531-32 (1982). It reaches discrimination against males and females. Regulations promulgated under the Act, found at 45 C.F.R. § 86.40, cover all types of sex discrimination, including discrimination based on pregnancy or marital status. As under Title VII, the interpretive guidelines provide that pregnancy must be treated the same as any other temporary disability. On the other hand, although the Title IX regulations previously required insurance coverage and benefits for abortion, the Civil Rights Restoration Act, 20 U.S.C. § 1687, enacted in 1988, contains a neutrality provision protecting any entity which refuses to provide or pay for any abortion services. However, the Act still states that penalties cannot be imposed on an individual who has received a legal abortion.

Note also that 20 U.S.C. § 1681 exempts from coverage certain religious educational institutions, military training schools, the admissions programs of traditionally sex-segregated schools, social fraternities and sororities, Boy or Girl Conferences sponsored by the American Legion, and beauty contest scholarship recipients. Could a school district operate sex-segregated high schools without violating Title IX?

1. SEXUAL HARASSMENT IN SCHOOLS

GEBSER V. LAGO VISTA INDEPENDENT SCHOOL DISTRICT
524 U.S. 274 (1998)

JUSTICE O'CONNOR delivered the opinion of the Court.

The question in this case is when a school district may be held liable in damages in an implied right of action under Title IX of the Education Amendments of 1972, 20 U.S.C. § 1681 *et seq.* (Title IX), for the sexual harassment of a student by one of the district's teachers. We conclude that damages may not be recovered in those circumstances unless an official of the school district who at a minimum has authority to institute corrective measures on the district's behalf has actual notice of, and is deliberately indifferent to, the teacher's misconduct.

I

In the spring of 1991, when petitioner Alida Star Gebser was an eighth-grade student at a middle school in respondent Lago Vista Independent School District (Lago Vista), she joined a high school book discussion group led by Frank Waldrop, a teacher at Lago Vista's high school.

Lago Vista received federal funds at all pertinent times. During the book discussion sessions, Waldrop often made sexually suggestive comments to the students. Gebser entered high school in the fall and was assigned to classes taught by Waldrop in both semesters. Waldrop continued to make inappropriate remarks to the students, and he began to direct more of his suggestive comments toward Gebser, including during the substantial amount of time that the two were alone in his classroom. He initiated sexual contact with Gebser in the spring, when, while visiting her home ostensibly to give her a book, he kissed and fondled her. The two had sexual intercourse on a number of occasions during the remainder of the school year. Their relationship continued through the summer and into the following school year, and they often had intercourse during class time, although never on school property.

Gebser did not report the relationship to school officials, testifying that while she realized Waldrop's conduct was improper, she was uncertain how to react and she wanted to continue having him as a teacher. In October 1992, the parents of two other students complained to the high school principal about Waldrop's comments in class. The principal arranged a meeting, at which, according to the principal, Waldrop indicated that he did not believe he had made offensive remarks but apologized to the parents and said it would not happen again. The principal also advised Waldrop to be careful about his classroom comments and told the school guidance counselor about the meeting, but he did not report the parents' complaint to Lago Vista's superintendent, who was the district's Title IX coordinator. A couple of months later, in January 1993, a police officer discovered Waldrop and Gebser engaging in sexual intercourse and arrested Waldrop. Lago Vista terminated his employment, and subsequently, the Texas Education Agency revoked his teaching license. During this time, the district had not promulgated or distributed an official grievance procedure for lodging sexual harassment complaints; nor had it issued a formal anti-harassment policy.

Gebser and her mother filed suit against Lago Vista and Waldrop in state court in November 1993, raising claims against the school district under Title IX, 42 U.S.C. § 1983, and state negligence law, and claims against Waldrop primarily under state law. They sought compensatory and punitive damages from both defendants. After the case was removed, the United States District Court for the Western District of Texas granted summary judgment in favor of Lago Vista on all claims, and remanded the allegations against Waldrop to state court. In rejecting the Title IX claim against the school district, the court reasoned that the statute "was enacted to counter policies of discrimination . . . in federally funded education programs," and that "[o]nly if school administrators have some type of notice of the gender discrimination and fail to respond in good faith can the discrimination be interpreted as a policy of the school district." Here, the court determined, the parents' complaint to the principal concerning Waldrop's comments in class was the only one Lago Vista had received about Waldrop, and that evidence was inadequate to raise a genuine issue on whether the school district had actual or constructive notice that Waldrop was involved in a sexual relationship with a student. Petitioners appealed only on the Title IX claim. The Court of Appeals for the Fifth Circuit affirmed.

II

The Court held in *Cannon v. University of Chicago* that Title IX is enforceable through an implied private right of action, a conclusion we do not revisit here. We subsequently established in *Franklin v. Gwinnett County Public Schools* that monetary damages are available in the implied private action. In *Franklin*, a high school student alleged that a teacher had sexually abused her on repeated occasions and that teachers and school administrators knew about the harassment but took no action, even to the point of dissuading her from initiating charges. We concluded that Title IX supports a private action for damages, at least "in a case such as this, in which intentional discrimination is alleged." *Franklin* thereby establishes that a school district can be held liable in damages in cases involving a teacher's sexual harassment of a student; the decision, however, does not purport to define the contours of that liability.

We face that issue squarely in this case. Petitioners, joined by the United States as *amicus curiae*, would invoke standards used by the Courts of Appeals in Title VII cases involving a supervisor's sexual harassment of an employee in the workplace. In support of that approach, they point to a passage in *Franklin* in which we stated: "Unquestionably, Title IX placed on the Gwinnett County Public Schools the duty not to discriminate on the basis of sex, and 'when a supervisor sexually harasses a subordinate because of the subordinate's sex, that supervisor "discriminate[s]" on the basis of sex.' We believe the same rule should apply when a teacher sexually harasses and abuses a student." *Meritor Savings Bank* directs courts to look to common-law agency principles when assessing an employer's liability under Title VII for sexual harassment of an employee by a supervisor. Petitioners and the United States submit that, in light of *Franklin's* comparison of teacher-student harassment with supervisor-employee harassment, agency principles should likewise apply in Title IX actions.

Specifically, they advance two possible standards under which Lago Vista would be liable for Waldrop's conduct. First, relying on a 1997 "Policy Guidance" issued by the Department of Education, they would hold a school district liable in damages under Title IX where a teacher is "'aided in carrying out the sexual harassment of students by his or her position of authority with the institution,'" irrespective of whether school district officials had any knowledge of the harassment and irrespective of their response upon becoming aware. That rule is an expression of respondeat superior liability, *i.e.,* vicarious or imputed liability, under which recovery in damages against a school district would generally follow whenever a teacher's authority over a student facilitates the harassment. Second, petitioners and the United States submit that a school district should at a minimum be liable for damages based on a theory of constructive notice, *i.e.,* where the district knew or "should have known" about harassment but failed to uncover and eliminate it. Both standards would allow a damages recovery in a broader range of situations than the rule adopted by the Court of Appeals, which hinges on actual knowledge by a school official with authority to end the harassment.

Whether educational institutions can be said to violate Title IX based solely on principles of *respondeat superior* or constructive notice was not resolved by *Franklin's* citation of *Meritor*. *Meritor's* rationale for concluding that agency principles guide the liability inquiry under Title

VII rests on an aspect of that statute not found in Title IX: Title VII, in which the prohibition against employment discrimination runs against "an employer," explicitly defines "employer" to include "any agent." Title IX contains no comparable reference to an educational institution's "agents," and so does not expressly call for application of agency principles.

In this case, moreover, petitioners seek not just to establish a Title IX violation but to recover damages based on theories of respondeat superior and constructive notice. It is that aspect of their action, in our view, which is most critical to resolving the case. Unlike Title IX, Title VII contains an express cause of action, and specifically provides for relief in the form of monetary damages. Congress therefore has directly addressed the subject of damages relief under Title VII and has set out the particular situations in which damages are available as well as the maximum amounts recoverable. With respect to Title IX, however, the private right of action is judicially implied, and there is thus no legislative expression of the scope of available remedies, including when it is appropriate to award monetary damages. In addition, although the general presumption that courts can award any appropriate relief in an established cause of action, coupled with Congress' abrogation of the States' Eleventh Amendment immunity under Title IX, led us to conclude in *Franklin* that Title IX recognizes a damages remedy, we did so in response to lower court decisions holding that Title IX does not support damages relief at all. We made no effort in *Franklin* to delimit the circumstances in which a damages remedy should lie.

III

Because the private right of action under Title IX is judicially implied, we have a measure of latitude to shape a sensible remedial scheme that best comports with the statute. That endeavor inherently entails a degree of speculation, since it addresses an issue on which Congress has not specifically spoken. To guide the analysis, we generally examine the relevant statute to ensure that we do not fashion the parameters of an implied right in a manner at odds with the statutory structure and purpose. Those considerations, we think, are pertinent not only to the scope of the implied right, but also to the scope of the available remedies. We suggested as much in *Franklin*, where we recognized "the general rule that all appropriate relief is available in an action brought to vindicate a federal right," but indicated that the rule must be reconciled with congressional purpose. The "general rule," that is, "yields where necessary to carry out the intent of Congress or to avoid frustrating the purposes of the statute involved."

Applying those principles here, we conclude that it would "frustrate the purposes" of Title IX to permit a damages recovery against a school district for a teacher's sexual harassment of a student based on principles of *respondeat superior* or constructive notice, *i.e.,* without actual notice to a school district official. Because Congress did not expressly create a private right of action under Title IX, the statutory text does not shed light on Congress' intent with respect to the scope of available remedies. Instead, "we attempt to infer how the [1972] Congress would have addressed the issue had the . . . action been included as an express provision in the" statute.

As a general matter, it does not appear that Congress contemplated unlimited recovery in damages against a funding recipient where the recipient is unaware of discrimination in its programs. When Title IX was enacted in 1972, the principal civil rights statutes containing an express right of action did not provide for recovery of monetary damages at all, instead allowing only injunctive and equitable relief. It was not until 1991 that Congress made damages available under Title VII, and even then, Congress carefully limited the amount recoverable in any individual case, calibrating the maximum recovery to the size of the employer. Adopting petitioners' position would amount, then, to allowing unlimited recovery of damages under Title IX where Congress has not spoken on the subject of either the right or the remedy, and in the face of evidence that when Congress expressly considered both in Title VII it restricted the amount of damages available. Congress enacted Title IX in 1972 with two principal objectives in mind: "to avoid the use of federal resources to support discriminatory practices" and "to provide individual citizens effective protection against those practices." The statute was modeled after Title VI of the Civil Rights Act of 1964, which is parallel to Title IX except that it prohibits race discrimination, not sex discrimination, and applies in all programs receiving federal funds, not only in education programs. The two statutes operate in the same manner, conditioning an offer of federal funding on a promise by the recipient not to discriminate, in what amounts essentially to a contract between the Government and the recipient of funds. That contractual framework distinguishes Title IX from Title VII, which is framed in terms not of a condition but of an outright prohibition. Title VII applies to all employers without regard to federal funding and aims broadly to "eradicat[e] discrimination throughout the economy." Title VII, moreover, seeks to "make persons whole for injuries suffered through past discrimination." Thus, whereas Title VII aims centrally to compensate victims of discrimination, Title IX focuses more on "protecting" individuals from discriminatory practices carried out by recipients of federal funds. That might explain why, when the Court first recognized the implied right under Title IX in *Cannon*, the opinion referred to injunctive or equitable relief in a private action, but not to a damages remedy.

Title IX's contractual nature has implications for our construction of the scope of available remedies. When Congress attaches conditions to the award of federal funds under its spending power, as it has in Title IX and Title VI, we examine closely the propriety of private actions holding the recipient liable in monetary damages for noncompliance with the condition. Our central concern in that regard is with ensuring "that the receiving entity of federal funds [has] notice that it will be liable for a monetary award." Justice White's opinion announcing the Court's judgment in *Guardians Ass'n*, for instance, concluded that the relief in an action under Title VI alleging unintentional discrimination should be prospective only, because where discrimination is unintentional, "it is surely not obvious that the grantee was aware that it was administering the program in violation of the [condition]." We confront similar concerns here. If a school district's liability for a teacher's sexual harassment rests on principles of constructive notice or *respondeat superior*, it will likewise be the case that the recipient of funds was unaware of the discrimination. It is sensible to assume that Congress did not envision a recipient's liability in damages in that situation.

Most significantly, Title IX contains important clues that Congress did not intend to allow recovery in damages where liability rests solely on principles of vicarious liability or constructive notice. Title IX's express means of enforcement—by administrative agencies—operates on an assumption of actual notice to officials of the funding recipient. The statute entitles agencies who disburse education funding to enforce their rules implementing the non-discrimination mandate through proceedings to suspend or terminate funding or through "other means authorized by law." Significantly, however, an agency may not initiate enforcement proceedings until it "has advised the appropriate person or persons of the failure to comply with the requirement and has determined that compliance cannot be secured by voluntary means."

In the event of a violation, a funding recipient may be required to take "such remedial action as [is] deem[ed] necessary to overcome the effects of [the] discrimination." While agencies have conditioned continued funding on providing equitable relief to the victim, the regulations do not appear to contemplate a condition ordering payment of monetary damages, and there is no indication that payment of damages has been demanded as a condition of finding a recipient to be in compliance with the statute. In *Franklin*, for instance, the Department of Education found a violation of Title IX but determined that the school district came into compliance by virtue of the offending teacher's resignation and the district's institution of a grievance procedure for sexual harassment complaints.

Presumably, a central purpose of requiring notice of the violation "to the appropriate person" and an opportunity for voluntary compliance before administrative enforcement proceedings can commence is to avoid diverting education funding from beneficial uses where a recipient was unaware of discrimination in its programs and is willing to institute prompt corrective measures. The scope of private damages relief proposed by petitioners is at odds with that basic objective. When a teacher's sexual harassment is imputed to a school district or when a school district is deemed to have "constructively" known of the teacher's harassment, by assumption the district had no actual knowledge of the teacher's conduct. Nor, of course, did the district have an opportunity to take action to end the harassment or to limit further harassment.

It would be unsound, we think, for a statute's express system of enforcement to require notice to the recipient and an opportunity to come into voluntary compliance while a judicially implied system of enforcement permits substantial liability without regard to the recipient's knowledge or its corrective actions upon receiving notice. Moreover, an award of damages in a particular case might well exceed a recipient's level of federal funding. Where a statute's express enforcement scheme hinges its most severe sanction on notice and unsuccessful efforts to obtain compliance, we cannot attribute to Congress the intention to have implied an enforcement scheme that allows imposition of greater liability without comparable conditions.

IV

Because the express remedial scheme under Title IX is predicated upon notice to an "appropriate person" and an opportunity to rectify any violation, we conclude, in the absence of further direction from Congress, that the implied damages remedy should be fashioned along the same lines. An "appropriate person" under § 1682 is, at a minimum, an official of the recipient entity with authority to take corrective action to end the discrimination. Consequently, in cases like this one that do not involve official policy of the recipient entity, we hold that a damages remedy will not lie under Title IX unless an official who at a minimum has authority to address the alleged discrimination and to institute corrective measures on the recipient's behalf has actual knowledge of discrimination in the recipient's programs and fails adequately to respond.

We think, moreover, that the response must amount to deliberate indifference to discrimination. The administrative enforcement scheme presupposes that an official who is advised of a Title IX violation refuses to take action to bring the recipient into compliance. The premise, in other words, is an official decision by the recipient not to remedy the violation. That framework finds a rough parallel in the standard of deliberate indifference. Under a lower standard, there would be a risk that the recipient would be liable in damages not for its own official decision but instead for its employees' independent actions. Comparable considerations led to our adoption of a deliberate indifference standard for claims under § 1983 alleging that a municipality's actions in failing to prevent a deprivation of federal rights was the cause of the violation.

Applying the framework to this case is fairly straightforward, as petitioners do not contend they can prevail under an actual notice standard. The only official alleged to have had information about Waldrop's misconduct is the high school principal. That information, however, consisted of a complaint from parents of other students charging only that Waldrop had made inappropriate comments during class, which was plainly insufficient to alert the principal to the possibility that Waldrop was involved in a sexual relationship with a student. Lago Vista, moreover, terminated Waldrop's employment upon learning of his relationship with Gebser. JUSTICE STEVENS points out in his dissenting opinion that Waldrop of course had knowledge of his own actions. Where a school district's liability rests on actual notice principles, however, the knowledge of the wrongdoer himself is not pertinent to the analysis.

Petitioners focus primarily on Lago Vista's asserted failure to promulgate and publicize an effective policy and grievance procedure for sexual harassment claims. They point to Department of Education regulations requiring each funding recipient to "adopt and publish grievance procedures providing for prompt and equitable resolution" of discrimination complaints, and to notify students and others "that it does not discriminate on the basis of sex in the educational programs or activities which it operates." Lago Vista's alleged failure to comply with the regulations, however, does not establish the requisite actual notice and deliberate indifference. And in any event, the failure to promulgate a grievance procedure does not itself constitute "discrimination" under Title IX. Of course, the Department of Education could enforce the requirement administratively: Agencies generally have authority to promulgate and enforce requirements that effectuate the statute's non-discrimination mandate, even if those requirements do not purport to represent a definition of discrimination under the statute. We have never held, however, that the implied private right of action under Title IX allows recovery in damages for violation of those sorts of administrative requirements.

V

The number of reported cases involving sexual harassment of students in schools confirms that harassment unfortunately is an all too common aspect of the educational experience. No one questions that a student suffers extraordinary harm when subjected to sexual harassment and abuse by a teacher, and that the teacher's conduct is reprehensible and undermines the basic purposes of the educational system. The issue in this case, however, is whether the independent misconduct of a teacher is attributable to the school district that employs him under a specific federal statute designed primarily to prevent recipients of federal financial assistance from using the funds in a discriminatory manner. Our decision does not affect any right of recovery that an individual may have against a school district as a matter of state law or against the teacher in his individual capacity under state law or under 42 U.S.C. § 1983. Until Congress speaks directly on the subject, however, we will not hold a school district liable in damages under Title IX for a teacher's sexual harassment of a student absent actual notice and deliberate indifference. We therefore affirm the judgment of the Court of Appeals.

Justice STEVENS, with Whom Justice SOUTER, Justice GINSBURG, and Justice BREYER join, dissenting.

As a basis for its decision, the majority relies heavily on the notion that because the private cause of action under Title IX is "judicially implied," the Court has "a measure of latitude" to use its own judgment in shaping a remedial scheme. This assertion of lawmaking authority is not faithful either to our precedents or to our duty to interpret, rather than to revise, congressional commands. Moreover, the majority's policy judgment about the appropriate remedy in this case thwarts the purposes of Title IX.

I

It is important to emphasize that in *Cannon v. University of Chicago*, the Court confronted a question of statutory construction. The decision represented our considered judgment about the intent of the Congress that enacted Title IX in 1972. After noting that Title IX had been patterned after Title VI of the Civil Rights Act of 1964, which had been interpreted to include a private right of action, we concluded that Congress intended to authorize the same private enforcement of Title IX.

In *Franklin v. Gwinnett County Public Schools*, we unanimously concluded that Title IX authorized a high school student who had been sexually harassed by a sports coach/teacher to recover damages from the school district. That conclusion was supported by two considerations. In his opinion for the Court, Justice White first relied on the presumption that Congress intends to authorize "all appropriate remedies" unless it expressly indicates otherwise. He then noted that two amendments to Title IX enacted after the decision in *Cannon* had validated *Cannon's* holding and supported the conclusion that "Congress did not intend to limit the remedies available in a suit brought under Title IX."

Because these constructions of the statute have been accepted by Congress and are unchallenged here, they have the same legal effect as if the private cause of action seeking damages had been explicitly, rather than implicitly, authorized by Congress. We should therefore seek guidance from the text of the statute and settled legal principles rather than from our views about sound policy.

II

Although the opinion the Court announces today is not entirely clear, it does not purport to overrule *Franklin*. Moreover, I do not understand the Court to question the conclusion that an intentional violation of Title IX, of the type we recognized in *Franklin*, has been alleged in this case. During her freshman and sophomore years of high school, petitioner Alida Star Gebser was repeatedly subjected to sexual abuse by her teacher, Frank Waldrop, whom she had met in the eighth grade when she joined his high school book discussion group. Waldrop's conduct was surely intentional and it occurred during, and as a part of, a curriculum activity in which he wielded authority over Gebser that had been delegated to him by respondent. Moreover, it is undisputed that the activity was subsidized, in part, with federal moneys.

The Court nevertheless holds that the law does not provide a damages remedy for the Title IX violation alleged in this case because no official of the school district with "authority to institute corrective measures on the district's behalf" had actual notice of Waldrop's misconduct. That holding is at odds with settled principles of agency law, under which the district is responsible for Waldrop's misconduct because "he was aided in accomplishing the tort by the existence of the agency relation."

The reason why the common law imposes liability on the principal in such circumstances is the same as the reason why Congress included the prohibition against discrimination on the basis of sex in Title IX: to induce school boards to adopt and enforce practices that will minimize the danger that vulnerable students will be exposed to such odious behavior. The rule that the Court has crafted creates the opposite incentive. As long as school boards can insulate themselves from knowledge about this sort of conduct, they can claim immunity from damages liability. Indeed, the rule that the Court adopts would preclude a damages remedy even if every teacher at the school knew about the harassment but did not have "authority to institute corrective measures on the district's behalf." It is not my function to determine whether this newly fashioned rule is wiser than the established common-law rule. It is proper, however, to suggest that the Court bears the burden of justifying its rather dramatic departure from settled law, and to explain why its opinion fails to shoulder that burden.

III

The Court advances several reasons why it would "frustrate the purposes" of Title IX to allow recovery against a school district that does not have actual notice of a teacher's sexual harassment of a student. First, the Court observes that at the time Title IX was enacted, "the principal civil rights statutes containing an express right of action did not provide for recovery of monetary damages at all." *Franklin*, however, forecloses this reevaluation of legislative intent; in that case, we "evaluate[d] the state of the law when the Legislature passed Title IX," and concluded that "the same contextual approach used to justify an implied right of action more than amply demonstrates the lack of any legislative intent to abandon the traditional presumption in favor of all available remedies."

Second, the Court suggests that the school district did not have fair notice when it accepted federal funding that it might be held liable "'for a monetary award'" under Title IX. The Court cannot mean, however, that respondent was not on notice that sexual harassment of a student by a teacher constitutes an "intentional" violation of Title IX for which damages are available, because we so held shortly before Waldrop began abusing Gebser. Given the fact that our holding in *Franklin* was unanimous, it is not unreasonable to assume that it could have been foreseen by counsel for the recipients of Title IX funds. Moreover, the nondiscrimination requirement set out in Title IX is clear, and this Court held that sexual harassment constitutes intentional sex discrimination long before the sexual abuse in this case began. Normally, of course, we presume that the citizen has knowledge of the law.

The majority's inappropriate reliance on Title IX's administrative enforcement scheme to limit the availability of a damages remedy leads the Court to require not only actual knowledge on the part of "an official who at a minimum has authority to address the alleged discrimination and to institute corrective measures on the recipient's behalf," but also that official's "refus[al] to take action," or "deliberate indifference" toward the harassment. Presumably, few Title IX plaintiffs who have been victims of intentional discrimination will be able to recover damages under this exceedingly high standard. The Court fails to recognize that its holding will virtually "render inutile causes of action authorized by Congress through a decision that no remedy is available."

IV

We are not presented with any question concerning the affirmative defenses that might eliminate or mitigate the recovery of damages for a Title IX violation. It has been argued, for example, that a school district that has adopted and vigorously enforced a policy that is designed to prevent sexual harassment and redress the harms that such conduct may produce should be exonerated from damages liability. The Secretary of Education has promulgated regulations directing grant recipients to adopt such policies and disseminate them to students.

[Justice GINSBURG, with whom Justice SOUTER and Justice BREYER join, dissenting, explicitly support an affirmative defense where a school district can show "that its internal remedies were adequately publicized and likely would have provided redress without exposing the complainant to undue risk, effort, or expense. Under such a regime, to the extent that a plaintiff unreasonably failed to avail herself of the school district's preventive and remedial measures, and consequently suffered avoidable harm."]

NOTES AND QUESTIONS

1. What will a student have to show in order to hold a school district liable in damages for sexual harassment by a teacher?

2. Compare the standard adopted in this case to that in Title VII cases, namely in *Faragher and Ellerth, supra* Ch. III. Is the difference justified? Would the school district have been liable under the *Faragher* approach?

3. Is the decision in this case consistent with Franklin? Explain.

DAVIS V. MONROE COUNTY BOARD OF EDUCATION
526 U.S. 629 (1999)

Justice O'CONNOR delivered the opinion of the Court.

Petitioner brought suit against the Monroe County Board of Education and other defendants, alleging that her fifth-grade daughter had been the victim of sexual harassment by another student in her class. Among petitioner's claims was a claim for monetary and injunctive relief under Title IX of the Education Amendments of 1972 (Title IX), 20 U.S.C. §1681 *et seq.* The District Court dismissed petitioner's Title IX claims on the ground that "student-on-student," or peer, harassment provides no ground for a private cause of action under the statute. The Court of Appeals for the Eleventh Circuit, sitting en banc, affirmed. We consider here whether a private damages action may lie against the school board in cases of student-on-student harassment. We conclude that it may, but only where the funding recipient acts with deliberate indifference to known acts of harassment in its programs or activities. Moreover, we conclude that such an action will lie only for harassment that is so severe, pervasive, and objectively offensive that it effectively bars the victim's access to an educational opportunity or benefit.

I

A

Petitioner's minor daughter, LaShonda, was allegedly the victim of a prolonged pattern of sexual harassment by one of her fifth-grade classmates at Hubbard Elementary School, a public school in Monroe County, Georgia. According to petitioner's complaint, the harassment began in December 1992, when the classmate, G.F., attempted to touch LaShonda's breasts and genital area and made vulgar statements such as, "'I want to get in bed with you'" and "'I want to feel your boobs.'" Similar conduct allegedly occurred on or about January 4 and January 20, 1993. LaShonda reported each of these incidents to her mother and to her classroom teacher, Diane Fort. Petitioner, in turn, also contacted Fort, who allegedly assured petitioner that the school principal, Bill Querry, had been informed of the incidents. Petitioner contends that, notwithstanding these reports, no disciplinary action was taken against G.F.

G.F.'s conduct allegedly continued for many months. In early February, G.F. purportedly placed a door stop in his pants and proceeded to act in a sexually suggestive manner toward LaShonda during physical education class. LaShonda reported G.F.'s behavior to her physical education teacher, Whit Maples. Approximately one week later, G.F. again allegedly engaged in harassing behavior, this time while under the supervision of another classroom teacher, Joyce Pippin. Again, LaShonda allegedly reported the incident to the teacher, and again the petitioner contacted the teacher to follow up. In mid-April 1993, G.F. allegedly rubbed his body against LaShonda in the school hallway in what LaShonda considered a sexually suggestive manner, and LaShonda again reported the matter to Fort.

The string of incidents finally ended in mid-May, when G.F. was charged with, and pleaded guilty to, sexual battery for his misconduct. The complaint alleges that LaShonda had suffered during the months of harassment, however; specifically her previously high grades allegedly dropped as she became unable to concentrate on her studies, and, in April 1993, her father discovered that she had written a suicide note. The complaint further alleges that, at one point, LaShonda told petitioner that she "'didn't know how much longer she could keep [G.F.] off her.'"

Nor was LaShonda G.F.'s only victim; it is alleged that other girls in the class fell prey to G.F.'s conduct. At one point, in fact, a group composed of LaShonda and other female students tried to speak with Principal Querry about G.F.'s behavior. According to the complaint, however, a teacher denied the students' request with the statement, "'if [Querry] wants you, he'll call you.'"

Petitioner alleges that no disciplinary action was taken in response to G.F.'s behavior toward LaShonda. In addition to her conversations with Fort and Pippen, petitioner alleges that she spoke with Principal Querry in mid-May 1993. When petitioner inquired as to what action the school intended to take against G.F., Querry simply stated, "'I guess I'll have to threaten him a little bit harder.'" Yet, petitioner alleges, at no point during the many months of his reported misconduct was G.F. disciplined for harassment. Indeed, Querry allegedly asked petitioner why LaShonda "'was the only one complaining.'" Nor, according to the complaint, was any effort made to separate G.F. and LaShonda. On the contrary, notwithstanding LaShonda's frequent complaints, only after more than three months of reported harassment was she even permitted to change her classroom seat so that she was no longer seated next to G.F. Moreover, petitioner alleges that, at the time of the events in question, the Monroe County Board of Education (Board) had not instructed its personnel on how to respond to peer sexual harassment and had not established a policy on the issue.

B

On May 4, 1994, petitioner filed suit in the United States District Court for the Middle District of Georgia against the Board, Charles Dumas, the school district's superintendent, and Principal Querry. The complaint alleged that the Board is a recipient of federal funding for purposes of Title IX, that "[t]he persistent sexual advances and harassment by the student G.F. upon [LaShonda] interfered with her ability to attend school and perform her studies and activities," and that "[t]he deliberate indifference by Defendants to the unwelcome sexual advances of a student upon LaShonda created an intimidating, hostile, offensive and abus[ive] school environment in violation of Title IX." The complaint sought compensatory and punitive damages, attorney's fees, and injunctive relief.

II

[A]t issue here is the question whether a recipient of federal education funding may be liable for damages under Title IX under any circumstances for discrimination in the form of student-on-student sexual harassment.

A

Petitioner urges that Title IX's plain language compels the conclusion that the statute is intended to bar recipients of federal funding from permitting this form of discrimination in their programs or activities. She emphasizes that the statute prohibits a student from being "*subjected to discrimination* under any education program or activity receiving Federal financial assistance." 20 U.S.C. §1681 (emphasis supplied). It is Title IX's "unmistakable focus on the benefitted class," rather than the perpetrator, that, in petitioner's view, compels the conclusion that the statute works to protects students from the discriminatory misconduct of their peers.

Invoking *Pennhurst*, respondents urge that Title IX provides no notice that recipients of federal educational funds could be liable in damages for harm arising from student-on-student harassment. Respondents contend, specifically, that the statute only proscribes misconduct by grant recipients, not third parties. Respondents argue, moreover, that it would be contrary to the very purpose of Spending Clause legislation to impose liability on a funding recipient for the misconduct of third parties, over whom recipients exercise little control.

We agree with respondents that a recipient of federal funds may be liable in damages under Title IX only for its own misconduct. The recipient itself must "exclud[e] [persons] from participating in, . . . den[y] [persons] the benefits of, or . . . subjec[t] [persons] to discrimination under" its "program[s] or activit[ies]" in order to be liable under Title IX. The Government's enforcement power may only be exercised against the funding recipient and we have not extended damages liability under Title IX to parties outside the scope of this power.

We disagree with respondents' assertion, however, that petitioner seeks to hold the Board liable for G.F.'s actions instead of its own. Here, petitioner attempts to hold the Board liable for its own decision to remain idle in the face of known student-on-student harassment in its schools. In *Gebser*, we concluded that a recipient of federal education funds may be liable in damages under Title IX where it is deliberately indifferent to known acts of sexual harassment by a teacher. Contrary to the dissent's suggestion, the misconduct of the teacher in *Gebser* was not "treated as the grant recipient's actions." Liability arose, rather, from "an official decision by the recipient not to remedy the violation." By employing the "deliberate indifference" theory already used to establish municipal liability under 42 U.S.C. §1983, we concluded in *Gebser* that recipients could be liable in damages only where their own deliberate indifference effectively "cause[d]" the discrimination. The high standard imposed in *Gebser* sought to eliminate any "risk that the recipient would be liable in damages not for its own official decision but instead for its employees' independent actions."

We consider here whether the misconduct identified in *Gebser*—deliberate indifference to known acts of harassment—amounts to an intentional violation of Title IX, capable of supporting a private damages action, when the harasser is a student rather than a teacher. We conclude that, in certain limited circumstances, it does. As an initial matter, in *Gebser* we expressly rejected the use of agency principles in the Title IX context, noting the textual differences between Title IX and Title VII. Additionally, the regulatory scheme surrounding Title IX has long provided funding recipients with notice that they may be liable for their failure to respond to the discriminatory acts of certain non-agents. The Department of Education requires recipients to monitor third parties for discrimination in specified circumstances and to refrain from particular forms of interaction with outside entities that are known to discriminate.

The common law, too, has put schools on notice that they may be held responsible under state law for failure to protect students from the tortious acts of third parties. *See* RESTATEMENT (SECOND) OF TORTS §320, and Comment a (1965). In fact, state courts routinely uphold claims alleging that schools have been negligent in failing to protect their students from the torts of their peers.

This is not to say the identity of the harasser is irrelevant. On the contrary, both the "deliberate indifference" standard and the language of Title IX narrowly circumscribe the set of parties whose known acts of sexual harassment can trigger some duty to respond on the part of funding recipients. Deliberate indifference makes sense as a theory of direct liability under Title IX only where the funding recipient has some control over the alleged harassment. A recipient cannot be directly liable for its indifference where it lacks the authority to take remedial action.

The language of Title IX itself—particularly when viewed in conjunction with the requirement that the recipient have notice of Title IX's prohibitions to be liable for damages—also cabins the range of misconduct that the statute proscribes. The statute's plain language confines the scope of prohibited conduct based on the recipients degree of control over the harasser and the environment in which the harassment occurs. If a funding recipient does not engage in harassment directly, it may not be liable for damages unless its deliberate indifference "subject[s]" its students to harassment. That is, the deliberate indifference must, at minimum, "cause [students] to undergo" harassment or "make them liable or vulnerable" to it. Moreover, because the harassment must occur "under" "the operations of" a funding recipient, the harassment must take place in a context subject to the school district's control.

These factors combine to limit a recipient's damages liability to circumstances wherein the recipient exercises substantial control over both the harasser and the context in which the known harassment occurs. Where, as here, the misconduct occurs during school hours and on school grounds—the bulk of G.F.'s misconduct, in fact, took place in the classroom—the misconduct is taking place "under" an "operation" of the funding recipient. In these circumstances, the recipient retains substantial control over the context in which the harassment occurs. More importantly, however, in this setting the Board exercises significant control over the harasser. We have observed, for example, "that the nature of [the State's] power [over public schoolchildren] is custodial and tutelary, permitting a degree of supervision and control that could not be exercised over free adults." We thus conclude that recipients of federal funding may be liable for "subject[ing]" their students to discrimination where the recipient is deliberately indifferent to known acts of student-on-student sexual harassment and the harasser is under the school's disciplinary authority.

At the time of the events in question here, in fact, school attorneys and administrators were being told that student-on-student harassment could trigger liability under Title IX. In March 1993, even as the events alleged in petitioner's complaint were unfolding, the National School Boards Association issued a publication, for use by "school attorneys and administrators in understanding the law regarding sexual harassment of employees and students," which observed that districts could be liable under Tile IX for their failure to respond to student-on-student harassment. Drawing on the Equal Employment Opportunity Commission guidelines interpreting Title VII, the publication informed the districts that, "if [a] school district has constructive notice of severe and repeated acts of sexual harassment by students against students, that may form the basis of a [T]itle IX claim." The publication even correctly anticipated a form of Gebser's actual notice requirement: "It is unlikely that courts will hold a school district liable for sexual harassment by students against students in the absence of actual knowledge or notice to district employees." Although we do not rely on this publication as an "indicum of congressional notice," we do find support for our reading of Title IX in the fact that school attorneys have rendered an analogous interpretation.

We stress that our conclusion here—that recipients may be liable for their deliberate indifference to known acts of peer sexual harassment—does not mean that recipients can avoid liability only by purging their schools of actionable peer harassment or that administrators must engage in particular disciplinary action. We thus disagree with respondents' contention that, if Title IX provides a cause of action for student-on-student harassment, "nothing short of expulsion of every student accused of misconduct involving sexual overtones would protect school systems from liability or damages." Likewise, the dissent erroneously imagines that victims of peer harassment now have a Title IX right to make particular remedial demands. In fact, as we have previously noted, courts should refrain from second guessing the disciplinary decisions made by school administrators.

School administrators will continue to enjoy the flexibility they require so long as funding recipients are deemed "deliberately indifferent" to acts of student-on-student harassment only where the recipient's response to the harassment or lack thereof is clearly unreasonable in light of the known circumstances. This is not a mere "reasonableness" standard, as the dissent assumes. In an appropriate case, there is no reason why courts, on a motion to dismiss, for summary judgment, or for a directed verdict, could not identify a response as not "clearly unreasonable" as a matter of law.

We believe that the standard set out here is sufficiently flexible to account both for the level of disciplinary authority available to the school and for the potential liability arising from certain forms of disciplinary action. A university might not, for example, be expected to exercise the same degree of control over its students that a grade school would enjoy, and it would be entirely reasonable for a school to refrain from a form of disciplinary action that would expose it to constitutional or statutory claims.

While it remains to be seen whether petitioner can show that the Board's response to reports of G.F.'s misconduct was clearly unreasonable in light of the known circumstances, petitioner may be able to show that the Board "subject[ed]" LaShonda to discrimination by failing to respond in any way over a period of five months to complaints of G.F.'s in-school misconduct from LaShonda and other female students.

B

Having previously determined that "sexual harassment" is "discrimination" in the school context under Title IX, we are constrained to conclude that student-on-student sexual harassment, if sufficiently severe, can likewise rise to the level of discrimination actionable under the statute. The statute's other prohibitions, moreover, help give content to the term "discrimination" in this context. Students are not only protected from discrimination, but also specifically shielded from being "excluded from participation in" or "denied the benefits of" any "education program or activity receiving Federal financial assistance." The statute makes clear that, whatever else it prohibits, students must not be denied access to educational benefits and opportunities on the basis of gender. We thus conclude that funding recipients are properly held liable in damages only where they are deliberately indifferent to sexual harassment, of which they have actual knowledge, that is so severe, pervasive, and objectively offensive that it can be said to deprive the victims of access to the educational opportunities or benefits provided by the school.

Whether gender-oriented conduct rises to the level of actionable "harassment" thus "depends on a constellation of surrounding circumstances, expectations, and relationships," including, but not limited to, the ages of the harasser and the victim and the number of individuals involved. Courts, moreover, must bear in mind that schools are unlike the adult workplace and that children may regularly interact in a manner that would be unacceptable among adults. Indeed, at least early on, students are still learning how to interact appropriately with their peers. It is thus understandable that, in the school setting, student often engage in insults, banter, teasing, shoving, pushing, and gender-specific conduct that is upsetting to the student subjected to it.

Damages are not available for simple acts of teasing and name-calling among school children, however, even where these comments target differences in gender. Rather, in the context of student-on-student harassment, damages are available only where the behavior is so severe, pervasive, and objectively offensive that it denies its victims the equal access to education that Title IX is designed to protect.

Moreover, the provision that the discrimination occur "under any education program or activity" suggests that the behavior be serious enough to have the systemic effect of denying the victim equal access to an educational program or activity. Although, in theory, a single instance of sufficiently severe one-on-one peer harassment could be said to have such an effect, we think it unlikely that Congress would have thought such behavior sufficient to rise to this level in light of the inevitability of student misconduct and the amount of litigation that would be invited by entertaining claims of official indifference to a single instance of one-on-one peer harassment. By limiting private damages actions to cases having a systemic effect on educational programs or activities, we reconcile the general principle that Title IX prohibits official indifference to known peer sexual harassment with the practical realities of responding to student behavior, realities that Congress could not have meant to be ignored. Even the dissent suggests that Title IX liability may arise when a funding recipient remains indifferent to severe, gender-based mistreatment played out on a "widespread level" among students.

The fact that it was a teacher who engaged in harassment in *Franklin* and *Gebser* is relevant. The relationship between the harasser and the victim necessarily affects the extent to which the misconduct can be said to breach Title IX's guarantee of equal access to educational benefits and to have a systemic effect on a program or activity. Peer harassment, in particular, is less likely to satisfy these requirements than is teacher-student harassment.

C

Applying this standard to the facts at issue here, we conclude that the Eleventh Circuit erred in dismissing petitioner's complaint.

NOTES AND QUESTIONS

1. What constitutes actionable peer harassment, *i.e.*, when does peer harassment rise to the level of "discrimination" within the meaning of Title IX? Can Davis meet this standard?

2. Assuming peer harassment is actionable, under what circumstances can the school district be held liable to a student who was harassed by another student?

3. Does Title IX reach harassment that targets gay/lesbian students?

4. In view of the decision in *Davis*, what steps should a school district take to limit its exposure to Title IX liability as a result of peer harassment?

5. Should *Davis* control claims of race-motivated peer harassment under Title VI?

2. APPLICATION TO SPORTS

Even though federal financial assistance rarely flows directly to an athletic department, due to passage of the Civil Rights Restoration Act, sex discrimination in the athletic programs of educational institutions receiving any federal funding is prohibited. The 1979 Intercollegiate Athletics Policy Interpretation, 44 Fed. Reg. 71,418 (1979), identifies three major categories that should be analyzed in determining compliance with Title IX: (a) accommodation of interests and abilities (sports offerings), (b) financial assistance, and (c) other program areas, *e.g.*, equipment and supplies, travel and per diem allowances, coaching, facilities, publicity, support services, scheduling, and recruitment. The next decision exemplifies the difficulty in determining whether an institution has "effectively accommodated" the interests of its male and female students.

BIEDIGER V. QUINNIPIAC UNIVERSITY
691 F.3D 85 (2D CIR. 2012)

REENA RAGGI, Circuit Judge:

Quinnipiac University appeals after a bench trial at which Quinnipiac was found to have violated Title IX of the Education Amendments of 1972 by failing to afford equal participation opportunities in varsity sports to female students. Quinnipiac argues that the injunction, which prohibits any such future discrimination, should be vacated because it is based on a Title IX ruling infected by errors in counting the varsity athletic participation opportunities afforded Quinnipiac's female students in the 2009–10 school year. Specifically, Quinnipiac faults the district court for excluding from its count of the total athletic participation opportunities afforded female students: (1) 11 roster positions on the women's indoor and outdoor track and field teams, held by members of Quinnipiac's women's cross-country team who were required to join the track teams even though they were unable to compete in 2009–10 because they were injured or "red-shirted";[1] and (2) all 30 roster positions on Quinnipiac's nascent women's competitive cheerleading team, based on a finding that the team did not afford the athletic participation opportunities of a varsity sport. Quinnipiac further contends that, even if these 41 roster positions should not count as varsity athletic participation opportunities for women, the district court erred in concluding that (3) the resulting 3.62% disparity between the percentage of all

---

[1] This is not to say that Congress could not give federal financial assistance in the form of property improvements, such as a runway. Although the word "financial" usually indicates "money," federal financial assistance may take nonmoney form.

participation opportunities in varsity sports afforded female students (58.25%) and the percentage of enrolled female undergraduates (61.87%) established a Title IX violation warranting the challenged injunctive relief.

We identify no merit in these arguments, and we affirm the challenged injunction substantially for the reasons stated by the district court in its comprehensive and well reasoned opinion.

I. Background

A. Quinnipiac's Decision to Eliminate Women's Volleyball Prompts This Title IX Action

This lawsuit has its origins in Quinnipiac's March 2009 announcement that in the 2009–10 academic year, it would eliminate its varsity sports teams for women's volleyball, men's golf, and men's outdoor track and field, while simultaneously creating a new varsity sports team for women's competitive cheerleading. Plaintiffs, five Quinnipiac women's volleyball players and their coach, Robin Sparks, filed this action in April 2009, charging the university with violating Title IX by denying women equal varsity athletic participation opportunities, and seeking an injunction that, among other things, prevented Quinnipiac from eliminating its women's volleyball team. After a hearing, the district court preliminarily enjoined Quinnipiac from withdrawing support from its volleyball team, finding that Quinnipiac systematically and artificially increased women's teams' rosters and decreased men's teams' rosters to achieve the appearance of Title IX compliance. In June 2010, the district court conducted a bench trial on plaintiffs' claim of disproportionate allocation of athletic participation opportunities and, finding in their favor, granted permanent injunctive relief.

B. Statutory and Regulatory Background

To discuss the district court's challenged ruling further, we must briefly review certain controlling law and regulations.

Title IX provides, in relevant part, that "[n]o person in the United States shall, on the basis of sex, be excluded from participation in, be denied the benefits of, or be subjected to discrimination under any education program or activity receiving Federal financial assistance." 20 U.S.C. § 1681(a). Although the statutory language makes no mention of athletics programs, the former Department of Health, Education and Welfare ("HEW") and its successor agency, the Department of Education ("DOE"), have interpreted Title IX to require recipients of federal financial assistance operating or sponsoring "interscholastic, intercollegiate, club or intramural athletics" to "provide equal athletic opportunity for members of both sexes." 34 C.F.R. § 106.41(c).

Section 106.41(c) provides a non-exhaustive list of factors relevant to determining whether equal athletic opportunities are available:

(1) Whether the selection of sports and levels of competition effectively accommodate the interests and abilities of members of both sexes; (2) The provision of equipment and supplies; (3) Scheduling of games and practice time; (4) Travel and per diem allowance; (5) Opportunity to receive coaching and academic tutoring; (6) Assignment and compensation of coaches and tutors; (7) Provision of locker rooms, practice and competitive facilities; (8) Provision of medical and training facilities and services; (9) Provision of housing and dining facilities and services; (10) Publicity.

Title IX claims of sex discrimination in athletics fall into two categories based on the § 106.41(c) factors to which the claims are addressed: effective accommodation claims focus on § 106.41(c)(1), and equal treatment claims focus on § 106.41(c)(2)-(10). At issue in this appeal is plaintiffs' effective accommodation claim.

In 1979, HEW published in the Federal Register a policy interpretation of § 106.41(c), which states that a school's compliance with the effective accommodation requirement will be assessed "in any one of the following ways":

(1) Whether intercollegiate level participation opportunities for male and female students are provided in numbers substantially proportionate to their respective enrollments; or

(2) Where the members of one sex have been and are underrepresented among intercollegiate athletes, whether the institution can show a history and continuing practice of program expansion which is demonstrably responsive to the developing interest and abilities of the members of that sex; or

(3) Where the members of one sex are underrepresented among intercollegiate athletes and the institution cannot show a continuing practice of program expansion such as that cited above, whether it can be demonstrated that the interests and abilities of the members of that sex have been fully and effectively accommodated by the present program.

1979 Policy Interpretation, 44 Fed. Reg. 71,413, 71,418 (Dec. 11, 1979). The 1979 Policy Interpretation thus affords a school three safe harbors in defending against an effective accommodation claim under § 106.41(c)(1).

In 1996, the DOE's Office of Civil Rights ("OCR"), which is responsible for enforcement of Title IX, clarified that the analysis for determining whether a university affords substantially proportionate participation opportunities to athletes of both sexes under the first prong of the three-part test—the prong relied on by Quinnipiac in defending against plaintiffs' Title IX effective accommodation claim—"begins with a determination of the number of participation opportunities afforded to male and female athletes in the intercollegiate athletic program." OCR, U.S. DOE, *Clarification of Intercollegiate Athletics Policy Guidance: The Three–Part Test*, at 2–3 (Jan. 15,

1996) ("1996 Clarification"). OCR explained that, "[a]s a general rule, all athletes who are listed on a team's squad or eligibility list and are on the team as of the team's first competitive event are counted as participants." Further, "an athlete who participates in more than one sport will be counted as a participant in each sport in which he or she participates." It is not necessary for an athlete to meet minimum criteria of playing time or athletic ability to count as a participant. As OCR explained, "athletes who practice but may not compete" nevertheless "receive numerous benefits and services, such as training and practice time, coaching, tutoring services, locker room facilities, and equipment, as well as important non-tangible benefits derived from being a member of an intercollegiate athletic team." Thus, "it is necessary to count all athletes who receive such benefits when determining the number of athletic opportunities provided to men and women." In a letter accompanying the 1996 Clarification, however, OCR sounded a note of caution: for an athlete to be counted, he or she must be afforded a participation opportunity that is "real, not illusory," in that it offers the same benefits as would be provided to other *bona fide* athletes.

In a 2008 letter, OCR explained that a genuine athletic participation opportunity must take place in the context of a "sport." If a school is a member of a recognized intercollegiate athletic organization, such as the National Collegiate Athletic Association ("NCAA"), that subjects the activity at issue to its organizational requirements, OCR will "presume" that the activity is a sport and that participation can be counted under Title IX. But if that presumption does not apply or has been rebutted, OCR will determine whether the activity qualifies as a sport by reference to several factors relating to "program structure and administration" and "team preparation and competition."

Eight years earlier, in 2000, OCR had issued two letters stating that cheerleading, whether of the sideline or competitive variety, was presumptively not a sport, and that team members could not be counted as athletes under Title IX. While the letters indicated OCR's willingness to review particular cheerleading programs on a case-by-case basis, the parties stipulated in the district court that, since 2000, OCR has never recognized an intercollegiate varsity cheerleading program to be a sport for Title IX purposes. Nor has Quinnipiac ever sought OCR recognition of its competitive cheerleading program as a sports activity.

Once the numbers of real athletic participation opportunities afforded men and women have been determined in light of these principles, the next step of Title IX effective-accommodation analysis considers whether the numbers are substantially proportionate to each sex's enrollment. OCR has not construed substantial proportionality to require exact proportionality. Rather, substantial proportionality is determined on a case-by-case basis in light of "the institution's specific circumstances and the size of its athletic program." As a baseline, OCR will consider substantial proportionality achieved if the number of additional participants necessary required for exact proportionality "would not be sufficient to sustain a viable team."

OCR affords schools considerable "flexibility and choice" in deciding how to provide substantially proportionate athletic opportunities to students of both sexes, including by eliminating teams, placing caps on its rosters, or "[e]xpanding . . . athletic opportunities through new sports."

C. The District Court Ruling

At trial, Quinnipiac maintained that it offered athletic participation opportunities to male and female undergraduates substantially proportionate to their respective enrollments. In support, it pointed to evidence showing that, of the 5,686 students enrolled in Quinnipiac's undergraduate programs in the 2009–10 academic year, 3,518 were female and 2,168 were male. Varsity rosters for the first day of team competitions in 2009–10 listed 440 varsity athletes, of whom 274 were female and 166 were male. Thus, Quinnipiac maintained that women represented 61.87% of the total student body and 62.27% of all varsity athletes, while men represented 38.13% of the student body and 37.73% of all varsity athletes.

Plaintiffs challenged Quinnipiac's count of its varsity athletes, arguing that (1) the university manipulated its team rosters to produce artificially undersized men's teams and artificially oversize women's teams; (2) counting the same women's membership on cross-country, indoor track, and outdoor track teams as three distinct athletic participation opportunities was unwarranted because Quinnipiac's indoor and outdoor track teams did not afford cross-country athletes genuine and distinct benefits; and (3) women who participated on the competitive cheerleading team should not be counted at all because the activity had not yet achieved the status of an intercollegiate varsity sport.

After trial, the district court issued a detailed memorandum of decision in favor of plaintiffs. Therein, the district court rejected plaintiffs' contention that, in setting roster targets for each of its teams, Quinnipiac had manipulated the rosters so as to undercount male participants and overcount female participants, or to set artificially high targets for women's teams that denied women participants genuine athletic opportunities. At the same time, the district court identified concerns about how Quinnipiac counted athletes participating on its women's cross-country, indoor track, and outdoor track teams, stating that it "recall[ed] roster manipulations similar to those" identified in its preliminary injunction opinion. The district court also decided that none of the 30 roster positions assigned to women's competitive cheerleading should be counted because the activity did not yet afford genuine athletic participation opportunities in a varsity sport.

Expanding Quinnipiac's reported roster positions for male athletes by one to reflect an additional participant on the men's ice hockey team revealed at trial, the district court counted a total of 400 varsity athletic participation opportunities. Of these 400, it found that 233—or 58.25%—were assigned to women and 167—or 41.75%—were assigned to men. The district court observed that "in strictly numerical terms," a 3.62% disparity between Quinnipiac's women's 58.25% varsity athletic participation and their 61.87% representation in the undergraduate population reflected only "a borderline case of disproportionate athletic opportunities for women." Nevertheless, the district court concluded that the disparity was significant enough to support judgment in favor of plaintiffs because (1) the disparity was caused by Quinnipiac's own actions and not by natural fluctuations in enrollment; and (2) it was reasonable to expect Quinnipiac to close the gap because the 38 roster positions needed for that purpose would be enough to field a viable women's athletic team, and such a team already existed in the form of the women's volleyball team.

Accordingly, the district court entered a declaratory judgment finding Quinnipiac to have violated Title IX and its implementing regulations by discriminating against women in failing to provide equal athletic participation opportunities to female students, and it permanently enjoined Quinnipiac from continuing to discriminate in this manner. The district court ordered Quinnipiac to submit a plan for complying with the injunction, which plan was to provide for continuation of the women's volleyball team during the 2010–11 athletic season.

II. Discussion

A.   Quinnipiac's Argument and the Standard of Review

Quinnipiac contends that the district court finding of sex discrimination is infected by three errors: (1) the exclusion of 11 positions on the women's indoor and outdoor track teams from its count of varsity athletic participation opportunities, (2) the exclusion of all 30 competitive cheerleading positions from its count of varsity athletic participation opportunities, and (3) the determination that an identified 3.62% disparity between women's representation in Quinnipiac's student body and on its varsity sports teams sufficed to show that women were not afforded substantially proportionate varsity athletic participation opportunities.

B. Deference to Agency Interpretation of Title IX's Implementing Regulations

In addressing Quinnipiac's arguments, we note at the outset that no party challenges the district court's reliance on agency policy statements and letters interpreting 34 C.F.R. § 106.41(c) (1). This court has already ruled that the 1979 Policy Interpretation of § 106.41(c) is entitled to a "particularly high" degree of judicial deference under *Chevron U.S.A. Inc. v. Natural Resources Defense Council, Inc.*, 467 U.S. 837 (1984), because Congress explicitly delegated to the administering agency "the task of prescribing standards for athletic programs under Title IX." We here conclude that the 1996 Clarification, the accompanying 1996 OCR Letter, and the 2000 and 2008 OCR Letters are likewise entitled to substantial deference, because they reflect reasonable agency interpretations of ambiguities in its own regulation, and there is no reason to think that the agency's interpretations do not reflect its "fair and considered judgment on the matter in question."

Title IX has been construed to prohibit the intentional exclusion of students from collegiate athletics programs on the basis of sex. A school's decision to provide students with athletic participation opportunities through separate sports programs for each sex thus necessarily raises a disparate treatment rather than disparate impact claim in that the school decides which athletic opportunities are available to particular students "on the basis of sex."[5] The critical question in this case is thus not whether Quinnipiac's disparate treatment of varsity athletes was based on their sex, but whether the treatment constituted unlawful discrimination under Title IX.

As OCR has interpreted § 1681(a), not every decision to maintain separate sports programs for male and female students constitutes proscribed discrimination. A choice to allocate specific athletic opportunities on the basis of sex will not violate Title IX provided that, in general, the participation opportunities afforded the two sexes are "equal." Plaintiffs here alleged that Quinnipiac did not treat men and women equally in allocating athletic participation opportunities because the opportunities afforded women (1) were not substantially proportionate to women's undergraduate enrollment, and (2) did not fully and effectively accommodate women's athletic interests and abilities. The three-part test did not reduce plaintiffs' burden to prove these elements of their disparate treatment claim. Rather, it afforded Quinnipiac three distinct opportunities to demonstrate that its sex-based treatment of athletes was not unlawful.

Here, Quinnipiac elected to defend against plaintiffs' discrimination claim *only* by reference to the first safe harbor created by the three-part test, arguing that its athletics program provided "substantially proportionate" athletic participation opportunities to women. For reasons we discuss *infra*, the district court reasonably found to the contrary, thus simultaneously rejecting Quinnipiac's defense and finding for plaintiffs on the first element of their disparate treatment claim. To the extent that plaintiffs further offered evidence that Quinnipiac's disproportionate provision of athletic participation opportunities failed fully and effectively to accommodate the athletic interests and abilities of its female undergraduates insofar as it eliminated the women's volleyball team, Quinnipiac did not dispute the point. Nor did it attempt to argue that the school has a history of expanding women's athletic participation opportunities.

In sum, as a matter of Quinnipiac's litigation strategy, resolution of this case effectively turned on whether Quinnipiac's sex based treatment of varsity athletes provided its female students with genuine athletic participation opportunities substantially proportionate to their enrollment. Because the district court found that it did not, plaintiffs carried their burden to prove unlawful disparate treatment.

C. Athletic Participation Opportunities for Women Runners: Discounting the Reported Numbers for Indoor and Outdoor Track

During the 2009–10 academic year, the roster for Quinnipiac's women's cross-country team listed 18 athletes; the roster for its women's indoor track team listed 30 athletes; and the roster for its women's outdoor track team listed 30 athletes. Quinnipiac faults the district court for concluding that this represented 67 rather than 78 genuine athletic participation opportunities

---

5   An athlete is "red-shirted" when he or she takes advantage of a National Collegiate Athletic Association ("NCAA") regulation permitting the athlete to remain on a team but not to compete for a year without losing a year of athletic eligibility. An athlete may red-shirt because of injury or to conserve a year's eligibility while practicing and improving skills.

for women runners. We identify no error of law or fact in the district court's carefully reasoned resolution of this issue.

Before the district court, plaintiffs argued that Quinnipiac should not be allowed to count as 54 athletic participation opportunities the cross-country, indoor track, and outdoor track roster positions held by the same 18 women. As the district court recognized, the issue admitted no easy resolution. The 1996 Clarification plainly states that "an athlete who participates in more than one sport will be counted as a participant in each sport in which . . . she participates." But the trial evidence reflected circumstances not addressed in the 1996 Clarification: Quinnipiac's women cross-country runners were not afforded a choice as to whether to participate in more than one sport; they were required to do so. Specifically, their participation on the cross-country team was conditioned on their membership on the indoor and outdoor track teams. No other Quinnipiac athletes were required to join multiple sports teams. Notably, male cross-country runners were not required to join men's indoor and outdoor track teams, as Quinnipiac had no such teams in 2009–10. Indeed, male cross-country runners were prohibited from representing Quinnipiac as individual entrants in indoor and outdoor track events. As the district court recognized, these circumstances raise questions as to whether simultaneous participation on the women's cross-country, indoor track, and outdoor track teams at Quinnipiac represented three genuine athletic opportunities, or whether cross-country runners' mandated participation on the indoor and outdoor track teams was simply a form of alternative off-season training for the cross-country runners, one that allowed Quinnipiac to inflate the rosters of its women's indoor and outdoor track teams.

In this respect, the district court carefully reviewed evidence that we only summarize: Quinnipiac had a highly competitive women's cross-country team, which, by the 2009–10 school year, had won the last five New England Conference championships; cross-country runners' mandated participation on the indoor and outdoor track teams afforded these runners more training time (albeit for a different type of running) during the cross-country off-season than NCAA rules would otherwise have allowed; Quinnipiac expanded its indoor and outdoor track teams' rosters to accommodate mandated participation by cross-country runners; despite the resulting large rosters, Quinnipiac's indoor and outdoor track teams participated in only the minimum number of track and field tournaments required by the NCAA and were never competitive for team awards as no Quinnipiac athletes entered field events; and Quinnipiac offered scholarship money only to those members of the indoor and outdoor track teams who also ran cross-country. The totality of these circumstances suggested that the 60 positions on Quinnipiac's indoor and outdoor track team rosters were not reflective of genuine participation opportunities in these sports, but were inflated to afford mandated year-round training for the 18 members of the women's cross-country team.

While identifying such a roster-manipulation concern, the district court nevertheless proceeded cautiously in drawing conclusions as to any Title IX violation. Notably, it decided that the evidence did *not* "justify discounting *all* of the cross-country runners' participation on the [women's] indoor and outdoor track teams." Such a ruling would have reduced by 36 the number of athletic participation opportunities that Quinnipiac claimed to afford female students. In explaining its decision, the district court observed that 13 of the 18 women cross-country runners had competed for Quinnipiac in four or more indoor track meets, accounting for 54.4% of the team's races. Meanwhile, 12 of the 18 women cross-country runners had competed for Quinnipiac in three or more outdoor track meets, accounting for 50.0% of the team's races. Finding that this reflected "a substantial contribution" by cross-country runners to Quinnipiac's indoor and outdoor track teams, the district court concluded that the school's "Title IX calculation should account for it," regardless of whether cross-country runners' participation in indoor and outdoor track was mandated. Thus, it rejected plaintiffs' argument that these cross-country runners should not also be viewed as having been afforded further athletic participation opportunities as members of the indoor and outdoor track teams.

At the same time, however, the district court persuasively explained why a smaller number of cross-county runners, required to join Quinnipiac's track teams but participating in no competitions—or in one case, only one competition—could not be viewed as having been afforded multiple genuine athletic participation opportunities. Specifically, five positions on the indoor track team and six positions on the outdoor track team were held by cross-country runners who did not—and effectively could not—avail themselves of distinct participation opportunities on the track teams because they were injured or red-shirted. Not only did these injured or red-shirted runners not compete in indoor or outdoor track events, they received no benefits from membership on these teams beyond those that they were already receiving as injured or red-shirted members of the cross-country team during that sport's off-season. Thus, the district court concluded that for injured and red-shirted cross-country runners, the athletic participation opportunities afforded by *mandated* membership on the indoor and outdoor track teams were "truly illusory."

What was not illusory, however, was Quinnipiac's ability to "pad[ ] its rosters" with female athletes who had "no hope of competing or otherwise participating meaningfully during the indoor and outdoor track seasons." As the district court aptly observed, it would be "unacceptable for Quinnipiac to pump up its women's track team rosters" by requiring every injured field hockey, soccer, and volleyball player to join these teams even though they "would never actually compete in the indoor and outdoor track seasons and, for that matter, would never want to enter a race." But, the district court found, "that is essentially what Quinnipiac is doing with its injured cross-country runners." Thus, the district court discounted Quinnipiac's claimed 30 athletic participation opportunities in indoor track by five, and its claimed 30 athletic participation opportunities in outdoor track by six. We conclude that this reduction in the total number of athletic participation opportunities for women runners in cross-country, indoor track, and outdoor track from Quinnipiac's claimed 78 to an actual 67 is fully supported by the record evidence and by the applicable law.

D. Athletic Participation Opportunities for Women in Competitive Cheerleading: The Determination That the Activity Does Not Yet Qualify as a "Sport"

Competitive cheerleading, which Quinnipiac decided to create as a new women's varsity sport team for 2009–10, is a late twentieth-century outgrowth of traditional sideline cheerleading. Whereas sideline cheerleaders generally strive to entertain audiences or solicit crowd reaction at sport or school functions, a competitive cheerleading team seeks to pit its skills against other teams for the purpose of winning. Thus, to distinguish the two activities, competitive cheerleaders do not attempt to elicit crowd response; generally do not use pom-poms, megaphones, signs, or other props associated with [sideline] cheerleading teams; . . . wear uniforms consisting of shorts and jerseys, much like what women's volleyball players don; and emphasize the more gymnastic elements of sideline cheerleading, such as aerial maneuvers, floor tumbling, and balancing exercises, to the exclusion of those activities intended to rally the watching audience.

The district court nevertheless concluded that the 30 roster positions that Quinnipiac assigned competitive cheerleading for 2009–10 could not be counted under Title IX because the activity did not yet afford the participation opportunities of a varsity "sport."

Preliminary to reaching this conclusion, the district court observed that competitive cheerleading is not yet recognized as a "sport," or even an "emerging sport," by the NCAA, action that would have triggered a presumption in favor of counting its participants under Title IX. Nor has DOE recognized competitive cheerleading as a sport; to the contrary, in two letters in 2000, OCR indicated competitive cheerleading is presumptively not a sport, while leaving open the possibility for a different conclusion with respect to a particular cheerleading program. There is, however, no record evidence of any competitive cheerleading program being recognized by DOE as a sport.

Mindful of these circumstances, the district court proceeded carefully to review the structure, administration, team preparation, and competition of Quinnipiac's competitive cheerleading program to determine whether it nevertheless qualified as a sport whose athletic participation opportunities should be counted for purposes of Title IX. Again, we only briefly summarize the district court's detailed findings, which find ample support in the record evidence. The district court found that in terms of the team's operating budget, benefits, services, and coaching staff, competitive cheerleading was generally structured and administered by Quinnipiac's athletics department in a manner consistent with the school's other varsity teams. With respect to factors relating to the team's preparation and competition, the district court found that the competitive cheerleading team's practice time, regimen, and venue were consistent with other varsity sports. Further, as with other varsity sports, the length of the competitive cheerleading season and the minimum number of competitions in which a team would participate were pre-determined by a governing athletic organization, the recently formed National Competitive Stunt and Tumbling Association, of which Quinnipiac was a founding member. Finally, the purpose of the team—to compete athletically at the intercollegiate varsity level—was akin to that of other varsity sports.

At the same time, however, the district court identified a number of circumstances that sufficiently distinguished Quinnipiac's competitive cheerleading program from traditional varsity sports as to "compel[ ] the decision that, for the 2009–10 season," the program could not "be counted as a varsity sport for purposes of Title IX." First, Quinnipiac did not—and, in 2009–10, could not—conduct any off-campus recruitment for its competitive cheerleading team, in marked contrast not only to the school's other varsity sports teams but also to a typical NCAA Division I sports program.

More important, no uniform set of rules applied to competitive cheerleading competition throughout the 2009–10 season. Indeed, in the ten competitions in which the Quinnipiac team participated during the regular season, it was judged according to five different scoring systems. Further, in these competitions, Quinnipiac did not face only varsity intercollegiate competitive cheerleading teams. Rather, it was challenged by "a motley assortment of competitors," including collegiate club opponents who did not receive varsity benefits, collegiate sideline cheerleading teams, and all-star opponents unaffiliated with a particular academic institution, some of whom may still have been high-school age. As the district court observed, "application of a uniform set of rules for competition and the restriction of competition to contests against other varsity opponents" are the "touchstones" of a varsity sports program.

The concerns raised by these irregularities in season competition were only aggravated by aspects of post-season play. Notably, competitive cheerleading offered no progressive playoff system leading to a championship game. Rather, it provided an open invitational, which neither excluded any team on the basis of its regular season performance nor ranked or seeded participating teams on that basis. Viewing the totality of these circumstances, the district court concluded that the competitive cheerleading team's post-season competition did not conform to expectations for a varsity sport.

Based on these findings, as well as those pertaining to regular season play, the district court concluded that Quinnipiac's competitive cheerleading team did not compete in circumstances indicative of varsity sports. Thus, it ruled that Quinnipiac's 30 roster positions for competitive cheerleading could not be counted for Title IX purposes because the activity did not yet afford women genuine participation opportunities in a varsity sport.

Like the district court, we acknowledge record evidence showing that competitive cheerleading can be physically challenging, requiring competitors to possess "strength, agility, and grace." Similarly, we do not foreclose the possibility that the activity, with better organization and defined rules, might some day warrant recognition as a varsity sport. But, like the district court, we conclude that the record evidence shows that "that time has not yet arrived."

E. Finding a Title IX Violation Based on a 3.62% Disparity

Having reduced Quinnipiac's claimed athletic participation opportunities for women by 41—representing 30 competitive cheerleaders and 11 cross-country runners required to join the indoor and outdoor track teams but unable to compete on those teams because of their injuries or red-shirt status—the district court correctly found that the school had a total of 400 varsity athletic participation opportunities, of which 233, or 58.25%, were assigned to women. Because enrollment data established that 61.87% of Quinnipiac's undergraduate population were women, this indicated a 3.62% disparity in the athletic opportunities that Quinnipiac afforded women. The district court concluded that this disparity was sufficient to support a finding that Quinnipiac had failed to afford female students varsity athletic participation opportunities substantially proportionate to their enrollment.

Quinnipiac argues that a 3.62% disparity is too small to support such a finding. In any event, it submits that the district court erred in holding Quinnipiac responsible for the disparity in light of fluctuations in enrollment and Quinnipiac's good faith reliance on the district court's statement at the time of the preliminary injunction decision that it would likely count all women members of the cross-country, indoor track, outdoor track, and competitive cheerleading teams as athletic participants for purposes of Title IX. Further, Quinnipiac contends that the district court erroneously accorded dispositive weight to the fact that the number of additional female roster spots needed to achieve exact proportionality—38—would have been sufficient for Quinnipiac to field an additional varsity team.

Quinnipiac's arguments fail to persuade. First, its emphasis on the relatively small percentage of disparity is unwarranted. The district court itself recognized that "in strictly numerical terms," a 3.62% disparity presents "a borderline case of disproportionate athletic opportunities." But as the 1996 Clarification makes clear, substantial proportionality is not determined by any bright-line statistical test. The Clarification instructs that substantial proportionality is properly determined on a "case-by-case basis" after a careful assessment of the school's "specific circumstances," including the causes of the disparity and the reasonableness of requiring the school to add additional athletic opportunities to eliminate the disparity. The district court's challenged ruling was based on precisely this analysis.

Specifically, the district court pointed to record evidence showing that the 3.62% identified disparity was almost entirely attributable to Quinnipiac's own careful control of its athletic rosters. Although Quinnipiac claims that, but for a 0.27% increase in female enrollment in 2009–10 beyond its control, the disparity would have been only 3.35%, the difference is not one that undermines the district court's conclusion that Quinnipiac's voluntary actions largely caused the disparity.

Finally, we do not understand the district court to have ruled, as Quinnipiac suggests, that no matter how small a disparity, if it can be closed by the creation of a new sports team, a school will be found not to have afforded substantially proportionate athletic opportunities. Rather, we understand the court to have discussed the possible creation of a new sports team only to explain why it was reasonable to expect Quinnipiac to add additional athletic opportunities for women to close the identified 3.62% disparity. In so concluding, the district court noted that, insofar as the gap reflected 38 positions, each of Quinnipiac's women's varsity teams had 30 or fewer roster spots, making it "certain that an independent sports team could be created from the shortfall of participation opportunities." Moreover, the district court observed that little effort was required for Quinnipiac to afford the additional participation opportunities of an independent sports team: "That independent sports team would be the eliminated women's volleyball squad, a team that, based on Quinnipiac's 2010–11 roster target, requires a mere 14 players to compete." Of course, the district court did not suggest that Quinnipiac's compliance with Title IX was dependent on it forever fielding a women's volleyball team. But the ease with which Quinnipiac could afford these particular additional varsity athletic opportunities was a "specific circumstance[ ]" that, pursuant to the 1996 Clarification, supported the conclusion that a 3.62% disparity in this case demonstrated that Quinnipiac was not affording substantially proportionate varsity athletic participation opportunities to its female students.

Accordingly, the district court's order enjoining Quinnipiac from continuing to discriminate against female students by failing to provide them with equal athletic participation opportunities is AFFIRMED.

NOTES AND QUESTIONS

1. How did Quinnipiac seek to comply with Title IX's equal accommodation mandate? Why did the court reject its "counting" of athletic opportunities?

2. Why did the court find that a mere 3.62% disparity between the percentage of women students and the percentage of women listed on varsity sports teams constituted a violation of Title IX?

3. In several cases male athletes have challenged university decisions to cut their teams in order to meet Title IX's mandate. See *Equity In Athletics, Inc. v. Department of Educ.*, 639 F.3d 91, 101–05 (4th Cir. 2011), *cert. denied*, 132 S. Ct. 1004 (2012) (rejecting the argument that, "because Title IX prohibits intentional discrimination as disparate treatment, any implementing regulation that is directed toward disparate impact violates the statute" since the "clear statutory language of Title IX . . . allows for some consideration of proportionality between participation and enrollment" and the three-part test provides universities with flexibility in achieving statutory compliance; further, the court rejected an argument that the three-part test violates the Equal Protection Clause by requiring compliance with an enrollment-based quota that does not serve a governmental purpose, consistent with every other appellate court that has considered the constitutionality of the test); *Miami University Wrestling Club v. Miami University*, 302 F.3d 608, 615 (6th Cir. 2002) (neither the DOE regulations nor the policy interpretation is unreasonable, arbitrary, capricious or manifestly contrary to Title IX and, therefore, the court defers to the 1979 Policy Interpretation; the plaintiffs, challenging the University's decision to eliminate the men's soccer, tennis and wrestling teams, in order to bring its athletic programs into compliance with Title IX and equalize the athletic opportunities for men and women, do not state a claim under Title IX); *Chalenor v. University of North*

Dakota, 291 F.3d 1042, 1044-47 (8th Cir. 2002) (in an action by male student wrestlers challenging the university's decision to eliminate its wrestling program, the court held that the DOE policy interpretation is entitled to controlling deference and the university could choose to pursue gender proportionality without showing that it had not already met one of the alternative criteria for effective accommodation); *Neal v. Board of Trustees of California State Universities*, 198 F.3d 763, 766-72 (9th Cir. 1999) (a university in which male students occupy a disproportionately high percentage of athletic roster spots is not prevented by Title IX, and its implementing regulations, from making gender-conscious decisions to reduce the proportion of roster spots assigned to men, in this case by reducing the number of spots on its men's wrestling team).

4. Title IX regulations also require that athletic scholarships be provided to athletes in numbers substantially proportionate to the number of students of each sex participating in sports at the institution. 34 C.F.R. § 106.37(c). In addition, the regulations require equal opportunity in terms of equipment, travel, coaching, the provision of lockers, training equipment, etc. 34 C.F.R. § 106.41(c).

3. RETALIATION

JACKSON V. BIRMINGHAM BOARD OF EDUCATION
544 U.S. 167 (2005)

Justice O'CONNOR delivered the opinion of the Court.

Roderick Jackson, a teacher in the Birmingham, Alabama, public schools, brought suit against the Birmingham Board of Education (Board) alleging that the Board retaliated against him because he had complained about sex discrimination in the high school's athletic program. Jackson claimed that the Board's retaliation violated Title IX of the Education Amendments of 1972, 20 U.S.C. § 1681, *et seq.* The District Court dismissed Jackson's complaint on the ground that Title IX does not prohibit retaliation, and the Court of Appeals for the Eleventh Circuit affirmed. We consider here whether the private right of action implied by Title IX encompasses claims of retaliation. We hold that it does where the funding recipient retaliates against an individual because he has complained about sex discrimination.

I

According to the complaint, Jackson has been an employee of the Birmingham school district for over 10 years. In 1993, the Board hired Jackson to serve as a physical education teacher and girls' basketball coach. Jackson was transferred to Ensley High School in August 1999. At

Ensley, he discovered that the girls' team was not receiving equal funding and equal access to athletic equipment and facilities. The lack of adequate funding, equipment, and facilities made it difficult for Jackson to do his job as the team's coach.

In December 2000, Jackson began complaining to his supervisors about the unequal treatment of the girls' basketball team, but to no avail. Jackson's complaints went unanswered, and the school failed to remedy the situation. Instead, Jackson began to receive negative work evaluations and ultimately was removed as the girls' coach in May 2001. Jackson is still employed by the Board as a teacher, but he no longer receives supplemental pay for coaching.

After the Board terminated Jackson's coaching duties, he filed suit in the United States District Court for the Northern District of Alabama. He alleged, among other things, that the Board violated Title IX by retaliating against him for protesting the discrimination against the girls' basketball team.

II

A

More than 25 years ago, in *Cannon v. University of Chicago*, we held that Title IX implies a private right of action to enforce its prohibition on intentional sex discrimination. In subsequent cases, we have defined the contours of that right of action. In *Franklin v. Gwinnett County Public Schools*, we held that it authorizes private parties to seek monetary damages for intentional violations of Title IX. We have also held that the private right of action encompasses intentional sex discrimination in the form of a recipient's deliberate indifference to a teacher's sexual harassment of a student, *Gebser v. Lago Vista Independent School Dist.*, or to sexual harassment of a student by another student, *Davis v. Monroe County Bd. of Ed.*

In all of these cases, we relied on the text of Title IX, which, subject to a list of narrow exceptions not at issue here, broadly prohibits a funding recipient from subjecting any person to "discrimination" "on the basis of sex." Retaliation against a person because that person has complained of sex discrimination is another form of intentional sex discrimination encompassed by Title IX's private cause of action. Retaliation is, by definition, an intentional act. It is a form of "discrimination" because the complainant is being subjected to differential treatment. Moreover, retaliation is discrimination "on the basis of sex" because it is an intentional response to the nature of the complaint: an allegation of sex discrimination. We conclude that when a funding recipient retaliates against a person because he complains of sex discrimination, this constitutes intentional "discrimination" "on the basis of sex," in violation of Title IX.

The Court of Appeals' conclusion that Title IX does not prohibit retaliation because the "statute makes no mention of retaliation" ignores the import of our repeated holdings construing "discrimination" under Title IX broadly. Though the statute does not mention sexual harassment, we have held that sexual harassment is intentional discrimination encompassed by Title IX's private right of action. Thus, a recipient's deliberate indifference to a teacher's sexual harassment of a student also "violate[s] Title IX's plain terms." Likewise, a recipient's deliberate indifference to sexual harassment of a student by another student also squarely constitutes "discrimination" "on the basis of sex." "Discrimination" is a term that covers a wide range of intentional unequal treatment; by using such a broad term, Congress gave the statute a broad reach.

Congress certainly could have mentioned retaliation in Title IX expressly, as it did in § 704 of Title VII of the Civil Rights Act of 1964. Title VII, however, is a vastly different statute from Title IX, and the comparison the Board urges us to draw is therefore of limited use. Title IX's cause of action is implied, while Title VII's is express. Title IX is a broadly written general prohibition on discrimination, followed by specific, narrow exceptions to that broad prohibition. By contrast, Title VII spells out in greater detail the conduct that constitutes discrimination in violation of that statute. Because Congress did not list *any* specific discriminatory practices when it wrote Title IX, its failure to mention one such practice does not tell us anything about whether it intended that practice to be covered.

Title IX was enacted in 1972, three years after our decision in *Sullivan v. Little Hunting Park, Inc.* In *Sullivan*, we held that 42 U.S.C. § 1982, which provides that "[a]ll citizens of the United States shall have the same right . . . as is enjoyed by white citizens . . . to inherit, purchase, lease, sell, hold, and convey real and personal property," protected a white man who spoke out against discrimination toward one of his tenants and who suffered retaliation as a result. Sullivan had rented a house to a black man and assigned him a membership share and use rights in a private park. The corporation that owned the park would not approve the assignment to the black lessee. Sullivan protested, and the corporation retaliated against him by expelling him and taking his shares. Sullivan sued the corporation, and we upheld Sullivan's cause of action under 42 U.S.C. § 1982 for "[retaliation] for the advocacy of [the black person's] cause." Thus, in *Sullivan* we interpreted a general prohibition on racial discrimination to cover retaliation against those who advocate the rights of groups protected by that prohibition.

Congress enacted Title IX just three years after *Sullivan* was decided, and accordingly that decision provides a valuable context for understanding the statute. As we recognized in *Cannon*, "it is not only appropriate but also realistic to presume that Congress was thoroughly familiar with [*Sullivan*] and that it expected its enactment [of Title IX] to be interpreted in conformity with [it]." Retaliation for Jackson's advocacy of the rights of the girls' basketball team in this case is "discrimination" "on the basis of sex," just as retaliation for advocacy on behalf of a black lessee in *Sullivan* was discrimination on the basis of race.

B

The Board contends that our decision in *Alexander v. Sandoval*, compels a holding that Title IX's private right of action does not encompass retaliation. *Sandoval* held that private parties may not invoke Title VI regulations to obtain redress for disparate-impact discrimination because Title VI itself prohibits only intentional discrimination. The Board cites a Department of Education regulation prohibiting retaliation "against any individual for the purpose of interfering with any right or privilege secured by [Title IX]," and contends that Jackson, like the petitioners in *Sandoval*, seeks an "impermissible extension of the statute" when he argues that Title

IX's private right of action encompasses retaliation. This argument, however, entirely misses the point. We do not rely on regulations extending Title IX's protection beyond its statutory limits; indeed, we do not rely on the Department of Education's regulation at all, because the statute *itself* contains the necessary prohibition. As we explain above, the text of Title IX prohibits a funding recipient from retaliating against a person who speaks out against sex discrimination, because such retaliation is intentional "discrimination" "on the basis of sex." We reach this result based on the statute's text. In step with *Sandoval*, we hold that Title IX's private right of action encompasses suits for retaliation, because retaliation falls within the statute's prohibition of intentional discrimination on the basis of sex.

C

Nor are we convinced by the Board's argument that, even if Title IX's private right of action encompasses discrimination, Jackson is not entitled to invoke it because he is an "indirect victi[m]" of sex discrimination. The statute is broadly worded; it does not require that the victim of the retaliation must also be the victim of the discrimination that is the subject of the original complaint. If the statute provided instead that "no person shall be subjected to discrimination on the basis of *such individual's sex*," then we would agree with the Board. However, Title IX contains no such limitation. Where the retaliation occurs because the complainant speaks out about sex discrimination, the "on the basis of sex" requirement is satisfied.

Congress enacted Title IX not only to prevent the use of federal dollars to support discriminatory practices, but also "to provide individual citizens effective protection against those practices." We agree with the United States that this objective "would be difficult, if not impossible, to achieve if persons who complain about sex discrimination did not have effective protection against retaliation." If recipients were permitted to retaliate freely, individuals who witness discrimination would be loathe to report it, and all manner of Title IX violations might go unremedied as a result.

Reporting incidents of discrimination is integral to Title IX enforcement and would be discouraged if retaliation against those who report went unpunished. Indeed, if retaliation were not prohibited, Title IX's enforcement scheme would unravel. Recall that Congress intended Title IX's private right of action to encompass claims of a recipient's deliberate indifference to sexual harassment. Accordingly, if a principal sexually harasses a student, and a teacher complains to the school board but the school board is indifferent, the board would likely be liable for a Title IX violation. But if Title IX's private right of action does not encompass retaliation claims, the teacher would have no recourse if he were subsequently fired for speaking out. Without protection from retaliation, individuals who witness discrimination would likely not report it, indifference claims would be short-circuited, and the underlying discrimination would go unremedied.

Title IX's enforcement scheme also depends on individual reporting because individuals and agencies may not bring suit under the statute unless the recipient has received "actual notice" of the discrimination. If recipients were able to avoid such notice by retaliating against all those who dare complain, the statute's enforcement scheme would be subverted. We should not assume that Congress left such a gap in its scheme.

Moreover, teachers and coaches such as Jackson are often in the best position to vindicate the rights of their students because they are better able to identify discrimination and bring it to the attention of administrators. Indeed, sometimes adult employees are "the only effective adversar[ies]" of discrimination in schools.

D

The Board is correct in pointing out that, because Title IX was enacted as an exercise of Congress' powers under the Spending Clause, "private damages actions are available only where recipients of federal funding had adequate notice that they could be liable for the conduct at issue." When Congress enacts legislation under its spending power, that legislation is "in the nature of a contract: in return for federal funds, the States agree to comply with federally imposed conditions."

The Board insists that we should not interpret Title IX to prohibit retaliation because it was not on notice that it could be held liable for retaliating against those who complain of Title IX violations. We disagree. Funding recipients have been on notice that they could be subjected to private suits for intentional sex discrimination under Title IX since 1979, when we decided *Cannon.* [T]he Board should have been put on notice by the fact that our cases since *Cannon,* such as *Gebser* and *Davis,* have consistently interpreted Title IX's private cause of action broadly to encompass diverse forms of intentional sex discrimination. Indeed, retaliation presents an even easier case than deliberate indifference. It is easily attributable to the funding recipient, and it is always—by definition—intentional. We therefore conclude that retaliation against individuals because they complain of sex discrimination is "intentional conduct that violates the clear terms of the statute," and that Title IX itself therefore supplied sufficient notice to the Board that it could not retaliate against Jackson after he complained of discrimination against the girls' basketball team.

The regulations implementing Title IX clearly prohibit retaliation and have been on the books for nearly 30 years. More importantly, the Courts of Appeals that had considered the question at the time of the conduct at issue in this case all had already interpreted Title IX to cover retaliation. The Board could not have realistically supposed that, given this context, it remained free to retaliate against those who reported sex discrimination. A reasonable school board would realize that institutions covered by Title IX cannot cover up violations of that law by means of discriminatory retaliation.

Justice THOMAS, with whom THE CHIEF JUSTICE, Justice SCALIA, and Justice KENNEDY join, dissenting.

The Court holds that the private right of action under Title IX of the Education Amendments of 1972, for sex discrimination that it implied in *Cannon v. University of Chicago,* extends to claims of retaliation. Its holding is contrary to the plain terms of Title IX, because retaliatory conduct is not discrimination on the basis of sex. Moreover, we require Congress to speak unambiguously in imposing conditions on funding recipients through its spending power. And, in cases in which a party asserts that a cause of action should be implied, we require that the statute itself evince a plain intent to provide such a cause of action. Section 901 of Title IX meets none of these requirements. I therefore respectfully dissent.

NOTES AND QUESTIONS

1. How is retaliation a form of intentional discrimination "on the basis of sex"?

2. Were recipients of federal financial assistance on notice, prior to the decision in *Jackson*, that they could be subjected to liability for retaliating against one who complains of sex discrimination? What role do the regulations prohibiting discrimination play in the analysis?

3. How is a retaliation claim "integral to Title IX enforcement"?

4. Could Jackson have brought his retaliation claim under Title VII?

C. REHABILITATION ACT OF 1973—§ 504

1.   INDIVIDUAL WITH A DISABILITY

SCHOOL BOARD OF NASSAU COUNTY V. ARLINE
480 U.S. 273 (1987)

Justice BRENNAN delivered the opinion of the Court.

Section 504 of the Rehabilitation Act of 1973, 29 U.S.C. § 794 (Act), prohibits a federally funded state program from discriminating against a handicapped individual solely by reason of his or her handicap. This case presents the questions whether a person afflicted with tuberculosis, a contagious disease, may be considered a "handicapped individual" within the meaning of § 504 of the Act, and, if so, whether such an individual is "otherwise qualified" to teach elementary school.

I

From 1966 until 1979, respondent Arline taught elementary school in Nassau County, Florida. She was discharged in 1979 after suffering a third relapse of tuberculosis within two years. After she was denied relief in state administrative proceedings, she brought suit in federal court, alleging that the School Board's decision to dismiss her because of her tuberculosis violated § 504 of the Act.

A trial was held in the District Court, at which the principal medical evidence was provided by Marianne McEuen, M.D., an assistant director of the Community Tuberculosis Control Service of the Florida Department of Health and Rehabilitative Services. According to the medical records reviewed by Dr. McEuen, Arline was hospitalized for tuberculosis in 1957. For the next twenty years, Arline's disease was in remission. Then, in 1977, a culture revealed that tuberculosis was again active in her system; cultures taken in March 1978 and in November 1978 were also positive.

In her trial memorandum, Arline argued that it was "not disputed that the [School Board dismissed her] solely on the basis of her illness. Since the illness in this case qualifies the Plaintiff as a 'handicapped person' it is clear that she was dismissed solely as a result of her handicap in violation of Section 504." The District Court held, however, that although there was "[n]o question that she suffers a handicap," Arline was nevertheless not "a handicapped person under the terms of that statute." The court found it "difficult . . . to conceive that Congress intended contagious diseases to be included within the definition of a handicapped person." The court then went on to state that, "even assuming" that a person with a contagious disease could be deemed a handicapped person, Arline was not "qualified" to teach elementary school.

II

In enacting and amending the Act, Congress enlisted all programs receiving federal funds in an effort "to share with handicapped Americans the opportunities for an education, transportation, housing, health care, and jobs that other Americans take for granted." To that end, Congress not only increased federal support for vocational rehabilitation, but also addressed the broader problem of discrimination against the handicapped by including § 504, an antidiscrimination provision patterned after Title VI of the Civil Rights of 1964. Section 504 of the Rehabilitation Act reads in pertinent part:

> No otherwise qualified handicapped individual in the United States, as defined in section 706(7) of this title, shall, solely by reason of his handicap, be excluded from participation in, be denied the benefits of, or be subjected to discrimination under any program or activity receiving Federal financial assistance. . . .

In 1974 Congress expanded the definition of "handicapped individual" for use in § 504 to read as follows:

[A]ny person who (i) has a physical or mental impairment which substantially limits one or more of such person's major life activities, (ii) has a record of such an impairment, or (iii) is regarded as having such an impairment. 29 U.S.C. § 706(7)(B).

The amended definition reflected Congress' concern with protecting the handicapped against discrimination stemming not only from simple prejudice, but from "archaic attitudes and laws" and from "the fact that the American people are simply unfamiliar with and insensitive to the difficulties confront[ing] individuals with handicaps." To combat the effects of erroneous but nevertheless prevalent perceptions about the handicapped, Congress expanded the definition of "handicapped individual" so as to preclude discrimination against "[a] person who has a record of, or is regarded as having, an impairment [but who] may at present have no actual incapacity at all." *Southeastern Community College v. Davis.*

In determining whether a particular individual is handicapped as defined by the Act, the regulations promulgated by the Department of Health and Human Services are of significant assistance. The regulations are particularly significant here because they define two critical terms used in the statutory definition of handicapped individual. "Physical impairment" is defined as follows:

[A]ny physiological disorder or condition, cosmetic disfigurement, or anatomical loss affecting one or more of the following body systems: neurological; musculoskeletal; special sense organs; respiratory, including speech organs; cardiovascular; reproductive, digestive, genito-urinary; hemic and lymphatic; skin; and endocrine. 45 C.F.R. § 84.3(j) (2)(i).

In addition, the regulations define "major life activities" as:

functions such as caring for one's self, performing manual tasks, walking, seeing, hearing, speaking, breathing, learning, and working." § 84.3(j)(2)(ii).

III

Within this statutory and regulatory framework, then, we must consider whether Arline can be considered a handicapped individual. According to the testimony of Dr. McEuen, Arline suffered tuberculosis "in an acute form in such a degree that it affected her respiratory system," and was hospitalized for this condition. Arline thus had a physical impairment as that term is defined by the regulations, since she had a "physiological disorder or condition . . . affecting [her] . . . respiratory [system]." This impairment was serious enough to require hospitalization, a fact more than sufficient to establish that one or more of her major life activities were substantially limited by her impairment. Thus, Arline's hospitalization for tuberculosis in 1957 suffices to establish that she has a "record of . . . impairment" within the meaning of 29 U.S.C. § 706(7) (B)(ii), and is therefore a handicapped individual.

Petitioners concede that a contagious disease may constitute a handicapping condition to the extent that it leaves a person with "diminished physical or mental capabilities" and concede that Arline's hospitalization for tuberculosis in 1957 demonstrates that she has a record of a physical impairment. Petitioners maintain, however, Arline's record of impairment is irrelevant in this case, since the School Board dismissed Arline not because of her diminished physical capabilities, but because of the threat that her relapses of tuberculosis posed to the health of others.

We do not agree with petitioners that, in defining a handicapped individual under § 504, the contagious effects of a disease can be meaningfully distinguished from the disease's physical effects on a claimant in a case such as this. Arline's contagiousness and her physical impairment each resulted from the same underlying condition, tuberculosis. It would be unfair to allow an employer to seize upon the distinction between the effects of a disease on others and the effects of a disease on a patient and use that distinction to justify discriminatory treatment.[7]

Nothing in the legislative history of § 504 suggests that Congress intended such a result. That history demonstrates that Congress was as concerned about the effect of an impairment on others as it was about its effect on the individual. Congress extended coverage, in 29 U.S.C. § 706(7)(B)(iii), to those individuals who are simply "regarded as having" a physical or mental impairment. The Senate Report provides as an example of a person who would be covered under this subsection "a person with some kind of visible physical impairment which in fact does not substantially limit that person's functioning." Such an impairment might not diminish a person's physical or mental capabilities, but could nevertheless substantially limit that person's ability to work as a result of the negative reactions of others to the impairment.

Allowing discrimination based on the contagious effects of a physical impairment would be inconsistent with the basic purpose of § 504, which is to ensure that handicapped individuals are not denied jobs or other benefits because of the prejudiced attitudes or the ignorance of others. By amending the definition of "handicapped individual" to include not only those who are actually physically impaired, but also those who are regarded as impaired and who, as a result, are substantially limited in a major life activity, Congress acknowledged that society's accumulated myths and fears about disability and disease are as handicapping as are the physical limitations that flow from actual impairment. Few aspects of a handicap give rise to the same level of public fear and misapprehension as contagiousness. Even those who suffer or have recovered from such noninfectious diseases as epilepsy or cancer have faced discrimination based on the irrational fear that they might be contagious. The Act is carefully structured to replace such reflexive

---

7   The United States argues that it is possible for a person to be simply a carrier of a disease, that is, to be capable of spreading a disease without having a "physical impairment" or suffering from any other symptoms associated with the disease. The United States contends that this is true in the case of some carriers of the Acquired Immune Deficiency Syndrome (AIDS) virus. From this premise the United States concludes that discrimination solely on the basis of contagiousness is never discrimination on the basis of a handicap. The argument is misplaced in this case, because the handicap here, tuberculosis, gave rise both to a physical impairment and to contagiousness. This case does not present, and we therefore do not reach, the questions whether a carrier of a contagious disease such as AIDS could be considered to have a physical impairment, or whether such a person could be considered, solely on the basis of contagiousness, a handicapped person as defined by the Act.

reactions to actual or perceived handicaps with actions based on reasoned and medically sound judgments: the definition of "handicapped individual" is broad, but only those individuals who are both handicapped and otherwise qualified are eligible for relief. The fact that *some* persons who have contagious diseases may pose a serious health threat to others under certain circumstances does not justify excluding from the coverage of the Act all persons with actual or perceived contagious diseases. Such exclusion would mean that those accused of being contagious would never have the opportunity to have their condition evaluated in light of medical evidence and a determination made as to whether they were "otherwise qualified." Rather, they would be vulnerable to discrimination on the basis of mythology—precisely the type of injury Congress sought to prevent. We conclude that the fact that a person with a record of a physical impairment is also contagious does not suffice to remove that person from coverage under § 504.

NOTES AND QUESTIONS

1. Since Ms. Arline was found to be an individual with a disability, is she entitled to an injunction reinstating her to the teaching position? See § 706(8)(D), which was enacted in response to *Arline*. What if the parents decide to withdraw their children from the school if she is reinstated? Would the refusal to reinstate then be "solely by reason of her disability?" Is this analogous to a "customer preference" defense in a Title VII case or a refusal to employ a pregnant elementary school teacher?

2. Is an employee discharged because of alcoholism an "individual with a disability" within the meaning of § 504? because of cancer? because of epilepsy? because of addiction to marijuana? Alcoholics [and drug abusers] are excluded by 29 U.S.C. § 706(8)(C) if their current use prevents them from performing the duties of a job or constitutes a threat to property or safety of others. *See also 42 U.S.C. § 12114 (ADA).*

3. A certified teacher of hearing-impaired elementary school students is diagnosed as having AIDS and immediately reassigned to an administrative position and barred from teaching. Is he an "individual with a disability" within the meaning of § 504? *See Chalk v. U.S. Dist. Court Cent. Dist. of California*, 840 F.2d 701 (9th Cir. 1988). If the teacher is able to perform all aspects of the job, what is the justification for the reassignment? In *Bragdon v. Abbott*, 524 U.S. 624 (1998), the Court held that HIV infection is a disability, even when it has not progressed to the symptomatic phase. Applying the Americans with Disabilities Act (ADA) definition of disability, which parallels the definition in § 504, the Court found that the condition constitutes a physical impairment from the moment of infection, that the impairment affects a major life activity—reproduction, and that the impairment represents a substantial limitation on reproduction. The case was remanded for a determination of whether the dentist could justify his decision to fill the plaintiff's cavity at a hospital, rather than his office, by showing "a direct threat to the health or safety of others."

SOUTHEASTERN COMMUNITY COLLEGE V. DAVIS
442 U.S. 397 (1979)

Mr. Justice POWELL delivered the opinion of the Court.

This case presents a matter of first impression for this Court: Whether § 504 of the Rehabilitation Act of 1973, which prohibits discrimination against an "otherwise qualified handicapped individual" in federally funded programs "solely by reason of his handicap," forbids professional schools from imposing physical qualifications for admission to their clinical training programs.

I

Respondent, who suffers from a serious hearing disability, seeks to be trained as a registered nurse. During the 1973-1974 academic year she was enrolled in the College Parallel program of Southeastern Community College, a state institution that receives federal funds. Respondent hoped to progress to Southeastern's Associate Degree Nursing program, completion of which would make her eligible for state certification as a registered nurse. In the course of her application to the nursing program, she was interviewed by a member of the nursing faculty. It became apparent that respondent had difficulty understanding questions asked, and on inquiry she acknowledged a history of hearing problems and dependence on a hearing aid. She was advised to consult an audiologist.

On the basis of an examination at Duke University Medical Center, respondent was diagnosed as having a "bilateral, sensori-neural hearing loss." A change in her hearing aid was recommended, as a result of which it was expected that she would be able to detect sounds "almost as well as a person would who has normal hearing." But this improvement would not mean that she could discriminate among sounds sufficiently to understand normal spoken speech.

Southeastern next consulted Mary McRee, Executive Director of the North Carolina Board of Nursing. On the basis of the audiologist's report, McRee recommended that respondent not be admitted to the nursing program. In McRee's view, respondent's hearing disability made it unsafe for her to practice as a nurse. In addition, it would be impossible for respondent to participate safely in the normal clinical training program, and those modifications that would be necessary to enable safe participation would prevent her from realizing the benefits of the program: "To adjust patient learning experiences in keeping with [respondent's] hearing limitations could, in fact, be the same as denying her full learning to meet the objectives of your nursing programs."

Respondent then filed suit alleging both a violation of § 504 of the Rehabilitation Act of 1973, 29 U.S.C. § 794, and a denial of equal protection and due process. After a bench trial, the District

Court entered judgment in favor of Southeastern. [The Court of Appeals for the Fourth Circuit reversed.]

II

Section 504 by its terms does not compel educational institutions to disregard the disabilities of handicapped individuals or to make substantial modifications in their programs to allow disabled persons to participate. Instead, it requires only that an "otherwise qualified handicapped individual" not be excluded from participation in a federally funded program "solely by reason of his handicap," indicating only that mere possession of a handicap is not a permissible ground for assuming an inability to function in a particular context.

The [Court of Appeals], however, believed that the "otherwise qualified" persons protected by § 504 include those who would be able to meet the requirements of a particular program in every respect except as to limitations imposed by their handicap. Taken literally, this holding would prevent an institution from taking into account any limitation resulting from the handicap, however disabling. It assumes, in effect, that a person need not meet legitimate physical requirements in order to be "otherwise qualified." We think the understanding of the District Court is closer to the plain meaning of the statutory language. An otherwise qualified person is one who is able to meet all of a program's requirements in spite of his handicap.

III

The remaining question is whether the physical qualifications Southeastern demanded of respondent might not be necessary for participation in its nursing program. It is not open to dispute that, as Southeastern's Associate Degree Nursing program currently is constituted, the ability to understand speech without reliance on lip-reading is necessary for patient safety during the clinical phase of the program. As the District Court found, this ability also is indispensable for many of the functions that a registered nurse performs.

Respondent contends nevertheless that § 504, properly interpreted, compels Southeastern to undertake affirmative action that would dispense with the need for effective oral communication. First, it is suggested that respondent can be given individual supervision by faculty members whenever she attends patients directly. Moreover, certain required courses might be dispensed with altogether for respondent. It is not necessary, she argues, that Southeastern train her to undertake all the tasks a registered nurse is licensed to perform. Rather, it is sufficient to make § 504 applicable if respondent might be able to perform satisfactorily some of the duties of a registered nurse or to hold some of the positions available to a registered nurse.

Respondent finds support for this argument in portions of the HEW regulations. In particular, a provision applicable to postsecondary educational programs requires covered institutions to make "modifications" in their programs to accommodate handicapped persons, and to provide "auxiliary aids" such as sign-language interpreters. Respondent argues that this regulation imposes an obligation to ensure full participation in covered programs by handicapped individuals and, in particular, requires Southeastern to make the kind of adjustments that would be necessary to permit her safe participation in the nursing program.

We note first that on the present record it appears unlikely respondent could benefit from any affirmative action that the regulation reasonably could be interpreted as requiring. Section 84.44(d)(2) [of the regulation], for example, explicitly excludes "devices or services of a personal nature" from the kinds of auxiliary aids a school must provide a handicapped individual. Yet the only evidence in the record indicates that nothing less than close, individual attention by a nursing instructor would be sufficient to ensure patient safety if respondent took part in the clinical phase of the nursing program. Furthermore, it also is reasonably clear that § 84.44(a) does not encompass the kind of curricular changes that would be necessary to accommodate respondent in the nursing program. In light of respondent's inability to function in clinical courses without close supervision, Southeastern, with prudence, could allow her to take only academic classes. Whatever benefits respondent might realize from such a course of study, she would not receive even a rough equivalent of the training a nursing program normally gives. Such a fundamental alteration in the nature of a program is far more than the "modification" the regulation requires.

Moreover, an interpretation of the regulations that required the extensive modifications necessary to include respondent in the nursing program would raise grave doubts about their validity. If these regulations were to require substantial adjustments in existing programs beyond those necessary to eliminate discrimination against otherwise qualified individuals, they would do more than clarify the meaning of § 504. Instead, they would constitute an unauthorized extension of the obligations imposed by that statute.

The language and structure of the Rehabilitation Act of 1973 reflect a recognition by Congress of the distinction between the evenhanded treatment of qualified handicapped persons and affirmative efforts to overcome the disabilities caused by handicaps. Section 501(b), governing the employment of handicapped individuals by the Federal Government, requires each federal agency to submit "an affirmative action program plan for the hiring, placement, and advancement of handicapped individuals. . . ." These plans "shall include a description of the extent to which and methods whereby the special needs of handicapped employees are being met." Similarly, § 503(a), governing hiring by federal contractors, requires employers to "take affirmative action to employ and advance in employment qualified handicapped individuals. . . ." The President is required to promulgate regulations to enforce this section.

Under § 501(c) of the Act, by contrast, state agencies such as Southeastern are only "encourage[d] . . . to adopt and implement such policies and procedures." Section 504 does not refer at all to affirmative action, and except as it applies to federal employers it does not provide for implementation by administrative action. A comparison of these provisions demonstrates that Congress understood accommodation of the needs of handicapped individuals may require affirmative action and knew how to provide for it in those instances where it wished to do so.

Although an agency's interpretation of the statute under which it operates is entitled to some deference, "this deference is constrained by our obligation to honor the clear meaning of a statute, as revealed by its language, purpose, and history." Here, neither the language, purpose, nor history of § 504 reveals an intent to impose an affirmative-action obligation on all recipients of federal funds. Accordingly, we hold that even if HEW has attempted to create such an obligation itself, it lacks the authority to do so.

IV

We do not suggest that the line between a lawful refusal to extend affirmative action and illegal discrimination against handicapped persons always will be clear. It is possible to envision situations where an insistence on continuing past requirements and practices might arbitrarily deprive genuinely qualified handicapped persons of the opportunity to participate in a covered program. Technological advances can be expected to enhance opportunities to rehabilitate the handicapped or otherwise to qualify them for some useful employment. Such advances also may enable attainment of these goals without imposing undue financial and administrative burdens upon a State. Thus, situations may arise where a refusal to modify an existing program might become unreasonable and discriminatory. Identification of those instances where a refusal to accommodate the needs of a disabled person amounts to discrimination against the handicapped continues to be an important responsibility of HEW.

In this case, however, it is clear that Southeastern's unwillingness to make major adjustments in its nursing program does not constitute such discrimination. The uncontroverted testimony of several members of Southeastern's staff and faculty established that the purpose of its program was to train persons who could serve the nursing profession in all customary ways. This type of purpose, far from reflecting any animus against handicapped individuals is shared by many if not most of the institutions that train persons to render professional service. It is undisputed that respondent could not participate in Southeastern's nursing program unless the standards were substantially lowered. Section 504 imposes no requirement upon an educational institution to lower or to effect substantial modifications of standards to accommodate a handicapped person.

One may admire respondent's desire and determination to overcome her handicap, and there well may be various other types of service for which she can qualify. In this case, however, we hold that there was no violation of § 504 when Southeastern concluded that respondent did not qualify for admission to its program. Nothing in the language or history of § 504 reflects an intention to limit the freedom of an educational institution to require reasonable physical qualifications for admission to a clinical training program. Nor has there been any showing in this case that any action short of a substantial change in Southeastern's program would render unreasonable the qualifications it imposed.

NOTES AND QUESTIONS

1. The Court states that "[a]n otherwise qualified person is one who is able to meet all of the program's requirements in spite of his handicap." Does this emasculate § 504? Can a person confined to a wheelchair be "excluded" from public transportation because of her inability to climb the steps?

2. The Court explains that "situations may arise where a refusal to modify an existing program might become unreasonable and discriminatory." How does this affect your response to question 1? Is cost an appropriate consideration, *e.g.*, if Davis could have fully participated in the nursing program with a sign-language interpreter (at a cost of $15,000 per year), does § 504 impose an obligation on the educational institution to provide such an interpreter? Would the school have to enroll Davis if she agreed to pay for the interpreter?

3. Compare the Court's analysis of § 504 with the statutory duty to accommodate disabilities under the ADA. How is the analysis different?

4. If Davis could fully participate in the educational program, but not the nursing profession, would her exclusion violate § 504? Could a law school exclude an applicant because of a disability that would preclude admission to the bar? Could a medical school exclude an applicant because of a disability that would preclude issuance of a license to practice medicine?

SCHOOL BOARD OF NASSAU COUNTY V. ARLINE
480 u.s. 273 (1987)

[Parts I-III of the opinion appear *supra* Ch. IV]

IV

The remaining question is whether Arline is otherwise qualified for the job of elementary school teacher. To answer this question in most cases, the District Court will need to conduct an individualized inquiry and make appropriate findings of fact. Such an inquiry is essential if § 504 is to achieve its goal of protecting handicapped individuals from deprivations based on prejudice, stereotypes, or unfounded fear, while giving appropriate weight to such legitimate concerns of grantees as avoiding exposing others to significant health and safety risks.[16] The basic factors to be considered in conducting this inquiry are well established.[17] In the context of the employment of a person handicapped with a contagious disease, we agree with amicus American Medical Association that this inquiry should include:

---

16 A person who poses a significant risk of communicating an infectious disease to others in the workplace will not be otherwise qualified for his or her job if reasonable accommodation will not eliminate that risk. The Act would not require a school board to place a teacher with active, contagious tuberculosis in a classroom with elementary school children.

17 "An otherwise qualified person is one who is able to meet all of the program's requirements in spite of his handicap." *Southeastern Community College v. Davis.* In the employment context, an otherwise qualified person is one who can perform "the essential functions" of the job in question. When a handicapped person is not able to perform the essential functions of the job, the court must also consider whether any "reasonable accommodation" by the employer would enable the handicapped person to perform those functions. Accommodation is not reasonable if it either imposes "undue financial and administrative burdens" on a grantee or requires "a fundamental alteration in the nature of the program."

[findings of] facts, based on reasonable medical judgments given the state of medical knowledge, about (a) the nature of the risk (how the disease is transmitted), (b) the duration of the risk (how long is the carrier infectious), (c) the severity of the risk (what is the potential harm to third parties) and (d) the probabilities the disease will be transmitted and will cause varying degrees of harm.

In making these findings, courts normally should defer to the reasonable medical judgments of public health officials. The next step in the "otherwise-qualified" inquiry is for the court to evaluate, in light of these medical findings, whether the employer could reasonably accommodate the employee under the established standards for that inquiry. *See supra*, note 17.

Because of the paucity of factual findings by the District Court, we, like the Court of Appeals, are unable at this stage of the proceedings to resolve whether Arline is "otherwise qualified" for her job. The District Court made no findings as to the duration and severity of Arline's condition, nor as to the probability that she would transmit the disease. Nor did the court determine whether Arline was contagious at the time she was discharged, or whether the School Board could have reasonably accommodated her.[19] Accordingly the resolution of whether Arline was otherwise qualified requires further findings of fact.

NOTES AND QUESTIONS

1. On remand the district court held that Arline was otherwise qualified for the job of elementary school teacher because tuberculosis was not easily communicated (her family members were not infected) and there was no medical evidence of "risk" after 1978. The court found she was entitled to full back pay plus benefits and reinstatement or front pay. 692 F. Supp. 1286 (M.D. Fla. 1988). If Arline's condition was infectious, would the school have to transfer her to another position?

2. A correctional officer at a county jail is diagnosed as having AIDS and promptly fired. Assuming the risk of transferring the disease to an inmate was real, but highly improbable, and that he was employed in a "program" receiving federal financial assistance, evaluate his claim under § 504. What arguments would you present on behalf of the defendant? Would the employer be required to transfer the officer to a desk job at the jail? What if no such job is available?

3. If a § 504 plaintiff is outside the definition of "individual with a disability" due to § 706(8)(D), does the court need to get to the "otherwise qualified" issue?

---

19 Employers have an affirmative obligation to make a reasonable accommodation for a handicapped employee. Although they are not required to find another job for an employee who is not qualified for the job he or she was doing, they cannot deny an employee alternative employment opportunities reasonably available under the employer's existing policies. See n. 17, *supra*.

ALEXANDER V. CHOATE
469 U.S. 287 (1985)

[The portion of the opinion addressing the intent/impact issue is found *supra* Ch. IV]

In 1980, Tennessee proposed reducing the number of annual days of inpatient hospital care covered by its state Medicaid program. The question presented is whether the effect upon the handicapped that this reduction will have is cognizable under § 504 of the Rehabilitation Act of 1973 or its implementing regulations. We hold that it is not.

III

To determine which disparate impacts § 504 might make actionable, the proper starting point is *Southeastern Community College v. Davis*, our major previous attempt to define the scope of § 504. *Davis* involved a plaintiff with a major hearing disability who sought admission to a college to be trained as a registered nurse, but who would not be capable of safely performing as a registered nurse even with fulltime personal supervision. [In *Davis* we] struck a balance between the statutory rights of the handicapped to be integrated into society and the legitimate interests of federal grantees in preserving the integrity of their programs: while a grantee need not be required to make "fundamental" or "substantial" modifications to accommodate the handicapped, it may be required to make "reasonable" ones.

The balance struck in *Davis* requires that an otherwise qualified handicapped individual must be provided with meaningful access to the benefit that the grantee offers. The benefit itself, of course, cannot be defined in a way that effectively denies otherwise qualified handicapped individuals the meaningful access to which they are entitled; to assure meaningful access, reasonable accommodations in the grantee's program or benefit may have to be made. In this case, respondents argue that the 14-day rule, or any annual durational limitation, denies meaningful access to Medicaid services in Tennessee.

A

The 14-day limitation will not deny respondents meaningful access to Tennessee Medicaid services or exclude them from those services. The new limitation does not invoke criteria that have a particular exclusionary effect on the handicapped; the reduction, neutral on its face, does not distinguish between those whose coverage will be reduced and those whose coverage will not on the basis of any test, judgment, or trait that the handicapped as a class are less capable of meeting or less likely of having. Moreover, it cannot be argued that "meaningful access" to state Medicaid services will be denied by the 14-day limitation on inpatient coverage; nothing in the record suggests that the handicapped in Tennessee will be unable to benefit meaningfully from the coverage they will receive under the 14-day rule.[22] The reduction in inpatient coverage will leave both handicapped and non-handicapped Medicaid users with identical and effective hospital services fully available for their use, with both classes of users subject to the same durational limitation. The 14-day limitation, therefore, does not exclude the handicapped from or deny them the benefits of the 14 days of care the State has chosen to provide.

To the extent respondents further suggest that their greater need for prolonged inpatient care means that, to provide meaningful access to Medicaid services, Tennessee must single out the handicapped for more than 14 days of coverage, the suggestion is simply unsound. At base, such a suggestion must rest on the notion that the benefit provided through state Medicaid programs is the amorphous objective of "adequate health care." But Medicaid programs do not guarantee that each recipient will receive that level of health care precisely tailored to his or her particular needs.

The federal Medicaid Act makes this point clear. The Act gives the States substantial discretion to choose the proper mix of amount, scope, and duration limitations on coverage, as long as care and services are provided in "the best interests of the recipients." The District Court found that the 14-day limitation would fully serve 95% of even handicapped individuals eligible for Tennessee Medicaid, and both lower courts concluded that Tennessee's proposed Medicaid plan would meet the "best interests" standard. That unchallenged conclusion indicates that Tennessee is free, as a matter of the Medicaid Act, to choose to define the benefit it will be providing as 14 days of inpatient coverage.

Section 504 seeks to assure evenhanded treatment and the opportunity for handicapped individuals to participate in and benefit from programs receiving federal assistance. The Act does not, however, guarantee the handicapped equal results from the provision of state Medicaid, even assuming some measure of equality of health could be constructed.

B

[N]othing in the pre- or post-1973 legislative discussion of § 504 suggests that Congress desired to make major inroads on the States' longstanding discretion to choose the proper mix of amount, scope, and duration limitations on services covered by state Medicaid.

The costs of such a requirement would be far from minimal, and thus Tennessee's refusal to pursue this course does not, as respondents suggest, inflict a "gratuitous" harm on the handicapped. On the contrary, to require that the sort of broad-based distributive decision at issue in this case always be made in the way most favorable, or least disadvantageous, to the handicapped, even when the same benefit is meaningfully and equally offered to them, would be to impose a virtually unworkable requirement on state Medicaid administrators.

---

22 The record does not contain any suggestion that the illnesses uniquely associated with the handicapped or occurring with greater frequency among them cannot be effectively treated, at least in part, with fewer than 14 days coverage. In addition, the durational limitation does not apply to only particular handicapped conditions and takes effect regardless of the particular cause of hospitalization.

It should be obvious that administrative costs of implementing such a regime would be well beyond the accommodations that are required under *Davis*. As a result, Tennessee need not redefine its Medicaid program to eliminate durational limitations on inpatient coverage, even if in doing so the State could achieve its immediate fiscal objectives in a way less harmful to the handicapped.

IV

The 14-day rule challenged in this case is neutral on its face, is not alleged to rest on a discriminatory motive, and does not deny the handicapped access to or exclude them from the particular package of Medicaid services Tennessee has chosen to provide. The State has made the same benefit—14 days of coverage—equally accessible to both handicapped and non-handicapped persons, and the State is not required to assure the handicapped "adequate health care" by providing them with more coverage than the non-handicapped. In addition, the State is not obligated to modify its Medicaid program by abandoning reliance on annual durational limitations on inpatient coverage. Assuming, then, that § 504 or its implementing regulations reach some claims of disparate-impact discrimination, the effect of Tennessee's reduction in annual inpatient coverage is not among them. For that reason, the Court of Appeals erred in holding that respondents had established a *prima facie* violation of § 504.

NOTES AND QUESTIONS

1. Does the 14-day limitation have a disparate impact on disabled individuals? Do the disabled have meaningful access to hospital care? Would the result have been different if the "program" was limited to 5 days despite a statistical showing that 75% of all disabled users of hospital services who received Medicaid required more than 5 days of care? Why?

2. Given the statistics cited in the opinion, do the disabled, in light of the 14-day limit, have equal access to hospital care in Tennessee? Why does § 504 not require Tennessee to extend coverage for the handicapped to the point where only 7.8% of the handicapped would require an additional period of inpatient care?

3. If Tennessee excluded from Medicaid coverage (for hospital care) a condition which affects only certain handicapped persons, would there be a violation of § 504? *See* footnote 22.

4. Title II of the ADA, 42 U.S.C. § 12131, *et seq.*, prohibits discrimination against individuals with disabilities in public services furnished by state and local government entities. Enforcement of Title II is in accordance with § 504. 42 U.S.C. § 12203. In *Olmstead v. L.C.,* 527 U.S. 581 (1999), the Court held that Title II requires states "to

provide community-based treatment for persons with mental disabilities when the State's treatment professionals determine that such placement is appropriate, the affected persons do not oppose such treatment, and the placement can be reasonably accommodated, taking into account the resources available to the State and the needs of others with mental disabilities."

3. EMPLOYMENT

After *Darrone, supra* Ch. IV, there is no longer any doubt that § 504 applies to employment. Pursuant to 29 U.S.C. § 794(d), the "standards used to determine whether this section has been violated in a complaint alleging employment discrimination under this section shall be the standards applied under Title I of the Americans with Disabilities Act." In addition to § 504 there are two sections of the Rehabilitation Act of 1973 which relate specifically to employment. Section 503 of the Act, 29 U.S.C. § 793, provides that all federal contracts in excess of $10,000, for the procurement of personal property and nonpersonal services, must "contain a provision requiring that the party contracting with the United States shall take affirmative action to employ and advance in employment qualified individuals with disabilities." This section is to be enforced through the Department of Labor, 29 U.S.C. § 793(b), and the courts have generally held that it does not give rise to a private cause of action. *See, e.g., D'amato v. Wisconsin Gas Co.*, 760 F.2d 1474, 1478 (7th Cir. 1985) (indicating that eight other circuits agree); *Jones v. United Parcel Service, Inc.*, 378 F. Supp. 2d 1312, 1313–14 (D. Kan. 2005).

Section 501 of the Act, 29 U.S.C. § 791(b), imposes an obligation on federal agencies to adopt affirmative action plans to insure that individuals with a disability have equal access to employment opportunities in these agencies. In contrast to § 503, § 501 can be enforced through private actions under § 505 of the Act, 29 U.S.C. § 794a, which sets forth the remedial scheme for § 504. While the interpretation of § 501 is generally consistent with the interpretation of § 504, § 501 and its implementing regulations require affirmative steps to accommodate the individuals with a disability. If such an individual is not qualified to perform the essential requirements of a job without the risk of injury to others, then it must be determined whether a "reasonable accommodation [can] be made, without undue hardship to the employer, sufficient to enable the applicant to perform the essential requirements of the job without a reasonable probability of substantial injury to the applicant or others." *Mantolete v. Bolger*, 767 F.2d 1416, 1423 (9th Cir. 1985).

LUCERO, Circuit Judge.

Clarice Sanchez, a long-time secretarial employee of the United States Forest Service ("Forest Service"), suffered irreversible brain damage after falling at work. As a result of her injury, Sanchez lost the left half of her field of vision. She requested a hardship transfer to Albuquerque, New Mexico, where she could better access ongoing medical treatment. After the Forest Service declined to accommodate her request, she brought suit under the Rehabilitation Act, 29 U.S.C. § 791. The district court granted summary judgment in favor of the Forest Service, concluding that Sanchez was not disabled within the meaning of the Act. We disagree and hold that Sanchez has raised a genuine issue of material fact regarding her disability. On appeal, the Forest Service urges us to affirm summary judgment on an alternative ground. However, we decline this invitation because we conclude that transfer accommodations for the purpose of medical treatment or therapy are not unreasonable per se.

I

While newly stationed in the Lufkin, Texas Forest Service office, Sanchez fell down a flight of stairs at work. She suffered irreversible brain damage, which caused a complete homonymous hemianopsia—a permanent injury to the nerves that transmit images from the eyes to the brain. As a result of this injury, Sanchez has only 50 percent of the total visual field in each eye. She is unable to see objects to the left line of center when her eyes are focused ahead. According to the American Medical Association, a complete homonymous hemianopsia is as disabling as a visual acuity loss to 20/200. Sanchez's vision loss is permanent and cannot be improved by lenses or surgery.

After seven weeks of recovery, Sanchez returned to work. Shortly thereafter, she requested a hardship transfer to the Albuquerque, New Mexico office because no doctors in Lufkin were qualified to provide specialized therapy to help her adjust to her injury. Sanchez also explained that she needed the support of her family and friends in Albuquerque and noted the lack of public transportation in Lufkin.

Although neither party contends that Sanchez was unable to perform her job, the record suggests that she experienced difficulties at work due to her condition. Sanchez testified that she struggled with reading, in part because her condition causes her to focus on the center of the page rather than starting at the left side of the page. Sanchez found reading numbers especially difficult and had to check her assignments several times to avoid errors. Because Sanchez could not tolerate bright lighting, the Forest Service provided her with special lights and an office in which she could adjust them. In addition, Sanchez suffered eye strain which prevented her from working on the computer or reading for more than forty-five minutes at a time. Transportation to the office was also a challenge. Family and friends initially helped to drive Sanchez; but she eventually began driving herself to work despite her doctor's orders, relying on back roads and otherwise avoiding traffic.

Sanchez's immediate supervisor in Lufkin made several inquiries about open positions in Albuquerque, to no avail. In September 2003, the Forest Service assigned Sanchez to a 120-day detail in Albuquerque. During this time, Sanchez saw a specialist who helped her learn techniques to make reading easier. But Forest Service employees in Albuquerque felt that Sanchez was disruptive and inefficient. They informed the Deputy Regional Forester that Sanchez's performance was unsatisfactory and at least one recommended that she not be permanently assigned to the Albuquerque office. Sanchez was not selected for either of two equivalent-pay positions in Albuquerque for which she met the minimum qualifications according to an agency computer system.

Back in Lufkin, Sanchez's work environment allegedly began to deteriorate. According to Sanchez, her supervisor and coworkers mocked her brain injury saying that she was "crazy," "not all there," and "not right in the head." She also alleges that her supervisor made gestures to this effect. Thus, in 2006, Sanchez took a pay cut to accept an accounting technician position with the Forest Service in Albuquerque.

She then filed this suit in federal district court, alleging that the Forest Service discriminated against her in violation of the Rehabilitation Act by failing to accommodate her and by subjecting her to a hostile work environment. After a period of discovery, both parties moved for summary judgment. In its motion, the Forest Service argued that Sanchez's impairment did not substantially limit her so as to qualify as a disability under the Rehabilitation Act. Sanchez provided deposition testimony and an affidavit describing the impact of the hemianopsia on her ability to see. She also submitted expert medical testimony from Dr. Clark Watts based on a review of her medical records. The district court, however, agreed with the Forest Service that Sanchez was not substantially limited by her impairment. It accordingly granted summary judgment in favor of the defendant and denied Sanchez's motion. Because the court determined that Sanchez was not disabled within the meaning of the Act, it did not resolve the Forest Service's argument in response to Sanchez's motion that the requested transfer accommodation fell outside of the scope of the Rehabilitation Act. Sanchez now appeals the district court's decision to grant summary judgment in favor of the Forest Service.

II

The Rehabilitation Act prohibits the federal government from discriminating against an "otherwise qualified individual with a disability." Part of the government's obligation is to provide reasonable accommodations to disabled employees. To prevail on a failure-to-accommodate claim a plaintiff must demonstrate that: (1) she is disabled; (2) she is "otherwise qualified"; and (3) she requested a plausibly reasonable accommodation. We review de novo the district court's determination that Sanchez failed to create a genuine dispute of fact on the first prong.

A

A "disability" is a "physical or mental impairment that substantially limits one or more major life activities." To prove that she is disabled, Sanchez must: (1) have a recognized impairment; (2) identify one or more appropriate major life activities; and (3) show that the impairment substantially limits one or more of those activities. "Whether a plaintiff has met the first two requirements are questions of law for the court. But whether the impairment substantially limits a major life activity is ordinarily a question of fact for the jury."

There is no dispute that Sanchez has a recognized impairment or that the life activity she has identified—seeing—falls within the Act. We thus focus on whether Sanchez has demonstrated at least a genuine dispute of material fact as to whether her condition "substantially limits" her ability to see. We conclude that she has done so.

An impairment is substantially limiting when it renders an individual significantly restricted in her ability to perform a major life activity "compared to the average person in the general population." In conducting this analysis, courts must take into account: (1) the nature and severity of the impairment; (2) the expected duration of the impairment; and (3) the permanent or long term impact resulting from the impairment.

As this definition suggests, it is not sufficient for a plaintiff to identify an impairment and leave the court to infer that it results in substantial limitations to a major life activity. At the summary judgment stage, Sanchez must point to some evidence showing that her impairment limits her seeing or some other major life activity. For a visually impaired plaintiff, this might include evidence of "loss of depth perception," "degree of visual acuity," "age at which [the individuals] suffered their vision loss," "extent of ... compensating adjustments in visual techniques," or the "ultimate scope of restrictions on visual abilities." Nonetheless, Sanchez's burden is not an "onerous" one. The ADA and Rehabilitation Acts "address[ ] substantial limitations on major life activities, not utter inabilities."

Applying these principles, we conclude that summary judgment was inappropriate. Sanchez provided a great deal of evidence attesting to the manner in which homonymous hemianopsia limited her ability to see as compared to the average person. Sanchez testified that her field of vision when looking straight ahead was half of what she could see prior to the injury. Sanchez additionally averred—and medical experts confirmed—that her vision loss is permanent and cannot be improved by lenses or surgery. Dr. Watts stated that individuals who suffer from a homonymous hemianopsia find it difficult to accommodate for their loss of vision, instead ignoring the side of their bodies on which the vision is lost.

According to the Forest Service, Sanchez can correct for her impairment by turning her head. But turning one's head merely shifts one's field of vision. Even with such adjustments, Sanchez's field of vision remains significantly limited in comparison to the average person. Thus, unlike some visually impaired individuals for whom corrective lenses are a solution, the record does not reveal any mitigating measures available to Sanchez that would allow her to "function identically to individuals without a similar impairment."

This evidence is sufficient to send to the jury the question of whether Sanchez was "substantially limited" in her ability to see as compared to the average person. However, Sanchez also submitted evidence showing that her limited ability to see rendered other aspects of her life more "difficult, slower, and more dangerous." She described challenges in reading and performing basic financial math. She testified to her tendency "to injure [her]self while performing basic cleaning and maintenance" at home, and explained that she relied on her daughter to fly from Albuquerque to Lufkin every few weeks to assist her with shopping and other tasks. She also presented evidence that it was unsafe for her to drive, and that she did so—against doctor's orders—only when and where she could avoid traffic.

Concluding that Sanchez was not disabled as a matter of law, the district court relied on the fact that she drives despite doctor's orders, reads with some difficulty, is "able to care for herself," and "walks and bicycles on a regular basis." This analysis misses the mark. The question is not whether Sanchez can do many of the same activities a person who is not visually impaired takes for granted. Rather, we must focus on the major life activity Sanchez has identified—seeing—and determine whether she has shown "the [substantial] extent of the limitation" on that activity "in terms of [her] own experience." We conclude that Sanchez has produced ample evidence that "the manner in which" she sees is substantially limited as compared to the average individual.

B

In the alternative, the Forest Service argues that the judgment of the district court should be affirmed because the Rehabilitation Act does not contemplate transfer accommodations for employees who require medical treatment despite being able to perform the essential functions of their jobs.

As an initial matter, we reject the Forest Service's suggestion that transfer accommodations are generally "not mandatory." This court has plainly held that "a reasonable accommodation may include reassignment to a vacant position if the employee is qualified for the job and it does not impose an undue burden on the employer."

Nevertheless, this circuit has thus far required transfer accommodations only if an employee, "because of disability, can no longer perform the essential functions of the job that she or he has held." We must therefore consider whether transfers for medical treatment also fall within the Rehabilitation Act's ambit. Several of our sibling circuits have concluded that the Act contemplates such accommodations.

The Seventh Circuit has perhaps the most expansive jurisprudence on point. That court has held that accommodations may be required to allow an employee to: "(1) perform the essential functions of the job in question, (2) pursue therapy or treatment for their handicap, or (3) enjoy the privileges and benefits of employment equal to those enjoyed by non-handicapped employees." Fedro v. Reno, 21 F.3d 1391, 1395–96 (7th Cir. 1994).

The Ninth's Circuit's decision in *Buckingham v. United States*, 998 F.2d 735 (9th Cir. 1993) is most analogous to the case at hand. There, a federal postal service worker with HIV requested a transfer from Columbus, Mississippi to a post office in Los Angeles where he could obtain medical treatment for his condition. Over the government's objection, the Ninth Circuit held that the transfer was not precluded from being a reasonable accommodation as a matter of law. In so holding, the court expressly rejected the argument that Buckingham's request was unreasonable because it was "not tied to his ability to perform the essential functions of his job."

Regulations promulgated by the Equal Employment Opportunity Commission ("EEOC") support our sibling circuits' interpretation. According to the EEOC, disability law cognizes not only those reasonable accommodations that "enable an individual with a disability who is qualified to perform the essential functions of that position," but also those that "enable a[n] ... employee with a disability to enjoy equal benefits and privileges of employment that are enjoyed by ... other similarly-situated employees without disabilities." 29 C.F.R. § 1630.2(*o*)(ii) & (iii). Accordingly, the EEOC interpretive regulations contemplate accommodations that are wholly unrelated to the essential functions of a job. An employer's duty to modify the work environment, for example, "even applies to nonwork facilities ... such as restrooms and break rooms." These regulations comport with this court's insistence that "[f]or federal employers, nondiscrimination requires more than mere 'equal treatment' of disabled employees and job applicants, and encompasses an affirmative duty to meet the needs of disabled workers and to broaden their employment opportunities."

Considering the case law from this court and others, we conclude that a transfer accommodation for medical care or treatment is not per se unreasonable, even if an employee is able to perform the essential functions of her job without it. An employer may, of course, avoid obligation under the Act by showing that a requested accommodation is an undue burden in a particular case. The Forest Service, however, has not argued below or before this court that transferring Sanchez would have imposed such a burden. Accordingly, we do not address this question. For the same reason, we do not opine as to whether reassignment was necessary for Sanchez to access treatment. Without resolving the reasonableness of a transfer accommodation in this particular case, we hold as a matter of law that transferring an employee for the purposes of treatment or therapy may be a reasonable accommodation under the Rehabilitation Act.

NOTES AND QUESTIONS

1. Why did the court reverse the district court's holding that Sanchez was not an "individual with a disability" within the meaning of the Act?

2. What was the basis for Sanchez's "failure to accommodate" claim? What will the Forest Service have to prove to avoid liability?

PROBLEM: THIRTY-TWO

Treadwell is a retired Air Force colonel, rated by the Veteran's Administration as being 100 percent disabled. It based this rating primarily on two handicaps, a nervous condition and a heart condition. In February 1979 Treadwell had quadruple coronary bypass surgery and a pacemaker was implanted. Shortly thereafter he sought a job with the Corps of Engineers as a seasonal park technician at Clark's Hill Lake in South Carolina.

After numerous internal communications, medical examinations and reports, and discussions of the job's requirements, an Office of Personnel Management medical officer approved the Corps' request to pass over Treadwell, citing his coronary bypass and use of a pacemaker.

The district court concluded Treadwell was unable to perform the essential functions of the job. Treadwell contends the district court did not require the Corps to show that the physical and environmental criteria were job related. Specifically, he asserts that neither the Corps nor the court enumerated precisely which duties he could not perform, failed to consider that the single activity consuming the vast majority of a park technician's time is fee collection, and overlooked the fact that 90 percent of the time on the job is spent traveling from campsite to campsite. The court's findings of fact, however, referred to a doctor's deposition testimony that he did not believe Treadwell could safely perform such duties as operating a motor boat alone, walking over rough terrain, or handling disorderly park visitors. The court's opinion concluded that the plaintiff could not physically perform other essential functions such as working alone. Thomas Lewis, the supervisor of park technicians, testified that each of the functional and environmental factors is essential to the position for which Treadwell applied at Clark's Hill Lake. Furthermore, the essential nature of a particular job function is not determined solely by the amount of time devoted to it. That a technician might be called upon to operate a motor boat alone only occasionally does not make that job function any less essential or make it unrelated to the job.

Finally, Treadwell argues that by using an improper standard to define the term "otherwise qualified individual," the district court failed to require the defendants to sufficiently show that reasonable accommodations either could not be made or would pose an undue hardship on the employer.

1. How does a plaintiff establish a prima facie case under § 504 and did Treadwell do so? What is the significance of the fact that Treadwell is able to perform around 95% of the job, but may not be able to safely perform 5%? How does the § 504 inquiry regarding qualifications differ from the Title VII inquiry?

2. If the plaintiff establishes a *prima facie* case, what burden shifts to the defendant? Did the defendant meet its burden here?

3. If the defendant is successful in meeting its burden, what must the plaintiff establish in order to prevail?

4. Would your answers to the first three questions differ if Treadwell had filed his action under the ADA? Explain.

5. Compare the employer's duty to accommodate under the Rehabilitation Act with the duty in Title VII cases where the plaintiff alleges discrimination based on religion.

Appendix

FEDERAL STATUTES

TITLE IX OF EDUCATION AMENDMENTS OF 1972

20 U.S.C. § 1681 [§ 901]

§ 1681. Sex

(a) **Prohibition against discrimination; exceptions.** No person in the United States shall, on the basis of sex, be excluded from participation in, be denied the benefits of, or be subjected to discrimination under any education program or activity receiving Federal financial assistance, except that:

(1) **Classes of educational institutions subject to prohibition.** In regard to admissions to educational institutions, this section shall apply only to institutions of vocational education, professional education, and graduate higher education, and to public institutions of undergraduate higher education;

(2) **Educational institutions commencing planned change in admissions.** In regard to admissions to educational institutions, this section shall not apply (A) for one year from June 23, 1972, nor for six years after June 23, 1972, in the case of an educational institution which has begun the process of changing from being an institution which admits only students of one sex to being an institution which admits students of both sexes, but only if it is carrying out a plan for such a change which is approved by the Secretary of Education or (B) for seven years from the date an educational institution begins the process of changing from being an institution which admits only students of only one sex to being an institution which admits students of both sexes, but only if it is carrying out a plan for such a change which is approved by the Secretary of Education, whichever is the later;

(3) **Educational institutions of religious organizations with contrary religious tenets.** This section shall not apply to an educational institution which is controlled by a religious organization if the application of this subsection would not be consistent with the religious tenets of such organization;

(4) **Educational institutions training individuals for military services or merchant marine.** This section shall not apply to an educational institution whose primary purpose is the training of individuals for the military services of the United States, or the merchant marine;

(5) Public educational institutions with traditional and continuing admissions policy. In regard to admissions this section shall not apply to any public institution of undergraduate higher education which is an institution that traditionally and continually from its establishment has had a policy of admitting only students of one sex;

(6) Social fraternities or sororities; voluntary youth service organizations. This section shall not apply to membership practices–

    (A) of a social fraternity or social sorority which is exempt from taxation under section 501(a) of Title 26, the active membership of which consists primarily of students in attendance at an institution of higher education, or

    (B) of the Young Men's Christian Association, Young Women's Christian Association, Girl Scouts, Boy Scouts, Camp Fire Girls, and voluntary youth service organizations which are so exempt, the membership of which has traditionally been limited to persons of one sex and principally to persons of less than nineteen years of age;

*   *   *

(b) Preferential or disparate treatment because of imbalance in participation or receipt of Federal benefits; statistical evidence of imbalance. Nothing contained in subsection (a) of this section shall be interpreted to require any educational institution to grant preferential or disparate treatment to the members of one sex on account of an imbalance which may exist with respect to the total number or percentage of persons of that sex participating in or receiving the benefits of any federally supported program or activity, in comparison with the total number or percentage of persons of that sex in any community, State, section, or other area: Provided, That this subsection shall not be construed to prevent the consideration in any hearing or proceeding under this chapter of statistical evidence tending to show that such an imbalance exists with respect to the participation in, or receipt of the benefits of, any such program or activity by the members of one sex.

(c) Educational institution defined. For purposes of this chapter an educational institution means any public or private preschool, elementary, or secondary school, or any institution of vocational, professional, or higher education, except that in the case of an educational institution composed of more than one school, college, or department which are administratively separate units, such term means each such school, college, or department.

20 U.S.C. § 1682 [§ 902]

§ 1682. Federal administrative enforcement; report to Congressional committees.

[same as 42 U.S.C. § 2000d-1, infra]

20 U.S.C. § 1687 [§ 908]

§ 1687. Interpretation of "program or activity."

[same as 42 U.S.C. § 2000d-4a, *infra*, with the following addition]

except that such term does not include any operation of an entity which is controlled by a religious organization if the application of section 1681 of this title to such operation would not be consistent with the religious tenets of such organization.

20 U.S.C. § 1688 [§ 909]

§ 1688. Neutrality with respect to abortion

Nothing in this chapter shall be construed to require or prohibit any person, or public or private entity, to provide or pay for any benefit or service, including the use of facilities, related to an abortion. Nothing in this section shall be construed to permit a penalty to be imposed on any person or individual because such person or individual is seeking or has received any benefit or service related to a legal abortion.

FAIR LABOR STANDARDS ACT

(PROVISIONS RELEVANT TO EPA AND ADEA)

29 U.S.C. § 203(d), (e), (r) & (s)

§ 203. Definitions

As used in this chapter–

(d) "Employer" includes any person acting directly or indirectly in the interest of an employer in relation to an employee and includes a public agency, but does not include any labor organization (other than when acting as an employer) or anyone acting in the capacity of officer or agent of such labor organization.

(e) (1) Except as provided in paragraphs (2), (3), and (4) the term "employee" means any individual employed by an employer.
(2) In the case of an individual employed by a public agency, such term means–(A) any individual employed by the Government of the United States–(i) as a civilian in the military

departments (as defined in section 102 of Title 5), **(ii)** in any executive agency (as defined in section 105 of such title), **(iii)** in any unit of the judicial branch of the Government which has positions in the competitive service, **(iv)** in a nonappropriated fund instrumentality under the jurisdiction of the Armed Forces, **(v)** in the Library of Congress or, **(vi)** the Government Publishing Office; **(B)** any individual employed by the United States Postal Service or the Postal Regulatory Commission; and **(C)** any individual employed by a State, political subdivision of a State, or an interstate governmental agency, other than such an individual–**(i)** who is not subject to the civil service laws of the State, political subdivision, or agency which employs him; and **(ii)** who–**(I)** holds a public elective office of that State, political subdivision, or agency, **(II)** is selected by the holder of such an office to be a member of his personal staff, **(III)** is appointed by such an officeholder to serve on a policymaking level, **(IV)** is an immediate adviser to such an officeholder with respect to the constitutional or legal powers of his office, or **(V)** is an employee in the legislative branch or legislative body of that State, political subdivision, or agency and is not employed by the legislative library of such State, political subdivision, or agency.

(3) For purposes of subsection (u) of this section, such term does not include any individual employed by an employer engaged in agriculture if such individual is the parent, spouse, child, or other member of the employer's immediate family.

*   *   *

(r) **(1)** "Enterprise" means the related activities performed (either through unified operation or common control) by any person or persons for a common business purpose, and includes all such activities whether performed in one or more establishments or by one or more corporate or other organizational units including departments of an establishment operated through leasing arrangements, but shall not include the related activities performed for such enterprise by an independent contractor. Within the meaning of this subsection, a retail or service establishment which is under independent ownership shall not be deemed to be so operated or controlled as to be other than a separate and distinct enterprise by reason of any arrangement, which includes, but is not necessarily limited to, an agreement **(A)** that it will sell, or sell only, certain goods specified by a particular manufacturer, distributor, or advertiser, or **(B)** that it will join with other such establishments in the same industry for the purpose of collective purchasing, or **(C)** that it will have the exclusive right to sell the goods or use the brand name of a manufacturer, distributor, or advertiser within a specified area, or by reason of the fact that it occupies premises leased to it by a person who also leases premises to other retail or service establishments.

(2) For purposes of paragraph (1), the activities performed by any person or persons–(A) in connection with the operation of a hospital, an institution primarily engaged in the care of the sick, the aged, the mentally ill or defective who reside on the premises of such institution, a school for mentally or physically handicapped or gifted children, a preschool, elementary or secondary school, or an institution of higher education (regardless of whether or not such hospital, institution, or school is operated for profit or not for profit), or (B) in connection with the operation of a street, suburban or interurban electric railway, or local trolley or motorbus carrier, if the rates and services of such railway or carrier are subject to regulation by a State or local agency (regardless of whether or not such railway or carrier is public or private or operated for profit or not for profit), or (C) in connection with the activities of a public agency, shall be deemed to be activities performed for a business purpose.

(s) (1) "Enterprise engaged in commerce or in the production of goods for commerce" means an enterprise that—(A)(i) has employees engaged in commerce or in the production of goods for commerce, or that has employees handling, selling, or otherwise working on goods or materials that have been moved in or produced for commerce by any person; and (ii) is an enterprise whose annual gross volume of sales made or business done is not less than $500,000 (exclusive of excise taxes at the retail level that are separately stated); (B) is engaged in the operation of a hospital, an institution primarily engaged in the care of the sick, the aged, or the mentally ill or defective who reside on the premises of such institution, a school for mentally or physically handicapped or gifted children, a preschool, elementary or secondary school, or an institution of higher education (regardless of whether or not such hospital, institution, or school is public or private or operated for profit or not for profit); or (C) is an activity of a public agency.

(2) Any establishment that has as its only regular employees the owner thereof or the parent, spouse, child or other member of the immediate family of such owner shall not be considered to be an enterprise engaged in commerce or in the production of goods for commerce or a part of such an enterprise. The sales of such an establishment shall not be included for the purpose of determining the annual gross volume of sales of any enterprise for the purpose of this subsection.

29 U.S.C. § 213(a)(3), (8) & (10)

§ 213. Exemptions

(a) Minimum wage and maximum hour requirements.

The provisions of section 206 (except subsection (d) in the case of paragraph (1) of this subsection) and section 207 of this title shall not apply with respect to–

* * *

(3) any employee employed by an establishment which is an amusement or recreational establishment, organized camp, or religious or nonprofit educational conference center, if (A) it does not operate for more than seven months in any calendar year, or (B) during the preceding calendar year, its average receipts for any six months of such year were not more than 33 1/3 per centum of its average receipts for the other six months of such year, except

that the exemption from sections 206 and 207 of this title provided by this paragraph does not apply with respect to any employee of a private entity engaged in providing services or facilities (other than, in the case of the exemption from section 206 of this title, a private entity engaged in providing services and facilities directly related to skiing) in a national park or a national forest, or on land in the National Wildlife Refuge System, under a contract with the Secretary of the Interior or the Secretary of Agriculture; or

* * *

(8) any employee employed in connection with the publication of any weekly, semiweekly, or daily newspaper with a circulation of less than four thousand the major part of which circulation is within the county where published or counties contiguous thereto; or

* * *

(10) any switchboard operator employed by an independently owned public telephone company which has not more than seven hundred and fifty stations;

* * *

29 U.S.C. § 215

§ 215. Prohibited acts; prima facie evidence.

(a) After the expiration of one hundred and twenty days from June 25, 1938, it shall be unlawful for any person–

* * *

(3) to discharge or in any other manner discriminate against any employee because such employee has filed any complaint or instituted or caused to be instituted any proceeding under or related to this chapter, or has testified or is about to testify in any such proceeding, or has served or is about to serve on an industry committee;

* * *

29 U.S.C. § 216(b)

§ 216. Penalties

* * *

(b) Damages; right of action; attorney fees and costs; termination of right of action.
Any employer who violates the provisions of section 206 or section 207 of this title shall be liable to the employee or employees affected in the amount of their unpaid minimum wages, or their unpaid overtime compensation, as the case may be, and in an additional equal amount as liquidated damages. Any employer who violates the provisions of section 215(a)(3) of this title shall be liable for such legal or equitable relief as may be appropriate to effectuate the purposes of section 215(a)(3) of this title, including without limitation employment, reinstatement, promotion, and the payment of wages lost and an additional equal amount as liquidated damages. An action to recover the liability prescribed in the preceding sentences may be maintained against any employer (including a public agency) in any Federal or State court of competent jurisdiction by any one or more employees for and in behalf of himself or themselves and other employees similarly situated. No employee shall be a party plaintiff to any such action unless he gives his consent in writing to become such a party and such consent is filed in the court in which such action is brought. The court in such action shall, in addition to any judgment awarded to the plaintiff or plaintiffs, allow a reasonable attorney's fee to be paid by the defendant, and costs of the action. . . .

(c) The Secretary is authorized to supervise the payment of the unpaid minimum wages or the unpaid overtime compensation owing to any employee or employees under section 206 or section 207 of this title, and the agreement of any employee to accept such payment shall upon payment in full constitute a waiver by such employee of any right he may have under subsection (b) of this section to such unpaid minimum wages or unpaid overtime compensation and an additional equal amount as liquidated damages. The Secretary may bring an action in any court of competent jurisdiction to recover the amount of unpaid minimum wages or overtime compensation and an equal amount as liquidated damages. The right provided by subsection (b) of this section to bring an action by or on behalf of any employee to recover the liability specified in the first sentence of such subsection and of any employee to become a party plaintiff to any such action shall terminate upon the filing of a complaint by the Secretary in an action under this subsection in which a recovery is sought of unpaid minimum wages or unpaid overtime compensation under sections 206 and 207 of this title or liquidated or other damages provided by this subsection owing to such employee by an employer liable under the provisions of subsection (b) of this section, unless such action is dismissed without prejudice on motion of the Secretary. Any sums thus recovered by the Secretary of Labor on behalf of an employee pursuant to this subsection shall be held in a special deposit account and shall be paid, on order of the Secretary of Labor, directly to the employee or employees affected. Any such sums not paid to an employee because of inability to do so within a period of three years shall be covered into the Treasury of the United States as miscellaneous receipts. In determining when an action is commenced by the Secretary of Labor under this subsection for the purposes of the statutes of limitations provided in section 255(a) of this title, it shall be considered to be commenced in the case of any individual claimant on the date when the complaint is filed if he is specifically named as a party plaintiff in the complaint, or if his name did not so appear, on the subsequent date on which his name is added as a party plaintiff in such action.

* * *

29 U.S.C. § 217

§ 217. Injunction proceedings

The district courts, together with the United States District Court for the District of the Canal Zone, the District Court of the Virgin Islands, and the District Court of Guam shall have jurisdiction, for cause shown, to restrain violations of section 215 of this title, including in the case of violations of section 215(a)(2) of this title the restraint of any withholding of payment of minimum wages or overtime compensation found by the court to be due to employees under this chapter (except sums which employees are barred from recovering, at the time of the commencement of the action to restrain the violations, by virtue of the provisions of section 255 of this title).

29 U.S.C. § 255

§ 255. Statute of limitations

Any action commenced on or after May 14, 1947, to enforce any cause of action for unpaid minimum wages, unpaid overtime compensation, or liquidated damages, under the Fair Labor Standards Act of 1938, . . .

(a) if the cause of action accrues on or after May 14, 1947—may be commenced within two years after the cause of action accrued, . . . except that a cause of action arising out of a willful violation may be commenced within three years after the cause of action accrued;

* * *

§ 260. Liquidated damages

In any action commenced prior to or on or after May 14, 1947 to recover unpaid minimum wages, unpaid overtime compensation, or liquidated damages, under the Fair Labor Standards Act of 1938, as amended [29 U.S.C. § 201 *et seq.*], if the employer shows to the satisfaction of the court that the act or omission giving rise to such action was in good faith and that he had reasonable grounds for believing that his act or omission was not a violation of the Fair Labor Standards Act of 1938, as amended, the court may, in its sound discretion, award no liquidated damages or award any amount thereof not to exceed the amount specified in section 216 of this title.

EQUAL PAY ACT

29 U.S.C. § 206(d)

§ 206(d)(1). Prohibition of sex discrimination

(d) **(1)** No employer having employees subject to any provisions of this section shall discriminate, within any establishment in which such employees are employed, between employees on the basis of sex by paying wages to employees in such establishment at a rate less than the rate at which he pays wages to employees of the opposite sex in such establishment for equal work on jobs the performance of which requires equal skill, effort, and responsibility, and which are performed under similar working conditions, except where such payment is made pursuant to **(i)** a seniority system; **(ii)** a merit system; **(iii)** a system which measures earnings by quantity or quality of production; or **(iv)** a differential based on any other factor other than sex: *Provided*, That an employer who is paying a wage rate differential in violation of this subsection shall not, in order to comply with the provisions of this subsection, reduce the wage rate of any employee.

(2) No labor organization, or its agents, representing employees of an employer having employees subject to any provisions of this section shall cause or attempt to cause such an employer to discriminate against an employee in violation of paragraph (1) of this subsection.

(3) For purposes of administration and enforcement, any amounts owing to any employee which have been withheld in violation of this subsection shall be deemed to be unpaid minimum wages or unpaid overtime compensation under this chapter.

(4) As used in this subsection, the term "labor organization" means any organization of any kind, or any agency or employee representation committee or plan, in which employees participate and which exists for the purpose, in whole or in part, of dealing with employers concerning grievances, labor disputes, wages, rates of pay, hours of employment, or conditions of work.

AGE DISCRIMINATION IN EMPLOYMENT ACT

29 U.S.C. § 623

§ 623. Prohibition of age discrimination

(a) **Employer practices.** It shall be unlawful for an employer–

(1) to fail or refuse to hire or to discharge any individual or otherwise discriminate against any individual with respect to his compensation, terms, conditions, or privileges of employment, because of such individual's age;

(2) to limit, segregate, or classify his employees in any way which would deprive or tend to deprive any individual of employment opportunities or otherwise adversely affect his status as an employee, because of such individual's age; or

(3) to reduce the wage rate of any employee in order to comply with this chapter.

[Subsections (b) and (c) impose similar limitations upon employment agencies and labor organizations.]

(d) **Opposition to unlawful practices; participation in investigations, proceedings, or litigation.** It shall be unlawful for an employer to discriminate against any of his employees or applicants for employment, for an employment agency to discriminate against any individual, or for a labor organization to discriminate against any member thereof or applicant for membership, because such individual, member or applicant for membership has opposed any practice made unlawful by this section, or because such individual, member or applicant for membership has made a charge, testified, assisted, or participated in any manner in an investigation, proceeding, or litigation under this chapter.

[Subsection (e) prohibits any publication indicating discrimination based on age.]

(f) **Lawful practice; age as occupational qualification; other reasonable factors; seniority system; employee benefit plans; discharge or discipline for good cause.** It shall not be unlawful for an employer, employment agency, or labor organization–

(1) to take any action otherwise prohibited under subsections (a), (b), (c), or (e) of this section where age is a bona fide occupational qualification reasonably necessary to the normal operation of the particular business, or where the differentiation is based on reasonable factors other than age, or where such practices involve an employee in a workplace in a foreign country, and compliance with such subsections would cause such employer, or a

corporation controlled by such employer, to violate the laws of the country in which such workplace is located;

(2) to take any action otherwise prohibited under subsection (a), (b), (c), or (e) of this section–

(A) to observe the terms of a bona fide seniority system that is not intended to evade the purposes of this chapter, except that no such seniority system shall require or permit the involuntary retirement of any individual specified by section 631(a) of this title because of the age of such individual; or

(B) to observe the terms of a bona fide employee benefit plan—

   (i) where, for each benefit or benefit package, the actual amount of payment made or cost incurred on behalf of an older worker is no less than that made or incurred on behalf of a younger worker, as permissible under section 1625.10, title 29, Code of Federal Regulations (as in effect on June 22, 1989); or

   (ii) that is a voluntary early retirement incentive plan consistent with the relevant purpose or purposes of this chapter.

Notwithstanding clause (i) or (ii) of subparagraph (B), no such employee benefit plan or voluntary early retirement incentive plan shall excuse the failure to hire any individual, and no such employee benefit plan shall require or permit the involuntary retirement of any individual specified by section 631(a) of this title, because of the age of such individual. An employer, employment agency, or labor organization acting under subparagraph (A), or under clause (i) or (ii) of subparagraph (B), shall have the burden of proving that such actions are lawful in any civil enforcement proceeding brought under this Act; or

(3) to discharge or otherwise discipline an individual for good cause.

[Subsection (h) addresses foreign corporations; subsection (j), provides an exception for firefighters and law enforcement officers; and subsections (k) and (l) address employee seniority systems and benefit plans.]

29 U.S.C. § 626

§ 626. Recordkeeping, investigation, and enforcement.

[Subsection (a) gives the EEOC (Commission) the power to investigate and require the keeping of records.]

(b) Enforcement; prohibition of age discrimination under fair labor standards; unpaid minimum wages and unpaid overtime compensation; liquidated damages; judicial relief; conciliation, conference, and persuasion. The provisions of this chapter shall be enforced in accordance with the powers, remedies, and procedures provided in sections

211(b), 216 (except for subsection (a) thereof), and 217 of this title, and subsection (c) of this section. Any act prohibited under section 623 of this title shall be deemed to be a prohibited act under section 215 of this title. Amounts owing to a person as a result of a violation of this chapter shall be deemed to be unpaid minimum wages or unpaid overtime compensation for purposes of sections 216 and 217 of this title: *Provided*, That liquidated damages shall be payable only in cases of willful violations of this chapter. In any action brought to enforce this chapter the court shall have jurisdiction to grant such legal or equitable relief as may be appropriate to effectuate the purposes of this chapter, including without limitation judgments compelling employment, reinstatement or promotion, or enforcing the liability for amounts deemed to be unpaid minimum wages or unpaid overtime compensation under this section. Before instituting any action under this section, the Commission shall attempt to eliminate the discriminatory practice or practices alleged, and to effect voluntary compliance with the requirements of this chapter through informal methods of conciliation, conference, and persuasion.

(c) Civil actions; persons aggrieved; jurisdiction; judicial relief; termination of individual action upon commencement of action by Secretary; jury trial.

(1) Any person aggrieved may bring a civil action in any court of competent jurisdiction for such legal or equitable relief as will effectuate the purposes of this chapter: *Provided*, That the right of any person to bring such action shall terminate upon the commencement of an action by the Commission to enforce the right of such employee under this chapter.

(2) In an action brought under paragraph (1), a person shall be entitled to a trial by jury of any issue of fact in any such action for recovery of amounts owing as a result of a violation of this chapter, regardless of whether equitable relief is sought by any party in such action.

(d) (1) Filing of charge with Commission; timeliness; conciliation, conference, and persuasion. No civil action may be commenced by an individual under this section until 60 days after a charge alleging unlawful discrimination has been filed with the Commission. Such a charge shall be filed—

   (A) within 180 days after the alleged unlawful practice occurred; or

   (B) in a case to which section 633(b) of this title applies, within 300 days after the alleged unlawful practice occurred, or within 30 days after receipt by the individual of notice of termination of proceedings under State law, whichever is earlier.

(2) Upon receiving such a charge, the Commission shall promptly notify all persons named in such charge as prospective defendants in the action and shall promptly seek to eliminate any alleged unlawful practice by informal methods of conciliation, conference, and persuasion.

(3) For purposes of this section, an unlawful practice occurs, with respect to discrimination in compensation in violation of this Act, when a discriminatory decision or other practice is adopted, when a person becomes subject to a discriminatory compensation decision or other practice, or when a person is affected by application of a discriminatory compensation decision or other practice, including each time wages, benefits, or other compensation is paid, resulting in whole or in part from such a decision or other practice.

(e) Reliance on administrative rulings; notice of dismissal or termination; civil action after receipt of notice.

Section 259 of this title shall apply to actions under this chapter. If a charge filed with the Commission under this chapter is dismissed or the proceedings of the Commission are otherwise terminated by the Commission, the Commission shall notify the person aggrieved. A civil action may be brought under this section by a person defined in section 630(a) of this title against the respondent named in the charge within 90 days after the date of the receipt of such notice.

(f) Waiver

(1) An individual may not waive any right or claim under this chapter unless the waiver is knowing and voluntary. Except as provided in paragraph (2), a waiver may not be considered knowing and voluntary unless at a minimum—

(A) the waiver is part of an agreement between the individual and the employer that is written in a manner calculated to be understood by such individual, or by the average individual eligible to participate;

(B) the waiver specifically refers to rights or claims arising under this chapter;

(C) the individual does not waive rights or claims that may arise after the date the waiver is executed;

(D) the individual waives rights or claims only in exchange for consideration in addition to anything of value to which the individual already is entitled;

(E) the individual is advised in writing to consult with an attorney prior to executing the agreement;

(F) (i) the individual is given a period of at least 21 days within which to consider the agreement; or

   (i)   if a waiver is requested in connection with an exit incentive or other employment termination program offered to a group or class of employees, the individual is given a period of at least 45 days within which to consider the agreement;

(G) the agreement provides that for a period of at least 7 days following the execution of such agreement, the individual may revoke the agreement, and the agreement shall not become effective or enforceable until the revocation period has expired;

(H) if a waiver is requested in connection with an exit incentive or other employment termination program offered to a group or class of employees, the employer (at the commencement of the period specified in subparagraph (F)) informs the individual in writing in a manner calculated to be understood by the average individual eligible to participate, as to—

     (i) any class, unit, or group of individuals covered by such program, any eligibility factors for such program, and any time limits applicable to such program; and

     (ii) the job titles and ages of all individuals eligible or selected for the program, and the ages of all individuals in the same job classification or organizational unit who are not eligible or selected for the program.

(2) A waiver in settlement of a charge filed with the Equal Employment Opportunity Commission, or an action filed in court by the individual or the individual's representative, alleging age discrimination of a kind prohibited under section 623 or 633a of this title may not be considered knowing and voluntary unless at a minimum—

     (A) subparagraphs (A) through (E) of paragraph (1) have been met; and

     (B) the individual is given a reasonable period of time within which to consider the settlement agreement.

(3) In any dispute that may arise over whether any of the requirements, conditions, and circumstances set forth in subparagraph (A), (B), (C), (D), (E), (F), (G), or (H) of paragraph (1), or subparagraph (A) or (B) of paragraph (2), have been met, the party asserting the validity of a waiver shall have the burden of proving in a court of competent jurisdiction that a waiver was knowing and voluntary pursuant to paragraph (1) or (2).

(4) No waiver agreement may affect the Commission's rights and responsibilities to enforce this chapter. No waiver may be used to justify interfering with the protected right of an employee to file a charge or participate in an investigation or proceeding conducted by the Commission.

29 U.S.C. § 627

§ 627. Notices to be posted

Every employer, employment agency, and labor organization shall post and keep posted in conspicuous places upon its premises a notice to be prepared or approved by the Equal Employment Opportunity Commission setting forth information as the Commission deems appropriate to effectuate the purposes of this chapter.

29 U.S.C. § 630

§ 630. Definitions

For the purposes of this chapter—

(a) The term "person" means one or more individuals, partnerships, associations, labor organizations, corporations, business trust, legal representatives, or any organized groups of persons.

(b) The term "employer" means a person engaged in an industry affecting commerce who has twenty or more employees for each working day in each of twenty or more calendar weeks in the current or preceding calendar year: *Provided*, That prior to June 30, 1968, employers having fewer than fifty employees shall not be considered employers. The term also means **(1)** any agent of such a person, and **(2)** a State or political subdivision of a State and any agency or instrumentality of a State or a political subdivision of a State, and any interstate agency, but such term does not include the United States, or a corporation wholly owned by the Government of the United States.

* * *

(f) The term "employee" means an individual employed by any employer except that the term "employee" shall not include any person elected to public office in any State or political subdivision of any State by the qualified voters thereof, or any person chosen by such officer to be on such officer's personal staff, or an appointee on the policymaking level or an immediate adviser with respect to the exercise of the constitutional or legal powers of the office. The exemption set forth in the preceding sentence shall not include employees subject to the civil service laws of a State government, governmental agency, or political subdivision. The term "employee" includes any individual who is a citizen of the United States employed by an employer in a workplace in a foreign country.

* * *

29 U.S.C. § 631

§ 631. Age limits

(a) Individuals at least 40 years of age. The prohibitions in this chapter shall be limited to individuals who are at least 40 years of age.

(b) Employees or applicants for employment in Federal Government. In the case of any personnel action affecting employees or applicants for employment which is subject to the provisions of section 633a of this title, the prohibitions established in section 633a of this title shall be limited to individuals who are at least 40 years of age.

(c) Bona fide executives or high policymakers

(1) Nothing in this chapter shall be construed to prohibit compulsory retirement of any employee who has attained 65 years of age and who, for the 2-year period immediately before retirement, is employed in a bona fide executive or a high policymaking position, if such employee is entitled to an immediate nonforfeitable annual retirement benefit from a pension, profit-sharing, savings, or deferred compensation plan, or any combination of such plans, of the employer of such employee, which equals, in the aggregate, at least $44,000.

(2) In applying the retirement benefit test of paragraph (1) of this subsection, if any such retirement benefit is in a form other than a straight life annuity (with no ancillary benefits), or if employees contribute to any such plan or make rollover contributions, such benefit shall be adjusted in accordance with regulations prescribed by the Equal Employment Opportunity Commission, after consultation with the Secretary of the Treasury, so that the benefit is the equivalent of a straight life annuity (with no ancillary benefits) under a plan to which employees do not contribute and under which no rollover contributions are made.

29 U.S.C. § 633(b)

§ 633. Federal-State relationship

(b) **Limitation of Federal action upon commencement of State proceedings.** In the case of an alleged unlawful practice occurring in a State which has a law prohibiting discrimination in employment because of age and establishing or authorizing a State authority to grant or seek relief from such discriminatory practice, no suit may be brought under section 7 of this Act [29 U.S.C. § 626] before the expiration of sixty days after proceedings have been commenced under the State law, unless such proceedings have been earlier terminated: *Provided,* That such sixty-day period shall be extended to one hundred and twenty days during the first year after the effective date of such State law. . . .

29 U.S.C. § 633a

§ 633a. Nondiscrimination on account of age in Federal Government employment

(a) **Federal agencies affected.** All personnel actions affecting employees or applicants for employment who are at least 40 years of age (except personnel actions with regard to aliens employed outside the limits of the United States) in military departments as defined in section 102 of Title 5, in executive agencies as defined in section 105 of Title 5 (including employees and applicants for employment who are paid from nonappropriated funds), in the United States Postal Service and the Postal Regulatory Commission, in those units in the government of the District of Columbia having positions in the competitive service, and in those units of the judicial branch of the Federal Government having positions in the competitive service, in the Smithsonian Institution, and in the Government Printing Office, the General Accountability Office, and the Library of Congress shall be made free from any discrimination based on age.

(b) Enforcement by Equal Employment Opportunity Commission and by Librarian of Congress in Library of Congress; remedies; rules, regulations, orders, and instructions of Commission: compliance by Federal agencies; powers and duties of Commission; notification of final action on complaint of discrimination; exemptions: bona fide occupational qualification. Except as otherwise provided in this subsection, the Equal Employment Opportunity Commission is authorized to enforce the provisions of subsection (a) of this section through appropriate remedies, including reinstatement or hiring of employees with or without backpay, as will effectuate the policies of this section. The Equal Employment Opportunity Commission shall issue such rules, regulations, orders, and instructions as it deems necessary and appropriate to carry out its responsibilities under this section. The Equal Employment Opportunity Commission shall— **(1)** be responsible for the review and evaluation of the operation of all agency programs designed to carry out the policy of this section, periodically obtaining and publishing (on at least a semiannual basis) progress reports from each department, agency, or unit referred to in subsection (a) of this section; **(2)** consult with and solicit the recommendations of interested individuals, groups, and organizations relating to nondiscrimination in employment on account of age; and **(3)** provide for the acceptance and processing of complaints of discrimination in Federal employment on account of age. The head of each such department, agency, or unit shall comply with such rules, regulations, orders, and instructions of the Equal Employment Opportunity Commission which shall include a provision that an employee or applicant for employment shall be notified of any final action taken on any complaint of discrimination filed by him thereunder. Reasonable exemptions to the provisions of this section may be established by the Commission but only when the Commission has established a maximum age requirement on the basis of a determination that age is a bona fide occupational qualification necessary to the performance of the duties of the position. With respect to employment in the Library of Congress, authorities granted in this subsection to the Equal Employment Opportunity Commission shall be exercised by the Librarian of Congress.

(c) Civil actions; jurisdiction; relief. Any person aggrieved may bring a civil action in any Federal district court of competent jurisdiction for such legal or equitable relief as will effectuate the purposes of this chapter.

(d) Notice to Commission; time of notice; Commission notification of prospective defendants; Commission elimination of unlawful practices. When the individual has not filed a complaint concerning age discrimination with the Commission, no civil action may be commenced by any individual under this section until the individual has given the Commission not less than thirty days' notice of an intent to file such action. Such notice shall be filed within one hundred and eighty days after the alleged unlawful practice occurred. Upon receiving a notice of intent to sue, the Commission shall promptly notify all persons named therein as prospective defendants in the action and take any appropriate action to assure the elimination of any unlawful practice.

(e) Duty of Government agency or official. Nothing contained in this section shall relieve any Government agency or official of the responsibility to assure nondiscrimination on account of age in employment as required under any provision of Federal law.

(f) Applicability of statutory provisions to personnel action of Federal departments, etc. Any personnel action of any department, agency, or other entity referred to in subsection (a) of this section shall not be subject to, or affected by, any provision of this chapter, other than the provisions of section 631(b) of this title and the provisions of this section.

REHABILITATION ACT OF 1973 AND RELATED PROVISIONS

29 U.S.C. § 705(20)

§ 705. Definitions

*   *   *

(20) Individual with a disability.

(A) In general
Except as otherwise provided in subparagraph (B), the term "individual with a disability" means any individual who
(i) has a physical or mental impairment which for such individual constitutes or results in a substantial impediment to employment and
(ii) can benefit in terms of an employment outcome from vocational rehabilitation services provided pursuant to subchapters I, III, or VI.

(B) Certain programs; limitations on major life activities.
Subject to subparagraphs [(C), (D), (E), and (F)], the term "individual with a disability" means, for purposes of [§ 791, 793 and 794], any person who has a disability as defined in [42 U.S.C. § 12102].

*   *   *

(C) Rights and advocacy provisions
(i) In General; exclusion of individuals engaging in drug use

For purposes of subchapter V of this chapter [29 U.S.C.A. § 790 et seq.], the term "individual with a disability" does not include an individual who is currently engaging in the illegal use of drugs, when a covered entity acts on the basis of such use.

(ii) Exception for individuals no longer engaging in drug use

Nothing in clause (i) shall be construed to exclude as an individual with a disability an individual who--

> **(I)** has successfully completed a supervised drug rehabilitation program and is no longer engaging in the illegal use of drugs, or has otherwise been rehabilitated successfully and is no longer engaging in such use;

> **(II)** is participating in a supervised rehabilitation program and is no longer engaging in such use; or

> **(III)** is erroneously regarded as engaging in such use, but is not engaging in such use; except that it shall not be a violation of this chapter [29 U.S.C.A. § 701 et seq.] for a covered entity to adopt or administer reasonable policies or procedures, including but not limited to drug testing, designed to ensure that an individual described in subclause (I) or (II) is no longer engaging in the illegal use of drugs.

> **(v)** For purposes of sections 793 and 794 of this title as such sections relate to employment, the term "individual with a disability" does not include any individual who is an alcoholic whose current use of alcohol prevents such individual from performing the duties of the job in question or whose employment, by reason of such current alcohol abuse, would constitute a direct threat to property or the safety of others.

(D) For the purpose of sections 793 and 794 of this title, as such sections relate to employment, such term does not include an individual who has a currently contagious disease or infection and who, by reason of such disease or infection, would constitute a direct threat to the health or safety of other individuals or who, by reason of the currently contagious disease or infection, is unable to perform the duties of the job.

29 U.S.C. § 791(b) [§ 501]

§ 791. Employment of individuals with disabilities

* * *

(b) Federal agencies; affirmative action program plans. Each department, agency, and instrumentality (including the United States Postal Service and the Postal Regulatory Commission) in the executive branch and the Smithsonian Institution shall, within one hundred and eighty days after September 26, 1973, submit to the Commission and to the Committee an affirmative action program plan for the hiring, placement, and advancement of individuals with disabilities in such department, agency, instrumentality, or institution.

Such plan shall include a description of the extent to which and methods whereby the special needs of employees who are individuals with disabilities are being met. . . .

29 U.S.C. § 793 [§ 503]

§ 793. Employment under Federal contracts

(c) Amount of contracts or subcontracts; provisions for employment and advancement of qualified individuals with disabilities; regulations. Any contract in excess of $10,000 entered into by any Federal department or agency for the procurement of personal property and nonpersonal services (including construction) for the United States shall contain a provision requiring that, the party contracting with the United States shall take affirmative action to employ and advance in employment qualified individuals with disabilities. The provisions of this section shall apply to any subcontract in excess of $10,000 entered into by a prime contractor in carrying out any contract for the procurement of personal property and nonpersonal services (including construction) for the United States. The President shall implement the provisions of this section by promulgating regulations within ninety days after September 26, 1973.

(d) Administrative enforcement; complaints; investigations; departmental action. If any individual with a disability believes any contractor has failed or refuses to comply with the provisions of a contract with the United States, relating to employment of individuals with disabilities, such individual may file a complaint with the Department of Labor. The Department shall promptly investigate such complaint and shall take such action thereon as the facts and circumstances warrant, consistent with the terms of such contract and the laws and regulations applicable thereto.

29 U.S.C. § 794 [§ 504]

§ 794. Nondiscrimination under Federal grants and programs.

(a) Promulgation of Rules and Regulations. No otherwise qualified individual with a disability in the United States, as defined in section 705(20) of this title, shall, solely by reason of her or his disability, be excluded from the participation in, be denied the benefits of, or be subjected to discrimination under any program or activity receiving Federal financial assistance or under any program or activity conducted by any Executive agency or by the United States Postal Service. [Each such agency is required to promulgate regulations.]

(b) Program or activity defined. For the purposes of this section, the term "program or activity" means [same as § 2000d-4a *infra*].

(c) Significant structural alterations by small providers. Small providers are not required by subsection (a) of this section to make significant structural alterations to their existing facilities for the purpose of assuring program accessibility, if alternative means of providing the services are available. The terms used in this subsection shall be construed with reference to the regulations existing on March 22, 1988.

(d) Standards used in determining violation of section. The standards used to determine whether this section has been violated in a complaint alleging employment discrimination under this section shall be the standards applied under title I of the Americans with Disabilities Act of 1990 (42 U.S.C. § 12111 *et seq.*) and the provisions of sections 501 through 504, and 510, of the Americans with Disabilities Act of 1990 (42 U.S.C. '§ 12201 to 12204 and 12210), as such sections relate to employment.

29 U.S.C. § 794a [§ 505]

§ 794a. Remedies and attorney fees

(a) (1) The remedies, procedures, and rights set forth in section 717 of the Civil Rights Act of 1964 (42 U.S.C. § 2000e-16), including the application of sections 706(f) through 706(k) (42 U.S.C. § 2000e-5(f) through (k)), shall be available, with respect to any complaint under section 791 of this title, to any employee or applicant for employment aggrieved by the final disposition of such complaint, or by the failure to take final action on such complaint. In fashioning an equitable or affirmative action remedy under such section, a court may take into account the reasonableness of the cost of any necessary work place accommodation, and the availability of alternatives therefor or other appropriate relief in order to achieve an equitable and appropriate remedy.

(2) The remedies, procedures, and rights set forth in Title VI of the Civil Rights Act of 1964 (42 U.S.C. § 2000d *et seq.*) (and in subsection (e)(3) of section 706 of such Act (42 U.S.C. 2000e-5), applied to claims of discrimination in compensation) shall be available to any person aggrieved by any act or failure to act by any recipient of Federal assistance or Federal provider of such assistance under section 794 of this title.

(b) In any action or proceeding to enforce or charge a violation of a provision of this subchapter, the court, in its discretion, may allow the prevailing party, other than the United States, a reasonable attorney's fee as part of the costs.

42 U.S.C. § 1981

§ 1981. Equal rights under the law

(a) **Statement of equal rights.** All persons within the jurisdiction of the United States shall have the same right in every State and Territory to make and enforce contracts, to sue, be parties, give evidence, and to the full and equal benefit of all laws and proceedings for the security of persons and property as is enjoyed by white citizens, and shall be subject to like punishment, pains, penalties, taxes, licenses, and exactions of every kind, and to no other.

(b) **Definition.** For purposes of this section, the term "make and enforce contracts" includes the making, performance, modification, and termination of contracts, and the enjoyment of all benefits, privileges, terms, and conditions of the contractual relationship.

(c) **Protection against impairment.** The rights protected by this section are protected against impairment by nongovernmental discrimination and impairment under color of State law.

§ 1981a. Damages in cases of intentional discrimination in employment

(a) **Right of recovery**

(1) **Civil rights.** In an action brought by a complaining party under section 706 or 717 of the Civil Rights Act of 1964 (42 U.S.C. § 2000e-5) [42 U.S.C. § 2000e-5 or 42 U.S.C. § 2000e-16] against a respondent who engaged in unlawful intentional discrimination (not an employment practice that is unlawful because of its disparate impact) prohibited under section 703, 704, or 717 of the Act (42 U.S.C. § 2000e-2 or § 2000e-3) [42 U.S.C. § 2000e-2, 42 U.S.C. § 2000e-3, or 42 U.S.C. § 2000e-16], and provided that the complaining party cannot recover under section 1981 of this title, the complaining party may recover compensatory and punitive damages as allowed in subsection (b) of this section, in addition to any relief authorized by section 706(g) of the Civil Rights Act of 1964 [42 U.S.C. § 2000e-5(g)], from the respondent.

(2) **Disability.** In an action brought by a complaining party under the powers, remedies, and procedures set forth in section 706 or 717 of the Civil Rights Act of 1964 [42 U.S.C. § 2000e-5 or 42 U.S.C. § 2000e-16] (as provided in section 107(a) of the Americans with Disabilities Act of 1990 (42 U.S.C. § 12117(a)), and section 794a(a)(1) of Title 29, respectively) against a respondent who engaged in unlawful intentional discrimination (not an employment practice that is unlawful because of its disparate impact) under section 791 of Title 29 and the regulations implementing section 791 of Title 29, or who violated the requirements of section 791 of Title 29 or the regulations implementing section 791 of Title 29 concerning the provision of a reasonable accommodation, or section 102 of the Americans with Disabilities

Act of 1990 (42 U.S.C. § 12112), or committed a violation of section 102(b)(5) of the Act [42 U.S.C. § 12112(b)(5)], against an individual, the complaining party may recover compensatory and punitive damages as allowed in subsection (b) of this section, in addition to any relief authorized by section 706(g) of the Civil Rights Act of 1964 [42 U.S.C. § 2000e-5(g)], from the respondent.

(3) Reasonable accommodation and good faith effort. In cases where a discriminatory practice involves the provision of a reasonable accommodation pursuant to section 102(b)(5) of the Americans with Disabilities Act of 1990 [42 U.S.C. § 12112(b)(5)] or regulations implementing section 791 of Title 29, damages may not be awarded under this section where the covered entity demonstrates good faith efforts, in consultation with the person with the disability who has informed the covered entity that accommodation is needed, to identify and make a reasonable accommodation that would provide such individual with an equally effective opportunity and would not cause an undue hardship on the operation of the business.

(b) Compensatory and punitive damages

(1) Determination of punitive damages. A complaining party may recover punitive damages under this section against a respondent (other than a government, government agency or political subdivision) if the complaining party demonstrates that the respondent engaged in a discriminatory practice or discriminatory practices with malice or with reckless indifference to the federally protected rights of an aggrieved individual.

(2) Exclusions from compensatory damages. Compensatory damages awarded under this section shall not include backpay, interest on backpay, or any other type of relief authorized under section 706(g) of the Civil Rights Act of 1964 [42 U.S.C. § 2000e-5(g)].

(3) Limitations. The sum of the amount of compensatory damages awarded under this section for future pecuniary losses, emotional pain, suffering, inconvenience, mental anguish, loss of enjoyment of life, and other nonpecuniary losses, and the amount of punitive damages awarded under this section, shall not exceed, for each complaining party—

(A) in the case of a respondent who has more than 14 and fewer than 101 employees in each of 20 or more calendar weeks in the current or preceding calendar year, $50,000;

(B) in the case of a respondent who has more than 100 and fewer than 201 employees in each of 20 or more calendar weeks in the current or preceding calendar year, $100,000; and

(C) in the case of a respondent who has more than 200 and fewer than 501 employees in each of 20 or more calendar weeks in the current or preceding calendar year, $200,000; and

(D) in the case of a respondent who has more than 500 employees in each of 20 or more calendar weeks in the current or preceding calendar year, $300,000.

(4) Construction. Nothing in this section shall be construed to limit the scope of, or the relief available under, section 1981 of this title.

(c) **Jury trial.** If a complaining party seeks compensatory or punitive damages under this section—

(1) any party may demand a trial by jury; and

(2) the court shall not inform the jury of the limitations described in subsection (b)(3) of this section.

(d) **Definitions**

As used in this section:

(1) **Complaining party.** The term "complaining party" means—

(A) in the case of a person seeking to bring an action under subsection (a)(1) of this section, the Equal Employment Opportunity Commission, the Attorney General, or a person who may bring an action or proceeding under title VII of the Civil Rights Act of 1964 (42 U.S.C. § 2000e *et seq.*); or

(B) in the case of a person seeking to bring an action under subsection (a)(2) of this section, the Equal Employment Opportunity Commission, the Attorney General, a person who may bring an action or proceeding under section 794a(a)(1) of Title 29, or a person who may bring an action or proceeding under title I of the Americans with Disabilities Act of 1990 (42 U.S.C. § 12101 *et seq.*).

(2) **Discriminatory practice.** The term "discriminatory practice" means the discrimination described in paragraph (1), or the discrimination or the violation described in paragraph (2), of subsection (a) of this section.

42 U.S.C. § 1982

§ 1982. Property rights of citizens

All citizens of the United States shall have the same right, in every State and Territory, as is enjoyed by white citizens thereof to inherit, purchase, lease, sell, hold, and convey real and personal property.

42 U.S.C. § 1983

§ 1983. Civil action for deprivation of rights

Every person who, under color of any statute, ordinance, regulation, custom, or usage, of any State or Territory or the District of Columbia, subjects, or causes to be subjected, any citizen of the United States or other person within the jurisdiction thereof to the deprivation of any rights, privileges, or immunities secured by the Constitution and laws, shall be liable to the party injured in an action at law, suit in equity, or other proper proceeding for redress, except that in any action brought against a judicial officer for an act or omission taken in such officer's judicial capacity, injunctive relief shall not be granted unless a declaratory decree was violated or declaratory relief was unavailable. For the purposes of this section, any Act of Congress applicable exclusively to the District of Columbia shall be considered to be a statute of the District of Columbia.

42 U.S.C. § 1985(3)

§ 1985. Conspiracy to interfere with civil rights

(3) Depriving persons of rights or privileges. If two or more persons in any State or Territory conspire or go in disguise on the highway or on the premises of another, for the purpose of depriving, either directly or indirectly, any person or class of persons of the equal protection of the laws, or of equal privileges and immunities under the laws; or for the purpose of preventing or hindering the constituted authorities of any State or Territory from giving or securing to all persons within such State or Territory the equal protection of the laws; or if two or more persons conspire to prevent by force, intimidation, or threat, any citizen who is lawfully entitled to vote, from giving his support or advocacy in a legal manner, toward or in favor of the election of any lawfully qualified person as an elector for President or Vice President, or as a Member of Congress of the United States; or to injure any citizen in person or property on account of such support or advocacy; in any case of conspiracy set forth in this section, if one or more persons engaged therein do, or cause to be done, any act in furtherance of the object of such conspiracy, whereby another is injured in his person or property, or deprived of having and exercising any right or privilege of a citizen of the United States, the party so injured or deprived may have an action for the recovery of damages occasioned by such injury or deprivation, against any one or more of the conspirators.

42 U.S.C. § 1986

§ 1986. Action for neglect to prevent

Every person who, having knowledge that any of the wrongs conspired to be done, and mentioned in section 1985 of this title, are about to be committed, and having power to prevent or aid in preventing the commission of the same, neglects or refuses so to do, if such wrongful act be committed, shall be liable to the party injured, or his legal representatives, for all damages caused by such wrongful act, which such person by reasonable diligence could have prevented; and such damages may be recovered in an action on the case; and any number of persons guilty of such wrongful neglect or refusal may be joined as defendants in the action; and if the death of any party be caused by any such wrongful act and neglect, the legal representatives of the deceased shall have such action therefor, and may recover not exceeding $5,000 damages therein, for the benefit of the widow of the deceased, if there be one, and if there be no widow, then for the benefit of the next of kin of the deceased. But no action under the provisions of this section shall be sustained which is not commenced within one year after the cause of action has accrued.

42 U.S.C. § 1988

§ 1988. Proceedings in vindication of civil rights; attorney's fees; expert fees

(a) **Applicability of statutory and common law.** The jurisdiction in civil and criminal matters conferred on the district courts by the provisions of Titles 13, 24 and 70 of the Revised Statutes for the protection of all persons in the United States in their civil rights, and for their vindication, shall be exercised and enforced in conformity with the laws of the United States, so far as such laws are suitable to carry the same into effect; but in all cases where they are not adapted to the object, or are deficient in the provisions necessary to furnish suitable remedies and punish offenses against law, the common law, as modified and changed by the constitution and statutes of the State wherein the court having jurisdiction of such civil or criminal cause is held, so far as the same is not inconsistent with the Constitution and laws of the United States, shall be extended to and govern the said courts in the trial and disposition of the cause, and, if it is of a criminal nature, in the infliction of punishment on the party found guilty.

(b) **Attorney's fees.** In any action or proceeding to enforce a provision of sections 1981, 1981a, 1982, 1983, 1985, and 1986 of this title, title IX of Public Law 92-318, the Religious Freedom Restoration Act of 1993, the Religious Land Use and Institutionalized Persons Act of 2000, title VI of the Civil Rights Act of 1964, or section 12361 of title 34, the court, in its discretion, may allow the prevailing party, other than the United States, a reasonable attorney's fee as part of the costs, except that in any action brought against a judicial officer for an act or omission taken in such officer's judicial capacity such officer shall not be held liable for any costs, including attorney's fees, unless such action was clearly in excess of such officer's jurisdiction.

(c) **Expert fees.** In awarding an attorney's fee under subsection (b) of this section in any action or proceeding to enforce a provision of section 1981 or 1981a of this title, the court, in its discretion, may include expert fees as part of the attorney's fee.

TITLE II: PUBLIC ACCOMMODATIONS

42 U.S.C. § 2000a [§ 201]

§ 2000a. Prohibition against discrimination or segregation in places of public accommodation

(a) **Equal access.** All persons shall be entitled to the full and equal enjoyment of the goods, services, facilities, privileges, advantages, and accommodations of any place of public accommodation, as defined in this section, without discrimination or segregation on the ground of race, color, religion, or national origin.

(b) **Establishments affecting interstate commerce or supported in their activities by State action as places of public accommodation; lodgings; facilities principally engaged in selling food for consumption on the premises; gasoline stations; places of exhibition or entertainment; other covered establishments.** Each of the following establishments which serves the public is a place of public accommodation within the meaning of this subchapter if its operations affect commerce, or if discrimination or segregation by it is supported by State action:

(1) any inn, hotel, motel, or other establishment which provides lodging to transient guests, other than an establishment located within a building which contains not more than five rooms for rent or hire and which is actually occupied by the proprietor of such establishment as his residence;

(2) any restaurant, cafeteria, lunchroom, lunch counter, soda fountain, or other facility principally engaged in selling food for consumption on the premises, including, but not limited to, any such facility located on the premises of any retail establishment; or any gasoline station;

(3) any motion picture house, theater, concert hall, sports arena, stadium or other place of exhibition or entertainment; and

(4) any establishment (A)(i) which is physically located within the premises of any establishment otherwise covered by this subsection, or (ii) within the premises of which is physically located any such covered establishment, and (B) which holds itself out as serving patrons of such covered establishment.

(c) **Operations affecting commerce; criteria; "commerce" defined.** The operations of an establishment affect commerce within the meaning of this subchapter if (1) it is one of the establishments described in paragraph (1) of subsection (b) of this section; (2) in the case of an establishment described in paragraph (2) of subsection (b) of this section, it serves or offers to serve interstate travelers of a substantial portion of the food which it serves, or gasoline or other products which it sells, has moved in commerce; **(3)** in the case of an establishment described in paragraph (3) of subsection (b) of this section, it customarily presents films, performances, athletic teams, exhibitions, or other sources of entertainment which move in commerce; and **(4)** in the case of an establishment described in paragraph (4) of subsection (b) of this section, it is physically located within the premises of, or there is physically located within its premises, an establishment the operations of which affect commerce within the meaning of this subsection. For purposes of this section, "commerce" means travel, trade, traffic, commerce, transportation, or communication among the several States, or between the District of Columbia and any State, or between any foreign country or any territory or possession and any State or the District of Columbia, or between points in the same State but through any other State or the District of Columbia or a foreign country.

(d) **Support by State action.** Discrimination or segregation by an establishment is supported by State action within the meaning of this subchapter if such discrimination or segregation **(1)** is carried on under color of any law, statute, ordinance, or regulation; or **(2)** is carried on under color of any custom or usage required or enforced by officials of the State or political subdivision thereof; or **(3)** is required by action of the State or political subdivision thereof.

(e) **Private establishments.** The provisions of this subchapter shall not apply to a private club or other establishment not in fact open to the public, except to the extent that the facilities of such establishment are made available to the customers or patrons of an establishment within the scope of subsection (b) of this section.

42 U.S.C. § 2000a-2 [§ 203]

§ 2000a-2. Prohibition against deprivation of, interference with, and punishment for exercising rights and privileges secured by section 2000a or 2000a-1 of this title.

No person shall **(a)** withhold, deny, or attempt to withhold or deny, or deprive or attempt to deprive any person of any right or privilege secured by section 2000a or 2000a-1 of this title, or **(b)** intimidate, threaten, or coerce, or attempt to intimidate, threaten, or coerce any person with the purpose of interfering with any right or privilege secured by section 2000a or 2000a-1 of this title, or **(c)** punish or attempt to punish any person for exercising or attempting to exercise any right or privilege secured by section 2000a or 2000a-1 of this title.

§ 2000a-3. Civil actions for injunctive relief

(a) **Persons aggrieved; intervention by Attorney General; legal representation; commencement of action without payment of fees, costs, or security.** Whenever any person has engaged or there are reasonable grounds to believe that any person is about to engage in any act or practice prohibited by section 2000a-2 of this title, a civil action for preventive relief, including an application for a permanent or temporary injunction, restraining order, or other order, may be instituted by the person aggrieved and, upon timely application, the court may, in its discretion, permit the Attorney General to intervene in such civil action if he certifies that the case is of general public importance. Upon application by the complainant and in such circumstances as the court may deem just, the court may appoint an attorney for such complainant and may authorize the commencement of the civil action without the payment of fees, costs, or security.

(b) **Attorney's fees; liability of United States for costs.** In any action commenced pursuant to this subchapter, the court, in its discretion, may allow the prevailing party, other than the United States, a reasonable attorney's fee as part of the costs, and the United States shall be liable for costs the same as a private person.

(c) **State or local enforcement proceedings; notification of State or local authority; stay of Federal proceedings.** In the case of an alleged act or practice prohibited by this subchapter which occurs in a State, or political subdivision of a State, which has a State or local law prohibiting such act or practice and establishing or authorizing a State or local authority to grant or seek relief from such practice or to institute criminal proceedings with respect thereto upon receiving notice thereof, no civil action may be brought under subsection (a) of this section before the expiration of thirty days after written notice of such alleged act or practice has been given to the appropriate State or local authority by registered mail or in person, provided that the court may stay proceedings in such civil action pending the termination of State or local enforcement proceedings.

(d) **References to Community Relations Service to obtain voluntary compliance; duration of reference; extension of period.** In the case of an alleged act or practice prohibited by this subchapter which occurs in a State, or political subdivision of a State, which has no State or local law prohibiting such act or practice, a civil action may be brought under subsection (a) of this section: *Provided,* That the court may refer the matter to the Community Relations Service established by subchapter VIII of this chapter for as long as the court believes there is a reasonable possibility of obtaining voluntary compliance, but for not more than sixty days: *Provided further,* That upon expiration of such sixty-day period, the court may extend such period for an additional period, not to exceed a cumulative total of one hundred and twenty days, if it believes there then exists a reasonable possibility of securing voluntary compliance.

42 U.S.C. § 2000a-4 [§ 205]

§ 2000a-4. Community Relations Service; investigations and hearings; executive session; release of testimony; duty to bring about voluntary settlements.

The Service is authorized to make a full investigation of any complaint referred to it by the court under section 2000a-3(d) of this title and may hold such hearings with respect thereto as may be necessary. The Service shall conduct any hearings with respect to any such complaint in executive session, and shall not release any testimony given therein except by agreement of all parties involved in the complaint with the permission of the court, and the Service shall endeavor to bring about a voluntary settlement between the parties.

42 U.S.C. § 2000a-5 [§ 206]

§ 2000a-5. Civil actions by Attorney General

(a) **Complaint.** Whenever the Attorney General has reasonable cause to believe that any person or group of persons is engaged in a pattern or practice of resistance to the full enjoyment of any of the rights secured by this subchapter, and that the pattern or practice is of such a nature and is intended to deny the full exercise of the rights herein described, the Attorney General may bring a civil action in the appropriate district court of the United States by filing with it a complaint (1) signed by him (or in his absence the Acting Attorney General), (2) setting forth facts pertaining to such pattern or practice, and (3) requesting such preventive relief, including an application for a permanent or temporary injunction, restraining order or other order against the person or persons responsible for such pattern or practice, as he deems necessary to insure the full enjoyment of the rights herein described.

(b) **Three-judge district court for cases of general public importance: hearing, determination, expedition of action, review by Supreme Court; single judge district court: hearing, determination, expedition of action.**

[Text of Subsection (b) is omitted.]

42 U.S.C. § 2000a-6 [§ 207]

§ 2000a-6. Jurisdiction; exhaustion of other remedies; exclusiveness of remedies; assertion of rights based on other Federal or State laws and pursuit of remedies for enforcement of such rights.

(a) The district courts of the United States shall have jurisdiction of proceedings instituted pursuant to this subchapter and shall exercise the same without regard to whether the aggrieved party shall have exhausted any administrative or other remedies that may be provided by law.

(b) The remedies provided in this subchapter shall be the exclusive means of enforcing the rights based on this subchapter, but nothing in this subchapter shall preclude any individual or any State or local agency from asserting any right based on any other Federal or State law not inconsistent with this subchapter, including any statute or ordinance requiring nondiscrimination in public establishments or accommodations, or from pursuing any remedy, civil or criminal, which may be available for the vindication or enforcement of such right.

TITLE VI: FEDERALLY ASSISTED PROGRAMS

42 U.S.C. § 2000d [§ 601]

§ 2000d. Prohibition against exclusion from participation in, denial of benefits of, and discrimination under Federally assisted programs on ground of race, color, or national origin.

No person in the United States shall, on the ground of race, color, or national origin, be excluded from participation in, be denied the benefits of, or be subjected to discrimination under any program or activity receiving Federal financial assistance.

42 U.S.C. § 2000d-1 [§ 602]

§ 2000d-1. Federal authority and financial assistance to programs or activities by way of grant, loan, or contract other than contract of insurance or guaranty; rules and regulations; approval by President; compliance with requirements; reports to Congressional committees; effective date of administrative action.

Each Federal department and agency which is empowered to extend Federal financial assistance to any program or activity, by way of grant, loan, or contract other than a contract of insurance or guaranty, is authorized and directed to effectuate the provisions of section 2000d of this title with respect to such program or activity by issuing rules, regulations, or orders of general applicability which shall be consistent with achievement of the objectives of the statute authorizing the financial assistance in connection with which the action is taken. No such rule, regulation, or order shall become effective unless and until approved by the President. Compliance with any requirement adopted pursuant to this section may be effected (1) by the termination of or refusal to grant or to continue assistance under such program or activity to any recipient as to whom there has been an express finding on the record, after opportunity for hearing, of a failure to comply with such requirement, but such termination or refusal shall be limited to the particular political entity, or part thereof, or other recipient as to whom such a finding has been made and, shall be limited in its effect to the particular program, or part thereof, in which such noncompliance has been so found, or (2) by any other means authorized by law: *Provided, however,* That no such action shall be taken until the department or agency concerned has advised the appropriate person or persons of the failure to comply with the requirement and has determined that compliance cannot be secured by voluntary means. In the case of any action, terminating, or refusing to grant or continue, assistance because of failure to comply with a requirement imposed pursuant to this section, the head of the Federal department or agency shall file with the committees of the House and Senate having legislative jurisdiction over the program or activity involved a full written report of the circumstances and the grounds for such action. No such action shall become effective until thirty days have elapsed after the filing of such report.

42 U.S.C. § 2000d-2 [§ 603]

§ 2000d-2. Judicial review; administrative procedure provisions.

Any department or agency action taken pursuant to section 2000d-1 of this title shall be subject to such judicial review as may otherwise be provided by law for similar action taken by such department or agency on other grounds. In the case of action, not otherwise subject to judicial review, terminating or refusing to grant or to continue financial assistance upon a finding of failure to comply with any requirement imposed pursuant to section 2000d-1 of this title, any person aggrieved (including any State or political subdivision thereof and any agency of either) may obtain judicial review of such action in accordance with chapter 7 of Title 5, and such action shall not be deemed committed to unreviewable agency discretion within the meaning of that chapter.

42 U.S.C. § 2000d-3 [§ 604]

§ 2000d-3. Construction of provisions not to authorize administrative action with respect to employment practices except where primary objective of Federal financial assistance is to provide employment.

Nothing contained in this subchapter shall be construed to authorize action under this subchapter by any department or agency with respect to any employment practice of any employer, employment agency, or labor organization except where a primary objective of the Federal financial assistance is to provide employment.

42 U.S.C. § 2000d-4a [§ 606]

§ 2000d-4a. "Program or activity" defined

For the purposes of this subchapter the term "program or activity" and the term "program" mean all of the operations ofC
(1) (A) a department, agency, special purpose district, or other instrumentality of a State or of a local government; or
   (B) the entity of such State or local government that distributes such assistance and each such department or agency (and each other State or local government entity) to which the assistance is extended, in the case of assistance to a State or local government;
(2) (A) a college, university, or other postsecondary institution, or a public system of higher education; or
   (B) a local educational agency (as defined in section 2854(a)(10) of Title 20), system of vocational education, or other school system;
(3) (A) an entire corporation, partnership, or other private organization, or an entire sole proprietorship—
      (i) if assistance is extended to such corporation, partnership, private organization, or sole proprietorship as a whole; or
      (ii) which is principally engaged in the business of providing education, health care, housing, social services, or parks and recreation; or
   (B) the entire plant or other comparable, geographically separate facility to which Federal financial assistance is extended, in the case of any other corporation, partnership, private organization, or sole proprietorship; or
(4) any other entity which is established by two or more of the entities described in paragraph (1), (2), or (3);
any part of which is extended Federal financial assistance.

42 U.S.C. § 2000d-7 [§ 609]

§ 2000d-7. Civil rights remedies equalization

(a) General provision

(1) A State shall not be immune under the Eleventh Amendment of the Constitution of the United States from suit in Federal court for a violation of section 794 of Title 29, title IX of the Education Amendments of 1972, the Age Discrimination Act of 1975 (42 U.S.C. § 6101 *et seq.*), title VI of the Civil Rights Act of 1964 (42 U.S.C. § 2000d *et seq.*), or the provisions of any other Federal statute prohibiting discrimination by recipients of Federal financial assistance.

(2) In a suit against a State for a violation of a statute referred to in paragraph (1), remedies (including remedies both at law and in equity) are available for such a violation to the same extent as such remedies are available for such a violation in the suit against any public or private entity other than a State.

(b) Effective date. The provisions of subsection (a) of this section shall take effect with respect to violations that occur in whole or in part after October 21, 1986.

TITLE VII: EQUAL EMPLOYMENT OPPORTUNITIES

42 U.S.C. § 2000e [§ 701]

§ 2000e. Definitions

For the purposes of this subchapter–

(a) The term "person" includes one or more individuals, governments, governmental agencies, political subdivisions, labor unions, partnerships, associations, corporations, legal representatives, mutual companies, joint-stock companies, trusts, unincorporated organizations, trustees, trustees in cases under Title 11, or receivers.

(b) The term "employer" means a person engaged in an industry affecting commerce who has fifteen or more employees for each working day in each of twenty or more calendar weeks in the current or preceding calendar year, and any agent of such a person, but such term does not include **(1)** the United States, a corporation wholly owned by the Government of the United States, an Indian tribe, or any department or agency of the District of Columbia subject by statute to procedures of the competitive service (as defined in section 2102 of Title 5), or **(2)** a bona fide private membership club (other than a labor organization) which is exempt from taxation under section 501(c) of title 26, except that during the first year after

March 24, 1972, persons having fewer than twenty-five employees (and their agents) shall not be considered employers.

(c) The term "employment agency" means any person regularly undertaking with or without compensation to procure employees for an employer or to procure for employees opportunities to work for an employer and includes an agent of such a person.

(d) The term "labor organization" means a labor organization engaged in an industry affecting commerce, and any agent of such an organization, and includes any organization of any kind, any agency, or employee representation committee, group, association, or plan so engaged in which employees participate and which exists for the purpose, in whole or in part, of dealing with employers concerning grievances, labor disputes, wages, rates of pay, hours, or other terms or conditions of employment, and any conference, general committee, joint or system board, or joint council so engaged which is subordinate to a national or international labor organization.

(e) A labor organization shall be deemed to be engaged in an industry affecting commerce if **(1)** it maintains or operates a hiring hall . . . or **(2)** the number of its members . . . is **(a)** twenty-five or more during the first year after March 24, 1972, or **(b)** fifteen or more thereafter, and such labor organization–
(1) is the certified representative of employees under the provisions of the National Labor Relations Act, as amended, or the Railway Labor Act, as amended; [or]
(2) although not certified, is a national or international labor organization or a local labor organization recognized or acting as the representative of employees of an employer or employers engaged in an industry affecting commerce.

* * *

(f) The term "employee" means an individual employed by an employer, except that the term "employee" shall not include any person elected to public office in any State or political subdivision of any State by the qualified voters thereof, or any person chosen by such officer to be on such officer's personal staff, or an appointee on the policy making level or an immediate adviser with respect to the exercise of the constitutional or legal powers of the office. The exemption set forth in the preceding sentence shall not include employees subject to the civil service laws of a State government, governmental agency or political subdivision. With respect to employment in a foreign country, such term includes an individual who is a citizen of the United States.
[Subsections (g) and (h) further refine the commerce requirement; subsection (i) defines the term "state".]

(j) The term "religion" includes all aspects of religious observance and practice, as well as belief, unless an employer demonstrates that he is unable to reasonably accommodate to an employee's or prospective employee's religious observance or practice without undue hardship on the conduct of the employer's business.

(k) The terms "because of sex" or "on the basis of sex" include, but are not limited to, because of or on the basis of pregnancy, childbirth, or related medical conditions; and women affected by pregnancy, childbirth, or related medical conditions shall be treated the same for all employment-related purposes, including receipt of benefits under fringe benefit programs, as other persons not so affected but similar in their ability or inability to work, and nothing in section 2000e-2(h) of this title shall be interpreted to permit otherwise. This subsection shall not require an employer to pay for health insurance benefits for abortion, except where the life of the mother would be endangered if the fetus were carried to term, or except where medical complications have arisen from an abortion: *Provided*, That nothing herein shall preclude an employer from providing abortion benefits or otherwise affect bargaining agreements in regard to abortion.

(l) (The term "complaining party" means the Commission, the Attorney General, or a person who may bring an action or proceeding under this subchapter.

(m) The term "demonstrates" means meets the burdens of production and persuasion.

(n) The term "respondent" means an employer, employment agency, labor organization, joint labor-management committee controlling apprenticeship or other training or retraining program, including an on-the-job training program, or Federal entity subject to section 2000e-16 of this title.

42 U.S.C. § 2000e-1 [§ 702]

§ 2000e-1. Foreign and religious employment

(a) Inapplicability of subchapter to certain aliens and employees of religious entities. This subchapter shall not apply to an employer with respect to the employment of aliens outside any State, or to a religious corporation, association, educational institution, or society with respect to the employment of individuals of a particular religion to perform work connected with the carrying on by such corporation, association, educational institution, or society of its activities.

(b) Compliance with statute as violative of foreign law. It shall not be unlawful under section 2000e-2 or 2000e-3 of this title for an employer (or a corporation controlled by an employer), labor organization, employment agency, or joint labor-management committee controlling apprenticeship or other training or retraining (including on-the-job training programs to take any action otherwise prohibited by such section, with respect to an employee in a workplace in a foreign country if compliance with such section would cause such employer (or such corporation), such organization, such agency, or such committee to violate the law of the foreign country in which such workplace is located.

(c) Control of corporation incorporated in a foreign country

(1) If an employer controls a corporation whose place of incorporation is a foreign country, any practice prohibited by such section 2000e-2 or 2000e-3 of this title engaged in by such corporation shall be presumed to be engaged in by such employer.

(2) Sections 2000e-2 and 2000e-3 of this title shall not apply with respect to the foreign operations of an employer that is a foreign person not controlled by an American employer.

(3) For purposes of this subsection, the determination of whether an employer controls a corporation shall be based on–

    (A) the interrelation of operations;

    (B) the common management;

    (C) the centralized control of labor relations; and

    (D) the common ownership or financial control,

of the employer and the corporation.

42 U.S.C. § 2000e-2 [§ 703]

§ 2000e-2. Unlawful employment practices

(a) **(a) Employer practices**. It shall be an unlawful employment practice for an employer–

    (1) to fail or refuse to hire or to discharge any individual, or otherwise to discriminate against any individual with respect to his compensation, terms, conditions, or privileges of employment, because of such individual's race, color, religion, sex, or national origin; or

    (2) to limit, segregate, or classify his employees or applicants for employment in any way which would deprive or tend to deprive any individual of employment opportunities or otherwise adversely affect his status as an employee, because of such individual's race, color, religion, sex, or national origin.

[Subsections (b) and (c) impose similar limitations upon employment agencies and labor organization and subsection (d) prohibits discrimination regarding training programs.]

(e) Businesses or enterprises with personnel qualified on basis of religion, sex, or national origin; educational institutions with personnel of particular religion. Notwithstanding any other provision of this subchapter, **(1)** it shall not be an unlawful employment practice for an employer to hire and employ employees, for an employment agency to classify, or refer for employment any individual, for a labor organization to classify its membership or to classify or refer for employment any individual, or for an employer, labor organization, or joint labor-management committee controlling apprenticeship or other training or retraining programs to admit or employ any individual in any such program, on the basis of his religion, sex, or national origin in those certain instances where religion, sex, or national origin is a bona fide occupational qualification reasonably necessary to the normal operation of that particular business or enterprise, and (2) it shall not be an unlawful employment practice for a school, college, university, or other educational institution or institution of learning to hire and employ employees of a particular religion if such school, college, university, or other educational institution or institution of learning is, in whole or in substantial part, owned, supported, controlled, or managed by a particular religion or by a particular religious corporation, association, or society, or if the curriculum of such school, college, university, or other educational institution or institution of learning is directed toward the propagation of a particular religion.

[Subsections (f) and (g) deal with national security exceptions.]

(h) Seniority or merit system; quantity or quality of production; ability tests; compensation based on sex and authorized by minimum wage provisions. Notwithstanding any other provision of this subchapter, it shall not be an unlawful employment practice for an employer to apply different standards of compensation, or different terms, conditions, or privileges of employment pursuant to a bona fide seniority or merit system, or a system which measures earnings by quantity or quality of production or to employees who work in different locations, provided that such differences are not the result of an intention to discriminate because of race, color, religion, sex, or national origin, nor shall it be an unlawful employment practice for an employer to give and to act upon the results of any professionally developed ability test provided that such test, its administration or action upon the results is not designed, intended or used to discriminate because of race, color, religion, sex or national origin. It shall not be an unlawful employment practice under this subchapter for any employer to differentiate upon the basis of sex in determining the amount of the wages or compensation paid or to be paid to employees of such employer if such differentiation is authorized by the provisions of section 206(d) of title 29.

[Subsection (i) allows preferential treatment for Indians.]

(j) Preferential treatment not to be granted on account of existing number or percentage imbalance. Nothing contained in this subchapter shall be interpreted to require any employer, employment agency, labor organization, or joint labor-management committee subject to this subchapter to grant preferential treatment to any individual or to any group because of the race, color, religion, sex, or national origin of such individual or group on account of an imbalance which may exist with respect to the total number or percentage of persons of any race, color, religion, sex, or national origin employed by any employer, referred or classified for employment by any employment agency or labor organization, admitted to membership or classified by any labor organization, or admitted to, or employed in, any apprenticeship or other training program, in comparison with the total number or percentage of persons of such race, color, religion, sex, or national origin in any community, State, section, or other area, or in the available work force in any community, State, section, or other area.

(k) Disparate impact as basis of practice

(1) (A) An unlawful employment practice based on disparate impact is established under this subchapter only if–

    (i) a complaining party demonstrates that a respondent uses a particular employment practice that causes a disparate impact on the basis of race, color, religion, sex, or national origin and the respondent fails to demonstrate that the challenged practice is job related for the position in question and consistent with business necessity; or

    (ii) the complaining party makes the demonstration described in subparagraph (C) with respect to an alternate employment practice and the respondent refuses to adopt such alternative employment practice.

(B) (i) with respect to demonstrating that a particular employment practice causes a disparate impact as described in subparagraph (A)(i), the complaining party shall demonstrate that each particular challenged employment practice causes a disparate impact, except that if the complaining party can demonstrate to the court that the elements of a respondent's decisionmaking process are not capable of separation for analysis, the decisionmaking process may be analyzed as one employment practice.

    (ii) If the respondent demonstrates that a specific employment practice does not cause the disparate impact, the respondent shall not be required to demonstrate that such practice is required by business necessity.

(C) The demonstration referred to by subparagraph (A)(ii) shall be in accordance with the law as it existed on June 4, 1989, with respect to the concept of "alternative employment practice."

(2) A demonstration that an employment practice is required by business necessity may not be used as a defense against a claim of intentional discrimination under this subchapter.

(3) Notwithstanding any other provision of this subchapter, a rule barring the employment of an individual who currently and knowingly uses or possesses a controlled substance, as defined in schedules I and II of section 102(6) of the Controlled Substances Act (21 U.S.C. § 802(6)), other than the use or possession of a drug taken under the supervision of a licensed health care professional, or any other use or possession authorized by the Controlled Substances Act or any other provision of Federal law, shall be considered an unlawful employment practice under this subchapter only if such rule is adopted or applied with an intent to discriminate because of race, color, religion, sex, or national origin.

(l) Alteration of test results. It shall be an unlawful employment practice for a respondent, in connection with the selection or referral of applicants or candidates for employment or promotion, to adjust the scores of, use different cutoff score or otherwise alter the results of, employment related tests on the basis of race, color, religion, sex, or national origin.

(m) Motivations for practice. Except as otherwise provided in this subchapter, an unlawful employment practice is established when the complaining party demonstrates that race, color, religion, sex, or national origin was a motivating factor for any employment practice, even though other factors also motivated the practice.

(n) Challenges to practice implementing litigated or consent judgments or orders.

(1) (A) Notwithstanding any other provision of law, and except as provided in paragraph (2), an employment practice that implements and is within the scope of a litigated or consent judgment or order that resolves a claim of employment discrimination under the Constitution or Federal civil rights laws may not be challenged under the circumstances described in subparagraph (B).

(B) A practice described in subparagraph (A) may not be challenged in a claim under the Constitution or Federal civil rights laws–

    (i) by a person who, prior to the entry of the judgment or order described in subparagraph (A), had–

        (I) actual notice of the proposed judgment or order sufficient to apprise such person that such judgment or order might adversely affect the interests and legal rights of such person and that an opportunity was available to present objections to such judgment or order by a future date certain; and

        (II) a reasonable opportunity to present objections to such judgment or order; or

    (ii) by a person whose interests were adequately represented by another person who had previously challenged the judgment or order on the same legal grounds and with a similar factual situation, unless there has been an intervening change in law or fact.

(2) (Nothing in this subsection shall be construed to–

(A) alter the standards for intervention under rule 24 of the Federal Rules of Civil Procedure or apply to the rights of parties who have successfully intervened pursuant to such rule in the proceeding in which the parties intervened;

(B) apply to the rights of parties to the action in which a litigated or consent judgment or order was entered, or of members of a class represented or sought to be represented in such action, or of members of a group on whose behalf relief was sought in such action by the Federal Government;

(C) prevent challenges to a litigated or consent judgment or order on the ground that such judgment or order was obtained through collusion or fraud, or is transparently invalid or was entered by a court lacking subject matter jurisdiction; or

(D) authorize or permit the denial to any person of the due process of law required by the Constitution.

(3) Any action not precluded under this subsection that challenges an employment consent judgment or order described in paragraph (1) shall be brought in the court, and if possible before the judge, that entered such judgment or order. Nothing in this subsection shall preclude a transfer of such action pursuant to section 1404 of Title 28.

42 U.S.C. § 2000e-3 [§ 704]

§ 2000e-3. Other unlawful employment practices

(a) Discrimination for making charges, testifying, assisting, or participating in enforcement proceedings. It shall be an unlawful employment practice for an employer to discriminate against any of his employees or applicants for employment, for an employment agency, or joint labor-management committee controlling apprenticeship or other training or retraining, including on-the-job training programs, to discriminate against any individual, or for a labor organization to discriminate against any member thereof or applicant for membership, because he has opposed any practice made an unlawful employment practice by this subchapter, or because he has made a charge, testified, assisted, or participated in any manner in an investigation, proceeding, or hearing under this subchapter.

(b) Printing or publication of notices or advertisements indicating prohibited preference, limitation, specification, or discrimination; occupational qualification exception. It shall be an unlawful employment practice for an employer, labor organization, employment agency, or joint labor-management committee controlling apprenticeship or other training or retraining, including on-the-job training programs, to print or publish or cause to be printed or published any notice or advertisement relating to employment by such an employer or membership in or any classification or referral for employment by such a labor organization, or relating to any classification or referral for employment by such an employment agency, or relating to admission to, or employment in, any program established to provide apprenticeship or other training by such a joint labor-management committee, indicating any preference, limitation, specification, or discrimination, based on race, color, religion, sex, or national origin, except that such a notice or advertisement may indicate a preference, limitation, specification, or discrimination based on religion, sex, or national origin when religion, sex, or national origin is a bona fide occupational qualification for employment.

§ 2000e-5. Enforcement provisions

(a) **Power of Commission to prevent unlawful employment practices.** The Commission is empowered, as hereinafter provided, to prevent any person from engaging in any unlawful employment practice as set forth in section 2000e-2 or 2000e-3 of this title.

(b) **Charges by persons aggrieved or member of Commission of unlawful employment practices by employers, etc.; filing; allegations; notice to respondent; contents of notice; investigation by Commission; contents of charges; prohibition on disclosure of charges; determination of reasonable cause; conference, conciliation, and persuasion for elimination of unlawful practices; prohibition on disclosure of informal endeavors to end unlawful practices; use of evidence in subsequent proceedings; penalties for disclosure of information; time for determination of reasonable cause.** Whenever a charge is filed by or on behalf of a person claiming to be aggrieved, or by a member of the Commission, alleging that an employer, employment agency, labor organization, or joint labor-management committee controlling apprenticeship or other training or retraining, including on-the-job training programs, has engaged in an unlawful employment practice, the Commission shall serve a notice of the charge (including the date, place and circumstances of the alleged unlawful employment practice) on such employer, employment agency, labor organization, or joint labor-management committee (hereinafter referred to as the "respondent") within ten days, and shall make an investigation thereof. Charges shall be in writing under oath or affirmation and shall contain such information and be in such form as the Commission requires. Charges shall not be made public by the Commission. If the Commission determines after such investigation that there is not reasonable cause to believe that the charge is true, it shall dismiss the charge and promptly notify the person claiming to be aggrieved and the respondent of its action. In determining whether reasonable cause exists, the Commission shall accord substantial weight to final findings and orders made by State or local authorities in proceedings commenced under State or local law pursuant to the requirements of subsections (c) and (d) of this section. If the Commission determines after such investigation that there is reasonable cause to believe that the charge is true, the Commission shall endeavor to eliminate any such alleged unlawful employment practice by informal methods of conference, conciliation, and persuasion.

(c) **State or local enforcement proceedings; notification of State or local authority; time for filing charges with Commission; commencement of proceedings.** In the case of an alleged unlawful employment practice occurring in a State, or political subdivision of a State, which has a State or local law prohibiting the unlawful employment practice alleged and establishing or authorizing a State or local authority to grant or seek relief from such practice or to institute criminal proceedings with respect thereto upon receiving notice thereof, no charge may be filed under subsection (b) of this section by the person aggrieved before the expiration of sixty days after proceedings have been commenced under the State or local law, unless such proceedings have been earlier terminated, provided that such sixty-day period shall be extended to one hundred and twenty days during the first year after the effective date of such State or local law. If any requirement for the commencement of such proceedings is imposed by a State or local authority other than a requirement of the filing of a written and signed statement of the facts upon which the proceeding is based, the proceeding shall be deemed to have been commenced for the purposes of this subsection at the time such statement is sent by registered mail to the appropriate State or local authority.

(e) **Time for filing charges; time for service of notice of charge on respondent; filing of charge by Commission with State or local agency.**

(1) A charge under this section shall be filed within one hundred and eighty days after the alleged unlawful employment practice occurred and notice of the charge (including the date, place and circumstances of the alleged unlawful employment practice) shall be served upon the person against whom such charge is made within ten days thereafter, except that in a case of an unlawful employment practice with respect to which the person aggrieved has initially instituted proceedings with a State or local agency with authority to grant or seek relief from such practice or to institute criminal proceedings with respect thereto upon receiving notice thereof, such charge shall be filed by or on behalf of the person aggrieved within three hundred days after the alleged unlawful employment practice occurred, or within thirty days after receiving notice that the State or local agency has terminated the proceedings under the State or local law, whichever is earlier, and a copy of such charge shall be filed by the Commission with the State or local agency.

(2) For purposes of this section, an unlawful employment practice occurs, with respect to a seniority system that has been adopted for an intentionally discriminatory purpose in violation of this subchapter (whether or not that discriminatory purpose is apparent on the face of the seniority provision), when the seniority system is adopted, when an individual becomes subject to the seniority system, or when a person aggrieved is injured by the application of the seniority system or provision of the system.

(3) (A) For purposes of this section, an unlawful employment practice occurs, with respect to discrimination in compensation in violation of this title, when a discriminatory compensation decision or other practice is adopted, when an individual becomes subject to a discriminatory compensation decision or other practice, or when an individual is affected by application of a discriminatory compensation decision or other practice, including each time wages, benefits, or other compensation is paid, resulting in whole or in part from such a decision or practice.

(B) In addition to any relief authorized by section 1977A of the Revised Statutes (42 U.S.C. 1981a), liability may accrue and an aggrieved person may obtain relief as provided in subsection (g)(1), including recovery of back pay for up to two years preceding the filing of the charge, where the unlawful employment practices that have occurred during the charge filing period are similar or related to unlawful employment practices with regard to discrimination in compensation that occurred outside the time for filing a charge.

[Subsection (3) is part of the "Lilly Ledbetter Fair Pay Act of 2009" and the amendments made by this Act, take effect as if enacted on May 28, 2007 and apply to all claims of discrimination in compensation under title VII of the Civil Rights Act of 1964, the Age Discrimination in Employment Act of 1967, title I and section 503 of the Americans with Disabilities Act of 1990, and sections 501 and 504 of the Rehabilitation Act of 1973, that are pending on or after that date.]

(f) Civil action by Commission, Attorney General, or person aggrieved; preconditions; procedure; appointment of attorney; payment of fees, costs, or security; intervention; stay of Federal proceedings; action for appropriate temporary or preliminary relief pending final disposition of charge; jurisdiction and venue of United States courts; designation of judge to hear and determine case; assignment of case for hearing; expedition of case; appointment of master.

(1) If within thirty days after a charge is filed with the Commission or within thirty days after expiration of any period of reference under subsection (c) or (d) of this section, the Commission has been unable to secure from the respondent a conciliation agreement acceptable to the Commission, the Commission may bring a civil action against any respondent not a government, governmental agency, or political subdivision named in the charge. In the case of a respondent which is a government, governmental agency, or political subdivision, if the Commission has been unable to secure from the respondent a conciliation agreement acceptable to the Commission, the Commission shall take no further action and shall refer the case to the Attorney General who may bring a civil action against such respondent in the appropriate United States district court. The person or persons aggrieved shall have the right to intervene in a civil action brought by the Commission or the Attorney General in a case involving a government, governmental agency, or political subdivision. If a charge filed with the Commission pursuant to subsection (b) of this section, is dismissed by the Commission, or if within one hundred and eighty days from the filing of such charge or the expiration of any period of reference under subsection (c) or (d) of this section, whichever is later, the Commission has not filed a civil action under this section or the Attorney General has not filed a civil action in a case involving a government, governmental agency, or political subdivision, or the Commission has not entered into a conciliation agreement to which the person aggrieved is a party, the Commission, or the Attorney General in a case involving a government, governmental agency, or political subdivision, shall so notify the person aggrieved and within ninety days after the giving of such notice a civil action may be brought against the respondent named in the charge **(A)** by the person claiming to be aggrieved or **(B)** if such charge was filed by a member of the Commission, by any person whom the charge alleges was aggrieved by the alleged unlawful mployment practice. Upon application by the complainant and in such circumstances as ̇ ̇e court may deem just, the court may appoint an attorney for such complainant and ̇ ̇ay authorize the commencement of the action without the payment of fees, costs, or security. . . .

(2) Whenever a charge is filed with the Commission and the Commission concludes on the basis of a preliminary investigation that prompt judicial action is necessary to carry out the purposes of this Act, the Commission, or the Attorney General in a case involving a government, governmental agency, or political subdivision, may bring an action for appropriate temporary or preliminary relief pending final disposition of such charge. Any temporary restraining order or other order granting preliminary or temporary relief shall be issued in accordance with rule 65 of the Federal Rules of Civil Procedure. It shall be the duty of a court having jurisdiction over proceedings under this section to assign cases for hearing at the earliest practicable date and to cause such cases to be in every way expedited.

(3) Each United States district court and each United States court of a place subject to the jurisdiction of the United States shall have jurisdiction of actions brought under this subchapter. Such an action may be brought in any judicial district in the State in which the unlawful employment practice is alleged to have been committed, in the judicial district in which the employment records relevant to such practice are maintained and administered, or in the judicial district in which the aggrieved person would have worked but for the alleged unlawful employment practice, but if the respondent is not found within any such district, such an action may be brought within the judicial district in which the respondent has his principal office.

*   *   *

(g) [Relief Available.]

(1) If the court finds that the respondent has intentionally engaged in or is intentionally engaging in an unlawful employment practice charged in the complaint, the court may enjoin the respondent from engaging in such unlawful employment practice, and order such affirmative action as may be appropriate, which may include, but is not limited to, reinstatement or hiring of employees, with or without back pay (payable by the employer, employment agency, or labor organization, as the case may be, responsible for the unlawful employment practice), or any other equitable relief as the court deems appropriate. Back pay liability shall not accrue from a date more than two years prior to the filing of a charge with the Commission. Interim earnings or amounts earnable with reasonable diligence by the person or persons discriminated against shall operate to reduce the back pay otherwise allowable.

(2) (A) No order of the court shall require the admission or reinstatement of an individual as a member of a union, or the hiring, reinstatement, or promotion of an individual as an employee, or the payment to him of any back pay, if such individual was refused admission, suspended, or expelled, or was refused employment or advancement or was suspended or discharged for any reason other than discrimination on account of race, color, religion, sex, or national origin or in violation of section 2000e-3(a) of this title.

(B) On a claim in which an individual proves a violation under section 2000e-2(m) of this title and a respondent demonstrates that the respondent would have taken the same action in the absence of the impermissible motivating factor, the court–

    (i) may grant declaratory relief, injunctive relief (except as provided in clause (ii)), and attorney's fees and costs demonstrated to be directly attributable only to the pursuit of a claim under section 2000e-2(m) of this title; and

    (ii) shall not award damages or issue an order requiring any admission, reinstatement, hiring, promotion, or payment, described in subparagraph (A).

(k) **Attorney's fee; liability of Commission and United States for costs.** In any action or proceeding under this subchapter the court, in its discretion, may allow the prevailing party, other than the Commission or the United States, a reasonable attorney's fee (including expert fees) as part of the costs, and the Commission and the United States shall be liable for costs the same as a private person.

42 U.S.C. § 2000e-10 [§ 711]

§ 2000e-10. Posting of notices; penalties.

(a) Every employer, employment agency, and labor organization, as the case may be, shall post and keep posted in conspicuous places upon its premises where notices to employees, applicants for employment, and members are customarily posted a notice to be prepared or approved by the Commission setting forth excerpts from or, summaries of, the pertinent provisions of this subchapter and information pertinent to the filing of a complaint.

(b) A willful violation of this section shall be punishable by a fine of not more than $100 for each separate offense.

42 U.S.C. § 2000e-11 [§ 712]

§ 2000e-11. Veteran's special rights or preference

Nothing contained in this subchapter shall be construed to repeal or modify any Federal, State, territorial, or local law creating special rights or preference for veterans.

42 U.S.C. § 2000e-12 [§ 713]

§ 2000e-12. Regulations; conformity of regulations with administrative procedure provisions; reliance on interpretations and instructions of Commission.

(a) The Commission shall have authority from time to time to issue, amend, or rescind suitable procedural regulations to carry out the provisions of this subchapter. Regulations issued under this section shall be in conformity with the standards and limitations of subchapter II of chapter 5 of Title 5.

(b) In any action or proceeding based on any alleged unlawful employment practice, no person shall be subject to any liability or punishment for or on account of (1) the commission by such person of an unlawful employment practice if he pleads and proves that the act or omission complained of was in good faith, in conformity with, and in reliance on any written interpretation or opinion of the Commission, or (2) the failure of such person to publish and file any information required by any provision of this subchapter if he pleads and proves that he failed to publish and file such information in good faith, in conformity with the instructions of the Commission issued under this subchapter regarding the filing of such information. Such a defense, if established, shall be a bar to the action or proceeding, notwithstanding that (A) after such act or omission, such interpretation or opinion is modified or rescinded or is determined by judicial authority to be invalid or of no legal effect, or (B) after publishing or filing the description and annual reports, such publication or filing is determined by judicial authority not to be in conformity with the requirements of this subchapter.

42 U.S.C. § 2000e-16 [§ 717]

§ 2000e-16. Employment by Federal Government

(a) **Discriminatory practices prohibited; employees or applicants for employment subject to coverage.** All personnel actions affecting employees or applicants for employment (except with regard to aliens employed outside the limits of the United States) in military departments as defined in section 102 of Title 5, in executive agencies as defined in section 105 of Title 5 (including employees and applicants for employment who are paid from appropriated funds), in the United States Postal Service and the Postal Rate Commission, in those units of the Government of the District of Columbia having positions in the competitive service, and in those units of the judicial branch of the Federal Government having positions in the competitive service, and in the Government Printing Office, the General Accounting Office, and in the Library of Congress shall be made free from any discrimination based on race, color, religion, sex, or national origin.

(b) **Role of Civil Service Commission; compliance of departments and agencies with rules and regulations.** Except as otherwise provided in this subsection, the Civil Service Commission shall have authority to enforce the provisions of subsection (a) of this section through appropriate remedies, including reinstatement or hiring of employees with or without back pay, as will effectuate the policies of this section, and shall issue such rules, regulations, orders and instructions as it deems necessary and appropriate to carry out its responsibilities under this section. The Civil Service Commission shall–

(1) be responsible for the annual review and approval of a national and regional equal employment opportunity plan which each department and agency and each appropriate unit referred to in subsection (a) of this section shall submit in order to maintain an affirmative program of equal employment opportunity for all such employees and applicants for employment;

(2) be responsible for the review and evaluation of the operation of all agency equal employment opportunity programs, periodically obtaining and publishing (on at least a semiannual basis) progress reports from each such department, agency, or unit; and

(3) consult with and solicit the recommendations of interested individuals, groups, and organizations relating to equal employment opportunity.

The head of each such department, agency, or unit shall comply with such rules, regulations, orders, and instructions which shall include a provision that an employee or applicant for employment shall be notified of any final action taken on any complaint of discrimination filed by him thereunder. The plan submitted by each department, agency, and unit shall include, but not be limited to–

(1) (1) provision for the establishment of training and education programs designed to provide a maximum opportunity for employees to advance so as to perform at their highest potential; and

(2) (2) a description of the qualifications in terms of training and experience relating to equal employment opportunity for the principal and operating officials of each such department, agency, or unit responsible for carrying out the equal employment opportunity program and of the allocation of personnel and resources proposed by such department, agency, or unit to carry out its equal employment opportunity program.

With respect to employment in the Library of Congress, authorities granted in this subsection to the Civil Service Commission shall be exercised by the Librarian of Congress.

(c) **Civil action by employee or applicant for employment for redress of grievances: time for bringing of action; head of department, agency, or unit as defendant.** Within 90 days of receipt of notice of final action taken by a department, agency, or unit referred to in subsection (a) of this section, or by the Civil Service Commission upon an appeal from a decision or order of such department, agency, or unit on a complaint of discrimination based on race, color, religion, sex or national origin, brought pursuant to subsection (a) of this section, Executive Order 11478 or any succeeding Executive orders, or after one hundred and eighty days from the filing of the initial charge with the department, agency, or unit or with the Civil Service Commission on appeal from a decision or order of such department, agency, or unit until such time as final action may be taken by a department, agency, or unit, an employee or applicant for employment, if aggrieved by the final disposition of his complaint, or by the failure to take final action on his complaint, may file a civil action as provided in section 2000e-5 of this title, in which civil action the head of the department, agency, or unit, as appropriate, shall be the defendant.

(d) Section 2000e-5(f) through (k) of this title applicable to civil actions. The provisions of section 2000e-5(f) through (k) of this title, as applicable, shall govern civil actions brought hereunder, and the same interest to compensate for delay in payment shall be available as in cases involving nonpublic parties.

(e) Government agency or official not relieved of responsibility to assure nondiscrimination in employment or equal employment opportunity. Nothing contained in this Act shall relieve any Government agency or official of its or his primary responsibility to assure nondiscrimination in employment as required by the Constitution and statutes or of its or his responsibilities under Executive Order 11478 relating to equal employment opportunity in the Federal Government.

FAIR HOUSING ACT

42 U.S.C. § 3604

§ 3604. Discrimination in the sale or rental of housing and other prohibited practices

As made applicable by section 3603 of this title and except as exempted by sections 3603(b) and 3607 of this title, it shall be unlawful—

(a) To refuse to sell or rent after the making of a bona fide offer, or to refuse to negotiate for the sale or rental of, or otherwise make unavailable or deny, a dwelling to any person because of race, color, religion, sex, familial status, or national origin.

(b) To discriminate against any person in the terms, conditions, or privileges of sale or rental of a dwelling, or in the provision of services or facilities in connection therewith, because of race, color, religion, sex, familial status, or national origin.

(c) To make, print, or publish, or cause to be made, printed, or published any notice, statement, or advertisement, with respect to the sale or rental of a dwelling that indicates any preference, limitation, or discrimination based on race, color, religion, sex, handicap, familial status, or national origin, or an intention to make any such preference, limitation, or discrimination.

(d) To represent to any person because of race, color, religion, sex, handicap, familial status, or national origin that any dwelling is not available for inspection, sale, or rental when such dwelling is in fact so available.

(e) For profit, to induce or attempt to induce any person to sell or rent any dwelling by representations regarding the entry or prospective entry into the neighborhood of a person or persons of a particular race, color, religion, sex, handicap, familial status, or national origin.

(f) **(1)** To discriminate in the sale or rental, or to otherwise make unavailable or deny, a dwelling to any buyer or renter because of a handicap of—
    (A) that buyer or renter,
    (B) a person residing in or intending to reside in that dwelling after it is so sold, rented, or made available; or
    (C) any person associated with that buyer or renter.
(2) To discriminate against any person in the terms, conditions, or privileges of sale or rental of a dwelling, or in the provision of services or facilities in connection with such dwelling, because of a handicap of—
    (A) that person; or
    (B) a person residing in or intending to reside in that dwelling after it is so sold, rented, or made available; or
    (C) any person associated with that person.
(3) (For purposes of this subsection, discrimination includes—
    (A) a refusal to permit, at the expense of the handicapped person, reasonable modifications of existing premises occupied or to be occupied by such person if such modifications may be necessary to afford such person full enjoyment of the premises except that, in the case of a rental, the landlord may where it is reasonable to do so condition permission for a modification on the renter agreeing to restore the interior of the premises to the condition that existed before the modification, reasonable wear and tear excepted.
    (B) a refusal to make reasonable accommodations in rules, policies, practices, or services, when such accommodations may be necessary to afford such person equal opportunity to use and enjoy a dwelling; or
    (C) in connection with the design and construction of covered multifamily dwellings for first occupancy after the date that is 30 months after September 13, 1988, a failure to design and construct those dwellings in such a manner that—
        (i) the public use and common use portions of such dwellings are readily accessible to and usable by handicapped persons;

(ii) all the doors designed to allow passage into and within all premises within such dwellings are sufficiently wide to allow passage by handicapped persons in wheelchairs; and

(iii) all premises within such dwellings contain the following features of adaptive design:

(I) an accessible route into and through the dwelling;

(II) light switches, electrical outlets, thermostats, and other environmental controls in accessible locations;

(III) reinforcements in bathroom walls to allow later installation of grab bars; and

(IV) usable kitchens and bathrooms such that an individual in a wheelchair can maneuver about the space.

42 U.S.C. § 3605

§ 3605. Discrimination in residential real estate-related transactions

(a) In general

It shall be unlawful for any person or other entity whose business includes engaging in residential real estate-related transactions to discriminate against any person in making available such a transaction, or in the terms or conditions of such a transaction, because of race, color, religion, sex, handicap, familial status, or national origin.

(b) "Residential real estate-related transaction" defined

As used in this section, the term "residential real estate-related transaction" means any of the following:

(1) The making or purchasing of loans or providing other financial assistance—

(A) **(A)** for purchasing, constructing, improving, repairing, or maintaining a dwelling; or

(B) **(B)** secured by residential real estate.

(2) The selling, brokering, or appraising of residential real property.

42 U.S.C. § 3606

§ 3606. Discrimination in the provision of brokerage services

After December 31, 1968, it shall be unlawful to deny any person access to or membership or participation in any multiple-listing service, real estate brokers' organization or other service, organization, or facility relating to the business of selling or renting dwellings, or to discriminate against him in the terms or conditions of such access, membership, or participation, on account of race, color, religion, sex, handicap, familial status, or national origin.

§ 3610. Administrative enforcement; preliminary matters

(a) Complaints and answers

(1) (A)(i) An aggrieved person may, not later than one year after an alleged discriminatory housing practice has occurred or terminated, file a complaint with the Secretary alleging such discriminatory housing practice. The Secretary, on the Secretary's own initiative, may also file such a complaint.

> **(ii)** Such complaints shall be in writing and shall contain such information and be in such form as the Secretary requires.
>
> **(iii)** The Secretary may also investigate housing practices to determine whether a complaint should be brought under this section.

[The remainder of this section describes in detail the administrative proceedings.]

42 U.S.C. § 3613.

§ 3613. Enforcement by private persons

(a) Civil action

(1) (A) An aggrieved person may commence a civil action in an appropriate United States district court or State court not later than 2 years after the occurrence or the termination of an alleged discriminatory housing practice, or the breach of a conciliation agreement entered into under this subchapter, whichever occurs last, to obtain appropriate relief with respect to such discriminatory housing practice or breach.

> **(B)** The computation of such 2-year period shall not include any time during which an administrative proceeding under this subchapter was pending with respect to a complaint or charge under this subchapter based upon such discriminatory housing practice. This subparagraph does not apply to actions arising from a breach of a conciliation agreement.

(2) An aggrieved person may commence a civil action under this subsection whether or not a complaint has been filed under section 3610(a) of this title and without regard to the status of any such complaint, but if the Secretary or a State or local agency has obtained a conciliation agreement with the consent of an aggrieved person, no action may be filed under this subsection by such aggrieved person with respect to the alleged discriminatory housing practice which forms the basis for such complaint except for the purpose of enforcing the terms of such an agreement.

(3) An aggrieved person may not commence a civil action under this subsection with respect to an alleged discriminatory housing practice which forms the basis of a charge issued by the Secretary if an administrative law judge has commenced a hearing on the record under this subchapter with respect to such charge.

(c) Relief which may be granted

(1) In a civil action under subsection (a) of this section, if the court finds that a discriminatory housing practice has occurred or is about to occur, the court may award to the plaintiff actual and punitive damages, and subject to subsection (d) of this section, may grant as relief, as the court deems appropriate, any permanent or temporary injunction, temporary restraining order, or other order (including an order enjoining the defendant from engaging in such practice or ordering such affirmative action as may be appropriate).

(2) In a civil action under subsection (a) of this section, the court, in its discretion, may allow the prevailing party, other than the United States, a reasonable attorney's fee and costs. The United States shall be liable for such fees and costs to the same extent as a private person.

42 U.S.C. § 3617

§ 3617. Interference, coercion, or intimidation

It shall be unlawful to coerce, intimidate, threaten, or interfere with any person in the exercise or enjoyment of, or on account of his having exercised or enjoyed, or on account of his having aided or encouraged any other person in the exercise or enjoyment of, any right granted or protected by section 3603, 3604, 3605, or 3606 of this title.

AMERICANS WITH DISABILITIES ACT

TITLE I: EMPLOYMENT

42 U.S.C. § 12102

§ 12102. Definitions

(1) Disability. The term "disability" means, with respect to an individual—

(A) a physical or mental impairment that substantially limits one or more major life activities of such individual;

(B) a record of such an impairment; or

(C) being regarded as having such an impairment (as described in paragraph (3)).

(2) Major Life Activities.

(A) In General. For purposes of paragraph (1), major life activities include, but are not limited to, caring for oneself, performing manual tasks, seeing, hearing, eating, sleeping, walking, standing, lifting, bending, speaking, breathing, learning, reading, concentrating, thinking, communicating, and working.

(B) Major Bodily Functions. For purposes of paragraph (1), a major life activity also includes the operation of a major bodily function, including but not limited to, functions of the immune system, normal cell growth, digestive, bowel, bladder, neurological, brain, respiratory, circulatory, endocrine, and reproductive functions.

(3) Regarded as Having Such an Impairment. For purposes of paragraph (1)(C):

(A) An individual meets the requirement of "being regarded as having such an impairment" if the individual establishes that he or she has been subjected to an action prohibited under this chapter because of an actual or perceived physical or mental impairment whether or not the impairment limits or is perceived to limit a major life activity.

(B) Paragraph (1)(C) shall not apply to impairments that are transitory and minor. A transitory impairment is an impairment with an actual or expected duration of 6 months or less.

(4) Rules of Construction Regarding the Definition of Disability. The definition of "disability" in paragraph (1) shall be construed in accordance with the following:

(A) The definition of disability in this Act shall be construed in favor of broad coverage of individuals under this Act, to the maximum extent permitted by the terms of this chapter.

(B) The term "substantially limits" shall be interpreted consistently with the findings and purposes of the ADA Amendments Act of 2008.

(C) An impairment that substantially limits one major life activity need not limit other major life activities in order to be considered a disability.

(D) An impairment that is episodic or in remission is a disability if it would substantially limit a major life activity when active.

(E) (i) The determination of whether an impairment substantially limits a major life activity shall be made without regard to the ameliorative effects of mitigating measures such as—

> **(I)** medication, medical supplies, equipment, or appliances, low-vision devices (which do not include ordinary eyeglasses or contact lenses), prosthetics including limbs and devices, hearing aids and cochlear implants or other implantable hearing devices, mobility devices, or oxygen therapy equipment and supplies;
>
> **(II)** use of assistive technology;
>
> **(III)** reasonable accommodations or auxiliary aids or services; or
>
> **(IV)** learned behavioral or adaptive neurological modifications.

(ii) The ameliorative effects of the mitigating measures of ordinary eyeglasses or contact lenses shall be considered in determining whether an impairment substantially limits a major life activity.

(iii) As used in this subparagraph—

    (I) the term "ordinary eyeglasses or contact lenses" means lenses that are intended to fully correct visual acuity or eliminate refractive error; and

    (II) the term "low-vision devices" means devices that magnify, enhance, or otherwise augment a visual image.

42 U.S.C. § 12111

§ 12111. Definitions

As used in this subchapter:

(1) Commission. The term "Commission" means the Equal Employment Opportunity Commission established by section 2000e-4 of this title.

(2) Covered entity. The term "covered entity" means an employer, employment agency, labor organization, or joint labor-management committee.

(3) Direct threat. The term "direct threat" means a significant risk to the health or safety of others that cannot be eliminated by reasonable accommodation.

(4) Employee. The term "employee" means an individual employed by an employer. With respect to employment in a foreign country, such term includes an individual who is a citizen of the United States.

(5) Employer

    (A) In general. The term "employer" means a person engaged in an industry affecting commerce who has 15 or more employees for each working day in each of 20 or more calendar weeks in the current or preceding calendar year, and any agent of such person, except that, for two years following the effective date of this subchapter, an employer means a person engaged in an industry affecting commerce who has 25 or more employees for each working day in each of 20 or more calendar weeks in the current or preceding year, and any agent of such person.

    (B) Exceptions. The term "employer" does not include–

        (i) the United States, a corporation wholly owned by the government of the United States, or an Indian tribe; or

        (ii) a bona fide private membership club (other than a labor organization) that is exempt from taxation under section 501(c) of Title 26.

(6) Illegal use of drugs

    (A) In general. The term "illegal use of drugs" means the use of drugs, the possession or distribution of which is unlawful under the Controlled Substances Act (21 U.S.C. § 812). Such term does not include the use of a drug taken under supervision by a licensed health care professional, or other uses authorized by the Controlled Substances Act [21 U.S.C. § 801 *et seq.*] or other provisions of Federal law.

(B) Drugs. The term "drug" means a controlled substance, as defined in schedules I through V of section 202 of the Controlled Substances Act [21 U.S.C. § 812].

(7) Person, etc. The terms "person," "labor organization," "employment agency," "commerce," and "in-dustry affecting commerce," shall have the same meaning given such terms in section 2000e of this title.

(8) Qualified individual. The term "qualified individual" means an individual who, with or without reasonable accommodation, can perform the essential functions of the employment position that such individual holds or desires. For the purposes of this subchapter, consideration shall be given to the employer's judgment as to what functions of a job are essential, and if an employer has prepared a written description before advertising or interviewing applicants for the job, this description shall be considered evidence of the essential functions of the job.

(9) Reasonable accommodation. The term "reasonable accommodation" may include–

(A) making existing facilities used by employees readily accessible to and usable by individuals with disabilities; and

(B) job restructuring, part-time or modified work schedules, reassignment to a vacant position, acquisition or modification of equipment or devices, appropriate adjustment or modifications of examinations, training materials or policies, the provision of qualified readers or interpreters, and other similar accommodations for individuals with disabilities.

(10) Undue hardship

(A) In general. The term "undue hardship" means an action requiring significant difficulty or expense, when considered in light of the factors set forth in subparagraph (B).

(B) Factors to be considered. In determining whether an accommodation would impose an undue hardship on a covered entity, factors to be considered include–

(i) the nature and cost of the accommodation needed under this chapter;

(ii) the overall financial resources of the facility or facilities involved in the provision of the reasonable accommodation; the number of persons employed at such facility; the effect on expenses and resources, or the impact otherwise of such accommodation upon the operation of the facility;

(iii) the overall financial resources of the covered entity; the overall size of the business of a covered entity with respect to the number of its employees; the number, type, and location of its facilities; and

(iv) the type of operation or operations of the covered entity, including the composition, structure, and functions of the workforce of such entity; the geographic separateness, administrative, or fiscal relationship of the facility or facilities in question to the covered entity.

42 U.S.C. § 12112

§ 12112. Discrimination

(a) **General rule.** No covered entity shall discriminate against a qualified individual on the basis of disability in regard to job application procedures, the hiring, advancement, or discharge of employees, employee compensation, job training, and other terms, conditions, and privileges of employment.

(b) **Construction.** As used in subsection (a) of this section, the term "discriminate against a qualified individual on the basis of disability" includes–

(1) limiting, segregating, or classifying a job applicant or employee in a way that adversely affects the opportunities or status of such applicant or employee because of the disability of such applicant or employee;

(2) participating in a contractual or other arrangement or relationship that has the effect of subjecting a covered entity's qualified applicant or employee with a disability to the discrimination prohibited by this subchapter (such relationship includes a relationship with an employment or referral agency, labor union, an organization providing fringe benefits to an employee of the covered entity, or an organization providing training and apprenticeship programs);

(3) utilizing standards, criteria, or methods of administration–

  (A) that have the effect of discrimination on the basis of disability; or

  (B) that perpetuate the discrimination of others who are subject to common administrative control;

(4) excluding or otherwise denying equal jobs or benefits to a qualified individual because of the known disability of an individual with whom the qualified individual is known to have a relationship or association;

(5) (A) not making reasonable accommodations to the known physical or metal limitations of an otherwise qualified individual with a disability who is an applicant or employee, unless such covered entity can demonstrate that the accommodation would impose an undue hardship on the operation of the business of such covered entity; or

  (B) denying employment opportunities to a job applicant or employee who is an otherwise qualified individual with a disability, if such denial is based on the need of such covered entity to make reasonable accommodation to the physical or mental impairments of the employee or applicant;

(6) using qualification standards, employment tests or other selection criteria that screen out or tend to screen out an individual with a disability or a class of individuals with disabilities unless the standard, test or other selection criteria, as used by the covered entity, is shown to be job-related for the position in question and is consistent with business necessity; and

(7) failing to select and administer tests concerning employment in the most effective manner to ensure that, when such test is administered to a job applicant or employee who

has a disability that impairs sensory, manual, or speaking skills, such test results accurately reflect the skills, aptitude, or whatever other factor of such applicant or employee that such test purports to measure, rather than reflecting the impaired sensory, manual, or speaking skills of such employee or applicant (except where such skills are the factors that the test purports to measure).

* * *

(d) **Medical examinations and inquiries**

(1) **In general.** The prohibition against discrimination as referred to in subsection (a) of this section shall include medical examinations and inquiries.

(2) **Preemployment**

(A) **Prohibited examination or inquiry.** Except as provided in paragraph (3), a covered entity shall not conduct a medical examination or make inquiries of a job applicant as to whether such applicant is an individual with a disability or as to the nature or severity of such disability.

(B) **Acceptable inquiry.** A covered entity may make preemployment inquiries into the ability of an applicant to perform job-related functions.

(3) **Employment entrance examination.** A covered entity may require a medical examination after an offer of employment has been made to a job applicant and prior to the commencement of the employment duties of such applicant, and may condition an offer of employment on the results of such examination, if–

(A) all entering employees are subjected to such an examination regardless of disability;

(B) information obtained regarding the medical condition or history of the applicant is collected and maintained on separate forms and in separate medical files and is treated as a confidential medical record, except that–

(i) supervisors and managers may be informed regarding necessary restrictions on the work or duties of the employee and necessary accommodations;

(ii) first aid and safety personnel may be informed, when appropriate, if the disability might require emergency treatment; and

(iii) government officials investigating compliance with this chapter shall be provided relevant information on request; and

(C) the results of such examination are used only in accordance with this subchapter.

(4) **Examination and inquiry**

(A) **Prohibited examinations and inquiries.** A covered entity shall not require a medical examination and shall not make inquiries of an employee as to whether such employee is an individual with a disability or as to the nature or severity of the disability, unless such examination or inquiry is shown to be job-related and consistent with business necessity.

(B) Acceptable examinations and inquiries. A covered entity may conduct voluntary medical examinations, including voluntary medical histories, which are part of an employee health program available to employees at that work site. A covered entity may make inquiries into the ability of an employee to perform job-related functions.

(C) Requirement. Information obtained under subparagraph (B) regarding the medical condition or history of any employee are subject to the requirements of subparagraphs (B) and (C) of paragraph (3).

42 U.S.C. § 12113

§ 12113. Defenses

(a) **In general.** It may be a defense to a charge of discrimination under this chapter that an alleged application of qualification standards, tests, or selection criteria that screen out or tend to screen out or otherwise deny a job or benefit to an individual with a disability has been shown to be job-related and consistent with business necessity, and such performance cannot be accomplished by reasonable accommodation, as required under this subchapter.

(b) **Qualification standards.** The term "qualification standards" may include a requirement that an individual shall not pose a direct threat to the health or safety of other individuals in the workplace.

(c) **Qualification standards and tests related to uncorrected vision.** Notwithstanding section 12102(4)(E)(ii), a covered entity shall not use qualification standards, employment tests, or other selection criteria based on an individual's uncorrected vision unless the standard, test, or other selection criteria, as used by the covered entity, is shown to be job-related for the position in question and consistent with business necessity.

(d) **Religious entities**

(1) **In general.** This subchapter shall not prohibit a religious corporation, association, educational institution, or society from giving preference in employment to individuals of a particular religion to perform work connected with the carrying on by such corporation, association, educational institution, or society of its activities.

(2) **Religious tenets requirement.** Under this subchapter, a religious organization may require that all applicants and employees conform to the religious tenets of such organization.

§ 12114. Illegal use of drugs and alcohol

(a) **Qualified individual with a disability.** For purposes of this subchapter, "a qualified individual with a disability" shall not include any employee or applicant who is currently engaging in the illegal use of drugs, when the covered entity acts on the basis of such use.

(b) **Rules of construction.** Nothing in subsection (a) of this section shall be construed to exclude as a qualified individual with a disability an individual who–

(1) has successfully completed a supervised drug rehabilitation program and is no longer engaging in the illegal use of drugs, or has otherwise been rehabilitated successfully and is no longer engaging in such use;

(2) is participating in a supervised rehabilitation program and is no longer engaging in such use; or

(3) is erroneously regarded as engaging in such use, but is not engaging in such use; except that it shall not be a violation of this chapter for a covered entity to adopt or administer reasonable policies or procedures, including but not limited to drug testing, designed to ensure that an individual described in paragraph (1) or (2) is no longer engaging in the illegal use of drugs.

(c) **Authority of covered entity.** A covered entity—

(1) may prohibit the illegal use of drugs and the use of alcohol at the workplace by all employees;

(2) may require that employees shall not be under the influence of alcohol or be engaging in the illegal use of drugs at the workplace;

(3) may require that employees behave in conformance with the requirements established under the Drug-Free Workplace Act of 1988 (41 U.S.C. § 701 *et seq.*);

(4) may hold an employee who engages in the illegal use of drugs or who is an alcoholic to the same qualification standards for employment or job performance and behavior that such entity holds other employees, even if any unsatisfactory performance or behavior is related to the drug use or alcoholism of such employee; and

(5) may, with respect to Federal regulations regarding alcohol and the illegal use of drugs, require that—

(A) employees comply with the standards established in such regulations of the Department of Defense, if the employees of the covered entity are employed in an industry subject to such regulations, including complying with regulations (if any) that apply to employment in sensitive positions in such an industry, in the case of employees of the covered entity who are employed in such positions (as defined in the regulations of the Department of Defense);

(B) employees comply with the standards established in such regulations of the Nuclear Regulatory Commission, if the employees of the covered entity are employed in an industry subject to such regulations, including complying with regulations (if any) that apply to employment in sensitive positions in such an industry, in the case of employees of the covered entity who are employed in such positions (as defined in the regulations of the Nuclear Regulatory Commission); and

(C) employees comply with the standards established in such regulations of the Department of Transportation, if the employees of the covered entity are employed in a transportation industry subject to such regulations, including complying with such regulations (if any) that apply to employment in sensitive positions in such an industry, in the case of employees of the covered entity who are employed in such positions (as defined in the regulations of the Department of Transportation).

(d) Drug testing

(1) In general. For purposes of this subchapter, a test to determine the illegal use of drugs shall not be considered a medical examination.

(2) Construction. Nothing in this subchapter shall be construed to encourage, prohibit, or authorize the conducting of drug testing for the illegal use of drugs by job applicants or employees or making employment decisions based on such test results.

(e) Transportation employees. Nothing in this subchapter shall be construed to encourage, prohibit, restrict, or authorize the otherwise lawful exercise by entities subject to the jurisdiction of the Department of Transportation of authority to–

(1) test employees of such entities in, and applicants for, positions involving safety-sensitive duties for the illegal use of drugs and for on-duty impairment by alcohol; and

(2) remove such persons who test positive for illegal use of drugs and on-duty impairment by alcohol pursuant to paragraph (1) from safety-sensitive duties in implementing subsection (c) of this section.

42 U.S.C. § 12117

§ 12117. Enforcement

(a) Powers, remedies, and procedures. The powers, remedies, and procedures set forth in sections 2000e-4, 2000e-5, 2000e-6, 2000e-8, and 2000e-9 of this title shall be the powers, remedies, and procedures this subchapter provides to the Commission, to the Attorney General, or to any person alleging discrimination on the basis of disability in violation of any provision of this chapter, or regulations promulgated under section 12116 of this title, concerning employment.

(b) Coordination. The agencies with enforcement authority for actions which allege employment discrimination under this subchapter and under the Rehabilitation Act of 1973 [29 U.S.C. § 701 *et seq.*] shall develop procedures to ensure that administrative complaints filed under this subchapter and under the Rehabilitation Act of 1973 [29 U.S.C. § 701 *et seq.*] are dealt with in a manner that avoids duplication of effort and prevents imposition of inconsistent or conflicting standards for the same requirements under this subchapter and the Rehabilitation Act of 1973.

TITLE III. PUBLIC ACCOMMODATIONS AND SERVICES OPERATED BY PRIVATE ENTITIES

42 U.S.C. § 12181

§ 12181. Definitions

As used in this subchapter:

(1) **Commerce.** The term "commerce" means travel, trade, traffic, commerce, transportation, or communication–

   (A) among the several States;

   (B) between any foreign country or any territory or possession and any State; or

   (C) between points in the same State but through another State or foreign country.

(2) **Commercial facilities.** The term "commercial facilities" means facilities–

   (A) that are intended for nonresidential use; and

   (B) whose operations will affect commerce.

Such term shall not include railroad locomotives, railroad freight cars, railroad cabooses, railroad cars described in section 242 or covered under this subchapter, railroad rights-of-way, or facilities that are covered or expressly exempted from coverage under the Fair Housing Act of 1968 (42 U.S.C. 3601 *et seq.*).

* * *

(6) **Private entity.** The term "private entity" means any entity other than a public entity (as defined in section 12131(1) of this title).

(7) **Public accommodation.** The following private entities are considered public accommodations for purposes of this subchapter, if the operations of such entities affect commerce–

   (A) an inn, hotel, motel, or other place of lodging, except for an establishment located within a building that contains not more than five rooms for rent or hire and that is actually occupied by the proprietor of such establishment as the residence of such proprietor;

(B) a restaurant, bar, or other establishment serving food or drink;

(C) a motion picture house, theater, concert hall, stadium, or other place of exhibition or entertainment;

(D) an auditorium, convention center, lecture hall, or other place of public gathering;

(E) a bakery, grocery store, clothing store, hardware store, shopping center, or other sales or rental establishment;

(F) a laundromat, dry-cleaner, bank, barber shop, beauty shop, travel service, shoe repair service, funeral parlor, gas station, office of an accountant or lawyer, pharmacy, insurance office, professional office of a health care provider, hospital, or other service establishment;

(G) a terminal, depot, or other station used for specified public transportation;

(H) a museum, library, gallery, or other place of public display or collection;

(I) a park, zoo, amusement park, or other place of recreation;

(J) a nursery, elementary, secondary, undergraduate, or postgraduate private school, or other place of education;

(K) a day care center, senior citizen center, homeless shelter, food bank, adoption agency, or other social service center establishment; and

(L) a gymnasium, health spa, bowling alley, golf course, or other place of exercise or recreation.

42 U.S.C. § 12182

§ 12182. Prohibition of discrimination by public accommodations

(a) General rule. No individual shall be discriminated against on the basis of disability in the full and equal enjoyment of the goods, services, facilities, privileges, advantages, or accommodations of any place of public accommodation by any person who owns, leases (or leases to), or operates a place of public accommodation.

(b) Construction

(1) General prohibition

(A) Activities

(i) Denial of participation. It shall be discriminatory to subject an individual or class of individuals on the basis of a disability or disabilities of such individual or class, directly, or through contractual, licensing, or other arrangements, to a denial of the opportunity of the individual or class to participate in or benefit from the goods, services, facilities, privileges, advantages, or accommodations of an entity.

(ii) Participation in unequal benefit. It shall be discriminatory to afford an individual or class of individuals, on the basis of a disability or disabilities of such individual or class, directly, or through contractual, licensing, or other arrangements with the opportunity to participate in or benefit from a good, service, facility, privilege, advantage, or accommodation that is not equal to that afforded to other individuals.

  (iii) Separate benefit. It shall be discriminatory to provide an individual or class of individuals, on the basis of a disability or disabilities of such individual or class, directly, or through contractual, licensing, or other arrangements with a good, service, facility, privilege, advantage, or accommodation that is different or separate from that provided to other individuals, unless such action is necessary to provide the individual or class of individuals with a good, service, facility, privilege, advantage, or accommodation, or other opportunity that is as effective as that provided to others.

  (iv) Individual or class of individuals. For purposes of clauses (i) through (iii) of this subparagraph, the term "individual or class of individuals" refers to the clients or customers of the covered public accommodation that enters into the contractual, licensing or other arrangement.

(B) Integrated settings. Goods, services, facilities, privileges, advantages, and accommodations shall be afforded to an individual with a disability in the most integrated setting appropriate to the needs of the individual.

(C) Opportunity to participate. Notwithstanding the existence of separate or different programs or activities provided in accordance with this section, an individual with a disability shall not be denied the opportunity to participate in such programs or activities that are not separate or different.

(D) Administrative methods. An individual or entity shall not, directly or through contractual or other arrangements, utilize standards or criteria or methods of administration–

  (i) that have the effect of discriminating on the basis of disability; or

  (ii) that perpetuate the discrimination of others who are subject to common administrative control.

(E) Association. It shall be discriminatory to exclude or otherwise deny equal goods, services, facilities, privileges, advantages, accommodations, or other opportunities to an individual or entity because of the known disability of an individual with whom the individual or entity is known to have a relationship or association.

(2) Specific prohibitions

(A) Discrimination. For purposes of subsection (a) of this section, discrimination includes–

  (i) the imposition or application of eligibility criteria that screen out or tend to screen out an individual with a disability or any class of individuals with disabilities from fully and equally enjoying any goods, services, facilities, privileges, advantages, or accommodations, unless such criteria can be shown to be necessary for the provision of the goods, services, facilities, privileges, advantages, or accommodations being offered;

(ii) a failure to make reasonable modifications in policies, practices, or procedures, when such modifications are necessary to afford such goods, services, facilities, privileges, advantages, or accommodations to individuals with disabilities, unless the entity can demonstrate that making such modifications would fundamentally alter the nature of such goods, services, facilities, privileges, advantages, or accommodations;

(iii) a failure to take such steps as may be necessary to ensure that no individual with a disability is excluded, denied services, segregated or otherwise treated differently than other individuals because of the absence of auxiliary aids and services, unless the entity can demonstrate that taking such steps would fundamentally alter the nature of the good, service, facility, privilege, advantage, or accommodation being offered or would result in an undue burden;

(iv) a failure to remove architectural barriers, and communication barriers that are structural in nature, in existing facilities, and transportation barriers in existing vehicles and rail passenger cars used by an establishment for transporting individuals (not including barriers that can only be removed through the retrofitting of vehicles or rail passenger cars by the installation of a hydraulic or other lift), where such removal is readily achievable; and

(v) where an entity can demonstrate that the removal of a barrier under 42 U.S.C. § 12182 clause (iv) is not readily achievable, a failure to make such goods, services, facilities, privileges, advantages, or accommodations available through alternative methods if such methods are readily achievable.

* * *

(3) **Specific construction.** Nothing in this subchapter shall require an entity to permit an individual to participate in or benefit from the goods, services, facilities, privileges, advantages and accommodations of such entity where such individual poses a direct threat to the health or safety of others. The term "direct threat" means a significant risk to the health or safety of others that cannot be eliminated by a modification of policies, practices, or procedures or by the provision of auxiliary aids or services.

42 U.S.C. § 12187

§ 12187. Exemptions for private clubs and religious organizations

The provisions of this subchapter shall not apply to private clubs or establishments exempted from coverage under title II of the Civil Rights Act of 1964 (42 U.S.C. 2000a) or to religious organizations or entities controlled by religious organizations, including places of worship.

§ 12188. Enforcement

(a) In general

(1) Availability of remedies and procedures. The remedies and procedures set forth in section 2000a-3(a) of this title are the remedies and procedures this subchapter provides to any person who is being subjected to discrimination on the basis of disability in violation of this subchapter or who has reasonable grounds for believing that such person is about to be subjected to discrimination in violation of section 12183 of this title. Nothing in this section shall require a person with a disability to engage in a futile gesture if such person has actual notice that a person or organization covered by this subchapter does not intend to comply with its provisions.

(2) Injunctive relief. In the case of violations of sections 12182(b)(2)(A)(iv) of this title and section 12183(a) of this title, injunctive relief shall include an order to alter facilities to make such facilities readily accessible to and usable by individuals with disabilities to the extent required by this subchapter. Where appropriate, injunctive relief shall also include requiring the provision of an auxiliary aid or service, modification of a policy, or provision of alternative methods, to the extent required by this subchapter.

(b) Enforcement by the Attorney General

(1) Denial of rights

(A) Duty to investigate

    (i) In general. The Attorney General shall investigate alleged violations of this subchapter, and shall undertake periodic reviews of compliance of covered entities under this subchapter.

    (ii) Attorney General certification. On the application of a State or local government, the Attorney General may, in consultation with the Architectural and Transportation Barriers Compliance Board, and after prior notice and a public hearing at which persons, including individuals with disabilities, are provided an opportunity to testify against such certification, certify that a State law or local building code or similar ordinance that establishes accessibility requirements meets or exceeds the minimum requirements of this chapter for the accessibility and usability of covered facilities under this subchapter. At any enforcement proceeding under this section, such certification by the Attorney General shall be rebuttable evidence that such State law or local ordinance does meet or exceed the minimum requirements of this chapter.

(B) Potential violation. If the Attorney General has reasonable cause to believe that–

    (i) any person or group of persons is engaged in a pattern or practice of discrimination under this subchapter; or

     (ii) any person or group of persons has been discriminated against under this subchapter and such discrimination raises an issue of general public importance, the Attorney General may commence a civil action in any appropriate United States district court.

(2) Authority of court. In a civil action under paragraph (1)(B), the court–

    (A) may grant any equitable relief that such court considers to be appropriate, including, to the extent required by this subchapter–

       (i) granting temporary, preliminary, or permanent relief;

       (ii) providing an auxiliary aid or service, modification of policy, practice, or procedure, or alternative method; and

       (iii) making facilities readily accessible to and usable by individuals with disabilities;

    (B) may award such other relief as the court considers to be appropriate, including monetary damages to persons aggrieved when requested by the Attorney General; and

    (C) may, to vindicate the public interest, assess a civil penalty against the entity in an amount–

       (i) not exceeding $50,000 for a first violation; and

       (ii) not exceeding $100,000 for any subsequent violation.

(3) Single violation. For purposes of paragraph (2)(C), in determining whether a first or subsequent violation has occurred, a determination in a single action, by judgment or settlement, that the covered entity has engaged in more than one discriminatory act shall be counted as a single violation.

(4) Punitive damages. For purposes of subsection (b)(2)(B) of this section, the term "monetary damages" and "such other relief" does not include punitive damages.

(5) Judicial consideration. In a civil action under paragraph (1)(B), the court, when considering what amount of civil penalty, if any, is appropriate, shall give consideration to any good faith effort or attempt to comply with this chapter by the entity. In evaluating good faith, the court shall consider, among other factors it deems relevant, whether the entity could have reasonably anticipated the need for an appropriate type of auxiliary aid needed to accommodate the unique needs of a particular individual with a disability.

TITLE IV. MISCELLANEOUS PROVISIONS

42 U.S.C. § 12202

§ 12202. State immunity

A State shall not be immune under the eleventh amendment to the Constitution of the United States from an action in Federal or State court of competent jurisdiction for a violation of this chapter. In any action against a State for a violation of the requirements of this chapter, remedies (including remedies both at law and in equity) are available for such a violation to the same extent as such remedies are available for such a violation in an action against any public or private entity other than a State.

42 U.S.C. § 12203

§ 12203. Prohibition against retaliation and coercion

(a) **Retaliation.** No person shall discriminate against any individual because such individual has opposed any act or practice made unlawful by this chapter or because such individual made a charge, testified, assisted, or participated in any manner in an investigation, proceeding, or hearing under this chapter.

(b) **Interference, coercion, or intimidation.** It shall be unlawful to coerce, intimidate, threaten, or interfere with any individual in the exercise or enjoyment of, or on account of his or her having exercised or enjoyed, or on account of his or her having aided or encouraged any other individual in the exercise or enjoyment of, any right granted or protected by this chapter.

(c) **Remedies and procedures.** The remedies and procedures available under sections 12117, 12133, and 12188 of this title shall be available to aggrieved persons for violations of subsections (a) and (b) of this section, with respect to subchapter I, subchapter II and subchapter III, respectively, of this chapter.

42 U.S.C. § 12205

§ 12205. Attorney's fees

In any action or administrative proceeding commenced pursuant to this chapter, the court or agency, in its discretion, may allow the prevailing party, other than the United States, a reasonable attorney's fee, including litigation expenses, and costs, and the United States shall be liable for the foregoing the same as a private individual.

UNITED STATES CONSTITUTION

(SELECTED PROVISIONS)

Amendment I [1791]

Congress shall make no law respecting an establishment of religion, or prohibiting the free exercise thereof; or abridging the freedom of speech, or of the press; or the right of the people peaceably to assemble, and to petition the Government for a redress of grievances.

Amendment IV [1791]

The right of the people to be secure in their persons, houses, papers, and effects, against unreasonable searches and seizures, shall not be violated, and no Warrants shall issue, but upon probable cause, supported by Oath or affirmation and particularly describing the place to be searched, and the persons or things to be seized.

Amendment V [1791]

No person shall be . . . deprived of life, liberty, or property, without due process of law; nor shall private property be taken for public use, without just compensation.

Amendment VIII [1791]

Excessive bail shall not be required, nor excessive fines imposed, nor cruel and unusual punishments inflicted.

Amendment XI [1798]

The Judicial power of the United States shall not be construed to extend to any suit in law or equity, commenced or prosecuted against one of the United States by Citizens of another State, or by Citizens of any Foreign State.

Amendment XIII [1865]

Section 1. Neither slavery nor involuntary servitude, except as a punishment for crime whereof the party shall have been duly convicted, shall exist within the United States, or any place subject to their jurisdiction.

Section 2. Congress shall have power to enforce this article by appropriate legislation.

Amendment XIV [1868]

>ection 1. All persons born or naturalized in the United States, and subject to the jurisdiction thereof, are citizens of the United States and of the State wherein they reside. No State shall make or enforce any law which shall abridge the privileges or immunities of citizens of the United States; nor shall any State deprive any person of life, liberty, or property, without due process of law; nor deny to any person within its jurisdiction the equal protection of the laws.
Section 5. The Congress shall have power to enforce, by appropriate legislation, the provisions of this article.

Amendment XV [1870]

Section 1. The right of citizens of the United States to vote shall not be denied or abridged by the United States or by any State on account of race, color, or previous condition of servitude.
Section 2. The Congress shall have power to enforce this article by appropriate legislation.